Lecture Notes in Computer Science 11209

More information about this series at http://www.springer.com/series/7412

Vittorio Ferrari · Martial Hebert
Cristian Sminchisescu · Yair Weiss (Eds.)

Computer Vision – ECCV 2018

15th European Conference
Munich, Germany, September 8–14, 2018
Proceedings, Part V

Editors
Vittorio Ferrari
Google Research
Zurich
Switzerland

Martial Hebert
Carnegie Mellon University
Pittsburgh, PA
USA

Cristian Sminchisescu
Google Research
Zurich
Switzerland

Yair Weiss
Hebrew University of Jerusalem
Jerusalem
Israel

ISSN 0302-9743 ISSN 1611-3349 (electronic)
Lecture Notes in Computer Science
ISBN 978-3-030-01227-4 ISBN 978-3-030-01228-1 (eBook)
https://doi.org/10.1007/978-3-030-01228-1

Library of Congress Control Number: 2018955489

LNCS Sublibrary: SL6 – Image Processing, Computer Vision, Pattern Recognition, and Graphics

This Springer imprint is published by the registered company Springer Nature Switzerland AG
The registered company address is: Gewerbestrasse 11, 6330 Cham, Switzerland

Foreword

It was our great pleasure to host the European Conference on Computer Vision 2018 in Munich, Germany. This constituted by far the largest ECCV event ever. With close to 2,900 registered participants and another 600 on the waiting list one month before the conference, participation more than doubled since the last ECCV in Amsterdam. We believe that this is due to a dramatic growth of the computer vision community combined with the popularity of Munich as a major European hub of culture, science, and industry. The conference took place in the heart of Munich in the concert hall Gasteig with workshops and tutorials held at the downtown campus of the Technical University of Munich.

One of the major innovations for ECCV 2018 was the free perpetual availability of all conference and workshop papers, which is often referred to as open access. We note that this is not precisely the same use of the term as in the Budapest declaration. Since 2013, CVPR and ICCV have had their papers hosted by the Computer Vision Foundation (CVF), in parallel with the IEEE Xplore version. This has proved highly beneficial to the computer vision community.

We are delighted to announce that for ECCV 2018 a very similar arrangement was put in place with the cooperation of Springer. In particular, the author's final version will be freely available in perpetuity on a CVF page, while SpringerLink will continue to host a version with further improvements, such as activating reference links and including video. We believe that this will give readers the best of both worlds; researchers who are focused on the technical content will have a freely available version in an easily accessible place, while subscribers to SpringerLink will continue to have the additional benefits that this provides. We thank Alfred Hofmann from Springer for helping to negotiate this agreement, which we expect will continue for future versions of ECCV.

September 2018

Horst Bischof
Daniel Cremers
Bernt Schiele
Ramin Zabih

Preface

Welcome to the proceedings of the 2018 European Conference on Computer Vision (ECCV 2018) held in Munich, Germany. We are delighted to present this volume reflecting a strong and exciting program, the result of an extensive review process. In total, we received 2,439 valid paper submissions. Of these, 776 were accepted (31.8%): 717 as posters (29.4%) and 59 as oral presentations (2.4%). All oral presentations were presented as posters as well. The program selection process was complicated this year by the large increase in the number of submitted papers, +65% over ECCV 2016, and the use of CMT3 for the first time for a computer vision conference. The program selection process was supported by four program co-chairs (PCs), 126 area chairs (ACs), and 1,199 reviewers with reviews assigned.

We were primarily responsible for the design and execution of the review process. Beyond administrative rejections, we were involved in acceptance decisions only in the very few cases where the ACs were not able to agree on a decision. As PCs, and as is customary in the field, we were not allowed to co-author a submission. General co-chairs and other co-organizers who played no role in the review process were permitted to submit papers, and were treated as any other author is.

Acceptance decisions were made by two independent ACs. The ACs also made a joint recommendation for promoting papers to oral status. We decided on the final selection of oral presentations based on the ACs' recommendations. There were 126 ACs, selected according to their technical expertise, experience, and geographical diversity (63 from European, nine from Asian/Australian, and 54 from North American institutions). Indeed, 126 ACs is a substantial increase in the number of ACs due to the natural increase in the number of papers and to our desire to maintain the number of papers assigned to each AC to a manageable number so as to ensure quality. The ACs were aided by the 1,199 reviewers to whom papers were assigned for reviewing. The Program Committee was selected from committees of previous ECCV, ICCV, and CVPR conferences and was extended on the basis of suggestions from the ACs. Having a large pool of Program Committee members for reviewing allowed us to match expertise while reducing reviewer loads. No more than eight papers were assigned to a reviewer, maintaining the reviewers' load at the same level as ECCV 2016 despite the increase in the number of submitted papers.

Conflicts of interest between ACs, Program Committee members, and papers were identified based on the home institutions, and on previous collaborations of all researchers involved. To find institutional conflicts, all authors, Program Committee members, and ACs were asked to list the Internet domains of their current institutions. We assigned on average approximately 18 papers to each AC. The papers were assigned using the affinity scores from the Toronto Paper Matching System (TPMS) and additional data from the OpenReview system, managed by a UMass group. OpenReview used additional information from ACs' and authors' records to identify collaborations and to generate matches. OpenReview was invaluable in refining conflict definitions and in generating quality matches. The only glitch is that, once the matches were generated, a small percentage of papers were unassigned because of discrepancies between the OpenReview conflicts and the conflicts entered in CMT3. We manually assigned these papers. This glitch is revealing of the challenge of using multiple systems at once (CMT3 and OpenReview in this case), which needs to be addressed in future.

After assignment of papers to ACs, the ACs suggested seven reviewers per paper from the Program Committee pool. The selection and rank ordering were facilitated by the TPMS affinity scores visible to the ACs for each paper/reviewer pair. The final assignment of papers to reviewers was generated again through OpenReview in order to account for refined conflict definitions. This required new features in the OpenReview matching system to accommodate the ECCV workflow, in particular to incorporate selection ranking, and maximum reviewer load. Very few papers received fewer than three reviewers after matching and were handled through manual assignment. Reviewers were then asked to comment on the merit of each paper and to make an initial recommendation ranging from definitely reject to definitely accept, including a borderline rating. The reviewers were also asked to suggest explicit questions they wanted to see answered in the authors' rebuttal. The initial review period was five weeks. Because of the delay in getting all the reviews in, we had to delay the final release of the reviews by four days. However, because of the slack included at the tail end of the schedule, we were able to maintain the decision target date with sufficient time for all the phases. We reassigned over 100 reviews from 40 reviewers during the review period. Unfortunately, the main reason for these reassignments was reviewers declining to review, after having accepted to do so. Other reasons included technical relevance and occasional unidentified conflicts. We express our thanks to the emergency reviewers who generously accepted to perform these reviews under short notice. In addition, a substantial number of manual corrections had to do with reviewers using a different email address than the one that was used at the time of the reviewer invitation. This is revealing of a broader issue with identifying users by email addresses that change frequently enough to cause significant problems during the timespan of the conference process.

The authors were then given the opportunity to rebut the reviews, to identify factual errors, and to address the specific questions raised by the reviewers over a seven-day rebuttal period. The exact format of the rebuttal was the object of considerable debate among the organizers, as well as with prior organizers. At issue is to balance giving the author the opportunity to respond completely and precisely to the reviewers, e.g., by including graphs of experiments, while avoiding requests for completely new material or experimental results not included in the original paper. In the end, we decided on the two-page PDF document in conference format. Following this rebuttal period, reviewers and ACs discussed papers at length, after which reviewers finalized their evaluation and gave a final recommendation to the ACs. A significant percentage of the reviewers did enter their final recommendation if it did not differ from their initial recommendation. Given the tight schedule, we did not wait until all were entered.

After this discussion period, each paper was assigned to a second AC. The AC/paper matching was again run through OpenReview. Again, the OpenReview team worked quickly to implement the features specific to this process, in this case accounting for the existing AC assignment, as well as minimizing the fragmentation across ACs, so that each AC had on average only 5.5 buddy ACs to communicate with. The largest number was 11. Given the complexity of the conflicts, this was a very efficient set of assignments from OpenReview. Each paper was then evaluated by its assigned pair of ACs. For each paper, we required each of the two ACs assigned to certify both the final recommendation and the metareview (aka consolidation report). In all cases, after extensive discussions, the two ACs arrived at a common acceptance decision. We maintained these decisions, with the caveat that we did evaluate, sometimes going back to the ACs, a few papers for which the final acceptance decision substantially deviated from the consensus from the reviewers, amending three decisions in the process.

We want to thank everyone involved in making ECCV 2018 possible. The success of ECCV 2018 depended on the quality of papers submitted by the authors, and on the very hard work of the ACs and the Program Committee members. We are particularly grateful to the OpenReview team (Melisa Bok, Ari Kobren, Andrew McCallum, Michael Spector) for their support, in particular their willingness to implement new features, often on a tight schedule, to Laurent Charlin for the use of the Toronto Paper Matching System, to the CMT3 team, in particular in dealing with all the issues that arise when using a new system, to Friedrich Fraundorfer and Quirin Lohr for maintaining the online version of the program, and to the CMU staff (Keyla Cook, Lynnetta Miller, Ashley Song, Nora Kazour) for assisting with data entry/editing in CMT3. Finally, the preparation of these proceedings would not have been possible without the diligent effort of the publication chairs, Albert Ali Salah and Hamdi Dibeklioğlu, and of Anna Kramer and Alfred Hofmann from Springer.

September 2018

Vittorio Ferrari
Martial Hebert
Cristian Sminchisescu
Yair Weiss

Organization

General Chairs

Horst Bischof	Graz University of Technology, Austria
Daniel Cremers	Technical University of Munich, Germany
Bernt Schiele	Saarland University, Max Planck Institute for Informatics, Germany
Ramin Zabih	CornellNYCTech, USA

Program Committee Co-chairs

Vittorio Ferrari	University of Edinburgh, UK
Martial Hebert	Carnegie Mellon University, USA
Cristian Sminchisescu	Lund University, Sweden
Yair Weiss	Hebrew University, Israel

Local Arrangements Chairs

Björn Menze	Technical University of Munich, Germany
Matthias Niessner	Technical University of Munich, Germany

Workshop Chairs

Stefan Roth	TU Darmstadt, Germany
Laura Leal-Taixé	Technical University of Munich, Germany

Tutorial Chairs

Michael Bronstein	Università della Svizzera Italiana, Switzerland
Laura Leal-Taixé	Technical University of Munich, Germany

Website Chair

Friedrich Fraundorfer	Graz University of Technology, Austria

Demo Chairs

Federico Tombari	Technical University of Munich, Germany
Joerg Stueckler	Technical University of Munich, Germany

Publicity Chair

Giovanni Maria Farinella	University of Catania, Italy

Industrial Liaison Chairs

Florent Perronnin	Naver Labs, France
Yunchao Gong	Snap, USA
Helmut Grabner	Logitech, Switzerland

Finance Chair

Gerard Medioni	Amazon, University of Southern California, USA

Publication Chairs

Albert Ali Salah	Boğaziçi University, Turkey
Hamdi Dibeklioğlu	Bilkent University, Turkey

Area Chairs

Kalle Åström	Lund University, Sweden
Zeynep Akata	University of Amsterdam, The Netherlands
Joao Barreto	University of Coimbra, Portugal
Ronen Basri	Weizmann Institute of Science, Israel
Dhruv Batra	Georgia Tech and Facebook AI Research, USA
Serge Belongie	Cornell University, USA
Rodrigo Benenson	Google, Switzerland
Hakan Bilen	University of Edinburgh, UK
Matthew Blaschko	KU Leuven, Belgium
Edmond Boyer	Inria, France
Gabriel Brostow	University College London, UK
Thomas Brox	University of Freiburg, Germany
Marcus Brubaker	York University, Canada
Barbara Caputo	Politecnico di Torino and the Italian Institute of Technology, Italy
Tim Cootes	University of Manchester, UK
Trevor Darrell	University of California, Berkeley, USA
Larry Davis	University of Maryland at College Park, USA
Andrew Davison	Imperial College London, UK
Fernando de la Torre	Carnegie Mellon University, USA
Irfan Essa	GeorgiaTech, USA
Ali Farhadi	University of Washington, USA
Paolo Favaro	University of Bern, Switzerland
Michael Felsberg	Linköping University, Sweden

Sanja Fidler	University of Toronto, Canada
Andrew Fitzgibbon	Microsoft, Cambridge, UK
David Forsyth	University of Illinois at Urbana-Champaign, USA
Charless Fowlkes	University of California, Irvine, USA
Bill Freeman	MIT, USA
Mario Fritz	MPII, Germany
Jürgen Gall	University of Bonn, Germany
Dariu Gavrila	TU Delft, The Netherlands
Andreas Geiger	MPI-IS and University of Tübingen, Germany
Theo Gevers	University of Amsterdam, The Netherlands
Ross Girshick	Facebook AI Research, USA
Kristen Grauman	Facebook AI Research and UT Austin, USA
Abhinav Gupta	Carnegie Mellon University, USA
Kaiming He	Facebook AI Research, USA
Martial Hebert	Carnegie Mellon University, USA
Anders Heyden	Lund University, Sweden
Timothy Hospedales	University of Edinburgh, UK
Michal Irani	Weizmann Institute of Science, Israel
Phillip Isola	University of California, Berkeley, USA
Hervé Jégou	Facebook AI Research, France
David Jacobs	University of Maryland, College Park, USA
Allan Jepson	University of Toronto, Canada
Jiaya Jia	Chinese University of Hong Kong, SAR China
Fredrik Kahl	Chalmers University, USA
Hedvig Kjellström	KTH Royal Institute of Technology, Sweden
Iasonas Kokkinos	University College London and Facebook, UK
Vladlen Koltun	Intel Labs, USA
Philipp Krähenbühl	UT Austin, USA
M. Pawan Kumar	University of Oxford, UK
Kyros Kutulakos	University of Toronto, Canada
In Kweon	KAIST, South Korea
Ivan Laptev	Inria, France
Svetlana Lazebnik	University of Illinois at Urbana-Champaign, USA
Laura Leal-Taixé	Technical University of Munich, Germany
Erik Learned-Miller	University of Massachusetts, Amherst, USA
Kyoung Mu Lee	Seoul National University, South Korea
Bastian Leibe	RWTH Aachen University, Germany
Aleš Leonardis	University of Birmingham, UK
Vincent Lepetit	University of Bordeaux, France and Graz University of Technology, Austria
Fuxin Li	Oregon State University, USA
Dahua Lin	Chinese University of Hong Kong, SAR China
Jim Little	University of British Columbia, Canada
Ce Liu	Google, USA
Chen Change Loy	Nanyang Technological University, Singapore
Jiri Matas	Czech Technical University in Prague, Czechia

Yasuyuki Matsushita	Osaka University, Japan
Dimitris Metaxas	Rutgers University, USA
Greg Mori	Simon Fraser University, Canada
Vittorio Murino	Istituto Italiano di Tecnologia, Italy
Richard Newcombe	Oculus Research, USA
Minh Hoai Nguyen	Stony Brook University, USA
Sebastian Nowozin	Microsoft Research Cambridge, UK
Aude Oliva	MIT, USA
Bjorn Ommer	Heidelberg University, Germany
Tomas Pajdla	Czech Technical University in Prague, Czechia
Maja Pantic	Imperial College London and Samsung AI Research Centre Cambridge, UK
Caroline Pantofaru	Google, USA
Devi Parikh	Georgia Tech and Facebook AI Research, USA
Sylvain Paris	Adobe Research, USA
Vladimir Pavlovic	Rutgers University, USA
Marcello Pelillo	University of Venice, Italy
Patrick Pérez	Valeo, France
Robert Pless	George Washington University, USA
Thomas Pock	Graz University of Technology, Austria
Jean Ponce	Inria, France
Gerard Pons-Moll	MPII, Saarland Informatics Campus, Germany
Long Quan	Hong Kong University of Science and Technology, SAR China
Stefan Roth	TU Darmstadt, Germany
Carsten Rother	University of Heidelberg, Germany
Bryan Russell	Adobe Research, USA
Kate Saenko	Boston University, USA
Mathieu Salzmann	EPFL, Switzerland
Dimitris Samaras	Stony Brook University, USA
Yoichi Sato	University of Tokyo, Japan
Silvio Savarese	Stanford University, USA
Konrad Schindler	ETH Zurich, Switzerland
Cordelia Schmid	Inria, France and Google, France
Nicu Sebe	University of Trento, Italy
Fei Sha	University of Southern California, USA
Greg Shakhnarovich	TTI Chicago, USA
Jianbo Shi	University of Pennsylvania, USA
Abhinav Shrivastava	UMD and Google, USA
Yan Shuicheng	National University of Singapore, Singapore
Leonid Sigal	University of British Columbia, Canada
Josef Sivic	Czech Technical University in Prague, Czechia
Arnold Smeulders	University of Amsterdam, The Netherlands
Deqing Sun	NVIDIA, USA
Antonio Torralba	MIT, USA
Zhuowen Tu	University of California, San Diego, USA

Tinne Tuytelaars	KU Leuven, Belgium
Jasper Uijlings	Google, Switzerland
Joost van de Weijer	Computer Vision Center, Spain
Nuno Vasconcelos	University of California, San Diego, USA
Andrea Vedaldi	University of Oxford, UK
Olga Veksler	University of Western Ontario, Canada
Jakob Verbeek	Inria, France
Rene Vidal	Johns Hopkins University, USA
Daphna Weinshall	Hebrew University, Israel
Chris Williams	University of Edinburgh, UK
Lior Wolf	Tel Aviv University, Israel
Ming-Hsuan Yang	University of California at Merced, USA
Todd Zickler	Harvard University, USA
Andrew Zisserman	University of Oxford, UK

Technical Program Committee

Hassan Abu Alhaija
Radhakrishna Achanta
Hanno Ackermann
Ehsan Adeli
Lourdes Agapito
Aishwarya Agrawal
Antonio Agudo
Eirikur Agustsson
Karim Ahmed
Byeongjoo Ahn
Unaiza Ahsan
Emre Akbaş
Eren Aksoy
Yağız Aksoy
Alexandre Alahi
Jean-Baptiste Alayrac
Samuel Albanie
Cenek Albl
Saad Ali
Rahaf Aljundi
Jose M. Alvarez
Humam Alwassel
Toshiyuki Amano
Mitsuru Ambai
Mohamed Amer
Senjian An
Cosmin Ancuti
Peter Anderson
Juan Andrade-Cetto
Mykhaylo Andriluka
Anelia Angelova
Michel Antunes
Pablo Arbelaez
Vasileios Argyriou
Chetan Arora
Federica Arrigoni
Vassilis Athitsos
Mathieu Aubry
Shai Avidan
Yannis Avrithis
Samaneh Azadi
Hossein Azizpour
Artem Babenko
Timur Bagautdinov
Andrew Bagdanov
Hessam Bagherinezhad
Yuval Bahat
Min Bai
Qinxun Bai
Song Bai
Xiang Bai
Peter Bajcsy
Amr Bakry
Kavita Bala
Arunava Banerjee
Atsuhiko Banno
Aayush Bansal
Yingze Bao
Md Jawadul Bappy
Pierre Baqué
Dániel Baráth
Adrian Barbu
Kobus Barnard
Nick Barnes
Francisco Barranco
Adrien Bartoli
E. Bayro-Corrochano
Paul Beardlsey
Vasileios Belagiannis
Sean Bell
Ismail Ben
Boulbaba Ben Amor
Gil Ben-Artzi
Ohad Ben-Shahar
Abhijit Bendale
Rodrigo Benenson
Fabian Benitez-Quiroz
Fethallah Benmansour
Ryad Benosman
Filippo Bergamasco
David Bermudez

Jesus Bermudez-Cameo
Leonard Berrada
Gedas Bertasius
Ross Beveridge
Lucas Beyer
Bir Bhanu
S. Bhattacharya
Binod Bhattarai
Arnav Bhavsar
Simone Bianco
Adel Bibi
Pia Bideau
Josef Bigun
Arijit Biswas
Soma Biswas
Marten Bjoerkman
Volker Blanz
Vishnu Boddeti
Piotr Bojanowski
Terrance Boult
Yuri Boykov
Hakan Boyraz
Eric Brachmann
Samarth Brahmbhatt
Mathieu Bredif
Francois Bremond
Michael Brown
Luc Brun
Shyamal Buch
Pradeep Buddharaju
Aurelie Bugeau
Rudy Bunel
Xavier Burgos Artizzu
Darius Burschka
Andrei Bursuc
Zoya Bylinskii
Fabian Caba
Daniel Cabrini Hauagge
Cesar Cadena Lerma
Holger Caesar
Jianfei Cai
Junjie Cai
Zhaowei Cai
Simone Calderara
Neill Campbell
Octavia Camps
Xun Cao
Yanshuai Cao
Joao Carreira
Dan Casas
Daniel Castro
Jan Cech
M. Emre Celebi
Duygu Ceylan
Menglei Chai
Ayan Chakrabarti
Rudrasis Chakraborty
Shayok Chakraborty
Tat-Jen Cham
Antonin Chambolle
Antoni Chan
Sharat Chandran
Hyun Sung Chang
Ju Yong Chang
Xiaojun Chang
Soravit Changpinyo
Wei-Lun Chao
Yu-Wei Chao
Visesh Chari
Rizwan Chaudhry
Siddhartha Chaudhuri
Rama Chellappa
Chao Chen
Chen Chen
Cheng Chen
Chu-Song Chen
Guang Chen
Hsin-I Chen
Hwann-Tzong Chen
Kai Chen
Kan Chen
Kevin Chen
Liang-Chieh Chen
Lin Chen
Qifeng Chen
Ting Chen
Wei Chen
Xi Chen
Xilin Chen
Xinlei Chen
Yingcong Chen
Yixin Chen
Erkang Cheng
Jingchun Cheng
Ming-Ming Cheng
Wen-Huang Cheng
Yuan Cheng
Anoop Cherian
Liang-Tien Chia
Naoki Chiba
Shao-Yi Chien
Han-Pang Chiu
Wei-Chen Chiu
Nam Ik Cho
Sunghyun Cho
TaeEun Choe
Jongmoo Choi
Christopher Choy
Wen-Sheng Chu
Yung-Yu Chuang
Ondrej Chum
Joon Son Chung
Gökberk Cinbis
James Clark
Andrea Cohen
Forrester Cole
Toby Collins
John Collomosse
Camille Couprie
David Crandall
Marco Cristani
Canton Cristian
James Crowley
Yin Cui
Zhaopeng Cui
Bo Dai
Jifeng Dai
Qieyun Dai
Shengyang Dai
Yuchao Dai
Carlo Dal Mutto
Dima Damen
Zachary Daniels
Kostas Daniilidis
Donald Dansereau
Mohamed Daoudi
Abhishek Das
Samyak Datta

Achal Dave
Shalini De Mello
Teofilo deCampos
Joseph DeGol
Koichiro Deguchi
Alessio Del Bue
Stefanie Demirci
Jia Deng
Zhiwei Deng
Joachim Denzler
Konstantinos Derpanis
Aditya Deshpande
Alban Desmaison
Frédéric Devernay
Abhinav Dhall
Michel Dhome
Hamdi Dibeklioğlu
Mert Dikmen
Cosimo Distante
Ajay Divakaran
Mandar Dixit
Carl Doersch
Piotr Dollar
Bo Dong
Chao Dong
Huang Dong
Jian Dong
Jiangxin Dong
Weisheng Dong
Simon Donné
Gianfranco Doretto
Alexey Dosovitskiy
Matthijs Douze
Bruce Draper
Bertram Drost
Liang Du
Shichuan Du
Gregory Dudek
Zoran Duric
Pınar Duygulu
Hazım Ekenel
Tarek El-Gaaly
Ehsan Elhamifar
Mohamed Elhoseiny
Sabu Emmanuel
Ian Endres
Aykut Erdem
Erkut Erdem
Hugo Jair Escalante
Sergio Escalera
Victor Escorcia
Francisco Estrada
Davide Eynard
Bin Fan
Jialue Fan
Quanfu Fan
Chen Fang
Tian Fang
Yi Fang
Hany Farid
Giovanni Farinella
Ryan Farrell
Alireza Fathi
Christoph Feichtenhofer
Wenxin Feng
Martin Fergie
Cornelia Fermuller
Basura Fernando
Michael Firman
Bob Fisher
John Fisher
Mathew Fisher
Boris Flach
Matt Flagg
Francois Fleuret
David Fofi
Ruth Fong
Gian Luca Foresti
Per-Erik Forssén
David Fouhey
Katerina Fragkiadaki
Victor Fragoso
Jan-Michael Frahm
Jean-Sebastien Franco
Ohad Fried
Simone Frintrop
Huazhu Fu
Yun Fu
Olac Fuentes
Christopher Funk
Thomas Funkhouser
Brian Funt
Ryo Furukawa
Yasutaka Furukawa
Andrea Fusiello
Fatma Güney
Raghudeep Gadde
Silvano Galliani
Orazio Gallo
Chuang Gan
Bin-Bin Gao
Jin Gao
Junbin Gao
Ruohan Gao
Shenghua Gao
Animesh Garg
Ravi Garg
Erik Gartner
Simone Gasparin
Jochen Gast
Leon A. Gatys
Stratis Gavves
Liuhao Ge
Timnit Gebru
James Gee
Peter Gehler
Xin Geng
Guido Gerig
David Geronimo
Bernard Ghanem
Michael Gharbi
Golnaz Ghiasi
Spyros Gidaris
Andrew Gilbert
Rohit Girdhar
Ioannis Gkioulekas
Georgia Gkioxari
Guy Godin
Roland Goecke
Michael Goesele
Nuno Goncalves
Boqing Gong
Minglun Gong
Yunchao Gong
Abel Gonzalez-Garcia
Daniel Gordon
Paulo Gotardo
Stephen Gould

Venu Govindu
Helmut Grabner
Petr Gronat
Steve Gu
Josechu Guerrero
Anupam Guha
Jean-Yves Guillemaut
Alp Güler
Erhan Gündoğdu
Guodong Guo
Xinqing Guo
Ankush Gupta
Mohit Gupta
Saurabh Gupta
Tanmay Gupta
Abner Guzman Rivera
Timo Hackel
Sunil Hadap
Christian Haene
Ralf Haeusler
Levente Hajder
David Hall
Peter Hall
Stefan Haller
Ghassan Hamarneh
Fred Hamprecht
Onur Hamsici
Bohyung Han
Junwei Han
Xufeng Han
Yahong Han
Ankur Handa
Albert Haque
Tatsuya Harada
Mehrtash Harandi
Bharath Hariharan
Mahmudul Hasan
Tal Hassner
Kenji Hata
Soren Hauberg
Michal Havlena
Zeeshan Hayder
Junfeng He
Lei He
Varsha Hedau
Felix Heide
Wolfgang Heidrich
Janne Heikkila
Jared Heinly
Mattias Heinrich
Lisa Anne Hendricks
Dan Hendrycks
Stephane Herbin
Alexander Hermans
Luis Herranz
Aaron Hertzmann
Adrian Hilton
Michael Hirsch
Steven Hoi
Seunghoon Hong
Wei Hong
Anthony Hoogs
Radu Horaud
Yedid Hoshen
Omid Hosseini Jafari
Kuang-Jui Hsu
Winston Hsu
Yinlin Hu
Zhe Hu
Gang Hua
Chen Huang
De-An Huang
Dong Huang
Gary Huang
Heng Huang
Jia-Bin Huang
Qixing Huang
Rui Huang
Sheng Huang
Weilin Huang
Xiaolei Huang
Xinyu Huang
Zhiwu Huang
Tak-Wai Hui
Wei-Chih Hung
Junhwa Hur
Mohamed Hussein
Wonjun Hwang
Anders Hyden
Satoshi Ikehata
Nazlı Ikizler-Cinbis
Viorela Ila
Evren Imre
Eldar Insafutdinov
Go Irie
Hossam Isack
Ahmet Işcen
Daisuke Iwai
Hamid Izadinia
Nathan Jacobs
Suyog Jain
Varun Jampani
C. V. Jawahar
Dinesh Jayaraman
Sadeep Jayasumana
Laszlo Jeni
Hueihan Jhuang
Dinghuang Ji
Hui Ji
Qiang Ji
Fan Jia
Kui Jia
Xu Jia
Huaizu Jiang
Jiayan Jiang
Nianjuan Jiang
Tingting Jiang
Xiaoyi Jiang
Yu-Gang Jiang
Long Jin
Suo Jinli
Justin Johnson
Nebojsa Jojic
Michael Jones
Hanbyul Joo
Jungseock Joo
Ajjen Joshi
Amin Jourabloo
Frederic Jurie
Achuta Kadambi
Samuel Kadoury
Ioannis Kakadiaris
Zdenek Kalal
Yannis Kalantidis
Sinan Kalkan
Vicky Kalogeiton
Sunkavalli Kalyan
J.-K. Kamarainen

Martin Kampel
Kenichi Kanatani
Angjoo Kanazawa
Melih Kandemir
Sing Bing Kang
Zhuoliang Kang
Mohan Kankanhalli
Juho Kannala
Abhishek Kar
Amlan Kar
Svebor Karaman
Leonid Karlinsky
Zoltan Kato
Parneet Kaur
Hiroshi Kawasaki
Misha Kazhdan
Margret Keuper
Sameh Khamis
Naeemullah Khan
Salman Khan
Hadi Kiapour
Joe Kileel
Chanho Kim
Gunhee Kim
Hansung Kim
Junmo Kim
Junsik Kim
Kihwan Kim
Minyoung Kim
Tae Hyun Kim
Tae-Kyun Kim
Akisato Kimura
Zsolt Kira
Alexander Kirillov
Kris Kitani
Maria Klodt
Patrick Knöbelreiter
Jan Knopp
Reinhard Koch
Alexander Kolesnikov
Chen Kong
Naejin Kong
Shu Kong
Piotr Koniusz
Simon Korman
Andreas Koschan
Dimitrios Kosmopoulos
Satwik Kottur
Balazs Kovacs
Adarsh Kowdle
Mike Krainin
Gregory Kramida
Ranjay Krishna
Ravi Krishnan
Matej Kristan
Pavel Krsek
Volker Krueger
Alexander Krull
Hilde Kuehne
Andreas Kuhn
Arjan Kuijper
Zuzana Kukelova
Kuldeep Kulkarni
Shiro Kumano
Avinash Kumar
Vijay Kumar
Abhijit Kundu
Sebastian Kurtek
Junseok Kwon
Jan Kybic
Alexander Ladikos
Shang-Hong Lai
Wei-Sheng Lai
Jean-Francois Lalonde
John Lambert
Zhenzhong Lan
Charis Lanaras
Oswald Lanz
Dong Lao
Longin Jan Latecki
Justin Lazarow
Huu Le
Chen-Yu Lee
Gim Hee Lee
Honglak Lee
Hsin-Ying Lee
Joon-Young Lee
Seungyong Lee
Stefan Lee
Yong Jae Lee
Zhen Lei
Ido Leichter
Victor Lempitsky
Spyridon Leonardos
Marius Leordeanu
Matt Leotta
Thomas Leung
Stefan Leutenegger
Gil Levi
Aviad Levis
Jose Lezama
Ang Li
Dingzeyu Li
Dong Li
Haoxiang Li
Hongdong Li
Hongsheng Li
Hongyang Li
Jianguo Li
Kai Li
Ruiyu Li
Wei Li
Wen Li
Xi Li
Xiaoxiao Li
Xin Li
Xirong Li
Xuelong Li
Xueting Li
Yeqing Li
Yijun Li
Yin Li
Yingwei Li
Yining Li
Yongjie Li
Yu-Feng Li
Zechao Li
Zhengqi Li
Zhenyang Li
Zhizhong Li
Xiaodan Liang
Renjie Liao
Zicheng Liao
Bee Lim
Jongwoo Lim
Joseph Lim
Ser-Nam Lim
Chen-Hsuan Lin

Shih-Yao Lin
Tsung-Yi Lin
Weiyao Lin
Yen-Yu Lin
Haibin Ling
Or Litany
Roee Litman
Anan Liu
Changsong Liu
Chen Liu
Ding Liu
Dong Liu
Feng Liu
Guangcan Liu
Luoqi Liu
Miaomiao Liu
Nian Liu
Risheng Liu
Shu Liu
Shuaicheng Liu
Sifei Liu
Tyng-Luh Liu
Wanquan Liu
Weiwei Liu
Xialei Liu
Xiaoming Liu
Yebin Liu
Yiming Liu
Ziwei Liu
Zongyi Liu
Liliana Lo Presti
Edgar Lobaton
Chengjiang Long
Mingsheng Long
Roberto Lopez-Sastre
Amy Loufti
Brian Lovell
Canyi Lu
Cewu Lu
Feng Lu
Huchuan Lu
Jiajun Lu
Jiasen Lu
Jiwen Lu
Yang Lu
Yujuan Lu
Simon Lucey
Jian-Hao Luo
Jiebo Luo
Pablo Márquez-Neila
Matthias Müller
Chao Ma
Chih-Yao Ma
Lin Ma
Shugao Ma
Wei-Chiu Ma
Zhanyu Ma
Oisin Mac Aodha
Will Maddern
Ludovic Magerand
Marcus Magnor
Vijay Mahadevan
Mohammad Mahoor
Michael Maire
Subhransu Maji
Ameesh Makadia
Atsuto Maki
Yasushi Makihara
Mateusz Malinowski
Tomasz Malisiewicz
Arun Mallya
Roberto Manduchi
Junhua Mao
Dmitrii Marin
Joe Marino
Kenneth Marino
Elisabeta Marinoiu
Ricardo Martin
Aleix Martinez
Julieta Martinez
Aaron Maschinot
Jonathan Masci
Bogdan Matei
Diana Mateus
Stefan Mathe
Kevin Matzen
Bruce Maxwell
Steve Maybank
Walterio Mayol-Cuevas
Mason McGill
Stephen Mckenna
Roey Mechrez
Christopher Mei
Heydi Mendez-Vazquez
Deyu Meng
Thomas Mensink
Bjoern Menze
Domingo Mery
Qiguang Miao
Tomer Michaeli
Antoine Miech
Ondrej Miksik
Anton Milan
Gregor Miller
Cai Minjie
Majid Mirmehdi
Ishan Misra
Niloy Mitra
Anurag Mittal
Nirbhay Modhe
Davide Modolo
Pritish Mohapatra
Pascal Monasse
Mathew Monfort
Taesup Moon
Sandino Morales
Vlad Morariu
Philippos Mordohai
Francesc Moreno
Henrique Morimitsu
Yael Moses
Ben-Ezra Moshe
Roozbeh Mottaghi
Yadong Mu
Lopamudra Mukherjee
Mario Munich
Ana Murillo
Damien Muselet
Armin Mustafa
Siva Karthik Mustikovela
Moin Nabi
Sobhan Naderi
Hajime Nagahara
Varun Nagaraja
Tushar Nagarajan
Arsha Nagrani
Nikhil Naik
Atsushi Nakazawa

P. J. Narayanan
Charlie Nash
Lakshmanan Nataraj
Fabian Nater
Lukáš Neumann
Natalia Neverova
Alejandro Newell
Phuc Nguyen
Xiaohan Nie
David Nilsson
Ko Nishino
Zhenxing Niu
Shohei Nobuhara
Klas Nordberg
Mohammed Norouzi
David Novotny
Ifeoma Nwogu
Matthew O'Toole
Guillaume Obozinski
Jean-Marc Odobez
Eyal Ofek
Ferda Ofli
Tae-Hyun Oh
Iason Oikonomidis
Takeshi Oishi
Takahiro Okabe
Takayuki Okatani
Vlad Olaru
Michael Opitz
Jose Oramas
Vicente Ordonez
Ivan Oseledets
Aljosa Osep
Magnus Oskarsson
Martin R. Oswald
Wanli Ouyang
Andrew Owens
Mustafa Özuysal
Jinshan Pan
Xingang Pan
Rameswar Panda
Sharath Pankanti
Julien Pansiot
Nicolas Papadakis
George Papandreou
N. Papanikolopoulos
Hyun Soo Park
In Kyu Park
Jaesik Park
Omkar Parkhi
Alvaro Parra Bustos
C. Alejandro Parraga
Vishal Patel
Deepak Pathak
Ioannis Patras
Viorica Patraucean
Genevieve Patterson
Kim Pedersen
Robert Peharz
Selen Pehlivan
Xi Peng
Bojan Pepik
Talita Perciano
Federico Pernici
Adrian Peter
Stavros Petridis
Vladimir Petrovic
Henning Petzka
Tomas Pfister
Trung Pham
Justus Piater
Massimo Piccardi
Sudeep Pillai
Pedro Pinheiro
Lerrel Pinto
Bernardo Pires
Aleksis Pirinen
Fiora Pirri
Leonid Pischulin
Tobias Ploetz
Bryan Plummer
Yair Poleg
Jean Ponce
Gerard Pons-Moll
Jordi Pont-Tuset
Alin Popa
Fatih Porikli
Horst Possegger
Viraj Prabhu
Andrea Prati
Maria Priisalu
Véronique Prinet
Victor Prisacariu
Jan Prokaj
Nicolas Pugeault
Luis Puig
Ali Punjani
Senthil Purushwalkam
Guido Pusiol
Guo-Jun Qi
Xiaojuan Qi
Hongwei Qin
Shi Qiu
Faisal Qureshi
Matthias Rüther
Petia Radeva
Umer Rafi
Rahul Raguram
Swaminathan Rahul
Varun Ramakrishna
Kandan Ramakrishnan
Ravi Ramamoorthi
Vignesh Ramanathan
Vasili Ramanishka
R. Ramasamy Selvaraju
Rene Ranftl
Carolina Raposo
Nikhil Rasiwasia
Nalini Ratha
Sai Ravela
Avinash Ravichandran
Ramin Raziperchikolaei
Sylvestre-Alvise Rebuffi
Adria Recasens
Joe Redmon
Timo Rehfeld
Michal Reinstein
Konstantinos Rematas
Haibing Ren
Shaoqing Ren
Wenqi Ren
Zhile Ren
Hamid Rezatofighi
Nicholas Rhinehart
Helge Rhodin
Elisa Ricci
Eitan Richardson
Stephan Richter

Gernot Riegler
Hayko Riemenschneider
Tammy Riklin Raviv
Ergys Ristani
Tobias Ritschel
Mariano Rivera
Samuel Rivera
Antonio Robles-Kelly
Ignacio Rocco
Jason Rock
Emanuele Rodola
Mikel Rodriguez
Gregory Rogez
Marcus Rohrbach
Gemma Roig
Javier Romero
Olaf Ronneberger
Amir Rosenfeld
Bodo Rosenhahn
Guy Rosman
Arun Ross
Samuel Rota Bulò
Peter Roth
Constantin Rothkopf
Sebastien Roy
Amit Roy-Chowdhury
Ognjen Rudovic
Adria Ruiz
Javier Ruiz-del-Solar
Christian Rupprecht
Olga Russakovsky
Chris Russell
Alexandre Sablayrolles
Fereshteh Sadeghi
Ryusuke Sagawa
Hideo Saito
Elham Sakhaee
Albert Ali Salah
Conrad Sanderson
Koppal Sanjeev
Aswin Sankaranarayanan
Elham Saraee
Jason Saragih
Sudeep Sarkar
Imari Sato
Shin'ichi Satoh
Torsten Sattler
Bogdan Savchynskyy
Johannes Schönberger
Hanno Scharr
Walter Scheirer
Bernt Schiele
Frank Schmidt
Tanner Schmidt
Dirk Schnieders
Samuel Schulter
William Schwartz
Alexander Schwing
Ozan Sener
Soumyadip Sengupta
Laura Sevilla-Lara
Mubarak Shah
Shishir Shah
Fahad Shahbaz Khan
Amir Shahroudy
Jing Shao
Xiaowei Shao
Roman Shapovalov
Nataliya Shapovalova
Ali Sharif Razavian
Gaurav Sharma
Mohit Sharma
Pramod Sharma
Viktoriia Sharmanska
Eli Shechtman
Mark Sheinin
Evan Shelhamer
Chunhua Shen
Li Shen
Wei Shen
Xiaohui Shen
Xiaoyong Shen
Ziyi Shen
Lu Sheng
Baoguang Shi
Boxin Shi
Kevin Shih
Hyunjung Shim
Ilan Shimshoni
Young Min Shin
Koichi Shinoda
Matthew Shreve
Tianmin Shu
Zhixin Shu
Kaleem Siddiqi
Gunnar Sigurdsson
Nathan Silberman
Tomas Simon
Abhishek Singh
Gautam Singh
Maneesh Singh
Praveer Singh
Richa Singh
Saurabh Singh
Sudipta Sinha
Vladimir Smutny
Noah Snavely
Cees Snoek
Kihyuk Sohn
Eric Sommerlade
Sanghyun Son
Bi Song
Shiyu Song
Shuran Song
Xuan Song
Yale Song
Yang Song
Yibing Song
Lorenzo Sorgi
Humberto Sossa
Pratul Srinivasan
Michael Stark
Bjorn Stenger
Rainer Stiefelhagen
Joerg Stueckler
Jan Stuehmer
Hang Su
Hao Su
Shuochen Su
R. Subramanian
Yusuke Sugano
Akihiro Sugimoto
Baochen Sun
Chen Sun
Jian Sun
Jin Sun
Lin Sun
Min Sun

Qing Sun
Zhaohui Sun
David Suter
Eran Swears
Raza Syed Hussain
T. Syeda-Mahmood
Christian Szegedy
Duy-Nguyen Ta
Tolga Taşdizen
Hemant Tagare
Yuichi Taguchi
Ying Tai
Yu-Wing Tai
Jun Takamatsu
Hugues Talbot
Toru Tamak
Robert Tamburo
Chaowei Tan
Meng Tang
Peng Tang
Siyu Tang
Wei Tang
Junli Tao
Ran Tao
Xin Tao
Makarand Tapaswi
Jean-Philippe Tarel
Maxim Tatarchenko
Bugra Tekin
Demetri Terzopoulos
Christian Theobalt
Diego Thomas
Rajat Thomas
Qi Tian
Xinmei Tian
YingLi Tian
Yonghong Tian
Yonglong Tian
Joseph Tighe
Radu Timofte
Massimo Tistarelli
Sinisa Todorovic
Pavel Tokmakov
Giorgos Tolias
Federico Tombari
Tatiana Tommasi
Chetan Tonde
Xin Tong
Akihiko Torii
Andrea Torsello
Florian Trammer
Du Tran
Quoc-Huy Tran
Rudolph Triebel
Alejandro Troccoli
Leonardo Trujillo
Tomasz Trzcinski
Sam Tsai
Yi-Hsuan Tsai
Hung-Yu Tseng
Vagia Tsiminaki
Aggeliki Tsoli
Wei-Chih Tu
Shubham Tulsiani
Fred Tung
Tony Tung
Matt Turek
Oncel Tuzel
Georgios Tzimiropoulos
Ilkay Ulusoy
Osman Ulusoy
Dmitry Ulyanov
Paul Upchurch
Ben Usman
Evgeniya Ustinova
Himanshu Vajaria
Alexander Vakhitov
Jack Valmadre
Ernest Valveny
Jan van Gemert
Grant Van Horn
Jagannadan Varadarajan
Gul Varol
Sebastiano Vascon
Francisco Vasconcelos
Mayank Vatsa
Javier Vazquez-Corral
Ramakrishna Vedantam
Ashok Veeraraghavan
Andreas Veit
Raviteja Vemulapalli
Jonathan Ventura
Matthias Vestner
Minh Vo
Christoph Vogel
Michele Volpi
Carl Vondrick
Sven Wachsmuth
Toshikazu Wada
Michael Waechter
Catherine Wah
Jacob Walker
Jun Wan
Boyu Wang
Chen Wang
Chunyu Wang
De Wang
Fang Wang
Hongxing Wang
Hua Wang
Jiang Wang
Jingdong Wang
Jinglu Wang
Jue Wang
Le Wang
Lei Wang
Lezi Wang
Liang Wang
Lichao Wang
Lijun Wang
Limin Wang
Liwei Wang
Naiyan Wang
Oliver Wang
Qi Wang
Ruiping Wang
Shenlong Wang
Shu Wang
Song Wang
Tao Wang
Xiaofang Wang
Xiaolong Wang
Xinchao Wang
Xinggang Wang
Xintao Wang
Yang Wang
Yu-Chiang Frank Wang
Yu-Xiong Wang

Zhaowen Wang
Zhe Wang
Anne Wannenwetsch
Simon Warfield
Scott Wehrwein
Donglai Wei
Ping Wei
Shih-En Wei
Xiu-Shen Wei
Yichen Wei
Xie Weidi
Philippe Weinzaepfel
Longyin Wen
Eric Wengrowski
Tomas Werner
Michael Wilber
Rick Wildes
Olivia Wiles
Kyle Wilson
David Wipf
Kwan-Yee Wong
Daniel Worrall
John Wright
Baoyuan Wu
Chao-Yuan Wu
Jiajun Wu
Jianxin Wu
Tianfu Wu
Xiaodong Wu
Xiaohe Wu
Xinxiao Wu
Yang Wu
Yi Wu
Ying Wu
Yuxin Wu
Zheng Wu
Stefanie Wuhrer
Yin Xia
Tao Xiang
Yu Xiang
Lei Xiao
Tong Xiao
Yang Xiao
Cihang Xie
Dan Xie
Jianwen Xie
Jin Xie
Lingxi Xie
Pengtao Xie
Saining Xie
Wenxuan Xie
Yuchen Xie
Bo Xin
Junliang Xing
Peng Xingchao
Bo Xiong
Fei Xiong
Xuehan Xiong
Yuanjun Xiong
Chenliang Xu
Danfei Xu
Huijuan Xu
Jia Xu
Weipeng Xu
Xiangyu Xu
Yan Xu
Yuanlu Xu
Jia Xue
Tianfan Xue
Erdem Yörük
Abhay Yadav
Deshraj Yadav
Payman Yadollahpour
Yasushi Yagi
Toshihiko Yamasaki
Fei Yan
Hang Yan
Junchi Yan
Junjie Yan
Sijie Yan
Keiji Yanai
Bin Yang
Chih-Yuan Yang
Dong Yang
Herb Yang
Jianchao Yang
Jianwei Yang
Jiaolong Yang
Jie Yang
Jimei Yang
Jufeng Yang
Linjie Yang
Michael Ying Yang
Ming Yang
Ruiduo Yang
Ruigang Yang
Shuo Yang
Wei Yang
Xiaodong Yang
Yanchao Yang
Yi Yang
Angela Yao
Bangpeng Yao
Cong Yao
Jian Yao
Ting Yao
Julian Yarkony
Mark Yatskar
Jinwei Ye
Mao Ye
Mei-Chen Yeh
Raymond Yeh
Serena Yeung
Kwang Moo Yi
Shuai Yi
Alper Yılmaz
Lijun Yin
Xi Yin
Zhaozheng Yin
Xianghua Ying
Ryo Yonetani
Donghyun Yoo
Ju Hong Yoon
Kuk-Jin Yoon
Chong You
Shaodi You
Aron Yu
Fisher Yu
Gang Yu
Jingyi Yu
Ke Yu
Licheng Yu
Pei Yu
Qian Yu
Rong Yu
Shoou-I Yu
Stella Yu
Xiang Yu

Yang Yu
Zhiding Yu
Ganzhao Yuan
Jing Yuan
Junsong Yuan
Lu Yuan
Stefanos Zafeiriou
Sergey Zagoruyko
Amir Zamir
K. Zampogiannis
Andrei Zanfir
Mihai Zanfir
Pablo Zegers
Eyasu Zemene
Andy Zeng
Xingyu Zeng
Yun Zeng
De-Chuan Zhan
Cheng Zhang
Dong Zhang
Guofeng Zhang
Han Zhang
Hang Zhang
Hanwang Zhang
Jian Zhang
Jianguo Zhang
Jianming Zhang
Jiawei Zhang
Junping Zhang
Lei Zhang
Linguang Zhang
Ning Zhang
Qing Zhang
Quanshi Zhang
Richard Zhang
Runze Zhang
Shanshan Zhang
Shiliang Zhang
Shu Zhang
Ting Zhang
Xiangyu Zhang
Xiaofan Zhang
Xu Zhang
Yimin Zhang
Yinda Zhang
Yongqiang Zhang
Yuting Zhang
Zhanpeng Zhang
Ziyu Zhang
Bin Zhao
Chen Zhao
Hang Zhao
Hengshuang Zhao
Qijun Zhao
Rui Zhao
Yue Zhao
Enliang Zheng
Liang Zheng
Stephan Zheng
Wei-Shi Zheng
Wenming Zheng
Yin Zheng
Yinqiang Zheng
Yuanjie Zheng
Guangyu Zhong
Bolei Zhou
Guang-Tong Zhou
Huiyu Zhou
Jiahuan Zhou
S. Kevin Zhou
Tinghui Zhou
Wengang Zhou
Xiaowei Zhou
Xingyi Zhou
Yin Zhou
Zihan Zhou
Fan Zhu
Guangming Zhu
Ji Zhu
Jiejie Zhu
Jun-Yan Zhu
Shizhan Zhu
Siyu Zhu
Xiangxin Zhu
Xiatian Zhu
Yan Zhu
Yingying Zhu
Yixin Zhu
Yuke Zhu
Zhenyao Zhu
Liansheng Zhuang
Zeeshan Zia
Karel Zimmermann
Daniel Zoran
Danping Zou
Qi Zou
Silvia Zuffi
Wangmeng Zuo
Xinxin Zuo

Contents – Part V

Poster Session

Poster Session

Snap Angle Prediction for 360° Panoramas

Bo Xiong[1(✉)] and Kristen Grauman[2]

[1] University of Texas at Austin, Austin, USA
bxiong@cs.utexas.edu
[2] Facebook AI Research, Austin, USA
grauman@fb.com

Abstract. 360° panoramas are a rich medium, yet notoriously difficult to visualize in the 2D image plane. We explore how intelligent rotations of a spherical image may enable content-aware projection with fewer perceptible distortions. Whereas existing approaches assume the viewpoint is fixed, intuitively some viewing angles within the sphere preserve high-level objects better than others. To discover the relationship between these optimal *snap angles* and the spherical panorama's content, we develop a reinforcement learning approach for the cubemap projection model. Implemented as a deep recurrent neural network, our method selects a sequence of rotation actions and receives reward for avoiding cube boundaries that overlap with important foreground objects. We show our approach creates more visually pleasing panoramas while using 5x less computation than the baseline.

Keywords: 360° panoramas · Content-aware projection
Foreground objects

1 Introduction

The recent emergence of inexpensive and lightweight 360° cameras enables exciting new ways to capture our visual surroundings. Unlike traditional cameras that capture only a limited field of view, 360° cameras capture the entire visual world from their optical center. Advances in virtual reality technology and promotion from social media platforms like YouTube and Facebook are further boosting the relevance of 360° data.

However, viewing 360° content presents its own challenges. Currently three main directions are pursued: manual navigation, field-of-view (FOV) reduction,

K. Grauman—On leave from University of Texas at Austin (grauman@cs.utexas.edu).

Electronic supplementary material The online version of this chapter (https://doi.org/10.1007/978-3-030-01228-1_1) contains supplementary material, which is available to authorized users.

V. Ferrari et al. (Eds.): ECCV 2018, LNCS 11209, pp. 3–20, 2018.
https://doi.org/10.1007/978-3-030-01228-1_1

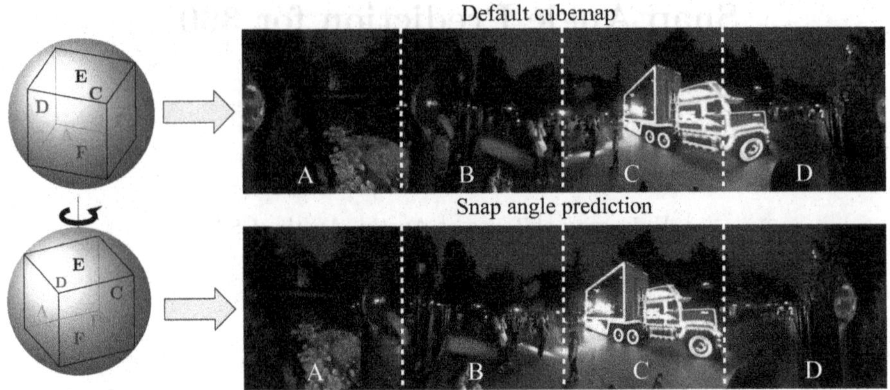

Fig. 1. Comparison of a cubemap before and after snap angle prediction (dotted lines separate each face). Unlike prior work that assumes a fixed angle for projection, we propose to predict the cube rotation that will best preserve foreground objects in the output. For example, here our method better preserves the truck (third picture C in the second row). We show four (front, right, left, and back) out of the six faces for visualization purposes. Best viewed in color or pdf.

and content-based projection. In manual navigation scenarios, a human viewer chooses which normal field-of-view subwindow to observe, e.g., via continuous head movements in a VR headset, or mouse clicks on a screen viewing interface. In contrast, FOV reduction methods generate normal FOV videos by learning to render the most interesting or capture-worthy portions of the viewing sphere [1–4]. While these methods relieve the decision-making burden of manual navigation, they severely limit the information conveyed by discarding all unselected portions. Projection methods render a wide-angle view, or the entire sphere, onto a single plane (e.g., equirectangular or Mercator) [5] or multiple planes [6]. While they avoid discarding content, any projection inevitably introduces distortions that can be unnatural for viewers. Content-based projection methods can help reduce perceived distortions by prioritizing preservation of straight lines, conformality, or other low-level cues [7–9], optionally using manual input to know what is worth preserving [10–14].

However, all prior automatic content-based projection methods implicitly assume that the *viewpoint* of the input 360° image is fixed. That is, the spherical image is processed in some default coordinate system, e.g., as the equirectangular projection provided by the camera manufacturer. This assumption limits the quality of the output image. Independent of the content-aware projection eventually used, a fixed viewpoint means some *arbitrary portions of the original sphere will be relegated to places where distortions are greatest*—or at least where they will require most attention by the content-aware algorithm to "undo".

We propose to eliminate the fixed viewpoint assumption. Our key insight is that an intelligently chosen viewing angle can immediately lessen distortions, even when followed by a conventional projection approach. In particular, we consider the widely used cubemap projection [6,15,16]. A cubemap visualizes the entire sphere by first mapping the sphere to a cube with rectilinear projection (where each face captures a 90° FOV) and then unfolding the faces of the cube. Often, an important object can be projected across two cube faces, destroying object integrity. In addition, rectilinear projection distorts content near cube face boundaries more. See Fig. 1, top. However, intuitively, some viewing angles—some cube orientations—are less damaging than others.

We introduce an approach to automatically predict *snap angles*: the rotation of the cube that will yield a set of cube faces that, among all possible rotations, most look like nicely composed human-taken photos originating from the given 360° panoramic image. While what comprises a "well-composed photo" is itself the subject of active research [17–21], we concentrate on a high-level measure of good composition, where the goal is to consolidate each (automatically detected) foreground object within the bounds of one cubemap face. See Fig. 1, bottom.

Accordingly, we formalize our snap angle objective in terms of minimizing the spatial mass of foreground objects near cube edges. We develop a reinforcement learning (RL) approach to infer the optimal snap angle given a 360° panorama. We implement the approach with a deep recurrent neural network that is trained end-to-end. The sequence of rotation "actions" chosen by our RL network can be seen as a *learned* coarse-to-fine adjustment of the camera viewpoint, in the same spirit as how people refine their camera's orientation just before snapping a photo.

We validate our approach on a variety of 360° panorama images. Compared to several informative baselines, we demonstrate that (1) snap angles better preserve important objects, (2) our RL solution efficiently pinpoints the best snap angle, (3) cubemaps unwrapped after snap angle rotation suffer less perceptual distortion than the status quo cubemap, and (4) snap angles even have potential to impact recognition applications, by orienting 360° data in ways that better match the statistics of normal FOV photos used for today's pretrained recognition networks.

2 Related Work

Spherical Image Projection Spherical image projection models project either a limited FOV [7,22] or the entire panorama [5,6,23]. The former group includes rectilinear and Pannini [7] projection; the latter includes equirectangular, stereographic, and Mercator projections (see [5] for a review). Rectilinear and Pannini prioritize preservation of lines in various ways, but always independent of the specific input image. Since any projection of the full sphere must incur distortion, multi-view projections can be perceptually stronger than a single global projection [23]. Cubemap [6], the subject of our snap angle approach, is a multi-view projection method; as discussed above, current approaches simply consider a cubemap in its default orientation.

Content-Aware Projection Built on spherical projection methods, content-based projections make image-specific choices to reduce distortion. Recent work [8] optimizes the parameters in the Pannini projection [7] to preserve regions with greater low-level saliency and straight lines. Interactive methods [10–13] require a user to outline regions of interest that should be preserved or require input from a user to determine projection orientation [14]. Our approach is content-based and fully automatic. Whereas prior automatic methods assume a fixed viewpoint for projection, we propose to actively predict snap angles for rendering. Thus, our idea is orthogonal to 360° content-aware projection. Advances in the projection method could be applied in concert with our algorithm, e.g., as post-processing to enhance the rotated faces further. For example, when generating cubemaps, one could replace rectilinear projection with others [7,8,10] and keep the rest of our learning framework unchanged. Furthermore, the proposed snap angles respect high-level image content—detected foreground objects—as opposed to typical lower-level cues like line straightness [10,12] or low-level saliency metrics [8].

Viewing Wide-Angle Panoramas Since viewing 360° and wide-angle data is non-trivial, there are vision-based efforts to facilitate. The system of [24] helps efficient exploration of gigapixel panoramas. More recently, several systems automatically extract normal FOV videos from 360° video, "piloting" a virtual camera by selecting the viewing angle and/or zoom level most likely to interest a human viewer [1–4].

Recurrent Networks for Attention Though treating very different problems than ours, multiple recent methods incorporate deep recurrent neural networks (RNN) to make sequential decisions about where to focus attention. The influential work of [25] learns a policy for visual attention in image classification. Active perception systems use RNNs and/or reinforcement learning to select places to look in a novel image [26,27], environment [28–30], or video [31–34] to detect certain objects or activities efficiently. Broadly construed, we share the general goal of efficiently converging on a desired target "view", but our problem domain is entirely different.

3 Approach

We first formalize snap angle prediction as an optimization problem (Sect. 3.1). Then present our learning framework and network architecture for snap angle prediction (Sect. 3.2).

We concentrate on the cubemap projection [6]. Recall that a cubemap maps the sphere to a cube with rectilinear projection (where each face captures a 90° FOV) and then unfolds the six faces of the cube. The unwrapped cube can be visualized as an unfolded box, with the lateral strip of four faces being spatially contiguous in the scene (see Fig. 1, bottom). We explore our idea with cubemaps for a couple reasons. First, a cubemap covers the entire 360° content and does not discard any information. Secondly, each cube face is very similar to a conventional FOV, and therefore relatively easy for a human to view and/or edit.

3.1 Problem Formulation

We first formalize snap angle prediction as an optimization problem. Let $P(I, \theta)$ denote a projection function that takes a panorama image I and a projection angle θ as input and outputs a cubemap after rotating the sphere (or equivalently the cube) by θ. Let function F be an objective function that takes a cubemap as input and outputs a score to measure the quality of the cubemap. Given a novel panorama image I, our goal is to minimize F by predicting the snap angle θ^*:

$$\theta^* = \operatorname*{argmin}_{\theta} F(P(I, \theta)). \tag{1}$$

The projection function P first transforms the coordinates of each point in the panorama based on the snap angle θ and then produces a cubemap in the standard manner.

Views from a horizontal camera position (elevation 0°) are more informative than others due to human recording bias. The bottom and top cube faces often align with the sky (above) and ground (below); "stuff" regions like sky, ceiling, and floor are thus common in these faces and foreground objects are minimal. Therefore, rotations in azimuth tend to have greater influence on the disruption caused by cubemap edges. Hence, without loss of generality, we focus on snap angles in azimuth only, and jointly optimize the front/left/right/back faces of the cube.

The coordinates for each point in a panorama can be represented by a pair of latitude and longitude (λ, φ). Let L denote a coordinate transformation function that takes the snap angle θ and a pair of coordinates as input. We define the coordinate transformation function L as:

$$L((\lambda, \varphi), \theta) = (\lambda, \varphi - \theta). \tag{2}$$

Note when the snap angle is 90°, the orientation of the cube is the same as the default cube except the order of front, back, right, and left is changed. We therefore restrict $\theta \in [0, \pi/2]$. We discretize the space of candidate angles for θ into a uniform $N = 20$ azimuths grid, which we found offers fine enough camera control.

We next discuss our choice of the objective function F. A cubemap in its default orientation has two disadvantages: (1) It does not guarantee to project each important object onto the same cube face; (2) Due to the nature of the perspective projection, objects projected onto cube boundaries will be distorted more than objects in the center. Motivated by these shortcomings, our goal is to produce cubemaps that *place each important object in a single face* and avoid placing objects at the cube boundaries/edges.

In particular, we propose to minimize the area of foreground objects near or on cube boundaries. Supposing each pixel in a cube face is automatically labeled as either object or background, our objective F measures *the fraction of pixels that are labeled as foreground near cube boundaries.* A pixel is near cube boundaries if it is less than $A\%$ of the cube length away from the left, right, or top boundary. We do not penalize objects near the bottom boundary since

Fig. 2. Pixel objectness [35] foreground map examples. White pixels in the pixel objectness map indicate foreground. Our approach learns to find cubemap orientations where the foreground objects are not disrupted by cube edges, i.e., each object falls largely within one face.

it is common to place objects near the bottom boundary in photography (e.g., potraits).

To infer which pixels belong to the foreground, we use "pixel objectness" [35]. Pixel objectness is a CNN-based foreground estimation approach that returns pixel-wise estimates for all foreground object(s) in the scene, no matter their category. While other foreground methods are feasible (e.g., [36–40]), we choose pixel objectness due to its accuracy in detecting foreground objects of any category, as well as its ability to produce a single pixel-wise foreground map which can contain multiple objects. Figure 2 shows example pixel objectness foreground maps on cube faces. We apply pixel objectness to a given projected cubemap to obtain its pixel objectness score. In conjunction, other measurements for photo quality, such as interestingness [20], memorability [18], or aesthetics [41], could be employed within F.

3.2 Learning to Predict Snap Angles

On the one hand, a direct regression solution would attempt to infer θ^* directly from I. However, this is problematic because good snap angles can be multi-modal, i.e., available at multiple directions in the sphere, and thus poorly suited for regression. On the other hand, a brute force solution would require projecting the panorama to a cubemap and then evaluating F for every possible projection angle θ, which is costly.

We instead address snap angle prediction with reinforcement learning. The task is a time-budgeted sequential decision process—an iterative adjustment of the (virtual) camera rotation that homes in on the least distorting viewpoint for

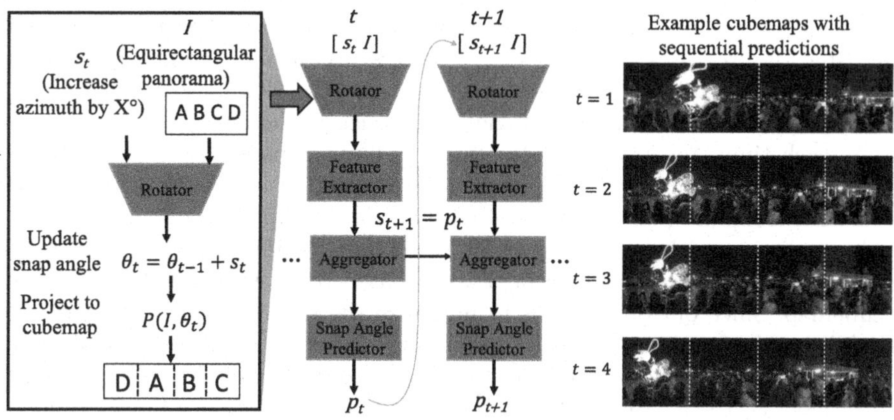

Fig. 3. We show the rotator (left), our model (middle), and a series of cubemaps produced by our sequential predictions (right). Our method iteratively refines the best snap angle, targeting a given budget of allowed computation.

cubemap projection. Actions are cube rotations and rewards are improvements to the pixel objectness score F. Loosely speaking, this is reminiscent of how people take photos with a coarse-to-fine refinement towards the desired composition. However, unlike a naive coarse-to-fine search, our approach learns to trigger different search strategies depending on what is observed, as we will demonstrate in results.

Specifically, let T represent the budget given to our system, indicating the number of rotations it may attempt. We maintain a history of the model's previous predictions. At each time step t, our framework takes a relative snap prediction s_t (for example, s_t could signal to update the azimuth by 45°) and updates its previous snap angle $\theta_t = \theta_{t-1} + s_t$. Then, based on its current observation, our system makes a prediction p_t, which is used to update the snap angle in the next time step. That is, we have $s_{t+1} = p_t$. Finally, we choose the snap angle with the lowest pixel objectness objective score from the history as our final prediction $\hat{\theta}$:

$$\hat{\theta} = \underset{\theta_t=\theta_1,\ldots,\theta_T}{\operatorname{argmin}} F(P(I, \theta_t)). \tag{3}$$

To further improve efficiency, one could compute pixel objectness *once* on a cylindrical panorama rather than recompute it for every cubemap rotation, and then proceed with the iterative rotation predictions above unchanged. However, learned foreground detectors [35,37–40] are trained on Web images in rectilinear projection, and so their accuracy can degrade with different distortions. Thus we simply recompute the foreground for each cubemap reprojection. See Sect. 4.1 for run-times.

Network We implement our reinforcement learning task with deep recurrent and convolutional neural networks. Our framework consists of four modules: a *rotator*, a *feature extractor*, an *aggregator*, and a *snap angle predictor*. At each time step, it processes the data and produces a cubemap (*rotator*), extracts learned features (*feature extractor*), integrates information over time (*aggregator*), and predicts the next snap angle (*snap angle predictor*).

At each time step t, the *rotator* takes as input a panorama I in equirectangular projection and a relative snap angle prediction $s_t = p_{t-1}$, which is the prediction from the previous time step. The *rotator* updates its current snap angle prediction with $\theta_t = \theta_{t-1} + s_t$. We set $\theta_1 = 0$ initially. Then the *rotator* applies the projection function P to I based on θ_t with Eq. 2 to produce a cubemap. Since our objective is to minimize the total amount of foreground straddling cube face boundaries, it is more efficient for our model to learn directly from the pixel objectness map than from raw pixels. Therefore, we apply pixel objectness [35] to each of the four lateral cube faces to obtain a binary objectness map per face. The rotator has the form: $\mathbb{I}^{W\times H\times 3} \times \Theta \rightarrow \mathbb{B}^{W_c\times W_c\times 4}$, where W and H are the width and height of the input panorama in equirectangular projection and W_c denotes the side length of a cube face. The *rotator* does not have any learnable parameters since it is used to preprocess the input data.

At each time step t, the *feature extractor* then applies a sequence of convolutions to the output of the *rotator* to produce a feature vector f_t, which is then fed into the *aggregator* to produce an aggregate feature vector $a_t = A(f_1, ..., f_t)$ over time. Our *aggregator* is a recurrent neural network (RNN), which also maintains its own hidden state.

Finally, the *snap angle predictor* takes the aggregate feature vector as input, and produces a relative snap angle prediction p_t. In the next time step $t+1$, the relative snap angle prediction is fed into the *rotator* to produce a new cubemap. The *snap angle predictor* contains two fully connected layers, each followed by a ReLU, and then the output is fed into a softmax function for the N azimuth candidates. The N candidates here are relative, and range from decreasing azimuth by $\frac{N}{2}$ to increasing azimuth by $\frac{N}{2}$. The *snap angle predictor* first produces a multinomial probability density function $\pi(p_t)$ over all candidate relative snap angles, then it samples one snap angle prediction proportional to the probability density function. See Fig. 3 for an overview of the network, and Supp. for all architecture details.

Training The parameters of our model consist of parameters of the *feature extractor*, *aggregator*, and *snap angle predictor*: $w = \{w_f, w_a, w_p\}$. We learn them to maximize the total reward (defined below) our model can expect when predicting snap angles. The *snap angle predictor* contains stochastic units and therefore cannot be trained with the standard backpropagation method. We therefore use REINFORCE [42]. Let $\pi(p_t|I, w)$ denote the parameterized policy, which is a pdf over all possible snap angle predictions. REINFORCE iteratively increases weights in the pdf $\pi(p_t|I, w)$ on those snap angles that have received higher rewards. Formally, given a batch of training data $\{I_i : i = 1, \ldots, M\}$, we can approximate the gradient as follows:

$$\sum_{i=1}^{M}\sum_{t=1}^{T}\nabla_w \log \pi(p_t^i|I_i, w)R_t^i \tag{4}$$

where R_t^i denotes the reward at time t for instance i.

Reward At each time step t, we compute the objective. Let $\hat{\theta}_t = \text{argmin}_{\theta=\theta_1,\ldots\theta_t} F(P(I,\theta))$ denote the snap angle with the lowest pixel objectness until time step t. Let $O_t = F(P(I,\hat{\theta}_t))$ denote its corresponding objective value. The reward for time step t is

$$\hat{R}_t = \min(O_t - F(P(I,\theta_t + p_t)), 0). \tag{5}$$

Thus, the model receives a reward proportional to the decrease in edge-straddling foreground pixels whenever the model updates the snap angle. To speed up training, we use a variance-reduced version of the reward $R_t = \hat{R}_t - b_t$ where b_t is the average amount of decrease in pixel objectness coverage with a random policy at time t.

4 Results

Our results address **four main questions**: (1) How efficiently can our approach identify the best snap angle? (Sect. 4.1); (2) To what extent does the foreground "pixel objectness" objective properly capture objects important to human viewers? (Sect. 4.2); (3) To what extent do human viewers favor snap-angle cubemaps over the default orientation? (Sect. 4.3); and (4) Might snap angles aid image recognition? (Sect. 4.4).

Dataset We collect a dataset of 360° images to evaluate our approach; existing 360° datasets are topically narrow [1,3,43], restricting their use for our goal. We use YouTube with the 360° filter to gather videos from four activity categories—Disney, Ski, Parade, and Concert. After manually filtering out frames with only text or blackness, we have 150 videos and 14,076 total frames sampled at 1 FPS.

Implementation Details We implement our model with Torch, and optimize with stochastic gradient and REINFORCE. We set the base learning rate to 0.01 and use momentum. We fix $A = 6.25\%$ for all results after visual inspection of a few human-taken cubemaps (not in the test set). See Supp. for all network architecture details.

4.1 Efficient Snap Angle Prediction

We first evaluate our snap angle prediction framework. We use all 14,076 frames, 75% for training and 25% for testing. We ensure testing and training data do *not* come from the same video. We define the following baselines:

- RANDOM ROTATE: Given a budget T, predict T snap angles randomly (with no repetition).
- UNIFORM ROTATE: Given a budget T, predict T snap angles uniformly sampled from all candidates. When $T = 1$, UNIFORM receives the CANONICAL view. This is a strong baseline since it exploits the human recording bias in the starting view. Despite the 360° range of the camera, photographers still tend to direct the "front" of the camera towards interesting content, in which case CANONICAL has some manual intelligence built-in.
- COARSE-TO-FINE SEARCH: Divide the search space into two uniform intervals and search the center snap angle in each interval. Then recursively search the better interval, until the budget is exhausted.
- PANO2VID(P2V) [1]-ADAPTED: We implement a snap angle variant inspired by the pipeline of Pano2Vid [1]. We replace C3D [44] features (which require video) used in [1] with F7 features from VGG [45] and train a logistic classifier to learn "capture-worthiness" [1] with Web images and randomly sampled panorama subviews (see Supp.). For a budget T, we evaluate T "glimpses" and choose the snap angle with the highest encountered capture-worthiness score. We stress that Pano2Vid addresses a different task: it creates a normal field-of-view video (discarding the rest) whereas we create a well-oriented omnidirectional image. Nonetheless, we include this baseline to test their general approach of learning a framing prior from human-captured data.
- SALIENCY: Select the angle that centers a cube face around the maximal saliency region. Specifically, we compute the panorama's saliency map [40] in equirectangular form and blur it with a Gaussian kernel. We then identify the $P \times P$ pixel square with the highest total saliency value, and predict the snap angle as the center of the square. Unlike the other methods, this baseline is not iterative, since the maximal saliency region does not change with rotations. We use a window size $P = 30$. Performance is not sensitive to P for $20 \leq P \leq 200$.

We train our approach for a spectrum of budgets T, and report results in terms of the amount of foreground disruption as a function of the budget. Each unit of the budget corresponds to one round of rotating, re-rendering, and predicting foregrounds. We score foreground disruption as the average $F(P(I, \theta_t^*))$ across all four faces.

Figure 4 (left) shows the results. Our method achieves the least disruptions to foreground regions among all the competing methods. UNIFORM ROTATE and COARSE-TO-FINE SEARCH perform better than RANDOM because they benefit from hand-designed search heuristics. Unlike UNIFORM ROTATE and COARSE-TO-FINE SEARCH, our approach is content-based and learns to trigger different search strategies depending on what it observes. When $T = 1$, SALIENCY is better than RANDOM but it underperforms our method and UNIFORM. SALIENCY likely has difficulty capturing important objects in panoramas, since the saliency model is trained with standard field-of-view images. Directly adapting PANO2VID [1] for our problem results in unsatisfactory results. A capture-worthiness classifier [1] is relatively insensitive to the placement of important objects/people and

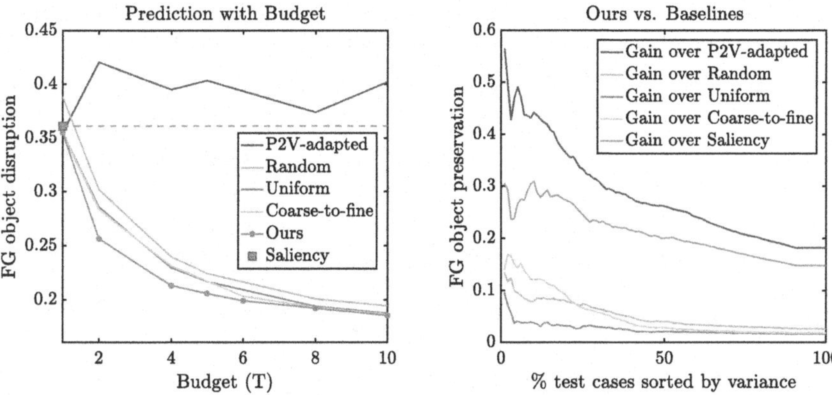

Fig. 4. Predicting snap angles in a timely manner. Left: Given a budget, our method predicts snap angles with the least foreground disruption on cube edges. Gains are larger for smaller budgets, demonstrating our method's efficiency. Right: Our gain over the baselines (for a budget $T = 4$) as a function of the test cases' decreasing "difficulty", i.e., the variance in ground truth quality for candidate angles. See text.

therefore less suitable for the snap angle prediction task, which requires detailed modeling of object placement on *all* faces of the cube.

Figure 4 (right) plots our gains sorted by the test images' decreasing "difficulty" for a budget $T = 4$. In some test images, there is a high variance, meaning certain snap angles are better than others. However, for others, all candidate rotations look similarly good, in which case all methods will perform similarly. The righthand plot sorts the test images by their variance (in descending order) in quality across all possible angles, and reports our method's gain as a function of that difficulty. Our method outperforms P2V-ADAPTED, SALIENCY, COARSE-TO-FINE SEARCH, RANDOM and UNIFORM by up to 56%, 31%, 17%, 14% and 10% (absolute), respectively. Overall Fig. 4 demonstrates that our method predicts the snap angle more efficiently than the baselines.

We have thus far reported efficiency in terms of abstract budget usage. One unit of budget entails the following: projecting a typical panorama of size 960×1920 pixels in equirectangular form to a cubemap (8.67 s with our Matlab implementation) and then computing pixel objectness (0.57 s). Our prediction method is very efficient and takes 0.003 seconds to execute for a budget $T = 4$ with a GeForce GTX 1080 GPU. Thus, for a budget $T = 4$, the savings achieved by our method is approximately 2.4 min (5x speedup) per image compared to exhaustive search. Note that due to our method's efficiency, even if the Matlab projections were 1000x faster for all methods, our 5x speedup over the baseline would remain the same. Our method achieves a good tradeoff between speed and accuracy.

Table 1. Performance on preserving the integrity of objects explicitly identified as important by human observers. Higher overlap scores are better. Our method outperforms all baselines.

	CANONICAL	RANDOM	SALIENCY	P2V-ADAPTED	OURS	UPPERBOUND
Concert	77.6%	73.9%	76.2%	71.6%	**81.5%**	86.3%
Ski	64.1%	72.5%	68.1%	70.1%	**78.6%**	83.5%
Parade	84.0%	81.2%	86.3%	85.7%	**87.6%**	96.8%
Disney	58.3%	57.7%	60.8%	60.8%	**65.5%**	77.4%
All	74.4%	74.2%	76.0%	75.0%	**81.1%**	88.3%

4.2 Justification for Foreground Object Objective

Next we justify empirically the pixel objectness cube-edge objective. To this end, we have human viewers identify important objects in the source panoramas, then evaluate to what extent our objective preserves them.

Specifically, we randomly select 340 frames among those where: (1) Each frame is at least 10-s apart from the rest in order to ensure diversity in the dataset; (2) The difference in terms of overall pixel objectness between our method and the canonical view method is non-neglible. We collect annotations via Amazon Mechanical Turk. Following the interface of [3], we present crowdworkers the panorama and instruct them to label any "important objects" with a bounding box—as many as they wish. See Supp. for interface and annotation statistics.

Here we consider PANO2VID(P2V) [1]-ADAPTED and SALIENCY as defined in Sect. 4.1 and two additional baselines: (1) CANONICAL VIEW: produces a cubemap using the camera-provided orientation; (2) RANDOM VIEW: rotates the input panorama by an arbitrary angle and then generates the cubemap. Note that the other baselines in Sect. 4.1 are not applicable here, since they are search mechanisms.

Consider the cube face X that contains the largest number of foreground pixels from a given bounding box after projection. We evaluate the cubemaps of our method and the baselines based on the overlap score (IoU) between the foreground region from the cube face X and the corresponding human-labeled important object, for each bounding box. This metric is maximized when all pixels for the same object project to the same cube face; higher overlap indicates better preservation of important objects.

Table 1 shows the results. Our method outperforms all baselines by a large margin. This supports our hypothesis that avoiding foreground objects along the cube edges helps preserve objects of interest to a viewer. Snap angles achieve this goal much better than the baseline cubemaps. The UPPERBOUND corresponds to the maximum possible overlap achieved if exhaustively evaluating *all* candidate angles, and helps gauge the difficulty of each category. Parade and Disney have the highest and lowest upper bounds, respectively. In Disney images, the camera is often carried by the recorders, so important objects/persons appear relatively large in the panorama and cannot fit in a single cube face, hence a lower upper bound score. On the contrary, in Parade images the camera is often placed in the crowd and far away from important objects, so each can be confined to a single face. The latter also explains why the baselines do best (though still weaker than ours) on Parade images. An ablation study decoupling the pixel objectness performance from snap angle performance pinpoints the effects of foreground quality on our approach (see Supp.).

Table 2. User study result comparing cubemaps outputs for perceived quality. Left: Comparison between our method and CANONICAL. Right: Comparison between our method and RANDOM.

	Prefer OURS	Tie	Prefer CANONICAL	Prefer OURS	Tie	Prefer RANDOM
Parade	54.8%	16.5%	28.7%	70.4%	9.6%	20.0%
Concert	48.7%	16.2%	35.1%	52.7%	16.2%	31.1%
Disney	44.8%	17.9%	37.3%	72.9%	8.5%	18.6%
Ski	64.3%	8.3%	27.4%	62.9%	16.1%	21.0%
All	53.8%	14.7%	31.5%	65.3%	12.3%	22.4%

Table 3. Memorability and aesthetics scores.

	Concert	Ski	Parade	Disney	All (normalized)
Image memorability [21]					
CANONICAL	**71.58**	69.49	67.08	70.53	46.8%
RANDOM	71.30	69.54	67.27	70.65	48.1%
SALIENCY	71.40	69.60	67.35	70.58	49.9%
P2V-ADAPTED	71.34	69.85	67.44	70.54	52.1%
OURS	71.45	**70.03**	**67.68**	**70.87**	**59.8%**
UPPER	72.70	71.19	68.68	72.15	–
Image aesthetics [17]					
CANONICAL	33.74	41.95	30.24	32.85	44.3%
RANDOM	32.46	41.90	30.65	32.79	42.4%
SALIENCY	34.52	41.87	30.81	32.54	47.9%
P2V-ADAPTED	34.48	41.97	30.86	**33.09**	48.8%
OURS	**35.05**	**42.08**	**31.19**	32.97	**52.9%**
UPPER	38.45	45.76	34.74	36.81	–

4.3 User Study: Perceived Quality

Having justified the perceptual relevance of the cube-edge foreground objective (Sect. 4.2), next we perform a user study to gauge perceptual quality of our results. Do snap angles produce cube faces that look like human-taken photos? We evaluate on the same image set used in Sect. 4.2.

We present cube faces produced by our method and one of the baselines at a time in arbitrary order and inform subjects the two sets are photos from the

Fig. 5. Qualitative examples of default CANONICAL cubemaps and our snap angle cubemaps. Our method produces cubemaps that place important objects/persons in the same cube face to preserve the foreground integrity. Bottom two rows show failure cases. In the bottom left, pixel objectness [35] does not recognize the round stage as foreground, and therefore our method splits the stage onto two different cube faces, creating a distorted heart-shaped stage. In the bottom right, the train is too large to fit in a single cube.

same scene but taken by different photographers. We instruct them to consider composition and viewpoint in order to decide which set of photos is more pleasing (see Supp.). To account for the subjectivity of the task, we issue each sample to 5 distinct workers and aggregate responses with majority vote. 98 unique MTurk crowdworkers participated in the study.

Table 2 shows the results. Our method outperforms the CANONICAL baseline by more than 22% and the RANDOM baseline by 42.9%. This result supports our claim that by preserving object integrity, our method produces cubemaps that align better with human perception of quality photo composition. Figure 5 shows qualitative examples. As shown in the first two examples (top two rows), our method is able to place an important person in the same cube face whereas the baseline splits each person and projects a person onto two cube faces. We also present two failure cases in the last two rows. In the bottom left, pixel objectness does not recognize the stage as foreground, and therefore our method places the stage on two different cube faces, creating a distorted heart-shaped stage. Please see Supp. for pixel objectness map input for failure cases.

So far, Table 1 confirms empirically that our foreground-based objective does preserve those objects human viewers deem important, and Table 2 shows that human viewers have an absolute preference for snap angle cubemaps over other projections. As a final test of snap angle cubemaps' perceptual quality, we score them using state-of-the-art metrics for *aesthetics* [17] and *memorability* [21]. Since both models are trained on images annotated by people (for their aesthetics and memorability, respectively), higher scores indicate higher correlation with these perceived properties (though of course no one learned metric can perfectly represent human opinion).

Table 3 shows the results. We report the raw scores s per class as well as the score over all classes, normalized as $\frac{s-s_{min}}{s_{max}-s_{min}}$, where s_{min} and s_{max} denote the lower and upper bound, respectively. Because the metrics are fairly tolerant to local rotations, there is a limit to how well they can capture subtle differences in cubemaps. Nonetheless, our method outperforms the baselines overall. Given these metrics' limitations, the user study in Table 2 offers the most direct and conclusive evidence for snap angles' perceptual advantage.

4.4 Cubemap Recognition from Pretrained Nets

Since snap angles provide projections that better mimic human-taken photo composition, we hypothesize that they also align better with conventional FOV images, compared to cubemaps in their canonical orientation. This suggests that snap angles may better align with Web photos (typically used to train today's recognition systems), which in turn could help standard recognition models perform well on 360° panoramas. We present a preliminary proof-of-concept experiment to test this hypothesis.

We train a multi-class CNN classifier to distinguish the four activity categories in our 360° dataset (Disney, Parade, etc.). The classifier uses ResNet-101 [46] pretrained on ImageNet [47] and fine-tuned on 300 training images per class downloaded from Google Image Search (see Supp.). Note that in all experiments until now, the category labels on the 360° dataset were invisible to our algorithm. We randomly select 250 panoramas per activity as a test set. Each panorama is projected to a cubemap with the different projection methods, and we compare the resulting recognition rates.

Table 4 shows the results. We report recognition accuracy in two forms: *Single*, which treats each individual cube face as a test instance, and *Pano*, which classifies the entire panorama by multiplying the predicted posteriors from all cube faces. For both cases, snap angles produce cubemaps that achieve the best recognition rate. This result hints at the potential for snap angles to be a bridge between pretrained normal FOV networks on the one hand and 360° images on the other hand. That said, the margin is slim, and the full impact of snap angles for recognition warrants further exploration.

Table 4. Image recognition accuracy (%). Snap angles help align the 360° data's statistics with that of normal FOV Web photos, enabling easier transfer from conventional pretrained networks.

	Canonical	Random	Ours
Single	68.5	69.4	**70.1**
Pano	66.5	67.0	**68.1**

5 Conclusions

We introduced the snap angle prediction problem for rendering 360° images. In contrast to previous work that assumes either a fixed or manually supplied projection angle, we propose to automatically predict the angle that will best preserve detected foreground objects. We present a framework to efficiently and accurately predict the snap angle in novel panoramas. We demonstrate the advantages of the proposed method, both in terms of human perception and several statistical metrics. Future work will explore ways to generalize snap angles to video data and expand snap angle prediction to other projection models.

Acknowledgements. This research is supported in part by NSF IIS-1514118 and a Google Faculty Research Award. We also gratefully acknowledge a GPU donation from Facebook.

References

1. Su, Y.C., Jayaraman, D., Grauman, K.: Pano2Vid: automatic cinematography for watching 360° videos. In: ACCV (2016)
2. Su, Y.C., Grauman, K.: Making 360° video watchable in 2D: learning videography for click free viewing. In: CVPR (2017)
3. Hu, H.N., Lin, Y.C., Liu, M.Y., Cheng, H.T., Chang, Y.J., Sun, M.: Deep 360 pilot: learning a deep agent for piloting through 360° sports videos. In: CVPR (2017)

4. Lai, W.S., Huang, Y., Joshi, N., Buehler, C., Yang, M.H., Kang, S.B.: Semantic-driven generation of hyperlapse from 360° video. IEEE Trans. Vis. Comput. Graph. **24**(9), 2610–2621 (2017)
5. Snyder, J.P.: Flattening the Earth: Two Thousand Years of Map Projections. University of Chicago Press (1997)
6. Greene, N.: Environment mapping and other applications of world projections. IEEE Comput. Graph. Appl. **6**(11), 21–29 (1986)
7. Sharpless, T.K., Postle, B., German, D.M.: Pannini: a new projection for rendering wide angle perspective images. In: International Conference on Computational Aesthetics in Graphics, Visualization and Imaging (2010)
8. Kim, Y.W., Jo, D.Y., Lee, C.R., Choi, H.J., Kwon, Y.H., Yoon, K.J.: Automatic content-aware projection for 360° videos. In: ICCV (2017)
9. Li, D., He, K., Sun, J., Zhou, K.: A geodesic-preserving method for image warping. In: CVPR (2015)
10. Carroll, R., Agrawala, M., Agarwala, A.: Optimizing content-preserving projections for wide-angle images. ACM Trans. Graph. **28**, 43 (2009)
11. Tehrani, M.A., Majumder, A., Gopi, M.: Correcting perceived perspective distortions using object specific planar transformations. In: ICCP (2016)
12. Carroll, R., Agarwala, A., Agrawala, M.: Image warps for artistic perspective manipulation. ACM Trans. Graph. **29**, 127 (2010)
13. Kopf, J., Lischinski, D., Deussen, O., Cohen-Or, D., Cohen, M.: Locally adapted projections to reduce panorama distortions. In: Computer Graphics Forum, Wiley Online Library (2009)
14. Wang, Z., Jin, X., Xue, F., He, X., Li, R., Zha, H.: Panorama to cube: a content-aware representation method. In: SIGGRAPH Asia Technical Briefs (2015)
15. https://code.facebook.com/posts/1638767863078802/under-the-hood-building-360-video/
16. https://www.blog.google/products/google-vr/bringing-pixels-front-and-center-vr-video/
17. Kong, S., Shen, X., Lin, Z., Mech, R., Fowlkes, C.: Photo aesthetics ranking network with attributes and content adaptation. In: Leibe, B., Matas, J., Sebe, N., Welling, M. (eds.) ECCV 2016. LNCS, vol. 9905, pp. 662–679. Springer, Cham (2016). https://doi.org/10.1007/978-3-319-46448-0_40
18. Isola, P., Xiao, J., Torralba, A., Oliva, A.: What makes an image memorable? In: CVPR (2011)
19. Xiong, B., Grauman, K.: Detecting snap points in egocentric video with a web photo prior. In: Fleet, D., Pajdla, T., Schiele, B., Tuytelaars, T. (eds.) ECCV 2014. LNCS, vol. 8693, pp. 282–298. Springer, Cham (2014). https://doi.org/10.1007/978-3-319-10602-1_19
20. Gygli, M., Grabner, H., Riemenschneider, H., Nater, F., Van Gool, L.: The interestingness of images. In: ICCV (2013)
21. Khosla, A., Raju, A.S., Torralba, A., Oliva, A.: Understanding and predicting image memorability at a large scale. In: ICCV (2015)
22. Chang, C.H., Hu, M.C., Cheng, W.H., Chuang, Y.Y.: Rectangling stereographic projection for wide-angle image visualization. In: ICCV (2013)
23. Zelnik-Manor, L., Peters, G., Perona, P.: Squaring the circle in panoramas. In: ICCV (2005)
24. Kopf, J., Uyttendaele, M., Deussen, O., Cohen, M.F.: Capturing and viewing gigapixel images. ACM Trans. Graph. **26**, 93 (2007)
25. Mnih, V., Heess, N., Graves, A., Kavukcuoglu, K.: Recurrent models of visual attention. In: NIPS (2014)

26. Caicedo, J.C., Lazebnik, S.: Active object localization with deep reinforcement learning. In: ICCV (2015)
27. Mathe, S., Pirinen, A., Sminchisescu, C.: Reinforcement learning for visual object detection. In: CVPR (2016)
28. Jayaraman, D., Grauman, K.: Look-ahead before you leap: end-to-end active recognition by forecasting the effect of motion. In: Leibe, B., Matas, J., Sebe, N., Welling, M. (eds.) ECCV 2016. LNCS, vol. 9909, pp. 489–505. Springer, Cham (2016). https://doi.org/10.1007/978-3-319-46454-1_30
29. Jayaraman, D., Grauman, K.: Learning to look around: intelligently exploring unseen environments for unknown tasks. In: CVPR (2018)
30. Jayaraman, D., Grauman, K.: End-to-end policy learning for active visual categorization. PAMI (2018)
31. Yeung, S., Russakovsky, O., Mori, G., Fei-Fei, L.: End-to-end learning of action detection from frame glimpses in videos. In: CVPR (2016)
32. Alwassel, H., Heilbron, F.C., Ghanem, B.: Action search: Learning to search for human activities in untrimmed videos. arXiv preprint arXiv:1706.04269 (2017)
33. Singh, B., Marks, T.K., Jones, M., Tuzel, O., Shao, M.: A multi-stream bi-directional recurrent neural network for fine-grained action detection. In: CVPR (2016)
34. Su, Y.-C., Grauman, K.: Leaving some stones unturned: dynamic feature prioritization for activity detection in streaming video. In: Leibe, B., Matas, J., Sebe, N., Welling, M. (eds.) ECCV 2016. LNCS, vol. 9911, pp. 783–800. Springer, Cham (2016). https://doi.org/10.1007/978-3-319-46478-7_48
35. Xiong, B., Jain, S.D., Grauman, K.: Pixel objectness: learning to segment generic objects automatically in images and videos. PAMI (2018)
36. Zitnick, C.L., Dollár, P.: Edge boxes: locating object proposals from edges. In: Fleet, D., Pajdla, T., Schiele, B., Tuytelaars, T. (eds.) ECCV 2014. LNCS, vol. 8693, pp. 391–405. Springer, Cham (2014). https://doi.org/10.1007/978-3-319-10602-1_26
37. Carreira, J., Sminchisescu, C.: CPMC: automatic object segmentation using constrained parametric min-cuts. PAMI **34**(7), 1312–1328 (2011)
38. Jiang, P., Ling, H., Yu, J., Peng, J.: Salient region detection by UFO: uniqueness, focusness, and objectness. In: ICCV (2013)
39. Pinheiro, P.O., Collobert, R., Dollár, P.: Learning to segment object candidates. In: NIPS (2015)
40. Liu, T., et al.: Learning to detect a salient object. PAMI **33**(2), 353–367 (2011)
41. Dhar, S., Ordonez, V., Berg, T.L.: High level describable attributes for predicting aesthetics and interestingness. In: CVPR (2011)
42. Williams, R.J.: Simple statistical gradient-following algorithms for connectionist reinforcement learning. Mach. Learn. **8**(3–4), 229–256 (1992)
43. Xiao, J., Ehinger, K.A., Oliva, A., Torralba, A.: Recognizing scene viewpoint using panoramic place representation. In: CVPR (2012)
44. Tran, D., Bourdev, L., Fergus, R., Torresani, L., Paluri, M.: Learning spatiotemporal features with 3D convolutional networks. In: ICCV (2015)
45. Simonyan, K., Zisserman, A.: Very deep convolutional networks for large-scale image recognition. CoRR abs/1409.1556 (2014)
46. He, K., Zhang, X., Ren, S., Sun, J.: Deep residual learning for image recognition. In: CVPR (2016)
47. Russakovsky, O., et al.: Imagenet large scale visual recognition challenge. IJCV **115**(3), 211–252 (2015)

Unsupervised Holistic Image Generation from Key Local Patches

Donghoon Lee[1(✉)], Sangdoo Yun[2], Sungjoon Choi[1], Hwiyeon Yoo[1], Ming-Hsuan Yang[3,4], and Songhwai Oh[1]

[1] Electrical and Computer Engineering and ASRI, Seoul National University, Seoul, South Korea
dorucia@gmail.com
[2] Clova AI Research, NAVER, Bundang-gu, South Korea
[3] Electrical Engineering and Computer Science, University of California at Merced, Merced, USA
[4] Google Cloud AI, Mountain View, USA

Abstract. We introduce a new problem of generating an image based on a small number of key local patches without any geometric prior. In this work, key local patches are defined as informative regions of the target object or scene. This is a challenging problem since it requires generating realistic images and predicting locations of parts at the same time. We construct adversarial networks to tackle this problem. A generator network generates a fake image as well as a mask based on the encoder-decoder framework. On the other hand, a discriminator network aims to detect fake images. The network is trained with three losses to consider spatial, appearance, and adversarial information. The spatial loss determines whether the locations of predicted parts are correct. Input patches are restored in the output image without much modification due to the appearance loss. The adversarial loss ensures output images are realistic. The proposed network is trained without supervisory signals since no labels of key parts are required. Experimental results on seven datasets demonstrate that the proposed algorithm performs favorably on challenging objects and scenes.

Keywords: Image synthesis · Generative adversarial networks

1 Introduction

The goal of image generation is to construct images that are as barely distinguishable from target images which may contain general objects, diverse scenes, or human drawings. Synthesized images can contribute to a number of applications such as the image to image translation [7], image super-resolution [13],

Electronic supplementary material The online version of this chapter (https://doi.org/10.1007/978-3-030-01228-1_2) contains supplementary material, which is available to authorized users.

V. Ferrari et al. (Eds.): ECCV 2018, LNCS 11209, pp. 21–37, 2018.
https://doi.org/10.1007/978-3-030-01228-1_2

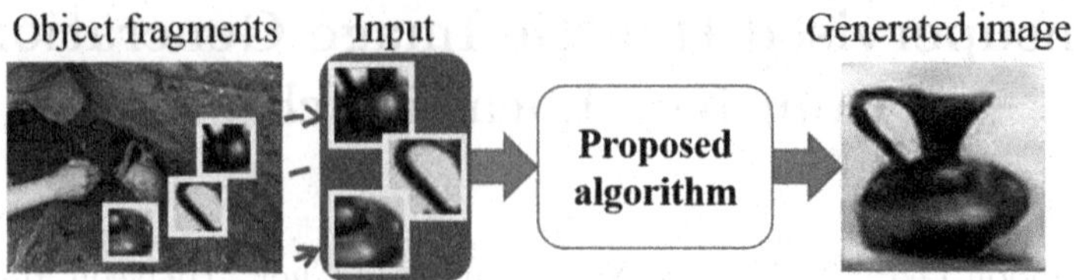

Fig. 1. The proposed algorithm is able to synthesize an image from key local patches without geometric priors, e.g., restoring broken pieces of ancient ceramics found in ruins. Convolutional neural networks are trained to predict locations of input patches and generate the entire image based on adversarial learning.

3D object modeling [36], unsupervised domain adaptation [15], domain transfer [39], future frame prediction [33], image inpainting [38], image editing [43], and feature recovering of astrophysical images [29].

In this paper, we introduce a new image generation problem: a holistic image generation conditioned on a small number of local patches of objects or scenes without any geometry prior. It aims to estimate what and where object parts are needed to appear and how to fill in the remaining regions. There are various applications for this problem. For example, in a surveillance system, objects are often occluded and we need to recover the whole appearance from limited information. For augmented reality, by rendering plausible scenes based on a few objects, the experience of users become more realistic and diverse. Combining parts of different objects can generate various images in a target category, e.g., designing a new car based on parts of BMW and Porsche models. Broken objects that have missing parts can be restored as shown in Fig. 1. While the problem is related to image completion and scene understanding tasks, it is more general and challenging than each of these problems due to following reasons.

First, spatial arrangements of input patches need to be inferred since the data does not contain explicit information about the location. To tackle this issue, we assume that inputs are key local patches which are informative regions of the target image. Therefore, the algorithm should learn the spatial relationship between key parts of an object or scene. Our approach obtains key regions without any supervision such that the whole algorithm is developed within the unsupervised learning framework.

Second, we aim to generate an image while preserving the key local patches. As shown in Fig. 1, the appearances of input patches are included in the generated image without significant modification. In other words, the inputs are not directly copied to the output image. It allows us to create images more flexibly such that we can combine key patches of different objects as inputs. In such cases, input patches must be deformed by considering each other.

Third, the generated image should look closely to a real image in the target category. Unlike the image inpainting problem, which mainly replaces small regions or eliminates minor defects, our goal is to reconstruct a holistic image based on limited appearance information contained in a few patches.

To address the above issues, we adopt the adversarial learning scheme [4] in this work. The generative adversarial network (GAN) contains two networks which are trained based on the min-max game of two players. A generator network typically generates fake images and aims to fool a discriminator, while a discriminator network seeks to distinguish fake images from real images. In our case, the generator network is also responsible for predicting the locations of input patches. Based on the generated image and predicted mask, we design three losses to train the network: a spatial loss, an appearance loss, and an adversarial loss, corresponding to the aforementioned issues, respectively.

While a conventional GAN is trained in an unsupervised manner, some recent methods formulate it in a supervised manner by using labeled information. For example, a GAN is trained with a dataset that has 15 or more joint positions of birds [25]. Such labeling task is labor intensive since GAN-based algorithms need a large amount of training data to achieve high-quality results. In contrast, experiments on seven challenging datasets that contain different objects and scenes, such as faces, cars, flowers, ceramics, and waterfalls, demonstrate that the proposed unsupervised algorithm generates realistic images and predict part locations well. In addition, even if inputs contain parts from different objects, our algorithm is able to generate reasonable images.

The main contributions are as follows. First, we introduce a new problem of rendering realistic image conditioned on the appearance information of a few key patches. Second, we develop a generative network to jointly predict the mask and image without supervision to address the defined problem. Third, we propose a novel objective function using additional fake images to strengthen the discriminator network. Finally, we provide new datasets that contain challenging objects and scenes.

2 Related Work

Image Generation. Image generation is an important problem that has been studied extensively in computer vision. With the recent advances in deep convolutional neural networks [12,31], numerous image generation methods have achieved the state-of-the-art results. Dosovitskiy et al. [3] generate 3D objects by learning transposed convolutional neural networks. In [10], Kingma et al. propose a method based on variational inference for stochastic image generation. An attention model is developed by Gregor et al. [5] to generate an image using a recurrent neural network. Recently, the stochastic PixelCNN [21] and PixelRNN [22] are introduced to generate images sequentially.

The generative adversarial network [4] is proposed for generating sharp and realistic images based on two competing networks: a generator and a discriminator. Numerous methods [28,42] have been proposed to improve the stability of the GAN. Radford et al. [24] propose deep convolutional generative adversarial networks (DCGAN) with a set of constraints to generate realistic images effectively. Based on the DCGAN architecture, Wang et al. [34] develop a model to generate the style and structure of indoor scenes (SSGAN), and Liu et al. [15]

present a coupled GAN which learns a joint distribution of multi-domain images, such as color and depth images.

Conditional GAN. Conditional GAN approaches [18,26,40] are developed to control the image generation process with label information. Mizra et al. [18] propose a class-conditional GAN which uses discrete class labels as the conditional information. The GAN-CLS [26] and StackGAN [40] embed a text describing an image into the conditional GAN to generate an image corresponding to the condition. On the other hand, the GAWWN [25] creates numerous plausible images based on the location of key points or an object bounding box. In these methods, the conditional information, e.g., text, key points, and bounding boxes, is provided in the training data. However, it is labor intensive to label such information since deep generative models require a large amount of training data. In contrast, key patches used in the proposed algorithm are obtained without the necessity of human annotation.

Numerous image conditional models based on GANs have been introduced recently [7,13,14,23,30,38,39,43]. These methods learn a mapping from the source image to target domain, such as image super-resolution [13], user interactive image manipulation [43], product image generation from a given image [39], image inpainting [23,38], style transfer [14] and realistic image generation from synthetic image [30]. Isola et al. [7] tackle the image-to-image translation problem including various image conversion examples such as day image to night image, gray image to color image, and sketch image to real image, by utilizing the U-net [27] and GAN. In contrast, the problem addressed in this paper is the holistic image generation based on only a small number of local patches. This challenging problem cannot be addressed by existing image conditional methods as the domain of the source and target images are different.

Unsupervised Image Context Learning. Unsupervised learning of the spatial context in an image [2,20,23] has attracted attention to learn rich feature representations without human annotations. Doersch et al. [2] train convolutional neural networks to predict the relative position between two neighboring patches in an image. The neighboring patches are selected from a grid pattern based on the image context. To reduce the ambiguity of the grid, Noroozi et al. [20] divide the image into a large number of tiles, shuffle the tiles, and then learn a convolutional neural network to solve the jigsaw puzzle problem. Pathak et al. [23] address the image inpainting problem which predicts missing pixels in an image, by training a context encoder. Through the spatial context learning, the trained networks are successfully applied to various applications such as object detection, classification and semantic segmentation. However, discriminative models [2,20] can only infer the spatial arrangement of input patches, and the image inpainting method [23] requires the spatial information of the missing pixels. In contrast, we propose a generative model which is capable of not only inferring the spatial arrangement of inputs but also generating the entire image.

Image Reconstruction from Local Information. Weinzaepfel et al. [35] reconstruct an image from local descriptors such as SIFT while the locations are

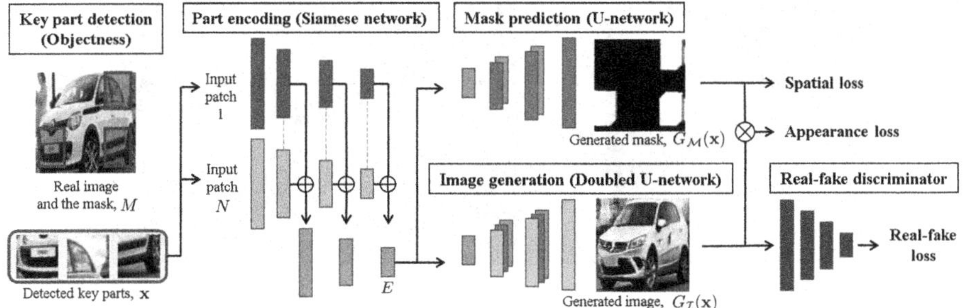

Fig. 2. Proposed network architecture. A bar represents a layer in the network. Layers of the same size and the same color have the same convolutional feature maps. Dashed lines in part encoding networks represent shared weights. An embedded vector is denoted as E. (Color figure online)

known. This method retrieves an image patch for each region of interest from a database based on the similarity of local descriptors. These patches are then warped into a single image and stitched seamlessly. Zhang et al. [41] extrapolate an image from a limited field of view to a panoramic image. An input image is aligned with a guidance panorama image such that the unseen viewpoint is predicted based on self-similarity.

3 Proposed Algorithm

Figure 2 shows the structure of the proposed network for image generation from a few patches. It is developed based on the concept of adversarial learning, where a generator and a discriminator compete with each other [4]. However, in the proposed network, the generator has two outputs: the predicted mask and generated image. Let $G_{\mathcal{M}}$ be a mapping from N observed image patches $\mathbf{x} = \{x_1, ..., x_N\}$ to a mask M, $G_{\mathcal{M}} : \mathbf{x} \rightarrow M$.[1] Also let $G_{\mathcal{I}}$ be a mapping from $\mathbf{x}$ to an output image y, $G_{\mathcal{I}} : \mathbf{x} \rightarrow y$. These mappings are performed based on three networks: a part encoding network, a mask prediction network, and an image generation network. The discriminator D is based on a convolutional neural network which aims to distinguish the real image from the image generated by $G_{\mathcal{I}}$. The function of each described module is essential in order to address the proposed problem. For example, it is not feasible to infer which region in the generated image should be similar to the input patches without the mask prediction network.

We use three losses to train the network. The first loss is the spatial loss $\mathcal{L}_S$. It compares the inferred mask and real mask which represents the cropped region of the input patches. The second loss is the appearance loss $\mathcal{L}_A$, which maintains input key patches in the generated image without much modification.

[1] Here, $\mathbf{x}$ is a set of image patches resized to the same width and height suitable for the proposed network and N is the number of image patches in $\mathbf{x}$.

Fig. 3. Examples of detected key patches on faces [16], vehicles [11], flowers [19], and waterfall scenes. Three regions with top scores from the EdgeBox algorithm are shown in red boxes after pruning candidates of an extreme size or aspect ratio. (Color figure online)

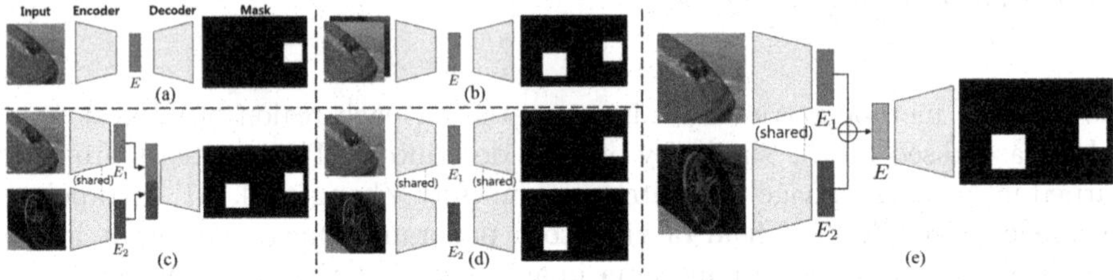

Fig. 4. Different structures of networks to predict a mask from input patches. We choose (e) as our encoder-decoder model.

The third loss is the adversarial loss $\mathcal{L}_R$ to distinguish fake and real images. The whole network is trained by the following min-max game:

$$\min_{G_\mathcal{M}, G_\mathcal{I}} \max_D \mathcal{L}_R(G_\mathcal{I}, D) + \lambda_1 \mathcal{L}_S(G_\mathcal{M}) + \lambda_2 \mathcal{L}_A(G_\mathcal{M}, G_\mathcal{I}), \tag{1}$$

where λ_1 and λ_2 are weights for the spatial loss and appearance loss, respectively.

3.1 Key Part Detection

We define key patches as informative local regions to generate the entire image. For example, when generating a face image, patches of eyes and a nose are more informative than those of the forehead and cheeks. Therefore, it would be better for the key patches to contain important parts that can describe objects in a target class. However, detecting such regions is a challenging problem as it requires to possess high-level concepts of the image. Although there exist methods to find most representative and discriminative regions [1,32], these schemes are limited to the detection or classification problems. In this paper, we only assume that key parts can be obtained based on the objectness score. The objectness score allows us to exclude most regions without textures or full of simple edges which unlikely contain key parts. In particular, we use the Edgebox algorithm [44] to detect key patches of general objects in an unsupervised manner. In addition, we discard detected patches with extreme sizes or aspect ratios. Figure 3 shows examples of detected key patches from various objects and scenes. Overall, the detected regions from these object classes are fairly informative. We sort candidate regions by the objectness score and feed the top N patches to the proposed network. In addition, the training images and corresponding key patches are augmented using a random left-right flip with the equal probability.

3.2 Part Encoding Network

The structure of the generator is based on the encoder-decoder network [6]. It uses convolutional layers as an encoder to reduce the dimension of the input data until the bottleneck layer. Then, transposed convolutional layers upsample the embedded vector to its original size. For the case with a single input, the network has a simple structure as shown in Fig. 4(a). For the case with multiple inputs as considered in the proposed network, there are many possible structures. In this work, we carefully examine four cases while noting that our goal is to encode information invariant to the ordering of image patches.

The first network is shown in Fig. 4(b), which uses depth-concatenation of multiple patches. This is a straightforward extension of the single input case. However, it is not suitable for the task considered in this work. Regardless of the order of input patches, the same mask should be generated when the patches have the same appearance. Therefore, the embedded vector E must be the same for all different orderings of inputs. Nevertheless, the concatenation causes the network to depend on the ordering, while key patches have an arbitrary order since they are sorted by the objectness score. In this case, the part encoding network cannot learn proper filters. The same issue arises in the model in Fig. 4(c). On the other hand, there are different issues with the network in Fig. 4(d). While it can resolve the ordering issue, it predicts a mask of each input independently, which is not desirable as we aim to predict masks jointly. The network should consider the appearance of both input patches to predict positions. To address the above issues, we propose to use the network in Fig. 4(e). It encodes multiple patches based on a Siamese-style network and summarizes all results in a single descriptor by the summation, i.e., $E = E_1 + ... + E_N$. Due to the commutative property, we can predict a mask jointly, even if inputs have an arbitrary order. In addition to the final bottleneck layer, we use all convolutional feature maps in the part encoding network to construct U-net [27] style architectures as shown in Fig. 2.

3.3 Mask Prediction Network

The U-net is an encoder-decoder network that has skip connections between i-th encoding layer and $(L - i)$-th decoding layer, where L is the total number of layers. It directly feeds the information from an encoding layer to its corresponding decoding layer. Therefore, combining the U-net and a generation network is effective when the input and output share the same semantic [7]. In this work, the shared semantic of input patches and the output mask is the target image.

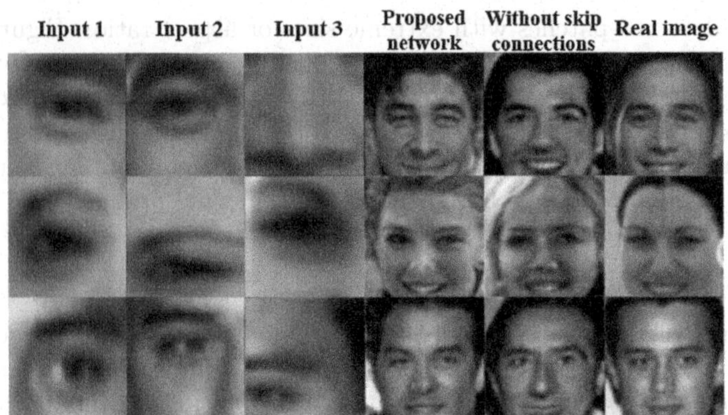

Fig. 5. Sample image generation results on the CelebA dataset using the network in Fig. 2. Generated images are sharper and realistic with the skip connections.

We pose the mask prediction as a regression problem. Based on the embedded part vector E, we use transposed convolutional layers with a fractional stride [24] to upsample the data. The output mask has the same size as the target image and has a value between 0 and 1 at each pixel. Therefore, we use the sigmoid activation function at the last layer.

The spatial loss, $\mathcal{L}_S$, is defined as follows:

$$\mathcal{L}_S(G_{\mathcal{M}}) = \mathbb{E}_{\mathbf{x}\sim p_{data}(\mathbf{x}),M\sim p_{data}(M)}[\|G_{\mathcal{M}}(\mathbf{x}) - M\|_1]. \quad (2)$$

We note that other types of losses, such as the l_2-norm, or more complicated network structures, such as GAN, have been evaluated for mask prediction, and similar results are achieved by these alternative options.

3.4 Image Generation Network

We propose a doubled U-net structure for the image generation task as shown in Fig. 2. It has skip connections from both the part encoding network and mask generation network. In this way, the image generation network can communicate with other networks. This is critical since the generated image should consider the appearance and locations of input patches. Figure 5 shows generated images with and without the skip connections. It shows that the proposed network improves the quality of generated images. In addition, it helps to preserve the appearances of input patches. Based on the generated image and predicted mask, we define the appearance loss $\mathcal{L}_A$ as follows:

$$\mathcal{L}_A(G_{\mathcal{M}}, G_{\mathcal{I}}) = \mathbb{E}_{\mathbf{x},y\sim p_{data}(\mathbf{x},y),M\sim p_{data}(M)}[\|G_{\mathcal{I}}(\mathbf{x}) \otimes G_{\mathcal{M}}(\mathbf{x}) - y \otimes M\|_1], \quad (3)$$

where $\otimes$ is an element-wise product.

3.5 Real-Fake Discriminator Network

A simple discriminator can be trained to distinguish real images from fake images. However, it has been shown that a naive discriminator may cause artifacts [30] or network collapses during training [17]. To address this issue, we propose a new objective function as follows:

$$
\begin{aligned}
\mathcal{L}_R(G_\mathcal{I}, D) = \mathbb{E}_{y \sim p_{data}(y)}[\log D(y)] + \\
& \mathbb{E}_{\mathbf{x}, y, y' \sim p_{data}(\mathbf{x}, y, y'), M \sim p_{data}(M)} \\
& [\log(1 - D(G_\mathcal{I}(\mathbf{x}))) + \\
& \log(1 - D(M \otimes G_\mathcal{I}(\mathbf{x}) + (1 - M) \otimes y)) + \log(1 - D((1 - M) \otimes G_\mathcal{I}(\mathbf{x}) + M \otimes y)) + \\
& \log(1 - D(M \otimes y' + (1 - M) \otimes y)) + \log(1 - D((1 - M) \otimes y' + M \otimes y))],
\end{aligned}
\tag{4}
$$

where y' is a real image randomly selected from the outside of the current mini-batch. When the real image y is combined with the generated image $G_\mathcal{I}(\mathbf{x})$ (line 4–5 in (4)), it should be treated as a fake image as it partially contains the fake image. When two different real images y and y' are combined (line 6–7 in (4)), it is also a fake image although both images are real. It not only enriches training data but also strengthens discriminator by feeding difficult examples.

4 Experiments

Experiments for the CelebA-HQ and CompCars datasets, images are resized to the have the minimum length of 256 pixels on the width or height. For other datasets, images are resized to 128 pixels. Then, key part candidates are obtained using the Edgebox algorithm [44]. We reject candidate boxes that are larger than 25% or smaller than 5% of the image size unless otherwise stated. After that, the non-maximum suppression is applied to remove candidates that are too close with each other. Finally, the image and top N candidates are resized to the target size, $256 \times 256 \times 3$ pixels for the CelebA-HQ and CompCars datasets or $64 \times 64 \times 3$ pixels for other datasets, and fed to the network. The λ_1 and λ_2 are decreased from 10^{-2} to 10^{-4} as the epoch increases. A detailed description of the proposed network structure is described in the supplementary material.

We train the network with a learning rate of 0.0002. As the epoch increases, we decrease λ_1 and λ_2 in (1). With this training strategy, the network focuses on predicting a mask in the beginning, while it becomes more important to generate realistic images in the end. The mini-batch size is 64, and the momentum of the Adam optimizer [9] is set to 0.5. During training, we first update the discriminator network and then update the generator network twice.

As this work introduces a new image generation problem, we carry out extensive experiments to demonstrate numerous potential applications and ablation studies as summarized in Table 1. Due to space limitation, we present some results in the supplementary material. All the source code and datasets will be made available to the public.

Table 1. Setups for numerous experiments in this work.

Experiment	Description
Image generation from key patches	The main experiment of this paper. It aims to generate an entire image from key local patches without knowing their spatial location (Figs. 6, 8 and supplementary materials)
Image generation from random patches	It relaxes the assumption of the input from key patches to random patches. It is more difficult problem than the original task. We show reasonable results with this challenging condition
Part combination	Generating images from patches of different objects. This is a new application of image synthesis as we can combine human faces or design new cars by a patch-level combination (Fig. 9)
Unsupervised feature learning	We perform a classification task based on the feature representation of our trained network. As such, we can classify objects by only using their parts as an input
An alternative objectvie function	It shows the effectiveness of the proposed objective function in (4) compared to the naive GAN loss. Generated images from our loss function is more realistic
An alternative network structure	We evaluate three different network architectures; auto-encoder based approach, conditional GAN based method, and the proposed network without mask prediction network
Different number of input patches	We change the number of input patches for the CelebA dataset. The proposed algorithm renders proper images for a different number of inputs
Degraded input patches	To consider practical scenarios, we degrade the input patches using a noise. Experimental results demonstrate that the trained network is robust to a small amount of noise
User study	As there is no rule of thumb to assess generated images, we carry out user study to evaluate the proposed algorithm quantitatively

4.1 Datasets

The CelebA dataset [16] contains 202,599 celebrity images with large pose variations and background clutters (see Fig. 8(a)). There are 10,177 identities with various attributes, such as eyeglasses, hat, and mustache. We use aligned and cropped face images of 108×108 pixels. The network is trained for 25 epochs.

Based on the CelebA dataset, we use the method [8] to generate a set of high-quality images. The CelebA-HQ dataset consists of 30,000 aligned images of $1,024 \times 1,024$ pixels for human face. The network is trained for 100 epochs.

There are two car datasets [11,37] used in this paper. The CompCars dataset [37] includes images from two scenarios: the web-nature and surveillance-nature

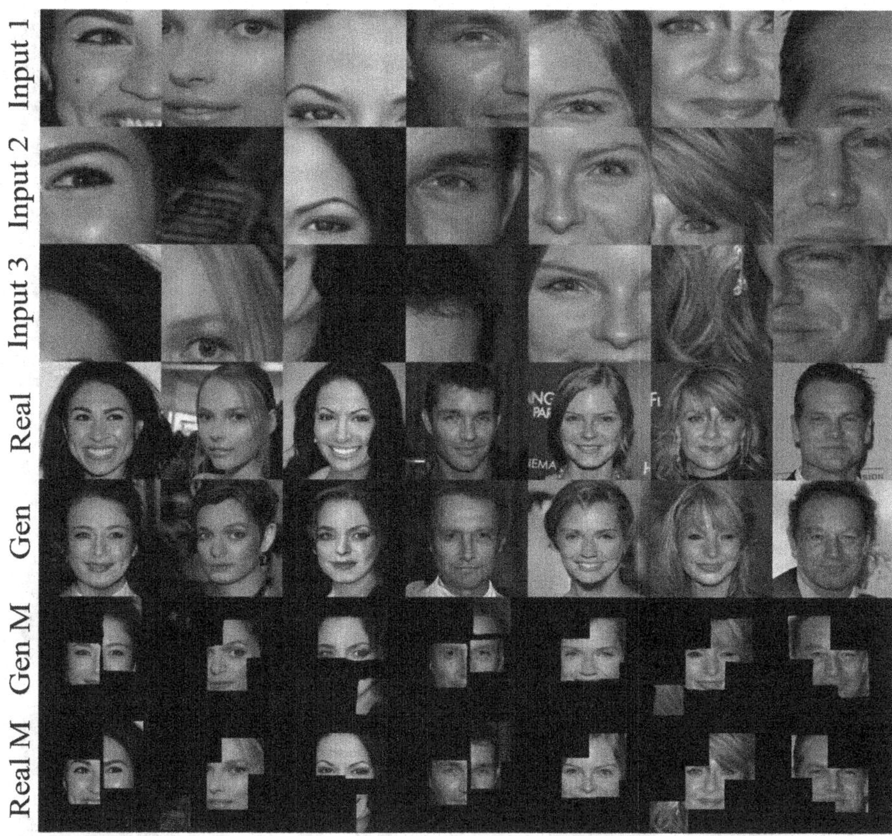

Fig. 6. Generated images and predicted masks on the CelebA-HQ dataset. Three key local patches (Input 1, Input 2, and Input 3) are from a real image (Real). Given inputs, images and masks are generated. We present masked generated images (Gen M) and masked ground truth images (Real M).

(see Fig. 8(c)). The web-nature data contains 136,726 images of 1,716 car models, and the surveillance-nature data contains 50,000 images. The network is trained for 50 epochs to generate 128 × 128 pixels images. To generate high-quality images (256 × 256 pixels), 30,000 training images are used and the network is trained for 300 epochs. The Stanford Cars dataset [11] contains 16,185 images of 196 classes of cars (see Fig. 8(d)). They have different lighting conditions and camera angles. Furthermore, a wide range of colors and shapes, e.g., sedans, SUVs, convertibles, trucks, are included. The network is trained for 400 epochs.

The flower dataset [19] consists of 102 flower categories (see Fig. 8(e)). There is a total of 8,189 images, and each class has between 40 and 258 images. The images contain large variations in the scale, pose, and lighting condition. We train the network for 800 epochs.

Fig. 7. Generated images and predicted masks on the CompCars dataset.

The waterfall dataset consists of 15,323 images taken from various viewpoints (see Fig. 8(b)). It has different types of waterfalls as images are collected from the internet. It also includes other objects such as trees, rocks, sky, and ground, as images are obtained from natural scenes. For this dataset, we allow tall candidate boxes, in which the maximum height is 70% of the image height, to catch long water streams. The network is trained for 100 epochs.

The ceramic dataset is made up of 9,311 side-view images (see Fig. 8(f)). Images of both Eastern-style and Western-style potteries are collected from the internet. The network is trained for 800 epochs.

4.2 Image Generation Results

Figures 6, 7, and 8 shows image generation results of different object classes. Each input has three key patches from a real image and we show both generated

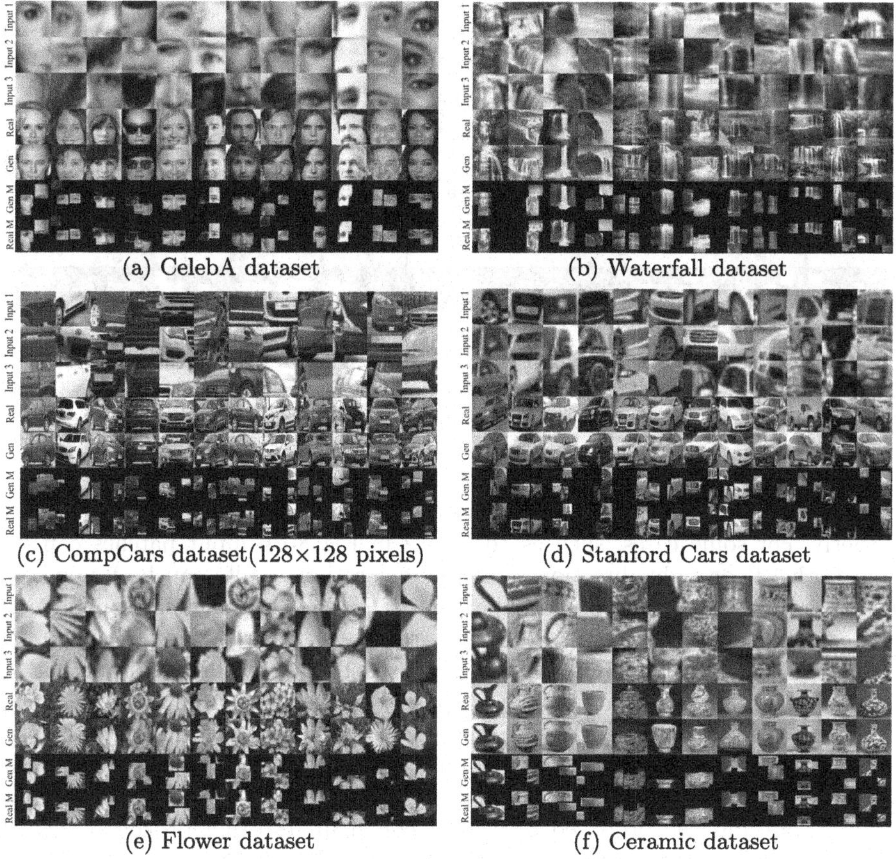

(a) CelebA dataset (b) Waterfall dataset

(c) CompCars dataset(128×128 pixels) (d) Stanford Cars dataset

(e) Flower dataset (f) Ceramic dataset

Fig. 8. Examples of generated masks and images on six datasets.

and original ones for visual comparisons. For all datasets, which contain challenging objects and scenes, the proposed algorithm is able to generate realistic images. Figures 6 and 7 show that the proposed algorithm is able to generate high-resolution images. In addition, input patches are well preserved around their original locations. As shown in the masked images, the proposed problem is a superset of the image inpainting task since known regions are assumed to available in the latter task. While the CelebA-HQ dataset provides high-quality images, we can generate more diverse results on the original CelebA dataset as shown in Fig. 8(a). The subject of the generated face images may have different gender (column 1 and 2), wear a new beanie or sunglasses (column 3 and 4), and become older, chubby, and with new hairstyles (column 5–8). Even when the input key patches are concentrated on the left or right sides, the proposed algorithm can generate realistic images (column 9 and 10). In the CompCars dataset, the shape of car images is mainly generated based on the direction of tire wheels, head lights, and windows. As shown in Figs. 7 and 8(c), the proposed algorithm

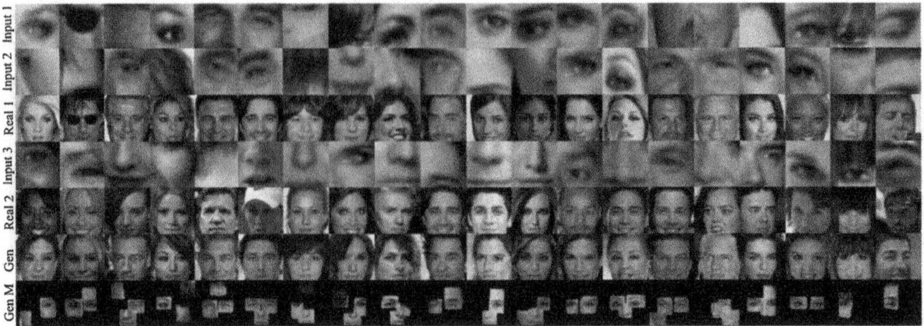

Fig. 9. Results on the CelebA dataset when input patches come from other images. Input 1 and Input 2 are patches from Real 1. Input 3 is a local region of Real 2. Given inputs, the proposed algorithm generates the image (Gen) and mask (Gen M).

can generate various poses and colors of cars while keeping the original patches properly. For some cases, such as column 2 in Fig. 8(c), input patches can be from both left or right directions and the generation results can be flipped. It demonstrates that the proposed algorithm is flexible since the correspondence between the generated mask and input patches, e.g., the left part of the mask corresponds to the left wheel patch, is not needed. Due to the small number of training samples compared to the CompCars dataset, the results of the Stanford Cars dataset are less sharp but still realistic. For the waterfall dataset, the network learns how to draw a new water stream (column 1), a spray from the waterfall (column 3), or other objects such as rock, grass, and puddles (column 10). In addition, the proposed algorithm can help restoring broken pieces of ceramics found in ancient ruins (see Fig. 8(f)).

Figure 9 shows generated images and masks when input patches are obtained from different persons. The results show that the proposed algorithm can handle a wide scope of input patch variations. For example, inputs contain different skin colors in the first column. In this case, it is not desirable to exactly preserve inputs since it will generate a face image with two different skin colors. The proposed algorithm generates an image with a reasonable skin color as well as the overall shape. Other cases include with or without sunglasses (column 2), different skin textures (column 3), hairstyle variations (column 4 and 5), and various expressions and orientations. Despite large variations, the proposed algorithm is able to generate realistic images.

5 Conclusions

We introduce a new problem of generating images based on local patches without geometric priors. Local patches are obtained using the objectness score to retain informative parts of the target image in an unsupervised manner. We propose a generative network to render realistic images from local patches. The part encoding network embeds multiple input patches using a Siamese-style convolutional neural network. Transposed convolutional layers with skip connections from the encoding network are used to predict a mask and generate an image. The discriminator network aims to classify the generated image and the real image. The whole network is trained using the spatial, appearance, and adversarial losses. Extensive experiments show that the proposed network generates realistic images of challenging objects and scenes. As humans can visualize a whole scene with a few visual cues, the proposed network can generate realistic images based on given unordered image patches.

Acknowledgements. The work of D. Lee, S. Choi, H. Yoo, and S. Oh is supported in part by Basic Science Research Program through the National Research Foundation of Korea (NRF) funded by the Ministry of Science and ICT (NRF-2017R1A2B2006136) and by 'The Cross-Ministry Giga KOREA Project' grant funded by the Korea government(MSIT) (No. GK18P0300, Real-time 4D reconstruction of dynamic objects for ultra-realistic service). The work of M.-H. Yang is supported in part by the National Natural Science Foundation of China under Grant #61771288, the NSF CAREER Grant #1149783, and gifts from Adobe and Nvidia.

References

1. Bansal, A., Shrivastava, A., Doersch, C., Gupta, A.: Mid-level elements for object detection. arXiv preprint arXiv:1504.07284 (2015)
2. Doersch, C., Gupta, A., Efros, A.A.: Unsupervised visual representation learning by context prediction. In: Proceedings of the IEEE International Conference on Computer Vision (2015)
3. Dosovitskiy, A., Tobias Springenberg, J., Brox, T.: Learning to generate chairs with convolutional neural networks. In: Proceedings of the IEEE Conference on Computer Vision and Pattern Recognition (2015)
4. Goodfellow, I., et al.: Generative adversarial nets. In: Advances in Neural Information Processing Systems (2014)
5. Gregor, K., Danihelka, I., Graves, A., Rezende, D.J., Wierstra, D.: DRAW: a recurrent neural network for image generation. In: Proceedings of the International Conference on Machine Learning (2015)
6. Hinton, G.E., Salakhutdinov, R.R.: Reducing the dimensionality of data with neural networks. Science **313**(5786), 504–507 (2006)
7. Isola, P., Zhu, J.Y., Zhou, T., Efros, A.A.: Image-to-image translation with conditional adversarial networks. In: Proceedings of the IEEE Conference on Computer Vision and Pattern Recognition (2017)
8. Karras, T., Aila, T., Laine, S., Lehtinen, J.: Progressive growing of GANs for improved quality, stability, and variation. In: Proceedings of the International Conference on Learning Representations (2018)
9. Kingma, D., Ba, J.: Adam: a method for stochastic optimization. In: Proceedings of the International Conference on Learning Representations (2014)
10. Kingma, D.P., Welling, M.: Auto-encoding variational bayes. arXiv preprint arXiv:1312.6114 (2013)
11. Krause, J., Stark, M., Deng, J., Fei-Fei, L.: 3D object representations for fine-grained categorization. In: Proceedings of the IEEE International Conference on Computer Vision Workshops (2013)

12. Krizhevsky, A., Sutskever, I., Hinton, G.E.: Imagenet classification with deep convolutional neural networks. In: Advances in Neural Information Processing Systems (2012)
13. Ledig, C., et al.: Photo-realistic single image super-resolution using a generative adversarial network. In: Proceedings of the IEEE Conference on Computer Vision and Pattern Recognition (2017)
14. Li, C., Wand, M.: Precomputed real-time texture synthesis with markovian generative adversarial networks. In: Leibe, B., Matas, J., Sebe, N., Welling, M. (eds.) ECCV 2016. LNCS, vol. 9907, pp. 702–716. Springer, Cham (2016). https://doi.org/10.1007/978-3-319-46487-9_43
15. Liu, M.Y., Tuzel, O.: Coupled generative adversarial networks. In: Advances in Neural Information Processing Systems (2016)
16. Liu, Z., Luo, P., Wang, X., Tang, X.: Deep learning face attributes in the wild. In: Proceedings of International Conference on Computer Vision (2015)
17. Metz, L., Poole, B., Pfau, D., Sohl-Dickstein, J.: Unrolled generative adversarial networks. In: Proceedings of the International Conference on Learning Representations (2017)
18. Mirza, M., Osindero, S.: Conditional generative adversarial nets. arXiv preprint arXiv:1411.1784 (2014)
19. Nilsback, M.E., Zisserman, A.: Automated flower classification over a large number of classes. In: Proceedings of the IEEE Conference on Computer Vision, Graphics & Image Processing (2008)
20. Noroozi, M., Favaro, P.: Unsupervised learning of visual representations by solving jigsaw puzzles. In: Leibe, B., Matas, J., Sebe, N., Welling, M. (eds.) ECCV 2016. LNCS, vol. 9910, pp. 69–84. Springer, Cham (2016). https://doi.org/10.1007/978-3-319-46466-4_5
21. Oord, A.V.D., Kalchbrenner, N., Espeholt, L., Vinyals, O., Graves, A., et al.: Conditional image generation with pixelcnn decoders. In: Advances in Neural Information Processing Systems (2016)
22. Oord, A.V.D., Kalchbrenner, N., Kavukcuoglu, K.: Pixel recurrent neural networks. In: Proceedings of the International Conference on Machine Learning (2016)
23. Pathak, D., Krähenbühl, P., Donahue, J., Darrell, T., Efros, A.A.: Context encoders: feature learning by inpainting. In: Proceedings of the IEEE Conference on Computer Vision and Pattern Recognition (2016)
24. Radford, A., Metz, L., Chintala, S.: Unsupervised representation learning with deep convolutional generative adversarial networks. arXiv preprint arXiv:1511.06434 (2015)
25. Reed, S., Akata, Z., Mohan, S., Tenka, S., Schiele, B., Lee, H.: Learning what and where to draw. In: Advances In Neural Information Processing Systems (2016)
26. Reed, S., Akata, Z., Yan, X., Logeswaran, L., Schiele, B., Lee, H.: Generative adversarial text to image synthesis. In: Proceedings of the International Conference on Machine Learning (2016)
27. Ronneberger, O., Fischer, P., Brox, T.: U-net: convolutional networks for biomedical image segmentation. In: Navab, N., Hornegger, J., Wells, W.M., Frangi, A.F. (eds.) MICCAI 2015. LNCS, vol. 9351, pp. 234–241. Springer, Cham (2015). https://doi.org/10.1007/978-3-319-24574-4_28
28. Salimans, T., Goodfellow, I., Zaremba, W., Cheung, V., Radford, A., Chen, X.: Improved techniques for training gans. In: Advances in Neural Information Processing Systems (2016)

29. Schawinski, K., Zhang, C., Zhang, H., Fowler, L., Santhanam, G.K.: Generative adversarial networks recover features in astrophysical images of galaxies beyond the deconvolution limit. Mon. Not. R. Astron. Soc. Lett. **467**(1), L110–L114 (2017)
30. Shrivastava, A., Pfister, T., Tuzel, O., Susskind, J., Wang, W., Webb, R.: Learning from simulated and unsupervised images through adversarial training. In: Proceedings of the IEEE Conference on Computer Vision and Pattern Recognition (2017)
31. Simonyan, K., Zisserman, A.: Very deep convolutional networks for large-scale image recognition. arXiv preprint arXiv:1409.1556 (2014)
32. Singh, S., Gupta, A., Efros, A.A.: Unsupervised discovery of mid-level discriminative patches. In: Fitzgibbon, A., Lazebnik, S., Perona, P., Sato, Y., Schmid, C. (eds.) ECCV 2012. LNCS, pp. 73–86. Springer, Heidelberg (2012). https://doi.org/10.1007/978-3-642-33709-3_6
33. Vondrick, C., Pirsiavash, H., Torralba, A.: Generating videos with scene dynamics. In: Advances In Neural Information Processing Systems (2016)
34. Wang, X., Gupta, A.: Generative image modeling using style and structure adversarial networks. In: Leibe, B., Matas, J., Sebe, N., Welling, M. (eds.) ECCV 2016. LNCS, vol. 9908, pp. 318–335. Springer, Cham (2016). https://doi.org/10.1007/978-3-319-46493-0_20
35. Weinzaepfel, P., Jégou, H., Pérez, P.: Reconstructing an image from its local descriptors. In: Proceedings of the IEEE Conference on Computer Vision and Pattern Recognition (2011)
36. Wu, J., Zhang, C., Xue, T., Freeman, B., Tenenbaum, J.: Learning a probabilistic latent space of object shapes via 3D generative-adversarial modeling. In: Advances in Neural Information Processing Systems (2016)
37. Yang, L., Luo, P., Change Loy, C., Tang, X.: A large-scale car dataset for fine-grained categorization and verification. In: Proceedings of the IEEE Conference on Computer Vision and Pattern Recognition (2015)
38. Yeh, R.A., Chen, C., Lim, T.Y., Schwing, A.G., Hasegawa-Johnson, M., Do, M.N.: Semantic image inpainting with deep generative models. In: Proceedings of the IEEE Conference on Computer Vision and Pattern Recognition (2017)
39. Yoo, D., Kim, N., Park, S., Paek, A.S., Kweon, I.S.: Pixel-level domain transfer. In: Leibe, B., Matas, J., Sebe, N., Welling, M. (eds.) ECCV 2016. LNCS, vol. 9912, pp. 517–532. Springer, Cham (2016). https://doi.org/10.1007/978-3-319-46484-8_31
40. Zhang, H., Xu, T., Li, H., Zhang, S., Huang, X., Wang, X., Metaxas, D.: StackGAN: text to photo-realistic image synthesis with stacked generative adversarial networks. In: Proceedings of the IEEE International Conference on Computer Vision (2017)
41. Zhang, Y., Xiao, J., Hays, J., Tan, P.: FrameBreak: dramatic image extrapolation by guided shift-maps. In: Proceedings of the IEEE Conference on Computer Vision and Pattern Recognition (2013)
42. Zhao, J., Mathieu, M., LeCun, Y.: Energy-based generative adversarial network. In: Proceedings of the International Conference on Learning Representations (2017)
43. Zhu, J.-Y., Krähenbühl, P., Shechtman, E., Efros, A.A.: Generative visual manipulation on the natural image manifold. In: Leibe, B., Matas, J., Sebe, N., Welling, M. (eds.) ECCV 2016. LNCS, vol. 9909, pp. 597–613. Springer, Cham (2016). https://doi.org/10.1007/978-3-319-46454-1_36
44. Zitnick, C.L., Dollár, P.: Edge boxes: locating object proposals from edges. In: Fleet, D., Pajdla, T., Schiele, B., Tuytelaars, T. (eds.) ECCV 2014. LNCS, vol. 8693, pp. 391–405. Springer, Cham (2014). https://doi.org/10.1007/978-3-319-10602-1_26

DF-Net: Unsupervised Joint Learning of Depth and Flow Using Cross-Task Consistency

Yuliang Zou[1(✉)], Zelun Luo[2], and Jia-Bin Huang[1]

[1] Virginia Tech, Blacksburg, USA
ylzou@vt.edu
[2] Stanford University, Stanford, USA

Abstract. We present an unsupervised learning framework for simultaneously training single-view depth prediction and optical flow estimation models using unlabeled video sequences. Existing unsupervised methods often exploit brightness constancy and spatial smoothness priors to train depth or flow models. In this paper, we propose to leverage geometric consistency as additional supervisory signals. Our core idea is that for rigid regions we can use the predicted scene depth and camera motion to synthesize 2D optical flow by backprojecting the induced 3D scene flow. The discrepancy between the rigid flow (from depth prediction and camera motion) and the estimated flow (from optical flow model) allows us to impose a cross-task consistency loss. While all the networks are jointly optimized during training, they can be applied independently at test time. Extensive experiments demonstrate that our depth and flow models compare favorably with state-of-the-art unsupervised methods.

1 Introduction

Single-view depth prediction and optical flow estimation are two fundamental problems in computer vision. While the two tasks aim to recover highly correlated information from the scene (i.e., the scene structure and the dense motion field between consecutive frames), existing efforts typically study each problem in isolation. In this paper, we demonstrate the benefits of exploring the geometric relationship between depth, camera motion, and flow for unsupervised learning of depth and flow estimation models.

With the rapid development of deep convolutional neural networks (CNNs), numerous approaches have been proposed to tackle dense prediction problems in an end-to-end manner. However, supervised training CNN for such tasks often involves in constructing large-scale, diverse datasets with dense pixelwise ground truth labels. Collecting such densely labeled datasets in real-world requires significant amounts of human efforts and is prone to error. Existing efforts of RGB-D dataset construction [18,45,53,54] often have limited scope (e.g., in terms

Electronic supplementary material The online version of this chapter (https://doi.org/10.1007/978-3-030-01228-1_3) contains supplementary material, which is available to authorized users.

V. Ferrari et al. (Eds.): ECCV 2018, LNCS 11209, pp. 38–55, 2018.
https://doi.org/10.1007/978-3-030-01228-1_3

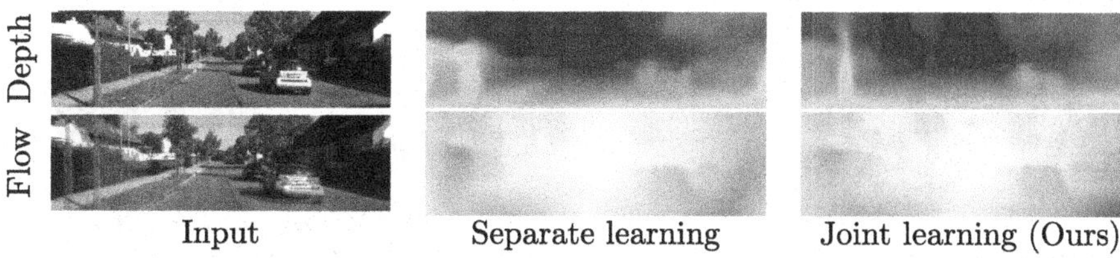

Fig. 1. Joint learning v.s. separate learning. Single-view depth prediction and optical flow estimation are two highly correlated tasks. Existing work, however, often addresses these two tasks in isolation. In this paper, we propose a novel cross-task consistency loss to couple the training of these two problems using unlabeled monocular videos. Through enforcing the underlying geometric constraints, we show substantially improved results for both tasks.

of locations, scenes, and objects), and hence are lack of diversity. For optical flow, dense motion annotations are even more difficult to acquire [37]. Consequently, existing CNN-based methods rely on synthetic datasets for training the models [5,12,16,24]. These synthetic datasets, however, do not capture the complexity of motion blur, occlusion, and natural image statistics from real scenes. The trained models usually do not generalize well to unseen scenes without fine-tuning on sufficient ground truth data in a new visual domain.

Several work [17,21,28] have been proposed to capitalize on large-scale real-world videos to train the CNNs in the unsupervised setting. The main idea lies to exploit the brightness constancy and spatial smoothness assumptions of flow fields or disparity maps as supervisory signals. These assumptions, however, often do not hold at motion boundaries and hence makes the training unstable.

Many recent efforts [59,60,65,73] explore the geometric relationship between the two problems. With the estimated depth and camera pose, these methods can produce dense optical flow by backprojecting the 3D scene flow induced from camera ego-motion. However, these methods implicitly assume *perfect* depth and camera pose estimation when "synthesizing" the optical flow. The errors in either depth or camera pose estimation inevitably produce inaccurate flow predictions.

In this paper, we present a technique for *jointly* learning a single-view depth estimation model and a flow prediction model using unlabeled videos as shown in Fig. 2. Our key observation is that the predictions from depth, pose, and optical flow should be *consistent* with each other. By exploiting this geometry cue, we present a novel cross-task consistency loss that provides additional supervisory signals for training both networks. We validate the effectiveness of the proposed approach through extensive experiments on several benchmark datasets. Experimental results show that our joint training method significantly improves the performance of both models (Fig. 1). The proposed depth and flow models compare favorably with state-of-the-art unsupervised methods.

We make the following contributions. (1) We propose an unsupervised learning framework to *simultaneously* train a depth prediction network and an optical flow network. We achieve this by introducing a cross-task consistency loss that enforces geometric consistency. (2) We show that through the proposed unsu-

Pixelwise ground truth

Unlabeled video sequences (ours)

Fig. 2. Supervised v.s. unsupervised learning. Supervised learning of depth or flow networks requires large amount of training data with pixelwise ground truth annotations, which are difficult to acquire in real scenes. In contrast, our work leverages the readily available *unlabeled* video sequences to jointly train the depth and flow models.

pervised training our depth and flow models compare favorably with existing unsupervised algorithms and achieve competitive performance with supervised methods on several benchmark datasets. (3) We release the source code and pre-trained models to facilitate future research: http://yuliang.vision/DF-Net/.

2 Related Work

Supervised Learning of Depth and Flow. Supervised learning using CNNs has emerged to be an effective approach for depth and flow estimation to avoid hand-crafted objective functions and computationally expensive optimization at test time. The availability of RGB-D datasets and deep learning leads to a line of work on single-view depth estimation [13,14,35,38,62,72]. While promising results have been shown, these methods rely on the *absolute* ground truth depth maps. These depth maps, however, are expensive and difficult to collect. Some efforts [8,74] have been made to relax the difficulty of collecting absolute depth by exploring learning from *relative/ordinal* depth annotations. Recent work also explores gathering training datasets from web videos [7] or Internet photos [36] using structure-from-motion and multi-view stereo algorithms.

Compared to ground truth depth datasets, constructing optical flow datasets of diverse scenes in real-world is even more challenging. Consequently, existing approaches [12,26,47] typically rely on synthetic datasets [5,12] for training. Due to the limited scalability of constructing diverse, high-quality training data, fully supervised approaches often require fine-tuning on sufficient ground truth labels in new visual domains to perform well. In contrast, our approach leverages the readily available real-world videos to jointly train the depth and flow models. The ability to learn from unlabeled data enables unsupervised pre-training for domains with limited amounts of ground truth data.

Self-supervised Learning of Depth and Flow. To alleviate the dependency on large-scale annotated datasets, several works have been proposed to exploit the classical assumptions of brightness constancy and spatial smoothness on the disparity map or the flow field [17,21,28,43,71]. The core idea is to treat the estimated depth and flow as latent layers and use them to differentiably warp the source frame to the target frame, where the source and target frames can either be the stereo pair or two consecutive frames in a video sequence. A photometric loss between the synthesized frame and the target frame can then serve as an unsupervised proxy loss to train the network. Using photometric loss alone, however, is not sufficient due to the ambiguity on textureless regions and occlusion boundaries. Hence, the network training is often unstable and requires careful hyper-parameter tuning of the loss functions. Our approach builds upon existing unsupervised losses for training our depth and flow networks. We show that the proposed cross-task consistency loss provides a sizable performance boost over individually trained models.

Methods Exploiting Geometry Cues. Recently, a number of work exploits the geometric relationship between depth, camera pose, and flow for learning depth or flow models [60,65,68,73]. These methods first estimate the depth of the input images. Together with the estimated camera poses between two consecutive frames, these methods "synthesize" the flow field of rigid regions. The synthesized flow from depth and pose can either be used for flow prediction in rigid regions [48,60,65,68] as is or used for view synthesis to train depth model using monocular videos [73]. Additional cues such as surface normal [67], edge [66], physical constraints [59] can be incorporated to further improve the performance.

These approaches exploit the inherent geometric relationship between structure and motion. However, the errors produced by either the depth or the camera pose estimation propagate to flow predictions. Our key insight is that for rigid regions the estimated flow (from flow prediction network) and the synthesized rigid flow (from depth and camera pose networks) should be consistent. Consequently, coupled training allows both depth and flow networks to learn from each other and enforce geometrically consistent predictions of the scene.

Structure from Motion. Joint estimation of structure and camera pose from multiple images of a given scene is a long-standing problem [15,46,64]. Conventional methods can recover (semi-)dense depth estimation and camera pose through keypoint tracking/matching. The outputs of these algorithms can potentially be used to help train a flow network, but not the other way around. Our work differs as we are also interested in learning a depth network to recover dense structure from a single input image.

Multi-task Learning. Simultaneously addressing multiple tasks through multi-task learning [52] has shown advantages over methods that tackle individual ones [70]. For examples, joint learning of video segmentation and optical flow through layered models [6,56] or feature sharing [9] helps improve accuracy at motion boundaries. Single-view depth model learning can also benefit from joint training with surface normal estimation [35,67] or semantic segmentation [13,30].

Our approach tackles the problems of learning both depth and flow models. Unlike existing multi-task learning methods that often require *direct supervision* using ground truth training data for each task, our approach instead leverage *meta-supervision* to couple the training of depth and flow models. While our models are jointly trained, they can be applied independently at test time.

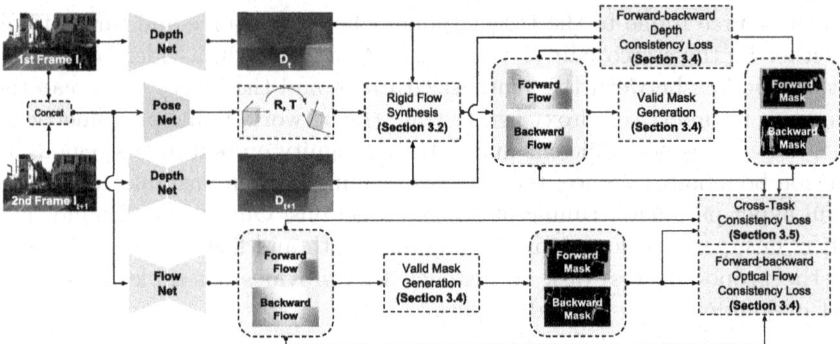

Fig. 3. Overview of our unsupervised joint learning framework. Our framework consists of three major modules: (1) a *Depth Net* for single-view depth estimation; (2) a *Pose Net* that takes two stacked input frames and estimates the relative camera pose between the two input frames; and (3) a *Flow Net* that estimates dense optical flow field between the two input frames. Given a pair of input images $\mathbf{I}_t$ and $\mathbf{I}_{t+1}$ sampled from an unlabeled video, we first estimate the depth of each frame, the 6D camera pose, and the dense forward and backward flows. Using the predicted scene depth and the estimated camera pose, we can synthesize 2D forward and backward optical flows (referred as *rigid flow*) by backprojecting the induced 3D forward and backward scene flows (Sect. 3.2). As we do not have ground truth depth and flow maps for supervision, we leverage standard photometric and spatial smoothness costs to regularize the network training (Sect. 3.3, not shown in this figure for clarity). To enforce the consistency of flow and depth prediction in both directions, we exploit the forward-backward consistency (Sect. 3.4), and adopt the valid masks derived from it to filter out invalid regions (e.g., occlusion/dis-occlusion) for the photometric loss. Finally, we propose a novel cross-network consistency loss (Sect. 3.5)—encouraging the optical flow estimation (from the *Flow Net*) and the rigid flow (from the *Depth and Pose Net*) to be consistent to each other within in valid regions.

3 Unsupervised Joint Learning of Depth and Flow

3.1 Method Overview

Our goal is to develop an unsupervised learning framework for *jointly* training the single-view depth estimation network and the optical flow prediction network using *unlabeled* video sequences. Figure 3 shows the high-level sketch of our proposed approach. Given two consecutive frames (I_t, I_{t+1}) sampled from an unlabeled video, we first estimate depth of frame I_t and I_{t+1}, and forward-backward optical flow fields between frame I_t and I_{t+1}. We then estimate the 6D camera pose transformation between the two frames (I_t, I_{t+1}).

With the predicted depth map and the estimated 6D camera pose, we can produce the 3D scene flow induced from camera ego-motion and backproject them onto the image plane to synthesize the 2D flow (Sect. 3.2). We refer this synthesized flow as *rigid flow*. Suppose the scenes are mostly static, the synthesized rigid flow should be consistent with the results from the estimated optical flow (produced by the optical flow prediction model). However, the prediction results from the two branches may not be consistent with each other. Our intuition is that the discrepancy between the rigid flow and the estimated flow provides additional supervisory signals for both networks. Hence, we propose a *cross-task consistency loss* to enforce this constraint (Sect. 3.5). To handle non-rigid transformations that cannot be explained by the camera motion and occlusion-disocclusion regions, we exploit the forward-backward consistency check to identify valid regions (Sect. 3.4). We avoid enforcing the cross-task consistency for those forward-backward inconsistent regions.

Our overall objective function can be formulated as follows:

$$L = L_{\text{photometric}} + \lambda_s L_{\text{smooth}} + \lambda_f L_{\text{forward-backward}} + \lambda_c L_{\text{cross}}. \tag{1}$$

All of the four loss terms are applied to both depth and flow networks. Also, all of the four loss terms are symmetric for forward and backward directions, for simplicity we only derive them for the forward direction.

3.2 Flow Synthesis Using Depth and Pose Predictions

Given the two input frames I_t and I_{t+1}, the predicted depth map $\hat{D}_t$, and relative camera pose $\hat{T}_{t\to t+1}$, here we wish to establish the dense pixel correspondence between the two frames. Let p_t denotes the 2D homogeneous coordinate of an pixel in frame I_t and K denotes the intrinsic camera matrix. We can compute the corresponding point of p_t in frame I_{t+1} using the equation [73]:

$$p_{t+1} = K\hat{T}_{t\to t+1}\hat{D}_t(p_t)K^{-1}p_t. \tag{2}$$

We can then obtain the synthesized forward rigid flow at pixel p_t in I_t by

$$F_{\text{rigid}}(p_t) = p_{t+1} - p_t \tag{3}$$

3.3 Brightness Constancy and Spatial Smoothness Priors

Here we briefly review two loss functions that we used in our framework to regularize network training. Leveraging the brightness constancy and spatial smoothness priors used in classical dense correspondence algorithms [4,23,40], prior work has used the photometric discrepancy between the warped frame and the target frame as an unsupervised proxy loss function for training CNNs without ground truth annotations.

Photometric Loss. Suppose that we have frame I_t and I_{t+1}, as well as the estimated flow $F_{t\to t+1}$ (either from the optical flow predicted from the flow model or the synthesized rigid flow induced from the estimated depth and camera pose), we can produce the warped frame $\bar{I}_t$ with the inverse warping from frame I_{t+1}. Note that the projected image coordinates p_{t+1} might not lie exactly on the image pixel grid, we thus apply a differentiable bilinear interpolation strategy used in the spatial transformer networks [27] to perform frame synthesis.

With the warped frame $\bar{I}_t$ from I_{t+1}, we formulate the brightness constancy objective function as

$$L_{\text{photometric}} = \sum_{p} \rho\big(I_t(p), \bar{I}_t(p)\big). \tag{4}$$

where $\rho(\cdot)$ is a function to measure the difference between pixel values. Previous work simply choose L_1 norm or the appearance matching loss [21], which is not invariant to illumination changes in real-world scenarios [61]. Here we adopt the ternary census transform based loss [43,55,69] that can better handle complex illumination changes.

Smoothness Loss. The brightness constancy loss is not informative in low-texture or homogeneous region of the scene. To handle this issue, existing work incorporates a smoothness prior to regularize the estimated disparity map or flow field. We adopt the spatial smoothness loss as proposed in [21].

3.4 Forward-Backward Consistency

According to the brightness constancy assumption, the warped frame should be similar to the target frame. However, the assumption does not hold for occluded and dis-occluded regions. We address this problem by using the commonly used forward-backward consistency check technique to identify invalid regions and do not impose the photometric loss on those regions.

Valid Masks. We implement the occlusion detection based on forward-backward consistency assumption [58] (i.e., traversing flow vector forward and then backward should arrive at the same position). Here we use a simple criterion proposed in [43]. We mark pixels as invalid whenever this constraint is violated. Figure 4 shows two examples of the marked invalid regions by forward-backward consistency check using the synthesized rigid flow (animations can be viewed in Adobe Reader).

Denote the valid region by V (either from rigid flow or estimated flow), we can modify the photometric loss term (4) as

$$L_{\text{photometric}} = \sum_{p \in V} \rho\big(I_t(p), \bar{I}_t(p)\big). \tag{5}$$

Forward-Backward Consistency Loss. In addition to using forward-backward consistency check for identifying invalid regions, we can further impose constraints on the valid regions so that the network can produce consistent predictions for both forward and backward directions. Similar ideas have been exploited in [25,43] for occlusion-aware flow estimation. Here, we apply the forward-backward consistency loss to both flow and depth predictions.

For flow prediction, the forward-backward consistency loss is of the form:

$$L_{\text{forward-backward, flow}} = \sum_{p \in V_{\text{flow}}} \|F_{t\to t+1}(p) + F_{t+1\to t}(p + F_{t\to t+1}(p))\|_1 \tag{6}$$

Input frames

Invalid masks by rigid flow

Fig. 4. Valid mask visualization. We estimate the invalid mask by checking the forward-backward consistency from the synthesized rigid flow, which can not only detect occluded regions, but also identify the moving objects (cars) as they cannot be explained by the estimated depth and pose. Animations can be viewed in Adobe Reader. (See supplementary material)

Similarly, we impose a consistency penalty for depth:

$$L_{\text{forward-backward, depth}} = \sum_{p \in V_{\text{depth}}} \|D_t(p) - \bar{D}_t(p)\|_1 \tag{7}$$

where $\bar{D}_t$ is warped from D_{t+1} using the synthesized rigid flow from t to $t+1$.

While we exploit robust functions for enforcing photometric loss, forward-backward consistency for each of the tasks, the training of depth and flow networks using unlabeled data remains non-trivial and sensitive to the choice of hyper-parameters [33]. Building upon the existing loss functions, in the following we introduce a novel cross-task consistency loss to further regularize the network training.

3.5 Cross-Task Consistency

In Sect. 3.2, we show that the motion of rigid regions in the scene can be explained by the ego-motion of the camera and the corresponding scene depth. On the one hand, we can estimate the rigid flow by backprojecting the induced 3D scene flow from the estimated depth and relative camera pose. On the other hand, we have direct estimation results from an optical flow network. Our core idea is the that these two flow fields should be consistent with each other for non-occluded and static regions. Minimizing the discrepancy between the two flow fields allows us to simultaneously update the depth and flow models.

We thus propose to minimize the endpoint distance between the flow vectors in the rigid flow (computed from the estimated depth and pose) and that in the estimated flow (computed from the flow prediction model). We denote the synthesized rigid flow as $F_{\text{rigid}} = (u_{\text{rigid}}, v_{\text{rigid}})$ and the estimated flow as $F_{\text{flow}} = (u_{\text{flow}}, v_{\text{flow}})$. Using the computed valid masks (Sect. 3.4), we impose the cross-task consistency constraints over valid pixels.

$$L_{\text{cross}} = \sum_{p \in V_{\text{depth}} \cap V_{\text{flow}}} \|F_{\text{rigid}}(p) - F_{\text{flow}}(p)\|_1 \tag{8}$$

4 Experimental Results

In this section, we validate the effectiveness of our proposed method for unsupervised learning of depth and flow on several standard benchmark datasets. More results can be found in the supplementary material. Our source code and pre-trained models are available on http://yuliang.vision/DF-Net/.

4.1 Datasets

Datasets for Joint Network Training. We use video clips from the train split of KITTI raw dataset [18] for joint learning of depth and flow models. Note that our training does not involve any depth/flow labels.

Datasets for Pre-training. To avoid the joint training process converging to trivial solutions, we (unsupervisedly) pre-train the flow network on the SYNTHIA dataset [51]. For pre-training both depth and pose networks, we use either KITTI raw dataset or the CityScapes dataset [11].

The SYNTHIA dataset [51] contains multi-view frames captured by driving vehicles in different scenarios and traffic conditions. We take all the four-view images of the left camera from all summer and winter driving sequences, which contains around 37K image pairs. The CityScapes dataset [11] contains real-world driving sequences, we follow Zhou et al. [73] and pre-process the dataset to generate around 75K training image pairs.

Datasets for Evaluation. For evaluating the performance of our depth network, we use the *test split* of the KITTI raw dataset. The depth maps for KITTI raw are sampled at irregularly spaced positions, captured using a rotating LIDAR scanner. Following the standard evaluation protocol, we evaluate the performance using only the regions with ground truth depth samples (bottom parts of the images). We also evaluate the generalization of our depth network on general scenes using the Make3D dataset [53].

For evaluating our flow network, we use the challenging KITTI flow 2012 [19] and KITTI flow 2015 [44] datasets. The ground truth optical flow is obtained from a 3D laser scanner and thus only covers about 50% of the pixels.

4.2 Implementation Details

We implement our approach in TensorFlow [1] and conduct all the experiments on a single Tesla K80 GPU with 12 GB memory. We set $\lambda_s = 3.0$, $\lambda_f = 0.2$, and $\lambda_c = 0.2$. For network training, we use the Adam optimizer [31] with $\beta_1 = 0.9$, $\beta_2 = 0.99$. In the following, we provide more implementation details in network architecture, network pre-training, and the proposed unsupervised joint training.

Network Architecture. For the pose network, we adopt the architecture from Zhou et al. [73]. For the depth network, we use the ResNet-50 [22] as our feature backbone with ELU [10] activation functions. For the flow network, we adopt the UnFlow-C structure [43]—a variant of FlowNetC [12]. As our network training is *model-agnostic*, more advanced network architectures (e.g., pose [20], depth [36], or flow [57]) can be used for further improving the performance.

Unsupervised Depth Pre-training. We train the depth and pose networks with a mini-batch size of 6 image pairs whose size is 576×160, from KITTI raw dataset or CityScapes dataset for 100K iterations. We use a learning rate is 2e-4. Each iteration takes around 0.8s (forward and backprop) during training.

Unsupervised Flow Pre-training. Following Meister et al. [43], we train the flow network with a mini-batch size of 4 image pairs whose size is 1152×320 from SYNTHIA dataset for 300K iterations. We keep the initial learning rate as 1e-4 for the first 100K iterations and then reduce the learning rate by half after each 100K iterations. Each iteration takes around 2.4 s (forward and backprop).

Unsupervised Joint Training. We jointly train the depth, pose, and flow networks with a mini-batch size of 4 image pairs from KITTI raw dataset for 100K iterations. Input size for the depth and pose networks is 576×160, while the input size for the flow network is 1152×320. We divide the initial learning rate by 2 for every 20K iterations. Our depth network produces depth predictions at 4 spatial scales, while the flow network produces flow fields at 5 scales. We enforce the cross-network consistency in the finest 4 scales. Each iteration takes around 3.6 s (forward and backprop) during training.

Image Resolution of Network Inputs/Outputs. As the input size of the UnFlow-C network [43] must be divisible by 64, we resize input image pairs of the two KITTI flow datasets to 1280×384 using bilinear interpolation. We then resize the estimated optical flow and rescale the predicted flow vectors to match the original input size. For depth estimation, we resize the input image to the

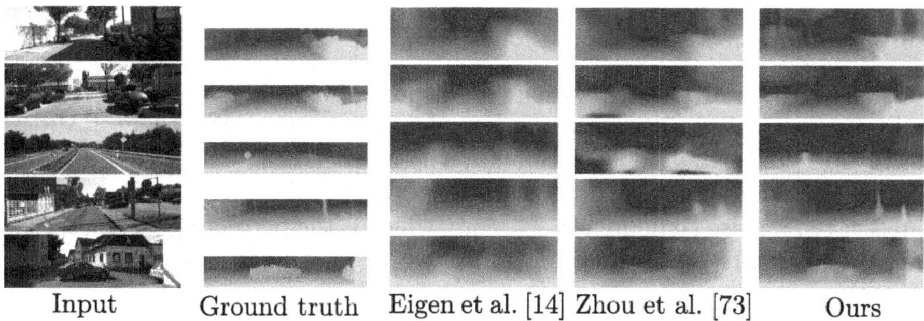

Fig. 5. Sample results on KITTI raw test set. The ground truth depth is interpolated from sparse point cloud for visualization only. Compared to Zhou et al. [73] and Eigen et al. [14], our method can better capture object contour and thin structures.

Table 1. Single-view depth estimation results on *test split* of KITTI raw dataset [18]. The methods trained on KITTI raw dataset [18] are denoted by K. Models with additional training data from CityScapes [11] are denoted by CS+K. (D) denotes depth supervision, (B) denotes stereo input pairs, (M) denotes monocular video clips. The best and the second best performance in each block are highlighted as bold and underline.

Method	Dataset	Error metric ↓				Accuracy metric ↑		
		Abs Rel	Sq Rel	RMSE	log RMSE	$\delta < 1.25$	$\delta < 1.25^2$	$\delta < 1.25^3$
Eigen et al. [14]	K (D)	0.203	1.548	6.307	0.246	0.702	0.890	0.958
Kuznietsov et al. [32]	K (B)/K (D)	**0.113**	**0.741**	**4.621**	**0.189**	**0.862**	**0.960**	**0.986**
Zhan et al. [71]	K (B)	0.144	1.391	5.869	0.241	0.803	0.928	0.969
Godard et al. [21]	K (B)	0.133	1.140	5.527	0.229	0.830	0.936	0.970
Godard et al. [21]	CS+K (B)	0.121	1.032	5.200	0.215	0.854	0.944	0.973
Zhou et al. [73]	K (M)	0.208	1.768	6.856	0.283	0.678	0.885	0.957
Yang et al. [67]	K (M)	0.182	1.481	6.501	0.267	0.725	0.906	0.963
Mahjourian et al. [41]	K (M)	0.163	1.240	6.220	0.250	0.762	0.916	0.968
Yang et al. [66]	K (M)	0.162	1.352	6.276	0.252	-	-	-
Yin et al. [68]	K (M)	0.155	1.296	5.857	0.233	0.793	0.931	**0.973**
Godard et al. [20]	K (M)	0.154	1.218	5.699	0.231	0.798	0.932	**0.973**
Ours (w/o forward-backward)	K (M)	0.160	1.256	5.555	0.226	0.796	0.931	**0.973**
Ours (w/o cross-task)	K (M)	0.160	1.234	5.508	0.225	0.800	0.932	0.972
Ours	K (M)	**0.150**	**1.124**	**5.507**	**0.223**	**0.806**	**0.933**	**0.973**
Zhou et al. [73]	CS+K (M)	0.198	1.836	6.565	0.275	0.718	0.901	0.960
Yang et al. [67]	CS+K (M)	0.165	1.360	6.641	0.248	0.750	0.914	0.969
Mahjourian et al. [41]	CS+K (M)	0.159	1.231	5.912	0.243	0.784	0.923	0.970
Yang et al. [66]	CS+K (M)	0.159	1.345	6.254	0.247	-	-	-
Yin et al. [68]	CS+K (M)	0.153	1.328	5.737	0.232	0.802	0.934	0.972
Ours (w/o forward-backward)	CS+K (M)	0.159	1.716	5.616	0.222	0.805	0.939	0.976
Ours (w/o cross-task)	CS+K (M)	0.155	**1.181**	5.301	0.218	0.805	0.939	0.977
Ours	CS+K (M)	**0.146**	1.182	**5.215**	**0.213**	**0.818**	**0.943**	**0.978**

same size of training input to predict the disparity first. We then resize and rescale the predicted disparity to the original size and compute the inverse the obtain the final prediction.

4.3 Evaluation Metrics

Following Zhou et al. [73], we evaluate our depth network using several error metrics (absolute relative difference, square related difference, RMSE, log RMSE). For optical flow estimation, we compute the average endpoint error (EPE) on pixels with the ground truth flow available for each dataset. On KITTI flow 2015 dataset [44], we also compute the F1 score, which is the percentage of pixels that have EPE greater than 3 pixels and 5% of the ground truth value.

4.4 Experimental Evaluation

Single-View Depth Estimation. We compare our depth network with state-of-the-art algorithms on the *test split* of the KITTI raw dataset provided by

Eigen et al. [14]. As shown in Table 1, our method achieves the state-of-the-art performance when compared with models trained with monocular video sequences. However, our method performs slightly worse than the models that exploit calibrated stereo image pairs (i.e., pose supervision) or with additional ground truth depth annotation. We believe that performance gap can be attributed to the error induced by our pose network. Extending our approach to *calibrated stereo videos* is an interesting future direction.

We also conduct an ablation study by removing the forward-backward consistency loss or cross-task consistency loss. In both cases our results show significant performance of degradation, highlighting the importance the proposed consistency loss. Figure 5 shows qualitative comparison with [14, 73], our method can better capture thin structure and delineate clear object contour.

To evaluate the generalization ability of our depth network on general scenes, we also apply our trained model to the Make3D dataset [53]. Table 2 shows that our method achieves the state-of-the-art performance compared with existing unsupervised models and is competitive with respect to supervised learning models (even without fine-tuning on Make3D datasets).

Table 2. Results on the Make3D dataset [54]. Our results were obtained by the model trained on Cityscapes + KITTI *without* fine-tuning on the training images in Make3D. Following the evaluation protocol of [21], the errors are only computed where depth is less than 70 m. The best and the second best performance in each block are highlighted as bold and underline

Method	Supervision	Error metric ↓			
		Abs Rel	Sq Rel	RMSE	log RMSE
Train set mean	-	0.876	12.98	12.27	0.307
Karsch et al. [29]	Depth	0.428	<u>5.079</u>	8.389	0.149
Liu et al. [39]	Depth	0.475	6.562	10.05	0.165
Laina et al. [34]	Depth	<u>0.204</u>	**1.840**	<u>5.683</u>	<u>0.084</u>
Li et al. [36]	Depth	**0.176**	-	**4.260**	**0.069**
Godard et al. [21]	Pose	0.544	10.94	11.76	**0.193**
Zhou et al. [73]	None	<u>0.383</u>	<u>5.321</u>	<u>10.47</u>	0.478
Ours	None	**0.331**	**2.698**	**6.89**	<u>0.416</u>

Optical Flow Estimation. We compare our flow network with conventional variational algorithms, supervised CNN methods, and several unsupervised CNN models on the KITTI flow 2012 and 2015 datasets. As shown in Table 3, our method achieves state-of-the-art performance on both datasets. A visual comparison can be found in Fig. 6. With optional fine-tuning on available ground truth labels on the KITTI flow datasets, we show that our approach achieves competitive performance sharing similar network architectures. This suggests that our method can serve as an unsupervised pre-training technique for learning optical flow in domains where the amounts of ground truth data are scarce.

Table 3. Quantitative evaluation on optical flow. Results on KITTI flow 2012 [19], KITTI flow 2015 [44] datasets. We denote "C" as the FlyingChairs dataset [12], "T" as the FlyingThings3D dataset [42], "K" as the KITTI raw dataset [18], "SYN" as the SYNTHIA dataset [51]. (S) indicates that the model is trained with ground truth annotation, while (U) indicates the model is trained in an unsupervised manner. The best and the second best performance in each block are highlighted as bold and underline.

Method	Dataset	KITTI 2012		KITTI 2015		
		Train	Test	Train	Train	Test
		EPE	EPE	EPE	F1	F1
LDOF [3]	-	10.94	12.4	18.19	38.05%	-
DeepFlow [63]	-	4.58	5.8	10.63	26.52%	29.18%
EpicFlow [50]	-	3.47	**3.8**	9.27	27.18%	**27.10%**
FlowField [2]	-	**3.33**	-	**8.33**	**24.43%**	-
FlowNetS [12]	C (S)	8.26	-	15.44	52.86%	-
FlowNetC [12]	C (S)	9.35	-	12.52	47.93%	-
SpyNet [47]	C (S)	9.12	-	20.56	44.78%	-
SemiFlowGAN [33]	C (S)/K (U)	7.16	-	16.02	38.77%	-
FlowNet2 [26]	C (S) + T (S)	**4.09**	-	**10.06**	**30.37%**	-
UnsupFlownet [28]	C (U) + K (U)	11.3	9.9	-	-	-
DSTFlow [49]	C (U)	16.98	-	24.30	52.00%	-
DSTFlow [49]	K (U)	10.43	12.4	16.79	36.00%	39.00%
Yin et al. [68]	K (U)	-	-	10.81	-	-
UnFlowC [43]	SYN (U) + K (U)	3.78	4.5	**8.80**	28.94%	29.46%
Ours (w/o forward-backward)	SYN (U) + K (U)	3.86	4.7	9.12	26.27%	26.90%
Ours (w/o cross-task)	SYN (U) + K (U)	4.70	5.8	8.95	28.37%	30.03%
Ours	SYN (U) + K (U)	**3.54**	**4.4**	8.98	**26.01%**	**25.70%**
FlowNet2-ft-kitti [26]	C (S) + T (S) + K (S)	(1.28)	1.8	(2.30)	(8.61%)	11.48%
UnFlowCSS-ft-kitti [43]	SYN (U) + K (U) + K (S)	**(1.14)**	**1.7**	**(1.86)**	**(7.40%)**	**11.11%**
UnFlowC-ft-kitti [43]	SYN (U) + K (U) + K (S)	(2.13)	3.0	(3.67)	(17.78%)	24.20%
Ours-ft-kitti	SYN (U) + K (U) + K (S)	(1.75)	3.0	(2.85)	(13.47%)	22.82%

Table 4. Pose estimation results on KITTI Odometry datest [19].

	Seq. 09	Seq. 10
ORB-SLAM (full)	0.014±0.008	0.012±0.011
ORB-SLAM (short)	0.064±0.141	0.064±0.130
Mean Odom	0.032±0.026	0.028±0.023
Zhou et al. [73]	0.021±0.017	0.020±0.015
Mahjourian et al. [41]	0.013±0.010	0.012±0.011
Yin et al. [68]	**0.012±0.007**	**0.012±0.009**
Ours	0.017±0.007	0.015±0.009

Pose Estimation. For completeness, we provide the performance evaluation of the pose network. We follow the same evaluation protocol as [73] and use a 5-frame based pose network. As shown in Table 4, our pose network shows competitive performance with respect to state-of-the-art visual SLAM methods

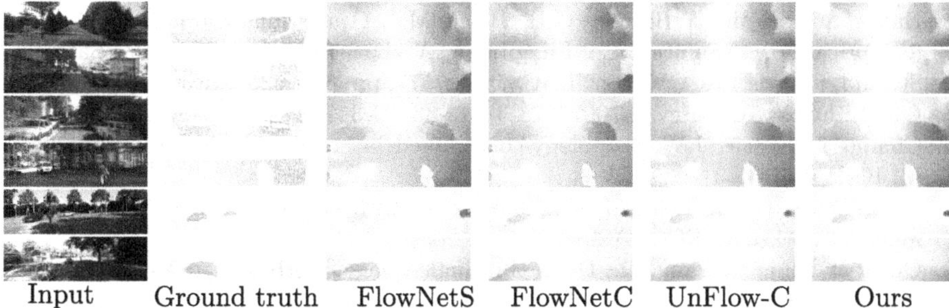

Fig. 6. Visual results on KITTI flow datasets. All the models are directly applied *without* fine-tuning on KITTI flow annotations. Our model delineates clearer object contours compared to both supervised/unsupervised methods.

or other unsupervised learning methods. We believe that a better pose network would further improve the performance of both depth or optical flow estimation.

5 Conclusions

We presented an unsupervised learning framework for both sing-view depth prediction and optical flow estimation using unlabeled video sequences. Our key technical contribution lies in the proposed cross-task consistency that couples the network training. At test time, the trained depth and flow models can be applied independently. We validate the benefits of joint training through extensive experiments on benchmark datasets. Our single-view depth prediction model compares favorably against existing unsupervised models using unstructured videos on both KITTI and Make3D datasets. Our flow estimation model achieves competitive performance with state-of-the-art approaches. By leveraging geometric constraints, our work suggests a promising future direction of advancing the state-of-the-art in multiple dense prediction tasks using unlabeled data.

Acknowledgement. This work was supported in part by NSF under Grant No. (#1755785). We thank NVIDIA Corporation for the donation of GPUs.

References

1. Abadi, M., et al.: TensorFlow: large-scale machine learning on heterogeneous distributed systems. arXiv preprint arXiv:1603.04467 (2016)
2. Bailer, C., Taetz, B., Stricker, D.: Flow fields: dense correspondence fields for highly accurate large displacement optical flow estimation. In: ICCV (2015)
3. Brox, T., Bregler, C., Malik, J.: Large displacement optical flow. In: CVPR (2009)
4. Bruhn, A., Weickert, J., Schnörr, C.: Lucas/Kanade meets Horn/Schunck: combining local and global optic flow methods. IJCV **61**(3), 211–231 (2005)

5. Butler, D.J., Wulff, J., Stanley, G.B., Black, M.J.: A naturalistic open source movie for optical flow evaluation. In: Fitzgibbon, A., Lazebnik, S., Perona, P., Sato, Y., Schmid, C. (eds.) ECCV 2012. LNCS, vol. 7577, pp. 611–625. Springer, Heidelberg (2012). https://doi.org/10.1007/978-3-642-33783-3_44
6. Chang, J., Fisher, J.W.: Topology-constrained layered tracking with latent flow. In: ICCV (2013)
7. Chen, W., Deng, J.: Learning single-image depth from videos using quality assessment networks. In: ECCV (2018)
8. Chen, W., Fu, Z., Yang, D., Deng, J.: Single-image depth perception in the wild. In: NIPS (2016)
9. Cheng, J., Tsai, Y.H., Wang, S., Yang, M.H.: SegFlow: joint learning for video object segmentation and optical flow. In: ICCV (2017)
10. Clevert, D.A., Unterthiner, T., Hochreiter, S.: Fast and accurate deep network learning by exponential linear units (ELUs). In: ICLR (2016)
11. Cordts, M., et al.: The cityscapes dataset for semantic urban scene understanding. In: CVPR (2016)
12. Dosovitskiy, A., et al.: FlowNet: learning optical flow with convolutional networks. In: ICCV (2015)
13. Eigen, D., Fergus, R.: Predicting depth, surface normals and semantic labels with a common multi-scale convolutional architecture. In: ICCV (2015)
14. Eigen, D., Puhrsch, C., Fergus, R.: Depth map prediction from a single image using a multi-scale deep network. In: NIPS (2014)
15. Furukawa, Y., Curless, B., Seitz, S.M., Szeliski, R.: Towards internet-scale multi-view stereo. In: CVPR (2010)
16. Gaidon, A., Wang, Q., Cabon, Y., Vig, E.: Virtual worlds as proxy for multi-object tracking analysis. In: CVPR (2016)
17. Garg, R., Carneiro, G., Reid, I.: Unsupervised CNN for single view depth estimation: geometry to the rescue. In: Leibe, B., Matas, J., Sebe, N., Welling, M. (eds.) ECCV 2016. LNCS, vol. 9912, pp. 740–756. Springer, Cham (2016). https://doi.org/10.1007/978-3-319-46484-8_45
18. Geiger, A., Lenz, P., Stiller, C., Urtasun, R.: Vision meets robotics: the KITTI dataset. IJRR **32**(11), 1231–1237 (2013)
19. Geiger, A., Lenz, P., Urtasun, R.: Are we ready for autonomous driving? The KITTI vision benchmark suite. In: CVPR (2012)
20. Godard, C., Mac Aodha, O., Brostow, G.: Digging into self-supervised monocular depth estimation. arXiv preprint arXiv:1806.01260 (2018)
21. Godard, C., Mac Aodha, O., Brostow, G.J.: Unsupervised monocular depth estimation with left-right consistency. In: CVPR (2017)
22. He, K., Zhang, X., Ren, S., Sun, J.: Deep residual learning for image recognition. In: CVPR (2016)
23. Horn, B.K., Schunck, B.G.: Determining optical flow. Artif. Intell. **17**(1–3), 185–203 (1981)
24. Huang, P.H., Matzen, K., Kopf, J., Ahuja, N., Huang, J.B.: DeepMVS: learning multi-view stereopsis. In: CVPR (2018)
25. Hur, J., Roth, S.: MirrorFlow: exploiting symmetries in joint optical flow and occlusion estimation. In: ICCV (2017)
26. Ilg, E., Mayer, N., Saikia, T., Keuper, M., Dosovitskiy, A., Brox, T.: Flownet 2.0: evolution of optical flow estimation with deep networks. In: CVPR (2017)
27. Jaderberg, M., Simonyan, K., Zisserman, A., Kavukcuoglu, K.: Spatial transformer networks. In: NIPS (2015)

28. Yu, J.J., Harley, A.W., Derpanis, K.G.: Back to basics: unsupervised learning of optical flow via brightness constancy and motion smoothness. In: Hua, G., Jégou, H. (eds.) ECCV 2016. LNCS, vol. 9915, pp. 3–10. Springer, Cham (2016). https://doi.org/10.1007/978-3-319-49409-8_1
29. Karsch, K., Liu, C., Kang, S.B.: Depth transfer: depth extraction from video using non-parametric sampling. TPAMI **36**(11), 2144–2158 (2014)
30. Kendall, A., Gal, Y., Cipolla, R.: Multi-task learning using uncertainty to weigh losses for scene geometry and semantics. In: NIPS (2017)
31. Kingma, D., Ba, J.: Adam: a method for stochastic optimization. In: ICLR (2014)
32. Kuznietsov, Y., Stückler, J., Leibe, B.: Semi-supervised deep learning for monocular depth map prediction. In: CVPR (2017)
33. Lai, W.S., Huang, J.B., Yang, M.H.: Semi-supervised learning for optical flow with generative adversarial networks. In: NIPS (2017)
34. Laina, I., Rupprecht, C., Belagiannis, V., Tombari, F., Navab, N.: Deeper depth prediction with fully convolutional residual networks. In: 3DV (2016)
35. Li, B., Shen, C., Dai, Y., van den Hengel, A., He, M.: Depth and surface normal estimation from monocular images using regression on deep features and hierarchical CRFs. In: CVPR (2015)
36. Li, Z., Snavely, N.: MegaDepth: learning single-view depth prediction from internet photos. In: CVPR (2018)
37. Liu, C., Freeman, W.T., Adelson, E.H., Weiss, Y.: Human-assisted motion annotation. In: CVPR (2008)
38. Liu, F., Shen, C., Lin, G.: Deep convolutional neural fields for depth estimation from a single image. In: CVPR (2015)
39. Liu, M., Salzmann, M., He, X.: Discrete-continuous depth estimation from a single image. In: CVPR (2014)
40. Lucas, B.D., Kanade, T., et al.: An iterative image registration technique with an application to stereo vision. In: IJCAI (1981)
41. Mahjourian, R., Wicke, M., Angelova, A.: Unsupervised learning of depth and ego-motion from monocular video using 3D geometric constraints. In: CVPR (2018)
42. Mayer, N., et al.: A large dataset to train convolutional networks for disparity, optical flow, and scene flow estimation. In: CVPR (2016)
43. Meister, S., Hur, J., Roth, S.: UnFlow: unsupervised learning of optical flow with a bidirectional census loss. In: AAAI (2018)
44. Menze, M., Geiger, A.: Object scene flow for autonomous vehicles. In: CVPR (2015)
45. Silberman, N., Hoiem, D., Kohli, P., Fergus, R.: Indoor segmentation and support inference from RGBD images. In: Fitzgibbon, A., Lazebnik, S., Perona, P., Sato, Y., Schmid, C. (eds.) ECCV 2012. LNCS, vol. 7576, pp. 746–760. Springer, Heidelberg (2012). https://doi.org/10.1007/978-3-642-33715-4_54
46. Newcombe, R.A., Lovegrove, S.J., Davison, A.J.: DTAM: Dense tracking and mapping in real-time. In: ICCV (2011)
47. Ranjan, A., Black, M.J.: Optical flow estimation using a spatial pyramid network. In: CVPR (2017)
48. Ranjan, A., Jampani, V., Kim, K., Sun, D., Wulff, J., Black, M.J.: Adversarial Collaboration: Joint unsupervised learning of depth, camera motion, optical flow and motion segmentation. arXiv preprint arXiv:1805.09806 (2018)
49. Ren, Z., Yan, J., Ni, B., Liu, B., Yang, X., Zha, H.: Unsupervised deep learning for optical flow estimation. In: AAAI (2017)
50. Revaud, J., Weinzaepfel, P., Harchaoui, Z., Schmid, C.: EpicFlow: edge-preserving interpolation of correspondences for optical flow. In: CVPR (2015)

51. Ros, G., Sellart, L., Materzynska, J., Vazquez, D., Lopez, A.M.: The synthia dataset: a large collection of synthetic images for semantic segmentation of urban scenes. In: CVPR (2016)
52. Ruder, S.: An overview of multi-task learning in deep neural networks. arXiv preprint arXiv:1706.05098 (2017)
53. Saxena, A., Chung, S.H., Ng, A.Y.: Learning depth from single monocular images. In: NIPS (2006)
54. Saxena, A., Chung, S.H., Ng, A.Y.: 3-D depth reconstruction from a single still image. IJCV **76**(1), 53–69 (2008)
55. Stein, F.: Efficient computation of optical flow using the census transform. In: Rasmussen, C.E., Bülthoff, H.H., Schölkopf, B., Giese, M.A. (eds.) DAGM 2004. LNCS, vol. 3175, pp. 79–86. Springer, Heidelberg (2004). https://doi.org/10.1007/978-3-540-28649-3_10
56. Sun, D., Wulff, J., Sudderth, E.B., Pfister, H., Black, M.J.: A fully-connected layered model of foreground and background flow. In: CVPR (2013)
57. Sun, D., Yang, X., Liu, M.Y., Kautz, J.: PWC-net: CNNs for optical flow using pyramid, warping, and cost volume. In: CVPR (2018)
58. Sundaram, N., Brox, T., Keutzer, K.: Dense point trajectories by GPU-accelerated large displacement optical flow. In: Daniilidis, K., Maragos, P., Paragios, N. (eds.) ECCV 2010. LNCS, vol. 6311, pp. 438–451. Springer, Heidelberg (2010). https://doi.org/10.1007/978-3-642-15549-9_32
59. Tung, H.Y.F., Harley, A., Seto, W., Fragkiadaki, K.: Adversarial inversion: inverse graphics with adversarial priors. In: ICCV (2017)
60. Vijayanarasimhan, S., Ricco, S., Schmid, C., Sukthankar, R., Fragkiadaki, K.: SFM-net: learning of structure and motion from video. arXiv preprint arXiv:1704.07804 (2017)
61. Vogel, C., Roth, S., Schindler, K.: An evaluation of data costs for optical flow. In: Weickert, J., Hein, M., Schiele, B. (eds.) GCPR 2013. LNCS, vol. 8142, pp. 343–353. Springer, Heidelberg (2013). https://doi.org/10.1007/978-3-642-40602-7_37
62. Wang, P., Shen, X., Lin, Z., Cohen, S., Price, B., Yuille, A.L.: Towards unified depth and semantic prediction from a single image. In: CVPR (2015)
63. Weinzaepfel, P., Revaud, J., Harchaoui, Z., Schmid, C.: DeepFlow: large displacement optical flow with deep matching. In: ICCV (2013)
64. Wu, C.: VisualSFM: a visual structure from motion system (2011)
65. Wulff, J., Sevilla-Lara, L., Black, M.J.: Optical flow in mostly rigid scenes. In: CVPR (2017)
66. Yang, Z., Wang, P., Wang, Y., Xu, W., Nevatia, R.: LEGO: learning edge with geometry all at once by watching videos. In: CVPR (2018)
67. Yang, Z., Wang, P., Xu, W., Zhao, L., Nevatia, R.: Unsupervised learning of geometry with edge-aware depth-normal consistency. In: AAAI (2018)
68. Yin, Z., Shi, J.: GeoNet: unsupervised learning of dense depth, optical flow and camera pose. In: CVPR (2018)
69. Zabih, R., Woodfill, J.: Non-parametric local transforms for computing visual correspondence. In: Eklundh, J.-O. (ed.) ECCV 1994. LNCS, vol. 801, pp. 151–158. Springer, Heidelberg (1994). https://doi.org/10.1007/BFb0028345
70. Zamir, A.R., Sax, A., Shen, W., Guibas, L., Malik, J., Savarese, S.: Taskonomy: disentangling task transfer learning. In: CVPR (2018)
71. Zhan, H., Garg, R., Weerasekera, C.S., Li, K., Agarwal, H., Reid, I.: Unsupervised learning of monocular depth estimation and visual odometry with deep feature reconstruction. In: CVPR (2018)

72. Zhang, Z., Schwing, A.G., Fidler, S., Urtasun, R.: Monocular object instance segmentation and depth ordering with CNNs. In: ICCV (2015)
73. Zhou, T., Brown, M., Snavely, N., Lowe, D.G.: Unsupervised learning of depth and ego-motion from video. In: CVPR (2017)
74. Zoran, D., Isola, P., Krishnan, D., Freeman, W.T.: Learning ordinal relationships for mid-level vision. In: ICCV (2015)

Neural Stereoscopic Image Style Transfer

Xinyu Gong[2], Haozhi Huang[1(✉)], Lin Ma[1], Fumin Shen[2], Wei Liu[1], and Tong Zhang[1]

[1] Tencent AI Lab, Shenzhen, China
huanghz08@gmail.com, forest.linma@gmail.com, tongzhang@tongzhang-ml.org, wl2223@columbia.edu

[2] University of Electronic Science and Technology of China, Chengdu, China
neoxygong@gmail.com, fumin.shen@gmail.com

Abstract. Neural style transfer is an emerging technique which is able to endow daily-life images with attractive artistic styles. Previous work has succeeded in applying convolutional neural networks (CNNs) to style transfer for monocular images or videos. However, style transfer for stereoscopic images is still a missing piece. Different from processing a monocular image, the two views of a stylized stereoscopic pair are required to be consistent to provide observers a comfortable visual experience. In this paper, we propose a novel dual path network for view-consistent style transfer on stereoscopic images. While each view of the stereoscopic pair is processed in an individual path, a novel feature aggregation strategy is proposed to effectively share information between the two paths. Besides a traditional perceptual loss being used for controlling the style transfer quality in each view, a multi-layer view loss is leveraged to enforce the network to coordinate the learning of both the paths to generate view-consistent stylized results. Extensive experiments show that, compared against previous methods, our proposed model can produce stylized stereoscopic images which achieve decent view consistency.

Keywords: Neural style transfer · Stereoscopic image

1 Introduction

With the advancement of technologies, more and more novel devices provide people various visual experiences. Among them, a device providing an immersive visual experience is one of the most popular, including virtual reality devices [8], augmented reality devices [21], 3D movie systems [11], and 3D televisions [17]. A common component shared by these devices is the stereo imaging technique, which creates the illusion of depth in a stereo pair by means of stereopsis for binocular vision. To provide more appealing visual experiences, lots of studies strive to apply engrossing visual effects to stereoscopic images [1,3,20]. Neural style transfer is one of the emerging techniques that can be used to achieve this goal.

Work done while Xinyu Gong was a Research Intern with Tencent AI Lab.

V. Ferrari et al. (Eds.): ECCV 2018, LNCS 11209, pp. 56–71, 2018.
https://doi.org/10.1007/978-3-030-01228-1_4

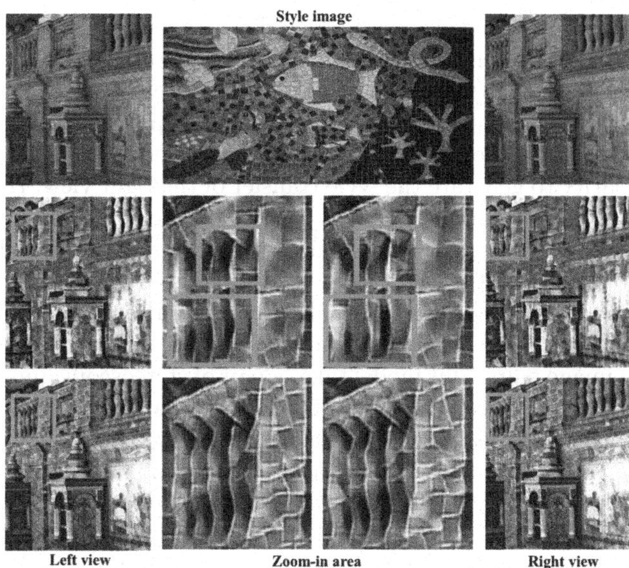

Fig. 1. Style transfer applied on stereoscopic images with and without view consistency. The first row shows two input stereoscopic images and one reference style image. The second row includes the stylized results generated by Johnson *et al.*'s method [12]. The middle columns show the zoom-in results, where apparent inconsistency appears in Johnson *et al.*'s method, while our results showed in the third row maintain high consistency.

Style transfer is a longstanding problem aiming to combine the content of one image with the style of another. Recently, Gatys *et al.* [6] revisited this problem and proposed an optimization-based solution utilizing features extracted by a pre-trained convolutional neural network, dubbed Neural Style Transfer, which generates the most fascinating results ever. Following this pioneering work, lots of efforts have been devoted to boosting speed [12,27], improving quality [28,31], extending to videos [4,7,9], and modeling multiple styles simultaneously [10,19,29]. However, the possibility of applying neural style transfer to stereoscopic images has not yet been sufficiently explored. For stereoscopic images, one straightforward solution is to apply single-image style transfer [12] to the left view and right view separately. However, this method will introduce severe view inconsistency which disturbs the original depth information incorporated in the stereo pair and thus brings observers an uncomfortable visual experience [15]. Here view inconsistency means that the stylized stereo pair has different stereo mappings from the input. This is because single image style transfer is highly unstable. A slight difference between the input stereo pair may be enormously amplified in the stylized results. An example is shown in the second row of Fig. 1, where stylized patterns of the same part in the two views are obviously inconsistent.

In the literature of stereoscopic image editing, a number of methods have been proposed to satisfy the need of maintaining view consistency. However, they introduce visible artifacts [23] and require precise stereo matchings [1], while being computationally expensive [20]. An intuitive approach is to run single-image style transfer on the left view, and then warp the result according to the estimated disparity to generate the style transfer of the right view. However, this will introduce extremely annoying black regions due to the occluded regions in a stereo pair. Even if filling the black regions with the right-view stylized result, severe edge artifacts are still inevitable.

In this paper, we propose a novel dual path convolutional neural network for the stereoscopic style transfer, which can generate view-consistent high-quality stylized stereo image pairs. Our model takes a pair of stereoscopic images as input simultaneously and stylizes each view of the stereo pair through an individual path. The intermediate features of one path are aggregated with the features from the other path via a trainable feature aggregation block. Specifically, a gating operation is directly learned by the network to guide the feature aggregation process. Various feature aggregation strategies are explored to demonstrate the superiority of our proposed feature aggregation block. Besides the traditional perceptual loss used in the style transfer for monocular images [12], a multi-layer view loss is leveraged to constrain the stylized outputs of both views to be consistent in multiple scales. Employing the proposed view loss, our network is able to coordinate the training of both the paths and guide the feature aggregation block to learn the optimal feature fusion strategy for generating view-consistent stylized stereo image pairs. Compared against previous methods, our method can produce view-consistent stylized results, while achieving competitive quality.

In general, the main contributions of our paper are as follows:

- We propose a novel dual path network for stereoscopic style transfer, which can simultaneously stylize a pair of stereoscopic images while maintaining view consistency.
- A multi-layer view loss is proposed to coordinate the training of the two paths of our network, enabling the model, specifically the dual path network, to yield view-consistent stylized results.
- A feature aggregation block is proposed to learn a proper feature fusion strategy for improving the view consistency of the stylized results.

2 Related Work

In this work, we try to generate view-consistent stylized stereo pairs via a dual path network, which is closely related to the existing literature on style transfer and stereoscopic image editing.

Neural Style Transfer. The first neural style transfer method was proposed by Gatys *et al.* [6], which iteratively optimizes the input image to minimize a content loss and a style loss defined on a pretrained deep neural network. Although this method achieves fascinating results for arbitrary styles, it is time consuming due to the optimization process. Afterwards, models based on feed-forward CNNs were proposed to boost the speed [12,27], which obtain real-time performance without sacrificing too much style quality. Recently, efforts have been devoted to extending singe-image neural style transfer to videos [4,10,24]. The main challenge for video neural style transfer lies in preventing flicker artifacts brought by temporal inconsistency. To solve this problem, Ruder *et al.* [24] introduced a temporal loss to the time-consuming optimization-based method proposed by Gatys *et al.* [6]. By incorporating temporal consistency into a feed-forward CNN in the training phase, Huang *et al.* [9] were able to generate temporally coherent stylized videos in real time. Gupta *et al.* [7] also accomplished real-time video neural style transfer by a recurrent convolutional network trained with a temporal loss. Besides the extensive literature on neural style transfer for images or videos, there is still a short of studies on stereoscopic style transfer. Applying single-image style transfer on stereoscopic images directly will cause view inconsistency, which provides observers an uncomfortable visual experience. In this paper, we propose a dual path network to share information between both views, which can accomplish view-consistent stereoscopic style transfer.

Stereoscopic Image Editing. The main difficulty of stereoscopic image editing lies in maintaining the view consistency. Basha *et al.* [1] successfully extended single image seam carving to stereoscopic images, by considering visibility relationships between pixels. A patch-based synthesis framework was presented by Luo *et al.* [20] for stereoscopic images, which suggests a joint patch-pair search to enhance the view consistency. Lee *et al.* [16] proposed a layer-based stereoscopic image resizing method, leveraging image warping to handle the view correlation. In [23], Northam *et al.* proposed a view-consistent stylization method for simple image filters, but introducing severe artifacts due to layer-wise operations. Kim *et al.* [13] presented a projection based stylization method for stereoscopic 3D lines, which maps stroke textures information through the linked parameterized stroke paths in each view. Stavrakis *et al.* [26] proposed a warping based image stylization method, warping the left view of the stylized image to the right and using a segment merging operation to fill the occluded regions. The above methods are either task specific or time-consuming, which are not able to generalize to the neural style transfer problem. In this paper, we incorporate view consistency into the training phase of a dual path convolutional neural network, thus generating view-consistent style transfer results with very high efficiency.

3 Proposed Method

Generally, our model is composed of two parts: a dual path stylizing network and a loss network (see Fig. 2). The dual path stylizing network takes a stereo pair and processes each view in an individual path. A feature aggregation block is embedded into the stylizing network to effectively share feature level information between the two paths. The loss network computes a perceptual loss and a multi-layer view loss to coordinate the training of both the paths of the stylizing network for generating view-consistent stylized results.

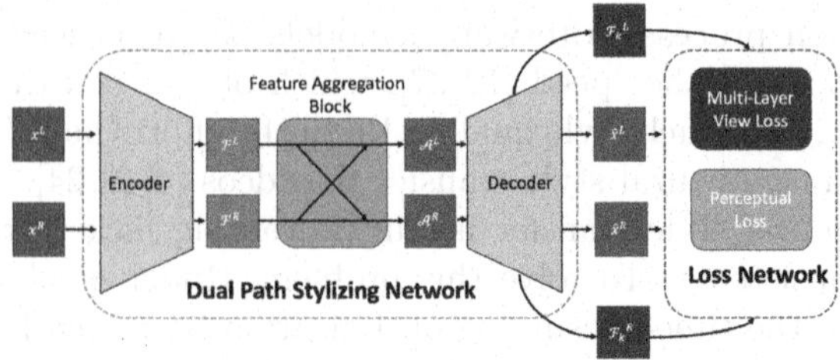

Fig. 2. An overview of our proposed model, which consists of a dual path stylizing network and a loss network. The dual path stylizing network takes a pair of stereoscopic images x^L and x^R as input, generating the corresponding stylized images $\widehat{x}^L$ and $\widehat{x}^R$. A feature aggregation block is proposed to share information between the two paths. The loss network calculates the perceptual loss and the multi-layer view loss to guide the training of the stylizing network.

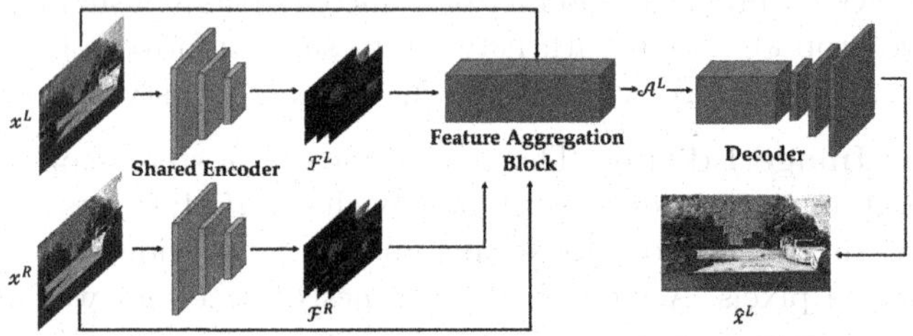

Fig. 3. The architecture of the stylizing network, consisting of an encoder, a feature aggregation block, and a decoder. Input images x^L and x^R are encoded to yield the feature maps $\mathcal{F}^L$ and $\mathcal{F}^R$. The feature aggregation block takes $\mathcal{F}^L$ and $\mathcal{F}^R$ as input and aggregates them into $\mathcal{A}^L$. Then $\mathcal{A}^L$ is decoded to yield the stylized result $\widehat{x}^L$.

3.1 Dual Path Stylizing Network

Our stylizing network is composed of three parts: an encoder, a feature aggregation block, and a decoder. The architecture of the stylizing network is shown in Fig. 3. For simplicity, we mainly illustrate the stylizing process of the left view, which is identical to that of the right view. First, the encoder, which is shared by both paths, takes the original images as input and extracts initial feature maps $\mathcal{F}^L$ and $\mathcal{F}^R$ for both views. Second, in the feature aggregation block, $\mathcal{F}^L$ and $\mathcal{F}^R$ are combined together to formulate an aggregated feature map $\mathcal{A}^L$. Finally, $\mathcal{A}^L$ is decoded to produce the stylized image of the left view $\widehat{x}^L$.

Encoder-Decoder. Our encoder downsamples the input images, and extracts the corresponding features progressively. The extracted features are then fed to the feature aggregation block. Finally, our decoder takes the aggregated feature map $\mathcal{A}^L$ as input, and decodes it into stylized images. Note that the encoder and decoder are shared by both views. The specific architectures of the encoder and decoder are shown in Sect. 4.1.

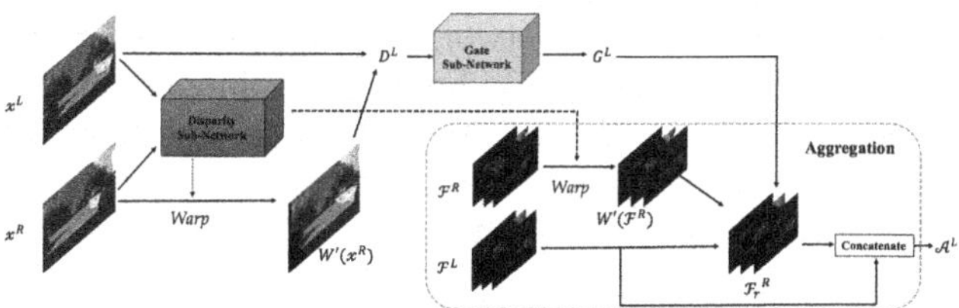

Fig. 4. The architecture of the feature aggregation block. The feature aggregation block takes the input stereo pair x^L and x^R and the corresponding encoder's outputs $\mathcal{F}^L$ and $\mathcal{F}^R$. Then, it computes the aggregated feature map $\mathcal{A}^L$. The proposed feature aggregation block consists of three key components: a disparity sub-network, a gate sub-network, and an aggregation.

Feature Aggregation Block. As aforementioned, separately applying a single-image style transfer algorithm on each view of a stereo image pair will cause view inconsistency. Thus, we introduce a feature aggregation block to integrate the features of both the paths, enabling our model to exploit more information from both views to preserve view consistency.

The architecture of the feature aggregation block is shown in Fig. 4. Taking the original stereoscopic images and the features extracted by the encoder as input, the feature aggregation block outputs an aggregated feature map $\mathcal{A}^L$, which absorbs information from both views.

Specifically, a disparity map is predicted by a pretrained disparity sub-network. The predicted disparity map is used to warp the initial right-view feature map $\mathcal{F}^R$ to align with the initial left-view feature map $\mathcal{F}^L$, obtaining the warped right-view feature map $W'(\mathcal{F}^R)$. Explicitly learning a warp operation in this way can reduce the complexity of extracting pixel correspondence information for the model. However, instead of directly concatenating the warped right-view feature map $W'(\mathcal{F}^R)$ with the initial left-view feature map $\mathcal{F}^L$, a gate sub-network is adopted to learn a gating operation for guiding the refinement of $W'(\mathcal{F}^R)$, to generate the refined right feature map $\mathcal{F}_r^R$. Finally, we concatenate $\mathcal{F}_r^R$ with $\mathcal{F}^L$ along the channel axis to obtain the aggregated feature map $\mathcal{A}^L$.

Disparity Sub-network. Our disparity sub-network takes the concatenation of both views of the stereoscopic pair as input, and outputs the estimated disparity map. It is pretrained on the *Driving* dataset [22] in a supervised way, which contains ground-truth disparity maps. To predict the disparity map for the left view, both views of the stereoscopic pair are concatenated along the channel axis to formulate $\{x^R, x^L\}$, which is thereafter fed to the disparity sub-network. Similarly, $\{x^L, x^R\}$ is the input for predicting the right disparity map. The specific architecture of our disparity sub-network is shown in Sect. 4.1. The architecture of our disparity sub-network is simple; however, it is efficient and does benefit the decrease of the view loss. It is undoubted that applying a more advanced disparity estimation network can boost the performance further at the cost of efficiency, which is out of the scope of this paper.

Gate Sub-network. The gate sub-network is proposed to generate a gate map for guiding the refinement of $W'(\mathcal{F}^R)$. First, using bilinear interpolation, we resize the input stereoscopic pair x^L, x^R to the same resolution as the initial left-view feature map $\mathcal{F}^L$, which is denoted as $r(x^L)$ and $r(x^R)$. Then we calculate the absolute difference between $r(x^L)$ and $W'(r(x^R))$:

$$D^L = \left|r(x^L) - W'(r(x^R))\right|. \tag{1}$$

Taking D^L as input, the gate sub-network predicts a single channel gate map G^L, which has the same resolution as $\mathcal{F}^L$. The range of the pixel values lies in $[0, 1]$, which will be used to refine the warped right-view feature map $W'(\mathcal{F}^R)$ later. The specific architecture of the gate sub-network is shown in Sect. 4.1.

Aggregation. Under the guidance of the gate map generated by the gate sub-network, we refine the warped right-view feature map $W'(\mathcal{F}^R)$ with the initial left-view feature map $\mathcal{F}^L$ to generate a refined right-view feature map:

$$\mathcal{F}_r^R = W'(\mathcal{F}^R) \odot G^L + \mathcal{F}^L \odot (1 - G^L), \tag{2}$$

where $\odot$ denotes element-wise multiplication. In our experiments, we find that concatenating $W'(\mathcal{F}^R)$ with $\mathcal{F}^L$ directly to formulate the final aggregated left-view feature map $\mathcal{A}^L$ will cause ghost artifacts in the stylized results. This is because the mismatching between $\mathcal{F}^L$ and $W'(\mathcal{F}^R)$, which is caused by occlusion and inaccurate disparity prediction, will incorrectly introduce right-view information to the left view. Using the gating operation can avoid this issue. Finally, the refined right-view feature map $\mathcal{F}_r^R$ is concatenated with the initial left-view feature map $\mathcal{F}^L$ to formulate the aggregated left-view feature map $\mathcal{A}^L$.

3.2 Loss Network

Different from the single-image style transfer [12], the loss network used by our method serves for two purposes. One is to evaluate the style quality of the outputs, and the other is to enforce our network to incorporate view consistency in the training phase. Thus, our loss network calculates a perceptual loss and a multi-layer view loss to guide the training of the stylizing network:

$$\mathcal{L}_{\text{total}} = \sum_{d \in \{L,R\}} \mathcal{L}_{\text{perceptual}}(s, x^d, \widehat{x}^d) + \lambda \mathcal{L}_{\text{view}}(\widehat{x}^L, \widehat{x}^R, \mathcal{F}_k^L, \mathcal{F}_k^R), \tag{3}$$

where $\mathcal{F}_k$ denotes the k-th layer feature map of the decoder in the stylizing network. s is the reference style image. The architecture of our loss network is shown in Fig. 5. While the perceptual losses of the two views are calculated separately, the multi-layer view loss is calculated based on the outputs and the features of both views. By training with the proposed losses, the stylizing network learns to coordinate the training of both the paths to leverage the information from both views, eventually generating stylized and view-consistent results.

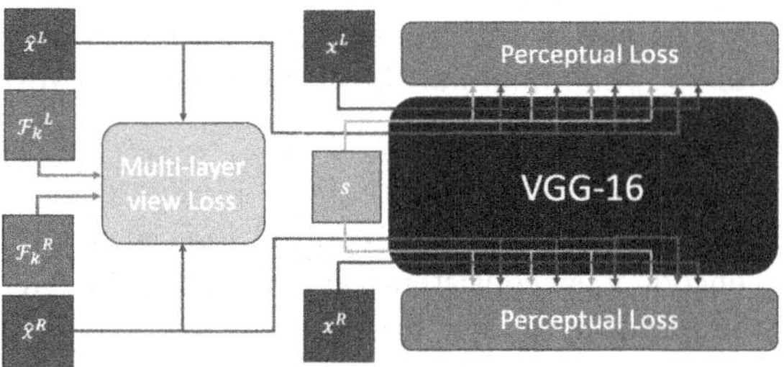

Fig. 5. The architecture of the loss network. The perceptual losses of the two views are calculated separately, while the multi-layer view loss is calculated based on the outputs and the features of both views.

Perceptual Loss. We adopt the definition of the perceptual loss in [12], which has been demonstrated effective in neural style transfer. The perceptual loss is employed to evaluate the stylizing quality of the outputs, which consists of a content loss and a style loss:

$$\mathcal{L}_{\text{perceptual}}(s, x^d, \widehat{x}^d) = \alpha \mathcal{L}_{\text{content}}(x^d, \widehat{x}^d) + \beta \mathcal{L}_{\text{style}}(s, \widehat{x}^d), \tag{4}$$

where α, β are the trade-off weights. We adopt a pretrained VGG-16 network [25] to extract features for calculating the perceptual loss.

The content loss is introduced to preserve the high-level content information of the inputs:

$$\mathcal{L}_{\text{content}}(x^d, \widehat{x}^d) = \sum_l \frac{1}{H^l W^l C^l} \left\| \mathcal{F}^l(x^d) - \mathcal{F}^l(\widehat{x}^d) \right\|_2^2, \tag{5}$$

where $\mathcal{F}^l$ denotes the feature map at layer l in the VGG-16 network. W^l, H^l, C^l are the height, width, and channel size of the feature map at layer l, respectively. The content loss constrains the feature maps of x^d and $\widehat{x}^d$ to be similar, where $d = \{L, R\}$ represents different views.

The style loss is employed to evaluate the stylizing quality of the generated images. Here we use the Gram matrix as the style representation, which has been demonstrated effective in [6]:

$$G_{ij}^l(x^d) = \frac{1}{H^l W^l} \sum_h^{H^l} \sum_w^{W^l} \mathcal{F}^l(x^d)_{h,w,i} \mathcal{F}^l(x^d)_{h,w,j}, \tag{6}$$

where G_{ij}^l denotes the i, j-th element of the Gram matrix of the feature map at layer l. The style loss is defined as the mean square error between the Gram matrices of the output and the reference style image:

$$\mathcal{L}_{\text{style}}(s, \widehat{x}^d) = \sum_l \frac{1}{C^l}^2 \left\| G^l(s) - G^l(\widehat{x}^d) \right\|_2^2. \tag{7}$$

Matching the Gram matrices of feature maps has also been demonstrated to be equivalent to minimizing the Maximum Mean Discrepancy (MMD) between the output and the style reference [18].

Multi-layer View Loss. Besides a perceptual loss, a novel multi-layer view loss is proposed to encode view consistency into our model in the training phase. The definition of the multi-layer view loss is:

$$\mathcal{L}_{\text{view}} = \mathcal{L}_{\text{view}}^{\text{img}} + \mathcal{L}_{\text{view}}^{\text{feat}}, \tag{8}$$

where the image-level view loss constrains the outputs to be view-consistent, and the feature-level view loss constrains the feature maps in the stylizing network to be consistent. The image-level view loss is defined as:

$$\begin{aligned} \mathcal{L}_{\text{view}}^{\text{img}} &= \frac{1}{\sum_{i,j} M_{i,j}^L} \left\| M^L \odot (\widehat{x}^L - W(\widehat{x}^R)) \right\|_2^2 \\ &+ \frac{1}{\sum_{i,j} M_{i,j}^R} \left\| M^R \odot (\widehat{x}^R - W(\widehat{x}^L)) \right\|_2^2, \end{aligned} \tag{9}$$

where M is the per-pixel confidence mask of the disparity map, which has the same shape as stylized images. The value of $M_{i,j}$ is either 0 or 1, where 0 in mismatched areas, and 1 in well-matched corresponding areas. $\widehat{x}^L$ and $\widehat{x}^R$ are stylized results. We use W to denote the warp operation using the ground-truth disparity map, provided by the Scene Flow Datasets [22]. Thus, $W(\widehat{x}^L)$ and $W(\widehat{x}^R)$ are a warped stylized stereo pair, using the ground-truth disparity map.

In order to enhance view consistency of stylized images further, we also enforce the corresponding activation values on intermediate feature maps of left and right content images to be identical. Thus, the feature-level view loss is introduced. Similarly, the feature-level view loss is defined as follow:

$$\begin{aligned} \mathcal{L}_{\text{view}}^{\text{feat}} &= \frac{1}{\sum_{i,j} m_{i,j}^L} \left\| m^L \odot [\mathcal{F}_k^L - W(\mathcal{F}_k^R)] \right\|_2^2 \\ &+ \frac{1}{\sum_{i,j} m_{i,j}^R} \left\| m^R \odot [\mathcal{F}_k^R - W(\mathcal{F}_k^L)] \right\|_2^2, \end{aligned} \tag{10}$$

where m is the resized version of M, sharing the same resolution as the k-th layer's feature map in the decoder. $\mathcal{F}_k^L$ and $\mathcal{F}_k^R$ are the feature maps fetched out from the k-th layer in the stylizing network. Similarly, $W(\mathcal{F}_k^L)$ and $W(\mathcal{F}_k^R)$ are the warped feature maps using the ground-truth disparity map.

4 Experiments

4.1 Implementation

The specific configuration of the encoder and the decoder of our model is shown in Table 1. We use *Conv* to denote Convolution-BatchNorm-Activation block.

Table 1. Model configuration.

Layer	Kernel	Stride	C_{in}	C_{out}	Acitivation
Encoder					
Conv	3×3	1	3	16	ReLU
Conv	3×3	2	16	32	ReLU
Conv	3×3	2	32	48	ReLU
Decoder					
Conv	3×3	1	96	96	ReLU
Conv	3×3	1	96	48	ReLU
Res × 5			48	48	ReLU
Deconv	3×3	0.5	48	32	ReLU
Deconv	3×3	0.5	32	16	ReLU
Conv	3×3	1	16	3	tanh

Layer	Kernel	Stride	C_{in}	C_{out}	Acitivation
Disparity Sub-network					
Conv	3×3	1	6	32	ReLU
Conv	3×3	2	32	64	ReLU
Conv	3×3	2	64	48	ReLU
Res × 5			48	48	ReLU
Deconv	3×3	0.5	48	24	ReLU
Deconv	3×3	0.5	24	8	ReLU
Conv	3×3	1	8	3	ReLU
Conv	3×3	1	3	1	-
Gate Sub-network					
Conv	3×3	1	3	6	ReLU
Conv	1×1	1	6	12	ReLU
Conv	1×1	1	12	6	ReLU
Conv	1×1	1	6	3	ReLU
Conv	1×1	1	3	1	tanh

C_{in} and C_{out} denote the channel numbers of the input and the output respectively. *Res* denotes the Residual block, following a similar configuration to [12]. *Deconv* denotes Deconvolution-BatchNorm-Activation block.

We use *Driving* in the Scene Flow Datasets [22] as our dataset, which contains $4.4k$ pairs of stereoscopic images. 440 pairs of them are used as testing samples, while the rest are used as training samples. Besides, we also use the stereo images from Flickr [5], *Driving* test set and Sintel [2] to show the visual quality of our results in Sect. 4.2. In addition, images from Waterloo-IVC 3D database [30] are used to conduct our user study. Testing on various datasets in this way demonstrates the generalization ability of our model. The loss network (VGG-16) is pretrained on the image classification task [25]. Note that during the training phase, the multi-layer view loss is calculated using the ground-truth disparity map provided by the Scene Flow Datasets [22] to warp fetched feature maps and stylized images. Specifically, we fetch feature maps at 7-th layer of decoder to calculate feature-level view loss according to our experiments.

The disparity sub-network is first pretrained and fixed thereafter. Then, we train the other parts of the stylizing network for 2 epochs. The input image resolution is 960×540. We set $\alpha = 1$, $\beta = 500$, $\lambda = 100$. The batch size is set to 1. The learning rate is fixed as $1e - 3$. For optimization we use Adam [14].

4.2 Qualitative Results

We apply the trained model to some stereoscopic pictures from Flickr [5] to show the visual qualities of different styles. In Fig. 6, stylized results in four different styles are presented, from which we can see that the semantic content of the input images are preserved, while the texture and color are transferred from the reference style images successfully. Besides, view consistency is also maintained.

4.3 Comparison

In this section, we compare our method with the single image style transfer method [12]. Though there are many alternative baseline designed for single

Fig. 6. Visual results of our proposed stereoscopic style transfer method. While the high-level contents of the inputs are well preserved, the style details are successfully transferred from the given style images. Meanwhile, view consistency is maintained.

image neural style transfer, both of them will suffer from similar view inconsistency artifacts as Johnson's method [12]. Hence, we only choose [12] as a representative. Also, we testify the effectiveness of the multi-layer view loss and the feature aggregation block.

As the evaluation metric, we define a term called the mean view loss MVL:

$$MVL = \frac{1}{N}\sum_{n=1}^{N} \mathcal{L}_{\text{view}}^{\text{img}}(I_n), \tag{11}$$

where N is the total number of test images, I_n is the n-th image in the test dataset, $\mathcal{L}_{\text{view}}^{\text{img}}$ is the image-level view loss defined in Eq. 9. In other words, MVL is employed to evaluate the average of the image-level view losses over the whole test dataset. Similarly, we also define mean style loss (MSL) and mean content loss (MCL):

$$MSL = \frac{1}{N}\sum_{n=1}^{N} \mathcal{L}_{\text{style}}(I_n), \tag{12}$$

$$MCL = \frac{1}{N}\sum_{n=1}^{N} \mathcal{L}_{\text{content}}(I_n). \tag{13}$$

For clarity, the single image style transfer method is named as *SingleImage*, where the single image method trained with image-level view loss is named as *SingleImage-IV*. Our full model with a feature aggregation block trained with a multi-layer view loss is named as *Stereo-FA-MV*. The variant model with a feature aggregation block but trained with an image-level view loss is named as *Stereo-FA-IV*. We evaluate the MVL, MSL and MCL of the above models across four styles: *Fish*, *Mosaic*, *Candy* and *Dream*, where the MSLs are coordinated into a similar level. In Table 2, we can see that the mean view loss MVL of

Table 2. MVL, MSL and MCL of five different models over 4 styles, where MSLs are coordinated into a similar level.

Model	*SingleImage*	*SingleImage-IV*	*Stereo-FA-IV*	*Stereo-FA-dp-IV*	*Stereo-FA-MV*
MSL	426	424	410	**407**	417
MVL	2033	1121	1028	1022	**1014**
MCL	**424153**	485089	481056	478413	445336

our full model *Stereo-FA-MV* is the smallest. The result of the single image style transfer method is the worst. Comparing *Stereo-FA-IV* with *SingleImage-IV*, we know that the feature aggregation block benefits the view consistency. Comparing *Stereo-FA-MV* with *Stereo-FA-IV*, we find that constraining the view loss in the feature level besides the image level improves the view consistency further. We also conduct the experiment with fine-tuning the whole network together instead of freezing the disparity sub-network *Stereo-FA-dp-IV*, which performs comparably with *Stereo-FA-IV*.

In order to give a more intuitive comparison, we visualize the view inconsistency maps of the single image style transfer method and our proposed method in Fig. 7. The view inconsistency map is defined as:

$$V^L = \sum_c \left|\widehat{x}_c^L - W(\widehat{x}^R)_c\right| \odot M^L, \tag{14}$$

where $\widehat{x}_c^L$ and $W(\widehat{x}^R)_c$ denote c-th channel of $\widehat{x}^L$ and $W(\widehat{x}^R)$ respectively. M is the per-pixel confidence mask of disparity map which is illustrated in Sect. 3.2. Note that W denotes the warp operation using the ground-truth disparity map, provided by the Scene Flow Datasets [22]. Compared with the results of *SingleImage*, a larger number of blue pixels in our results indicate that our method can preserve the view consistency better.

Moreover, a user study is conducted to compare *SingleImage* with our method. Specifically, a total number of 21 participants take part in our experiment. Ten stereo pairs are randomly picked up from the Waterloo-IVC 3D database [30]. For each of the stereo pair, we apply style transfer using three different style images (*candy, fish, mosaic*). As a result, 3×10 stylized stereoscopic pairs are generated for each model. Each time, a participant is shown the stylized results of the two methods on a 3D TV with a pair of 3D glasses, and asked to vote for the preferred one (which is more view-comfortable). Specifically, the original stereo pairs are shown before the stylized results of the two methods, in order to give participants the correct sense of depth as references. Table 3 shows the final results. 73% votes are cast to the stylized results generated by our method, which demonstrates that our method achieves better view consistency and provides more satisfactory visual experience.

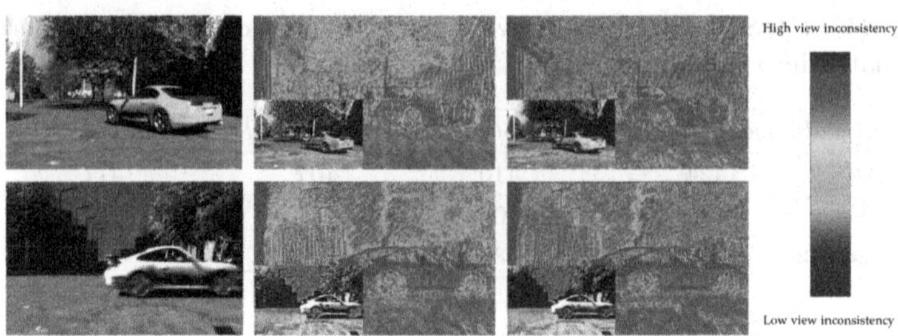

Fig. 7. Visualization of the view inconsistency. The second column shows view inconsistency maps of the single-image style transfer method [12]. The third column shows our results. The last column is the color map of view inconsistency maps. Obviously, our results are more view-consistent.

Table 3. User preferences.

Style	Prefer ours	Prefer Johnson *et al.*'s	Equal
Candy	**143**	29	38
Fish	**166**	14	30
Mosaic	**152**	24	34

4.4 Ablation Study on Feature Aggregation

To testify the effectiveness of the proposed feature aggregation block, we set up an ablation study. Our feature aggregation block consists of three key operations: warping, gating and concatenation. We test 3 variant models with different settings of these key operations for obtaining the final aggregated feature maps $\mathcal{A}^L$ and $\mathcal{A}^R$. For simplicity, we only describe the process of obtaining $\mathcal{A}^L$.

The first model is *SingleImage-IV*, where the single image method trained with image-level view loss and perceptual loss. In the second model *CON-IV*, $\mathcal{A}^L$ is obtained by concatenating $\mathcal{F}^R$ with $\mathcal{F}^L$. The last model *W-G-CON-IV* uses our proposed feature aggregation block, which is equal to *Stereo-FA-IV* as mentioned before. Here we consider warping-gating as an indivisible operation, as the warping operation will inevitably introduce hollow areas in the occluded region, and the gating operation is used to localize the hollow areas and guide a feature aggregation process to fill the holes. All models above are trained with the perceptual loss and view loss, using *Fish*, *Mosaic*, *Candy* and *Dream* as the reference style images.

Table 4 shows the mean view loss of the 3 variant models. Comparing *CON-IV* with *SingleImage-IV*, we can see that concatenating $\mathcal{F}^R$ with $\mathcal{F}^L$ does help the decrease of the *MVL*, which demonstrates that the concatenated skip connection is essential. Comparing *W-G-CON-IV* with *CON-IV*, *W-G-CON-IV* achieves better performance. This is because that $\mathcal{F}_r^R$ is aligned with $\mathcal{F}^L$ along the channel axis, which relieves the need of learning pixel correspondences.

Table 4. MVL, MSL and MCL of three different feature aggregation blocks. Our proposed feature aggregation block architecture achieves the smallest MVL and MCL, indicating the best view consistency and content preservation.

Model	*SingleImage-IV*	*CON-IV*	*W-G-CON-IV*
MSL	424	**328**	410
MVL	1121	1068	**1028**
MCL	485089	489555	**481056**

Fig. 8. Visualization of gate maps. The left and middle columns are two input stereo pairs. The right column shows the left-view gate map generated by the gate sub-network.

In order to give an intuitive understanding of the gate maps, we visualize several gate maps in Fig. 8. Recalling that the Eq. 2, the refined feature map $\mathcal{F}_r^R$ is a linear combination of the initial feature map $\mathcal{F}^L$ and the warped feature map $W'(\mathcal{F}^R)$, under the guidance of the gate map. For simplicity, we only illustrate the gate maps for the left view. Generated gate maps are shown in the right column. The black regions in the gate maps indicate the mismatching between $\mathcal{F}^L$ and $W'(\mathcal{F}^R)$. Here, the mismatching is caused by occlusion and inaccurate disparity estimation. For the mismatched areas, the gate sub-network learns to predict 0 values to enforce the refined feature map $\mathcal{F}_r^R$ directly copy values from $\mathcal{F}^L$ to avoid inaccurately incorporating information from the occluded regions in the right view.

5 Conclusion

In this paper, we proposed a novel dual path network to deal with style transfer on stereoscopic images. While each view of an input stereo pair has been processed in an individual path to transfer the style from a reference image, a novel feature aggregation block was proposed to propagate the information from one path to another. Multiple feature aggregation strategies were investigated and compared to demonstrate the advantage of our proposed feature aggregation block. To coordinate the learning of both the paths for gaining better view consistency, a multi-layer view loss was introduced to constrain the stylized outputs of both views to be consistent in multiple scales. The extensive experiments demonstrate that our method is able to yield stylized results with better view consistency than those achieved by the previous methods.

References

1. Basha, T., Moses, Y., Avidan, S.: Geometrically consistent stereo seam carving. In: Proceedings of ICCV (2011)
2. Butler, D.J., Wulff, J., Stanley, G.B., Black, M.J.: A naturalistic open source movie for optical flow evaluation. In: Fitzgibbon, A., Lazebnik, S., Perona, P., Sato, Y., Schmid, C. (eds.) ECCV 2012. LNCS, vol. 7577, pp. 611–625. Springer, Heidelberg (2012). https://doi.org/10.1007/978-3-642-33783-3_44
3. Chang, C.H., Liang, C.K., Chuang, Y.Y.: Content-aware display adaptation and interactive editing for stereoscopic images. IEEE Trans. Multimed. **13**(4), 589–601 (2011)
4. Chen, D., Liao, J., Yuan, L., Yu, N., Hua, G.: Coherent online video style transfer. In: Proceedings of ICCV (2017)
5. Flickr: Flickr. https://www.flickr.com
6. Gatys, L.A., Ecker, A.S., Bethge, M.: Image style transfer using convolutional neural networks. In: Proceedings of CVPR (2016)
7. Gupta, A., Johnson, J., Alahi, A., Fei-Fei, L.: Characterizing and improving stability in neural style transfer. In: Proceedings of ICCV (2017)
8. HTC: HTC Vive. https://www.vive.com/us/
9. Huang, H., et al.: Real-time neural style transfer for videos. In: Proceedings of CVPR (2017)
10. Huang, X., Belongie, S.: Arbitrary style transfer in real-time with adaptive instance normalization. In: Proceedings of ICCV (2017)
11. IMAX: IMAX. https://www.imax.com
12. Johnson, J., Alahi, A., Fei-Fei, L.: Perceptual losses for real-time style transfer and super-resolution. In: Leibe, B., Matas, J., Sebe, N., Welling, M. (eds.) ECCV 2016. LNCS, vol. 9906, pp. 694–711. Springer, Cham (2016). https://doi.org/10.1007/978-3-319-46475-6_43
13. Kim, Y., Lee, Y., Kang, H., Lee, S.: Stereoscopic 3D line drawing. ACM Trans. Graph. (TOG) **32**(4), 57 (2013)
14. Kingma, D., Ba, J.: Adam: a method for stochastic optimization. arXiv preprint arXiv:1412.6980 (2014)
15. Kooi, F.L., Toet, A.: Visual comfort of binocular and 3D displays. Displays **25**(2), 99–108 (2004)
16. Lee, K.Y., Chung, C.D., Chuang, Y.Y.: Scene warping: layer-based stereoscopic image resizing. In: Proceedings of CVPR (2012)
17. LG: 4K HDR Smart TV. http://www.lg.com/us/tvs/lg-OLED65G6P-oled-4k-tv
18. Li, Y., Wang, N., Liu, J., Hou, X.: Demystifying neural style transfer. arXiv preprint arXiv:1701.01036 (2017)
19. Li, Y., Fang, C., Yang, J., Wang, Z., Lu, X., Yang, M.H.: Diversified texture synthesis with feed-forward networks. arXiv preprint arXiv:1703.01664 (2017)
20. Luo, S.J., Sun, Y.T., Shen, I.C., Chen, B.Y., Chuang, Y.Y.: Geometrically consistent stereoscopic image editing using patch-based synthesis. IEEE Trans. Vis. Comput. Graph. **21**, 56–67 (2015)

21. Microsoft: Microsoft HoloLens. https://www.microsoft.com/en-gb/hololens
22. Mayer, N., et al.: A large dataset to train convolutional networks for disparity, optical flow, and scene flow estimation. In: Proceedings of CVPR (2016)
23. Northam, L., Asente, P., Kaplan, C.S.: Consistent stylization and painterly rendering of stereoscopic 3D images. In: Proceedings of NPAR (2012)
24. Ruder, M., Dosovitskiy, A., Brox, T.: Artistic style transfer for videos. In: Rosenhahn, B., Andres, B. (eds.) GCPR 2016. LNCS, vol. 9796, pp. 26–36. Springer, Cham (2016). https://doi.org/10.1007/978-3-319-45886-1_3
25. Simonyan, K., Zisserman, A.: Very deep convolutional networks for large-scale image recognition. arXiv preprint arXiv:1409.1556 (2014)
26. Stavrakis, E., Bleyer, M., Markovic, D., Gelautz, M.: Image-based stereoscopic stylization. In: IEEE International Conference on Image Processing, ICIP 2005, vol. 3, pp. III–5. IEEE (2005)
27. Ulyanov, D., Lebedev, V., Vedaldi, A., Lempitsky, V.S.: Texture networks: feed-forward synthesis of textures and stylized images. In: Proceedings of ICML (2016)
28. Ulyanov, D., Vedaldi, A., Lempitsky, V.: Instance normalization: the missing ingredient for fast stylization. arXiv preprint arXiv:1607.08022 (2016)
29. Wang, H., Liang, X., Zhang, H., Yeung, D.Y., Xing, E.P.: ZM-net: real-time zero-shot image manipulation network. arXiv preprint arXiv:1703.07255 (2017)
30. Wang, J., Rehman, A., Zeng, K., Wang, S., Wang, Z.: Quality prediction of asymmetrically distorted stereoscopic 3D images. IEEE Trans. Image Process. **24**(11), 3400–3414 (2015)
31. Wang, X., Oxholm, G., Zhang, D., Wang, Y.F.: Multimodal transfer: a hierarchical deep convolutional neural network for fast artistic style transfer. In: Proceedings of CVPR (2017)

Transductive Centroid Projection for Semi-supervised Large-Scale Recognition

Yu Liu[1,2](✉), Guanglu Song[2], Jing Shao[2], Xiao Jin[2], and Xiaogang Wang[1,2]

[1] The Chinese University of Hong Kong, Shatin, Hong Kong
{yuliu,xgwang}@ee.cuhk.edu.hk
[2] Sensetime Group Limited, Beijing 100084, China
{songguanglu,shaojing,jinxiao}@sensetime.com

Abstract. Conventional deep semi-supervised learning methods, such as recursive clustering and training process, suffer from cumulative error and high computational complexity when collaborating with Convolutional Neural Networks. To this end, we design a simple but effective learning mechanism that merely substitutes the last fully-connected layer with the proposed Transductive Centroid Projection (TCP) module. It is inspired by the observation of the weights in the final classification layer (called *anchors*) converge to the central direction of each class in hyperspace. Specifically, we design the TCP module by dynamically adding an *ad hoc anchor* for each cluster in one mini-batch. It essentially reduces the probability of the inter-class conflict and enables the unlabelled data functioning as labelled data. We inspect its effectiveness with elaborate ablation study on seven public face/person classification benchmarks. Without any bells and whistles, TCP can achieve significant performance gains over most state-of-the-art methods in both fully-supervised and semi-supervised manners.

Keywords: Person Re-ID · Face recognition
Deep semi-supervised learning

1 Introduction

The explosion of the Convolutional Neural Networks (CNNs) brings a remarkable evolution in the field of image understanding, especially some real-world tasks such as face recognition [1–5] and person re-identification (Re-ID) [6–11]. Much of this progress was sparked by the creation of large-scale datasets as well as the new and robust learning strategies for feature learning. For instance, MS-Celeb-1M [12] and MARS [13] provide more than 10-million face images and 1-million pedestrian images respectively with rough annotation. Moreover, in the industrial environment, it may take only a few weeks to collect billions of face/pedestrian gallery from a city-level surveillance system. But it is hard to label such billion-level data. Utilizing these large-scale unlabelled data to benefit the classification tasks remains non-trivial.

V. Ferrari et al. (Eds.): ECCV 2018, LNCS 11209, pp. 72–89, 2018.
https://doi.org/10.1007/978-3-030-01228-1_5

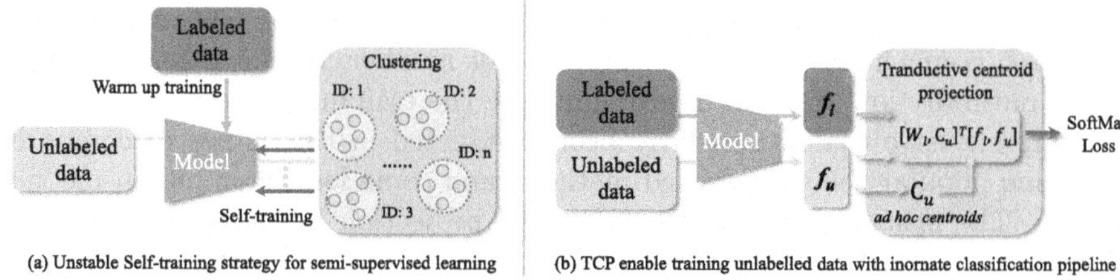

Fig. 1. A comparison between (a) self-training process with recursive clustering-finetuning (b) un/semi-supervised learning with transductive centroid projection

Most of recent unsupervised or semi-supervised learning approaches for face recognition or Re-ID [14–20] are based on self-training, *i.e.* the model clusters the training data and then the clustered results are used to fine-tune the model iteratively until converges, as shown in Fig. 1(a). The typical downsides in this process lie in two aspects. First, the recursive training framework is time-consuming. And second, since the clustering algorithms used in such approaches always generate ID-clusters with high precision scores but somewhat low recall score, that guarantee the clean clusters without inner errors, it may cause *inter-class conflict*, *i.e.* instances belonging to one identity are divided into different clusters, which hampers the fine-tuning stage. To this end, a question arises: how to utilize unlabelled data in a stable training process, such as a CNN modle with softmax classification loss function, without any recursion and avoid the inter-class conflict?

In this study, we design a novel Transductive Centroid Projection layer to efficiently incorporate the training of the unlabelled clusters accompanied by the learning of the labelled samples, and can be readily extended to an unsupervised manner by setting the labelled data to $\varnothing$.

It is enlightened from the latent space learned by the common used Softmax loss. In deep neural network, each column in the projection matrix $\mathbf{W}$ of the final fully-connected layer indicates the *normal direction* of the decision hyperplane. We call each column as *anchor* in this paper. For a labelled data, the *anchor* of its class already exists in $\mathbf{W}$, and thus we can train the network by maximizing the inner product of its feature and its anchor. However, the unlabelled data doesn't even have a class, so it cannot directly provide the decision hyperplane. To utilize unlabelled samples with conventional deep classification network, we need to find a way to simulate the their *anchors*.

Motivated by the observation that the *anchor* approximates the centroid direction as shown in Fig. 2, the transductive centroid projection layer could dynamically estimate the class centroids for the unlabelled clusters in each mini-batch, and treat them as the new anchors for unlabelled data which are then absorbed to the projection matrix so as to enable classification for both labelled and unlabelled data. As visualized in Fig. 1(b), the projection matrix $\mathbf{W}$ of the classification layer in original CNN is replaced by the joint matrix of $\mathbf{W}$ and *ad hoc* centroids $\mathbf{C}$. In this manner, labelled data and unlabelled data function the same during training. As analyzed in Sect. 3.3, since the *ad hoc* centroids in each mini-batch is much fewer than the total cluster number, the inter-class conflict ratio is naturally low and can hardly influence the training process.

Comprehensive evaluations have been conducted in this paper to compare with some popular semi-supervised methods and some loss functions in metric learning. The proposed transductive centroid projection has a superior performance on stabilizing unsupervised/semi-supervised and optimizing the learned feature representation.

To sum up, the contribution of this paper is threefold:

(1) *Observation interpretation* - We investigate the observation that the directions of anchor (*i.e.* weight $\mathbf{w}_n$) gradually coincides with the centroid as model converges, both theoretically and empirically.
(2) *A novel Transductive Centroid Projection layer* - Based on the observation above, we propose an innovative un/semi-supervised learning mechanism to wisely integrate the unlabelled data into the recognition to boost its discriminative ability by introducing a new layer named as Transductive Centroid Projection (TCP). Without any iterative processing like self-training and label propagation, the proposed TCP can be simply trained and steadily embedded into arbitrary CNN structure with any classification loss.
(3) *Superior performance on face recognition and ReID benchmarks* - We apply TCP to the task of face recognition and person re-identification, and conduct extensive evaluations to thoroughly examine its superiority to both semi-supervised learning and supervised learning approaches.

1.1 Related Works

Semi-supervised Learning. An effective way for deep semi-supervised learning is the label propagation with self-training [21] by trusting the predicted label from the model trained on labeled data or clustered by clustering model [22–25], for close set or open set respectively. It will hamper the model convergence if the threshold is not precisely set. Other methods like Generative models [26], semi-supervised Support Vector Machines [27] and some graph-based semi-supervised learning methods [28] hold clear mathematical framework but are hard to be incorporated with deep learning methods.

Semi-supervised Face/Person Recognition. In [16], a couple dictionaries are jointly learned from both labelled and unlabelled data. LSRO [8] adopts GAN [29] to generate person patches to normalize data distribution and propose a loss named LSRO to supervise the generated patches. Some works [18,19] adopt local metric loss functions (*e.g.* triplet loss [2]) to avoid the inter-class conflict. These methods with local optimization function, however, are usually unstable and hard to converge, especially for large-scale data. Some other methods [19] adopt softmax loss to optimize global classes and suffer from the inter-class conflict. Most of these methods focus on transfer learning, self-training and data distribution normalization. In this work, we mainly pay attention to a basic

Table 1. Experimental settings on three tasks with different data scales to validate the observation

Task	#Class	Backbone	#Feature dim.	Feature space
MNIST	10	LeNet [30]	2	Fig. 2(a)
CIFAR-100	100	ResNet-18 [31]	128	Fig. 2(b)
MS1M-100K	100,000	Inception-ResNet [32]	128	Fig. 2(c)

question, namely how to wisely train a simple CNN model by fully leveraging both labelled and unlabelled data, without self-training or transfer learning.

2 Observation Inside the Softmax Classifier

In a typical straightforward CNN, let $\mathbf{f} \in \mathbb{R}^D$ denote the feature vector of one sample generated by prior layers, where D is the feature dimension. The linear activation $\mathbf{y} \in \mathbb{R}^N$ referring to N class labels is therefore accompanied with the weight $\mathbf{W} \in \mathbb{R}^{D \times N}$ and bias $\mathbf{b} \in \mathbb{R}^N$,

$$\mathbf{y} = \mathbf{W}^T \mathbf{f} + \mathbf{b}. \tag{1}$$

In this work we degenerate this classifier layer from affine to linear projection by setting the bias term $\mathbf{b} \equiv \mathbf{0}$. Supervised by softmax loss and optimized by SGD, we can usually observe the following phenomenon: The anchor $\mathbf{w}_i = \mathbf{W}_{[i]} \in \mathbb{R}^D$ for class i points to the direction of the data centroid of class i, when the model has successfully converged. We first show this observation in three toy examples from a low-dimensional space to a high one. Then we try to interpret it by gradient view.

2.1 Toy Examples

To investigate the aforementioned observation from small-scale to large-scale tasks and from low dimensional to high dimensional latent space, we empirically analyze three tasks with different data scales, feature dimension and network structure, *i.e.* character classification on MNIST [33] with 10 classes, object classification on CIFAR-100 [34] with 100 classes, and face recognition on MS1M [35] with $100,000$ classes[1]. Table 1 records the detailed settings for these experiments. To each task, there are two `FC` layers after its backbone structure, in which `FC1` learns an internal feature vector $\mathbf{f}$ and `FC2` acts as the projection onto the class space. All tasks employ the softmax loss. Figure 2 depicts the feature spaces extracted from different datasets, in which the 2-D features in MNIST are directly plotted and the 128-D features in CIFAR-100 and MS1M are compressed by Barnes-Hut t-SNE [36].

[1] The original MS1M dataset has one million face identities with several noises samples. Here we only take the first $100,000$ identities for the convenience of illustration.

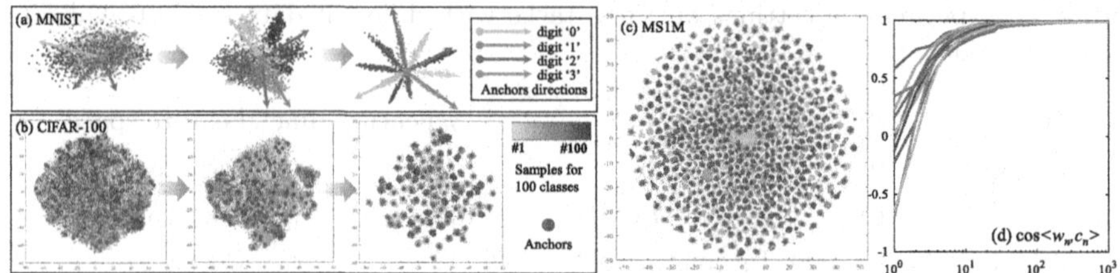

Fig. 2. Visualization of feature spaces on different tasks, *i.e.* (a) MNIST, (b) CIFAR-100 and (c) MS1M, where the features of CIFAR-100 and MS1M are visualized by Barnes-Hut *t*-SNE [36], and (d) depicts the evolution of cosine distance between anchor direction and class centroid with respect to the training iteration on MNIST

MNIST – Figure 2(a) describes the feature visualization in three stages: 0, 2 and 10 epochs. We set the feature dimension $D = 2$ for $\mathbf{f}$ so as to explore the distribution in low dimensional case. The training of this model progressively increases the congregation between features in each class and inter-discrepancy between classes. We pick four classes and show their directions $\mathbf{W}_{[n]}$ from the projection matrix $\mathbf{W}$, named as *anchor*. All anchors have random directions at the initial stage of training, and they gradually move towards the direction of their respective centroids.

CIFAR-100 and MS1M – To examine this observation in a much larger data scale and higher dimension case, we further apply CIFAR-100 and MS1M for an ample demonstration. Different from MNIST, the feature dimension for $\mathbf{f}$ is $D = 128$ and *t*-SNE is used for dimensionality reduction without losing cosine metric. Similar to the phenomenon as observed in MNIST, features in each class tend to be progressively clustered together while features from different classes own more distinct margins in between. Meanwhile the anchors marked by red dots almost locate around its corresponding class centroids. The anchors of a well trained MS1M model also co-locate with the class centroids.

In addition, for a quantified assessment, we compute the cosine similarity $\mathcal{C}(\mathbf{w}_n, \mathbf{c}_n)$ between the anchor $\mathbf{w}_n = \mathbf{W}_{[n]}$ and the class centroid $\mathbf{c}_n$ for the nth class out of 10 classes in total on MNIST. Figure 2(d) exhibits $\mathcal{C}(\mathbf{w}_n, \mathbf{c}_n)$ with respect to the training iterations. Almost all classes converge to a distance of 1 within one epoch, *i.e.* the direction of the anchor shifts to the same direction of the class centroid.

To conclude, the anchor direction $\mathbf{W}_{[n]}$ is always consistent with the direction of the corresponding class centroid over different dataset scales with various lengths of the feature dimension in $\mathbf{f}$.

2.2 Investigate in Gradients

We investigate the reason why the directions of anchor and centroid will be gradually consistent, from the perspective of gradient descent in the training

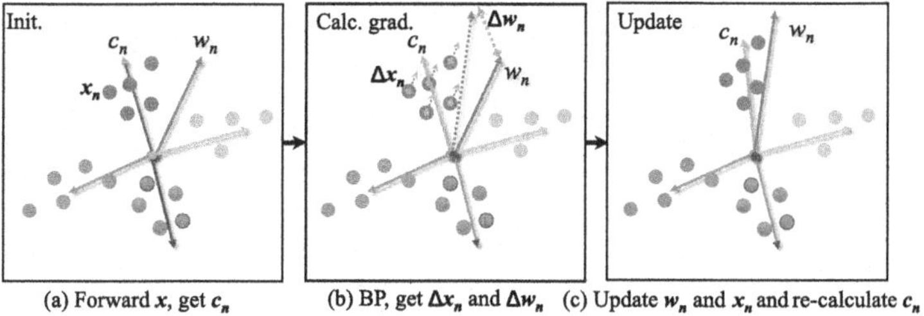

Fig. 3. The evolution of the anchor w_n and features x_n for class n within one iteration. After this iteration, the directions between anchor w_n and centroid c_n get closer

procedure. Considering the input of linear projection $\mathbf{f}$ which belongs to the n-th chass and the output $\mathbf{y} = \mathbf{W}^T\mathbf{f}$, the softmax probability of $\mathbf{f}$ belongs to n-th chass can be calculated by:

$$p_n = softmax(y) = \frac{\exp(\mathbf{y}_n)}{\sum_{i=1}^{N}\exp(\mathbf{y}_i)} \tag{2}$$

We want to minimize the negative log-likelihood, *i.e.* softmax loss ℓ:

$$\arg\min_{\theta} \ell = \arg\min_{\theta} -log(p), \tag{3}$$

where θ denotes the set of all parameters in CNN. Now we can infer the gradients of softmax loss $\ell_{\mathbf{f}}$ with respect to the anchor $\mathbf{w}_n$ given the single sample $\mathbf{f}$:

$$\nabla_{\mathbf{w}_n}\ell_{\mathbf{f}} = \frac{\partial \ell_{\mathbf{f}}}{\partial \mathbf{w}_n} = -\sum_{\mathbf{f}\in\mathcal{I}}\left(\mathbb{I}[\mathbf{f}\in\mathcal{I}_n] - \frac{\exp(\mathbf{y}_n)}{\sum_{i=1}^{N}\exp(\mathbf{y}_i)}\right)\cdot\mathbf{f}, \tag{4}$$

in which the samples of class n is denoted as $\mathcal{I}_n$, and $\mathbf{y}_n$ is the nth element in $\mathbf{y}$. $\mathbb{I}$ refers to the indicator which is 1 when $\mathbf{f}$ is in $\mathcal{I}_n$, and 0 *vice versa.*

Now considering samples in one mini-batch, the gradient $\nabla_{\mathbf{w}_n}\ell$ with respect to results in the summation of all feature samples in the class n with a negative contribution from the summation of feature samples from the rest classes:

$$\nabla_{\mathbf{w}_n}\ell = -\sum_{\mathbf{f}\in\mathcal{I}_n}\left(1 - \frac{\exp(\mathbf{y}_n)}{\sum_{n=1}^{N}\exp(\mathbf{y}_n)}\right)\cdot\mathbf{f} + \sum_{\mathbf{f}\notin\mathcal{I}_n}\frac{\exp(\mathbf{y}_n)}{\sum_{n=1}^{N}\exp(\mathbf{y}_n)}\cdot\mathbf{f}.$$

In each iteration, the update value of $\mathbf{w}_n$ equal to

$$\varDelta\mathbf{w}_n = -\eta\dot{\nabla}_{\mathbf{w}_n}\ell = \eta\sum_{\mathbf{f}\in\mathcal{I}_n}\left(1 - \frac{\exp(\mathbf{y}_n)}{\sum_{n=1}^{N}\exp(\mathbf{y}_n)}\right)\cdot\mathbf{f} - \eta\sum_{\mathbf{f}\notin\mathcal{I}_n}\frac{\exp(\mathbf{y}_n)}{\sum_{n=1}^{N}\exp(\mathbf{y}_n)}\cdot\mathbf{f}.$$

Where η denote the learning rate. The former term can be assumed as the scaled summation of the data samples in class n, thus is approximately proportional to the class centroid $\mathbf{c}_n$. And the feature samples are usually evenly distributed in

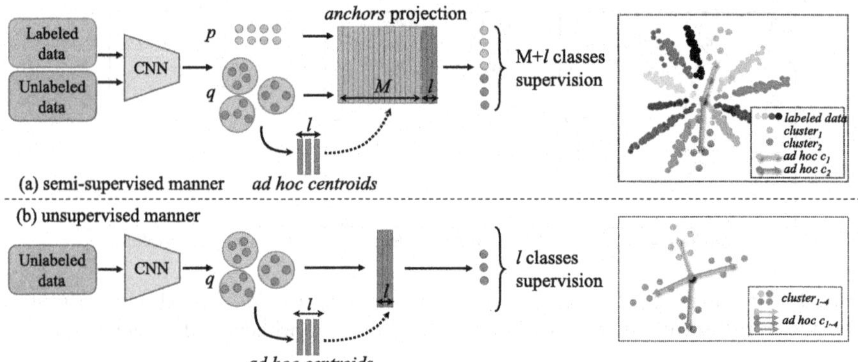

Fig. 4. A comparison between (a) semi-supervised learning with the proposed *transductive centroid projection* and (b) unsupervised learning framework

the feature space, the summation of the negative feature samples for class n will also approximately follow the negative direction of the centroid $\mathbf{c}_n$. Therefore, the gradient $\nabla_{\mathbf{w}_n}\ell$ approximately points to the centroid direction $\mathbf{c}_n$ in one time step, thus finally the anchor $\mathbf{w}_n$ will also follow the direction of the centroid with sufficient accumulation of the gradients. Figure 3 describes the moving direction of anchor $\mathbf{w}_n$ with the gradient $\Delta\mathbf{w}_n = -\nabla_{\mathbf{w}_n}\ell$ and the direction of samples x_n with the gradient $\Delta\mathbf{x}_n = -\nabla_{\mathbf{x}_n}\ell$ marked in red dot lines. For a class n, the samples and anchors are marked with yellow dots and arrow line, respectively. When the network back-propagates, the direction of $\mathbf{w}_n$ is updated towards the class centroid $\mathbf{c}_n$ in tangential direction whilst the samples $\mathbf{x_n} \in \mathcal{I}_n$ are also gradually transformed to the direction of $\mathbf{w}_n$, which leads to $\sum_{j=1}^{o} x_{nj} = c_n \rightarrow w_n$.

3 Approach

Inspired by the observation stated in the previous section, we propose a novel learning mechanism to wisely congregate the unlabelled data into the recognition system to enhance its discriminative ability. Let $\mathcal{X}^{\mathrm{L}}$ denote the labelled dataset with M classes and $\mathcal{X}^{\mathrm{U}}$ the unlabelled dataset. We first cluster the $\mathcal{X}^{\mathrm{U}}$ by [24] and get N clusters. According to the property $w_n \approx c_n$ discussed in the previous section, the *ad hoc* centroid $\mathbf{c}^{\mathrm{U}}$ from an unlabelled cluster can be used to build up the corresponding *anchor* vector $\mathbf{w}^{\mathrm{U}}$, which means that it is possible to utilize the *ad hoc* centroid for a faithful classification of the unlabelled cluster.

3.1 Transductive Centroid Projection (TCP)

In one training step, we construct the mini-batch $\mathcal{B} = \{\mathcal{X}_p^{\mathrm{L}}, \mathcal{X}_q^{\mathrm{U}}\}$ by the labelled data $\mathcal{X}_p^{\mathrm{L}} \subset \mathcal{X}^{\mathrm{L}}$ and unlabelled data $\mathcal{X}_q^{\mathrm{U}} \subset \mathcal{X}^{\mathrm{U}}$, with $p = \mathrm{card}(\tilde{\mathcal{X}}^{\mathrm{L}})$ and $q = \mathrm{card}(\tilde{\mathcal{X}}^{\mathrm{U}})$ denote the number of selected labelled and unlabelled data in this batch, respectively. We randomly select $\mathcal{X}_p^{\mathrm{L}}$ from the labelled dataset as usual, but the unlabelled data are constructed by randomly selecting l unlabelled clusters with o samples in each cluster, *i.e.* $q = l \times o$. Note that the selected l clusters are dynamically changed for each mini-batch. Therefore, this mini-batch $\mathcal{B}$ is then fed into the network and the extracted features before the TCP layer are reformulated as $\mathbf{f} = [\mathbf{f}^{\mathrm{L}}, \mathbf{f}^{\mathrm{U}}]^{\top} \in \mathbb{R}^{(p+q)\times D}$, where D is the feature dimension and $\mathbf{f}^{\mathrm{L}}, \mathbf{f}^{\mathrm{U}}$ denote the feature vectors for labelled and unlabelled data, respectively.

The projection matrix for the TCP layer is reformulated as $\mathbf{W} = [\mathbf{W}^M, \mathbf{W}^l] \in \mathbb{R}^{(M+l)\times(p+q)}$, in which the first M columns are reserved for the anchors of labeled classes and the rest l columns are substituted by the *ad hoc* centroid vectors $\{\mathbf{c}_\iota^{\mathrm{U}}\}_{\iota=1}^{l}$ from the selected unlabeled data. Note that $\mathbf{c}_\iota^{\mathrm{U}}$ is calculated through the selected samples $\{\mathbf{f}_{\iota,i}^{\mathrm{U}}\}_{i=1}^{o}$ of the cluster ι in this mini-batch as

$$\mathbf{c}_\iota^{\mathrm{U}} = \alpha \sum_{i=1}^{o} \frac{\mathbf{f}_{\iota,i}^{\mathrm{U}}}{\|\mathbf{f}_{\iota,i}^{\mathrm{U}}\|_2}, \text{ where } \alpha = \frac{1}{M}\sum_{j=1}^{M} \|\mathbf{c}_j^{\mathrm{L}}\|_2. \tag{5}$$

The scale factor α is the average magnitude of the centroids for the labeled clusters. The output of the TCP layer is thereby obtained by $\mathbf{y} = \mathbf{W}^{\top}\mathbf{f}$ without the bias term, which is then fed into the `softmax` loss layer.

Compared to the training in a purely unsupervised manner, the semi-supervised learning procedure in this paper (as shown in Fig. 4(a)) applies the proposed transductive centroid projection layer which not only optimizes the inference towards the labeled data but also indirectly gains the recognition ability for the unlabeled clusters. Actually, it can be easily transferred to the unsupervised learning paradigm by setting $M = 0$ as shown in Fig. 4(b), or the supervised learning framework when there is no unlabeled data as $l = 0$.

3.2 Scale Factor α Matters

As stated in Sect. 3.1, the scale factor α is applied to normalize the *ad hoc* centroids for the unlabeled data. For the purpose of training stability and fast convergence, a suitable scaling criterion is to let the mapped activation $\mathbf{y}^{\mathrm{U}}$ for unlabeled data have a scale similar to the labeled one $\mathbf{y}^{\mathrm{L}}$. Indeed, the ℓ_2 norm of each centroid inherently offers a reasonable prior scale in mapping the input features $\mathbf{f}^{\mathrm{L}}$ to the output activation $\mathbf{y}^{\mathrm{L}}$. Therefore, by scaling the *ad hoc* centroids for the unlabeled data with an average scale $\alpha = \frac{1}{M}\sum_{j=1}^{M}\|\mathbf{c}_j^{\mathrm{L}}\|_2$ as the labeled centroids, activations for unlabeled data will have a similar distribution as the labeled activations, thus ensuring the stability and fast convergence during training.

3.3 Avoid Inter-class Conflict in Large Mini-Batch

A larger batch size theoretically induces a better training performance in conventional recognition tasks. However, in TCP, it might be possible that a larger

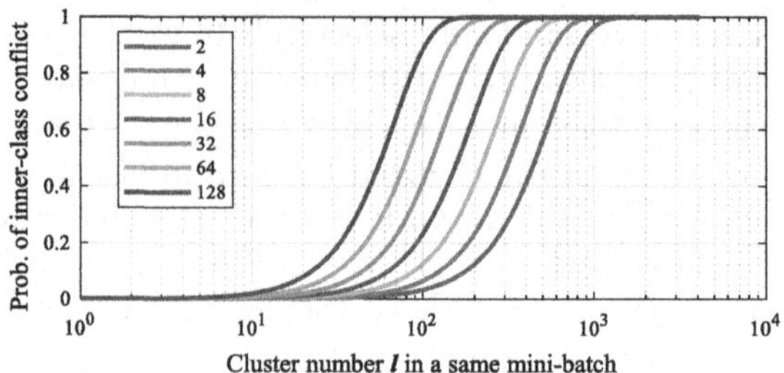

Fig. 5. The probability of each single cluster owning a unique class label in a mini-batch decreases with respect to the batch size. Seven ratios $N/\tilde{N}$ are marked in different colors (Color figure online)

batch size will introduce multiple clusters with a same class label for the unlabelled data. Let the classes be evenly distributed in the unlabeled clusters, and assume that N clusters in the unlabelled data actually belong to $\tilde{N}$ classes, the probability that every cluster has a unique class label in the mini-batch $\mathcal{B}$ is $P(l) = (1 - \frac{N/\tilde{N}-1}{N})^l$, where l is the number of selected clusters. This probability decreases as the batch size increases, as shown in Fig. 5.

In our experiment, the ratio $N/\tilde{N} \simeq 8$ for person re-id and $N/\tilde{N} \simeq 3$ for face recognition. To guarantee the probability $P(l) > 0.99$, the number of cluster l selected in a mini-batch should not be larger than 40. To further increase the number of unlabelled clusters in the mini-batch as much as possible, we provide two strategies as follows:

Selection of Clusters – Based on the assumption that the probability of inter-class conflict reduces along with the time interval during data collection, to avoid the conflict in training stage, the l clusters should be picked with an minimum interval T_l. In the experiment, we find that $T_l \geq 120$ s presents a good performance.

Selection of Samples – The diversity of samples extracted from consecutive frames in one cluster is always too small to aid intra-class feature learning. To this end, we make a constraint on sample selection by setting the interval between each sampled frame larger than T_o. In the experiment, we set T_o as 1 s.

Based on the aforementioned strategies, we find that only 19 out of 10, 000 mini-batches on Re-ID and 7 out of 10, 000 mini-batches on face recognition have duplicated identities when setting $l = 48$ in our training dataset.

3.4 Discussion: Stability and Efficiency

We further discuss the superiority of the proposed TCP layer comparing with some other metric learning losses, such as triplet loss [2] and contrastive loss [37], that can also avoid inter-class conflict by elaborate batch selection. Both of these losses suffer from dramatic data expansion when forming the sample pairs or sample triplets from the training set. Take triplet loss as an example, n unlabelled samples constitute $\frac{1}{3}n$ triplet sets and the metric only restricts on $\frac{2}{3}n$ distances

Table 2. The list of eight datasets for training with their respective image and identity numbers

	CUHK03	CUHK01	PRID	VIPeR	3DPeS	i-LIDS	SenseReId	Market-1501	Total
# Tr. ID	1,467	971	385	632	193	119	16,377	751	20,895
# Tr. Imgs	21,012	1,552	2,997	506	420	194	160,396	10,348	197,425

in each iteration, *i.e.* the anchor to the negative sample and the anchor to the positive sample in each single triplet. It makes the triplet term suffer severe disturbance during training. Alternatively, in the proposed TCP layer, $n = p+q$ samples are compared with all the M anchors by labelled data as well as the l ad hoc centroids of the unlabeled data to achieve $(M+l) \times (p+q)$ comparisons, which is quadratically larger than other metric learning methods. It thus ensures a stable training process and a quick convergence.

4 Experimental Settings and Implementation Details

Labeled Data and Unlabeled Data. For both of person re-identification and face recognition, the training data consist of two parts: labeled data $\mathcal{D}^{\mathrm{L}}$ and unlabeled data $\mathcal{D}^{\mathrm{U}}$.

In experiments for Re-ID, following the pipeline of DGD [38] and Spindle [39], we take the combined training samples from eight datasets described in Table 2 together as $\mathcal{D}^{\mathrm{L}}$. Note that MARS [13] is excluded from the training set since it is an extension of Market-1501. For $\mathcal{D}^{\mathrm{U}}$ construction, we collect videos with a total length of four hours from three different scenes with four cameras. The person clusters are obtained by the POI tracker [40] and clustered by [24] without further alignment, where those shorter than one second are removed. The unlabeled dataset, named as Person Tracker Re-Identification dataset (PT-ReID)[2], contains $158,446$ clusters and $1,324,019$ frames in total. For ablation study, we further manually annotate the PT-ReID, named as Labeled PT-ReID dataset (L-PT-ReID), and get a total of $2,495$ identities.

In experiments for face recognition, we combine a labelled MS-Celeb-1M [35] with some collected photos from internet as $\mathcal{D}^{\mathrm{L}}$, which in total contains $\sim 10M$ images and $1.6M$ identities. For $\mathcal{D}^{\mathrm{U}}$ we collect $11.0M$ face frames from surveillance videos and cluster them into $500K$ clusters. All faces are detected and aligned by [41].

Evaluation Benchmarks. For Re-ID, The proposed method is evaluated on six significant publicly benchmarks, including the image-based Market-1501 [42], CUHK01 [43], CUHK03 [44], and the video-based MARS [13], iLIDS-VID [45] as well as Prid2011 [46]. For face recognition, we evaluate the method on NIST IJB-C [47], which contains 138000 face images, 11000 face videos, and 10000 non-face images. To the best of our knowledge, it is the latest and the most challenging

[2] The dataset will be released.

Table 3. Comparison results of different baselines with the proposed TCP (last row) on Market-1501 dataset. All pipelines are trained by a plain ResNet-101 without any bells and whistles. The top four are single-task learning with single data source (*i.e.* $\mathcal{D}^{\mathrm{L}}$ or $\mathcal{D}^{\mathrm{U}}$), while the following five take both data sources with multi-task learning

Methods	Top-1	Top-5	Top-10	Top-20	MAP
$\mathbf{S}^{\mathrm{L}}$	87.7	93.5	95.1	96.6	79.4
$\mathbf{S}^{\mathrm{U}}$	22.8	32.2	36.6	41.8	8.6
$\mathbf{S}^{\mathrm{U}}_{\mathrm{self}}$	65.0	77.0	82.9	93.5	61.3
$\mathbf{S}^{\mathrm{U}}_{\mathrm{labeled}}$	66.4	78.0	83.4	98.0	67.6
$\mathbf{M}^{\mathrm{U+L}}$	37.4	46.6	51.5	67.0	21.0
$\mathbf{M}^{\mathrm{U+L}}_{\mathrm{self}}$	68.8	79.9	84.6	94.5	55.0
$\mathbf{M}^{\mathrm{U+L}}_{\mathrm{labeled}}$	86.0	90.8	92.7	94.8	75.8
$\mathbf{M}^{\mathrm{U+L}}_{\mathrm{tr\text{-}loss}}$	83.5	89.5	93.5	95.9	79.3
$\mathbf{M}^{\mathrm{U+L}}_{\mathrm{TCP}}$	89.6	94.1	95.6	96.8	83.5
TCP	**90.4**	**94.5**	**95.7**	**96.9**	**84.4**

benchmarks for face verification. Notice that we found more than one hundred wrong annotations in this dataset, which introduce significant confusion for recall rate on some small false positive rate (FPR $\leq$ 1e-3), so we remove these pairs in evaluation[3].

Evaluation Metrics. For Re-ID, the widely used Cumulative Match Curve (CMC) is adopted in both ablation study and comparison experiments. In addition, we apply Mean Average Precision (MAP) as another metric for evaluations on Market-1501 [42] and MARS [13] dataset. For face recognition, the receiver operating characteristic (ROC) curve is adopted as in most of the other works. On all datasets, we compute cosine distance between each pair of query image and any image from the gallery, and return the ranked gallery list.

Training Details. As a common practice in most deep learning frameworks for visual tasks, we initialize our model with the parameters pre-trained on ImageNet. Specifically, we employ resnet-101 as the backbone structure in all experiments which is followed by an additional `fc` layer after `pool5` to generate 128-D features. Dropout [48] is used to randomly drop out a channel with the ratio of 0.5. The input size is normalized as 224×224 and the training batch size is $3,840$, in which $p = 2,880, q = 960, l = 96$ and $o = 10$. Warm up technology [49] is used to achieve stability when training with large batch size.

5 Ablation Study

Since the training data, network structure and pre-processing for the data vary from method to method, we first analyse the effectiveness of the proposed method

[3] The list will be made available.

with quantitative comparisons to different baselines in Sect. 5.1 and visualize the feature space in Sect. 5.2. All the ablation study are conducted on Market-1501, a large-scale clean dataset with strong generalizability.

5.1 Component Analysis

Since the semi-supervised learning contains two data sources, *i.e.* labeled data $\mathcal{D}^{\mathrm{L}}$ and unlabeled data $\mathcal{D}^{\mathrm{U}}$, the proposed TCP is compared with nine typical configuration baselines listed in Table 3. These baselines can be divided into two types: single-task learning with only one data source and multi-task learning with multiple data sources.

The top four are single-task learning with single data source: (1) $\mathbf{S}^{\mathrm{L}}$ only uses $\mathcal{D}^{\mathrm{L}}$ supervised by the annotated ground truth IDs with softmax loss; (2) $\mathbf{S}^{\mathrm{U}}$ only uses $\mathcal{D}^{\mathrm{U}}$ supervised by taking the cluster IDs as the pseudo ground truth with softmax loss; (3) $\mathbf{S}^{\mathrm{U}}_{\mathrm{self}}$ with self-training on unlabeled data, where self-training is a classical semi-supervised learning method. We first train the CNN with $\mathcal{D}^{\mathrm{L}}$ which is used to extract features of $\mathcal{D}^{\mathrm{U}}$, and then obtain the pseudo ground truth by a cluster algorithm. The pseudo ground truth is taken as the supervision for training on $\mathcal{D}^{\mathrm{U}}$; and (4) $\mathbf{S}^{\mathrm{U}}_{\mathrm{labeled}}$ - We further annotate the real ground truth of unlabeled data and compare it with the model trained with pseudo ground truth.

The latter five are multi-task learning and three of them are a combination of the above single-task baselines as follows: (5) $\mathbf{M}^{\mathrm{U+L}}$ combines $\mathbf{S}^{\mathrm{L}}$ and $\mathbf{S}^{\mathrm{U}}$; (6) $\mathbf{M}^{\mathrm{U+L}}_{\mathrm{self}}$ is a combination of $\mathbf{S}^{\mathrm{L}}$ and $\mathbf{S}^{\mathrm{U}}_{\mathrm{self}}$; and (7) $\mathbf{M}^{\mathrm{U+L}}_{\mathrm{labeled}}$ is a combination of $\mathbf{S}^{\mathrm{L}}$ and $\mathbf{S}^{\mathrm{U}}_{\mathrm{labeled}}$. The last two take the annotated ground truth to supervise the branch with labeled data and compare the performance of operating triplet loss with our TCP on unlabeled data as (8) $\mathbf{M}^{\mathrm{U+L}}_{\mathrm{tr\text{-}loss}}$ with triplet loss, where the selection strategy for triplets also follow the Online Batch Selection described in Sect. 3.3, and (9) $\mathbf{M}^{\mathrm{U+L}}_{\mathrm{TCP}}$ utilizes the proposed TCP which is regarded as training in a unsupervised manner.

The proposed method TCP is neither single-task nor multi-task learning, but with the labeled and unlabeled data trained simultaneously in a semi-supervised manner. The results clearly prove that either single-task or multi-task learning will pull down the performance which are concluded as follows:

Clustered Data Contain Noisy and Fake Ground Truth. Compared with the näive baseline $\mathbf{S}^{\mathrm{U}}$ that directly uses cluster IDs as the supervision, the self-training $\mathbf{S}^{\mathrm{U}}_{\mathrm{self}}$ outperforms it by 42%. Similarly, by fusing labeled data, the $\mathbf{M}^{\mathrm{U+L}}_{\mathrm{self}}$ is superior to $\mathbf{M}^{\mathrm{U+L}}$ with 31.4%. It shows that (1) the source cluster data contains many fake ground truth and (2) many cluster fragments cause the same identity to be clustered to different ID ground truth.

It's Hard to Manually Refine Unlabelled Cluster Data. We further annotate the cluster data to get the real ground truth of unlabeled data. Although $\mathbf{S}^{\mathrm{U}}_{\mathrm{labeled}}$ outperforms $\mathbf{S}^{\mathrm{U}}$ with pseudo ground truth again demonstrating the noise of cluster, both $\mathbf{S}^{\mathrm{U}}_{\mathrm{labeled}}$ and $\mathbf{M}^{\mathrm{U+L}}_{\mathrm{labeled}}$ drop performance compared to training on labeled data $\mathbf{S}^{\mathrm{L}}$. It shows that there is a significant disparity between two source

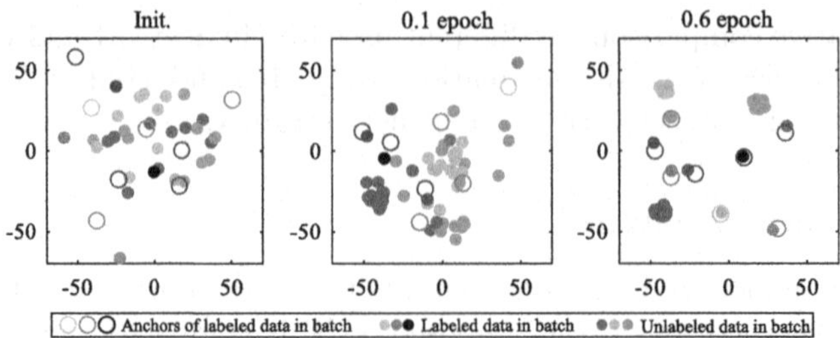

Fig. 6. Feature and anchor distribution converge during semi-supervised training with the proposed TCP layer

data domains, and it is non-trivial to get a clean annotation set due to the time gap between different clusters.

Self-training and Triplet-Loss are Not Optimal. Both self-training $\mathbf{M}_{\text{self}}^{\text{U+L}}$ and triplet-loss $\mathbf{M}_{\text{tr-loss}}^{\text{U+L}}$ provide solutions to overcome the problems caused by the pseudo ground truth of clusters data, significantly performing the näive combination of unlabeled and labeled data $\mathbf{M}^{\text{U+L}}$, however, their results are still lower than that of our method by 21.6% and 6.9% respectively. As discussed in Sect. 3.4, the triplet-loss only consider $\frac{2}{3}N$ distances that cannot fully exploit the information in each batch data, while self-training profoundly depends on the robustness of the pre-trained model with labeled data that cannot be guaranteed to intrinsically solve the problem.

The Superiority of TCP. By employing TCP, both the unsupervised learning $\mathbf{M}_{\text{TCP}}^{\text{U+L}}$ and semi-supervised learning TCP, not surprisingly, outperform all of the above baseline variants by a large margin. It proves the superiority of the proposed online batch selection and the centroid projection mechanism which comprehensively utilize all labeled as well as unlabeled data by optimizing $(M + l) \times (p + q)$ distances.

5.2 Feature Hyperspace on Person Re-ID

The feature spaces learned on MNIST, CIFAR-100 and MS1M are discussed in Sect. 2.1. Here we examine whether the same observations and conclusions also occur on person re-identification with the proposed TCP layer, by visualizing the distribution related to the mini-batches on a single GPU in different training stages. For a clear visualization, we show the mini-batch with 8 labeled samples where each belongs to a distinct class and 24 unlabeled samples from 3 classes each of which has 8 samples in Fig. 6. As the number of epoch increases, the anchors of labeled data converge towards their corresponding sample centroids while those of unlabeled data keep still in the centroids. Until the network converges, the anchors of both labeled and unlabeled data are in the centroid of each class and thus the unlabeled data can be regarded as the auto-annotated data to enlarge the training data span.

Table 4. Experimental results (%) of the proposed and other comparisons on six person re-identification datasets. The best are in bold while the second best are underlined

Market1501	**Top-1**	**Top-5**	**Top-10**	**Top-20**	**MAP**	**CUHK01**	**Top-1**	**Top-5**	**Top-10**	**Top-20**
Best [50]	84.1	92.7	94.9	96.8	63.4	Best [39]	79.9	94.4	97.1	98.6
Basel	82.7	92.3	95.0	96.0	58.1	Basel	83.0	96.2	98.1	99.3
TCP	86.1	94.0	95.0	96.2	66.2	TCP	90.0	98.0	99.0	**99.4**
TCP + Re-rank	**90.4**	**94.5**	**95.7**	**96.9**	**84.4**	TCP + Re-rank	**91.6**	**98.3**	**99.1**	**99.4**
MARS	**Top-1**	**Top-5**	**Top-10**	**Top-20**	**MAP**	**iLIDS-VID**	**Top-1**	**Top-5**	**Top-10**	**Top-20**
Best [51]	73.9	-	-	-	**68.4**	Best [52]	62.0	86.0	94.0	98.0
Basel	77.2	90.4	93.3	95.1	47.7	Basel	64.5	91.8	96.9	98.8
TCP	80.7	91.6	**94.4**	95.7	53.7	TCP	69.4	**95.1**	**98.3**	**99.3**
TCP + Re-rank	**82.9**	**91.8**	93.7	96.4	67.6	TCP + Re-rank	**71.7**	**95.1**	**98.3**	**99.3**
CUHK03	**Top-1**	**Top-5**	**Top-10**	**Top-20**	-	**PRID2011**	**Top-1**	**Top-5**	**Top-10**	**Top-20**
Best [50]	88.7	98.6	99.2	99.6	-	Best [52]	77.0	95.0	99.0	99.0
Basel	91.7	99.1	99.6	99.8		Basel	84.6	95.4	99.0	99.6
TCP	94.4	99.7	99.9	**100.0**	-	TCP	92.1	98.1	**99.6**	**100.0**
TCP + Re-rank	**98.2**	**100.0**	**100.0**	**100.0**	-	TCP + Re-rank	**93.6**	**98.9**	**99.6**	**100.0**

Table 5. Experimental results (%) on IJB-C and LFW datasets

Benchmark	IJB-C							LFW
Index	tpr@1e-1	tpr@1e-2	tpr@1e-3	tpr@1e-4	tpr@1e-5	tpr@1e-6	tpr@1e-7	Acc
Best [32]	-	-	-	-	-	-	-	99.80
$\mathbf{S}^{U}$	98.65	95.08	84.14	64.98	40.42	21.89	9.94	98.24
$\mathbf{S}^{L}$	99.70	98.98	97.37	94.62	90.49	83.68	76.37	99.78
$\mathbf{S}^{U+L}_{self}$	98.97	98.80	98.16	96.60	93.67	88.64	80.69	99.80
TCP	**99.97**	**99.81**	**99.16**	**97.58**	**94.63**	**89.21**	**82.90**	**99.82**

6 Evaluation on Seven Benchmarks

6.1 Person Re-Identification Benchmarks

We first evaluate our method on the six Re-ID benchmarks. Notice that since the data pre-processing, training setting and network structure vary in different state-of-the-art methods, we only list recent best performing methods in the tables just for reference. The test procedure on iLIDS-VID and PRID2011 is the average of 10-fold cross validation result, whereas on MARS we use a fixed split following the official protocol [13]. As shown in Table 4, 'Basel.' denote the $\mathbf{S}^{L}$ setting in Sect. 5. The proposed TCP, compared with a variety of recent methods, achieves the best performance on the Market-1501, CUHK03 and CUHK01 datasets. The performance will be further improved with an additional re-rank skill (Table 5).

6.2 Face Recognition Benchmarks

IJB-C [47] is the most challenging face recognition benchmark for now. Since it has just been released for a few months, few work report its result on it. We report the true positive rates on seven different levels of false positive rates (from 1e-1 to 1e-7) in Fig. 5. Comparison has been made between the proposed TCP with some baselines as described in Sect. 5. The best accuracy of existing works on the widely used LFW dataset is also reported for reference. The result of the proposed TCP outperforms all the baselines especially the self-training one, the training process of which takes more than 4-times the time of TCP.

7 Conclusion

By observing the latent space learned by softmax loss in CNN, we propose a semi-supervised method named TCP which can be steadily embedded in CNN and followed by any classification loss functions. Extensive experiments and ablation study demonstrate its superiority in utilizing full information across labelled and unlabelled data to achieve state-of-the-art performance on six person re-identification datasets and one face recognition dataset.

References

1. Taigman, Y., Yang, M., Ranzato, M., Wolf, L.: Deepface: closing the gap to human-level performance in face verification. In: Proceedings of the IEEE Conference on Computer Vision and Pattern Recognition, pp. 1701–1708 (2014)
2. Schroff, F., Kalenichenko, D., Philbin, J.: Facenet: a unified embedding for face recognition and clustering. In: Proceedings of the IEEE Conference on Computer Vision and Pattern Recognition, pp. 815–823 (2015)
3. Sun, Y., Wang, X., Tang, X.: Deep learning face representation from predicting 10,000 classes. In: Proceedings of the IEEE Conference on Computer Vision and Pattern Recognition, pp. 1891–1898 (2014)
4. Sun, Y., Liang, D., Wang, X., Tang, X.: Deepid3: face recognition with very deep neural networks. arXiv preprint arXiv:1502.00873 (2015)
5. Liu, Y., Li, H., Wang, X.: Rethinking feature discrimination and polymerization for large-scale recognition. arXiv preprint arXiv:1710.00870 (2017)
6. Song, G., Leng, B., Liu, Y., Hetang, C., Cai, S.: Region-based quality estimation network for large-scale person re-identification. arXiv preprint arXiv:1711.08766 (2017)
7. Liu, Y., Yan, J., Ouyang, W.: Quality aware network for set to set recognition. In: CVPR, vol. 2, p. 8 (2017)
8. Zheng, Z., Zheng, L., Yang, Y.: Unlabeled samples generated by gan improve the person re-identification baseline in vitro. In: The IEEE International Conference on Computer Vision (ICCV), October 2017
9. Zhou, Z., Huang, Y., Wang, W., Wang, L., Tan, T.: See the forest for the trees: joint spatial and temporal recurrent neural networks for video-based person re-identification. In: The IEEE Conference on Computer Vision and Pattern Recognition (CVPR), July 2017

10. Zhao, L., Li, X., Zhuang, Y., Wang, J.: Deeply-learned part-aligned representations for person re-identification. In: The IEEE International Conference on Computer Vision (ICCV), October 2017
11. Li, W., Zhu, X., Gong, S.: Person re-identification by deep joint learning of multi-loss classification. arXiv preprint arXiv:1705.04724 (2017)
12. Guo, Y., Zhang, L., Hu, Y., He, X., Gao, J.: MS-Celeb-1M: a dataset and benchmark for large-scale face recognition. In: Leibe, B., Matas, J., Sebe, N., Welling, M. (eds.) ECCV 2016. LNCS, vol. 9907, pp. 87–102. Springer, Cham (2016). https://doi.org/10.1007/978-3-319-46487-9_6
13. Zheng, L., et al.: MARS: a video benchmark for large-scale person re-identification. In: Leibe, B., Matas, J., Sebe, N., Welling, M. (eds.) ECCV 2016. LNCS, vol. 9910, pp. 868–884. Springer, Cham (2016). https://doi.org/10.1007/978-3-319-46466-4_52
14. Weston, J., Ratle, F., Mobahi, H., Collobert, R.: Deep learning via semi-supervised embedding. In: Montavon, G., Orr, G.B., Müller, K.-R. (eds.) Neural Networks: Tricks of the Trade. LNCS, vol. 7700, pp. 639–655. Springer, Heidelberg (2012). https://doi.org/10.1007/978-3-642-35289-8_34
15. Lee, D.H.: Pseudo-label: the simple and efficient semi-supervised learning method for deep neural networks. In: Workshop on Challenges in Representation Learning, ICML, vol. 3, p. 2 (2013)
16. Liu, X., Song, M., Tao, D., Zhou, X., Chen, C., Bu, J.: Semi-supervised coupled dictionary learning for person re-identification. In: Proceedings of the IEEE Conference on Computer Vision and Pattern Recognition, pp. 3550–3557 (2014)
17. Odena, A.: Semi-supervised learning with generative adversarial networks. arXiv preprint arXiv:1606.01583 (2016)
18. Fan, H., Zheng, L., Yang, Y.: Unsupervised person re-identification: clustering and fine-tuning. arXiv preprint arXiv:1705.10444 (2017)
19. Yang, J., Parikh, D., Batra, D.: Joint unsupervised learning of deep representations and image clusters. In: Proceedings of the IEEE Conference on Computer Vision and Pattern Recognition, pp. 5147–5156 (2016)
20. Wang, X., et al.: Unsupervised joint mining of deep features and image labels for large-scale radiology image categorization and scene recognition. In: 2017 IEEE Winter Conference on Applications of Computer Vision (WACV), pp. 998–1007. IEEE (2017)
21. Zhu, X., Ghahramani, Z.: Learning from labeled and unlabeled data with label propagation (2002)
22. MacQueen, J., et al.: Some methods for classification and analysis of multivariate observations. In: Proceedings of the Fifth Berkeley Symposium on Mathematical Statistics and Probability, vol. 1, pp. 281–297, Oakland, CA, USA (1967)
23. Gowda, K.C., Krishna, G.: Agglomerative clustering using the concept of mutual nearest neighbourhood. Pattern Recognit. **10**(2), 105–112 (1978)
24. Gdalyahu, Y., Weinshall, D., Werman, M.: Self-organization in vision: stochastic clustering for image segmentation, perceptual grouping, and image database organization. IEEE Trans. Pattern Anal. Mach. Intell. **23**(10), 1053–1074 (2001)
25. Kurita, T.: An efficient agglomerative clustering algorithm using a heap. Pattern Recognit. **24**(3), 205–209 (1991)
26. Cozman, F.G.: Semi-supervised learning of mixture models. In: ICML (2003)
27. Bennett, K.P.: Semi-supervised support vector machines. In: NIPS, pp. 368–374 (1999)
28. Liu, W., Wang, J., Chang, S.F.: Robust and scalable graph-based semisupervised learning. Proc. IEEE **100**(9), 2624–2638 (2012)

29. Goodfellow, I., et al.: Generative adversarial nets. In: Advances in Neural Information Processing Systems, pp. 2672–2680 (2014)
30. LeCun, Y., Bottou, L., Bengio, Y., Haffner, P.: Gradient-based learning applied to document recognition. Proc. IEEE **86**(11), 2278–2324 (1998)
31. He, K., Zhang, X., Ren, S., Sun, J.: Deep residual learning for image recognition. In: Proceedings of the IEEE Conference on Computer Vision and Pattern Recognition, pp. 770–778 (2016)
32. Szegedy, C., Ioffe, S., Vanhoucke, V., Alemi, A.A.: Inception-v4, inception-resnet and the impact of residual connections on learning. In: AAAI, vol. 4., p. 12 (2017)
33. Lecun, Y., Cortes, C.: The MNIST database of handwritten digits (2010)
34. Krizhevsky, A., Hinton, G.: Learning multiple layers of features from tiny images (2009)
35. Guo, Y., Zhang, L., Hu, Y., He, X., Gao, J.: Ms-celeb-1m: challenge of recognizing one million celebrities in the real world. Electron. Imaging **2016**(11), 1–6 (2016)
36. Maaten, L.V., Hinton, G.: Visualizing data using t-SNE. J. Mach. Learn. Res. **9**(Nov), 2579–2605 (2008)
37. Hadsell, R., Chopra, S., LeCun, Y.: Dimensionality reduction by learning an invariant mapping. In: 2006 IEEE Computer Society Conference on Computer Vision and Pattern Recognition, vol. 2, pp. 1735–1742. IEEE (2006)
38. Xiao, T., Li, H., Ouyang, W., Wang, X.: Learning deep feature representations with domain guided dropout for person re-identification. In: Proceedings of the IEEE Conference on Computer Vision and Pattern Recognition, pp. 1249–1258 (2016)
39. Zhao, H., et al.: Spindle Net: person re-identification with human body region guided feature decomposition and fusion. In: Proceedings of the IEEE Conference on Computer Vision and Pattern Recognition, pp. 1077–1085 (2017)
40. Yu, F., Li, W., Li, Q., Liu, Y., Shi, X., Yan, J.: POI: multiple object tracking with high performance detection and appearance feature. In: Hua, G., Jégou, H. (eds.) ECCV 2016. LNCS, vol. 9914, pp. 36–42. Springer, Cham (2016). https://doi.org/10.1007/978-3-319-48881-3_3
41. Liu, Y., Li, H., Yan, J., Wei, F., Wang, X., Tang, X.: Recurrent scale approximation for object detection in CNN. In: IEEE International Conference on Computer Vision, vol. 5 (2017)
42. Zheng, L., Shen, L., Tian, L., Wang, S., Wang, J., Tian, Q.: Scalable person re-identification: a benchmark. In: Proceedings of the IEEE International Conference on Computer Vision, pp. 1116–1124 (2015)
43. Li, W., Zhao, R., Wang, X.: Human reidentification with transferred metric learning. In: Lee, K.M., Matsushita, Y., Rehg, J.M., Hu, Z. (eds.) ACCV 2012. LNCS, vol. 7724, pp. 31–44. Springer, Heidelberg (2013). https://doi.org/10.1007/978-3-642-37331-2_3
44. Li, W., Zhao, R., Xiao, T., Wang, X.: Deepreid: deep filter pairing neural network for person re-identification. In: CVPR (2014)
45. Wang, T., Gong, S., Zhu, X., Wang, S.: Person re-identification by video ranking. In: Fleet, D., Pajdla, T., Schiele, B., Tuytelaars, T. (eds.) ECCV 2014. LNCS, vol. 8692, pp. 688–703. Springer, Cham (2014). https://doi.org/10.1007/978-3-319-10593-2_45
46. Hirzer, M., Beleznai, C., Roth, P.M., Bischof, H.: Person re-identification by descriptive and discriminative classification. In: Proceedings Scandinavian Conference on Image Analysis (SCIA) (2011)
47. The iarpa janus benchmark-c face challenge (ijb-c). https://www.nist.gov/programs-projects/face-challenges. Accessed 15 Mar 2018

48. Srivastava, N., Hinton, G.E., Krizhevsky, A., Sutskever, I., Salakhutdinov, R.: Dropout: a simple way to prevent neural networks from overfitting. J. Mach. Learn. Res. **15**(1), 1929–1958 (2014)
49. Goyal, P., et al.: Accurate, large minibatch SGD: training imagenet in 1 hour. arXiv preprint arXiv:1706.02677 (2017)
50. Su, C., Li, J., Zhang, S., Xing, J., Gao, W., Tian, Q.: Pose-driven deep convolutional model for person re-identification. In: The IEEE International Conference on Computer Vision (ICCV), October 2017
51. Zhong, Z., Zheng, L., Cao, D., Li, S.: Re-ranking person re-identification with k-reciprocal encoding. In: The IEEE Conference on Computer Vision and Pattern Recognition (CVPR), July 2017
52. Xu, S., Cheng, Y., Gu, K., Yang, Y., Chang, S., Zhou, P.: Jointly attentive spatial-temporal pooling networks for video-based person re-identification. In: The IEEE International Conference on Computer Vision (ICCV), October 2017

Generalized Loss-Sensitive Adversarial Learning with Manifold Margins

Marzieh Edraki and Guo-Jun Qi(✉)

Laboratory for MAchine Perception and LEarning (MAPLE), University of Central Florida, Orlando, FL 32816, USA
m.edraki@knights.ucf.edu, guojunq@gmail.com, guojun.qi@ucf.edu,
http://maple.cs.ucf.edu/

Abstract. The classic Generative Adversarial Net and its variants can be roughly categorized into two large families: the unregularized versus regularized GANs. By relaxing the non-parametric assumption on the discriminator in the classic GAN, the regularized GANs have better generalization ability to produce new samples drawn from the real distribution. It is well known that the real data like natural images are not uniformly distributed over the whole data space. Instead, they are often restricted to a low-dimensional manifold of the ambient space. Such a manifold assumption suggests the distance over the manifold should be a better measure to characterize the distinct between real and fake samples. Thus, we define a pullback operator to map samples back to their data manifold, and a manifold margin is defined as the distance between the pullback representations to distinguish between real and fake samples and learn the optimal generators. We justify the effectiveness of the proposed model both theoretically and empirically.

Keywords: Regularized GAN · Image generation
Semi-supervised classification · Lipschitz regularization

1 Introduction

Since the Generative Adversarial Nets (GAN) was proposed by Goodfellow et al. [4], it has attracted much attention in literature with a number of variants have been proposed to improve its data generation quality and training stability. In brief, the GANs attempt to train a generator and a discriminator that play an adversarial game to mutually improve one another [4]. A discriminator is trained to distinguish between real and generated samples as much as possible, while a generator attempts to generate good samples that can fool the discriminator. Eventually, an equilibrium is reached where the generator can produce high quality samples that cannot be distinguished by a well trained discriminator.

The classic GAN and its variants can be roughly categorized into two large families: the unregularized versus regularized GANs. The former contains the original GAN and many variants [11,24], where the consistency between the

V. Ferrari et al. (Eds.): ECCV 2018, LNCS 11209, pp. 90–104, 2018.
https://doi.org/10.1007/978-3-030-01228-1_6

distribution of their generated samples and real data is established based on the non-parametric assumption that their discriminators have infinite modeling ability. In other words, the unregularized GANs assume the discriminator can take an arbitrary form so that the generator can produce samples following any given distribution of real samples.

On the contrary, the regularized GANs focus on some regularity conditions on the underlying distribution of real data, and it has some constraints on the discriminators to control their modeling abilities. The two most representative models in this category are Loss-Sensitive GAN (LS-GAN) [11] and Wasserstein GAN (WGAN) [1]. Both are enforcing the Lipschitz constraint on training their discriminators. Moreover, it has been shown that the Lipschitz regularization on the loss function of the LS-GAN yields a generator that can produce samples distributed according to any Lipschitz density, which is a regularized form of distribution on the supporting manifold of real data.

Compared with the family of unregularized GANs, the regularized GANs sacrifice their ability to generate an unconstrained distribution of samples for better training stability and generalization performances. For examples, both LS-GAN and WGAN can produce uncollapsed natural images without involving batch-normalization layers, and both address vanishing gradient problem in training their generators. Moreover, the generalizability of the LS-GAN has also been proved with the Lipschitz regularity condition, showing the model can generalize to produce data following the real density with only a reasonable number of training examples that are polynomial in model complexity. In other words, the generalizability asserts the model will not be overfitted to merely memorize training examples; instead it will be able to extrapolate to produce unseen examples beyond provided real examples.

Although the regularized GANs, in particular LS-GAN [11] considered in this paper, have shown compelling performances, there are still some unaddressed problems. The loss function of LS-GAN is designed based on a margin function defined over ambient space to separate the loss of real and fake samples. While the margin-based constraint on training the loss function is intuitive, directly using the ambient distance as the loss margin may not accurately reflect the dissimilarity between data points.

It is well known that the real data like natural images do not uniformly distribute over the whole data space. Instead, they are often restricted to a low-dimensional manifold of the ambient space. Such manifold assumption suggests the "geodesic" distance over the manifold should be a better measure of the margin to separate the loss functions between real and fake examples. For this purpose, we will define a pullback mapping that can invert the generator function by mapping a sample back to the data manifold. Then a manifold margin is defined as the distance between the representation of data points on the manifold to approximate their distance. The loss function, the generator and the pullback mapping are jointly learned by a threefold adversarial game. We will prove that the fixed point characterized by this game will be able to yield a generator that can produce samples following the real distribution of samples.

2 Related Work

The original GAN [4,14,17] can be viewed as the most classic unregularized model with its discriminator based on a non-parametric assumption of infinite modeling ability. Since then, great research efforts have been made to efficiently train the GAN by different criteria and architectures [15,19,22].

In contrast to unregularized GANs, Loss-Sensitive GAN (LS-GAN) [11] was recently presented to regularize the learning of a loss function in Lipschitz space, and proved the generalizability of the resultant model. [1] also proposed to minimize the Earth-Mover distance between the density of generated samples and the true data density, and they show the resultant Wasserstein GAN (WGAN) can address the vanishing gradient problem that the classic GAN suffers from. Coincidentally, the learning of WGAN is also constrained in a Lipschitz space.

Recent efforts [2,3] have also been made to learn a generator along with a corresponding encoder to obtain the representation of input data. The generator and encoder are simultaneously learned by jointly distinguishing between not only real and generated samples but also their latent variables in an adversarial process. Both methods still focus on learning unregularized GAN models without regularization constraints.

Researchers also leverage the learned representations by deep generative networks to improve the classification accuracy when it is too difficult or expensive to label sufficient training examples. For example, Qi et al. [13] propose a localized GAN to explore data variations in proximity of datapoints for semi-supervised learning. It can directly calculate Laplace-Beltra operator, which makes it amenable to handle large-scale data without resorting to a graph Laplacian approximation. [6] presents variational auto-encoders [7] by combining deep generative models and approximate variational inference to explore both labeled and unlabeled data. [17] treats the samples from the GAN generator as a new class, and explore unlabeled examples by assigning them to a class different from the new one. [15] proposes to train a ladder network [22] by minimizing the sum of supervised and unsupervised cost functions through back-propagation, which avoids the conventional layer-wise pre-training approach. [19] presents an approach to learn a discriminative classifier by trading-off mutual information between observed examples and their predicted classes against an adversarial generative model. [3] seeks to jointly distinguish between not only real and generated samples but also their latent variables in an adversarial process. These methods have shown promising results for classification tasks by leveraging deep generative models.

3 The Formulation

3.1 Loss Functions and Margins

The Loss-Sensitive Adversarial Learning (LSAL) aims to generate data by learning a generator G that transforms a latent vector $\mathbf{z} \in \mathcal{Z}$ of random variables drawn from a distribution $P_Z(\mathbf{z})$ to a real sample $\mathbf{x} \triangleq G(\mathbf{z}) \in \mathcal{X}$, where $\mathcal{Z}$ and

$\mathcal{X}$ are the noise and data spaces respectively. Usually, the space $\mathcal{Z}$ is of a lower dimensionality than $\mathcal{X}$, and the generator mapping G can be considered as an embedding of $\mathcal{Z}$ into a low-dimensional manifold $G(\mathcal{Z}) \subset \mathcal{X}$. In this sense, each $\mathbf{z}$ can be considered as a compact representation of $G(\mathbf{z}) \in \mathcal{X}$ on the manifold $G(\mathcal{Z})$.

Then, we can define a loss function L over the data domain $\mathcal{X}$ to characterize if a sample $\mathbf{x}$ is real or not. The smaller the loss L, the more likely $\mathbf{x}$ is a real sample. To learn L, a margin $\Delta_x(\mathbf{x}, \mathbf{x}')$ that measures the dissimilarity between samples will be defined to separate the loss functions between a pair of samples $\mathbf{x}$ and $\mathbf{x}'$, so that the loss of a real sample should be smaller than that of a fake sample $\mathbf{x}'$ by at least $\Delta_x(\mathbf{x}, \mathbf{x}')$. Since the margin $\Delta_x(\mathbf{x}, \mathbf{x}')$ is defined over the samples in their original ambient space $\mathcal{X}$ directly, we called it *ambient margin.*

In the meantime, we can also define a manifold margin $\Delta_z(\mathbf{z}, \mathbf{z}')$ over the manifold representations to separate the losses between real and generated samples. This is because the ambient margin alone may not well reflect the difference between samples, in particular considering real data like natural images often only occupy a small low-dimensional manifold embedded in the ambient space. Alternatively, the manifold will better capture the difference between data points to separate their losses on the manifold of real data.

To this end, we propose to learn another pullback mapping Q that projects a sample $\mathbf{x}$ back to the latent vector $\mathbf{z} \triangleq Q(\mathbf{x})$ that can be viewed as the low-dimensional representation of $\mathbf{x}$ over the underlying data manifold. Then, we can use the distance $\Delta_z(\mathbf{z}, \mathbf{z}')$ between latent vectors to approximate the geodesic distance between the projected points on the data manifold, and use it to define the *manifold margin* to separate the loss functions of different data points.

3.2 Learning Objectives

Formally, let us consider a loss function $L(\mathbf{x}, \mathbf{z})$ defined over a joint space $\mathcal{X} \times \mathcal{Z}$ of data and latent vectors. For a real sample $\mathbf{x}$ and its corresponding latent vector $Q(\mathbf{x})$, its loss function $L(\mathbf{x}, Q(\mathbf{x}))$ should be smaller than $L(G(\mathbf{z}), \mathbf{z})$ of a fake sample $G(\mathbf{z})$ and its latent vector $\mathbf{z}$. The required margin between them is defined as a combination of margins over data samples and latent vectors

$$\Delta_{\mu,\nu}(\mathbf{x}, \mathbf{z}) \triangleq \mu \Delta_x(\mathbf{x}, G(\mathbf{z})) + \nu \Delta_z(Q(\mathbf{x}), \mathbf{z}) \tag{1}$$

where the first term is the ambient margin separating loss functions between data points in the ambient space $\mathcal{X}$, while the second term is the manifold margin that separates loss functions based on the distance between latent vectors.

When a fake sample is far away from a real one, a larger margin will be imposed between them to separate their losses; otherwise, a smaller margin will be used to separate the losses. This allows the model to focus on improving the poor samples that are still far away from real samples, instead of wasting efforts on improving those well-generated data that are already close to real examples.

Then we will use the following objective functions to learn the fixed points of loss function L^*, the generator G^* and the pullback mapping Q^* by solving the following optimization problems.

(I) Learning L with fixed G^* and Q^*:

$$L^* = \arg\min_L \mathcal{S}(L, G^*, Q^*) \triangleq \mathbb{E}_{\substack{\mathbf{x}\sim P_x(\mathbf{x})\\ \mathbf{z}\sim P_Z(\mathbf{z})}} C\big[\Delta_{\mu,\nu}(\mathbf{x},\mathbf{z}) + L(\mathbf{x}, Q^*(\mathbf{x})) - L(G^*(\mathbf{z}), \mathbf{z})\big]$$

(II) Learning G with fixed L^* and Q^*:

$$G^* = \arg\min_G \mathcal{T}(L^*, G, Q^*) \triangleq \mathbb{E}_{\mathbf{z}\sim P_Z(\mathbf{z})} L^*(G(\mathbf{z}), \mathbf{z})$$

(III) Learning Q with fixed L^* and G^*:

$$Q^* = \arg\max_Q \mathcal{R}(L^*, G^*, Q) \triangleq \mathbb{E}_{\mathbf{x}\sim P_X(\mathbf{x})} L^*(\mathbf{x}, Q(\mathbf{x}))$$

where (1) the expectations in the above three objective functions are taken with respect to the probability measure P_X of real samples $\mathbf{x}$ and/or the probability measure P_Z of latent vectors $\mathbf{z}$. (2) the function $C[\cdot]$ is the cost function measuring the degree of the loss function L violating the required margin $\Delta_{\mu,\nu}(\mathbf{x},\mathbf{z})$, and it should satisfy the following two conditions:

$$C[a] = a \ \text{ for } \ a \geq 0, \ \text{ and } \ C[a] \geq a \ \text{ for } \ \text{any } a \in \mathbb{R}.$$

For example, the hinge loss $[a]_+ = \max(0, a)$ satisfies these two conditions, and it results in a LSAL model by penalizing the violation of margin requirement. Any rectifier linear function $\mathrm{ReLU}(a) = \max(a, \eta a)$ with a slope $\eta \leq 1$ also satisfies these two conditions.

Later on, we will prove the LSAL model satisfying these two conditions can produce samples following the true distribution of real data, i.e., the distributional consistency between real and generated samples.

(3) Problem (II) and (III) learn the generator G and pullback mapping Q in an adversarial fashion: G is learned by minimizing the loss function L^* since real samples and their latent vectors should have a smaller loss. In contrast, Q is learned by maximizing the loss function L^* – the reason will become clear in the theoretical justification of the following section when proving the distributional consistency between real and generated samples.

4 Theoretical Justification

In this section, we will justify the learning objectives of the proposed LSAL model by proving the distributional consistency between real and generated samples.

Formally, we will show that the joint distribution $P_{GZ}(\mathbf{x},\mathbf{z}) = P_Z(\mathbf{z})P_{X|Z}(\mathbf{x}|\mathbf{z})$ of generated sample $\mathbf{x} = G(\mathbf{z})$ and the latent vector $\mathbf{z}$ matches the joint distribution $P_{QX}(\mathbf{x},\mathbf{z}) = P_X(\mathbf{x})P_{Z|X}(\mathbf{z}|\mathbf{x})$ of the real sample $\mathbf{x}$ and its latent vector $\mathbf{z} = Q(\mathbf{x})$, i.e., $P_{GZ} = P_{QX}$. Then, by marginalizing out $\mathbf{z}$, we will be able to show the marginal distribution $P_{GZ}(\mathbf{x}) = \int_{\mathbf{z}} P_{GZ}(\mathbf{x},\mathbf{z})d\mathbf{z}$ of generated samples is consistent with $P_X(\mathbf{x})$ of the real samples. Hence, the main result justifying the distributional consistency for the LSAL model is Theorem 1 below.

4.1 Auxiliary Functions and Their Property

First, let us define two auxiliary functions that will be used in the proof:

$$f_{QX}(\mathbf{x},\mathbf{z}) = \frac{dP_{QX}}{dP_{GQ}},\ f_{GZ}(\mathbf{x},\mathbf{z}) = \frac{dP_{GZ}}{dP_{GQ}} \tag{2}$$

where $P_{GQ} = P_{GZ} + P_{QX}$, and the above two derivatives defining the auxiliary functions are the Radon-Nikodym derivative that exists since P_{QX} and P_{GZ} are absolutely continuous with respect to P_{GQ}. Here, we will need the following property regarding these two functions in our theoretical justification.

Lemma 1. *If $f_{QX}(\mathbf{x},\mathbf{z}) \geq f_{GZ}(\mathbf{x},\mathbf{z})$ for P_{GQ}-almost everywhere, we must have $P_{GZ} = P_{QX}$.*

Proof. To show $P_{GZ} = P_{QX}$, consider an arbitrary subset $R \subseteq \mathcal{X} \times \mathcal{Z}$. We have

$$\begin{aligned} P_{QX}(R) &= \int_R dP_{QX} = \int_R \frac{dP_{QX}}{dP_{GQ}} dP_{GQ} = \int_R f_{QX} dP_{GQ} \\ &\geq \int_R f_{GZ} dP_{GQ} = \int_R \frac{dP_{GZ}}{dP_{GQ}} dP_{GQ} = \int_R dP_{GZ} = P_{GZ}(R). \end{aligned} \tag{3}$$

Similarly, we can show the following inequality on $\Omega \setminus R$ with $\Omega = \mathcal{X} \times \mathcal{Z}$

$$P_{QX}(\Omega \setminus R) \geq P_{GZ}(\Omega \setminus R).$$

Since $P_{QX}(R) = 1 - P_{QX}(\Omega \setminus R)$ and $P_{GZ}(R) = 1 - P_{GZ}(\Omega \setminus R)$, we have

$$P_{QX}(R) = 1 - P_{QX}(\Omega \setminus R) \leq 1 - P_{GZ}(\Omega \setminus R) = P_{GZ}(R). \tag{4}$$

Putting together Eqs. (3) and (4), we have $P_{QX}(R) = P_{GZ}(R)$ for an arbitrary R, and thus $P_{QX} = P_{GZ}$, which completes the proof.

4.2 Main Result on Consistency

Now we can prove the consistency between generated and real samples with the following Lipschitz regularity condition on f_{QX} and f_{GZ}.

Assumption 1. *Both $f_{QX}(\mathbf{x},\mathbf{z})$ and $f_{GZ}(\mathbf{x},\mathbf{z})$ have bounded Lipschitz constants in $(\mathbf{x},\mathbf{z})$.*

It is noted that the bounded Lipschitz condition for both functions is only applied to the support of $(\mathbf{x},\mathbf{z})$. In other words, we only require the Lipschitz condition hold on the joint space $\mathcal{X} \times Z$ of data and latent vectors.

Then, we can prove the following main theorem.

Theorem 1. *Under Assumption 1, $P_{QX} = P_{GZ}$ for P_{GQ}-almost everywhere with the optimal generator G^* and the pullback mapping Q^*. Moreover, $f_{QX} = f_{GZ} = \frac{1}{2}$ at the optimum.*

The second part of the theorem follows from the first part. since $P_{QX} = P_{GZ}$ for the optimum G^* and Q^*, $f_{QX} = \frac{dP_{QX}}{dP_{GQ}} = \frac{dP_{QX}}{d(P_{QX}+P_{GZ})} = \frac{1}{2}$. Similarly, $f_{GZ} = \frac{1}{2}$. This shows f_{QX} and f_{GZ} are both Lipschitz at the fixed point depicted by Problem (I)–(III).

Here we give the proof of this theorem step-by-step in detail. The proof will shed us some light on the roles of the ambient and manifold margins as well as the Lipschitz regularity in guaranteeing the distributional consistency between generated and real samples.

Proof. **Step 1:** First, we will show that

$$\mathcal{S}(L^*, G^*, Q^*) \geq \mathbb{E}_{\mathbf{x},\mathbf{z}}[\Delta^*_{\mu,\nu}(\mathbf{x},\mathbf{z})], \tag{5}$$

where $\Delta^*_{\mu,\nu}(\mathbf{x},\mathbf{z})$ is defined in Eq. (1) with G and Q being replaced with their optimum G^* and Q^*.

This can be proved following the deduction below

$$\mathcal{S}(L^*, G^*, Q^*) \geq \mathbb{E}_{\mathbf{x},\mathbf{z}}[\Delta^*_{\mu,\nu}(\mathbf{x},\mathbf{z})] + \mathbb{E}_{\mathbf{x}} L^*(\mathbf{x}, Q^*(\mathbf{x})) - \mathbb{E}_{\mathbf{z}} L^*(G^*(\mathbf{z}), \mathbf{z})$$

This follows from $C[a] \geq a$. Continuing the deduction, we have the RHS of the last inequality equals

$$\begin{aligned}
&\mathbb{E}_{\mathbf{x},\mathbf{z}}[\Delta^*_{\mu,\nu}(\mathbf{x},\mathbf{z})] + \int_{\mathbf{x},\mathbf{z}} L^*(\mathbf{x},\mathbf{z}) dP_{Z|X}(\mathbf{z} = Q^*(\mathbf{x})|\mathbf{x}) dP_X(\mathbf{x}) \\
&- \int_{\mathbf{x},\mathbf{z}} L^*(\mathbf{x},\mathbf{z}) dP_{X|Z}(\mathbf{x} = G^*(\mathbf{z})|\mathbf{z}) dP_Z(\mathbf{z}) \\
&\geq \mathbb{E}_{\mathbf{x},\mathbf{z}}[\Delta^*_{\mu,\nu}(\mathbf{x},\mathbf{z})] + \int_{\mathbf{x},\mathbf{z}} L^*(\mathbf{x},\mathbf{z}) dP_Z(\mathbf{z}) dP_X(\mathbf{x}) - \int_{\mathbf{x},\mathbf{z}} L^*(\mathbf{x},\mathbf{z}) dP_X(\mathbf{x}) dP_Z(\mathbf{z}) \\
&= \mathbb{E}_{\mathbf{x},\mathbf{z}}[\Delta^*_{\mu,\nu}(\mathbf{x},\mathbf{z})],
\end{aligned}$$

which follows from the Problem (II) and (III) where G^* and Q^* minimizes and maximizes L^* respectively. Hence, the second and third terms in the LHS are lower bounded when $P_{Z|X}(\mathbf{z} = Q^*(\mathbf{x})|\mathbf{x})$ and $P_{X|Z}(\mathbf{x} = G^*(\mathbf{z})|\mathbf{z})$ are replaced with $P_Z(\mathbf{z})$ and $P_X(\mathbf{x})$ respectively.

Step 2: we will show that $f_{QX} \geq f_{GZ}$ for P_{GQ}-almost everywhere so that we can apply Lemma 1 to prove the consistency.

With Assumption 1, we can define the following Lipschitz continuous loss function

$$L(\mathbf{x},\mathbf{z}) = \alpha[-f_{QX}(\mathbf{x},\mathbf{z}) + f_{GZ}(\mathbf{x},\mathbf{z})]_+ \tag{6}$$

with a sufficiently small $\alpha > 0$. Thus, $L(\mathbf{x},\mathbf{z})$ will also be Lipschitz continuous whose Lipschitz constants are smaller than μ and ν in $\mathbf{x}$ and $\mathbf{z}$ respectively. This will result in the following inequality

$$\Delta^*_{\mu,\nu}(\mathbf{x},\mathbf{z}) + L(\mathbf{x}, Q^*(\mathbf{x})) - L(G^*(\mathbf{z}), \mathbf{z}) \geq 0.$$

Then, by $C[a] = a$ for $a \geq 0$, we have

$$\begin{aligned}\mathcal{S}(L, Q^*, G^*) &= \mathbb{E}_{\mathbf{x},\mathbf{z}}[\Delta^*_{\mu,\nu}(\mathbf{x},\mathbf{z})] + \int_{\mathbf{x},\mathbf{z}} L(\mathbf{x},\mathbf{z})dP_{QX} - \int_{\mathbf{x},\mathbf{z}} L(\mathbf{x},\mathbf{z})dP_{GZ} \\ &= \mathbb{E}_{\mathbf{x},\mathbf{z}}[\Delta^*_{\mu,\nu}(\mathbf{x},\mathbf{z})] + \int_{\mathbf{x},\mathbf{z}} L(\mathbf{x},\mathbf{z})f_{QX}(\mathbf{x},\mathbf{z})dP_{GQ} - \int_{\mathbf{x},\mathbf{z}} L(\mathbf{x},\mathbf{z})f_{GZ}(\mathbf{x},\mathbf{z})dP_{GQ}\end{aligned}$$

where the last equality follows from Eq. (2). By substituting (6) into the RHS of the above equality, we have

$$\mathcal{S}(L, Q^*, G^*) = \mathbb{E}_{\mathbf{x},\mathbf{z}}[\Delta^*_{\mu,\nu}(\mathbf{x},\mathbf{z})] - \alpha \int_{\mathbf{x},\mathbf{z}} [-f_{QX}(\mathbf{x},\mathbf{z}) + f_{GZ}(\mathbf{x},\mathbf{z})]^2_+ dP_{GQ}$$

Let us assume that $f_{QX}(\mathbf{x},\mathbf{z}) < f_{GZ}(\mathbf{x},\mathbf{z})$ holds on a subset $(\mathbf{x},\mathbf{z})$ of nonzero measure with respect to P_{GQ}. Then since $\alpha > 0$, we have

$$\mathcal{S}(L^*, Q^*, G^*) \leq \mathcal{S}(L, Q^*, G^*) < \mathbb{E}_{\mathbf{x},\mathbf{z}}[\Delta^*_{\mu,\nu}(\mathbf{x},\mathbf{z})]$$

The first inequality arises from Problem (I) where L^* minimizes $\mathcal{S}(L, Q^*, G^*)$. Obviously, this contradicts with (5), thus we must have $f_{QX}(\mathbf{x},\mathbf{z}) \geq f_{GZ}(\mathbf{x},\mathbf{z})$ for P_{GQ}-almost everywhere. This completes the proof of Step 2.
Step 3: Now the theorem can be proved by combining Lemma 1 and the result from Step 2.

As a corollary, we can show that the optimal Q^* and G^* are mutually inverse.

Corollary 1. *With optimal Q^* and G^*, ${Q^*}^{-1} = G^*$ almost everywhere. In other words, $Q^*(G^*(\mathbf{z})) = z$ for P_Z-almost every $\mathbf{z} \in \mathcal{Z}$ and $G^*(Q^*(\mathbf{x})) = x$ for P_X-almost every $\mathbf{x} \in \mathcal{X}$.*

The corollary is a consequence of the proved distributional consistency $P_{QX} = P_{GZ}$ for optimal Q^* and G^* as shown in [2]. This implies that the optimal pullback mapping $Q^*(\mathbf{x})$ forms a latent representation of $\mathbf{x}$ as the inverse of the optimal generator function G^*.

5 Semi-supervised Learning

LSAL can also be used to train a semi-supervised classifier [12,21,25] by exploring a large amount of unlabeled examples when the labeled samples are scarce. To serve as a classifier, the loss function $L(\mathbf{x},\mathbf{z},\mathbf{y})$ can be redefined over a joint space of $\mathcal{X} \times \mathcal{Z} \times \mathcal{Y}$ where $\mathcal{Y}$ is the label space. Now the loss function measures the cost of assigning jointly a sample $\mathbf{x}$ and its manifold representation $Q(\mathbf{x})$ to a label y^* by minimizing $L(\mathbf{x},\mathbf{z},\mathbf{y})$ over $\mathcal{Y}$ below

$$y^* = \arg\min_{y \in \mathcal{Y}} L(\mathbf{x},\mathbf{z},\mathbf{y}) \tag{7}$$

To train the Loss function of LSAL in a semi-supervised fashion, We define the following objective function

$$\mathcal{S}(L, G, Q) = \mathcal{S}_l(L, G, Q) + \lambda\, \mathcal{S}_u(L, G, Q) \tag{8}$$

where $\mathcal{S}_l$ is the objective function for labeled examples while $\mathcal{S}_u$ is for unlabeled samples, and λ is a positive coefficient balancing between the contributions of labeled and unlabeled data.

Since our goal is to classify a pair of $(\mathbf{x}, Q(\mathbf{x}))$ to one class in the label space $\mathcal{Y}$, we can define the loss function L by the negative log-softmax output from a network. So we have

$$L(\mathbf{x}, \mathbf{z}, \mathbf{y}) = -\log \frac{\exp(a_y(\mathbf{x}, \mathbf{z}))}{\sum_{y'} \exp(a_{y'}(\mathbf{x}, \mathbf{z}))}$$

which $a_y(\mathbf{x}, \mathbf{z})$ is the activation output of class $\mathbf{y}$. By the LSAL formulation, given a label example $(\mathbf{x}, \mathbf{y})$, the $L(\mathbf{x}, Q(\mathbf{x}), \mathbf{y})$ should be smaller than $L(G(\mathbf{z}), \mathbf{z}, \mathbf{y})$ by at least a margin of $\Delta_{\mu,\nu}(\mathbf{x}, \mathbf{z})$. So the objective S_l is defined as

$$\begin{aligned} &\mathcal{S}_l(L, G^*, Q^*) \triangleq \\ &\mathbb{E}_{\substack{\mathbf{x},\mathbf{y} \sim \mathbf{P}_{data}(\mathbf{x},\mathbf{y}) \\ \mathbf{z} \sim \mathbf{P}_Z(\mathbf{z})}} C\big[\Delta_{\mu,\nu}(\mathbf{x}, \mathbf{z}) + L(\mathbf{x}, Q^*(\mathbf{x}), \mathbf{y}) - L(G^*(\mathbf{z}), \mathbf{z}, \mathbf{y})\big] \end{aligned} \tag{9}$$

For the unlabeled samples, we rely on the fact that the best guess of the label for a sample $\mathbf{x}$ is the one that minimizes $L(\mathbf{x}, \mathbf{z}, \mathbf{y})$ over the label space $\mathbf{y} \in \mathcal{Y}$. So the loss function for an unlabeled sample can be defined as

$$L_u(\mathbf{x}, \mathbf{z}) \triangleq \min_y L(\mathbf{x}, \mathbf{z}, \mathbf{y}) \tag{10}$$

We also update the $L(\mathbf{x}, \mathbf{z}, \mathbf{y})$ to $-\log \frac{\exp(a_y(\mathbf{x},\mathbf{z}))}{1+\sum_{y'} \exp(a_{y'}(\mathbf{x},\mathbf{z}))}$. Equipped with the new L_u, we can define the loss-sensitive objective for unlabeled samples as

$$\begin{aligned} &\mathcal{S}_u(L, G^*, Q^*) \triangleq \\ &\mathbb{E}_{\substack{\mathbf{x},\mathbf{y} \sim \mathbf{P}_{data}(\mathbf{x},\mathbf{y}) \\ \mathbf{z} \sim \mathbf{P}_Z(\mathbf{z})}} C\big[\Delta_{\mu,\nu}(\mathbf{x}, \mathbf{z}) + L_u(\mathbf{x}, Q^*(\mathbf{x}), \mathbf{y}) - L_u(G^*(\mathbf{z}), \mathbf{z}, \mathbf{y})\big] \end{aligned}$$

Like in the LSAL, G^* and Q^* can be found by solving the following optimization problems.

- Learning G with fixed L^* and Q^*:

$$G^* = \arg\min_G \mathcal{T}(L^*, G, Q^*) \triangleq \mathbb{E}_{\substack{\mathbf{y} \sim P_Y(\mathbf{y}) \\ \mathbf{z} \sim P_Z(\mathbf{z})}} L_u^*(G(\mathbf{z}), \mathbf{z}) + L^*(G(\mathbf{z}), \mathbf{z}, \mathbf{y})$$

- Learning Q with fixed L^* and G^*:

$$Q^* = \arg\max_Q \mathcal{R}(L^*, G^*, Q) \triangleq \mathbb{E}_{\mathbf{x},\mathbf{y} \sim P_{data}(\mathbf{x},\mathbf{y})} L_u^*(\mathbf{x}, Q(\mathbf{x})) + L^*(\mathbf{x}, Q(\mathbf{x}), \mathbf{y})$$

In experiments, we will evaluate the semi-supervised LSAL model in image classification task.

6 Experiments

We evaluated the performance of the LSAL model on four datasets, namely Cifar10 [8], SVHN [10], CelebA [23] and 64 × 64 cropped center ImageNet [16]. We compared the image generation ability of the LSAL, both qualitatively and quantitatively, with other state-of-the-art GAN models. We also trained LSAL model in semi-supervised fashion for image classification task.

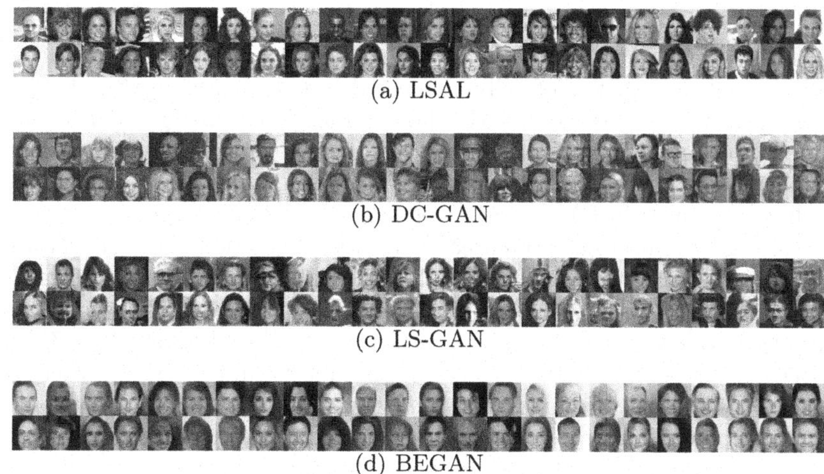

Fig. 1. Generated samples by various methods. Size 64×64 on CelebA data-set. Best seen on screen.

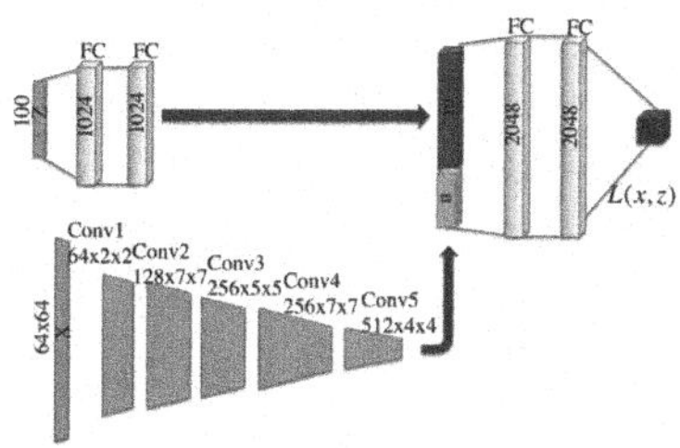

Fig. 2. Network architecture for the loss function $L(\mathbf{x}, \mathbf{z})$. All convolution layers have a stride of two to halve the size of their input feature maps.

6.1 Architecture and Training

While this work does not aim to test new idea of designing architectures for the GANs, we adopt the exisiting architectures to make the comparison with other models as fair as possible. Three convnet models have been used to represent the generator $G(\mathbf{z})$, the pullback mapping $Q(\mathbf{x})$ and the loss function $L(\mathbf{x}, \mathbf{z})$. We use hinge loss as our cost function $C[\cdot] = \max(0, \cdot)$. Similar to DCGAN [14], we use strided-convolutions instead of pooling layers to down-sample feature maps and fractional-convolutions for the up-sampling purpose. Batch-normalization [5] (BN) also has been used before Rectified Linear (ReLU) activation function in the generator and pullback mapping networks while weight-normalization [18] (WN) is applied to the convolutional layers of the loss function. We also apply the dropout [20] with a ratio of 0.2 over all fully connected layers. The loss function $L(\mathbf{x}, \mathbf{z})$ is computed over the joint space $\mathcal{X} \times \mathcal{Z}$, so its input consists of two parts: the first part is a convnet that maps an input image $\mathbf{x}$ to an n-dim vector representation; the second part is a sequence of fully connected layers that successively maps the latent vector $\mathbf{z}$ to an m-dim vector too. Then an $(n+m)$-dim vector is generated by concatenation of these two vectors and goes further through a sequence of fully connected layers to compute the final loss value. For the semi-supervised LSAL, the loss function $L(\mathbf{x}, \mathbf{z}, \mathbf{y})$ is also defined over the label space $\mathcal{Y}$. In this case, the loss function network defined above can have multiple outputs, each for one label in $\mathcal{Y}$. The main idea of loss function network is illustrated in Fig. 2. LSAL code also is available here.

The Adam optimizer has been used to train all of the models on four datasets. For image generation task, we use the learning rate of 10^{-4} and the first and second moment decay rate of $\beta_1 = 0.5$ and $\beta_2 = 0.99$. In the semi-supervised classification task, the learning rate is set to 6×10^{-4} and decays by 5% every 50 epochs till it reaches 3×10^{-4}. For both Cifar10 and SVHN datasets, the coefficient λ of unlabeled samples, and the hyper parameters μ and ν for manifold and ambient margins are chosen based on the validation set of each dataset. The L1-norm has been used in all of the experiments for both margins.

Table 1. Comparison of Inception score for various GAN models on Cifar10 data-set. Inception score of real data represents the upper bound of the score.

Model	Inception score
Real data	11.24 ±0.12
ALI [3]	4.98 ±0.48
LS-GAN [11]	5.83 ±0.22
LSAL	6.43 ±0.53

Finally, it is noted that, from theoretical perspective, we do not need to do any kind of pairing between generated and real samples in showing the distributional consistency in Sect. 4. Thus, we can randomly choose a real image rather than a "ground truth" counterpart (e.g., the most similar image) to pair with a generated sample. The experiments below also empirically demonstrate the random sampling strategy works well in generating high-quality images as well as training competitive semi-supervised classifiers.

6.2 Image Generation Results

Qualitative Comparison: To show the performance of the LSAL model, we qualitatively compared the generated images by proposed model on CelebA dataset with other state of the art GANs models. As illustrated in Fig. 1, the LSAL can produce details of face images as compared to other methods. Faces have well defined borders and nose and eyes have real shape while in LS-GAN Fig. 1(c) and DC-GAN Fig. 1(b) most of generated samples don't have clear face borders and samples of BEGAN model Fig. 1(d) lack stereoscopic features. Figure 3 shows the samples generated by LSAL for Cifar10, SVHN, and

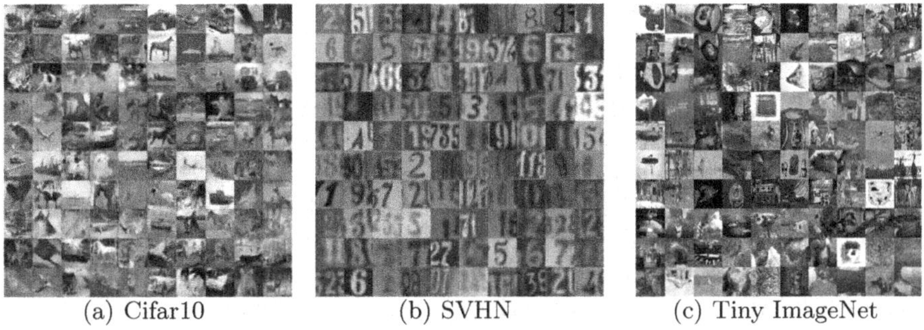

(a) Cifar10 (b) SVHN (c) Tiny ImageNet

Fig. 3. Generated samples by LSAL on different data-sets. Samples of (a) Cifar10 and (b) SVHN are of size 32×32. Samples of (c) Tiny ImageNet are of size 64×64.

tiny ImageNet datasets. We also walk through the manifold space $\mathcal{Z}$, projected by the pullback mapping Q. To this end, pullback mapping network Q has been used to find the manifold representations $\mathbf{z}_1$ and $\mathbf{z}_2$ of two randomly selected samples from the validation set. Then G has been used to generate new samples for $\mathbf{z}$'s on the linear interpolate of $\mathbf{z}_1$ and $\mathbf{z}_2$. As illustrated in Fig. 4, the transition between pairs of images are smooth and meaningful.

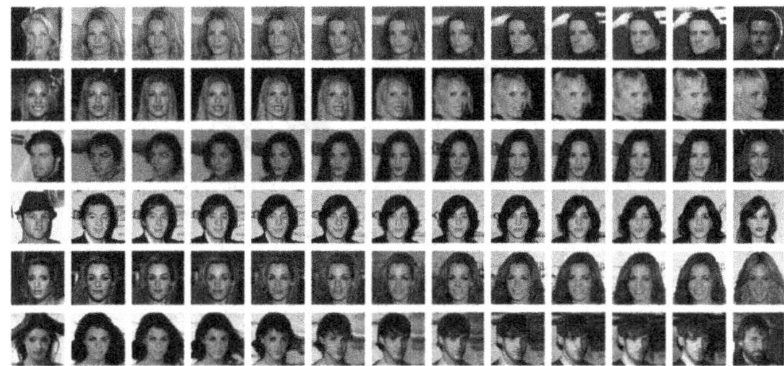

Fig. 4. Generated images for the interpolation of latent representations learned by pullback mapping Q for CelebA data-set. First and last column are real samples from validation set.

Quantitative Comparison: To quantitively assess the quality of LSAL generated samples, we used *Inception Score* proposed by [17]. We chose this metric as it had been widely used in literature so we can fairly compare with the other models directly. We applied the Inception model to images generated by various GAN models trained on Cifar10. The comparison of Inception scores on 50,000 images generated by each model is reported in Table 1.

6.3 Semi-supervised Classification

Using semi-supervised LSAL to train an image classifier, we achieved competitive results in comparison to other GAN models. Table 3 shows the error rate of the semi-supervised LSAL along with other semi-supervised GAN models when only 1,000 labeled examples were used in training on SVHN with the other examples unlabeled. For Cifar10, LSAL was trained with various numbers of labeled examples. In Table 2, we show the error rates of the LSAL with 1,000, 2,000, 4,000, and 8,000 labeled images. The results show the proposed semi-supervised LSAL successfully outperforms the other methods.

Table 2. Comparison of classification error on Cifar10

# of labeled samples	1000	2000	4000	8000
Model		Classification error		
Ladder network [15]			20.40	
CatGAN [19]			19.58	
CLS-GAN [11]			17.3	
Improved GAN [17]	21.83 ± 2.01	19.61 ± 2.32	18.63 ± 2.32	17.72 ± 1.82
ALI [3]	19.98 ± 0.89	19.09 ± 0.44	17.99 ± 1.62	17.05 ± 1.49
LSAL	$\mathbf{18.83 \pm 0.44}$	$\mathbf{17.97 \pm 0.74}$	$\mathbf{16.22 \pm 0.31}$	$\mathbf{14.17 \pm 0.62}$

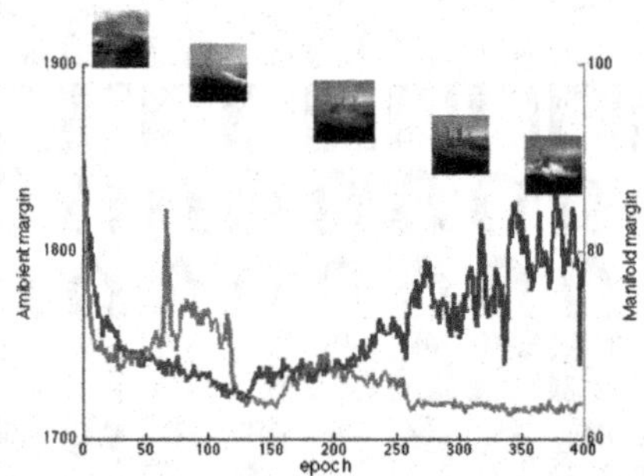

Fig. 5. Trends of manifold and ambient margins over epochs on the Cifar10 dataset. Example images are generated at epoch 10, 100, 200, 300, 400.

6.4 Trends of Ambient and Manifold Margins

We also illustrate the trends of ambient and manifold margins as the learning algorithm proceeds over epochs in Fig. 5. The curves were obtained by training the LSAL model on Cifar10 with 4,000 labeled examples, and both margins are averaged over mini-batches of real and fake pairs sampled in each epoch.

From the illustrated curves, we can see that the manifold margin continues to decrease and eventually stabilize after about 270 epochs. As manifold margin decreases, we find the quality of generated images continues to improve even

Table 3. Comparison of classification error on SVHN test set for semi-supervised learning using 1000 labeled examples.

Model	Classification error
Skip deep generative model [9]	16.61 $\pm$ 0.24
Improved GAN [17]	8.11 $\pm$ 1.3
ALI [3]	7.42 $\pm$ 0.65
CLS-GAN [11]	5.98 $\pm$ 0.27
LSAL	$\mathbf{5.46 \pm 0.24}$

though the ambient margin fluctuates over epochs. This shows the importance of manifold margin that motivates the proposed LSAL model. It also demonstrates the manifold margin between real and fake images should be a better indicator we can use for the quality of generated images.

7 Conclusion

In this paper, we present a novel regularized LSAL model, and justify it from both theoretical and empirical perspectives. Based on the assumption that the real data are distributed on a low-dimensional manifold, we define a pullback operator that maps a sample back to the manifold. A manifold margin is defined as the distance between the pullback representations to distinguish between real and fake samples and learn the optimal generators. The resultant model also demonstrates it can produce high quality images as compared with the other state-of-the-art GAN models.

Acknowledgement. The research was partly supported by NSF grant #1704309 and IARPA grant #D17PC00345. We also appreciate the generous donation of GPU cards by NVIDIA in support of our research.

References

1. Arjovsky, M., Chintala, S., Bottou, L.: Wasserstein gan. arXiv preprint arXiv:1701.07875, January 2017
2. Donahue, J., Krähenbühl, P., Darrell, T.: Adversarial feature learning. arXiv preprint arXiv:1605.09782 (2016)
3. Dumoulin, V., et al.: Adversarially learned inference. arXiv preprint arXiv:1606.00704 (2016)
4. Goodfellow, I., et al.: Generative adversarial nets. In: Advances in Neural Information Processing Systems, pp. 2672–2680 (2014)
5. Ioffe, S., Szegedy, C.: Batch normalization: accelerating deep network training by reducing internal covariate shift. In: International conference on machine learning, pp. 448–456 (2015)

6. Kingma, D.P., Mohamed, S., Rezende, D.J., Welling, M.: Semi-supervised learning with deep generative models. In: Advances in Neural Information Processing Systems, pp. 3581–3589 (2014)
7. Kingma, D.P., Welling, M.: Auto-encoding variational bayes. arXiv preprint arXiv:1312.6114 (2013)
8. Krizhevsky, A.: Learning multiple layers of features from tiny images (2009)
9. Maaløe, L., Sønderby, C.K., Sønderby, S.K., Winther, O.: Auxiliary deep generative models. arXiv preprint arXiv:1602.05473 (2016)
10. Netzer, Y., Wang, T., Coates, A., Bissacco, A., Wu, B., Ng, A.Y.: Reading digits in natural images with unsupervised feature learning (2011)
11. Qi, G.J.: Loss-sensitive generative adversarial networks on lipschitz densities. arXiv preprint arXiv:1701.06264, January 2017
12. Qi, G.J., Aggarwal, C.C., Huang, T.S.: On clustering heterogeneous social media objects with outlier links. In: Proceedings of the Fifth ACM International Conference on Web Search and Data Mining, pp. 553–562. ACM (2012)
13. Qi, G.J., Zhang, L., Hu, H., Edraki, M., Wang, J., Hua, X.S.: Global versus localized generative adversarial nets. In: Proceedings of IEEE Conference on Computer Vision and Pattern Recognition (2018)
14. Radford, A., Metz, L., Chintala, S.: Unsupervised representation learning with deep convolutional generative adversarial networks. arXiv preprint arXiv:1511.06434 (2015)
15. Rasmus, A., Berglund, M., Honkala, M., Valpola, H., Raiko, T.: Semi-supervised learning with ladder networks. In: Advances in Neural Information Processing Systems, pp. 3546–3554 (2015)
16. Russakovsky, O., et al.: ImageNet large scale visual recognition challenge. Int. J. Comput. Vis. (IJCV) **115**(3), 211–252 (2015). https://doi.org/10.1007/s11263-015-0816-y
17. Salimans, T., Goodfellow, I., Zaremba, W., Cheung, V., Radford, A., Chen, X.: Improved techniques for training gans. In: Advances in Neural Information Processing Systems, pp. 2226–2234 (2016)
18. Salimans, T., Kingma, D.P.: Weight normalization: a simple reparameterization to accelerate training of deep neural networks. In: Advances in Neural Information Processing Systems, pp. 901–909 (2016)
19. Springenberg, J.T.: Unsupervised and semi-supervised learning with categorical generative adversarial networks. arXiv preprint arXiv:1511.06390 (2015)
20. Srivastava, N., Hinton, G., Krizhevsky, A., Sutskever, I., Salakhutdinov, R.: Dropout: a simple way to prevent neural networks from overfitting. J. Mach. Learn. Res. **15**(1), 1929–1958 (2014)
21. Tang, J., Hua, X.S., Qi, G.J., Wu, X.: Typicality ranking via semi-supervised multiple-instance learning. In: Proceedings of the 15th ACM International Conference on Multimedia, pp. 297–300. ACM (2007)
22. Valpola, H.: From neural PCA to deep unsupervised learning. In: Advances in Independent Component Analysis and Learning Machines, pp. 143–171 (2015)
23. Yang, S., Luo, P., Loy, C.C., Tang, X.: From facial parts responses to face detection: a deep learning approach. In: Proceedings of the IEEE International Conference on Computer Vision, pp. 3676–3684 (2015)
24. Zhao, J., Mathieu, M., LeCun, Y.: Energy-based generative adversarial network. arXiv preprint arXiv:1609.03126 (2016)
25. Zhu, X.: Semi-supervised learning. In: Seel, N.M. (ed.) Encyclopedia of Machine Learning, pp. 892–897. Springer, Heidelberg (2011)

Into the Twilight Zone: Depth Estimation Using Joint Structure-Stereo Optimization

Aashish Sharma(✉) and Loong-Fah Cheong

Department of ECE, National University of Singapore, Singapore, Singapore
aashish.sharma@u.nus.edu, eleclf@nus.edu.sg

Abstract. We present a joint Structure-Stereo optimization model that is robust for disparity estimation under low-light conditions. Eschewing the traditional denoising approach – which we show to be ineffective for stereo due to its artefacts and the questionable use of the PSNR metric, we propose to instead rely on structures comprising of piecewise constant regions and principal edges in the given image, as these are the important regions for extracting disparity information. We also judiciously retain the coarser textures for stereo matching, discarding the finer textures as they are apt to be inextricably mixed with noise. This selection process in the structure-texture decomposition step is aided by the stereo matching constraint in our joint Structure-Stereo formulation. The resulting optimization problem is complex but we are able to decompose it into sub-problems that admit relatively standard solutions. Our experiments confirm that our joint model significantly outperforms the baseline methods on both synthetic and real noise datasets.

Keywords: Stereo matching · Depth estimation · Low-light vision
Structure extraction · Joint optimization

1 Introduction

Disparity estimation from stereo plays an imperative role in 3D reconstruction, which is useful for many real-world applications such as autonomous driving. In the past decade, with the development of fast and accurate methods [1,2] and especially with the advent of deep learning [3–5], there has been a significant improvement in the field. Despite this development, binocular depth estimation under low-light conditions still remains a relatively unexplored area. Presence of severe image noise, multiple moving light sources, varying glow and glare, unavailability of reliable low-light stereo datasets, are some of the numerous grim challenges that possibly explain the slow progress in this field. However, given its significance in autonomous driving, it becomes important to develop algorithms that can perform robust stereo matching under these conditions. Given that the challenges are manifold, we focus in this paper on the primary issue that plagues

V. Ferrari et al. (Eds.): ECCV 2018, LNCS 11209, pp. 105–121, 2018.
https://doi.org/10.1007/978-3-030-01228-1_7

stereo matching under low-light: that images inevitably suffer from low contrast, loss of saturation, and substantial level of noise which is dense and often non-Gaussian [6]. The low signal to noise ratio (SNR) under low-light is in a sense unpreventable since the camera essentially acts like a gain-control amplifier.

While the aforementioned problem may be alleviated somewhat by using longer exposure time, this additionally causes other imperfections such as motion blur [7]. Multi-spectral imaging involving specialized hardware such as color-infrared or color-monochrome camera pair [7] can be used, but their usability is often restricted owing to high manufacturing and installation costs. Rather than relying on modifying the image acquisition process, our research interest is more that of coming to grips with the basic problems: how to recover adequate disparity information from a given pair of low-light stereo images under typical urban conditions, and to discover the crucial recipes for success.

One obvious way to handle noise could be to use denoising to clean up the images before stereo matching. However, denoising in itself either suffers from ineffectiveness in the higher noise regimes (e.g., NLM [8], ROF [9]), or creates undesirable artefacts (e.g., BM3D [10]), both of which are detrimental for stereo matching. Even some of the recent state-of-the-art deep learning solutions, such as MLP [11], SSDA [12] and DnCNN [13], only show equal or marginally better performances over BM3D [10] in terms of image Peak Signal to Noise Ratio (PSNR). On the most basic level, these denoising algorithms are designed for a single image and thus may not remove noise in a manner that is consistent across the stereo pair, which is again detrimental for stereo matching. Another fundamental issue is raised by a recent paper "Dirty Pixels" [6] which demonstrated empirically that PSNR might not be a suitable criteria for evaluation of image quality if the aim is to perform high-level vision tasks such as classification, and even low PSNR images (but optimized for the vision task ahead) can outperform their high PSNR unoptimized counterparts. This debunks the general belief of a linear relationship between improving the PSNR and improving the competency of the associated vision task. We argue that the same phenomenon holds for the task of stereo matching, for which case we offer the following reasoning: unlike PSNR, in stereo matching, not all pixels are equal in terms of their impact arising from a denoising artefact. In image regions with near-uniform intensity, the energy landscape of the objective function for stereo matching is very shallow; any small artefacts caused by denoising algorithms in these regions can have a disproportionally large influence on the stereo solution. On the other hand, in textured regions, we can afford to discard some of the finer textures (thus losing out in PSNR) but yet suffer no loss in disparity accuracy, provided there are sufficient coarser textures in the same region to provide the necessary information for filling in. This latter condition is often met in outdoor images due to the well-known scale invariance properties of natural image statistics [14].

Our algorithm is founded upon the foregoing observations. Our first key idea originates from how we humans perceive depth in low-light, which is mainly

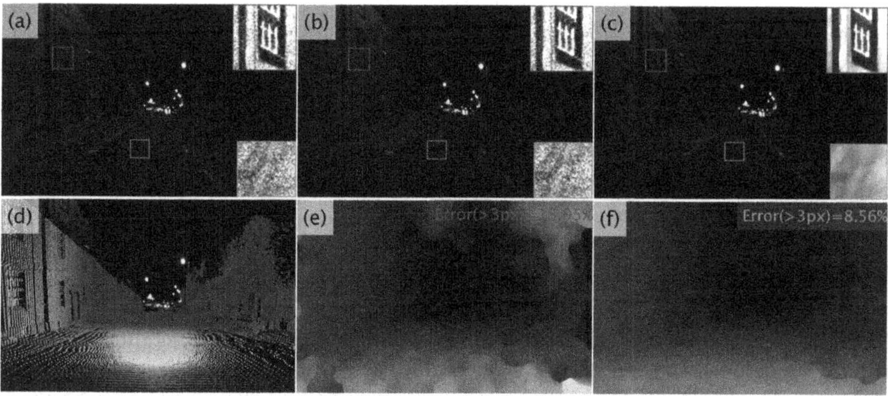

Fig. 1. (a) Sample low-light image from the Oxford dataset [15]. From the two patches (boosted with [16]), we can observe that in low-light, fine textures are barely distinguishable from dense noise, and only coarser textures and object boundaries are recoverable; (b) Denoising result from DnCNN [13] showing its ineffectiveness under low-contrast dense noise; (c) Structures from our model showing recovery of sharp object boundaries and coarse textures; (d) Image (a) with projected disparity ground truth (for visualization); (e) Disparity result from 'DnCNN [13]+MS [17]', (f) Disparity result from our model. Our result is more accurate, robust and has lesser artefacts, showing our model's robustness for stereo matching under low-light conditions.

through the principal scene structures such as object boundaries and coarser textures. The main underlying physiological explanation for the preceding is the increased spatiotemporal pooling of photoreceptor responses for increased sensitivity, under which low-light vision becomes necessarily coarser and slower. It means that for highly noisy images perturbed by randomly oriented elements, only the principal contours (i.e. lower spatial frequency contours) become salient because their elements are coaligned with a smooth global trajectory, as described by the Gestalt law of good continuation. In an analogous manner, we postulate that since fine details in low-light are barely irrevocable from noise (e.g., the fine textures on the building and road in the inset boxes of Fig. 1a), we should instead rely on structures consisting of piecewise constant regions and principal edges (from both object boundaries and coarse textures) to obtain scene depth (see the coarse textures extracted in the inset boxes of Fig. 1c)[1]. For this purpose, we adopt the nonlinear $TV - L_2$ decomposition algorithm

[1] Most night-time outdoor and traffic lighting scenarios in a city are amidst such a wash of artificial lights that our eyes never fully transition to scotopic vision. Instead, they stay in the mesopic range, where both the cones and rods are active (mesopic light levels range from ~0.001–3 cd/m^2). This range of luminance where some coarse textures in the interiors of objects are still visible to the human eyes will occupy our main interest, whereas extremely impoverished conditions such as a moonless scene (where even coarse textures are not discernible) will be tangential to our enquiry.

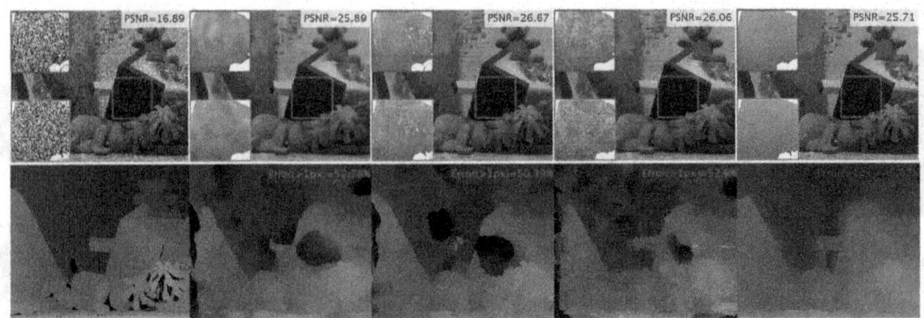

Fig. 2. Going column-wise: (i) Noisy 'Teddy' [18] image with corresponding left-right (red-green) patches (boosted with [16]); Denoised with (ii) BM3D [10] (inconsistent artefacts across the patches); (iii) DnCNN [13] (inconsistent denoising), (iv) SS-PCA [19] (inconsistent and ineffective denoising); (v) Structures from our model (consistent and no artefacts); (vi) Disparity ground truth; Result from (vii) 'BM3D [10]+MS [17]', (viii) 'DnCNN [13]+MS [17]', (ix) SS-PCA [19], and (x) Our model. All the baseline methods show high error in the patch area, while our method produces more accurate result in there while keeping sharp edges in other parts. Also note that our structures have the lowest PSNR, but still the highest disparity performance among all the methods. (Color figure online)

[9] to perform both denoising and extraction of the principal structures[2]. This variational style of denoising ensures that (1) the near-uniform intensity regions will remain flat, critical for disparity accuracy, and (2) those error-prone high-frequency fine details will be suppressed, whereas the coarser textures, which are more consistently recoverable across the images, will be retained. These attributes contribute significantly to the success of our disparity estimation (see results obtained by 'DnCNN [13]+MS [17]', Fig. 1e and our algorithm, Fig. 1f).

Our second key idea is to jointly optimize the $TV - L_2$ decomposition and the disparity estimation task. The motivation is twofold. Firstly, a careful use of $TV - L_2$ decomposition as a denoising step [9] is required since any denoising algorithm may not only remove the noise but also the useful texture information, leading to a delicate tradeoff. Indeed, without additional information, patch-based image denoising theory suggests that existing methods have practically converged to the theoretical bound of the achievable PSNR performance [20]. An additional boost in performance can be expected if we are given an alternative view and the disparity between these two images, since this allows us to take advantage of the self-similarity and redundancy of the adjacent frame. This depends on us knowing the disparity between the two images, and such dependency calls for a joint approach. In our joint formulation, the self-similarity constraint is captured by the well-known Brightness Constancy Constraint (BCC) and Gradient Constancy Constraint (GCC) terms appearing as coupling terms

[2] Note that we purposely avoid calling the $TV - L_2$ decomposition as structure-texture decomposition, since for our application, the term "structure" is always understood to contain the coarser textures (such as those in the inset boxes of Fig. 1c).

in the $TV - L_2$ decomposition sub-problem. The second motivation is equally important: by solving the $TV - L_2$ decomposition problem concurrently with the disparity estimation problem, we make sure that the denoising is done in a way that is consistent across the stereo pair (see Fig. 2), that is, it is optimized for stereo disparity estimation rather than for some generic metric such as PSNR.

The joint formulation has significant computational ramifications. Our stereo matching cost for a pixel is aggregated over a window for increased robustness. This results in significant coupling of variables when we are solving the $TV - L_2$ decomposition sub-problem which means that the standard solutions for $TV - L_2$ are no longer applicable. We provide an alternative formulation such that the sub-problems still admit fairly standard solutions. We conduct experiments on our joint model to test our theories. We show that our model with its stereo-optimized structures, while yielding low PSNR, is still able to considerably surpass the baseline methods on both synthetic and real noise datasets. We then discuss some of the limitations of our algorithm, followed by a conclusion.

2 Related Work

As our paper is to specifically solve the problem of stereo matching under noisy conditions, we skip providing a comprehensive review of general stereo matching. Interested readers may refer to [21] and [22] for general stereo overview and stereo with radiometric variations respectively. Similarly, our work is not specifically concerned with denoising per se; readers may refer to [23] for a review in image denoising, and to [24] for some modern development in video denoising. Some works that target video denoising using stereo/flow correspondences include [25–27], but they are either limited by their requirement of large number of frames [27], or their dependency on pre-computed stereo/flow maps [26], which can be highly inaccurate for low SNR cases. [28] reviewed various structure-texture image decomposition models[3], and related them to denoising.

The problem of stereo matching under low-light is non-trivial and challenging. Despite its significance, only a few works can be found in the literature to have attempted this problem. To the best of our knowledge, there are only three related works [19,29,30] we could find till date. All the three works propose a joint framework of denoising and disparity, with some similarities and differences. They all propose to improve NLM [8] based denoising by finding more number of similar patches in the other image using disparity, and then improving disparity from the new denoised results. [29,30] use an Euclidean based similarity metric which has been shown in [19] to be very ineffective in highly noisy conditions. Hence, the two methods perform poorly after a certain level of noise. [19] handles this problem by projecting the patches into a lower dimensional space using PCA, and also uses the same projected patches for computing the stereo matching cost.

[3] Among these models, we choose $TV - L_2$ based on the recommendations given in [28](Pg.18), which advocates it when no *a-priori* knowledge of the texture/noise pattern is given at hand, which is likely to be the case for real low-light scenes.

Our work is more closely related to [19] in terms of iterative joint optimization, but with a few key differences. Firstly, we do not optimize PSNR to improve the stereo quality, which, as we have argued, might not have a simple relationship with PSNR. Secondly, we rely on the coarse scale textures and object boundaries for guiding the stereo, and not on NLM based denoising which might be ineffective in high noise. Thirdly, underpinning our joint Stereo-Structure optimization is a single global objective function that is mathematically consistent and physically well motivated, unlike the iterative denoising-disparity model proposed by [19] which has multiple components processed in sequence.

3 Joint Structure-Stereo Model

Let $I_{n1}, I_{n2} \in \mathbb{R}^{h \times w \times c}$ be respectively the two given rectified right-left noisy stereo images each of resolution $h \times w$ with c channels. Let $I_{s1}, I_{s2} \in \mathbb{R}^{h \times w \times c}$ be the underlying structures to obtain, and $D_2 \in \mathbb{Z}_{\geq 0}^{h \times w}$ be the disparity of the left view (note that we use $D_2 = 0$ to mark invalid/unknown disparity).

Our joint model integrates the two problems of structure extraction and stereo estimation into a single unified framework and takes the energy form:

$$\begin{aligned} E_{ALL}(I_{s1}, I_{s2}, D_2) = {} & E_{StructureData}(I_{s1}, I_{s2}) + \lambda_S \cdot E_{StructureSmooth}(I_{s1}, I_{s2}) \\ & + \lambda_{SD} \cdot E_{StereoData}(I_{s1}, I_{s2}, D_2) + \lambda_{SS} \cdot E_{StereoSmooth}(D_2) \end{aligned} \tag{1}$$

where $\lambda_\times$ are parameters controlling strengths of the individual terms. We then decompose the overall energy form Eq. (1) into two sub-problems and solve them alternatingly until convergence:

$$\begin{aligned} E_{Structure}(I_{s1}, I_{s2}, D_2^*) = {} & E_{StructureData}(I_{s1}, I_{s2}) + \lambda_S \cdot E_{StructureSmooth}(I_{s1}, I_{s2}) \\ & + \lambda_{SD} \cdot E_{StereoData}(I_{s1}, I_{s2}, D_2^*) \end{aligned} \tag{2}$$

$$\begin{aligned} E_{Stereo}(I_{s1}^*, I_{s2}^*, D_2) = {} & \lambda_{SD} \cdot E_{StereoData}(I_{s1}^*, I_{s2}^*, D_2) \\ & + \lambda_{SS} \cdot E_{StereoSmooth}(D_2) \end{aligned} \tag{3}$$

The superscript (*) represents that the variable is treated as a constant in the given sub-problem. Let us next describe the two sub-problems in Eqs. (2) and (3) in detail, and then discuss their solutions and the joint optimization procedure.

3.1 Structure Sub-problem

The first two terms of $E_{Structure}$ in Eq. (2) represent the associated data and smoothness costs for TV regularization, and are defined as

$$E_{StructureData}(I_{s1}, I_{s2}) = \sum_p \left((I_{s1}(p) - I_{n1}(p))^2 + (I_{s2}(p) - I_{n2}(p))^2 \right) \tag{4}$$

$$E_{StructureSmooth}(I_{s1}, I_{s2}) = \sum_p \left(\mathbf{RTV}(I_{s1}(p)) + \mathbf{RTV}(I_{s2}(p)) \right) \tag{5}$$

where $\mathbf{RTV}(\cdot)$ or Relative Total Variation introduced in [31] is a more robust formulation of the TV penalty function $|\nabla(\cdot)|$, and is defined as $\mathbf{RTV}(\cdot) = \frac{\sum_{q \in N_p} g_\sigma(p,q) \cdot |\nabla(\cdot)|}{|\sum_{q \in N_p} g_\sigma(p,q) \cdot \nabla(\cdot)| + \epsilon_s}$ where N_p is a small fixed-size window around p, $g_\sigma(p,q)$ is a Gaussian weighing function parametrized by σ, and ϵ_s is a small value constant to avoid numerical overflow. For noisy regions or fine textures, the denominator term in $\mathbf{RTV}(\cdot)$ summing up noisy random gradients generates small values while the numerator summing up their absolute versions generates large values, incurring a high smoothness penalty. For smooth regions or edges of both object boundaries and coarse textures, both the terms generate similar values incurring smaller penalties. This leads to the robustness of the $\mathbf{RTV}(\cdot)$ function.

The last term of *E_Structure* stems from the stereo matching constraint that provides additional information to the structure sub-problem and is defined as

$$E_{StereoData}(I_{s1}, I_{s2}, D_2^*) = \sum_p \left(\alpha \cdot \sum_{q \in W_p} \left(I_{s2}(q) - I_{s1}\left(q - D_2^*(q)\right)\right)^2 + \sum_{q \in W_p} \min\left(\left| \nabla I_{s2}(q) - \nabla I_{s1}(q - D_2^*(q)) \right|, \theta \right) \right) \tag{6}$$

where the first term represents the BCC cost with a quadratic penalty function, scaled by α and summed over a fixed-size window W_p, while the second term represents the GCC cost with a truncated L_1 penalty function (with an upper threshold parameter θ), also aggregated over W_p.

3.2 Stereo Sub-problem

The first term of E_{Stereo} in Eq. (3) represents the stereo matching cost and is essentially Eq. (6) just with a change of dependent (D_2) and constant variables (I_{s1}^*, I_{s2}^*). The second term represents the smoothness cost for disparity and is defined as

$$E_{StereoSmooth}(D_2) = \sum_p \sum_{q \in N4_p} \begin{cases} \lambda_{SS1}, & \text{if } \left[|D_2(p) - D_2(q)| = 1 \right] \\ \lambda_{SS2}, & \text{if } \left[|D_2(p) - D_2(q)| > 1 \right] \end{cases} \tag{7}$$

where $N4_p$ represents the 4-neighbourhood of p, $[\cdot]$ is the Iverson bracket and $\lambda_{SS2} \geq \lambda_{SS1} \geq 0$ represent the regularization parameters.

Our E_{Stereo} formulation is very similar to the classic definition of the Semi-Global Matching (SGM) objective function [1] and also closely matches with the definition proposed in SGM-Stereo [32]. However, we do not use the Hamming-Census based BCC cost used in [32] mainly to avoid additional complexities in optimizing the structure sub-problem.

Algorithm 1. Optimize E_{ALL}

Initialize: $I_{s1} = I_{n1}$; $I_{s2} = I_{n2}$; $D_2 = D_{init}$
repeat
Solve the structure sub-problem:
Fix $D_2^* = D_2$, optimize $E_{structure}$ w.r.t (I_{s1}, I_{s2}) using Algorithm 2
Solve the stereo sub-problem:
Fix $(I_{s1}^*, I_{s2}^*) = (I_{s1}, I_{s2})$, optimize E_{stereo} w.r.t D_2 using SGM [1]
until converged
Post-Processing D_2: Left-Right consistency [1] + Weighted Median Filtering [1]

4 Optimization

The overall energy E_{ALL} is a challenging optimization problem. We propose to solve the problem by first decomposing it into two sub-problems $E_{Structure}$ and E_{Stereo} as shown above, and then iteratively solve them using an alternating minimization approach. The overall method is summarized in Algorithm 1.[4]

We now derive the solution for $E_{structure}$. We again decompose Eq. (2) into two sub-equations, one for each image. We have for I_{s2}

$$E_{Is2}(I_{s1}^*, I_{s2}) \simeq E_{StructureData}(I_{s2}) + \lambda_S \cdot E_{StructureSmooth}(I_{s2}) + \lambda_{SD} \cdot E_{StereoData}(I_{s1}^*, I_{s2}, D_2^*) \quad (8)$$

and similarly, $E_{Is1}(I_{s1}, I_{s2}^*)$ for I_{s1}. We can observe that the stereo constraint now acts as a coupling term between the two sub-equations, thus bringing to bear the redundancy from the adjacent frame and help extract more stereo-consistent structures. Now, for solving Eq. (8), we first substitute for the individual terms, write it as a combination of two parts $\mathbf{f}(\cdot)$ and $\mathbf{g}(\cdot)$ containing the convex and non-convex parts respectively, and then solve it via the alternating direction method of multipliers (ADMM). Specifically, $E_{Is2}(I_{s1}^*, I_{s2}) = \mathbf{f}(I_{s2}) + \mathbf{g}(I_{s2})$, where

$$\begin{aligned}\mathbf{f}(I_{s2}) &= \sum_p \Big((I_{s2}(p) - I_{n2}(p))^2 + \lambda_S \cdot \mathbf{RTV}(I_{s2}(p)) + \\ &\quad \lambda_{SD} \cdot \alpha \cdot \sum_{q \in W_p} \big(I_{s2}(q) - I_{s1}^*(q - D_2^*(q))\big)^2 \Big) \\ \mathbf{g}(I_{s2}) &= \sum_p \Big(\lambda_{SD} \cdot \sum_{q \in W_p} \min\Big(\big|\nabla I_{s2}(q) - \nabla I_{s1}^*(q - D_2^*(q))\big|, \theta \Big) \Big)\end{aligned} \quad (9)$$

where we use the approximated convex quadratic formulation of the $\mathbf{RTV}(\cdot)$ function from [31] to include it in $\mathbf{f}(\cdot)$. Now, representing $\widetilde{I_{s1}^*} = \mathbf{W}_{D_2^*}(I_{s1}^*)$ where $\mathbf{W}_{D_2^*}(\cdot)$ represents our warping function parametrized by D_2^*, and with some algebraic manipulations of $\mathbf{f}(\cdot)$, it can be defined in vector form $(\vec{\cdot})$ as

[4] D_{init} is obtained using our own algorithm but with $\lambda_{SD} = 0$ (no stereo constraint).

$$\mathbf{f}(\overrightarrow{I_{s2}}) = (\overrightarrow{I_{s2}} - \overrightarrow{I_{n2}})^T(\overrightarrow{I_{s2}} - \overrightarrow{I_{n2}}) + \lambda_S \cdot \overrightarrow{I_{s2}}^T \mathbb{L}_{I_{s2}} \overrightarrow{I_{s2}} + \lambda_{SD} \cdot \alpha \cdot \left((\overrightarrow{I_{s2}} - \overrightarrow{\widetilde{I^*_{s1}}})^T \Lambda (\overrightarrow{I_{s2}} - \overrightarrow{\widetilde{I^*_{s1}}}) \right) \quad (10)$$

where $\mathbb{L}_{I_{s2}}$ and Λ are some matrix operators defined later. From Eq. (10), we can see that $\mathbf{f}(\cdot)$ is a simple quadratic function and is easy to optimize. Now, for $\mathbf{g}(\cdot)$, the complication is more severe because of the windowed operation combined with a complicated penalty function, thereby coupling different columns of I_{s2} together, which means that the proximal solution for $\mathbf{g}(\cdot)$ is no longer given by iterative shrinkage and thresholding (or more exactly, its generalized version for truncated L_1 [33]). To resolve this, we swap the order of summations, obtaining

$$\mathbf{g}(I_{s2}) = \sum_{i=[-|W_p|/2, -|W_p|/2]}^{[+|W_p|/2, +|W_p|/2]} \lambda_{SD} \sum_p \min \left(\left| \nabla \mathbf{S}_i(I_{s2}(p)) - \nabla \mathbf{S}_i(\widetilde{I^*_{s1}}) \right|, \theta \right) \quad (11)$$

where $\mathbf{S}_i(\cdot)$ represents our shift function such that $\mathbf{S}_{[dx,dy]}(\cdot)$ shifts the variable by dx and dy in the x-axis and y-axis respectively. Next, if we represent $\nabla \mathbf{S}_i(\cdot)$ by a function say $\mathbf{A}_i(\cdot)$, and $-\nabla \mathbf{S}_i(\widetilde{I^*_{s1}})$ by a variable say B_i, we can show that

$$\begin{aligned} \min_{I_{s2}} \; E_{Is2}(I^*_{s1}, I_{s2}) &= \min_{I_{s2}} \; \mathbf{f}(I_{s2}) + \sum_i \mathbf{g}_s \left(\mathbf{A}_i(I_{s2}) + B_i \right) \\ &= \min_{I_{s2}} \; \mathbf{f}(I_{s2}) + \sum_i \mathbf{g}_s(Z_i) \quad \text{s.t} \quad Z_i = \mathbf{A}_i(I_{s2}) + B_i \end{aligned} \quad (12)$$

where $\mathbf{g}_s(\cdot)$ represents $\lambda_{SD} \cdot \sum_p \mathbf{min}(|\cdot|, \theta)$ penalty function, for which we have a closed form solution [33]. Next, since $\nabla(\cdot), \mathbf{S}_i(\cdot)$ $\mathbf{W}_{D^*_2}(\cdot)$ are all linear functions representable by matrix operations, we can define Eq. (12) in vector form ($\vec{\cdot}$) as

$$\min_{\overrightarrow{I_{s2}}} \; \mathbf{f}(\overrightarrow{I_{s2}}) + \sum_i \mathbf{g}_s(\overrightarrow{Z_i}) \quad \text{s.t} \quad \overrightarrow{Z_i} = A_i \overrightarrow{I_{s2}} + \overrightarrow{B_i} \quad (13)$$

where A_i and $\overrightarrow{B_i}$ are operators/variables independent of $\overrightarrow{I_{s2}}$, also defined later. We see that Eq. (8) reduces to a constrained minimization problem Eq. (13). The new equation is similar to the ADMM variant discussed in (Sect. 4.4.2, [34]) (of the form $\mathbf{f}(\overrightarrow{I_{s2}}) + \mathbf{g}_s(A\overrightarrow{I_{s2}})$) except that our second term comprises of a summation of multiple $\mathbf{g}_s(\overrightarrow{Z_i})$ over i rather than a single $\mathbf{g}_s(\overrightarrow{Z})$, with dependency among the various $\overrightarrow{Z_i}$ caused by $\overrightarrow{Z_i} = A_i \overrightarrow{I_{s2}} + \overrightarrow{B_i}$. Each of these "local variables" $\overrightarrow{Z_i}$ should be equal to the common global variable $\overrightarrow{I_{s2}}$; this is an instance of Global Variable Consensus Optimization (Sect. 7.1.1, [35]). Hence, following [34,35], we write Eq. (13) first in its Augmented Lagrangian form defined as

$$\begin{aligned} \min_{\overrightarrow{I_{s2}}, \overrightarrow{Z_i}, \overrightarrow{U_i}} \; \mathcal{L}(\overrightarrow{I_{s2}}, \; \overrightarrow{Z_i}, \; \overrightarrow{U_i}) &= \min_{\overrightarrow{I_{s2}}, \overrightarrow{Z_i}, \overrightarrow{Y_i}} \; \mathbf{f}(\overrightarrow{I_{s2}}) + \sum_i \mathbf{g}_s(\overrightarrow{Z_i}) \\ &+ \rho \cdot \sum_i \overrightarrow{U_i}^T (A_i \overrightarrow{I_{s2}} + \overrightarrow{B_i} - \overrightarrow{Z_i}) + \frac{\rho}{2} \cdot \sum_i \left\| A_i \overrightarrow{I_{s2}} + \overrightarrow{B_i} - \overrightarrow{Z_i} \right\|_2^2 \end{aligned} \quad (14)$$

where $\overrightarrow{U_i}$ represent the scaled dual variables and $\rho > 0$ is the penalty parameter. Now substituting for the individual terms and minimizing Eq. (14) over the three variables, we can get the following update rules

$$\begin{aligned}
\overrightarrow{I_{s2}}^{k+1} &:= \Big(\big(2\mathbb{1} + 2\lambda_S \mathbb{L}_{I_{s2}} + \lambda_{SD}\alpha(\mathbb{1} - W_2)^T(\Lambda + \Lambda^T)(\mathbb{1} - W_2)\big) + \rho \sum_i A_i^T A_i\Big)^{-1} \\
&\quad \Big(\big(2\overrightarrow{I_{n2}} + \lambda_{SD}\alpha(\mathbb{1} - W_2)^T(\Lambda + \Lambda^T)W_1\overrightarrow{I_{s1}^*}\big) - \underbrace{\rho \sum_i A_i^T(\overrightarrow{B_i} - \overrightarrow{Z_i}^k + \overrightarrow{U_i}^k)\Big)}_{\text{consensus}} \\
\overrightarrow{Z_i}^{k+1} &:= \mathbf{prox}_{\frac{1}{\rho}\mathbf{g}_s}(A_i\overrightarrow{I_{s2}}^{k+1} + \overrightarrow{B_i} + \overrightarrow{U_i}^k) \\
\overrightarrow{U_i}^{k+1} &:= \overrightarrow{U_i}^k + A_i\overrightarrow{I_{s2}}^{k+1} + \overrightarrow{B_i} - \overrightarrow{Z_i}^{k+1}
\end{aligned} \tag{15}$$

The update rules have an intuitive meaning. The local variables $\overrightarrow{Z_i}, \overrightarrow{U_i}$ are updated using the global variable $\overrightarrow{I_{s2}}$, which then seeks consensus among all the local variables until they have stopped changing. Now, let's define the individual terms. In Eq. (15), $\mathbb{1}$ is an identity matrix; $\mathbb{L}_{I_{s\times}} = G_x^T U_x V_x G_x + G_y^T U_y V_y G_y$ is a weight matrix [31] such that G_x, G_y are Toeplitz matrices containing the discrete gradient operators, and $U_{(\cdot)}, V_{(\cdot)}$ are diagonal matrices given by

$$U_{(\cdot)}(q,q) = \sum_{q \in N_p} \frac{g_\sigma(p,q)}{|\sum_{q \in N_p} g_\sigma(p,q) \cdot \partial_{(\cdot)} I_{s\times}^k(q)| + \epsilon_s}, \quad V_{(\cdot)}(q,q) = \frac{1}{|\partial_{(\cdot)} I_{s\times}^k(q)|} \tag{16}$$

W_1, W_2 are warping operators such that $\overrightarrow{\widetilde{I_{s1}^*}} = W_1\overrightarrow{I_{s1}^*} + W_2\overrightarrow{I_{s2}}$, and are given by

$$W_1(p,q) = \begin{cases} 1, & \text{if } q = p - (h \cdot \overrightarrow{D_2^*}(p)) \\ 0, & \text{if } \overrightarrow{D_2^*}(p) = 0 \end{cases}, \quad W_2(p,p) = \begin{cases} 1, & \text{if } \overrightarrow{D_2^*}(p) = 0 \\ 0, & \text{otherwise} \end{cases} \tag{17}$$

Thus, W_1 warps $\overrightarrow{I_{s1}^*}$ towards $\overrightarrow{I_{s2}}$ for all the points except where $\overrightarrow{D_2^*}(p) = 0$ (invalid/unknown disparity), where we simply use the diagonal W_2 to fill-up data from $\overrightarrow{I_{s2}}$ and avoid using our stereo constraint. Then we have $\Lambda = \sum_i S_i^T S_i$, where S_i represents our shift operator (analogous to the definition of $\mathbf{S}_i(\cdot)$ above) defined as $S_{[dx,dy]}(p,q) = 1, \text{if } q = \big(p - dy - (h \cdot dx)\big) \, \forall p \notin V(dx,dy)$, and 0 otherwise; $V(dx,dy)$ is a set containing border pixels present in the first or last $|dx|^{\text{th}}$ column $(1 \leq |dx| \leq w)$ and $|dy|^{\text{th}}$ row $(1 \leq |dy| \leq h)$ depending upon whether $dx, dy > 0$ or $dx, dy < 0$, $A_i = (G_x + G_y)S_i(\mathbb{1} - W_2)$ and lastly $\overrightarrow{B_i} = -(G_x + G_y)S_i W_1 \overrightarrow{I_{s1}}^*$.

Now following a similar procedure for the other image I_{s1}, we can derive the following update rules

Algorithm 2. Optimize $E_{Structure}$

Obtain warping operators W_1, W_2 from D_2^* using Eq.(17); let $G_{xy} = G_x + G_y$
repeat
  Solve $E_{Is2}(I_{s1}^*, I_{s2})$: Obtain $\mathbb{L}_{I_{s2}}$ from Eq. (16)
  1. For each i: compute S_i, $A_i = G_{xy}S_i(\mathbb{1} - W_2)$, and $\overrightarrow{B_i} = -G_{xy}S_iW_1\overrightarrow{I_{s1}}^*$
  2. Solve for I_{s2} using the update rules in Eq. (15), and assign it to I_{s2}^*
  Solve $E_{Is1}(I_{s1}, I_{s2}^*)$: Obtain $\mathbb{L}_{I_{s1}}$ from Eq. (16)
  1. For each i: compute S_i, $A_i = -G_{xy}S_iW_1$, and $\overrightarrow{B_i} = G_{xy}S_i(\mathbb{1} - W_2)\overrightarrow{I_{s2}}^*$
  2. Solve for I_{s1} using the update rules in Eq. (18), and assign it to I_{s1}^*
until converged

$$
\begin{aligned}
\overrightarrow{I_{s1}}^{k+1} :=& \Big((2\mathbb{1} + 2\lambda_S \mathbb{L}_{I_{s1}} + \lambda_{SD}\alpha(-W_1)^T(\Lambda + \Lambda^T)(-W_1)) + \rho \sum_i A_i^T A_i \Big)^{-1} \\
& \Big((2\overrightarrow{I_{n1}} + \lambda_{SD}\alpha W_1^T(\Lambda + \Lambda^T)(\mathbb{1} - W_2)\overrightarrow{I_{s2}^*}) - \rho \sum_i A_i^T(\overrightarrow{B_i} - \overrightarrow{Z_i}^k + \overrightarrow{U_i}^k) \Big) \\
\overrightarrow{Z_i}^{k+1} :=& \ \mathbf{prox}_{\frac{1}{\rho}\mathbf{g}_s}(A_i\overrightarrow{I_{s1}}^{k+1} + \overrightarrow{B_i} + \overrightarrow{U_i}^k) \qquad (18) \\
\overrightarrow{U_i}^{k+1} :=& \ \overrightarrow{U_i}^k + A_i\overrightarrow{I_{s1}}^{k+1} + \overrightarrow{B_i} - \overrightarrow{Z_i}^{k+1}
\end{aligned}
$$

with $A_i = -(G_x + G_y)S_iW_1$ and $\overrightarrow{B_i} = (G_x + G_y)S_i(\mathbb{1} - W_2)\overrightarrow{I_{s2}}^*$. Finally, we have the definition of $\mathbf{prox}_{\frac{1}{\rho}\mathbf{g}_s}(\cdot)$ given by $\mathbf{prox}_{\frac{1}{\rho}\mathbf{g}_s}(v) = \begin{cases} x_1, & \text{if } \mathbf{h}(x_1) \leq \mathbf{h}(x_2) \\ x_2, & \text{otherwise} \end{cases}$ where $x_1 = \text{sign}(v)\max\big(|(v|, \theta)\big)$, $x_2 = \text{sign}(v)\min(\max(|(v)| - (\lambda_{SD}/\rho), 0), \theta)$, and $\mathbf{h}(x) = 0.5(x - v)^2 + (\lambda_{SD}/\rho)\min(|x|, \theta)$. This completes our solution for $E_{Structure}$, also summarized in Algorithm 2. The detailed derivations for Eqs. (10), (11) and (15) are provided in the supplementary paper for reference.

5 Experiments

In this section, we evaluate our algorithm through a series of experiments. Since there are not many competing algorithms, we begin with creating our own baseline methods first. We select the two best performing denoising algorithms, BM3D [10] and DnCNN [13] till date, to perform denoising as a pre-processing step, and then use MeshStereo [17], a recent high performance stereo algorithm, to generate the disparity maps. The codes are downloaded from the authors' websites. We refer to these two baseline methods as 'BM3D+MS' and 'DnCNN+MS' respectively. Our third baseline method is a recently proposed joint denoising-disparity algorithm [19], which we refer to as 'SS-PCA'. Due to unavailability of the code, this method is based on our own implementation.

For our first experiment, we test our algorithm against the baseline methods on the Middlebury(Ver3) dataset [18] corrupted with Gaussian noise at levels: 25, 50, 55 and 60, i.e. we consider one low and three high noise cases, the latter resulting in low SNR similar to those encountered in night scenes. To ensure a fair comparison, we select three images 'Playroom', 'Recycle' and 'Teddy', from

Table 1. Image-wise evaluation on the Middlebury dataset with added Gaussian noise at levels: [25, 50, 55, 60]. Error threshold $\delta = 1$px. Bold font indicates lowest error.

Image	BM3D+MS				DnCNN+MS				SS-PCA				Ours			
	25	50	55	60	25	50	55	60	25	50	55	60	25	50	55	60
'Adirondack'	37.57	52.95	56.98	62.02	**35.80**	47.99	51.37	56.13	60.01	66.40	80.57	84.67	38.76	**44.85**	**49.00**	**50.74**
'Jadeplant'	66.17	79.52	76.84	80.42	68.49	77.43	**76.45**	**78.90**	**64.42**	**75.78**	78.30	81.75	72.29	78.92	77.76	80.40
'Motorcycle'	40.75	50.86	51.66	52.80	**37.63**	50.46	50.61	49.62	41.74	47.81	50.63	54.16	40.44	**45.17**	**43.21**	**44.17**
'Pipes'	41.35	58.08	60.47	63.07	**37.07**	**47.62**	**53.28**	**53.20**	39.52	50.73	56.97	61.31	45.82	54.48	55.90	60.56
'Playroom'	46.82	55.35	57.23	55.72	**41.46**	49.21	54.77	57.64	57.82	62.96	71.65	75.56	43.87	**48.87**	**50.36**	**52.74**
'Recycle'	48.65	61.28	62.91	63.43	**44.20**	57.72	60.52	60.22	51.64	64.45	66.04	69.20	50.42	**57.72**	**57.38**	**54.83**
'Shelves'	60.18	69.24	71.44	70.56	**55.82**	66.05	64.68	66.64	63.28	68.03	74.96	73.99	58.89	**62.58**	**63.07**	**63.93**
'Teddy'	30.15	49.20	52.78	58.79	**27.01**	44.05	50.39	49.46	32.65	44.14	52.89	52.75	31.39	**40.86**	**45.07**	**45.71**

Table 2. Overall evaluation on the Middlebury dataset with added Gaussian noise at levels: [25, 50, 55, 60] for error threshold δ. Bold font indicates lowest error.

δ	BM3D+MS				DnCNN+MS				SS-PCA				Ours			
	25	50	55	60	25	50	55	60	25	50	55	60	25	50	55	60
1px	46.45	59.55	61.29	63.35	**43.43**	55.06	57.76	58.97	51.39	60.04	66.48	69.17	47.74	**54.19**	**55.22**	**56.59**
3px	22.68	30.57	33.72	34.63	**22.04**	29.62	32.67	32.68	30.41	35.32	42.02	43.67	25.12	**29.00**	**29.45**	**30.48**
5px	**16.22**	22.01	24.17	25.07	16.82	21.53	24.36	23.94	23.14	26.07	31.48	32.93	18.21	**20.94**	**20.60**	**21.81**

the dataset and tune the parameters of BM3D and SS-PCA to generate the best possible PSNR results for every noise level, while for DnCNN, we pick its blind model trained on a large range of noise levels. Furthermore, we keep the same disparity post-processing steps for all the algorithms including ours to ensure fairness. Our stereo evaluation metric is based on the percentage of bad pixels, i.e. percentage (%) of pixels with disparity error above a fixed threshold δ. For our algorithm, we set the parameters $\{\lambda_S, \epsilon_s, \lambda_{SD}, \alpha, \theta, \rho, \lambda_{SS}, \lambda_{SS1}, \lambda_{SS2}\} = \{650.25, 5, 1, 0.003, 15, 0.04, 1, 100, 1600\}$, $|W_p| = 25(= 5 \times 5)$, and use $\sigma = 1.0, 2.0, 2.5$ and 3.0 for the four noise levels respectively. The number of outermost iteration is fixed to 5 while all the inner iterations follow $(\Delta E_{\times}^{k+1}/E_{\times}^{k}) < 10^{-4}$ for convergence. Our evaluation results are summarized in Tables 1 and 2.

For our second experiment, we perform our evaluation on the real outdoor Oxford RobotCar [15] dataset, specifically those clips in the 'night' category. These clips contain a large amount of autonomous driving data collected under typical urban and suburban lighting in the night, with a wide range of illumination variations. It comes with rectified stereo images and their corresponding raw sparse depth ground truth. We create two sets of data, 'Set1' containing 10 poorly-lit images (such as in Fig. 1a), and 'Set2' containing 20 well-lit images (selection criteria is to maximize variance in the two sets in terms of scene content therefore no consecutive/repetitive frames; scenes with moving objects are also discarded due to unreliability of ground truth); together they span a range of conditions such as varying exposure, sodium vs LED lightings, amount of textures, image saturation, and error sources such as specularities (specific details in supplementary). We set the parameters $\{\lambda_S, \lambda_{SD}, \lambda_{SS}\} = \{50.25, 0.1, 0.1\}$ while

Table 3. Comparison with the baseline methods on the Oxford RobotCar dataset. Error threshold is specified by δ. Bold font indicates lowest error.

	DnCNN+MS					Ours				
	$\delta = 1$px	$\delta = 2$px	$\delta = 3$px	$\delta = 4$px	$\delta = 5$px	$\delta = 1$px	$\delta = 2$px	$\delta = 3$px	$\delta = 4$px	$\delta = 5$px
Set1	63.86	41.66	30.96	24.40	19.66	**58.76**	**33.75**	**23.03**	**16.99**	**12.31**
Set2	58.96	28.82	16.71	10.73	7.35	**57.76**	**28.80**	**16.10**	**10.29**	**6.82**
Set2 (f.t)	58.96	28.82	16.71	10.73	7.35	**56.45**	**26.43**	**14.54**	**9.20**	**6.08**

keeping other parameters exactly the same as before for both the sets, and compare our algorithm only against 'DnCNN+MS' since there are no corresponding noise-free images available to tune the other baseline algorithms for maximizing their PSNR performance. Our evaluation results are summarized in Table 3 ('Set2 (f.t)' denotes evaluation with parameters further fine tuned on 'Set2').

From the experimental results, we can see that for all the highly noisy (or low SNR) cases, our algorithm consistently outperforms the baseline methods quite significantly with improvements as high as 5–10% in terms of bad pixels percentage. Our joint formulation generates stereo-consistent structures (unlike denoising, see Fig. 2) which results in more accurate and robust stereo matching under highly noisy conditions. The overall superiority of our method is also quite conspicuous qualitatively (see Fig. 3). We achieve a somewhat poorer recovery for 'Jadeplant' and 'Pipes', the root problem being the sheer amount of spurious corners in the scenes which is further aggravated by the loss of interior texture in our method. For low noise levels, there is sufficient signal (with finer textures) recovery by the baseline denoising algorithms, thus yielding better disparity solutions than our structures which inevitably give away the fine details. Thus, our algorithm really comes to the forth for the high noise (or low SNR) regimes. For the real data, our algorithm again emerges as the clear winner (see Table 3 and middle block of Fig. 3). First and foremost, we should note that the parameters used for 'Set1' and 'Set2' are based on those tuned on two sequences in 'Set1'. The fact these values are transferable to a different dataset ('Set2') with rather different lighting conditions showed that the parameter setting works quite well under a wide range of lighting conditions (depicted in the middle block of Fig. 3). Qualitatively, the proficiency of our algorithm in picking up 3D structures in the very dark areas, some even not perceivable to human eyes, is very pleasing (see red boxes in the middle block of Fig. 3, row 1: wall on the left, rows 2 and 3: tree and fence). It is also generally able to delineate relatively crisp structures and discern depth differences (e.g. the depth discontinuities between the two adjoining walls in row 4), in contrast to the patchwork quality of the disparity returned by 'DnCNN+MS'. Finally, our algorithm also seems to be rather robust against various error sources such as glow from light sources, under-to-over exposures. Clearly, there will be cases of extreme darkness and such paucity of information, against which we cannot prevail (bottom block of Fig. 3, top-right: a scene with sole distant street lamp). Other cases of failures are also depicted in the bottom block of this figure, namely, lens flare and high glare in the scene.

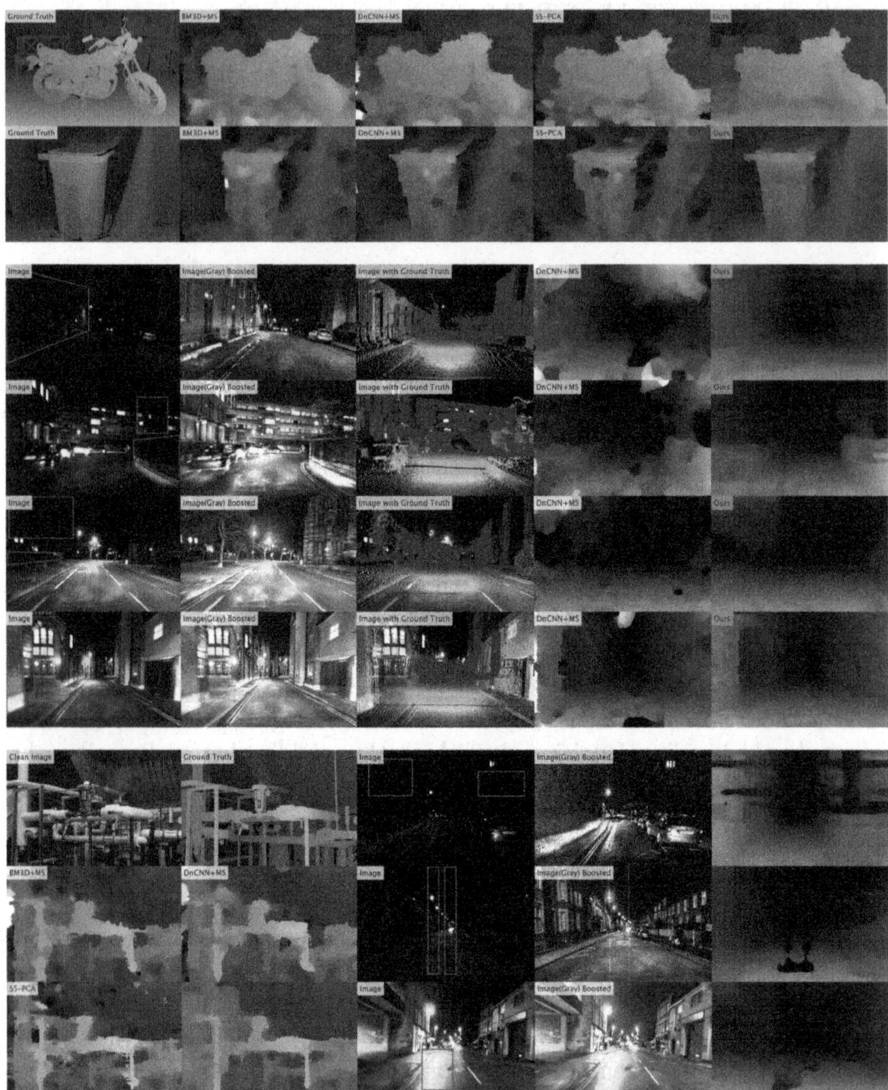

Fig. 3. Qualitative analysis of our algorithm against the baseline methods. For Middlebury (first two rows), we observe more accurate results with sharper boundaries (see 'Recycle' image, second row). For the Oxford dataset (middle four rows), our algorithm generates superior results and is quite robust under varying illumination and exposure conditions, and can even pick up barely visible objects like fence or trees (see areas corresponding to red boxes in middle second and third row). Our algorithm also has certain limitations in extremely dim light information-less conditions (see red boxes, third last row) or in the presence of lens flare or high glow/glare in the scene (bottom two rows), generating high errors in disparity estimation. (Color figure online)

6 Discussion and Conclusion

We have showed that under mesopic viewing condition, despite the presence of numerous challenges, disparity information can still be recovered with adequate accuracy. We have also argued that for denoising, PSNR is not meaningful; instead there should be a close coupling with the disparity estimation task to yield stereo-consistent denoising. For this purpose, we have proposed a unified energy objective that jointly removes noise and estimates disparity. With careful design, we transform the complex objective function into a form that admits fairly standard solutions. We have showed that our algorithm has substantially better performance over both synthetic and real data, and is also stable under a wide range of low-light conditions.

The above results were obtained based on the assumptions that effects of glare/glow could be ignored. Whilst there has been some stereo works that deal with radiometric variations (varying exposure and lighting conditions), the compounding effect of glare/glow on low-light stereo matching has not been adequately investigated. This shall form the basis of our future work.

Acknowledgement. The authors are thankful to Robby T. Tan, Yale-NUS College, for all the useful discussions. This work is supported by the DIRP Grant R-263-000-C46-232.

References

1. Hirschmuller, H.: Accurate and efficient stereo processing by semi-global matching and mutual information. In: IEEE Computer Society Conference on Computer Vision and Pattern Recognition, CVPR 2005, vol. 2, pp. 807–814. IEEE (2005)
2. Bleyer, M., Rhemann, C., Rother, C.: Patchmatch stereo-stereo matching with slanted support windows. In: BMVC, vol. 11, pp. 1–11 (2011)
3. Zbontar, J., LeCun, Y.: Computing the stereo matching cost with a convolutional neural network. In: Proceedings of the IEEE Conference on Computer Vision and Pattern Recognition, pp. 1592–1599 (2015)
4. Luo, W., Schwing, A.G., Urtasun, R.: Efficient deep learning for stereo matching. In: Proceedings of the IEEE Conference on Computer Vision and Pattern Recognition, pp. 5695–5703 (2016)
5. Kendall, A., et al.: End-to-end learning of geometry and context for deep stereo regression. CoRR, abs/1703.04309 (2017)
6. Diamond, S., Sitzmann, V., Boyd, S., Wetzstein, G., Heide, F.: Dirty pixels: optimizing image classification architectures for raw sensor data. arXiv preprint arXiv:1701.06487 (2017)
7. Jeon, H.G., Lee, J.Y., Im, S., Ha, H., So Kweon, I.: Stereo matching with color and monochrome cameras in low-light conditions. In: Proceedings of the IEEE Conference on Computer Vision and Pattern Recognition, pp. 4086–4094 (2016)
8. Buades, A., Coll, B., Morel, J.M.: A non-local algorithm for image denoising. In: IEEE Computer Society Conference on Computer Vision and Pattern Recognition, CVPR 2005, vol. 2, pp. 60–65. IEEE (2005)
9. Rudin, L.I., Osher, S., Fatemi, E.: Nonlinear total variation based noise removal algorithms. Physica D: Nonlinear Phenom. **60**(1–4), 259–268 (1992)

10. Dabov, K., Foi, A., Katkovnik, V., Egiazarian, K.: Image denoising by sparse 3-D transform-domain collaborative filtering. IEEE Trans. Image Process. **16**(8), 2080–2095 (2007)
11. Burger, H.C., Schuler, C.J., Harmeling, S.: Image denoising: can plain neural networks compete with BM3D? In: 2012 IEEE Conference on Computer Vision and Pattern Recognition (CVPR), pp. 2392–2399. IEEE (2012)
12. Xie, J., Xu, L., Chen, E.: Image denoising and inpainting with deep neural networks. In: Advances in Neural Information Processing Systems, pp. 341–349 (2012)
13. Zhang, K., Zuo, W., Chen, Y., Meng, D., Zhang, L.: Beyond a Gaussian denoiser: residual learning of deep CNN for image denoising. IEEE Trans. Image Process. **26**(7), 3142–3155 (2017)
14. Ruderman, D.L., Bialek, W.: Statistics of natural images: scaling in the woods. In: Advances in Neural Information Processing Systems, pp. 551–558 (1994)
15. Maddern, W., Pascoe, G., Linegar, C., Newman, P.: 1 year, 1000 km: the Oxford RobotCar dataset. Int. J. Robot. Res. (IJRR) **36**(1), 3–15 (2017)
16. Guo, X.: Lime: a method for low-light image enhancement. In: Proceedings of the 2016 ACM on Multimedia Conference, pp. 87–91. ACM (2016)
17. Zhang, C., Li, Z., Cheng, Y., Cai, R., Chao, H., Rui, Y.: Meshstereo: a global stereo model with mesh alignment regularization for view interpolation. In: Proceedings of the IEEE International Conference on Computer Vision, pp. 2057–2065 (2015)
18. Scharstein, D., et al.: High-Resolution stereo datasets with subpixel-accurate ground truth. In: Jiang, X., Hornegger, J., Koch, R. (eds.) GCPR 2014. LNCS, vol. 8753, pp. 31–42. Springer, Cham (2014). https://doi.org/10.1007/978-3-319-11752-2_3
19. Jiao, J., Yang, Q., He, S., Gu, S., Zhang, L., Lau, R.W.: Joint image denoising and disparity estimation via stereo structure PCA and noise-tolerant cost. Int. J. Comput. Vis. **124**(2), 204–222 (2017)
20. Levin, A., Nadler, B., Durand, F., Freeman, W.T.: Patch complexity, finite pixel correlations and optimal denoising. In: Fitzgibbon, A., Lazebnik, S., Perona, P., Sato, Y., Schmid, C. (eds.) ECCV 2012. LNCS, vol. 7576, pp. 73–86. Springer, Heidelberg (2012). https://doi.org/10.1007/978-3-642-33715-4_6
21. Scharstein, D., Szeliski, R.: A taxonomy and evaluation of dense two-frame stereo correspondence algorithms. Int. J. Comput. Vis. **47**(1–3), 7–42 (2002)
22. Hirschmuller, H., Scharstein, D.: Evaluation of stereo matching costs on images with radiometric differences. IEEE Trans. Pattern Anal. Mach. Intell. **31**(9), 1582–1599 (2009)
23. Buades, A., Coll, B., Morel, J.M.: Image denoising methods. A new nonlocal principle. SIAM Rev. **52**(1), 113–147 (2010)
24. Wen, B., Li, Y., Pfister, L., Bresler, Y.: Joint adaptive sparsity and low-rankness on the fly: an online tensor reconstruction scheme for video denoising. In: IEEE International Conference on Computer Vision (ICCV) (2017)
25. Li, N., Li, J.S.J., Randhawa, S.: 3D image denoising using stereo correspondences. In: 2015 IEEE Region 10 Conference, TENCON 2015, pp. 1–4. IEEE (2015)
26. Liu, C., Freeman, W.T.: A high-quality video denoising algorithm based on reliable motion estimation. In: Daniilidis, K., Maragos, P., Paragios, N. (eds.) ECCV 2010. LNCS, vol. 6313, pp. 706–719. Springer, Heidelberg (2010). https://doi.org/10.1007/978-3-642-15558-1_51
27. Zhang, L., Vaddadi, S., Jin, H., Nayar, S.K.: Multiple view image denoising. In: IEEE Conference on Computer Vision and Pattern Recognition, CVPR 2009, pp. 1542–1549. IEEE (2009)

28. Aujol, J.F., Gilboa, G., Chan, T., Osher, S.: Structure-texture image decomposition—modeling, algorithms, and parameter selection. Int. J. Comput. Vis. **67**(1), 111–136 (2006)
29. Xu, Y., Long, Q., Mita, S., Tehrani, H., Ishimaru, K., Shirai, N.: Real-time stereo vision system at nighttime with noise reduction using simplified non-local matching cost. In: 2016 IEEE Intelligent Vehicles Symposium (IV), pp. 998–1003. IEEE (2016)
30. Heo, Y.S., Lee, K.M., Lee, S.U.: Simultaneous depth reconstruction and restoration of noisy stereo images using non-local pixel distribution. In: IEEE Conference on Computer Vision and Pattern Recognition, CVPR 2007, pp. 1–8. IEEE (2007)
31. Xu, L., Yan, Q., Xia, Y., Jia, J.: Structure extraction from texture via relative total variation. ACM Trans. Graph. (TOG) **31**(6), 139 (2012)
32. Yamaguchi, K., McAllester, D., Urtasun, R.: Efficient joint segmentation, occlusion labeling, stereo and flow estimation. In: Fleet, D., Pajdla, T., Schiele, B., Tuytelaars, T. (eds.) ECCV 2014. LNCS, vol. 8693, pp. 756–771. Springer, Cham (2014). https://doi.org/10.1007/978-3-319-10602-1_49
33. Gong, P., Zhang, C., Lu, Z., Huang, J., Ye, J.: A general iterative shrinkage and thresholding algorithm for non-convex regularized optimization problems. In: International Conference on Machine Learning, pp. 37–45 (2013)
34. Parikh, N., Boyd, S., et al.: Proximal algorithms. Found. Trends® Optim. **1**(3), 127–239 (2014)
35. Boyd, S., Parikh, N., Chu, E., Peleato, B., Eckstein, J., et al.: Distributed optimization and statistical learning via the alternating direction method of multipliers. Found. Trends® Mach. Learn. **3**(1), 1–122 (2011)

Recycle-GAN: Unsupervised Video Retargeting

Aayush Bansal[1(✉)], Shugao Ma[2], Deva Ramanan[1], and Yaser Sheikh[1,2]

[1] Carnegie Mellon University, Pittsburgh, USA
aayushb@cs.cmu.edu
[2] Facebook Reality Lab, Pittsburgh, USA
http://www.cs.cmu.edu/~aayushb/Recycle-GAN/

Abstract. We introduce a data-driven approach for unsupervised video retargeting that translates content from one domain to another while preserving the style native to a domain, i.e., if contents of John Oliver's speech were to be transferred to Stephen Colbert, then the generated content/speech should be in Stephen Colbert's style. Our approach combines both spatial and temporal information along with adversarial losses for content translation and style preservation. In this work, we first study the advantages of using spatiotemporal constraints over spatial constraints for effective retargeting. We then demonstrate the proposed approach for the problems where information in both space and time matters such as face-to-face translation, flower-to-flower, wind and cloud synthesis, sunrise and sunset.

1 Introduction

We present an unsupervised data-driven approach for video retargeting that enables the transfer of sequential content from one domain to another while preserving the style of the target domain. Such a content translation and style preservation task has numerous applications including human motion and face translation from one person to other, teaching robots from human demonstration, or converting black-and-white videos to color. This work also finds application in creating visual content that is hard to capture or label in real world settings, e.g., aligning human motion and facial data of two individuals for virtual reality, or labeling night data for a self-driving car. Above all, the notion of content translation and style preservation transcends pixel-to-pixel operation to a more semantic and abstract human understandable concepts, thereby paving way for advance machines that can directly collaborate with humans.

The current approaches for retargeting can be broadly classified into three categories. The first set of work is specifically designed for domains such as human faces [5,41,42]. While these approaches work well when faces are fully visible, they fail when applied to occluded faces (virtual reality) and lack generalization to other domains. The work on paired image-to-image translation [23] attempted for generalization across domain but requires manual supervision for

V. Ferrari et al. (Eds.): ECCV 2018, LNCS 11209, pp. 122–138, 2018.
https://doi.org/10.1007/978-3-030-01228-1_8

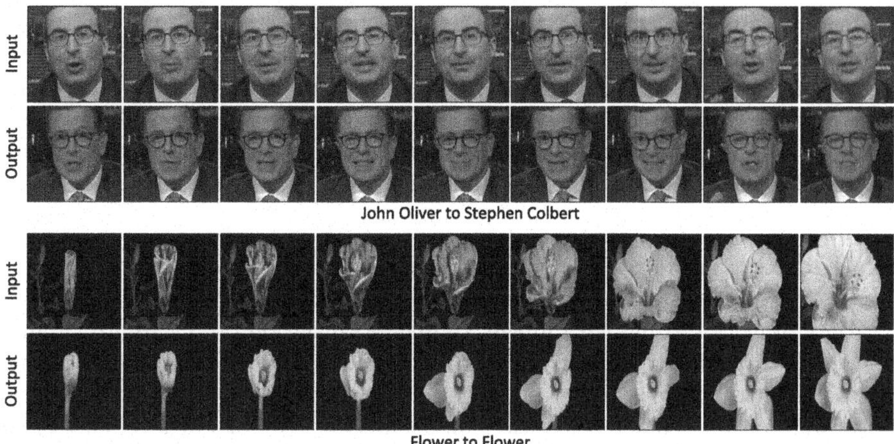

Fig. 1. Our approach for video retargeting used for faces and flowers. The top row shows translation from John Oliver to Stephen Colbert. The bottom row shows how a synthesized flower follows the blooming process with the input flower. The corresponding videos are available on the project webpage.

labeling and alignment. This requirement makes it hard for the use of such approaches as manual alignment or labeling many (in-the-wild) domains is not possible. The third category of work attempts unsupervised and unpaired image translation [26,53]. These work enforce a cyclic consistency [51] on unpaired 2D images and learn transformation from one domain to another. However, the use of unpaired images alone is not sufficient for video retargeting. Primarily, it is not able to pose sufficient constraints on optimization and often leads to bad local minima or a perceptual mode collapse making it hard to generate the required output in the target domain. Secondly, the use of the spatial information alone in 2D images makes it hard to learn the *style* of a particular domain as stylistic information requires temporal knowledge as well.

In this work, we make two specific observations: (i) the use of temporal information provides more constraints to the optimization for transforming one domain to other and helps in learning a better local minima; (ii) the combined influence of spatial and temporal constraints helps in learning the style characteristic of an identity in a given domain. More importantly, we do not require manual labels as temporal information is freely available in videos (available in abundance on web). Shown in Fig. 1 are the example of translation for human faces and flowers. Without any manual supervision and domain-specific knowledge, our approach learns this *retargeting* from one domain to the other using publicly available video data on the web from both domains.

Our Contributions: We introduce a new approach that incorporates spatiotemporal cues along with conditional generative adversarial networks [15] for video retargeting. We demonstrate the advantages of spatiotemporal constraints over the spatial constraints alone for image-to-labels, and labels-to-image in varying environmental settings. We then show the importance of proposed approach in learning better association between two domains, and its importance for self-supervised content alignment of the visual data. Inspired by the ever-existing nature of space-time, we qualitatively demonstrate the effectiveness of our approach for various natural processes such as face-to-face translation, flower-to-flower, synthesizing clouds and winds, aligning sunrise and sunset.

2 Related Work

A variety of work dealing with image-to-image translation [11,17,23,40,53] and style translation [4,10,19] exists. In fact a large body of work in computer vision and computer graphics is about an image-to-image operation. While the primary efforts were on inferencing semantic [30], geometric [1,9], or low-level cues [48], there is a renewed interest in synthesizing images using data-driven approaches by the introduction of generative adversarial networks [15]. This formulation have been used to generate images from cues such as a low-resolution image [8, 28], class labels [23], and various other input priors [21,35,49]. These approaches, however, require an input-output pair to train a model. While it is feasible to label data for a few image-to-image operations, there are numerous tasks for which it is non-trivial to generate input-output pairs for training supervision. Recently, Zhu et al. [53] proposed to use the cycle-consistency constraint [51] in adversarial learning framework to deal with this problem of unpaired data, and demonstrate effective results for various tasks. The cycle-consistency [26,53] enabled many image-to-image translation tasks without any expensive manual labeling. Similar ideas have also found application in learning depth cues in an unsupervised manner [14], machine translation [47], shape correspondences [20], point-wise correspondences [51,52], or domain adaptation [18].

The variants of Cycle-GAN [53] have been applied to various temporal domains [14,18]. However, these work consider only the spatial information in 2D images, and ignore the temporal information for optimization. We observe two major limitations: (1). **Perceptual Mode Collapse:** there are no guarantees that cycle consistency would produce perceptually unique data to the inputs. In Fig. 2, we show the outputs of a model trained for Donald Trump to Barack Obama, and an example for image2labels and labels2image. We find that for different inputs of Donald Trump, we get perceptually similar output of Barack Obama. However, we observe that these outputs have some unique encoding that enables to reconstruct image similar to input. We see similar behavior for image2labels and labels2image in Fig. 2-(b); (2). **Tied Spatially to Input:** Due to the reconstruction loss on the input itself, the optimization is forced to learn a solution that is closely tied to the input. While this is reasonable for the problems where only spatial transformation matters (such as horse-to-zebra, apples-to-oranges, or paintings etc.), it is important for the problems where temporal and stylistic information is required for synthesis (prominently face-to-face translation). In this work, we propose a new formulation that utilizes both spatial and temporal constraints along with the adversarial loss to overcome these

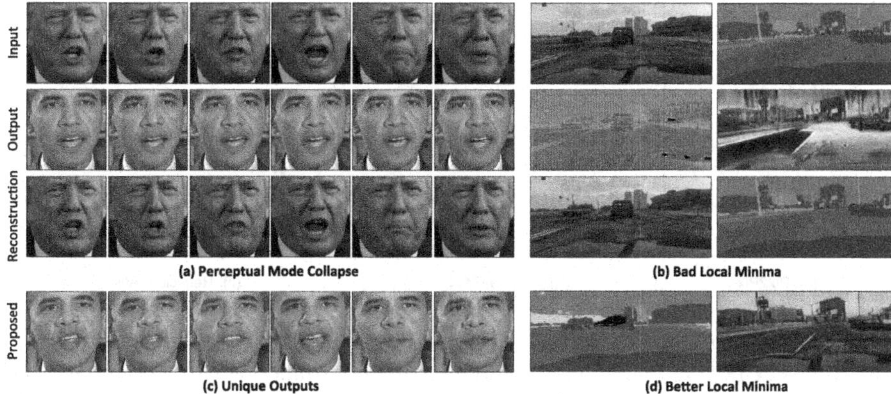

Fig. 2. Spatial cycle consistency is not sufficient: We show two examples illustrating why spatial cycle consistency alone is not sufficient for the optimization. (a) shows an example of *perceptual* mode-collapse while using Cycle-GAN [53] for Donald Trump to Barack Obama. First row shows the input of Donald Trump, and second row shows the output generated. The third row shows the output of reconstruction that takes the second row as input. The second row looks similar despite different inputs; and the third row shows output similar to first row. On a very close observation, we found that a few pixels in second row were different (but not perceptually significant) and that was sufficient to get the different reconstruction; (b) shows another example for image2labels and labels2image. While the generator is not able to generate the required output for the given input in both the cases, it is still able to perfectly reconstruct the input. Both the examples suggest that the spatial cyclic loss is not sufficient to ensure the required output in another domain because the overall optimization is focussed on reconstructing the input. However as shown in (c) and (d), **we get better outputs with our approach combining the spatial and temporal constraints**. Videos for face comparison are available on project webpage.

two problems. Shown in Fig. 2-(c, d) are the outputs of proposed approach overcoming the above mentioned problems. We posit this is due to more constraints available for an under-constrained optimization.

The use of GANs [15] and variational auto-encoder [27] have also found a way for synthesizing videos and temporal information. Walker et al. [45] use temporal information to predict future trajectories from a single image. Recent work [16,44,46] used temporal models to predict long term future poses from a single 2D image. MoCoGAN [43] decomposes motion and content to control video generation. Similarly, Temporal GAN [39] employs a temporal generator and an image generator that generates a set of latent variables and image sequences respectively. While relevant, the prior work is mostly focused about predicting the future intent from single images at test time or generating videos from a random noise. Concurrently, MoCoGAN [43] shows example of image-to-video translation using their formulation. However, our focus is on a general video-to-video translation where the input video can control the output in a spirit similar to image-to-image translation. To this end, we can generate hi-res videos

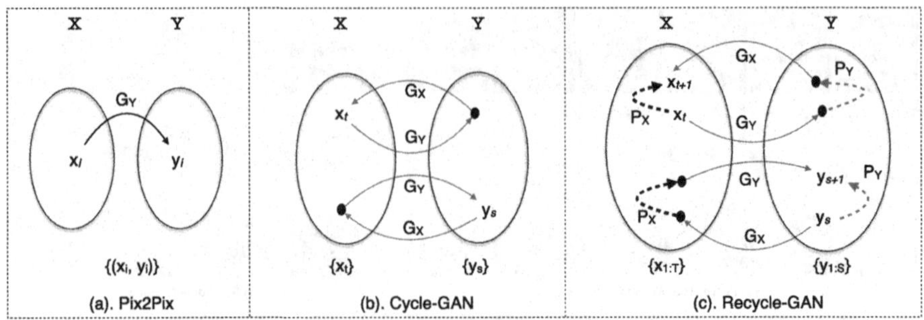

Fig. 3. We contrast our work with two prominent directions in image-to-image translation. (a) **Pix2Pix** [23]: Paired data is available. A simple function (Eq. 1) can be learnt via regression to map $X \rightarrow Y$. (b) **Cycle-GAN** [53]: The data is not paired in this setting. Zhu et al. [53] proposed to use cycle-consistency loss (Eq. 3) to deal with the problem of unpaired data. (c) **Recycle-GAN**: The approaches so far have considered independent 2D images only. Suppose we have access to unpaired but *ordered streams* $(x_1, x_2, \ldots, x_t, \ldots)$ and $(y_1, y_2 \ldots, y_s, \ldots)$. We present an approach that combines spatiotemporal constraints (Eq. 5). See Sect. 3 for more details.

of arbitrary length from our approach whereas the prior work [39,43] has shown to generate only 16 frames of 64×64.

Spatial and Temporal Constraints: The spatial and temporal information is known to be an integral sensory component that guides human action [12]. There exists a wide literature utilizing these two constraints for various computer vision tasks such as learning better object detectors [34], action recognition [13] etc. In this work, we take a first step to exploit spatiotemporal constraints for video retargeting and unpaired image-to-image translation.

Learning Association: Much of computer vision is about learning association, be it learning high-level image classification [38], object relationships [32], or point-wise correspondences [2,24,29,31]. However, there has been relatively little work on learning association for aligning the content of different videos. In this work, we use our model trained with spatiotemporal constraints to align the semantical content of two videos in a self-supervised manner, and do automatic alignment of the visual data without any additional supervision.

3 Method

Assume we wish to learn a mapping $G_Y : X \rightarrow Y$. The classic approach tunes G_Y to minimize reconstruction error on paired data samples $\{(x_i, y_i)\}$ where $x_i \in X$ and $y_i \in Y$:

$$\min_{G_Y} \sum_i ||y_i - G_Y(x_i)||^2. \tag{1}$$

Adversarial Loss: Recent work [15,23] has shown that one can improve the learned mapping by tuning it with a discriminator D_Y that is adversarially trained to distinguish between real samples of y from generated samples $G_Y(x)$:

$$\min_{G_Y} \max_{D_Y} L_g(G_Y, D_Y) = \sum_s \log D_Y(y_s) + \sum_t \log(1 - D_Y(G_Y(x_t))), \tag{2}$$

Importantly, we use a formulation that does *not* require paired data and only requires access to individual samples $\{x_t\}$ and $\{y_s\}$, where different subscripts are used to emphasize the lack of pairing.

Cycle Loss: Zhu et al. [53] use cycle consistency [51] to define a reconstruction loss when the pairs are not available. Popularly known as Cycle-GAN (Fig. 3-b), the objective can be written as:

$$L_c(G_X, G_Y) = \sum_t ||x_t - G_X(G_Y(x_t))||^2. \tag{3}$$

Recurrent Loss: We have so far considered the setting when static data is available. Instead, assume that we have access to unpaired but *ordered streams* $(x_1, x_2, \ldots, x_t, \ldots)$ and $(y_1, y_2 \ldots, y_s, \ldots)$. Our motivating application is learning a mapping between two videos from different domains. One option is to ignore the stream indices, and treat the data as an unpaired *and unordered* collection of samples from X and Y (e.g., learn mappings between shuffled video frames). We demonstrate that much better mapping can be learnt by taking advantage of the temporal ordering. To describe our approach, we first introduce a recurrent temporal predictor P_X that is trained to predict future samples in a stream given its past:

$$L_\tau(P_X) = \sum_t ||x_{t+1} - P_X(x_{1:t})||^2, \tag{4}$$

where we write $x_{1:t} = (x_1 \ldots x_t)$.

Recycle Loss: We use this temporal prediction model to define a new cycle loss across domains and *time* (Fig. 3-c) which we refer as a recycle loss:

$$L_r(G_X, G_Y, P_Y) = \sum_t ||x_{t+1} - G_X(P_Y(G_Y(x_{1:t})))||^2, \tag{5}$$

where $G_Y(x_{1:t}) = (G_Y(x_1), \ldots, G_Y(x_t))$. Intuitively, the above loss requires *sequences* of frames to map back to themselves. We demonstrate that this is a much richer constraint when learning from unpaired data streams in Fig. 4.

Recycle-GAN: We now combine the recurrent loss, recycle loss, and adversarial loss into our final Recycle-GAN formulation:

$$\min_{G,P} \max_{D} L_{rg}(G, P, D) = L_g(G_X, D_X) + L_g(G_Y, D_Y) +$$
$$\lambda_{rx} L_r(G_X, G_Y, P_Y) + \lambda_{ry} L_r(G_Y, G_X, P_X) + \lambda_{\tau x} L_\tau(P_X) + \lambda_{\tau y} L_\tau(P_Y).$$

Inference: At test time, given an input video with frames $\{x_t\}$, we would like to generate an output video. The simplest strategy would be directly using the trained G_Y to generate a video frame-by-frame $y_t = G_Y(x_t)$. Alternatively, one could use the temporal predictor P_Y to smooth the output:

$$y_t = \frac{G_Y(x_t) + P_Y(G_Y(x_{1:t-1}))}{2},$$

where the linear combination could be replaced with a nonlinear function, possibly learned with the original objective function. However, for simplicity, we produce an output video by simple single-frame generation. This allows our framework to be applied to both videos and single images at test-time, and produces fairer comparison to spatial approach.

Implementation Details: We adopt much of the training details from Cycle-GAN [53] to train our spatial translation model, and Pix2Pix [23] for our temporal prediction model. The generative network consists of two convolution (down-sampling with stride-2), six residual blocks, and finally two upsampling convolution (each with a stride 0.5). We use the same network architecture for G_X, and G_Y. The resolution of the images for all the experiments is set to 256×256. The discriminator network is a 70×70 PatchGAN [23,53] that is used to classify a 70×70 image patch if it is real or fake. We set all $\lambda_s = 10$. To implement our temporal predictors P_X and P_Y, we concatenate the last two frames as input to a network whose architecture is identical to U-Net architecture [23,37].

4 Experiments

We now study the influence of spatiotemporal constraints over spatial cyclic constraints. Because our key technical contribution is the introduction of temporal constraints in learning unpaired image mappings, the natural baseline is Cycle-GAN [53], a widely adopted approach for exploiting spatial cyclic consistency alone for an unpaired image translation. We first present quantitative results on domains where ground-truth correspondence between input and output videos are known (e.g., a video where each frame is paired with a semantic label map). Importantly, this correspondence pairing is *not available* to either Cycle-GAN or Recycle-GAN, but used only for evaluation. We then present qualitative results on a diverse set of videos with unknown correspondence, including video translations across different human faces and temporally-intricate events found in nature (flowers blooming, sunrise/sunset, time-lapsed weather progressions).

4.1 Quantitative Analysis

We use publicly available Viper [36] dataset for image2labels and labels2image to evaluate our findings. This dataset is collected using computer game with varying realistic content and provides densely annotated pixel-level labels. Out of the 77 different video sequences consisting of varying environmental conditions, we use

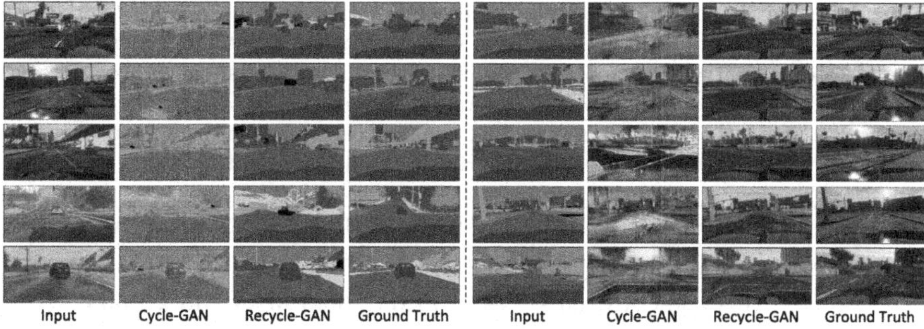

Fig. 4. We compare the performance of our approach for image2labels and labels2image with Cycle-GAN [53] on a held out data of Viper dataset [36] for various environmental conditions.

57 sequences for training our model and baselines. The held-out 20 sequences are used for evaluation. The goal for this evaluation is not to achieve the state-of-the-art performance but to compare and understand the advantage of spatiotemporal cyclic consistency over the spatial cyclic consistency [53]. We selected the model that correspond to minimum reconstruction loss for our approach.

While the prior work [23,53] has mostly used Cityscapes dataset [7], we could not use it for our evaluation. Primarily the labelled images in Cityscapes are not continuous video sequences, and the information in the consecutive frames is drastically different from the initial frame. As such it is not trivial to use a temporal predictor. We used Viper as a proxy for Cityscapes because the task is similar and that dataset contains dense video annotations. Additionally, a concurrent work [3] on unsupervised video-to-video translation also use Viper dataset for evaluation. However, they restrict to a small subset of sequences from daylight and walking only whereas we use all the varying environmental conditions available in the dataset.

Image2Labels: In this setting, we use the real world image as input to generator that output segmentation label maps. We compute three statistics to compare the output of two approaches: (1). Mean Pixel Accuracy (**MP**); (2). Average Class Accuracy (**AC**); (3). Intersection over Union (**IoU**). These statistics are computed using the ground truth for the held-out sequences under varying environmental conditions. Table 1 contrast the performance of our approach (Recycle-GAN) with Cycle-GAN. We observe that Recycle-GAN achieves significantly better performance than Cycle-GAN over all criteria and under all conditions.

Labels2Image: In this setting, we use the segmentation label map as an input to generator and output an image that is close to a real image. The goal of this evaluation is to compare the quality of output images obtained from both approaches. We follow Pix2Pix [23] for this evaluation. We use the generated images from each of the algorithm with a pre-trained FCN-style segmentation model. We then compute the performance of synthesized images against the real

Table 1. Image2Labels (Semantic Segmentation): We use the Viper [36] dataset to evaluate the performance improvement when using spatiotemporal constraints as opposed to only spatial cyclic consistency [53]. We report results using three criteria: (1). Mean Pixel Accuracy (**MP**); (2). Average Class Accuracy (**AC**); and (3). Intersection over union (**IoU**). We observe that our approach achieves significantly better performance than prior work over all the criteria in all the conditions.

Criterion	Approach	Day	Sunset	Rain	Snow	Night	All
MP	Cycle-GAN	35.8	38.9	51.2	31.8	27.4	35.5
	Recycle-GAN (ours)	**48.7**	**71.0**	**60.9**	**57.1**	**45.2**	**56.0**
AC	Cycle-GAN	7.8	6.7	7.4	7.0	4.7	7.1
	Recycle-GAN (ours)	**11.9**	**12.2**	**10.5**	**11.1**	**6.5**	**11.3**
IoU	Cycle-GAN	4.9	3.9	4.9	4.0	2.2	4.2
	Recycle-GAN (ours)	**7.9**	**9.6**	**7.1**	**8.2**	**4.1**	**8.2**

Table 2. Normalized FCN score for Labels2Image: We use a pre-trained FCN-style model to evaluate the quality of synthesized images over real images using the Viper [36] dataset. Higher performance on this criteria suggest that the output of a particular approach produces images that look closer to the real images.

Approach	Day	Sunset	Rain	Snow	Night	All
Cycle-GAN	0.33	0.27	**0.39**	0.29	0.37	0.30
Recycle-GAN (ours)	0.33	**0.51**	0.37	**0.43**	**0.40**	**0.39**

images to compute a normalized FCN-score. Higher performance on this criterion suggest that generated image is closer to the real images. Table 2 compares the performance of our approach with Cycle-GAN. We observe that our approach achieves overall better performance and sometimes competitive in different conditions when compared with Cycle-GAN for this task. Figure 4 qualitatively compares our approach with Cycle-GAN.

In these experiments, we make two observations: (i) Cycle-GAN learnt a good translation model within a few initial iterations (seeing only a few examples) but this model degraded as reconstruction loss started to decrease. We believe that minimizing reconstruction loss alone on input lead it to a bad local minima, and having a combined spatiotemporal constraint avoided this behavior; (ii) Cycle-GAN learns better translation model for Cityscapes as opposed to Viper. Cityscapes consists of images from mostly daylight and agreeable weather. This is not the case with Viper as it is rendered, and therefore has a large and varied distribution of different sunlight and weather conditions such as day, night, snow, rain etc. This makes it harder to learn a good mapping because for each labelled input, there are potentially many output images. We find that standard conditional GANs suffer from mode collapse in such scenarios, producing "average" outputs (as pointed by prior works [2]). Our experiments suggest that spatiotemporal constraints help ameliorate such challenging translation problems.

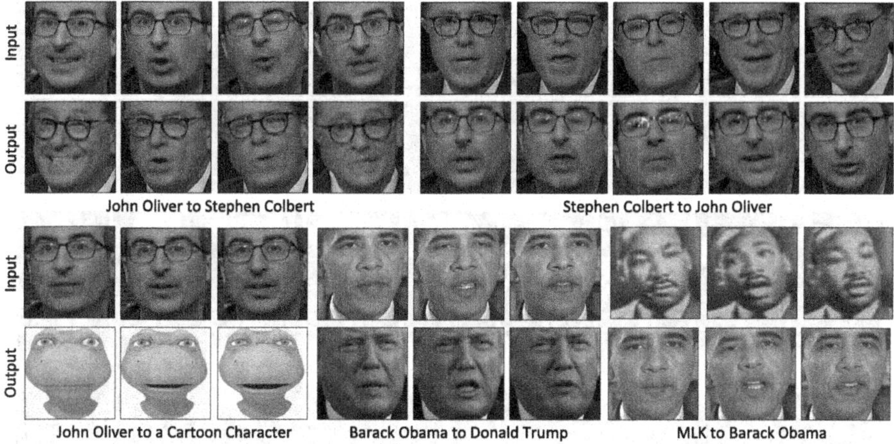

Fig. 5. Face to Face: The top row shows multiple examples of face-to-face between John Oliver and Stephen Colbert using our approach. The bottom row shows example of translation from John Oliver to a cartoon character, Barack Obama to Donald Trump, and Martin Luther King Jr. (MLK) to Barack Obama. Without any input alignment or manual supervision, our approach could capture stylistic expressions for these public figures. As an example, John Oliver's dimple while smiling, the shape of mouth characteristic of Donald Trump, and the facial mouth lines and smile of Stephen Colbert. More results and videos are available on our project webpage.

4.2 Qualitative Analysis

Face to Face: We use the publicly available videos of various public figures for the face-to-face translation task. The faces are extracted using the facial keypoints generated using the OpenPose Library [6] and a minor manual efforts are made to remove false positives. Figure 5 shows an example of face-to-face translation between John Oliver and Stephen Colbert, Barack Obama to Donald Trump, and Martin Luther King Jr. (MLK) to Barack Obama, and John Oliver to a cartoon character. Note that without any additional supervisory signal or manual alignment, our approach can learn to do face-to-face translation and captures stylistic expression for these personalities, such as the dimple on the face of John Oliver while smiling, the characteristic shape of mouth of Donald Trump, facial expression of Bill Clinton, and the mouth lines for Stephen Colbert.

Flower to Flower: Extending from faces and other traditional translations, we demonstrate our approach for flowers. We use various flowers, and extracted their time-lapse from publicly available videos. The time-lapses show the blooming of different flowers but without any sync. We use our approach to align the content, i.e. both flowers bloom or die together. Figure 6 shows how our video retargeting approach can be viewed as an approach for learning association between the events of different flowers life.

Fig. 6. Flower to Flower: We shows two examples of flower-to-flower translation. Note the smooth transition from Left to Right. These results can be best visualized using videos on our project webpage.

4.3 Video Manipulation via Retargeting

Clouds and Wind Synthesis: Our approach can be used to synthesize a new video that has the required environmental condition such as clouds and wind without the need for physical efforts of recapturing. We use the given video and video data from required environmental condition as two domains in our experiment. The conditional video and trained translation model is then used to generate a required output.

For this experiment, we collected the video data for various wind and cloud conditions, such as calm day or windy day. Using our approach, we can convert a calm-day to a windy-day, and a windy-day to a calm-day, without modifying the aesthetics of the place. Shown in Fig. 7 is an example of synthesizing clouds and winds on a windy day at a place when the only information available was a video captured at same place with a light breeze. More videos for these clouds and wind synthesis are available on our project webpage.

Sunrise and Sunset: We extracted the sunrise and sunset data from various web videos, and show how our approach could be used for both video manipulation and content alignment. This is similar to settings in our experiments on clouds and wind synthesis. Figure 8 shows an example of synthesizing a sunrise video from an original sunset video by conditioning it on a sunrise video. We also show examples of alignment of various sunrise and sunset scenes.

Fig. 7. Synthesizing Clouds & Winds: We use our approach to synthesize clouds and winds. The top row shows example frames of a video captured on a day with light breeze. We condition it on video data from a windy data (shown in second row) by learning a transformation between two domains using our approach. The last row shows the output synthesized video with the clouds and trees moving faster (giving a notion of wind blowing). Refer to the videos on our project webpage for better visualization and more examples.

Note: We refer the reader to our project webpage for different videos synthesized using our approach, and extension of our work utilizing both 2D images and videos by combining Cycle-loss and Recycle-loss in a generative adversarial formulation.

4.4 Human Studies

We performed human studies on the synthesized output, particularly faces and flowers, following the protocol of MoCoGAN [43] who also evaluate videos. However, our analysis consist of three parts: (1). In the first study, we showed synthesized videos individually from both Cycle-GAN and ours to 15 sequestered human subjects, and asked them if it is a real video or a generated video. The subjects misclassified 28.3% times generated videos from our approach as real, and 7.3% times for Cycle-GAN. (2). In the second study, we show the synthesized videos from Cycle-GAN and our approach simultaneously, and asked them to tell which one looks more natural and realistic. Human subjects chose the videos synthesized from our approach 76% times, 8% times Cycle-GAN, and 16% times they were confused. (3). In the final study, we showed the video-to-video translation. This is an extension of (2), except now we also include input and ask which looks like a more realistic and natural translation. We showed each video to 15 human subjects. The human subjects selected our approach 74.7% times, 13.3% times they selected Cycle-GAN, and 12% times they were confused. From the human study, we can clearly see that combining spatial and temporal constraints lead to better retargeting.

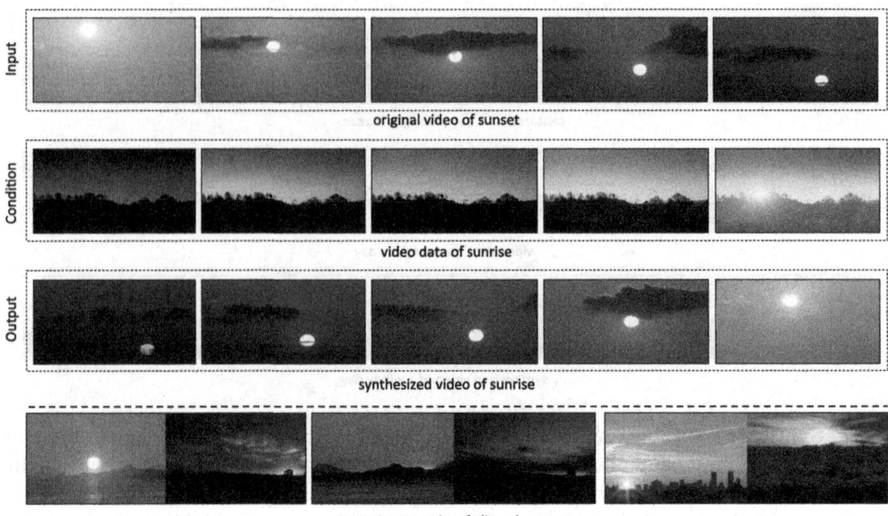

Fig. 8. Sunrise & Sunset: We use our approach to manipulate and align the videos of sunrise and sunset. The top row shows example frames from a sunset video. We condition it on video data of sunrise (shown in second row) by learning a transformation between two domains using our approach. The third row shows example frames of new synthesized video of sunrise. Finally, the last row shows random examples of input-output pair from different sunrise and sunset videos. Videos and more examples are available on our project webpage.

4.5 Failure Example: Learning Association Beyond Data Distribution

We show an example of transformation from a real bird to a origami bird to demonstrate a case where our approach failed to learn the association. The real bird data was extracted using web videos, and we used the origami bird from the synthesis of Kholgade et al. [25]. Shown in Fig. 9 is the synthesis of origami bird conditioned on the real bird. While the real bird is sitting, the origami bird stays and attempts to imitate the actions of real bird. The problem comes when the bird begins to fly. The initial frames when the bird starts to fly are fine. After some time the origami bird reappears. From an association perspective, the origami bird should not have reappeared. Looking back at the training data, we found that the original origami bird data does not have a example of frame without the origami bird, and therefore our approach is not able to associate an example when the real bird is no more visible. Perhaps, our approach could only learn to interpolate over a given data distribution and fails to capture anything beyond it. One possible way to address this problem is by using a lot of training data such that the data distribution encapsulates all possible scenarios and can lead to an effective interpolation.

Fig. 9. Failure Example: We present the failure in association/synthesis for our approach using a transformation from a *real* bird to an *origami* bird. While the origami bird (output) is trying to imitate the real bird (input) when it is sitting (Column 1–4), and also flies away when the real bird flies (Column 5–6). We observe that it reappears after sometime (red bounding box in Column 7) in a flying mode while the real bird didn't exist in the input. Our algorithm is not able to make transition of association when the real bird is completely invisible, and so it generated a random flying origami. (Color figure online)

5 Discussion and Future Work

In this work, we explore the influence of spatiotemporal constraints in learning video retargeting and image translation. Unpaired video/image translation is a challenging task because it is unsupervised, lacking any correspondences between training samples from the input and output space. We point out that many natural visual signals are inherently spatiotemporal in nature, which provides strong temporal constraints for free to help learn such mappings. This results in significantly better mappings. We also point that unpaired and unsupervised video retargeting and image translation is an under-constrained problem, and so more constraints using auxiliary tasks from the visual data itself (as used for other vision tasks [33,50]) could help in learning better transformation models.

Recycle-GANs learn both a mapping function and a recurrent temporal predictor. Thus far, our results make use of only the mapping function, so as to facilitate fair comparisons with previous work. But it is natural to synthesize target videos by making use of both the single-image translation model and the temporal predictor. Additionally, the notion of style in video retargeting can be incorporated more precisely by using spatiotemporal generative models as this would allow to even learn the speed of generated output. E.g. Two people may have different ways of content delivery and that one person can take longer than other to say the same thing. A true notion of style should be able to generate even this variation in amount of time for delivering speech/content. We believe that better spatiotemporal neural network architecture could attempt this problem in near future. Finally, our work could also utilize the concurrent approach from Huang et al. [22] to learn a one-to-many translation model.

References

1. Bansal, A., Russell, B., Gupta, A.: Marr revisited: 2D–3D model alignment via surface normal prediction. In: CVPR (2016)
2. Bansal, A., Sheikh, Y., Ramanan, D.: PixelNN: example-based image synthesis. In: ICLR (2018)
3. Bashkirova, D., Usman, B., Saenko, K.: Unsupervised video-to-video translation. CoRR abs/1806.03698 (2018)
4. Brand, M., Hertzmann, A.: Style machines. ACM Trans. Graph. (2000)
5. Cao, C., Hou, Q., Zhou, K.: Displaced dynamic expression regression for real-time facial tracking and animation. ACM Trans. Graph. **33**, 43 (2014)
6. Cao, Z., Simon, T., Wei, S.E., Sheikh, Y.: Realtime multi-person 2D pose estimation using part affinity fields. In: CVPR (2017)
7. Cordts, M., et al.: The cityscapes dataset for semantic urban scene understanding. In: CVPR (2016)
8. Denton, E.L., Chintala, S., Szlam, A., Fergus, R.: Deep generative image models using a Laplacian pyramid of adversarial networks. In: NIPS (2015)
9. Eigen, D., Fergus, R.: Predicting depth, surface normals and semantic labels with a common multi-scale convolutional architecture. In: ICCV (2015)
10. Freeman, W.T., Tenenbaum, J.B.: Learning bilinear models for two-factor problems in vision. In: CVPR (1997)
11. Gatys, L.A., Ecker, A.S., Bethge, M.: Image style transfer using convolutional neural networks. In: CVPR (2016)
12. Gibson, J.J.: The ecological approach to visual perception (1979)
13. Girdhar, R., Ramanan, D., Gupta, A., Sivic, J., Russell, B.: ActionVLAD: learning spatio-temporal aggregation for action classification. In: CVPR (2017)
14. Godard, C., Mac Aodha, O., Brostow, G.J.: Unsupervised monocular depth estimation with left-right consistency. In: CVPR (2017)
15. Goodfellow, I.J., et al.: Generative adversarial networks. In: NIPS (2014)
16. He, J., Lehrmann, A., Marino, J., Mori, G., Sigal, L.: Probabilistic video generation using holistic attribute control. In: ECCV (2018)
17. Hertzmann, A., Jacobs, C.E., Oliver, N., Curless, B., Salesin, D.H.: Image analogies. ACM Trans. Graph. (2001)
18. Hoffman, J., et al.: Cycada: cycle-consistent adversarial domain adaptation. In: ICML (2018)
19. Hsu, E., Pulli, K., Popović, J.: Style translation for human motion. ACM Trans. Graph. **24**, 1082–1089 (2005)
20. Huang, Q.X., Guibas, L.: Consistent shape maps via semidefinite programming. In: Eurographics Symposium on Geometry Processing (2013)
21. Huang, X., Li, Y., Poursaeed, O., Hopcroft, J.E., Belongie, S.J.: Stacked generative adversarial networks. In: CVPR (2017)
22. Huang, X., Liu, M.Y., Belongie, S., Kautz, J.: Multimodal unsupervised image-to-image translation. In: ECCV (2018)
23. Isola, P., Zhu, J.Y., Zhou, T., Efros, A.A.: Image-to-image translation with conditional adversarial networks. In: CVPR (2017)
24. Kanazawa, A., Jacobs, D.W., Chandraker, M.: WarpNet: weakly supervised matching for single-view reconstruction. In: CVPR (2016)
25. Kholgade, N., Simon, T., Efros, A., Sheikh, Y.: 3D object manipulation in a single photograph using stock 3D models. ACM Trans. Graph. **33**, 127 (2014)

26. Kim, T., Cha, M., Kim, H., Lee, J.K., Kim, J.: Learning to discover cross-domain relations with generative adversarial networks. In: ICML (2017)
27. Kingma, D.P., Welling, M.: Auto-encoding variational bayes. arXiv preprint arXiv:1312.6114 (2013)
28. Ledig, C., et al.: Photo-realistic single image super-resolution using a generative adversarial network. In: CVPR (2017)
29. Liu, C., Yuen, J., Torralba, A.: Sift flow: dense correspondence across scenes and its applications. IEEE Trans. Pattern Anal. Mach. Intell. **33**, 978–994 (2011)
30. Long, J., Shelhamer, E., Darrell, T.: Fully convolutional models for semantic segmentation. In: CVPR (2015)
31. Long, J., Zhang, N., Darrell, T.: Do convnets learn correspondence? In: NIPS (2014)
32. Malisiewicz, T., Efros, A.A.: Beyond categories: the visual memex model for reasoning about object relationships. In: NIPS (2009)
33. Meister, S., Hur, J., Roth, S.: UnFlow: unsupervised learning of optical flow with a bidirectional census loss. In: AAAI (2018)
34. Misra, I., Shrivastava, A., Hebert, M.: Watch and learn: semi-supervised learning of object detectors from videos. In: CVPR (2015)
35. Radford, A., Metz, L., Chintala, S.: Unsupervised representation learning with deep convolutional generative adversarial networks. CoRR abs/1511.06434 (2015)
36. Richter, S.R., Hayder, Z., Koltun, V.: Playing for benchmarks. In: International Conference on Computer Vision (ICCV) (2017)
37. Ronneberger, O., Fischer, P., Brox, T.: U-Net: convolutional networks for biomedical image segmentation. In: Navab, N., Hornegger, J., Wells, W.M., Frangi, A.F. (eds.) MICCAI 2015. LNCS, vol. 9351, pp. 234–241. Springer, Cham (2015). https://doi.org/10.1007/978-3-319-24574-4_28
38. Russakovsky, O., et al.: ImageNet large scale visual recognition challenge. IJCV **115**, 211–252 (2015)
39. Saito, M., Matsumoto, E., Saito, S.: Temporal generative adversarial nets with singular value clipping. In: ICCV (2017)
40. Shrivastava, A., Pfister, T., Tuzel, O., Susskind, J., Wang, W., Webb, R.: Learning from simulated and unsupervised images through adversarial training. In: CVPR (2017)
41. Thies, J., Zollhofer, M., Niessner, M., Valgaerts, L., Stamminger, M., Theobalt, C.: Real-time expression transfer for facial reenactment. ACM Trans. Graph. (2015)
42. Thies, J., Zollhofer, M., Stamminger, M., Theobalt, C., Niessner, M.: Face2face: real-time face capture and reenactment of RGB videos. In: CVPR (2016)
43. Tulyakov, S., Liu, M.Y., Yang, X., Kautz, J.: Mocogan: decomposing motion and content for video generation. In: CVPR (2018)
44. Villegas, R., Yang, J., Zou, Y., Sohn, S., Lin, X., Lee, H.: Learning to generate long-term future via hierarchical prediction. In: ICML (2017)
45. Walker, J., Doersch, C., Gupta, A., Hebert, M.: An uncertain future: forecasting from static images using variational autoencoders. In: Leibe, B., Matas, J., Sebe, N., Welling, M. (eds.) ECCV 2016. LNCS, vol. 9911, pp. 835–851. Springer, Cham (2016). https://doi.org/10.1007/978-3-319-46478-7_51
46. Walker, J., Marino, K., Gupta, A., Hebert, M.: The pose knows: video forecasting by generating pose futures. In: ICCV (2017)
47. Xia, Y., et al.: Dual learning for machine translation. In: NIPS (2016)
48. Xie, S., Tu, Z.: Holistically-nested edge detection. In: ICCV (2015)
49. Zhang, H., et al.: Stackgan: text to photo-realistic image synthesis with stacked generative adversarial networks. In: ICCV (2017)

50. Zhou, T., Brown, M., Snavely, N., Lowe, D.G.: Unsupervised learning of depth and ego-motion from video. In: CVPR (2017)
51. Zhou, T., Krähenbühl, P., Aubry, M., Huang, Q., Efros, A.A.: Learning dense correspondence via 3D-guided cycle consistency. In: CVPR (2016)
52. Zhou, T., Lee, Y.J., Yu, S.X., Efros, A.A.: FlowWeb: joint image set alignment by weaving consistent, pixel-wise correspondences. In: CVPR (2015)
53. Zhu, J., Park, T., Isola, P., Efros, A.A.: Unpaired image-to-image translation using cycle-consistent adversarial networks. In: ICCV (2017)

Fine-Grained Video Categorization with Redundancy Reduction Attention

Chen Zhu[1(✉)], Xiao Tan[2], Feng Zhou[3], Xiao Liu[2], Kaiyu Yue[2], Errui Ding[2], and Yi Ma[4]

[1] University of Maryland, College Park, USA
chenzhu@cs.umd.edu

[2] Department of Computer Vision Technology (VIS), Baidu Inc., Beijing, China
{tanxiao01,liuxiao12,yuekaiyu,dingerrui}@baidu.com

[3] Baidu Research, Sunnyvale, USA
zhoufeng09@baidu.com

[4] University of California, Berkeley, USA
yima@eecs.berkeley.edu

Abstract. For fine-grained categorization tasks, videos could serve as a better source than static images as videos have a higher chance of containing discriminative patterns. Nevertheless, a video sequence could also contain a lot of redundant and irrelevant frames. How to locate critical information of interest is a challenging task. In this paper, we propose a new network structure, known as Redundancy Reduction Attention (RRA), which learns to focus on multiple discriminative patterns by suppressing redundant feature channels. Specifically, it firstly summarizes the video by weight-summing all feature vectors in the feature maps of selected frames with a spatio-temporal soft attention, and then predicts which channels to suppress or to enhance according to this summary with a learned non-linear transform. Suppression is achieved by modulating the feature maps and threshing out weak activations. The updated feature maps are then used in the next iteration. Finally, the video is classified based on multiple summaries. The proposed method achieves outstanding performances in multiple video classification datasets. Furthermore, we have collected two large-scale video datasets, YouTube-Birds and YouTube-Cars, for future researches on fine-grained video categorization. The datasets are available at http://www.cs.umd.edu/~chenzhu/fgvc.

Keywords: Fine-grained video categorization · Attention mechanism

1 Introduction

Fine-grained visual recognition, such as recognizing bird species [30,36] and car models [6,18], has long been of interest to computer vision community. In such tasks, categories may differ only in subtle details, e.g., Yellow-billed Cuckoo and Black-billed Cuckoo, collected in the popular benchmark CUB-200-2011 [30],

V. Ferrari et al. (Eds.): ECCV 2018, LNCS 11209, pp. 139–155, 2018.
https://doi.org/10.1007/978-3-030-01228-1_9

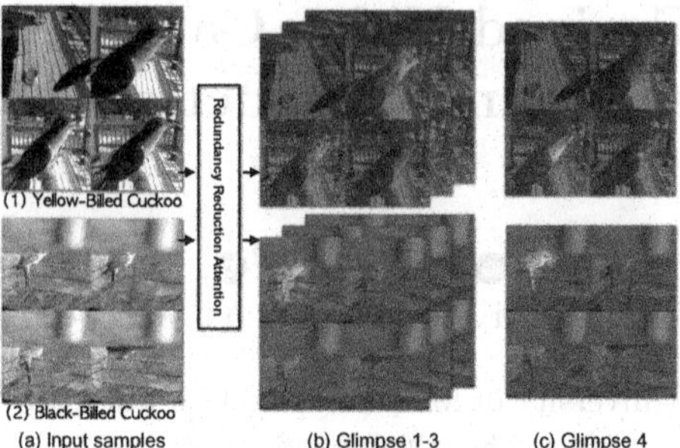

Fig. 1. Visualization of two real cases on our YouTube-Birds validation set with our RRA model. The heat maps are computed with Eq. 7 which represents the model's attention on the pixels. This instance has 4 sampled frames and 4 glimpses. Glimpses 2 and 3 are hidden to save space. The target in the input frames for the network may be missing or deformed after preprocessing, as in (1) and (2). Our model counters such problems by: (1) Focusing on most discriminative locations among all input frames with soft attention, which helps (1) to ignore the "empty" frame. (2) Iteratively depressing uninformative channels, which helps (2) to correct the mis-recognition to House Wren in glimpses 1–3 due to deformation, and recognize correctly with discriminative patterns (head) in glimpse 4. (Color figure online)

look almost the same except for the color of their bills and the patterns under their tails. Hence, lots of works emphasize the importance of discriminative patterns, adopting part annotations [34,35] and attention mechanisms [4,36]. Progress has been evident on existing datasets, but photos reflecting Cuckoos' bill color or their tail are not always easy to take, as birds seldom keep still and move fast. The discriminative patterns may also become insignificant during the preprocessing process, as shown in Fig. 1. Recognizing such non-discriminative images is an ill-posed problem. Instead, videos usually come with abundant visual details, motions and audios of their subjects, which have a much higher chance of containing discriminative patterns and are more suitable than single images for fine-grained recognition in daily scenarios. Nevertheless, videos have higher temporal and spatial redundancy than images. The discriminative patterns of interest are usually present only in a few frames and occupy only a small fraction of the frames. Other redundant frames or backgrounds may dilute the discriminative patterns and cause the model to overfit irrelevant information.

In this work, we propose a novel neural network structure, called Redundancy Reduction Attention (RRA), to address the aforementioned redundancy problem. It is inspired by the observation that different feature channels respond to different patterns, and learning to reduce the activations of non-discriminative channels leads to substantial performance improvement [10,36]. In the same spirit, we allow our model to learn to reduce the redundancy and to focus on discriminative patterns by weakening or even blocking non-discriminative channels. Specifically, the model summarizes and updates the feature maps of all input frames iteratively. In each iteration, a soft attention mask is applied over each feature vector of all input feature maps to weight-sum the feature maps into a summary feature vector, and then a learned non-linear transform predicts the increment or decrement of each channel according to the summary feature vector. The increment or decrement is replicated spatially and temporally to each feature vector in the feature maps, and a BN-ReLU block will re-weight and threshold the modified feature maps. With such structures, our model learns to focus on discriminative local features through soft attention while ignoring redundant channels to make each glimpse[1] informative.

Because existing fine-grained video datasets are small [25] or weakly-labeled [15], we have collected two new large video datasets to remedy for the lack of better fine-grained video datasets. The two datasets are for fine-grained bird species and car model categorization, and are named YouTube Birds and YouTube Cars, respectively. As their names indicate, the videos are obtained from YouTube. They share the same taxonomy as CUB-200-2011 dataset [30] and Stanford Cars dataset [18], and are annotated via crowd sourcing. YouTube-Cars has 15220 videos of 196 categories, and YouTube-Birds has 18350 videos of 200 categories. To the best of our knowledge, our two datasets are the largest fine-grained video datasets with clean labels.

To sum up, the main contributions of this work are: (1) Proposing a novel redundancy reduction attention module to deal with the redundancy problems in videos explicitly. (2) Collecting two published fine-grained video categorization datasets. (3) Achieving state-of-the-art results on ActivityNet [3], Kinetics [16], as well as our newly collected datasets.

2 Related Works

2.1 Fine-Grained Visual Categorization

State-of-the-art fine-grained categorization approaches mostly employ deep convolutional networks pretrained on ImageNet to extract image features. Some works seek for increasing the capacity of the features e.g., the popular bilinear features [21] and recently proposed polynomial kernels [1] resort to higher-order statistics of convolutional activations to enhance the representativeness of the network. Despite its success, such statistics treat the whole image equally. There are other methods trying to explicitly capture the discriminative parts. Some of them leverage the manual annotations of key regions [30,34,35] to learn part detectors to help fine-grained classifiers, which requires heavy human involvements. In order to get rid of the labor intensive procedure, attention mechanism is deployed to highlights relevant parts without annotations, which boosts subsequent modules. A seminal work called STN [12] utilizes localization networks to predict the region of interest along with its deformation parameters such that the region can be more flexible than the rigid bounding box. [4] improves STN by adopting multiple glimpses to gradually zoom into the most discriminative region, but refining the same region does not fully exploit the rich information

[1] Refers to $\hat{\mathbf{x}}$ in Eq. 1, similar to [19].

in videos. MA-CNN [36] learns to cluster spatially-correlated feature channels, localize and classify with discriminative parts from the clustered channels.

2.2 Video Classification

It has been found that the accuracy of video classification with only convolutional features of a single frame is already competitive [15,24]. A natural extension to 2D ConvNets is 3D ConvNets [13] that convolves both spatially and temporally. P3D ResNet [24] decomposes a 3D convolution filter into the tensor product of a temporal and a spatial convolution filter initialized with pre-trained 2D ConvNets, which claims to be superior to previous 3D ConvNets. I3D [2] inflates pretrained 2D ConvNets into 3D ConvNets, achieving state-of-the-art accuracies on major video classification datasets. RNNs is an alternative to capture dependencies in the temporal dimension [20,28].

Many of the best-performing models so far adopt a two-stream ensembling [27], which trains two networks on the RGB images and optical flow fields separately, and fuse the predictions of them for classification. TSN [32] improves [27] by fusing the scores of several equally divided temporal segments.

Another direction is to consider the importance of regions or frames. Attentional Pooling [7] interprets the soft-attention-based classifier as a low-rank second order pooling. Attention Clusters [22] argues that integrating a cluster of independent local glimpses is more essential than considering long-term temporal patterns. [37] proposes a key volume mining approach which learns to identify key volumes and classify simultaneously. AdaScan [14] predicts the video frames' discrimination importance while passing through each frame's features sequentially, and computes the importance-weighted sum of the features. [26] utilizes a 3-layer LSTM to predict an attention map on one frame at each step. The aforementioned two methods only use previous frames to predict the importance or attention and ignore the incoming frames. In addition, all methods mentioned above lack of a mechanism which can wisely distinguish the informative locations and frames in videos jointly. To be noted, Attend and Interact [23] considers the interaction of objects, while we focus on extracting multiple complementary attentions by suppressing redundant features.

3 Methods

Figure 2 shows the overall structure of the proposed network. The same structure can be used to handle both RGB and optical flow inputs, except for changing the first convolution layer to adapt to stacked optical flows. Generally, our model learns to focus on the most discriminative visual features for classification through soft attention and channel suppression. For the inputs, we take a frame from each uniformly sliced temporal clip to represent the video. For training, each clip is represented by a random sample of its frames to increase variety of training data. For testing, frames are taken at the same index of each clip. Before going into details, we list some notations to be used throughout the

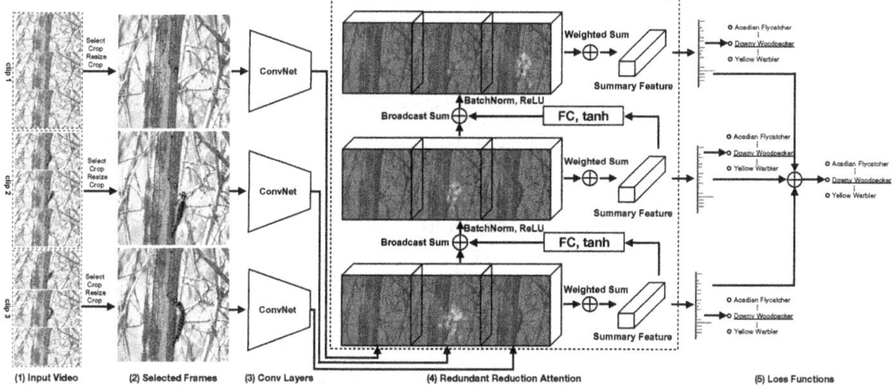

Fig. 2. The general structure of the proposed model. Input sequences are divided into clips of the same length. One frame or flow stack is sampled from each clip. The CNNs extract feature maps from the sampled frames, then the RRA modules iteratively updates the feature maps. Each summary feature vector gives one classification score via the classifiers, and the scores are averaged as the final prediction.

paper. Denote the width and the height of feature maps as w and h. $\mathbf{x}_i \in \mathbb{R}^{c \times hw}$ is the convolutional feature map of the i-th frame, $\mathbf{X} = [\mathbf{x}_1, \ldots, \mathbf{x}_n] \in \mathbb{R}^{c \times nhw}$ is the matrix composed of feature maps of all the n frames. $\bar{\mathbf{X}}$ is the redundancy-reduced $\mathbf{X}$ to be described in Sect. 3.1. We use $A \oplus B$ to denote the operation of replication followed by an element-wise sum, where the replication transforms A and B to have the same dimensions. The superscript ^{k} represents k-th iteration.

3.1 Redundancy Reduction Attention

Due to duplication of contents, the spatio-temporal feature representation $\mathbf{X}$ is highly redundant. In this section, we introduce a new network structure shown in Fig. 3 which is able to attend to the most discriminative spatio-temporal features and suppress the redundant channels of feature maps.

The soft attention mechanism [5,33] is able to select the most discriminative regional features. We extend it to the spatio-temporal domain to infer the most discriminative features of the video for categorization and reduce redundancy. As shown in our ablation experiments, unlike the spatial-only attention, it prevents the most discriminative features from being averaged out by background features. The attention weights $\mathbf{a} \in \mathbb{R}^{nhw}$ are modeled as $\mathbf{a} = \mathrm{softmax}(\bar{\mathbf{X}}^T \mathbf{W}_a)$, where $\mathbf{W}_a \in \mathbb{R}^c$ is learnable, and $\bar{\mathbf{X}}$ is defined in Eq. 2. The feature vectors of $\mathbf{X}$ are then weight-summed by $\mathbf{a}$ to get the summary vector:

$$\hat{\mathbf{x}} = \bar{\mathbf{X}}\mathbf{a}. \tag{1}$$

Since videos contain rich context for classification, it is natural to think of extracting multiple discriminative features with multiple attentions. However,

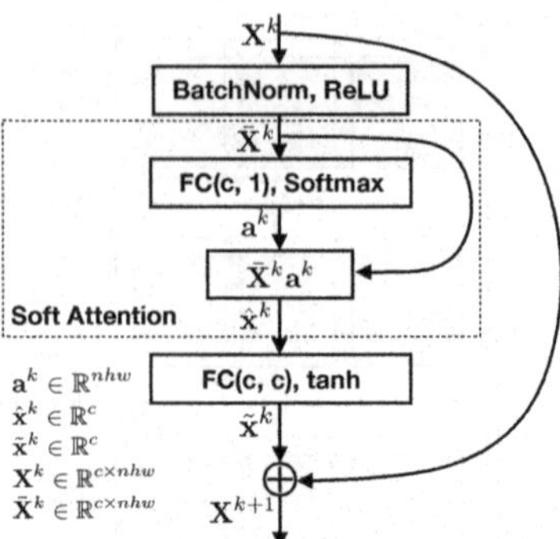

Fig. 3. Structure of one RRA module. RRA network is constructed by concatenating such modules. The final addition is a broadcasting operator.

we do not want the summaries to duplicate. We herein introduce a simple but effective approach which iteratively suppresses redundant feature channels while extracting complementary discriminative features, named Redundancy Reduction Attention (RRA). By reduction we refer to decreasing the magnitude of the activations. In k-th step, the channel-wise reduction $\tilde{\mathbf{x}}^k$ is inferred from the non-linear transform of the summary $\bar{\mathbf{x}}^k$. In the case of Fig. 3, the non-linear transform is selected as a fully connected layer followed by a tanh activation. Reduction is achieved by adding $\tilde{\mathbf{x}}^k$ to the ReLU activation feature map $\mathbf{X}^k$, which is further augmented by the BatchNorm-ReLU [11] block to threshold out activations below the average to get the redundancy-reduced feature map $\bar{\mathbf{X}}^{k+1}$:

$$\bar{\mathbf{X}}^{k+1} = \mathrm{ReLU}(\mathrm{BatchNorm}(\mathbf{X}^k \oplus \tilde{\mathbf{x}}^k)) \tag{2}$$

Since the range of $\tilde{\mathbf{x}}^k$ is $(-1, 1)$, $\tilde{\mathbf{x}}^k$ can not only suppress redundant channels but also enhance the informative channels to produce a more preferable feature map $\mathbf{X}^{k+1}$. As demonstrated in the experiments, using tanh as the activation for $\tilde{\mathbf{x}}^k$ is better than the -ReLU(x) alternative. A visualization of the suppression process is shown in Fig. 4.

3.2 Loss Functions

We utilize a Softmax classifier to predict the video's label distribution $\hat{\mathbf{y}}$ from the summary feature $\hat{\mathbf{x}}$ as $\hat{\mathbf{y}} = \mathrm{softmax}(\mathbf{W}_c\hat{\mathbf{x}} + \boldsymbol{b}_c)$. A cross entropy loss is applied to minimize the KL divergence between the ground truth distribution $\mathbf{y}$ and $\hat{\mathbf{y}}$:

$$L(\hat{\mathbf{y}}, \mathbf{y}) = -\sum_i \mathbf{y}_i \log \hat{\mathbf{y}}_i \tag{3}$$

For models with more than one RRA module (iterations), fusing the summary vectors for classification is a natural choice. We have explored three approaches to achieve the fusion.

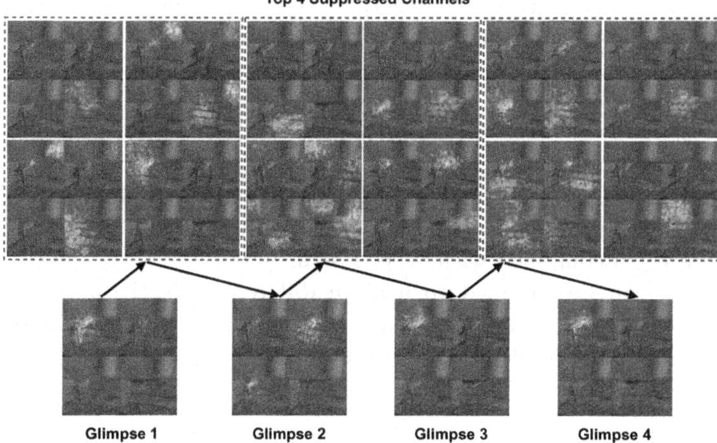

Fig. 4. One instance of redundancy suppression. Input frames are the same as Fig. 1. The top four suppressed channels are selected as the smallest four entrys' indices in $\tilde{\mathbf{x}}^k$, which are channels given the most decrements. We then compute I_{vis} in Sect. 3.3 by setting a_i as all decreased entries from $\mathbf{X}^k$ to $\bar{\mathbf{X}}^{k+1}$ in these channels, and setting w_i as their respective decrements. The suppressions does not overlap with the next target, and are on meaningful patterns. Red colors indicate higher suppression. (Color figure online)

Concatenation Loss L_c: Equivalent to the multi-glimpse models such as [5] which concatenates the glimpse features into a higher dimensional feature vector, we compute each glimpse score $\mathbf{s}^k = \mathbf{W}_c^k \hat{\mathbf{x}}^k + \boldsymbol{b}_c^k$ first, and minimize the cross entropy loss $L_c = L(\hat{\mathbf{y}}_{cat}, \mathbf{y})$ of their sum

$$\hat{\mathbf{y}}_{cat} = \text{softmax}(\sum_{k=1}^{K} \mathbf{s}^k). \tag{4}$$

This approach is broadly used, but since the scores are not normalized, they do not necessary have the same scale. If one glimpse gives extremely high magnitude, then other glimpses will be drowned, and the softmax loss may also reach saturation where the gradient vanishes, which harms the performance. In our experiments, we also find this loss suboptimal.

Individual Loss L_i: To overcome the normalization problem of L_c, we directly supervise on each of the individual glimpses. That is, we can apply cross entropy loss on each glimpse's categorical distribution $\hat{\mathbf{y}}^k$ and minimize their sum,

$$L_i = \sum_{k=1}^{K} L(\hat{\mathbf{y}}^k, \mathbf{y}). \tag{5}$$

This loss and its combinations perform the best in our experiments.

Ensemble Loss L_e: Since we have actually trained several classifiers with L_i, we could ensemble results from different glimpses as

$$\bar{\mathbf{y}} = \frac{1}{K}\sum_{k=1}^{K}\hat{\mathbf{y}}^k, \tag{6}$$

and compute $L_e = L(\bar{\mathbf{y}}, \mathbf{y})$. This is in fact optimizing the ensemble score directly. In our experiments, this loss does not perform well alone, but improves the performance when combined with other losses.

The losses can be summed to achieve different objectives. Although not explored in this paper, weights can also be applied on each loss, and even as trainable parameters reflecting the importance of each glimpse when computing L_e and the final scores.

3.3 Visualizing Attention over the Input

To check whether the network has really learned to focus on discriminative parts, we visualize each pixel's influence on the distribution of attention **a**. Since $||\mathbf{a}||_1 = 1$, $L_{vis} = \frac{1}{2}||\mathbf{a}||_2^2$ reflects **a**'s difference from mean pooling. We expect its distribution to highlight the discriminative patterns, which is probably far from mean pooling. Further, its derivative w.r.t. a input pixel $\mathbf{p} \in \mathbb{R}^3$ is $\frac{\partial L_{vis}}{\partial \mathbf{p}} = \sum_{i=1}^{nhw} \frac{\partial L_{vis}}{\partial a_i}\frac{\partial a_i}{\partial \mathbf{p}} = \sum_{i=1}^{nhw} w_i \frac{\partial a_i}{\partial \mathbf{p}}$ where $w_i = a_i$. It not only reflects **p**'s influence on a_i with $\frac{\partial a_i}{\partial \mathbf{p}}$, but also reflects how much attention is paid to this influence by the weight w_i. With this equation, we can also set w_i to other values to weigh the influences. Finally, we quantize the attention-weighed influence by the ℓ^1 norm of this derivative

$$I_{vis} = \left\| \frac{\partial L_{vis}}{\partial \mathbf{p}} \right\|_1, \tag{7}$$

and use a color map on I_{vis} to enhance the visual difference. A Gaussian filter is applied to make high values more distinguishable.

4 Novel Fine-Grained Video Datasets

In order to provide a good benchmark for fine-grained video categorization, we built two challenging video datasets, YouTube Birds and YouTube Cars, which consist of 200 different bird species and 196 different car models respectively. The taxonomy of the two datasets are the same as CUB-200-2011 [30] and Stanford Cars [18] respectively. Figure 1 shows some sample frames from the two datasets. Compared with the two reference datasets, subjects in our datasets have more view point and scale changes. YouTube Birds also doubles the size of IBC127 [25], a video dataset with 8,014 videos and 127 fine-grained bird categories. Table 2 lists the specifications of the annotated datasets. N_c is number of categories. N_{train} and N_{test} are number of training and testing videos. n_v and m_v are minimum and maximum number of videos for a category (Table 1).

Table 1. Sample frames from YouTube Birds and YouTube Cars datasets. Top 2 rows are from YouTube Birds, bottom 2 rows are from YouTube Cars.

Table 2. Specifications of YouTube Birds and YouTube Cars.

Set	N_c	N_{train}	N_{test}	n_v	m_v
Birds	200	12666	5684	6	249
Cars	196	10259	4961	6	207

Videos of both datasets were collected through YouTube video search. We limited the resolution of videos to be no lower than 360p and the duration to be no more than 5 min. We used a crowd sourcing system to annotate the videos. Before annotating, we firstly filter the videos with bird and car detectors to ensure at least one of the sample frames contains a bird or a car. For each video, the workers were asked to annotate whether each of its sample frames (8 to 15 frames per video) belong to the presumed category by comparing with the positive images (10 to 30 per category) of that category. As long as there is one sample frame from the video belong to the presumed category, the video will be kept. According to the annotations, about 29% and 50% of the frames of YouTube Birds/YouTube Cars contain a bird/car. However, since one video may contain multiple subjects from different categories, there may be more than one category in the same video. To make evaluation easier, we removed all videos appearing in more than one category. Videos of each category were split into training and test sets in a fixed ratio. More details are in the project page.

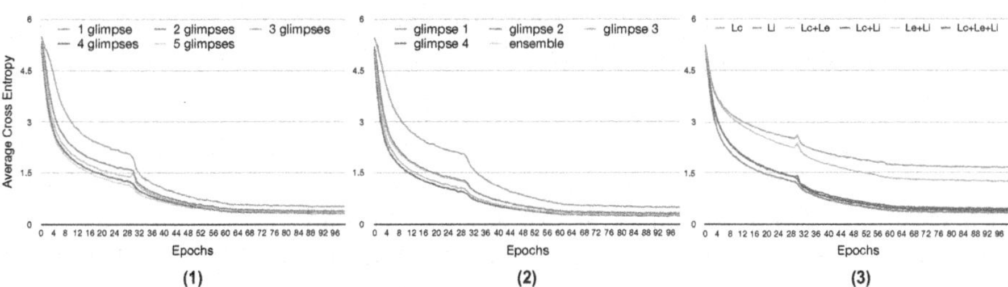

Fig. 5. Average loss curves throughout epochs on ActivityNet v1.3 training set. (1): loss curves w.r.t. different number of glimpses. As the number of glimpse increases, it converges quicker, and indicates better generalization on validation set. (2): loss curves of each glimpse and the ensemble score in the 4-glimpse model with only L_i. (3): loss curves of different loss functions. The L_e curve is ignored - the curve is ascending.

5 Experimental Results

We evaluated the proposed method for general video categorization and fine-grained video categorization. For general tasks, we selected activity recognition and performed experiments on RGB frames of ActivityNet v1.3 [3] and both RGB and flow of Kinetics [16]. For fine-grained tasks, we performed experiments on our novel datasets YouTube Birds and YouTube Cars.

We first introduce the two public datasets and our experimental settings, and then analyze our model with controlled experiments. Finally we compare our method with state-of-the-art methods.

Table 3. Ablation analysis of loss functions on ActivityNet v1.3 validation set. mAP_e stands for the mAP of ensemble score, mAP_c stands for the mAP of concatenation score.

Loss	mAP_c	mAP_e	Loss	mAP_c	mAP_e
L_c	80.27	77.84	L_i	82.60	82.97
L_e	25.75	36.24	$L_c + L_i$	82.41	82.80
$L_c + L_e$	81.48	80.45	$L_e + L_i$	82.90	**83.42**
$L_c + L_i + L_e$	82.28	82.59	-	-	-

5.1 Settings

ActivityNet v1.3 [3]**:** It has 200 activity classes, with 10,024/4,926/5,044 training/validation/testing videos. Each video in the dataset may have multiple activity instances. There are 15,410/7,654 annotated activity instances in the training/validation sets respectively. The videos were downsampled to 4 fps. We trained on the 15,410 annotated activity instances in the training set, and kept the top 3 scores for each of the 4,926 validation videos. We report the performances given by the official evaluation script.

Kinetics [16]**:** This dataset contains 306,245 video clips with 400 human action classes. Each clip is around 10 s, and is taken from different YouTube videos. Each class has 250–1000 clips, 50 validation clips and 100 testing clips. The optical flows were extracted using TV-L1 algorithm implemented in OpenCV. We did not downsample the frames on this dataset. The results were tested with official scripts on the validation set.

YouTube Birds and YouTube Cars: We only experiment on the RGB frames of the 2 datasets. Videos in YouTube Birds and YouTube Cars were downsampled to 2 fps and 4 fps respectively. We split the datasets as in Table 2.

Training: We trained the model in an end-to-end manner with PyTorch. The inputs to our model are the label and 4 randomly sampled RGB frames or flow stacks (with 5 flow fields) from 4 equally divided temporal segments. We adopted the same multi-scale cropping and random flipping to each frame as TSN for data augmentation. We used ImageNet pretrained ResNet-152 [9] provided by

PyTorch and ImageNet pretrained Inception-V3 [29] provided by Wang et al. [32] for fair comparisons. We used Adam [17] optimizer, with an initial learning rate 0.0002 and a learning rate decay factor 0.1 for both RGB and flow networks. Batch size is set to 256 on all datasets. For ActivityNet, YouTube Birds and YouTube Cars, we decayed the learning rate every 30 epochs and the total number of epochs was set to 120, while on Kinetics, we decayed learning rate every 13000 and 39000 iterations for RGB and flow networks respectively. The pre-trained convolutional layers were frozen until 30 epochs later on ActivityNet, YouTube Birds and YouTube Cars, and 5 epochs later on Kinetics. Dropout is added before each classification FC layer and set to 0.7/0.5 for RGB/flow respectively.

Testing: We followed the standard TSN testing protocol, where each video was divided into 25 temporal segments. One sample frame was taken from the middle of each temporal segment, and the sample was duplicated into 5 crops (top-left, top-right, bottom-left, bottom-right, center) in 2 directions (original + horizontal flipping), i.e., inputs were 250 images for each video.

5.2 Ablation Studies

First, we evaluated the performance of RRA model on ActivityNet v1.3 with different loss functions as proposed in Sect. 3.2. We enumerated all possible combinations of the 3 losses. For combinations with more than one loss, all losses are equally weighted. All variants used ResNet-152 as the base network, and were configured to have 4 glimpses. Table 3 lists the mAP of the concatenation score (Eq. 4), and the ensemble score (Eq. 6). We can see that when combined with another loss, L_e generally improves the performance. L_c, on the contrary, undermines the accuracy when combined with L_i or $L_i + L_e$. However, training with L_e alone does not converge. It is probably because without individual supervision for each glimpse, training all glimpses jointly is difficult to achieve. In addition, since L_c directly supervises on the concatenate score, L_c and $L_c + L_e$ have higher mAP_c than mAP_e. From the mAP values, we can see that for our model, L_i is the best single loss, and $L_e + L_i$ is the best combination.

Figure 5(3) shows the average loss of each epoch on the ActivityNet training set with different kinds of losses. We can see that adding L_e does not change the curves of L_i and $L_c + L_i$ so much, though it does improve the performance when added to them. To be noted, L_i achieved top-1 accuracy of 83.03 with frozen BN, a trick used in TSN. However, in our experiments, frozen BN does not improve the $L_e + L_i$ objective.

We also compared our model with parallel glimpses model. A k parallel glimpses model predicts k glimpses and concatenates the summary feature vectors for classification. More glimpses generally improve the performance, which is quite reasonable. And without surprise, our model is better than parallel glimpse models. The best mAP of 4 parallel glimpse model on ActivityNet v1.3 is 82.39, while the mAP our best RRA model is 83.42.

Second, we evaluated RRA model with different number of glimpses. In this experiment, the base network is ResNet-152, and the loss is $L_i + L_e$. Figure 5(1)

Table 4. Ablation mAPs on the ActivityNet v1.3 validation set, with ResNet-152. *Left*: changing number of glimpses from 1 to 5. *Right*: modifying RRA module into: 1. spatio-temporal average pooling instead of attention; 2. spatial attention and temporal average pooling; 3. no BN; 4. no ReLU; 5. no tanh; 6. -ReLU(x) instead of tanh(x). All the settings are the same as the 83.42 mAP model except for the specified variations.

#Glimpses	1	2	3	4	5
mAP	80.89	82.14	82.12	**83.42**	82.94

No.	1	2	3	4	5	6
mAP	80.20	81.97	82.41	83.15	82.75	82.75

shows the average training cross entropy of the ensemble score under different number of glimpses. Generally, with more glimpses, it converges more rapidly, and when glimpse number reaches 4, further increase in glimpse number brings much less acceleration in convergence, and the validation mAP starts to drop, as shown in Table 4 (Left). So in most of our experiments, we have set it to 4. Figure 5(2) shows the cross entropy of each glimpse's individual score, and the cross entropy of ensemble scores, which helps to explain why adding more glimpses accelerates the convergence of the ensemble score. Glimpses at later iterations converge more rapidly, which indicates redundancy is removed and they have extracted more discriminative features for classification. With more accurate glimpses, the ensemble score also becomes better, hence converging faster. To check the difference between the glimpses, the top-1 accuracy for each glimpse and their ensembling of the 4-glimpse model is 77.49, 79.09, 78.71, 78.92 and 78.81 respectively.

Third, we evaluate the role of each component in Fig. 3 by removing or changing one of them and validate the mAP on ActivityNet v1.3. The results are shown in Table 4 (Right). Attention plays the most important role, without which the mAP drops by 3.22. If replace the spatio-temporal attention with spatial attention and temporal average pooling, the mAP is better than average pooling, but still worse than spatio-temporal attention. The tanh activation is more suitable as the activation for the reduction as replacing it with a linear transform (removing it directly) or -ReLU(x) decreases the mAP by 0.67. Batch normalization and ReLU are also important components.

5.3 Comparison with State-of-the-Arts

After validating the configurations of the model, we fix the loss function as $L_i + L_e$, the number of glimpses to 4, then train and test on our two datasets along with the two action recognition datasets.

Table 5 (left) shows results on ActivityNet v1.3, where the results of state-of-the-art methods all come from published papers or tech reports. With only RGB frames, our network already out competes 3D CNN-like methods, including the recently proposed P3D [24] which uses ImageNet pretrained ResNets to help initialization. To be noted, our model on ActivityNet v1.3 only used 4 fps RGB frames for both training and validation due to physical limitations.

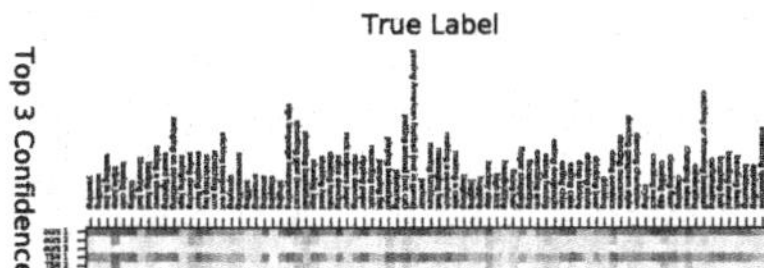

Ground Truth	Ours	TSN	Highest Confusion	Ours	TSN	Ours	TSN
beatboxing	0.456	0.344	playing harmonica	0.106	0.079	0.350	0.265
celebrating	0.420	0.307	applauding	0.079	0.072	0.341	0.235
cartwheeling	0.467	0.393	gymnastics tumbling	0.065	0.075	0.402	0.318
cooking egg	0.540	0.435	scram bling eggs	0.201	0.257	0.339	0.178
drinking	0.330	0.238	drinking beer	0.125	0.114	0.205	0.124
drinking shots	0.253	0.169	drinking beer	0.087	0.097	0.166	0.072

Fig. 6. *Left*: top-3 confidences for the classes. Darker color indicates higher confidence, and all highest-confidence predictions are correct. *Right*: confidences of the ground truth (first 3 columns) and the most-confusing class (next 3 columns), and the gaps (last 2 columns). Our model's mAP is 73.7 while the TSN's is 72.5. Both models' highest confidence is less than 0.5 in these cases.

Table 5. *Left*: Results on the ActivityNet v1.3 validation dataset, with ResNet-152. *Right*: Top-1 accuracies on the Kinetics dataset, with ResNet-152.

Method	top-1	mAP	top-3
IDT [31]	64.70	68.69	77.98
C3D [24]	65.80	67.68	81.16
P3D [24]	75.12	78.86	87.71
Ours	**78.81**	**83.42**	**91.88**

Method	RGB	Flow	Fusion
3D ResNet [8]	58.0	-	-
I3D [2]*	71.1	63.4	74.2
TSN [32]	72.5	62.8	**76.6**
Ours	**73.7**	**63.9**	76.1

Table 6. Comparing with methods on YouTube Birds and YouTube Cars.

Method	Birds	Cars
BN-Inception	60.13	61.96
I3D(Res50)	40.68	40.92
TSN [32]	72.361	74.340
Ours	**73.205**	**77.625**

We further evaluate our model on the challenging Kinetics dataset with both RGB and optical flow inputs. Table 5 (right) shows the comparison with state-of-the-art results on Kinetics dataset. Results of 3D ResNet, TSN and ours are on the validation set while I3D is on the test set. Results of TSN come from their latest project page. Our fusion result is achieved by adding RGB and flow scores directly. Our method surpasses TSN on both RGB and optical flow by significant margins, but the fusion result is a bit lower, which might due to sampling the same frames for both RGB and flow at validation.

To demonstrate the reduction of confusion brought by our model, in Fig. 6 we show some of TSN and our model's top-3 average confidences from the confusion matrix on confusing classes of the Kinetics dataset. Our model has a systematically higher average confidence on the correct classes and a clearer gap between correct and wrong classes.

Finally, Table 6 shows results on YouTube Birds and YouTube Cars. The BN-Inception model randomly takes one frame from each video during training and takes the middle frame for testing. Similarly, I3D(Res50) [2] is initialized by inflating an ImageNet-pretrained ResNet-50. It takes 32 consecutive frames at a random time or in the middle of the video for training and testing respectively. For TSN, we use its official implementation in PyTorch and the ImageNet pretrained Inception-V3 model provided by its authors for fair comparison. Our model also used the same Inception-V3 model for initialization. Our method surpasses TSN on these two datasets, since categories in fine-grained tasks often share many features in common and hence require a higher level of redundant

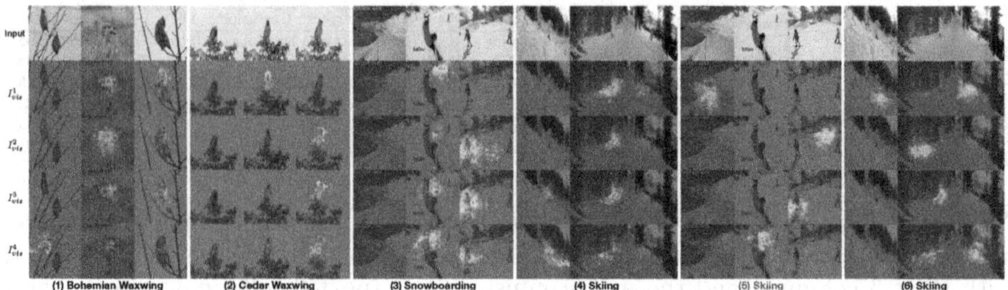

Fig. 7. Qualitative results. Red color on heat maps indicate higher attention. (1, 2) come from YouTube Birds, the rest come from ActivityNet. Green words are correct answers, red words are wrong answers. The answer of (5) should be SnowBoarding. (1)(2): Results of our model. The 2 birds are very similar, except for their bellies and tails. Our model firstly focus on texture of wings and faces (I_{vis}^1) to recognize general species, and then colors of bellies (I_{vis}^4) to distinguish the 2 species. (3, 4): Results of our model. The first glimpse/middle two/last glimpse tend to focus on backgrounds/human pose/both background and pose. (5, 6): Results of parallel attentions. In (5), all 4 glimpses happen to focus on background and the prediction is wrong since the glimpses are independent. (Color figure online)

reduction and to focus more on the informative locations and frames. A even larger margin is especially evident on YouTube Cars for the similar reason.

5.4 Qualitative Results

Figure 7 shows qualitative visualizations on YouTube Birds and ActivityNet v1.3 to demonstrate how the attention modules work. The heat maps are drawn with Eq. 7. We select two similar classes for each dataset. Our model attends to the correct region in all cases, while parallel attention fails in one case. The visualizations also demonstrate the complementarity of the glimpses given by our model. In (3, 4), its first glimpse tends to be more general, focusing on the surroundings, which is only a weak indicator of actions since both actions are on snow fields. Thanks to the specifically designed redundancy reduction structure, activations of channels representing background features have been weakened after the first iteration. Later glimpses focus more on the human pose, more helpful to identifying activities. However, it is the combination of background and human pose that gives more accurate predictions, so both are attended in the end. Comparing Fig. 7(3, 4) with (5, 6), the advantage of our model is evident. It may happen by chance for the parallel glimpses model that all glimpses focus on the background and being redundant, leading to a wrong prediction. However, in our model, the glimpses can cooperate and get rid of this problem.

6 Conclusion

We have demonstrated the Redundancy Reduction Attention (RRA) structure, which aims to extract features of multiple discriminative patterns for fine-grained video categorization. It consists of a spatio-temporal soft attention which summarizes the video, and a suppress-thresholding structure which decreases the redundant activations. Experiments on four video classification datasets demonstrate the effectiveness of the proposed structure. We also release two video datasets for fine-grained categorization, which will be helpful to the community in the future.

References

1. Cai, S., Zuo, W., Zhang, L.: Higher-order integration of hierarchical convolutional activations for fine-grained visual categorization. In: The IEEE International Conference on Computer Vision (ICCV), October 2017
2. Carreira, J., Zisserman, A.: Quo vadis, action recognition? A new model and the kinetics dataset. arXiv preprint arXiv:1705.07750 (2017)
3. Caba Heilbron, F., Escorcia, V., Ghanem, B., Carlos Niebles, J.: ActivityNet: a large-scale video benchmark for human activity understanding. In: Proceedings of the IEEE Conference on Computer Vision and Pattern Recognition, pp. 961–970 (2015)
4. Fu, J., Zheng, H., Mei, T.: Look closer to see better: recurrent attention convolutional neural network for fine-grained image recognition. In: The IEEE Conference on Computer Vision and Pattern Recognition (CVPR), July 2017
5. Fukui, A., Park, D.H., Yang, D., Rohrbach, A., Darrell, T., Rohrbach, M.: Multimodal compact bilinear pooling for visual question answering and visual grounding. arXiv preprint arXiv:1606.01847 (2016)
6. Gebru, T., Hoffman, J., Fei-Fei, L.: Fine-grained recognition in the wild: a multitask domain adaptation approach. In: The IEEE International Conference on Computer Vision (ICCV), October 2017
7. Girdhar, R., Ramanan, D.: Attentional pooling for action recognition. In: Advances in Neural Information Processing Systems, pp. 34–45 (2017)
8. Hara, K., Kataoka, H., Satoh, Y.: Learning spatio-temporal features with 3D residual networks for action recognition. arXiv preprint arXiv:1708.07632 (2017)
9. He, K., Zhang, X., Ren, S., Sun, J.: Deep residual learning for image recognition. In: Proceedings of the IEEE Conference on Computer Vision and Pattern Recognition, pp. 770–778 (2016)
10. Hu, J., Shen, L., Sun, G.: Squeeze-and-excitation networks. arXiv preprint arXiv:1709.01507 (2017)
11. Ioffe, S., Szegedy, C.: Batch normalization: accelerating deep network training by reducing internal covariate shift. In: International Conference on Machine Learning, pp. 448–456 (2015)
12. Jaderberg, M., Simonyan, K., Zisserman, A., et al.: Spatial transformer networks. In: Advances in Neural Information Processing Systems, pp. 2017–2025 (2015)
13. Ji, S., Xu, W., Yang, M., Yu, K.: 3D convolutional neural networks for human action recognition. IEEE Trans. Pattern Anal. Mach. Intell. **35**(1), 221–231 (2013)
14. Kar, A., Rai, N., Sikka, K., Sharma, G.: AdaScan: adaptive scan pooling in deep convolutional neural networks for human action recognition in videos. In: The IEEE Conference on Computer Vision and Pattern Recognition (CVPR), July 2017
15. Karpathy, A., Toderici, G., Shetty, S., Leung, T., Sukthankar, R., Fei-Fei, L.: Large-scale video classification with convolutional neural networks. In: Proceedings of the IEEE conference on Computer Vision and Pattern Recognition, pp. 1725–1732 (2014)

16. Kay, W., et al.: The kinetics human action video dataset. arXiv preprint arXiv:1705.06950 (2017)
17. Kingma, D., Ba, J.: Adam: a method for stochastic optimization. arXiv preprint arXiv:1412.6980 (2014)
18. Krause, J., Stark, M., Deng, J., Fei-Fei, L.: 3D object representations for fine-grained categorization. In: Proceedings of the IEEE International Conference on Computer Vision Workshops, pp. 554–561 (2013)
19. Larochelle, H., Hinton, G.E.: Learning to combine foveal glimpses with a third-order Boltzmann machine. In: Advances in Neural Information Processing Systems, pp. 1243–1251 (2010)
20. Li, Z., Gavrilyuk, K., Gavves, E., Jain, M., Snoek, C.G.: VideoLSTM convolves, attends and flows for action recognition. Comput. Vis. Image Underst. **166**, 41–50 (2017)
21. Lin, T.Y., RoyChowdhury, A., Maji, S.: Bilinear CNN models for fine-grained visual recognition. In: Proceedings of the IEEE International Conference on Computer Vision, pp. 1449–1457 (2015)
22. Long, X., Gan, C., de Melo, G., Wu, J., Liu, X., Wen, S.: Attention clusters: purely attention based local feature integration for video classification. In: Proceedings of the IEEE Conference on Computer Vision and Pattern Recognition, pp. 7834–7843 (2018)
23. Ma, C.Y., Kadav, A., Melvin, I., Kira, Z., AlRegib, G., Graf, H.P.: Attend and interact: higher-order object interactions for video understanding. arXiv preprint arXiv:1711.06330 (2017)
24. Qiu, Z., Yao, T., Mei, T.: Learning spatio-temporal representation with pseudo-3D residual networks. In: Proceedings of the IEEE Conference on Computer Vision and Pattern Recognition, pp. 5533–5541 (2017)
25. Saito, T., Kanezaki, A., Harada, T.: IBC127: video dataset for fine-grained bird classification. In: 2016 IEEE International Conference on Multimedia and Expo (ICME), pp. 1–6. IEEE (2016)
26. Sharma, S., Kiros, R., Salakhutdinov, R.: Action recognition using visual attention. arXiv preprint arXiv:1511.04119 (2015)
27. Simonyan, K., Zisserman, A.: Two-stream convolutional networks for action recognition in videos. In: Advances in Neural Information Processing Systems, pp. 568–576 (2014)
28. Sun, L., Jia, K., Chen, K., Yeung, D.Y., Shi, B.E., Savarese, S.: Lattice long short-term memory for human action recognition. arXiv preprint arXiv:1708.03958 (2017)
29. Szegedy, C., Vanhoucke, V., Ioffe, S., Shlens, J., Wojna, Z.: Rethinking the inception architecture for computer vision. In: Proceedings of the IEEE Conference on Computer Vision and Pattern Recognition, pp. 2818–2826 (2016)
30. Wah, C., Branson, S., Welinder, P., Perona, P., Belongie, S.: The Caltech-UCSD Birds-200-2011 dataset. Technical report (2011)
31. Wang, H., Schmid, C.: Action recognition with improved trajectories. In: Proceedings of the IEEE International Conference on Computer Vision, pp. 3551–3558 (2013)
32. Wang, L., et al.: Temporal Segment networks: towards good practices for deep action recognition. In: Leibe, B., Matas, J., Sebe, N., Welling, M. (eds.) ECCV 2016. LNCS, vol. 9912, pp. 20–36. Springer, Cham (2016). https://doi.org/10.1007/978-3-319-46484-8_2
33. Xu, K., et al.: Show, attend and tell: neural image caption generation with visual attention. In: International Conference on Machine Learning, pp. 2048–2057 (2015)

34. Zhang, H., et al.: SPDA-CNN: unifying semantic part detection and abstraction for fine-grained recognition. In: Proceedings of the IEEE Conference on Computer Vision and Pattern Recognition, pp. 1143–1152 (2016)
35. Zhang, N., Donahue, J., Girshick, R., Darrell, T.: Part-based R-CNNs for fine-grained category detection. In: Fleet, D., Pajdla, T., Schiele, B., Tuytelaars, T. (eds.) ECCV 2014. LNCS, vol. 8689, pp. 834–849. Springer, Cham (2014). https://doi.org/10.1007/978-3-319-10590-1_54
36. Zheng, H., Fu, J., Mei, T., Luo, J.: Learning multi-attention convolutional neural network for fine-grained image recognition. In: The IEEE International Conference on Computer Vision (ICCV), October 2017
37. Zhu, W., Hu, J., Sun, G., Cao, X., Qiao, Y.: A key volume mining deep framework for action recognition. In: Proceedings of the IEEE Conference on Computer Vision and Pattern Recognition, pp. 1991–1999 (2016)

Open Set Domain Adaptation by Backpropagation

Kuniaki Saito[1(✉)], Shohei Yamamoto[1], Yoshitaka Ushiku[1], and Tatsuya Harada[1,2]

[1] The University of Tokyo, Tokyo, Japan
{ksaito,yamamoto,ushiku,harada}@mi.t.u-tokyo.ac.jp
[2] RIKEN, Tokyo, Japan

Abstract. Numerous algorithms have been proposed for transferring knowledge from a label-rich domain (source) to a label-scarce domain (target). Most of them are proposed for closed-set scenario, where the source and the target domain completely share the class of their samples. However, in practice, a target domain can contain samples of classes that are not shared by the source domain. We call such classes the "unknown class" and algorithms that work well in the open set situation are very practical. However, most existing distribution matching methods for domain adaptation do not work well in this setting because unknown target samples should not be aligned with the source. In this paper, we propose a method for an open set domain adaptation scenario, which utilizes adversarial training. This approach allows to extract features that separate unknown target from known target samples. During training, we assign two options to the feature generator: aligning target samples with source known ones or rejecting them as unknown target ones. Our method was extensively evaluated and outperformed other methods with a large margin in most settings.

Keywords: Domain adaptation · Open set recognition
Adversarial learning

1 Introduction

Deep neural networks have demonstrated significant performance on many image recognition tasks [1]. One of the main problems of such methods is that basically, they cannot recognize samples as unknown, whose class is absent during training. We call such a class as an "unknown class" and the categories provided during training is referred to as the "known class." If these samples can be recognized as unknown, we can arrange noisy datasets and pick out the samples of interest from them. Moreover, if robots working in the real-world can detect unknown

Electronic supplementary material The online version of this chapter (https://doi.org/10.1007/978-3-030-01228-1_10) contains supplementary material, which is available to authorized users.

V. Ferrari et al. (Eds.): ECCV 2018, LNCS 11209, pp. 156–171, 2018.
https://doi.org/10.1007/978-3-030-01228-1_10

objects and ask annotators to give labels to them, these robots will be able to easily expand their knowledge. Therefore, the open set recognition is a very important problem.

In domain adaptation, we aim to train a classifier from a label-rich domain (source domain) and apply it to a label-scarce domain (target domain). Samples in different domains have diverse characteristics which degrade the performance of a classifier trained in a different domain. Most works on domain adaptation assume that samples in the target domain necessarily belong to the class of the source domain. However, this assumption is not realistic. Consider the setting of an unsupervised domain adaptation, where only unlabeled target samples are provided. We cannot know that the target samples necessarily belong to the class of the source domain because they are not given labels. Therefore, open set recognition algorithm is also required in domain adaptation. For this problem, the task called open set domain adaptation was recently proposed [2] where the target domain contains samples that do not belong to the class in the source domain as shown in the left of Fig. 1. The goal of the task is to classify unknown target samples as "unknown" and to classify known target samples into correct known categories. They [2] utilized unknown source samples to classify unknown target samples as unknown. However, collecting unknown source samples is also expensive because we must collect diverse and many unknown source samples to obtain the concept of "unknown." Then, in this paper, we present a more challenging open set domain adaptation (OSDA) that does not provide any unknown source samples, and we propose a method for it. That is, we propose a method where we have access to only known source samples and unlabeled target samples for open set domain adaptation as shown in the right of Fig. 1.

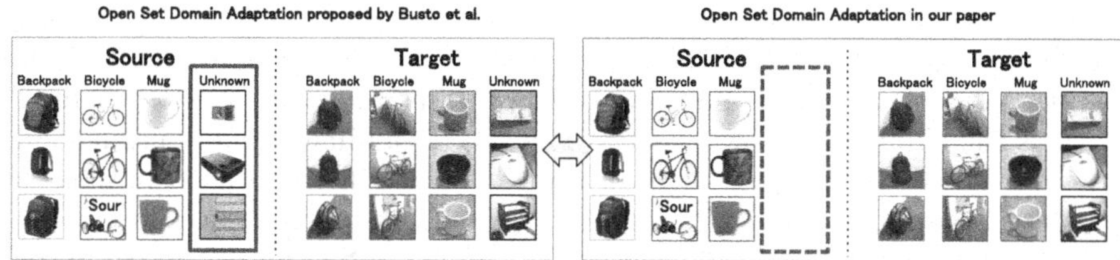

Fig. 1. A comparison between existing open set domain adaptation setting and our setting. Left: Existing setting of open set domain adaptation [2]. It is assumed that access is granted to the unknown source samples although the class of unknown source does not overlap with that of unknown target. Right: Our setting. We do not assume the accessibility to the unknown samples in the source domain. We propose a method that can be applied even when such samples are absent.

How can we solve the problem? We think that there are mainly two problems. First, in this situation, we do not have knowledge about which samples are the unknown samples. Thus, it seems difficult to delineate a boundary between known and unknown classes. The second problem is related to the domain's difference. Although we need to align target samples with source samples to reduce this domain's difference, unknown target samples cannot be aligned due to the absence of unknown samples in the source domain. The existing distribution matching method is aimed at matching the distribution of the target with that of the source. However, this method cannot be applied to our problem. In OSDA, we must reject unknown target samples without aligning them with the source.

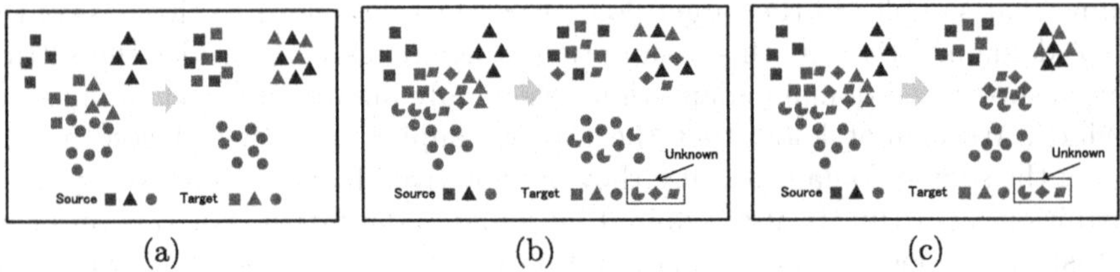

Fig. 2. (a): Closed set domain adaptation with distribution matching method. (b): Open set domain adaptation with distribution matching method. Unknown samples are aligned with known source samples. (c): Open set domain adaptation with our proposed method. Our method enables to learn features that can reject unknown target samples.

To solve the problems, we propose a new approach of adversarial learning that enables generator to separate target samples into known and unknown classes. A comparison with existing methods is shown in Fig. 2. Unlike the existing distribution alignment methods that only match the source and target distribution, our method facilitates the rejection of unknown target samples with high accuracy as well as the alignment of known target samples with known source samples. We assume that we have two players in our method, i.e., the feature generator and the classifier. The feature generator generates features from inputs, and the classifier takes the features and outputs $K+1$ dimension probability, where K indicates the number of known classes. The $K+1$ th dimension of output indicates the probability for the unknown class. The classifier is trained to make a boundary between source and target samples whereas the feature generator is trained to make target samples far from the boundary. Specifically, we train the classifier to output probability t for unknown class, where $0 < t < 1$. We can build a decision boundary for unknown samples by weakly training a classifier to classify target samples as unknown. To deceive the classifier, the feature generator has two options to increase or to decrease the probability. As such, we assign two options to the feature generator: aligning them with samples in the source domain or rejecting them as unknown.

The contribution of our paper is as follows.

1. We present the open set domain adaptation where unknown source samples are not provided. The setting is more challenging than the existing setting.
2. We propose a new adversarial learning method for the problem. The method enables training of the feature generator to learn representations which can separate unknown target samples from known ones.

3. We evaluate our method on adaptation for digits and objects datasets and demonstrate its effectiveness. Additionally, the effectiveness of our method was demonstrated in standard open set recognition experiments where we are provided unlabeled unknown samples during training.

2 Related Work

In this section, we briefly introduce methods for domain adaptation and open set recognition.

2.1 Domain Adaptation

Domain adaptation for image recognition has attracted attention for transferring the knowledge between different domains and reducing the cost for annotating a large number of images in diverse domains. Benchmark datasets are released [3], and many methods for unsupervised domain adaptation and semi-supervised domain adaptation have been proposed [4–11]. As previously indicated, unsupervised and semi-supervised domain adaptation focus on the situation where different domains completely share the class of their samples, which may not be practical especially in unsupervised domain adaptation.

One of the effective methods for unsupervised domain adaptation are distribution matching based methods [4,6,12–14]. Each domain has unique characteristics of their features, which decrease the performance of classifiers trained on a different domain. Therefore, by matching the distributions of features between different domains, they aim to extract domain-invariantly discriminative features. This technique is widely used in training neural networks for domain adaptation tasks [4,15]. The representative of the methods harnesses techniques used in Generative Adversarial Networks (GAN) [16]. GAN trains a classifier to judge whether input images are fake or real images whereas the image generator is trained to deceive it. In domain adaptation, similar to GAN, the classifier is trained to judge whether the features of the middle layers are from a target or a source domain whereas the feature generator is trained to deceive it. Variants of the method and extensions to the generative models for domain adaptation have been proposed [13,17–20]. Maximum Mean Discrepancy (MMD) [21] is also a representative way to measure the distance between domains. The distance is utilized to train domain-invariantly effective neural networks, and its variants are proposed [6,7,22,23].

The problem is that these methods do not assume that the target domain has categories that are not included in the source domain. The methods are not supposed to perform well on our open set domain adaptation scenario. This is because all target samples including unknown classes will be aligned with source samples. Therefore, this makes it difficult to detect unknown target samples.

In contrast, our method enables to categorize unknown target samples into unknown class, although we are not provided any labeled target unknown samples during training. We will compare our method with MMD and domain classifier based methods in experiments. We utilize the technique of distribution matching methods technique to achieve open set recognition. However, the main difference is that our method allows the feature generator to reject some target samples as outliers.

2.2 Open Set Recognition

A wide variety of research has been conducted to reject outliers while correctly classifying inliers during testing. Multi-class open set SVM is proposed by [24]. They propose to reject unknown samples by training SVM that assign probabilistic decision scores. The aim is to reject unknown samples using a threshold probability value. In addition, method of harnessing deep neural networks for open set recognition was proposed [25]. They introduced OpenMax layer, which estimates the probability of an input being from an unknown class. Moreover, to give supervision of the unknown samples, a method to generate these samples was proposed [26]. The method utilizes GAN to generate unknown samples and use it to train neural networks, then combined it with OpenMax layer. In order to recognize unknown samples as unknown during testing, these methods defined a threshold value to reject unknown samples. Also, they do not assume that they can utilize unlabeled samples including known and unknown classes during training.

In our work, we propose a method that enables us to deal with the open set recognition problem in the setting of the domain adaptation. In this setting, the distribution of the known samples in the target domain is different from that of the samples in the source domain, which makes the task more difficult.

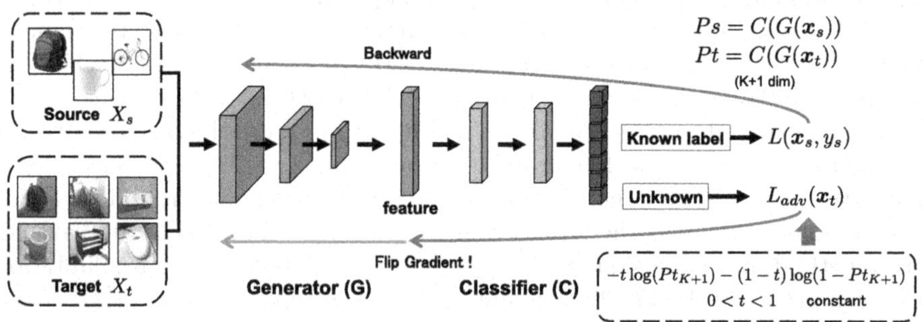

Fig. 3. The proposed method for open set domain adaptation. The network is trained to correctly classify source samples. For target samples, the classifier is trained to output t for the probability of the unknown class whereas the generator is trained to deceive it.

3 Method

First, we provide an overview of our method, then we explain the actual training procedure and provide an analysis of our method by comparing it with existing open set recognition algorithm. The overview is shown in Fig. 3.

3.1 Problem Setting and Overall Idea

We assume that a labeled source image $\boldsymbol{x}_s$ and a corresponding label y_s drawn from a set of labeled source images $\{X_s, Y_s\}$ are available, as well as an unlabeled target image $\boldsymbol{x}_t$ drawn from unlabeled target images X_t. The source images are drawn only from known classes whereas target images can be drawn from unknown class. In our method, we train a feature generation network G, which takes inputs $\boldsymbol{x}_s$ or $\boldsymbol{x}_t$, and a network C, which takes features from G and classifies them into $K+1$ classes, where the K denotes the number of known categories. Therefore, C outputs a $K+1$-dimensional vector of logits $\{l_1, l_2, l_3 ... l_{K+1}\}$ per one sample.

The logits are then converted to class probabilities by applying the softmax function. Namely, the probability of $\boldsymbol{x}$ being classified into class j is denoted by $p(y=j|\boldsymbol{x}) = \frac{\exp(l_j)}{\sum_{k=1}^{K+1}\exp(l_k)}$. $1 \sim$ K dimensions indicate the probability for the known classes whereas $K+1$ dimension indicates that for the unknown class. We use the notation $p(\boldsymbol{y}|\boldsymbol{x})$ to denote the $K+1$-dimensional probabilistic output for input $\boldsymbol{x}$.

Our goal is to correctly categorize known target samples into corresponding known class and recognize unknown target samples as unknown. We have to construct a decision boundary for the unknown class, although we are not given any information about the class. Therefore, we propose to make a pseudo decision boundary for unknown class by weakly training a classifier to recognize target samples as unknown class. Then, we train a feature generator to deceive the classifier. The important thing is that feature generator has to separate unknown target samples from known target samples. If we train a classifier to output $p(y=K+1|\boldsymbol{x}_t) = 1.0$ and train the generator to deceive it, then ultimate objective of the generator is to completely match the distribution of the target with that of the source. Therefore, the generator will only try to decrease the value of the probability for unknown class. This method is used for training Generative Adversarial Networks for semi-supervised learning [27] and should be useful for unsupervised domain adaptation. However, this method cannot be directly applied to separate unknown samples from known samples.

Then, to solve the difficulty, we propose to train the classifier to output $p(y=K+1|\boldsymbol{x}_t) = t$, where $0 < t < 1$. We train the generator to deceive the classifier. That is, the objective of the generator is to maximize the error of the classifier. In order to increase the error, the generator can choose to increase the value of the probability for an unknown class, which means that the sample is rejected as unknown. For example, consider when t is set as a very small value, it should be easier for generator to increase the probability for an unknown class than to decrease it to maximize the error of the classifier. Similarly, it can choose to decrease it to make $p(y=K+1|\boldsymbol{x}_t)$ lower than t, which means that the sample is aligned with source. In summary, the generator will be able to choose whether a target sample should be aligned with the source or should be rejected. In all our experiments, we set the value of t as 0.5. If t is larger than 0.5, the sample is necessarily recognized as unknown. Thus, we assume that this value can be a good boundary between known and unknown. In our experiment, we will analyze the behavior of our model when this value is varied.

Algorithm 1. Minibatch training of the proposed method.

for the number of training iterations **do**
- Sample minibatch of m source samples $\{\{\boldsymbol{x}_s, y_s\}^{(1)}, \ldots, \{\boldsymbol{x}_s, y_s\}^{(m)}\}$ from $\{X_s, Y_s\}$.
- Sample minibatch of m target samples $\{\boldsymbol{x}_t^{(1)}, \ldots, \boldsymbol{x}_t^{(m)}\}$ from X_t.

Calculate $L_s(\boldsymbol{x}_s, y_s)$ by cross-entropy loss and $L_{adv}(\boldsymbol{x}_t)$ following Eq. 3.
Update the parameter of G and C following Eq. 4, Eq. 5. We used gradient reversal layer for this operation.

end for

3.2 Training Procedure

We begin by demonstrating how we trained the model with our method. First, we trained both the classifier and the generator to categorize source samples correctly. We use a standard cross-entropy loss for this purpose.

$$L_s(\boldsymbol{x}_s, y_s) = -\log(p(y = y_s|\boldsymbol{x}_s)) \tag{1}$$

$$p(y = y_s|\boldsymbol{x}_s) = (C \circ G(\boldsymbol{x}_s))_{y_s} \tag{2}$$

In order to train a classifier to make a boundary for an unknown sample, we propose to utilize a binary cross entropy loss.

$$L_{adv}(\boldsymbol{x}_t) = -t\log(p(y = K+1|\boldsymbol{x}_t)) - (1-t)\log(1 - p(y = K+1|\boldsymbol{x}_t)), \tag{3}$$

where t is set as 0.5 in our experiment. The overall training objective is,

$$\min_C L_s(\boldsymbol{x}_s, y_s) + L_{adv}(\boldsymbol{x}_t) \tag{4}$$

$$\min_G L_s(\boldsymbol{x}_s, y_s) - L_{adv}(\boldsymbol{x}_t) \tag{5}$$

The classifier attempts to set the value of $p(y = K+1|\boldsymbol{x}_t)$ equal to t whereas the generator attempts to maximize the value of $L_{adv}(\boldsymbol{x}_t)$. Thus, it attempts to make the value of $p(y = K+1|\boldsymbol{x}_t)$ different from t. In order to efficiently calculate the gradient for $L_{adv}(\boldsymbol{x}_t)$, we utilize a gradient reversal layer proposed by [4]. The layer enables flipping of the sign of the gradient during the backward process. Therefore, we can update the parameters of the classifier and generator simultaneously. The algorithm is shown in Algorithm 1.

3.3 Comparison with Existing Methods

We think that there are three major differences from existing methods. Since most existing methods do not have access to unknown samples during training, they cannot train feature extractors to learn features to reject them. In contrast, in our setting, unknown target samples are included in training samples. Under the condition, our method can train feature extractors to reject unknown samples. In addition, existing methods such as open set SVM reject unknown samples if the probability of any known class for a testing sample is not larger than the threshold value. The value is a pre-defined one and does not change across testing samples. However, with regard to our method, we can consider that the threshold value changes across samples because our model assigns different classification outputs to different samples. Thirdly, the feature extractor is informed of the pseudo decision boundary between known and unknown classes. Thus, feature extractors can recognize the distance between each target sample and the boundary for the unknown class. It attempts to make it far from the boundary. It makes representations such that the samples similar to the known source samples are aligned with known class whereas ones dissimilar to known source samples are separated from them.

4 Experiments

We conduct experiments on Office [3], VisDA [28] and digits datasets.

4.1 Implementation Detail

We trained the classifier and generator using the features obtained from AlexNet [1] and VGGNet [29] pre-trained on ImageNet [30]. In the experiments on both Office and VisDA dataset, we did not update the parameters of the pre-trained networks. We constructed fully-connected layers with 100 hidden units after the FC8 layers. Batch Normalization [31] and Leaky-ReLU layer were employed for stable training. We used momentum SGD with a learning rate 1.0×10^{-3}, where the momentum was set as 0.9. Other details are shown in our supplementary material due to a limit of space.

We implemented three baselines in the experiments. The first baseline is an open set SVM (OSVM) [24]. OSVM utilizes the threshold probability to recognize samples as unknown if the predicted probability is lower than the threshold for any class. We first trained CNN only using source samples, then, use it as a feature extractor. Features are extracted from the output of generator networks when using OSVM. OSVM does not require unknown samples during training. Therefore, we trained OSVM only using source samples and tested them on the target samples. The second one is a combination of Maximum Mean Discrepancy(MMD) [21] based training method for neural networks [6] and OSVM. MMD is used to match the distribution between different domains in unsupervised domain adaptation. For an open set recognition, we trained the networks with MMD and trained OSVM using the features obtained by the networks. A comparison with this baseline should indicate how our proposed method is different from existing distribution matching methods. The third one is a combination of a domain classifier based method, BP [4] and OSVM. BP is also a representative of a distribution matching method. As was done for MMD, we first trained BP and extracted features to train OSVM. We used the same network architecture to train the baseline models. The experiments were run a total of 3 times for each method, and the average score was reported. We report the standard deviation only in Table 2 because of the limit of space.

4.2 Experiments on Office

11 Class Classification. Firstly, we evaluated our method using Office following the protocol proposed by [2]. The dataset consists of 31 classes, and 10 classes were selected as shared classes. The classes are also common in the Caltech dataset [8]. In alphabetical order, 21–31 classes are used as unknown samples in the target domain. The classes 11–20 are used as unknown samples in the source domain in [2]. However, we did not use it because our method does not require such samples. We have to correctly classify samples in the target domain into 10 shared classes or unknown class. In total, 11 class classification was performed. Accuracy averaged over all classes is denoted as OS in all Tables. $\mathrm{OS} = \frac{1}{K+1}\sum_{k=1}^{K+1} Acc_k$, where K indicates number of known classes and $K+1$ th class is an unknown class. We also show the accuracy measured only on the known classes of the target domain (OS*). $\mathrm{OS}^* = \frac{1}{K}\sum_{k=1}^{K} Acc_k$. Following [2], we show the accuracy averaged over the classes in the OS and OS*. We also compared our method with a method proposed by [2]. Their method is developed for a situation where unknown samples in the source domain are available. However, they applied their method using OSVM when unknown source samples were absent. In order to better understand the performance of our method, we also show the results which utilized the unknown source samples during training. The values are cited from [2].

The results are shown in Table 1. Compared with the baseline methods, our method exhibits better performance in almost all scenarios. The accuracy of the OS is almost always better than that of OS*, which means that many known target samples are regarded as unknown. This is because OSVM is trained to detect outliers and is likely to classify target samples as unknown. When comparing the performance of OSVM and MMD+OSVM, we can see that the usage of MMD does not always boost the performance. The existence of unknown target samples seems to perturb the correct feature alignment. Visualizations of features are shown in our supplementary material.

Number of Unknown Samples and Accuracy. We further investigate the accuracy when the number of target samples varies in the adaptation from DSLR to Amazon. We randomly chose unknown target samples from Amazon and varied the ratio of the unknown samples. The accuracy of OS is shown in Fig. 4(a). When the ratio changes, our method seems to perform well.

Table 1. Accuracy (%) of each method in 10 shared class situation. A, D and W correspond to Amazon, DSLR and Webcam respectively.

	Adaptation scenario													
	A-D		A-W		D-A		D-W		W-A		W-D		AVG	
	OS	OS*	OS	OS*	OS	OS*	OS	OS*	OS	OS*	OS	OS*	OS	OS*
Method w/ unknown classes in source domain (AlexNet)														
BP [4]	78.3	77.3	75.9	73.8	57.6	54.1	89.8	88.9	64.0	61.8	98.7	98.0	77.4	75.7
ATI-λ [2]	79.8	79.2	77.6	76.5	71.3	70.0	93.5	93.2	76.7	76.5	98.3	99.2	82.9	82.4
Method w/o unknown classes in source domain (AlexNet)														
OSVM	59.6	59.1	57.1	55.0	14.3	5.9	44.1	39.3	13.0	4.5	62.5	59.2	40.6	37.1
MMD+OSVM	47.8	44.3	41.5	36.2	9.9	0.9	34.4	28.4	11.5	2.7	62.0	58.5	34.5	28.5
BP+OSVM	40.8	35.6	31.0	24.3	10.4	1.5	33.6	27.3	11.5	2.7	49.7	44.8	29.5	22.7
ATI-λ [2]+OSVM	72.0	-	65.3	-	**66.4**	-	82.2	-	71.6	-	92.7	-	75.0	-
Ours	**76.6**	**76.4**	**74.9**	**74.3**	62.5	**62.3**	**94.4**	**94.6**	**81.4**	**81.2**	**96.8**	**96.9**	**81.1**	**80.9**
Method w/o unknown classes in source domain (VGGNet)														
OSVM	82.1	83.9	75.9	75.8	38.0	33.1	57.8	54.4	54.5	50.7	83.6	83.3	65.3	63.5
MMD+OSVM	84.4	**85.8**	75.6	75.7	41.3	35.9	61.9	58.7	50.1	45.6	84.3	83.4	66.3	64.2
BP+OSVM	83.1	84.7	76.3	76.1	41.6	36.5	61.1	57.7	53.7	49.9	82.9	82.0	66.4	64.5
Ours	**85.8**	**85.8**	**85.3**	**85.1**	**88.7**	**89.6**	**94.6**	**95.2**	**83.4**	**83.1**	**97.1**	**97.3**	**89.1**	**89.4**

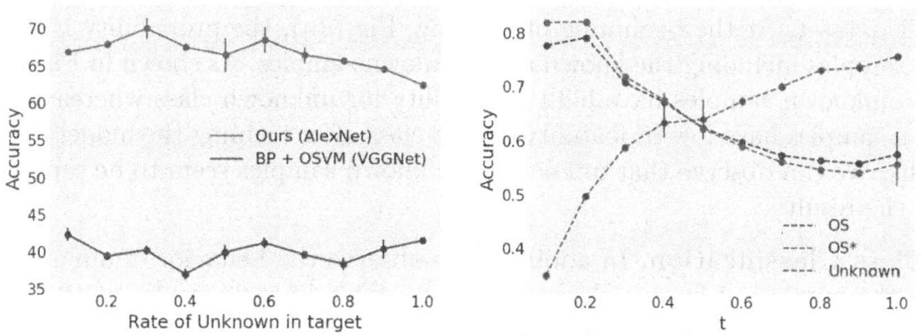

(a) Ratio of unknown samples

(b) Value of t and accuracy

Fig. 4. (a): The behavior of our method when we changed the ratio of unknown samples. As we increase the number of unknown target samples, the accuracy decreases. (b): The change of accuracy with the change of the value t. The accuracy for unknown target samples is denoted as green line. As t increases, target samples are likely classified as "unknown". However, the entire accuracy OS and OS* decrease. (Color figure online)

Value of t. We observe the behavior of our model when the training signal, t in Eq. 3 is varied. As we mentioned in the method section, When t is equal to 1, the objective of the generator is to match the whole distribution of the target features with that of the source, which is exactly the same as an existing distribution matching method. Accordingly, the accuracy should degrade in this

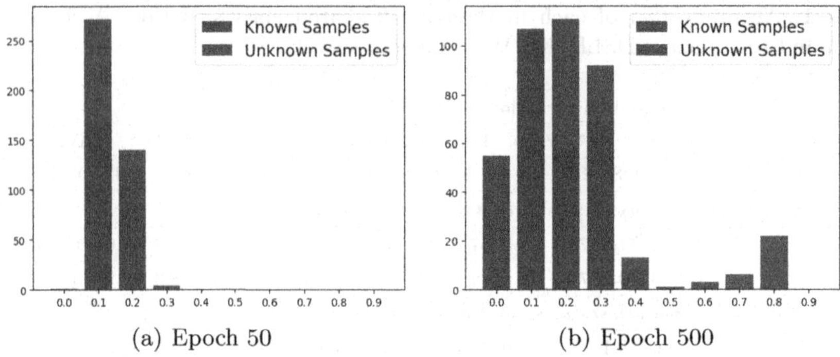

(a) Epoch 50 (b) Epoch 500

Fig. 5. (a)(b): Frequency diagram of the probability of target samples for unknown class in adaptation from Webcam to DSLR.

case. According to Fig. 5(b), as we increase the value of t, the accuracies of OS and OS* decrease and the overall accuracy increases. This result means that the model does not learn representations where unknown samples can be distinguished from known samples.

Probability for Unknown Class. In Fig. 5(a)(b), frequency diagram of the probability for an unknown class is shown in the adaptation from Webcam to DSLR dataset. At the beginning of training, Fig. 5(a), the probability is low in most samples including the known and unknown samples. As shown in Fig. 5(b), many unknown samples have high probability for unknown class whereas many known samples have low probability for the class after training the model for 500 epochs. We can observe that unknown and known samples seem to be separated from the result.

21 Class Classification. In addition, we observe the behavior of our method when the number of known classes increases. We add the samples of 10 classes which were not used in the previous setting. The 10 classes are the ones used as unknown samples in the source domain in [2]. In total, we conducted 21 class classification experiments in this setting. We also evaluate our method on VGG Network. With regard to other details of the experiment, we followed the setting of the previous experiment. The results are shown in Table 2. Compared to the baseline methods, the superiority of our method is clear. The usefulness of MMD and BP is not observed for this setting too. An examination of the result of adaptation from Amazon to Webcam (A-W) reveals that the accuracy of other methods is better than our approach based on OS* and OS. However, "ALL" of the measurements are inferior to our method. The value of "ALL" indicates the accuracy measured for all the samples without averaging over classes. Thus, the result means that existing methods are likely to recognize target samples as one of known classes in this setting. From the results, the effectiveness of our method is verified when the number of class increases.

Table 2. Accuracy (%) of experiments on Office dataset in 20 shared class situation. We used VGG Network to obtain the results.

	Adaptation Scenario								
	A-D			A-W			D-A		
	OS	OS*	ALL	OS	OS*	ALL	OS	OS*	ALL
OSVM	73.6±0.4	**75.8**±0.6	57.6	**72.0**±0.5	**74.1**±0.5	58.0	44.9±0.1	43.9±0.1	51.1
MMD + OSVM	72.1±0.9	73.9±1.0	57.8	69.1±0.8	71.2±0.9	54.9	29.8±0.6	26.5±0.6	50.3
BP + OSVM	70.4±0.2	72.1±0.3	57.1	70.9±0.5	72.9±0.4	57.6	30.9±0.2	27.6±0.2	51.3
Ours	**74.8**±0.5	74.6 ±0.5	**73.9**	66.8±3.5	66.1±3.7	**69.7**	**64.6**±1.2	**65.9**±4.9	**68.5**

	D-W			W-A			W-D			AVG		
	OS	OS*	ALL	OS	OS*	ALL	OS	OS*	ALL	OS	OS*	ALL
OSVM	63.1±1.1	61.9±1.2	69.9	34.0±0.9	31.8±1.3	48.3	82.9±2.3	82.9±1.7	84.2	61.8	61.7	61.5
MMD + OSVM	58.3±0.6	56.6±0.6	68.8	39.7±2.1	37.1±2.4	55.9	84.5±1.2	84.2±1.3	87.2	58.9	58.2	62.3
BP+OSVM	63.2±2.8	61.7±3.0	71.3	40.0±2.7	37.4±3.0	56.0	83.5±0.8	83.1±0.8	86.4	59.8	59.1	63.2
Ours	**83.1**±0.6	**82.5**±0.6	**84.9**	**65.9**±0.1	**65.3**±0.2	**69.0**	**92.8**±0.2	**93.3**±0.2	**90.3**	**74.7**	**74.6**	**76.1**

4.3 Experiments on VisDA Dataset

We further evaluate our method on adaptation from synthetic images to real images. VisDA dataset [28] consists of 12 categories in total. The source domain images are collected by rendering 3D models whereas the target domain images consist of real images. We used the training split as the source domain and validation one as the target domain. We choose 6 categories (bicycle, bus, car, motorcycle, train and truck) from them and set other 6 categories as the unknown class (aeroplane, horse, knife, person, plant and skateboard). The training procedure of the networks is the same as that used for Office dataset.

Table 3. Accuracy (%) on VisDA dataset. The accuracy per class is shown.

Method	Bcycle	Bus	Car	Mcycle	Train	Truck	Unknwn	Avg	Avg knwn
AlexNet									
OSVM	4.8	45.0	44.2	43.5	59.0	10.5	57.4	37.8	34.5
OSVM+MMD	0.2	30.9	49.1	54.8	56.1	8.1	61.3	37.2	33.2
OSVM+BP	9.1	50.5	**53.9**	79.8	69.0	8.1	42.5	44.7	45.1
Ours	**48.0**	**67.4**	39.2	**80.2**	**69.4**	**24.9**	**80.3**	**58.5**	**54.8**
VGGNet									
OSVM	31.7	51.6	66.5	70.4	**88.5**	20.8	38.0	52.5	54.9
OSVM+MMD	39.0	50.1	64.2	79.9	86.6	16.3	44.8	54.4	56.0
OSVM+BP	31.8	56.6	**71.7**	77.4	87.0	22.3	41.9	55.5	57.8
Ours	**51.1**	**67.1**	42.8	**84.2**	81.8	**28.0**	**85.1**	**62.9**	**59.2**

The results are shown in Table 3. Our method outperformed the other methods in most cases. *Avg* indicates the accuracy averaged over all classes. *Avg known* indicates the accuracy averaged over only known classes. In both evaluation metrics, our method showed better performance, which means that our method is better both at matching distributions between known samples and

Table 4. Examples of recognition results on VisDA dataset.

Ground Truth Class → Predicted Class			
Known → Unknown ×	**Unknown → Known ×**	**Known → Known √**	**Unknown → Unknown √**
Train → Unknown 	Unknown → Motorcycle 	Truck → Truck 	Unknown → Unknown 
Motorcycle → Unknown 	Unknown → Motorcycle 	Bicycle → Bicycle 	Unknown → Unknown 
Car → Unknown 	Unknown → Motorcycle 	Motorcycle → Motorcycle 	Unknown → Unknown 

rejecting unknown samples in open set domain adaptation setting. In this setting, the known classes and unknown class should have different characteristics because known classes are picked up from vehicles and unknown samples are from others. Thus, in our method, the accuracy for the unknown class is better than that for the known classes. We further show the examples of images in Table 4. Some of the known samples are recognized as unknown. As we can see from the three images, most of them contain multiple classes of objects or are hidden by other objects. Then, look at the second columns from the left. The images are categorized as motorcycle though they are unknown. The images of motorcycle often contain persons and the appearance of the person and horse have similar features to such images. In the third and fourth columns, we demonstrate the correctly classified known and unknown samples. If the most part of the image is occupied by the object of interest, the classification seems to be successful.

4.4 Experiments on Digits Dataset

We also evaluate our method on digits dataset. We used SVHN [32], USPS [33] and MNIST for this experiment. In this experiment, we conducted 3 scenarios in total. Namely, adaptation from SVHN to MNIST, USPS to MNIST and MNIST to USPS. These are common scenarios in unsupervised domain adaptation. The numbers from 0 to 4 were set as known categories whereas the other numbers were set as unknown categories. In this experiment, we also compared

Table 5. Accuracy (%) of experiments on digits datasets.

Method	SVHN-MNIST				USPS-MNIST				MNIST-USPS				Average			
	OS	OS*	ALL	UNK	OS	OS*	ALL	UNK	OS	OS*	ALL	UNK	OS	OS*	ALL	UNK
OSVM	54.3	63.1	37.4	10.5	43.1	32.3	63.5	97.5	79.8	77.9	84.2	**89.0**	59.1	57.7	61.7	65.7
MMD+OSVM	55.9	64.7	39.1	12.2	62.8	58.9	69.5	82.1	80.0	79.8	81.3	81.0	68.0	68.8	66.3	58.4
BP+OSVM	62.9	**75.3**	39.2	0.7	84.4	**92.4**	72.9	0.9	33.8	40.5	21.4	44.3	60.4	69.4	44.5	15.3
Ours	**63.0**	59.1	**71.0**	**82.3**	**92.3**	91.2	**94.4**	**97.6**	**92.1**	**94.9**	**88.1**	78.0	**82.4**	**81.7**	**84.5**	**85.9**

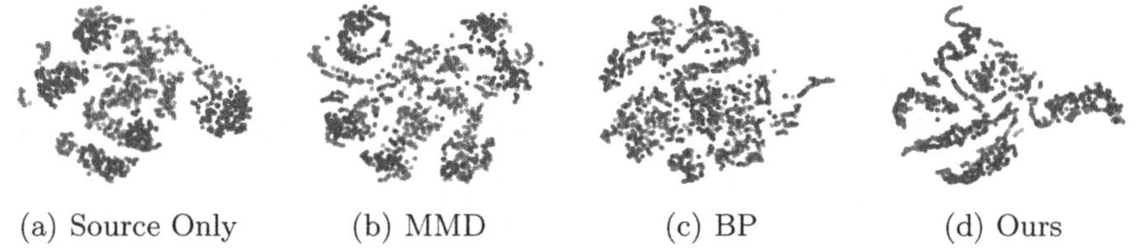

(a) Source Only (b) MMD (c) BP (d) Ours

Fig. 6. Feature visualization of adaptation from USPS to MNIST. Visualization of source and target features. **Blue points** are source features. **Red points** are target known features. **Green points** are target unknown features. (Color figure online)

our method with two baselines, OSVM and MMD combined with OSVM. With regard to OSVM, we first trained the network using source known samples and extracted features using the network, then applied OSVM to the features. When training CNN, we used Adam [34] with a learning rate 2.0×10^{-5}.

Adaptation from SVHN to MNIST. In this experiment, we used all SVHN training samples with numbers in the range from 0 to 4 to train the network. We used all samples in the training splits of MNIST.

Adaptation Between USPS and MNIST. When using the datasets as a source domain, we used all training samples with number from 0 to 4. With regard to the target datasets, we used all training samples.

Result. The quantitative results are shown in Table 5. Our proposed method outperformed other methods. In particular, with regard to the adaptation between USPS and MNIST, our method achieves accurate recognition. In contrast, the adaptation performance on for SVHN to MNIST is worse compared to the adaptation between USPS and MNIST. Large domain difference between SVHN and MNIST causes the bad performance. We also visualized the learned features in Fig. 6. Unknown classes (5–9) are separated using our method whereas known classes are aligned with source samples. The method based on distribution matching such as BP [4] fails in adaptation for this open set scenario. When examining the learned features, we can observe that BP attempts to match all of the target features with source features. Consequently, unknown target samples are made difficult to detect, which is obvious from the quantitative results for BP. The accuracy of UNK in BP+OSVM is much worse than the other methods.

5 Conclusion

In this paper, we proposed a novel adversarial learning method for open set domain adaptation. Our proposed method enables the generation of features that can separate unknown target samples from known target samples, which is definitely different from existing distribution matching methods. Moreover, our approach does not require unknown source samples. Through extensive experiments, the effectiveness of our method has been verified. Improving our method for the open set recognition will be our future work.

Acknowledgements. The work was partially supported by CREST, JST, and was partially funded by the ImPACT Program of the Council for Science, Technology, and Innovation (Cabinet Office, Government of Japan). We would like to thank Kate Saenko for her great advice on our paper.

References

1. Krizhevsky, A., Sutskever, I., Hinton, G.E.: ImageNet classification with deep convolutional neural networks. In: NIPS (2012)
2. Busto, P.P., Gall, J.: Open set domain adaptation. In: ICCV (2017)
3. Saenko, K., Kulis, B., Fritz, M., Darrell, T.: Adapting visual category models to new domains. In: Daniilidis, K., Maragos, P., Paragios, N. (eds.) ECCV 2010. LNCS, vol. 6314, pp. 213–226. Springer, Heidelberg (2010). https://doi.org/10.1007/978-3-642-15561-1_16
4. Ganin, Y., Lempitsky, V.: Unsupervised domain adaptation by backpropagation. In: ICML (2015)
5. Gong, B., Grauman, K., Sha, F.: Connecting the dots with landmarks: discriminatively learning domain-invariant features for unsupervised domain adaptation. In: ICML (2013)
6. Long, M., Cao, Y., Wang, J., Jordan, M.I.: Learning transferable features with deep adaptation networks. In: ICML (2015)
7. Long, M., Zhu, H., Wang, J., Jordan, M.I.: Unsupervised domain adaptation with residual transfer networks. In: NIPS (2016)
8. Gong, B., Shi, Y., Sha, F., Grauman, K.: Geodesic flow kernel for unsupervised domain adaptation. In: CVPR (2012)
9. Saito, K., Ushiku, Y., Harada, T.: Asymmetric tri-training for unsupervised domain adaptation. In: ICML (2017)
10. Sener, O., Song, H.O., Saxena, A., Savarese, S.: Learning transferrable representations for unsupervised domain adaptation. In: NIPS (2016)
11. Ghifary, M., Kleijn, W.B., Zhang, M., Balduzzi, D., Li, W.: Deep reconstruction-classification networks for unsupervised domain adaptation. In: Leibe, B., Matas, J., Sebe, N., Welling, M. (eds.) ECCV 2016. LNCS, vol. 9908, pp. 597–613. Springer, Cham (2016). https://doi.org/10.1007/978-3-319-46493-0_36
12. Tzeng, E., Hoffman, J., Zhang, N., Saenko, K., Darrell, T.: Deep domain confusion: maximizing for domain invariance. arXiv preprint arXiv:1412.3474 (2014)
13. Bousmalis, K., Silberman, N., Dohan, D., Erhan, D., Krishnan, D.: Unsupervised pixel-level domain adaptation with generative adversarial networks. In: CVPR (2017)

14. Saito, K., Watanabe, K., Ushiku, Y., Harada, T.: Maximum classifier discrepancy for unsupervised domain adaptation. arXiv preprint arXiv:1712.02560 (2017)
15. Hoffman, J., Wang, D., Yu, F., Darrell, T.: FCNs in the wild: pixel-level adversarial and constraint-based adaptation. arXiv preprint arXiv:1612.02649 (2016)
16. Goodfellow, I., et al.: Generative adversarial nets. In: NIPS (2014)
17. Bousmalis, K., Trigeorgis, G., Silberman, N., Krishnan, D., Erhan, D.: Domain separation networks. In: NIPS (2016)
18. Tzeng, E., Hoffman, J., Saenko, K., Darrell, T.: Adversarial discriminative domain adaptation. In: CVPR (2017)
19. Taigman, Y., Polyak, A., Wolf, L.: Unsupervised cross-domain image generation. In: ICLR (2016)
20. Liu, M.Y., Breuel, T., Kautz, J.: Unsupervised image-to-image translation networks. In: NIPS (2017)
21. Gretton, A., Borgwardt, K.M., Rasch, M., Schölkopf, B., Smola, A.J.: A kernel method for the two-sample-problem. In: NIPS (2007)
22. Long, M., Wang, J., Jordan, M.I.: Deep transfer learning with joint adaptation networks. In: ICML (2017)
23. Yan, H., Ding, Y., Li, P., Wang, Q., Xu, Y., Zuo, W.: Mind the class weight bias: weighted maximum mean discrepancy for unsupervised domain adaptation. In: CVPR (2017)
24. Jain, L.P., Scheirer, W.J., Boult, T.E.: Multi-class open set recognition using probability of inclusion. In: Fleet, D., Pajdla, T., Schiele, B., Tuytelaars, T. (eds.) ECCV 2014. LNCS, vol. 8691, pp. 393–409. Springer, Cham (2014). https://doi.org/10.1007/978-3-319-10578-9_26
25. Bendale, A., Boult, T.E.: Towards open set deep networks. In: CVPR (2016)
26. Ge, Z., Demyanov, S., Chen, Z., Garnavi, R.: Generative openmax for multi-class open set classification. In: BMVC (2017)
27. Salimans, T., Goodfellow, I., Zaremba, W., Cheung, V., Radford, A., Chen, X.: Improved techniques for training GANs. In: NIPS (2016)
28. Peng, X., Usman, B., Kaushik, N., Hoffman, J., Wang, D., Saenko, K.: VisDA: the visual domain adaptation challenge. arXiv preprint arXiv:1710.06924 (2017)
29. Simonyan, K., Zisserman, A.: Very deep convolutional networks for large-scale image recognition. arXiv preprint arXiv:1409.1556 (2014)
30. Deng, J., Dong, W., Socher, R., Li, L.J., Li, K., Fei-Fei, L.: ImageNet: a large-scale hierarchical image database. In: CVPR (2009)
31. Ioffe, S., Szegedy, C.: Batch normalization: accelerating deep network training by reducing internal covariate shift. In: ICML (2015)
32. Netzer, Y., Wang, T., Coates, A., Bissacco, A., Wu, B., Ng, A.Y.: Reading digits in natural images with unsupervised feature learning. In: NIPS Workshop on Deep Learning and Unsupervised Feature Learning (2011)
33. LeCun, Y., Bottou, L., Bengio, Y., Haffner, P.: Gradient-based learning applied to document recognition. Proc. IEEE **86**(11), 2278–2324 (1998)
34. Kingma, D., Ba, J.: Adam: a method for stochastic optimization. arXiv preprint arXiv:1412.6980 (2014)

Deep Feature Pyramid Reconfiguration for Object Detection

Tao Kong[1(✉)], Fuchun Sun[1], Wenbing Huang[2], and Huaping Liu[1]

[1] Department of Computer Science and Technology, Beijing National Research Center for Information Science and Technology (BNRist), Tsinghua University, Beijing, China
kt14@mails.tsinghua.edu.cn, {fcsun,hpliu}@mail.tsinghua.edu.cn
[2] Tencent AI Lab, Shenzhen, China
hwenbing@126.com

Abstract. State-of-the-art object detectors usually learn multi-scale representations to get better results by employing feature pyramids. However, the current designs for feature pyramids are still inefficient to integrate the semantic information over different scales. In this paper, we begin by investigating current feature pyramids solutions, and then reformulate the feature pyramid construction as the feature reconfiguration process. Finally, we propose a novel reconfiguration architecture to combine low-level representations with high-level semantic features in a highly-nonlinear yet efficient way. In particular, our architecture which consists of global attention and local reconfigurations, is able to gather task-oriented features across different spatial locations and scales, globally and locally. Both the global attention and local reconfiguration are lightweight, in-place, and end-to-end trainable. Using this method in the basic SSD system, our models achieve consistent and significant boosts compared with the original model and its other variations, without losing real-time processing speed.

Keywords: Object detection · Feature pyramids
Global-local reconfiguration

1 Introduction

Detecting objects at vastly different scales from images is a fundamental challenge in computer vision [1]. One traditional way to solve this issue is to build feature pyramids upon image pyramids directly. Despite the inefficiency, this kind of approaches have been applied for object detection and many other tasks along with hand-engineered features [7,12].

We focus on detecting objects with deep ConvNets in this paper. Aside from being capable of representing higher-level semantics, ConvNets are also robust to variance in scale, thus making it possible to detect multi-scale objects from features computed on a single scale input [16,38]. However, recent works suggest

V. Ferrari et al. (Eds.): ECCV 2018, LNCS 11209, pp. 172–188, 2018.
https://doi.org/10.1007/978-3-030-01228-1_11

that taking pyramidal representations into account can further boost the detection performance [15,19,29]. This is due to its principle advantage of producing multi-scale feature representations in which all levels are semantically strong, including the high-resolution features.

There are several typical works exploring the feature pyramid representations for object detection. The Single Shot Detector (SSD) [33] is one of the first attempts on using such technique in ConvNets. Given one input image, SSD combines the predictions from multiple feature layers with different resolutions to naturally handle objects of various sizes. However, SSD fails to capture deep semantics for shallow-layer feature maps, since the bottom-up pathway in SSD can learn strong features only for deep layers but not for the shallow ones. This causes the key bottleneck of SSD for detecting small instances.

To overcome the disadvantage of SSD and make the networks more robust to object scales, recent works (e.g., FPN [29], DSSD [14], RON [25] and TDM [43]) propose to combine low-resolution and semantically-strong features with high-resolution and semantically-weak features via lateral connections in a top-down pathway. In contrast to the bottom-up fashion in SSD, the lateral connections pass the semantic information down to the shallow layers one by one, thus enhancing the detection ability of shallow-layer features. Such technology is successfully used in object detection [14,30], segmentation [18], pose estimation [5,46], etc.

Ideally, the pyramid features in ConvNets should: (1) reuse multi-scale features from different layers of a single network, and (2) improve features with strong semantics at all scales. The FPN works [29] satisfy these conditions by lateral connections. Nevertheless, the FPN, as demonstrated by our analysis in Sect. 3, is actually equivalent to a linear combination of the feature hierarchy. Yet, the linear combination of features is too simple to capture highly-nonlinear patterns for more complicate and practical cases. Several works are trying to develop more suitable connection manners [24,45,47], or to add more operations before combination [27].

The basic motivation of this paper is to enable the networks learn information of interest for each pyramid level in a more flexible way, given a ConvNet's feature hierarchy. To achieve this goal, we explicitly reformulate the feature pyramid construction process as feature reconfiguration functions in a highly-nonlinear yet efficient way. To be specific, our pyramid construction employs a global attention to emphasize global information of the full image followed by a local reconfiguration to model local patch within the receptive field. The resulting pyramid representation is capable of spreading strong semantics to all scales. Compared to previous studies including SSD and FPN-like models, our pyramid construction is more advantageous in two aspects: (1) the global-local reconfigurations are non-linear transformations, thus depicting more expressive power; (2) the pyramidal precessing for all scales are performed simultaneously and are hence more efficient than the layer-by-layer transformation (e.g. in lateral connections).

In our experiments, we compare different feature pyramid strategies within SSD architecture, and demonstrate the proposed method works more competitive in terms of accuracy and efficiency. The main contributions of this paper are summarized as follows:

- We propose the global attention and local reconfiguration for building feature pyramids to enhance multi-scale representations with semantically strong information;
- We compare and analysis popular feature pyramid methodologies within the standard SSD framework, and demonstrate that the proposed reconfiguration works more effective;
- The proposed method achieves the state-of-the-art results on standard object detection benchmarks (i.e., PASCAL VOC 2007, PASCAL VOC 2012 and MS COCO) without losing real-time processing speed.

2 Related Work

Hand-Engineered Feature Pyramids: Prior to the widely development of deep convolutional networks, hand-craft features such as HOG [44] and SIFT [34] are popular for feature extraction. To make them scale-invariant, these features are computed over image pyramids [9,13]. Several attempts have been performed on image pyramids for the sake of efficient computation [4,7,8]. The sliding window methods over multi-scale feature pyramids are usually applied in object detection [10,13].

Deep Object Detectors: Benefited by the success of deep ConvNets, modern object detectors like R-CNN [17] and Overfeat [40] lead dramatic improvement for object detection. Particularly, OverFeat adopts a similar strategy to early face detectors by applying a ConvNet as the sliding window detector on image pyramids; R-CNN employs a region proposal-based strategy and classifies each scale-normalized proposal with a ConvNet. The SPP-Net [19] and Fast R-CNN [16] speed up the R-CNN approach with RoI-Pooling that allows the classification layers to reuse the CNN feature maps. Since then, Faster R-CNN [38] and R-FCN [6] replace the region proposal step with lightweight networks to deliver a complete end-to-end system. More recently, Redmon et al. [36,37] propose a method named YOLO to predict bounding boxes and associate class probabilities in a single step.

Deep Feature Pyramids: To make the detection more reliable, researchers usually adopt multi-scale representations by inputting images with multiple resolutions during training and testing [3,19,20]. Clearly, the image pyramid methods are very time-consuming as them require to compute the features on each of image scale independently and thus the ConvNet features can not be reused. Recently, a number of approaches improve the detection performance by combining predictions from different layers in a single ConvNet. For instance, the

HyperNet [26] and ION [3] combine features from multiple layers before making detection. To detect objects of various sizes, the SSD [33] spreads out default boxes of different scales to multiple layers of different resolutions within a single ConvNets. So far, the SSD is a desired choice for object detection satisfying the speed-vs-accuracy trade-off [23]. More recently, the lateral connection (or reverse connection) is becoming popular and used in object detection [14,25,29]. The main purpose of lateral connection is to enrich the semantic information of shallow layers via the top-down pathway. In contrast to such layer-by-layer connection, this paper develops a flexible framework to integrate the semantic knowledge of multiple layers in a global-local scheme.

3 Method

In this section, we firstly revisit the SSD detector, then consider the recent improvements of lateral connection. Finally, we present our feature pyramid reconfiguration methodology (Fig. 1).

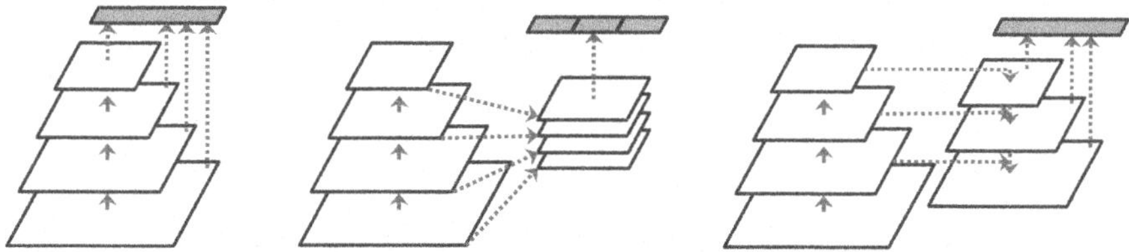

Fig. 1. Different feature pyramid construction frameworks. left: SSD uses pyramidal feature hierarchy computed by a ConvNet as if it is a featurized image pyramid; middle: Some object segmentation works produce final detection feature maps by directly combining features from multiple layers; right: FPN-like frameworks enforce shallow layers by top-down pathway and lateral connections.

ConvNet Feature Hierarchy: The object detection models based on ConvNets usually adopt a backbone network (such as VGG-16, ResNets). Consider a single image x_0 that is passed through a convolutional network. The network comprises L layers, each of which is implemented by a non-linear transformation $\mathcal{F}_l(\cdot)$, where l indexes the layer. $\mathcal{F}_l(\cdot)$ is a combination transforms such as convolution, pooling, ReLU, etc. We denote the output of the lth layer as x_l. The total backbone network outputs are expressed as $X_{net} = \{x_1, x_2, ..., x_L\}$.

Without feature hierarchy, object detectors such as Faster R-CNN [38] use one deep and semantic layer such as x_L to perform object detection. In SSD [33], the prediction feature map sets can be expressed as

$$X_{pred} = \{x_P, x_{P+1}, \dots, x_L\}, \tag{1}$$

where $P \gg 1$[1]. Here, the deep feature maps x_L learn high-semantic abstraction. When $P < l < L$, x_l becomes shallower thus has more low-level features. SSD

[1] For VGG-16 based model, $P = 23$ since we begin to predict from *conv4_3* layer.

uses deeper layers to detect large instances, while uses the shallow and high-resolution layers to detect small ones[2]. The high-resolution maps with limited-semantic information harm their representational capacity for object recognition. It misses the opportunity to reuse deeper and semantic information when detecting small instances, which we show is the key bottleneck to boost the performance.

Lateral Connection: To enrich the semantic information of shallow layers, one way is to add features from the deeper layers[3]. Taking the FPN manner [29] as an example, we get

$$\begin{aligned} x_L^{'} &= x_L, \\ x_{L-1}^{'} &= \alpha_{L-1} \cdot x_{L-1} + \beta_{L-1} \cdot x_L, \\ x_{L-2}^{'} &= \alpha_{L-2} \cdot x_{L-2} + \beta_{L-2} \cdot x_{L-1}^{'}, \\ &= \alpha_{L-2} \cdot x_{L-2} + \beta_{L-2}\alpha_{L-1} \cdot x_{L-1} + \beta_{L-2}\beta_{L-1} \cdot x_L, \end{aligned} \tag{2}$$

where α, β are weights. Without loss of generality,

$$x_l^{'} = \sum_{l=P}^{L} w_l \cdot x_l, \tag{3}$$

where w_l is the generated final weights for l^{th} layer output after similar polynomial expansions. Finally, the features used for detection are expressed as:

$$X_{pred}^{'} = \{x_P^{'}, x_{P+1}^{'}, \ldots, x_L^{'}\}. \tag{4}$$

From Eq. 3 we see that the final features $x_l^{'}$ is equivalent to the linear combination of $x_l, x_{l+1}, \ldots, x_L$. The linear combination with deeper feature hierarchy is one way to improve information of a specific shallow layer. And the linear model can achieve a good extent of abstraction when the samples of the latent concepts are linearly separable. However, the feature hierarchy for detection often lives on a non-linear manifold, therefore the representations that capture these concepts are generally highly non-linear function of the input [22,28,32]. It's representation power, as we show next, is not enough for the complex task of object detection.

3.1 Deep Feature Reconfiguration

Given the deep feature hierarchy $X = [x_P, x_{P+1}, \ldots, x_L]$ of a ConvNet, the key problem of object detection framework is to generate suitable features for each

[2] Here the 'small' means that the proportion of objects in the image is small, not the actual instance size.

[3] When the resolutions of the two layers are not the same, usually upsample and linear projection are carried out before combination.

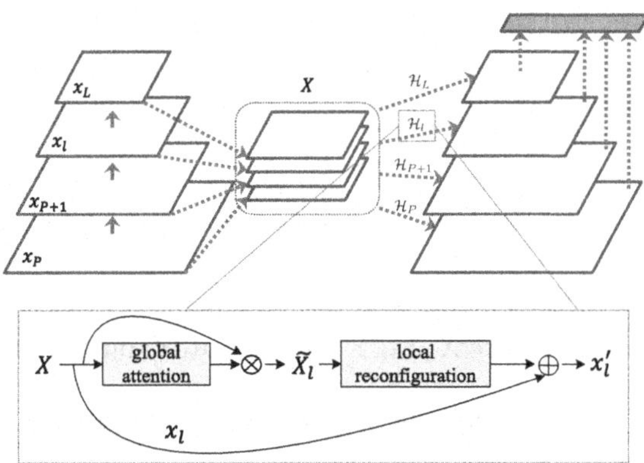

Fig. 2. Top: Overview of the proposed feature pyramid building networks. We firstly combine multiple feature maps, then generate features at a specific level, finally detect objects at multiple scales. Down: A building block illustrating the global attention and local reconfiguration.

level of detector. In this paper, the feature generating process at l^{th} level is viewed as a non-linear transformation of the given feature hierarchy (Fig. 2):

$$x_l^{'} = \mathcal{H}_l(X) \tag{5}$$

where X is the feature hierarchy considered for multi-scale detection. For ease of implementation, we concatenate the multiple inputs of $\mathcal{H}_l(\cdot)$ in Eq. 5 into a single tensor before following transformations[4].

Given no priors about the distributions of the latent concepts of the feature hierarchy, it is desirable to use a universal function approximator for feature extraction of each scale. The function should also keep the spatial consistency, since the detector will activate at the corresponding locations. *The final features for each level are non-linear transformations for the feature hierarchy, in which learnable parameters are shared between different spatial locations.*

In this paper, we formulate the feature transformation process $\mathcal{H}_l(\cdot)$ as global attention and local reconfiguration problems. Both global attention and local reconfiguration are implemented by a light-weight network so they could be embedded into the ConvNets and learned end-to-end. The global and local operations are also complementary to each other, since they deal with the feature hierarchy from different scales.

Global Attention for Feature Hierarchy. Given the feature hierarchy, the aim of the global part is to emphasise informative features and suppress less useful ones globally for a specific scale. In this paper, we apply the Squeeze-and-Excitation block [22] as the basic module. One Squeeze-and-Excitation block

[4] For a target scale which has $W \times H$ spatial resolution, adaptive sampling is carried out before concatenation.

consists of two steps, *squeeze* and *excitation*. For the lth level layer, the *squeeze* stage is formulated as a global pooling operation on each channel of X which has $W \times H \times C$ dimensions:

$$z_l^c = \frac{1}{W \times H} \sum_{i=1}^{W} \sum_{j=1}^{H} x_l^c(i,j) \tag{6}$$

where $x_l^c(i,j)$ specifies one element at c^{th} channel, i^{th} column and j^{th} row. If there are C channels in feature X, Eq. 8 will generate C output elements, denoted as $\mathbf{z}_l$.

The excitation stage is two fully-connected layers followed by sigmoid activation with input $\mathbf{z}_l$:

$$\mathbf{s}_l = \sigma(W_l^1 \delta(W_2^l \mathbf{z}_l)) \tag{7}$$

where δ refers to the ReLU function, σ is the sigmoid activation, $W_l^1 \in R^{\frac{c}{r}}$ and $W_2^2 \in R^c$. r is set to 16 to make dimensionality-reduction. The final output of the block is obtained by rescaling the input X with the activations:

$$\tilde{\mathbf{x}}_l^c = s_l^c \otimes \mathbf{x}^c \tag{8}$$

then $\tilde{X}_l = [\tilde{x}_l^P, \tilde{x}_l^{P+1}, \ldots, \tilde{x}_l^L]$, $\otimes$ denotes channel-wise multiplication. More details can be referred to the SENets [22] paper.

The original SE block is developed for explicitly modelling interdependencies between channels, and shows great success in object recognition [2]. In contrast, we apply it to emphasise channel-level hierarchy features and suppress less useful ones. By dynamically adopting conditions on the input hierarchy, SE Block helps to boost feature discriminability and select more useful information globally.

Local Reconfiguration. The local reconfiguration network maps the feature hierarchy patch to an output feature patch, and is shared among all local receptive fields. The output feature maps are obtained by sliding the operation over the input. In this work, we design a residual learn block as the instantiation of the micro network, which is a universal function approximator and trainable by back-propagation (Fig. 3).

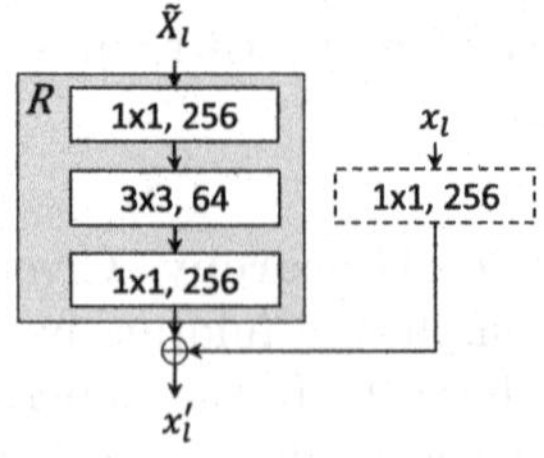

Fig. 3. A building block illustrating the local reconfiguration for level l.

Formally, one local reconfiguration is defined as:

$$x_l^{'} = R(\tilde{X}_l) + W_l x_l \tag{9}$$

where W_l is a linear projection to match the dimensions[5]. $R(\cdot)$ represents the residual mapping that improves the semantics to be learned.

Discussion. A direct way to generate feature pyramids is just use the term $R(\cdot)$ in Eq. 9. However, as demonstrated in [20], it is easier to optimize the residual mapping than to optimize the desired underlying mapping. Our experiments in Sect. 4.1 also prove this hypothesize.

We note there are some differences between our residual learn module and that proposed in ResNets [20]. Our hypothesize is that the semantic information is distributed among feature hierarchy and the residual learn block could select additional information by optimization. While the purpose of the residual learn in [20] is to gain accuracy by increasing network depth. Another difference is that the input of the residual learning is the feature hierarchy, while in [20], the input is one level of convolutional output.

The form of the residual function $R(\cdot)$ is also flexible. In this paper, we involve a function that has three layers (Fig. 3), while more layers are possible. The element-wise addition is performed on two feature maps, channel by channel. Because all levels of the pyramid use shared operations for detection, we fix the feature dimension (numbers of channels, denoted as d) in all the feature maps. We set $d = 256$ in this paper and thus all layers used for prediction have 256-channel outputs.

4 Experiments

We conduct experiments on three widely used benchmarks: PASCAL VOC 2007, PASCAL VOC 2012 [11] and MS COCO datasets [31]. All network backbones are pretrained on the ImageNet1k classification set [39] and fine-tuned on the detection dataset. We use the pre-trained VGG-16 and ResNets models that are publicly available[6]. Our experiments are based on re-implementation of SSD [33], Faster R-CNN [38] and Feature Pyramid Networks [29] using PyTorch [35]. For the SSD framework, all layers in $\boldsymbol{X}$ are resized to the spatial size of layer conv8_2 in VGG and conv6_x in ResNet-101 to keep consistency with DSSD. For the Faster R-CNN pipeline, the resized spatial size is as same as the conv4_3 layer in both VGG and ResNet-101 backbones.

4.1 PASCAL VOC 2007

Implementation Details. All models are trained on the VOC 2007 and VOC 2012 trainval sets, and tested on the VOC 2007 test set. For *one-stage* SSD, we

[5] When dimensions are the same, there is no need to use it, denoted as dotted line in Fig. 3.

[6] https://github.com/pytorch/vision.

set the learn rate to 10^{-3} for the first 160 epochs, and decay it to 10^{-4} and 10^{-5} for another 40 and 40 epochs. We use the default batch size 32 in training, and use VGG-16 as the backbone networks for all the ablation study experiments on the PASCAL VOC dataset. For *two-stage* Faster R-CNN experiments, we follow the training strategies introduced in [38]. We also report the results of ResNets used in these models.

Baselines. For fair comparisons with original SSD and its feature pyramid variations, we conduct two baselines: Original SSD and SSD with feature lateral connections. In Table 1, the original SSD scores 77.5%, which is the same as that reported in [33]. Adding lateral connections in SSD improves results to 78.5% (SSD+lateral). When using the global and local reconfiguration strategy proposed above, the result is improved to 79.6%, which is 1.6% better than SSD with lateral connection. In the next, we discuss the ablation study in more details.

Table 1. Effectiveness of various designs with SSD300.

Method	Backbone	FPS	mAP(%)
SSD (Caffe) [33]	VGG-16	46	77.5
SSD (ours-re)	VGG-16	44	77.5
SSD+lateral	VGG-16	37	78.5
SSD+Local only	VGG-16	40	79.0
SSD+Local only(no res)	VGG-16	40	78.6
SSD+Global-Local	VGG-16	39.5	**79.6**

How Important Is Global Attention? In Table 1, the fourth row shows the results of our model without the global attention. With this modification, we remove the global attention part and directly add local transformation into the feature hierarchy. Without global attention, the result drops to 79.0% mAP (-0.6%). The global attention makes the network to focus more on features with suitable semantics and helps detecting instance with variation.

Comparison with the Lateral Connections. Adding global and local reconfiguration to SSD improves the result to 79.6%, which is 2.1% better than SSD and 1.1% better than SSD with lateral connection. This is because there are large semantic gaps between different levels on the bottom-up pyramid. And the global and local reconfigurations help the detectors to select more suitable feature maps. This issue cannot be simply remedied by just lateral connections. We note that only adding local reconfiguration, the result is better than lateral connection (+0.5%).

Only Use the Term $R(\cdot)$. One way to generate the final feature pyramids is just use the term $R(\cdot)$. in Eq. 9. Compared with residual learn block, the result drops 0.4%. The residual learn block can avoid the gradients of the objective function to directly flow into the backbone network, thus gives more opportunity to better model the feature hierarchy.

Use All Feature Hierarchy or Just Deeper Layers? In Eq. 3, the lateral connection only considers feature maps that are deeper (and same) than corresponding levels. To better compare our method with lateral connection, we conduct a experiment that only consider the deep layers too. Other settings are the same with the previous baselines. We find that just using deeper features drops accuracy by a small margin (−0.2%). We think the difference is that when using the total feature hierarchy, the deeper layers also have more opportunities to re-organize its features, and has more potential for boosting results, similar conclusions are also drawn from the most recent work of PANet [32].

Accuracy vs. Speed. We present the inference speed of different models in the third column of Table 1. The speed is evaluated with batch size 1 on a machine with NVIDIA Titan X, CUDA 8.0 and cuDNN v5. Our model has a 2.7% accuracy gain with 39.5 *fps*. Compared with the lateral connection based SSD, our model shows higher accuracy and faster speed. In lateral connection based model, the pyramid layers are generated serially, thus last constructed layer considered for detection becomes the speed bottleneck ($x_P^{'}$ in Eq. 4). In our design, all final pyramid maps are generated simultaneously, and is more efficient.

Under Faster R-CNN Pipeline. To validate the generation of the proposed feature reconfiguration method, we conduct experiment under *two-stage* Faster R-CNN pipeline. In Table 2, Faster R-CNN with ResNet-101 get mAP of 78.9%. Feature Pyramid Networks with lateral connection improve the result to 79.8% (+0.9%). When replacing the lateral connection with global-local transformation, we get score of 80.6% (+1.8%). This result indicate that our global-and-local reconfiguration is also effective in *two-stage* object detection frameworks and could improve its performance.

Comparison with Other State-of-the-Arts. Table 3 shows our results on VOC2007 test set based on SSD [33]. Our model with 300 × 300 achieves 79.6% mAP, which is much better than baseline method SSD300 (77.5%) and on par with SSD512. Enlarging the input image to 512 × 512 improves the result to 81.1%. Notably our model is much better than other methods which try to include context information such as MRCNN [10] and ION [3]. When replace the backbone network from VGG-16 to ResNet-101, our model with 512 × 512 scores 82.4% without bells and whistles, which is much better than the one-stage DSSD [14] and two-stage R-FCN [6].

Table 2. Effectiveness of various designs within Faster R-CNN.

Method	Backbone	mAP(%)
Faster [38]	VGG-16	73.2
Faster [6]	ResNet-101	76.4
Faster(ours-re)	ResNet-50	77.6
Faster(ours-re)	ResNet-101	78.9
Faster+FPNs	ResNet-50	78.8
Faster+FPNs	ResNet-101	79.8
Faster+Global-Local	ResNet-50	79.4
Faster+Global-Local	ResNet-101	**80.6**

Table 3. PASCAL VOC 2007 test detection results. All models are trained with 07 + 12 (07 trainval + 12 trainval). The entries with the best APs for each object category are bold-faced.

Method	backbone	mAP(%)	aero	bike	bird	boat	bottle	bus	car	cat	chair	cow	table	dog	horse	mbike	person	plant	sheep	sofa	train	tv
Faster[39]	VGG-16	73.2	76.5	79.0	70.9	65.5	52.1	83.1	84.7	86.4	52.0	81.9	65.7	84.8	84.6	77.5	76.7	38.8	73.6	73.9	83.0	72.6
ION[3]	VGG-16	76.5	79.2	79.2	77.4	69.8	55.7	85.2	84.2	89.8	57.5	78.5	73.8	87.8	85.9	81.3	75.3	49.7	76.9	74.6	85.2	82.1
MRCNN[16]	VGGNet	78.2	80.3	84.1	78.5	70.8	68.5	88.0	85.9	87.8	60.3	85.2	73.7	87.2	86.5	85.0	76.4	48.5	76.3	75.5	85.0	81.0
Faster[39]	ResNet-101	76.4	79.8	80.7	76.2	68.3	55.9	85.1	85.3	89.8	56.7	87.8	69.4	88.3	88.9	80.9	78.4	41.7	78.6	79.8	85.3	72.0
R-FCN[6]	ResNet-101	80.5	79.9	87.2	81.5	72.0	**69.8**	86.8	88.5	89.8	**67.0**	88.1	74.5	89.8	**90.6**	79.9	81.2	53.7	81.8	**81.5**	85.9	79.9
SSD300[34]	VGG-16	77.5	79.5	83.9	76.0	69.6	50.5	87.0	85.7	88.1	60.3	81.5	77.0	86.1	87.5	83.9	79.4	52.3	77.9	79.5	87.6	76.8
SSD512[34]	VGG-16	79.5	84.8	85.1	81.5	73.0	57.8	87.8	88.3	87.4	63.5	85.4	73.2	86.2	86.7	83.9	82.5	55.6	81.7	79.0	86.6	80.0
StairNet[46]	VGG-16	78.8	81.3	85.4	77.8	72.1	59.2	86.4	86.8	87.5	62.7	85.7	76.0	84.1	88.4	86.1	78.8	54.8	77.4	79.0	88.3	79.2
RON320[26]	VGG-16	76.6	79.4	84.3	75.5	69.5	56.9	83.7	84.0	87.4	57.9	81.3	74.1	84.1	85.3	83.5	77.8	49.2	76.7	77.3	86.7	77.2
DSSD321[15]	ResNet-101	78.6	81.9	84.9	80.5	68.4	53.9	85.6	86.2	88.9	61.1	83.5	78.7	86.7	88.7	86.7	79.7	51.7	78.0	80.9	87.2	79.4
DSSD513[15]	ResNet-101	81.5	86.6	86.2	**82.6**	74.9	62.5	**89.0**	88.7	88.8	65.2	87.0	78.7	88.2	89.0	87.5	83.7	51.1	86.3	81.6	85.7	**83.7**
Ours300	VGG-16	79.6	84.5	85.5	77.2	72.1	53.9	87.6	87.9	89.4	63.8	86.1	76.1	87.3	88.8	86.7	80.0	54.6	80.5	81.2	88.9	80.2
Ours512	VGG-16	81.1	90.0	87.0	79.9	75.1	60.3	88.8	**89.6**	89.6	65.8	**88.4**	79.4	87.5	90.1	85.6	81.9	54.8	79.0	80.8	87.2	79.9
Ours300	ResNet-101	80.2	89.3	84.9	79.9	**75.6**	55.4	88.2	88.6	88.6	63.3	87.9	78.8	87.3	87.7	85.5	80.5	55.4	81.1	79.6	87.8	78.5
Ours512	ResNet-101	**82.4**	**92.0**	**88.2**	81.1	71.2	65.7	88.2	87.9	**92.2**	65.8	86.5	**79.4**	**90.3**	90.4	89.3	**88.6**	**59.4**	**88.4**	75.3	**89.2**	78.5

To understand the performance of our method in more detail, we use the detection analysis tool from [21]. Figure 4 shows that our model can detect various object categories with high quality. The recall is higher than 90%, and is much higher with the 'weak' (0.1 jaccard overlap) criteria.

4.2 PASCAL VOC 2012

For VOC2012 task, we follow the setting of VOC2007 and with a few differences described here. We use 07++12 consisting of VOC2007 trainval, VOC2007 test, and VOC2012 trainval for training and VOC2012 test for testing. We see the same performance trend as we observed on VOC 2007 test. The results, as shown in Table 4, demonstrate the effectiveness of our models. Compared with SSD [33] and other variants, the proposed network is significantly better (+2.7% with 300×300).

Compared with DSSD with ResNet-101 backbone, our model gets similar results with VGG-16 backbone. The most recently proposed RUN [27] improves the results of SSD with skip-connection and unified prediction. The method add several residual blocks to improve the non-linear ability before prediction. Compared with RUN, our model is more direct and with better detection

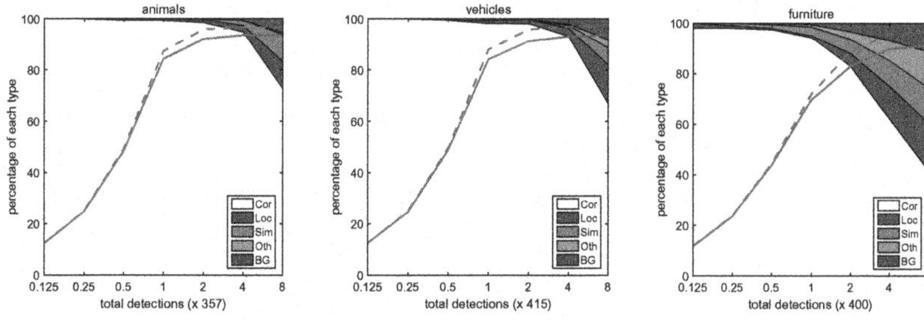

Fig. 4. Visualization of performance for our model with VGG-16 and 300 × 300 input resolution on animals, vehicles, and furniture from VOC2007 test. The Figures show the cumulative fraction of detections that are correct (Cor) or false positive due to poor localization (Loc), confusion with similar categories (Sim), with others (Oth), or with background (BG). The solid red line reflects the change of recall with the 'strong' criteria (0.5 jaccard overlap) as the number of detections increases. The dashed red line uses the 'weak' criteria (0.1 jaccard overlap).

Table 4. PASCAL VOC 2012 test detection results. All models are trained with 07++12 (07 trainval+test + 12 trainval). The entries with the best APs for each object category are bold-faced

Method	network	mAP(%)	aero	bike	bird	boat	bottle	bus	car	cat	chair	cow	table	dog	horse	mbike	person	plant	sheep	sofa	train	tv
Faster[39]	ResNet-101	73.8	86.5	81.6	77.2	58.0	51.0	78.6	76.6	93.2	48.6	80.4	59.0	92.1	85.3	84.8	80.7	48.1	77.3	66.5	84.7	65.6
R-FCN[6]	ResNet-101	77.6	86.9	83.4	**81.5**	63.8	62.4	81.6	81.1	93.1	58.0	83.8	60.8	92.7	86.0	84.6	84.4	59.0	80.8	68.6	86.1	72.9
ION[3]	VGG-16	76.4	87.5	84.7	76.8	63.8	58.3	82.6	79.0	90.9	57.8	82.0	64.7	88.9	86.5	84.7	82.3	51.4	78.2	69.2	85.2	73.5
SSD300[34]	VGG-16	75.8	88.1	82.9	74.4	61.9	47.6	82.7	78.8	91.5	58.1	80.0	64.1	89.4	85.7	85.5	82.6	50.2	79.8	73.6	86.6	72.1
SSD512[34]	VGG-16	78.5	90.0	85.3	77.7	64.3	58.5	85.1	84.3	92.6	61.3	83.4	65.1	89.9	88.5	88.2	85.5	54.4	82.4	70.7	87.1	75.6
DSSD321[15]	ResNet-101	76.3	87.3	83.3	75.4	64.6	46.8	82.7	76.5	92.9	59.5	78.3	64.3	91.5	86.6	86.6	82.1	53.3	79.6	75.7	85.2	73.9
DSSD513[15]	ResNet-101	80.0	92.1	86.6	80.3	68.7	58.2	84.3	85.0	**94.6**	63.3	85.9	65.6	**93.0**	88.5	87.8	86.4	57.4	85.2	73.4	87.8	76.8
YOLOv2[38]	Darknet-19	75.4	86.6	85.0	76.8	61.1	55.5	81.2	78.2	91.8	56.8	79.6	61.7	89.7	86.0	85.0	84.2	51.2	79.4	62.9	84.9	71.0
DSOD[42]	DenseNet	76.3	89.4	85.3	72.9	62.7	49.5	83.6	80.6	92.1	60.8	77.9	65.6	88.9	85.5	86.8	84.6	51.1	77.7	72.3	86.0	72.2
RUN300[28]	VGG-16	77.1	88.2	84.4	76.2	63.8	53.1	82.9	79.5	90.9	60.7	82.5	64.1	89.6	86.5	86.6	83.3	51.5	83.0	74.0	87.6	74.4
RUN512[28]	VGG-16	79.8	**90.0**	87.3	80.2	67.4	62.4	84.9	**85.6**	92.9	61.8	84.9	66.2	90.9	89.1	88.0	86.5	55.4	**85.0**	72.6	87.7	76.8
StairNet[46]	VGG-16	76.4	87.7	83.1	74.6	64.2	51.3	83.6	78.0	92.0	58.9	81.8	**66.2**	89.6	86.0	84.9	82.6	50.9	80.5	71.8	86.2	73.5
Ours300	VGG-16	77.5	89.5	85.0	77.7	64.3	54.6	81.6	80.0	91.6	60.0	82.5	64.7	89.9	85.4	86.1	84.1	53.2	81.0	74.2	87.9	75.9
Ours512	VGG-16	80.0	89.6	**87.4**	80.9	68.3	61.0	83.5	83.9	92.4	63.8	85.9	63.9	89.9	89.2	88.9	86.2	56.3	84.4	75.5	89.7	78.5
Ours300	ResNet-101	78.7	89.4	85.7	80.2	65.1	58.6	84.3	81.8	91.9	63.6	84.2	65.6	89.6	85.9	86.0	85.0	54.4	81.9	**75.9**	87.8	77.5
Ours512	ResNet-101	**81.1**	87.4	85.7	81.4	**71.1**	**64.3**	**85.1**	84.8	92.2	**66.3**	**87.6**	66.1	90.3	**90.1**	**89.6**	**87.2**	**60.0**	84.4	75.7	**89.7**	**80.1**

performance. Our final result using ResNet-101 scores 81.1%, which is much better than the state-of-the-art methods.

4.3 MS COCO

To further validate the proposed framework on a larger and more challenging dataset, we conduct experiments on MS COCO [31] and report results from test-dev evaluation server. The evaluation metric of MS COCO dataset is different from PASCAL VOC. The average mAP over different IoU thresholds, from 0.5 to 0.95 (written as 0.5:0.95) is the overall performance of methods. We use the 80k training images and 40k validation images [31] to train our model, and validate the performance on the test-dev dataset which contains 20k images. For ResNet-101 based models, we set batch-size as 32 and 20 for 320 × 320 and 512 × 512 model separately, due to the memory issue (Table 5).

Table 5. MS COCO test-dev2015 detection results.

Method	Train data	Input size	Network	Average precision		
				0.5	0.75	0.5:0.95
Two-stage						
OHEM++[42]	trainval	$\sim 1000 \times 600$	VGG-16	45.9	26.1	25.5
Faster [38]	trainval	$\sim 1000 \times 600$	VGG-16	42.7	-	21.9
R-FCN [6]	trainval	$\sim 1000 \times 600$	ResNet-101	51.9	-	29.9
CoupleNet [48]	trainval35k	$\sim 1000 \times 600$	ResNet-101	**54.8**	37.2	34.4
One-stage						
SSD300 [33]	trainval35k	300×300	VGG-16	43.1	25.8	25.1
SSD512 [33]	trainval35k	512×512	VGG-16	48.5	30.3	28.8
SSD513 [14]	trainval35k	513×513	ResNet-101	50.4	33.1	31.2
DSSD321 [14]	trainval35k	321×321	ResNet-101	46.1	29.2	28.0
DSSD513 [14]	trainval35k	513×513	ResNet-101	53.3	35.2	33.2
RON320 [25]	trainval	320×320	VGG-16	47.5	25.9	26.2
YOLOv2 [37]	trainval35k	544×544	DarkNet-19	44.0	19.2	21.6
RetinaNet [30]	trainval35k	500×500	ResNet-101	53.1	36.8	34.4
Ours300	trainval	300×300	VGG-16	48.2	29.1	28.4
Ours512	trainval	512×512	VGG-16	50.9	32.2	31.5
Ours300	trainval	300×300	ResNet-101	50.5	32.0	31.3
Ours512	trainval	512×512	ResNet-101	54.3	**37.3**	**34.6**

Table 6. MS COCO test-dev2015 detection results on small (AP_s), medium (AP_m) and large (AP_l) objects.

Methods	AP_s	AP_m	AP_l	AP
SSD513	10.2	34.5	49.8	31.2
DSSD513	13.0	35.4	51.1	33.2
Ours512	14.7	38.1	51.9	34.6

With the standard COCO evaluation metric, SSD300 scores 25.1% AP, and our model improves it to 28.4% AP (+3.3%), which is also on par with DSSD with ResNet-101 backbone (28.0%). When change the backbone to ResNet-101, our model gets 31.3% AP, which is much better than the DSSD321 (+3.3%). The accuracy of our model can be improved to 34.6% by using larger input size of 512×512, which is also better than the most recently proposed RetinaNet [30] that adds lateral connection and focal loss for better object detection.

Table 6 reports the multi-scale object detection results of our method under SSD framework using ResNet-101 backbone. It is observed that our method achieves better detection accuracies than SSD and DSSD for the objects of all scales (Fig. 5).

Fig. 5. Qualitative detection examples on VOC 2007 test set with SSD300 (77.5% mAP) and Ours-300 (79.6% mAP) models. For each pair, the left is the result of SSD and right is the result of ours. We show detections with scores higher than 0.6. Each color corresponds to an object category in that image. (Color figure online)

5 Conclusions

A key issue for building feature pyramid representations under a ConvNet is to reconfigure and reuse the feature hierarchy. This paper deal with this problem with global-and-local transformations. This representation allows us to explicitly model the feature reconfiguration process for the specific scales of objects. We conduct extensive experiments to compare our method to other feature pyramid variations. Our study suggests that despite the strong representations of deep ConvNet, there is still room and potential to building better pyramids to further address multiscale problems.

Acknowledgement. This work was jointly supported by the National Science Fundation of China (NSFC) and the German Research Foundation (DFG) joint project NSFC 61621136008/DFG TRR-169 and the National Natural Science Foundation of China (Grant No: 61327809, 61210013).

References

1. Adelson, E.H., Anderson, C.H., Bergen, J.R., Burt, P.J., Ogden, J.M.: Pyramid methods in image processing. RCA Eng. **29**(6), 33–41 (1984)
2. Badrinarayanan, V., Kendall, A., Cipolla, R.: SegNet: a deep convolutional encoder-decoder architecture for image segmentation. IEEE Trans. Pattern Anal. Mach. Intell. **39**(12), 2481–2495 (2017)
3. Bell, S., Lawrence Zitnick, C., Bala, K., Girshick, R.: Inside-outside net: detecting objects in context with skip pooling and recurrent neural networks. In: Proceedings of the IEEE Conference on Computer Vision and Pattern Recognition, pp. 2874–2883 (2016)
4. Benenson, R., Mathias, M., Timofte, R., Van Gool, L.: Pedestrian detection at 100 frames per second. In: 2012 IEEE Conference on Computer Vision and Pattern Recognition (CVPR), pp. 2903–2910. IEEE (2012)
5. Chen, Y., Wang, Z., Peng, Y., Zhang, Z., Yu, G., Sun, J.: Cascaded pyramid network for multi-person pose estimation. arXiv preprint arXiv:1711.07319 (2017)
6. Dai, J., Li, Y., He, K., Sun, J.: R-FCN: object detection via region-based fully convolutional networks. In: Advances in neural information processing systems, pp. 379–387 (2016)
7. Dollár, P., Appel, R., Belongie, S., Perona, P.: Fast feature pyramids for object detection. IEEE Trans. Pattern Anal. Mach. Intell. **36**(8), 1532–1545 (2014)
8. Dollár, P., Appel, R., Kienzle, W.: Crosstalk cascades for frame-rate pedestrian detection. In: Fitzgibbon, A., Lazebnik, S., Perona, P., Sato, Y., Schmid, C. (eds.) ECCV 2012. LNCS, pp. 645–659. Springer, Heidelberg (2012). https://doi.org/10.1007/978-3-642-33709-3_46
9. Dollar, P., Belongie, S.J., Perona, P.: The fastest pedestrian detector in the west. In: BMVC, vol. 2, p. 7 (2010)
10. Dollar, P., Wojek, C., Schiele, B., Perona, P.: Pedestrian detection: an evaluation of the state of the art. IEEE Trans. Pattern Anal. Mach. Intell. **34**(4), 743–761 (2012)
11. Everingham, M., Van Gool, L., Williams, C.K., Winn, J., Zisserman, A.: The pascal visual object classes (VOC) challenge. Int. J. Comput. Vis. **88**(2), 303–338 (2010)
12. Felzenszwalb, P., McAllester, D., Ramanan, D.: A discriminatively trained, multiscale, deformable part model. In: 2008 IEEE Conference on Computer Vision and Pattern Recognition. CVPR 2008, pp. 1–8. IEEE (2008)
13. Felzenszwalb, P.F., Girshick, R.B., McAllester, D., Ramanan, D.: Object detection with discriminatively trained part-based models. IEEE Trans. Pattern Anal. Mach. Intell. **32**(9), 1627–1645 (2010)
14. Fu, C.Y., Liu, W., Ranga, A., Tyagi, A., Berg, A.C.: DSSD: deconvolutional single shot detector. arXiv preprint arXiv:1701.06659 (2017)
15. Gidaris, S., Komodakis, N.: Object detection via a multi-region and semantic segmentation-aware CNN model. In: Proceedings of the IEEE International Conference on Computer Vision, pp. 1134–1142 (2015)
16. Girshick, R.: Fast R-CNN. In: Proceedings of the IEEE International Conference on Computer Vision, pp. 1440–1448 (2015)
17. Girshick, R., Donahue, J., Darrell, T., Malik, J.: Rich feature hierarchies for accurate object detection and semantic segmentation. In: Proceedings of the IEEE conference on computer vision and pattern recognition, pp. 580–587 (2014)
18. He, K., Gkioxari, G., Dollár, P., Girshick, R.: Mask R-CNN. arXiv preprint arXiv:1703.06870 (2017)

19. He, K., Zhang, X., Ren, S., Sun, J.: Spatial pyramid pooling in deep convolutional networks for visual recognition. IEEE Trans. Pattern Anal. Mach. Intell. **37**(9), 1904–1916 (2015)
20. He, K., Zhang, X., Ren, S., Sun, J.: Deep residual learning for image recognition. In: Proceedings of the IEEE conference on computer vision and pattern recognition, pp. 770–778 (2016)
21. Hoiem, D., Chodpathumwan, Y., Dai, Q.: Diagnosing error in object detectors. In: Fitzgibbon, A., Lazebnik, S., Perona, P., Sato, Y., Schmid, C. (eds.) ECCV 2012. LNCS, vol. 7574, pp. 340–353. Springer, Heidelberg (2012). https://doi.org/10.1007/978-3-642-33712-3_25
22. Hu, J., Shen, L., Sun, G.: Squeeze-and-excitation networks. arXiv preprint arXiv:1709.01507 (2017)
23. Huang, J., et al.: Speed/accuracy trade-offs for modern convolutional object detectors. In: Proceedings of the IEEE Conference on Computer Vision and Pattern Recognition, pp. 7310–7311 (2017)
24. Jeong, J., Park, H., Kwak, N.: Enhancement of SSD by concatenating feature maps for object detection. arXiv preprint arXiv:1705.09587 (2017)
25. Kong, T., Sun, F., Yao, A., Liu, H., Lu, M., Chen, Y.: RON: reverse connection with objectness prior networks for object detection. In: IEEE Conference on Computer Vision and Pattern Recognition, vol. 1, p. 2 (2017)
26. Kong, T., Yao, A., Chen, Y., Sun, F.: HyperNet: towards accurate region proposal generation and joint object detection. In: Proceedings of the IEEE Conference on Computer Vision and Pattern Recognition, pp. 845–853 (2016)
27. Lee, K., Choi, J., Jeong, J., Kwak, N.: Residual features and unified prediction network for single stage detection. arXiv preprint arXiv:1707.05031 (2017)
28. Lin, M., Chen, Q., Yan, S.: Network in network. arXiv preprint arXiv:1312.4400 (2013)
29. Lin, T.Y., Dollár, P., Girshick, R., He, K., Hariharan, B., Belongie, S.: Feature pyramid networks for object detection. arXiv preprint arXiv:1612.03144 (2016)
30. Lin, T.Y., Goyal, P., Girshick, R., He, K., Dollár, P.: Focal loss for dense object detection. arXiv preprint arXiv:1708.02002 (2017)
31. Lin, T.-Y., et al.: Microsoft COCO: common objects in context. In: Fleet, D., Pajdla, T., Schiele, B., Tuytelaars, T. (eds.) ECCV 2014. LNCS, vol. 8693, pp. 740–755. Springer, Cham (2014). https://doi.org/10.1007/978-3-319-10602-1_48
32. Liu, S., Qi, L., Qin, H., Shi, J., Jia, J.: Path aggregation network for instance segmentation. arXiv preprint arXiv:1803.01534 (2018)
33. Liu, W., et al.: SSD: single shot multibox detector. In: Leibe, B., Matas, J., Sebe, N., Welling, M. (eds.) ECCV 2016. LNCS, vol. 9905, pp. 21–37. Springer, Cham (2016). https://doi.org/10.1007/978-3-319-46448-0_2
34. Lowe, D.G.: Distinctive image features from scale-invariant keypoints. Int. J. Comput. Vis. **60**(2), 91–110 (2004)
35. Paszke, A., et al.: Automatic differentiation in pyTorch (2017)
36. Redmon, J., Divvala, S., Girshick, R., Farhadi, A.: You only look once: unified, real-time object detection. In: Proceedings of the IEEE Conference on Computer Vision and Pattern Recognition, pp. 779–788 (2016)
37. Redmon, J., Farhadi, A.: YOLO9000: better, faster, stronger. arXiv preprint arXiv:1612.08242 (2016)
38. Ren, S., He, K., Girshick, R., Sun, J.: Faster R-CNN: towards real-time object detection with region proposal networks. In: Advances in Neural Information Processing Systems, pp. 91–99 (2015)

39. Russakovsky, O., et al.: Imagenet large scale visual recognition challenge. Int. J. Comput. Vis. **115**(3), 211–252 (2015)
40. Sermanet, P., Eigen, D., Zhang, X., Mathieu, M., Fergus, R., LeCun, Y.: OverFeat:integrated recognition, localization and detection using convolutional networks. arXiv preprint arXiv:1312.6229 (2013)
41. Shen, Z., Liu, Z., Li, J., Jiang, Y.G., Chen, Y., Xue, X.: DSOD: learning deeply supervised object detectors from scratch. In: The IEEE International Conference on Computer Vision (ICCV), vol. 3, p. 7 (2017)
42. Shrivastava, A., Gupta, A., Girshick, R.: Training region-based object detectors with online hard example mining. In: Proceedings of the IEEE Conference on Computer Vision and Pattern Recognition, pp. 761–769 (2016)
43. Shrivastava, A., Sukthankar, R., Malik, J., Gupta, A.: Beyond skip connections: top-down modulation for object detection. arXiv preprint arXiv:1612.06851 (2016)
44. Wang, X., Han, T.X., Yan, S.: An HOG-LBP human detector with partial occlusion handling. In: CVPR (2009)
45. Woo, S., Hwang, S., Kweon, I.S.: StairNet: top-down semantic aggregation for accurate one shot detection. arXiv preprint arXiv:1709.05788 (2017)
46. Yang, W., Li, S., Ouyang, W., Li, H., Wang, X.: Learning feature pyramids for human pose estimation. In: The IEEE International Conference on Computer Vision (ICCV), vol. 2 (2017)
47. Zhang, S., Wen, L., Bian, X., Lei, Z., Li, S.Z.: Single-shot refinement neural network for object detection. arXiv preprint arXiv:1711.06897 (2017)
48. Zhu, Y., Zhao, C., Wang, J., Zhao, X., Wu, Y., Lu, H.: CoupleNet: coupling global structure with local parts for object detection. In: Proceedings of International Conference on Computer Vision (ICCV) (2017)

Goal-Oriented Visual Question Generation via Intermediate Rewards

Junjie Zhang[1,3], Qi Wu[2(✉)], Chunhua Shen[2], Jian Zhang[1], Jianfeng Lu[3], and Anton van den Hengel[2]

[1] School of Electrical and Data Engineering, University of Technology Sydney, Sydney, Australia
junjie.zhang@student.uts.edu.au, jian.zhang@uts.edu.au

[2] Australian Insititute for Machine Learning, The University of Adelaide, Adelaide, Australia
{qi.wu01,chunhua.shen,anton.vandenhengel}@adelaide.edu.au

[3] School of Computer Science and Engineering, Nanjing University of Science and Technology, Nanjing, China
lujf@njust.edu.cn

Abstract. Despite significant progress in a variety of vision-and-language problems, developing a method capable of asking intelligent, goal-oriented questions about images is proven to be an inscrutable challenge. Towards this end, we propose a Deep Reinforcement Learning framework based on three new intermediate rewards, namely *goal-achieved*, *progressive* and *informativeness* that encourage the generation of succinct questions, which in turn uncover valuable information towards the overall goal. By directly optimizing for questions that work quickly towards fulfilling the overall goal, we avoid the tendency of existing methods to generate long series of inane queries that add little value. We evaluate our model on the GuessWhat?! dataset and show that the resulting questions can help a standard 'Guesser' identify a specific object in an image at a much higher success rate.

Keywords: Goal-oriented · VQG · Intermediate rewards

1 Introduction

Although visual question answering (VQA) [2,23,24] has attracted more attention, visual question generation (VQG) is a much more difficult task. Obviously, generating facile, repetitive questions represents no challenge at all, but generating a series of questions that draw out useful information towards an overarching goal, however, demands consideration of the image content, the goal, and the conversation thus far. It could, generally, also be seen as requiring consideration of the abilities and motivation of the other participant in the conversation.

J. Zhang—The work was done while visiting The University of Adelaide.

Q. Wu—The first two authors contributed to this work equally.

V. Ferrari et al. (Eds.): ECCV 2018, LNCS 11209, pp. 189–204, 2018.
https://doi.org/10.1007/978-3-030-01228-1_12

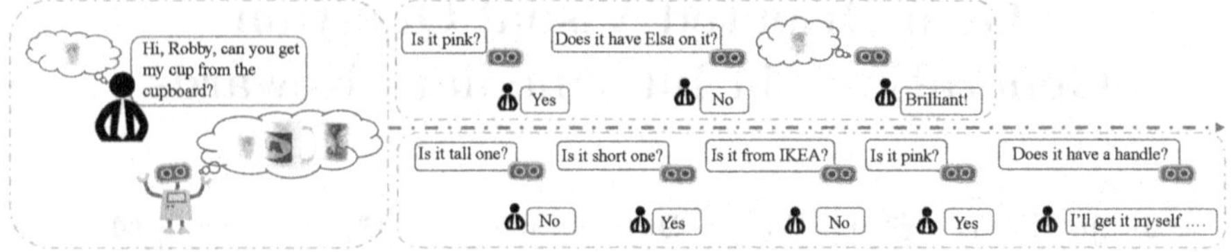

Fig. 1. Two illustrative examples of potential conversations between a human and a robot. The bottom conversation clearly makes people frustrated while the top one makes people happy because the robot achieves the goal in a quicker way via less but informative questions.

A well-posed question extracts the most informative answer towards achieving a particular goal, and thus reflects the knowledge of the asker, and their estimate of the capabilities of the answerer. Although the information would be beneficial in identifying a particular object in an image, there is little value in an agent asking a human about the exact values of particular pixels, the statistics of their gradients, or the aspect ratio of the corresponding bounding box. The fact that the answerer is incapable of providing the requested information makes such questions pointless. Selecting a question that has a significant probability of generating an answer that helps achieve a particular goal is a complex problem.

Asking questions is an essential part of the human communication. Any intelligent agent that seeks to interact flexibly and effectively with humans thus needs to be able to ask questions. The ability to ask intelligent questions is even more important than receiving intelligent, actionable answers. A robot, for example in Fig. 1, has been given a task and realized that it is missing critical information required to carry it out, needs to ask a question. It will have a limited number of attempts before the human gets frustrated and carries out the task themselves. This scenario applies equally to any intelligent agent that seeks to interact with humans, as we have surprisingly little tolerance for agents that are unable to learn by asking questions, and for those that ask too many.

As a result of the above, VQG has started to receive attention, but primarily as a vision-to-language problem [10,13,25]. Methods that approach the problem in this manner tend to generate arbitrary sequences of questions that are somewhat related to the image [14], but which bare no relationship to the goal. This reflects the fact that these methods have no means of measuring whether the answers generated to assist in making progress towards the goal. Instead, in this paper, we ground the VQG problem as a goal-oriented version of the game - GuessWhat?!, introduced in [22]. The method presented in [22] to play the GuessWhat game is made up of three components: the `Questioner` asks questions to the `Oracle`, and the `Guesser` tries to identify the object that the `Oracle` is referring to, based on its answers. The quality of the generated questions is thus directly related to the success rate of the final task.

Goal-oriented training that uses a game setting has been used in the visual dialog generation previously [4]. However, it focuses on generating more human-like dialogs, not on helping the agent achieve the goal through better question generation. Moreover, previous work [18] only uses the final goal as the reward to train the dialog generator, which might be suitable for dialog generation but is a rather weak and undirected signal by which to control the quality, effectiveness, and informativeness of the generated question in a goal-oriented task. In other words, in some cases, we want to talk to a robot because we want it to finish a specific task but not to hold the meaningless boring chat. Therefore, in this paper, we use intermediate rewards to encourage the agent to ask short but informative questions to achieve the goal. Moreover, in contrast to previous works that only consider the overall goal as the reward, we assign different intermediate rewards for each posed question to control the quality.

This is achieved through fitting the goal-oriented VQG into a reinforcement learning (RL) paradigm and devising three different intermediate rewards, which are our main contributions in this paper, to explicitly optimize the question generation. The first *goal-achieved* reward is designed to encourage the agent to achieve the final goal (pick out the object that the `Oracle` is 'thinking') via asking multiple questions. However, different from only considering whether the goal is achieved, additional rewards are awarded if the agent can use fewer questions to achieve it. This is a reasonable setting because you do not need a robot that can finish a task but has to ask you hundreds of questions. The second reward we proposed is the *progressive* reward, which is established to encourage questions that generated by the agent can progressively increase the probability of the right answer. This is an intermediate reward for the individual question, and the reward is decided by the change of the ground-truth answer probability. A negative reward will be given if the probability decreases. The last reward is the *informativeness* reward, which is used to restrict the agent not to ask 'useless' questions, for example, a question that leads to the identical answer for all the candidate objects (this question cannot eliminate any ambiguous). We show the whole framework in Fig. 2.

We evaluate our model on the GuessWhat?! dataset [22], with the pre-trained standard `Oracle` and `Guesser`, we show that our novel `Questioner` model outperforms the baseline and state-of-the-art model by a large margin. We also evaluate each reward respectively, to measure the individual contribution. Qualitative results show that we can produce more informative questions.

2 Related Works

Visual Question Generation. Recently, the visual question generation problem has been brought to the computer vision community, aims at generating visual-related questions. Most of the works treat the VQG as a standalone problem and follow an image captioning style framework, *i.e.*, translate an image into a sentence, in this case, a question. For example, in [13], Mora *et al.* use a CNN-LSTM model to generate questions and answers directly from the image visual content. Zhang *et al.* [25] focus on generating questions of grounded images. They use Densecap [8] as region captioning generator to guide the question generation.

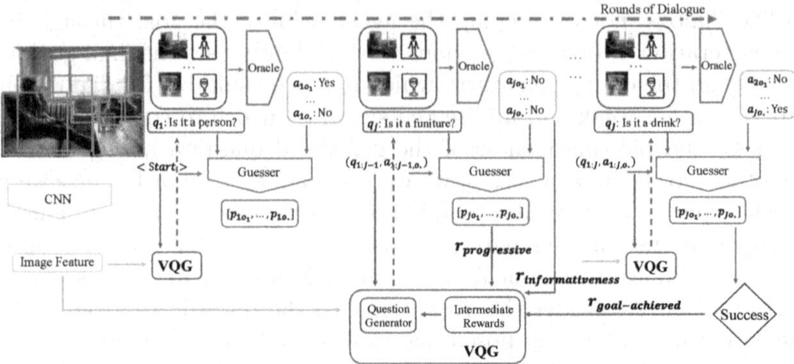

Fig. 2. The framework of the proposed VQG agent plays in the whole game environment. A target object o^* is assigned to the Oracle, but it is unknown to VQG and Guesser. Then VQG generates a series of questions, which are answered by Oracle. During training, we let Oracle answer the question based on all the objects at each round, and measure the *informativeness* reward, and we also let Guesser generate probability distribution to measure the *progressive* reward. Finally, we consider the number of rounds J and set the *goal-achieved* reward based on the status of success. These intermediate rewards are adopted for optimizing the VQG agent by the REINFORCE.

In [14], Mostafazadeh *et al.* propose a dataset to generate natural questions about images, which are beyond the literal description of image content. Li *et al.* [10] view the VQA and VQG as a dual learning process by jointly training them in an end-to-end framework. Although these works can generate meaningful questions that are related to the image, the motivation of asking these questions are rather weak since they are not related to any goals. Another issue of the previous works is that it is hard to conduct the quality measurement on this type of questions. Instead, in our work, we aim to develop an agent that can learn to ask realistic questions, which can contribute to achieving a specific goal.

Goal-Oriented Visual Dialogue generation has attracted many attentions at most recently. In [5], Das *et al.* introduce a reinforcement learning mechanism for visual dialogue generation. They establish two RL agents corresponding to question and answer generation respectively, to finally locate an unseen image from a set of images. The question agent predicts the feature representation of the image and the reward function is given by measuring how close the representation is compared to the true feature. However, we focus on encouraging the agent to generate questions that directed towards the final goal, and we adopt different kinds of intermediate rewards to achieve that in the question generation process. Moreover, the question generation agent in their model only asks questions based on the dialogue history, which does not involve visual information. In [18], Strub *et al.* propose to employ reinforcement learning to solve question generation of the GuessWhat game by introducing the final status of success as the sole reward. We share the similar backbone idea, but there are several technical differences. One of the most significant differences is that the previous work only considers using whether achieving the final goal as the reward but we assign different intermediate rewards for each posed question to push VQG agent to ask short but informative questions to achieve the goal. The experimental results and analysis in Sect. 4 show that our model not only outperforms the state-of-art but also achieves higher intelligence, *ie.*, using as few questions as possible to finish the task.

Reinforcement Learning for V2L. Reinforcement learning [9,20] has been adopted in several vision-to-language (V2L) problems, including image captioning [11,16,17], VQA [1,7,26], and aforementioned visual dialogue system [5,12] *etc.* In [16], Ren *et al.* use a policy network and a value network to collaboratively generate image captions, while different optimization methods for RL in image captioning are explored in [11] and [17], called SPIDEr and self-critical sequence training. Zhu *et al.* [26] introduce knowledge source into the iterative VQA and employ RL to learn the query policy. In [1], authors use RL to learn the parameters of QA model for both images and structured knowledge bases. These works solve V2L related problems by employing RL as an optimization method, while we focus on using RL with carefully designed intermediate rewards to train the VQG agent for goal-oriented tasks.

Reward Shaping. Our work is also somewhat related to the reward shaping, which focuses on solving the sparsity of the reward function in the reinforcement learning. In [19], Su *et al.* examine three RNN based approaches as potential functions for reward shaping in spoken dialogue systems. In [6], El Asri *et al.* propose two diffuse reward functions to apply to the spoken dialogue system by evaluating the states and transitions respectively. Different from these prior works that condition their model on discourse-based constraints for a purely linguistic (rather than visuo-linguistic) dataset. The tasks we target, our architectural differences, and the dataset and metrics we employ are distinct.

3 Goal-Oriented VQG

We ground our goal-oriented VQG problem on a *Guess What* game, specifically, on the GuessWhat?! dataset [22]. GuessWhat?! is a three-role interactive game, where all roles observe the same image of a rich visual scene that contains multiple objects. We view this game as three parts: `Oracle`, `Questioner` and `Guesser`. In each game, a random object in the scene is assigned to the `Oracle`, where this process is hidden to the `Questioner`. Then the `Questioner` can ask a series of yes/no questions to locate this object. The list of objects is also hidden to the `Questioner` during the question-answer rounds. Once the `Questioner` has gathered enough information, the `Guesser` can start to guess. The game is considered as successful if the `Guesser` selects the right object.

The `Questioner` part of the game is a goal-oriented VQG problem, each question is generated based on the visual information of the image and the previous rounds of question-answer pairs. The goal of VQG is to successfully finish the game, in this case, to locate the right object. In this paper, we fit the goal-oriented VQG into a reinforcement learning paradigm and propose three different intermediate rewards, namely the *goal-achieved* reward, *progressive* reward, and *informativeness* reward, to explicitly optimize the question generation. The *goal-achieved* reward is established to lead the dialogue to achieve the final goal, the *progressive* reward is used to push the intermediate generation process towards the optimal direction, while the *informativeness* reward is used to ensure the quality of generated questions. To better express the generation process, we first introduce the notations of GuessWhat?! game.

Each game is defined as a tuple (I, D, O, o^*), where I is the observed image, D is the dialogue with J rounds of question-answer pairs $(q_j, a_j)_{j=1}^{J}$, $O = (o_n)_{n=1}^{N}$ is the list of N objects in the image I, where o^* is the target object. Each question $q_j = (w_m^j)_{m=1}^{M_j}$ is a sequence of M_j tokens, which are sampled from the pre-defined vocabulary V. The V is composed of word tokens, a question stop token <?> and a dialogue stop token <End>. The answer $a_j \in \{$<Yes>,<No>,<NA> $\}$ is set to be yes, no or not applicable. For each object o, it has an object category $c_o \in \{1 \dots C\}$ and a segment mask.

3.1 Learning Environment

We build the learning environment to generate visual dialogues based on the GuessWhat?! dataset. Since we focus on the goal-oriented VQG, for a fair comparison, the `Oracle` and `Guesser` are produced by referring to the original baseline models in GuessWhat?! [22]. We also introduce the VQG supervised learning model, which is referred as the baseline for the rest of the paper.

The `Oracle` requires generating answers for all kinds of questions about any objects within the image scene. The bounding box (obtained from the segment mask) of the object o are encoded to represent the spatial feature, where $o_{spa} = [x_{min}, y_{min}, x_{max}, y_{max}, x_{center}, y_{center}, w, h]$ indicates the box coordinates, width and height. The category c_o is embedded using a learned look-up table, while the current question is encoded by an LSTM. All three features are concatenated into a single vector and fed into a one hidden layer MLP followed by a softmax layer to produce the answer probability $p(a|o_{spa}, c_o, q)$.

Given an image I and a series of question-answer pairs, the `Guesser` requires predicting right object o^* from a list of objects. We consider the generated dialogue as one flat sequence of tokens and encode it with an LSTM. The last hidden state is extracted as the feature to represent the dialogue. We also embed all the objects' spatial features and categories by an MLP. We perform a dot-product between dialogue and object features with a softmax operation to produce the final prediction.

Given an image I and a history of the question-answer pairs $(q, a)_{1:j-1}$, the VQG requires generating a new question q_j. We build the VQG baseline based on an RNN generator. The RNN recurrently produces a series of state vectors $s_{1:m}^j$ by transitioning from the previous state s_{m-1}^j and the current input token w_m^j. We use an LSTM as the transition function f, that is, $s_m^j = f(s_{m-1}^j, w_m^j)$. In our case, the state vector s is conditioned on the whole image and all the previous question-answer tokens. We add a softmax operation to produce the probability distribution over the vocabulary V, where $p(w_m^j|I,(q,a)_{1:j-1},w_{1:m-1}^j)$. This baseline is conducted by employing the supervised training. We train the VQG by minimizing the following negative log loss function:

$$\begin{aligned} L &= -\log p(q_{1:J}|I,a_{1:J}) \\ &= -\sum_{j=1}^{J}\sum_{m=1}^{M_j}\log p(w_m^j|I,w_{1:m-1}^j,(q,a)_{1:j-1}) \end{aligned} \tag{1}$$

During the test stage, the question can be sampled from the model by starting from state s_1^j; a new token w_m^j is sampled from the probability distribution, then embedded and fed back to the LSTM. We repeat this operation until the end of question token is encountered.

3.2 Reinforcement Learning of VQG

We use our established `Oracle`, `Guesser` and VQG baseline model to simulate a complete GuessWhat?! game. Given an image I, an initial question q_1 is generated by sampling from the VQG baseline until the stop question token is encountered. Then the `Oracle` receives the question q_1 along with the assigned object category o^* and its spatial information o^*_{spa}, and output the answer a_1, the question-answer pair (q_1,a_1) is appended to the dialogue history. We repeat this loop until the end of the dialogue token is sampled, or the number of questions reaches the maximum. Finally, the `Guesser` takes the whole dialogue D and the object list O as inputs to predict the object. We consider the goal reached if o^* is selected. Otherwise, it failed.

To more efficiently optimize the VQG towards the final goal and generate informative questions, we adopt three intermediate rewards (which will be introduced in the following sections) into the RL framework.

`State, Action & Policy.` We view the VQG as a Markov Decision Process (MDP), the `Questioner` is noted as the agent. For the dialogue generated based on the image I at time step t, the state of agent is defined as the image visual content with the history of question-answer pairs and the tokens of current question generated so far: $S_t=(I,(q,a)_{1:j-1},(w_1^j,\dots,w_m^j))$, where $t=\sum_{k=1}^{k=j-1}M_k+m$. The action A_t of agent is to select the next output token w_{m+1}^j from the vocabulary V. Depending on the actions that agent takes, the transition between two states falls into one of the following cases:

(1) w_{m+1}^j =<?>: The current question is finished, the `Oracle` from the environment will answer a_j, which is appended to the dialogue history. The next state $S_{t+1}=(I,(q,a)_{1:j})$.
(2) w_{m+1}^j =<End>: The dialogue is finished, the `Guesser` from the environment will select the object from the list O.
(3) Otherwise, the new generated token w_{m+1}^j keeps appending to the current question q_j, the next state $S_{t+1}=(I,(q,a)_{1:j-1},(w_1^j,\dots,w_m^j,w_{m+1}^j))$.

The maximum length of question q_j is M_{max}, and the maximum rounds of the dialogue is J_{max}. Therefore, the number of time steps T of any dialogue are $T \leq M_{max} * J_{max}$. We model the VQG under the stochastic policy $\pi_\theta(A|S)$, where θ represents the parameters of the deep neural network we used in the VQG baseline that produces the probability distributions for each state. The goal of the policy learning is to estimate the parameter θ.

After we set up the components of MDP, the most significant aspect of the RL is to define the appropriate reward function for each state-action pair (S_t, A_t). As we emphasized before, the goal-oriented VQG aims to generate the questions that lead to achieving the final goal. Therefore, we build three kinds of intermediate rewards to push the VQG agent to be optimized towards the optimal direction. The whole framework is shown in Fig. 2.

`Goal-Achieved Reward`. One basic rule of the appropriate reward function is that it cannot conflict with the final optimal policy [15]. The primary purpose of the VQG agent is to gather enough information as soon as possible to help `Guesser` to locate the object. Therefore, we define the first reward to reflect whether the final goal is achieved. But more importantly, we take the number of rounds into consideration to accelerate the questioning part and let the reward be nonzero when the game is successful.

Given the state S_t, where the <End> token is sampled or the maximum round J_{max} is reached, the reward of the state-action pair is defined as:

$$r_g(S_t, A_t) = \begin{cases} 1+\lambda \cdot J_{max}/J, & \text{If } \texttt{Guesser}(S_t) = o^* \\ 0, & \text{Otherwise} \end{cases} \tag{2}$$

We set the reward as one plus the weighted maximum number of rounds J_{max} against the actual rounds J of the current dialogue if the dialogue is successful, and zero otherwise. This is based on that we want the final goal to motivate the agent to generate useful questions. The intermediate process is considered into the reward as the rounds of the question-answer pairs J, which guarantees the efficiency of the generation process; the fewer questions are generated, the more reward VQG agent can get at the end of the game (if and only if the game succeed). This is a quite useful setting in the realistic because we do want to use fewer orders to guide the robot to finish more tasks. λ is a weight to balance between the contribution of the successful reward and the dialogue round reward.

`Progressive Reward`. Based on the observation of the human interactive dialogues, we find that the questions of a successful game, are ones that progressively achieve the final goal, *i.e.* as long as the questions being asked and answered, the confidence of referring to the target object becomes higher and higher. Therefore, at each round, we define an intermediate reward for state-action pair as the improvement of target probability that `Guesser` outputs. More specific, we interact with the `Guesser` at each round to obtain the probability of predicting the target object. If the probability increases, it means that the generated question q_j is a positive question that leads the dialogue towards the right direction.

We set an intermediate reward called *progressive* reward to encourage VQG agent to progressively generate these positive questions. At each round j, we record the probability $p_j(o^*|I, (q, a)_{1:j})$ returned by `Guesser`, and compare it with the last round $j-1$. The difference between the two probabilities is used as the intermediate reward. That is:

$$r_p(S_t, A_t) = p_j(o^*|I, (q, a)_{1:j}) - p_{j-1}(o^*|I, (q, a)_{1:j-1}) \tag{3}$$

Despite the total reward summed over all time steps are the initial and final states due to the cancellation of intermediate terms, during the REINFORCE optimization, the state-action value function that returns the cumulative rewards of each step are different. In this way, the question is considered high-quality and has a positive reward, if it leads to a higher probability to guess the right object. Otherwise, the reward is negative.

`Informativeness Reward.` When we human ask questions (especially in a guess what game), we expect an answer that can help us to eliminate the confusion and distinguish the candidate objects. Hence, imagine that if a posed question that leads to the same answer for all the candidate object, this question will be useless. For example, all the candidate objects are 'red' and if we posed a question that 'Is it red?', we will get the answer 'Yes.' However, this question-answer pair cannot help us to identify the target. We want to avoid this kind of questions because they are non-informative. In this case, we need to evaluate the question based on the answer from the `Oracle`.

Given generated question q_j, we interact with the `Oracle` to answer the question. Since the `Oracle` takes the image I, the current question q_j, and the target object o^* as inputs, and outputs the answer a_j, we let the `Oracle` answer question q_j for all objects in the image. If more than one answer is different from others, we consider q_j is useful for locating the right object. Otherwise, it does not contribute to the final goal. Therefore, we set the reward positive, which we called *informativeness* reward, for these useful questions.

Formally, during each round, the `Oracle` receives the image I, the current question q_j and the list of objects O, and then outputs the answer set $a_{jO} = \{a_{jo_1}, \ldots, a_{jo_N}\}$, where each element corresponds to each object. Then the *informativeness* reward is defined as:

$$r_i(S_t, A_t) = \begin{cases} \eta, & \text{If all } a_{jo_n} \text{ are not identical} \\ 0, & \text{Otherwise} \end{cases} \tag{4}$$

By giving a positive reward to the state-action pair, we improve the quality of the dialogue by encouraging the agent to generate more informative questions.

`Training with Policy Gradient.` Now we have three different kinds of rewards that take the intermediate process into consideration, for each state-action pair (S_t, A_t), we add three rewards together as the final reward function:

$$r(S_t, A_t) = r_g(S_t, A_t) + r_p(S_t, A_t) + r_i(S_t, A_t) \tag{5}$$

Considering the large action space in the game setting, we adopt the policy gradient method [21] to train the VQG agent with proposed intermediate rewards. The goal of policy gradient is to update policy parameters with respect

Algorithm 1. Training procedure of the VQG agent.

Input: `Oracle`(Ora), `Guesser`(Gus), VQG, batch size H

for Each update **do**
  # Generate episodes τ
  for $h = 1$ to H **do**
    select image I_h and one target object $o_h^* \in O_h$
    # Generate question-answer pairs $(q, a)_{1:j}^h$
    for $j = 1$ to J_{max} **do**
      $q_j^h = VQG(I_h, (q, a)_{1:j-1}^h)$
      # N is the number of total objects
      for $n = 1$ to N **do**
        $a_{jo_{hn}}^h = Ora(I_h, q_j^h, o_{hn})$
      if all $a_{jo_{hn}}^h$ are not identical **then**
        $r_i(S_t, A_t) = \eta$
      else $r_i(S_t, A_t) = 0$
      $r(S_t, A_t) = r_i(S_t, A_t)$
      $p_j(o_h^*|\cdot) = Gus(I_h, (q, a)_{1:j}^h, O_h)$
      if $j > 1$ **then**
        $r_p(S_t, A_t) = p_j(o_h^*|\cdot) - p_{j-1}(o_h^*|\cdot)$
        $r(S_t, A_t) = r(S_t, A_t) + r_p(S_t, A_t)$
      if <End>$\in q_j^h$ **then**
        break;
    $p(o^h|\cdot) = Gus(I_h, (q, a)_{1:j}^h, O_h)$
    if $argmax_{o_h} p(o^h|\cdot) = o_h^*$ **then**
      $r_g(S_t, A_t) = 1 + \lambda \cdot J_{max}/j$
    else $r_g(S_t, A_t) = 0$
    $r(S_t, A_t) = r(S_t, A_t) + r_g(S_t, A_t)$
  Define $\tau = (I_h, (q, a)_{1:j_h}^h, r_h)_{1:H}$
  Evaluate $\nabla J(\theta)$ as Eq. 9 and update VQG agent
  Evaluate $\nabla L(\varphi)$ as Eq. 10 and update b_φ baseline

to the expected return by gradient descent. Since we are in the episodic environment, given the policy π_θ, which is the generative network of the VQG agent, in this case, the policy objective function takes the form:

$$J(\theta) = E_{\pi_\theta}[\sum_{t=1}^{T} r(S_t, A_t)] \tag{6}$$

The parameters θ then can be optimized by following the gradient update rule. In REINFORCE algorithm [9], the gradient of $J(\theta)$ can be estimated from a batch of episodes τ that are sampled from the policy π_θ:

$$\nabla J(\theta) \approx \left\langle \sum_{t=1}^{T} \sum_{A_t \in V} \nabla_\theta \log \pi_\theta(S_t, A_t)(Q^{\pi_\theta}(S_t, A_t) - b_\varphi) \right\rangle_\tau \tag{7}$$

where $Q^{\pi_\theta}(S_t, A_t)$ is the state-action value function that returns the expectation of cumulative reward at (S_t, A_t):

$$Q^{\pi_\theta}(S_t, A_t) = E_{\pi_\theta}[\sum_{t'=t}^{T} r(S_{t'}, A_{t'})] \tag{8}$$

by substituting the notations with VQG agent, we have the following policy gradient:

$$\nabla J(\theta) \approx \left\langle \sum_{j=1}^{J} \sum_{m=1}^{M_j} \nabla_\theta \log \pi_\theta(w_m^j | I, (q,a)_{1:j-1}, w_{1:m-1}^j) \right. \\ \left. (Q^{\pi_\theta}(I, (q,a)_{1:j-1}, w_{1:m-1}^j, w_m^j) - b_\varphi) \right\rangle_\tau \tag{9}$$

b_φ is a baseline function to help reduce the gradient variance, which can be chosen arbitrarily. We use a one-layer MLP that takes state S_t as input in VQG agent and outputs the expected reward. The baseline b_φ is trained with mean squared error as:

$$\min_\varphi L(\varphi) = \left\langle [b_\varphi(S_t) - \sum_{t'=t}^{T} r(S_{t'}, A_{t'})]^2 \right\rangle_\tau \tag{10}$$

The whole training procedure is shown in Algorithm 1.

4 Experiment

In this section, we present our VQG results and conduct comprehensive ablation analysis about each intermediate reward. As mentioned above, the proposed method is evaluated on the GuessWhat?! game dataset [22] with pre-trained standard `Oracle` and `Guesser`. By comparing with the baseline and the state-of-the-art model, we show that the proposed model can efficiently generate informative questions, which serve the final goal.

4.1 Dataset and Evaluation Metric

The GuessWhat?! Dataset [22] is composed of 155,281 dialogues grounded on the 66,537 images with 134,074 unique objects. There are 821,955 question-answer pairs in the dialogues with vocabulary size 4,900. We use the standard split of training, validation and test in [18,22]. Following [18], we report the accuracies of the games as the evaluation metric. Given a J-round dialogue, if the target object o^* is located by `Guesser`, the game is noted as successful, which indicates that the VQG agent has generated the qualified questions to serve the final goal. There are two kinds of test runs on the training set and test set respectively, named `NewObject` and `NewImage`. NewObject is randomly sampling target objects from the training images (but we restrict only to use new objects that are not seen before), while NewImage is sampling objects from the test images (unseen). We report three inference methods namely sampling, greedy and beam-search (beam size is 5) for these two test runs.

4.2 Implementation Details

The standard `Oracle`, `Guesser` and VQG baseline are reproduced by referring to [18]. The error of trained `Oracle`, `Guesser` on test set are 21.1% and 35.8% respectively. The VQG baseline is referred as Baseline in Table 1[1].

[1] These results are reported on https://github.com/GuessWhatGame by original authors.

Table 1. Results on training images (NewObject) and test images (NewImage).

Method	NewObject			NewImage		
	Sampling	Greedy	Beam-Search	Sampling	Greedy	Beam-Search
Baseline [22]	41.6	43.5	47.1	39.2	40.8	44.6
Sole-r [18]	58.5	60.3	60.2	56.5	58.4	58.4
VQG-r_g	60.6	61.7	61.4	58.2	59.3	59.4
VQG-r_g+r_p	62.1	62.9	63.1	59.3	60.6	60.5
VQG-r_g+r_i	61.3	62.4	62.7	58.5	59.7	60.1
VQG-r_g+r_p+r_i	63.2	63.6	63.9	59.8	60.7	60.8

We initialize the training environment with the standard `Oracle`, `Guesser` and VQG baseline, then start to train the VQG agent with proposed reward functions. We train our models for 100 epochs with stochastic gradient descent (SGD) [3]. The learning rate and batch size are 0.001 and 64, respectively. The baseline function b_φ is trained with SGD at the same time. During each epoch, each training image is sampled once, and one of the objects inside it is randomly assigned as the target. We set the maximum round $J_{max} = 5$ and maximum length of question $M_{max} = 12$. The weight of the dialog round reward is set to $\lambda = 0.1$. The progressive reward is set as $\eta = 0.1$[2].

4.3 Results and Ablation Analysis

In this section, we give the overall analysis on proposed intermediate reward functions. To better show the effectiveness of each reward, we conduct comprehensive ablation studies. Moreover, we also carry out a human interpretability study to evaluate whether human subjects can understand the generated questions and how well the human can use these question-answer pairs to achieve the final goal. We note VQG agent trained with *goal-achieved* reward as VQG-r_g, trained with *goal-achieved* and *progressive* rewards as VQG-r_g+r_p, trained with *goal-achieved* and *informativeness* rewards as VQG-r_g+r_i. The final agent trained with all three rewards is noted as VQG-r_g+r_p+r_i.

`Overall Analysis.` Table 1 show the comparisons between VQG agent optimized by proposed intermediate rewards and the state-of-the-art model proposed in [18] noted as Sole-r, which uses indicator of whether reaching the final goal as the sole reward function. As we can see, with proposed intermediate rewards and their combinations, our VQG agents outperform both compared models on all evaluation metrics. More specifically, our final VQG-r_g+r_p+r_i agent surpasses the Sole-r 4.7%, 3.3% and 3.7% accuracy on NewObject sampling, greedy and beam-search respectively, while obtains 3.3%, 2.3% and 2.4% higher accuracy on NewImage sampling, greedy and beam-search respectively. Moreover, all of our agents outperform the supervised baseline by a significant margin.

To fully show the effectiveness of our proposed intermediate rewards, we train three VQG agents using r_g, r_g+r_p, and r_g+r_i rewards respectively, and conduct

[2] We use a grid search to select the hyper-parameters λ and η, we find 0.1 produces the best results..

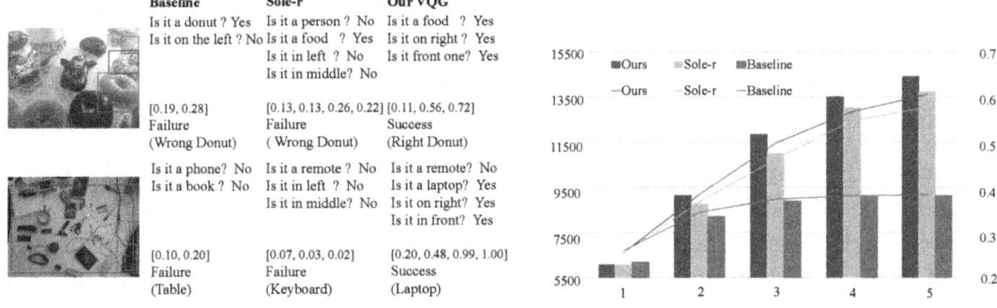

Fig. 3. Left figure: Some qualitative results of our agent (green), and the comparisons with the baseline (blue) and Sole-r model (brown). The elements in the middle array indicate the successful probabilities after each round. Right figure: The comparisons of success ratio between our agent and Sole-r, as well the baseline model, at the different dialogue round. The left and right y-axises indicate the number and ratio of successful dialogues respectively, which corresponds to the bar and line charts. (Color figure online)

ablation analysis. As we can see, the VQG-r_g already outperforms both the baseline and the state-of-the-art model, which means that controlling dialogue round can push the agent to ask more wise questions. With the combination of r_p and r_i reward respectively, the performance of VQG agent further improved. We find that the improvement gained from r_p reward is higher than r_i reward, which suggests that the intermediate *progressive* reward contributes more in our experiment. Our final agent combines all rewards and achieves the best results. Figure 3 shows some qualitative results.

`Dialogue Round.` We conduct an experiment to investigate the relationship between the dialogue round and the game success ratio. More specifically, we let `Guesser` to select the object at each round and calculate the success ratio at the given round, the comparisons of different models are shown in Fig. 3. As we can see, our agent can achieve the goal at fewer rounds compared to the other models, especially at the round three.

`Progressive Trend.` To prove our VQG agent can learn a progressive trend on generated questions, we count the percentage of the successful game that has a progressive (ascending) trend on the target object, by observing the probability distributions generated by `Guesser` at each round. Our agent achieves 60.7%, while baseline and Sole-r are 50.8% and 57.3% respectively, which indicates that our agent is better at generating questions in a progressive trend considering we introduce the progressive reward r_p. Some qualitative results of the 'progressive trend' are shown in the Fig. 3, *i.e.*, the probability of the right answer is progressively increasing. Moreover, we also compute the target probability differences between the initial and final round and then divided by the number of rounds J, *i.e.*, $(p_J(o^*) - p_1(o^*))/J$. This value is the 'slope' of the progress, which reflects whether an agent can make progress in a quicker way. Our model achieves 0.10 on average, which outperforms the baseline 0.05 and Sole-r 0.08. This shows that with the proposed reward, our agent can reach the final goal with a higher 'jump' on the target probability. By combining the progressive reward with other two rewards, the agent is designed to reach the final goal in a progressive manner within limited rounds, which eliminates the infinitesimal increase case.

`Question Informativeness.` We investigate the informativeness of the questions generated by different models. We let `Oracle` answer questions for all the objects at each round, and count the percentage of high-quality questions in the successful game. We define that a high-quality question is a one does not lead to the same answer for all the candidate objects. The experimental results show that our VQG agent has 87.7% high-quality questions, which is higher than the baseline 84.7% and Sole-r 86.3%. This confirms the contribution of the r_i reward.

4.4 Human Study

We conduct human studies to see how well the human can benefit from the questions generated by these models. We show 100 images with generated question-answer pairs from different agents to eight human subjects.

For the *goal-achieved* reward, we let human subjects guess the target object, i.e., replacing the Guesser as a human. Eight subjects are asked to play on the same split, and the game is successful if more than half of the subjects give the right answer. Subjects achieve the highest success rate 75% based on our agent, while achieving 53% and 69% on the baseline and Sole-r respectively. The human study along with the ablation studies validate the significance of our proposed goal-achieved reward. For the *progressive* reward, each game generated by different agents is rated by the human subjects on a scale of 1 to 5, if the generated questions gradually improve the probability of guessing the target object from the human perspective, i.e., it can help human progressively achieve the final goal, the higher score will be given by the subject. We then compute the average scores from the eight subjects. Based on the experimental results, our agent achieves 3.24 on average, which is higher than baseline 2.02 and Sole-r 2.76. This indicates that the questions generated by our agent can lead to the goal in a more progressive way. For the *informativeness* reward, we evaluate the informativeness of each generated question by asking human subjects to rate it on a scale of 1 to 5, if this question is useful for guessing the target object from the human perspective, i.e., it can eliminate the confusion and distinguish the candidate objects for the human, the higher score will be given by the subject. We then average the scores from eight subjects for each question. Based on the experimental results, our agent achieves 3.08 on average, while baseline and Sole-r achieves 2.45 and 2.76 respectively. The advanced result shows that our agent can generate more informative questions for the human.

5 Conclusions

The ability to devise concise questions that lead to two parties to a dialog satisfying a shared goal as effectively as possible has important practical applications and theoretical implications. By introducing suitably crafted intermediate rewards into a deep reinforcement learning framework, we have shown that it is possible to achieve this result, at least for a particular class of goal. The method we have devised not only achieves the final goal reliably and succinctly but also outperforms the state-of-art. The technique of intermediate rewards we proposed here can also be applied to related goal-oriented tasks, for example, in the robot navigation, we want the robot to spend as few movements as possible to reach the destination, or in a board game, we design AI to win quickly. Our intermediate rewards can be used in these scenarios to develop an efficient AI agent.

References

1. Andreas, J., Rohrbach, M., Darrell, T., Klein, D.: Learning to compose neural networks for question answering. In: NAACL HLT 2016, The 2016 Conference of the North American Chapter of the Association for Computational Linguistics: Human Language Technologies, San Diego California, USA, 12–17 June 2016, pp. 1545–1554 (2016)
2. Antol, S., et al.: VQA: visual question answering. In: Proceedings of the IEEE International Conference on Computer Vision, pp. 2425–2433 (2015)
3. Bottou, L.: Large-scale machine learning with stochastic gradient descent. In: Lechevallier, Y., Saporta, G. (eds.) Proceedings of COMPSTAT 2010, pp. 177–186. Springer, Heidelberg (2010). https://doi.org/10.1007/978-3-7908-2604-3_16
4. Das, A., et al.: Visual dialog. CoRR abs/1611.08669 (2016)
5. Das, A., Kottur, S., Moura, J.M.F., Lee, S., Batra, D.: Learning cooperative visual dialog agents with deep reinforcement learning. In: Proceedings of IEEE International Conferernce on Computer Vision, pp. 2970–2979 (2017)
6. El Asri, L., Laroche, R., Pietquin, O.: Reward shaping for statistical optimisation of dialogue management. In: Dediu, A.-H., Martín-Vide, C., Mitkov, R., Truthe, B. (eds.) SLSP 2013. LNCS (LNAI), vol. 7978, pp. 93–101. Springer, Heidelberg (2013). https://doi.org/10.1007/978-3-642-39593-2_8
7. Hu, R., Andreas, J., Rohrbach, M., Darrell, T., Saenko, K.: Learning to reason: end-to-end module networks for visual question answering. In: Proceedings of IEEE International Conferernce on Computer Vision, pp. 804–813 (2017)
8. Johnson, J., Karpathy, A., Fei-Fei, L.: DenseCap: fully convolutional localization networks for dense captioning. In: Proceedings of the IEEE Conference on Computer Vision and Pattern Recognition, pp. 4565–4574 (2016)
9. Kaelbling, L.P., Littman, M.L., Moore, A.W.: Reinforcement learning: a survey. J. Arti. Intell. Res. **4**, 237–285 (1996)
10. Li, Y., Duan, N., Zhou, B., Chu, X., Ouyang, W., Wang, X.: Visual question generation as dual task of visual question answering. CoRR abs/1709.07192 (2017)
11. Liu, S., Zhu, Z., Ye, N., Guadarrama, S., Murphy, K.: Optimization of image description metrics using policy gradient methods. CoRR abs/1612.00370 (2016)
12. Lu, J., Kannan, A., Yang, J., Parikh, D., Batra, D.: Best of both worlds: transferring knowledge from discriminative learning to a generative visual dialog model. In: Proceedings of Advances in Neural Information Processing Systems, pp. 313–323 (2017)
13. Mora, I.M., de la Puente, S.P., Giro-i Nieto, X.: Towards automatic generation of question answer pairs from images (2016)

14. Mostafazadeh, N., Misra, I., Devlin, J., Mitchell, M., He, X., Vanderwende, L.: Generating natural questions about an image. In: Proceedings of Conference Association for Computational Linguistics (2016)
15. Ng, A.Y., Harada, D., Russell, S.: Policy invariance under reward transformations: theory and application to reward shaping. In: Proceedings of the International Conference on Machine Learning, vol. 99, pp. 278–287 (1999)
16. Ren, Z., Wang, X., Zhang, N., Lv, X., Li, L.J.: Deep reinforcement learning-based image captioning with embedding reward. In: Proceedings of the IEEE Confererrnce on Computer Vision and Pattern Recognition (2017)
17. Rennie, S.J., Marcheret, E., Mroueh, Y., Ross, J., Goel, V.: Self-critical sequence training for image captioning. In: Proceedings of the IEEE Confererrnce on Computer Vision and Pattern Recognition, pp. 1179–1195 (2017)
18. Strub, F., de Vries, H., Mary, J., Piot, B., Courville, A.C., Pietquin, O.: End-to-end optimization of goal-driven and visually grounded dialogue systems. In: Proceedings of the International Joint Conferences on Artificial Intelligence (2017)
19. Su, P., Vandyke, D., Gasic, M., Mrksic, N., Wen, T., Young, S.J.: Reward shaping with recurrent neural networks for speeding up on-line policy learning in spoken dialogue systems. In: Proceedings of the SIGDIAL 2015 Conference, The 16th Annual Meeting of the Special Interest Group on Discourse and Dialogue, pp. 417–421 (2015)
20. Sutton, R.S., Barto, A.G.: Reinforcement Learning: An Introduction, vol. 1. MIT press, Cambridge (1998)
21. Sutton, R.S., McAllester, D.A., Singh, S.P., Mansour, Y.: Policy gradient methods for reinforcement learning with function approximation. In: Advances in Neural Information Processing Systems, pp. 1057–1063 (2000)
22. de Vries, H., Strub, F., Chandar, S., Pietquin, O., Larochelle, H., Courville, A.C.: Guesswhat?! visual object discovery through multi-modal dialogue. In: Proceedings of IEEE Conference on Computer Vision and Pattern Recognition (2017)
23. Wu, Q., Wang, P., Shen, C., Dick, A., van den Hengel, A.: Ask me anything: free-form visual question answering based on knowledge from external sources. In: Proceedings of the IEEE Conference on Computer Vision and Pattern Recognition, June 2016
24. Xu, H., Saenko, K.: Ask, attend and answer: exploring question-guided spatial attention for visual question answering. In: Leibe, B., Matas, J., Sebe, N., Welling, M. (eds.) ECCV 2016. LNCS, vol. 9911, pp. 451–466. Springer, Cham (2016). https://doi.org/10.1007/978-3-319-46478-7_28
25. Zhang, S., Qu, L., You, S., Yang, Z., Zhang, J.: Automatic generation of grounded visual questions. In: Proceedings of the International Joint Conference on Artificial Intelligence, pp. 4235–4243 (2017)
26. Zhu, Y., Lim, J.J., Fei-Fei, L.: Knowledge acquisition for visual question answering via iterative querying. In: Proceedings of the IEEE Conference on Computer Vision and Pattern Recognition (2017)

DeepGUM: Learning Deep Robust Regression with a Gaussian-Uniform Mixture Model

Stéphane Lathuilière[1,3(✉)], Pablo Mesejo[1,2], Xavier Alameda-Pineda[1], and Radu Horaud[1]

[1] Inria Grenoble Rhône-Alpes, Montbonnot-Saint-Martin, France
{stephane.lathuiliere,pablo.mesejo,xavier.alameda-pineda, radu.horaud}@inria.fr
[2] University of Granada, Granada, Spain
[3] University of Trento, Trento, Italy

Abstract. In this paper we address the problem of how to robustly train a ConvNet for regression, or deep robust regression. Traditionally, deep regression employ the L_2 loss function, known to be sensitive to outliers, i.e. samples that either lie at an abnormal distance away from the majority of the training samples, or that correspond to wrongly annotated targets. This means that, during back-propagation, outliers may bias the training process due to the high magnitude of their gradient. In this paper, we propose DeepGUM: a deep regression model that is robust to outliers thanks to the use of a Gaussian-uniform mixture model. We derive an optimization algorithm that alternates between the unsupervised detection of outliers using expectation-maximization, and the supervised training with *cleaned* samples using stochastic gradient descent. DeepGUM is able to adapt to a continuously evolving outlier distribution, avoiding to manually impose any threshold on the proportion of outliers in the training set. Extensive experimental evaluations on four different tasks (facial and fashion landmark detection, age and head pose estimation) lead us to conclude that our novel robust technique provides reliability in the presence of various types of noise and protection against a high percentage of outliers.

Keywords: Robust regression · Deep neural networks Mixture model · Outlier detection

1 Introduction

For the last decade, deep learning architectures have undoubtably established the state of the art in computer vision tasks such as image classification [18,38]

Electronic supplementary material The online version of this chapter (https://doi.org/10.1007/978-3-030-01228-1_13) contains supplementary material, which is available to authorized users.

V. Ferrari et al. (Eds.): ECCV 2018, LNCS 11209, pp. 205–221, 2018.
https://doi.org/10.1007/978-3-030-01228-1_13

Fig. 1. A Gaussian-uniform mixture model is combined with a ConvNet architecture to downgrade the influence of wrongly annotated targets (outliers) on the learning process.

or object detection [15,33]. These architectures, e.g. ConvNets, consist of several convolutional layers, followed by a few fully connected layers and by a classification softmax layer with, for instance, a cross-entropy loss. ConvNets have also been used for regression, i.e. predict continuous as opposed to categorical output values. Classical regression-based computer vision methods have addressed human pose estimation [39], age estimation [30], head-pose estimation [9], or facial landmark detection [37], to cite a few. Whenever ConvNets are used for learning a regression network, the softmax layer is replaced with a fully connected layer, with linear or sigmoid activations, and L_2 is often used to measure the discrepancy between prediction and target variables. It is well known that L_2-loss is strongly sensitive to outliers, potentially leading to poor generalization performance [17]. While robust regression is extremely well investigated in statistics, there has only been a handful of methods that combine robust regression with deep architectures.

This paper proposes to mitigate the influence of outliers when deep neural architectures are used to learn a regression function, ConvNets in particular. More precisely, we investigate a methodology specifically designed to cope with two types of outliers that are often encountered: (i) samples that lie at an abnormal distance away from the other training samples, and (ii) wrongly annotated training samples. On the one hand, abnormal samples are present in almost any measurement system and they are known to bias the regression parameters. On the other hand, deep learning requires very large amounts of data and the annotation process, be it either automatic or manual, is inherently prone to errors. These unavoidable issues fully justify the development of robust deep regression.

The proposed method combines the representation power of ConvNets with the principled probabilistic mixture framework for outlier detection and rejection, e.g. Fig. 1. We propose to use a Gaussian-uniform mixture (GUM) as the last layer of a ConvNet, and we refer to this combination as DeepGUM. The mixture model hypothesizes a Gaussian distribution for inliers and a uniform distribution for outliers. We interleave an EM procedure within stochastic gradient descent (SGD) to downgrade the influence of outliers in order to robustly estimate the network parameters. We empirically validate the effectiveness of the proposed method with four computer vision problems and associated datasets:

facial and fashion landmark detection, age estimation, and head pose estimation. The standard regression measures are accompanied by statistical tests that discern between random differences and systematic improvements.

The remainder of the paper is organized as follows. Section 2 describes the related work. Section 3 describes in detail the proposed method and the associated algorithm. Section 4 describes extensive experiments with several applications and associated datasets. Section 5 draws conclusions and discusses the potential of robust deep regression in computer vision.

2 Related Work

Robust regression has long been studied in statistics [17,24,31] and in computer vision [6,25,36]. Robust regression methods have a high *breakdown point*, which is the smallest amount of outlier contamination that an estimator can handle before yielding poor results. Prominent examples are the least trimmed squares, the Theil-Sen estimator or heavy-tailed distributions [14]. Several robust training strategies for artificial neural networks are also available [5,27].

M-estimators, sampling methods, trimming methods and robust clustering are among the most used robust statistical methods. M-estimators [17] minimize the sum of a positive-definite function of the residuals and attempt to reduce the influence of large residual values. The minimization is carried our with weighted least squares techniques, with no proof of convergence for most M-estimators. Sampling methods [25], such as least-median-of-squares or random sample consensus (RANSAC), estimate the model parameters by solving a system of equations defined for a randomly chosen data subset. The main drawback of sampling methods is that they require complex data-sampling procedures and it is tedious to use them for estimating a large number of parameters. Trimming methods [31] rank the residuals and down-weight the data points associated with large residuals. They are typically cast into a (non-linear) weighted least squares optimization problem, where the weights are modified at each iteration, leading to iteratively re-weighted least squares problems. Robust statistics have also been addressed in the framework of mixture models and a number of robust mixture models were proposed, such as Gaussian mixtures with a uniform noise component [2,8], heavy-tailed distributions [11], trimmed likelihood estimators [12,28], or weighted-data mixtures [13]. Importantly, it has been recently reported that modeling outliers with an uniform component yields very good performance [8,13].

Deep robust classification was recently addressed, e.g. [3] assumes that observed labels are generated from true labels with unknown noise parameters: a probabilistic model that maps true labels onto observed labels is proposed and an EM algorithm is derived. In [41] is proposed a probabilistic model that exploits the relationships between classes, images and noisy labels for large-scale image classification. This framework requires a dataset with explicit clean- and noisy-label annotations as well as an additional dataset annotated with a noise type for each sample, thus making the method difficult to use in practice. Classification algorithms based on a distillation process to learn from noisy data was recently proposed [21].

Recently, deep regression methods were proposed, e.g. [19,26,29,37,39]. Despite the vast robust statistics literature and the importance of regression in computer vision, at the best of our knowledge there has been only one attempt to combine robust regression with deep networks [4], where robustness is achieved by minimizing the Tukey's bi-weight loss function, i.e. an M-estimator. In this paper we take a radical different approach and propose to use robust mixture modeling within a ConvNet. We conjecture that while *inlier noise* follows a Gaussian distribution, *outlier errors* are uniformly distributed over the volume occupied by the data. Mixture modeling provides a principled way to characterize data points individually, based on posterior probabilities. We propose an algorithm that interleaves a robust mixture model with network training, i.e. alternates between EM and SGD. EM evaluates data-posterior probabilities which are then used to weight the residuals used by the network loss function and hence to downgrade the influence of samples drawn from the uniform distribution. Then, the network parameters are updated which in turn are used by EM. A prominent feature of the algorithm is that it requires neither annotated outlier samples nor prior information about their percentage in the data. This is in contrast with [41] that requires explicit inlier/outlier annotations and with [4] which uses a fixed hyperparameter ($c = 4.6851$) that allows to exclude from SGD samples with high residuals.

3 Deep Regression with a Robust Mixture Model

We assume that the inlier noise follows a Gaussian distribution while the outlier error follows a uniform distribution. Let $\boldsymbol{x} \in \mathbb{R}^M$ and $\boldsymbol{y} \in \mathbb{R}^D$ be the input image and the output vector with dimensions M and D, respectively, with $D \ll M$. Let $\boldsymbol{\phi}$ denote a ConvNet with parameters $\boldsymbol{w}$ such that $\boldsymbol{y} = \boldsymbol{\phi}(\boldsymbol{x}, \boldsymbol{w})$. We aim to train a model that detects outliers and downgrades their role in the prediction of a network output, while there is no prior information about the percentage and spread of outliers. The probability of $\boldsymbol{y}$ conditioned by $\boldsymbol{x}$ follows a Gaussian-uniform mixture model (GUM):

$$p(\boldsymbol{y}|\boldsymbol{x};\boldsymbol{\theta},\boldsymbol{w}) = \pi\, \mathcal{N}(\boldsymbol{y};\boldsymbol{\phi}(\boldsymbol{x};\boldsymbol{w}),\boldsymbol{\Sigma}) + (1-\pi)\, \mathcal{U}(\boldsymbol{y};\gamma), \tag{1}$$

where π is the prior probability of an inlier sample, γ is the normalization parameter of the uniform distribution and $\boldsymbol{\Sigma} \in \mathbb{R}^{D\times D}$ is the covariance matrix of the multivariate Gaussian distribution. Let $\boldsymbol{\theta} = \{\pi, \gamma, \boldsymbol{\Sigma}\}$ be the parameter set of GUM. At training we estimate the parameters of the mixture model, $\boldsymbol{\theta}$, and of the network, $\boldsymbol{w}$. An EM algorithm is used to estimate the former together with the responsibilities r_n, which are plugged into the network's loss, minimized using SGD so as to estimate the later.

3.1 EM Algorithm

Let a training dataset consist of N image-vector pairs $\{\boldsymbol{x}_n, \boldsymbol{y}_n\}_{n=1}^N$. At each iteration, EM alternates between evaluating the expected complete-data log-likelihood (E-step) and updating the parameter set $\boldsymbol{\theta}$ conditioned by the network parameters (M-step). In practice, the E-step evaluates the posterior probability (responsibility) of an image-vector pair n to be an inlier:

$$r_n(\boldsymbol{\theta}^{(i)}) = \frac{\pi^{(i)}\mathcal{N}(\boldsymbol{y}_n; \boldsymbol{\phi}(\boldsymbol{x}_n, \boldsymbol{w}^{(c)}), \boldsymbol{\Sigma}^{(i)})}{\pi^{(i)}\mathcal{N}(\boldsymbol{y}_n; \boldsymbol{\phi}(\boldsymbol{x}_n, \boldsymbol{w}^{(c)}), \boldsymbol{\Sigma}^{(i)}) + (1-\pi^{(i)})\gamma^{(i)}}, \tag{2}$$

where (i) denotes the EM iteration index and $\boldsymbol{w}^{(c)}$ denotes the currently estimated network parameters. The posterior probability of the n-th data pair to be an outlier is $1 - r_n(\boldsymbol{\theta}^{(i)})$. The M-step updates the mixture parameters $\boldsymbol{\theta}$ with:

$$\boldsymbol{\Sigma}^{(i+1)} = \sum_{n=1}^{N} r_n(\boldsymbol{\theta}^{(i)})\boldsymbol{\delta}_n^{(i)}\boldsymbol{\delta}_n^{(i)\top}, \tag{3}$$

$$\pi^{(i+1)} = \sum_{n=1}^{N} r_n(\boldsymbol{\theta}^{(i)})/N, \tag{4}$$

$$\frac{1}{\gamma^{(i+1)}} = \prod_{d=1}^{D} 2\sqrt{3\left(C_{2d}^{(i+1)} - \left(C_{1d}^{(i+1)}\right)^2\right)}, \tag{5}$$

where $\boldsymbol{\delta}_n^{(i)} = \boldsymbol{y}_n - \boldsymbol{\phi}(\boldsymbol{x}_n; \boldsymbol{w}^{(c)})$, and C_1 and C_2 are the first- and second-order centered data moments computed using ($\delta_{nd}^{(i)}$ denotes the d-th entry of $\boldsymbol{\delta}_n^{(i)}$):

$$C_{1d}^{(i+1)} = \frac{1}{N}\sum_{n=1}^{N} \frac{(1 - r_n(\boldsymbol{\theta}^{(i)}))}{1-\pi^{(i+1)}}\delta_{nd}^{(i)}, \; C_{2d}^{(i+1)} = \frac{1}{N}\sum_{n=1}^{N} \frac{(1 - r_n(\boldsymbol{\theta}^{(i)}))}{1-\pi^{(i+1)}}\left(\delta_{nd}^{(i)}\right)^2. \tag{6}$$

The iterative estimation of γ as just proposed has an advantage over using a constant value based on the volume of the data, as done in robust mixture models [8]. Indeed, γ is updated using the actual volume occupied by the outliers, which increases the ability of the algorithm to discriminate between inliers and outliers.

Another prominent advantage of DeepGUM for robustly predicting multi-dimensional outputs is its flexibility for handling the granularity of outliers. Consider for example to problem of locating landmarks in an image. One may want to devise a method that disregards outlying landmarks and not the whole image. In this case, one may use a GUM model for each landmark category. In the case of two-dimensional landmarks, this induces $D/2$ covariance matrices of size 2 (D is the dimensionality of the target space). Similarly one may use an coordinate-wise outlier model, namely D scalar variances. Finally, one may use an image-wise outlier model, i.e. the model detailed above. This flexibility is an attractive property of the proposed model as opposed to [4] which uses a coordinate-wise outlier model.

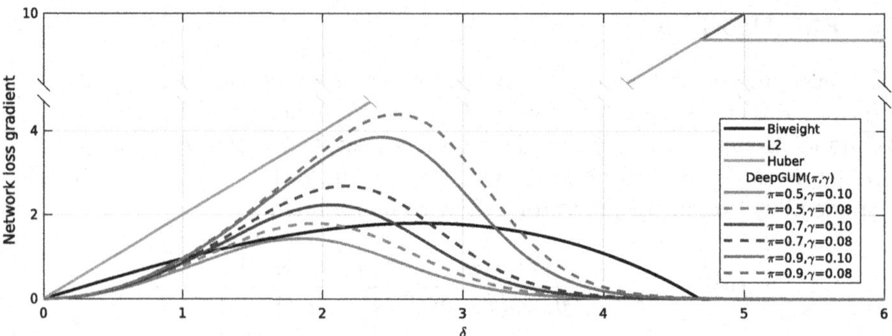

Fig. 2. Loss gradients for Biweight (black), Huber (cyan), L_2 (magenta), and DeepGUM (remaining colors). Huber and L_2 overlap up to $\delta = 4.6851$ (the plots are truncated along the vertical coordinate). DeepGUM is shown for different values of π and γ, although in practice they are estimated via EM. The gradients of DeepGUM and Biweight vanish for large residuals. DeepGUM offers some flexibility over Biweight thanks to π and γ. (Color figure online)

3.2 Network Loss Function

As already mentioned we use SGD to estimate the network parameters $\boldsymbol{w}$. Given the updated GUM parameters estimated with EM, $\boldsymbol{\theta}^{(c)}$, the regression loss function is weighted with the responsibility of each data pair:

$$\mathcal{L}_{\text{DEEPGUM}} = \sum_{n=1}^{N} r_n(\boldsymbol{\theta}^{(c)}) ||\boldsymbol{y}_n - \boldsymbol{\phi}(\boldsymbol{x}_n; \boldsymbol{w})||_2^2. \tag{7}$$

With this formulation, the contribution of a training pair to the loss gradient vanishes (i) if the sample is an inlier with small error ($\|\boldsymbol{\delta}_n\|_2 \to 0, r_n \to 1$) or (ii) if the sample is an outlier ($r_n \to 0$). In both cases, the network will not back propagate any error. Consequently, the parameters $\boldsymbol{w}$ are updated only with inliers. This is graphically shown in Fig. 2, where we plot the loss gradient as a function of a one-dimensional residual δ, for DeepGUM, Biweight, Huber and L_2. For fair comparison with Biweight and Huber, the plots correspond to a unit variance (i.e. standard normal, see discussion following Eq. (3) in [4]). We plot the DeepGUM loss gradient for different values of π and γ to discuss different situations, although in practice all the parameters are estimated with EM. We observe that the gradient of the Huber loss increases linearly with δ, until reaching a stable point (corresponding to $c = 4.6851$ in [4]). Conversely, the gradient of both DeepGUM and Biweight vanishes for large residuals (i.e. $\delta > c$). Importantly, DeepGUM offers some flexibility as compared to Biweight. Indeed, we observe that when the amount of inliers increases (large π) or the spread of outliers increases (small γ), the importance given to inliers is higher, which is a desirable property. The opposite effect takes place for lower amounts of inliers and/or reduced outlier spread.

Algorithm 1. DeepGUM training

input: $\mathcal{T} = (\boldsymbol{x}_n^{\mathrm{T}}, \boldsymbol{y}_n^{\mathrm{T}})_{n=1}^{N_{\mathrm{T}}}$, $\mathcal{V} = \{\boldsymbol{x}_n^{\mathrm{V}}, \boldsymbol{y}_n^{\mathrm{V}}\}_{n=1}^{N_{\mathrm{V}}}$, and $\epsilon > 0$ (convergence threshold).
initialization: Run SGD on $\mathcal{T}$ to minimize (7) with $r_n = 1, \forall n$, until the convergence criterion on $\mathcal{V}$ is reached.
repeat
  EM algorithm: Unsupervised outlier detection
  repeat
    Update the r_n's with (2).
    Update the mixture parameters with (3), (4), (5).
  until The parameters $\boldsymbol{\theta}$ are stable.
  SGD: Deep regression learning
  repeat
    Run SGD to minimize $\mathcal{L}_{\text{DEEPGUM}}$ in (7).
  until Early stop with a patience of K epochs.
until $\mathcal{L}_{\text{DEEPGUM}}$ grows on $\mathcal{V}$.

3.3 Training Algorithm

In order to train the proposed model, we assume the existence of a training and validation datasets, denoted $\mathcal{T} = \{\boldsymbol{x}_n^{\mathrm{T}}, \boldsymbol{y}_n^{\mathrm{T}}\}_{n=1}^{N_{\mathrm{T}}}$ and $\mathcal{V} = \{\boldsymbol{x}_n^{\mathrm{V}}, \boldsymbol{y}_n^{\mathrm{V}}\}_{n=1}^{N_{\mathrm{V}}}$, respectively. The training alternates between the unsupervised EM algorithm of Sect. 3.1 and the supervised SGD algorithm of Sect. 3.2, i.e. Algorithm 1. EM takes as input the training set, alternates between responsibility evaluation, (2) and mixture parameter update, (3), (4), (5), and iterates until convergence, namely until the mixture parameters do not evolve anymore. The current mixture parameters are used to evaluate the responsibilities of the validation set. The SGD algorithm takes as input the training and validation sets as well as the associated responsibilities. In order to prevent over-fitting, we perform early stopping on the validation set with a patience of K epochs.

Notice that the training procedure requires neither specific annotation of outliers nor the ratio of outliers present in the data. The procedure is initialized by executing SGD, as just described, with all the samples being supposed to be inliers, i.e. $r_n = 1, \forall n$. Algorithm 1 is stopped when $\mathcal{L}_{\text{DEEPGUM}}$ does not decrease anymore. It is important to notice that we do not need to constrain the model to avoid the trivial solution, namely all the samples are considered as outliers. This is because after the first SGD execution, the network can discriminate between the two categories. In the extreme case when DeepGUM would consider all the samples as outliers, the algorithm would stop after the first SGD run and would output the initial model.

Since EM provides the data covariance matrix $\boldsymbol{\Sigma}$, it may be tempting to use the Mahalanobis norm instead of the L_2 norm in (7). The covariance matrix is narrow along output dimensions with low-amplitude noise and wide along dimensions with high-amplitude noise. The Mahalanobis distance would give equal importance to low- and high-amplitude noise dimensions which is not desired. Another interesting feature of the proposed algorithm is that the posterior r_n weights the learning rate of sample n as its gradient is simply multiplied by r_n.

Therefore, the proposed algorithm automatically selects a learning rate for each individual training sample.

4 Experiments

The purpose of the experimental validation is two-fold. First, we empirically validate DeepGUM with three datasets that are naturally corrupted with outliers. The validations are carried out with the following applications: fashion landmark detection (Sect. 4.1), age estimation (Sect. 4.2) and head pose estimation (Sect. 4.3). Second, we delve into the robustness of DeepGUM and analyze its behavior in comparison with existing robust deep regression techniques by corrupting the annotations with an increasing percentage of outliers on the facial landmark detection task (Sect. 4.4).

We systematically compare DeepGUM with the standard L_2 loss, the Huber loss and the Biweight loss (used in [4]). In all these cases, we use the VGG-16 architecture [35] pre-trained on ImageNet [32]. We also tried to use the architecture proposed in [4], but we were unable to reproduce the results reported in [4] on the LSP and Parse datasets, using the code provided by the authors. Therefore, for the sake of reproducibility and for a fair comparison between different robust loss functions, we used VGG-16 in all our experiments. Following the recommendations from [20], we fine-tune the last convolutional block and both fully connected layers with a mini-batch of size 128 and learning rate set to 10^{-4}. The fine-tuning starts with 3 epochs of L_2 loss, before exploiting either the Biweight, Huber of DeepGUM loss. When using any of these three losses, the network output is normalized with the median absolute deviation (as in [4]), computed on the entire dataset after each epoch. Early stopping with a patience of $K = 5$ epochs is employed and the data is augmented using mirroring.

In order to evaluate the methods, we report the mean absolute error (MAE) between the regression target and the network output over the test set. Inspired by [20], we complete the evaluation with statistical tests that allow to point out when the differences between methods are systematic and statistically significant or due to chance. Statistical tests are run per-image regression errors and therefore can only be applied to the methods for which the code is available, and not to average errors reported in the literature; in the latter case, only MAE are made available. In practice, we use the non-parametric Wilcoxon signed-rank test [40] to assess whether the null hypothesis (the median difference between pairs of observations is zero) is true or false. We denote the statistical significance with *, ** or ***, corresponding to a p-value (the conditional probability of, given the null hypothesis is true, getting a test statistic as extreme or more extreme than the calculated test statistic) smaller than $p = 0.05$, $p = 0.01$ or $p = 0.001$, respectively. We only report the statistical significance of the methods with the lowest MAE. For instance, A^{***} means that *the probability that method* A *is equivalent to any other method is less than* $p = 0.001$.

Table 1. Mean absolute error on the upper-body subset of FLD, per landmark and in average. The landmarks are left (L) and right (R) collar (C), sleeve (S) and hem (H). The results of DFA are from [23] and therefore do not take part in the statistical comparison.

Method	Upper-body landmarks						
	LC	RC	LS	RS	LH	RH	Avg.
DFA [23] (L_2)	15.90	15.90	30.02	29.12	23.07	22.85	22.85
DFA [23] (5 VGG)	10.75	10.75	20.38	19.93	15.90	16.12	15.23
L_2	12.08	12.08	18.87	18.91	16.47	16.40	15.80
Huber [16]	14.32	13.71	20.85	19.57	20.06	19.99	18.08
Biweight [4]	13.32	13.29	21.88	21.84	18.49	18.44	17.88
DeepGUM	11.97***	11.99***	18.59***	18.50***	16.44***	16.29***	15.63***

4.1 Fashion Landmark Detection

Visual fashion analysis presents a wide spectrum of applications such as cloth recognition, retrieval, and recommendation. We employ the fashion landmark dataset (FLD) [22] that includes more than $120K$ images, where each image is labeled with eight landmarks. The dataset is equally divided in three subsets: upper-body clothes (6 landmarks), full-body clothes (8 landmarks) and lower-body clothes (4 landmarks). We randomly split each subset of the dataset into test ($5K$), validation ($5K$) and training ($\sim 30K$). Two metrics are used: the mean absolute error (MAE) of the landmark localization and the percentage of failures (landmarks detected further from the ground truth than a given threshold). We employ *landmark-wise* r_n.

Table 1 reports the results obtained on the upper-body subset of the fashion landmark dataset (additional results on full-body and lower-body subsets are included in the supplementary material). We report the mean average error (in pixels) for each landmark individually, and the overall average (last column). While for the first subset we can compare with the very recent results reported in [23], for the other there are no previously reported results. Generally speaking, we outperform all other baselines in average, but also in each of the individual landmarks. The only exception is the comparison against the method utilizing five VGG pipelines to estimate the position of the landmarks. Although this method reports slightly better performance than DeepGUM for some columns of Table 1, we recall that we are using one single VGG as front-end, and therefore the representation power cannot be the same as the one associated to a pipeline employing five VGG's trained for tasks such as pose estimation and cloth classification that clearly aid the fashion landmark estimation task.

Interestingly, DeepGUM yields better results than L_2 regression and a major improvement over Biweight [4] and Huber [16]. This behavior is systematic for all fashion landmarks and statistically significant (with $p < 0.001$). In order to better understand this behavior, we computed the percentage of outliers detected by DeepGUM and Biweight, which are 3% and 10% respectively (after convergence).

Fig. 3. Sample fashion landmarks detected by DeepGUM.

Method	MAE
L_2	5.75
Huber [16]	5.59
Biweight [4]	5.55
Dex [30]	5.25
DexGUM***	5.14
DeepGUM***	5.08

14 14 14 16 20 23

49 51 60 60 60 62

Fig. 4. Results on the CACD dataset: (left) mean absolute error and (right) images considered as outliers by DeepGUM, the annotation is displayed below each image.

We believe that within this difference (7% corresponds to $2.1K$ images) there are mostly "difficult" inliers, from which the network could learn a lot (and does it in DeepGUM) if they were not discarded as happens with Biweight. This illustrates the importance of rejecting the outliers while keeping the inliers in the learning loop, and exhibits the robustness of DeepGUM in doing so. Figure 3 displays a few landmarks estimated by DeepGUM.

4.2 Age Estimation

Age estimation from a single face image is an important task in computer vision with applications in access control and human-computer interaction. This task is closely related to the prediction of other biometric and facial attributes, such as gender, ethnicity, and hair color. We use the cross-age celebrity dataset (CACD) [7] that contains 163,446 images from 2,000 celebrities. The images are collected from search engines using the celebrity's name and desired year (from 2004 to 2013). The dataset splits into 3 parts, 1,800 celebrities are used for training, 80 for validation and 120 for testing. The validation and test sets are manually cleaned whereas the training set is noisy. In our experiments, we report results using *image-wise* r_n.

Apart from DeepGUM, L_2, Biweight and Huber, we also compare to the age estimation method based on deep expectation (Dex) [30], which was the winner of the Looking at People 2015 challenge. This method uses the VGG-16 architecture and poses the age estimation problem as a classification problem followed by a softmax expected value refinement. Regression-by-classification strategies have also been proposed for memorability and virality [1,34]. We report results with two different approaches using Dex. First, our implementation of the original Dex model. Second, we add the GUM model on top the Dex architecture; we termed this architecture DexGUM.

The table in Fig. 4 reports the results obtained on the CACD test set for age estimation. We report the mean absolute error (in years) for size different methods. We can easily observe that DeepGUM exhibits the best results: 5.08 years of MAE (0.7 years better than L_2). Importantly, the architectures using GUM (DeepGUM followed by DexGUM) are the ones offering the best performance. This claim is supported by the results of the statistical tests, which say that DexGUM and DeepGUM are statistically better than the rest (with $p < 0.001$), and that there are no statistical differences between them. This is further supported by the histogram of the error included in the supplementary material. DeepGUM considered that 7% of images were outliers and thus these images were undervalued during training. The images in Fig. 4 correspond to outliers detected by DeepGUM during training, and illustrate the ability of DeepGUM to detect outliers. Since the dataset was automatically annotated, it is prone to corrupted annotations. Indeed, the age of each celebrity is automatically annotated by subtracting the date of birth from the picture time-stamp. Intuitively, this procedure is problematic since it assumes that the automatically collected and annotated images show the right celebrity and that the times-tamp and date of birth are correct. Our experimental evaluation clearly demonstrates the benefit of a robust regression technique to operate on datasets populated with outliers.

4.3 Head Pose Estimation

The McGill real-world face video dataset [9] consists of 60 videos (a single participant per video, 31 women and 29 men) recorded with the goal of studying unconstrained face classification. The videos were recorded in both indoor and outdoor environments under different illumination conditions and participants move freely. Consequently, some frames suffer from important occlusions. The yaw angle (ranging from $-90°$ to $90°$) is annotated using a two-step labeling procedure that, first, automatically provides the most probable angle as well as a degree of confidence, and then the final label is chosen by a human annotator among the plausible angle values. Since the resulting annotations are not perfect it makes this dataset suitable to benchmark robust regression models. As the training and test sets are not separated in the original dataset, we perform a 7-fold cross-validation. We report the fold-wise MAE average and standard deviation as well as the statistical significance corresponding to the concatenation of the test results of the 7 folds. Importantly, only a subset of the dataset is publicly available (35 videos over 60).

In Table 2, we report the results obtained with different methods and employ a dagger to indicate when a particular method uses the entire dataset (60 videos)

Table 2. Mean average error on the McGill dataset. The results of the first half of the table are directly taken from the respective papers and therefore no statistical comparison is possible. †Uses extra training data.

Method	MAE	RMSE
Xiong et al. [42]†	-	29.81 ± 7.73
Zhu and Ramanan [43]†	-	35.70 ± 7.48
Demirkus et al. [9]†	-	12.41 ± 1.60
Drouard et al. [10]	12.22 ± 6.42	23.00 ± 9.42
L_2	8.60 ± 1.18	12.03 ± 1.66
Huber [16]	8.11 ± 1.08	11.79 ± 1.59
Biweight [4]	7.81 ± 1.31	11.56 ± 1.95
DeepGUM***	7.61 ± 1.00	11.37 ± 1.34

for training. We can easily notice that DeepGUM exhibits the best results compared to the other ConvNets methods (respectively 0.99°, 0.50° and 0.20° lower than L_2, Huber and Biweight in MAE). The last three approaches, all using deep architectures, significantly outperform the current state-of-the-art approach [10]. Among them, DeepGUM is significantly better than the rest with $p < 0.001$.

4.4 Facial Landmark Detection

We perform experiments on the LFW and NET facial landmark detection datasets [37] that consist of 5590 and 7876 face images, respectively. We combined both datasets and employed the same data partition as in [37]. Each face is labeled with the positions of five key-points in Cartesian coordinates, namely left and right eye, nose, and left and right corners of the mouth. The detection error is measured with the Euclidean distance between the estimated and the ground truth position of the landmark, divided by the width of the face image, as in [37]. The performance is measured with the failure rate of each landmark, where errors larger than 5% are counted as failures. The two aforementioned datasets can be considered as outlier-free since the average failure rate reported in the literature falls below 1%. Therefore, we artificially modify the annotations of the datasets for facial landmark detection to find the breakdown point of DeepGUM. Our purpose is to study the robustness of the proposed deep mixture model to outliers generated in controlled conditions. We use three different types of outliers:

- Normally Generated Outliers (*NGO*): A percentage of landmarks is selected, regardless of whether they belong to the same image or not, and shifted a distance of d pixels in a uniformly chosen random direction. The distance d follows a Gaussian distribution, $\mathcal{N}(25, 2)$. *NGO* simulates errors produced by human annotators that made a mistake when clicking, thus annotating in a slightly wrong location.

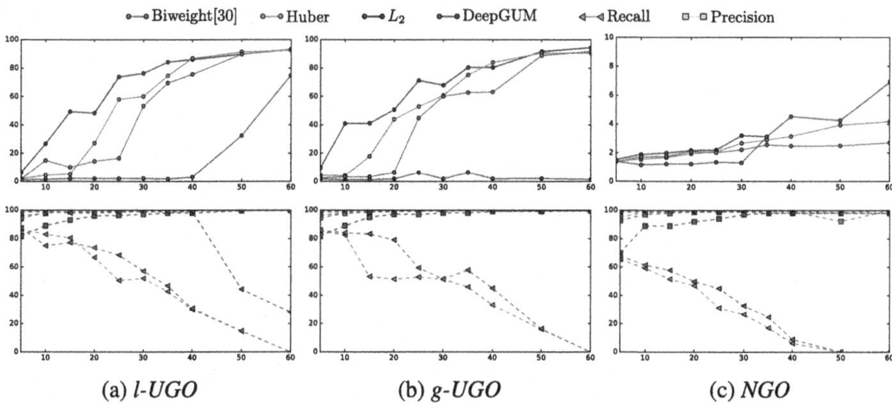

(a) *l-UGO* (b) *g-UGO* (c) *NGO*

Fig. 5. Evolution of the failure rate (top) when augmenting the noise for the 3 types of outliers considered. We also display the corresponding precisions and recalls in percentage (bottom) for the outlier class. Best seen in color. (color figure online)

- Local - Uniformly Generated Outliers (*l-UGO*): It follows the same philosophy as *NGO*, sampling the distance d from a uniform distribution over the image, instead of a Gaussian. Such errors simulate human errors that are not related to the human precision, such as not selecting the point or misunderstanding the image.
- Global - Uniformly Generated Outliers (*g-UGO*): As in the previous case, the landmarks are corrupted with uniform noise. However, in *g-UGO* the landmarks to be corrupted are grouped by image. In other words, we do not corrupt a subset of all landmarks regardless of the image they belong to, but rather corrupt all landmarks of a subset of the images. This strategy simulates problems with the annotation files or in the sensors in case of automatic annotation.

The first and the second types of outlier contamination employ *landmark-wise* r_n, while the third uses *image-wise* r_n.

The plots in Fig. 5 report the failure rate of DeepGUM, Biweight, Huber and L_2 (top) on the clean test set and the outlier detection precision and recall of all except for L_2 (bottom) for the three types of synthetic noise on the corrupted training set. The precision corresponds to the percentage of training samples classified as outliers that are true outliers; and the recall corresponds to the percentage of outliers that are classified as such. The first conclusion that can be drawn directly from this figure are that, on the one hand, Biweight and Huber systematically present a lower recall than DeepGUM.

In other words, DeepGUM exhibits the highest reliability at identifying and, therefore, ignoring outliers during training. And, on the other hand, DeepGUM tends to present a lower failure rate than Biweight, Huber and L_2 in most of the scenarios contemplated.

Regarding the four most-left plots, *l-UGO* and *g-UGO*, we can clearly observe that, while for limited amounts of outliers (i.e. <10%) all methods report comparable performance, DeepGUM is clearly superior to L_2, Biweight and Huber for larger amounts of outliers. We can also safely identify a breakdown point of DeepGUM on *l-UGO* at ~40%. This is inline with the reported precision and recall for the outlier detection task. While for Biweight and Huber, both decrease when increasing the number of outliers, these measures are constantly around 99% for DeepGUM (before 40% for *l-UGO*). The fact that the breakdown point of DeepGUM under *g-UGO* is higher than 50% is due to fact that the a priori model of the outliers (i.e. uniform distribution) corresponds to the way the data is corrupted.

For *NGO*, the corrupted annotation is always around the ground truth, leading to a failure rate smaller than 7% for all methods. We can see that all four methods exhibit comparable performance up to 30% of outliers. Beyond that threshold, Biweight outperforms the other methods in spite of presenting a progressively lower recall and a high precision (i.e. Biweight identifies very few outliers, but the ones identified are true outliers). This behavior is also exhibited by Huber. Regarding DeepGUM, we observe that in this particular setting the results are aligned with L_2. This is because the SGD procedure is not able to find a better optimum after the first epoch and therefore the early stopping mechanism is triggered and SFD output the initial network, which corresponds to L_2. We can conclude that the strategy of DeepGUM, consisting in removing all points detected as outliers, is not effective in this particular experiment. In other words, having more noisy data is better than having only few clean data in this particular case of 0-mean highly correlated noise. Nevertheless, we consider an attractive property of DeepGUM the fact that it can automatically identify these particular cases and return an acceptable solution.

5 Conclusions

This paper introduced a deep robust regression learning method that uses a Gaussian-uniform mixture model. The novelty of the paper resides in combining a probabilistic robust mixture model with deep learning in a jointly trainable fashion. In this context, previous studies only dealt with the classical L_2 loss function or Tukey's Biweight function, an M-estimator robust to outliers [4]. Our proposal yields better performance than previous deep regression approaches by proposing a novel technique, and the derived optimization procedure, that alternates between the unsupervised task of outlier detection and the supervised task of learning network parameters. The experimental validation addresses four different tasks: facial and fashion landmark detection, age estimation, and head pose estimation. We have empirically shown that DeepGUM (i) is a robust deep regression approach that does not need to rigidly specify *a priori* the distribution (number and spread) of outliers, (ii) exhibits a higher breakdown point than existing methods when the outliers are sampled from a uniform distribution (being able to deal with more than 50% of outlier contamination without providing incorrect results), and (iii) is capable of providing comparable or better results than current state-of-the-art approaches in the four aforementioned tasks. Finally, DeepGUM could be easily used to remove undesired samples that arise from tedious manual annotation. It could also deal with highly unusual training samples inherently present in automatically collected huge datasets, a problem that is currently addressed using error-prone and time-consuming human supervision.

Acknowledgments. This work was supported by the European Research Council via the ERC Advanced Grant VHIA (Vision and Hearing in Action) #113340.

References

1. Alameda-Pineda, X., Pilzer, A., Xu, D., Sebe, N., Ricci, E.: Viraliency: pooling local virality. In: IEEE Conference on Computer Vision and Pattern Recognition (2017)
2. Banfield, J.D., Raftery, A.E.: Model-based Gaussian and non-Gaussian clustering. Biometrics, 803–821 (1993)
3. Bekker, A.J., Goldberger, J.: Training deep neural-networks based on unreliable labels. In: ICASSP, pp. 2682–2686 (2016)
4. Belagiannis, V., Rupprecht, C., Carneiro, G., Navab, N.: Robust optimization for deep regression. In: ICCV (2015)
5. Beliakov, G., Kelarev, A.V., Yearwood, J.: Robust artificial neural networks and outlier detection. Technical report. CoRR abs/1110.0169 (2011)
6. Black, M.J., Rangarajan, A.: On the unification of line processes, outlier rejection, and robust statistics with applications in early vision. IJCV **19**(1), 57–91 (1996)
7. Chen, B.-C., Chen, C.-S., Hsu, W.H.: Cross-age reference coding for age-invariant face recognition and retrieval. In: Fleet, D., Pajdla, T., Schiele, B., Tuytelaars, T. (eds.) ECCV 2014. LNCS, vol. 8694, pp. 768–783. Springer, Cham (2014). https://doi.org/10.1007/978-3-319-10599-4_49
8. Coretto, P., Hennig, C.: Robust improper maximum likelihood: tuning, computation, and a comparison with other methods for robust Gaussian clustering. JASA **111**, 1648–1659 (2016)
9. Demirkus, M., Precup, D., Clark, J.J., Arbel, T.: Hierarchical temporal graphical model for head pose estimation and subsequent attribute classification in real-world videos. CVIU **136**, 128–145 (2015)
10. Drouard, V., Horaud, R., Deleforge, A., Ba, S., Evangelidis, G.: Robust head-pose estimation based on partially-latent mixture of linear regressions. TIP **26**, 1428–1440 (2017)
11. Forbes, F., Wraith, D.: A new family of multivariate heavy-tailed distributions with variable marginal amounts of tailweight: application to robust clustering. Stat. Comput. **24**(6), 971–984 (2014)
12. Galimzianova, A., Pernus, F., Likar, B., Spiclin, Z.: Robust estimation of unbalanced mixture models on samples with outliers. TPAMI **37**(11), 2273–2285 (2015)
13. Gebru, I.D., Alameda-Pineda, X., Forbes, F., Horaud, R.: EM algorithms for weighted-data clustering with application to audio-visual scene analysis. IEEE TPAMI **38**(12), 2402–2415 (2016)
14. Gelman, A., Carlin, J., Stern, H., Rubin, D.: Bayesian Data Analysis. Chapman & Hall/CRC Texts in Statistical Science. Taylor & Francis, Abingdon (2003)

15. Girshick, R., Donahue, J., Darrell, T., Malik, J.: Rich feature hierarchies for accurate object detection and semantic segmentation. In: CVPR (2014)
16. Huber, P.J.: Robust estimation of a location parameter. Ann. Math. Stat. **35**, 73–101 (1964)
17. Huber, P.: Robust Statistics. Wiley, Hoboken (2004)
18. Krizhevsky, A., Sutskever, I., Hinton, G.E.: ImageNet classification with deep convolutional neural networks. In: NIPS (2012)
19. Lathuilière, S., Juge, R., Mesejo, P., Muñoz Salinas, R., Horaud, R.: Deep mixture of linear inverse regressions applied to head-pose estimation. In: CVPR (2017)
20. Lathuilière, S., Mesejo, P., Alameda-Pineda, X., Horaud, R.: A comprehensive analysis of deep regression. arXiv preprint arXiv:1803.08450 (2018)
21. Li, Y., Yang, J., Song, Y., Cao, L., Luo, J., Li, J.: Learning from Noisy Labels with Distillation. arXiv preprint arXiv:1703.02391 (2017)
22. Liu, Z., Luo, P., Qiu, S., Wang, X., Tang, X.: Deepfashion: powering robust clothes recognition and retrieval with rich annotations. In: CVPR (2016)
23. Liu, Z., Yan, S., Luo, P., Wang, X., Tang, X.: Fashion landmark detection in the wild. In: Leibe, B., Matas, J., Sebe, N., Welling, M. (eds.) ECCV 2016. LNCS, vol. 9906, pp. 229–245. Springer, Cham (2016). https://doi.org/10.1007/978-3-319-46475-6_15
24. Maronna, R.A., Martin, D.R., Yohai, V.J.: Robust Statistics. Wiley, Hoboken (2006)
25. Meer, P., Mintz, D., Rosenfeld, A., Kim, D.Y.: Robust regression methods for computer vision: a review. IJCV **6**(1), 59–70 (1991)
26. Mukherjee, S., Robertson, N.: Deep head pose: gaze-direction estimation in multimodal video. TMM **17**(11), 2094–2107 (2015)
27. Neuneier, R., Zimmermann, H.G.: How to train neural networks. In: Montavon, G., Orr, G.B., Müller, K.-R. (eds.) Neural Networks: Tricks of the Trade. LNCS, vol. 7700, 2nd edn, pp. 369–418. Springer, Heidelberg (2012). https://doi.org/10.1007/978-3-642-35289-8_23
28. Neykov, N., Filzmoser, P., Dimova, R., Neytchev, P.: Robust fitting of mixtures using the trimmed likelihood estimator. CSDA **52**(1), 299–308 (2007)
29. Ranjan, R., Patel, V.M., Chellappa, R.: Hyperface: a deep multi-task learning framework for face detection, landmark localization, pose estimation, and gender recognition. CoRR abs/1603.01249 (2016)
30. Rothe, R., Timofte, R., Van Gool, L.: Deep expectation of real and apparent age from a single image without facial landmarks. IJCV (2016)
31. Rousseeuw, P.J., Leroy, A.M.: Robust Regression and Outlier Detection, vol. 589. Wiley, Hoboken (2005)
32. Russakovsky, O., et al.: Imagenet large scale visual recognition challenge. IJCV **115**(3), 211–252 (2015)
33. Sermanet, P., Eigen, D., Zhang, X., Mathieu, M., Fergus, R., Lecun, Y.: Overfeat: integrated recognition, localization and detection using convolutional networks. In: ICLR (2014)
34. Siarohin, A., Zen, G., Majtanovic, C., Alameda-Pineda, X., Ricci, E., Sebe, N.: How to make an image more memorable?: a deep style transfer approach. In: ACM International Conference on Multimedia Retrieval (2017)
35. Simonyan, K., Zisserman, A.: Very deep convolutional networks for large-scale image recognition. CoRR abs/1409.1556 (2014)
36. Stewart, C.V.: Robust parameter estimation in computer vision. SIAM Rev. **41**(3), 513–537 (1999)

37. Sun, Y., Wang, X., Tang, X.: Deep convolutional network cascade for facial point detection. In: CVPR (2013)
38. Szegedy, C., et al.: Going deeper with convolutions. In: CVPR (2015)
39. Toshev, A., Szegedy, C.: DeepPose: human pose estimation via deep neural networks. In: CVPR (2014)
40. Wilcoxon, F.: Individual comparisons by ranking methods. Biom. Bull. **1**, 80–83 (1945)
41. Xiao, T., Xia, T., Yang, Y., Huang, C., Wang, X.: Learning from massive noisy labeled data for image classification. In: CVPR (2015)
42. Xiong, X., De la Torre, F.: Supervised descent method and its applications to face alignment. In: CVPR, pp. 532–539 (06 2013)
43. Zhu, X., Ramanan, D.: Face detection, pose estimation, and landmark localization in the wild. In: CVPR, pp. 2879–2886 (2012)

Estimating the Success of Unsupervised Image to Image Translation

Sagie Benaim[1(✉)], Tomer Galanti[1], and Lior Wolf[1,2]

[1] The Blavatnik School of Computer Science, Tel Aviv University, Tel Aviv, Israel
sagieb@mail.tau.ac.il, sagiebenaim@gmail.com
[2] Facebook AI Research, Tel Aviv, Israel

Abstract. While in supervised learning, the validation error is an unbiased estimator of the generalization (test) error and complexity-based generalization bounds are abundant, no such bounds exist for learning a mapping in an unsupervised way. As a result, when training GANs and specifically when using GANs for learning to map between domains in a completely unsupervised way, one is forced to select the hyperparameters and the stopping epoch by subjectively examining multiple options. We propose a novel bound for predicting the success of unsupervised cross domain mapping methods, which is motivated by the recently proposed Simplicity Principle. The bound can be applied both in expectation, for comparing hyperparameters and for selecting a stopping criterion, or per sample, in order to predict the success of a specific cross-domain translation. The utility of the bound is demonstrated in an extensive set of experiments employing multiple recent algorithms. Our code is available at https://github.com/sagiebenaim/gan_bound.

Keywords: Unsupervised learning · Generalization bounds
Image to image translation · GANs

1 Introduction

In unsupervised learning, the process of selecting hyperparameters and the lack of clear stopping criteria are a constant source of frustration. This issue is commonplace for GANs [11] and the derived technologies, in which the training process optimizes multiple losses that balance each other. Practitioners are often uncertain regarding the results obtained when evaluating GAN-based methods, and many avoid using these altogether. One solution is to employ more stable methods such as [4]. However, these methods do not always match the results obtained by GANs. In this work, we offer, for an important family of

S. Benaim and T. Galanti—Equal contribution.

Electronic supplementary material The online version of this chapter (https://doi.org/10.1007/978-3-030-01228-1_14) contains supplementary material, which is available to authorized users.

V. Ferrari et al. (Eds.): ECCV 2018, LNCS 11209, pp. 222–238, 2018.
https://doi.org/10.1007/978-3-030-01228-1_14

GAN methodologies, an algorithm for selecting the hyperparameters, as well as a stopping criterion.

Specifically, we focus on predicting the success of algorithms that map between two image domains in an unsupervised manner. Multiple GAN-based methods have recently demonstrated convincing results, despite the apparent inherent ambiguity, which is described in Sect. 2. We derive what is, as far as we know, the first error bound for unsupervised cross domain mapping.

In addition to the novel capability of predicting the success, in expectation, of a mapping that was trained using one of the unsupervised mapping methods, we can predict the success of mapping every single sample individually. This is remarkable for two reasons: (i) even supervised generalization bounds do not deliver this capability; and (ii) we deal with complex multivariate regression problems (mapping between images) and not with classification problems, in which pseudo probabilities are often assigned.

In Sect. 2, we formulate the problem and present background on the Simplicity Principle of [9]. Then, in Sect. 3, we derive the prediction bounds and introduce multiple algorithms. Section 4 presents extensive empirical evidence for the success of our algorithms, when applied to multiple recent methods. This includes a unique combination of the hyperband method [16], which is perhaps the leading method in hyperparameter optimization, in the supervised setting, with our bound. This combination enables the application of hyperband in unsupervised learning, where, as far as we know, no hyperparameter selection method exists.

1.1 Related Work

Generative Adversarial Networks. GAN [11] methods train a generator network G that synthesizes samples from a target distribution, given noise vectors, by jointly training a second, adversarial, network D. Conditional GANs employ a vector of parameters that directs the generator, in addition to (or instead of) the noise vector. These GANs can generate images from a specific class [19] or based on a textual description [22], or invert mid-level network activations [6]. Our bound also applies in these situations. However, this is not the focus of our experiments, which target image mapping, in which the created image is based on an input image [2,13,15,18,25,30,33].

Unsupervised Mapping. The validation of our bound focuses on recent cross-domain mapping methods that employ no supervision, except for sample images from the two domains. This ability was demonstrated recently [2,15,30,33] in image to image translation and slightly earlier for translating between natural languages [28].

The DiscoGAN [15] method, similar to other methods [30,33], learns mappings in both directions, i.e., from domain A to domain B and vice versa. Our experiments also employ the DistanceGAN method [2], which unlike the circularity based methods, is applied only in one direction (from A to B). The constraint used by this method is that the distances for a pair of inputs $x_1, x_2 \in A$ before and after the mapping, by the learned mapping G, are highly correlated, i.e., $||x_1 - x_2|| \sim ||G(x_1) - G(x_2)||$.

Weakly Supervised Mapping. Our bound can also be applied to GAN-based methods that match between the source domain and the target domain by also incorporating a fixed pre-trained feature map f and requiring f-constancy, i.e, that the activations of f are the same for the input samples and for mapped samples [25,27]. During training, the various components of the loss (GAN, f-constancy, and a few others) do not provide a clear signal when to stop training or which hyperparameters to use.

Generalization Bounds for Unsupervised Learning. Only a few generalization bounds for unsupervised learning were suggested in the literature. In [23], PAC-Bayesian generalization bounds are presented for density estimation. [21] gives an algorithm for estimating a bounded density using a finite combination of densities from a given class. This algorithm has estimation error bounded by $O(1/\sqrt{n})$. Our work studies the error of a mapping and not the KL-divergence with respect to a target distribution. Further, our bound is data-dependent and not based on the complexity of the hypothesis class.

Hyperparameter Optimization. Hyperparameters are constants and configurations that are being used by a learning algorithm. Hyperparameter selection is the process of selecting the hyperparameters that will produce better learning. This includes optimizing the number of epochs, size and depth of the neural network being trained, learning rate, etc. Many of the earlier hyperparameter methods that go beyond a random- or a grid-search were Bayesian in nature [3,7,12,24,26]. The hyperband method [16], which is currently leading various supervised learning benchmarks, is based on the multi-arm bandit problem. It employs partial training and dynamically allocates more resources to successful configurations. All such methods crucially rely on a validation error to be available for a given configuration, which means that these can only be used in the supervised settings. Our work enables, for the first time, the usage of such methods also in the unsupervised setting, by using our bound in lieu of the validation error for predicting the ground truth error.

2 Problem Setup

In Sect. 2.1 we define the alignment problem. Section 2.2 illustrates the Simplicity Principle which was introduced in [9] and was verified with an extensive set of experiments. Section 2.3 and everything that follows are completely novel. The section proposes the Occam's razor property, which extends the definition of the Simplicity Principle, and which is used in Sect. 3 to derive the main results and algorithms.

2.1 The Alignment Problem

The learning algorithm is provided with two unlabeled datasets: one includes i.i.d samples from a first distribution and the second, i.i.d samples from a second distribution.

$$S_A := \{x_i\}_{i=1}^m \overset{\text{i.i.d}}{\sim} D_A^m \text{ and } S_B := \{y_i\}_{i=1}^n \overset{\text{i.i.d}}{\sim} D_B^n \tag{1}$$

D_A and D_B are distributions over $\mathcal{X}_A$ and $\mathcal{X}_B$ (resp.). In this paper we focus on the deterministic case, i.e, there is a target function, y_{AB}, which is one of the functions that map the first domain to the second, such that $y_{AB} \circ D_A = D_B$ ($g \circ D$ is defined to be the distribution of $g(x)$ where $x \sim D$). The theory can be extended to the non-deterministic case, where there are multiple possible target functions [8]. The goal of the learner is to fit a function $G \in \mathcal{H}$, for some hypothesis class $\mathcal{H}$ that is closest to y_{AB}, i.e, $\inf_{G\in\mathcal{H}} R_{D_A}[G, y_{AB}]$, where $R_D[f_1, f_2] = \mathop{\mathbb{E}}_{x\sim D}[\ell(f_1(x), f_2(x))]$, for a loss function $\ell : \mathbb{R}^M \times \mathbb{R}^M \to \mathbb{R}$ and distribution D.

It is not clear that such fitting is possible, without additional information. Assume, for example, that there is a natural order on the samples in $\mathcal{X}_B$. A mapping that maps an input sample $x \in \mathcal{X}_A$ to the sample that is next in order to $y_{AB}(x)$, could be just as feasible. More generally, one can permute the samples in $\mathcal{X}_A$ by some function Π that replaces each sample with another sample that has a similar likelihood and learn G that satisfies $G = \Pi \circ y_{AB}$. This difficulty is referred to in [9] as "the alignment problem".

In multiple recent contributions [15,28,30,33], circularity is employed. Circularity requires the recovery of both y_{AB} and $y_{BA} = y_{AB}^{-1}$ simultaneously. Namely, functions G and G' are learned jointly by minimizing the following objective:

$$\text{disc}(G\circ D_A, D_B) + \text{disc}(G'\circ D_B, D_A) + R_{D_A}[G'\circ G, \text{Id}_A] + R_{D_B}[G\circ G', \text{Id}_B] \tag{2}$$

where

$$\begin{aligned} \text{disc}(D_1, D_2) &:= \sup_{c_1,c_2\in\mathcal{C}} \left|R_{D_1}[c_1, c_2] - R_{D_2}[c_1, c_2]\right| \\ &= \sup_{c_1,c_2\in\mathcal{C}} \left|\mathbb{E}_{x\sim D_1}[\ell(c_1(x), c_2(x))] - \mathbb{E}_{x\sim D_2}[\ell(c_1(x), c_2(x))]\right| \end{aligned} \tag{3}$$

denotes the discrepancy between distributions D_1 and D_2, $\mathcal{C}$ is a selected class of functions and $\text{Id}_A : \mathcal{X}_A \to \mathcal{X}_A$ and $\text{Id}_B : \mathcal{X}_B \to \mathcal{X}_B$ are the identity functions over $\mathcal{X}_A$ and $\mathcal{X}_B$ (resp.). The discrepancy is similar to the WGAN divergence [1], where instead of 1-Lipschitz discriminators, we use discriminators of the form $\ell(c_1(x), c_2(x))$, where $c_1, c_2 \in \mathcal{C}$. This discrepancy is implemented by a GAN, as in [10].

As shown in [9], the circularity constraint does not eliminate the uncertainty in its entirety. In DistanceGAN [2], the circularity was replaced by a multidimensional scaling type of constraint, which enforces a high correlation between the distances in the two domains. However, since these constraints hold only approximately, the ambiguity is not completely eliminated.

2.2 The Simplicity Principle

In order to understand how the recent unsupervised image mapping methods work despite the inherent ambiguity, [9] recently showed that the target

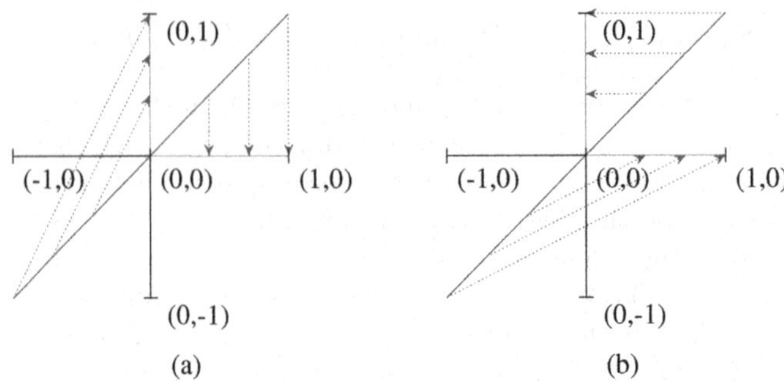

Fig. 1. An illustrative example, where the two domains are the blue and green areas. There are infinitely many mappings that preserve the uniform distribution on the two domains. However, only two stand out as "semantic". These two, which are depicted in red, are exactly the two mappings that can be captured by a minimal neural network with ReLU activations. (a) the mapping y^1_{AB}. (b) the mapping y^2_{AB} (see Eq. 4). (Color figure online)

("semantic") mapping y_{AB} is typically the distribution preserving mapping ($h \circ D_A = D_B$) with the lowest complexity. It was shown that such mappings are expected to be unique.

As a motivating example to the key role of minimal mappings, consider the domain A of uniformly distributed points $(x_1, x_2)^\top \in \mathbb{R}^2$, where $x_1 = x_2 \in [-1, 1]$. Let B be the domain of uniformly distributed points in $\{(x_1, x_2)^\top | x_1 \in [0, 1], x_2 = 0\} \cup \{(x_1, x_2)^\top | x_2 \in [0, 1], x_1 = 0\}$. We note that there are infinitely many mappings from domain A to B that, given inputs in A, result in the uniform distribution of B and satisfy the circularity constraint (Eq. 2).

However, it is easy to see that when restricting the hypothesis class to neural networks with one layer of size 2, and ReLU activations σ, there are only two options left. In this case, $h(x) = \sigma_a(Wx)$, for $W \in \mathbb{R}^{2\times 2}, b \in \mathbb{R}^2$. The only admissible solutions are of the form $W = \begin{pmatrix} a & 1-a \\ b & -1-b \end{pmatrix}$ or $W' = \begin{pmatrix} a & -1-a \\ b & 1-b \end{pmatrix}$, which are identical, for every $a, b \in \mathbb{R}$, to one of the following functions:

$$y^1_{AB}((x,x)^\top) = \begin{cases} (x,0)^\top & \text{if } x \geq 0 \\ (0,-x)^\top & \text{if } x \leq 0 \end{cases} \text{ and } y^2_{AB}((x,x)^\top) = \begin{cases} (0,x)^\top & \text{if } x \geq 0 \\ (-x,0)^\top & \text{if } x \leq 0 \end{cases} \tag{4}$$

Therefore, by restricting the hypothesis space to be minimal, we eliminate all alternative solutions, except two. These two are exactly the two mappings that would commonly be considered "more semantic" than any other mapping, see Fig. 1. Another motivating example can be found in [9].

2.3 Occam's Razor

We note that the Simplicity Principle, presented in [9], is highly related to the principle known as Occam's razor. In this section we provide a definition of the

Occam's razor property which extends the formulation of the Simplicity Principle used in [9]. Our formulation is not limited to Kolmogorov-like complexity of multi-layered neural networks as in [9] and is more general.

Given two domains $A = (\mathcal{X}_A, D_A)$ and $B = (\mathcal{X}_B, D_B)$, a mapping $y_{AB} : \mathcal{X}_A \to \mathcal{X}_B$ satisfies the Occam's razor property between domains A and B, if it has minimal complexity among the functions $h : \mathcal{X}_A \to \mathcal{X}_B$ that satisfy $h \circ D_A \approx D_B$. Minimal complexity is defined by the nesting of hypothesis classes, which forms a partial order, and not as a continuous score. For example, if $\mathcal{H}_j$ is the set of neural networks of a specific architecture and $\mathcal{H}_i$ is the set of neural networks of the architecture obtained after deleting one of the hidden neurons, then, $\mathcal{H}_i \subset \mathcal{H}_j$. Intuitively, minimal complexity would mean that there is no sub-class that can implement a mapping $h : \mathcal{X}_A \to \mathcal{X}_B$ such that $h \circ D_A \approx D_B$. For this purpose, we define, $\mathcal{P}(\mathcal{H}; \epsilon) := \{G \in \mathcal{H} \mid \text{disc}(G \circ D_A, D_B) \leq \epsilon\}$.

Definition 1 (Occam's razor property). Let $A = (\mathcal{X}_A, D_A)$ and $B = (\mathcal{X}_B, D_B)$ be two domains and $\mathcal{U} = \{\mathcal{H}_i\}_{i \in I}$ be a family of hypothesis classes. A mapping $y_{AB} : \mathcal{X}_A \to \mathcal{X}_B$ satisfies an (ϵ_1, ϵ_2)-Occam's razor property if for every $\mathcal{H} \in \mathcal{U}$ such that $\mathcal{P}(\mathcal{H}; \epsilon_1) \neq \emptyset$, we have: $\inf_{G \in \mathcal{P}(\mathcal{H}; \epsilon_1)} R_{D_A}[G, y_{AB}] \leq \epsilon_2$.

Informally, according to Definition 1, a function satisfies the Occam's razor property, if it can be approximated by even the lowest-complexity hypothesis classes that successfully map between the domains A and B. If y_{AB} has the (ϵ_1, ϵ_2)-Occam's razor property, then it is ϵ_2-close to a function in every minimal hypothesis class $\mathcal{H} \in \mathcal{U}$ such that $\mathcal{P}(\mathcal{H}; \epsilon_1) \neq \emptyset$. As the hypothesis class $\mathcal{H}$ grows, so does $\mathcal{P}(\mathcal{H}; \epsilon_1)$, i.e., $\mathcal{H}_i \subset \mathcal{H}_j$ implies that $\mathcal{P}(\mathcal{H}_i; \epsilon_1) \subset \mathcal{P}(\mathcal{H}_j; \epsilon_1)$. Therefore, the growing $\mathcal{P}(\mathcal{H}; \epsilon_1)$ would always contain at least one function that is ϵ_2-close to y_{AB}. Nevertheless, as the hypothesis class grows, $\mathcal{P}(\mathcal{H}; \epsilon_1)$ can potentially contain many functions f that satisfy $f \circ D_A \approx D_B$ and differ from each other, causing an increased amount of ambiguity. In addition, we note that uniqueness is not assumed, and the property may hold for multiple mappings.

3 Estimating the Ground Truth Error

In this section, we introduce a bound on the generalization risk between a given function $G_1 \in \mathcal{H}$ and an unknown target function y_{AB}, i.e., $R_{D_A}[G_1, y_{AB}]$. This bound is based on a bias-variance decomposition and sums two terms: the bias error and the approximation error. The bias error is the maximal risk possible with a member G_2 of the class $\mathcal{P}(\mathcal{H}; \epsilon_1)$, i.e., $\sup_{G_2 \in \mathcal{P}(\mathcal{H}; \epsilon_1)} R_{D_A}[G_1, G_2]$. The approximation error is the minimal possible risk between a member G of the class $\mathcal{P}(\mathcal{H}; \epsilon_1)$ with respect to y_{AB}, i.e., $\inf_{G \in \mathcal{P}(\mathcal{H}; \epsilon_1)} R_{D_A}[G, y_{AB}]$.

3.1 Derivation of the Bound and the Algorithms

The bound is a consequence of using a loss ℓ that satisfies the triangle inequality. Losses of this type include the L_1 loss, which is often used in cross domain mapping. The L_2 loss and the perceptual loss [14] satisfy the triangle inequality up to a factor of three, which would incur the addition of a factor into the bound. The following Lemma 1 provides an upper bound on the generalization risk.

Lemma 1. *Let* $A = (\mathcal{X}_A, D_A)$ *and* $B = (\mathcal{X}_B, D_B)$ *be two domains,* $\mathcal{U} = \{\mathcal{H}_i\}_{i \in I}$ *be a family of hypothesis classes and* $\epsilon_1 > 0$*. In addition, assume that* ℓ *is a loss function that satisfies the triangle inequality. Then, for all* $\mathcal{H} \in \mathcal{U}$ *such that* $\mathcal{P}(\mathcal{H}; \epsilon_1) \neq \emptyset$ *and two functions* y_{AB} *and* G_1*, we have:*

$$R_{D_A}[G_1, y_{AB}] \leq \sup_{G_2 \in \mathcal{P}(\mathcal{H};\epsilon_1)} R_{D_A}[G_1, G_2] + \inf_{G \in \mathcal{P}(\mathcal{H};\epsilon_1)} R_{D_A}[G, y_{AB}] \tag{5}$$

Proof. Let $G^* = \arg\inf_{G \in \mathcal{P}(\mathcal{H};\epsilon_1)} R_{D_A}[G, y_{AB}]$. By the triangle inequality, we have:

$$\begin{aligned} R_{D_A}[G_1, y_{AB}] \leq & R_{D_A}[G_1, G^*] + R_{D_A}[G^*, y_{AB}] \\ \leq & \sup_{G_2 \in \mathcal{P}(\mathcal{H};\epsilon_1)} R_{D_A}[G_1, G_2] + \inf_{G \in \mathcal{P}(\mathcal{H};\epsilon_1)} R_{D_A}[G, y_{AB}] \end{aligned} \tag{6}$$

□

If y_{AB} satisfies Occam's razor, then the approximation error is lower than ϵ_2 and by Eq. 5 in Lemma 1 the following bound is obtained:

$$R_{D_A}[G_1, y_{AB}] \leq \sup_{G_2 \in \mathcal{P}(\mathcal{H};\epsilon_1)} R_{D_A}[G_1, G_2] + \epsilon_2 \tag{7}$$

Equation 7 provides us with an accessible bound for the generalization risk. The right hand side can be directly approximated by training a neural network G_2 that has a discrepancy lower than ϵ_1 and has the maximal risk with regards to G_1, i.e.,

$$\sup_{G_2 \in \mathcal{H}} R_{D_A}[G_1, G_2] \text{ s.t: } \text{disc}(G_2 \circ D_A, D_B) \leq \epsilon_1 \tag{8}$$

In general, it is computationally impossible to compute the exact solution h_2 to Eq. 8 since in most cases we cannot explicitly compute the set $\mathcal{P}(\mathcal{H}; \epsilon_1)$. Therefore, inspired by Lagrange relaxation, we employ the following relaxed version of Eq. 8:

$$\min_{G_2 \in \mathcal{H}} \text{disc}(G_2 \circ D_A, D_B) - \lambda R_{D_A}[G_1, G_2] \tag{9}$$

where $\lambda > 0$ is a trade-off parameter. Therefore, instead of computing Eq. 8, we maximize the dual form in Eq. 9 with respect to G_2. In addition, we optimize λ to be the maximal values such that $\text{disc}(G_2 \circ D_A, D_B) \leq \epsilon_1$ is still satisfied. The expectation over $x \sim D_A$ (resp $x \sim D_B$) in the risk and discrepancy are replaced, as is often done, with the sum over the training samples in domain A (resp B). Based on this, we present a stopping criterion in Algorithm 1, and a method for hyperparameter selection in Algorithm 2. Equation 9 is manifested in Step 4 of the former and Step 6 of the latter is the selection criterion that appears as the last line of both algorithms.

Algorithm 1. Deciding when to stop training G_1

Require: S_A and S_B: unlabeled training sets; $\mathcal{H}$: a hypothesis class; ϵ_1: a threshold; λ: a trade-off parameter; T_2: a fixed number of epochs for G_2; T_1: a maximal number of epochs.

Initialize $G_1^0 \in \mathcal{H}$ and $G_2^0 \in \mathcal{H}$ randomly.
for $i = 1, ..., T_1$ **do**
  Train G_1^{i-1} for one epoch to minimize $\text{disc}(G_1^{i-1} \circ D_A, D_B)$, obtaining G_1^i.
  Train G_2^i for T_2 epochs to minimize $\text{disc}(G_2^i \circ D_A, D_B) - \lambda R_{D_A}[G_1^i, G_2^i]$.
  $\triangleright$ T_2 provides a fixed comparison point.
end for
return G_1^t such that: $t = \arg\min_{i \in [T]} R_{D_A}[G_1^i, G_2^i]$.

Algorithm 2. Model Selection

Require: S_A and S_B: unlabeled training sets; $\mathcal{U} = \{\mathcal{H}_i\}_{i \in I}$: a family of hypothesis classes; ϵ: a threshold; λ: a trade-off parameter.

Initialize $J = \emptyset$.
for $i \in I$ **do**
  Train $G_1^i \in \mathcal{H}_i$ to minimize $\text{disc}(G_1^i \circ D_A, D_B)$.
  if $\text{disc}(G_1^i \circ D_A, D_B) \leq \epsilon$ **then**
    Add i to J.
    Train $G_2^i \in \mathcal{H}_i$ to minimize $\text{disc}(G_2^i \circ D_A, D_B) - \lambda R_{D_A}[G_1^i, G_2^i]$.
  end if
end for
return G_1^i such that: $i = \arg\min_{j \in J} R_{D_A}[G_1^j, G_2^j]$.

3.2 Bound on the Loss of Each Sample

We next extend the bound to estimate the error $\ell(G_1(x), y_{AB}(x))$ of mapping by G_1 a specific sample $x \sim D_A$. Lemma 2 follows very closely to Lemma 1. It gives rise to a simple method for bounding the loss of G_1 on a specific sample x. Note that the second term in the bound does not depend on G_1 and is expected to be small, since it denotes the capability of overfitting on a single sample x.

Lemma 2. *Let $A = (\mathcal{X}_A, D_A)$ and $B = (\mathcal{X}_B, D_B)$ be two domains and $\mathcal{H}$ a hypothesis class. In addition, let ℓ be a loss function satisfying the triangle inequality. Then, for any target function y_{AB} and $G_1 \in \mathcal{H}$, we have:*

$$\ell(G_1(x), y_{AB}(x)) \leq \sup_{G_2 \in \mathcal{P}(\mathcal{H};\epsilon)} \ell(G_1(x), G_2(x)) + \inf_{G \in \mathcal{P}(\mathcal{H};\epsilon)} \ell(G(x), y_{AB}(x)) \quad (10)$$

Similarly to the analysis done in Sect. 3, Eq. 10 provides us with an accessible bound for the generalization risk. The RHS can be directly approximated by training a neural network G_2 of a discrepancy lower than ϵ and has maximal loss with regards to G_1, i.e.,

$$\sup_{G_2 \in \mathcal{H}} \ell(G_1(x), G_2(x)) \text{ s.t: } \text{disc}(G_2 \circ D_A, D_B) \leq \epsilon \quad (11)$$

Algorithm 3. Bounding the loss of G_1 on sample x

Require: S_A and S_B: unlabeled training sets; $\mathcal{H}$: a hypothesis class; $G_1 \in \mathcal{H}$: a mapping; λ: a trade-off parameter; x: a specific sample.
1: Train $G_2 \in \mathcal{H}$ to minimize $\text{disc}(G_2 \circ D_A, D_B) - \lambda\ell(G_1(x), G_2(x))$.
2: **return** $\ell(G_1(x), G_2(x))$.

With similar considerations as in Sect. 3, we replace Eq. 11 with the following objective:

$$\min_{G_2 \in \mathcal{H}} \text{disc}(G_2 \circ D_A, D_B) - \lambda\ell(G_1(x), G_2(x)) \tag{12}$$

As before, the expectation over $x \sim D_A$ and $x \sim D_B$ in the discrepancy are replaced with the sum over the training samples in domain A and B (resp.).

In practice, we modify Eq. 12 such that x is weighted to half the weight of all samples, during the training of G_2. This emphasizes the role of x and allows us to train G_2 for less epochs. This is important, as a different G_2 must be trained for measuring the error of each sample x.

3.3 Deriving an Unsupervised Variant of Hyperband Using the Bound

In order to optimize multiple hyperparameters simultaneously, we create an unsupervised variant of the hyperband method [16]. Hyperband requires the evaluation of the loss for every configuration of hyperparameters. In our case, our loss is the risk function, $R_{D_A}[G_1, y_{AB}]$. Since we cannot compute the actual risk, we replace it with our bound $\sup_{G_2 \in \mathcal{P}(\mathcal{H};\epsilon_1)} R_{D_A}[G_1, G_2]$.

In particular, the function 'run_then_return_val_loss' in the hyperband algorithm (Algorithm 1 of [16]), which is a plug-in function for loss evaluation, is provided with our bound from Eq. 7 after training G_2, as in Eq. 9. Our variant of this function is listed in Algorithm 4. It employs two additional procedures that are used to store the learned models G_1 and G_2 at a certain point in the training process and to retrieve these to continue the training for a set amount of epochs. The retrieval function is simply a map between a vector of hypermarkets and a tuple of the learned networks and the number of epochs T when stored. For a new vector of hyperparameters, it returns $T = 0$ and two randomly initialized networks, with architectures that are determined by the given set of hyperparameters. When a network is retrieved, it is then trained for a number of epochs that is the difference between the required number of epochs T, which is given by the hyperband method, and the number of epochs it was already trained, denoted by T_{last}.

4 Experiments

We test the three algorithms on two unsupervised alignment methods: DiscoGAN [15] and DistanceGAN [2]. In DiscoGAN, we train G_1 (and G_2), using

Algorithm 4. Unsupervised run_then_return_val_loss for hyperband

Require: S_A, S_B, and λ as before. T: Number of epochs. θ: Set of hyperparameters

$[G_1, G_2, T_{\text{last}}] = \text{return\_stored\_functions}(\theta)$

Train G_1 for $T - T_{\text{last}}$ epochs to minimize $\text{disc}(G_1 \circ D_A, D_B)$.

Train G_2 for $T - T_{\text{last}}$ epochs to minimize $\text{disc}(G_2 \circ D_A, D_B) - \lambda R_{D_A}[G_1, G_2]$.

store_functions(θ, $[G_1, G_2, T]$)

return $R_{D_A}[G_1, G_2]$.

Table 1. Pearson correlations and the corresponding p-values (in parentheses) of the ground truth error with: (i) the bound, (ii) the GAN losses, and (iii) the circularity losses or (iv) the distance correlation loss. *The cycle loss $A \to B \to A$ is shown for DiscoGAN and the distance correlation loss is shown for DistanceGAN.

Alg.	Method	Dataset	Bound	GAN_A	GAN_B	$Cycle_A/\mathcal{L}_D$*	$Cycle_B$
Alg. 1	Disco-GAN [15]	Shoes2Edges	**1.00** (<1E-16)	-0.15 (3E-03)	-0.28 (1E-08)	0.76(<1E-16)	0.79(<1E-16)
		Bags2Edges	**1.00** (<1E-16)	-0.26 (6E-11)	-0.57 (<1E-16)	0.85 (<1E-16)	0.84 (<1E-16)
		Cityscapes	**0.94** (<1E-16)	-0.66 (<1E-16)	-0.69 (<1E-16)	-0.26 (1E-07)	0.80 (<1E-16)
		Facades	**0.85** (<1E-16)	-0.46 (<1E-16)	0.66 (<1E-16)	0.92 (<1E-16)	0.66 (<1E-16)
		Maps	**1.00** (<1E-16)	-0.81 (<1E-16)	0.58 (<1E-16)	0.20 (9E-05)	-0.14 (5E-03)
	Distance-GAN [2]	Shoes2Edges	**0.98** (<1E-16)	-	-0.25 (2E-16)	-0.14 (1E-05)	-
		Bags2Edges	**0.93** (<1E-16)	-	-0.08 (2E-02)	0.34 (<1E-16)	-
		Cityscapes	**0.59** (<1E-16)	-	0.22 (1E-11)	-0.41 (<1E-16)	-
		Facades	**0.48** (<1E-16)	-	0.03 (5E-01)	-0.01 (9E-01)	-
		Maps	**1.00** (<1E-16)	-	-0.73 (<1E-16)	0.39 (4E-16)	-
Alg. 2	Disco-GAN [15]	Shoes2Edges	**0.95** (1E-03)	0.73 (7E-02)	0.51 (2E-01)	0.05 (9E-01)	0.05 (9E-01)
		Bags2Edges	**0.99** (2E-06)	0.64 (2E-01)	0.54 (3E-01)	-0.26 (7E-01)	-0.20 (7E-01)
		Cityscapes	**0.99** (1E-03)	0.69 (9E-02)	0.85 (2E-02)	-0.53 (2E-01)	-0.42 (4E-01)
		Facades	**0.94** (1E-03)	-0.33 (4E-01)	0.88 (4E-02)	0.66 (8E-02)	-0.45 (3E-01)
		Maps	**1.00** (1E-03)	0.62 (1E-01)	0.54 (2E-01)	0.60 (2E-01)	0.07 (9E-01)
	Distance-GAN [2]	Shoes2Edges	**0.96** (1E-04)	-	0.33 (5E-01)	-0.87 (6E-03)	-
		Bags2Edges	**0.98** (1E-05)	-	-0.11 (8E-01)	0.23 (6E-01)	-
		Cityscapes	**0.92** (1E-03)	-	0.66 (8E-02)	-0.49 (2E-01)	-
		Facades	**0.84** (2E-02)	-	0.75 (5E-02)	0.37 (4E-01)	-
		Maps	**0.95** (1E-03)	-	-0.43 (3E-01)	-0.15 (7E-01)	-
Alg. 3	Disco-GAN [15]	Shoes2Edges	**0.92** (<1E-16)	-0.12 (5E-01)	0.02 (9E-01)	0.29 (6E-02)	0.15 (4E-01)
		Bags2Edges	**0.96** (<1E-16)	0.25 (1E-01)	0.08 (6E-01)	0.08 (6E-01)	0.05 (7E-01)
		Cityscapes	**0.78** (4E-04)	0.24 (4E-01)	-0.16 (6E-01)	-0.04 (9E-01)	0.03 (9E-01)
		Facades	**0.80** (6E-10)	0.13 (4E-01)	0.16 (3E-01)	0.20 (2E-01)	0.09 (5E-01)
		Maps	**0.66** (1E-03)	0.08 (7E-01)	0.12 (6E-01)	0.17 (5E-01)	-0.25 (3E-01)
	Distance-GAN [2]	Shoes2Edges	**0.98** (<1E-16)	-	-0.05 (7E-01)	0.84 (<1E-16)	-
		Bags2Edges	**0.92** (<1E-16)	-	-0.28 (2E-01)	0.45 (3E-02)	-
		Cityscapes	**0.51** (4E-04)	-	0.10 (5E-01)	0.28 (2E-2)	-
		Facades	**0.72** (<1E-16)	-	-0.01 (1E00)	0.08 (6E-01)	-
		Maps	**0.94** (1E-06)	-	0.20 (2E-01)	0.30 (6E-02)	-

two GANs and two circularity constraints; in DistanceGAN, one GAN and one distance correlation loss are used. The published parameters for each dataset are used, except when applying our model selection method, where we vary the number of layers and when using hyperband, where we vary the learning rate and the batch size as well. In the experiments we employ the L_1 loss between G_1 and G_2 and between G_1 and y. In the supplementary we also use the perceptual loss. When running the experiments, the discrepancy is implemented by a

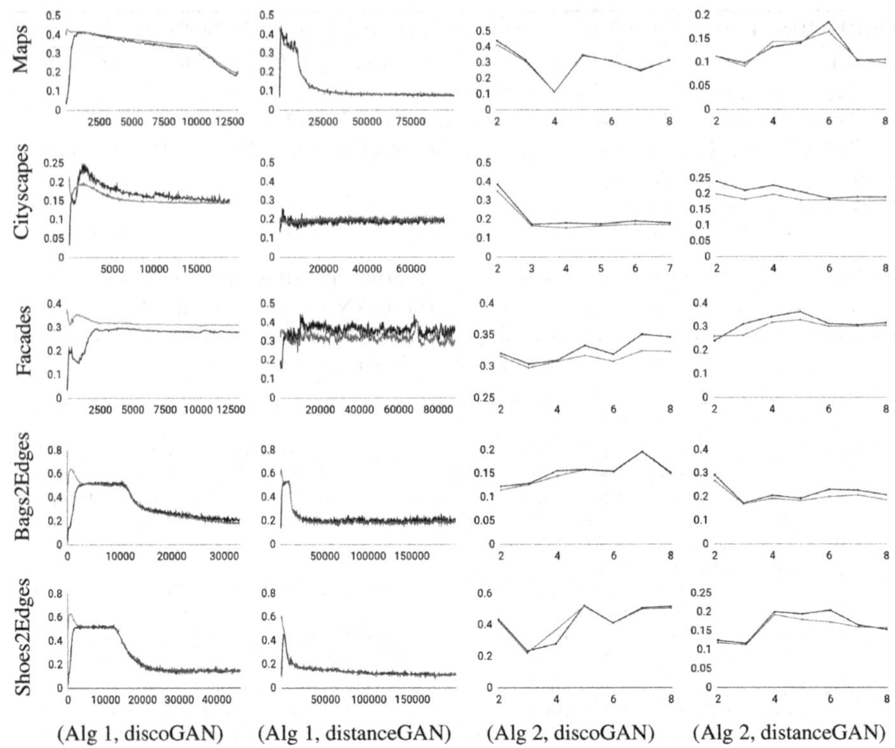

Fig. 2. Results of Algorithms 1 and 2. Ground truth errors are in red and bound in black. x-axis is the iteration or number of layers. y-axis is expected risk. For Algorithm 1 it takes a few epochs for G_1 to have a small enough discrepancy, until which the bound is ineffective. (Color figure online)

GAN, i.e., the error of the discriminator d measures the discrepancy. The exact architectures are given in the supplementary.

Five datasets were used in the experiments: (i) aerial photographs to maps, trained on data scraped from Google Maps [13], (ii) the mapping between photographs from the cityscapes dataset and their per-pixel semantic labels [5], (iii) architectural photographs to their labels from the CMP Facades dataset [20], (iv) handbag images [32] to their binary edge images as obtained from the HED edge detector [29], and (v) a similar dataset for the shoe images from [31].

Throughout the experiments, fixed values are used as the low-discrepancy threshold ($\epsilon_1 = 0.2$). The tradeoff parameter between the dissimilarity term and the fitting term during the training of G_2 is set, per dataset, to be the maximal value such that the fitting of G_2 provides a solution that has a discrepancy lower than the threshold, $\text{disc}(G_2 \circ D_A, D_B) \leq \epsilon_1$. This is done once, for the default parameters of G_1, as given in the original DiscoGAN and DistanceGAN [2,15].

The results of all experiments are summarized in Table 1, which presents the correlation and p-value between the ground truth error, as a function of the inde-

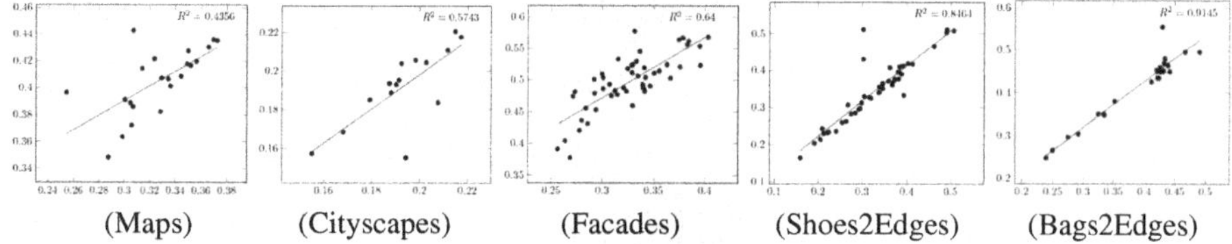

Fig. 3. Results of Algorithm 3. Results shown for DiscoGAN. Results for DistanceGAN are shown in supplementary due to lack of space. The ground truth errors (x-axis) vs. bound (y-axis) are shown per point. The coefficient of determination is shown (top right).

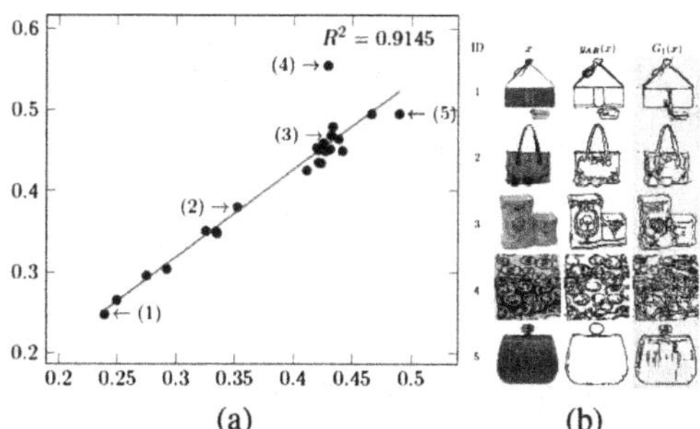

Fig. 4. Results of Algorithm 3 on DiscoGAN bags2edges. (a) The ground truth errors vs. the bound per point are shown. This is the same as Fig. 3 top right plot with added information identifying specific points. (b) The source (x), ground truth ($y_{AB}(x)$) and mapping ($G_1(x)$) of the marked points.

pendent variable, and the bound. The independent variable is either the training epoch, the architecture, or the sample, depending on the algorithm tested. For example, in Algorithm 2 we wish to decide on the best architecture, the independent variable is the number of layers. A high correlation (low p-value) between the bound and the ground truth error, both as a function of the number of layers, indicates the validity of the bound and the utility of the algorithm. Similar correlations are shown with the GAN losses and the reconstruction losses (DiscoGAN) or the distance correlation loss (DistanceGAN), in order to demonstrate that these are much less correlated with the ground truth error. In the plots of Fig. 2, we omit the other scores in order to reduce clutter.

Figure 2 (all four columns), can be used to quantify the gain from using the two algorithms. The "regret" when using the algorithm is simply the ground truth error at the minimal value of the bound minus the minimal ground truth error.

Stopping Criterion(Algorithm 1). For testing the stopping criterion suggested in Algorithm 1, we compared, at each time point, two scores that are averaged over all training samples: $||G_1(x) - G_2(x)||_1$, which is our bound, and

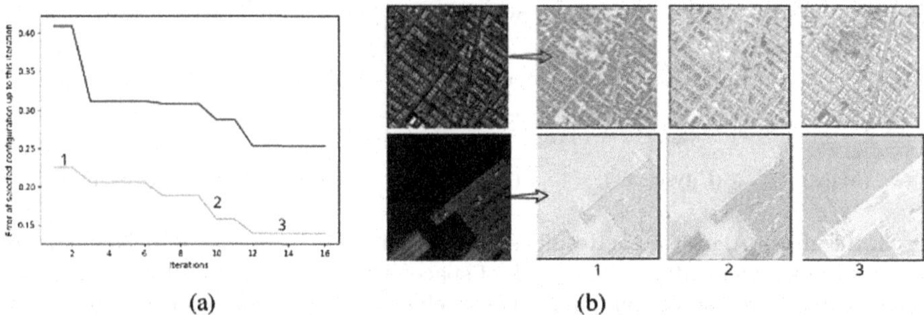

(a) (b)

Fig. 5. Applying unsupervised hyperband for selecting the best configuration for UNIT for the Maps dataset. (a) blue and orange lines are bound and ground truth error as in Fig. 6. (b) Images produced for 3 different configurations as indicated on the plot in (a). (Color figure online)

the ground truth error $||G_1(x) - y_{AB}(x)||_1$, where $y_{AB}(x)$ is the ground truth image that matches x in domain B.

Note that similar to the experiments with ground truth in the literature [2, 15,33], the ground truth error is measured in the label space and not in the image domain. The mapping in the other direction y_{BA} is not one to one.

The results are depicted in the main results table (Table 1) as well as in Fig. 2 for both DiscoGAN (first column) and DistanceGAN (second column). As can be seen, there is an excellent match between the mean ground truth error of the learned mapping G_1 and the predicted error. No such level of correlation is present when considering the GAN losses or the reconstruction losses (for DiscoGAN), or the distance correlation loss of DistanceGAN. Specifically, the very low p-values in the first column of Table 1 show that there is a clear correlation between the ground truth error and our bound for all datasets. For the other columns, the values in question are chosen to be the losses used for G_1. The lower scores in these columns show that none of these values are as correlated with the ground truth error, and so cannot be used to estimate this error.

In the experiment of Algorithm 1 for DiscoGAN, which has a large number of sample points, the cycle from B to A and back to B is significantly correlated with the ground truth error with very low p-values in four out of five datasets. However, its correlation is significantly lower than that of our bound.

In Fig. 2, the Facades graph shows a different behavior than the other graphs. This is because the Facades dataset is inherently ambiguous and presents multiple possible mappings from A to B. Each mapping satisfies the Occam's razor property separately.

Selecting Architecture using Algorithm 2. Next we vary the number of layers of G and consider its effect on the risk by measuring the bound and the ground truth error (which cannot be computed in an unsupervised way); A large correlation between our bound and the ground truth error is observed, see Table 1 and Fig. 2, columns 3 and 4. We can therefore optimize the number of

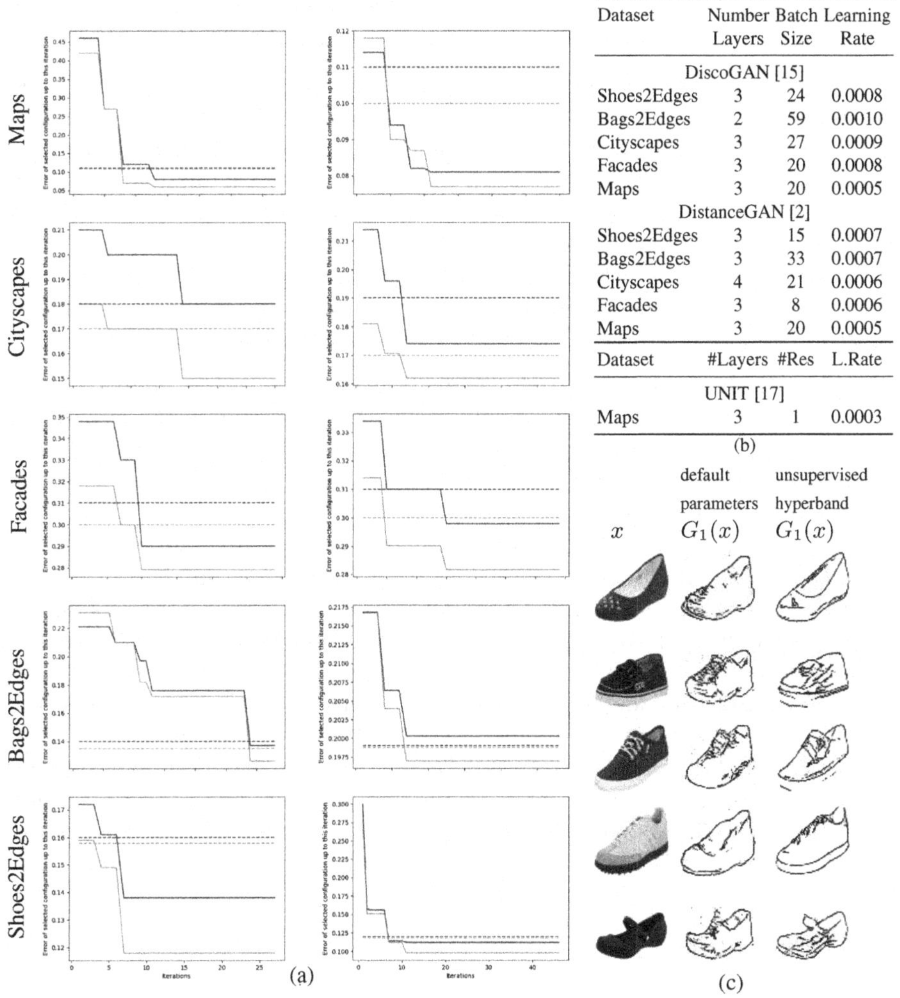

Dataset	Number Layers	Batch Size	Learning Rate
DiscoGAN [15]			
Shoes2Edges	3	24	0.0008
Bags2Edges	2	59	0.0010
Cityscapes	3	27	0.0009
Facades	3	20	0.0008
Maps	3	20	0.0005
DistanceGAN [2]			
Shoes2Edges	3	15	0.0007
Bags2Edges	3	33	0.0007
Cityscapes	4	21	0.0006
Facades	3	8	0.0006
Maps	3	20	0.0005
Dataset	#Layers	#Res	L.Rate
UNIT [17]			
Maps	3	1	0.0003

(b)

Fig. 6. Applying unsupervised hyperband for selecting the best configuration. For DiscoGAN and DistanceGAN we optimized of the number of encoder and decoder layers, batch size and learning rate while for UNIT, we optimized for the number of encoder and decoder Layers, number of resnet layers and learning rate. (a) For each dataset, the first plot is of DiscoGAN and the second is of DistanceGAN. Hyperband optimizes according to the bound values indicated in blue. The corresponding ground truth errors are shown in orange. Dotted lines represent the best configuration errors, when varying only the number of layers without hyperband (blue for bound and orange for ground truth error). Each graph shows the error of the best configuration selected by hyperband as a function the number of hyperband iterations. (b) The corresponding hyperparameters of the best configuration as selected by hyperband. (c) Images produced for DiscoGAN's shoes2edges: 1st column is the input, the 2nd is the result of DiscoGAN's default configuration, 3rd is the result of the configuration selected by our unsupervised Hyperband. (Color figure online)

layers based on our bound. With a much smaller number of sample points, the p-values are generally higher than in the previous experiment.

Predicting Per-Sample Loss with Algorithm 3. Finally, we consider the per sample loss. The results are reported numerically in Table 1 and plotted in Figs. 3 and 4. As can be seen, there is a high degree of correlation between the measured bound and the ground truth error. Therefore, our method is able to reliably predict the per-sample success of a multivariate mapping learned in a fully unsupervised manner.

Remarkably, this correlation also seems to hold when considering the time axis, i.e., we can combine Algorithms 1 and 3 and select the stopping epoch that is best for a specific sample. The results are shown in the supplementary.

Selecting Architecture with the Modified Hyperband Algorithm. Our bound is used in Sect. 3.3 to create an unsupervised variant of the hyperband method. In comparison to Algorithm 2, this allows for the optimization of multiple hyperparameters at once, while enjoying the efficient search strategy of the hyperband method.

Figure 6 demonstrates the applicability of our unsupervised hyperband-based method for different datasets, employing both DiscoGAN and DistanceGAN. The graphs show the error and the bound obtained for the selected configuration after up to 35 hyperband iterations. As can be seen, in all cases, the method is able to recover a configuration that is significantly better than what is recovered, when only optimizing for the number of layers. To further demonstrate the generality of our method, we applied it on the UNIT [17] architecture. As the runtime of UNIT is much higher than DiscoGAN and DistanceGAN, this did not allow for extensive experimentation. We therefore focused on the most useful application of applying hyperband on a relatively complex dataset, specifically Maps. Figures 5 and 6b show the convergence on the hyperband method.

5 Conclusions

We extend the envelope of what is known to be possible in unsupervised learning by showing that we can reliably predict the error of a cross-domain mapping that was trained without matching samples. This is true both in expectation, with application to hyperparameter selection, and per sample, thus supporting dynamic confidence-based run time behavior, and (future work) unsupervised boosting during training.

The method is based on measuring the maximal distance within the set of low discrepancy mappings. This measure becomes the bound by applying what we define as the Occam's razor property, which is a general form of the Simplicity Principle. Therefore, the clear empirical success observed in our experiments supports the recent hypothesis that simplicity plays a key role in unsupervised learning.

For an extended version of this work, which is more rigorous than what can be provided here, and which also handles the non-deterministic case, please see [8].

Acknowledgements. This project has received funding from the European Research Council (ERC) under the European Union's Horizon 2020 research and innovation programme (grant ERC CoG 725974). The contribution of Sagie Benaim is part of Ph.D. thesis research conducted at Tel Aviv University.

References

1. Arjovsky, M., Chintala, S., Bottou, L.: Wasserstein generative adversarial networks. In: Proceedings of the 34th International Conference on Machine Learning, ICML 2017, pp. 214–223 (2017)
2. Benaim, S., Wolf, L.: One-sided unsupervised domain mapping. In: NIPS (2017)
3. Bergstra, J., Bengio, Y.: Random search for hyper-parameter optimization. J. Mach. Learn. Res. **13**, 281–305 (2012)
4. Bojanowski, P., Joulin, A., Lopez-Paz, D., Szlam, A.: Optimizing the latent space of generative networks. arXiv preprint arXiv:1707.05776 (2017)
5. Cordts, M., et al.: The cityscapes dataset for semantic urban scene understanding. In: CVPR (2016)
6. Dosovitskiy, A., Brox, T.: Generating images with perceptual similarity metrics based on deep networks. arXiv preprint arXiv:1602.02644 (2016)
7. Eggensperger, K., Feurer, M., Hutter, F., Bergstra, J., Snoek, J., Hoos, H.H.: Towards an empirical foundation for assessing Bayesian optimization of hyperparameters. In: NIPS workshop on Bayesian Optimization in Theory and Practice (2013)
8. Galanti, T., Benaim, S., Wolf, L.: Generalization bounds for unsupervised cross-domain mapping with WGANs. arXiv preprint arXiv:1807.08501 (2018)
9. Galanti, T., Wolf, L., Benaim, S.: The role of minimal complexity functions in unsupervised learning of semantic mappings. International Conference on Learning Representations (2018)
10. Ganin, Y., et al.: Domain-adversarial training of neural networks. J. Mach. Learn. Res. **17**(1), 2030–2096 (2016)
11. Goodfellow, I., et al.: Generative adversarial nets. In: NIPS (2014)
12. Hutter, F., Hoos, H.H., Leyton-Brown, K.: Sequential model-based optimization for general algorithm configuration. In: Coello, C.A.C. (ed.) LION 2011. LNCS, vol. 6683, pp. 507–523. Springer, Heidelberg (2011). https://doi.org/10.1007/978-3-642-25566-3_40
13. Isola, P., Zhu, J.Y., Zhou, T., Efros, A.A.: Image-to-image translation with conditional adversarial networks. In: CVPR (2017)
14. Johnson, J., Alahi, A., Fei-Fei, L.: Perceptual Losses for real-time style transfer and super-resolution. In: Leibe, B., Matas, J., Sebe, N., Welling, M. (eds.) ECCV 2016. LNCS, vol. 9906, pp. 694–711. Springer, Cham (2016). https://doi.org/10.1007/978-3-319-46475-6_43
15. Kim, T., Cha, M., Kim, H., Lee, J., Kim, J.: Learning to discover cross-domain relations with generative adversarial networks. arXiv preprint arXiv:1703.05192 (2017)
16. Li, L., Jamieson, K.G., DeSalvo, G., Rostamizadeh, A., Talwalkar, A.: Efficient hyperparameter optimization and infinitely many armed bandits. arXiv preprint arXiv:1603.06560 (2016)
17. Liu, M.Y., Breuel, T., Kautz, J.: Unsupervised image-to-image translation networks. In: NIPS (2017)

18. Liu, M.Y., Tuzel, O.: Coupled generative adversarial networks. In: NIPS, pp. 469–477 (2016)
19. Mirza, M., Osindero, S.: Conditional generative adversarial nets. arXiv preprint arXiv:1411.1784 (2014)
20. Tyleček, R., Šára, R.: Spatial pattern templates for recognition of objects with regular structure. In: Weickert, J., Hein, M., Schiele, B. (eds.) GCPR 2013. LNCS, vol. 8142, pp. 364–374. Springer, Heidelberg (2013). https://doi.org/10.1007/978-3-642-40602-7_39
21. Rakhlin, A., Panchenko, D., Mukherjee, S.: Probability and statistics risk bounds for mixture density estimation. ESAIM: Prob. Stat. **9** (2005)
22. Reed, S., Akata, Z., Yan, X., Logeswaran, L., Schiele, B., Lee, H.: Generative adversarial text to image synthesis. In: ICML (2016)
23. Seldin, Y., Tishby, N.: PAC-Bayesian generalization bound for density estimation with application to co-clustering. In: AISTATS (2009)
24. Snoek, J., Larochelle, H., Adams, R.P.: Practical Byesian optimization of machine learning algorithms. In: NIPS (2012)
25. Taigman, Y., Polyak, A., Wolf, L.: Unsupervised cross-domain image generation. In: International Conference on Learning Representations (ICLR) (2017)
26. Thornton, C., Hutter, F., Hoos, H.H., Leyton-Brown, K.: Auto-weka: combined selection and hyperparameter optimization of classification algorithms. In: KDD (2013)
27. Wolf, L., Taigman, Y., Polyak, A.: Unsupervised creation of parameterized avatars. In: The IEEE International Conference on Computer Vision (ICCV), October 2017
28. Xia, Y., et al.: Dual learning for machine translation. arXiv preprint arXiv:1611.00179 (2016)
29. Xie, S., Tu, Z.: Holistically-nested edge detection. In: ICCV (2015)
30. Yi, Z., Zhang, H., Tan, P., Gong, M.: DualGAN: unsupervised dual learning for image-to-image translation. arXiv preprint arXiv:1704.02510 (2017)
31. Yu, A., Grauman, K.: Fine-grained visual comparisons with local learning. In: CVPR (2014)
32. Zhu, J.-Y., Krähenbühl, P., Shechtman, E., Efros, A.A.: Generative visual manipulation on the natural image manifold. In: Leibe, B., Matas, J., Sebe, N., Welling, M. (eds.) ECCV 2016. LNCS, vol. 9909, pp. 597–613. Springer, Cham (2016). https://doi.org/10.1007/978-3-319-46454-1_36
33. Zhu, J.Y., Park, T., Isola, P., Efros, A.A.: Unpaired image-to-image translation using cycle-consistent adversarial networks. arXiv preprint arXiv:1703.10593 (2017)

Parallel Feature Pyramid Network for Object Detection

Seung-Wook Kim, Hyong-Keun Kook, Jee-Young Sun, Mun-Cheon Kang, and Sung-Jea Ko(✉)

School of Electrical Engineering, Korea University, Seoul, South Korea
{swkim,hkkook,mckang}@dali.korea.ac.kr, sjko@korea.ac.kr, jysun@dali.korea.ac.kr

Abstract. Recently developed object detectors employ a convolutional neural network (CNN) by gradually increasing the number of feature layers with a pyramidal shape instead of using a featurized image pyramid. However, the different abstraction levels of CNN feature layers often limit the detection performance, especially on small objects. To overcome this limitation, we propose a CNN-based object detection architecture, referred to as a parallel feature pyramid (FP) network (PFPNet), where the FP is constructed by widening the network width instead of increasing the network depth. First, we adopt spatial pyramid pooling and some additional feature transformations to generate a pool of feature maps with different sizes. In PFPNet, the additional feature transformation is performed in parallel, which yields the feature maps with similar levels of semantic abstraction across the scales. We then resize the elements of the feature pool to a uniform size and aggregate their contextual information to generate each level of the final FP. The experimental results confirmed that PFPNet increases the performance of the latest version of the single-shot multi-box detector (SSD) by mAP of 6.4% AP and especially, 7.8% $\mathrm{AP}_{\mathrm{small}}$ on the MS-COCO dataset.

Keywords: Real-time object detection · Feature pyramid

1 Introduction

Multi-scale object detection is a difficult and fundamental challenge in computer vision. Recently, object detection has achieved a considerable progress thanks to a decade of advances in convolutional neural networks (CNNs).

The early CNN-based object detectors utilize a deep CNN (DCNN) model as part of an object detection system. OverFeat [38] applies a CNN-based classifier to an image pyramid in a sliding window manner [5,7]. The regions with CNN features (R-CNN) method [10] adopts a region-based approach (also known as a two-stage scheme), where the image regions of object candidates are provided for a CNN-based classifier. Recent region-based detectors such as Fast R-CNN [9] and Faster R-CNN [35] utilize a single-scale feature map, which is transformed

V. Ferrari et al. (Eds.): ECCV 2018, LNCS 11209, pp. 239–256, 2018.
https://doi.org/10.1007/978-3-030-01228-1_15

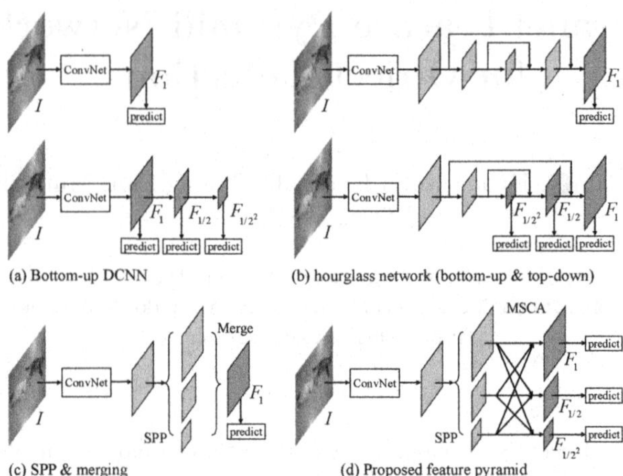

Fig. 1. Variant DCNN models that use a single-scale feature layer for visual recognition and their extensions to feature pyramids: bottom-up DCNN models (a), hourglass networks (b), and SPP-based networks (c); our network model (d) can be viewed as an extended version of (c) for multi-scale object detection.

by a DCNN model, as shown in Fig. 1(a) (top). In [35], using this single-scale feature, a complete object detection system is formed as an end-to-end CNN model and exhibits state-of-the-art performance.

Inspired by the pyramidal shape of the DCNN feature layers, some researchers have attempted to exploit multiple feature layers to improve the detection performance [2,27]. As shown in Fig. 1(a) (bottom), the single-shot multi-box detector (SSD) [27] utilizes a feature pyramid (FP), each level of which comprises DCNN layers responsible for detecting objects within a certain size range. In addition, SSD, a single-stage detector, is a region-free detector that does not require a region proposal process. By using the FP and a single-stage scheme, SSD exhibits detection performance that is comparable to region-based detectors and high computational efficiency competitive to YOLO [31], which uses a single-scale feature map. However, the object detectors with this FP would poorly perform on the lower feature layers because of their lack of object-level information.

It has been shown that the lower- and upper-level features are complementary to each other and their combinations are beneficial for segmentation [30], keypoint estimation [29], and object detection [22]. In the hourglass model (see Fig. 1(b)), to generate a single high-level feature map, the object knowledge contained in the upper layer is forwarded to the lower layers by appending a top-down module. The low-resolution of the upper layers can ensure invariance to pixel variations, which is helpful for identifying object instances, but it can cause difficulties in pixel-level tasks such as pixel labeling and box regression [13,28]. Thus, the lateral connections are added between the bottom-up and top-down layers to transfer the information on object details to the top-down layers. A recent trend in single-stage methods is to bring such benefits of the hourglass network into FP-based object detectors [8,20,23,25,43]. The deconvolutional single shot detector (DSSD) [8] forms an hourglass structure that can exploit both the object-level information insensitive to pose and appearance from the upper layers and the richer spatial information from the lower layers. By appending a top-down module to SSD, DSSD can raise the performance of the region-free object detectors to the level of region-based ones. However, the top-down modules incur additional computational costs, so the speed of region-free methods is no longer their advantage. In recent, the RetinaNet [25] and RefineDet [43] simplify the feature layers of the top-down and lateral paths, and achieve state-of-the-art performance while operating in real time.

In this study, we propose a parallel FP network (PFPNet) to construct an FP by widening the network width instead of increasing its depth. As shown in Fig. 1(d), we first employ the spatial pyramid pooling (SPP) [14] to generate a wide FP pool with the feature maps of different sizes. Next, we apply additional feature abstraction to the feature maps of the FP pool in parallel, which makes all of them have similar levels of semantic abstraction. The multi-scale context aggregation (MSCA) modules then resize these feature maps to a uniform size and aggregate their contextual information to produce each level of the final FP.

To the best of our knowledge, PFPNet is the first attempt to apply the SPP module to a region-free multi-scale object detector using a CNN-based FP. Previous studies have demonstrated that multi-scale representation using the SPP module can greatly improve the performance in terms of object detection [14] and segmentation [44]. These studies utilize the SPP module to produce a single high-level feature vector with a fixed size or a feature map with a fine resolution for making predictions as shown in Fig. 1(c). By contrast, we utilize the SPP module to produce an FP where the predictions are independently made on each level. In summary, this study makes three main contributions:

- We employ the SPP module to generate pyramid-shaped feature maps via widening the network width instead of increasing its depth.
- By using the MSCA module similar to an inception module [41], our model effectively combines the context information at vastly different scales. Since the feature maps of our FP have a similar abstraction level, the difference in performance among the levels of the FP can be effectively reduced.
- We obtained remarkable performance on the public datasets. Using an input size of 512×512, PFPNet achieved the mean average precision (mAP) of 82.3% on the Pascal VOC 2007, 80.3% on the PASCAL VOC 2012, and 35.2% on the MS-COCO, thereby outperforming the state-of-the-art object detectors. Using an input size of 320×320 and 512×512, PFPNet operates at 33 and 24 frames per second (FPS), respectively, on a single Titan X GPU. For small-scale objects, PFPNet increases the performance of the latest version of the SSD [26] by the AP of 7.8% on the MS-COCO dataset.

2 Parallel Feature-Pyramid Network

First, we explain our motivation for designing the proposed architecture for object detection. In [34], Ren *et al.* stated that useful feature maps for robust object detection should have the following properties: (1) the feature maps need to contain the fine details that represent the structure of objects well; (2) the feature maps must be extracted by using a sufficiently deep transformation function, *i.e.*, the high-level object knowledge should be encoded in the feature maps; (3) the feature maps should have meaningful context information to support predictions of the exact location and the class labels of "hard-to-detect" objects such as occluded, small, blurred, and saturated objects.

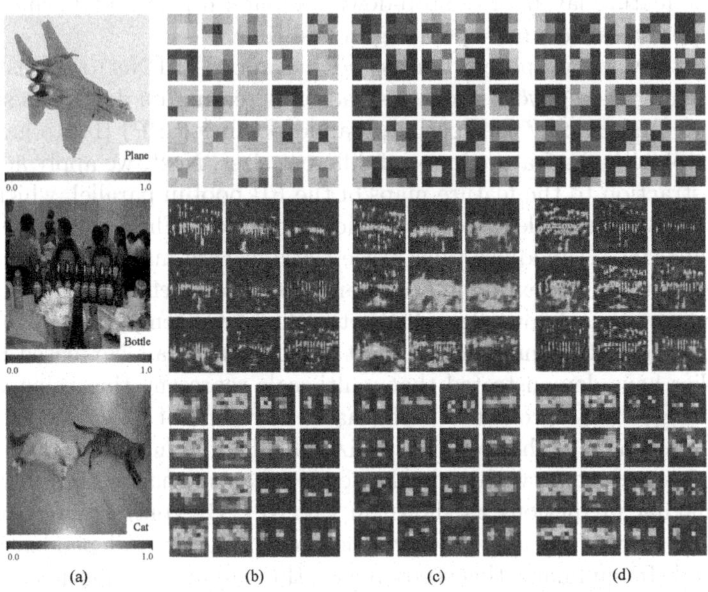

Fig. 2. Examples of input images (a) and their corresponding feature maps using SSD [27] (b), FPN [23] (c), and PFPNet (d). All the models use VGGNet-16 as their backbone network. The objects are detected at the visualized scales of the feature maps (in the second row, the feature maps represent the scale of the beer bottles).

Let us recall FPs discussed in Sect. 1. The feature maps in the FP based on the bottom-up DCNN might not satisfy the first property for the upper-level feature maps obtained by the deep transformation functions; on the other hand, the lower-level feature maps obtained by the shallow transformation functions may not meet the second property, which impairs the detection performance on small objects. Furthermore, each feature map is only responsible for the output at its corresponding scale, so contextual information at different scales cannot be effectively incorporated. A simple way to overcome these limitations is to utilize the transformation functions with a proper depth to retain both the fine spatial information and the high-level semantic object information. As shown in Fig. 1(d), if the FP is arranged in a row, we can apply such transformation functions with the same depth to generate every level of the FP. We then aggregate different types of contextual information using the proposed MSCA modules to produce the final feature maps which satisfy the third property required for good feature maps mentioned above.

Figure 2 shows the images of objects with various sizes and their feature maps at the scales corresponding to the objects. As discussed earlier, for SSD, the visualized channels of the upper-level feature map for a plane are well activated, but the activation values are not sparse, which could diminish the box regression performance. For small bottles, fine details can be observed, but the activations are not consistent despite the similar shape of the bottles. Some studies [20,42] have shown that masking the activation values concentrated in the object regions can improve the performance of visual recognition tasks. Thus, sparse channel values on the object region can provide more accurate object information for large objects. For FPN [23], which is an hourglass model, and PFPNet, the visualized channels for a plane are well activated and sparser than those for SSD. For small bottles, the channel values of FPN are more activated than those of SSD, but the details somewhat disappear owing to the blurred information from the top-down path. On the other hand, the visualized channels in PFPNet retain not only the fine details of the objects, but also the consistent high activation values overlapping with the exact object location. For the medium-sized objects (the cats in the bottom row), all the feature channels of SSD, FPN, and PFPNet have feature values that are well activated and concentrated in the object region. This observation shows that the proper depth of the transformation function can enhance the quality of feature representation, and the experimental results in Sect. 3 demonstrate the effectiveness of the proposed structure. In the following, we provide details of the proposed PFPNet.

Base Network. PFPNet is based on VGGNet-16 [40]. In PFPNet, the final fully-connected (fc) layers in VGGNet-16 are replaced with convolutional (Conv) layers by sub-sampling their parameters, and this modified VGGNet-16 were pre-trained on the ILSVRC dataset [37].

Bottleneck Layer. For a feature transformation, we use bottleneck layers [16]. In the bottleneck layer, to improve the computational efficiency, a 1×1 convolution is applied prior to a 3×3 convolution to reduce the number of channels. The batch normalization [17] without scale/shift and the rectified linear unit (ReLU) [12] are used for input normalization and activation. In the bottleneck layer, the 1×1 convolution produces the feature maps with $C/2$ channels, where C is the number of the output channels of the bottleneck layer.

FP Pool. The pooling [21] layer, which is widely used in visual classification tasks [15,40,41], not only reduces the spatial size of the feature maps to a specific size, but it can also aggregate the contextual prior in a sub-region. In [14,44], the SPP layer with various sizes of pooling sub-regions is utilized to construct an FP for object detection and segmentation.

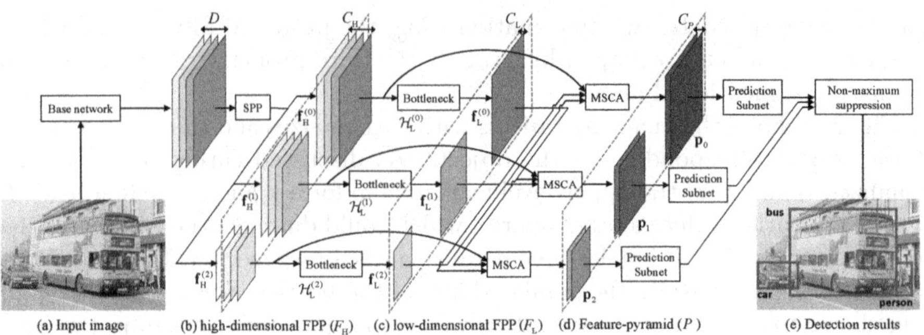

(a) Input image (b) high-dimensional FPP (F_H) (c) low-dimensional FPP (F_L) (d) Feature-pyramid (P) (e) Detection results

Fig. 3. Overview of PFPNet with $N = 3$. For an input image (a), the base network is employed to obtain the input for PFPNet. The high-dimensional FP pool (F_{H}) (b) is formed by using the SPP module, and the low-dimensional FP pool (F_{L}) (c) is obtained by applying the further transformation to the elements of (b). From these feature pools, the MSCA modules generate the final FP (P) (d) for multi-scale detection. Finally, the FP is fed into the Conv prediction Subnets to obtain the detection results (e).

Inspired by these previous studies, we use the SPP layer to construct an FP pool that is enriched with both the spatial information and multi-scale semantic object-information. Figure 3 illustrates the architecture of PFPNet for multi-scale object detection. Let the base network produces the $W \times H$ output feature map having D output channels. By using the SPP module, we first form the high-dimensional FP pool, $F_{\mathrm{H}} = \{\mathbf{f}_{\mathrm{H}}^{(0)}, \mathbf{f}_{\mathrm{H}}^{(1)}, \cdots, \mathbf{f}_{\mathrm{H}}^{(N-1)}\}$, where $\mathbf{f}_{\mathrm{H}}^{(n)}$, the feature map with a spatial size of $\frac{W}{2^n} \times \frac{H}{2^n}$, denotes the nth level of F_{H}, and N denotes the number of pyramid levels. Thus, we obtain downsampled feature maps with the channel number of $C_{\mathrm{H}} = D$ by successively decreasing the spatial size by half. We apply the bottleneck layers, denoted as $\mathcal{H}_{\mathrm{L}}^{(n)}(\cdot)$, to each level in parallel to further extract the appropriate contextual feature for each scale and to reduce the channel number of contextual representation. We let $F_{\mathrm{L}} = \{\mathbf{f}_{\mathrm{L}}^{(0)}, \mathbf{f}_{\mathrm{L}}^{(1)}, \cdots, \mathbf{f}_{\mathrm{L}}^{(N-1)}\}$ represent the low-dimensional FP pool, which is the output of the transformation of F_{H} with a reduced channel number, $C_{\mathrm{L}} = D/(N-1)$.

MSCA. Incorporating context information at different scales can facilitate several visual classification tasks [1,13,18,28]. Combining the feature maps by summation is a common approach for collecting contextual information from multiple features [15]. However, Huang *et al.* [16] recently insisted that the summation could weaken the information flow in a network. They introduced an alternative approach, which involves concatenating the feature maps directly to retain the maximum information flow between feature layers. Several architectures for object detection adopted this approach. For instance, in [1], higher-level DCNN layers are fused into a single feature map via concatenation. In [18], multiple feature-layers based on the DCNN or the hourglass network are concatenated as well to exploit the contextual information at different scales.

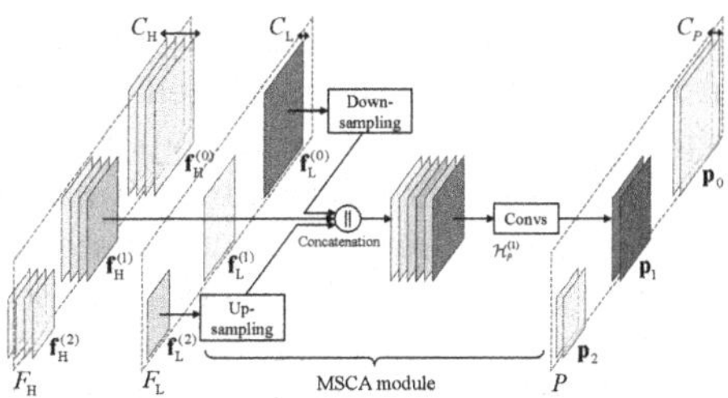

Fig. 4. Multi-scale context aggregation (MSCA) module.

PFPNet also use concatenation to collect the contextual information in the FP pool. Figure 4 shows an example of how the MSCA module produces a level of the final FP, $P = \{\mathbf{p}_0, \mathbf{p}_1, \cdots, \mathbf{p}_{N-1}\}$. Consider that we generate the level n of the FP, $\mathbf{p}_n$, with a size of $\frac{W}{2^n} \times \frac{H}{2^n}$. We assume that the level n of the FP pool contains primary information about the objects in $\mathbf{p}_n$, and the other levels supplement the information for the objects as context priors at different scales. Therefore, we bring $\mathbf{f}_{\mathrm{H}}^{(n)}$ from the high-dimensional FP pool, F_{H}, as the primary information, while we gather the larger- and smaller-sized feature maps from the low-dimensional FP pool, F_{L}, as the supplementary information. To match the sizes of the feature maps from F_{L}, we directly upsample the feature maps with smaller sizes ($>n$) via bilinear interpolation and downsample those with larger sizes ($<n$) via non-overlapping average pooling. Finally, these feature maps are combined via concatenation as described in [44]. The single feature map from F_{H} accounts for half the contents of the concatenated feature map and the $N-1$ feature maps in F_{L} with $D/(N-1)$ channels comprise the other half, *i.e.*, the concatenated feature map has $2D$ channels. We utilize another transformation by using bottleneck module or a series of 3×3 convolutions, denoted as $\mathcal{H}_P^{(n)}(\cdot)$, to refine and aggregate the collected information in the concatenated feature maps, and finally obtain $\mathbf{p}_n$ with C_P channels. Since the MSCA modules reuse the feature maps in F_{L}, we can effectively exploit the multi-scale context information with the improved use of computational resources.

In the MSCA module, the feature map from F_{H} is combined with other feature maps of F_{L} by using the skip connection. This can ease difficult optimization process due to a wide and complex structure of the MSCA module having a number of parameters. We conducted an experiment in which the skip connection was omitted and the concatenated feature map was built using only the feature maps of F_{L}. In this case, to form F_{L}, we let the number of output channels of $\mathcal{H}_{\mathrm{L}}(\cdot)$ be $2D/N$ so that the concatenated feature maps have $2D$ channels. In the experiment, this setting not only increased the number of parameters for $\mathcal{H}_{\mathrm{L}}(\cdot)$, but also decreased the performance of the proposed network slightly, as we expected.

Details of PFPNet. We use 3×3 Conv layers to predict the locations of objects and their class labels. For box regression sub-network (Subnet), a 3×3

Conv layer with $4A$ filters is applied to each level of the FP to calculate the relative offset between the anchor and the predicted bounding box, where A is the number of anchors per location of the feature map. For classification, another 3×3 Conv layer with $(K+1)A$ filters followed by softmax is applied to predict the probability of an object being present at each spatial position for each of the A anchors and K object classes. Since we focus on the contribution of the proposed FP to object detection, we use simple Subnets using a single-layer 3×3 convolution to ensure fair comparisons with SSD [27] and RefineDet [43].

The anchors allow us to allocate the output space to the multiple levels of the FP. For fair comparisons with SSD and RefineDet, we employ two anchor types: the pre-defined anchor boxes identical to those used in [26], denoted by a suffix "-S", and the anchor boxes predicted by the anchor refinement module (ARM) presented in [43], denoted by a suffix"-R". For PFPNet-S, we adopt most of the settings presented in [26,27] such as anchor design, a matching scheme, and input sizes. We use the input sizes of 300×300 and 512×512, which are denoted as PFPNet-S300 and PFPNet-S512, respectively. For PFPNet-S, a bottleneck module is used for a transformation function $\mathcal{H}_P^{(n)}(\cdot)$, and all of the new Conv layers were initialized using the Gaussian filler with the standard deviation of 0.01. For PFPNet-R, we employ the ARM proposed in [43]. The ARM is a prediction Subnet, which outputs the coordinate information and objectness of the refined anchors. If the objectness of a refined anchor is larger than a threshold θ (θ is empirically set to 0.01), the refined anchor is then used as an input anchor for the final prediction Subnets; otherwise, it will be discarded. As described in [43], we employ PFPNet with the input sizes of 320×320 and 512×512, which are denoted as PFPNet-R320 and PFPNet-R512, respectively. The levels of the final pyramid P has $C_P = 256$ channels, and two 3×3 Conv layers followed by ReLU are applied as a transformation function $\mathcal{H}_P^{(n)}(\cdot)$ for PFPNet-R. All of the new Conv layers were initialized using the Xavier method [11].

We employ the multi-task loss defined in [27] for PFPNet-S and that in [43] for PFPNet-R to optimize the model parameters. Following SSD, the smooth L_1 loss is used to calculate the loss function for bounding box regression. Our experiments were conducted on a single NVIDIA Titan X GPU. For PFPNet-S300 and PFPNet-R320, we use the stochastic gradient descent (SGD) with a mini-batch size of 32 images, and for PFPNet with the size of 512, we employ the SGD with a mini-batch size of 28 images owing to the memory limit. We use a momentum of 0.9 and weight decay of 5×10^{-4}.

3 Experiments

3.1 Datasets

We utilize three datasets, namely Pascal VOC 2007, VOC 2012 [6], and MS COCO (COCO) [24] datasets. Both VOC 2007 and VOC 2012 datasets contain 20 object classes. VOC 2007 is divided into two subsets, *trainval* (5,011 images) and *test* (4,952 images) sets, which are fully annotated with the ground truth bounding boxes of objects. VOC 2012 comprises the *trainval* set (11,540 images), which is annotated, and the *test* set (10,991 images), which has no disclosed label. COCO has 80 object categories for object detection. In our experiments using COCO, we use the *trainval35k* subset [1] for training, which is a union of 80k images from *train* and a random subset of 35k images from the 40k *val* images. We present the results obtained using the *test-dev* subset of the COCO dataset.

3.2 Experimental Setup

We compare performance of PFPNet with state-of-the-art region-based detectors, Faster R-CNN [35,36] and its variations [15,23,39], HyperNet [19], ION [1], R-FCN [3], Deformable R-FCN [4], and CoupleNet [45], as well as some region-free detectors, the YOLO [31], YOLOv2 [32], and SSD [27]. Note that, for SSD, we use the versions of the latest implementations [26]. For comparisons with the multi-scale region-free detector using the hourglass model, we employed RON [20], R-SSD [18], DSSD [8], RetinaNet [25], and RefineDet [43]. The suffix "+" represents the results obtained with a multi-scale testing.

3.3 PASCAL VOC 2007

Training and Evaluation Metric. In this experiment, the union of VOC 2007 *trainval* and VOC 2012 *trainval* sets denoted as VOC07+12 is used to train all of the networks. For VOC 2007 *test* set, the detection performance is evaluated using the mean AP (mAP) where a predicted bounding box is correct if its intersection over union (IoU) with the ground truth bounding box is higher than 0.5. We train our network for 110k iterations with an initial learning rate of 10^{-3}, which is divided by 10 at 80k iterations and again at 100k iterations.

Table 1. Impact of hyperparameters.

	# pyramid levels (N)					Reduced channel number (C_{L})		
	2	3	**4**	5	6	64	128	**256**
mAP (%)	79.08	80.08	**80.72**	80.68	80.15	80.16	80.34	**80.72**

Ablation Study for the Impact of the Hyperparameters. We conduct experiments to clarify the impact of the hyperparameters, N and C_{L}. As shown in Table 1, for the pyramid levels (with $C_{\mathrm{L}} = 256$), PFPNet shows the best result of 80.72% where $N = 4$. For the reduced channel number of the low-dimensional feature pool F_{L} (with $N = 4$), $C_{\mathrm{L}} = 256$ shows the best mAP value.

Table 2. Performance comparisons of different FPs.

Method	PFPNet-R320			RefineDet320		FPN320		SSD (baseline)
ARM	✓			✓		✓		
MSCA module	✓	✓						
mAP (%)	80.7	78.5	77.9	80.0	77.3	79.6	77.6	76.2

Ablation Study for Wide FP and MSCA Module. To verify the effectiveness of the wide FP and MSCA module, we conduct an experiment with or without using the MSCA modules. The prediction Subnets are applied directly to the feature maps of F_{L}. As listed in Table 2, the wide FP obtained by using the SPP layer (*i.e.*, the mAP of 77.9%) increases the performance by 1.7% mAP as compared to the baseline. With the MSCA module, we find that mAP is further increased from 77.9% to 78.5%.

Performance Comparisons with Other FPs. To demonstrate the effectiveness of the proposed FP, we test four different FPs. For the FP based on the bottom-up model, we use SSD [27] as a baseline. For the FP based on the hourglass model, we adopt two different models, the single-stage detector using the feature pyramid network (FPN) [23] and RefineDet [43]. VGGNet-16 [40] is used as a base network, where the input size was 320×320. For a fair comparison, we use the same parameter settings. Every tested model has four pyramid levels ($N = 4$), and the number of anchors was $A = 3$ where the aspect ratios $\{\frac{1}{2}, 1, 2\}$ are employed. Single-layer 3×3 convolutions are utilized as prediction Subnets. For the proposed FP and the FPs based on hourglass models, we additionally evaluate the performance w/ or w/o ARM [43]. As shown in Table 2, PFPNet-R, RefineDet, and FPN can effectively increase the mAPs as compared to the baseline. Without ARM, FPN shows better performance than RefineDet (77.6% *vs.* 77.3%). As indicated in [8,32], well designed anchors boost the performance of object detectors. Since ARM adaptively refines the anchor boxes, it has increased the performance of all the models by more than 2% points. Specifically, the mAPs of PFPNet-R, RefineDet, and FPN are increased by 2.2%, 2.7%, and 2.0%, respectively. As a result, by using the ARM, the proposed FP exhibits the best performance (80.7% mAP) among the compared models.

Results. Table 3 shows the performance of PFPNet and other conventional detectors. Recent region-free methods based on the hourglass model such as R-SSD512 [18], DSSD513 [8], and RefineDet512 [43] exhibit the performance competitive to the region-based detectors on this set. For the input size of 300×300, PFPNet-S300 shows the result similar to RefineDet320, which is the first method achieving the mAP of above 80% with such a small-resolution input. PFPNet-R320, *i.e.*, PFPNet using the ARM which was also used in RefineDet, obtains the mAP of 80.7%. Note that, for the larger input size of 512×512, PFPNet-S512

Table 3. Detection results on PASCAL VOC 2007 and VOC 2012 test sets.

Method	Backbone	Input resolution	# Boxes	FPS	mAP (%)	
					VOC 2007	VOC 2012
Faster R-CNN [35]	VGGNet-16	∼1000 × 600	300	5	73.2	70.4
HyperNet [19]	VGGNet-16	∼1000 × 600	100	0.9	76.3	71.4
Faster R-CNN [36]	ResNet-101	∼1000 × 600	300	2.4	76.4	73.8
ION * [1]	VGGNet-16	∼1000 × 600	4000	1.3	79.2	76.4
R-FCN [3]	ResNet-101	∼1000 × 600	300	9	80.5	77.6
CoupleNet [45]	ResNet-101	∼1000 × 600	300	8	82.7	80.4
YOLO [31]	GoogleNet [41]	448 × 448	98	45	63.4	57.9
RON384 [20]	VGGNet-16	384 × 384	30600	15	75.4	73.0
SSD300 [26]	VGGNet-16	300 × 300	8732	46	77.2	75.8
R-SSD300 [18]	VGGNet-16	300 × 300	8732	35	78.5	76.4
YOLOv2 [32]	DarkNet-19	544 × 544	845	40	78.6	73.4
DSSD321 [8]	ResNet-101	321 × 321	17080	10	78.6	76.3
SSD512 [26]	VGGNet-16	512 × 512	24564	19	79.8	78.5
R-SSD512 [18]	VGGNet-16	512 × 512	24564	17	80.8	-
DSSD513 [8]	ResNet-101	513 × 513	43688	6	81.5	80.0
RefineDet320 [43]	VGGNet-16	320 × 320	6375	40	80.0	78.1
RefineDet512 [43]	VGGNet-16	512 × 512	16320	24	81.8	80.1
RefineDet320+ [43]	VGGNet-16	-	-	-	83.1	82.7
RefineDet512+ [43]	VGGNet-16	-	-	-	83.8	83.5
PFPNet-S300	VGGNet-16	300 × 300	8732	39	79.9	76.8[a]
PFPNet-R320	VGGNet-16	320 × 320	6375	33	80.7	77.7[b]
PFPNet-S512	VGGNet-16	512 × 512	24564	26	81.8	79.7[c]
PFPNet-R512	VGGNet-16	512 × 512	16320	24	82.3	80.3[d]
PFPNet-R320+	VGGNet-16	-	-	-	83.5	83.0[e]
PFPNet-R512+	VGGNet-16	-	-	-	**84.1**	**83.7**[f]

*ION adopted iterative bbox regression and voting, and regularizing with segmentation labels.

[a] http://host.robots.ox.ac.uk:8080/anonymous/HUJBN7.html

[b] http://host.robots.ox.ac.uk:8080/anonymous/GATL5Q.html

[c] http://host.robots.ox.ac.uk:8080/anonymous/SNRWPN.html

[d] http://host.robots.ox.ac.uk:8080/anonymous/GKGYPV.html

[e] http://host.robots.ox.ac.uk:8080/anonymous/B5AKH8.html

[f] http://host.robots.ox.ac.uk:8080/anonymous/M7K1BM.html

achieves the same result as RefineDet512. As shown in Table 3, PFPNet-R512 exhibits the best mAP among the region-free methods, and both PFPNet-R320 and PFPNet-R512 perform better than most of the region-based methods except CoupleNet [45], which adopts the residual network (ResNet)-101 as its base network and uses an larger input size (1000 × 600) as compared with PFPNet-R512. Since the input size dramatically affects the detection performance, we also tested PFPNet-R320+ and PFPNet-R512+, which utilizes the multi-scale testing, to reduce the impact of input sizes. PFPNet-R320+ and PFPNet-R512+ achieves the mAPs of 83.5% and 84.1%, respectively. As compared with the real-time object detectors such as SSD, YOLOv2, R-SSD, and RefineDet, PFPNet not only has the real-time speed, but also exhibits the best mAPs. The time complexity and detection performance of PFPNet-S, even without using ARM, are similar to those of RefineDet. PFPNet-R320 and PFPNet-R512 operate at 33 FPS and 24 FPS, respectively.

3.4 PASCAL VOC 2012

In this experiment, we used a subset, called VOC07++12, consisting of VOC 2007 *trainval* and *test* sets, and VOC 2012 *trainval* set, for a training, as described in [27,35]. Using the VOC07++12 set, we trained PFPNet for 240k iterations in total. Starting with an initial learning rate of 10^{-3}, the learning rate is decreased by a factor of 10 at 160k and again at 200k iterations.

Table 3 shows the detection performance of PFPNet and other conventional detectors based on the comp4 (outside data) track from the public leaderboard on PASCAL VOC 2012. For the input size of 300×300, PFPNet-S300 obtains the mAP of 76.8%, which is better than most of the region-based methods using the input size of 1000×600 and region-free ones using the similar input size to PFPNet-S300. PFPNet-R320 shows the mAP of 77.7%, which is better than the performance of most region-free detectors with similar input sizes except RefineDet320 [43]. For the input size of 512×512, PFPNet-S512 and PFPNet-R512 exhibit the mAPs of 79.7% and 80.3%, respectively. PFPNet-R512 outperforms other compared models except CoupleNet [45]. To reduce the impact of input sizes for a fair comparison, the multi-scale testing is applied, and as can be seen in Table 3, PFPNet-R320+ and PFPNet-R512+ yield the state-of-the-art mAPs of 83.0% and 83.7%, respectively.

3.5 MS COCO

To validate PFPNet on a more challenging dataset, we conducted experiments using the COCO dataset. The performance evaluation metric for the COCO dataset is slightly different from that for the VOC dataset. The AP over different IoU thresholds from 0.5 to 0.95 is denoted as $\mathrm{AP}_{50:95}$, to present the overall performance of the detection models. The APs with IoU thresholds of 0.5 and 0.75 are denoted as AP_{50} and AP_{75}, respectively. In addition, the MS COCO evaluation server provides the AP for diverse scales. The object scales are determined by measuring the number of pixels in the object's segmentation mask, S, as follows: small objects (AP_{S}): $S < 32^2$; medium objects (AP_{M}): $32^2 < S < 96^2$; large objects (AP_{L}): $S > 96^2$. Using the COCO *trainval35k* sets, we trained our model for 400k iterations in total, starting with an initial learning rate of 10^{-3}, and then decreasing it by a factor of 10 at 280k and again at 360k iterations.

As shown in Table 4, PFPNet-S300 and PFPNet-R320 produce the APs of 29.6% and 31.8%, which outperform the VGGNet-16-based models using an input size of around 300. PFPNet-R320 even produces the better results than

Table 4. Detection results on MS COCO test-dev set.

Method	Backbone	Train set	$AP_{50:95}$	AP_{50}	AP_{75}	AP_S	AP_M	AP_L
Faster R-CNN [35]	VGGNet-16	trainval	21.9	42.7	-	-	-	-
ION* [1]	VGGNet-16	train	33.1	55.7	34.6	14.5	35.2	47.2
R-FCN [3]	ResNet-101	trainval	29.9	51.9	-	10.8	32.8	45.0
CoupleNet [45]	ResNet-101	trainval	34.4	54.8	37.2	13.4	38.1	50.8
Faster R-CNN+++ [15]	ResNet-101-C4	trainval	34.9	55.7	37.4	15.6	38.7	50.9
Faster R-CNN w/ FPN [23]	ResNet-101-FPN	trainval35k	36.2	59.1	39.0	18.2	39.0	48.2
Faster R-CNN w/ TDM [39]	Inception-ResNet-v2-TDM	trainval	37.3	57.8	39.8	17.1	40.3	52.1
Deformable R-FCN [4]	Aligned-Inception-ResNet	trainval	37.5	58.0	40.8	19.4	40.1	52.5
YOLOv2 [32]	DarkNet-19	trainval35k	21.6	44.0	19.2	5.0	22.4	35.5
SSD300 [26]	VGGNet-16	trainval35k	25.1	43.1	25.8	6.6	25.9	41.4
RON384++ [20]	VGGNet-16	trainval	27.4	49.5	27.1	-	-	-
DSSD321 [8]	ResNet-101	trainval35k	28.0	46.1	29.2	7.4	28.1	47.6
SSD512 [26]	VGGNet-16	trainval35k	28.8	48.5	30.3	10.9	31.8	43.5
RefineDet320 [43]	VGGNet-16	trainval35k	29.4	49.2	31.3	10.0	32.0	44.4
RetinaNet400 [25]	ResNet-50	trainval35k	30.5	47.8	32.7	11.2	33.8	46.1
RetinaNet400 [25]	ResNet-101	trainval35k	31.9	49.5	34.1	11.6	35.8	48.5
RefineDet320 [43]	ResNet-101	trainval35k	32.0	51.4	34.2	10.5	34.7	50.4
RetinaNet500 [25]	ResNet-50	trainval35k	32.5	50.9	34.8	13.9	35.8	46.7
RefineDet512 [43]	VGGNet-16	trainval35k	33.0	54.5	35.5	16.3	36.3	44.3
DSSD513 [8]	ResNet-101	trainval35k	33.2	53.3	35.2	13.0	35.4	51.1
RetinaNet500 [25]	ResNet-101	trainval35k	34.4	53.1	36.8	14.7	38.5	49.1
RefineDet320+ [43]	VGGNet-16	trainval35k	35.2	56.1	37.7	19.5	37.2	47.0
RefineDet512 [43]	ResNet-101	trainval35k	36.4	57.5	39.5	16.6	39.9	51.4
RefineDet512+ [43]	VGGNet-16	trainval35k	37.6	58.7	40.8	22.7	40.3	48.3
RefineDet320+ [43]	ResNet-101	trainval35k	38.6	59.9	41.7	21.1	41.7	52.3
RetinaNet800** [25]	ResNet-101-FPN	trainval35k	39.1	59.1	42.3	21.8	42.7	50.2
RetinaNet800** [25]	ResNeXt-101-FPN	trainval35k	40.8	61.1	44.1	24.1	44.2	51.2
RefineDet512+ [43]	ResNet-101	trainval35k	**41.8**	**62.9**	**45.7**	**25.6**	**45.1**	**54.1**
PFPNet-S300	VGGNet-16	trainval35k	29.6	49.6	31.1	10.6	32.0	44.9
PFPNet-R320	VGGNet-16	trainval35k	31.8	52.9	33.6	12.0	35.5	46.1
PFPNet-S512	VGGNet-16	trainval35k	33.4	54.8	35.8	16.3	36.7	46.7
PFPNet-R512	VGGNet-16	trainval35k	35.2	57.6	37.9	18.7	38.6	45.9
PFPNet-R320+	VGGNet-16	trainval35k	37.8	60.0	40.7	22.2	40.4	49.1
PFPNet-R512+	VGGNet-16	trainval35k	39.4	61.5	42.6	25.3	42.3	48.8

* ION adopted iterative bbox regression and voting, and regularizing with segmentation labels.
** RetinaNet800 was trained with scale jitter and for 1.5× longer than RetinaNet500.

R-FCN using ResNet-101 [15], and the similar results to RetinaNet400 using ResNet-101 with the larger input size of 400 × 400. Without using the ARM, PFPNet-S512 shows the comparable performance to the hourglass models using the similar input size such as RetinaNet500 [23], DSSD513 [8], which are based on ResNet-101, and RefineDet512 [43]. With the ARM, PFPNet-R512 achieves the AP of 35.2%. By using VGGNet-16, ARM, and the same input sizes, PFPNet-R320 and PFPNet-R512 increase the overall APs of RefineDet by 2.4% and 2.2%, respectively. As can be seen in Table 4, the performance of PFPNet-R512 is much better than the state-of-the-art region-free detectors with an input size of around 512, and superior to most of the region-based detectors except Faster R-CNN w/ FPN [23], Faster R-CNN w/ TDM [39], and Deformable R-FCN [39], which use complex ResNet-based backbones with a large input size of 1000×600. To reduce the impact of input sizes for a fair comparison, we also employed the multi-scale testing on this set. PFPNet-R320+ obtains the even higher AP than all of the compared region-based object detectors, and PFPNet-R512+ attains the best AP of 39.4% among the compared object detection models based on VGGNet. As compared with the detectors based on recent backbone networks, PFPNet shows comparable detection performance, especially on small objects.

Note that PFPNet-S512 and PFPNet-R512 show the particularly good AP values at a small scale (16.3% and 18.7%) among the compared models. Detecting the small-scaled objects is one of the most challenging problem for both the region-based and region-free methods. The experimental results demonstrate that the feature representation power can be improved by using the proposed FP architecture, especially at a small scale, as discussed in Sect. 2. As provided in [24], more than 70% of COCO dataset is composed of objects, the sizes of which are smaller than 10% of the input size (cf. the VOC dataset has less than 50% of objects with such sizes). In addition, the images of COCO dataset possess more valuable contextual information than those of VOC dataset, which can be estimated by investigating the average number of object categories per image (3.4 vs. 1.4). Since the proposed MSCA modules aggregate the multi-scale context, the COCO dataset has more information available than VOC dataset. As a result, PFPNet has great advantages in detecting small-scale objects and utilizing the multi-scale context information, which yields a significant improvement on COCO dataset.

Speed Versus Accuracy Trade-Off. Figure 5 shows the speed versus AP of single-stage detectors on COCO test-dev dataset. As compared with RetinaNet and RefineDet models yielding similar APs to PFPNet, PFPNet operates more than twice as fast. For the similar speed, PFPNet outperforms SSD [26], RefineDet [43], and recently-released YOLOv3 [33].

In addition, we obtain the performance on VOC 2012 test set using the fine-tuned models pretrained on COCO. The models were first trained on COCO

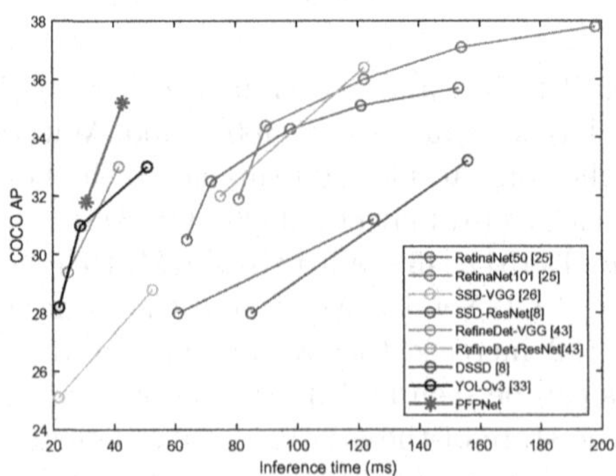

Fig. 5. Speed (ms) versus accuracy (AP) of single-stage detectors on COCO test-dev.

trainval35k set, and then fine-tuned on VOC07++12 set. The mAP results of PFPNet-R320 and PFPNet-R512 are 84.5% and 85.7%, respectively. With the same backbone and train set, PFPNet-R320 and PFPNet-R512 increase the mAPs of RefineDet [43] by 1.8% and 0.7%, respectively. By using the multi-scale test scheme, PFPNet-R (87.8% mAP) was ranked 7th place on the leaderboard among the overall architectures at the time of submission.

4 Conclusions

In this paper, we proposed an effective FP for object detection. In contrast to the conventional FPs, we designed the FP having a wide structure. This allows transformation functions to have a proper and uniform depth. Thus, all elements of the FP could retain both the fine-structure of objects and the high-level object knowledge. By using the proposed MSCA module, we efficiently reused the elements in the FP pool to collect the various contextual information at the different scale and produce the final FP. A single-shot object detection method developed using the wide FP, called PFPNet, achieved 82.3% on the Pascal VOC 2007, 80.3% on the PASCAL VOC 2012, and 35.2% on the MS-COCO, in terms of the mAP. By employing the multi-scale testing, PFPNet exhibits the state-of-the-art performance. In particular, PFPNet has the advantage in detecting small-scale objects with the AP_S of 18.7% on the MS-COCO dataset.

Although we concentrated on object detection, we believe that the feature representation using the proposed wide FP will be beneficial for a variety of other computer vision tasks.

Acknowledgements. This work was supported by Institute for Information & communications Technology Promotion (IITP) grant funded by the Korea government (MSIP) (2014-0-00077, Development of global multi-target tracking and event prediction techniques based on real-time large-scale video analysis).

References

1. Bell, S., Zitnick, C.L., Bala, K., Girshick, R.: Inside-outside net: detecting objects in context with skip pooling and recurrent neural networks. In: Proceedings of the IEEE Computer Vision and Pattern Recognition (2016)
2. Cai, Z., Fan, Q., Feris, R.S., Vasconcelos, N.: A unified multi-scale deep convolutional neural network for fast object detection. In: Leibe, B., Matas, J., Sebe, N., Welling, M. (eds.) ECCV 2016. LNCS, vol. 9908, pp. 354–370. Springer, Cham (2016). https://doi.org/10.1007/978-3-319-46493-0_22
3. Dai, J., Li, Y., He, K., Sun, J.: R-fcn: Object detection via region-based fully convolutional networks. In: Proceedings of Advances in Neural Information Processing Systems (2016)
4. Dai, J., et al.: Deformable convolutional networks. In: Proceedings of IEEE International Conference on Computer Vision (2017)
5. Dollár, P., Appel, R., Belongie, S., Perona, P.: Fast feature pyramids for object detection. IEEE Trans. Pattern Anal. Mach. Intell. **36**(8), 1532–1545 (2014)

6. Everingham, M., Gool, L.V., Williams, C.K.I., Winn, J., Zisserman, A.: The Pascal visual object classes (VOC) challenge. Int. J. Comput. Vis. **88**(2), 303–338 (2010)
7. Felzenszwalb, P.F., Girshick, R.B., McAllester, D., Ramanan, D.: Object detection with discriminatively trained part-based models. IEEE Trans. Pattern Anal. Mach. Intell. **32**(9), 1627–1645 (2010)
8. Fu, C.Y., Liu, W., Ranga, A., Tyagi, A., Berg, A.C.: DSSD: Deconvolutional single shot detector. arXiv preprint arXiv:1701.06659 (2017)
9. Girshick, R.: Fast R-CNN. In: Proceedings of IEEE International Conference on Computer Vision (2015)
10. Girshick, R., Donahue, J., Darrell, T., Malik, J.: Rich feature hierarchies for accurate object detection and semantic segmentation. In: Proceedings of IEEE Computer Vision and Pattern Recognition (2014)
11. Glorot, X., Bengio, Y.: Understanding the difficulty of training deep feedforward neural networks. In: AISTATS (2010)
12. Glorot, X., Bordes, A., Bengio, Y.: Deep sparse rectifier neural networks. In: AISTATS (2011)
13. Hariharan, B., Arbelaez, P., Girshick, R., Malik, J.: Hypercolumns for object segmentation and fine-grained localization. In: Proceedings of the IEEE Conference on Computer Vision and Pattern Recognition (2015)
14. He, K., Zhang, X., Ren, S., Sun, J.: Spatial pyramid pooling in deep convolutional networks for visual recognition. IEEE Trans. Pattern Anal. Mach. Intell. **37**(9), 1904–1916 (2015)
15. He, K., Zhang, X., Ren, S., Sun, J.: Deep residual learning for image recognition (2016)
16. Huang, G., Liu, Z., van der Maaten, L., Weinberger, K.Q.: Densely connected convolutional networks. In: Proceedings of IEEE Conference on Computer Vision and Pattern Recognition (2017)
17. Ioffe, S., Szegedy, C.: Batch normalization : accelerating deep network training by reducing internal covariate shift. In: Proceedings of International Conference on Machine Learning (2015)
18. Jeong, J., Park, H., Kwak, N.: Enhancement of SSD by concatenating feature maps for object detection. In: Proceedings of British Machine Vision Conference (2017)
19. Kong, T., Yao, A., Chen, Y., Sun, F.: Hypernet: towards accurate region proposal generation and joint object detection. In: Proceedings of Conference on Computer Vision and Pattern Recognition (2016)
20. Kong, T., Sun, F., Yao, A., Liu, H., Lu, M., Chen, Y.: Ron: reverse connection with objectness prior networks for object detection. In: IEEE Conference on Computer Vision and Pattern Recognition (2017)
21. LeCun, Y., Bottou, L., Bengio, Y., Haffner, P.: Gradient-based learning applied to document recognition. Proc. IEEE **86**(11), 2278–2324 (1998)
22. Li, H., Liu, Y., Ouyang, W., Wang, X.: Zoom out-and-in network with map attention decision for region proposal and object detection. arXiv preprint arXiv:1709.04347 (2017)
23. Lin, T.Y., Dollár, P., Girshick, R., He, K., Hariharan, B., Belongie, S.: Feature pyramid networks for object detection. In: Proceedings of IEEE Conference on Computer Vision and Pattern Recognition (2017)
24. Lin, T.-Y., et al.: Microsoft COCO: common objects in context. In: Fleet, D., Pajdla, T., Schiele, B., Tuytelaars, T. (eds.) ECCV 2014. LNCS, vol. 8693, pp. 740–755. Springer, Cham (2014). https://doi.org/10.1007/978-3-319-10602-1_48

25. Lin, T.Y., Goyal, P., Girshick, R., He, K., Dollár, P.: Focal loss for dense object detection. In: Proceedings of IEEE International Conference on Computer Vision (2017)
26. Liu, W., et al.: SSD: Single shot multibox detector. arXiv preprint arXiv:1512.02325 (2015)
27. Liu, W., et al.: SSD: single shot multibox detector. In: Leibe, B., Matas, J., Sebe, N., Welling, M. (eds.) ECCV 2016. LNCS, vol. 9905, pp. 21–37. Springer, Cham (2016). https://doi.org/10.1007/978-3-319-46448-0_2
28. Long, J., Shelhamer, E., Darrell, T.: Fully convolutional networks for semantic segmentation. In: Proceedings of IEEE Conference on Computer Vision and Pattern Recognition (2015)
29. Newell, A., Yang, K., Deng, J.: Stacked hourglass networks for human pose estimation. In: Leibe, B., Matas, J., Sebe, N., Welling, M. (eds.) ECCV 2016. LNCS, vol. 9912, pp. 483–499. Springer, Cham (2016). https://doi.org/10.1007/978-3-319-46484-8_29
30. Pinheiro, P.O., Lin, T.-Y., Collobert, R., Dollár, P.: Learning to refine object segments. In: Leibe, B., Matas, J., Sebe, N., Welling, M. (eds.) ECCV 2016. LNCS, vol. 9905, pp. 75–91. Springer, Cham (2016). https://doi.org/10.1007/978-3-319-46448-0_5
31. Redmon, J., Divvala, S., Girshick, R., Farhadi, A.: You only look once: unified, real-time object detection. In: Proceedings of IEEE Conference on Computer Vision and Pattern Recognition (2016)
32. Redmon, J., Farhadi, A.: Yolo9000: better, faster, stronger. In: Proceedings of IEEE Conference on Computer Vision and Pattern Recognition (2017)
33. Redmon, J., Farhadi, A.: Yolov3: an incremental improvement. arXiv preprint arXiv:1804.02767 (2018)
34. Ren, J., et al.: Accurate single stage detector using recurrent rolling convolution. In: Proceedings of IEEE Conference on Computer Vision and Pattern Recognition (2017)
35. Ren, S., He, K., Girshick, R., Sun, J.: Faster R-CNN: towards real-time object detection with region proposal networks. In: Proceedings of Advances in Neural Information Processing Systems (2015)
36. Ren, S., He, K., Girshick, R., Sun, J.: Faster R-CNN: towards real-time object detection with region proposal networks. IEEE Trans. Pattern Anal. Mach. Intell. **39**(6), 1137–1149 (2017)
37. Russakovsky, O., et al.: Imagenet large scale visual recognition challenge. Int. J. Comput. Vis. **115**(3), 211–252 (2015)
38. Sermanet, P., Eigen, D., Zhang, X., Mathieu, M., Fergus, R., LeCun, Y.: Overfeat: Integrated recognition, localization and detection using convolutional networks. In: Proceedings of International Conference on Learning Representations
39. Shrivastava, A., Sukthankar, R., Malik, J., Gupta, A.: Beyond skip connections: top-down modulation for object detection. arXiv preprint arXiv:1612.06851 (2016)
40. Simonyan, K., Zisserman, A.: Very deep convolutional networks for large-scale image recognition (2014)
41. Szegedy, C., et al.: Going deeper with convolutions. In: Proceedings of IEEE Conference on Computer Vision and Pattern Recognition (2015)
42. Wang, F., et al.: Residual attention network for image classification. In: Proceedings of IEEE Conference on Computer Vision and Pattern Recognition (2017)
43. Zhang, S., Wen, L., Bian, X., Lei, Z., Li, S.Z.: Single-shot refinement neural network for object detection. arXiv preprint arXiv:1711.06897 (2017)

44. Zhao, H., Shi, J., Qi, X., Wang, X., Jia, J.: Pyramid scene parsing network. In: Proceedings of IEEE Conference on Computer Vision and Pattern Recognition (2017)
45. Zhu, Y., Zhao, C., Wang, J., Zhao, X., Wu, Y., Lu, H.: Couplenet: coupling global structure with local parts for object detection. In: Proceedings of IEEE International Conference on Computer Vision (2017)

Joint Map and Symmetry Synchronization

Yifan Sun[1], Zhenxiao Liang[1,2], Xiangru Huang[1], and Qixing Huang[1(✉)]

[1] The University of Texas at Austin, Austin, USA
{yifan,liangzx,xrhuang,huangqx}@cs.utexas.edu
[2] Tsinghua University, Beijing, China

Abstract. Most existing techniques in map computation (e.g., in the form of feature or dense correspondences) assume that the underlying map between an object pair is unique. This assumption, however, easily breaks when visual objects possess self-symmetries. In this paper, we study the problem of jointly optimizing symmetry groups and pairwise maps among a collection of symmetric objects. We introduce a lifting map representation for encoding both symmetry groups and maps between symmetry groups. Based on this representation, we introduce a computational framework for joint symmetry and map synchronization. Experimental results show that this approach outperforms state-of-the-art approaches for symmetry detection from a single object as well as joint map optimization among an object collection.

Keywords: Correspondences · Symmetry group · Cycle-consistency Optimization

1 Introduction

Establishing maps across visual objects is a long standing problem in visual computing with rich applications in structure-from-motion [3,9], joint segmentation [48,49], and label/attribute transfer [2,31,50], among others. While early works focus on computing maps between pairs of objects in isolation (c.f. [21]), a recent trend is to jointly compute consistent maps across a collection of objects [5,16,17,19,20,24,29,37,38,42,51,66,67]. This is motivated from the fact that (i) many applications (e.g., multi-view structure-from-motion [8,54] and co-segmentation [56,60]) require consistent correspondences, and (ii) optimizing consistent maps enables us to improve maps computed between pairs of objects in isolation (c.f. [16]). The promise of these approaches is that pairwise maps between dissimilar objects can often be improved by composing maps along paths of similar objects.

Electronic supplementary material The online version of this chapter (https://doi.org/10.1007/978-3-030-01228-1_16) contains supplementary material, which is available to authorized users.

V. Ferrari et al. (Eds.): ECCV 2018, LNCS 11209, pp. 257–275, 2018.
https://doi.org/10.1007/978-3-030-01228-1_16

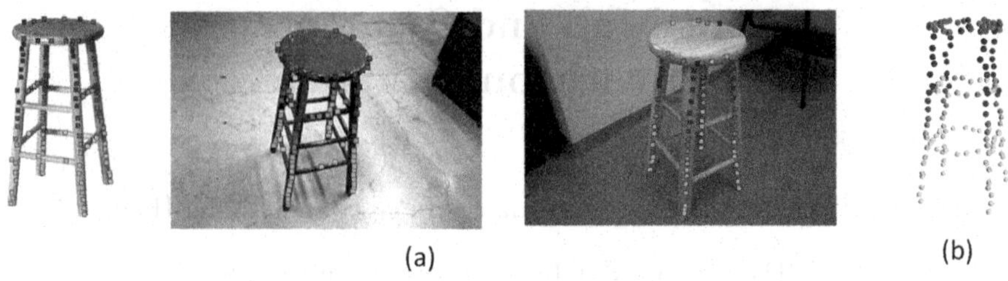

Fig. 1. Category specific reconstruction from internet images. (a) Subset of input images with matched edge feature points [12]. (b) Reconstruction using our approach. Color-coding highlights the recovered symmetry group. (Color figure online)

However, all existing joint map optimization techniques place the assumption that there is only one underlying map between two visual objects. It turns out this assumption does not hold in many scenarios. In particular, when the underlying objects are symmetric, there are multiple plausible maps between each object pair. This introduces issues both for map computation between pairs of objects and for optimizing consistent maps across multiple objects. To address this issue, a straightforward approach is to detect the underlying self-symmetry group of each object first, and then perform matching in factored or quotient spaces (c.f. [39]). This approach, however, is not optimal, since symmetry detection is quite challenging (especially for images where the symmetric parts may be occluded), and errors introduced in the symmetry detection phase cannot be recovered in the joint matching phase.

In this paper, we consider the problem of jointly optimizing the underlying symmetry groups and consistent pairwise maps. We call this problem joint symmetry and map synchronization. The motivation comes from the fact that symmetry detection and map computation are highly correlated. Besides the fact that computing the underlying symmetry groups facilitates map computation, maps can also propagate symmetry groups across objects, allowing us to rectify a noisy symmetry group computed from one object by propagating clean symmetry groups computed from other objects.

To formulate joint symmetry and map synchronization, we propose a representation that encodes symmetry groups and pair-wise maps using the product operator (also known as lifting in the literature [18,23,27,58]). We prove that for many symmetry groups in our physical world (e.g., reflection symmetry and n-fold rotational symmetry among others), this representation admits exact symmetry group decoding. In addition, we show that the computational cost incurred by the product operator can be effectively addressed via reduced functional basis [38]. Using this representation, we introduce a continuous optimization formulation for joint symmetry and map synchronization. The input consists of symmetry groups and pair-wise maps independently computed using off-the-shelf techniques in each domain. The output consists of consistent symmetry groups and pair-wise maps. Our approach exhibits a few appealing properties. First, the input symmetry groups and pair-wise maps may be noisy and incomplete (e.g., one input self-symmetry for a subset of objects and one object map per pair among a subset of object pairs), and our approach automatically rectifies, propagates and completes symmetry groups and pair-wise maps. Moreover, when we have sufficient data, we do not need to specify the type of the underlying symmetry group. It can be automatically determined by the input data, i.e., by aggregating self-symmetries among the input objects.

We evaluated our approach on a diverse set of object collections ranging from 2D images to 3D models. Experimental results show that our approach outperforms state-of-the-art methods in joint map computation from an object collection and symmetry group detection from each object in isolation.

2 Related Works

Map Synchronization. An emerging focus in object matching is to optimize maps jointly among an object collection. The intuition is that the map between a pair of dissimilar objects can be obtained by composing maps along a path of similar object pairs. A way to formalize this intuition is through the cycle-consistency constraint, i.e., composite maps along cycles should be identity maps. This has led to the problem of map synchronization, which takes as input maps computed between pairs of objects in isolation and outputs improved maps that are consistent along cycles. In [16], Huang and Guibas established a connection between the cycle-consistency constraint and the fact that data matrices that store cycle-consistent pair-wise maps in blocks are low-rank and/or positive semi-definite. This work has stimulated several recent works that formulate map synchronization as low-rank matrix recovery using convex optimization [5,16] and non-convex optimization [7,20,51,67]. Our approach also falls into this category. However, the focus is on establishing a matrix representation for joint map and symmetry synchronization.

Co-symmetry Detection and Matching. Symmetry detection can be considered a variant of shape matching, which seeks to compute self-maps that preserve extrinsic [22,36,44,52] or intrinsic [25,28,40,45,46,62–65] distances. In this regard, symmetry detection shares a similar limitation with pair-wise matching, namely, existing methods tend to break when the underlying symmetries become more and more approximate. To address this issue, we propose to optimize symmetry groups jointly among an object collection to improve the resulting symmetry group on each object. To the best of our knowledge, existing works on this topic have focused on individual pairs of objects so far. [33] proposed to detect a reflection symmetry axis for boosting the performance of correspondence computation. [39] introduced the first approach for factorizing out the underlying symmetry group when establishing shape maps. However, the approach only considers a pair of objects and does not utilize lifting. In addition, the formulation requires specifying the underlying symmetry group, or in other words, it does not perform joint inference of symmetries and maps. [57] developed an approach for joint structure recovery and matching of man-made 3D shapes. The approach

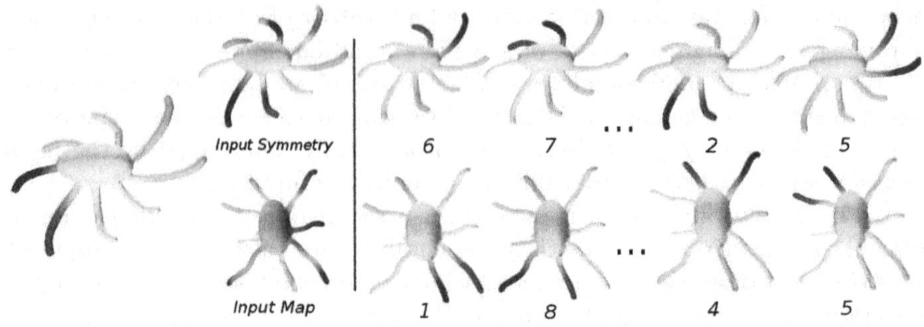

Fig. 2. This figure is better viewed in color. Corresponding points have the same colors. (Left) This input consists of one self-map per-shape and one pair-wise map per-pair. Here we show one shape among 20 shapes and one pair among 380 pairs. (Right) The output of our algorithm on the same shape and shape pair, respectively. Note that our approach not only improves symmetry groups and pair-wise maps, but we also complete the missing ones by propagating self-symmetries and maps. (Color figure online)

is based on graph matching, and thus requires part-based representations as input.

Matching via Lifting. Our symmetry group encoding scheme is motivated from the idea of lifting for convex relaxations of second-order MAP inference [18, 27]. When using indicators associated with the first-order potential functions, the second-order potential functions become quadratic in these indicator variables. The idea of lifting is to introduce an additional variable for each quadratic term. Using these additional variables (which form the lifted space), the objective function becomes linear and easy to solve. The lifting idea has also been used for object matching [14,23,58]. The novelty of our representation includes (1) the decoding scheme, (2) the types of symmetry groups that can be exactly recovered (to be introduced later), and (3) various properties of this encoding scheme, which will be used in formulating joint map and symmetry synchronization.

3 Problem Statement and Approach Overview

This section formally states the joint map and symmetry synchronization problem that is studied in this paper and presents an overview of our approach.

Problem Statement. Suppose we are given n relevant objects $S_1, \cdots, S_n$. In this paper, we focus on the case where objects are discrete point sets (e.g., image pixels [32] and feature/sample points extracted from images [34] or shapes [30]), and where a map or a self-map is given by a set of point-wise correspondences.

We assume these objects are generated from an underlying universal object $\overline{S}_0$ (also a point set), which possesses a symmetry group. The generation process consists of taking a subset and/or deformation. This setting covers many practical scenarios. For example, $\{S_i\}$ could be partial observations of an underlying object (e.g., in multi-view structure from motion). As another example, $\{S_i\}$ could also be objects that fall into the same category (See Fig. 2). The input to our approach consists of noisy pair-wise maps $P_{ij}^{in} : S_i \rightarrow S_j, (i,j) \in \mathcal{E}$ computed using off-the-shelf methods along a pre-computed edge set $\mathcal{E}$. In particular, $\mathcal{E}$ includes self loops, each of which is associated with a pre-computed self-map $P_{ii}^{in} : S_i \rightarrow S_i$. The output of our approach consists of the universal object $\overline{S}_0$, its symmetry group $\mathcal{G}$ (we write $\mathcal{G}$ instead of $\mathcal{G}_0$ to make the notations uncluttered), and an embedding map $P_{i0} : S_i \rightarrow \overline{S}_0$ for each object S_i. As we will see later, the pairwise maps from S_i to S_j are induced from $\{P_{i0}, 1 \leq i \leq n\}$ and $\mathcal{G}$.

An important feature of our approach is that it takes as input incomplete observations (e.g., one pair-wise map per object pair despite the fact that the underlying symmetry group suggests multiple plausible pair-wise maps). The promise of our approach comes from the fact that when looking at the input maps among an object collection as a whole, each element of the underlying symmetry group and the corresponding all pair-wise maps are densely sampled, providing sufficient observations for recovery.

Approach Overview. The main idea of our approach is to develop a matrix representation of symmetry groups and maps, which allows us to formulate joint map and symmetry synchronization as optimizing matrices. A simple approach is to use a binary correspondence matrix to encode correspondences in symmetry groups and pair-wise maps. As we will discuss later, this representation is insufficient when the size of a symmetry group is bigger than 2. To address this issue, we propose to use the product operator for encoding. We show that our proposed encoding is lossless for many symmetry groups. Using the same idea, we then show how to define and encode embedding maps $P_{i0}, 1 \leq i \leq n$ and pair-wise maps $P_{ij}, 1 \leq i,j \leq n$. Based on this encoding, we propose an optimization framework for recovering the underlying embedding maps $P_{i0}, 1 \leq i \leq n$ and self-symmetry group $\mathcal{G}$. To address the computational overhead incurred by the tensor operator, we show how to perform joint map and symmetry synchronization using reduced basis (c.f. [38]).

4 Symmetry and Map Representation via Lifting

In this section, we show how to effectively encode symmetry groups and pair-wise maps under the point-based representation. Section 4.1 describes how to encode symmetry groups. Section 4.2 introduces how to encode maps between symmetric objects that are partially similar.

4.1 Symmetry Groups

Consider an object S that consists of m points. A self-map is given by a permutation $P \in [0,1]^{m \times m}$, where each row and column has exactly one non-zero entry. With $\mathcal{P}_m$ we denote the space of all permutations. Let $\mathcal{G} \subset \mathcal{P}_m$ denote a symmetry group associated with S. For a thorough introduction to symmetry groups, we refer to [11] for more details.

In this paper, we are interested in symmetry groups where the largest orbit size is equal to the group size:

Definition 1. *Let $o_{\mathcal{G}}(i) \subset \{1, \cdots, m\}$ denote the orbit*[1] *of the i-th element under a symmetry group $\mathcal{G}$. We call $\mathcal{G}$ a cyclic group if*

$$|\mathcal{G}| = \max_{1 \leq i \leq m} |o_{\mathcal{G}}(i)|. \tag{1}$$

Note that cyclic groups cover a rich family of symmetry groups in our physical world. For example, standard reflection, n-fold rotational symmetry, and translation symmetries (both in the intrinsic and extrinsic sense) can be described as cyclic groups under suitable placements of samples.

When considering matrix representations of $\mathcal{G}$, a straight-forward approach is to use a correspondence matrix (of dimension $m \times m$) to encode all correspondences induced from the symmetry group. The downside of this encoding, however, is that when $|\mathcal{G}| > 2$, there may exist multiple symmetry groups that correspond to the same encoding. One such example is given in Appendix A. To address this issue, we propose to consider the following encoding using the tensor operator:

$$Q := \sum_{P \in \mathcal{G}} P \otimes P \quad \in \{0, 1\}^{m^2 \times m^2}. \tag{2}$$

A key property of Q is that when $\mathcal{G}$ is a cyclic group, then it can be recovered from the elements of Q:

Proposition 1. *If a symmetry group $\mathcal{G}$ is a cyclic group, then it can be exactly recovered from the elements of Q.*

To prove Proposition 1 (details are deferred to Appendix B.2) and for later usage, we define the following linear operator that shuffles the elements of Q:

Definition 2. *Consider a matrix $A \in \mathbb{R}^{m_1^2 \times m_2^2}$. Let $A_{a,b}$ denote (a, b)-th element of matrix A. Define $\mathcal{F} : \mathbb{R}^{m_1^2 \times m_2^2} \to \mathbb{R}^{m_1 m_2 \times m_1 m_2}$ as*

$$\mathcal{F}(A)_{i_1 m_2 + i_2, j_1 m_2 + j_2} = A_{i_1 m_1 + j_1, i_2 m_2 + j_2}, \quad 0 \leq i_1, j_1 \leq m_1 - 1, 0 \leq i_2, j_2 \leq m_2 - 1.$$

It is easy to check that $\mathcal{F}(Q)$ is low-rank:

Fact 1. *Let $\mathrm{vec}(P) = (\mathbf{p}_1^T, \cdots, \mathbf{p}_m^T)^T \in \mathbb{R}^{m^2}$ be the vector that unfolds the columns of $P = (\mathbf{p}_1, \cdots, \mathbf{p}_m) \in \mathbb{R}^{m \times m}$. Then*

$$\mathcal{F}(Q) = \sum_{P \in \mathcal{G}} \mathrm{vec}(P) \cdot \mathrm{vec}(P)^T. \tag{3}$$

Proof. See Appendix B.1. □

[1] Intuitively, the orbit collects correspondences induced from a symmetry group.

4.2 Maps Between Symmetry Groups

We proceed to define and encode maps between symmetry objects. To handle the case, where two objects being matched are subsets of an underlying complete object, we first define maps from a partial object to a complete object. Later, we show how to extend this setting to properly defined maps between partially similar objects.

Let us consider a source object S_1 and a target object $\overline{S}_0$ (which denotes the underlying universal object in this paper). To define the map from S_1 to $\overline{S}_0$, we introduce a latent object $\overline{S}_1$ that is (i) a superset of S_1, and (ii) a copy of $\overline{S}_0$, i.e., $|\overline{S}_1| = |\overline{S}_0|$, and the symmetry group $\mathcal{G}_1$ of $\overline{S}_1$ is isomorphic to $\mathcal{G}$ of $\overline{S}_0$. Our goal is to define the map from S_1 to $\overline{S}_0$ through the inclusion map $E_1 : S_1 \rightarrow \overline{S}_1$ and a properly defined map from $\overline{S}_1$ to $\overline{S}_0$:

Definition 3. *Let $f_1 : \mathcal{G} \rightarrow \mathcal{G}_1$ be the group isomorphism. We say a map $\overline{P}_{10}$: $\overline{S}_1 \rightarrow \overline{S}_0$ is proper if*

$$\overline{P}_{10} \cdot f_1(P) = P \cdot \overline{P}_{10}, \quad \forall P \in \mathcal{G}. \tag{4}$$

In other words, $\overline{P}_{10}$ is proper if it is consistent with the underlying symmetry groups. It is clear that each map $\overline{P}_{10}$ induces an equivalence class $\{P\overline{P}_{10}, P \in \mathcal{G}\}$. Now we are ready to define proper maps from S_1 to $\overline{S}_0$:

Definition 4. *We say a map $P_{10} : S_1 \rightarrow \overline{S}_0$ is proper if there exist $\overline{S}_1 \supset S_1$ and a proper map $\overline{P}_{10} : \overline{S}_1 \rightarrow \overline{S}_0$ such that*

$$P_{10} = \overline{P}_{10} \cdot E_1. \tag{5}$$

Note that P_{10} also induces an equivalent class $\mathcal{M}_{10} := \{PP_{10}, P \in \mathcal{G}\}$. We again use the product operator to encode $\mathcal{M}_{10}$:

$$Q_{10} = \sum_{P_{10} \in \mathcal{M}_{10}} P_{10} \otimes P_{10}. \tag{6}$$

Similar to symmetry groups, we have the following recovering condition:

Proposition 2. *When $\mathcal{G}$ is a cyclic group and S_1 contains one element of a maximal orbit of $\overline{S}_1$, then $\mathcal{M}_{10}$ can be exactly recovered from the elements of Q_{10} described in (6).*

The proof is similar to that of Proposition 1 and is deferred to Appendix B.3. Now we are ready to define maps between a partially similar object pair (S_1, S_2):

Definition 5. *We say a map $P_{12} : S_1 \rightarrow S_2$ is proper, if there exist proper maps $P_{i0} : S_i \rightarrow \overline{S}_0$, so that*

$$P_{12} = P_{20}^T P_{10}. \tag{7}$$

Note that each proper map P_{12} induces an equivalence class

$$\mathcal{M}_{12} := \{P_{20}^T P P_{10}, P \in \mathcal{G}\}. \quad (8)$$

It is easy to check that $\mathcal{M}_{12}$ is independent of the particular choice of $P_{i0}, 1 \leq i \leq 2$.

Again, we encode $\mathcal{M}_{12}$ using the tensor product:

$$Q_{12} := \sum_{P_{12} \in \mathcal{M}_{12}} P_{12} \otimes P_{12} \overset{(8)}{=} (P_{20} \otimes P_{20})^T Q_{00} (P_{10} \otimes P_{10}). \quad (9)$$

Finally, we introduce a property of $\mathcal{F}(Q_{12})$, which we will use later:

Proposition 3. *When* $|o_{\mathcal{G}}(i)| = |\mathcal{G}|, 1 \leq i \leq m$, *then each* $vec(P_{12})$ *is an eigenvector of* $\mathcal{F}(Q_{12})$, *i.e.,*

$$\mathcal{F}(Q_{12})\text{vec}(P_{12}) = \|\text{vec}(P_{12})\|^2 \cdot \text{vec}(P_{12}), \quad \forall P_{12} \in \mathcal{M}_{12}. \quad (10)$$

The proof is straight-forward, as two different members of $\mathcal{M}_{12}$, their non-zero entries do not overlap. In practice, the number of elements where $|o_{\mathcal{G}}(i)| < |\mathcal{G}|$ remains small (e.g., points on 1D reflection axis versus points on the entire image). This means (10) is at least approximately satisfied.

5 Functional-Based Joint Map and Symmetry Synchronization

In this section, we introduce a computational framework for joint map and symmetry synchronization. Section 5.1 describes a generalized representation for symmetry groups and maps using reduced basis. Section 5.2 then introduces an efficient approach using this reduced representation.

5.1 Symmetry and Map Representation Using Reduced Basis

Laplacian Reduced Basis. We begin with reviewing the reduced basis representation for encoding maps between discrete objects [38, 47, 61]. Consider an object S with m points, we associate S with an orthogonal matrix $B \in \mathbb{R}^{m \times k}$, which projects S onto the feature space spanned by the columns of B. Following [38, 61], we use the first k eigenvectors of Laplacian matrices, e.g., graph Laplacian for images and Laplace-Beltrami for 3D meshes. Note that it is possible to use other basis computation methods such as partial functional map [47]. We leave this as a future work.

Given two objects S_1 and S_2 and the associated basis B_1 and B_2, we represent a map from S_1 to S_2 in the feature space as a matrix $X_{12} \in \mathbb{R}^{k \times k}$ (called functional map in the literature ([38]). Given a point-based map $P_{12} : S_1 \to S_2$, we can derive the corresponding functional map as

$$X_{12} := \underset{X}{\text{argmin}} \ \|XB_1^T - B_2^T P_{12}\|_{\mathcal{F}}^2 = B_2^T P_{12} B_1. \tag{11}$$

In the other direction, we convert a functional map X_{12} into a point-map P_{12} via nearest neighbor query with respect to rows of B_1 and B_2. More precisely, for the i-th point of S_1, we compute the index of its target point as $j^\star = \underset{j}{\text{argmin}} \ \|B_2^T P_{12}\mathbf{e}_j - X_{12}B_1^T\mathbf{e}_i\|$,[2] where $A\mathbf{e}_i$ extracts the i-th column of A.

Given the underlying point-based map P_{12}, this functional map encoding scheme is accurate if there exists a linear map X_{12} such that $B_2^T P_{12} \approx X_{12}B_1^T$. In our experiments, we found using $k = 25$ Laplacian basis provides a fairly accurate encoding between discrete objects. We will also analyze the effects of varying k in the supplemental material.

Encoding Using Reduced Functional Basis. Using reduced basis to encode symmetry groups and maps between symmetry groups is quite similar to that in the point-based representation. Let B_0 be a basis of $\overline{S}_0$ (As we see later, our algorithm will recover both $\overline{S}_0$ and the reduced basis B_0. With $X_{00} = B_0^T P B_0$, $X_{10} = B_0^T P_{10} B_1^T$ and $X_{12} = B_2^T P_{12} B_1$ we denote the functional map representations of P, P_{10} and P_{12}, respectively. With this setup, we rewrite the functional representations of (2), (6) and (9) as

$$Y_{00} := \sum_{P \in \mathcal{G}} (X_{00} \otimes X_{00}), \quad Y_{10} := \sum_{P_{10} \in \mathcal{M}_{10}} (X_{10} \otimes X_{10}), \tag{12}$$

$$Y_{12} := (X_{20} \otimes X_{20})^T Y_{00} (X_{10} \otimes X_{10}). \tag{13}$$

Encoding using reduced Laplacian basis shares many properties as using the point-based representation. As discussed in Proposition 3, $\text{vec}(P_{12})$ is approximately an eigen-vector of Q_{12}. We find that under mild conditions (See Appendix B.5 for a discussion), this property also holds under the reduced basis:

$$\mathcal{F}(Y_{12})\text{vec}(X_{12}) \approx \|\text{vec}(X_{12})\|^2 \text{vec}(X_{12}). \tag{14}$$

Decoding via Alternating Minimization. Once we have obtained an encoding Y_{i0} under reduced basis, we recover the underlying functional maps and point-based maps via alternating minimization (c.f. [38]). Motivated from Fact 1, the functional maps are forced to lie within the leading eigenspace of $\mathcal{F}(Y_{i0})$. Due to space constraint, the details are left in Appendix C.

5.2 Joint Map and Symmetry Synchronization

In this section, we describe our approach for joint map and symmetry synchronization using the representation developed above. At this stage, we assume we

[2] It is also possible to enforce injectivity by solving a linear assignment.

have computed reduced basis $B_i, 1 \leq i \leq n$. We also assume we have computed initial functional maps $X_{ij}^{in}, (i,j) \in \mathcal{E}$ along an edge set $\mathcal{E}$. Both the input maps and the edge set are specified by off-the-shelf approaches, and we will discuss them in Sect. 6. Our goal is to recover the underlying universal object $\overline{S}_0$, its symmetry group G_0, and the maps $P_{i0} : S_i \rightarrow \overline{S}_0$. Our approach consists of a synchronization step and an extraction step.

Synchronization. We introduce a $n \times n$ block matrix $Y \in \mathbb{R}^{nk^2 \times nk^2}$ that encodes each Y_{ij} in the block of Y, i.e., Y_{ij} corresponds to j-th row and i-th column of Y. Similar to the point-based representation, Y is low-rank. To see this, we introduce $Z_i = Y_{00}^{\frac{1}{2}}(X_{i0} \otimes X_{i0}), 1 \leq i \leq n$. Let $Z = (Z_1^T, \cdots, Z_n^T)^T$. Then (13) gives rise to

$$Y = ZZ^T. \tag{15}$$

We propose to utilize numerical optimization to obtain Y and Z. Specifically, by combing (15) and (14), we arrive at the following objective function for recovery:

$$\min_{Y,Z} \sum_{(i,j)\in\mathcal{E}} \|\mathcal{F}(Y_{ij})\mathrm{vec}(X_{ij}^{in}) - \|\mathrm{vec}(X_{ij}^{in})\|^2 \mathrm{vec}(X_{ij}^{in})\| + \lambda \|Y - ZZ^T\|_{\mathcal{F}}^2 \tag{16}$$

where $\mathcal{F}$ is the Frobenius norm. Note that we use the block-wise L1-norm to suppress the noise in the input. We set $\lambda = \frac{1}{\sqrt{n}}$ in our experiments. In this paper, we combine spectral initialization and reweighted non-linear least squares to solve (16). The details are deferred to Appendix D.

Decoding. Since our goal is to recover the underlying object $\overline{S}_0$, merely recovering pair-wise maps Y_{ij} is insufficient. In contrast, we seek to recover $X_{i0}, 1 \leq i \leq n$ and Y_{00}. Let $Z^\star$ be the optimal solution to (16). If $Z^\star$ is an exact recovery, then there exists $V \in \mathbb{R}^{k^2 \times k^2}$, so that

$$V \cdot Z_i^{\star T} = X_{i0} \otimes X_{i0}, \qquad 1 \leq i \leq n, \quad Y_{00} = {V^{-1}}^T V^{-1}. \tag{17}$$

For decoding, we set up the following objective function to recover V and $X_{i0}, 1 \leq i \leq n$:

$$\min_{V, X_{i0}, 1 \leq i \leq n} \sum_{i=1}^{n} \|V \cdot Z_i^{\star T} - X_{i0} \otimes X_{i0}\|_{\mathcal{F}}^2 + \mu \|V - I_{k^2}\|_{\mathcal{F}}^2 \tag{18}$$

where the second term is introduced to avoid obtaining the trivial solution $V = 0, X_{i0} = 0, 1 \leq i \leq n$. In our experiment, we used $\mu = 10^{-3}$. We again perform alternating minimization to solve (18). Please refer to Appendix E for details.

As X_{i0} aligns the feature space associated with S_i with that of the latent universal object S_0, we apply clustering on the columns of $X_{i0}B_i^T, 1 \leq i \leq n$ to

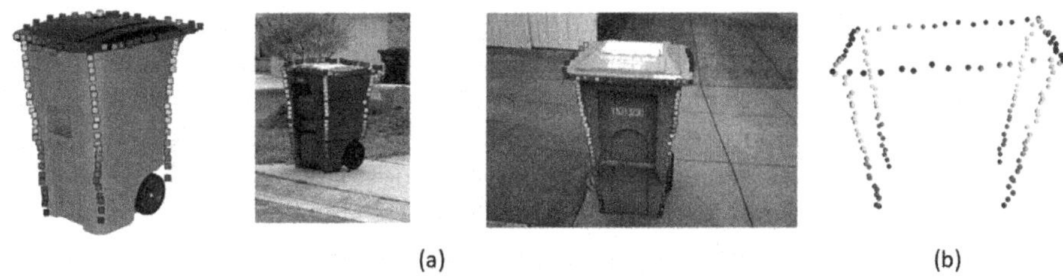

Fig. 3. Category specific reconstruction from internet images. (a) Subset of input images with matched edge feature points [12]. (b) Reconstruction using our approach. Color-coding highlights the recovered symmetry group. (Color figure online)

recover B_0, which also specifies S_0. In our experiments, we used single-linkage clustering and set the total number of clusters as m. We discard all clusters whose size are smaller than 3. Each cluster center corresponds to one column of B_0. Finally, we apply the decoding scheme described in (20) to recover the underlying symmetry group G.

6 Results

In this section, we evaluate our approach for joint map and symmetry synchronization on 2D images (Sect. 6.1) and 3D shapes (Sect. 6.2).

6.1 Experimental Evaluations on 2D Images

Experimental Setup. As illustrated in Figs. 1 and 3, we consider the application of reconstructing a generic sparse 3D pointcloud from multi-views of similar but different objects [4,59,67] (i.e., category-specific reconstruction). A crucial task for the reconstruction is to establish consistent feature correspondences across multiple images. We share this general motivation in our experiments, but focus on symmetric objects. In this regard, we collect two datasets. The first dataset consists of 16 images of similar stool objects that possess a four-way rotational symmetry (See Fig. 1). The second dataset consists of 16 images of similar trash container objects (See Fig. 3). For both datasets, we annotate key-points for evaluating feature correspondences. The full datasets and annotated feature correspondences are included in Appendix H. The same as [4,59,67], we assume the underlying objects are segmented out. In addition, we also evaluated on Sedan and SUV from [67]. We use these two datasets to compare our approach against standard joint map optimization approaches that do not explicitly consider the underlying symmetry group.

We follow the procedure described in [67], which applies structural forests [12] and graph matching [6] to generate the feature points and perform pair-wise matching, respectively. The reduced basis we utilize are the first $k = 25$ eigenvectors of unnormalized graph Laplacian of the graphs used in pair-wise matching

(See [6] for more details). For Stool and TrashContainer, we also apply this procedure to match each image with itself, which gives a self-map. To test whether the improvement of our algorithm on symmetry detection is consistent with respect to different input symmetries, we also evaluated on applying [13] for symmetry detection (we used the same procedure to exclude identity maps). Regarding the edge set $\mathcal{E}$, we connect each image with 8-closest images in terms of affinity scores for Stool and TrashContainer. The same as [67], we let $\mathcal{E}$ connect all image pairs for Sedan and SUV.

We consider four state-of-the-art synchronization techniques [7,19,66,67] for baseline evaluation. In particular, [19] synchronizes consistent functional maps; [66] optimizes point-based correspondences by enforcing three-cycles; [67] applies a fast low-rank matrix recovery approach to optimize consistent point-wise correspondences. [7] uses non-convex optimization to obtain consistent point-wise correspondences. The same as [67], we report the percentage of feature correspondences whose error with respect to annotated feature correspondences fall within a varying threshold δ. Note that for Stool and TrashContainer, we evaluate with respect to the closest map (in terms of cumulative feature correspondence error) induced by the underlying symmetry group. This is in contrast to evaluating the quality of each individual correspondence with respect to symmetric correspondences, where the closest correspondences may be inconsistent with each other. Table 1 collects the statistics of each method when $\delta = 0.1\max(w, h)$, where w and h are width and height of an input image.

Joint Map and Symmetry Detection Improves Symmetry Detection. As shown in Table 1(Top), our approach can drastically improve the input symmetry detection. For the first set of input symmetries (i.e., using [6]), our approach improves from 71.2% and 68.7% on Stool and TrashContainer, respectively, to 84.5% and 81.2%, respectively. For the second set of input symmetries (i.e., using [13]), our approach improves from 65.9% and 63.1% on Stool and TrashContainer, respectively, to 79.8% and 77.4%, respectively. Figure 4(Left) shows that the improvements are consistent when varying the error threshold.

Analysis of Correspondence Quality. Our approach outperforms baseline approaches considerably. Specifically, on Stool and TrashContainer, our approach achieved 80.6% and 75.2%, respectively. In contrast, the top-performing state-of-the-art methods only had 68.2% (from [67]) and 62.8% (from [19]), respectively. Figure 4(Middle) shows that the improvements are also consistent when varying the error threshold. One explanation is that due to the underlying symmetry, there are multiple plausible maps between each object pair. However, all existing methods are forced to output a single consistent map. In this case, it turns out their output tends to average multiple plausible maps, and the resulting correspondences may not be consistent across different feature points from the same image. It follows that their output may be far from the underlying map even after factoring out the underlying symmetry group.

Table 1. Comparisons with respect to human annotated feature points. We report percentage of correspondences whose error are below $0.1d$, where $d = \max(w, h)$ for images and d is the shape diameter for 3D shapes, respectively. (Top) Symmetry detection. Images:Sym-IN [6] and SymII-IN [13]. Shapes:Sym-IN [25] and SymII-IN [40]. (Middle) Evaluation of object maps after factoring out the underlying self-symmetry group. Baseline approaches: Huang14:[19], Zhou15a:[66], Zhou15b:[67], Cosmo17:[7]. (Bottom). Evaluation of object maps in the original space.

	Stool	TC	Sedan	SUV	Octop.	Arma.	Ant	Bird	Fish	4leg	Glass.	Hand	Human	Plane	**Mean**
Sym-In	71.2	68.7	na	na	52.4	72.9	69.1	59.3	54.5	64.0	78.2	55.1	89.3	61.2	67.0
Sym-Out	84.5	81.2	na	na	76.1	91.2	81.0	67.2	71.3	79.2	90.1	69.2	94.5	73.2	79.7
SymII-In	65.9	63.1	na	na	48.3	68.1	66.4	57.4	51.5	63.2	71.7	49.2	81.3	60.0	63.2
SymII-Out	79.8	77.4	na	na	68.0	81.2	77.3	74.2	70.1	80.7	86.5	57.1	90.3	72.4	76.6
Input	60.7	58.5	na	na	44.9	69.5	64.1	53.0	48.1	58.0	76.3	51.7	83.8	35.7	60.1
Huang14	68.2	60.6	na	na	58.1	69.4	69.0	54.3	42.8	76.9	71.1	66.3	90.9	42.4	64.8
Zhou15a	63.2	59.8	na	na	na	na	na	na	na	na	na	na	na	na	na
Zhou15b	64.6	62.8	na	na	56.5	70.1	71.1	51.3	43.7	71.9	66.7	68.1	86.1	44.4	63.7
Cosmo17	61.9	59.7	na	na	54.9	68.2	71.6	51.8	42.8	71.9	64.7	67.0	86.4	44.4	63.2
Ours	**80.6**	**75.2**	na	na	**74.6**	**81.2**	**76.3**	**62.9**	**54.1**	**80.1**	**78.3**	**71.1**	**92.1**	**53.7**	**72.2**
Input	na	na	78.7	77.6	na	65.7	47.8	39.8	45.6	56.6	54.1	47.5	69.4	30.2	50.7
Huang14	na	na	85.9	87.1	na	69.6	59.0	52.2	42.3	76.5	59.3	66.2	90.9	**39.4**	61.7
Zhou15a	na	na	86.1	85.2	na	na	na	na	na	na	na	na	na	na	na
Zhou15b	na	na	87.7	86.2	na	68.2	59.3	47.6	46.1	70.3	59.2	59.7	88.1	38.5	59.7
Cosmo17	na	na	84.5	83.4	na	67.1	61.4	44.9	42.8	71.3	57.9	61.4	85.8	37.9	58.9
Ours	na	na	**91.2**	**90.8**	na	**74.9**	**64.1**	**54.8**	**51.2**	**83.2**	**65.7**	**68.2**	**93.2**	38.0	**65.9**

To see the usefulness of the output of our approach, we perform SFM on each dataset of Stool and TrashContainer in isolation. Specifically, we run rigid reconstruction from optimized feature correspondences with an orthographic camera model and annotated viewpoints. As illustrated in Figs. 1 and 3, our approach can recover 3D point clouds that reflect the overall shapes of the Stool and TrashContainer. In contrast, the method of [67] was not successful on these two datasets.

We proceed to quantitatively compare our approach with baseline approaches on Sedan and SUV. In this case, we simply set the diagonal blocks as identity matrices in our approach. As shown in Table 1 and Fig. 4(Right), our approach outperforms existing approaches. The benefits come from the product operator, which enables the joint matching procedure to detect consistent correspondence pairs obtained in the graph matching phase. Similar to using pair-wise consistency for boosting the performance of graph matching, these consistent correspondence pairs enhance optimized correspondences.

Timing. Our approach is efficient. In average, the running time of our approach on each dataset is 137.0 s using a Matlab implementation on a single-core 3.2 G CPU with 32 G memory. This includes 12.5 s for converting point-based maps into functional maps, 95.6 s for joint map and symmetry optimization, and 28.9 s for converting functional maps back to the original point-based maps.

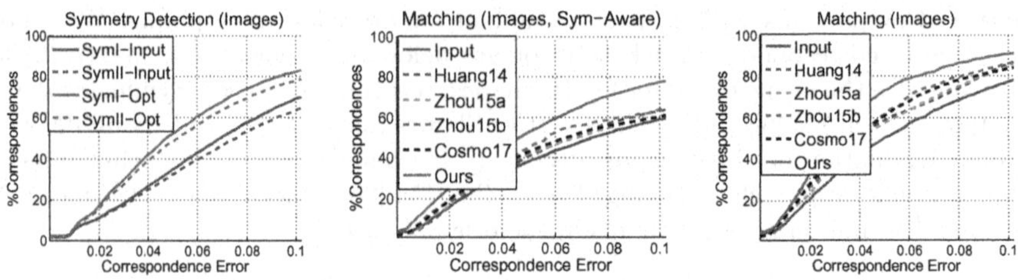

Fig. 4. Quantitative evaluations of joint map and symmetry synchronization on 2D images. (Left) Symmetry detection on Stool and TrashContainer. (Middle) Object matching evaluation in the quotient space on Stool and TrashContainer. (Right) Object matching evaluation in the original space on Sedan and SUV.

6.2 Experimental Evaluations on 3D Shapes

Experimental Setup. We perform experimental evaluation on SHREC07–Watertight [15], which is a challenging dataset for evaluating shape maps. Specifically, SHREC07-Watertight contains 400 shapes across 20 categories. Among them, we choose 10 categories (i.e., Ant, Armadillo, Bird, Fish, Fourleg, Glasses, Hand, Human, Plane, and Octopus) that are suitable for inter-shape mapping. In particular, Octopus contains a non-trivial rotational symmetry group. Each other category contains a reflection symmetry. All categories have human-annotated correspondences for experimental evaluation. As for symmetry detection, we employ [25]. We also tested on [40] to see if the improvements are consistent with respect to different input symmetries. For pair-wise maps, we employ blended intrinsic maps [26]. We consider the same set of baseline approaches described in Sect. 6.1 except [66], which is specifically designed for image matching. In terms of evaluation protocol, we report the percentage of feature correspondences whose geodesic errors fall into a varying threshold in $[0, 0.1d]$, where d is the diameter of each shape in geodesic distance.

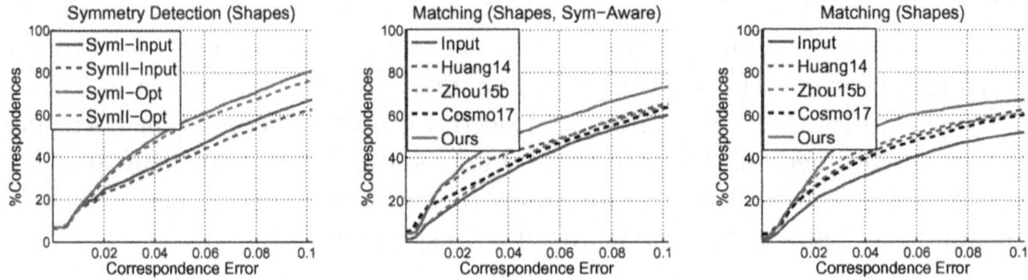

Fig. 5. Quantitative evaluations of joint map and symmetry synchronization on SHREC07-Watertight. (Left) Symmetry detection. (Middle) Object matching evaluation in the quotient space. (Right) Object matching evaluation in the original space.

Analysis of Results. We first evaluate our approach on the performance of symmetry detection. As show in Table 1, our approach improves the quality of input symmetries obtained from [25], by 23.7% and 12.5% on Octopus and remaining models, respectively. Replacing the input symmetries by the ones computed from [40], the improvements become 19.7% and 13.3% on Octopus and remaining categories, respectively. As shown in Fig. 5(Left), the improvements are also consistent when varying the cutoff threshold. This again shows the huge potential of detecting symmetries jointly among an object collection.

Table 1 and Fig. 5 compare our approach with baseline approaches for joint map optimization. Our approach outperforms baseline approaches both in the quotient space (i.e., after factoring out the self-symmetry) and in the original space. In particular, the relative improvements between our approach and baseline approaches in the quotient space are higher than those in the original space. This justifies the promise of joint map and symmetry optimization.

Timing. We employ a full observation graph on each category. The average running time on the same Desktop for each category is 560.1 s, where functional map conversion, joint map and symmetry recovery and point-based map extraction take 38.2 s, 313.1 s and 208.8 s, respectively.

7 Conclusions

In this paper, we have described an approach for joint map and symmetry synchronization. Our approach builds on a novel symmetry and map representation using the tensor operator. Based on the this representation, we introduce a non-convex optimization scheme for recovering consistent symmetry groups and pair-wise maps from noisy input. Experimental results demonstrate that our approach is better than state-of-the-art methods for joint map synchronization without symmetry detection and symmetry detection from each object in isolation.

Acknowledgement. Qixing Huang would like to acknowledge support of this research from NSF DMS-1700234, a Gift from Snap Research, and a hardware Donation from NVIDIA.

References

1. Bajaj, C., Gao, T., He, Z., Huang, Q., Liang, Z.: SMAC: simultaneous mapping and clustering using spectral decompositions. In: Proceedings of the 35th International Conference on Machine Learning, ICML 2018, Stockholmsmässan, Stockholm, Sweden, 10–15 July 2018, pp. 334–343 (2018). http://proceedings.mlr.press/v80/bajaj18a.html
2. Berg, A.C., Berg, T.L., Malik, J.: Shape matching and object recognition using low distortion correspondences. In: CVPR, vol. 1, pp. 26–33. IEEE Computer Society (2005)

3. Bregler, C., Hertzmann, A., Biermann, H.: Recovering non-rigid 3D shape from image streams. In: CVPR, pp. 2690–2696. IEEE Computer Society (2000)
4. Carreira, J., Kar, A., Tulsiani, S., Malik, J.: Virtual view networks for object reconstruction. In: Computer Vision and Pattern Regognition (CVPR) (2015)
5. Chen, Y., Guibas, L.J., Huang, Q.: Near-optimal joint object matching via convex relaxation. In: Proceedings of the 31th International Conference on Machine Learning, ICML 2014, Beijing, China, 21–26 June 2014, pp. 100–108 (2014). Proceedings of Machine Learning Research, NY, USA
6. Cho, M., Lee, J., Lee, K.M.: Reweighted random walks for graph matching. In: Daniilidis, K., Maragos, P., Paragios, N. (eds.) ECCV 2010. LNCS, vol. 6315, pp. 492–505. Springer, Heidelberg (2010). https://doi.org/10.1007/978-3-642-15555-0_36
7. Cosmo, L., Rodolà, E., Albarelli, A., Mémoli, F., Cremers, D.: Consistent partial matching of shape collections via sparse modeling. Comput. Graph. Forum **36**(1), 209–221 (2017)
8. Crandall, D., Owens, A., Snavely, N., Huttenlocher, D.: SfM with MRFs: discrete-continuous optimization for large-scale structure from motion. IEEE Trans. Pattern Anal. Mach. Intell. (PAMI) **35**(12), 2841–2853 (2013)
9. Dai, Y., Li, H., He, M.: A simple prior-free method for non-rigid structure-from-motion factorization. Int. J. Comput. Vis. **107**(2), 101–122 (2014)
10. Daubechies, I., DeVore, R.A., Fornasier, M., Güntürk, C.S.: Iteratively re-weighted least squares minimization: proof of faster than linear rate for sparse recovery. In: 42nd Annual Conference on Information Sciences and Systems, CISS 2008, Princeton, NJ, USA, 19–21 March 2008, pp. 26–29 (2008). https://doi.org/10.1109/CISS.2008.4558489
11. Diaconis, P.: Group representations in probability and statistics. Institute of Mathematical Statistics Lecture Notes-Monograph Series, 11. Institute of Mathematical Statistics, Hayward, CA (1988)
12. Dollár, P., Zitnick, C.L.: Structured forests for fast edge detection. In: Proceedings of the 2013 IEEE International Conference on Computer Vision, ICCV 2013, pp. 1841–1848. IEEE Computer Society, Washington (2013). https://doi.org/10.1109/ICCV.2013.231
13. Duchenne, O., Bach, F.R., Kweon, I., Ponce, J.: A tensor-based algorithm for high-order graph matching. IEEE Trans. Pattern Anal. Mach. Intell. **33**(12), 2383–2395 (2011)
14. Dym, N., Maron, H., Lipman, Y.: Ds++: a flexible, scalable and provably tight relaxation for matching problems. ACM Trans. Graph. **36**(6), 184:1–184:14 (2017). https://doi.org/10.1145/3130800.3130826
15. Giorgi, D., Biasotti, S., Paraboschi, L.: Shape retrieval contest 2007: Watertight models track (2007)
16. Huang, Q.X., Guibas, L.: Consistent shape maps via semidefinite programming. Comput. Graph. Forum **32**(5), 177–186 (2013)
17. Huang, Q., Zhang, G., Gao, L., Hu, S., Butscher, A., Guibas, L.J.: An optimization approach for extracting and encoding consistent maps in a shape collection. ACM Trans. Graph. **31**(6), 167:1–167:11 (2012)
18. Huang, Q., Chen, Y., Guibas, L.: Scalable semidefinite relaxation for maximum a posterior estimation. In: Proceedings of the 31st International Conference on Machine Learning, PMLR, vol. 32, no. 2, pp. 64–72 (2014)
19. Huang, Q., Wang, F., Guibas, L.: Functional map networks for analyzing and exploring large shape collections. ACM Trans. Graph. **33**(4), 36:1–36:11 (2014)

20. Huang, X., Liang, Z., Bajaj, C., Huang, Q.: Translation synchronization via truncated least squares. In: NIPS (2017)
21. van Kaick, O., Zhang, H., Hamarneh, G., Cohen-Or, D.: A survey on shape correspondence. Comput. Graph. Forum **30**(6), 1681–1707 (2011)
22. Kerber, J., Bokeloh, M., Wand, M., Seidel, H.P.: Scalable symmetry detection for urban scenes. Comput. Graph. Forum **32**(1), 3–15 (2013)
23. Kezurer, I., Kovalsky, S.Z., Basri, R., Lipman, Y.: Tight relaxation of quadratic matching. Comput. Graph. Forum **34**(5), 115–128 (2015)
24. Kim, V.G., Li, W., Mitra, N.J., DiVerdi, S., Funkhouser, T.: Exploring collections of 3D models using fuzzy correspondences. ACM Trans. Graph. **31**(4), 54:1–54:11 (2012). https://doi.org/10.1145/2185520.2185550
25. Kim, V.G., Lipman, Y., Chen, X., Funkhouser, T.A.: Möbius transformations for global intrinsic symmetry analysis. Comput. Graph. Forum **29**(5), 1689–1700 (2010)
26. Kim, V.G., Lipman, Y., Funkhouser, T.: Blended intrinsic maps. ACM Trans. Graph. **30**(4), 79:1–79:12 (2011)
27. Kumar, M.P., Kolmogorov, V., Torr, P.H.S.: An analysis of convex relaxations for MAP estimation of discrete MRFS. J. Mach. Learn. Res. **10**, 71–106 (2009). https://doi.org/10.1145/1577069.1577072
28. Lasowski, R., Tevs, A., Seidel, H., Wand, M.: A probabilistic framework for partial intrinsic symmetries in geometric data. In: ICCV, pp. 963–970. IEEE Computer Society, Kyoto (2009)
29. Leonardos, S., Zhou, X., Daniilidis, K.: Distributed consistent data association via permutation synchronization. In: ICRA, pp. 2645–2652. IEEE (2017)
30. Lipman, Y., Funkhouser, T.: MÖbius voting for surface correspondence. ACM Trans. Graph. **28**(3), 72:1–72:12 (2009). https://doi.org/10.1145/1531326.1531378
31. Liu, C., Yuen, J., Torralba, A.: Nonparametric scene parsing via label transfer. IEEE Trans. Pattern Anal. Mach. Intell. **33**(12), 2368–2382 (2011)
32. Liu, C., Yuen, J., Torralba, A.: Sift flow: dense correspondence across scenes and its applications. IEEE Trans. Pattern Anal. Mach. Intell. **33**(5), 978–994 (2011)
33. Liu, T., Kim, V.G., Funkhouser, T.A.: Finding surface correspondences using symmetry axis curves. Comput. Graph. Forum **31**(5), 1607–1616 (2012)
34. Lowe, D.G.: Distinctive image features from scale-invariant keypoints. Int. J. Comput. Vis. **60**(2), 91–110 (2004). https://doi.org/10.1023/B:VISI.0000029664.99615.94
35. Markovsky, I.: Low Rank Approximation: Algorithms, Implementation, Applications. Springer, London (2011). https://doi.org/10.1007/978-1-4471-2227-2
36. Mitra, N.J., Guibas, L.J., Pauly, M.: Partial and approximate symmetry detection for 3D geometry. ACM Trans. Graph. **25**(3), 560–568 (2006)
37. Nguyen, A., Ben-Chen, M., Welnicka, K., Ye, Y., Guibas, L.J.: An optimization approach to improving collections of shape maps. Comput. Graph. Forum **30**(5), 1481–1491 (2011). https://doi.org/10.1111/j.1467-8659.2011.02022.x
38. Ovsjanikov, M., Ben-Chen, M., Solomon, J., Butscher, A., Guibas, L.J.: Functional maps: a flexible representation of maps between shapes. ACM Trans. Graph. **31**(4), 30:1–30:11 (2012). https://doi.org/10.1145/2185520.2185526
39. Ovsjanikov, M., Mérigot, Q., Patraucean, V., Guibas, L.J.: Shape matching via quotient spaces. Comput. Graph. Forum **32**(5), 1–11 (2013). https://doi.org/10.1111/cgf.12167
40. Ovsjanikov, M., Sun, J., Guibas, L.J.: Global intrinsic symmetries of shapes. Comput. Graph. Forum **27**(5), 1341–1348 (2008)

41. Pachauri, D., Kondor, R., Sargur, G., Singh, V.: Permutation diffusion maps (pdm) with application to the image association problem in computer vision. In: Proceedings of the 27th International Conference on Neural Information Processing Systems, NIPS 2014, vol. 1, pp. 541–549. MIT Press, Cambridge (2014). http://dl.acm.org/citation.cfm?id=2968826.2968887
42. Pachauri, D., Kondor, R., Singh, V.: Solving the multi-way matching problem by permutation synchronization. In: Burges, C.J.C., Bottou, L., Welling, M., Ghahramani, Z., Weinberger, K.Q. (eds.) Advances in Neural Information Processing Systems vol. 26, pp. 1860–1868. Curran Associates, Inc. (2013)
43. Pachauri, D., Kondor, R., Singh, V.: Solving the multi-way matching problem by permutation synchronization. In: Proceedings of the 26th International Conference on Neural Information Processing Systems, NIPS 2013, vol. 2, pp. 1860–1868. Curran Associates Inc., USA (2013). http://dl.acm.org/citation.cfm?id=2999792.2999820
44. Podolak, J., Shilane, P., Golovinskiy, A., Rusinkiewicz, S., Funkhouser, T.: A planar-reflective symmetry transform for 3D shapes. ACM Trans. Graph. **25**(3), 549–559 (2006)
45. Raviv, D., Bronstein, A.M., Bronstein, M.M., Kimmel, R.: Full and partial symmetries of non-rigid shapes. Int. J. Comput. Vis. **89**(1), 18–39 (2010)
46. Raviv, D., Bronstein, M.M., Sapiro, G., Bronstein, A.M., Kimmel, R.: Diffusion symmetries of non-rigid shapes. In: Proceedings of 3DPVT (2010)
47. Rodolà, E., Cosmo, L., Bronstein, M.M., Torsello, A., Cremers, D.: Partial functional correspondence. CoRR abs/1506.05274 (2015). http://arxiv.org/abs/1506.05274
48. Rubinstein, M., Joulin, A., Kopf, J., Liu, C.: Unsupervised joint object discovery and segmentation in internet images. In: CVPR, pp. 1939–1946. IEEE Computer Society (2013). http://dblp.uni-trier.de/db/conf/cvpr/cvpr2013.html#RubinsteinJKL13
49. Rubio, J.C., Serrat, J., López, A.M., Paragios, N.: Unsupervised co-segmentation through region matching. In: CVPR, pp. 749–756. IEEE Computer Society (2012)
50. Russell, B., Torralba, A., Liu, C., Fergus, R., Freeman, W.T.: Object recognition by scene alignment. In: Platt, J.C., Koller, D., Singer, Y., Roweis, S.T. (eds.) Advances in Neural Information Processing Systems, vol. 20. pp. 1241–1248. Curran Associates, Inc. (2007)
51. Shen, Y., Huang, Q., Srebro, N., Sanghavi, S.: Normalized spectral map synchronization. In: NIPS, pp. 4925–4933. Curran Associates, Barcelona (2016)
52. Shi, Z., Alliez, P., Desbrun, M., Bao, H., Huang, J.: Symmetry and orbit detection via lie-algebra voting. Comput. Graph. Forum **35**(5), 217–227 (2016)
53. Singer, A., Wu, H.T.: Spectral convergence of the connection laplacian from random samples. Inf. Inference: J. IMA **35**(6), 58–123 (2017)
54. Snavely, N., Seitz, S.M., Szeliski, R.: Photo tourism: exploring photocollections in 3D. ACM Trans. Graph. **25**(3), 835–846 (2006). https://doi.org/10.1145/1141911.1141964
55. Tam, G.K.L., Martin, R.R., Rosin, P.L., Lai, Y.K.: Diffusion pruning for rapidly and robustly selecting global correspondences using local isometry. ACM Trans. Graph. **33**(1), 4:1–4:17 (2014)
56. Taniai, T., Sinha, S.N., Sato, Y.: Joint recovery of dense correspondence and cosegmentation in two images. In: 2016 IEEE Conference on Computer Vision and Pattern Recognition, CVPR 2016, Las Vegas, NV, USA, June 27–30, 2016, pp. 4246–4255 (2016). https://doi.org/10.1109/CVPR.2016.460

57. Tevs, A., Huang, Q., Wand, M., Seidel, H.P., Guibas, L.: Relating shapes via geometric symmetries and regularities. ACM Trans. Graph. **33**(4), 119:1–119:12 (2014). https://doi.org/10.1145/2601097.2601220
58. Vestner, M., Litman, R., Rodola, E., Bronstein, A., Cremers, D.: Product manifold filter: non-rigid shape correspondence via kernel density estimation in the product space. In: The IEEE Conference on Computer Vision and Pattern Recognition (CVPR), July 2017
59. Vicente, S., Carreira, J., Agapito, L., Batista, J.: Reconstructing PASCAL VOC. In: CVPR, pp. 41–48. IEEE Computer Society (2014)
60. Wang, F., Huang, Q., Guibas, L.: Image co-segmentation via consistent functional maps. In: Proceedings of the 14th International Conference on Computer Vision (ICCV) (2013)
61. Wang, F., Huang, Q., Guibas, L.J.: Image co-segmentation via consistent functional maps. In: IEEE International Conference on Computer Vision, ICCV 2013, Sydney, Australia, 1–8 December 2013, pp. 849–856. Computer Vision Foundation, Sydney (2013)
62. Wang, H., Huang, H.: Group representation of global intrinsic symmetries. Comput. Graph. Forum **36**, 51–61 (2017)
63. Wang, H., Simari, P., Su, Z., Zhang, H.: Spectral global intrinsic symmetry invariant functions. In: Proceedings of Graphics Interface 2014, GI 2014, pp. 209–215. Canadian Information Processing Society, Toronto (2014). http://dl.acm.org/citation.cfm?id=2619648.2619683
64. Xu, K.: Multi-scale partial intrinsic symmetry detection. ACM Trans. Graph. **31**(6), 181:1–181:11 (2012)
65. Xu, K., et al.: Partial intrinsic reflectional symmetry of 3D shapes. ACM Trans. Graph. **28**(5), 138:1–138:10 (2009)
66. Zhou, T., Lee, Y.J., Yu, S.X., Efros, A.A.: Flowweb: joint image set alignment by weaving consistent, pixel-wise correspondences. In: IEEE Conference on Computer Vision and Pattern Recognition, CVPR 2015, Boston, MA, USA, 7–12 June 2015, pp. 1191–1200 (2015)
67. Zhou, X., Zhu, M., Daniilidis, K.: Multi-image matching via fast alternating minimization. In: ICCV, pp. 4032–4040. IEEE Computer Society, Santiago (2015)

MT-VAE: Learning Motion Transformations to Generate Multimodal Human Dynamics

Xinchen Yan[1(✉)], Akash Rastogi[1], Ruben Villegas[1], Kalyan Sunkavalli[2], Eli Shechtman[2], Sunil Hadap[2], Ersin Yumer[3], and Honglak Lee[1,4]

[1] University of Michigan, Ann Arbor, USA
xcyan@umich.edu
[2] Adobe Research, San Jose, USA
[3] Argo AI, San Francisco, USA
[4] Google Brain, Mountain View, USA

Abstract. Long-term human motion can be represented as a series of *motion modes*—motion sequences that capture short-term temporal dynamics—with transitions between them. We leverage this structure and present a novel *Motion Transformation Variational Auto-Encoders (MT-VAE)* for learning motion sequence generation. Our model jointly learns a feature embedding for motion modes (that the motion sequence can be reconstructed from) and a feature transformation that represents the transition of one motion mode to the next motion mode. Our model is able to generate multiple diverse and plausible motion sequences in the future from the same input. We apply our approach to both facial and full body motion, and demonstrate applications like analogy-based motion transfer and video synthesis.

1 Introduction

Modeling the dynamics of human motion—both facial and full body motion—is a fundamental problem in computer vision, graphics, and machine intelligence, with applications ranging from virtual characters [1,2], video-based animation and editing [3–5], and human-robot interfaces [6]. Human motion is known to be highly structured and can be modeled as a sequence of atomic units that we refer to as *motion modes*. A motion mode captures the *short-term* temporal dynamics of a human action (e.g., smiling or walking), including its related stylistic attributes (e.g., how wide is the smile, how fast is the walk). Over the *long-term*, a human action sequence can be segmented into a series of motion modes with transitions between them (e.g., a transition from a neutral expression to smiling

X. Yan—Work partially done during internship with Adobe Research.

Electronic supplementary material The online version of this chapter (https://doi.org/10.1007/978-3-030-01228-1_17) contains supplementary material, which is available to authorized users.

V. Ferrari et al. (Eds.): ECCV 2018, LNCS 11209, pp. 276–293, 2018.
https://doi.org/10.1007/978-3-030-01228-1_17

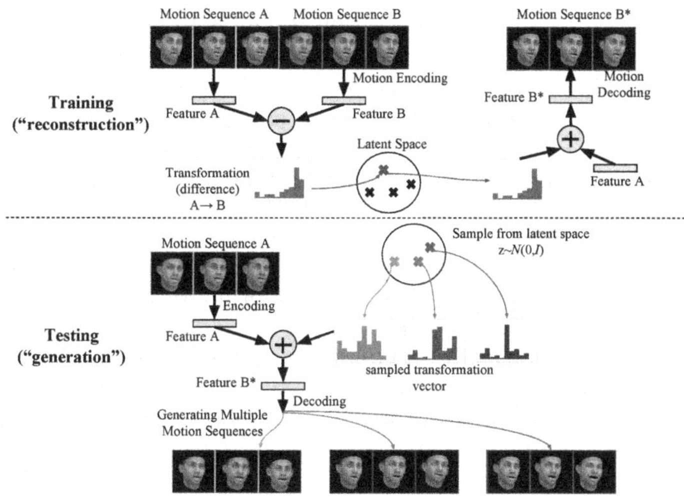

Fig. 1. Top: Learning motion sequence generation using *Motion Transformation VAE*. Bottom: Generating multiple future motion sequences from the transformation space.

to laughing). This structure is well known (referred to as basis motions [7] or walk cycles) and widely used in computer animation.

This paper leverages this structure to learn to generate human motion sequences, i.e., given a short human action sequence (present motion mode), we want to synthesize the action going forward (future motion mode). We hypothesize that (1) each motion mode can be represented as a low-dimensional feature vector, and (2) transitions between motion modes can be modeled as *transformations* of these features. As shown in Fig. 1, we present a novel model termed *Motion Transformation Variational Auto-Encoders (MT-VAE)* for learning motion sequence generation. Our MT-VAE is implemented using an LSTM encoder-decoder that embeds each short sub-sequence into a feature vector that can be decoded to reconstruct the motion. We further assume that the transition between current and future modes can be captured by a certain transformation. In the paper, we demonstrate that the proposed MT-VAE learns a motion feature representation in an unsupervised way.

A challenge with human motion is that it is inherently multimodal, i.e., the same initial motion mode could transition into different motion modes (e.g., a smile could transition to a frown, or a smile while looking left, or a wider smile, etc.). A deterministic model would not be able to learn these variations and may collapse to a single-mode distribution. Our MT-VAE supports a stochastic sampling of the feature transformations to generate multiple plausible output motion modes from a single input. This allows us to model transitions that may be rare (or potentially absent) in the training set.

We demonstrate our approach on both facial and full human body motions. In both domains, we conduct extensive ablation studies and comparisons with previous work showing that our generation results are more plausible (i.e., better preserve the structure of human dynamics) and diverse (i.e., explore multiple motion modes). We further demonstrate applications like (1) analogy-based motion transfer (e.g., transferring the act of smiling from one pose to another pose) and (2) future video synthesis (i.e., generating multiple possible future videos given input frames with human motions). Our key contributions are summarized as follows:

- We propose a generative motion model that consists of a sequence-level motion feature embedding and feature transformations, and show that it can be trained in an unsupervised manner.
- We show that stochastically sampling the transformation space is able to generate future motion dynamics that are diverse and plausible.
- We demonstrate applications of the learned model to challenging tasks like motion transfer and future video synthesis for both facial and human body motions.

2 Related Work

Understanding and modeling human motion dynamics has been a long-standing problem for decades [8–10]. Due to the high dimensionality of video data, early work mainly focused on learning hierarchical spatio-temporal representations for video event and action recognition [11–13]. In recent years, predicting and synthesizing motion dynamics using deep neural networks has become a popular research topic. Walker et al. [14], Fischer et al. [15] learn to synthesize dense flow in the future from a single image. Walker et al. [16] extended the deterministic prediction framework by modeling the flow uncertainty using variational auto-encoders. Chao et al. [17] proposed a recurrent neural network to generate movement of 3D human joints from a single observation with a 3D in-network projection layer. Taking one step further, Villegas et al. [18], Walker et al. [19] explored hierarchical structure (e.g., 2D human joints) for motion prediction in the future using recurrent neural networks. Li et al. [20] proposed an auto-conditional recurrent framework to generate long-term human motion dynamics through time. Besides human motion, face synthesis and editing is another interesting topic in vision and graphics. Methods for reenacting and interpolating face sequences in video have been developed [3,21–23] based on a 3D morphable face representation [24]. Very recently, Suwajanakorn et al. [5] introduced a speech-driven face synthesis system that learns to generate lip motions with a recurrent neural network.

Besides the flow representation, motion synthesis has been explored in a broader context, namely, video generation. For example, synthesizing video sequence in the future from a single or multiple video frames as initialization. Early works employed patch-based method for short-term video generation using mean squared mean squared loss [25] or perceptual loss [26]. Given an atomic action as additional condition, previous works extended with action-conditioned (i.e., rotation, location, etc.) architectures that enable better semantic control in video generation [27–30]. Due to the difficulty in holistic video frame prediction, the idea of disentangling video factors into motion and content is explored in [31–36]. Video generation has also been approached with architectures that output multinomial distribution vectors over the possible pixel values for each pixel in the generated frame [37].

The notion of feature transformations has also been exploited for other tasks. Mikolov et al. [38] showcased the composition additive property of word vectors learned in an unsupervised way from language data; Kulkarni et al. [39], Reed et al. [40] suggested that additive transformation can be achieved via reconstruction or prediction task by learning from parallel paired image data. In the video domain, Wang et al. [41] studied a transformation-aware representation for semantic human action classification; Zhou et al. [42] investigated time-lapse video generation given additional class labels.

Multimodal conditional generation has recently been explored for images [43, 44], sketch drawings [45], natural language [46,47], and video prediction [48,49]. As noted in previous work, learning to generate diverse and plausible visual data is very challenging for the following reasons: first, mode collapse may occur without one-to-many pairs. Collecting sequence data where one-to-many pairs exist is non-trivial. Second, posterior collapse could happen when the generation model is based on a recurrent neural network.

3 Problem Formulation and Methods

We start by giving an overview of our problem. We are given a sequence of T observations $S_A = [x_1, x_2, \cdots, x_T]$, where $x_t \in \mathbb{R}^D$ is a D dimensional vector representing the observation at time t. These observations encode the structure of the moving object and can be represented in different ways, for e.g., as keypoint locations or shape and pose parameters. *Changes* in these observations encode the motion that we are interested in modeling. We refer to the entire sequence as a *motion mode*. Given a motion mode, $S_A \in \mathbb{R}^{T \times D}$, we aim to build a model that is capable of predicting a future motion mode, $S_B = [y_1, y_2, \cdots, y_T]$, where $y_t \in \mathbb{R}^D$ represents the predicted t-th step in the *future*, i.e., $y_1 = x_{T+1}$. We first start with a discussion of two potential baseline models that could be used for this task (Sect. 3.1), and then present our method (Sect. 3.2).

3.1 Preliminaries

Prediction LSTM for Sequence Generation. Figure 2(a) shows a simple encoder-decoder LSTM [25,50] as a baseline for the motion prediction task. At time t, the encoder LSTM takes the motion x_t as input and updates its internal representation. After going through the entire motion mode S_A, it outputs a fixed-length feature $e_A \in \mathbb{R}^{N_e}$ as an intermediate representation. We initialize the internal representation of decoder LSTM using the feature e_A computed. At time t of the decoding stage, the decoder LSTM predicts the motion y_t. This way, the decoder LSTM gradually predicts the entire motion mode

$S_B^* = [y_1, y_2, \cdots, y_T]$ in the future within T steps. We denote the encoder LSTM as function $f : \mathbb{R}^{T \times D} \to \mathbb{R}^{N_e}$ and the decoder LSTM as function $g : \mathbb{R}^{N_e} \to \mathbb{R}^{T \times D}$. As a design choice, we initialize the decoder LSTM with additional input x_T for smoother prediction.

Vanilla VAE for Sequence Generation. As the deterministic LSTM model fails to reflect the multimodal nature of human motion, we consider a statistical model, $p_\theta(S_B|S_A)$, parameterized by θ. Given the observed sequence S_A, the model estimates a probability for the possible future sequence S_B instead of a single outcome. To model the multimodality (i.e., S_A can transition to different S_B's), a latent variable z (sampled from prior distribution) is introduced to capture the inherent uncertainty. The future sequence S_B is generated as follows:

1. Sample latent variable $z \sim \mathcal{N}(\mathbf{0}, \mathbf{I})$;
2. Given S_A and z, generate a sequence of length T: $S_B \sim p_\theta(S_B|z, S_A)$;

Following previous work on VAEs [16,19,33,43,51–53], the objective is to maximize the variational lower-bound of the conditional log-probability $\log p_\theta(S_B|S_A)$:

$$\mathcal{L}_{\text{VAE}} = -KL(q_\phi(z|S_B, S_A)||p_\theta(z)) + \mathbb{E}_{q_\phi(z|S_B,S_A)}\big[\log p_\theta(S_B|S_A, z)\big] \quad (1)$$

In Eq. 1, $q_\phi(z|S_B, S_A)$ is referred as an auxiliary posterior that approximates the true posterior $p_\theta(z|S_B, S_A)$. Specifically, the prior $p_\theta(z)$ is assumed to be $\mathcal{N}(\mathbf{0}, \mathbf{I})$. The posterior $q_\phi(z|S_B, S_A)$ is a multivariate Gaussian distribution with mean and variance μ_ϕ and σ_ϕ^2, respectively. Intuitively, the first term in Eq. 1 regularizes the auxiliary posterior $q_\phi(z|S_B, S_A)$ with prior $p_\theta(z)$. The second term $\log p_\theta(S_B|S_A, z)$ can be considered as an auto-encoding loss, where we refer to $q_\phi(z|S_B, S_A)$ as an encoder or recognition model, and $p_\theta(S_B|z, S_A)$ as a decoder or generation model.

As shown in Fig. 2(b), the vanilla VAE model adopts similar LSTM encoder and decoder for sequence processing. In contrast to Prediction LSTM model, the vanilla VAE decoder takes both motion feature e_A and latent variable z into account. Ideally, this allows to generate diverse motion sequences by drawing different samples from the latent space. However, the semantic role of the latent variable z in this vanilla VAE model is not straight-forward and may not effectively represent long-term trends (e.g., dynamics in a specific motion mode or during change of modes).

3.2 Motion-to-Motion Transformations in Latent Space

To further improve motion sequence generation beyond vanilla VAE, we propose to explicitly enforce the structure of motion modes in the latent space. We assume that (1) each motion mode can be represented as low-dimensional feature vector, and (2) transitions between motion modes can be modeled as *transformations* of these features. Our design is also supported by early studies on hierarchical motion modeling and prediction [8,54,55].

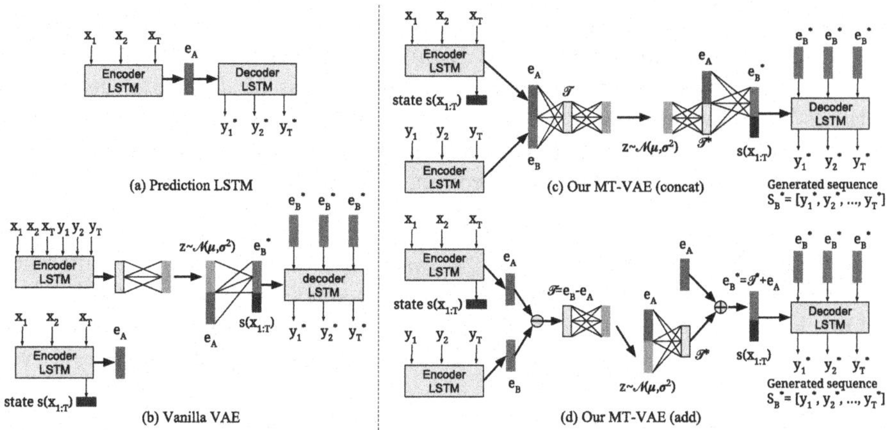

Fig. 2. Illustrations of different models for motion sequence generation. $s(x_{1:T})$ indicates the hidden state of the Encoder LSTM at time T.

We present a *Motion Transformation VAE (or MT-VAE)* (Fig. 2(c)) with four components:

1. An LSTM encoder $f : \mathbb{R}^{T \times D} \rightarrow \mathbb{R}^{N_e}$ maps the input sequences into motion features through $e_A = f(S_A)$ and $e_B = f(S_B)$, respectively.
2. A latent encoder $h_{e \rightarrow z} : \mathbb{R}^{2 \times N_e} \rightarrow \mathbb{R}^{N_z}$ computes the transformation in the latent space $z = h_{e \rightarrow z}([e_A, e_B])$ by concatenating motion features e_A and e_B. Here, N_z indicates the latent space dimension.
3. A latent decoder $h_{z \rightarrow e} : \mathbb{R}^{N_z + N_e} \rightarrow \mathbb{R}^{N_e}$ synthesizes the motion feature in the future from latent transformation z and current motion feature e_A via $e_B^* = h_{z \rightarrow e}([z, e_A])$.
4. An LSTM decoder $g : \mathbb{R}^{N_e} \rightarrow \mathbb{R}^{T \times D}$ synthesizes the future sequence given motion feature: $S_B^* = g(e_B^*)$.

Similar to the Prediction LSTM, we use an LSTM encoder/decoder to map motion modes into feature space. The MT-VAE further maps these features into *latent transformations* and stochastically samples these transformations. As we demonstrate, this change makes the model more expressive and leads to more plausible results. Finally, in the sequence decoding stage of MT-VAE, we feed the synthesized motion feature e_B^* as input to the decoder LSTM, with internal state initialized using the same motion feature e_B^* with an additional input x_t.

3.3 Additive Transformations in Latent Space

Although MT-VAE explicitly models motion transformations in latent space, this space might be unconstrained because the transformations are computed from vector concatenation of motion features e_A and e_B in our latent encoder $h_{e \rightarrow z}$. To better regularize the transformation space, we present an additive variant of

MT-VAE, that is depicted in Fig. 2(d). To distinguish between the two variants, we call the previous model *MT-VAE (concat)* and this model *MT-VAE (add)*, respectively. Our model is inspired by recent success of *deep analogy-making* methods [31,40] where a relation (or transformation) between two examples can be represented as a difference in the embedding space. In this model, we strictly constrain the latent encoding and decoding steps as follows:

1. Our latent encoder $h_{\mathcal{T}\rightarrow z} : \mathbb{R}^{N_e} \rightarrow \mathbb{R}^{N_z}$ computes the difference between two motion features e_A and e_B via $\mathcal{T} = e_B - e_A$; then it maps the difference feature $\mathcal{T}$ into a transformation in the latent space via $z = h_{\mathcal{T}\rightarrow z}(\mathcal{T})$.
2. Our latent decoder $h_{z\rightarrow\mathcal{T}} : \mathbb{R}^{N_z+N_e} \rightarrow \mathbb{R}^{N_e}$ reconstructs the difference feature $\mathcal{T}^*$ from latent variable z and current motion feature e_A via $\mathcal{T}^* = h_{z\rightarrow\mathcal{T}}(z, e_A)$.
3. Finally, we apply a simple additive interaction to reconstruct the motion feature via $e_B^* = e_A + \mathcal{T}^*$;

In step one, we infer the latent variable using $h_{\mathcal{T}\rightarrow z}$ from the difference of e_A and e_B (instead of a applying a linear layer on concatenated vectors). Intuitively, the latent code is expected to capture the mode transition from the current motion to the future motion rather than a concatenation of two modes. In step two, we reconstruct the transformation from the latent variable via $h_{z\rightarrow\mathcal{T}}(z, e_A)$ where z is obtained from recognition model. In this design, the feature difference is dependent on both latent transformation z and current motion feature e_A. Alternatively, we can make our latent decoder $h_{z\rightarrow\mathcal{T}}$ context-free by removing input from motion feature e_A. This way, the latent decoder is supposed to hallucinate the motion difference solely from the latent space. We provide this ablation study in Sect. 4.1.

Besides the architecture-wise regularization, we introduce two additional objectives while training our model.

Cycle Consistency. As mentioned previously, our training objective $\mathcal{L}_{\text{VAE}}$ in Eq. 1 is composed of a KL term and a reconstruction term at each frame. The KL term regularizes the latent space, while the reconstruction term ensures that the data can be explained by our generative model. However, we do not have direct regularization in the feature space. We therefore introduce a cycle-consistency loss in Eq. 2 (for MT-VAE (concat)) and Eq. 3 (for MT-VAE (add)). Figure 3 illustrates the cycle consistency in details.

$$\mathcal{L}_{\text{cycle}}^{\text{concat}} = ||z^* - z||, \text{ where } z^* = h_{e\rightarrow z}([e_A, h_{z\rightarrow e}(z, e_A)]) \text{ and } z \sim \mathcal{N}(\mathbf{0}, \mathbf{I}) \quad (2)$$

$$\mathcal{L}_{\text{cycle}}^{\text{add}} = ||z^* - z||, \text{ where } z^* = h_{\mathcal{T}\rightarrow z}(h_{z\rightarrow\mathcal{T}}(z, e_A)) \text{ and } z \sim \mathcal{N}(\mathbf{0}, \mathbf{I}) \quad (3)$$

In our preliminary experiments, we also investigated a consistency loss with a bigger cycle (involving the actual motion sequences) during training but we found it ineffective as a regularization term in our setting. We hypothesize that vanishing or exploding gradients make the cycle-consistency objective less effective, which is a known issue when training recurrent neural networks.

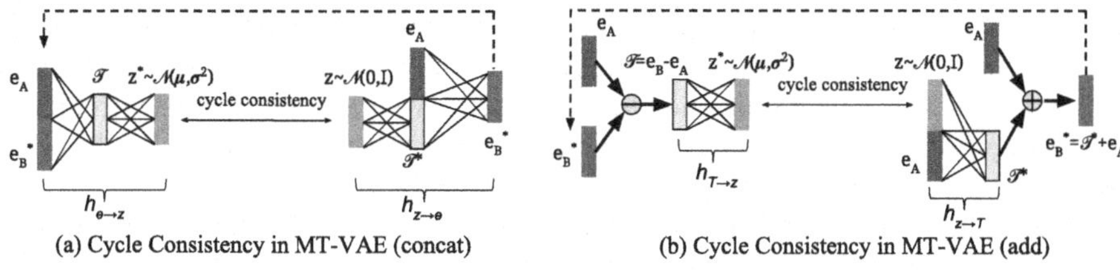

Fig. 3. Illustrations of cycle consistency in MT-VAE variations.

Motion Coherence. Specific to our motion generation task, we introduce a motion coherence loss in Eq. 4 that encourages a smooth transition in velocity in the first K steps of prediction. We define the velocity $v_1 = y_1 - x_T$ and $v_k = y_k - y_{k-1}$ when $k \geq 2$. Intuitively, such loss prevents the generated sequence from deviating too far from the future sequence sampled from the prior.

$$\mathcal{L}_{\text{motion}} = \frac{1}{K}\sum_{t=1}^{K} ||v_t^* - v_t||, \text{ where } g(e_B^z) = [y_1^*, \cdots, y_T^*] \text{ and } z \sim \mathcal{N}(\mathbf{0}, \mathbf{I}) \quad (4)$$

Finally, we summarize our overall loss in Eq. 5, where λ_{cycle} and λ_{motion} are two balancing hyper-parameters for cycle consistency and motion coherence, respectively.

$$\mathcal{L}_{\text{MT-VAE}} = \mathcal{L}_{\text{VAE}} + \lambda_{\text{cycle}}\mathcal{L}_{\text{cycle}} + \lambda_{\text{motion}}\mathcal{L}_{\text{motion}} \quad (5)$$

4 Experiments

Datasets. The evaluation is conducted on the datasets involving two representative human motion modeling tasks: Affect-in-the-wild (Aff-Wild) [56] for facial motions and Human3.6M [57] for full body motions. To better focus on face motion modeling (e.g., expressions and head movements), we leveraged the 3D morphable face model [24,58] (e.g., face identity, face expression, and pose) in our experiments. We fitted 198-dim identity coefficients, 29-dim expression coefficients, and 6-dim pose parameters to each frame with a pre-trained 3DMM-CNN [59] model, followed by a face fitting algorithm [60] based on optimization. Human3.6M is a large-scale database containing more than 800 human motion sequences captured by 11 professional actors (3.6 million frames in total) in an indoor environment. For experiments on Human3.6M, we used the raw 2D trajectories of 32 keypoints and further normalized the data into coordinates within the range $[-1, 1]$.

Architecture Design. Our MT-VAE model consists of four components: sequence encoder network, sequence decoder network, latent encoder network, and latent decoder network. We build our sequence encoder and decoder using Long Short-term Memory units (LSTMs) [50]. We used 1-layer LSTM with 1,024 hidden units for both networks. Given past and future motion features extracted from our sequence encoder network, we build three fully-connected layers with skip connections within our latent encoding network. We adopted a similar architecture (three fully-connected layers with skip connections) for our latent decoder network.

Due to the page limit, please see the implementation details in the supplementary document. Also, please see the website for more visualizations: https://goo.gl/2Q69Ym.

4.1 Multimodal Motion Generation

We evaluate our model's capacity to generate diverse and plausible future motion patterns for a given sequence on the Aff-Wild and Human3.6M test sets. Given sequence S_A as initialization, we generated multiple motion trajectories in the future using our proposed sampling and generation process. For the Prediction LSTM model, we only sample one motion trajectory in the future since the predicted future is deterministic.

Table 1. Quantitative evaluations for multimodal motion generation. We compare against two simple data-driven baselines for quantitative comparison: *Last-step Motion* that recursively applies the motion (velocity only) from the last step observed; *Sequence Motion* that recursively adds the average sequence velocity from the observed frames.

(a) Results on Aff-Wild with facial expression coefficients.

Method / Metric	R-MSE ↓ ($\times 10^{-1}$)		S-MSE ↓ ($\times 10^{-1}$)		Test CLL ↑ ($\times 10^3$)
	train	test	train	test	
Last-step Motion	—	—	63.8 ± 1.31	74.7 ± 5.59	0.719 ± 0.077
Sequence Motion	—	—	18.4 ± 0.25	19.1 ± 1.02	1.335 ± 0.057
Prediction LSTM [18]	—	—	1.53 ± 0.01	3.03 ± 0.06	2.232 ± 0.003
Vanilla VAE [48]	0.32 ± 0.00	1.28 ± 0.02	0.79 ± 0.00	1.79 ± 0.03	2.749 ± 0.012
Our MT-VAE (concat)	0.22 ± 0.00	0.73 ± 0.01	1.04 ± 0.00	1.76 ± 0.03	2.817 ± 0.023
Our MT-VAE (add)	0.20 ± 0.00	**0.47** ± 0.01	1.02 ± 0.00	**1.54** ± 0.04	**3.147** ± 0.018

(b) Results on Human3.6M with 2D joints.

Method / Metric	R-MSE ↓		S-MSE ↓		Test CLL ↑ ($\times 10^4$)
	train	test	train	test	
Last-step Motion	—	—	35.2 ± 0.49	32.1 ± 0.80	0.390 ± 0.004
Sequence Motion	—	—	37.8 ± 0.49	35.2 ± 0.73	0.406 ± 0.003
Prediction LSTM [18]	—	—	1.69 ± 0.02	11.2 ± 0.17	0.602 ± 0.002
Vanilla VAE [48]	0.36 ± 0.00	1.05 ± 0.02	3.18 ± 0.02	3.88 ± 0.05	0.993 ± 0.011
Our MT-VAE (concat)	0.36 ± 0.00	0.97 ± 0.02	2.26 ± 0.03	**2.84** ± 0.05	1.033 ± 0.010
Our MT-VAE (add)	0.25 ± 0.00	**0.75** ± 0.01	2.37 ± 0.02	**2.87** ± 0.05	**1.141** ± 0.009

Quantitative Evaluations. We evaluate our model and baselines quantitatively using the minimum squared error metric and conditional log-likelihood metric, which have been used in evaluating conditional generative models [16,43,48, 53]. As defined in Eq. 6, *Reconstruction* minimum squared error (or R-MSE) measures the squared error of the closest reconstruction to ground-truth when sampling latent variables from the recognition model. This is a measure of the quality of reconstruction given both current and future sequences. As defined in Eq. 7, *Sampling* minimum squared error (or S-MSE) measures the squared error of the closest sample to ground-truth when sampling latent variables from prior. This is a measure of how close our samples are to the reference future sequences.

$$\text{R-MSE} = \min_{1 \leq k \leq K} \|S_B - S_B^*(z^{(k)})\|^2, \text{ where } z^{(k)} \sim q_\phi(z|S_A, S_B). \tag{6}$$

$$\text{S-MSE} = \min_{1 \leq k \leq K} \|S_B - S_B^*(z^{(k)})\|^2, \text{ where } z^{(k)} \sim p_\theta(z). \tag{7}$$

In terms of generation diversity and quality, a good generative model is expected to achieve low R-MSE and S-MSE values, given sufficient number of samples. Note that *posterior collapse* issue is usually featured by low S-MSE but high R-MSE, as latent z sampled from the recognition model is being ignored to some extent. In addition, we measure the test conditional log-likelihood of the ground-truth sequences under our model via Parzen window estimation (with a bandwidth determined based on the validation set). We believe that Parzen window estimation is a reasonable approach for our setting as the dimensionality of data (sequence of keypoints) is not too high (unlike in the case of high-resolution videos). For each example, we used 50 samples to compute R-MSE metric, and 500 samples to compute S-MSE and conditional log-likelihood metrics. On Aff-Wild, we evaluate the models on 32-step expression coefficients prediction (29 $\times$ 32 = 928 dimensions in total). On Human3.6M, we evaluate the models on 64-step 2D joints prediction (64 $\times$ 64 = 4096 dimensions in total). Please note that such measurements are approximate, as we do not evaluate the model performance for every sub-sequence (e.g., essentially, every frame can serve as a starting point). Instead, we repeat the evaluations every 16 frames on Aff-Wild dataset and every 100 frames on Human3.6M dataset.

As we see in Table 1, data-driven approaches that simply repeat the motion computed from last-step velocity or averaged over the observed sequence performed poorly on both datasets. In contrast, the Prediction LSTM [18] baseline greatly reduces the S-MSE metric compared to simple data-driven approaches, due to the deep sequence encoder and decoder architecture in modeling more complex motion dynamics through time. Among all three models using latent variables, our MT-VAE (add) model achieve the best quantitative performance. Compared to MT-VAE (concat) that adopts vector concatenation, our additive version achieves lower reconstruction error with similar sampling eror. This suggests that the MT-VAE (add) model is able to regularize the learning of motion transformation further.

Qualitative Results. We provide qualitative side-by-side comparisons across different models in Fig. 4. For Aff-Wild, we render 3D face models using the

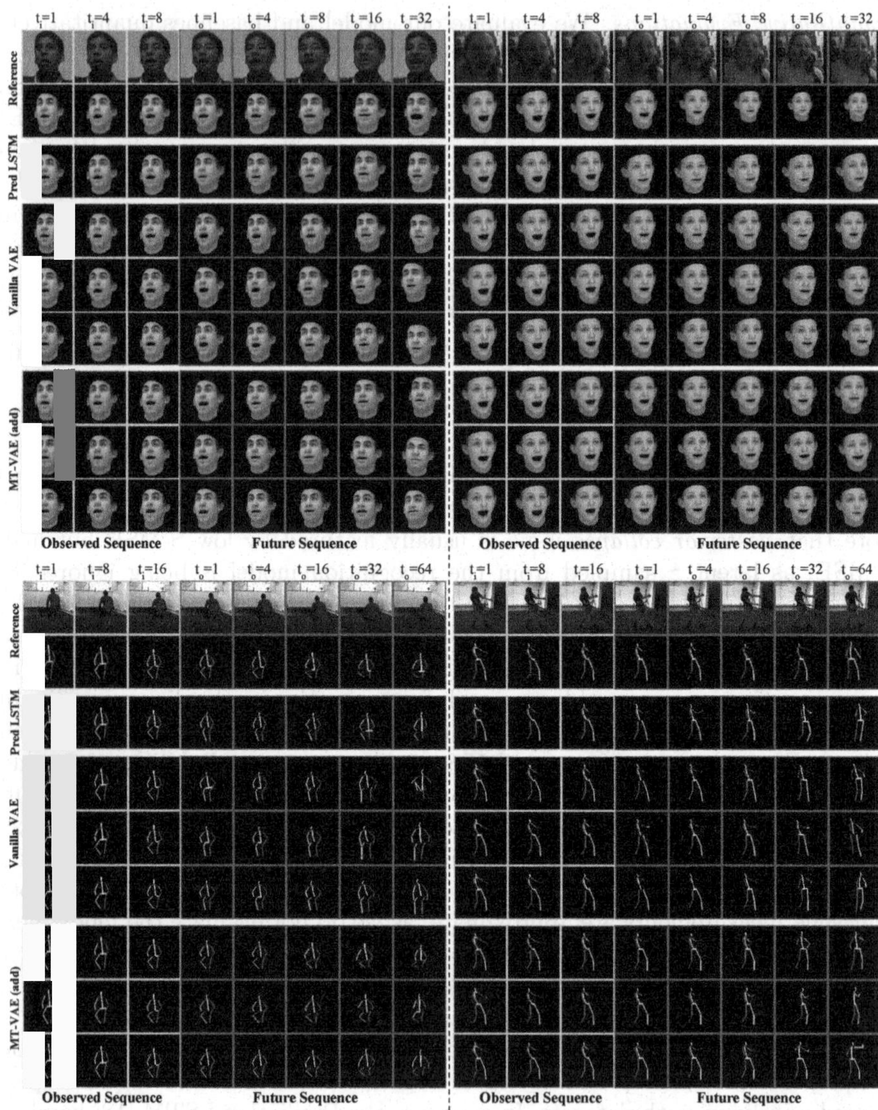

Fig. 4. Multimodal Sequence Generation. Given an input sequence (green boundary), we generate future sequences (red boundary). We predict 32 frames given 8 frames for face motion, and 64 frames given 16 frames for human body motion. Given the initial frames as condition, we demonstrate (top to bottom) the ground truth sequence, Prediction LSTM, Vanilla VAE, and our MT-VAE model. Overall, our model produces (1) diverse and structured motion patterns and (2) more natural transitions from the last frame observed to the first frame generated (See the subtle mouth shape and scale change from the last observed frame to the first generated one). (Color figure online)

generated expression-pose parameters along with the original identity parameters. For Human3.6M, we directly visualize the generated 2D keypoints. As shown in the generated sequences, our MT-VAE model is able to generate multiple diverse and plausible sequences in the future. In comparison, the sequences generated by Vanilla VAE are less realistic. For example, given a sitting down motion (lower-left part in Fig. 4) as initialization, the vanilla model fails to predict the motion trend (sitting down), while creating some artifacts (e.g., scale change) in the future prediction. Also note that MT-VAE produces more natural transitions from the last observed frame to the first generated one (see mouth shapes in the face motion examples and distances between two legs in full-body examples). This demonstrates that MT-VAE learns a more robust and structure-preserving representation of motion sequences compared to other baselines.

Crowd-sourced Human Evaluations. We conducted crowd-sourced human evaluations via Amazon Mechanical Turk (AMT) on 50 videos (10 Turkers per video) from Human3.6M dataset. This evaluation presents the past action, and 5 generated future actions for each method to a human evaluator and asks the person to select the most (1) realistic and (2) diverse results. In this evaluation, we also added comparisons to a recently published work [49] on stochastic video prediction, which we refer to as SVG. Table 2 presents the percentage of users who selected each method for each task. The Prediction LSTM produces the most realistic but the least diverse result; Babaeizadeh et al. [48] produces the most diverse but the least realistic result; Our MT-VAE model (we use the additive variant here) achieves a good balance between realism and diversity.

Table 2. Crowd-sourced Human Evaluations on Human3.6M. *We did not include Prediction LSTM for the diversity evaluation, as it makes deterministic prediction.

Metric	Vanilla VAE [48]	SVG [49]	Our MT-VAE (add)	Pred LSTM [18]
Realism (%)	19.2	23.8	26.4	30.6
Diversity (%)	51.6	22.3	26.1	0.0*

Table 3. Ablation Study on Different variants of MT-VAE (add) model: We evaluate models trained without motion coherence objective, without cycle consistency objective, and the model with context-free latent decoder.

Method/Metric	R-MSE (test) $\downarrow$	S-MSE (test) $\downarrow$	Test CLL $\uparrow$ ($\times 10^4$)
MT-VAE (add)	0.75 $\pm$ 0.01	2.87 $\pm$ 0.05	1.141 $\pm$ 0.009
MT-VAE (add) w/o Motion coherence	1.01 $\pm$ 0.02	2.93 $\pm$ 0.04	1.012 $\pm$ 0.014
MT-VAE (add) w/o Cycle consistency	1.18 $\pm$ 0.03	2.71 $\pm$ 0.05	0.927 $\pm$ 0.019
MT-VAE (add) Context-free decoder	0.31 $\pm$ 0.05	4.05 $\pm$ 0.05	1.299 $\pm$ 0.007

Ablation Study. We analyze variations of our MT-VAE (add) models on Human3.6M. As we see in Table 3, removing the cycle consistency or motion coherence results in a drop in reconstruction performance. This shows that cycle consistency and motion coherence encourage the motion feature to preserve motion structure and hence be more discriminative in nature. We also evaluate a *context-free* version of the MT-VAE (add) model, where the transformation vector $\mathcal{T}^*$ is not conditioned on input feature e_A. This version produces poor S-MSE value since it is challenging for the additive latent decoder to hallucinate transformation vector $\mathcal{T}^*$ solely from latent variable z.

4.2 Analogy-Based Motion Transfer

We evaluate our model on an additional task of *transfer by analogy*. In this analogy-making experiment, we are given three motion sequences A, B (which is the subsequent motion of A), and C (which is a different motion sequence). The objective is to recognize the *transition* from A to B and transfer it to C. This experiment can demonstrate whether our learned latent space models the mode transition across motion sequences. Moreover, this task has numerous graphics applications like transferring expressions and their styles, video dubbing, gait style transfer, and video-driven animation [22].

In this experiment, we compare Prediction LSTM, Vanilla VAE, and our MT-VAE variants. For the stochastic models, we compute the latent variable z from motion sequence A and B via the latent encoder, i.e., $z = h_{\mathcal{T}\to z}(e_B - e_A)$, and then decode using motion sequence C as $e_D^* = h_{z\to\mathcal{T}}(z, e_C)$. For Prediction LSTM model, we directly performed the analogy-making in the feature space $e_D^* = e_B - e_A + e_C$ since there is no notion of a latent space in that model. As shown in Fig. 5, our MT-VAE model is able to combine the transformation learned from A to B transitions with the structure in sequence C. The other baselines failed at either adapting the mode transition from A to B or preserving the structure in C. The analogy-based motion transfer task is significantly more challenging than motion generation, since the combination of three reference motion sequences A, B, and C may never appear in the training data. Yet, our model is able to synthesize realistic motions. Please note that motion modes may not explicitly correspond to semantic motions, as we learn the motion transformation in an unsupervised manner.

4.3 Towards Multimodal Hierarchical Video Generation

As an application, we showcase that our multimodal motion generation framework can be directly used for generating diverse and realistic pixel-level video frames in the future. We trained the keypoint-conditioned image generation model [18] that takes both previous image frame A and predicted motion structure B (e.g., rendered face or human joints) as input and hallucinates image C by combining the image content adapted from A but with motion adapted

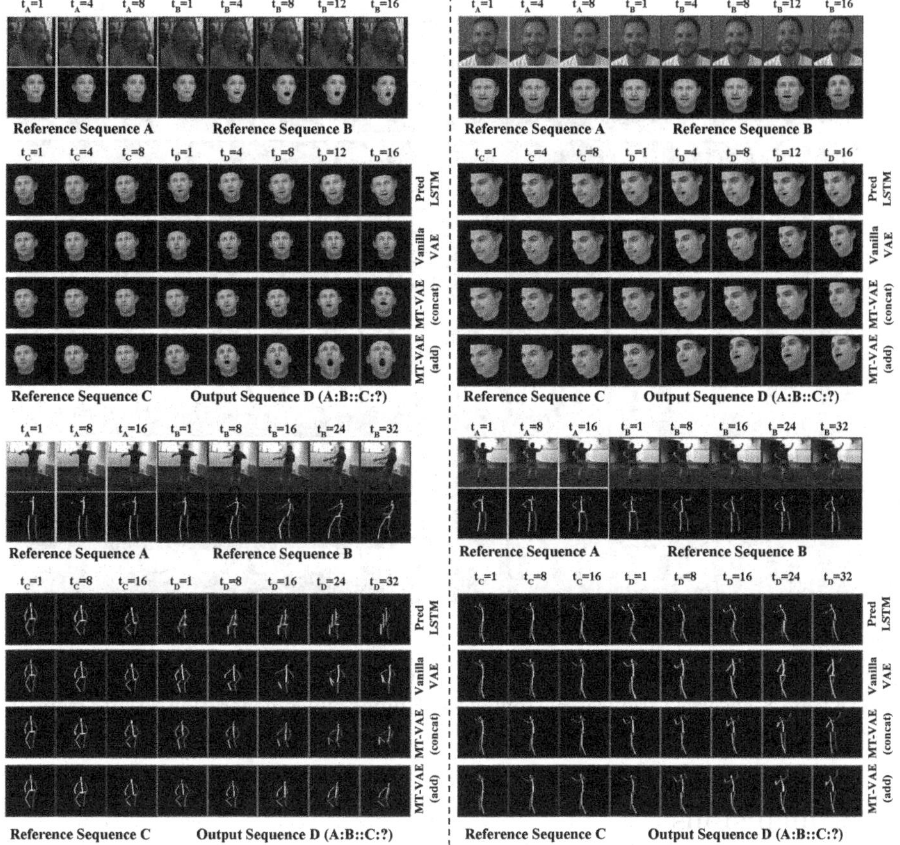

Fig. 5. Analogy-based motion transfer. Given three motion sequences A, B, and C from test set, the objective is to extract the motion mode transition from A to B and then apply it to animate the future starting from sequence C. For fair comparison, we set the encoder Gaussian distribution parameter σ to zero during evaluation.

from B. In Fig. 6, we show a comparison of video generated in a deterministic way by Prediction LSTM (i.e., single future), and in a stochastic way driven by the predicted motion sequence (i.e., multiple futures) from our MT-VAE (add) model. We use our generated motion sequences for performing video generation experiments on the Aff-Wild (with 8 input frames observed) and Human3.6M (with 16 input frames observed).

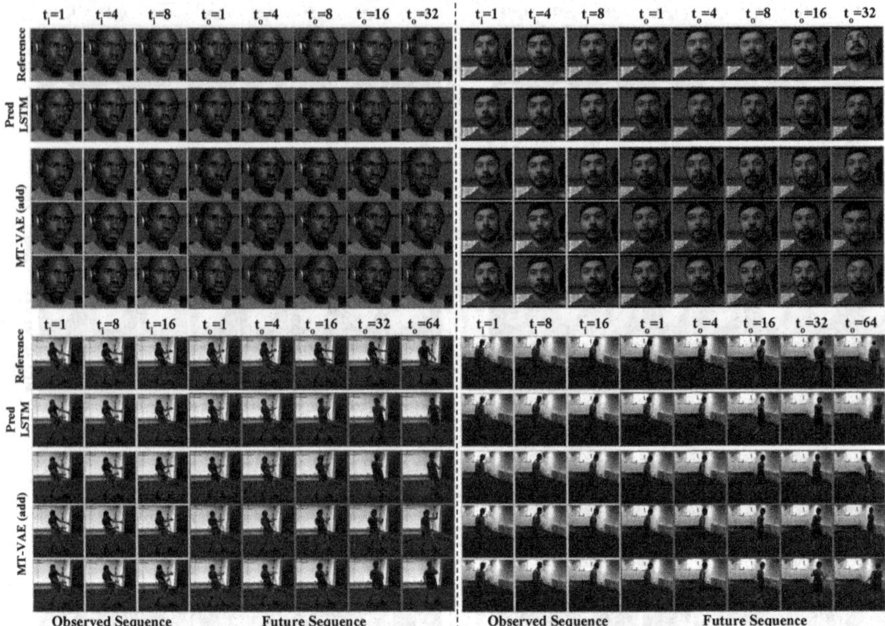

Fig. 6. Multimodal Hierarchical video generation. Top rows: Face video generation results from 8 observed frames. Bottom rows: Human video generation results from 16 observed frames.

5 Conclusions

Our goal in this work is to learn a conditional generative model for human motions. This is an extremely challenging problem in the general case and can require significant amount of training data to generate realistic results. Our work demonstrates that this can be accomplished with minimal supervision by enforcing a strong structure on the problem. In particular, we model long-term human dynamics as a set of motion modes with transitions between them, and construct a novel network architecture that strongly regularizes this space and allows for stochastic sampling. We have demonstrated that this same idea can be used to model both facial and full body motion, independent of the representation used (i.e., shape parameters, keypoints).

Acknowledgements. We thank Zhixin Shu and Haoxiang Li for their assistance with face tracking and fitting codebase. We thank Yuting Zhang, Seunghoon Hong, and Lajanugen Logeswaran for helpful comments and discussions. This work was supported in part by Adobe Research Fellowship to X. Yan, a gift from Adobe, ONR N00014-13-1-0762, and NSF CAREER IIS-1453651.

References

1. de Aguiar, E., Stoll, C., Theobalt, C., Ahmed, N., Seidel, H.P., Thrun, S.: Performance capture from sparse multi-view video. ACM Trans. Graph. **27**(3), 98:1–98:10 (2008)
2. Beeler, T., et al.: High-quality passive facial performance capture using anchor frames. ACM Trans. Graph. **30**(4), 75:1–75:10 (2011)
3. Yang, F., Wang, J., Shechtman, E., Bourdev, L., Metaxas, D.: Expression flow for 3D-aware face component transfer. ACM Trans. Graph. (TOG), **30**, 60 (2011)
4. Suwajanakorn, S., Seitz, S.M., Kemelmacher-Shlizerman, I.: What makes tom hanks look like tom hanks. In: Proceedings of the IEEE International Conference on Computer Vision, pp. 3952–3960 (2015)
5. Suwajanakorn, S., Seitz, S.M., Kemelmacher-Shlizerman, I.: Synthesizing obama: learning lip sync from audio. ACM Trans. Graph. (TOG) **36**(4), 95 (2017)
6. Sermanet, P., Lynch, C., Hsu, J., Levine, S.: Time-contrastive networks: self-supervised learning from multi-view observation. arXiv preprint arXiv:1704.06888 (2017)
7. Rose, C., Guenter, B., Bodenheimer, B., Cohen, M.F.: Efficient generation of motion transitions using spacetime constraints. In: SIGGRAPH (1996)
8. Bregler, C.: Learning and recognizing human dynamics in video sequences. In: 1997 IEEE Computer Society Conference on Computer Vision and Pattern Recognition, Proceedings, pp. 568–574. IEEE (1997)
9. Efros, A.A., Berg, A.C., Mori, G., Malik, J.: Recognizing action at a distance. In: Null, p. 726. IEEE (2003)
10. Gorelick, L., Blank, M., Shechtman, E., Irani, M., Basri, R.: Actions as space-time shapes. IEEE Trans. Pattern Anal. Mach. Intell. **29**(12), 2247–2253 (2007)
11. Laptev, I.: On space-time interest points. Int. J. Comput. Vis. **64**(2–3), 107–123 (2005)
12. Wang, H., Kläser, A., Schmid, C., Liu, C.L.: Action recognition by dense trajectories. In: 2011 IEEE Conference on Computer Vision and Pattern Recognition (CVPR), pp. 3169–3176. IEEE (2011)
13. Wang, J., Liu, Z., Wu, Y., Yuan, J.: Mining actionlet ensemble for action recognition with depth cameras. In: 2012 IEEE Conference on Computer Vision and Pattern Recognition (CVPR), pp. 1290–1297. IEEE (2012)
14. Walker, J., Gupta, A., Hebert, M.: Dense optical flow prediction from a static image. In: 2015 IEEE International Conference on Computer Vision (ICCV), pp. 2443–2451. IEEE (2015)
15. Fischer, P., et al.: Flownet: Learning optical flow with convolutional networks. arXiv preprint arXiv:1504.06852 (2015)
16. Walker, J., Doersch, C., Gupta, A., Hebert, M.: An uncertain future: forecasting from static images using variational autoencoders. In: Leibe, B., Matas, J., Sebe, N., Welling, M. (eds.) ECCV 2016. LNCS, vol. 9911, pp. 835–851. Springer, Cham (2016). https://doi.org/10.1007/978-3-319-46478-7_51
17. Chao, Y.W., Yang, J., Price, B., Cohen, S., Deng, J.: Forecasting human dynamics from static images. In: CVPR (2017)
18. Villegas, R., Yang, J., Zou, Y., Sohn, S., Lin, X., Lee, H.: Learning to generate long-term future via hierarchical prediction. In: ICML (2017)
19. Walker, J., Marino, K., Gupta, A., Hebert, M.: The pose knows: Video forecasting by generating pose futures. In: 2017 IEEE International Conference on Computer Vision (ICCV), pp. 3352–3361. IEEE (2017)
20. Li, Z., Zhou, Y., Xiao, S., He, C., Huang, Z., Li, H.: Auto-conditioned recurrent networks for extended complex human motion synthesis. In: ICLR (2018)

21. Yang, F., Bourdev, L., Shechtman, E., Wang, J., Metaxas, D.: Facial expression editing in video using a temporally-smooth factorization. In: 2012 IEEE Conference on Computer Vision and Pattern Recognition (CVPR), pp. 861–868. IEEE (2012)
22. Thies, J., Zollhofer, M., Stamminger, M., Theobalt, C., Nießner, M.: Face2face: real-time face capture and reenactment of RGB videos. In: Proceedings of the IEEE Conference on Computer Vision and Pattern Recognition, pp. 2387–2395 (2016)
23. Averbuch-Elor, H., Cohen-Or, D., Kopf, J., Cohen, M.F.: Bringing portraits to life. ACM Trans. Graph. **36**(6), 196 (2017). (Proceeding of SIGGRAPH Asia 2017)
24. Blanz, V., Vetter, T.: A morphable model for the synthesis of 3D faces. In: Proceedings of the 26th Annual Conference on Computer Graphics and Interactive Techniques, pp. 187–194. ACM Press/Addison-Wesley Publishing Co. (1999)
25. Srivastava, N., Mansimov, E., Salakhudinov, R.: Unsupervised learning of video representations using lstms. In: International Conference on Machine Learning, pp. 843–852 (2015)
26. Mathieu, M., Couprie, C., LeCun, Y.: Deep multi-scale video prediction beyond mean square error. In: ICLR (2016)
27. Hinton, G.E., Krizhevsky, A., Wang, S.D.: Transforming auto-encoders. In: Honkela, T., Duch, W., Girolami, M., Kaski, S. (eds.) ICANN 2011. LNCS, vol. 6791, pp. 44–51. Springer, Heidelberg (2011). https://doi.org/10.1007/978-3-642-21735-7_6
28. Oh, J., Guo, X., Lee, H., Lewis, R.L., Singh, S.: Action-conditional video prediction using deep networks in atari games. In: NIPS (2015)
29. Finn, C., Goodfellow, I.J., Levine, S.: Unsupervised learning for physical interaction through video prediction. In: NIPS (2016)
30. Yang, J., Reed, S.E., Yang, M.H., Lee, H.: Weakly-supervised disentangling with recurrent transformations for 3D view synthesis. In: Advances in Neural Information Processing Systems, pp. 1099–1107 (2015)
31. Villegas, R., Yang, J., Hong, S., Lin, X., Lee, H.: Decomposing motion and content for natural video sequence prediction. ICLR **1**(2), 7 (2017)
32. Denton, E.L., Birodkar, V.: Unsupervised learning of disentangled representations from video. In: Advances in Neural Information Processing Systems, pp. 4417–4426 (2017)
33. Xue, T., Wu, J., Bouman, K., Freeman, B.: Visual dynamics: probabilistic future frame synthesis via cross convolutional networks. In: NIPS, pp. 91–99 (2016)
34. Vondrick, C., Pirsiavash, H., Torralba, A.: Generating videos with scene dynamics. In: NIPS, pp. 613–621 (2016)
35. Tulyakov, S., Liu, M.Y., Yang, X., Kautz, J.: Mocogan: decomposing motion and content for video generation. arXiv preprint arXiv:1707.04993 (2017)
36. Wichers, N., Villegas, R., Erhan, D., Lee, H.: Hierarchical long-term video prediction without supervision. In: ICML
37. Kalchbrenner, N., et al.: Video pixel networks. arXiv preprint arXiv:1610.00527 (2016)
38. Mikolov, T., Sutskever, I., Chen, K., Corrado, G.S., Dean, J.: Distributed representations of words and phrases and their compositionality. In: Advances in Neural Information Processing Systems, pp. 3111–3119 (2013)
39. Kulkarni, T.D., Whitney, W.F., Kohli, P., Tenenbaum, J.: Deep convolutional inverse graphics network. In: Advances in Neural Information Processing Systems, pp. 2539–2547 (2015)
40. Reed, S.E., Zhang, Y., Zhang, Y., Lee, H.: Deep visual analogy-making. In: Advances in Neural Information Processing Systems, pp. 1252–1260 (2015)

41. Wang, X., Farhadi, A., Gupta, A.: Actions transformations. In: Proceedings of the IEEE Conference on Computer Vision and Pattern Recognition, pp. 2658–2667 (2016)
42. Zhou, Y., Berg, T.L.: Learning temporal transformations from time-lapse videos. In: Leibe, B., Matas, J., Sebe, N., Welling, M. (eds.) ECCV 2016. LNCS, vol. 9912, pp. 262–277. Springer, Cham (2016). https://doi.org/10.1007/978-3-319-46484-8_16
43. Sohn, K., Yan, X., Lee, H.: Learning structured output representation using deep conditional generative models. In: Advances in Neural Information Processing Systems, pp. 3483–3491 (2015)
44. Zhu, J.Y., et al.: Toward multimodal image-to-image translation. In: Advances in Neural Information Processing Systems, pp. 465–476 (2017)
45. Ha, D., Eck, D.: A neural representation of sketch drawings. In: ICLR (2018)
46. Bowman, S.R., Vilnis, L., Vinyals, O., Dai, A.M., Jozefowicz, R., Bengio, S.: Generating sentences from a continuous space. arXiv preprint arXiv:1511.06349 (2015)
47. Hu, Z., Yang, Z., Liang, X., Salakhutdinov, R., Xing, E.P.: Controllable text generation. arXiv preprint arXiv:1703.00955 (2017)
48. Babaeizadeh, M., Finn, C., Erhan, D., Campbell, R.H., Levine, S.: Stochastic variational video prediction. In: ICLR (2018)
49. Denton, E., Fergus, R.: Stochastic video generation with a learned prior. In: ICML (2018)
50. Hochreiter, S., Schmidhuber, J.: Long short-term memory. Neural Comput. **9**(8), 1735–1780 (1997)
51. Kingma, D.P., Welling, M.: Auto-encoding variational bayes. arXiv preprint arXiv:1312.6114 (2013)
52. Gregor, K., Danihelka, I., Graves, A., Rezende, D., Wierstra, D.: Draw: a recurrent neural network for image generation. In: International Conference on Machine Learning, pp. 1462–1471 (2015)
53. Yan, X., Yang, J., Sohn, K., Lee, H.: Attribute2Image: conditional image generation from visual attributes. In: Leibe, B., Matas, J., Sebe, N., Welling, M. (eds.) ECCV 2016. LNCS, vol. 9908, pp. 776–791. Springer, Cham (2016). https://doi.org/10.1007/978-3-319-46493-0_47
54. Smith, K.A., Vul, E.: Sources of uncertainty in intuitive physics. Top. Cogn. Sci. **5**(1), 185–199 (2013)
55. Lan, T., Chen, T.-C., Savarese, S.: A hierarchical representation for future action prediction. In: Fleet, D., Pajdla, T., Schiele, B., Tuytelaars, T. (eds.) ECCV 2014. LNCS, vol. 8691, pp. 689–704. Springer, Cham (2014). https://doi.org/10.1007/978-3-319-10578-9_45
56. Zafeiriou, S., Kollias, D., Nicolaou, M.A., Papaioannou, A., Zhao, G., Kotsia, I.: Aff-wild: valence and arousal in-the-wild challenge
57. Ionescu, C., Papava, D., Olaru, V., Sminchisescu, C.: Human3. 6m: large scale datasets and predictive methods for 3D human sensing in natural environments. IEEE Trans. Pattern Anal. Mach. Intell. **36**(7), 1325–1339 (2014)
58. Paysan, P., Knothe, R., Amberg, B., Romdhani, S., Vetter, T.: A 3D face model for pose and illumination invariant face recognition. Genova, Italy. IEEE (2009)
59. Tran, A.T., Hassner, T., Masi, I., Medioni, G.: Regressing robust and discriminative 3D morphable models with a very deep neural network. In: Computer Vision and Pattern Recognition (CVPR) (2017)
60. Zhu, X., Lei, Z., Liu, X., Shi, H., Li, S.Z.: Face alignment across large poses: A 3D solution. In: Proceedings of the IEEE Conference on Computer Vision and Pattern Recognition, pp. 146–155 (2016)

Rethinking the Form of Latent States in Image Captioning

Bo Dai[1(✉)], Deming Ye[2], and Dahua Lin[1]

[1] CUHK-SenseTime Joint Lab, The Chinese University of Hong Kong, Shatin, Hong Kong
{db014,dhlin}@ie.cuhk.edu.hk
[2] Department of Computer Science and Technology, Tsinghua University, Beijing, China
ydm18@mails.tsinghua.edu.cn

Abstract. RNNs and their variants have been widely adopted for image captioning. In RNNs, the production of a caption is driven by a sequence of latent states. Existing captioning models usually represent latent states as vectors, taking this practice for granted. We rethink this choice and study an alternative formulation, namely using two-dimensional maps to encode latent states. This is motivated by the curiosity about a question: *how the spatial structures in the latent states affect the resultant captions?* Our study on MSCOCO and Flickr30k leads to two significant observations. First, the formulation with 2D states is generally more effective in captioning, consistently achieving higher performance with comparable parameter sizes. Second, 2D states preserve spatial locality. Taking advantage of this, we *visually* reveal the internal dynamics in the process of caption generation, as well as the connections between input visual domain and output linguistic domain.

1 Introduction

Image captioning, a task of generating short descriptions for given images, has received increasing attention in recent years. Latest works on this task [1–4] mostly adopt the encoder-decoder paradigm, where a recurrent neural network (RNN) or one of its variants, *e.g.* GRU [5] and LSTM [6], is used for generating the captions. Specifically, the RNN maintains a series of *latent states*. At each step, it takes the visual features together with the preceding word as input, updates the latent state, then estimates the conditional probability of the next word. Here, the latent states serve as pivots that connect between the visual and the linguistic domains.

Following the standard practice in language models [5,7], existing captioning models usually formulate the latent states as *vectors* and the connections between them as fully-connected transforms. Whereas this is a natural choice

B. Dai and D. Ye—Equal contribution.

V. Ferrari et al. (Eds.): ECCV 2018, LNCS 11209, pp. 294–310, 2018.
https://doi.org/10.1007/978-3-030-01228-1_18

for purely linguistic tasks, it becomes a question when the visual domain comes into play, *e.g.* in the task of image captioning.

Along with the rise of deep learning, convolutional neural networks (CNN) have become the dominant models for many computer vision tasks [8,9]. *Convolution* has a distinctive property, namely *spatial locality*, *i.e.* each output element corresponds to a local region in the input. This property allows the spatial structures to be maintained by the feature maps across layers. The significance of spatial locality for vision tasks have been repeatedly demonstrated in previous work [8,10–13].

Image captioning is a task that needs to bridge both the linguistic and the visual domains. Thus for this task, it is important to capture and preserve properties of the visual content in the latent states. This motivates us to explore an alternative formulation for image captioning, namely representing the latent states with 2D maps and connecting them via convolutions. As opposed to the standard formulation, this variant is capable of preserving spatial locality, and therefore it may strengthen the role of visual structures in the process of caption generation.

We compared both formulations, namely the standard one with vector states and the alternative one that uses 2D states, which we refer to as *RNN-2DS*. Our study shows: (1) The spatial structures significantly impact the captioning process. Editing the latent states, *e.g.* suppressing certain regions in the states, can lead to substantially different captions. (2) Preserving the spatial structures in the latent states is beneficial for captioning. On two public datasets, MSCOCO [14] and Flickr30k [15], RNN-2DS achieves notable performance gain consistently across different settings. In particular, a simple RNN-2DS without gating functions already outperforms more sophisticated networks with vector states, *e.g.* LSTM. Using 2D states in combination with more advanced cells, *e.g.* GRU, can further boost the performance. (3) Using 2D states makes the captioning process amenable to visual interpretation. Specifically, we take advantage of the spatial locality and develop a simple yet effective way to identify the connections between latent states and visual regions. This enables us to visualize the dynamics of the states as a caption is being generated, as well as the connections between the visual domain and the linguistic domain.

In summary, our contributions mainly lie in three aspects. First, we rethink the form of latent states in image captioning models, for which existing work simply follows the standard practice and adopts the vectorized representations. To our best knowledge, this is the first study that systematically explores two dimensional states in the context of image captioning. Second, our study challenges the prevalent practice, which reveals the significance of spatial locality in image captioning and suggests that the formulation with 2D states and convolution is more effective. Third, leveraging the spatial locality of the alternative formulation, we develop a simple method that can visualize the dynamics of the latent states in the decoding process.

2 Related Work

Image Captioning. Image captioning has been an active research topic in computer vision. Early techniques mainly rely on detection results. Kulkarni *et al.* [16] proposed to first detect visual concepts including objects and visual relationships [17], and then generate captions by filling sentence templates. Farhadi *et al.* [18] proposed to generate captions for a given image by retrieving from training captions based on detected concepts.

In recent years, the methods based on neural networks are gaining ground. Particularly, the encoder-decoder paradigm [1], which uses a CNN [19] to encode visual features and then uses an LSTM net [6] to decode them into a caption, was shown to outperform classical techniques and has been widely adopted. Along with this direction, many variants have been proposed [2,20–22], where Xu *et al.* [2] proposed to use a dynamic attention map to guide the decoding process. And Yao *et al.* [22] additionally incorporate visual attributes detected from the images, obtaining further improvement. While achieving significant progress, all these methods rely on *vectors* to encode visual features and to represent latent states.

Multi-dimensional RNN. Existing works that aim at extending RNN to more dimensions roughly fall into three categories:

(1) RNNs are applied on *multi-dimensional grids*, *e.g.* the 2D grid of pixels, via recurrent connections along different dimensions [23,24]. Such extensions have been used in image generation [25] and CAPTCHA recognition [26].
(2) Latent states of RNN cells are stacked across multiple steps to form feature maps. This formulation is usually used to capture temporal statistics, *e.g.* those in language processing [27,28] and audio processing [29]. For both categories above, the latent states are still represented by *1D vectors*. Hence, they are essentially different from this work.
(3) Latent states themselves are represented as multi-dimensional arrays. The RNN-2DS studied in this paper belongs to the third category, where latent states are represented as 2D feature maps. The idea of extending RNN with 2D states has been explored in various vision problems, such as rainfall prediction [30], super-resolution [11], instance segmentation [12], and action recognition [13]. It is worth noting that all these works focused on tackling visual tasks, where both the inputs and the outputs are in 2D forms. To our best knowledge, this is the first work that studies recurrent networks with 2D states in image captioning. A key contribution of this work is that it reveals the significance of 2D states in connecting the visual and the linguistic domains.

Interpretation. There are studies to analyze recurrent networks. Karpathy *et al.* [31] try to interpret the latent states of conventional LSTM models for natural language understanding. Similar studies have been conducted by Ding *et al.* [32] for neural machine translation. However, these studies focused on linguistic analysis, while our study tries to identify the connections between linguistic and visual domains by leveraging the spatial locality of the 2D states.

Our visualization method on 2D latent states also differs from the attention module [2] fundamentally, in both theory and implementation. (1) Attention is a *mechanism* specifically designed to guide the focus of a model, while the 2D states are a form of *representation*. (2) Attention is usually implemented as a sub-network. In our work, the 2D states by themselves do not introduce any attention mechanism. The visualization method is mainly for the purpose of interpretation, which helps us better understand the internal dynamics of the decoding process. To our best knowledge, this is accomplished for the first time for image captioning.

3 Formulations

To begin with, we review the encoder-decoder framework [1] which represents latent states as 1D vectors. Subsequently, we reformulate the latent states as multi-channel 2D feature maps for this framework. These formulations are the basis for our comparative study.

3.1 Encoder-Decoder for Image Captioning

The encoder-decoder framework generates a caption for a given image in two stages, namely *encoding* and *decoding*. Specifically, given an image I, it first encodes the image into a feature vector $\mathbf{v}$, with a *Convolutional Neural Network (CNN)*, such as VGGNet [19] or ResNet [8]. The feature vector $\mathbf{v}$ is then fed to a *Recurrent Neural Network (RNN)* and decoded into a sequence of words $(w_1, \ldots, w_T)$. For decoding, the RNN implements a recurrent process driven by latent states, which generates the caption through multiple steps, each yielding a word. Specifically, it maintains a set of latent states, represented by a vector $\mathbf{h}_t$ that would be updated along the way. The computational procedure can be expressed by the formulas below:

$$\mathbf{h}_0 = \mathbf{0}, \quad \mathbf{h}_t = g(\mathbf{h}_{t-1}, \mathbf{x}_t, \mathbf{I}), \tag{1}$$

$$\mathbf{p}_{t|1:t-1} = \text{Softmax}(\mathbf{W}_p \mathbf{h}_t), \tag{2}$$

$$w_t \sim \mathbf{p}_{t|1:t-1}. \tag{3}$$

The procedure can be explained as follows. First, the latent state $\mathbf{h}_0$ is initialized to be zeros. At the t-th step, $\mathbf{h}_t$ is updated by an RNN cell g, which takes three inputs: the previous state $\mathbf{h}_{t-1}$, the word produced at the preceding step (represented by an embedded vector $\mathbf{x}_t$), and the visual feature $\mathbf{v}$. Here, the cell function g can take a simple form:

$$g(\mathbf{h}, \mathbf{x}, \mathbf{v}) = \tanh\left(\mathbf{W}_h \mathbf{h} + \mathbf{W}_x \mathbf{x} + \mathbf{W}_v \mathbf{v}\right). \tag{4}$$

More sophisticated cells, such as GRU [5] and LSTM [6], are also increasingly adopted in practice. To produce the word w_t, the latent state $\mathbf{h}_t$ will be transformed into a probability vector $\mathbf{p}_{t|1:t-1}$ via a fully-connected linear transform

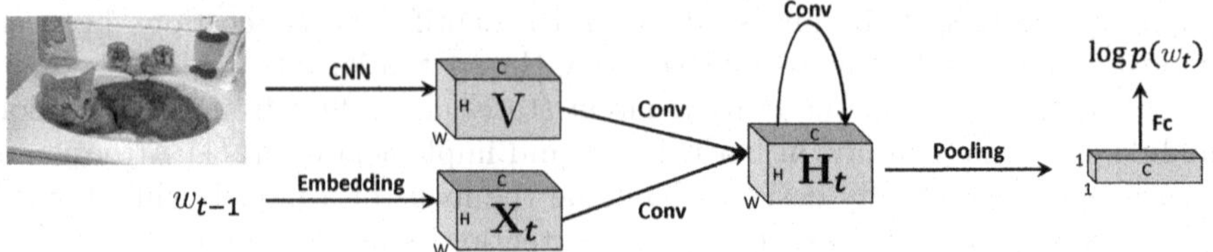

Fig. 1. The overall structure of the encoder-decoder framework with RNN-2DS. Given an image I, a CNN first turns it into a multi-channel feature map $\mathbf{V}$ that preserves high-level spatial structures. $\mathbf{V}$ will then be fed to an RNN-2DS, where the latent state $\mathbf{H}_t$ is also represented by multi-channel maps and the state transition is via convolution. At each step, the 2D states are transformed into a 1D vectors and then decoded into conditional probabilities of words.

$\mathbf{W}_p \mathbf{h}_t$ followed by a softmax function. Here, $\mathbf{p}_{t|1:t-1}$ can be considered as the probabilities of w_t conditioned on previous states.

Despite the differences in their architectures, all existing RNN-based captioning models represent latent states as *vectors* without explicitly preserving the spatial structures. In what follows, we will discuss the alternative choice that represents latent states as 2D multi-channel feature maps.

3.2 From 1D to 2D

From a technical standpoint, a natural way to maintain spatial structures in latent states is to formulate them as 2D maps and employ convolutions for state transitions, which we refer to as RNN-2DS.

Specifically, as shown in Fig. 1, the visual feature $\mathbf{V}$, the latent state $\mathbf{H}_t$, and the word embedding $\mathbf{X}_t$ are all represented as 3D tensors of size $C \times H \times W$. Such a tensor can be considered as a multi-channel map, which comprises C channels, each of size $H \times W$. Unlike the normal setting where the visual feature is derived from the activation of a fully-connected layer, $\mathbf{V}$ here is derived from the activation of a convolutional layer that preserves spatial structures. And $\mathbf{X}_t$ is the 2D word embedding for w_{t-1}, of size $C \times H \times W$. To reduce the number of parameters, we use a lookup table of smaller size $C_x \times H_x \times W_x$ to fetch the raw word embedding, which will be enlarged to $C \times H \times W$ by two convolutional layers[1]. With these representations, state updating can then be formulated using *convolutions*. For example, Eq. (4) can be converted into the following form:

$$\mathbf{H}_t = \text{relu}\left(\mathbf{K}_h \circledast \mathbf{H}_{t-1} + \mathbf{K}_x \circledast \mathbf{X}_t + \mathbf{K}_v \circledast \mathbf{V}\right). \tag{5}$$

Here, $\circledast$ denotes the convolution operator, and $\mathbf{K}_h$, $\mathbf{K}_x$, and $\mathbf{K}_v$ are convolution kernels of size $C \times C \times H_k \times W_k$. It is worth stressing that the modification

[1] In our experiments, the raw word embedding is of size $4 \times 15 \times 15$, and is scaled up to match the size of latent states via two convolutional layers respectively with kernel sizes $32 \times 4 \times 5 \times 5$ and $C \times 32 \times 5 \times 5$.

presented above is very flexible and can easily incorporate more sophisticated cells. For example, the original updating formulas of GRU are

$$\begin{aligned}
\mathbf{r}_t &= \sigma(\mathbf{W}_{rh}\mathbf{h}_{t-1} + \mathbf{W}_{rx}\mathbf{x}_t + \mathbf{W}_{rv}\mathbf{v}), \\
\mathbf{z}_t &= \sigma(\mathbf{W}_{zh}\mathbf{h}_{t-1} + \mathbf{W}_{zx}\mathbf{x}_t + \mathbf{W}_{zv}\mathbf{v}), \\
\tilde{\mathbf{h}}_t &= \tanh(\mathbf{r}_t \circ (\mathbf{W}_{hh}\mathbf{h}_{t-1}) + \mathbf{W}_{hx}\mathbf{x}_t + \mathbf{W}_{hv}\mathbf{v}), \\
\mathbf{h}_t &= \mathbf{z}_t \circ \mathbf{h}_{t-1} + (1 - \mathbf{z}_t) \circ \tilde{\mathbf{h}}_t,
\end{aligned} \tag{6}$$

where σ is the sigmoid function, and $\circ$ is the element-wise multiplication operator. In a similar way, we can convert them to the 2D form as

$$\begin{aligned}
\mathbf{R}_t &= \sigma(\mathbf{K}_{rh} \circledast \mathbf{H}_{t-1} + \mathbf{K}_{rx} \circledast \mathbf{X}_t + \mathbf{K}_{rv} \circledast \mathbf{V}), \\
\mathbf{Z}_t &= \sigma(\mathbf{K}_{zh} \circledast \mathbf{H}_{t-1} + \mathbf{K}_{zx} \circledast \mathbf{X}_t + \mathbf{K}_{zv} \circledast \mathbf{V}), \\
\tilde{\mathbf{H}}_t &= \mathrm{relu}(\mathbf{R}_t \circ (\mathbf{K}_{hh} \circledast \mathbf{H}_{t-1}) + \mathbf{K}_{hx} \circledast \mathbf{X}_t + \mathbf{K}_{hv} \circledast \mathbf{V}), \\
\mathbf{H}_t &= \mathbf{Z}_t \circ \mathbf{H}_{t-1} + (1 - \mathbf{Z}_t) \circ \tilde{\mathbf{H}}_t.
\end{aligned} \tag{7}$$

Given the latent states $\mathbf{H}_t$, the word w_t can be generated as follows. First, we compress $\mathbf{H}_t$ (of size $C \times H \times W$) into a C-dimensional vector $\mathbf{h}_t$ by mean pooling across spatial dimensions. Then, we transform $\mathbf{h}_t$ into a probability vector $\mathbf{p}_{t|1:t-1}$ and draw w_t therefrom, following Eqs. (2) and (3). Note that the pooling operation could be replaced with more sophisticated modules, such as an attention module, to summarize the information from all locations for word prediction. We choose the pooling operation as it adds zero extra parameters, which makes the comparison between 1D and 2D states fair.

Since this reformulation is generic, besides the encoder-decoder framework, it can be readily extended to other captioning models that adopt RNNs as the language module, *e.g.* Att2in [3] and Review Net [33].

4 Qualitative Studies on 2D States

Thanks to the preserved spatial locality, the use of 2D states makes the framework amenable to some qualitative analysis. Taking advantage of this, we present three studies in this section: (1) We manipulate the 2D states and investigate how it impacts the generated captions. The results of this study would corroborate the statement that 2D states help to preserve spatial structures. (2) Leveraging the spatial locality, we identify the associations between the activations of latent states and certain subregions of the input image. Based on the dynamic associations between state activations and the corresponding subregions, we can visually reveal the internal dynamics of the decoding process. (3) Through latent states we also interpret the connections between the visual and the linguistic domains.

4.1 State Manipulation

We study how the spatial structures of the 2D latent states influence the resultant captions by controlling the accessible parts of the latent states.

Fig. 2. This figure lists several images with generated captions relying on various parts of RNN-2DS's states. The accessible part is marked with blue color in each case. (Color figure online)

As discussed in Sect. 3.2, the prediction at t-th step is based on $\mathbf{h}_t$, which is pooled from $\mathbf{H}_t$ across H and W. In other words, $\mathbf{h}_t$ summarizes the information from the entire area of $\mathbf{H}_t$. In this experiment, we replace the original region $(1, 1, H, W)$ with a subregion between the corners (x_1, y_1) and (x_2, y_2) to get a modified summarizing vector $\mathbf{h}'_t$ as

$$\mathbf{h}'_t = \frac{1}{(y_2 - y_1 + 1)(x_2 - x_1 + 1)} \sum_{i=y_1}^{y_2} \sum_{j=x_1}^{x_2} \mathbf{H}_t|_{(i,j)}. \tag{8}$$

Here, $\mathbf{h}'_t$ only captures a subregion of the image, on which the probabilities for the word w_t is computed. We expect that this caption only partially reflects the visual semantics.

Figure 2 shows several images together with the captions generated using different subregions of the 2D states. Take the bottom-left image in Fig. 2 for an instance, when using only the upper half of the latent states, the decoder generates a caption focusing on the cat, which indeed appears in the upper half of the image. Similarly, using only the lower half of the latent states results in a caption that talks about the book located in the lower half of the image. In other words, depending on a specific subregion of the latent states, a decoder

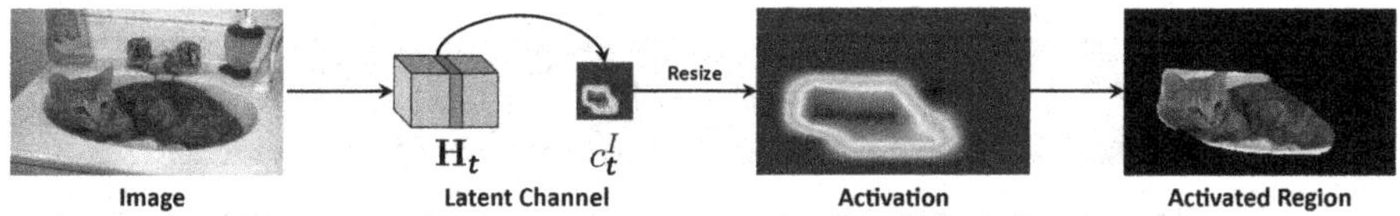

Fig. 3. This figure shows our procedure of finding the activated region of a latent channel at the t-th step.

with 2D states tends to generate a caption that conveys the visual content of the corresponding area in the input image. This observation suggests that the 2D latent states do preserve the spatial structures of the input image.

Manipulating latent states differs essentially from the passive data-driven attention module [2] commonly adopted in captioning models. It is a controllable operation, and does not require a specific module to achieve such functionality. With this operation, we can extend a captioning model with 2D states to allow *active* management of the focus, which, for example, can be used to generate multiple complementary sentences for an image. While the attention module can be considered as an automatic manipulation on latent states, the combination of 2D states and the attention mechanism worths exploring in the future work.

4.2 Revealing Decoding Dynamics

This study intends to analyze internal dynamics of the decoding process, *i.e.* how the latent states evolve in a series of decoding steps. We believe that it can help us better understand how a caption is generated based on the visual content. The spatial locality of the 2D states allows us to study this in an efficient and effective way.

We use *activated regions* to align the activations of the latent states at different decoding steps with the subregions in the input image. Specifically, we treat the channels of 2D states as the basic units in our study, which are 2D maps of activation values. Given a state channel c at the t-th decoding step, we resize it to the size of the input image I via bicubic interpolation. The pixel locations in I whose corresponding interpolated activations are above a certain threshold[2] are considered to be *activated*. The collection of all such pixel locations is referred to as the *activated region* for the state channel c at the t-th decoding step, as shown in Fig. 3.

With activated regions computed respectively at different decoding steps for one state channel, we may visually reveal the internal dynamics of the decoding process at that channel. Figure 4 shows several images and their generated captions, along with the activated regions of some channels following the decoding processes. These channels are selected as they are associated with nouns in the generated captions, which we will introduce in the next section. Via this study we found that (1) The activated regions of channels often capture salient visual

[2] See released code for more details.

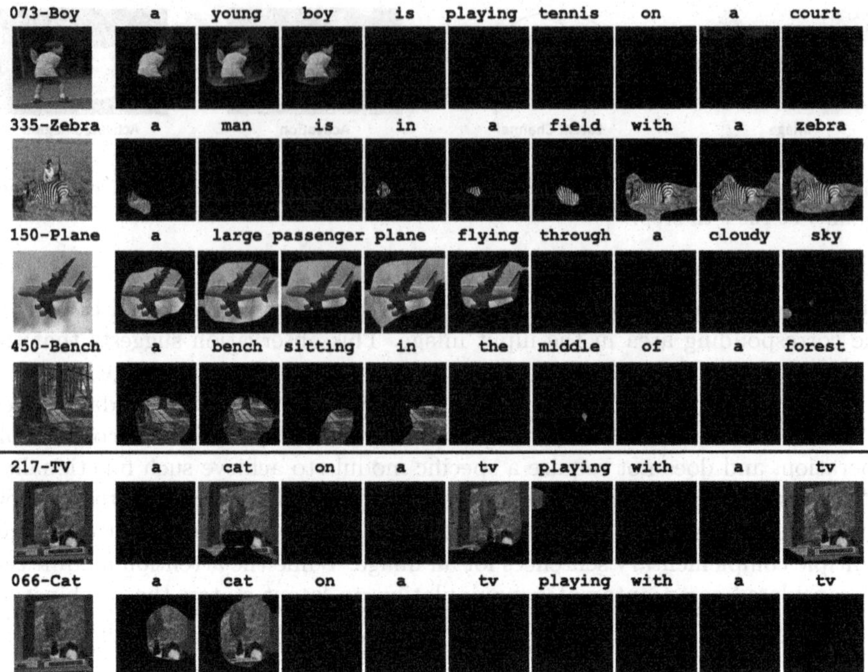

Fig. 4. This figure shows the changes of several channels, in terms of the activated regions, during the decoding processes. On the last two cases, changes of two channels in the same decoding process are shown and compared. (Best viewed in high resolution)

entities in the image, and also reflect the surrounding context occasionally. (2) During a decoding process, different channels have different dynamics. For a channel associated with a noun, the activated regions of its associated channel become significant as the decoding process approaches the point where the noun is produced, and the channel becomes deactivated afterwards.

The revealed dynamics can help us better understand the decoding process, which also point out some directions for future study. For instance, in Fig. 4, the visual semantics are distributed to different channels, and the decoder moves its focus from one channel to another. The mechanism that triggers such movements remains needed to be explored.

4.3 Connecting Visual and Linguistic Domains

Here we investigate how the visual domain is connected to the linguistic domain. As the latent states serve as pivots that connect both domains, we try to use the activations of the latent states to identify the detailed connections.

First, we find the associations between the latent states and the words. Similar to Sect. 4.2, we use state channels as the basic units here, so that we can use the activated regions which connect the latent states to the input image.

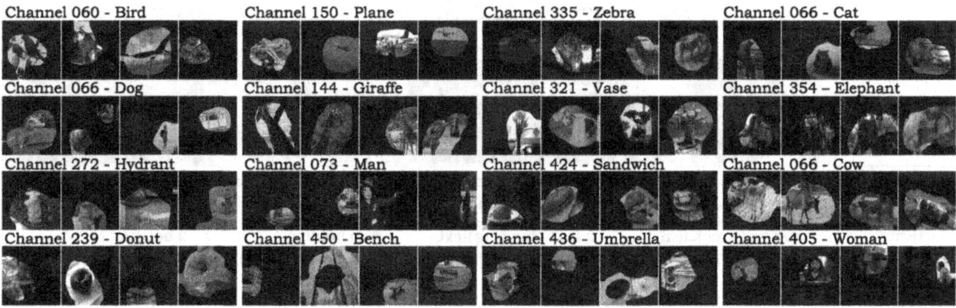

Fig. 5. Sample words and their associated channels in *RNN-2DS-(*512, 7, 7*)*. For each word, 5 activated regions of its associated channel on images that contain this word in the generated captions are shown. The activated regions are chosen at the steps where the words are produced. (Best viewed in high resolution)

In Sect. 4.2, we have observed that a channel associated with a certain word is likely to remain active until the word is produced, and its activation level will drop significantly afterwards thus preventing that word from being generated again. Hence, one way to judge whether a channel is associated with a word is to estimate the difference in its level of activations before and after the word is generated. The channel that yields *maximum difference* can be considered as the one associated with the word[3].

Words and Associated Channels. For each word in the vocabulary, we could find its associated channel as described above, and study the corresponding activated regions, as shown in Fig. 5. We found that (1) Only nouns have strong associations with the state channels, which is consistent with the fact that spatial locality is highly-related with the visual entities described as nouns. (2) Some channels have multiple associated nouns. For example, *Channel*-066 is associated with *"cat"*, *"dog"*, and *"cow"*. This is not surprising – since there are more nouns in the vocabulary than the number of channels, some nouns have to share channels. Here, it is worth noting that the nouns that share a channel tend to be visually relevant. This shows that the latent channels can capture meaningful visual structures. (3) Not all channels have associated words. Some channels may capture abstract notions instead of visual elements. The study of such channels is an interesting direction in the future.

Match of Words and Associated Channels. On top of the activated regions, we could also estimate the match between a word and its associated channel. Specifically, noticing the activated regions visually look like the attention maps in [34], we borrow the measurement of attention correctness from [34], to estimate the match. *Attention correctness* computes the similarity between a human-annotated segmentation mask of a word, and the activated region of its asso-

[3] See released code for more details.

Original	a red and red bird perched on a branch	a man getting ready to board a plane	a man standing in front of a fence with a bird	a vase filled with pink and yellow flowers
Deactivate word-associated channel	a red and green leaf filled with lots of fruit	a man standing next to a boarding gate	a man holding a baseball bat over his shoulder	a bouquet of red flowers sitting on a table

Fig. 6. This figure lists some images with generated captions before and after some word-associated channel being deactivated. The word that associates with the deactivated channel is marked in red. (Color figure online)

ciated channel, at the step the word is produced. The computation is done by summing up the normalized activations within that mask. On MSCOCO [14], we evaluated the attention correctness on 80 nouns that have human-annotated masks. As a result, the averaged attention correctness is 0.316. For reference, following the same setting except for replacing the activated regions with the attention maps, AdaptiveAttention [4], a state-of-the-art captioning model, got a result of 0.213.

Deactivation of Word-Associated Channels. We also verify the match of the found associations between the state channels and the words alternatively via an ablation study, where we compare the generated captions with and without the involvement of a certain channel. Specifically, on images that contain the target word w in the generated captions, we re-run the decoding process, in which we deactivate the associated channel of w by clipping its value to zero at all steps, then compare the generated captions with previous ones. As shown in Fig. 6, deactivating a word-associated channel leads to the miss of the corresponding words in the generated captions, even though the input still contains the visual semantics for those words. This ablation study corroborates the validity of our found associations.

5 Comparison on Captioning Performance

In this section, we compare the encoder-decoder framework with 1D states and 2D states. Specifically, we run our studies on MSCOCO [14] and Flickr30k [15], where we at first introduce the settings, followed by the results.

5.1 Settings

MSCOCO [14] contains 122, 585 images. We follow the splits in [35], using 112, 585 images for training, 5, 000 for validation, and the remaining 5, 000 for testing. Flickr30K [15] contains 31, 783 images in total, and we follow splits in

[35], which has 1,000 images respectively for validation and testing, and the rest for training. In both datasets, each image comes with 5 ground-truth captions. To obtain a vocabulary, we turn words to lowercase and remove those with non-alphabet characters. Then we replace words that appear less than 6 times with a special token *UNK*, resulting in a vocabulary of size 9,487 for MSCOCO, and 7,000 for Flickr30k. Following the common convention [35], we truncated all ground-truth captions to have at most 18 words.

All captioning methods in our experiments are based on the encoder-decoder paradigm [1]. We use ResNet-152 [8] pretrained on ImageNet [9] as the encoder in all methods. In particular, we take the output of the layer `res5c` as the visual feature $\mathbf{V}$. We use the combination of the cell type and the state shape to refer to each type of the decoder. *e.g.* *LSTM-1DS-(L)* refers to a standard LSTM-based decoder with latent states of size L, and *GRU-2DS-*(C, H, W) refers to an RNN-2DS decoder with GRU cells as in Eq. (7), whose latent states are of size $C \times H \times W$. Moreover, all RNN-2DS models adopt a raw word-embedding of size $4 \times 15 \times 15$, except when a different size is explicitly specified. The convolution kernels $\mathbf{K}_h$, $\mathbf{K}_x$, and $\mathbf{K}_v$ share the same size $C \times C \times 3 \times 3$.

The focus of this paper is the representations of latent states. To ensure fair comparison, no additional modules including the attention module [2] are added to the methods. Moreover, no other training strategies are utilized, such as the scheduled sampling [36], except for the maximum likelihood objective, where we use the ADAM optimizer [37]. During training, we first fix the CNN encoder and optimize the decoder with learning rate 0.0004 in the first 20 epochs, and then jointly optimize both the encoder and decoder, until the performance on the validation set saturates.

For evaluation, we report the results using metrics including BLEU-4 (B4) [38], METEOR (MT) [39], ROUGE (RG) [40], CIDER (CD) [41], and SPICE (SP) [42].

5.2 Comparative Results

First, we compared *RNN-2DS* with *LSTM-1DS*. The former has 2D states with the simplest type of cells while the latter has 1D states with sophisticated LSTM cells. As the capacity of a model is closely related to the number of parameters, to ensure a fair comparison, each config of *RNN-2DS* is compared to an *LSTM-1DS* config *with a similar number of parameters*. In this way, the comparative results will signify the differences in the inherent expressive power of both formulations.

The resulting curves in terms of different metrics are shown in Fig. 7, in which we can see that *RNN-2DS* outperforms *LSTM-1DS* consistently, across different parameter sizes and under different metrics. These results show that *RNN-2DS*, with the states that preserve spatial locality, can capture both visual and linguistic information more efficiently.

We also compared different types of decoders with similar numbers of parameters, namely *RNN-1DS*, *GRU-1DS*, *LSTM-1DS*, *RNN-2DS*, *GRU-2DS*, and *LSTM-2DS*. Table 1 shows the results of these decoders on both datasets, from

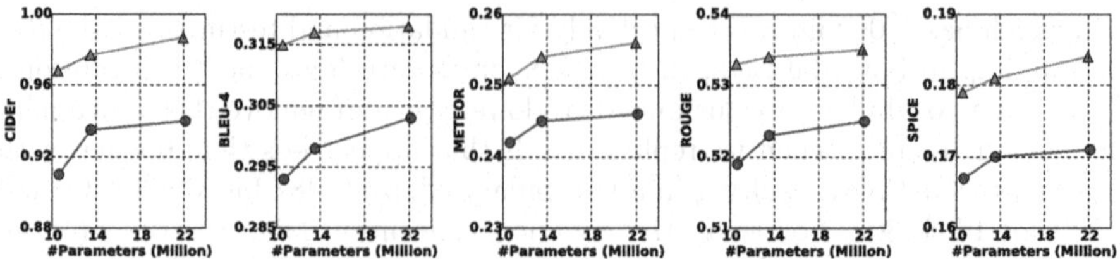

Fig. 7. The results, in terms of different metrics, obtained using RNN-2DS (green) and LSTM-1DS (red) on the MSCOCO offline test set with similar parameter sizes. Specifically, RNN-2DS of sizes 10.57M, 13.48M and 21.95M have compared to LSTM-1DS of sizes 10.65M, 13.52M and 22.14M. (Color figure online)

Table 1. The results obtained using different decoders on the offline and online test sets of MSCOCO, and the test set of Flickr30k, where METEOR (MT) [39] is omitted due to space limitation, and no SPICE (SP) [42] is reported by the online test set of MSCOCO.

Model	#Param	COCO-offline				COCO-online			Flickr30k			
		CD	B4	RG	SP	CD	B4	RG	CD	B4	RG	SP
RNN-1DS-(595)	13.58M	0.914	0.293	0.520	0.168	0.868	0.286	0.515	0.353	0.195	0.427	0.117
GRU-1DS-(525)	13.53M	0.920	0.295	0.520	0.169	0.889	0.291	0.518	0.360	0.195	0.428	0.117
LSTM-1DS-(500)	13.52M	0.935	0.298	0.523	0.170	0.904	0.295	0.523	0.381	0.202	0.437	0.120
RNN-2DS-(256,7,7)	13.48M	0.977	0.317	0.534	0.181	0.930	0.305	0.527	0.420	0.217	0.442	0.125
GRU-2DS-(256,7,7)	17.02M	1.001	0.323	0.539	0.186	0.962	0.316	0.535	0.438	0.218	0.445	0.131
LSTM-2DS-(256,7,7)	18.79M	0.994	0.319	0.538	0.187	0.958	0.313	0.531	0.427	0.220	0.444	0.132

which we observe: (1) *RNN-2DS* outperforms *RNN-1DS*, *GRU-1DS*, and *LSTM-1DS*, indicating that embedding latent states in 2D forms is more effective. (2) *GRU-2DS*, which is also based on the proposed formulation but adds several gate functions, surpasses other decoders and yields the best result. This suggests that the techniques developed for conventional RNNs including gate functions and attention modules [2] are very likely to benefit RNNs with 2D states as well.

Figure 8 includes some qualitative samples, in which we can see the captions generated by *LSTM-1DS* rely heavily on the language priors, which sometimes contain the phrases that are not consistent with the visual content but appear frequently in training captions. On the contrary, the sentences from *RNN-2DS* and *GRU-2DS* are more relevant to the visual content.

5.3 Ablation Study

Table 2 compares the performances obtained with different design choices in *RNN-2DS*, including pooling methods, activation functions, and sizes of word embeddings, kernels and latent states The results show that mean pooling outperforms max pooling by a significant margin, indicating that information from all locations is significant. The table also shows the best combination of modeling choices for RNN-2DS: mean pooling, ReLU, the word embeddings of size $4 \times 15 \times 15$, the kernel of size 3×3, and the latent states of size $256 \times 7 \times 7$.

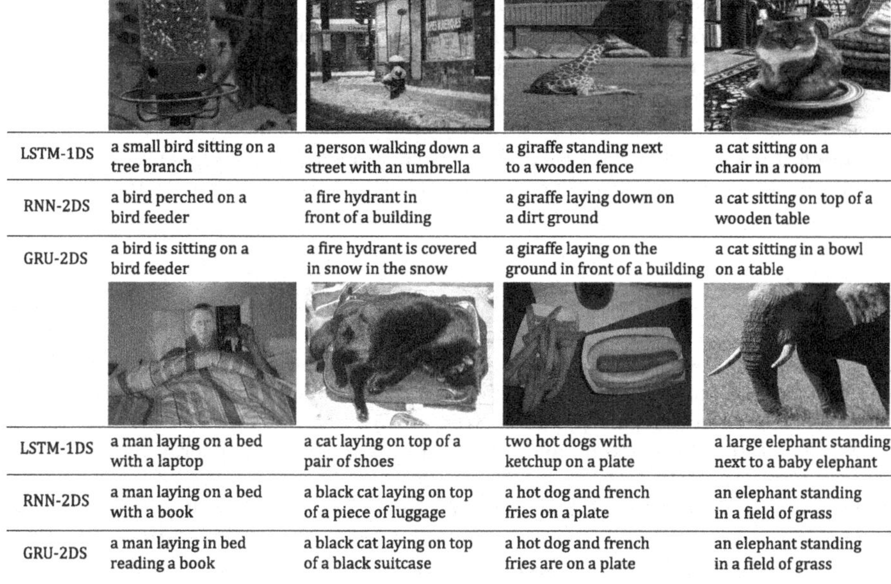

LSTM-1DS
a small bird sitting on a tree branch
a person walking down a street with an umbrella
a giraffe standing next to a wooden fence
a cat sitting on a chair in a room
RNN-2DS
a bird perched on a bird feeder
a fire hydrant in front of a building
a giraffe laying down on a dirt ground
a cat sitting on top of a wooden table
GRU-2DS
a bird is sitting on a bird feeder
a fire hydrant is covered in snow in the snow
a giraffe laying on the ground in front of a building
a cat sitting in a bowl on a table
LSTM-1DS
a man laying on a bed with a laptop
a cat laying on top of a pair of shoes
two hot dogs with ketchup on a plate
a large elephant standing next to a baby elephant
RNN-2DS
a man laying on a bed with a book
a black cat laying on top of a piece of luggage
a hot dog and french fries on a plate
an elephant standing in a field of grass
GRU-2DS
a man laying in bed reading a book
a black cat laying on top of a black suitcase
a hot dog and french fries are on a plate
an elephant standing in a field of grass

Fig. 8. This figure shows some qualitative samples of captions generated by different decoders, where words in red indicate they are inconsistent with the image. (Color figure online)

Table 2. The results obtained on the MSCOCO offline test set using RNN-2DS with different choices on pooling functions, activation functions, word-embeddings, kernels and latent states. Except for the first row, each row only lists the choice that is different from the first row. "-" means the same.

Pooling	Activation	Word-Embedding	Kernel	Latent-State	CD	B4	MT	RG	SP
Mean	ReLU	$4 \times 15 \times 15$	3×3	$256 \times 7 \times 7$	0.977	0.317	0.254	0.534	0.181
-	tanh	-	-	-	0.924	0.302	0.244	0.522	0.174
Max	-	-	-	-	0.850	0.279	0.233	0.507	0.166
-	-	$1 \times 15 \times 15$	-	-	0.965	0.313	0.251	0.532	0.180
-	-	$7 \times 15 \times 15$	-	-	0.951	0.309	0.250	0.529	0.179
-	-	-	1×1	-	0.927	0.298	0.247	0.522	0.177
-	-	-	5×5	-	0.951	0.308	0.250	0.529	0.177
-	-	-	-	$256 \times 5 \times 5$	0.934	0.300	0.245	0.523	0.173
-	-	-	-	$256 \times 11 \times 11$	0.927	0.300	0.246	0.523	0.176

6 Conclusions and Future Work

In this paper, we studied the impact of embedding latent states as 2D multi-channel feature maps in the context of image captioning. Compared to the standard practice that embeds latent states as 1D vectors, 2D states consistently achieve higher captioning performances across different settings. Such representations also preserve the spatial locality of the latent states, which helps reveal the internal dynamics of the decoding process, and interpret the connections between visual and linguistic domains. We plan to combine the decoder having 2D states with other modules commonly used in captioning community, including the attention module [2], for further exploration.

Acknowledgement. This work is partially supported by the Big Data Collaboration Research grant from SenseTime Group (CUHK Agreement No. TS1610626), the General Research Fund (GRF) of Hong Kong (No. 14236516).

References

1. Vinyals, O., Toshev, A., Bengio, S., Erhan, D.: Show and tell: a neural image caption generator. In: Proceedings of the IEEE Conference on Computer Vision and Pattern Recognition, pp. 3156–3164 (2015)
2. Xu, K., et al.: Show, attend and tell: Neural image caption generation with visual attention. In: ICML, vol. 14, pp. 77–81 (2015)
3. Rennie, S.J., Marcheret, E., Mroueh, Y., Ross, J., Goel, V.: Self-critical sequence training for image captioning. arXiv preprint arXiv:1612.00563 (2016)
4. Lu, J., Xiong, C., Parikh, D., Socher, R.: Knowing when to look: Adaptive attention via a visual sentinel for image captioning. arXiv preprint arXiv:1612.01887 (2016)
5. Cho, K., et al.: Learning phrase representations using RNN encoder-decoder for statistical machine translation. arXiv preprint arXiv:1406.1078 (2014)
6. Hochreiter, S., Schmidhuber, J.: Long short-term memory. Neural Comput. **9**(8), 1735–1780 (1997)
7. Graves, A.: Generating sequences with recurrent neural networks. arXiv preprint arXiv:1308.0850 (2013)
8. He, K., Zhang, X., Ren, S., Sun, J.: Deep residual learning for image recognition. arXiv preprint arXiv:1512.03385 (2015)
9. Russakovsky, O., et al.: ImageNet large scale visual recognition challenge. Int. J. Comput. Vis. (IJCV) **115**(3), 211–252 (2015)
10. Bau, D., Zhou, B., Khosla, A., Oliva, A., Torralba, A.: Network dissection: quantifying interpretability of deep visual representations. arXiv preprint arXiv:1704.05796 (2017)
11. Huang, Y., Wang, W., Wang, L.: Bidirectional recurrent convolutional networks for multi-frame super-resolution. In: Advances in Neural Information Processing Systems, pp. 235–243 (2015)
12. Romera-Paredes, B., Torr, P.H.S.: Recurrent instance segmentation. In: Leibe, B., Matas, J., Sebe, N., Welling, M. (eds.) ECCV 2016. LNCS, vol. 9910, pp. 312–329. Springer, Cham (2016). https://doi.org/10.1007/978-3-319-46466-4_19
13. Li, Z., Gavrilyuk, K., Gavves, E., Jain, M., Snoek, C.G.: Videolstm convolves, attends and flows for action recognition. Comput. Vis. Image Underst. **166**, 41–50 (2017)
14. Lin, T.-Y., et al.: Microsoft COCO: common objects in context. In: Fleet, D., Pajdla, T., Schiele, B., Tuytelaars, T. (eds.) ECCV 2014. LNCS, vol. 8693, pp. 740–755. Springer, Cham (2014). https://doi.org/10.1007/978-3-319-10602-1_48
15. Young, P., Lai, A., Hodosh, M., Hockenmaier, J.: From image descriptions to visual denotations: new similarity metrics for semantic inference over event descriptions. Trans. Assoc. Comput. Linguist. **2**, 67–78 (2014)

16. Kulkarni, G., et al.: Babytalk: understanding and generating simple image descriptions. IEEE Trans. Pattern Anal. Mach. Intell. **35**(12), 2891–2903 (2013)
17. Dai, B., Zhang, Y., Lin, D.: Detecting visual relationships with deep relational networks. In: 2017 IEEE Conference on Computer Vision and Pattern Recognition (CVPR), pp. 3298–3308. IEEE (2017)
18. Farhadi, A., et al.: Every picture tells a story: generating sentences from images. In: Daniilidis, K., Maragos, P., Paragios, N. (eds.) ECCV 2010. LNCS, vol. 6314, pp. 15–29. Springer, Heidelberg (2010). https://doi.org/10.1007/978-3-642-15561-1_2
19. Simonyan, K., Zisserman, A.: Very deep convolutional networks for large-scale image recognition. arXiv preprint arXiv:1409.1556 (2014)
20. Dai, B., Fidler, S., Urtasun, R., Lin, D.: Towards diverse and natural image descriptions via a conditional GAN. In: Proceedings of the IEEE International Conference on Computer Vision (2017)
21. Dai, B., Lin, D.: Contrastive learning for image captioning. In: Advances in Neural Information Processing Systems, pp. 898–907 (2017)
22. Yao, T., Pan, Y., Li, Y., Qiu, Z., Mei, T.: Boosting image captioning with attributes. arXiv preprint arXiv:1611.01646 (2016)
23. Graves, A., Fernández, S., Schmidhuber, J.: Multi-dimensional recurrent neural networks. In: de Sá, J.M., Alexandre, L.A., Duch, W., Mandic, D. (eds.) ICANN 2007. LNCS, vol. 4668, pp. 549–558. Springer, Heidelberg (2007). https://doi.org/10.1007/978-3-540-74690-4_56
24. Zuo, Z., et al.: Convolutional recurrent neural networks: Learning spatial dependencies for image representation. In: Proceedings of the IEEE Conference on Computer Vision and Pattern Recognition Workshops, pp. 18–26 (2015)
25. Wu, Z., Lin, D., Tang, X.: Deep Markov random field for image modeling. In: Leibe, B., Matas, J., Sebe, N., Welling, M. (eds.) ECCV 2016. LNCS, vol. 9912, pp. 295–312. Springer, Cham (2016). https://doi.org/10.1007/978-3-319-46484-8_18
26. Rui, C., Jing, Y., Rong-gui, H., Shu-guang, H.: A novel LSTM-RNN decoding algorithm in CAPTCHA recognition. In: 2013 Third International Conference on Instrumentation, Measurement, Computer, Communication and Control (IMCCC), pp. 766–771. IEEE (2013)
27. Wang, C., Jiang, F., Yang, H.: A hybrid framework for text modeling with convolutional rnn. In: Proceedings of the 23rd ACM SIGKDD International Conference on Knowledge Discovery and Data Mining, pp. 2061–2069. ACM (2017)
28. Fu, X., Ch'ng, E., Aickelin, U., See, S.: CRNN: a joint neural network for redundancy detection. In: 2017 IEEE International Conference on Smart Computing (SMARTCOMP), pp. 1–8. IEEE (2017
29. Keren, G., Schuller, B.: Convolutional RNN: an enhanced model for extracting features from sequential data. In: 2016 International Joint Conference on Neural Networks (IJCNN), pp. 3412–3419. IEEE (2016)
30. Xingjian, S., Chen, Z., Wang, H., Yeung, D.Y., Wong, W.K., Woo, W.C.: Convolutional LSTM network: a machine learning approach for precipitation nowcasting. In: Advances in Neural Information Processing Systems, pp. 802–810 (2015)
31. Karpathy, A., Johnson, J., Fei-Fei, L.: Visualizing and understanding recurrent networks. arXiv preprint arXiv:1506.02078 (2015)
32. Ding, Y., Liu, Y., Luan, H., Sun, M.: Visualizing and understanding neural machine translation. In: Proceedings of the 55th Annual Meeting of the Association for Computational Linguistics (Volume 1: Long Papers). vol. 1, pp. 1150–1159 (2017)

33. Yang, Z., Yuan, Y., Wu, Y., Cohen, W.W., Salakhutdinov, R.R.: Review networks for caption generation. In: Advances in Neural Information Processing Systems, pp. 2361–2369 (2016)
34. Liu, C., Mao, J., Sha, F., Yuille, A.L.: Attention correctness in neural image captioning. In: AAAI, pp. 4176–4182 (2017)
35. Karpathy, A., Fei-Fei, L.: Deep visual-semantic alignments for generating image descriptions. In: Proceedings of the IEEE Conference on Computer Vision and Pattern Recognition, pp. 3128–3137 (2015)
36. Bengio, S., Vinyals, O., Jaitly, N., Shazeer, N.: Scheduled sampling for sequence prediction with recurrent neural networks. In: Advances in Neural Information Processing Systems, pp. 1171–1179 (2015)
37. Kingma, D., Ba, J.: Adam: a method for stochastic optimization. arXiv preprint arXiv:1412.6980 (2014)
38. Papineni, K., Roukos, S., Ward, T., Zhu, W.J.: Bleu: a method for automatic evaluation of machine translation. In: Proceedings of the 40th Annual Meeting on Association for Computational Linguistics, pp. 311–318. Association For Computational Linguistics (2002)
39. Lavie, M.D.A.: Meteor universal: language specific translation evaluation for any target language. ACL 2014, p. 376 (2014)
40. Lin, C.Y.: Rouge: a package for automatic evaluation of summaries. In: Text Summarization Branches Out: Proceedings of the ACL 2004 Workshop, Barcelona, Spain, vol. 8 (2004)
41. Vedantam, R., Lawrence Zitnick, C., Parikh, D.: Cider: consensus-based image description evaluation. In: Proceedings of the IEEE Conference on Computer Vision and Pattern Recognition, pp. 4566–4575 (2015)
42. Anderson, P., Fernando, B., Johnson, M., Gould, S.: SPICE: semantic propositional image caption evaluation. In: Leibe, B., Matas, J., Sebe, N., Welling, M. (eds.) ECCV 2016. LNCS, vol. 9909, pp. 382–398. Springer, Cham (2016). https://doi.org/10.1007/978-3-319-46454-1_24

Transductive Semi-Supervised Deep Learning Using Min-Max Features

Weiwei Shi[1], Yihong Gong[1(✉)], Chris Ding[2], Zhiheng Ma[1], Xiaoyu Tao[1], and Nanning Zheng[1]

[1] Institute of Artificial Intelligence and Robotics, Xi'an Jiaotong University, Xi'an, China
{shiweiwei.math,mazhiheng,txy666793}@stu.xjtu.edu.cn,
{ygong,nnzheng}@mail.xjtu.edu.cn

[2] University of Texas at Arlington, Arlington, USA
chqding@uta.edu

Abstract. In this paper, we propose Transductive Semi-Supervised Deep Learning (TSSDL) method that is effective for training Deep Convolutional Neural Network (DCNN) models. The method applies transductive learning principle to DCNN training, introduces confidence levels on unlabeled image samples to overcome unreliable label estimates on outliers and uncertain samples, and develops the Min-Max Feature (MMF) regularization that encourages DCNN to learn feature descriptors with better between-class separability and within-class compactness. TSSDL method is independent of any DCNN architectures and complementary to the latest Semi-Supervised Learning (SSL) methods. Comprehensive experiments on the benchmark datasets CIFAR10 and SVHN have shown that the DCNN model trained by the proposed TSSDL method can produce image classification accuracies compatible to the state-of-the-art SSL methods, and that combining TSSDL with the Mean Teacher method can produce the best classification accuracies on the two benchmark datasets.

Keywords: Transductive Semi-Supervised Deep Learning (TSSDL) Min-Max Feature (MMF) regularization
Deep Convolutional Neural Network (DCNN) · Confidence levels

1 Introduction

To date, Deep Convolutional Neural Networks (DCNNs) have shown state-of-the-art performances in numerous computer vision applications, such as image classification [1–5], object detection [6,7], face recognition [8–10], image retrieval [11–14], etc. One of the main driving forces of these great accomplishments is the availability of large scale image datasets that contain millions of labeled training samples. However, creating a large scale, high quality training set by human labeling is very time-consuming, expensive, or even prohibitive

V. Ferrari et al. (Eds.): ECCV 2018, LNCS 11209, pp. 311–327, 2018.
https://doi.org/10.1007/978-3-030-01228-1_19

(e.g. training set for image semantic segmentation). On the other hand, there are an unlimited number of unlabeled images on the Internet, which can be easily obtained by web crawlers and search engines. In recent years, there have been increased research efforts that employ Semi-Supervised Learning (SSL) approaches to train DCNNs with both labeled and unlabeled image samples. Such research efforts have a great potential to dramatically reduce the cost of training DCNN models with high performance accuracies.

Many traditional SSL methods are based on the so-called label propagation approach [15–18], which measures similarities between training samples, and propagates labels of labeled samples to nearby unlabeled ones. Another line of research works are known as Transductive Semi-Supervised Learning (TSSL) [19–23], in which labels of unlabeled samples are treated as variables, and are determined through the iterative training process. At the end of the training process, a classifier is learned from both the labeled and unlabeled training samples. As additional unlabeled samples are used for training, classifiers generated by SSL and TSSL methods usually outperform their counterparts generated by supervised learning methods given the same amount of labeled training samples.

There are two common problems associated with the traditional SSL and TSSL methods. First, these methods generally require high-quality feature descriptors to measure the similarity distances among the training samples from the very beginning of the training process. This requirement makes them difficult to be applied to DCNN training, because feature descriptors generated by a DCNN model are of low quality at early training stages, and improve gradually along the iterative training process. Second, traditional SSL and TSSL methods treat every unlabeled sample equally, which makes the model learning process vulnerable to outliers and uncertain data samples. This problem will become more severe for training DCNNs, because initial feature descriptors generated by DCNNs are of low quality and unstable, which may mislead the training process into a wrong direction.

Recent research works [24–28] have explored supervisory information from unlabeled image samples by adding different perturbations to each image, and enforcing the label consistency between different perturbed versions of the image. The temporal ensembling (TempEns) work [25] enhances the perturbation-based methods by maintaining an Exponential Moving Average (EMA) of label predictions on each training sample, and penalizing the prediction of the network-in-training which is inconsistent with the corresponding EMA prediction. The Mean Teacher method [26] further improves TempEns by using EMA on DCNN model weights instead of label predictions. These two latest methods have achieved state-of-the-art image classification accuracies in the SSL field.

In this paper, we propose a novel Transductive Semi-Supervised Deep Learning (TSSDL) method that is effective for training DCNN models. The proposed TSSDL method is comprised of three major components. First, we extend the traditional TSSL methods to make it applicable to DCNN training. We also treat the labels of unlabeled samples as variables, and try to determine their optimal labels together with the optimal DCNN parameter set by minimizing the proposed loss function through the iterative training process. To the best of our knowledge, this is the first attempt in the literature to apply the transductive learning principle to DCNN model training. Second, to overcome the problem that low-quality feature descriptors generated by the DCNN model at early training stages may mislead the training process into a wrong direction, we introduce the confidence level r_i for each unlabeled sample $\mathbf{X}_i$, which indicates how reliable is the label vector $\mathbf{y}_i$ of $\mathbf{X}_i$ predicted by the current version of DCNN model. r_i is computed based on the assumption that $\mathbf{y}_i$ will be more reliable if $\mathbf{X}_i$ is located in densely populated regions, and vice versa. This is because label predictions for unlabeled samples in densely populated regions tend to be more accurate than those in sparsely populated ones. Third, we develop the Min-Max Feature (MMF) regularization that enforces features learned by the DCNN model to have the following properties: If two images possess the same label, then the distance between their feature descriptors must be minimized; otherwise, the distance must be larger than a predefined margin. The MMF regularization can be considered as an important extension to the traditional label propagation methods which mandates not only that images with the same label be close to each other in the feature space, but also that images with different labels be separated from each other by a predefined margin. These two mandates serve to force the DCNN model to learn better feature descriptors from the given labeled and unlabeled training samples.

The proposed TSSDL method is independent of any DCNN architectures, and is complementary to the latest SSL methods. Comprehensive experimental evaluations on the benchmark datasets CIFAR10 and SVHN have shown that the DCNN model trained by the proposed TSSDL method can produce image classification accuracies that are compatible to the state-of-the-art SSL methods, and that combining TSSDL with the Mean Teacher method can produce the best classification accuracies on the two benchmark datasets.

To sum up, our main contributions include:

- We extend the traditional TSSL methods to make it applicable to DCNN model training.
- We introduce the confidence level for each unlabeled sample to discount influences from outliers and uncertain samples.
- We develop the MMF regularization to make the DCNN model learn feature descriptors such that images with the same label will be close to each other in the feature space, and that images with different labels will be separated by a predefined margin.

The remaining of this paper is organized as follows: Sect. 2 reviews related works. Section 3 describes our method. Section 4 presents the experimental evaluations and analysis, and Sect. 5 concludes our work.

2 Related Work

In the past, many semi-supervised learning (SSL) methods [19,20,29–32] have been proposed in the literature. A large group of traditional SSL methods are based on the label propagation approach, which infers labels for unlabeled samples by measuring similarities between training samples, and propagating labels of labeled samples to nearby unlabeled ones.

Another line of research works are known as Trasductive Semi-Supervised Learning (TSSL) [19–22]. The key characteristic of TSSL is that labels of unlabeled samples are viewed as optimization variables, and are iteratively updated in the training process. As the learning proceeds, predicted labels of unlabeled samples become more consistent among themselves, and with labels of labeled samples.

Traditional SSL and the TSSL methods assume that feature descriptors of training samples are known and fixed, and their performance accuracies are highly dependent on the quality of the provided feature descriptors. This requirement makes them difficult to be applied to DCNN model training, because in deep learning, feature descriptors are learned during the training process. They are of low quality at early stages, and are gradually improved along the training process.

In recent years, there have been increased research efforts to develop SSL methods for DCNN model training. Some works use unlabeled data to pre-train DCNN models in an unsupervised way, and then fine-tune the models on labeled data [33–36]. Other works use unlabeled data in the entire training process instead of just pre-training. For example, Hoffer *et al.* [37] used the regularization term of entropy minimization to enforce that one sample is assigned to one class to reduce the overlaps between different classes. Weston *et al.* [38] proposed an unsupervised embedding for DCNN training. Kingma *et al.* [39] proposed the deep generative models for SSL. Based on the expectation-maximization algorithm, Papandreou *et al.* [39] developed a DCNN training method for SSL semantic image segmentation. Abbasnejad *et al.* [40] proposed the infinite variational autoencoder for SSL. Haeusser *et al.* [41] proposed a SSL method by association.

There also exist research studies [42–45] that use Generative Adversarial Networks (GAN) to generate additional training samples by optimizing an adversarial game between the discriminator and the generator. Samples generated by GAN can be viewed as a kind of "data augmentation".

A line of works more closely related to our method are the regularizations of features learned by DCNNs. For example, Sajjadi *et al.* [24] proposed to use perturbations (such as random data augmentation, dropout) on images to learn robust features. Miyato *et al.* [27] proposed a virtual adversarial training (VAT) method with the virtual adversarial loss, which improves the robustness of the model's predictions against adversarial perturbations. Rasmus *et al.* [46] proposed a SSL method with ladder networks [47]. Π model [25] evaluates the network twice for each training sample under two different i.i.d perturbations at every iteration of the training process, and enforces the label predictions on the two perturbed versions of the training sample to be consistent. Temporal ensembling (TempEns) [25] enhances the Π model by maintaining an exponential moving average (EMA) of label predictions on each training sample, and using it as the target prediction for the sample. It penalizes the prediction of the network-in-training which is inconsistent with its corresponding target prediction. Mean Teacher [26] further improves TempEns by using EMA on model weights instead of label predictions. To date, TempEns and Mean Teacher have achieved the state-of-the-art image classification accuracies in the SSL field.

However, the latest SSL methods described above only consider the perturbations around each single data point, while ignore the relationships between data points. In other words, these methods have not fully utilized the information, such as the structural information in the unlabeled data. It is known that data points belonging to the same class tend to form clusters. This has motivated us to develop the MMF regularization to utilize the structural information among unlabeled data points.

3 Methodology

3.1 Preliminaries

Let $\mathcal{D} = \mathcal{L} \bigcup \mathcal{U}$ be the entire training set, where $\mathcal{L} = \{(\mathbf{X}_i, \mathbf{y}_i)\}_{i=1}^{L}$, $\mathcal{U} = \{\mathbf{X}_i\}_{i=L+1}^{L+U}$ denote the labeled and unlabeled sample sets, respectively, and $\mathbf{X}_i$ is the ith training sample. If $\mathbf{X}_i \in \mathcal{L}$, then $\mathbf{y}_i = [y_i^1, y_i^2, \cdots, y_i^K]^\top \in \{0,1\}^K$ is the corresponding one-hot ground-truth label vector, where $y_i^j = 1$ if $\mathbf{X}_i$ belongs to the jth class, and $y_i^j = 0$ otherwise. K refers to the number of classes, L, U are the numbers of labeled and unlabeled training samples, respectively. Usually $L \ll U$. Let $N = L + U$ be the total number of training samples.

3.2 Transductive Semi-supervised Deep Learning (TSSDL)

When training a DCNN model using a Supervised Learning (SL) method, the typical loss function can be written as:

$$\ell^{\text{SL}}(\mathcal{X}, \mathcal{Y}; \theta) = \sum_{i=1}^{L} \ell_0(\mathbf{X}_i, \mathbf{y}_i; \theta), \tag{1}$$

where $\mathcal{X} = \{\mathbf{X}_i\}_{i=1}^{L}$, $\mathcal{Y} = \{\mathbf{y}_i\}_{i=1}^{L}$, θ is the entire parameter set of the DCNN model, and $\ell_0(\mathbf{X}_i, \mathbf{y}_i; \theta)$ is the loss for sample $\mathbf{X}_i$. Here, $\mathcal{Y}$ is the manually provided ground-truth label vector set for the training set $\mathcal{X}$, and is fixed throughout the entire training process. If the softmax loss is used, which is a popular choice for most image classification tasks, then Eq. (1) can be rewritten as:

$$\ell^{\text{SL}}(\mathcal{X}, \mathcal{Y}; \theta) = \sum_{i=1}^{L} \text{CEsoftmax}(\mathbf{W}\mathbf{f}(\mathbf{X}_i; \theta), \mathbf{y}_i), \tag{2}$$

where $\mathbf{f}(\mathbf{X}_i; \theta)$ is the output of the DCNN's penultimate layer for sample $\mathbf{X}_i$, which can be considered as the learned feature descriptors of $\mathbf{X}_i$, and $\mathbf{W}$ is the parameters of the last fully-connected layer of the DCNN.

Here CEsoftmax$(\mathbf{a}, \mathbf{b})$ = Cross-Entropy(softmax$(\mathbf{a}), \mathbf{b})$. The goal is to learn an optimal parameter set θ^* that minimizes the loss function: $\theta^* = \arg\min_\theta \ell^{\mathrm{SL}}(\mathcal{X}, \mathcal{Y}; \theta)$.

In contrast, the proposed TSSDL method uses the following loss function to train a DCNN model:

$$\ell^{\mathrm{TSSDL}}(\mathcal{X}, \tilde{\mathcal{Y}}; \theta, \mathcal{R}) = \sum_{i=1}^{N} r_i \cdot \mathrm{CEsoftmax}(\mathbf{Wf}(\mathbf{X}_i; \theta), \tilde{\mathbf{y}}_i), \tag{3}$$

where $\tilde{\mathcal{Y}} = \{\tilde{\mathbf{y}}_i\}_{i=1}^N$ is the estimated set of label vectors for the training set $\mathcal{X} = \{\mathbf{X}_i\}_{i=1}^N$, and each element r_i of $\mathcal{R} = \{r_i\}_{i=1}^N$ is the confidence level for sample $\mathbf{X}_i$, which indicates how reliable is the estimated label vector $\tilde{\mathbf{y}}_i$ of $\mathbf{X}_i$, and is computed in a self-consistent way (to be explained below). If $\mathbf{X}_i \in \mathcal{L}$, $\tilde{\mathbf{y}}_i$ is fixed to its ground-truth label vector $\tilde{\mathbf{y}}_i = \mathbf{y}_i$ throughout the entire training process. For unlabeled training sample $\mathbf{X}_i \in \mathcal{U}$, $\tilde{\mathbf{y}}_i$ is the estimate of its label vector by the current version of the network, and is treated as an optimization variable. As the transductive learning process progresses to its convergence, $\tilde{\mathbf{y}}_i$ gets iterative updates, and converges to the final predicted label vector for $\mathbf{X}_i$. The transductive learning process aims to learn optimal sets of θ^*, $\tilde{\mathcal{Y}}^*$ and $\mathcal{R}^*$ that jointly minimize the loss function:

$$(\tilde{\mathcal{Y}}^*, \theta^*, \mathcal{R}^*) = \arg\min_{\tilde{\mathcal{Y}}, \theta, \mathcal{R}} \ell^{\mathrm{TSSDL}}(\mathcal{X}, \tilde{\mathcal{Y}}; \theta, \mathcal{R}). \tag{4}$$

It is noteworthy to point out that the proposed TSSDL method is different from traditional Transductive Semi-Supervised Learning (TSSL) methods in the following two aspects:

(1) Traditional TSSL methods require a fixed feature descriptor $\mathbf{f}(\mathbf{X}_i)$ for each training sample $\mathbf{X}_i$, whereas the proposed TSSDL method keeps learning, and gradually optimizes $\mathbf{f}(\mathbf{X}_i)$ throughout the training process.
(2) Traditional TSSL methods treat every unlabeled sample $\mathbf{X}_i \in \mathcal{U}$ equally, which makes the learning process vulnerable to outliers and uncertain samples. In contract, the proposed TSSDL method introduces the confidence level r_i for each sample $\mathbf{X}_i$ to discount influences from those adverse samples.

We compute the confidence level r_i for $\mathbf{X}_i$ as follows. For each labeled sample $\mathbf{X}_i \in \mathcal{L}$, we always set its confidence level $r_i = 1$. For each unlabeled sample $\mathbf{X}_i \in \mathcal{U}$, we compute r_i based on the intuition that: (i) outliers and highly uncertain samples usually reside in sparsely populated areas in the feature space; and (ii) samples located in densely populated areas are more likely to be assigned correct labels. Let $\{\mathbf{f}_1, \cdots, \mathbf{f}_N\}$ be the learned feature descriptors of $\{\mathbf{X}_1, \cdots, \mathbf{X}_N\}$ outputted by the current version of the DCNN model (i.e., $\mathbf{f}_i = \mathbf{f}(\mathbf{X}_i; \theta)$). We define the proximity value d_i for $\mathbf{X}_i$ as follows:

$$d_i = \sum_{\mathbf{f}_j \in \mathcal{N}(\mathbf{f}_i)} \|\mathbf{f}_i - \mathbf{f}_j\|_2, \tag{5}$$

where $\mathcal{N}(\mathbf{f}_i)$ is the set of k-nearest neighbors (kNN) of $\mathbf{f}_i$. Clearly, a small d_i corresponds to a sample $\mathbf{X}_i$ that is located in a densely populated region, and is more likely to receive the correct label, and vice versa. Therefore, the confidence level r_i of $\mathbf{X}_i$ can be defined as:

$$r_i = 1 - \frac{d_i}{d_{max}}, \; d_{max} = \max\{d_1, \cdots, d_N\}. \tag{6}$$

Note that each loop when the network parameter set θ is updated, the learned feature descriptor set $\{\mathbf{f}_1, \cdots, \mathbf{f}_N\}$ will be changed. Therefore, we need to recompute the confidence level set $\mathcal{R} = \{r_i\}_{i=1}^N$ using the renewed feature descriptors after each loop of the training process.

3.3 Learning Robust Min-Max Features (RMMF)

Another main component of the proposed TSSDL method is to make the given DCNN model learn the Robust Min-Max Features (RMMF) to further improve the image classification accuracies. This goal is accomplished by adding two regularization terms to the loss function Eq. (3), one for learning the Min-Max Features, and the other for learning the Robust Features. The following part of this section provides detailed descriptions of the two regularization terms.

The Min-Max Feature (MMF) regularization aims to accomplish such properties that in the learned feature space: (i) the distances of images within the same class are minimized; and (ii) the distances of images between different classes are larger than a predefined margin. Based on this statement, we can define the MMF regularization term as follows:

$$R^{\mathrm{MMF}}(\mathcal{X}, \tilde{\mathcal{Y}}; \theta, \mathcal{R}) =$$
$$\sum_{i,j=1}^{N} r_i r_j \big(\|\mathbf{f}_i - \mathbf{f}_j\|^2 \delta(\tilde{\mathbf{y}}_i, \tilde{\mathbf{y}}_j) - \min(0, \|\mathbf{f}_i - \mathbf{f}_j\|^2 - h)(1 - \delta(\tilde{\mathbf{y}}_i, \tilde{\mathbf{y}}_j))\big), \tag{7}$$

where $\delta(\tilde{\mathbf{y}}_i, \tilde{\mathbf{y}}_j) = 1$ if $\tilde{\mathbf{y}}_i = \tilde{\mathbf{y}}_j$, and 0 otherwise. h is the predefined margin, and all other symbols have the same meanings as in Eq. (3).

As briefly explained in Sect. 2, the Robust Feature (RF) regularization turns out to be useful for improving image classification accuracies [24,25,48]. The main idea is as follows: For each sample $\mathbf{X}_i$, its two perturbed versions $\mathbf{X}_i + \eta_i, \mathbf{X}_i + \eta_i'$ are generated by adding two different random data perturbations η_i, η_i' to $\mathbf{X}_i$, and we require that the difference between the feature descriptors of $\mathbf{X}_i + \eta_i, \mathbf{X}_i + \eta_i'$ be minimized. Translating this statement into equation, we have:

$$R^{\mathrm{RF}}(\mathcal{X}; \theta) = \sum_{i=1}^{N} \|\mathbf{f}(\mathbf{X}_i + \eta_i; \theta) - \mathbf{f}(\mathbf{X}_i + \eta_i'; \theta)\|^2. \tag{8}$$

Note that since $\mathbf{X}_i + \eta_i, \mathbf{X}_j + \eta_i'$ are the two perturbed versions of $\mathbf{X}_i$, as they pass forward along the DCNN with dropout enabled, the dropout for $\mathbf{X}_i + \eta_i$ is mostly different from the dropout for $\mathbf{X}_i + \eta_i'$. Thus the perturbations include data augmentation and dropout within the network. This is a stronger effect and leads to a stronger robustness.

In summary, by combining the above two regularization terms, we enforce the DCNN model to learn the Robust Min-Max Features:

$$R^{\mathrm{RMMF}}(\mathcal{X}, \tilde{\mathcal{Y}}; \theta, \mathcal{R}) = \lambda_1 R^{\mathrm{MMF}}(\mathcal{X}, \tilde{\mathcal{Y}}; \theta, \mathcal{R}) + \lambda_2 R^{\mathrm{RF}}(\mathcal{X}; \theta), \tag{9}$$

where λ_1 and λ_2 are the parameters to control the tradeoff between the two terms. The overall loss function of the proposed TSSDL method takes the following form:

$$\ell^{\mathrm{TSSDL}}(\mathcal{X}, \tilde{\mathcal{Y}}; \theta, \mathcal{R}) = \sum_{i=1}^{N} r_i \cdot \mathrm{CEsoftmax}(\mathbf{Wf}(\mathbf{X}_i; \theta), \tilde{\mathbf{y}}_i) + R^{\mathrm{RMMF}}(\mathcal{X}, \tilde{\mathcal{Y}}; \theta, \mathcal{R}). \tag{10}$$

3.4 Optimization of TSSDL Method

Next, we describe the optimization of the loss function Eq. (10). The entire training algorithm for the proposed TSSDL method is shown in Algorithm 3.1. In the following, we provide details of the Steps 4 and 5 in Algorithm 3.1.

Step 4. Fixing the network parameter θ and the confidence level set $\mathcal{R}$, we wish to obtain the optimal label vector set $\tilde{\mathcal{Y}}$. In fact, we only need to obtain the optimal solution of $\tilde{\mathbf{y}}_i$ for each unlabeled sample $\mathbf{X}_i$, $(i = L+1, \cdots, N)$. For simplicity without any confusion, we use $\mathbf{y}_i$ instead of $\tilde{\mathbf{y}}_i$. Let $\mathbf{p}_i = [p_{1i}, p_{2i}, \cdots, p_{Ki}]$ be the prediction score vector of image $\mathbf{X}_i$ (i.e., $\mathbf{p}_i$ is the softmax normalization of the output of the DCNN model's last layer), where p_{ji} represents the prediction score of image $\mathbf{X}_i$ on the jth class.

The relevant term in Eq. (10) is the first term, which can be expressed as:

$$\sum_{\mathbf{X}_i \in \mathcal{U}} r_i \cdot \mathrm{CEsoftmax}(\mathbf{Wf}(\mathbf{X}_i; \theta), \tilde{\mathbf{y}}_i) = -\log \prod_{\mathbf{X}_i \in \mathcal{U}} \left(p_{1i}^{y_i^1} p_{2i}^{y_i^2} \cdots p_{Ki}^{y_i^K} \right)^{r_i}, \tag{11}$$

where we express $\mathbf{y}_i = [y_i^1, \cdots, y_i^K]$ in the component form. Clearly, different data instances i decouple, thus the optimization for Eq. (11) becomes $|\mathcal{U}|$ independent subproblems:

$$\max_{\mathbf{y}_i} \log \left(p_{1i}^{y_i^1} p_{2i}^{y_i^2} \cdots p_{Ki}^{y_i^K} \right)^{r_i} \tag{12}$$

Since $r_i \geq 0$, this optimization becomes:

$$\max_{y_i^1 \cdots y_i^K} \sum_{k=1}^{K} y_i^k \log(p_{ki}) \tag{13}$$

$$\text{subject to} \sum_{k=1}^{K} y_i^k = 1, \; y_i^k \geq 0 \tag{14}$$

Algorithm 3.1. Training algorithm for our proposed TSSDL method.

Input: Training set $\mathcal{D} = \mathcal{L} \bigcup \mathcal{U}$, parameters λ_1, λ_2, the number of loops $Tmax$ (we set $Tmax = 3$).
Output: Network parameter set θ of the DCNN.

1: Train the DCNN on labeled data $\mathcal{L}$ using a supervised learning way.
2: **for** $loop = 1$ to $Tmax$ **do**
3: Fixing θ, update the confidence level set $\mathcal{R} = \{r_i\}_{i=1}^N$ using Eq. (6).
4: Fixing θ and $\mathcal{R}$, optimize $\tilde{\mathcal{Y}}$.
5: Fixing $\mathcal{R}$ and $\tilde{\mathcal{Y}}$, optimize θ on the entire training set $\mathcal{D}$ with the loss function Eq. (10) using mini-batch based stochastic gradient descent from scratch, until the trained DCNN has converged.
6: **end for**

The optimal solution to this problem is given by $y_i^s = 1$ if $s = \arg\max_k p_{ki}$, $y_i^s = 0$ otherwise ($s = 1, \cdots, K$). Thus the optimal solution to Eq. (12) is given by

$$\begin{cases} y_i^s = 1 & \text{if} \quad s = \arg\max_k p_{ki} \\ y_i^s = 0 & \text{otherwise} \end{cases} \tag{15}$$

In summary, the optimal solution to Step 4 is given by Eq. (15).

Step 5. This is the DCNN back-propagation (BP) algorithm using stochastic gradient. The gradient of first term of Eq. (10) is computed in standard way. The gradient of R^{RF} is readily computed in terms of $\frac{\partial \mathbf{f}_i}{\partial \theta}$. Gradient of R^{MMF} can be easily computed numerically: $\frac{\partial R^{\text{MMF}}}{\partial \theta} = \sum_{i=1}^N \frac{\partial R^{\text{MMF}}}{\partial \mathbf{f}_i} \frac{\partial \mathbf{f}_i}{\partial \theta}$ and

$$\frac{\partial R^{\text{MMF}}}{\partial \mathbf{f}_i} = \sum_{j=1}^N r_i r_j 2(\mathbf{f}_i - \mathbf{f}_j)\left[\delta(\tilde{\mathbf{y}}_i, \tilde{\mathbf{y}}_j) - \psi(\|\mathbf{f}_i - \mathbf{f}_j\|^2 - h)(1 - \delta(\tilde{\mathbf{y}}_i, \tilde{\mathbf{y}}_j))\right], \tag{16}$$

where $\psi(a) = 1$ if $a < 0$. Otherwise $\psi(a) = 0$. $\frac{\partial \mathbf{f}_i}{\partial \theta}$ is part of the CNN back-propagation, thus easily handled.

3.5 TSSDL Mean-Teacher (TSSDL-MT) Method

In our experiment, we also implemented a TSSDL variant that is the combination of TSSDL and the Mean Teacher methods (TSSDL-MT in short) [26]. Its loss function is defined as:

$$\begin{aligned} \ell^{\text{TSSDL-MT}}(\mathcal{X}, \tilde{\mathcal{Y}}; \theta, \mathcal{R}) = \sum_{i=1}^N r_i \cdot \text{CEsoftmax}(\mathbf{W}\mathbf{f}(\mathbf{X}_i; \theta), \tilde{\mathbf{y}}_i) + \\ \lambda_1 R^{\text{MMF}}(\mathcal{X}, \tilde{\mathcal{Y}}; \theta, \mathcal{R}) + \lambda_2 \sum_{i=1}^N \|\mathbf{f}(\mathbf{X}_i + \eta_i; \theta) - \mathbf{f}(\mathbf{X}_i + \eta_i'; \theta')\|^2, \end{aligned} \tag{17}$$

where $\theta'_t = \alpha\theta'_{t-1} + (1-\alpha)\theta_t$, α is an exponential moving average (EMA) parameter. The base model using θ is the student model, and θ' is the teacher model. The optimization of the TSSDL-MT method is similar to that of the TSSDL method, and we abide by the same setting of α as that of [26].

4 Experiments

4.1 Experimental Setups

We evaluate the proposed TSSDL method on two benchmark datasets CIFAR10 [49] and SVHN [50]. We choose these two datasets because many recent SSL methods also used them for performance evaluations, which makes it possible to compare TSSDL with these methods. For fair comparison, we use the same 13-layer DCNN architecture, perturbations, and hyper-parameters (such as weight decay, learning rate, drop ratio, etc.) as the Π model [25] and the Mean Teacher model [26]. We conduct all the experiments using TensorFlow [51], and all the models under comparisons are trained from scratch without pre-training. Based on our experiments, we set the margin $h = 1$, $\lambda_1 = 10^{-3}$, $\lambda_2 = 100$ for the TSSDL model, and $\lambda_2 = 1$ for the TSSDL-MT model.

To further reveal how the two regularization terms R^{MMF}, R^{RF} contribute to the performance improvement, in addition to the TSSDL and TSSDL-MT, we also implement the following four variants of the proposed TSSDL method:

- TDCNN: The network is trained without using the two regularization terms R^{MMF} and R^{RF}.
- TMMF: The network is trained without using the regularization term R^{RF}.
- TRF: The network is trained without using the regularization term R^{MMF}.
- Fully Supervised: The network is trained using the standard fully supervised training algorithm with the loss function $\ell^{\text{SL}}(\mathcal{X}, \mathcal{Y}; \theta)$ in Eq. (2) instead of $\ell^{\text{TSSDL}}(\mathcal{X}, \tilde{\mathcal{Y}}; \theta, \mathcal{R})$ in Eq. (3).

4.2 Datasets

The details of the CIFAR10 [49] and SVHN [50] datasets, and their usages for the experimental evaluations are explained as follows.

CIFAR10 Dataset. It contains 10 classes of 60000 natural images, which are split into 50000, 10000 images to form the training and test sets, respectively. All the images are 32×32 RGB images. We followed the same training and testing protocols as [26] in the experimental evaluations, where 1000, 2000, 4000, and all the 50000 images (i.e., 100, 200, 400, and 5000 samples per class) are selected from the training set as the labeled training samples, respectively, and the remaining samples in the training set are used as the unlabeled training samples.

SVHN Dataset. It contains 73257 training and 26032 test images. All images are 32×32 RGB images. In each image, there can be multiple digits, but the task is to recognize the digit in the image center. Again, following the same training and testing protocols as [26], we select 250, 500, 1000 (i.e., 25, 50, 100 samples per class), and all the 73257 images from the training set as the labeled training samples, respectively, and use the remaining samples in the training set as the unlabeled ones in the experimental evaluations.

Table 1. Top-1 error rates (%) on CIFAR10 test set, averaged over 10 runs.

Method	No. of labeled samples (L)			
	1000	2000	4000	50000 (all)
Ladder networks [46]	–	–	20.40 ± 0.47	–
Entropy [37]	–	–	20.3 ± 0.5	–
GAN [42]	21.83 ± 2.01	19.61 ± 2.09	18.63 ± 2.32	–
Sajjadi *et al.* [24]	–	–	11.29 ± 0.24	–
VAT [27]	–	–	11.36	5.81
Π model [25]	–	–	12.36 ± 0.31	5.56 ± 0.10
TempEns [25]	–	–	12.16 ± 0.24	5.60 ± 0.10
Mean Teacher [26]	21.55 ± 1.48	15.73 ± 0.31	12.31 ± 0.28	5.94 ± 0.15
Fully supervised [26]	46.43 ± 1.21	33.94 ± 0.73	20.66 ± 0.57	6.45 ± 0.15
TDCNN	32.67 ± 1.93	22.99 ± 0.79	16.17 ± 0.37	6.45 ± 0.15
TMMF	26.73 ± 1.11	17.48 ± 0.66	13.11 ± 0.33	5.80 ± 0.17
TRF	27.36 ± 1.30	18.02 ± 0.60	13.30 ± 0.27	6.16 ± 0.11
TSSDL	21.13 ± 1.17	14.65 ± 0.33	10.90 ± 0.23	5.20 ± 0.14
TSSDL-MT	$\mathbf{18.41 \pm 0.92}$	$\mathbf{13.54 \pm 0.32}$	$\mathbf{9.30 \pm 0.55}$	$\mathbf{5.19 \pm 0.14}$

4.3 Comparison to State-of-the-Art Methods

Tables 1 and 2 report the experimental results of all the evaluated methods on the CIFAR10 and SVHN test sets, respectively. The four data columns in the righthand side of Table 1 correspond to the top-1 error rates of the respective models trained using 1000, 2000, 4000, and all the labeled training samples in the CIFAR10 training set, respectively, while the four data columns in Table 2 correspond to the top-1 error rates of the respective models trained using 250, 500, 1000, and all the labeled training samples in the SVHN training set, respectively. All the results are averaged over 10 runs with different seeds for data splits. The two tables also include the results of the state-of-the-art SSL methods described in Sect. 2. We use the same abbreviations for these SSL methods as in Sect. 2 to report their results. The experimental results in the two tables can be summarized as follows.

- TSSDL and all its variants dramatically outperform the "Fully Supervised" counterpart, proving that the proposed TSSDL method is effective for using

Table 2. Top-1 error rates (%) on SVHN test set, averaged over 10 runs.

Method	No. of labeled samples (L)			
	250	500	1000	73257 (all)
GAN [42]	–	18.44 ± 4.8	8.11 ± 1.3	–
VAT [27]	–	–	5.42	–
Haeusser *et al.* [41]	–	6.25 ± 0.32	5.14 ± 0.17	3.09 ± 0.06
Π model [25]	–	6.65 ± 0.53	4.82 ± 0.17	2.54 ± 0.04
TempEns [25]	–	5.12 ± 0.13	4.42 ± 0.16	2.74 ± 0.06
Mean Teacher [26]	4.35 ± 0.50	4.18 ± 0.27	3.95 ± 0.19	2.50 ± 0.05
Fully supervised [28]	42.65 ± 2.68	22.08 ± 0.73	14.46 ± 0.71	2.81 ± 0.07
TDCNN	22.90 ± 1.91	13.79 ± 1.24	8.77 ± 0.82	2.81 ± 0.07
TMMF	12.99 ± 1.02	7.23 ± 0.76	4.25 ± 0.33	2.30 ± 0.06
TRF	9.93 ± 1.15	6.83 ± 0.66	4.95 ± 0.26	2.65 ± 0.04
TSSDL	5.02 ± 0.26	4.32 ± 0.30	3.80 ± 0.27	2.42 ± 0.05
TSSDL-MT	$\mathbf{4.09 \pm 0.42}$	$\mathbf{3.90 \pm 0.27}$	$\mathbf{3.35 \pm 0.27}$	$\mathbf{2.10 \pm 0.07}$

Table 3. Top-1 error rates (%) on SVHN test set with extra unlabeled training data, averaged over 10 runs. The number of labeled samples is 500. $N_u = 73257 - 500$ is the number of unlabeled samples in the original training set.

Method	No. of unlabeled samples		
	N_u	$N_u + 100000$	$N_u + 500000$
TSSDL-MT	3.90 ± 0.27	2.96 ± 0.22	2.27 ± 0.09

the unlabeled samples to improve image classification accuracies of the DCNN model.

- Compared with the baseline TDCNN, adding either the MMF or the RF regularization terms to the loss function can remarkably reduce the error rates on the two test sets.
- TMMF and TRF produce compatible error rates. Combining them together (i.e., TSSDL) achieves the second best performance accuracies on CIFAR10 and compatible results on SVHN with the Mean Teacher method. This is a strong evidence that the proposed MMRF regularization is quite effective for making the DCNN model learn better feature descriptors for the image classification task.
- The TSSDL-MT method that combines TSSDL with the Mean Teacher method remarkably outperforms all the methods under comparisons.

4.4 Increasing Extra Unlabeled Samples for SVHN

Tables 1 and 2 indicate that the proposed TSSDL method can effectively use massive unlabeled training samples to improve image classification accuracies.

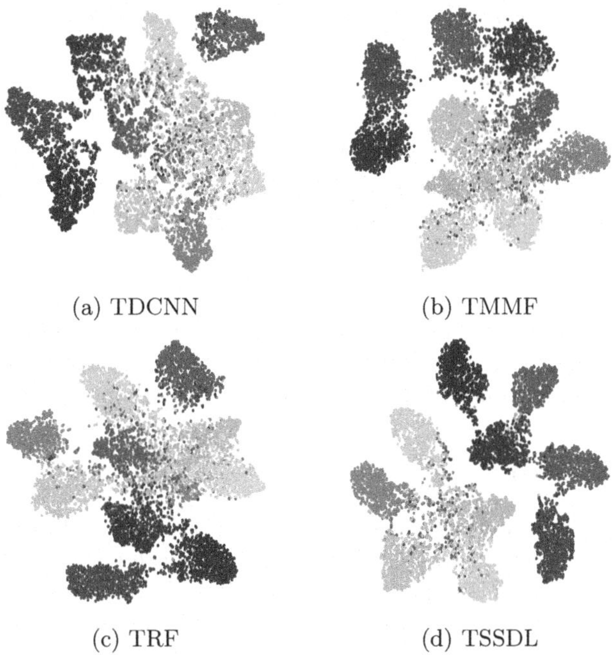

Fig. 1. Feature visualization of the CIFAR10 test set with (a) TDCNN, (b) TMMF, (c) TRF and (d) TSSDL, respectively. Each dot in the figure corresponds to an image, and different colors represent different classes. (Color figure online)

Here, we make an additional experiment on SVHN to test whether TSSDL can achieve a better image classification accuracy by using more unlabeled training samples. Apart from the original training set, SVHN also contains an extra set of 531131 images. Similar to [26], we pick only 500 images from the original training set as the labeled samples, and use the rest of the original training set together with the entire extra set to form the pool of unlabeled samples. Let $N_u = 73257 - 500$ be the number of unlabeled samples in the original training set. We run experiments with TSSDL-MT by using 0, 100000, and 500000 extra unlabeled samples (plus 500 labeled samples and N_u unlabeled samples in the primary training set), respectively. Table 3 shows that: (i) TSSDL-MT does further improve the classification accuracy by using extra unlabeled samples; and (ii) the degree of improvement is positively related to the number of extra unlabeled samples.

4.5 Feature Visualization

We utilize t-SNE [52] to visualize the learned feature descriptors extracted by the TDCNN, TMMF, TRF and TSSDL methods ($L = 4000$) on the CIFAR10 test set, respectively (see Fig. 1). It can be observed that: (i) feature descriptors learned by TMMF are better than that of TDCNN, and (ii) feature descriptors

Table 4. Top-1 error rates (%) on CIFAR10 and SVHN test sets.

Method	L for CIFAR10			L for SVHN		
	1000	2000	4000	250	500	1000
Fully supervised	46.43	33.94	20.66	42.65	22.08	14.46
TSSDL-No confidence	50.38	35.67	18.10	46.74	19.10	10.10
TSSDL	21.13	14.65	10.90	5.02	4.32	3.80

learned by TSSDL are the best in terms of between-class separability and within-class compactness. This agrees with the evaluation results in Tables 1 and 2, serving as another evidence for the effectiveness of the proposed TSSDL method.

4.6 Ablation Study

Table 4 lists the ablation study results on CIFAR10 and SVHN. It shows that TSSDL without the confidence levels yields much worse results, especially when the number of labeled samples (L) is small. Indeed, transductive learning together with confidences are an inseparable combination for DCNN application. The proposed TSSDL method is not a simple application of transductive learning to DCNNs. Transductive learning relies on computing distances between feature vectors. Traditional transductive learning requires fixed, high-quality features, while with DCNN, features are of low quality at the beginning and evolve over time during training. We introduce confidence estimates on inferred labels to avoid the training process from getting into a wrong direction. Table 4 shows that the confidences play an essential role for successful transductive learning application to DCNNs.

5 Conclusions

In this paper, we propose Transductive Semi-Supervised Deep Learning (TSSDL) method that is effective for training Deep Convolutional Neural Network (DCNN) models. The method applies transductive learning principle to DCNN training, introduces confidence levels on unlabeled data samples to overcome unreliable label estimates on outliers and uncertain samples, and uses the Min-Max Feature (MMF) regularization that encourages DCNN to learn features of same-class images be close, and features of different classes be separated by a predefined margin. Extensive experiments on the benchmark datasets CIFAR10 and SVHN have shown that the DCNN model trained by the proposed TSSDL method can produce image classification accuracies that are compatible to the state-of-the-art SSL methods, and that combining TSSDL with the Mean Teacher method can produce the best classification accuracies on the two benchmark datasets. Experiments (Tables 1 and 2) show that as the number of labeled data increase, TSSDL performance improves consistently. Experiments

(Table 3) also show that as number of unlabeled data increases while the number of labeled data is fixed, TSSDL performance improves consistently. Feature visualizations (Fig. 1) show that the Min-Max feature regularization enforces TSSDL to learn feature descriptors with better between-class separability and within-class compactness, thus better discriminative ability.

Acknowledgments. This work is supported by National Basic Research Program of China (973 Program) under Grant No. 2015CB351705, and the National Natural Science Foundation of China (NSFC) under Grant No. 61332018.

References

1. Yang, J., Yu, K., Gong, Y., Huang, T.: Linear spatial pyramid matching using sparse coding for image classification. In: Proceedings of the IEEE Conference on Computer Vision and Pattern Recognition, pp. 1794–1801 (2009)
2. Krizhevsky, A., Sutskever, I., Hinton, G.E.: ImageNet classification with deep convolutional neural networks. In: Advances in Neural Information Processing Systems, pp. 1097–1105 (2012)
3. He, K., Zhang, X., Ren, S., Sun, J.: Deep residual learning for image recognition. In: Proceedings of the IEEE Conference on Computer Vision and Pattern Recognition, pp. 770–778 (2016)
4. Wu, S., Ji, Q., Wang, S., Wong, H.S., Yu, Z., Xu, Y.: Semi-supervised image classification with self-paced cross-task networks. IEEE Trans. Multimed. **20**(4), 851–865 (2018)
5. Shi, W., Gong, Y., Wang, J.: Improving CNN performance with min-max objective. In: Proceedings of the International Joint Conference on Artificial Intelligence, pp. 2004–2010 (2016)
6. Girshick, R.: Fast R-CNN. In: Proceedings of the IEEE International Conference on Computer Vision, pp. 1440–1448 (2015)
7. Ren, S., He, K., Girshick, R., Sun, J.: Faster R-CNN: towards real-time object detection with region proposal networks. In: Advances in Neural Information Processing Systems, pp. 91–99 (2015)
8. Schroff, F., Kalenichenko, D., Philbin, J.: FaceNet: a unified embedding for face recognition and clustering. In: Proceedings of the IEEE Conference on Computer Vision and Pattern Recognition, pp. 815–823 (2015)
9. Sun, Y., Liang, D., Wang, X., Tang, X.: DeepID3: face recognition with very deep neural networks. arXiv preprint arXiv:1502.00873 (2015)
10. Shi, W., Gong, Y., Tao, X., Wang, J., Zheng, N.: Improving CNN performance accuracies with min-max objective. IEEE Trans. Neural Netw. Learn. Syst. **29**(7), 2872–2885 (2018)
11. Zhao, F., Huang, Y., Wang, L., Tan, T.: Deep semantic ranking based hashing for multi-label image retrieval. In: Proceedings of the IEEE Conference on Computer Vision and Pattern Recognition, pp. 1556–1564 (2015)
12. Yu, M., Liu, L., Shao, L.: Binary set embedding for cross-modal retrieval. IEEE Trans. Neural Netw. Learn. Syst. **28**(12), 2899–2910 (2017)
13. Liu, Q., Liu, G., Li, L., Yuan, X.T., Wang, M., Liu, W.: Reversed spectral hashing. IEEE Trans. Neural Netw. Learn. Syst. **29**(6), 2441–2449 (2018)
14. Huang, L.K., Yang, Q., Zheng, W.S.: Online hashing. IEEE Trans. Neural Netw. Learn. Syst. **29**(6), 2309–2322 (2018)

15. Zhu, X., Ghahramani, Z.: Learning from labeled and unlabeled data with label propagation. Technical report CMU-CALD-02-107, Carnegie Mellon University (2002)
16. Whitney, M., Sarkar, A.: Bootstrapping via graph propagation. In: Proceedings of the 50th Annual Meeting of the Association for Computational Linguistics: Long Papers-Volume 1, pp. 620–628 (2012)
17. Gong, C., Tao, D., Liu, W., Liu, L., Yang, J.: Label propagation via teaching-to-learn and learning-to-teach. IEEE Trans. Neural Netw. Learn. Syst. **28**(6), 1452–1465 (2017)
18. Pei, X., Chen, C., Guan, Y.: Joint sparse representation and embedding propagation learning: a framework for graph-based semisupervised learning. IEEE Trans. Neural Netw. Learn. Syst. **28**(12), 2949–2960 (2017)
19. Joachims, T.: Transductive inference for text classification using support vector machines. In: Proceedings of the International Conference on Machine Learning, vol. 99, pp. 200–209 (1999)
20. Joachims, T.: Transductive learning via spectral graph partitioning. In: Proceedings of the International Conference on Machine Learning, pp. 290–297 (2003)
21. Zhang, Y.M., Huang, K., Geng, G.G., Liu, C.L.: MTC: a fast and robust graph-based transductive learning method. IEEE Trans. Neural Netw. Learn. Syst. **26**(9), 1979–1991 (2015)
22. Wang, Z., et al.: Progressive graph-based transductive learning for multi-modal classification of brain disorder disease. In: Ourselin, S., Joskowicz, L., Sabuncu, M.R., Unal, G., Wells, W. (eds.) MICCAI 2016. LNCS, vol. 9900, pp. 291–299. Springer, Cham (2016). https://doi.org/10.1007/978-3-319-46720-7_34
23. Görnitz, N., Lima, L.A., Varella, L.E., Müller, K.R., Nakajima, S.: Transductive regression for data with latent dependence structure. IEEE Trans. Neural Netw. Learn. Syst. **29**(7), 2743–2756 (2018)
24. Sajjadi, M., Javanmardi, M., Tasdizen, T.: Regularization with stochastic transformations and perturbations for deep semi-supervised learning. In: Advances in Neural Information Processing Systems, pp. 1163–1171 (2016)
25. Laine, S., Aila, T.: Temporal ensembling for semi-supervised learning. arXiv preprint arXiv:1610.02242 (2016)
26. Tarvainen, A., Valpola, H.: Mean teachers are better role models: weight-averaged consistency targets improve semi-supervised deep learning results. In: Advances in Neural Information Processing Systems, pp. 1195–1204 (2017)
27. Miyato, T., Maeda, S.i., Koyama, M., Ishii, S.: Virtual adversarial training: a regularization method for supervised and semi-supervised learning. arXiv preprint arXiv:1704.03976 (2017)
28. Luo, Y., Zhu, J., Li, M., Ren, Y., Zhang, B.: Smooth neighbors on teacher graphs for semi-supervised learning. arXiv preprint arXiv:1711.00258 (2017)
29. de Sa, V.R.: Learning classification with unlabeled data. In: Advances in Neural Information Processing Systems, pp. 112–119 (1994)
30. Blum, A., Mitchell, T.: Combining labeled and unlabeled data with co-training. In: Proceedings of the Eleventh Annual Conference on Computational Learning Theory, pp. 92–100 (1998)
31. Cozman, F.G., Cohen, I., Cirelo, M.C.: Semi-supervised learning of mixture models. In: Proceedings of the International Conference on Machine Learning, pp. 99–106 (2003)
32. Rosenberg, C., Hebert, M., Schneiderman, H.: Semi-supervised self-training of object detection models. In: Application of Computer Vision, pp. 29–36 (2005)

33. LeCun, Y., Kavukcuoglu, K., Farabet, C.: Convolutional networks and applications in vision. In: Proceedings of 2010 IEEE International Symposium on Circuits and Systems, pp. 253–256 (2010)
34. Jarrett, K., Kavukcuoglu, K., LeCun, Y., et al.: What is the best multi-stage architecture for object recognition? In: Proceedings of the IEEE International Conference on Computer Vision, pp. 2146–2153 (2009)
35. Agrawal, P., Carreira, J., Malik, J.: Learning to see by moving. In: Proceedings of the IEEE International Conference on Computer Vision, pp. 37–45 (2015)
36. Doersch, C., Gupta, A., Efros, A.A.: Unsupervised visual representation learning by context prediction. In: Proceedings of the IEEE International Conference on Computer Vision, pp. 1422–1430 (2015)
37. Hoffer, E., Ailon, N.: Semi-supervised deep learning by metric embedding. arXiv preprint arXiv:1611.01449 (2016)
38. Weston, J., Ratle, F., Collobert, R.: Deep learning via semi-supervised embedding. In: Proceedings of the International Conference on Machine learning, pp. 1168–1175 (2008)
39. Kingma, D.P., Mohamed, S., Rezende, D.J., Welling, M.: Semi-supervised learning with deep generative models. In: Advances in Neural Information Processing Systems, pp. 3581–3589 (2014)
40. Abbasnejad, M.E., Dick, A., van den Hengel, A.: Infinite variational autoencoder for semi-supervised learning. In: Proceedings of the IEEE Conference on Computer Vision and Pattern Recognition, pp. 781–790 (2017)
41. Haeusser, P., Mordvintsev, A., Cremers, D.: Learning by association-a versatile semi-supervised training method for neural networks. In: Proceedings of the IEEE Conference on Computer Vision and Pattern Recognition, pp. 89–98 (2017)
42. Salimans, T., Goodfellow, I., Zaremba, W., Cheung, V., Radford, A., Chen, X.: Improved techniques for training GANs. In: Advances in Neural Information Processing Systems, pp. 2234–2242 (2016)
43. Springenberg, J.T.: Unsupervised and semi-supervised learning with categorical generative adversarial networks. arXiv preprint arXiv:1511.06390 (2015)
44. Chongxuan, L., Xu, T., Zhu, J., Zhang, B.: Triple generative adversarial nets. In: Advances in Neural Information Processing Systems, pp. 4091–4101 (2017)
45. Dai, Z., Yang, Z., Yang, F., Cohen, W.W., Salakhutdinov, R.R.: Good semi-supervised learning that requires a bad GAN. In: Advances in Neural Information Processing Systems, pp. 6513–6523 (2017)
46. Rasmus, A., Berglund, M., Honkala, M., Valpola, H., Raiko, T.: Semi-supervised learning with ladder networks. In: Advances in Neural Information Processing Systems, pp. 3546–3554 (2015)
47. Valpola, H.: From neural PCA to deep unsupervised learning. In: Advances in Independent Component Analysis and Learning Machines, pp. 143–171 (2015)
48. Dosovitskiy, A., Springenberg, J.T., Riedmiller, M., Brox, T.: Discriminative unsupervised feature learning with convolutional neural networks. In: Advances in Neural Information Processing Systems, pp. 766–774 (2014)
49. Krizhevsky, A., Hinton, G.: Learning multiple layers of features from tiny images. Master's thesis, University of Toronto (2009)
50. Netzer, Y., Wang, T., Coates, A., Bissacco, A., Wu, B., Ng, A.Y.: Reading digits in natural images with unsupervised feature learning. In: Neural Information Processing Systems (NIPS) Workshop on Deep Learning and Unsupervised Feature Learning, vol. 2011, p. 5 (2011)
51. Abadi, M., et al.: TensorFlow: large-scale machine learning on heterogeneous distributed systems. arXiv preprint arXiv:1603.04467 (2016)
52. Maaten, L., Hinton, G.: Visualizing data using t-SNE. J. Mach. Learn. Res. **9**(Nov), 2579–2605 (2008)

SAN: Learning Relationship Between Convolutional Features for Multi-scale Object Detection

Yonghyun Kim[1(✉)], Bong-Nam Kang[2], and Daijin Kim[1]

[1] Department of Computer Science and Engineering, POSTECH, Pohang, Korea
{gkyh0805,bnkang,dkim}@postech.ac.kr

[2] Department of Creative IT Engineering, POSTECH, Pohang, Korea

Abstract. Most of the recent successful methods in accurate object detection build on the convolutional neural networks (CNN). However, due to the lack of scale normalization in CNN-based detection methods, the activated channels in the feature space can be completely different according to a scale and this difference makes it hard for the classifier to learn samples. We propose a Scale Aware Network (SAN) that maps the convolutional features from the different scales onto a scale-invariant subspace to make CNN-based detection methods more robust to the scale variation, and also construct a unique learning method which considers purely the relationship between channels without the spatial information for the efficient learning of SAN. To show the validity of our method, we visualize how convolutional features change according to the scale through a channel activation matrix and experimentally show that SAN reduces the feature differences in the scale space. We evaluate our method on VOC PASCAL and MS COCO dataset. We demonstrate SAN by conducting several experiments on structures and parameters. The proposed SAN can be generally applied to many CNN-based detection methods to enhance the detection accuracy with a slight increase in the computing time.

Keywords: Scale Aware Network · Object detection · Multi scale Neural network

1 Introduction

Accurate and efficient detection of multi-scale objects is an important goal in object detection. Multi-scale objects are detected by a single detector [5,7,8,33] that uses an image pyramid with scale normalization, or by a multi-scale detector [2] that uses a separate detector for each of several scales. However, detection methods that are based on a convolutional neural network (CNN) can detect multi-scale objects by pooling regions of interest (RoIs) [13,21,28] to extract convolutional features of the same size in RoIs of different sizes, or by learning grid cells [26,27] that represent the surrounding area, or by assigning

V. Ferrari et al. (Eds.): ECCV 2018, LNCS 11209, pp. 328–343, 2018.
https://doi.org/10.1007/978-3-030-01228-1_20

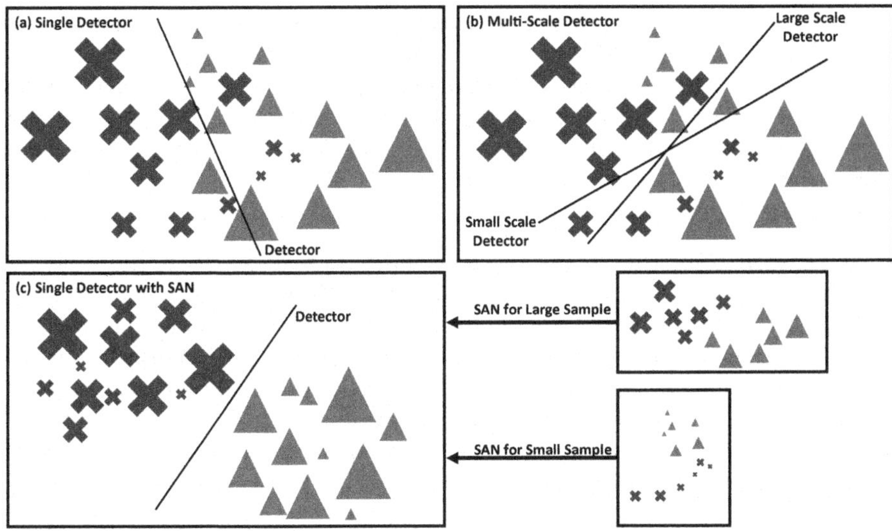

Fig. 1. Different strategies for multi-scale object detection. The blue cross and green triangular marks represent background and object samples, respectively, and the size of the mark is proportional to the size of the sample (Color figure online)

different scales according to the level of the feature map [22,24], without scale normalization.

The process of scale normalization can cause differences in feature space between samples if they have different resolutions. By mapping samples from different resolutions to a common subspace [35] or by calibrating the gradient features from different resolutions to the gradient features at the reference resolution [37], the variation between samples is reduced and the detection accuracy is improved.

However, CNN-based detection methods generally do not perform scale normalization, so new differences arise due to scale rather than to resolution. CNN-based methods that use RoI pooling or grid cells may represent the sizes of cell differently according to the size of RoIs, so this scale variation can lead to extraction of completely different shapes of features rather than to a small difference in the resolution variation. Several strategies can be used to detect multi-scale objects (Fig. 1). A single detector strategy (Fig. 1a) is used in many detection methods; it has a simple structure and can learn a single classifier from the whole set of training samples, but it may not consider the scale space sufficiently. The multi-scale detector strategy (Fig. 1b) learns multiple detectors for different scale spaces, but may have difficulty in learning the classifications if the scale space for each detector has too few samples.

We propose a Scale Aware Network (SAN) that maps the convolutional features from the different scales onto a scale-invariant subspace to learn a single classifier with consideration of the scale space (Fig. 1c). SAN learns the relationships between convolutional features in the scale space to reduce the feature differences and improves the detection accuracy. We study the effect of the scale difference in CNN by using a channel activation matrix that represents the relationship between scale change and channel activation, then design a structure for SAN and a unique learning method based on channel routing mechanism that considers the relationship between channels without the spatial information.

We make three main contributions:

- We develop SAN that maps the convolutional features from the different scales onto a scale-invariant subspace. We study the relationship between scale change and channel activation and, based on this, we design a unique learning method which considers purely the relationship between channels without the spatial information. The proposed SAN reduces the feature differences in the scale space and improves the detection accuracy.
- We empirically demonstrate SAN for object detection by conducting several experiments on structures and parameters for SAN. We visualize how convolutional features change according to the scale through a channel activation matrix and experimentally prove that SAN reduces the feature differences in the scale space.
- The proposed SAN essentially improves the quality of convolutional features in the scale space, thus it can be generally applied to many CNN-based detection methods to enhance the detection accuracy with a slight increase in the computing time.

This paper is organized as follow. We review related works in Sect. 2. We discuss the effect of the scale difference in CNN and present the proposed SAN and the training mechanism for SAN in Sect. 3. We show experimental results for object detection and empirically demonstrate SAN in Sect. 4. We conclude in Sect. 5.

2 Related Works

Multi-scale Detection. The image pyramid [1,15], which is one of the most popular approaches to multi-scale detection, has been applied to many applications such as pedestrian detection [5–8], human pose estimation [36], and object detection [10]. Because the image pyramid is constructed by resampling a given image to multiple scales, the differences in image statistics can occur depending on the degree of resampling. Several researchers studied natural image statistics and the relationship between two resampled images [11,29,30]. The difference in resolution caused by resampling degrades the detection accuracy. The variation between samples can be reduced by mapping samples from different resolutions onto a common subspace [35] or by calibrating the gradient features from different resolutions to the gradient features at the reference resolution [37], and the reduced variance makes it easy for the classifier to learn samples. In this work, we discuss the feature difference in CNN caused by the scale variance and make CNN-based detection methods more robust to the scale variation.

Detection Networks. The development of deep neural networks has achieved tremendous performance improvements in the field of object detection. Especially, Faster R-CNN [28], which is one of the representative object detection algorithms, generates candidate proposals using a region proposal network and classifies the proposals to the background and foreground classes using RoI pooling. Region-based fully convolutional networks (R-FCN) [21] improved speed by designing the structure of networks as fully convolutional by excluding RoI-wise sub-networks. PSRoI pooling in R-FCN solved the translation dilemma without a deep RoI-wise sub-network. R-FCN achieved the same detection performance as Faster R-CNN at faster speed. Deformable R-FCN [4] suggests deformable convolution and RoI pooling, which are a generalization of atrous convolution. SAN is trained using the relationship between convolutional features extracted by RoI pooling in the scale variation. We improve the accuracy of object detection by applying the proposed SAN between the last layer of ResNet-101 and the 1×1 convolutional layers for detection of R-FCN and Deformable R-FCN.

Residual Network. The residual network [17], one of the most widely used backbone networks in recent years, was proposed to solve the problem that learning becomes difficult as the network becomes deeper. The residual learning prevents the deeper networks from having a higher training error than the shallower networks by adding shortcut connections that are identity mapping. ResNet-101 is constructed using this residual learning with 101 layers. In this work, the detection network is based on a fully convolutional network that excludes the average pooling, 1000-d fully connected and softmax layers from ResNet-101. We modify a stride of the last convolution block *res5* from 1 to 2 for doubling the receptive fields in detection. The dilation is changed from 1 to 2 for all 3×3 convolution to compensate this modification.

Resolution Aware Detection Model. Many existing detectors find objects of various sizes by sliding a detection model on an image pyramid. The window used as the input of the detector is normalized to a pre-defined size, but there is a resolution difference in the resampling process. A resolution aware detection model [35] reduces the resolution difference by considering the relationships between the samples obtained at different resolutions, and trains a detection model and a resolution aware transformation to map features from different resolutions to a common subspace. Since the detector learns only the samples on the common subspace, the variation between samples can be reduced and higher detection accuracy can be achieved. The concepts, which reduce the variance of samples, are widely used to improve the performance of a classifier [12,19]. A typical way of reducing the variance is partitioning samples by pose [18,20,34], rotation [36] or resolution [25,35]. They reduced the coverage of a classifier by reducing the variance of samples, and the decreased coverage improved the performance of a classifier. In a similar manner, the proposed SAN suggests a method of mapping to a scale-invariant subspace in consideration of the relationship between different scales, not the resolution, to overcome the lack of scale normalization in CNN.

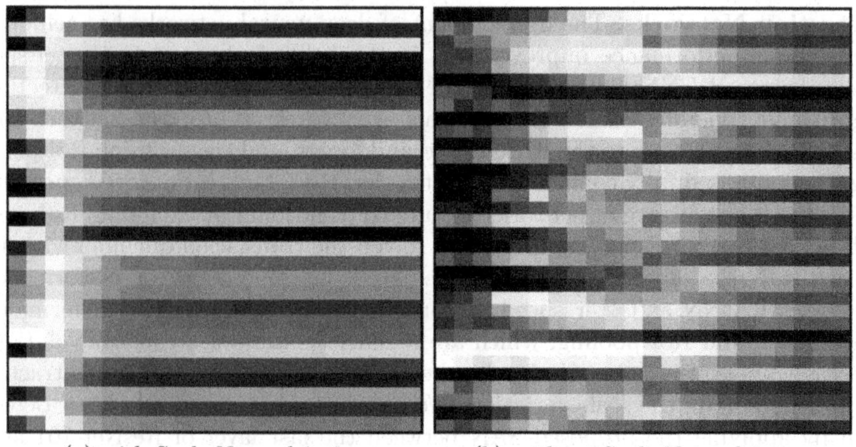

(a) with Scale Normalziation (b) without Scale Normalziation

Fig. 2. The channel activation matrix for the scale variation shows the comparison of RoI pooling with and without scale normalization. The x-axis represents the scale of an image and the y-axis represents the channel index. The closer the block is to white, the more the activation of the corresponding channel in the block

3 Scale Aware Network

Overview. We propose a Scale Aware Network (SAN) that maps the convolutional features from the different scales onto a scale-invariant subspace to make CNN-based detection methods more robust to the scale variation. CNN-based detectors have higher detection accuracy than the conventional detectors without any scale normalization. The conventional detectors, which mainly use hand-crafted features, detect multi-scale objects by classifying the scale normalized patches. The features obtained from the scale normalized patches have a small differences in the resolution variation caused by resizing, but the sizes of the objects and parts in the images remain unchanged. However, the convolutional features can completely change the activated channels rather than vary only slightly due to the lack of scale normalization.

Channel Activation Matrix. High dimensionality complicates the task of visually observing how convolutional features change according to the scale. The channel activation matrix (CAM) shows how convolutional features are affected by the scale variation by comparing values only of the channels that are primarily activated. Comparison of CAM for RoI Pooling with and without scale normalization (Fig. 2) shows the difference of the channel-wise output of the last residual block *res5c* in ResNet-101 according to the scale variation. We calculate CAM by redundantly extracting 10 channels that show large activation for resized images from 8×8 to 448×448. CAM for convolutional features with scale normalization (Fig. 2a) shows uniform channel activation in most of the scale space except that the resolution is severely impaired when the scale is too

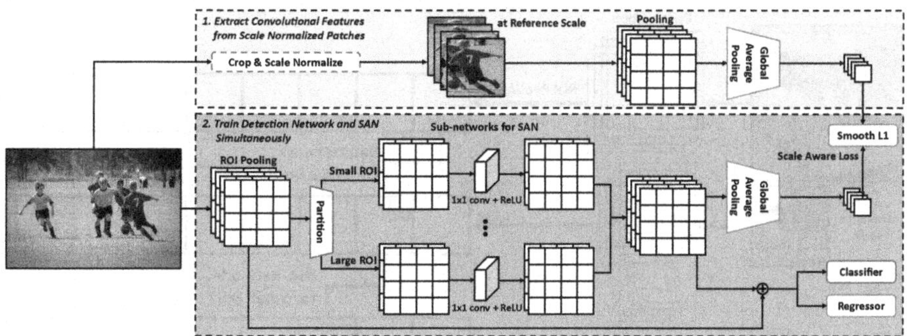

Fig. 3. Architecture of SAN. In learning, an additional stage is required for SAN to extract convolutional features from scale normalized patches. The detection network and SAN is trained using the extracted features, simultaneously. In inference, SAN simulates the scale normalization without it

small. In contrast, CAM for convolutional features without scale normalization (Fig. 2b) shows non-uniform channel activation across the scale space, and its value varies with the change in scale. Due to non-uniformity in the scale space, the scale variation can degrade the detection accuracy.

Architecture. SAN consists of several sub-networks corresponding to the different sizes of RoI. By exploiting these sub-networks, SAN learns the relationship between convolutional features obtained from the scale-normalized patch and RoI pooling of the input image (Fig. 3). Each sub-network consists of a 1×1 convolution of which the number of channels equals to the input feature and the following ReLU. We partition RoIs in a mini-batch into three intervals of size at the reference scale experimentally: $(0^2, 160^2]$, $(160^2, 288^2)$, $[288^2, \infty)$ at 224^2 for VOC Pascal and $(0^2, 64^2]$, $(64^2, 192^2)$, $[192^2, \infty)$ at 128^2 for MS COCO. The partitioned features are corrected by using the corresponding sub-network of SAN, then merged into one mini-batch. The detector uses element-wise sum of the original feature and the SAN feature to enrich the feature representation, just as the low-level features in FPN [22]. SAN can be adapted to many other types of CNN-based detection framework with a simple network extension.

Channel Routing Mechanism. The different receptive fields at various scales cause the discordance of the spatial information. The discordance makes SAN difficult to learn the expected scale normalization precisely. Thus, we use a global average pooling to learn only the information of channels by excluding the discordance of the spatial information. We interpret this learning method as a concept of routing: SAN transforms a channel activation at the specific scale to a channel activation at the reference scale (Fig. 4).

Loss Functions. The entire detection framework is divided into two parts according to the influence of loss: (1) SAN: SAN trained with a combination of classification, box regression, and scale-aware losses, and (2) Network without SAN: networks excluding SAN trained using only classification and box regres-

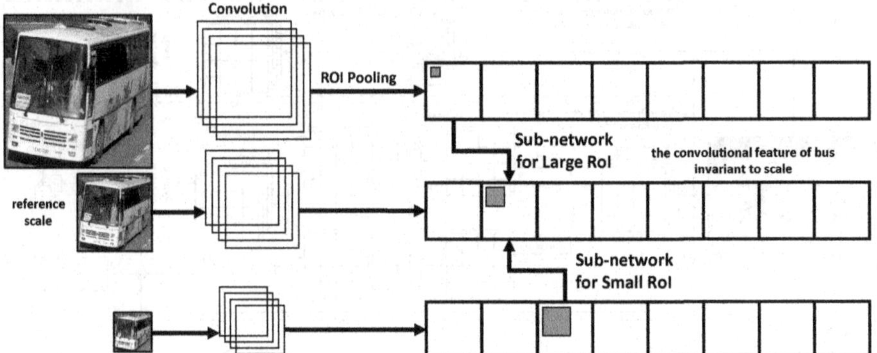

Fig. 4. A mechanism of channel routing. The smaller the size of the image, the lower the resolution in the feature space. Therefore, several channels can imply the same meaning according to the scale. Because of the difference in spatiality caused by the difference in receptive fields, learning should be done with the concept of channel routing without the spatial information

sion loss [13,21,28]. Scale-aware loss is designed to reduce the difference between features over scales, so it can cause an error in detection when applied to the entire network. In the case of SAN, both the scale invariance and the detection accuracy must be considered, so all three losses are applied. The multi-task loss for SAN is defined as:

$$\mathcal{L}(p, u, t^u, v, r, \widetilde{r}) = L_{cls}(p, u) + [u \geq 1]L_{reg}(t^u, v) + L_{san}(r, \widetilde{r}). \tag{1}$$

Here, p is a discrete probability distribution over $K+1$ categories and u is a ground-truth class. t^k is a tuple of bounding-box regression for each of the K classes, indexed by k, and v is a tuple of ground-truth bounding-box regression. r is a channel-wise convolutional feature extracted from RoI and $\widetilde{r}$ is a channel-wise convolutional feature for a scale-normalized patch from RoI. The classification loss, $L_{cls}(p, u) = -\log p_u$, is logarithmic loss for ground-truth class u. The regression loss, $L_{reg}(t^u, v) = \sum_{i \in \{x,y,w,h\}} \textbf{smooth}_{L_1}[t_i^u - v_i]$, measures the difference between t^u and v using the robust L_1 function [13]. The scale-aware loss L_{san} represents the difference between r and $\widetilde{r}$ using the robust L_1 function, and defined as:

$$L_{san}(r, \widetilde{r}) = \sum_{c \in C} \textbf{smooth}_{L_1}[r_c - \widetilde{r}_c]. \tag{2}$$

In this work, we extract the convolutional features $\widetilde{r}$ for the scale-normalized patches from only 16 randomly selected RoIs in a mini-batch due to the computing time.

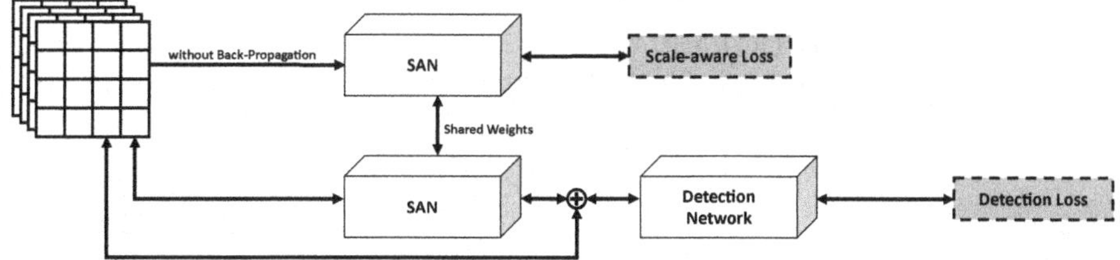

Fig. 5. A learning trick for SAN. The entire network uses two SANs sharing the weight as the siamese architecture to control the influence of losses

4 Experiments

Structure. We experimentally demonstrate the effectiveness of SAN based on R-FCN [21]. In this work, the backbone of R-FCN is ResNet-101 [17], which consists of 100 convolutional layers followed by global average pooling and a 1000 class fully-connected layer. We leave only the convolutional layers to compute feature maps by removing the average pooling layer and the fully-connected layer. We attach a 1×1 convolutional layer as a feature extraction layer, which consists of 1024 channels and is initialized from a gaussian distribution, to the end of the last residual block in ResNet-101. We apply a convolutional layers for classification and box regression, and extract a 7×7 score and regression map for given RoI using PSRoI pooling. Then, the probability of classes and the bounding boxes for the corresponding RoI are predicted through average voting. SAN, which is applied between the feature extraction layer and the detection layer, consists of several sub-networks corresponding to the different sizes of RoI and each sub-network consists of a 1×1 convolution of which the number of channels equals to the input feature and the following ReLU.

Learning. The detection network is trained by stochastic gradient descent (SGD) with the online hard example mining (OHEM) [32]. We use the pre-trained ResNet-101 model on ImageNet [31]. We train the network for 29k iterations with a learning rate of 10^{-3} dividing it by 10 at 20k iterations, a weight decay of 0.0005, and a momentum of 0.9 for VOC PASCAL and 240k iterations with a learning rate of 10^{-3} dividing it by 10 at 160k iterations, a weight decay of 0.0005, and a momentum of 0.9 for MS COCO. A mini-batch consists of 2 images, which are resized such that its shorter side of image is 600 pixels. We use 300 proposals per image for training and testing.

Learning Trick for SAN. We divide the entire detection framework into two parts according to the influence of loss to exclude the effect of scale-aware loss on the detection framework. However, since it is difficult to separate only the loss corresponding to SAN from the already aggregated loss, we use a learning trick based on the siamese architecture [3]. We configure the siamese architecture of two SAN with shared weights for scale-aware and detection loss, respectively (Fig. 5). By not propagating the error from the siamese network for scale-aware

Table 1. Comparison on VOC PASCAL and MS COCO. SAN_0 stands for SAN without scale-aware loss and *SAN* stands for the full extension of SAN with scale-aware loss

	VOC 07+12/07	MS COCO `trainval35k/minival`				
	mAP	mAP	$mAP_{@0.5}$	$mAP_{@S}$	$mAP_{@M}$	$mAP_{@L}$
Faster RCNN [28]	79.3	30.3	52.1	9.9	32.2	47.4
FPN [22]	-	37.8	60.8	22.0	41.5	49.8
R-FCN [21]	79.4	35.3	58.7	16.4	39.5	53.8
Deformable R-FCN [4]	82.1	41.2	62.9	19.4	46.6	61.2
R-FCN-SAN_0	80.1	-	-	-	-	-
Deformable R-FCN-SAN_0	82.4	-	-	-	-	-
Faster RCNN-*SAN*	79.9	-	-	-	-	-
R-FCN-*SAN*	80.6	36.3	59.6	16.7	40.5	55.5
Deformable R-FCN-*SAN*	82.8	43.3	65.1	21.0	48.8	64.6

loss, we prevent the performance degradation caused by scale-aware loss and make SAN consider both scale invariance and detection. Without this learning trick, the extension with SAN can reduces the detection accuracy.

Experiments on PASCAL VOC. We evaluate the proposed SAN on PASCAL VOC dataset [9] that has 20 object categories. We train the models on the union set of VOC 2007 `trainval` and VOC 2012 `trainval` (16k images), and evaluate on VOC 2007 `test` set (5k images). We attach SAN to baseline under these conditions: the reference scale of 224^2, the three partitions of $(0^2, 160^2]$, $(160^2, 288^2)$, $[288^2, \infty)$. SAN improves the mean Average Precision (mAP) by 1.2 points with a slight increase from 120 ms to 130 ms in the computing time, over a single-scale baseline of R-FCN on ResNet-101 (Fig. 8 and Tables 1 and 6).

Experiments on MS COCO. We evaluate the proposed SAN on MS COCO dataset [23] that has 80 object categories. We train the models on the union set of 80k training set and a 35k subset of validation set (`trainval35k`), and evaluate on a 5k subset of validation set (`minival`). We attach SAN to baseline under these conditions: the reference scale of 128^2, the three partitions of $(0^2, 64^2]$, $(64^2, 192^2)$, $[192^2, \infty)$. SAN improves the COCO-style mAP, which is the average AP across thresholds of IoU from 0.5 to 0.95 with an interval of 0.05, by 2.1 points over a single-scale baseline of Deformable R-FCN on ResNet-101 (Table 1).

Partitioning. It is important for SAN to define scale partitioning for the selection of the sub-network of SAN and the reference scale for training of SAN. The scale statistics for VOC PASCAL 2007 shows different medians and standard deviations of scales depending on the classes, but 231^2 scale is the most common (Fig. 6). SAN is trained by using the convolutional features obtained by normalizing the RoI areas to the reference scale. We conduct the experiment on three reference scales of $\{160^2, 224^2, 288^2\}$ around the common scale 231^2 and several partitions around the reference scale (Table 2). The best detection accuracy is obtained when the reference scale is 224^2 and the scale space is partitioned into

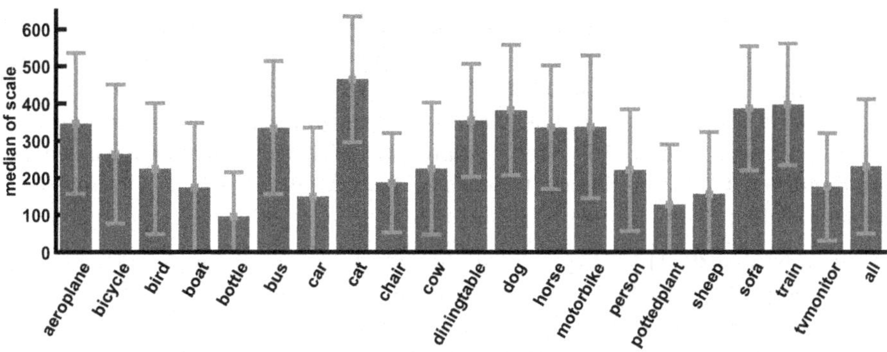

Fig. 6. The medians and standard deviations of scales according to the classes

Table 2. Varying partitions

$N_{partitions}$	Reference scale	Partitioning	mAP (%)
1 (R-FCN)	-	-	79.37
2	160^2	$(0^2, 160^2], [160^2, \infty)$	80.08
2	224^2	$(0^2, 224^2], [224^2, \infty)$	80.44
2	288^2	$(0^2, 288^2], [288^2, \infty)$	80.29
3	224^2	$(0^2, 160^2], (160^2, 288^2), [288^2, \infty)$	80.57
3	224^2	$(0^2, 112^2], (112^2, 448^2), [448^2, \infty)$	80.55
3	224^2	$(0^2, 112^2], (112^2, 224^2), [224^2, \infty)$	80.16

Table 3. Gaussian vs. Identity initialization

Initialization method	$N_{partitions}$	mAP (%)
Gaussian	2	79.85
Gaussian	3	79.97
Identity	2	80.44
Identity	3	80.57

three sections: $(0^2, 160^2]$, $(160^2, 288^2)$, $[288^2, \infty)$. The metric of MS COCO is defined over instance size: small ($Area < 32^2$), medium ($32^2 < Area < 96^2$) and large ($96^2 < Area$), and these partitions is doubled considering the process of resizing in detection network. The best detection accuracy is obtained with the partitions of $(0^2, 64^2]$, $(64^2, 192^2)$, $[192^2, \infty)$ at the reference scale 128^2 for MS COCO.

Initialization. The initialization methods for the sub-networks belonging to SAN is an important issue. Unlike ResNet-101 for the detection network, SAN does not have any pre-trained weights, but we have the clue to the initialization:

the role of SAN is reducing the difference between convolutional features for the scale difference. Because SAN should output almost the same convolutional features in adjacent scales, we need to initialize the weights to an identity matrix and biases to zero instead of the widely used initialization methods; gaussian, xavier [14], and MSRA [16]. We compare this with the gaussian initialization and figure out that it is difficult to learn SAN without the initialization with an identity matrix (Table 3).

Pooling Method. Apart from the pooling method used in the detection frameworks, the pooling method is also needed for the learning of SAN. We compare the average pooling (`AVE`) extracting the average value of a given area and the max pooling (`MAX`) extracting the maximum value of a given area (Table 4). In the case of R-FCN, SAN learned with the average pooling shows slightly higher detection accuracy than SAN learned with the max pooling.

Mini-Batch. To train SAN, we need the convolutional features for a scale normalized image at the reference scale. However, since the additional convolutional operations are a time-consuming process, we selectively extract only a part of a mini-batch by normalizing it with a square of 224^2. We shows the effect of the number of samples on the detection accuracy and the best results are obtained with 16 samples (Table 5).

Table 4. Average vs Max pooling

$N_{partitions}$	Pooling method	mAP (%)
2	`AVE`	80.44
3	`AVE`	80.57
3	`MAX`	80.35

Table 5. Varying mini-batch

$N_{partitions}$	N_x	mAP (%)
2	16	80.44
3	4	80.37
3	8	80.57
3	16	80.57

Effectiveness of SAN. We define the convolutional feature at the reference scale as a scale-invariant feature and measure RMSE between the convolutional features $z_{i,s}$ for sample i at scale s and the reference scale s_0, to demonstrate the effectiveness of SAN. RMSEs for a convolutional feature without and with SAN are defined as

$$\mathrm{RMSE}(i, s|s_0) = \sqrt{\frac{1}{N_c} \sum_{\{x,y,c\} \in i} [z_{i,s}(x,y,c) - z_{i,s_0}(x,y,c)]^2}, \tag{3}$$

$$\mathrm{RMSE}(i, s|s_0, f) = \sqrt{\frac{1}{N_c} \sum_{\{x,y,c\} \in i} [f_s(z_{i,s}(x,y,c)) - z_{i,s_0}(x,y,c)]^2}, \tag{4}$$

respectively, where N_c is the number of channels and f_s is the sub-network of SAN. The convolutional feature $z_{i,s}$ is extracted using global average pooling to exclude the difference of spatial information. We experimentally prove the validity of SAN by showing that SAN reduces RMSEs for all classes in VOC PASCAL (Fig. 7).

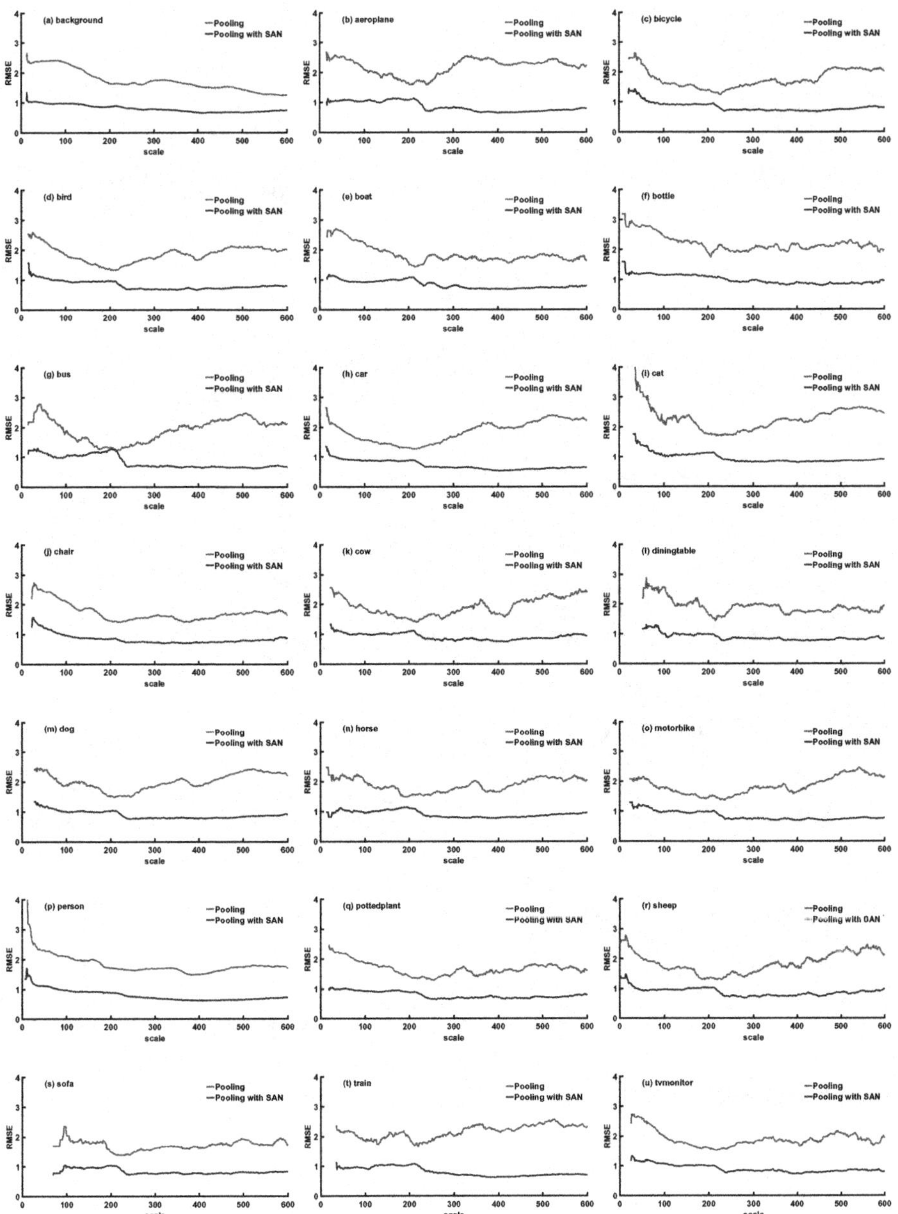

Fig. 7. The distribution for RMSE, which is a root mean squared error between the convolutional features extracted by RoI pooling with and without SAN, for 21 classes in VOC PASCAL

Fig. 8. Examples of object detection results on PASCAL VOC 2007 test set using R-FCN with SAN (80.57% mAP). The network is based on ResNet-101, and the training data is 07+12 trainval. A score threshold of 0.6 is used for displaying. The running time per image is 130 ms on NVidia Titan X Pascal GPU

Table 6. Detailed detection results on PASCAL VOC 2007 test set

Method	data	mAP	aero	bike	bird	boat	bottle	bus	car	cat	chair	cow	table	dog	horse	mbike	person	plant	sheep	sofa	train	tv
R-FCN	07+12	79.37	82.21	84.88	78.87	71.29	68.67	88.54	87.10	89.11	67.86	87.06	69.92	89.02	87.32	81.30	79.73	52.16	78.17	80.91	83.43	79.88
R-FCN(SAN)	07+12	80.57	82.02	84.33	79.74	72.52	70.16	87.33	87.72	89.45	68.74	87.51	75.65	88.40	88.18	83.79	81.05	53.71	81.75	81.04	87.21	81.13

5 Conclusion

We propose a Scale Aware Network (SAN) that maps the convolutional features from the different scales onto a scale-invariant subspace to make CNN-based detection methods more robust to the scale variation, and also construct a unique learning method which considers purely the relationship between channels without the spatial information for the efficient learning of SAN. To show the validity of our method, we visualize how convolutional features change according to the scale through a channel activation matrix and experimentally show that SAN reduces the feature differences in the scale space. We evaluate our method on VOC PASCAL and MS COCO dataset. Our method improves the mean Average Precision (mAP) by 1.2 points from R-FCN for VOC PASCAL and the COCO-style mAP by 2.1 point from Deformable R-FCN for MS COCO. We demonstrate SAN for object detection by conducting several experiments on structures and parameters. The proposed SAN essentially improves the quality of convolutional features in the scale space, and can be generally applied to many CNN-based detection methods to enhance the detection accuracy with a slight increase in the computing time.

As a future study, we will improve the performance by applying SAN to whole network including RPN, and try to study more deeply the relationship between convolutional features and scale normalization. In addition, we plan to improve not only the object detection but also the general influence of the scale that can exist in many areas of computer vision.

Acknowledgement. This work was supported by IITP grant funded by the Korea government (MSIT) (IITP-2014-3-00059, Development of Predictive Visual Intelligence Technology, IITP-2017-0-00897, SW Starlab support program, and IITP-2018-0-01290, Development of Open Informal Dataset and Dynamic Object Recognition Technology Affecting Autonomous Driving).

References

1. Adelson, E.H., Anderson, C.H., Bergen, J.R., Burt, P.J., Ogden, J.M.: Pyramid methods in image processing. RCA Eng. **29**, 33–41 (1984)
2. Benenson, R., Mathias, M., Timofte, R., Van Gool, L.: Pedestrian detection at 100 frames per second. In: IEEE Computer Society Conference on Computer Vision and Pattern Recognition (CVPR) (2012)
3. Chopra, S., Hadsell, R., LeCun, Y.: Learning a similarity metric discriminatively, with application to face verification. In: IEEE Computer Society Conference on Computer Vision and Pattern Recognition (CVPR) (2005)
4. Dai, J., et al.: Deformable convolutional networks. In: IEEE International Conference on Computer Vision (ICCV) (2017)
5. Dalal, N., Triggs, B.: Histograms of oriented gradients for human detection. In: IEEE Computer Society Conference on Computer Vision and Pattern Recognition (CVPR) (2005)
6. Ding, Y., Xiao, J.: Contextual boost for pedestrian detection. In: IEEE Computer Society Conference on Computer Vision and Pattern Recognition (CVPR) (2012)

7. Dollár, P., Appel, R., Belongie, S., Perona, P.: Fast feature pyramids for object detection. IEEE Trans. Pattern Anal. Mach. Intell. (TPAMI) **36**, 1532–1545 (2014)
8. Dollár, P., Tu, Z., Perona, P., Belongie, S.: Integral channel features. In: British Machine Vision Conference (BMVC) (2009)
9. Everingham, M., Van Gool, L., Williams, C.K., Winn, J., Zisserman, A.: The Pascal visual object classes (VOC) challenge. Int. J. Comput. Vis. (IJCV) **88**, 303–338 (2010)
10. Felzenszwalb, P.F., Girshick, R.B., McAllester, D., Ramanan, D.: Object detection with discriminatively trained part-based models. IEEE Trans. Pattern Anal. Mach. Intell. (TPAMI) **32**, 1627–1645 (2010)
11. Field, D.J.: Relations between the statistics of natural images and the response properties of cortical cells. JOSA A **4**, 2379–2394 (1987)
12. Geman, S., Bienenstock, E., Doursat, R.: Neural networks and the bias/variance dilemma. Neural Comput. **4**, 1–58 (1992)
13. Girshick, R.: Fast R-CNN. In: IEEE International Conference on Computer Vision (ICCV) (2015)
14. Glorot, X., Bengio, Y.: Understanding the difficulty of training deep feedforward neural networks. In: International Conference on Artificial Intelligence and Statistics (AISTATS) (2010)
15. Gonzalez, R.C.: Digital Image Processing. Pearson Education India, Noida (2009)
16. He, K., Zhang, X., Ren, S., Sun, J.: Delving deep into rectifiers: Surpassing human-level performance on imagenet classification. In: IEEE International Conference on Computer Vision (ICCV) (2015)
17. He, K., Zhang, X., Ren, S., Sun, J.: Deep residual learning for image recognition. In: IEEE Computer Society Conference on Computer Vision and Pattern Recognition (CVPR) (2016)
18. Huang, C., Ai, H., Li, Y., Lao, S.: Vector boosting for rotation invariant multi-view face detection. In: IEEE International Conference on Computer Vision (ICCV) (2005)
19. James, G., Witten, D., Hastie, T., Tibshirani, R.: An introduction to statistical learning. Springer, New York (2013). https://doi.org/10.1007/978-1-4614-7138-7
20. Jones, M., Viola, P.: Fast multi-view face detection. Mitsubishi Electric Research Lab TR-20003-96 (2003)
21. Li, Y., He, K., Sun, J., et al.: R-FCN: Object detection via region-based fully convolutional networks. In: Advances in Neural Information Processing Systems (NIPS) (2016)
22. Lin, T.Y., Dollár, P., Girshick, R., He, K., Hariharan, B., Belongie, S.: Feature pyramid networks for object detection. In: IEEE Computer Society Conference on Computer Vision and Pattern Recognition (CVPR) (2017)
23. Lin, T.-Y., et al.: Microsoft COCO: common objects in context. In: Fleet, D., Pajdla, T., Schiele, B., Tuytelaars, T. (eds.) ECCV 2014. LNCS, vol. 8693, pp. 740–755. Springer, Cham (2014). https://doi.org/10.1007/978-3-319-10602-1_48
24. Liu, W., et al.: SSD: single shot multibox detector. In: Leibe, B., Matas, J., Sebe, N., Welling, M. (eds.) ECCV 2016. LNCS, vol. 9905, pp. 21–37. Springer, Cham (2016). https://doi.org/10.1007/978-3-319-46448-0_2
25. Park, D., Ramanan, D., Fowlkes, C.: Multiresolution models for object detection. In: Daniilidis, K., Maragos, P., Paragios, N. (eds.) ECCV 2010. LNCS, vol. 6314, pp. 241–254. Springer, Heidelberg (2010). https://doi.org/10.1007/978-3-642-15561-1_18

26. Redmon, J., Divvala, S., Girshick, R., Farhadi, A.: You only look once: unified, real-time object detection. In: IEEE Computer Society Conference on Computer Vision and Pattern Recognition (CVPR) (2016)
27. Redmon, J., Farhadi, A.: YOLO9000: better, faster, stronger. In: IEEE Computer Society Conference on Computer Vision and Pattern Recognition (CVPR) (2017)
28. Ren, S., He, K., Girshick, R., Sun, J.: Faster R-CNN: towards real-time object detection with region proposal networks. In: Advances in Neural Information Processing Systems (NIPS) (2015)
29. Ruderman, D.L.: The statistics of natural images. Netw. Comput. Neural Syst. **5**, 517–548 (1994)
30. Ruderman, D.L., Bialek, W.: Statistics of natural images: scaling in the woods. In: Physical Review Letters (1994)
31. Russakovsky, O., et al.: ImageNet large scale visual recognition challenge. Int. J. Comput. Vis. (IJCV) **115**, 211–252 (2015)
32. Shrivastava, A., Gupta, A., Girshick, R.: Training region-based object detectors with online hard example mining. In: IEEE Computer Society Conference on Computer Vision and Pattern Recognition (CVPR) (2016)
33. Viola, P., Jones, M.J.: Robust real-time face detection. Int. J. Comput. Vis. (IJCV) **57**, 137–154 (2004)
34. Wu, B., Ai, H., Huang, C., Lao, S.: Fast rotation invariant multi-view face detection based on real AdaBoost. In: IEEE International Conference on Automatic Face and Gesture Recognition (FG) (2004)
35. Yan, J., Zhang, X., Lei, Z., Liao, S., Li, S.Z.: Robust multi-resolution pedestrian detection in traffic scenes. In: IEEE Computer Society Conference on Computer Vision and Pattern Recognition (CVPR) (2013)
36. Yang, Y., Ramanan, D.: Articulated human detection with flexible mixtures of parts. IEEE Trans. Pattern Anal. Mach. Intell. (TPAMI) **35**, 2878–2890 (2013)
37. Kim, Y., Kang, B.N., Kim, D.: Detector with focus: normalizing gradient in image pyramid. In: International Conference on Image Processing (ICIP) (2017)

Hashing with Binary Matrix Pursuit

Fatih Cakir[1(✉)], Kun He[2], and Stan Sclaroff[2]

[1] FirstFuel Software, Lexington, MA, USA
fcakirs@gmail.com
[2] Department of Computer Science, Boston University, Boston, MA, USA
{hekun,sclaroff}@cs.bu.edu

Abstract. We propose theoretical and empirical improvements for two-stage hashing methods. We first provide a theoretical analysis on the quality of the binary codes and show that, under mild assumptions, a residual learning scheme can construct binary codes that fit any neighborhood structure with arbitrary accuracy. Secondly, we show that with high-capacity hash functions such as CNNs, binary code inference can be greatly simplified for many standard neighborhood definitions, yielding smaller optimization problems and more robust codes. Incorporating our findings, we propose a novel two-stage hashing method that significantly outperforms previous hashing studies on widely used image retrieval benchmarks.

1 Introduction

A main challenge for "learning to hash" methods lies in the discrete nature of the problem. Most approaches are formulated as non-linear mixed integer programming problems which are computationally intractable. Common optimization remedies include discarding the binary constraints and solving for continuous embeddings [1–5]. At test time the embeddings are typically thresholded to obtain the desired binary codes. However, even the relaxed problem is highly non-convex requiring nontrivial optimization procedures (*e.g.*, [6]), and the thresholded embeddings are prone to large quantization errors, necessitating additional measures (*e.g.*, [7]).

One prominent alternative to the relaxation approach is *two-stage hashing*, which decomposes the optimization problem into two stages: binary code inference (i) and hash function learning (ii). For a training set, binary codes are inferred in the inference stage, which are then used as target vectors in the hash function learning stage. Such methods closely abide to the discrete nature of the problem as the binary codes are directly incorporated into the optimization procedure. In two-stage hashing, most of the attention is drawn to the more challenging binary code inference step. Typically, this task is itself decomposed

Electronic supplementary material The online version of this chapter (https://doi.org/10.1007/978-3-030-01228-1_21) contains supplementary material, which is available to authorized users.

V. Ferrari et al. (Eds.): ECCV 2018, LNCS 11209, pp. 344–361, 2018.
https://doi.org/10.1007/978-3-030-01228-1_21

into a stage-wise problem where binary codes are learned in an iterative fashion. While theoretical guarantees for the underlying iterative scheme are usually provided, the overall quality of the binary codes is often overlooked. It is desirable to also determine the quality of the constructed binary codes.

In this paper, our first contribution is to provide an analysis on the quality of learned binary codes in two-step hashing. We focus on the frequently considered matrix fitting formulation (*e.g.*, [6,8–11]), in which a "neighborhood structure" is defined through an affinity matrix and the task is to generate binary codes so as to preserve the affinity values. We first demonstrate that ordinary Hamming distances are unable to fully preserve the neighborhood. Then, with a weighted Hamming metric, we prove that a residual learning scheme can construct binary codes that can preserve any neighborhood with arbitrary accuracy under mild assumptions. Our analysis reveals that distance scaling, as well as fixing the dimensionality of the Hamming space, which are often employed in many hashing studies [6,12–14], are both unnecessary.

On the other hand, one common inconvenience in two-stage hashing methods is that, steps (i) and (ii) are often interleaved, so as to enable bit correction during training [11,15,16]. Bit correction has shown to improve retrieval performance, especially when the hash mapping constitutes simple functions such as linear hyperplanes and decision stumps [9]. In contrast, we show that such an interleaved process is unnecessary with high capacity hash functions such as Convolutional Neural Networks (CNNs).

A further benefit of removing interleaving is that the affinity matrix can be constructed directly according to the definition of the neighborhood structure, instead of the pairwise similarities between training instances. For example, when preserving semantic similarity, the neighborhood is generally defined through class label agreement. Defining the affinity with respect to labels rather than instances yields a much smaller optimization problem for the inference task (i), and provides robustness for the subsequent hash function learning (ii). In contrast, instance-based inference schemes result in larger optimization problems, often necessitating subsampling to reduce the scale.

With these insights in mind, we implement our novel two-stage hashing method with standard CNN architectures, and conduct experiments on multiple image retrieval datasets. The affinity matrix in our formulation may or may not be derived from class labels, and can constitute binary or multi-level affinities. In fact, we consider a variety of experiments that include multi-class (CIFAR-10 [17], ImageNet100 [18]), multi-label (NUSWIDE [19]) and unlabeled (22K LabelMe [20]) datasets. We achieve new state-of-the-art performance for all of these datasets. In summary, our contributions are:

1. We provide a technical analysis on the quality of the inferred binary codes demonstrating that under mild assumptions we can fit any neighborhood with arbitrary accuracy. Our analysis is relevant to the formulations used in many two-stage hashing methods (*e.g.*, [8,9,11,21,22]).
2. We demonstrate that with high-capacity hash functions such as CNNs, the bit correction task is expendable. As a result, binary code inference can be

performed on items that directly define the neighborhood, yielding more robust target vectors and improving the retrieval performance. We achieve state-of-the-art performance in four standard image retrieval benchmarks.

2 Related Work

We only review hashing studies most relevant to our problem. For a general survey, please refer to [23].

The two-stage strategy for hashing was pioneered by Lin *et al.* [21] in which the authors reduced the binary code inference task into a series of binary quadratic programming (BQP) problems. The target codes are optimized in an iterative fashion and traditional machine learning classifiers such as Support Vector Machines (SVMs) and linear hyperplanes that fit the target vectors are employed as the hash functions. In [9], the authors proposed a graph-cut algorithm to solve the BQP problem and employed boosted decision trees as the hash functions. The graph-cut algorithm has shown to yield a solution well bounded with respect to the optimal value [24]. The authors also demonstrated that, with shallow models an interleaved process of binary code inference and hash function learning allowed bit correction and improved the retrieval performance. Differently, Xia *et al.* [8] proposed using a coordinate descent algorithm with Newton's method to solve the BQP problem and utilized CNNs as the hash mapping. Do *et al.* [11] solved the the BQP problem using semidefinite relaxation and Lagrangian approaches. They also investigate the quality of the relaxed solution and prove that it is within a factor of the global minimum. Zhuang *et al.* [22] demonstrated that the same BQP approach can be extended to solve a triplet-based loss function. Other work reminiscent of these two-stage methods include hashing techniques that employ alternating optimization to minimize the original optimization problem [10,15,16,25].

While error-bounds and convergences properties of the underlying iterative scheme is usually provided, none of the aforementioned studies provide a technical guarantee on the overall quality of the constructed binary codes. In this study we provide such an analysis. Our technical analysis has connections to low-rank matrix learning [26–29] in which we construct binary codes in a gradient descent or *matrix pursuit* methodology. Differently, we constrain ourselves with binary rank-one matrices, which are required for Hamming distance computations. Also, while not all two-stage hashing studies follow an interleaved process (*e.g.*, [21,30,31]), to the best of our knowledge, all construct the affinity matrix using training instances. This warrants an in-depth look to the necessity of such a process when high-capacity hash functions are employed.

Our hashing formulation follows the matrix fitting formulation which is almost exclusively used in two-stage methods. This formulation was originally proposed in [6] and has been widely adopted in subsequent hashing studies (*e.g.*, [8,9,11,21,32]). Whereas the major contribution in this paper lies in establishing convergence properties of the binary code inference task, our formulation also has subtle and key differences to [6] and other two-stage methods. Specifically, we allow weighted hamming distances with optimally learned weights given the inferred binary codes. We perform inference directly on items that define the neighborhood, enabling more robust target vector construction as will be shown. In retrieval experiments, we compare against recent hashing studies, including [4,14,16,33–39], and achieve state-of-the-art performances.

3 Formulation

In this section, we first discuss the two stages of our hashing formulation: binary code inference and hash mapping learning. An analysis on affinity matrix construction comes next. All proofs are provided in the supplementary material.

3.1 Binary Code Inference

In this section, we explain our inference step (i). We are given a metric space $(\mathcal{X}, d)$ where $\mathcal{X} = \{\mathbf{x}_1, \cdots, \mathbf{x}_n\}$ denotes a set of items and $d : \mathcal{X} \times \mathcal{X} \to \mathbb{R}_{\geq 0}$ is a metric. Note that $\mathbf{x}$ can correspond to instances, labels, multi-labels or any item that is involved in defining the neighborhood. Given the assumption that the neighborhood is defined through metric d, we learn the hash mapping $\Phi : \mathcal{X} \to \mathbb{H}^b$ by optimizing the *neighborhood preservation fit*:

$$\min_{\Phi} \sum_{i,j} [\gamma d(\mathbf{x}_i, \mathbf{x}_j) - d_h(\Phi(\mathbf{x}_i), \Phi(\mathbf{x}_j))]^2, \tag{1}$$

where d_h is the Hamming distance and γ is a suitably selected scaling parameter. In order to scale distances to the range of d_h, we set $\gamma = b/d_{\max}$ where $d_{\max} = \max_{\mathbf{x},\mathbf{y} \in \mathcal{X}} d(\mathbf{x}, \mathbf{y})$ is known.[1] Solving Eq. 1 entails discrete loss minimization, which in general is a non-linear mixed-integer programming problem. Instead, two-stage methods decompose the solution into two steps, the first involving a binary integer program to find a set of binary codes, or auxilliary variables $\{\mathbf{u}_i \in \mathbb{H}^b\}_{i=1}^n$ that minimize Eq. 1. This program can be formulated as:

$$\min_{\mathbf{u}} \sum_{i,j} [\gamma d(\mathbf{x}_i, \mathbf{x}_j) - d_h(\mathbf{u}_i, \mathbf{u}_j)]^2 = \min_{\mathbf{u}} \frac{1}{4} \sum_{i,j} [\mathbf{u}_i^\top \mathbf{u}_j - s(\mathbf{x}_i, \mathbf{x}_i)]^2, \tag{2}$$

where $s(\mathbf{x}_i, \mathbf{x}_j) = b - 2\gamma d(\mathbf{x}_i, \mathbf{x}_j), \forall i, j \in \mathcal{X}$. While the LHS of Eq. 2 is a distance equivalence problem, the RHS is an affinity matching task. Such affinity based preservation objectives have also been considered previously [1,6,14,33].

In our formulation, we consider weighted Hamming distances by weighting each bit in $\mathbf{u}$. The weighted Hamming distance has been used in past studies to provide more granular similarities compared to its unweighted counterpart (*e.g.*, [40–44]). While this hashing scheme still enjoys low memory footprint and fast distance computations, weighting the individual bits enables us to construct binary codes that better preserve affinity values, as will be shown later.

---

[1] Our later analysis in this section only requires $d_{\max}$ to be bounded.

We reformulate Eq. 2 by defining weight vector $\boldsymbol{\alpha} = [\alpha_1, \cdots, \alpha_b]^\top$:

$$\frac{1}{4}\sum_{i,j}[(\boldsymbol{\alpha} \odot \mathbf{u}_i)^\top \mathbf{u}_j - s(\mathbf{x}_i, \mathbf{x}_i)]^2 \propto \frac{1}{2}\|\mathcal{U} - \mathcal{R}\|_F^2 = f(\mathcal{U}), \tag{3}$$

where $\odot$ denotes the Hadamard product, $\mathcal{U}_{ij} = (\boldsymbol{\alpha} \odot \mathbf{u}_i)^\top \mathbf{u}_j, \mathcal{R}_{ij} = s(\mathbf{x}_i, \mathbf{x}_j), \forall i,j \in \mathcal{X}$ and $\|\cdot\|_F$ denotes the Frobenius norm. We note that the *affinity matrix* $\mathcal{R}$ is real and symmetric as per its construction from metric d.

Let $\mathbf{V} = [\mathbf{u}_1, \cdots, \mathbf{u}_n]^\top \in \mathbb{H}^{n\times b}$ denote the *binary code matrix*, then $\mathcal{U}$ can be written as the weighted sum of b rank-one matrices $\sum_{k=1}^{b} \alpha_k \mathbf{v}_k \mathbf{v}_k^\top$ where $\mathbf{v}_k \in \{-1, 1\}^n$ is the k-th column in $\mathbf{V}$. Given this fact, our binary inference problem can be reformulated as:

$$\min\ f(\mathcal{U}), \quad \text{s.t. } \mathcal{U} = \sum_{k=1}^{b} \alpha_k \mathbf{v}_k \mathbf{v}_k^\top, \ \mathbf{v} \in \{-1, +1\}^n. \tag{4}$$

The additive property of $\mathcal{U}$ is attractive, since it suggests that the problem could be solved by a *stepwise* algorithm that adds the $\mathbf{v}_k$'s one by one. In particular, we will apply the projected gradient descent algorithm to solve Eq. 4. Starting with an initial value, $\mathcal{U}_0 = \mathbf{0}$, an update step can be formulated as:

$$\mathcal{U}_t \leftarrow \mathcal{U}_{t-1} + \alpha_t \mathbf{v}_t \mathbf{v}_t^\top, \tag{5}$$

where

$$\mathbf{v}_t = \underset{\mathbf{v}\in\{-1,+1\}^n}{\arg\max}\ \langle \mathbf{v}\mathbf{v}^\top, -\nabla f(\mathcal{U}_{t-1})\rangle \tag{6}$$

finds the projection of the negative gradient direction $-\nabla f(\mathcal{U}_{t-1})$ in the subspace spanned by rank-one binary matrices, and α_t is a step size. This projection is important for maintaining the additive property in Eq. 4.

Since $\langle \mathbf{v}\mathbf{v}^\top, \nabla f\rangle = \mathbf{v}^\top \nabla f \mathbf{v}$, Eq. 6 is a BQP problem which in general is NP-hard. Here, we take a spectral relaxation approach which is also used in past methods (*e.g.*, [6,21,33]). A closed-form solution to Eq. 6 exists if the binary vector $\mathbf{v}$ is relaxed to continuous values. Specifically, if $Q = -\nabla f(\mathcal{U})$, the following relaxation yields the Rayleigh Quotient [45]:

$$\max_{\mathbf{v}^\top \mathbf{v}=n} \mathbf{v}^\top Q \mathbf{v} = n\lambda_{\max}(Q), \tag{7}$$

where $\lambda_{\max}$ denotes the largest eigenvalue, and the optimal solution, $\mathbf{v}^*$, is the corresponding eigenvector. The binarized value of $\mathbf{v}^*$, $\text{sgn}(\mathbf{v}^*)$, is an approximate solution for Eq. 6. This solution can optionally be used as an initial point for BQP solvers in further maximizing Eq. 6, (*e.g.*, [46–48]). Note that the main technical results to be given are independent of the particular BQP solver.

The negative gradient $-\nabla f(\mathcal{U}_{t-1}) = \mathcal{R} - \sum_{k=1}^{t-1} \mathbf{v}_k \mathbf{v}_k^\top$, also a symmetric matrix, can be considered as the *residual* at iteration $t-1$. At each iteration, we find the most correlated rank-one matrix with this residual and move our solution in that direction. If the step size α_t is set to 1 for all t, then $\mathcal{U}$ can be decomposed as the product of the binary code matrices $\mathbf{V}\mathbf{V}^\top$, yielding ordinary Hamming distances. However, with constant step sizes, the below property states that there exist certain affinity matrices $\mathcal{R}$ such that no $\mathcal{U}$ exists that *fits* $\mathcal{R}$.

Property 1. *Let Q_t be the residual $-\nabla f(\mathcal{U}_t)$ at iteration t. There exists a $\mathcal{R}$ such that $\forall t$, $\|Q_t\|_F > 0$.*

Such a result motivates us to relax the constraint on the step size parameter α_t. If α is relaxed to any real value, then what we have essentially is weighted Hamming distances and we demonstrate that one can monotonically decrease the residual $\mathcal{R}$ in this case. We now provide our main theorem:

Theorem 2. *If $\alpha_t \in \mathbb{R}$, then the gradient descent algorithm Eqs. 5–6 satisfies*

$$\|Q_t\|_F \leq \eta^{t-1}\|Q_{t-1}\|_F, \quad \forall t \tag{8}$$

where $\eta \in [0, 1]$.

Theorem 2 states that the norm of the residual is only monotonically non-increasing. However, it may not strictly decrease, since the solution $\mathbf{v}_t$ of Eq. 6 can actually be orthogonal to the gradient, *i.e.*, $\mathbf{v}_t^\top Q_{t-1}\mathbf{v}_t$ might be zero. If we ensure non-orthogonal directions are selected at each iteration, then the residual strictly decreases, as the following corollary states.

Corollary 3. *If $\mathbf{v}_t^\top Q_{t-1}\mathbf{v}_t \neq 0$, $\forall t$ then the residual norm $\|Q_t\|_F$ strictly decreases.*

Although the directions $\mathbf{v}_t\mathbf{v}_t^\top$ are greedily selected with step sizes α_t, one can refine step sizes of all past directions at each iteration. This generally leads to much faster convergence. More formally, we can refine the step size parameters by solving the following regression problem:

$$\boldsymbol{\alpha}^* = \arg\min_{\alpha_1,\cdots,\alpha_t} \frac{1}{2}\|\sum_{k=1}^{t} \alpha_k \mathbf{v}_k\mathbf{v}_k^\top - \mathcal{R}\|_F^2. \tag{9}$$

Fortunately, Eq. 9 is an ordinary least squares problem admitting a closed-form solution. Let $\widehat{\mathbf{v}}_k = \text{vec}(\mathbf{v}_k\mathbf{v}_k^\top)$ and $\widehat{\mathbf{r}} = \text{vec}(\mathcal{R})$ where $\text{vec}(\cdot)$ denotes the vectorization operator. Given $\widehat{\mathbf{V}}_t = [\widehat{\mathbf{v}}_1, \cdots, \widehat{\mathbf{v}}_t]$, the minimizer of Eq. 9 is

$$\boldsymbol{\alpha}_t^* = (\widehat{\mathbf{V}}_t^\top \widehat{\mathbf{V}}_t)^{-1}\widehat{\mathbf{V}}_t^\top \widehat{\mathbf{r}}, \tag{10}$$

where $\boldsymbol{\alpha}_t^* = [\alpha_1^*, \cdots, \alpha_t^*]^\top$. The solution requires $\mathcal{O}(t^3) + \mathcal{O}(t^2n^2) + \mathcal{O}(tn^2)$ operations with $n = |\mathcal{X}|$. If $n > \sqrt{t}$, the time complexity is dominated by the $\mathcal{O}(t^2n^2)$ term. Note that in practice, typical values for t, the number of bits, are small (<100) and can be considered a constant factor.

We now provide a property indicating that this refinement of the step-sizes does not break the monotonicity as defined in Theorem 2 and Corollary 3.

Algorithm 1. Binary code inference

input : $\mathcal{X} = \{\mathbf{x}_1, \cdots, \mathbf{x}_n\}$, $d : \mathcal{X} \times \mathcal{X} \rightarrow \mathbb{R}_{\geq 0}$. Boolean variable `regress`. (Optional) Procedure `Improve`$(Q, \mathbf{v}_0)$ to improve the solution $\mathbf{v}^\top Q \mathbf{v}$ s.t. $\mathbf{v} = \{-1, 1\}^n$ where $\mathbf{v}_0$ is an initial solution. $\mathcal{U} = \mathbf{0}$.

output: Code matrix $\mathbf{V} = [\mathbf{u}_1, \cdots, \mathbf{u}_n]^\top$, weight vector $\boldsymbol{\alpha} = [\alpha_1, \cdots, \alpha_T]^\top$

$\gamma = \frac{1}{d_{\max}}$, $\mathcal{R}_{ij} = 1 - 2\gamma d(\mathbf{x}_i, \mathbf{x}_j)$ (if `regress`), $\mathcal{R}_{ij} = s(\mathbf{x}_i, \mathbf{x}_j) \times b$ (if $\neg$`regress`)
for $t \leftarrow 1, ..., T$ **do**
  $\mathbf{v}_t \leftarrow$ eigenvector corresponding to the largest eigenvalue of $-\nabla f(\mathcal{U}_{t-1})$
  $\mathbf{v}_t \leftarrow \text{sgn}(\mathbf{v}_t)$, $\alpha_t \leftarrow 1$
  $\mathbf{v}_t \leftarrow$ `Improve`$(-\nabla f(\mathcal{U}_{t-1}), \mathbf{v}_t)$ (optional)
  if *regress* **then** // $\alpha_t \in \mathbb{R}$
    Set $[\alpha_1, \cdots, \alpha_t]^\top$ using Eq. 10
  end
  $\mathcal{U}_t \leftarrow \sum_t \alpha_t \mathbf{v}_t \mathbf{v}_t^\top$, $V_{\cdot,t} \leftarrow \mathbf{v}_t$ // Append $\mathbf{v}_t$ to $\mathbf{V}$
end

Property 4. *Let Q_t be the residual matrix at iteration t and α_t set according to Theorem 2. Let $\widehat{Q}_t$ be the residual after refining the step-sizes $\boldsymbol{\alpha}_t = [\alpha_1, \cdots, \alpha_t]^\top$ using Eq. 10. Then $\|\widehat{Q}_t\|_F \leq \|Q_t\|_F$.*

After learning $\mathcal{U} = \sum_{k=1}^{T} \alpha_k \mathbf{v}\mathbf{v}^t = \mathbf{A} \odot \mathbf{V}\mathbf{V}^\top$ where $A_{k,\cdot} = [\alpha_1, \cdots, \alpha_t], \forall k$ we obtain our binary code matrix $\mathbf{V} = [\mathbf{u}_1, \cdots, \mathbf{u}_n]^\top$ that contains the target codes for each element $\{\mathbf{x}_1, \cdots, \mathbf{x}_n\} \in \mathcal{X}$. This ends our inference step (i). We summarize our inference scheme in Alg. Binary code inference.

Remarks. We consider two different binary inference schemes: `constant` where the binary codes are constructed with constant step sizes yielding ordinary Hamming distances; and, `regress` where each bit is weighted yielding the weighted Hamming distance. For `regress`, since $(\boldsymbol{\alpha} \odot \mathbf{u}_i)^\top \mathbf{u}_j = b(1 - 2d(\mathbf{x}_i, \mathbf{x}_j)/d_{\max})$ in Eq. 3, we can embed the constant b into the weight vector variable $\boldsymbol{\alpha}$. As a result, in contrast to hashing methods where the Hamming space dimensionality b must be specified (*e.g.*, to set margin and scaling parameters [6,10,14]), our method only requires $d_{\max}$ to be bounded. On the other hand, regular Hamming distance, or `constant`, requires scaling with b beforehand. The approximate solution of Eq. 7 can be improved by using off-the-shelf BQP solvers. In Alg. Binary code inference, we refer to such solvers as the subroutine `Improve`$(\cdot)$. In this paper, we consider using a simple heuristic [46], which merely requires a positive objective value for Eq. 6.

We now proceed with step (ii): hash mapping learning.

3.2 Hash Mapping Learning

Recall that we inferred target codes $\mathbf{u} \in \mathbb{H}^b$ for each item $\mathbf{x} \in \mathcal{X}$, where $\mathbf{x}$ may correspond to data instances, classes, multi-labels *etc.*, depending on the neighborhood definition. For example, when the dataset is unsupervised and the neighborhood is defined merely through data instances, then $\mathcal{X}$ may correspond to the feature space with $d(\mathbf{x}_i, \mathbf{x}_j)$ being the Euclidean distance. For multi-class datasets, $\mathcal{X}$ and $d(\mathbf{x}_i, \mathbf{x}_j)$ may represent the set of classes and the distance values between pairs of classes, respectively. For multi-label datasets, $\mathcal{X}$ may correspond to the set of possible label combinations. Our binary inference scheme constructs target codes to items that *directly* define the neighborhood. In the experiments section, we cover various scenarios.

If $\mathcal{X}$ does not represent the feature space, then after the binary inference step (i), the target codes get assigned to data instances in a one-to-many fashion, depending on the relationship between the target code and data instance. For sake of clarity, we assume $\mathcal{X}$ is the feature space in this section.

We employ a collection of hash functions to learn the mapping, where a function $f : \mathcal{X} \to \{-1, 1\}$ accounts for the generation of a bit in the binary code. Many types of hash functions are considered in the literature. For simplicity, we consider the thresholded scoring function:

$$f(\mathbf{x}) \triangleq \mathrm{sgn}(\psi(\mathbf{x})), \tag{11}$$

where ψ can be either a shallow model such as a linear function, or a deep neural network. In experiments, we consider both types of embeddings. $\Phi(\mathbf{x}) = [f_1(\mathbf{x}), \cdots, f_b(\mathbf{x})]^\top$ then becomes a vector-valued function to be learned.

Recall that we inferred target codes $\mathbf{u} \in \mathbb{H}^b$ for each element $\mathbf{x} \in \mathcal{X}$. Having the target codes at our disposal, we now would like to find Φ such that the Hamming distances between $\Phi(\mathbf{x})$ and the corresponding target codes $\mathbf{u}$ are minimized. Hence, the objective can be formulated as:

$$\sum_{i=1}^{n} d_h(\Phi(\mathbf{x}_i), \mathbf{u}_i). \tag{12}$$

The Hamming distance is defined as $d_h(\Phi(\mathbf{x}_i), \mathbf{u}_i) = \sum_t [\![f_t(\mathbf{x}_i) \neq u_{it}]\!]$ where both d_h and the functions f_t are non-differentiable. Fortunately, we can relax f_t by dropping the *sgn* function in Eq. 11 and derive an upper bound on the Hamming loss. Note that $d_h(\Phi(\mathbf{x}_i), \mathbf{u}_i) = \sum_t [\![f_t(\mathbf{x}_i) \neq u_{it}]\!] \leq \sum_t l(-u_{it}\psi_t(\mathbf{x}_i))$ with a suitably selected convex margin-based function l. Thus, by substituting this surrogate function into Eq. 12, we can directly minimize this upper bound using stochastic gradient descent. We use the hinge loss as the upper bound l.

As similar to other two-stage hashing methods, at the heart of our formulation are the target vectors which are inferred as to fit the affinity matrix $\mathcal{R}$. Next, we take a closer look on how to construct this affinity matrix.

3.3 Affinity Matrix Construction

The affinity matrix can be defined through pairwise similarities of items that directly define the neighborhood, which may not correspond to training instances. Despite this flexibility of the formulation, previous related hashing studies generally consider using training instances.

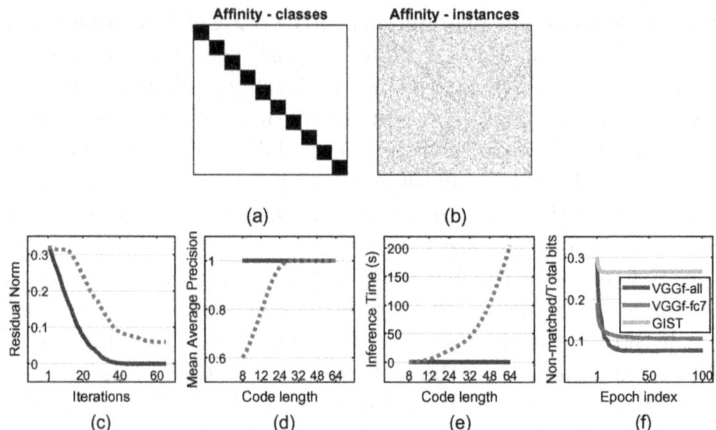

Fig. 1. In a series of experiments, we compare two sets of binary codes constructed with two different affinity matrices: class (a) and instance based (b). (c)–(e) contrasts the binary codes with respect to residual norm, mAP and inference time. Results for binary codes inferred from the class and instance affinity matrices are denoted with (—) and (····), respectively. We also learn hash functions with varying complexities to fit the inferred binary codes and plot the fraction of non-matched bits to the total number bits (f).

For certain neighborhoods, constructing the affinity matrix with training instances might yield suboptimal binary codes. To illustrate this case, consider Fig. 1 where we compare two sets of binary codes inferred from two different affinity matrices in a series of experiments. The neighborhood definition in these experiments is a standard one, typically found in nearly all hashing work. Specifically, we assume 10 classes and define the class affinity matrix as shown in Fig. 1(a). We also consider a hypothetical set of 1000 instances, each assigned to one of these 10 classes, and construct the affinity matrix as shown in Fig. 1(b) which we simply refer as the instance affinity matrix. Similarity of the instances are based on their class id's and deduced from the class affinity matrix. We infer binary codes under varying lengths as to reconstruct the class and instance affinity matrices. As explained in Sect. 3.2, instances are assigned the binary code of their respective classes for the class based inference. The experiments are repeated 5 times and average results are reported.

We first highlight the residual matrix Q_t norm in Fig. 1(c). Note that the residual norm of the class based inference converges to zero with fewer iterations: 40 bit codes are able to reconstruct the class affinity matrix with minimal discrepancy. On the other hand, lengthier codes are required to fully reconstruct the instance affinity matrix. We also provide the retrieval performance for the two sets of binary codes. Mean Average Precision (mAP) is the evaluation criterion. For this experiment, 100 instances are sampled from the instance set as queries, while the rest constitute the retrieval set. As demonstrated in Fig. 1(d), their is a dramatic difference in mAP values especially with compact codes.

The difference can be as large as 0.40. This type of sub-optimality for the binary codes inferred through the instance affinity matrix have also been observed previously (*e.g.*, [22]). Lastly, Fig. 1(e) gives the training time for the two inference schemes. While the inference time depends on the particular BQP solver, the number of decision variables nevertheless scales quadratically with the number of items in $\mathcal{X}$, as seen by the dramatic difference in the training time between the two inference schemes, especially with lengthier codes. Depending on the instance matrix size, the difference can easily scale up requiring subsampling to reduce the scale of the optimization task.

Given the evident disadvantages, why is the affinity matrix constructed from instances? The primary reason is because in most two-stage hashing methods the inference and hash function learning steps are interleaved for *on-the-fly* bit correction purposes. This requires the affinity matrix to correspond to pairwise instance similarities as the inferred bits will *immediately* be used for training the hash functions. However, given recent advances in deep learning, high-capacity predictors are becoming available, nullifying the need for bit correction. Consequently, one can opt to solve a smaller and more robust optimization problem defined on items that directly define the neighborhood.

To illustrate this point we learn hash functions of varying complexities to fit the set of binary codes,[2] and plot the fraction of non-matched bits to total number bits during hash function learning. We use the training set of CIFAR-10 and train the hash functions to fit the inferred 32-bit binary codes (total: $32 \times 50{,}000$ bits). We consider single layer neural networks on GIST [49] and fc7 features of a VGG-F network [50] pretrained on ImageNet [19], in addition to fine-tuning all the VGG-F layers. Figure 1(f) gives the results. Notice that as the capacity of the hash function increases the ratio of non-matched bits decrease significantly. While this ratio is above 0.25 with a single layer neural net on GIST, the single layer neural net trained on fc7 features yields just above 10% unmatched bits. When we fine-tune all layers of a VGG-F network this percentage reduces well below 10%. We can induce that with more complex architectures the ratio will diminish even more so.

We incorporate these insights into our formulation and conduct retrieval experiments against competing methods in the next section, where we achieve new state-of-the-art performances.

4 Experiments

We conduct experiments on widely used image retrieval benchmarks: CIFAR-10 [17], NUSWIDE [18], 22K LabelMe [20] and ImageNet100 [19].

CIFAR-10 is a dataset for image classification and retrieval, containing 60K images from 10 different categories. We follow the setup of [2,14,22,38]. This setup corresponds to two distinct partitions of the dataset. In the first case

[2] These binary codes are obtained from the class based inference scheme, though similar behavior is exhibited with codes obtained with instance based inference.

(*cifar-1*), we sample 500 images per category, resulting in 5,000 training examples to learn the hash mapping. The test set contains 100 images per category (1000 in total). The remaining images are then used to populate the hash table. In the second case (*cifar-2*), we sample 1000 images per category to construct the test set (10,000 in total). The remaining items are both used to learn the hash mapping and populate the hash table. Two images are considered neighbors if they belong to the same class.

NUSWIDE is a dataset containing 269K images. Each image can be associated with multiple labels, corresponding with 81 ground truth concepts. Following the setup in [2,14,22,38], we only consider images annotated with the 21 most frequent labels. In total, this corresponds to 195,834 images. The experimental setup also has two distinct partitionings: *nus-1* and *nus-2*. For both cases, a test set is constructed by randomly sampling 100 images per label (2,100 images in total). To learn the hash mapping, 500 images per label are randomly sampled in *nus-1* (10,500 in total). The remaining images are then used to populate the hash table. In the second case, *nus-2*, all the images excluding the test set are used in learning the hash mapping and populating the hash table. Two images are considered neighbors if they share a single label. We also specify a richer neighborhood by allowing multi-level affinities. In this scenario, two images have an affinity value equal to the number of common labels they share.

22K LabelMe consists of 22K images, each represented with a 512-dimensionality GIST descriptor. Following [3,12], we randomly partition the dataset into two: a training and test set consisting of 20K and 2K instances, respectively. A 5K subset of the training set is used in learning the hash mapping. As this dataset is unsupervised, we use the l_2 norm in determining the neighborhood. Similar to NUSWIDE, we allow multi-level affinities for this dataset. We consider four distance percentiles deduced from the training set and assign multi-level affinity values between the instances.

ImageNet100 is a subset of ImageNet [19] containing 130K images from 100 classes. We follow [4] and sample 100 images per class for training. All images in the selected classes from the ILSVRC 2012 validation set are used as the test set. Two images are considered neighbors if they belong to the same class.

Experiments without using multi-level affinities in defining the neighborhood are evaluated using a variant of Mean Average Precision (mAP), depending on the protocol we follow. We collectively group these as *binary affinity* experiments. *Multi-level affinity* experiments are evaluated using Normalized Discounted Cumulative Gain (NDCG), a metric standard in information retrieval for measuring ranking quality with multi-level similarities. In both experiments, Hamming distances are used to retrieve and rank data instances.

We term our method HBMP (**H**ashing with **B**inary **M**atrix **P**ursuit), and compare it against state-of-the-art hashing methods. These methods include: Spectral Hashing (**SH**) [33], Iterative Quantization (**ITQ**) [34], Supervised Hashing with Kernels (**SHK**) [6], Fast Hashing with Decision Trees (**FastHash**) [9], Structured Hashing (**StructHash**) [37], Supervised Discrete Hashing (**SDH**)

[16], Efficient Training of Very Deep Neural Networks (**VDSH**) [36], Deep Supervised Hashing with Pairwise Labels (**DPSH**) [38], Deep Supervised Hashing with Triplet Labels (**DTSH**) [14] and Mutual Information Hashing (**MIHash**) [39,51]. These competing methods have been shown to outperform earlier and other works such as [1,2,8,12,13,41,52].

For CIFAR-10 and NUSWIDE experiments, we fine tune the VGG-F architecture. For ImageNet100 experiments, we fine-tune the AlexNet architecture. Both deep learning models are pretrained using the ImageNet dataset. For *non-deep* methods, we use the output of the penultimate layer of both architectures. For the 22K LabelMe benchmark, we learn shallow models on top of the GIST descriptor. For deep learning based hashing methods, this corresponds to using a single fully connected neural network layer.

4.1 Results

We provide results for experiments with *binary similarities* with mAP as the evaluation criterion, and then for *multi-level similarities* with NDCG. In CIFAR-10, set $\mathcal{X}$, in which the binary inference is performed upon, represents the 10 classes. For NUSWIDE, as the neighborhood is defined using the multi-labels, it is then intuitive for set $\mathcal{X}$ to represent label combinations. In our case, we consider unique label combinations in the training set resulting in $\mathcal{X} = 4850$ items for binary inference. For the 22K LabelMe dataset, the items directly correspond to training instances. We provide results for the `regress` binary inference scheme, denoted simply as HBMP. A comparison between `constant` and `regress` is given in the supplementary material.

Table 1. Binary affinity experiments on CIFAR-10 and NUSWIDE datasets with *cifar-1* and *nus-1* partitionings. The underlying deep learning architecture is VGG-F. HBMP outperforms competing methods on CIFAR-10, and shows improvements, especially with lengthier codes on NUSWIDE.

VGG-F	CIFAR-10 (mAP)				NUSWIDE (mAP@5K)			
Method	12 Bits	24 Bits	32 Bits	48 Bits	12 Bits	24 Bits	32 Bits	48 Bits
SH [33]	0.183	0.164	0.161	0.161	0.621	0.616	0.615	0.612
ITQ [34]	0.237	0.246	0.255	0.261	0.719	0.739	0.747	0.756
SHK [6]	0.488	0.539	0.548	0.563	0.768	0.804	0.815	0.824
SDH [16]	0.478	0.557	0.584	0.592	**0.780**	0.804	0.816	0.824
FastHash [9]	0.553	0.607	0.619	0.636	0.779	0.807	0.816	0.825
StructHash [37]	0.664	0.693	0.691	0.700	0.748	0.772	0.790	0.801
VDSH [36]	0.538	0.541	0.545	0.548	0.769	0.796	0.803	0.807
DPSH [38]	0.713	0.727	0.744	0.757	0.758	0.793	0.818	0.830
DTSH [14]	0.710	0.750	0.765	0.774	0.773	0.813	0.820	0.838
MIHash [39]	0.738	0.775	0.791	0.816	0.773	**0.820**	**0.831**	**0.843**
HBMP	**0.799**	**0.804**	**0.830**	**0.831**	0.757	0.805	0.822	0.840

Table 2. Binary affinity experiments on CIFAR-10 and NUSWIDE datasets with *cifar-2* and *nus-2* partitionings (with VGG-F architecture). HBMP achieves new state-of-the-art performances, significantly improving over competing methods.

VGG-F	CIFAR-10 (mAP)				NUSWIDE (mAP@50K)			
Method	16 Bits	24 Bits	32 Bits	48 Bits	16 Bits	24 Bits	32 Bits	48 Bits
DRSH [52]	0.608	0.611	0.617	0.618	0.609	0.618	0.621	0.631
DRSCH [53]	0.615	0.622	0.629	0.631	0.715	0.722	0.736	0.741
DPSH [38]	0.903	0.885	0.915	0.911	0.715	0.722	0.736	0.741
DTSH [14]	0.915	0.923	0.925	0.926	0.756	0.776	0.785	0.799
MIHash [39]	0.927	0.938	0.942	0.943	0.798	0.814	0.819	0.820
HBMP	**0.942**	**0.944**	**0.945**	**0.945**	**0.804**	**0.829**	**0.841**	**0.855**

Binary Affinity Experiments. Table 1 gives results for the *cifar-1* and *nus-1* experimental settings in which mAP and mAP@5K values are reported for the CIFAR-10 and NUSWIDE datasets, respectively. Deep-learning based hashing methods such as DPSH, DTSH and MIHash outperform most non-deep hashing solutions. This is not surprising as feature representations are simultaneously learned along the hash mapping in these methods. Certain two-stage methods, *e.g.*, FastHash, remain competitive and top deep learning methods including DTSH and MIHash for various hash code lengths, especially for NUSWIDE. Our two-stage method, HBMP, outperforms all competing methods in majority of the cases, including MIHash, DTSH and DPSH with very large improvement margins. Specifically for CIFAR-10, the best competing method is MIHash, a recent study that learns the hash mapping using a mutual information formulation. The improvement over MIHash is over **6%** for certain hash code lengths, *e.g.*, for 12 bits **0.799** *vs.* 0.738 mAP. Our method significantly improves over SHK as well, which also proposes a matrix fitting formulation but learns its hash mapping in an interleaved manner. This validates defining the binary code inference over items that directly define the neighborhood, *i.e.* classes for CIFAR-10.

For the NUSWIDE dataset, the binary inference is done over the set of label combinations in the training data. HBMP demonstrates either comparable results or outperforms the state-of-the-art hashing methods. A relevant recent two-stage hashing method is [22] in which the same settings (*cifar-1* and *nus-1*) are used but with fine-tuning a VGG − 16 architecture. Their CIFAR-10 and NUSWIDE results have at most 0.80 mAP and 0.75 mAP@5K values, respectively, for all hash code lengths. HBMP, on the other hand, achieves these performance values with the inferior VGG-F architecture.

To further emphasize the merits of HBMP, we consider the experimental settings *cifar-2* and *nus-2* and compare against recent deep-learning hashing methods. In this setting, we again fine-tune the VGG-F architecture pretrained on ImageNet. Table 2 gives the results. Notice that our method significantly outperforms all techniques, and yields new state-of-the-art results for CIFAR-10 and NUSWIDE.

Retrieval results for ImageNet100 are given in Table 3. In these experiments, we only compare against MIHash, the overall best competing method in past experiments and HashNet [4], another very recent deep learning based hashing study. As demonstrated, HBMP establishes the new state-of-the-art in image retrieval for this benchmark. HBMP outperforms both methods significantly, *e.g.*, with 64-bits, we demonstrate 4–6% improvement. This further validates the quality of the binary codes produced with HBMP.

Table 3. mAP@1K values on ImageNet100 using AlexNet. HBMP outperforms the two state-of-the-art formulations using mutual information [39] and continuation methods [4].

AlexNet	ImageNet100 (mAP@1K)			
Method	16 Bits	32 Bits	48 Bits	64 Bits
HashNet [4]	0.506	0.630	0.663	0.683
MIHash [39]	0.569	0.661	0.685	0.694
HBMP	**0.574**	**0.692**	**0.712**	**0.742**

Multilevel Affinity Experiments. In these experiments, we allow multi-level similarities between items of set $\mathcal{X}$ and use NDCG as the evaluation criterion. For NUSWIDE, we consider the number of shared labels as affinity values. For 22K LabelMe dataset, we consider using distance percentiles $\{2\%, 5\%, 10\%, 20\%\}$ deduced from the training set to assign inversely proportional affinity values between the training instances. This emphasizes multi-level rankings among neighbors in the original feature space. In 22K LabelMe, we use a single fully connected layer as the hash mapping for the deep-learning based methods.

Table 4 gives results. For NUSWIDE, HBMP outperforms all state-of-the-art methods including MIHash. In 22K LabelMe, HBMP either achieves state-of-the-art performance, or is a close second. An interesting observation is that, when the feature learning aspect is removed due to the use of precomputed GIST features, non-deep methods such as FastHash and StructHash outperform deep-learning hashing methods DPSH and DTSH. While FastHash and StruchHash enjoy non-linear hash functions such as boosted decision trees, this also indicates that the prowess of DPSH and DTSH might come primarily through feature learning. On the other hand, both HBMP and MIHash show top performances with a single fully connected layer as the hash mapping, indicating that they produce binary codes that more accurately reflect the neighborhood. Regarding 22K LabelMe, for HBMP, set $\mathcal{X}$ corresponds to training instances, as similarly in other methods. This suggests that the performance improvement of HBMP is not merely due to the fact that the binary inference is performed upon items that directly define the neighborhood, but also due to our formulation that learns a Hamming metric with optimally selected bit weights.

Table 4. Multi-level affinity experiments on NUSWIDE and 22K LabelMe using VGG-F and GIST, respectively. The partitioning used for NUSWIDE is *nus-1*. The evaluation criterion is Normalized Discounted Cumulative Gain (NDCG). HBMP improves over the state-of-the-art in majority of the cases.

	NUSWIDE (VGG-F, NDCG)				22K LabelMe (GIST, NDCG)			
Method	16 Bits	32 Bits	48 Bits	64 Bits	16 Bits	24 Bits	32 Bits	48 Bits
FastHash [9]	0.885	0.896	0.899	0.902	0.672	0.716	0.740	0.757
StructHash [37]	0.889	0.893	0.894	0.898	0.704	0.768	0.802	0.824
DPSH [38]	0.895	0.905	0.909	0.909	0.677	0.740	0.755	0.765
DTSH [14]	0.896	0.905	0.911	0.913	0.620	0.685	0.694	0.702
MIHash [39]	0.886	0.903	0.909	0.912	0.713	0.822	**0.855**	**0.873**
HBMP	**0.914**	**0.924**	**0.927**	**0.930**	**0.823**	**0.829**	0.849	0.866

5 Conclusion

We have proposed improvements to a commonly used formulation in two-stage hashing methods. We first provided a theoretical result on the quality of the binary codes showing that, under mild assumptions, we can construct binary codes that fit the neighborhood with arbitrary accuracy. Secondly, we analyzed the sub-optimality of binary codes constructed as to fit an affinity matrix that is not defined on items directly related to the neighborhood. Incorporating our findings, we proposed a novel two-stage hashing method that significantly outperforms previous hashing studies on multiple benchmarks.

Acknowledgments. The authors thank Sarah Adel Bargal for helpful discussions. This work is primarily conducted at Boston University, supported in part by a BU IGNITION award, and equipment donated by NVIDIA.

References

1. Wang, J., Kumar, S., Chang, S.-F.: Semi-supervised hashing for large-scale search. In: IEEE Transactions on Pattern Analysis and Machine Intelligence (PAMI) (2012)
2. Lai, H., Pan, Y., Liu, Y., Yan, S.: Simultaneous feature learning and hash coding with deep neural networks. In: Proceedings of the IEEE Conference on Computer Vision and Pattern Recognition (CVPR) (2015)
3. Cakir, F., Sclaroff, S.: Adaptive hashing for fast similarity search. In: IEEE International Conference on Computer Vision (ICCV). IEEE (2015)
4. Cao, Z., Long, M., Wang, J., Yu, P.S.: HashNet: deep learning to hash by continuation. In: Proceedings of IEEE International Conference on Computer Vision (ICCV) (2017)
5. He, K., Cakir, F., Bargal, S.A., Sclaroff, S.: Hashing as tie-aware learning to rank. In: Proceedings of IEEE Conference on Computer Vision and Pattern Recognition (CVPR) (2018)
6. Liu, W., Wang, J., Ji, R., Jiang, Y.G., Chang, S.-F.: Supervised hashing with kernels. In:Proceedings of IEEE Conference on Computer Vision and Pattern Recognition (CVPR) (2012)

7. Liu, H., Wang, R., Shan, S., Chen, X.: Deep supervised hashing for fast image retrieval. In: Proceedings of IEEE Conference on Computer Vision and Pattern Recognition (CVPR), June 2016
8. Xia, R., Pan, Y., Lai, H., Liu, C., Yan, S.: Supervised hashing for image retrieval via image representation learning. In: Conference on Artificial Intelligence (AAAI) (2014)
9. Lin, G., Shen, C., Shi, Q., van den Hengel, A., Suter, D.: Fast supervised hashing with decision trees for high-dimensional data. In: Proceedings of the IEEE Conference on Computer Vision and Pattern Recognition (CVPR) (2014)
10. Shi, X., Xing, F., Cai, J., Zhang, Z., Xie, Y., Yang, L.: Kernel-based supervised discrete hashing for image retrieval. In: Proceedings of European Conference on Computer Vision (ECCV) (2016)
11. Do, T.T., Doan, A.D., Nguyen, D.T., Cheung, N.M.: Binary hashing with semidefinite relaxation and augmented lagrangian. In: Proceedings of European Conference on Computer Vision (ECCV) (2016)
12. Kulis, B., Darrell, T.: Learning to hash with binary reconstructive embeddings. In: Proceedings of Advances in Neural Information Processing Systems (NIPS) (2009)
13. Norouzi, M., Fleet, D.J.: Minimal loss hashing for compact binary codes. In: Proceedings of International Conference on Machine Learning (ICML) (2011)
14. Wang, X., Shi, Y., Kitani, K.M.: Deep supervised hashing with triplet labels. In: Lai, S.-H., Lepetit, V., Nishino, K., Sato, Y. (eds.) ACCV 2016. LNCS, vol. 10111, pp. 70–84. Springer, Cham (2017). https://doi.org/10.1007/978-3-319-54181-5_5
15. Ge, T., He, K., Sun, J.: Graph cuts for supervised binary coding. In: Fleet, D., Pajdla, T., Schiele, B., Tuytelaars, T. (eds.) ECCV 2014. LNCS, vol. 8695, pp. 250–264. Springer, Cham (2014). https://doi.org/10.1007/978-3-319-10584-0_17
16. Shen, F., Shen, C., Liu, W., Shen, H.T.: Supervised discrete hashing. In: Proceedings of the IEEE Conference on Computer Vision and Pattern Recognition (CVPR) (2015)
17. Krizhevsky, A., Hinton, G.: Learning multiple layers of features from tiny images. University of Toronto Technical Report (2009)
18. Chua, T.S., Tang, J., Hong, R., Li, H., Luo, Z., Zheng, Y.T.: NUS-WIDE: a real-world web image database from national university of Singapore. In: ACM Conference on Image and Video Retrieval (CIVR) (2009)
19. Deng, J., Dong, W., Socher, R., Li, L.J., Li, K., Li, F.-F.: ImageNet: a large-scale hierarchical image database. In: Proceedings of the IEEE Conference on Computer Vision and Pattern Recognition (CVPR) (2009)
20. Russell, B., Torralba, A., Murphy, K., Freeman, W.T.: LabelMe: a database and web-based tool for image annotation. Int. J. Comput. Vis. (IJCV) **77**, 157–173 (2008)
21. Suter, D., Lin, G., Shen, C., van den Hengel, A.: A general two-step approach to learning-based hashing. In: Proceedings of the IEEE International Conference on Computer Vision (ICCV) (2013)
22. Zhuang, B., Lin, G., Shen, C., Reid, I.: Fast training of triplet-based deep binary embedding networks. In: Proceedings of the IEEE International Conference on Computer Vision and Pattern Recognition (CVPR) (2016)
23. Wang, J., Zhang, T., Song, J., Sebe, N., Shen, H.T.: A survey on learning to hash. In: IEEE Transactions on Pattern Analysis and Machine Intelligence (PAMI) (2018)
24. Boykov, Y., Veksler, O., Zabih, R.: Fast approximate energy minimization via graph cuts. In: IEEE Transactions on Pattern Analysis and Machine Intelligence (PAMI) (2001)

25. Liu, W., Cun, M., Kumar, S., Chang, S.-F.: Discrete graph hashing. In: Proceedings of Advances in Neural Information Processing Systems (NIPS) (2014)
26. Shalev-Shwartz, S., Gonen, A., Shamir, O.: Large-scale convex minimization with a low-rank constraint. In: Proceedings of International Conference on Machine Learning (ICML) (2011)
27. Zhang, X., Schuurmans, D., Yu, Y.L.: Accelerated training for matrix-norm regularization: a boosting approach. In: Proceedings of Advances in Neural Information Processing Systems (NIPS) (2012)
28. Wang, Z., Lai, M.J., Lu, Z., Fan, W., Davulcu, H., Ye, J.: Rank-one matrix pursuit for matrix completion. In: Proceedings of International Conference on Machine Learning (ICML) (2014)
29. Yao, Q., Kwok, J.T.: Learning of generalized low-rank models: a greedy approach. In: Proceedings of International Joint Conference on Artificial Intelligence (IJCAI) (2016)
30. Zhang, D., Wang, J., Cai, D., Lu, J.: Self-taught hashing for fast similarity search. In: Proceedings of ACM SIGIR Conference on Research and Development in Information Retrieval (SIGIR) (2010)
31. Xia, R., Pan, Y., Lai, H., Liu, C., Yan, S.: Supervised hashing for image retrieval via image resentation learning. In: Conference on Artificial Intelligence (AAAI) (2014)
32. Yang, Q., Huang, L.-K., Zheng, W.-S., Ling, Y.: Smart hashing update for fast response. In: Proceedings International Joint Conference on Artificial Intelligence (IJCAI) (2013)
33. Weiss, Y., Torralba, A., Fergus, R.: Spectral hashing. In: Proceedings of Advances in Neural Information Processing Systems (NIPS) (2008)
34. Gong, Y., Lazebnik, S.: Iterative quantization: a procrustean approach to learning binary codes. In: Proceedings IEEE Conference on Computer Vision and Pattern Recognition (CVPR) (2011)
35. Wang, J., Kumar, S., Chang, S.-F.: Sequential projection learning for hashing with compact codes. In: Proceedings International Conference on Machine Learning (ICML) (2010)
36. Zhang, Z., Chen, Y., Saligrama, V.: Efficient training of very deep neural networks for supervised hashing. In: Proceedings of IEEE Conference on Computer Vision and Pattern Recognition (CVPR) (2016)
37. Lin, G., Liu, F., Shen, C., Jianxin, W., Shen, H.T.: Structured learning of binary codes with column generation for optimizing ranking measures. Int. J. Comput. Vis. (IJCV) **123**, 287–308 (2016)
38. Li, W.J., Wang, S., Kang, W.C.: Feature learning based deep supervised hashing with pairwise labels. In: Proceedings of International Joint Conference on Artificial Intelligence (IJCAI) (2016)
39. Fatih, C., He, K., Bargal, S.A., Sclaroff, S.: MIHash: online hashing with mutual information. In: IEEE International Conference on Computer Vision (ICCV) (2017)
40. Wang, X.J., Zhang, L., Jing, F., Ma, W.Y.: AnnoSearch: image auto-annotation by search. In: Proceedings of IEEE Conference on Computer Vision and Pattern Recognition (CVPR) (2006)
41. Weiss, Y., Fergus, R., Torralba, A.: Multidimensional spectral hashing. In: Fitzgibbon, A., Lazebnik, S., Perona, P., Sato, Y., Schmid, C. (eds.) ECCV 2012. LNCS, vol. 7576, pp. 340–353. Springer, Heidelberg (2012). https://doi.org/10.1007/978-3-642-33715-4_25

42. Li, X., Lin, G., Shen, C., van den Hengel, A., Dick, A.: Learning hash functions using column generation. In: Proceedings of International Conference on Machine Learning (ICML) (2013)
43. Zhang, L., Zhang, Y., Tang, J., Lu, K., Tian, Q.: Binary code ranking with weighted hamming distance. In: Proceedings of IEEE Conference on Computer Vision and Pattern Recognition (CVPR) (2013)
44. Jiang, Y.G., Wang, J., Xue, X., Chang, S.-F.: Query-adaptive image search with hash codes. IEEE Trans. Multimed. **15**, 442–453 (2013)
45. Horn, R.A., Johnson, C.R.: Matrix Analysis. Cambrigde University Press, Cambrigde (1983)
46. Merz, P., Freisleben, B.: Greedy and local search heuristics for unconstrained binary quadratic programming. J. Heuristics **8**, 197–213 (2002)
47. Buchheim, C., De Santis, M., Palagi, L., Piacentini, M.: An exact algorithm for nonconvex quadratic integer minimization using ellipsoidal relaxations. SIAM J. Optim. **23**, 1867–1889 (2013)
48. Wang, P., Shen, C., van den Hengel, A., Torr, P.: Large-scale binary quadratic optimization using semidefinite relaxation and applications. IEEE Trans. Pattern Anal. Mach. Intell. (PAMI) **39**, 470–485 (2017)
49. Oliva, A., Torralba, A.: Modeling the shape of the scene: a holistic representation of the spatial envelope. Int. J. Comput. Vis. (IJCV) **42**, 145–175 (2001)
50. Chatfield, K., Simonyan, K., Vedaldi, A., Zisserman, A.: Return of the devil in the details: delving deep into convolutional nets. In: Proceedings of British Machine Vision Conference (BMVC) (2014)
51. Cakir, F., He, K., Bargal, S.A., Sclaroff, S.: Hashing with mutual information. arXiv preprint arXiv:1803.00974 (2018)
52. Zhao, F., Huang, Y., Wang, L., Tan, T.: Deep semantic ranking based hashing for multi-label image retrieval. In: Proceedings of IEEE Conference on Computer Vision and Pattern Recognition (CVPR) (2015)
53. Zhang, R., Lin, L., Zhang, R., Zuo, W., Zhang, L.: Bit-scalable deep hashing with regularized imilarity learning for image retrieval and person re-identification. IEEE Trans. Image Process. **24**, 4766–4779 (2015)

MaskConnect: Connectivity Learning by Gradient Descent

Karim Ahmed(✉) and Lorenzo Torresani

Department of Computer Science, Dartmouth College, Hanover, NH, USA
karim@cs.dartmouth.edu, LT@dartmouth.edu

Abstract. Although deep networks have recently emerged as the model of choice for many computer vision problems, in order to yield good results they often require time-consuming architecture search. To combat the complexity of design choices, prior work has adopted the principle of modularized design which consists in defining the network in terms of a composition of topologically identical or similar building blocks (a.k.a. modules). This reduces architecture search to the problem of determining the number of modules to compose and how to connect such modules. Again, for reasons of design complexity and training cost, previous approaches have relied on simple rules of connectivity, e.g., connecting each module to only the immediately preceding module or perhaps to all of the previous ones. Such simple connectivity rules are unlikely to yield the optimal architecture for the given problem.

In this work we remove these predefined choices and propose an algorithm to learn the connections between modules in the network. Instead of being chosen a priori by the human designer, the connectivity is learned simultaneously with the weights of the network by optimizing the loss function of the end task using a modified version of gradient descent. We demonstrate our connectivity learning method on the problem of multi-class image classification using two popular architectures: ResNet and ResNeXt. Experiments on four different datasets show that connectivity learning using our approach yields consistently higher accuracy compared to relying on traditional predefined rules of connectivity. Furthermore, in certain settings it leads to significant savings in number of parameters.

Keywords: Connectivity learning · Image categorization

1 Introduction

Deep neural networks have emerged as one of the most prominent models for problems that require the learning of complex functions and that involve large

Electronic supplementary material The online version of this chapter (https://doi.org/10.1007/978-3-030-01228-1_22) contains supplementary material, which is available to authorized users.

V. Ferrari et al. (Eds.): ECCV 2018, LNCS 11209, pp. 362–378, 2018.
https://doi.org/10.1007/978-3-030-01228-1_22

amounts of training data. While deep learning has recently enabled dramatic performance improvements in many application domains, the design of deep architectures is still a challenging and time-consuming endeavor. The difficulty lies in the many architecture choices that impact—often significantly—the performance of the system. In the specific domain of image categorization, which is the focus of this paper, significant research effort has been invested in the empirical study of how depth, filter sizes, number of feature maps, and choice of nonlinearities affect performance [1–6]. Recently, several authors have proposed to simplify the architecture design by defining convolutional neural networks (CNNs) in terms of composition of topologically identical or similar building blocks or *modules*. This strategy was arguably first popularized by the VGG nets [7] which were built by stacking a series of convolutional layers having identical filter size (3×3). Other examples are ResNets [8] which are constructed by stacking residual blocks of fixed topology, ResNeXt models [9] which use multi-branch residual block modules, DenseNets [10] which use dense blocks as building blocks, or Multi-Fiber networks [11] which use parallel branches ("fibers") connected by routers ("transistors").

While the principle of modularized design has greatly simplified the challenge of building effective architectures for image analysis, the choice of how to combine and aggregate the computations of these building blocks still rests on the shoulders of the human designer. To avoid a combinatorial explosion of options, prior work has relied on simple, uniform rules of aggregation and composition. For example, in ResNets and DenseNets each building block is connected only to the preceding one, via identity mapping, convolution or pooling. ResNeXt models [9] use a set of simplifying assumptions: the branching factor C (also referred to as *cardinality*) is fixed to the same constant in all layers of the network, all branches of a module are fed the same input, and the outputs of parallel branches are aggregated by a simple additive operation that provides the input to the next module. While these simple rules of connectivity render network design more manageable, they are unlikely to yield the optimal connectivity for the given problem.

In this paper we remove these predefined choices and propose an algorithm that learns to combine and aggregate building blocks of a neural network by directly optimizing connectivity of modules with respect to the given task. In this new regime, the network connectivity naturally arises as a result of training rather than being hand-defined by the human designer. While in principle this involves a search over an exponential number of connectivity configurations, our method can efficiently optimize the training loss with respect to connectivity using a variant of backpropagation. This is achieved by means of *connectivity masks*, i.e., learned binary parameters that act as "switches" determining the final connectivity in our network. The masks are learned together with the convolutional weights of the network, as part of a joint optimization with respect to the given loss function for the problem.

We evaluate our method on the problem of multi-class image classification using two popular modular architectures: ResNet and ResNeXt. We demonstrate that models with our learned connectivity consistently outperform the networks based on predefined rules of connectivity for the same budget of residual blocks (and parameters). An interesting byproduct of our approach is that, in certain settings, it can automatically identify modules that are superfluous, i.e., unnecessary or detrimental for the end objective. At the end of the optimization, these unused modules can be pruned away without impacting the learned hypothesis while reducing substantially the runtime and the number of parameters to store.

By recasting the training procedure as an optimization over learning weights *and* connectivity, our method effectively searches over a larger space of solutions. This yields networks achieving higher accuracy than those constrained to use predefined connectivities. The average training time overhead is moderate, ranging between 13% (for ResNet models) and 39% (for ResNeXt models) compared to learning using fixed connectivity which, however, yields lower accuracy. Finally we point out that, although our experiments are carried out using ResNet and RexNeXt models, our approach is general and applicable without major modifications to other forms of network architectures and other tasks beyond image categorization. In principle our method can also be used to learn connectivity among layers of a traditional (i.e., non-modular) neural network or a CNN. However, modern networks typically include a very large number of layers (hundreds or even thousands [12]), which would make our approach very costly. Learning connectivity among modules is more manageable as each module encapsulates many layers and thus the total number of modules is typically small even for deep networks.

2 Related Work

Despite their wide adoption, deep networks often require laborious model search in order to yield good results. As a result, significant research effort has been devoted to the design of algorithms for automatic model selection. However, most of this prior work falls within the genre of hyper-parameter optimization [13–15] rather than architecture or connectivity learning. Evolutionary search has been proposed as an interesting framework to learn both the structure as well as the connections in a neural network [16–24]. Architecture search has also been recently formulated as a reinforcement learning problem with impressive results [25]. Several authors have proposed learning connectivity by pruning unimportant weights from the network [26–30]. However, these prior methods operate in stages where initially a network with full connectivity is learned and then connections are greedily removed according to an importance criterion. Compare to all these prior approaches, our work provides the advantage of learning the connectivity by direct global optimization of the loss function of the problem at hand rather than by greedy optimization of an auxiliary proxy criterion or by costly evolutionary search. Our technical approach shares similarities with the "Shake-Shake" regularization [31]. This procedure was demonstrated on two-branch ResNeXt models and consists in randomly scaling tensors produced by parallel branches during training while at test time the network uses uniform weighting of tensors. Conversely, our algorithm *learns* an optimal binary scaling of the parallel tensors with respect to the training objective and uses the resulting network with sparse connectivity at test time. While our algorithm is limited to optimizing the connectivity structure within a predefined architecture, Adams et al. [32] proposed a nonparametric Bayesian approach that searches over an infinite network using MCMC. Our approach can be viewed as a middle ground between two extremes: using hand-defined networks versus learning/searching the full architecture from scratch. The advantage is that our connectivity learning can be done without adding a significant training time overhead (only 13–39% depending on the architecture) compared to using fixed connectivity. The disadvantage is that the space of models considered by our approach is a lot more constrained than in the case of general architecture search. Saxena and Verbeek [33] introduced convolutional neural fabric which are learnable 3D trellises that locally connect response maps at different layers of a CNN. Similarly to our work, they enable optimization over an exponentially large family of connectivities, albeit different from those considered here. Finally, our approach is also related to conditional computation methods [34–43], which learn to drop out blocks of units. However, unlike these techniques, our algorithm learns a fixed, sparse connectivity that does *not* change with the input and thus it keeps the runtime cost and the number of used parameters constant.

3 Technical Approach

3.1 Modular Architecture

We begin by defining the modular architecture that will be used by our framework. In order to present our method in its full generality, we will describe it in the context of a *general* modular architecture, which we will then instantiate in the form of the two models used in our experiments (ResNet and ResNeXt).

We assume that the general modular architecture consists of a stack of L modules. (When using ResNet the modules will be residual blocks, while for ResNeXt each module will consist of multiple parallel branches.) We denote with $\mathbf{x}_j$ the input to the j-th module for $j = 1, \ldots, L$. The input of each module is an activation tensor computed from one the previous modules. We assume that the module implements a function $\mathcal{G}(.)$ parameterized by learnable weights θ_j. The weights may for example represent the coefficients of convolutional filters. Thus, the output $\mathbf{y}_j$ computed by the j-th module is given by $\mathbf{y}_j = \mathcal{G}(\mathbf{x}_j; \theta_j)$. In prior modular architectures, such as ResNet, ResNeXt and DenseNet, the connectivity between modules is hand-defined a priori according to a very simple rule: the input of a module is the output of the preceding module. In other words, $\mathbf{x}_j \leftarrow \mathbf{y}_{j-1}$. While this makes network design straightforward, it greatly limits the topology of architectures considered for the given task. In the next subsection we describe how to parameterize the architecture to remove these constraints and to enable connectivity learning in modular networks.

3.2 Masked Architecture

We now introduce learnable *masks* defining the connectivity in the network. Specifically, we want to allow each module j to take input from one or more of the preceding modules $k = 1, \ldots, j-1$. To achieve this we define for each module a binary mask vector that controls the input pathway of that module. The binary mask vectors are learned jointly with the weights of the network. Let $\mathbf{m}_j = [m_{j,1}, m_{j,2}, \ldots, m_{j,j-1}]^\top \in \{0,1\}^{j-1}$ be the binary mask vector defining the *active* input connections feeding the j-th module. If $m_{j,k} = 1$, then the activation volume produced by the k-th module is fed as input to the j-th module. If $m_{j,k} = 0$, then the output from the k-th module is ignored by the j-th module. The tensors from the *active* input connections are all added together (in an element-wise fashion) to form the input to the module. Thus, if we denote again with $\mathbf{y}_k$ the output activation tensor computed by the k-th module, the input $\mathbf{x}_j$ to the j-th module will be given by the following equation:

$$\mathbf{x}_j = \sum_{k=1}^{j-1} m_{j,k} \cdot \mathbf{y}_k \tag{1}$$

Then, the output of this module will be obtained through the usual computation, i.e., $\mathbf{y}_j = \mathcal{G}(\mathbf{x}_j; \theta_j)$. We note that under this model we no longer have predefined connectivity among modules. Instead, the mask $\mathbf{m}_j$ now determines *selectively* for each module which outputs from the previous modules will be aggregated and form the input to the block. In this paper we constrain the aggregations of outputs from the active connections to be in the form of simple additions as this does not require new parameters. When different modules yield feature maps of different sizes, we use zero-padding shortcuts to increase the dimensions of feature tensors to the largest size (as in [8]). These shortcuts are parameter free. We leave to future work the investigation of more sophisticated, parameterized aggregation schemes.

We point out that depending on the constraints defined over $\mathbf{m}_j$, different interesting models can be realized. For example, by introducing the constraint that $\sum_k m_{j,k} = 1$ for each block j, then each module will receive input from only one of the preceding modules (since each $m_{j,k}$ must be either 0 or 1). At the other end of the spectrum, if we set $m_{j,k} = 1$ for all modules j, k, then all connections would be active. In our experiments we will demonstrate that the best results are typically achieved for values in between these two extremes, i.e., by connecting each module to K previous modules where K is an integer-valued hyperparameter such that $1 < K < (j-1)$. We refer to this hyperparameter as the *fan-in* of a module. As discussed in the next section, the mask vector $\mathbf{m}_j$ for each block is learned simultaneously with all the other weights in the network via backpropagation. Finally, we note that it may be possible for a module in the network to become unused. This happens when, as a result of the optimization, module k is such that $m_{j,k} = 0$ for all j. In this case, at the end of the optimization, we prune the module in order to reduce the number of parameters to store and to speed up inference (note that this does not affect the function computed by the network). In the next subsection we discuss our method for jointly learning the weights and the masks in the network.

3.3 MaskConnect: Learning to Connect

We refer to our learning algorithm as MaskConnect. It performs joint optimization of a given learning objective ℓ with respect to both the weights of the network (θ) as well as the masks ($\mathbf{m}$). Since in this paper we apply our method to the problem of image categorization, we use the traditional multi-class cross-entropy objective for the loss ℓ. However, our approach can be applied without change to other loss functions and other tasks benefitting from connectivity learning.

In MaskConnect the weights have real values, as in traditional networks, while the masks have binary values. This renders the optimization challenging. To learn these binary parameters, we adopt a modified version of backpropagation, inspired by the algorithm proposed by Courbariaux et al. [44] to train neural networks with binary weights. During training we store and update a real-valued version $\tilde{\mathbf{m}}_j \in [0,1]^{j-1}$ of the masks, with entries clipped to lie between 0 and 1.

In general, the training via backpropagation consists of three steps: (1) forward propagation, (2) backward propagation, and (3) parameters update. At each iteration, we stochastically binarize the real-valued masks into binary-valued vectors $\mathbf{m}_j \in \{0,1\}^{j-1}$ which are then used for the forward propagation and backward propagation (steps 1 and 2). Instead, during the parameters update (step 3), the method updates the real-valued masks $\tilde{\mathbf{m}}_j$. The weights θ of the convolutional and fully connected layers are optimized using standard backpropagation. We discuss below the details of our mask training procedure, under the constraint that at any time there can be only K active entries in the binary mask $\mathbf{m}_j$, where K is a predefined integer hyperparameter with $1 \leq K \leq j-1$. In other words, we impose the following constraints:

$$m_{j,k} \in \{0,1\} \ \forall j,k, \quad \text{and} \quad \sum_{k=1}^{j-1} m_{j,k} = K \ \forall j.$$

These constraints imply that each module receives input from exactly K previous modules.

Forward Propagation. During the forward propagation, our algorithm first normalizes the real-valued entries in the mask of each block j to sum up to 1, such that $\sum_{k=1}^{j-1} \tilde{m}_{j,k} = 1$. This is done so that $\text{Mult}(\tilde{m}_{j,1}, \tilde{m}_{j,2}, \dots, \tilde{m}_{j,j-1})$ defines a proper multinomial distribution over the $j-1$ possible input connections into module j. Then, the binary mask $\mathbf{m}_j$ is stochastically generated by drawing K *distinct* samples $a_1, a_2, \dots, a_K \in \{1, \dots, (j-1)\}$ from the multinomial distribution over the connections. Finally, the entries corresponding to the K samples are activated in the binary mask vector, i.e., $m_{j,a_k} \leftarrow 1$, for $k = 1, \dots, K$. The input activation volume to the module j is then computed according to Eq. 1 from the sampled binary masks. We note that the sampling from the Multinomial distribution ensures that the connections with largest $\tilde{m}_{j,k}$ values will be more likely to be chosen, while at the same time the stochasticity of this process allows different connectivities to be explored, particularly during early stages of the learning when the real-valued masks still have fairly uniform distributions.

Backward Propagation. In the backward propagation step, the gradient $\partial \ell / \partial y_k$ with respect to each output is obtained via back-propagation from $\partial \ell / \partial x_j$ and the binary masks $m_{j,k}$.

Mask Update. In the parameter update step our algorithm computes the gradient with respect to the binary masks for each module. Then, using these computed gradients and the given learning rate, it updates the real-valued masks via gradient descent. At this time we clip the updated real-valued masks to constrain them to remain within the valid interval $[0, 1]$ (as in [44]).

Pseudocode for our training procedure is given in the supplementary material. After joint training over θ and $\mathbf{m}$, we have found beneficial to (1) freeze the binary masks to the top-K values for each mask (i.e., by setting as active connections in $\mathbf{m}_j$ those corresponding to the K largest values in $\tilde{\mathbf{m}}_j$) and then (2) fine-tune the weights θ of the network with respect to these fixed binary masks.

In the next subsections we discuss how we instantiated our general approach for the two architectures considered in our experiments: ResNet and ResNeXt.

3.4 MaskConnect Applied to ResNet

The application of our algorithm to ResNets is quite straightforward. ResNets are modular networks obtained by stacking residual blocks. A residual block implements a residual function $\mathcal{F}(.)$ with reference to the layer input. Figure 1(a) (left) illustrates an example of these modular components where the 3 layers in the block implement the residual function $\mathcal{F}(\mathbf{x}; \theta)$. A shortcut connections adds the residual block output $\mathcal{F}(\mathbf{x})$ to its input $\mathbf{x}$. Thus the complete function $\mathcal{G}(.)$ implemented by a residual block computes $\mathcal{G}(\mathbf{x}; \theta) = \mathcal{F}(\mathbf{x}; \theta) + \mathbf{x}$. The ResNets originally introduced in [8] use a hand-defined connectivity that passes the output of a block to the immediately subsequent block, i.e., $\mathbf{x}_{j+1} \leftarrow \mathcal{F}(\mathbf{x}_j; \theta_j) + \mathbf{x}_j$. Here we propose to use MaskConnect to learn the input connections for each individual residual block in the network. This changes the input provided to block $j+1$ in the network to be $\mathbf{x}_{j+1} \leftarrow \sum_{k=1}^{j} m_{j+1,k} \left[\mathcal{F}(\mathbf{x}_k; \theta_k) + \mathbf{x}_k\right]$, where binary parameters $m_{j+1,k}$ are learned automatically by our approach simultaneously with the weights θ subject to the constraint that $\sum_{k=1}^{j} m_{j+1,k} = K$. This implies that under our model each residual block now receives input from exactly K out of the preceding blocks. The output tensors from the K selected blocks are aggregated using element-wise addition and passed as input to the module. Our experiments present results for varying values of fan-in hyperparameter K, which controls the density of connectivity.

3.5 MaskConnect Applied to Multi-branch ResNeXt

The adaptation of MaskConnect to ResNeXt architectures is slightly more complex, as ResNeXt is based on a multi-branch topology. ResNeXt was motivated

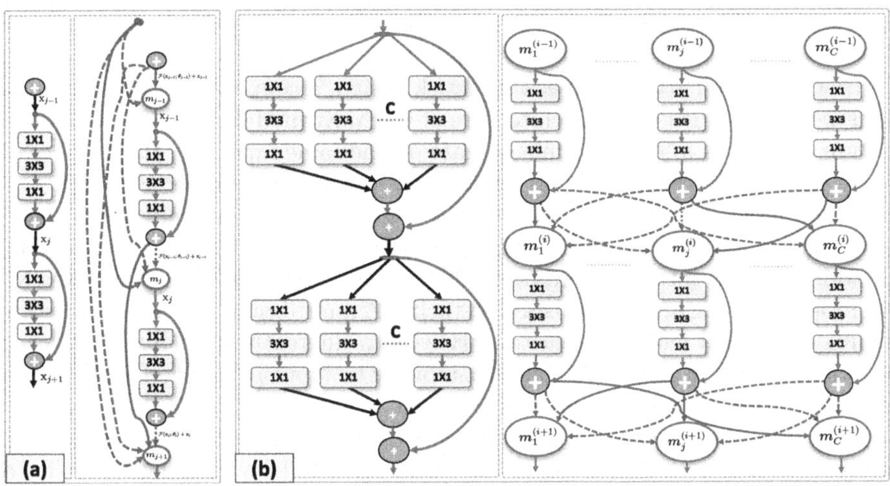

Fig. 1. Application of MaskConnect to two forms of modular network: **(a)** ResNet [45] and **(b)** multi-branch ResNeXt [9]. In traditional ResNet (a) (left) the connections between blocks are fixed (black links) so that each block receives input from only the preceding block. Our approach (a) (right) learns the optimal input connections (solid red links) for each individual block from a collection of potential connections (solid and dotted red links). Similarly, in traditional ResNeXt (b) (left) each module consists of C parallel residual blocks which are all aggregated and fed to the next module (black links). MaskConnect (b) (right) replaces the fixed aggregation points of RexNeXt with learnable masks $\mathbf{m}$ defining the active input connections (solid red links) for each individual residual block. (Color figure online)

by the observation that it is beneficial to arrange residual blocks not only along the depth dimension but also to implement parallel multiple threads of computation feeding from the same input layer. The outputs of the parallel residual blocks are then summed up together with the original input and passed on to the next module. The resulting multi-branch module is illustrated in Fig. 1(b) (left). More formally, let $\mathcal{F}(\mathbf{x}; \theta_j^{(i)})$ be the transformation implemented by the j-th residual block in module i-th of the network, where $j = 1, \ldots, C$ and $i = 1, \ldots, L$, with L denoting the total number of modules stacked on top of each other to form the complete network. The hyperparameter C is called the cardinality of the module and defines the number of parallel branches within each module. The hyperparameter L controls the total depth of the network. Then, in traditional ResNeXt, the output of the i-th module is computed as:

$$\mathbf{y}_i = \mathbf{x}_i + \sum_{j=1}^{C} \mathcal{F}(\mathbf{x}_i; \theta_j^{(i)}) \tag{2}$$

In [9] it was experimentally shown that increasing the cardinality C is a more effective way of improving accuracy compared to increasing depth or the number of filters. In other words, given a fixed budget of parameters, ResNeXt nets were shown to consistently outperform single-branch ResNets.

However, in an attempt to ease network design, a couple of restrictive limitations were embedded in the architecture of ResNeXt modules: (1) the C parallel feature extractors in each module operate on the same input; (2) the number of active branches is constant at all depth levels of the network.

MaskConnect allows us to remove these restrictions without adding any significant burden on the process of manual network design, with the exception of a single additional integer hyperparameter (K) for the entire network. As in ResNeXt, our proposed architecture consists of a stack of L multi-branch modules, each containing C parallel feature extractors. However, differently from ResNeXt, each branch in a module can take a different input. The input pathway of each branch is controlled by a binary mask vector. Let $\mathbf{m}_j^{(i)} = [m_{j,1}^{(i)}, m_{j,2}^{(i)}, \ldots, m_{j,C}^{(i)}]^\top \in \{0,1\}^C$ be the binary mask vector defining the *active* input connections feeding the j-th residual block in module i. We note that under this model we no longer have fixed aggregation nodes summing up *all* outputs computed from a module. Instead, the mask $\mathbf{m}_j^{(i)}$ now determines *selectively* for each block which branches from the previous module will be aggregated to form the input to the next block. Under this new scheme, the parallel branches in a module receive different inputs and as such are likely to yield more diverse features.

As before, different constraints over $\mathbf{m}_j^{(i)}$ will give rise to different forms of architecture. By introducing the constraint that $\sum_k m_{j,k}^{(i)} = 1$ for all blocks j, then each residual block will receive input from only one branch (since each $m_{j,k}^{(i)}$ must be either 0 or 1). If instead we set $m_{j,k}^{(i)} = 1$ for all blocks j, k in each module i, then all connections would be active and we would obtain again the fixed ResNeXt architecture. In our experiments we present results obtained by varying the fan-in hyperparameter K such that $1 < K < C$. We also note that it may be possible for a residual block in the network to become unused, as a result of the optimization over the mask values. Thus, at any point in the network the total number of active parallel threads can be any number smaller than or equal to C. This implies that a variable branching factor is learned adaptively for the different depths in the network.

4 Experiments

We tested our approach on the task of image categorization using two different examples of modularized architecture: ResNet [8] and ResNeXt [9]. We used the following datasets for our evaluation: CIFAR-10 [46], CIFAR-100 [46], Mini-ImageNet [47], as well as the full ImageNet [48]. In this paper we include the results achieved on CIFAR-100 and ImageNet [48], while the results for CIFAR-10 [46] and Mini-ImageNet [47] (showing consistent improvements up to nearly 4% over fixed connectivity) can be found in the supplementary material.

Table 1. CIFAR-100 accuracies achieved by models trained using the connectivity of **ResNet** [45] (Fixed-Prev), a fixed random connectivity (Fixed-Random), and the connectivity learned by our approach (Learned)

Model	Connectivity	Accuracy (%)
ResNet-38	Fixed-Prev, K = 1 [45]	68.54
	Fixed-Random, K = 10	62.67
	Learned, K = 10	**70.40**
ResNet-74	Fixed-Prev, K = 1 [45]	70.64
	Fixed-Random, K = 15	66.93
	Learned, K = 15	**72.81**
ResNet-110	Fixed-Prev, K = 1 [45]	71.21
	Fixed-Random, K = 20	67.22
	Learned, K = 20	**73.15**

4.1 CIFAR-100

CIFAR-100 contains images of size 32×32. It consists of 50,000 training images and 10,000 test images. Each image is labeled as belonging to one of 100 possible classes.

CIFAR-100 Results Based on the *ResNet* Architecture

Effect of Fan-In (K). The fan-in hyperparameter (K) defines the number of *active* input connections feeding each residual block. We study the effect of the fan-in on the performance of models built and trained using our proposed approach. We use residual blocks consisting of two 3×3 convolutional layers. We use a model obtained by stacking $L = 18$ residual blocks with total depth of $D = 2 + 2L = 38$ layers. We trained and tested this architecture using different fan-in values: $K = 1, .., 17$. All these models have the same learning capacity as varying K does not affect the number of parameters. The results are shown in Fig. 2. We notice that the best accuracy is achieved using $K = 10$. Using a very low or very high fan-in yields lower accuracy. However, the algorithm does not appear to be overly sensitive to the fan-in hyperparameter, as a wide range of values for K (from $K = 7$ to $K = 13$) produce accuracy close to the best.

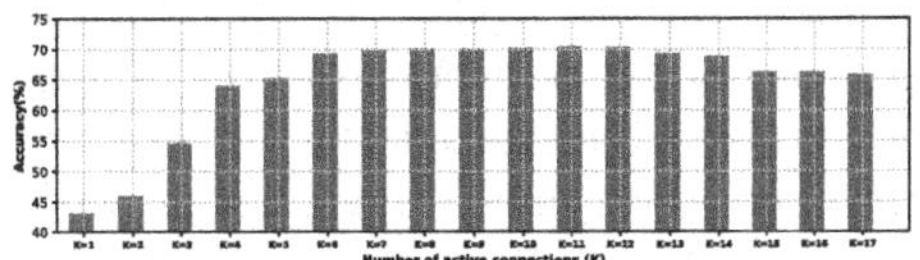

Fig. 2. Varying the fan-in (K), i.e., the number of learned active connections to each residual block. The plot reports accuracy achieved by MaskConnect on CIFAR-100 using a **ResNet-38** architecture ($L = 18$ blocks). All models have the same number of parameters (0.57M). The best accuracy is achieved at $K = 10$.

Varying the Model. We trained several ResNet models differing in depth, using both MaskConnect as as well as the traditional predefined connectivity. For these experiments we use a stack of L residual blocks with two 3 x 3 convolutional layers for each block. We choose $L \in \{18, 36, 54\}$ to build networks with depths $D = 2 + 2L$ equal to 38, 74, and 110 layers, respectively. We show the classification accuracy achieved by different models in Table 1. We report the results achieved using MaskConnect with fan-in $K = 10$, $K = 15$, $K = 20$ for models of depth $D = 38$, $D = 74$, $D = 110$, respectively. Fixed-Prev denotes the performance of ResNet, where each block is connected to only the previous block ($K = 1$). We also include the accuracy achieved by choosing a random connectivity (Fixed-Random) using the same fan-in values K as our approach and training the parameters while keeping the random connectivity fixed. This baseline is useful to show that our model achieves higher accuracy over traditional ResNet not because of the higher number of connections (i.e., $K > 1$), but rather because it learns the connectivity. Indeed, the results in Table 1 show that learning the connectivity using MaskConnect yields consistently higher accuracy than using multiple random connections or a single connection to the previous block.

CIFAR-100 Results Based on Multi-branch *ResNeXt*

Effect of Fan-In (K). Even for ResNeXt, we start by studying the effect of the fan-in hyperparameter (K). For this experiment we use a model obtained by stacking $L = 6$ multi-branch residual modules, each having cardinality $C = 8$ (number of branches in each module). We use residual blocks consisting of 3 convolutional layers with a bottleneck implementing dimensionality reduction on the number of feature channels, as shown in Fig. 1(b). The bottleneck for this experiment was set to $w = 4$. Since each residual block consists of 3 layers, the total depth of the network in terms of learnable layers is $D = 2 + 3L = 20$.

We trained and tested this architecture using different fan-in values: $K = 1, ..., 8$. Again, varying K does not alter the number of parameters. The results are shown in Fig. 3. We can see that the best accuracy is achieved by connecting each residual block to $K = 4$ branches out of the total $C = 8$ in each module. Note that when setting $K = C$, there is no need to learn the masks. In this case each mask is simply replaced by an element-wise addition of the outputs from all the branches. This renders the model equivalent to ResNeXt [9], which has fixed connectivity. Based on the results of Fig. 3, in all our experiments below we use $K = 4$ (since it gives the best accuracy) but also $K = 1$ since it gives high sparsity which, as we will see shortly, implies savings in number of parameters.

Varying the Models. In Table 2 we show the classification accuracy achieved with ResNeXt models of different depth and cardinality (the details of each model are listed in the Supplementary Material). For each architecture we also include the accuracy achieved with full (as opposed to learned) connectivity, which corresponds to ResNeXt. These results show that learning the connectivity produces consistently higher accuracy than using fixed connectivity, with accuracy gains of up to 2.2% compared to the state-of-the-art ResNeXt model. Furthermore, we can notice that the accuracy of models based on random connectivity (Fixed-Random) is considerably lower compared to our approach, despite having the

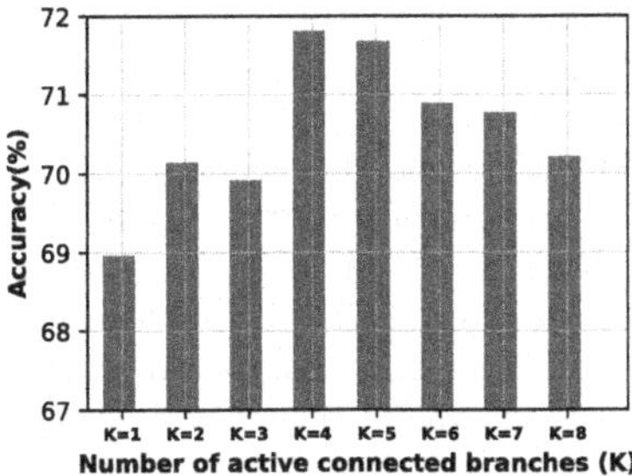

Fig. 3. Varying the fan-in (K) of our model, i.e., the number of active input branches to each residual block. The plot reports accuracy achieved on CIFAR-100 using a network stack of $L = 6$ **ResNeXt** modules having cardinality $C = 8$ and bottleneck width $w = 4$. All models have the same number of parameters (0.28M).

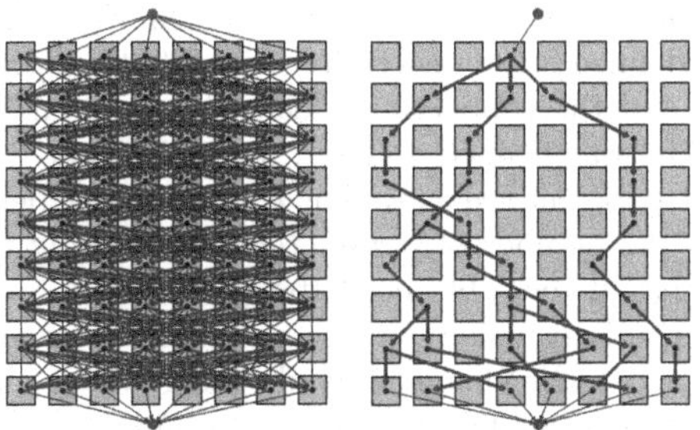

Fig. 4. A visualization of the fixed connectivity of **ResNext** (left) vs the connectivity learned by our method (right) using $K = 1$. Each green square is a residual block, each row of $C = 8$ square is a multi-branch module. Arrows indicate pathways connecting residual blocks of adjacent modules. It can be noticed that MaskConnect learns sparse connections. The squares without in/out edges are those pruned at the end of learning. This gives rise to a branching factor that varies along the depth of the net. (Color figure online)

same connectivity density ($K = 4$). This shows that the improvements of our approach over ResNeXt are not due to sparser connectivity but they are rather due to *learned* connectivity. We note that these improvements in accuracy come at little computational training cost: the average training time overhead for learning masks and weights is about 39% using our unoptimized implementation compared to learning only the weights given a fixed connectivity.

Parameter Savings. Our proposed approach provides the benefit of automatically identifying residual blocks that are unnecessary. At the end of the training, the unused residual blocks can be pruned away. This yields savings in the number of parameters to store and in test-time computation. In Table 2, columns *Train* and *Test* under *Params* show the original number of parameters (used during training) and the number of parameters after pruning (used at test-time). Note that for the biggest architecture, our approach using $K = 1$ yields a parameter saving of 40% compared to ResNeXt with full connectivity (20.5M vs 34.4M), while achieving the same accuracy. Thus, in summary, using fan-in $K = 4$ gives models that have the same number of parameters as ResNeXt but they yield higher accuracy; using fan-in $K = 1$ gives a significant saving in number of parameters and accuracy on par with ResNeXt.

Visualization of the Learned Connectivity. Figure 4 provides an illustration of the connectivity learned by MaskConnect for $K = 1$ versus the fixed connectivity

Table 2. CIFAR-100 accuracies achieved by two **ResNeXt** architectures trained using predefined full connectivity (Fixed-Full) [9], random connectivity (Fixed-Random, $K = 4$), and the connectivity learned by our algorithm (Learned, $K = 1$, $K = 4$). Each model was trained 4 times, using different random initializations. We report the best test performance as well as the mean test performance computed from the 4 runs. We list the number of parameters used during training (Params-Train) and the number of parameters obtained after pruning the unused blocks (Params-Test). Our learned connectivity using $K = 4$ produces accuracy gains of up to 2.2% compared to the strong ResNeXt model, while using $K = 1$ yields results equivalent to ResNeXt but it induces a significant reduction in number of parameters at test time (e.g., a saving of 40% for model {29, 64, 8})

Architecture	Connectivity	Params		Accuracy (%)
{Depth (D), Bottleneck width (w), Cardinality (C)}		*Train*	*Test*	*Best (mean ± std)*
{29, 8, 8}	Fixed-Full, K=8 [9]	0.86M	0.86M	73.52 (73.37 ± 0.13)
	Learned, K = 1	0.86M	0.65M	**73.91** (73.76 ± 0.14)
	Learned, K = 4	0.86M	0.81M	**75.89** (75.77 ± 0.12)
	Fixed-Random, K = 4	0.86M	0.85M	72.85 (72.66 ± 0.24)
{29, 64, 8}	Fixed-Full, K=8 [9]	34.4M	34.4M	82.23 (82.12 ± 0.12)
	Learned, K = 1	34.4M	20.5M	**82.31** (82.15 ± 0.15)
	Learned, K = 4	34.4M	32.1M	**84.05** (83.94 ± 0.11)
	Fixed-Random, K = 4	34.4M	34.3M	81.96 (81.73 ± 0.20)

of ResNeXt for model $\{D = 29, w = 8, C = 8\}$. While ResNeXt feeds the same input to all blocks of a module, our algorithm learns different input pathways for each block and yields a branching factor that varies along depth.

4.2 ImageNet

Finally, we evaluate our approach on the large-scale ImageNet 2012 dataset [48], which includes images of 1000 classes. We train our approach on the training set (1.28M images) and evaluate it on the validation set (50K images).

ImageNet Results Based on the *ResNet* Architecture. For this experiment we use a stack of $L = 16$ residual blocks with 3 convolutional layers with a bottleneck architecture. Thus, the total number of layers is $D = 2 + 3L = 50$. Compared to the traditional ResNet using fixed connectivity, the same network trained using MaskConnect with fan-in $K = 10$ yields a top-1 accuracy gain of 1.94% (78.09% vs 76.15%).

ImageNet Results Based on Multi-branch *ResNeXt*. In Table 3, we report the top accuracies for three different ResNeXt architectures. For these experiments we set $K = C/2$. We can observe that for all three architectures, our learned connectivity yields an improvement in accuracy over fixed full connectivity [9].

Table 3. ImageNet accuracies (single crop) achieved by different architectures using the predefined connectivity of **ResNeXt** (Fixed-Full) versus the connectivity learned by our algorithm (Learned)

Architecture {Depth (D), Bottleneck width (w), Cardinality (C)}	Connectivity	Accuracy	
		Top-1	*Top-5*
{50, 4, 32}	Fixed-Full, K = 32 [9]	77.8	93.3
	Learned, K = 16	**79.1**	**94.1**
{101, 4, 32}	Fixed-Full, K = 32 [9]	78.8	94.1
	Learned, K = 16	**79.5**	**94.5**
{101, 4, 64}	Fixed-Full, K = 64 [9]	79.6	94.7
	Learned, K = 32	**79.8**	**94.8**

5 Conclusions

In this paper we introduced an algorithm to learn the connectivity of deep modular networks. The problem is formulated as a single joint optimization over the weights and connections between modules in the model. We tested our approach on challenging image categorization benchmarks where it led to significant accuracy improvements over the state-of-the-art ResNet and ResNeXt models using fixed connectivity. An added benefit of our approach is that it can automatically identify superfluous blocks, which can be pruned after training without impact on accuracy for more efficient testing and for reducing the number of parameters to store.

While our experiments were carried out on two particular architectures (ResNet and ResNeXt) and a specific form of building block (residual block), we expect the benefits of our approach to extend to other modules and network structures. For example, it could be applied to learn the connectivity of skip-connections in DenseNets [10], which are currently based on predefined connectivity rules. In this paper, our masks perform non-parametric additive aggregation of the branch outputs. It would be interesting to experiment with learnable (parametric) aggregations of the outputs from the individual branches. Our approach is limited to learning connectivity within a given, fixed architecture. Future work will explore the use of learnable masks for full architecture discovery.

Acknowledgements. This work was funded in part by NSF award CNS-120552. We gratefully acknowledge NVIDIA and Facebook for the donation of GPUs used for portions of this work.

References

1. Glorot, X., Bordes, A., Bengio, Y.: Deep sparse rectifier neural networks. In: Proceedings of the Fourteenth International Conference on Artificial Intelligence and Statistics, AISTATS 2011, Fort Lauderdale, USA, 11–13 April 2011, pp. 315–323 (2011)
2. Krizhevsky, A., Sutskever, I., Hinton, G.E.: ImageNet classification with deep convolutional neural networks. In: Advances in Neural Information Processing Systems 25, Lake Tahoe, Nevada, United States, pp. 1106–1114 (2012)
3. Sermanet, P., Eigen, D., Zhang, X., Mathieu, M., Fergus, R., LeCun, Y.: OverFeat: integrated recognition, localization and detection using convolutional networks. In: International Conference on Learning Representations (ICLR) (2013)
4. Maas, A.L., Hannun, A.Y., Ng, A.Y.: Rectifier nonlinearities improve neural network acoustic models. Proc. ICML **30**, 1 (2013)
5. Zeiler, M.D., Fergus, R.: Visualizing and understanding convolutional networks. In: Fleet, D., Pajdla, T., Schiele, B., Tuytelaars, T. (eds.) ECCV 2014. LNCS, vol. 8689, pp. 818–833. Springer, Cham (2014). https://doi.org/10.1007/978-3-319-10590-1_53
6. Szegedy, C., et al.: Going deeper with convolutions. In: IEEE Conference on Computer Vision and Pattern Recognition, CVPR 2015, Boston, MA, USA, 7–12 June 2005, pp. 1–9 (2015)
7. Simonyan, K., Zisserman, A.: Very deep convolutional networks for large-scale image recognition. In: International Conference on Learning Representations (ICLR) (2015)
8. He, K., Zhang, X., Ren, S., Sun, J.: Deep residual learning for image recognition. In: 2016 IEEE Conference on Computer Vision and Pattern Recognition (CVPR) (2016)
9. Xie, S., Girshick, R.B., Dollár, P., Tu, Z., He, K.: Aggregated residual transformations for deep neural networks. In: IEEE Conference on Computer Vision and Pattern Recognition, CVPR (2017)
10. Huang, G., Liu, Z., Weinberger, K.Q.: Densely connected convolutional networks. In: IEEE Conference on Computer Vision and Pattern Recognition, CVPR (2017)
11. Chen, Y., Kalantidis, Y., Li, J., Yan, S., Feng, J.: Multi-fiber networks for video recognition. In: European Conference on Computer Vision (ECCV) (2018)
12. He, K., Zhang, X., Ren, S., Sun, J.: Identity mappings in deep residual networks. In: Leibe, B., Matas, J., Sebe, N., Welling, M. (eds.) ECCV 2016. LNCS, vol. 9908, pp. 630–645. Springer, Cham (2016). https://doi.org/10.1007/978-3-319-46493-0_38
13. Bergstra, J., Bengio, Y.: Random search for hyper-parameter optimization. J. Mach. Learn. Res. **13**, 281–305 (2012)
14. Snoek, J., Larochelle, H., Adams, R.P.: Practical bayesian optimization of machine learning algorithms. In: Advances in Neural Information Processing Systems 25, Lake Tahoe, Nevada, United States, pp. 2960–2968 (2012)
15. Snoek, J., et al.: Scalable Bayesian optimization using deep neural networks. In: Proceedings of the 32nd International Conference on Machine Learning, ICML 2015, Lille, France, 6–11 July 2015, pp. 2171–2180 (2015)
16. Pham, H., Guan, M.Y., Zoph, B., Le, Q.V., Dean, J.: Efficient neural architecture search via parameter sharing. arXiv preprint arXiv:1802.03268 (2018)
17. Such, F.P., Madhavan, V., Conti, E., Lehman, J., Stanley, K.O., Clune, J.: Deep neuroevolution: genetic algorithms are a competitive alternative for training deep neural networks for reinforcement learning. arXiv preprint arXiv:1712.06567 (2017)

18. Salimans, T., Ho, J., Chen, X., Sidor, S., Sutskever, I.: Evolution strategies as a scalable alternative to reinforcement learning. arXiv preprint arXiv:1703.03864 (2017)
19. Liu, H., Simonyan, K., Vinyals, O., Fernando, C., Kavukcuoglu, K.: Hierarchical representations for efficient architecture search. arXiv preprint arXiv:1711.00436 (2017)
20. Xie, L., Yuille, A.L.: Genetic CNN. In: ICCV, pp. 1388–1397 (2017)
21. Wierstra, D., Gomez, F.J., Schmidhuber, J.: Modeling systems with internal state using Evolino. In: Genetic and Evolutionary Computation Conference, GECCO 2005, Proceedings, Washington DC, USA, 25–29 June 2005, pp. 1795–1802 (2005)
22. Floreano, D., Dürr, P., Mattiussi, C.: Neuroevolution: from architectures to learning. Evol. Intell. **1**(1), 47–62 (2008)
23. Real, E., et al.: Large-scale evolution of image classifiers. CoRR abs/1703.01041 (2017)
24. Fernando, C., et al.: PathNet: evolution channels gradient descent in super neural networks. CoRR abs/1701.08734 (2017)
25. Zoph, B., Le, Q.V.: Neural architecture search with reinforcement learning. In: International Conference on Learning Representations (ICLR) (2017)
26. LeCun, Y., Denker, J.S., Solla, S.A.: Optimal brain damage. In: Advances in Neural Information Processing Systems 2, NIPS Conference, Denver, Colorado, USA, 27–30 November 1989, pp. 598–605 (1989)
27. Han, S., Mao, H., Dally, W.J.: Deep compression: compressing deep neural network with pruning, trained quantization and Huffman coding. In: International Conference on Learning Representations (ICLR) (2015)
28. Han, S., Pool, J., Tran, J., Dally, W.J.: Learning both weights and connections for efficient neural network. In: Advances in Neural Information Processing Systems 28, Montreal, Quebec, Canada, pp. 1135–1143 (2015)
29. Guo, Y., Yao, A., Chen, Y.: Dynamic network surgery for efficient DNNs. In: Advances in Neural Information Processing Systems 29: Annual Conference on Neural Information Processing Systems 2016, 5–10 December 2016, Barcelona, Spain, pp. 1379–1387 (2016)
30. Han, S., et al.: DSD: regularizing deep neural networks with dense-sparse-dense training flow. In: International Conference on Learning Representations (ICLR) (2016)
31. Gastaldi, X.: Shake-shake regularization. CoRR abs/1705.07485 (2017)
32. Adams, R.P., Wallach, H.M., Ghahramani, Z.: Learning the structure of deep sparse graphical models. In: Proceedings of the Thirteenth International Conference on Artificial Intelligence and Statistics, AISTATS 2010, Chia Laguna Resort, Sardinia, Italy, 13–15 May 2010, pp. 1–8 (2010)
33. Saxena, S., Verbeek, J.: Convolutional neural fabrics. In: Advances in Neural Information Processing Systems 29: Annual Conference on Neural Information Processing Systems 2016, 5–10 December 2016, Barcelona, Spain, pp. 4053–4061 (2016)
34. Wu, Z., et al.: BlockDrop: dynamic inference paths in residual networks. In: Proceedings of the IEEE Conference on Computer Vision and Pattern Recognition, pp. 8817–8826 (2018)
35. Bengio, Y., Léonard, N., Courville, A.: Estimating or propagating gradients through stochastic neurons for conditional computation. arXiv preprint arXiv:1308.3432 (2013)
36. Bengio, E., Bacon, P.L., Pineau, J., Precup, D.: Conditional computation in neural networks for faster models. arXiv preprint arXiv:1511.06297 (2015)

37. Bengio, Y.: Deep learning of representations: looking forward. In: Dediu, A.-H., Martín-Vide, C., Mitkov, R., Truthe, B. (eds.) SLSP 2013. LNCS (LNAI), vol. 7978, pp. 1–37. Springer, Heidelberg (2013). https://doi.org/10.1007/978-3-642-39593-2_1
38. Shazeer, N., et al.: Outrageously large neural networks: the sparsely-gated mixture-of-experts layer. arXiv preprint arXiv:1701.06538 (2017)
39. Davis, A., Arel, I.: Low-rank approximations for conditional feedforward computation in deep neural networks. arXiv preprint arXiv:1312.4461 (2013)
40. Eigen, D., Ranzato, M., Sutskever, I.: Learning factored representations in a deep mixture of experts. arXiv preprint arXiv:1312.4314 (2013)
41. Denoyer, L., Gallinari, P.: Deep sequential neural network. arXiv preprint arXiv:1410.0510 (2014)
42. Cho, K., Bengio, Y.: Exponentially increasing the capacity-to-computation ratio for conditional computation in deep learning. arXiv preprint arXiv:1406.7362 (2014)
43. Almahairi, A., Ballas, N., Cooijmans, T., Zheng, Y., Larochelle, H., Courville, A.: Dynamic capacity networks. In: International Conference on Machine Learning, pp. 2549–2558 (2016)
44. Courbariaux, M., Bengio, Y., David, J.: BinaryConnect: training deep neural networks with binary weights during propagations. In: Advances in Neural Information Processing Systems 28, Montreal, Quebec, Canada, pp. 3123–3131 (2015)
45. He, K., Zhang, X., Ren, S., Sun, J.: Deep residual learning for image recognition. CoRR abs/1512.03385 (2015)
46. Krizhesvsky, A.: Learning multiple layers of features from tiny images. Technical report (2009). https://www.cs.toronto.edu/~kriz/learning-features-2009-TR.pdf
47. Vinyals, O., Blundell, C., Lillicrap, T., Kavukcuoglu, K., Wierstra, D.: Matching networks for one shot learning. In: Advances in Neural Information Processing Systems 29, Barcelona, Spain, pp. 3630–3638 (2016)
48. Deng, J., Dong, W., Socher, R., Li, L., Li, K., Li, F.: ImageNet: a large-scale hierarchical image database. In: 2009 IEEE Computer Society Conference on Computer Vision and Pattern Recognition (CVPR 2009), 20–25 June 2009, Miami, Florida, USA, pp. 248–255 (2009)

Online Multi-Object Tracking with Dual Matching Attention Networks

Ji Zhu[1,2], Hua Yang[1(✉)], Nian Liu[3], Minyoung Kim[4], Wenjun Zhang[1], and Ming-Hsuan Yang[5,6]

[1] Shanghai Jiao Tong University, Shanghai, China
jizhu1023@gmail.com, {hyang,zhangwenjun}@sjtu.edu.cn
[2] Visbody Inc., Shanghai, China
[3] Northwestern Polytechnical University, Xi'an, China
liunian228@gmail.com
[4] Massachusetts Institute of Technology, Cambridge, USA
minykim@mit.edu
[5] University of California, Merced, USA
mhyang@ucmerced.edu
[6] Google Inc., Menlo Park, USA

Abstract. In this paper, we propose an online Multi-Object Tracking (MOT) approach which integrates the merits of single object tracking and data association methods in a unified framework to handle noisy detections and frequent interactions between targets. Specifically, for applying single object tracking in MOT, we introduce a cost-sensitive tracking loss based on the state-of-the-art visual tracker, which encourages the model to focus on hard negative distractors during online learning. For data association, we propose Dual Matching Attention Networks (DMAN) with both spatial and temporal attention mechanisms. The spatial attention module generates dual attention maps which enable the network to focus on the matching patterns of the input image pair, while the temporal attention module adaptively allocates different levels of attention to different samples in the tracklet to suppress noisy observations. Experimental results on the MOT benchmark datasets show that the proposed algorithm performs favorably against both online and offline trackers in terms of identity-preserving metrics.

Keywords: Multi-Object Tracking · Cost-sensitive tracking loss
Dual Matching Attention Network

1 Introduction

Multi-Object Tracking (MOT) aims to estimate trajectories of multiple objects by finding target locations and maintaining target identities across frames.

Electronic supplementary material The online version of this chapter (https://doi.org/10.1007/978-3-030-01228-1_23) contains supplementary material, which is available to authorized users.

V. Ferrari et al. (Eds.): ECCV 2018, LNCS 11209, pp. 379–396, 2018.
https://doi.org/10.1007/978-3-030-01228-1_23

In general, existing MOT methods can be categorized into offline and online methods. Offline MOT methods use both past and future frames to generate trajectories while online MOT methods only exploit the information available up to the current frame. Although offline methods have some advantages in handling ambiguous tracking results, they are not applicable to real-time vision tasks.

Recent MOT methods mainly adopt the tracking-by-detection strategy and handle the task by linking detections across frames using data association algorithms. However, these approaches heavily rely on the quality of detection results. If the detection is missing or inaccurate, the target object is prone to be lost. To alleviate such issues, recent methods [10, 53] exploit single object tracking methods for MOT. A single object tracker uses the detection in the first frame and online updates the model to find the target in following frames. However, it is prone to drift when the target is occluded. In this paper, we combine the merits of single object tracking and data association in a unified framework. In most frames, a single object tracker is used to track each target object. Data association is applied when the tracking score is below a threshold, which indicates the target object may be occluded or undergo large appearance changes.

The main challenge to use a single object tracker for MOT is to cope with frequent interactions between targets and intra-class distractors. Existing single object tracking methods usually suffer from the data imbalance issue between positive and negative samples for online model updates. In the search area of a tracker, only a few locations near the target center correspond to positive samples while all the samples drawn at other positions are negative samples. Most locations from the background region are easy negatives, which may cause inefficient training and weaken the discriminative strength of the model. This problem is exacerbated in the context of MOT task. If a model is overwhelmed by the easy background negatives, the tracker is prone to drift when similar distractors appear in the search area. Thus, it is imperative to focus on a small number of hard examples during online updates to alleviate the drifting problems.

For data association, we need to compare the current detected target with a sequence of previous observations in the trajectory. One of the most commonly tracked objects in MOT is pedestrian where the data association problem is also known as re-identification with challenging factors including pose variation, similar appearance, and frequent occlusion. In numerous public person re-identification datasets (e.g., [30–32]), pedestrians given by manually annotated bounding boxes are well separated. However, detected regions in the context of MOT may be noisy with large misalignment errors or missing parts as shown in Fig. 1(a). Furthermore, inaccurate and occluded observations in the previous trajectory likely result in noisy updates and make the appearance model less effective. These factors motivate us to design an appearance model for effective data association in two aspects. First, to cope with misaligned and missing parts in detections, the proposed model should focus on corresponding local regions between observations, as presented in Fig. 1(a). Second, to avoid being affected by contaminated samples, the proposed model should assign different weights to different observations in the trajectory, as shown in Fig. 1(b).

We make the following contributions in this work:

- We propose a spatial attention network to handle noisy detections and occlusions for MOT. When comparing two images, the proposed network generates dual spatial attention maps (as shown in Fig. 1(a)) based on the cross similarity between each location of the image pair, which enables the model to focus on matching regions between the paired images without any part-level correspondence annotation.
- We design a temporal attention network to adaptively allocate different degrees of attention to different observations in the trajectory. This module considers not only the similarity between the target detection and the observations in the trajectory but also the consistency of all observations to filter out unreliable samples in the trajectory.
- We apply the single object tracker in MOT and introduce a novel cost-sensitive tracking loss based on the state-of-the-art tracker. The proposed loss enables the tracker to focus training on a sparse set of hard samples which enhances the robustness to nearby distractors in MOT scenarios.
- We carry out extensive experiments against the state-of-the-art MOT methods on the MOT benchmark datasets with ablation studies to demonstrate the effectiveness of the proposed algorithm.

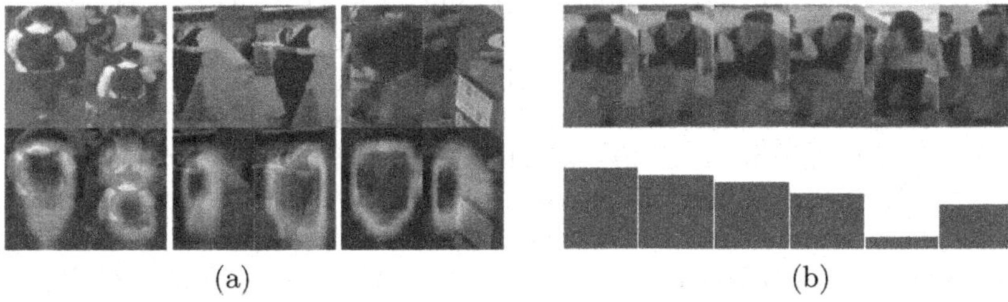

Fig. 1. Sample detections in the MOT16 dataset [35]. (a) Top row: image pairs with misalignments, missing parts, and occlusion. Bottom row: spatial attention maps for each image pair. (b) Top row: target trajectory containing noisy samples. Bottom row: temporal attention weights for corresponding images in the trajectory.

2 Related Work

Multi-Object Tracking. Existing MOT methods tackle the task by linking the detections across consecutive frames based on the tracking-by-detection paradigm. Numerous approaches [37,39,45,47,48,51,58] use detections from past and future frames for batch processing. Typically, these methods model the MOT task as a global optimization problem in various forms such as network flow [14,51,58], and multi-cut [46–48]. In contrast, online MOT methods [10,27,53] do not rely on detections from future frames and may not perform well when target objects are heavily occluded or mis-detected. Thus, a robust appearance model is crucial for associating detections for online MOT. Recently, several online approaches [2,10,27,36,42] using deep learning models have been proposed. Leal-Taixé et al. [27] adopt a Siamese CNN to learn local features from both RGB images and optical flow maps. In [42], Sadeghian et al. propose to exploit the LSTM network to account for appearance modeling, which takes images in the tracklet step-by-step and predicts the similarity score. In this work, we introduce attention mechanisms to handle inaccurate detections and occlusions. We show that the proposed online algorithm achieves favorable identity-preserving performance against the state-of-the-art offline methods, even though the offline methods have the advantage of exploiting global information across frames.

Attention Model. A number of methods adopt attention mechanisms for various tasks such as image captioning [8,17,55], visual question answering [54,57], and image classification [50]. A visual attention mechanism enables the model to focus on the most relevant regions of the input to extract more discriminative features. In this work, we integrate both spatial and temporal attention mechanisms into the proposed MOT algorithm. Our approach differs from the state-of-the-art STAM metohd [10], which adopts the spatial-temporal attention mechanism for online MOT, in three aspects. First, the spatial attention in the STAM corresponds to the visibility map. Since the visibility map is estimated directly from the detected image patch without comparison with the observations in the tracklet, it becomes unreliable when a distractor is close to the target. In contrast, we exploit the interplay of the detection and tracklet to generate dual spatial attention maps, which is demonstrated to be more robust to noisy detections and occlusions. Second, the STAM needs to synthetically generate occluded samples and the corresponding ground truth to initialize model training while our spatial attention map can be learned implicitly without any pixel-level annotation. Third, as the temporal attention value in [10] is generated independently for each sample in the tracklet based on the estimated occlusion status, it is less effective when the distractor appears in the tracklet. We take the consistency of the overall tracklet into account and assign a lower attention weight to a noisy sample that is different from most samples in the tracklet.

Data Imbalance. Data imbalance exists in numerous computer vision tasks where one class contains much fewer samples than others, which causes issues in training classifiers or model updates. One common solution [18,44] is to adopt hard negative mining during training. Recently, several methods [6,34] re-weight the contribution of each sample based on the observed loss and demonstrate significant improvements on segmentation and detection tasks. In this work, we propose a cost-sensitive tracking loss which puts more emphasis on hard samples with large loss to alleviate drifting problems.

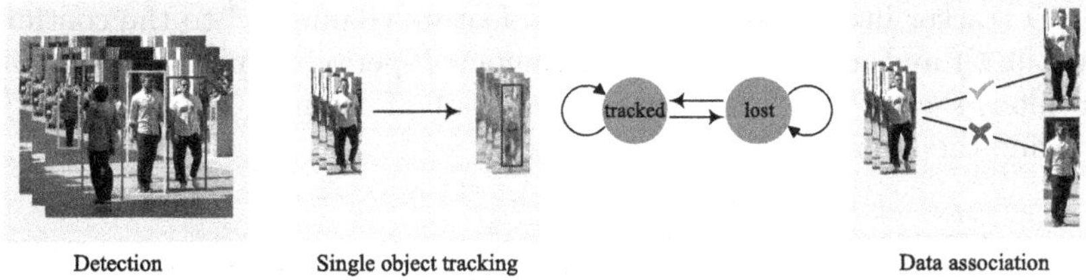

Fig. 2. Proposed online MOT pipeline. This pipeline mainly consists of three tasks: detection, single object tracking, and data association. The state of each target switches between tracked and lost depending on the tracking reliability. Single object tracking is applied to generate the tracklets for the tracked targets while data association compares the tracklets with candidate detections to make assignments for the lost targets.

3 Proposed Online MOT Algorithm

We exploit both single object tracking and data association to maintain target identities. Figure 2 illustrates the proposed online MOT pipeline. Given target detections in each frame, we apply a single object tracker to keep tracking each target. The target state is set as tracked until the tracking result becomes unreliable (e.g., the tracking score is low or the tracking result is inconsistent with the detection result). In such a case, the target is regarded as lost. We then suspend the tracker and perform data association to compute the similarity between the tracklet and detections that are not covered by any tracked target. Once the lost target is linked to a detection through data association, we update the state as tracked and restore the tracking process.

3.1 Single Object Tracking

Since significant progress has been made on single object tracking in recent years, we apply the state-of-the-art single object tracker in MOT. However, the tracker is prone to drift due to frequent interactions between different objects. To alleviate this problem, we propose a cost-sensitive tracking loss.

Baseline Tracker. We employ the method based on the Efficient Convolution Operators (ECO) [12] as the baseline tracker. The ECO tracker achieves the state-of-the-art performance on visual tracking benchmarks [25,33,38,52] and its fast variant ECO-HC based on hand-crafted features (HOG [11] and Color Names [49]) operates at 60 frames per second (FPS) on a single CPU, which is suitable for the online MOT task.

We first briefly review the ECO formulation as it is used as part of the proposed MOT algorithm. For clarity, we present the one-dimension domain formulation like [12,13]. Denote $\mathbf{x} = \{(\mathbf{x}^1)^\top, \cdots, (\mathbf{x}^D)^\top\}$ as a feature map with D feature channels extracted from an image patch. Each feature channel $\mathbf{x}^d \in \mathbb{R}^{N_d}$ has a resolution N_d. Different from conventional correlation filter based trackers, the ECO tracker interpolates the discrete feature channel $\mathbf{x}^d$ to the continuous domain $[0, T)$ and aims to learn a continuous T-periodic multi-channel convolution filter $f = \{f^1, \cdots, f^D\}$ from a batch of M training samples $\{\mathbf{x}_j\}_1^M$ by minimizing the following objective function:

$$E(f) = \sum_{j=1}^{M} \alpha_j \left\| S_f\{\mathbf{x}_j\}(t) - y_j(t) \right\|_{L^2} + \sum_{d=1}^{D} \left\| w(t) f^d(t) \right\|_{L^2}, \quad t \in [0, T). \quad (1)$$

Here, the factor α_j denotes the weight of the sample $\mathbf{x}_j$. The convolution operator S_f maps the sample $\mathbf{x}_j$ to a score function $S_f\{\mathbf{x}_j\}(t)$, which predicts the confidence score of the target at the location $t \in [0, T)$ in the image. The label function $y_j(t)$ is the desired output of the operator S_f applied to $\mathbf{x}_j$. The regularization term uses a weight function $w(t)$ to suppress boundary effects.

The objective function (1) can be transformed to a least squares problem in the Fourier domain, which is equivalent to solve the following normal equation:

$$(\mathbf{A}^{\mathrm{H}} \mathbf{\Gamma} \mathbf{A} + \mathbf{W}^{\mathrm{H}} \mathbf{W}) \hat{\mathbf{f}} = \mathbf{A}^{\mathrm{H}} \mathbf{\Gamma} \hat{\mathbf{y}}. \quad (2)$$

Here, the superscript ^{H} denotes the conjugate-transpose of a matrix. We let $\hat{\mathbf{f}} = [(\hat{\mathbf{f}}^1)^\top, \cdots, (\hat{\mathbf{f}}^D)^\top]^\top$ denote the non-zero Fourier coefficient vector of the filter f, and let $\hat{\mathbf{y}}$ denote the corresponding label vector in the Fourier domain. The diagonal matrix $\mathbf{\Gamma} = \alpha_1 \mathbf{I} \oplus \cdots \alpha_M \mathbf{I}$ contains the weight α_j for each sample $\mathbf{x}_j$. The matrix $\mathbf{A} = [(\mathbf{A}_1)^\top, \cdots, (\mathbf{A}_M)^\top]^\top$ is computed from the values of samples $\{\mathbf{x}_j\}_1^M$, while the block-diagonal matrix $\mathbf{W} = \mathbf{W}^1 \oplus \cdots \mathbf{W}^D$ corresponds to the penalty function w in (1). More details can be found in [12,13].

Cost-Sensitive Tracking Loss. Given an image patch, the ECO tracker utilizes all circular shifted versions of the patch to train the filter. Detection scores of all shifted samples compose the confidence map. Figure 3(a) shows the desired confidence map for the bottom image patch. The red bounding box in the patch corresponds to the target region. Most locations in the patch are labeled to near zero while only a few locations close to the target center make up positive samples. Figure 3(b) shows the score map predicted by the ECO tracker. Beside the

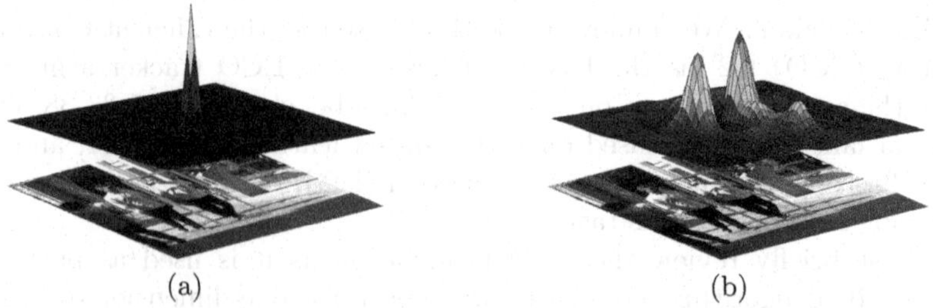

Fig. 3. Visualization of the confidence map. The heat map in (a) presents the desired confidence map for the bottom image patch while that in (b) shows the score map predicted by the ECO tracker. (Color figure online)

target location, the center of the object next to the target also gets high confidence score in the middle heat map. Hence, these negative samples centered at intra-class distractors are regarded as hard samples and should be penalized more heavily to prevent the tracker from drifting to the distractor. However, in the ECO formulation (1), the contributions of all shifted samples in the same search area are weighted equally. Since most negative samples come from the background, the training process may be dominated by substantial background information and consequently degenerate the discriminative power of model on hard samples centered at intra-class distractors.

To alleviate data imbalance, we propose a cost-sensitive loss to put emphasis on hard samples. Specifically, we add a factor $q(t)$ in the data term of (1) as

$$E(f) = \sum_{j=1}^{M} \alpha_j \left\| q(t)(S_f\{\mathbf{x}_j\}(t) - y_j(t)) \right\|_{L^2} + \sum_{d=1}^{D} \left\| w(t) f^d(t) \right\|_{L^2}. \tag{3}$$

Here, we define the modulating factor $q(t)$ as:

$$q(t) = \left| \frac{S_f\{\mathbf{x}_j\}(t) - y_j(t)}{\max_t |S_f\{\mathbf{x}_j\}(t) - y_j(t)|} \right|^2. \tag{4}$$

Hence, the modulating factor $q(t)$ re-weights the contributions of circular shifted samples based on their losses.

To make this loss function tractable to solve, we use the filter learned in the last model update step to compute $q(t)$. Thus, $q(t)$ can be precomputed before each training step. Similar to (1), we transform (3) to the objective function in the Fourier domain and perform optimization by solving the following equation:

$$\left((\mathbf{QA})^{\mathrm{H}} \mathbf{\Gamma} (\mathbf{QA}) + \mathbf{W}^{\mathrm{H}} \mathbf{W} \right) \hat{\mathbf{f}} = (\mathbf{QA})^{\mathrm{H}} \mathbf{\Gamma} \mathbf{Q} \hat{\mathbf{y}}, \tag{5}$$

where $\mathbf{Q}$ denotes the operation matrix in the Fourier domain, which corresponds to the factor $q(t)$. Like (2), this equation can also be iteratively solved by the Conjugate Gradient (CG) method with the same efficiency as the original ECO formulations. Due to the space limit, the concrete derivation and solution of the proposed cost-sensitive loss are provided in the supplementary material.

3.2 Data Association with Dual Matching Attention Network

When the tracking process becomes unreliable, we suspend the tracker and set the target to a lost state. Then we exploit the data association algorithm to determine whether to keep the target state as lost or transfer it to tracked. It is intuitive to use the tracking score s (i.e., the highest value in the confidence map) of the target to measure the tracking reliability. However, if we only rely on the tracking score, a false alarm detection on the background is prone to be consistently tracked with high confidence. Since a tracked target which does not get any detection for several frames is likely to be a false alarm, we utilize the overlap between bounding boxes given by the tracker and detector to filter out false alarms. Specifically, we set $o(t_l, \mathcal{D}_l)$ to 1 if the maximum overlap ratio between the tracked target $t_l \in \mathcal{T}_l$ and the detections $\mathcal{D}_l$ in l frames before is higher than 0.5. Otherwise, $o(t_l, \mathcal{D}_l)$ is set to 0. We consider the mean value of $\{o(t_l, \mathcal{D}_l)\}_1^L$ in the past L tracked frames o_{mean} as another measurement to decide the tracking state. Thus, the state of the target is defined as:

$$\text{state} = \begin{cases} \text{tracked}, & \text{if } s > \tau_s \text{ and } o_{mean} > \tau_o, \\ \text{lost}, & \text{otherwise}. \end{cases} \quad (6)$$

Before computing the appearance similarity for data association, we exploit motion cues to select candidate detections. When the target gets lost, we first keep the scale of the bounding box at the last frame $k-1$ and use a linear motion model to predict its location at the current frame k. Denote $\mathbf{c}_{k-1} = [x_{k-1}, y_{k-1}]$ as the center coordinate of the target at frame $k-1$, the velocity $\mathbf{v}_{k-1}$ of the target at frame $k-1$ is computed as:

$$\mathbf{v}_{k-1} = \frac{1}{K}(\mathbf{c}_{k-1} - \mathbf{c}_{k-K}), \quad (7)$$

where K denotes the frame interval for computing the velocity. Then the target coordinate in the current frame k is predicted as $\tilde{\mathbf{c}}_k = \mathbf{c}_{k-1} + \mathbf{v}_{k-1}$.

Given the predicted location of the target, we consider detections surrounding the predicted location which are not covered by any tracked target (i.e., the distance is smaller than a threshold τ_d) as candidate detections. We measure the appearance affinity between these detections and the observations in the target trajectory. Then we select the detection with the highest affinity and set a affinity threshold τ_a to decide whether to link the lost target to this detection.

The challenge is that both detections and observations in the tracklet may undergo misalignment and occlusion. To address these problems, we propose Dual Matching Attention Networks (DMAN) with both spatial and temporal attention mechanisms. Figure 4 illustrates the architecture of our network.

Spatial Attention Network. We propose a spatial attention network using the Siamese architecture to handle noisy detections and occlusions as shown in Fig. 4. In this work, we use the truncated ResNet-50 network [20] as the shared base network and apply L^2-normalization to output features along the channel dimension. The spatial attention map is applied to the features from the last convolutional layer of the ResNet-50 because representations from the top layer can capture high-level information that is useful for matching semantic regions. We denote the extracted feature map as $\mathbf{X} \in \mathbb{R}^{H \times W \times C}$ and consider $\mathbf{X}$ as a set of L^2-normalized C-dimension feature vectors:

$$\mathbf{X} = \{\mathbf{x}_1, \cdots, \mathbf{x}_N\}, \quad \mathbf{x}_i \in \mathbb{R}^C, \quad (8)$$

where $N = H \times W$. Each feature vector $\mathbf{x}_i$ corresponds to a spatial location on the feature map. Then we denote the feature maps extracted from the image pair as $\mathbf{X}^\alpha = \{\mathbf{x}_1^\alpha, \cdots, \mathbf{x}_N^\alpha\}$ and $\mathbf{X}^\beta = \left\{\mathbf{x}_1^\beta, \cdots, \mathbf{x}_N^\beta\right\}$, respectively. The intuition is that

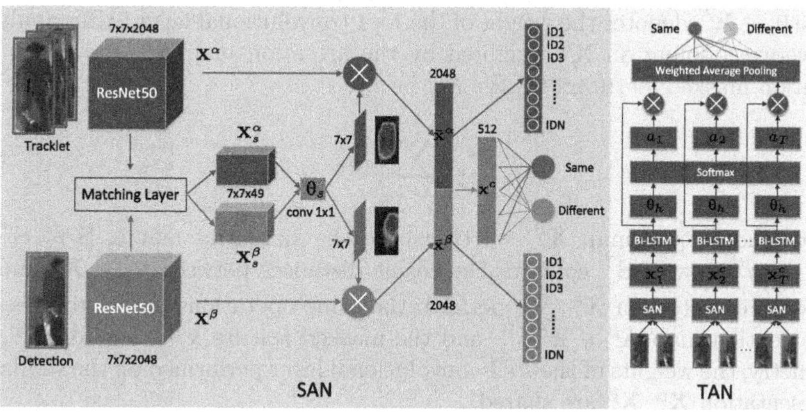

Fig. 4. Network architecture of the proposed DMAN. It consists of the Spatial Attention Network (SAN) and Temporal Attention Network (TAN). Given a candidate detection and a sequence of the target tracklet as inputs, the SAN repeatedly compares the detection with each sample in the tracklet to extract the combined features $\{\mathbf{x}^c\}_1^T$. Taking these features as inputs, the TAN integrates the information from the overall tracklet to infer whether the detection and the tracklet belong to the same target.

we should pay more attention to common local patterns of the two feature maps. However, since the two images are usually not well aligned due to inaccurate bounding boxes and pose change, the corresponding feature located in $\mathbf{X}^\alpha$ may not appears at the same location in $\mathbf{X}^\beta$. Thus, we generate the attention map for each input separately. To infer the attention value for the ith location in the feature map $\mathbf{X}^\alpha$, we need to compare $\mathbf{x}_i^\alpha \in \mathbf{X}^\alpha$ with all the feature slices appearing in the paired feature map $\mathbf{X}^\beta$.

We exploit a non-parametric matching layer to compute the cosine similarity $S_{ij} = (\mathbf{x}_i^\alpha)^\top \mathbf{x}_j^\beta$ between each $\mathbf{x}_i^\alpha$ and $\mathbf{x}_j^\beta$ and output the similarity matrix $\mathbf{S} \in \mathbb{R}^{N \times C}$ as

$$\mathbf{S} = \begin{bmatrix} (\mathbf{x}_1^\alpha)^\top \\ \vdots \\ (\mathbf{x}_N^\alpha)^\top \end{bmatrix} \cdot \begin{bmatrix} \mathbf{x}_1^\beta, \cdots, \mathbf{x}_N^\beta \end{bmatrix} = \begin{bmatrix} (\mathbf{s}_1)^\top \\ \vdots \\ (\mathbf{s}_N)^\top \end{bmatrix}, \tag{9}$$

where the vector $\mathbf{s}_i = [S_{i1}, \cdots, S_{iN}]^\top \in \mathbb{R}^N$ contains the elements in the ith row of $\mathbf{S}$, which indicate the cosine distances between $\mathbf{x}_i^\alpha \in \mathbf{X}^\alpha$ and all the feature vectors in $\mathbf{X}^\beta$. The similarity matrix $\mathbf{S} \in \mathbb{R}^{N \times N}$ is reshaped into a $H \times W \times N$ feature cube $\mathbf{X}_s^\alpha \in \mathbb{R}^{H \times W \times N}$ to form a similarity representation for the feature map $\mathbf{X}^\alpha$. Then we input $\mathbf{X}_s^\alpha$ to a convolutional layer with 1×1 kernel and perform a softmax over the output to generate the attention map $\mathbf{A}^\alpha \in \mathbb{R}^{H \times W}$ for $\mathbf{X}^\alpha$. The attention value a_i^α in $\mathbf{A}^\alpha$ for the ith location in $\mathbf{X}^\alpha$ is defined as:

$$a_i^\alpha = \frac{\exp\left(\theta_s^\top \mathbf{s}_i\right)}{\sum_{i=1}^N \exp\left(\theta_s^\top \mathbf{s}_i\right)}, \tag{10}$$

where $\theta_s \in \mathbb{R}^N$ denotes the weight of the 1×1 convolutional layer. After applying an average pooling on $\mathbf{X}^\alpha$ weighted by the attention map $\mathbf{A}^\alpha$, we obtain the attention-masked feature $\bar{\mathbf{x}}^\alpha \in \mathbb{R}^C$ as:

$$\bar{\mathbf{x}}^\alpha = \sum_{i=1}^{N} a_i^\alpha \mathbf{x}_i^\alpha. \tag{11}$$

For the feature map $\mathbf{X}^\beta$, we transpose the similarity matrix $\mathbf{S}$ to $\mathbf{S}^\top$ so that the jth row of $\mathbf{S}^\top$ contains the cosine distances between $\mathbf{x}_j^\beta \in \mathbf{X}^\beta$ and all the feature vectors in $\mathbf{X}^\alpha$. We perform the same operations on $\mathbf{S}^\top$ to generate the attention map $\mathbf{A}^\beta \in \mathbb{R}^{H\times W}$ and the masked feature $\bar{\mathbf{x}}^\beta \in \mathbb{R}^C$ for $\mathbf{X}^\beta$. For symmetry, the weights of the 1×1 convolutional layer performed on the similarity representation $\mathbf{X}_s^\alpha, \mathbf{X}_s^\beta$ are shared.

We exploit both the identification loss and verification loss to jointly train the network so that the network needs to simultaneously predict the identity of each image in the input pair and the similarity score between the two images during training. For identification, we apply the cross entropy loss on the masked features $\bar{\mathbf{x}}^\alpha$ and $\bar{\mathbf{x}}^\beta$, respectively. For verification, we concatenate $\bar{\mathbf{x}}^\alpha$ and $\bar{\mathbf{x}}^\beta$ to a single feature and input it to a 512-dimension fully-connected layer, which outputs the combined feature $\mathbf{x}^c \in \mathbb{R}^{512}$. A binary classifier with cross entropy loss is then performed on $\mathbf{x}^c$ for prediction.

Temporal Attention Network. When comparing the candidate detection with a sequence of observations in the tracklet, it is straightforward to apply average pooling on the feature vectors of all the observations in the tracklet for verification. However, as shown in Fig. 1(b), the tracklet may contain noisy observations. Simply assigning equal weights to all the observations may degrade the model performance. To handle unreliable samples in the tracklet, we exploit the temporal attention mechanism to adaptively allocate different degrees of importance to different samples in the tracklet. Figure 4 shows the structure of the proposed temporal attention network.

The temporal attention network takes the set of features $\{\mathbf{x}_1^c, \cdots, \mathbf{x}_T^c\}$ extracted from the spatial attention network as inputs. Here, the feature vector $\mathbf{x}_i^c$ is obtained by comparing the candidate detection with the ith sample in the T-length tracklet. To determine noisy samples in the tracket, the model should not only rely on the similarity between the detection and each sample in the tracklet (which has been encoded in each $\mathbf{x}_i^c$), but also consider the consistency of all samples. Thus, we utilize a Bi-directional Long-Short Term Memory (Bi-LSTM) network to predict the attention value a_t:

$$a_t = \frac{\exp\left(\theta_h^\top \left[\mathbf{h}_t^l; \mathbf{h}_t^r\right]\right)}{\sum_{t=1}^{T} \exp\left(\theta_h^\top \left[\mathbf{h}_t^l; \mathbf{h}_t^r\right]\right)}, \quad t = 1, \cdots, T, \tag{12}$$

where $\mathbf{h}_t^l, \mathbf{h}_t^r$ are the bi-directional hidden representations of the Bi-LSTM model and θ_h is the weight of the layer to generate attention values. The attention score

a_t is a scalar value which is used to weight the hidden representations $\mathbf{h}_t^l, \mathbf{h}_t^r$ of each observation for feature pooling as follows:

$$\bar{\mathbf{h}} = \sum_{i=1}^{T} a_t \left[\mathbf{h}_t^l; \mathbf{h}_t^r\right]. \tag{13}$$

Taking the pooled feature $\bar{\mathbf{h}}$ as input, the binary classification layer predicts the similarity score between the input detection and paired tracklet.

Finally, we make the assignments between candidate detections and lost targets based on the pairwise similarity scores of detections and tracklets.

Training Strategy. We utilize the ground-truth detections and identity information provided in the MOT16 training set to generate image pairs and detection-tracklet pairs for network training. However, the training data contains only limited identities and the sequence of each identity consists of consecutive samples with large redundancies. Hence, the proposed network is prone to overfit the training set. To alleviate this problem, we adopt a two-step training strategy. We first train the spatial attention network on randomly generated image pairs. Then we fix the weights of the spatial attention network and use the extracted features as inputs to train the temporal attention network. In addition, we augment the training set by randomly cropping and rescaling the input images. To simulate noisy tracklets in practice, we also add noisy samples to the training tracklet sequences by randomly replacing one or two images in the tracklet with images from other identities. Since some targets in the training set contain only a few samples, we randomly sample each identity with the equal probability to alleviate the effect of class imbalance.

Trajectory Management. For trajectory initialization, we set a threshold τ_i and discard the target which is lost or not covered by a detection in any of the first τ_i frames. For trajectory termination, we end the target if it keeps lost for over τ_t frames or just exits out of view. In addition, we collect M most recent observations of the target and generate the T-length tracklet for data association by uniformly sampling from the collected samples to reduce data redundancy.

4 Experiments

Datasets. We evaluate the proposed online MOT algorithm on the MOT16 [35] and MOT17 benchmark datasets. The MOT16 dataset consists of 14 video sequences (7 for training, 7 for testing). The MOT17 dataset contains the same video sequences as the MOT16 dataset while additionally providing three sets of detections (DPM [19], Faster-RCNN [40], and SDP [56]) for more comprehensive evaluation of the tracking algorithms.

Evaluation Metrics. We consider the metrics used by the MOT benchmarks [28,35] for evaluation, which includes Multiple Object Tracking Accuracy (MOTA) [4], Multiple Object Tracking Precision (MOTP) [4], ID F1 score [41] (IDF, the ratio of correct detections over the average number of ground-truth and computed detections), ID Precision [41] (IDP, the fraction of detections that are correctly identified), ID Recall [41] (IDR, the fraction of ground-truth detections that are correctly identified), the ratio of Mostly Tracked targets (MT), the ratio of Mostly Lost targets (ML), the number of False Negatives (FN), the number of False Positives (FP), the number of ID Switches (IDS), the number of fragments (Frag). Note that IDF, IDP, and IDR are recently introduced by Ristani et al. [41] and added to the MOT benchmarks to measure the identity-preserving ability of trackers. We also show the Average Ranking (AR) score suggested by the MOT benchmarks. It is computed by averaging all metric rankings, which can be considered as a reference to compare the overall MOT performance.

Implementation Details. The proposed method is implemented using MATLAB and Tensorflow [1]. For single object tracking, we exploit the same features as the ECO-HC [12] (i.e., HOG and Color Names). For data association, we use the convolution blocks of the ResNet-50 pre-trained on the ImageNet dataset [15] as the shared base network. All input images are resized to 224 × 224. The length of the tracklet is set to $T = 8$, and the maximum number of collected samples in the trajectory is set to $M = 100$. We use the Adam [24] optimizer to train both the spatial attention network and the temporal attention network. Learning rates of both networks are set to 0.0001. Let F denote the frame rate of the video, the interval for computing the target velocity is set to $K = 0.3F$. The trajectory initialization threshold is set to $\tau_i = 0.2F$, while the termination threshold is set to $\tau_t = 2F$. The tracking score threshold is set to $\tau_s = 0.2$, and the appearance affinity score threshold is set to $\tau_a = 0.6$. All the values of these threshold parameters are set according to the MOTA performance on the MOT16 training set. The source code will be made available to the public.

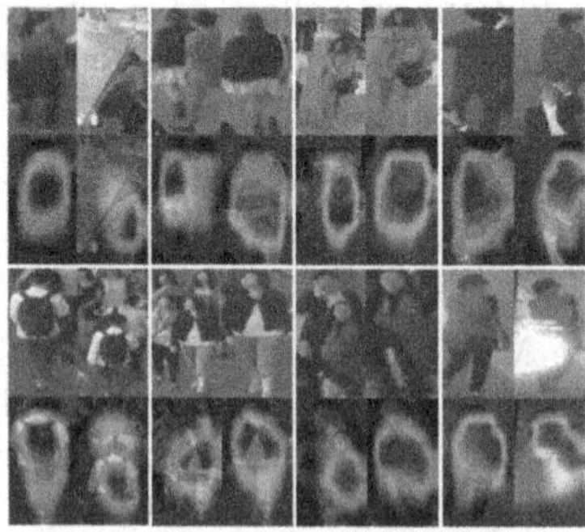

(a) Spatial attention maps

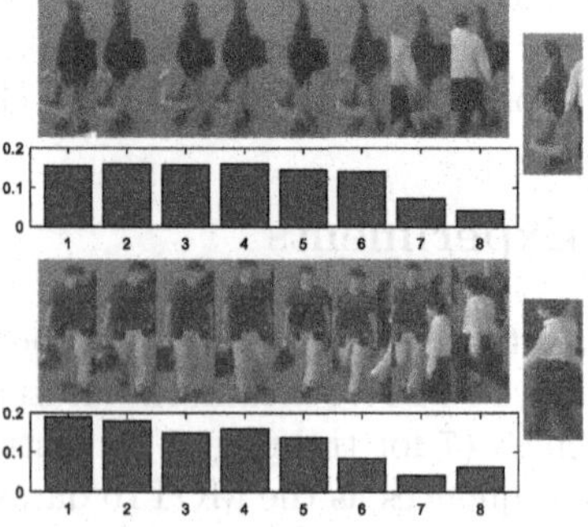

(b) Temporal attention values

Fig. 5. Visualization of spatial and temporal attention.

4.1 Visualization of the Spatial and Temporal Attention

Figure 5 shows the visualization results of the proposed spatial and temporal attention mechanisms. In Fig. 5(a), each group consists of four images. The top row of each group shows an image pair from the same target while the bottom row presents corresponding spatial attention maps. Although these image pairs undergo misalignment, scale change, and occlusion, the proposed spatial attention network is still able to locate the matching parts of each pair. Compared with the visibility maps shown in [10], our attention maps focus more explicitly on target regions and suppress both distractors and backgrounds, which enhances the discriminative power of the model on hard positive pairs.

Figure 5(b) shows the attention scores predicted by the proposed temporal attention network. The sequence on the left of each row is the tracklet for association while the image on the right of each row corresponds to the candidate detection. The bar chart below the tracklet shows the attention value for each observation. In the top row, the detection and the tracklet belong to the same target. However, the tracklet contains noisy observations caused by occlusion. As shown in the bar chart, the proposed temporal attention network assigns relative low attention scores to occluded observations to suppress their effects on data association. In the bottom row, the detection and the tracklet belong to different targets. Although the last two images in the tracklet contain the same target in the detected patch, the proposed network correctly assigns low attention scores to the last two images by taking the overall sequence into account. These two examples in Fig. 5(b) demonstrate the effectiveness of the proposed temporal attention mechanism on both hard positive and hard negative samples.

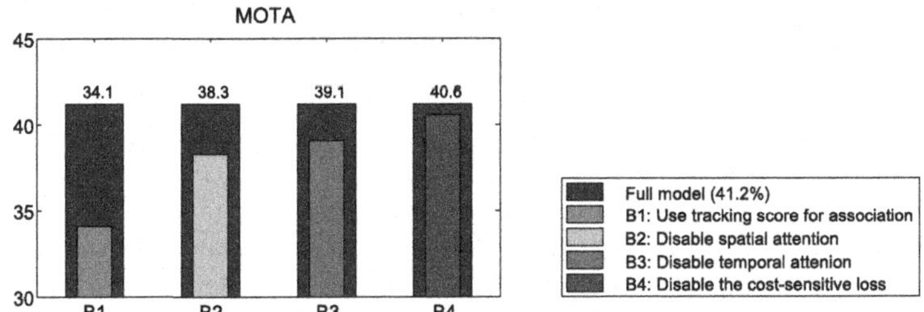

Fig. 6. Contributions of each component.

4.2 Ablation Studies

To demonstrate the contribution of each module in our algorithm, we set up four baseline approaches by disabling each module at one time. Each baseline approach is described as follows:

B1: We disable the proposed DMAN and rely on the cost-sensitive tracker to link the detections. Specifically, we apply the convolution filter of the tracker

on the candidate detection and directly use the maximum score in the confidence map as the appearance affinity for data association.
B2: We disable the spatial attention module and use the standard Siamese CNN architecture for identity verification of image pairs.
B3: We replace our temporal attention pooling with average pooling to integrate the hidden representations of the Bi-LSTM in multiple time steps.
B4: We use the baseline tracker without the cost-sensitive tracking loss.

Figure 6 shows the MOTA score of each baseline approach compared with our full model (41.2%) on the MOT16 training dataset. As we can see, all proposed modules make contributions to the performance. The MOTA score drops significantly by 7.1% when we directly use the tracking score for data association, which shows the advantage of the proposed DMAN. The degradation in B2 and B3 demonstrates the effectiveness of the proposed attention mechanisms. Finally, the cost-sensitive tracking loss shows a slight improvement in term of MOTA.

4.3 Performance on the MOT Benchmark Datasets

We evaluate our approach on the test sets of both the MOT16 and MOT17 benchmark against the state-of-the-art methods. Tables 1 and 2 present the quantitative performance on the MOT16 and MOT17 datasets, respectively.

As shown in Table 1, our method achieves a comparable MOTA score and performs favorably against the state-of-the-art methods in terms of IDF, IDP, IDR, MT, and FN on the MOT16 dataset. We improve 4.8% in IDF, 3.9% in IDP, 4% in IDR, and 2.8% in MT compared with the second best published online MOT tracker and achieves the best performance in IDF and IDP among both online and offline methods, which demonstrates the merits of our approach

Table 1. Tracking performance on the MOT16 dataset.

Mode	Method	MOTA ↑	MOTP ↑	IDF ↑	IDP ↑	IDR ↑	MT ↑	ML ↓	FP ↓	FN ↓	IDS ↓	Frag ↓	AR ↓
Online	OVBT [3]	38.4	75.4	37.8	55.4	28.7	7.5%	47.3%	11,517	99,463	1,321	2,140	49.8
	EAMTT [43]	38.8	75.1	42.4	65.2	31.5	7.9%	49.1%	8,114	102,452	965	1,657	37.4
	oICF [22]	43.2	74.3	49.3	73.3	37.2	11.3%	48.5%	6,651	96,515	381	1,404	33.3
	CDA_DDAL [2]	43.9	74.7	45.1	66.5	34.1	10.7%	44.4%	6,450	95,175	676	1,795	31.8
	STAM [10]	46.0	74.9	50.0	71.5	38.5	14.6%	43.6%	6,895	91,117	473	1,422	29.6
	AMIR [42]	47.2	75.8	46.3	68.9	34.8	14.0%	41.6%	2,681	92,856	774	1,675	21.8
	Ours	46.1	73.8	54.8	77.2	42.5	17.4%	42.7%	7,909	89,874	532	1,616	19.3
Offline	QuadMOT [45]	44.1	76.4	38.3	56.3	29.0	14.6%	44.9%	6,388	94,775	745	1,096	31.9
	EDMT [7]	45.3	75.9	47.9	65.3	37.8	17.0%	39.9%	11,122	87,890	639	946	20.3
	MHT_DAM [23]	45.8	76.3	46.1	66.3	35.3	16.2%	43.2%	6,412	91,758	590	781	23.7
	JMC [47]	46.3	75.7	46.3	66.3	35.6	15.5%	39.7%	6,373	90,914	657	1,114	21.1
	NOMT [9]	46.4	76.6	53.3	73.2	41.9	18.3%	41.4%	9,753	87,565	359	504	16.3
	MCjoint [21]	47.1	76.3	52.3	73.9	40.4	20.4%	46.9%	6,703	89,368	370	598	18.6
	NLLMPa [29]	47.6	78.5	47.3	67.2	36.5	17.0%	40.4%	5,844	89,093	629	768	16.8
	LMP [48]	48.8	79.0	51.3	71.1	40.1	18.2%	40.1%	6,654	86,245	481	595	14.8

in maintaining identity. Similarly, Table 2 shows that the proposed method performs favorably against the other online trackers in MOTA and achieves the best performance in terms of identity-preserving metrics (IDF, IDP, IDR, IDS) among all methods on the MOT17 dataset. In addition, we achieve the best AR score among all the online trackers on both the MOT16 and MOT17 datasets.

Table 2. Tracking performance on the MOT17 dataset.

Mode	Method	MOTA ↑	MOTP ↑	IDF ↑	IDP ↑	IDR ↑	MT ↑	ML ↓	FP ↓	FN ↓	IDS ↓	Frag ↓	AR ↓
Online	GM_PHD [16]	36.4	76.2	33.9	54.2	24.7	4.1%	57.3%	23,723	330,767	4,607	11,317	23.0
	GMPHD_KCF [26]	39.6	74.5	36.6	49.6	29.1	8.8%	43.3%	50,903	284,228	5,811	7,414	23.5
	E2EM	47.5	76.5	48.8	68.4	37.9	16.5%	37.5%	20,655	272,187	3,632	12,712	13.1
	Ours	48.2	75.9	55.7	75.9	44.0	19.3%	38.3%	26,218	263,608	2,194	5,378	11.4
Offline	IOU [5]	45.5	76.9	39.4	56.4	30.3	15.7%	40.5%	19,993	281,643	5,988	7,404	16.4
	EDMT [7]	50.0	77.3	51.3	67.0	41.5	21.6%	36.3%	32,279	247,297	2,264	3,260	9.9
	MHT_DAM [23]	50.7	77.5	47.2	63.4	37.6	20.8%	36.9%	22,875	252,889	2,314	2,865	10.8

5 Conclusions

In this work, we integrate the merits of single object tracking and data association methods in a unified online MOT framework. For single object tracking, we introduce a novel cost-sensitive loss to mitigate the effects of data imbalance. For data association, we exploit both the spatial and temporal attention mechanisms to handle noisy detections and occlusions. Experimental results on public MOT benchmark datasets demonstrate the effectiveness of the proposed approach.

Acknowledgments. This work is supported in part by National Natural Science Foundation of China (NSFC, Grant No. 61771303, 61671289, and 61521062), Science and Technology Commission of Shanghai Municipality (STCSM, Grant No. 17DZ1205602, 18DZ1200102, and 18DZ2270700), SJTU-YITU/Thinkforce Joint Lab of Visual Computing and Application, and Visbody. J. Zhu and N. Liu are supported by a scholarship from China Scholarship Council. M. Kim is supported by the Panasonic Silicon Valley Laboratory. M.-H. Yang acknowlegdes the support from NSF (Grant No. 1149783) and gifts from Adobe and NVIDIA.

References

1. Abadi, M., et al.: TensorFlow: large-scale machine learning on heterogeneous distributed systems. arXiv preprint arXiv:1603.04467 (2016)
2. Bae, S.H., Yoon, K.J.: Confidence-based data association and discriminative deep appearance learning for robust online multi-object tracking. TPAMI **40**, 595–610 (2017)
3. Ban, Y., Ba, S., Alameda-Pineda, X., Horaud, R.: Tracking multiple persons based on a variational bayesian model. In: Hua, G., Jégou, H. (eds.) ECCV 2016. LNCS, vol. 9914, pp. 52–67. Springer, Cham (2016). https://doi.org/10.1007/978-3-319-48881-3_5

4. Bernardin, K., Stiefelhagen, R.: Evaluating multiple object tracking performance: the CLEAR MOT metrics. JIVP **2008**, 1 (2008)
5. Bochinski, E., Eiselein, V., Sikora, T.: High-speed tracking-by-detection without using image information. In: AVSS Workshop (2017)
6. Bulo, S.R., Neuhold, G., Kontschieder, P.: Loss max-pooling for semantic image segmentation. In: CVPR (2017)
7. Chen, J., Sheng, H., Zhang, Y., Xiong, Z.: Enhancing detection model for multiple hypothesis tracking. In: CVPR Workshop (2017)
8. Chen, X., Lawrence Zitnick, C.: Mind's eye: a recurrent visual representation for image caption generation. In: CVPR (2015)
9. Choi, W.: Near-online multi-target tracking with aggregated local flow descriptor. In: ICCV (2015)
10. Chu, Q., Ouyang, W., Li, H., Wang, X., Liu, B., Yu, N.: Online multi-object tracking using CNN-based single object tracker with spatial-temporal attention mechanism. In: ICCV (2017)
11. Dalal, N., Triggs, B.: Histograms of oriented gradients for human detection. In: CVPR (2005)
12. Danelljan, M., Bhat, G., Khan, F.S., Felsberg, M.: ECO: efficient convolution operators for tracking. In: CVPR (2017)
13. Danelljan, M., Robinson, A., Shahbaz Khan, F., Felsberg, M.: Beyond correlation filters: learning continuous convolution operators for visual tracking. In: Leibe, B., Matas, J., Sebe, N., Welling, M. (eds.) ECCV 2016. LNCS, vol. 9909, pp. 472–488. Springer, Cham (2016). https://doi.org/10.1007/978-3-319-46454-1_29
14. Dehghan, A., Tian, Y., Torr, P.H., Shah, M.: Target identity-aware network flow for online multiple target tracking. In: CVPR (2015)
15. Deng, J., Dong, W., Socher, R., Li, L.J., Li, K., Fei-Fei, L.: ImageNet: a large-scale hierarchical image database. In: CVPR (2009)
16. Eiselein, V., Arp, D., Pätzold, M., Sikora, T.: Real-time multi-human tracking using a probability hypothesis density filter and multiple detectors. In: AVSS (2012)
17. Fang, H., et al.: From captions to visual concepts and back. In: CVPR (2015)
18. Felzenszwalb, P.F., Girshick, R.B., McAllester, D.: Cascade object detection with deformable part models. In: CVPR (2010)
19. Felzenszwalb, P.F., Girshick, R.B., McAllester, D., Ramanan, D.: Object detection with discriminatively trained part-based models. TPAMI **32**(9), 1627–1645 (2010)
20. He, K., Zhang, X., Ren, S., Sun, J.: Deep residual learning for image recognition. In: CVPR (2016)
21. Keuper, M., Tang, S., Zhongjie, Y., Andres, B., Brox, T., Schiele, B.: A multi-cut formulation for joint segmentation and tracking of multiple objects. arXiv preprint arXiv:1607.06317 (2016)
22. Kieritz, H., Becker, S., Hübner, W., Arens, M.: Online multi-person tracking using integral channel features. In: AVSS (2016)
23. Kim, C., Li, F., Ciptadi, A., Rehg, J.M.: Multiple hypothesis tracking revisited. In: ICCV (2015)
24. Kingma, D., Ba, J.: Adam: a method for stochastic optimization. arXiv preprint arXiv:1412.6980 (2014)
25. Kristan, M., et al.: The visual object tracking VOT2014 challenge results. In: Agapito, L., Bronstein, M.M., Rother, C. (eds.) ECCV 2014. LNCS, vol. 8926, pp. 191–217. Springer, Cham (2015). https://doi.org/10.1007/978-3-319-16181-5_14
26. Kutschbach, T., Bochinski, E., Eiselein, V., Sikora, T.: Sequential sensor fusion combining probability hypothesis density and kernelized correlation filters for multi-object tracking in video data. In: AVSS (2017)

27. Leal-Taixé, L., Canton-Ferrer, C., Schindler, K.: Learning by tracking: Siamese CNN for robust target association. In: CVPR Workshop (2016)
28. Leal-Taixé, L., Milan, A., Reid, I., Roth, S., Schindler, K.: MOTchallenge 2015: towards a benchmark for multi-target tracking. arXiv preprint arXiv:1504.01942 (2015)
29. Levinkov, E., et al.: Joint graph decomposition & node labeling: problem, algorithms, applications. In: CVPR (2017)
30. Li, W., Wang, X.: Locally aligned feature transforms across views. In: CVPR (2013)
31. Li, W., Zhao, R., Wang, X.: Human reidentification with transferred metric learning. In: Lee, K.M., Matsushita, Y., Rehg, J.M., Hu, Z. (eds.) ACCV 2012. LNCS, vol. 7724, pp. 31–44. Springer, Heidelberg (2013). https://doi.org/10.1007/978-3-642-37331-2_3
32. Li, W., Zhao, R., Xiao, T., Wang, X.: DeepReID: deep filter pairing neural network for person re-identification. In: CVPR (2014)
33. Liang, P., Blasch, E., Ling, H.: Encoding color information for visual tracking: algorithms and benchmark. TIP **24**(12), 5630–5644 (2015)
34. Lin, T.Y., Goyal, P., Girshick, R., He, K., Dollár, P.: Focal loss for dense object detection. In: ICCV (2017)
35. Milan, A., Leal-Taixé, L., Reid, I., Roth, S., Schindler, K.: MOT16: a benchmark for multi-object tracking. arXiv preprint arXiv:1603.00831 (2016)
36. Milan, A., Rezatofighi, S.H., Dick, A.R., Reid, I.D., Schindler, K.: Online multi-target tracking using recurrent neural networks. In: AAAI (2017)
37. Milan, A., Roth, S., Schindler, K.: Continuous energy minimization for multitarget tracking. TPAMI **36**(1), 58–72 (2014)
38. Mueller, M., Smith, N., Ghanem, B.: A benchmark and simulator for UAV tracking. In: Leibe, B., Matas, J., Sebe, N., Welling, M. (eds.) ECCV 2016. LNCS, vol. 9905, pp. 445–461. Springer, Cham (2016). https://doi.org/10.1007/978-3-319-46448-0_27
39. Pirsiavash, H., Ramanan, D., Fowlkes, C.C.: Globally-optimal greedy algorithms for tracking a variable number of objects. In: CVPR (2011)
40. Ren, S., He, K., Girshick, R., Sun, J.: Faster R-CNN: towards real-time object detection with region proposal networks. In: NIPS (2015)
41. Ristani, E., Solera, F., Zou, R., Cucchiara, R., Tomasi, C.: Performance measures and a data set for multi-target, multi-camera tracking. In: Hua, G., Jégou, H. (eds.) ECCV 2016. LNCS, vol. 9914, pp. 17–35. Springer, Cham (2016). https://doi.org/10.1007/978-3-319-48881-3_2
42. Sadeghian, A., Alahi, A., Savarese, S.: Tracking the untrackable: learning to track multiple cues with long-term dependencies. In: ICCV (2017)
43. Sanchez-Matilla, R., Poiesi, F., Cavallaro, A.: Online multi-target tracking with strong and weak detections. In: Hua, G., Jégou, H. (eds.) ECCV 2016. LNCS, vol. 9914, pp. 84–99. Springer, Cham (2016). https://doi.org/10.1007/978-3-319-48881-3_7
44. Shrivastava, A., Gupta, A., Girshick, R.: Training region-based object detectors with online hard example mining. In: CVPR (2016)
45. Son, J., Baek, M., Cho, M., Han, B.: Multi-object tracking with quadruplet convolutional neural networks. In: CVPR (2017)
46. Tang, S., Andres, B., Andriluka, M., Schiele, B.: Subgraph decomposition for multi-target tracking. In: CVPR (2015)
47. Tang, S., Andres, B., Andriluka, M., Schiele, B.: Multi-person tracking by multicut and deep matching. In: Hua, G., Jégou, H. (eds.) ECCV 2016. LNCS, vol. 9914, pp. 100–111. Springer, Cham (2016). https://doi.org/10.1007/978-3-319-48881-3_8

48. Tang, S., Andriluka, M., Andres, B., Schiele, B.: Multiple people tracking by lifted multicut and person re-identification. In: CVPR (2017)
49. Van De Weijer, J., Schmid, C., Verbeek, J., Larlus, D.: Learning color names for real-world applications. TIP **18**, 1512–1523 (2009)
50. Wang, F., et al.: Residual attention network for image classification. In: CVPR (2017)
51. Wang, X., Türetken, E., Fleuret, F., Fua, P.: Tracking interacting objects using intertwined flows. TPAMI **38**(11), 2312–2326 (2016)
52. Wu, Y., Lim, J., Yang, M.H.: Object tracking benchmark. TPAMI **37**(9), 1834–1848 (2015)
53. Xiang, Y., Alahi, A., Savarese, S.: Learning to track: online multi-object tracking by decision making. In: ICCV (2015)
54. Xu, H., Saenko, K.: Ask, attend and answer: exploring question-guided spatial attention for visual question answering. In: Leibe, B., Matas, J., Sebe, N., Welling, M. (eds.) ECCV 2016. LNCS, vol. 9911, pp. 451–466. Springer, Cham (2016). https://doi.org/10.1007/978-3-319-46478-7_28
55. Xu, K., et al.: Show, attend and tell: neural image caption generation with visual attention. In: ICML (2015)
56. Yang, F., Choi, W., Lin, Y.: Exploit all the layers: fast and accurate CNN object detector with scale dependent pooling and cascaded rejection classifiers. In: CVPR (2016)
57. Yang, Z., He, X., Gao, J., Deng, L., Smola, A.: Stacked attention networks for image question answering. In: CVPR (2016)
58. Zhang, L., Li, Y., Nevatia, R.: Global data association for multi-object tracking using network flows. In: CVPR (2008)

Connecting Gaze, Scene, and Attention: Generalized Attention Estimation via Joint Modeling of Gaze and Scene Saliency

Eunji Chong(✉), Nataniel Ruiz, Yongxin Wang, Yun Zhang, Agata Rozga, and James M. Rehg

School of Interactive Computing, Georgia Institute of Technology, Atlanta, GA, USA
{eunjichong,nataniel.ruiz,ywang751,yzhang467,agata,rehg}@gatech.edu

Abstract. This paper addresses the challenging problem of estimating the general visual attention of people in images. Our proposed method is designed to work across multiple naturalistic social scenarios and provides a full picture of the subject's attention and gaze. In contrast, earlier works on gaze and attention estimation have focused on constrained problems in more specific contexts. In particular, our model explicitly represents the gaze direction and handles out-of-frame gaze targets. We leverage three different datasets using a multi-task learning approach. We evaluate our method on widely used benchmarks for single-tasks such as gaze angle estimation and attention-within-an-image, as well as on the new challenging task of generalized visual attention prediction. In addition, we have created extended annotations for the MMDB and GazeFollow datasets which are used in our experiments, which we will publicly release.

Keywords: Visual attention · Gaze estimation · Saliency

1 Introduction

As humans, we are exquisitely sensitive to the gaze of others. We can rapidly infer if another person is making eye contact, follow their gaze to identify their gaze target, categorize quick glances to objects, and even identify when someone is not paying attention [19]. Automatically detecting and quantifying these types of visual attention from images and video remains a complex, open challenge. Although gaze estimation has long been an active area of research, most work has focused on relatively constrained versions of the problem in specific predetermined contexts. For example, [18,31] predict the gaze target *given* that the person is looking at a point on a smartphone screen, [23] predicts fixation on an object *given* that the person is looking at salient object within the frame, [7,30] predict eye contact *given* that the camera is located near the subject's eyes, and [24] predicts the focus of a person's gaze across views in commercial

V. Ferrari et al. (Eds.): ECCV 2018, LNCS 11209, pp. 397–412, 2018.
https://doi.org/10.1007/978-3-030-01228-1_24

Fig. 1. We present a model which aims to understand different aspects of the generalized attention prediction problem which are exemplified above. In (a) subjects are looking at a salient object in the scene, in (b) the subject is looking somewhere outside of the frame and in (c) the subject is looking at or around the camera. Our model predicts the 3D gaze vector of subjects in each of these images, along with the location of the gaze fixation in the image, if it exists. Our model explicitly determines if the subject's gaze target lies outside the frame.

movies which include camera views that follow the actor's attention. It remains a significant challenge to design a system that can model the visual attention of subjects in unconstrained scenarios, without the preconditions utilized by prior works. We call this the problem of *generalized visual attention prediction.*

The three examples in Fig. 1 illustrate the difficulty of the challenge. In Fig. 1(a), the subjects are looking at a salient object in the scene, while in Fig. 1(b) the subject is looking somewhere outside of the scene, and Fig. 1(c) they are looking at the camera. The case of Fig. 1(a) is addressed by the pioneering work of Recasens et al. [23], which tackles this problem by obtaining human annotations of subject gaze targets, leveraging the finding from [4,5,21] which indicate that annotators very often agree on which object is salient in the scene. Their approach, however, was not designed to handle cases Fig. 1(b) and (c) since the dataset annotation process forces human annotators to label a point in the image as the fixation location. In other words the dataset does not distinguish between subjects looking at a point inside of the image or looking somewhere outside of the image. A purely saliency based approach would also fail: notice that there are salient objects in Fig. 1(b), an American flag, and Fig. 1(c), a mug, which can confound such an approach.

Figure 1(c) corresponds to the case of screen-based eye tracking [11,18], in which subjects look at images on a screen and are captured by a calibrated camera that permits the estimation of the gaze location. The scenario in Fig. 1(a) corresponds to gaze following and has been addressed in [23]. Figure 1(b) represents a challenging case, which has not been addressed by prior work, in which the gaze target lies outside the frame and therefore cannot be identified explicitly without additional information.

It is challenging to design an attention model which can deal with these three different scenarios reliably. We tackle this problem by developing a novel generalized visual attention estimation method which jointly learns a subject-dependent saliency map and a 3D gaze vector represented by yaw and pitch. This allows us to estimate the final fixation likelihood map.

Our method is designed so that the fixation likelihood map becomes close to zero when the subject is looking outside the frame, as in cases (b) and (c). When the subject is looking at a target which is visible in the image, as in case (a), then the fixation likelihood map predicts where the subject is likely to be attending. The model simultaneously estimates the 3D gaze angle to provide a complete picture of the subject's attention and gaze. As a result, our approach produces interpretable results spanning all three of the cases in Fig. 1.

Our Contribution. The major contribution of this work is our method for *generalized visual attention prediction*, which works across most natural scenarios. To effectively train our model, we exploit three public datasets that were originally collected for different tasks. Specifically, we use the EYEDIAP dataset [11] to learn a precise gaze angle representation, a modified version of the GazeFollow dataset [23] to learn a gaze-relevant scene saliency representation, and the SynHead dataset [13] to complement the first two datasets as it includes large face pose variations and subject attention outside of the image frame.

As a result of our multi-task learning approach, our model achieves state-of-the-art results on the GazeFollow [23] task, which consists in identifying the location of the scene the subject is looking at. Our model also competes with state-of-the-art models on the 3D gaze estimation task from the EYEDIAP dataset [11]. Most importantly, we evaluate our full model on a new challenging task that automatically quantifies dense visual attention in naturalistic social interactions. We report our results on the Multimodal Dyadic Behavior (MMDB) dataset [25], a dataset of video recordings of the social and communicative behavior of toddlers. This dataset has frame-level annotations of subject's visual targets among many other nonverbal behaviors. We are the first to report attention estimation results on this dataset. We compare our results to several baselines, demonstrating the superior performance of our method.

2 Related Work

Gaze Estimation: Gaze estimation aims to predict the gaze of a human subject. Our work is related to third person gaze estimation and tracking methods which seek to estimate either the three dimensional direction of the gaze or the fixation point of the gaze on a screen. Krafka et al. [18] predict the coordinates of the gaze on a smartphone screen and present a dataset which addresses this problem. Funes Mora et al. [11] present EYEDIAP, a dataset designed for the evaluation of gaze estimation which was collected in a controlled lab environment. They devise an RGB-D method which predicts the 3D vector of the gaze of the subject. There exist datasets which address similar tasks, such as MPIIGaze [31], as well as synthetic datasets of eye images for gaze estimation [27,29]. In addition to predicting the 3D gaze vector, our work predicts a fixation likelihood map of the scene as well as whether the person is looking at a location inside or outside of the image.

Visual Saliency: The objective of visual saliency prediction is to estimate locations in an image which attract the attention of humans looking *at* the image. Since the seminal work of Itti et al. [16] visual saliency prediction has been extensively studied. Recently deep learning methods have shown superior performance on this task due to their ability to learn features and to incorporate both local and global context into the prediction [20,28,33]. Our work in generalized visual attention prediction is influenced by the task of visual saliency since people tend to look at salient objects inside a scene, yet it is distinct because we consider cases where the subject is not looking at any object in the scene. A method driven primarily by saliency detection would not succeed in the latter case. Furthermore, real-world scenes are more likely to generate a wide range of 3D gaze directions in comparison to a screen-based eye-tracking scenario.

Gaze Following: The paper by Recasens et al. [23] presents a new computer vision problem which inspired this work. The problem can be described as follows: given a single image containing one or more people, predict the location that each person in the scene is looking at. They presented a novel dataset which contains manual annotations of where the subjects are looking in each image. Our work differs in that we consider cases where the subjects are looking *outside* of the frame, and we predict the gaze direction in these cases even though the gaze target is not visible. In addition to predicting a fixation likelihood map for the image, we predict the 3D gaze vector of each subject. Gorji and Clark [12] study a problem at the intersection of visual saliency and gaze following, which consists of incorporating signals from regions of an image which guide attention to a certain part of the image. For example, when subjects in an image look at an object, this amplifies the apparent saliency of the object. Again, our problem differs in that we do not predict visual saliency but we predict the subject's gaze fixation and gaze direction.

Attention Modeling: Prior works have presented different methods for measuring third-person visual attention using an environment-mounted camera. By assuming body or head orientation is a good proxy for visual orientation, [3] projects attention on the street by tracking pedestrians in 3D, [8,26] model the focus of attention in crowded social scene, and [6] predicts the object in the scene that a person is interacting with which is usually indicated by hand manipulation or pointing. Our work is certainly related, although it differs because we explicitly consider the gaze of the subject.

3 Method

Figure 2 is an overview of our deep neural network model and its input and output. The model takes three inputs: the whole image, a crop of the subject's face, and the location of her face. Given the input, the model estimates 1. the subject's gaze angle in terms of yaw and pitch degrees ("where" component of visual attention), 2. the subject-dependent saliency in terms of a heatmap ("what" component of visual attention), and 3. how likely the subject is fixating at the estimated gaze target in the scene (overall "strength" of visual attention).

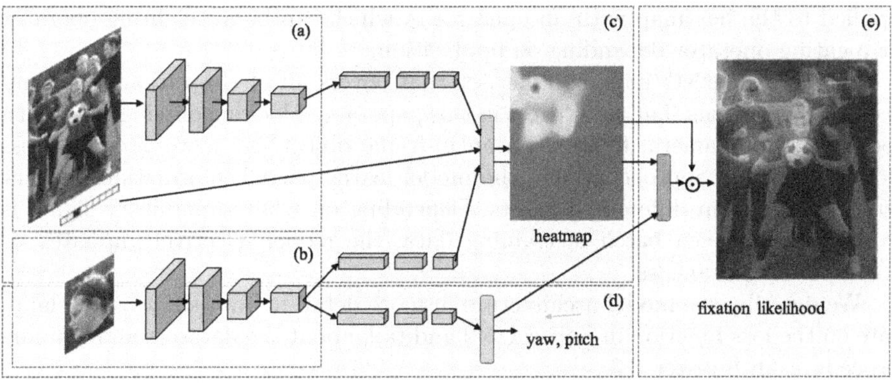

Fig. 2. *Overview of our approach.* Full scene image, a person's face location whose visual attention we want to predict, and the corresponding close-up face image is provided as input. Scene and face images go through separate convolutional layers in such a way that (a), (b) and (c) contribute to person-centric saliency, and (b) and (d) contribute to gaze angle prediction. In the very last layer, the final feature vectors for these two tasks are combined to estimate how likely the person is actually fixating at a gaze target within the observable scene. (Color figure online)

The model has two fully-convolutional pathways, one connected to the whole image (Fig. 2a) and the other connected to the face image (Fig. 2b). The reasoning behind having two separate pathways is inspired by the way humans infer another person's visual attention, as first exploited by [23]. For example, when we interpret a person's attention from an image, we infer their gaze direction and consider whether there are any salient objects in the image along the estimated direction. Based on this hypothesis, [23] connects two independent conv pathways together to learn the heatmap (Fig. 2c). We take this approach further and extend their model by explicitly training for the gaze angle (Fig. 2d) with a convolutional pathway that is connected to the face image, using a multi-task learning framework. Adding the gaze angle output as an auxiliary task has several advantages, including the additional supervisory signal that we can devise based on the relationship between gaze heatmap and angle, which pushes performance in heatmap estimation even further.

Lastly, we define the likelihood of fixation: a single-valued measure of how likely it is that the subject is looking at the estimated target region inside the frame. It is modeled by a fully connected layer (Fig. 2e). Using this last output, the model can produce a much more complete estimation of a person's visual attention. Think of the case of Fig. 1b or c, where the person is looking outside the image frame. In such cases, we want the heatmap to be as close to zero as possible since the person is not attending to any point inside of the image. By training this last layer to produce higher value for when it is more certain that the heatmap region is attended to and lower value otherwise, the value can be applied to the heatmap with an operator $\odot$ which can be a weighting operator or a gating operator depending on application.

Since there exists no single dataset that covers all of the various gaze and scene combinations that we address in this paper (e.g., looking outside the frame, looking at the camera, fixation on an in-frame object, etc.), we adopt a cross domain learning approach where the model learns partial information relevant to each task from different datasets. Depending on what supervisory signal is available in a given batch of training data, the model selectively updates its corresponding branches.

We describe the model architecture in more detail in Subsect. 3.1. We elaborate on the loss function in Subsect. 3.2 and talk about the datasets and training procedures in Subsect. 3.3.

3.1 Model

The inputs given to the model are the entire image, the subject's cropped face and the location of the face of the subject whose attention we want to estimate. The two images are resized to 227×227 so that the face can be observed in higher resolution by the network. Face position is available in terms of the (x, y) full image coordinates. These coordinates are quantized into a 13×13 grid and then flattened to a 169 dimensional 1-hot vector.

The model consists of two convolutional (conv) pathways: a face pathway (Fig. 2d) and a scene pathway (Fig. 2c). ResNet 50 [14] is used as a backbone network for the conv pathways (Fig. 2a and b). Specifically we use all conv layers of ResNet50 for each of our conv pathways. After each ResNet50 block we add three conv layers (1×1, followed by 3×3, followed by 1×1) with ReLu and batch norm - with stride 1 and no padding. The blue conv layers represented in (c) have filter depth of 512, 128 and 1 respectively. The purple and red conv layers after the face pathway (represented in (c) and (d)) have filter depth of 512, 128 and 16. These conv layers serve to reduce the dimensionality of the features extracted by the ResNet50 backbone networks.

In the face pathway, the feature vector computed with the face input image goes through a fully connected layer to predict the gaze angle represented using yaw and pitch intrinsic Euler angles. In the scene pathway, the feature vectors extracted from the whole image as well as from the face image are concatenated with the face position input vector to learn the person-centric heatmap. Similarly to face position, the ground truth used for learning the heatmap is available as a gaze target position in (x, y) coordinates which is quantized into 10 grids in each dimension.

Lastly, the input vectors to the last layer of each pathway are concatenated and go into the final fully connected layer to estimate the "strength" of the fixation i.e. how likely it is that the person is actually fixating at a gaze target within the observable scene. The training label for this value is equal to 1 for a fixation inside of the image and 0 when the subject is looking outside of the scene. We also explore alternative model architectures and restrict our training to a subset of the three datasets. Experiments are reported in Sect. 4.4.

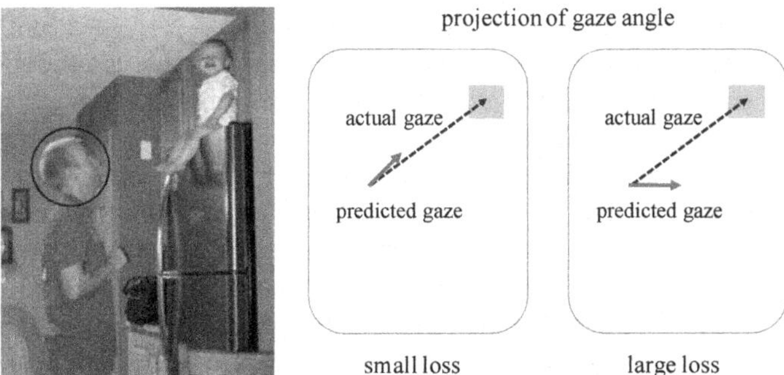

Fig. 3. Our project and compare loss is illustrated here. If the estimated angle is close to the actual one, the projected gaze angle on the image should also be close to the vector connecting the head position to the gaze target. (Color figure online)

3.2 Loss

As our model predicts gaze angle, saliency map and the fixation likelihood, we need to apply appropriate loss functions for each task. For the angle regression task we use an *L1 loss*, and for the other two tasks we use a *cross entropy loss.* Moreover, we recognize that the gaze angle and fixation target predictions are closely related. Based on their relationship additional constraints can be imposed to augment the training loss signal. Namely, when the subject is looking at a target, the actual gaze is a ray from the subject's head to the gaze target. This ray can be projected onto the image. It becomes a 2D vector coming from the subject's head to the target exemplified by the blue vector in Fig. 3. If the estimated angle is close to the actual one, the projected gaze angle on the image (orange vector in Fig. 3) should also be close to the blue vector. The proximity of the two vectors is measured using the cosine distance. We call this the *project and compare loss.*

3.3 Cross-Domain Datasets and Training Procedure

The largest challenge in training our model is the lack of availability of training examples. Although there are a couple of existing datasets that are suitable for training certain parts of our network, no single dataset contains all of the information that we need to train the full model. Therefore, we leverage three

Fig. 4. Examples of datasets used to train our model. Left two: SynHead, middle two: EYEDIAP, right two: GazeFollow.

different datasets, namely, GazeFollow [23], EYEDIAP [11], and SynHead [13]. We selectively train different sub-parts of our network at a time depending on the available supervisory information within a training batch. See Fig. 4 to see sample images from each dataset.

GazeFollow [23] is a real-world image dataset with manual annotations of the locations where people are looking. The images are taken from other major datasets such as MS COCO [22] and PASCAL [10]. As a result, the images cover a wide range of scenes, people, and gaze directions. However, the actual 3D gaze angles are not available. Furthermore, images where subjects are looking outside of the image frame are not distinguished and all images have a fixation annotation inside of the frame. Although it is mentioned in [23] that if the annotators indicated that the person was looking outside the image, the image would be discarded, we notice that there are a considerable number of images in which persons appear to be looking outside of the frame. Therefore, we added additional annotations to this dataset in the form of a binary indicator label for "looking inside" or "looking outside" for every image. In total, we identified 14,564 images correspond to the "looking outside" case which is approximately 11.6% of the total training samples. We have publicly released our additional annotations along with this paper.

EYEDIAP [11] dataset is designed for the evaluation of the gaze estimation task. It has videos of 16 different subjects with full face and background visible in a laboratory environment. Each subject was asked to look at a specific target point on a monitor screen and the 3D gaze angle was annotated by leveraging camera calibration and face depth measurement from depth camera. This dataset contains precise 3D gaze angles for frames where the person is fixating the target point. The dataset also contains video of the subjects looking at a 3D ball target instead of 2D screen target point, but we exclude these ball sessions from our experiments in order to conduct a fairer comparison with prior work. We randomly hold out four subjects for test and use the rest of the sessions for training. Since subjects were looking at a screen, all of the frames can be considered as looking outside the image. However, since the dataset has been collected in a controlled setting the backgrounds are primarily white and there is not a lot of variety in lighting or pose. Also, measured gaze angles range between $-40°$ to $40°$ which is rather limited.

NVIDIA SynHead [13] is a synthetic dataset created for the head pose estimation task. The dataset contains 510,960 frames of 70 head motion tracks rendered using 10 individual head models. The gaze of the head is fixed and aligned with the head pose, thus we use the labeled 3D head pose as the gaze angle ground truth. One of the advantages of a synthetic dataset is the ability to insert different images in the background. We randomly generated 15% from the total frames augmented with provided natural scene backgrounds and regard all as "looking outside" examples. The main reason we include SynHead in training is because it complements the EYEDIAP dataset, as the angle ranges are larger, between $-90°$ and $90°$, and it can include more diverse backgrounds. Since head pose estimation is not a focus of this paper we do not set aside a test set and use SynHead entirely for training. Dataset details are also summarized in Table 1.

Table 1. Datasets used in our experiments and the number of samples in the training and testing split, as well as the percentage of each split containing people looking in/out.

Dataset	Training set		Test set	
		In vs out		In vs out
GazeFollow [23]	125,557	88.4% vs 11.6%	4,782	100% vs 0%
EYEDIAP [11]	72,613	0% vs 100%	18,153	0% vs 100%
SynHead [13]	75,400	0% vs 100%	-	-
MMDB [25]	-	-	4,965	41.4% vs 58.6%

Training Procedure. Since each dataset is relevant only to certain subtasks, we only update the relevant parts of the network based on which dataset the training sample is from, while freezing other irrelevant layers during back-propagation. Specifically, when learning gaze angle estimation, we only update the angle pathway (b) and (d) in Fig. 2, when learning saliency we update the scene pathway (a), (b) and (c) while freezing all other layers. Similarly, when training fixation likelihood we only update the layer (e) in Fig. 2. We found that this selective back-propagation scheme is critical in achieving good performance.

In every batch, we draw random samples from all of the datasets shuffled together and perform three separate back-propagation for the three outputs as just described. In the beginning, both convolutional pathways were initialized using a ResNet50 model pre-trained on the ImageNet classification task [9]. We use the Adam optimization algorithm with a learning rate of $2.5e-4$ and a batch size of 36. Training usually converges within 12 epochs. All of our implementation and experiments are done in PyTorch [1].

4 Evaluation

In this section we evaluate our model by comparing each output with a number of existing methods and baselines. We first evaluate the person-dependent saliency map in Sect. 4.1, gaze angle estimation in Subsect. 4.2 and general attention estimation in Subsect. 4.3. Lastly, we evaluate our method by changing model architectures and training dataset in Subsect. 4.4.

4.1 Person-Dependent Saliency Prediction

We evaluate the performance of saliency map estimation using the suggested test split of the GazeFollow dataset. The test split contains all "looking inside" cases and each test image has multiple gaze target annotations. Following the same evaluation method by [23], we compute the Area Under Curve (AUC) score of the Receiver Operating Characteristic (ROC) curve in which the ground truth

Fig. 5. Qualitative results of our model's gaze-saliency prediction on the GazeFollow dataset. Input image is given on the 1st and 3rd row, the output heatmap and estimated gaze is overlaid below.

Table 2. Gaze-saliency evaluation on the GazeFollow test set

Method	AUC	L2 distance	Min distance
Random	0.504	0.484	0.391
Center	0.633	0.313	0.230
Judd [17]	0.711	0.337	0.250
GazeFollow [23]	0.878	0.190	0.113
Our	*0.896*	*0.187*	*0.112*

target positions are the true labels and heatmap value on corresponding positions are prediction confidence score. Our method achieves a score of 0.896 achieving state-of-the-art performance. Along with AUC we also report results in L2, min distance and angle metric. Please refer to [23] for details about the metric. The numbers are summarized in Table 2 along with a number of baselines reported in [23]. Qualitative results are presented in Fig. 5.

4.2 Gaze Angle Prediction

We report the 3D gaze estimation accuracy based on the yaw and pitch output of our model on the chosen EYEDIAP test split. Table 3 shows the angular errors in which we achieve less than 0.5° of difference to the state-of-the-art appearance-based gaze estimation method. It is worth noticing that the middle two values come from [32] which are computed by five-fold cross validation with the entire EYEDIAP dataset whereas our method is evaluated on a single train/test split.

Table 3. Gaze angle evaluation on EYEDIAP

Method	Angular error (degree)
Wood [29]	11.3°
iTracker [18]	8.3°
Zhang [32]	*6.0°*
Our	6.4°

Although we did not choose to perform full cross validation, we conclude that it reaches reasonable accuracy on the benchmark. Note also that our method is trained on multiple tasks whereas all other methods are trained solely on the gaze angle prediction task.

4.3 Generalized Attention Prediction During Naturalistic Social Interactions

The primary inspiration for our work stems from the need for the ability to quantify various types of visual attention behavior, which is one of the most important nonverbal social cues used in our daily life. Moreover, this is of particular interest among researchers who study child development since gaze behavior of young children is closely related to their social development and developmental disorders such as Autism [15]. The MMDB dataset is one of the largest datasets that contains children's social and communicative behaviors, collected in order to facilitate data-driven analysis of child behavior based on video. The dataset contains a wide range of nonverbal behavior such as hand gestures, smile, and gaze. It has frame-level human annotations of each behavior. As for gaze, each frame is annotated when the child is looking at a ball, book or the examiner. This is done by human annotation based on multiple views, therefore the child's gaze target can be visible or not depending on the viewpoint. Since the annotation does not indicate in which view the gaze target is visible, we added additional annotation ourselves and identified if the target is visible in a child-facing camera view to construct labels for the general attention estimation problem. We publicly release this annotation text file along with our paper.

We evaluate our method on the generalized attention prediction task. We design a gaze target grid classification task, where each test image is divided into $N \times N$ grids. If the subject is looking inside of the image then the grid square which contains the gaze target is assigned a label of 1 while others are assigned labels of 0. If the subject is looking somewhere outside of the frame then all grid squares are assigned the 0 label. Using our method's fixation likelihood map we predict the positive gaze grid square. We test the GazeFollow model [23] which is the closest work to our method in terms of having the ability to predict gaze target location. One of its limitations is the inability to correctly predict the "outside" case, where the subject is looking outside of the frame. As a result, our method achieves much higher precision in addition to increased recall as shown in Table 4.

Table 4. Evaluation on MMDB - gaze target grid classification

Grid size	Method	Precision	Recall
2×2	GazeFollow [23]	0.344	0.715
	Our	0.744	0.851
5×5	GazeFollow [23]	0.210	0.437
	Our	0.614	0.683

Additionally, we constructed various baseline tests consisting of a classifier based on a subset of features constructed for saliency, gaze and head pose. Specifically, we tested with SVM and Random Forest using a subset of {[23], [32], [2]} as features. In other words, each classifier has been trained for detection of looking inside with the training set described in Table 1, using aforementioned features, and tested on the MMDB images. We report the results in Table 5. Note that the MMDB dataset was not used for training across all methods including ours. Moreover, we evaluate the value of multi-dataset training in solving the general attention problem. As shown in the last three rows of Table 5, joint training of gaze and saliency is critical in solving the general attention estimation task because without the gaze angle estimate it is ineffective to determine whether the subject is looking inside or outside the frame (Fig. 6).

Table 5. Evaluation of fixation likelihood on MMDB

Method	Average precision
SVM with GazeFollow [23]	0.311
SVM with GazeFollow [23]+gaze [32]	0.531
SVM with GazeFollow [23]+headpose [2]	0.620
SVM with gaze [32]+headpose [2]	0.405
SVM with GazeFollow [23]+gaze [32]+headpose [2]	0.624
Random Forest with GazeFollow [23]	0.707
Random Forest with GazeFollow [23]+gaze [32]	0.727
Random Forest with GazeFollow [23]+headpose [2]	0.785
Random Forest with gaze [32]+headpose [2]	0.512
Random Forest with GazeFollow [23]+gaze [32]+headpose [2]	0.773
Our, trained only with GazeFollow dataset	0.737
Our, trained only with GazeFollow and EYEDIAP dataset	0.820
Our final	*0.902*

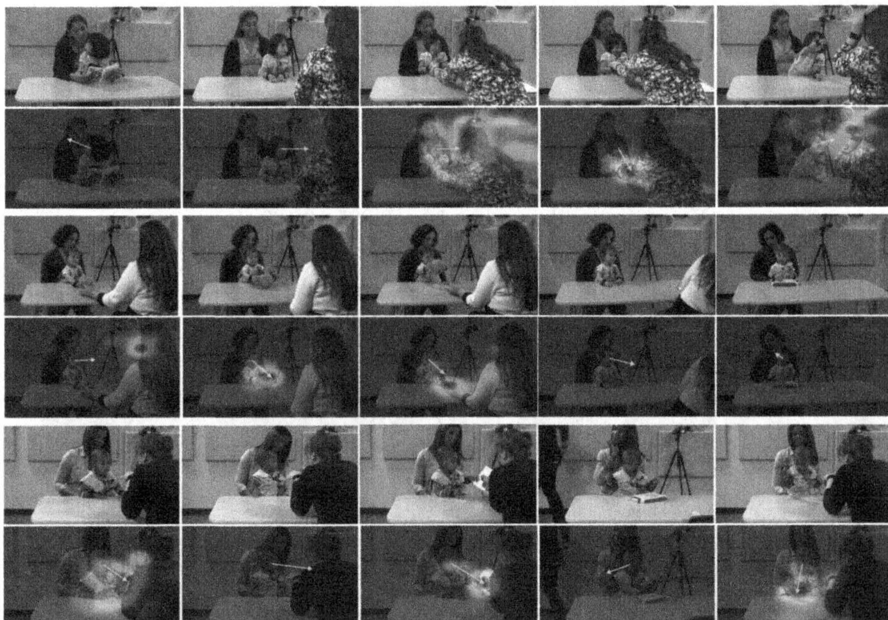

Fig. 6. Example result of our method on the MMDB dataset. The dataset contains various types of gaze behavior including fixations on a target both within and out of frame. Our method produces low heatmap when the fixation target is outside and high heatmap when the target becomes clear.

4.4 Alternative Model and Diagnostics

Finally, we run additional experiments to study how the performance of our model is affected by different training datasets and architectural choice by evaluating it on the GazeFollow benchmark. As shown in Table 6, omitting EYEDIAP or SynHead training dataset did not have much impact on the attention-within-an-image heatmap estimation whereas changing model architecture considerably affected the scores. For example, using a single ResNet50 pathway which pools facial features using ROI-pooling shows significantly degraded performance which supports our decision to use a scene pathway as well as a face pathway. Interestingly, the project-and-compare loss was not as helpful as initially expected, and we think that this is because the coverage range of pose in the SynHead and EYEDIAP datasets is limited (within $\pm$ 90) which is not the case in the GazeFollow dataset.

Qualitatively, we were able to observe that, even though our method is designed to measure fixation outside, it can make mistakes when the target is within the frame but occluded by other object. Also, when the subject is closer to the camera than some salient object in the background, the method sometimes estimates those as fixation candidate due to the lack of scene depth understanding. Examples are illustrated in Fig. 7.

Table 6. Additional model evaluation and diagnostics on the GazeFollow test split

Method	AUC	L2 distance
No EYEDIAP	0.887	0.197
No SynHead	0.895	0.191
No EYEDIAP and SynHead	0.891	0.194
No project-and-compare loss	0.895	0.189
Map resolution 15 × 15	0.778	0.194
ROI-pooling	0.700	0.325
Our final	*0.896*	*0.187*

Fig. 7. Challenging cases due to occlusion and the lack of depth understanding.

5 Conclusion

In this paper we presented the new challenging problem of generalized visual attention prediction which encapsulates several constrained attention prediction and gaze estimation problems that have been the focus of many previous works. We proposed a multi-task learning approach and neural architecture leveraging three different datasets which tackles this problem and works across multiple naturalistic social scenarios. In order to train our architecture we have supplemented these datasets with new annotations and we release these annotations to the public. Our model achieves state-of-the-art performance on the single-task gaze-saliency prediction and competes with state-of-the-art methods on gaze estimation benchmarks while achieving promising performance on the generalized attention prediction problem on the MMDB dataset. Future work in this area can lead to breakthroughs in attention prediction applications which are valuable in numerous scientific and commercial areas. A suggested first step would be to improve existing datasets with additional annotations or collect datasets tailored for this problem.

Acknowledgement. This study was funded in part by the Simons Foundation under grant 247332.

References

1. PyTorch: Tensors and dynamic neural networks in python with strong GPU acceleration. https://github.com/pytorch/pytorch. Accessed 11 Mar 2017
2. Baltrušaitis, T., Robinson, P., Morency, L.P.: OpenFace: an open source facial behavior analysis toolkit. In: 2016 IEEE Winter Conference on Applications of Computer Vision (WACV), pp. 1–10. IEEE (2016)
3. Benfold, B., Reid, I.: Guiding visual surveillance by tracking human attention. In: British Machine Vision Conference, September 2009
4. Borji, A., Cheng, M.M., Jiang, H., Li, J.: Salient object detection: a benchmark. IEEE Trans. Image Process. **24**(12), 5706–5722 (2015)
5. Borji, A., Sihite, D.N., Itti, L.: What stands out in a scene? A study of human explicit saliency judgment. Vis. Res. **91**, 62–77 (2013)
6. Chen, C.Y., Grauman, K.: Subjects and their objects: localizing interactees for a person-centric view of importance. Int. J. Comput. Vis. **126**, 1–22 (2016)
7. Chong, E., et al.: Detecting gaze towards eyes in natural social interactions and its use in child assessment. Proc. ACM Interact. Mob. Wearable Ubiquit. Technol. **1**(3), 43 (2017)
8. Cristani, M., et al.: Social interaction discovery by statistical analysis of f-formations. In: Proceedings of BMVC (2011)
9. Deng, J., Dong, W., Socher, R., Li, L.J., Li, K., Fei-Fei, L.: ImageNet: a large-scale hierarchical image database. In: 2009 IEEE Conference on Computer Vision and Pattern Recognition, CVPR 2009, pp. 248–255. IEEE (2009)
10. Everingham, M., Van Gool, L., Williams, C.K., Winn, J., Zisserman, A.: The pascal visual object classes (VOC) challenge. Int. J. Comput. Vis. **88**(2), 303–338 (2010)
11. Funes Mora, K.A., Monay, F., Odobez, J.M.: EYEDIAP: a database for the development and evaluation of gaze estimation algorithms from RGB and RGB-D cameras. In: Proceedings of the ACM Symposium on Eye Tracking Research and Applications. ACM, March 2014. https://doi.org/10.1145/2578153.2578190
12. Gorji, S., Clark, J.J.: Attentional push: a deep convolutional network for augmenting image salience with shared attention modeling in social scenes. In: Proceedings of the IEEE Conference on Computer Vision and Pattern Recognition, pp. 2510–2519 (2017)
13. Gu, J., Yang, X., De Mello, S., Kautz, J.: Dynamic facial analysis: from Bayesian filtering to recurrent neural network. In: The IEEE Conference on Computer Vision and Pattern Recognition (CVPR), July 2017
14. He, K., Zhang, X., Ren, S., Sun, J.: Deep residual learning for image recognition. arXiv preprint arXiv:1512.03385 (2015)
15. Hutman, T., Chela, M.K., Gillespie-Lynch, K., Sigman, M.: Selective visual attention at twelve months: signs of autism in early social interactions. J. Autism Dev. Disord. **42**(4), 487–498 (2012)
16. Itti, L., Koch, C., Niebur, E.: A model of saliency-based visual attention for rapid scene analysis. IEEE Trans. Pattern Anal. Mach. Intell. **20**(11), 1254–1259 (1998)
17. Judd, T., Ehinger, K., Durand, F., Torralba, A.: Learning to predict where humans look. In: 2009 IEEE 12th international conference on Computer Vision, pp. 2106–2113. IEEE (2009)
18. Krafka, K., et al.: Eye tracking for everyone. In: IEEE Conference on Computer Vision and Pattern Recognition (CVPR) (2016)
19. Land, M., Tatler, B.: Looking and Acting: Vision and Eye Movements in Natural Behaviour. Oxford University Press, Oxford (2009)

20. Li, G., Yu, Y.: Visual saliency based on multiscale deep features. In: Conference on Computer Vision and Pattern Recognition (2015)
21. Li, Y., Hou, X., Koch, C., Rehg, J.M., Yuille, A.L.: The secrets of salient object segmentation. In: Proceedings of the IEEE Conference on Computer Vision and Pattern Recognition, pp. 280–287 (2014)
22. Lin, T.-Y., et al.: Microsoft COCO: common objects in context. In: Fleet, D., Pajdla, T., Schiele, B., Tuytelaars, T. (eds.) ECCV 2014. LNCS, vol. 8693, pp. 740–755. Springer, Cham (2014). https://doi.org/10.1007/978-3-319-10602-1_48
23. Recasens, A., Khosla, A., Vondrick, C., Torralba, A.: Where are they looking? In: Advances in Neural Information Processing Systems (NIPS) (2015)
24. Recasens, A., Vondrick, C., Khosla, A., Torralba, A.: Following gaze in video. In: The IEEE International Conference on Computer Vision (ICCV), October 2017
25. Rehg, J., et al.: Decoding children's social behavior. In: Proceedings of the IEEE Conference on Computer Vision and Pattern Recognition, pp. 3414–3421 (2013)
26. Soo Park, H., Shi, J.: Social saliency prediction. In: Proceedings of the IEEE Conference on Computer Vision and Pattern Recognition, pp. 4777–4785 (2015)
27. Sugano, Y., Matsushita, Y., Sato, Y.: Learning-by-synthesis for appearance-based 3D gaze estimation. In: Proceedings of the IEEE Conference on Computer Vision and Pattern Recognition, pp. 1821–1828 (2014)
28. Wang, L., Lu, H., Ruan, X., Yang, M.H.: Deep networks for saliency detection via local estimation and global search. In: 2015 IEEE Conference on Computer Vision and Pattern Recognition (CVPR), pp. 3183–3192. IEEE (2015)
29. Wood, E., Baltrusaitis, T., Zhang, X., Sugano, Y., Robinson, P., Bulling, A.: Rendering of eyes for eye-shape registration and gaze estimation. In: Proceedings of the IEEE International Conference on Computer Vision, pp. 3756–3764 (2015)
30. Zhang, X., Sugano, Y., Bulling, A.: Everyday eye contact detection using unsupervised gaze target discovery. In: 30th Annual Symposium on User Interface Software and Technology. ACM (2017)
31. Zhang, X., Sugano, Y., Fritz, M., Bulling, A.: Appearance-based gaze estimation in the wild. In: Proceedings of the IEEE Conference on Computer Vision and Pattern Recognition (CVPR), pp. 4511–5420, June 2015
32. Zhang, X., Sugano, Y., Fritz, M., Bulling, A.: It's written all over your face: full-face appearance-based gaze estimation. In: Proceedings of IEEE International Conference on Computer Vision and Pattern Recognition Workshops (CVPRW) (2017)
33. Zhao, R., Ouyang, W., Li, H., Wang, X.: Saliency detection by multi-context deep learning. In: Proceedings of the IEEE Conference on Computer Vision and Pattern Recognition, pp. 1265–1274 (2015)

Videos as Space-Time Region Graphs

Xiaolong Wang(✉) and Abhinav Gupta

Robotics Institute, Carnegie Mellon University, Pittsburgh, USA
xiaolonw@cs.cmu.edu

Abstract. How do humans recognize the action "opening a book"? We argue that there are two important cues: modeling temporal shape dynamics and modeling functional relationships between humans and objects. In this paper, we propose to represent videos as space-time region graphs which capture these two important cues. Our graph nodes are defined by the object region proposals from different frames in a long range video. These nodes are connected by two types of relations: (i) similarity relations capturing the long range dependencies between correlated objects and (ii) spatial-temporal relations capturing the interactions between nearby objects. We perform reasoning on this graph representation via Graph Convolutional Networks. We achieve state-of-the-art results on the Charades and Something-Something datasets. Especially for Charades with complex environments, we obtain a huge 4.4% gain when our model is applied in complex environments.

1 Introduction

Consider a simple action such as "opening a book" as shown in Fig. 1. When we humans see the sequence of images, we can easily recognize the action category; yet our current vision systems (with hundreds of layers of 3D convolutions) struggle on this simple task. Why is that? What is missing in current video recognition frameworks?

Let's first take a closer look at the sequence shown in Fig. 1. How do humans recognize the action in the video corresponds to "opening a book"? We argue that there are two key ingredients to solving this problem: First, the shape of the book and how it changes over time (i.e., the object state changes from closed to open) is a crucial cue. Exploiting this cue requires temporally linking book regions across time and modeling actions as transformations. But just modeling temporal dynamics of objects is not sufficient. The state of objects change after interaction with human or other objects. Thus we also need to model human-object and object-object interactions as well for action recognition.

However, our current deep learning approaches fail to capture these two key ingredients. For example, the state-of-the-art approaches based on two-stream ConvNets [1,2] are still learning to classify actions based on individual video frame or local motion vectors. Local motion clearly fails to model the dynamics of shape changes. To tackle this limitation, recent work has also focused on modeling long term temporal information with Recurrent Neural Networks [3–6]

V. Ferrari et al. (Eds.): ECCV 2018, LNCS 11209, pp. 413–431, 2018.
https://doi.org/10.1007/978-3-030-01228-1_25

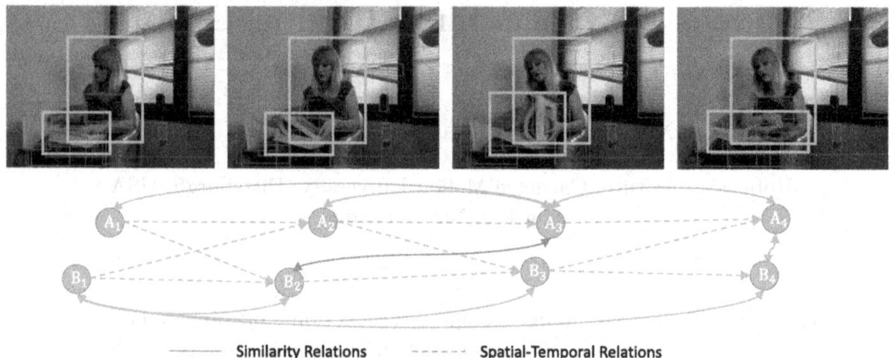

Fig. 1. How do you recognize simple actions such as opening book? We argue action understanding requires appearance modeling but also capturing temporal dynamics (how shape of book changes) and functional relationships. We propose to represent videos as space-time region graphs followed by graph convolutions for inference.

and 3D Convolutions [7–10]. However, all these frameworks focus on the features extracted from the whole scenes and fail to capture long-range temporal dependencies (transformations) or region-based relationships. In fact, most of the actions are classified based on the background information instead of capturing the key objects (e.g., the book in "opening a book") as observed in [11].

On the other hand, there have been several efforts to specifically model the human-object or object-object interactions [12,13]. This direction have been recently revisited with ConvNets in an effort to improve object detection [14–16], visual relationship detection [17] and action recognition [18], etc. However, the relationship reasoning is still performed in static images failing to capture temporal dynamics of these interactions. Thus, it is very hard for these approaches to capture the changes of object states over time as well as the causes and effects of these changes.

In this paper, we propose to perform long-range temporal modeling of human-object and object-object relationships via a graph-based reasoning framework. Unlike existing approaches which focus on local motion vectors, our model takes in a long range video sequence (e.g., more than 100 frames or 5 s). We represent the input video as a **space-time region graph** where each node in the graph represent region of interest in the video. Region nodes are connected by two types of edges: appearance-similarity and spatio-temporal proximity. Specifically, **(i) Similarity Relations**: regions which have similar appearance or semantically related are connected together. With similarity relations, we can model how the states of the same object change and the long range dependencies between any two objects in any frames. **(ii) Spatial-Temporal Relations**: objects which overlap in space and close in time are connected together via these edges. With spatial-temporal relations, we can capture the interactions between nearby objects as well as the temporal ordering of object state changes.

Given the graph representation, we perform reasoning on the graph and infer the action by applying the Graph Convolution Networks (GCNs) [19]. We conduct our experiments in the challenging Charades [20] and 20BN-Something-Something [21] datasets. Both datasets are extremely challenging as the actions cannot be easily inferred by the background of the scene and the 2D appearance of the objects or humans. Our model shows significant improvements over state-of-the-art results of action recognition. Especially in the Charades dataset, we obtain 4.4% boost.

Our contributions include: (a) A novel graph representation with variant relationships between objects in a long range video; (b) A Graph Convolutional Network for reasoning with multiple relation edges; (c) state-of-the-art performance with a significant gain in action recognition in complex environments.

2 Related Work

Video Understanding Models. Spatio-temporal reasoning is one of the core research areas in the field of video understanding and action recognition. However, most of the early work has focused on using spatio-temporal appearance features. For example, a large effort has been spent on manually designing the video features [22–31]. Some of the hand-designed features such as the Improved Dense Trajectory (IDT) [23] are still widely applied and show very competitive results in different video related tasks. However, instead of designing hand-crafted features, recent researches have focused towards learning deep representations from the video data [1,2,32–37]. One of the most popular model is the two-Stream ConvNets [1] where temporal information is model by a network with 10 optical flow frames as inputs (<1 s). To better model longer-term information, a lot of work has been focused on using Recurrent Neural Networks (RNNs) [3–5,38–43] and 3D ConvNets [8,9,44–48]. However, these frameworks focus on extracting features from the whole scenes and can hardly model the relationships between different object instances in space and time.

Visual Relationships. Reasoning about the pairwise relationships has been proven to be very helpful in a variety of computer vision tasks [12,13,49–51]. For example, object detection in cluttered scenes can be significantly improved by modeling the human-object interactions [13]. Recently, the visual relationships have been widely applied together with deep networks in the area of visual question answering [52], object recognition [14–16] and intuitive physics [53, 54]. In action recognition, a lot of effort has been made on modeling pairwise human-object and object-object relationships [55–57]. However, the interaction reasoning framework in these efforts focuses on static images and the temporal information is usually modeled by a RNN on image level features. Thus, these approaches still cannot capture how a certain object state changes over time.

An attempt at modeling pairwise relations in space and time has been recently made in the Non-local Neural Networks [58]. However, the Non-local operator is applied in every pixel in the feature space (from low layers to higher layers), while our reasoning is based on a graph with object level features. Moreover, the non-local operator does not process any temporal ordering information, while this is explicit modeled in our spatial-temporal relations.

Graphical Models. The long range relationships in images and videos are usually captured by graphical models. One popular direction is using the Conditional Random Fields (CRF) [59,60]. In the context of deep learning, especially for semantic segmentation, the CRF model is often applied on the outputs of the ConvNets by performing mean-field inference [61–66]. Instead of using mean-field inference, variant simpler feedforward graph based neural network have been proposed recently [19,67–71]. In this paper, we apply the Graph Convolutional Networks (GCNs) [19] which was originally proposed for applications in Natural Language Processing. Our GCN is built by stacking multiple layers of graph convolutions with similarity relations and spatial-temporal relations. The outputs of the GCNs are updated features for each object node, which can be used to perform classification.

Our work is also related to video recognition with object cues [72–74] and object graph models [75–78]. For example, Structural-RNN [77] is proposed to model the spatial-temporal relations between objects (adjacent in time) for video recognition tasks. Different from these works, our space-time graph representation encodes not only local relations but also long range dependencies between any pairs of objects across space and time. By using graph convolutions with long range relations, it enables efficient message passing between starting states and ending states of the objects. This global graph reasoning framework provides significant boost over the state-of-the-art.

3 Overview

Our goal is to represent the video as a graph of objects and perform reasoning on the graph for action recognition. The overview of our model is visualized in Fig. 2. Our model takes inputs as a long clip of video frames (more than 5 s) and forward them to a 3D Convolutional Neural Network [8,58]. The output of this 3D ConvNet is a feature map with the dimensions $\mathrm{T} \times \mathrm{H} \times \mathrm{W} \times d$, where T represents the temporal dimension, $\mathrm{H} \times \mathrm{W}$ represents the spatial dimensions and d represents the channel number.

Besides extracting the video features, we also apply a Region Proposal Network (RPN) [79] to extract the object bounding boxes (We have not visualized the RPN in Fig. 2 for simplicity). Given the bounding boxes for each of the T feature frames, we apply RoIAlign [80,81] to extract the features for each bounding box. Note that the RoIAlign is applied on each feature frame independently. The feature vector for each object has d dimensions (first aligned to $7 \times 7 \times d$ and then maxpooled to $1 \times 1 \times d$). We denote the object number as N, thus the feature dimension is $\mathrm{N} \times d$ after RoIAlign.

We now construct a graph which contains N nodes corresponding to N object proposals aggregated over T frames. There are mainly two types of relations in the graph: similarity relations and spatial-temporal relations. For simplicity, we

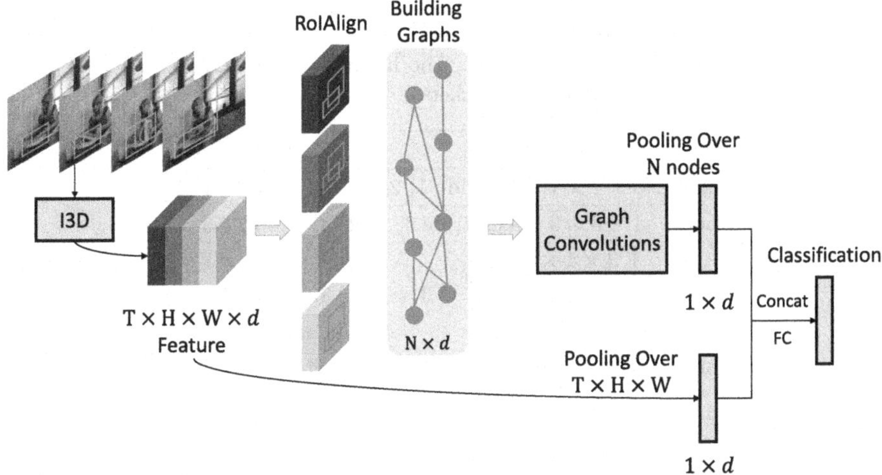

Fig. 2. Model Overview. Our model uses 3D convolutions to extract visual features followed by RoIAlign extracting d-dimension feature for each object proposal. These features are provided as inputs to the Graph Convolutional Network which performs information propagation based on spatiotemporal edges. Finally, a d-dimension feature is extracted and appended to another d-dimension video feature to perform classification.

decompose this big graph into two sub-graphs with the same nodes but two different relations: the similarity graph and the spatial-temporal graph.

With the graph representations, we apply the Graph Convolutional Networks (GCNs) to perform reasoning. The output for the GCNs are in the same dimension as the input features which is $\mathrm{N} \times d$. We perform average pooling over all the object nodes to obtain a d-dimension feature. Besides the GCN features, we also perform average pooling on the whole video representation ($\mathrm{T} \times \mathrm{H} \times \mathrm{W} \times d$) to obtain the same d-dimension feature as a global feature. These two features are then concatenated together for video level classification.

4 Graph Representations in Videos

In this section, we first introduce the feature extraction process with 3D ConvNets and then describe the similarity graph as well as the spatial-temporal graph.

4.1 Video Representation

Video Backbone Model. Given a long clip of video (around 5 s), we sample 32 video frames from it with the same temporal duration between every two frames. We extract the features on these frames via a 3D ConvNet. Table 1 shows our backbone model based on the ResNet-50 architecture (motivated by [58]). The

Table 1. Our baseline ResNet-50 I3D model. We use $\mathrm{T} \times \mathrm{H} \times \mathrm{W}$ to represent the dimensions of filter kernels and 3D output feature maps. For filter kernels, we also have number of channels following $\mathrm{T} \times \mathrm{H} \times \mathrm{W}$. The input is in $32 \times 224 \times 224$ dimensions and the residual blocks are shown in brackets.

Layer		Output size
conv_1	$5 \times 7 \times 7$, 64, stride 1, 2, 2	$32 \times 112 \times 112$
pool_1	$1 \times 3 \times 3$ max, stride 1, 2, 2	$32 \times 56 \times 56$
Res_2	$\begin{bmatrix} 3 \times 1 \times 1, 64 \\ 1 \times 3 \times 3, 64 \\ 1 \times 1 \times 1, 256 \end{bmatrix} \times 3$	$32 \times 56 \times 56$
pool_2	$3 \times 1 \times 1$ max, stride 2, 1, 1	$16 \times 56 \times 56$
res_3	$\begin{bmatrix} 3 \times 1 \times 1, 128 \\ 1 \times 3 \times 3, 128 \\ 1 \times 1 \times 1, 512 \end{bmatrix} \times 4$	$16 \times 28 \times 28$
res_4	$\begin{bmatrix} 3 \times 1 \times 1, 256 \\ 1 \times 3 \times 3, 256 \\ 1 \times 1 \times 1, 1024 \end{bmatrix} \times 6$	$16 \times 14 \times 14$
res_5	$\begin{bmatrix} 3 \times 1 \times 1, 512 \\ 1 \times 3 \times 3, 512 \\ 1 \times 1 \times 1, 2048 \end{bmatrix} \times 3$	$16 \times 14 \times 14$
Global average pool, fc		$1 \times 1 \times 1$

model takes input as 32 video frames with 224×224 dimensions and the output of the last convolutional layer is a $16 \times 14 \times 14$ feature map (i.e., 16 frames in the temporal dimension and 14×14 in the spatial dimension). The baseline in this paper adopts the same architecture, where the classification is simply performed by using a global average pooling on the final convolutional features following by a fully connected layer.

This backbone model is called Inflated 3D ConvNet (I3D) [8,48,58] as one can turn a 2D ConvNet into a 3D ConvNet by inflating the kernels during initialization. That is, a 3D kernel with $t \times k \times k$ dimensions can be inflated from a 2D $k \times k$ kernel by copying the weights t times and rescaling by $1/t$. Please refer to [8,48,58] for more initialization details.

Region Proposal Network. We apply the Region Proposal Network (RPN) in [79,82] to generate the object bounding boxes of interest on each video frame. More specifically, we use the RPN with ResNet-50 backbone and FPN [83]. The RPN is pre-trained with the MSCOCO object detection dataset [84] and there is no weight sharing between the RPN and our I3D video backbone model. Note that the bounding boxes extracted by the RPN are class-agnostic.

To extract object features on top of the last convolutional layer, we project the bounding boxes from the 16 input RGB frames (sampled from the 32 input

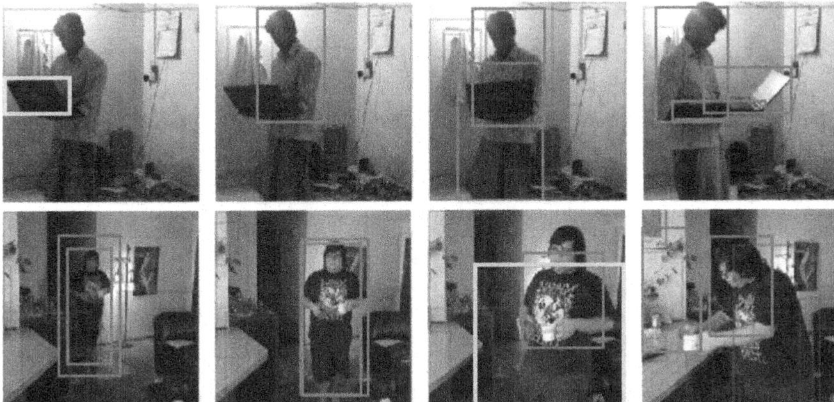

Fig. 3. Similarity Graph $\mathbf{G}^{sim}$. Above figure shows our similarity graph not only captures similarity in visual space but also correlations (similarity in functional space). The query box is shown in orange, the nearest neighbors are shown in blue. The transparent green boxes are the other unselected object proposals. (Color figure online)

frames for I3D, with the sampling rates of 1 frame every 2 frames) to the 16 output feature frames. Taking the video features and projected bounding boxes, we apply RoIAlign [81] to extract the feature for each object proposal. In RoIAlign, each output frame is processed independently. The RoIAlign generates a $7 \times 7 \times d$ output features for each object which is then max-pooled to $1 \times 1 \times d$ dimensions.

4.2 Similarity Graph

We measure the similarity between objects in the feature space to construct the similarity graph. In this graph, we connect pairs of semantically related objects together. More specifically, we will have a high confidence edge between two instances which are: (i) the same object in different states in different video frames or (ii) highly correlated for recognizing the actions. Note that the similarity edges are computed between any pairs of objects.

Formally, assuming we have the features for all the object proposals in the video as $\mathbf{X} = \{\mathbf{x}_1, \mathbf{x}_2, \ldots, \mathbf{x}_\mathrm{N}\}$, where N represents the number of object proposals and each object proposal feature $\mathbf{x}_i$ is a d dimensional vector. The pairwise similarity or the affinity between every two proposals can be represented as,

$$F(\mathbf{x}_i, \mathbf{x}_j) = \phi(\mathbf{x}_i)^T \phi'(\mathbf{x}_j), \tag{1}$$

where ϕ and ϕ' represents two different transformations of the original features. More specifically, we have $\phi(\mathbf{x}) = \mathbf{w}\mathbf{x}$ and $\phi'(\mathbf{x}) = \mathbf{w}'\mathbf{x}$. The parameters $\mathbf{w}$ and $\mathbf{w}'$ are both $d \times d$ dimensions weights which can be learned via back propagation. By adding the transformation weights $\mathbf{w}$ and $\mathbf{w}'$, it allows us to not only learn the correlations between different states of the same object instance across frame, but also the relations between different objects. We visualize the top nearest

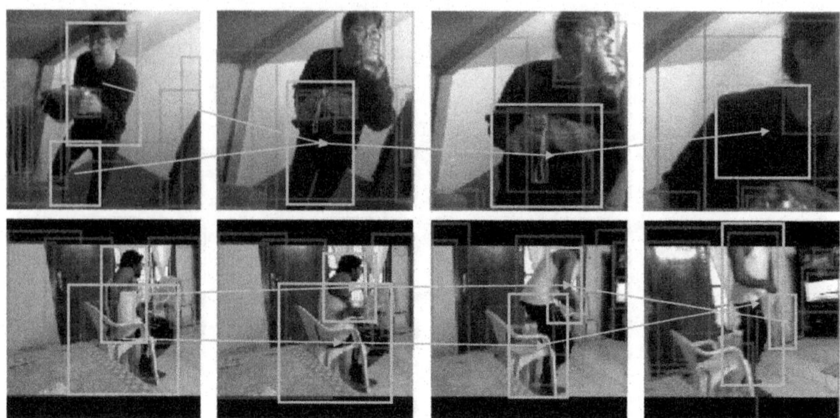

Fig. 4. Spatial-Temporal Graph $\mathbf{G}^{front}$. Highly overlapping object proposals across neighboring frames are linked by directed edge. We plot some example trajectories with blue boxes and the direction shows the arrow of time. (Color figure online)

neighbors for the object proposals in Fig. 3. In the first example, we can see the nearest neighbors of the laptop not only include the other laptop instances in other frames, but also the human who is operating it.

After computing the affinity matrix with Eq. 1, we perform normalization on each row of the matrix so that the sum of all the edge values connected to one proposal i will be 1. Motivated by the recent works [58,85], we adopt the softmax function for normalization to obtain the similarity graph,

$$\mathbf{G}_{ij}^{sim} = \frac{\exp F(\mathbf{x}_i, \mathbf{x}_j)}{\sum_{j=1}^{\mathrm{N}} \exp F(\mathbf{x}_i, \mathbf{x}_j)}. \tag{2}$$

4.3 Spatial-Temporal Graph

Although the similarity graph captures even the long term dependencies between any two object proposals, it does not capture the relative spatial relation between objects and the ordering of the state changes. To encode these spatial and temporal relations between objects, we propose to use spatial-temporal graphs, where objects in nearby locations in space and time are connected together.

Given a object proposal in frame t, we calculate the value of Intersection Over Unions (IoUs) between this object bounding box and all other object bounding boxes in frame $t+1$. We denote the IoU between object i in frame t and object j in frame $t+1$ as σ_{ij}. If σ_{ij} is larger than 0, we will link object i to object j using a directed edge $i \rightarrow j$ with value σ_{ij}. After assigning the edge values, we normalize the sum of the edge values connected to each proposal i to be 1 by

$$\mathbf{G}_{ij}^{front} = \frac{\sigma_{ij}}{\sum_{j=1}^{\mathrm{N}} \sigma_{ij}}, \tag{3}$$

where $\mathbf{G}^{front}$ is taken as the adjacency matrix for a spatial-temporal graph. We visualize some of the object proposals and the trajectories in Fig. 4.

Besides building the forward graph which connects objects from frame t to frame $t+1$, we also construct a backward graph in a similar way which connect objects from frame $t+1$ to frame t. We denote the adjacency matrix of this backward graph as $\mathbf{G}^{back}$. Specifically, for the overlapping object i in frame t and object j in frame $t+1$, we construct an edge $i \leftarrow j$ and assign the values to $\mathbf{G}^{back}_{ji}$ according to the IoU values. By building the spatial-temporal graphs in a bidirectional manner, we can obtain richer structure information and enlarge the number of propagation neighborhoods during graph convolutions.

5 Convolutions on Graphs

To perform reasoning on the graph, we apply the Graph Convolutional Networks (GCNs) proposed in [19]. Different from standard convolutions which operates on a local regular grid, the graph convolutions allow us to compute the response of a node based on its neighbors defined by the graph relations. Thus performing graph convolutions is equal to performing message passing inside the graphs. The outputs of the GCNs are updated features of each object node, which can be aggregated together for video classification. We can represent one layer of graph convolutions as,

$$\mathbf{Z} = \mathbf{G}\mathbf{X}\mathbf{W}, \tag{4}$$

where $\mathbf{G}$ represents one of the adjacency graph we have introduced ($\mathbf{G}^{sim}$, $\mathbf{G}^{front}$ or $\mathbf{G}^{back}$) with $\mathrm{N} \times \mathrm{N}$ dimensions, $\mathbf{X}$ is the input features of the object nodes in the graph with $\mathrm{N} \times d$ dimensions, and $\mathbf{W}$ is the weight matrix of the layer with dimension $d \times d$ in our case. Thus the output of one graph convolutional layer $\mathbf{Z}$ is still in $N \times d$ dimensions. The graph convolution operation can be stacked into multiple layers. After each layer of graph convolutions, we apply two non-linear functions including the Layer Normalization [86] and then ReLU before the feature $\mathbf{Z}$ is forwarded to the next layer.

To combine multiple graphs in GCNs, we can simply extend Eq. 4 as,

$$\mathbf{Z} = \sum_i \mathbf{G}_i\mathbf{X}\mathbf{W}_i, \tag{5}$$

where $\mathbf{G}_i$ indicates different types of graphs, and the weights for different graphs $\mathbf{W}_i$ are not shared. Note that in this way, each hidden layer of the GCN is updated though the relationships from different graphs. However, we find that the direct combination of 3 graphs ($\mathbf{G}^{sim}$, $\mathbf{G}^{front}$ and $\mathbf{G}^{back}$) with Eq. 5 actually hurts the performance compared to the situation with a single similarity graph.

The reason is that our similarity graph $\mathbf{G}^{sim}$ contains learnable parameters (Eq. 1) and requires back propagation for updating, while the other two graphs do not require learning. Fusing these graphs together in every GCN layer increases the optimization difficulties. Thus we create two branches of graph convolutional networks, and only fuse the results from two GCNs in the end: one GCN adopts

Eq. 4 with $\mathbf{G}^{sim}$ and the other GCN adopts Eq. 5 with $\mathbf{G}^{front}$ and $\mathbf{G}^{back}$. These two branches of GCNs perform convolutions separately for L layers and the final layer features are summed together, which is in $\mathrm{N} \times d$ dimensions.

Video Classification. As illustrated in Fig. 2, the updated features after graph convolutions are forwarded to an average pooling layer, which calculates the mean of all the proposal features and leads to a $1 \times d$ dimensions representation. Besides the GCN features, we also perform average pooling on the whole video representation and obtain the another $1 \times d$ dimensions global features. These two features are then concatenated together for video classification.

6 Experiments

We perform the experiments on two recent challenging datasets: Charades [20] and Something-Something [21]. We first introduce the implementation details.

Training. The training of our backbone models involves pre-training on 2 different datasets following [8,58]. The model is first pre-trained as a 2D ConvNet with the ImageNet dataset [87] and then inflated into a 3D ConvNet (i.e., I3D) as [8]. We then fine-tuned the 3D ConvNet with the Kinetics action recognition dataset [88] following the same training scheme for longer sequences (around 5 s video) in [58]. Given this initialization, we now introduce how to further fine-tune the network on our target datasets as following.

As specified in Table 1, our network takes 32 video frames as inputs. These 32 video frames are sampled in the frame rate of 6fps, thus the temporal length of the video clip is around 5 s. The spatial dimensions for input is 224×224. Following [89], the input frames are randomly cropped from a randomly scaled video whose shorter side is sampled in $[256, 320]$ dimensions. To reduce the number of GCN parameters, we add one more $1 \times 1 \times 1$ convolutional layer on top of the I3D baseline model, which reduces the output channel number from 2048 to $d = 512$. As Charades and Something-Something dataset are in similar scales in number of video frames, we adopt the same learning rate schedule.

Our baseline I3D model is trained with a 4-GPU machine. The total batch size is 8 clips during training. Note that we freeze the parameters in all Batch Normalization layers during training. Our model is trained for 100K iterations in total, with learning rate 0.00125 in the first 90K iterations and it is reduced by a factor of 10 during training the last 10K iterations. Dropout [90] is applied on the last global pooling layer with a ratio of 0.3.

We set the layer number of our Graph Convolutional Network to 3. The first two layers are randomly initialized and the last layer is initialized as zero inspired by [91]. To train the GCN together with the I3D backbone, we propose to apply stage-wise training. We first finetune the I3D model as mentioned above, then we apply RoIAlign and GCN on top of the final convolutional features as shown in Fig. 2. We fix the I3D features and train the GCN with the same learning rate schedules as for training the backbone. Then we train the I3D and GCN together end-to-end for 30K more iterations with the reduced learning rate.

Table 2. Ablations on Charades. We show the mean Average Precision (mAP%).

model, R50, I3D	mAP
baseline	31.8
Proposal+AvgPool	32.1
Spatial-Temporal GCN	34.2
Similarity GCN	35.0
Joint GCN	**36.2**

(a) GCN ablation studies.

model, R50, I3D	mAP
baseline	31.8
Non-local	33.5
Joint GCN	36.2
Non-local + Joint GCN	**37.5**

(b) Comparing our approach with Non-local Net.

Task Specific Settings. We apply different loss functions when training for Charades and Something-Something datasets. For Something-Something dataset, we apply the softmax loss function. For Charades, we apply binary sigmoid loss to handle the multi-label property. We also extract different numbers of object bounding boxes with RPN in two different datasets. For Charades, the scenes are more cluttered and we extract 50 object proposals for each frame. However, for Something-Something, there is usually only one or two objects in the center of video frame. We find that extracting 10 object proposals per frame is enough.

Inference. We perform fully-convolutional inference in space as [58,89] during inference. The shorter side of each video frame is scaled to 256 while maintaining the aspect ratios. During testing one whole video, we sample 10 clips for Charades and 2 clips for Something-Something according to the average video length in two different datasets. Scores from multiple clips are aggregated by Max-Pooling.

6.1 Experiments on Charades

In the Charades experiments, we follow the official split with 8K training videos and 1.8K validation videos. The average video duration is 30 s. There are 157 action classes and multiple actions can happen at the same time.

How Much Each Graph Helps? We first perform analysis on each component of our framework, with the backbone of ResNet-50 I3D, as illustrated in Table 2a. We first show that the result of I3D baseline without any proposal extractions and graph convolutions is 31.8% mAP on the validation set.

One simple extension on this baseline is: obtain the region proposals with RPN, extract the features for each proposal and perform average pooling over them as an extra feature. We concatenate the video level feature and the proposal feature together for classification. However, we can only obtain 0.3% boost with this approach. Thus, a naive aggregation of proposal features does not help much.

We then perform evaluations using GCNs with the similarity graph and the spatial-temporal graph individually. We observe that our GCN with only spatial-temporal graph can obtain a 2.4% boost over the baseline and achieve 34.2%. With the similarity graph, we can achieve a better performance of 35.0%. By

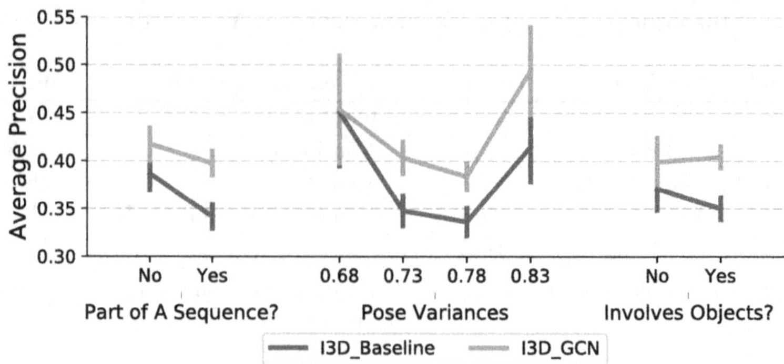

Fig. 5. Error analysis. We compare our approach against baseline I3D approach across three different attributes. Our approach improves significantly when action is part of sequence, involves interaction with objects and has high pose variance.

combining two graphs together and train GCNs with multiple relations, our method achieves 36.2% mAP which is a significant boost of 4.4% over the baseline.

Robustness to Proposal Numbers. We also analyze how the number of object proposals generated by the RPN affect our method. Note that our method achieves 36.2% with extracting 50 object proposals per video frame. If we use 25 (100) proposals per frame, the mAP of our method is 35.9% (36.1%) mAP. Thus our approach is actually very stable with the changes of RPN.

Model Complexity. Given this large improvement in performance, the extra computation cost of the GCN over the baseline is actually very small. In the Charades dataset, our graph is defined based on 800 object nodes per video (with 16 output frames and 50 object proposals per frame). The FLOPs of the baseline I3D model is 153×10^9 and the total FLOPs of our model (I3D + Joint GCN) is 158×10^9. Thus there is only around 3% increase in FLOPs.

Comparing to the Non-local Net. One of the related work is the recent proposed Non-local Neural Networks [58], where they propose to perform spatial-temporal reasoning on different layers of feature maps. As shown in Table 2b, the Non-local operations gives 1.7% improvements over the baseline and our approach performs 2.7% better than the Non-local Net. These two approaches are actually complementary to each other. By replacing the I3D backbone with Non-local Net, we have another 1.3% boost, leading to 37.5%.

Error Analysis. Given this significant improvements, we will also like to find out in what cases our methods improve over the baselines most. Following the attributes set up in [11], we show 3 different situations where our approach get more significant gains over the baselines in Fig. 5. Specifically, for each video in Charades, besides the action class labels, it is also labeled with different attributes (e.g., whether the actions are happening in a sequence?).

Table 3. Classification mAP (%) in the **Charades** dataset [20]. NL indicates Non-Local.

Model	Backbone	Modality	mAP
2-Stream [93]	VGG16	RGB + flow	18.6
2-Stream + LSTM [93]	VGG16	RGB + flow	17.8
Asyn-TF [93]	VGG16	RGB + flow	22.4
MultiScale TRN [36]	Inception	RGB	25.2
I3D [8]	Inception	RGB	32.9
I3D [58]	ResNet-101	RGB	35.5
NL I3D [58]	ResNet-101	RGB	37.5
NL I3D + GCN	ResNet-50	RGB	37.5
I3D + GCN	ResNet-101	RGB	39.1
NL I3D + GCN	ResNet-101	RGB	**39.7**

Part of A Sequence? This attribute specifies whether an action category is part of a sequence of actions. For example, "holding a cup" and then "sitting down" are usually in a sequence of actions, while "running" often happens in isolation. As shown in the left plots in Fig. 5, the baseline I3D method fails dramatically when an action is part of a sequence of actions, while our approach is more stable. If an action is not happening in isolation, we have more than 5% gain over the baseline.

Pose Variances. This attribute is computed by averaging the Procrustes distance [92] between any two poses in an action category. If the average distance is large, it means the poses change a lot in an action. As visualized in the middle plots in Fig. 5, we can see that our approach has similar performance as the baseline when the pose variance is small. However, the performance of the baseline drops dramatically again as the variance of pose becomes larger (from 0.68 to 0.73) in the action, while the slope of our curve is much smaller. The performance of both approaches improve as the pose variability reaches 0.83, where our approach has around 8%–9% boost over the baseline.

Involves Objects? This attribute specifies whether an object is involved in the action. For example, "drinking from a cup" involves the object cup while "running" does not require interactions with objects. As shown in the right plots in Fig. 5, we can see the baseline perform worse when the actions require interactions with objects. Interestingly, our approach actually performs slightly better when objects are involved.

Thus our approach is better in modeling a long sequence of actions as well as actions that require object interactions, and robust to pose changes.

Training with a Larger Backbone. Besides the ResNet-50 backbone architecture, we also verify our method on a much larger backbone model which is applied in [58]. This backbone is larger than our baseline in 3 aspects: (i) instead

Table 4. Classification accuracy (%) in the **Something-Something** dataset [21].

Model	Backbone	*Val*		*Test*
		top-1	top-5	top-1
C3D [21]	C3D [7]	-	-	27.2
MultiScale TRN [36]	Inception	34.4	63.2	33.6
I3D	ResNet-50	41.6	72.2	-
I3D + GCN	ResNet-50	43.3	75.1	-
NL I3D	ResNet-50	44.4	76.0	-
NL I3D + GCN	ResNet-50	46.1	76.8	45.0

of using ResNet-50, this backbone is based on the ResNet-101 architecture; (ii) instead of using 224 × 224 spatial inputs, this backbone takes in 288 × 288 images; (iii) instead of sampling 32 frames with 6 fps, this backbone performs sampling more densely by using 128 frames with 24 fps as inputs. Note that the temporal output dimension of both our baseline model and this ResNet-101 backbone are still the same (16 dimensions). With all the modifications on the backbone architecture, the FLOPs are 3 times as many as our ResNet-50 baseline model.

We show the results together with all the state-of-the-art methods in Table 3. The Non-local Net [58] with ResNet-101 backbone achieves the mAP of 37.5%. We can actually obtain the same performance with our method by using a much smaller ResNet-50 backbone (with around 1/3 FLOPs). By applying our method with the ResNet-101 backbone, our method (I3D + GCN) can still give 3.6% improvements and reaches 39.1%. This is another evidence showing that our method is modeling very different things from just increasing the spatial inputs and the depth of the ConvNets. By combining the non-local operation together with our approach, we obtain the final performance of 39.7%.

6.2 Experiments on Something-Something

In the Something-Something dataset, there are 86K training videos, around 12K validation videos and 11K testing videos. The number of classes is 174. The data in the Something-Something dataset is very different from the Charades dataset. In Charades, most of the actions are performed by agents in a cluttered indoor scene. However, in Something-Something, all videos are object centric and there is usually only one or two hands in actions. The background in the Something-Something dataset is also very clean in most cases.

We report our results in Table 4. The baseline I3D approach achieves 41.6% in top-1 accuracy and 72.2% in top-5 accuracy. By applying our method with the I3D backbone (I3D + Joint GCN), we achieve 1.7% improvements in the top-1 accuracy. We observe that the improvement of top-1 accuracy here is not as huge as the gains we have in the Charades dataset. The reason is mainly because the videos are already well calibrated with objects in the center of the frames.

We have also combined our method with the Non-local Net. As shown in Table 4, the Non-local I3D method achieves 44.4% in top-1 accuracy. By combining our approach with the Non-local Net, we achieve another 1.7% gain in top-1 accuracy, which leads to the state-of-the-art results 46.1%. We also test our final model on the test set by submitting to the official website. By using a single RGB model, we achieve the best result 45.0% in the leaderboard.

Acknowledgement. This work was supported by ONR MURI N000141612007, Sloan Fellowship, Okawa Fellowship to AG and Facebook Fellowship, NVIDIA Fellowship, Baidu Scholarship to XW. We would like to thank Xinlei Chen, Gunnar Sigurdsson, Yin Li, Ross Girshick and Kaiming He for helpful discussions.

References

1. Simonyan, K., Zisserman, A.: Two-stream convolutional networks for action recognition in videos. In: Neural Information Processing Systems (NIPS) (2014)
2. Wang, L., et al.: Temporal segment networks: towards good practices for deep action recognition. In: Leibe, B., Matas, J., Sebe, N., Welling, M. (eds.) ECCV 2016. LNCS, vol. 9912, pp. 20–36. Springer, Cham (2016). https://doi.org/10.1007/978-3-319-46484-8_2
3. Yue-Hei Ng, J., Hausknecht, M., Vijayanarasimhan, S., Vinyals, O., Monga, R., Toderici, G.: Beyond short snippets: deep networks for video classification. In: Computer Vision and Pattern Recognition (CVPR) (2015)
4. Donahue, J., et al.: Long-term recurrent convolutional networks for visual recognition and description. In: Computer Vision and Pattern Recognition (CVPR) (2015)
5. Li, F., et al.: Temporal modeling approaches for large-scale Youtube-8M video understanding. arXiv preprint arXiv:1707.04555 (2017)
6. Miech, A., Laptev, I., Sivic, J.: Learnable pooling with context gating for video classification. arXiv preprint arXiv:1706.06905 (2017)
7. Tran, D., Bourdev, L., Fergus, R., Torresani, L., Paluri, M.: Learning spatiotemporal features with 3D convolutional networks. In: International Conference on Computer Vision (ICCV) (2015)
8. Carreira, J., Zisserman, A.: Quo vadis, action recognition? A new model and the kinetics dataset. In: Computer Vision and Pattern Recognition (CVPR) (2017)
9. Tran, D., Wang, H., Torresani, L., Ray, J., LeCun, Y., Paluri, M.: A closer look at spatiotemporal convolutions for action recognition. In: CVPR (2018)
10. Xie, S., Sun, C., Huang, J., Tu, Z., Murphy, K.: Rethinking spatiotemporal feature learning for video understanding. arXiv:1712.04851 (2017)
11. Sigurdsson, G.A., Russakovsky, O., Gupta, A.: What actions are needed for understanding human actions in videos? In: ICCV (2017)
12. Gupta, A., Kembhavi, A., Davis, L.S.: Observing human-object interactions: using spatial and functional compatibility for recognition. Trans. Pattern Anal. Mach. Intell. (TPAMI) **31**, 1775–1789 (2009)
13. Yao, B., Fei-Fei, L.: Modeling mutual context of object and human pose in human-object interaction activities. In: Computer Vision and Pattern Recognition (CVPR) (2010)
14. Yatskar, M., Zettlemoyer, L., Farhadi, A.: Situation recognition: visual semantic role labeling for image understanding. In: CVPR (2016)

15. Hu, H., Gu, J., Zhang, Z., Dai, J., Wei, Y.: Relation networks for object detection. In: Computer Vision and Pattern Recognition (CVPR) (2018)
16. Gkioxari, G., Girshick, R., Dollár, P., He, K.: Detecting and recognizing human-object intaractions. In: CVPR (2018)
17. Lu, C., Krishna, R., Bernstein, M., Fei-Fei, L.: Visual relationship detection with language priors. In: Leibe, B., Matas, J., Sebe, N., Welling, M. (eds.) ECCV 2016. LNCS, vol. 9905, pp. 852–869. Springer, Cham (2016). https://doi.org/10.1007/978-3-319-46448-0_51
18. Gkioxari, G., Girshick, R., Malik, J.: Contextual action recognition with R*CNN. In: ICCV (2015)
19. Kipf, T.N., Welling, M.: Semi-supervised classification with graph convolutional networks. In: International Conference on Learning Representations (ICLR) (2017)
20. Sigurdsson, G.A., Varol, G., Wang, X., Farhadi, A., Laptev, I., Gupta, A.: Hollywood in homes: crowdsourcing data collection for activity understanding. In: Leibe, B., Matas, J., Sebe, N., Welling, M. (eds.) ECCV 2016. LNCS, vol. 9905, pp. 510–526. Springer, Cham (2016). https://doi.org/10.1007/978-3-319-46448-0_31
21. Goyal, R., et al.: The "something something" video database for learning and evaluating visual common sense. arXiv:1706.04261 (2017)
22. Laptev, I.: On space-time interest points. IJCV **64**, 107–123 (2005)
23. Wang, H., Schmid, C.: Action recognition with improved trajectories. In: International Conference on Computer Vision (ICCV) (2013)
24. Klaser, A., Marszalek, M., Schmid, C.: A spatio-temporal descriptor based on 3D-gradients. In: BMVC (2008)
25. Dalal, N., Triggs, B., Schmid, C.: Human detection using oriented histograms of flow and appearance. In: Leonardis, A., Bischof, H., Pinz, A. (eds.) ECCV 2006. LNCS, vol. 3952, pp. 428–441. Springer, Heidelberg (2006). https://doi.org/10.1007/11744047_33
26. Laptev, I., Marszalek, M., Schmid, C., Rozenfeld, B.: Learning realistic human actions from movies. In: CVPR (2008)
27. Sadanand, S., Corso, J.J.: Action bank: a high-level representation of activity in video. In: CVPR (2012)
28. Wang, Y., Mori, G.: Hidden part models for human action recognition: probabilistic vs. max-margin. TPAMI **33**, 1310–1323 (2011)
29. Zhu, J., Wang, B., Yang, X., Zhang, W., Tu, Z.: Action recognition with actons. In: ICCV (2013)
30. Peng, X., Zou, C., Qiao, Y., Peng, Q.: Action recognition with stacked fisher vectors. In: Fleet, D., Pajdla, T., Schiele, B., Tuytelaars, T. (eds.) ECCV 2014. LNCS, vol. 8693, pp. 581–595. Springer, Cham (2014). https://doi.org/10.1007/978-3-319-10602-1_38
31. Lan, Z., Lin, M., Li, X., Hauptmann, A.G., Raj, B.: Beyond Gaussian pyramid: multi-skip feature stacking for action recognition. In: CVPR (2015)
32. Karpathy, A., Toderici, G., Shetty, S., Leung, T., Sukthankar, R., Fei-Fei, L.: Large-scale video classification with convolutional neural networks. In: CVPR (2014)
33. Wang, L., Qiao, Y., Tang, X.: Action recognition with trajectory-pooled deep-convolutional descriptors. In: CVPR (2015)
34. Taylor, G.W., Fergus, R., LeCun, Y., Bregler, C.: Convolutional learning of spatio-temporal features. In: Daniilidis, K., Maragos, P., Paragios, N. (eds.) ECCV 2010. LNCS, vol. 6316, pp. 140–153. Springer, Heidelberg (2010). https://doi.org/10.1007/978-3-642-15567-3_11

35. Le, Q.V., Zou, W.Y., Yeung, S.Y., Ng, A.Y.: Learning hierarchical invariant spatio-temporal features for action recognition with independent subspace analysis. In: CVPR (2011)
36. Zhou, B., Andonian, A., Torralba, A.: Temporal relational reasoning in videos (2017)
37. Wang, X., Farhadi, A., Gupta, A.: Actions transformations. In: CVPR (2016)
38. Srivastava, N., Mansimov, E., Salakhutdinov, R.: Unsupervised learning of video representations using LSTMs. arXiv:1502.04681 (2015)
39. Sun, C., Shetty, S., Sukthankar, R., Nevatia, R.: Temporal localization of fine-grained actions in videos by domain transfer from web images. In: ACM Multimedia (2015)
40. Wu, Z., Wang, X., Jiang, Y.G., Ye, H., Xue, X.: Modeling spatial-temporal clues in a hybrid deep learning framework for video classification. arXiv:1504.01561 (2015)
41. Gan, C., Yao, T., Yang, K., Yang, Y., Mei, T.: You lead, we exceed: labor-free video concept learning by jointly exploiting web videos and images. In: CVPR (2016)
42. Bian, Y., et al.: Revisiting the effectiveness of off-the-shelf temporal modeling approaches for large-scale video classification. arXiv:1708.03805 (2017)
43. Pan, P., Xu, Z., Yang, Y., Wu, F., Zhuang, Y.: Hierarchical recurrent neural encoder for video representation with application to captioning. In: CVPR (2016)
44. Ji, S., Xu, W., Yang, M., Yu, K.: 3D convolutional neural networks for human action recognition. TPAMI **35**, 221–231 (2013)
45. Tran, D., Bourdev, L., Fergus, R., Torresani, L., Paluri, M.: Learning spatiotemporal features with 3D convolutional networks. In: ICCV (2015)
46. Xie, S., Girshick, R., Dollár, P., Tu, Z., He, K.: Aggregated residual transformations for deep neural networks. In: Computer Vision and Pattern Recognition (CVPR) (2017)
47. Qiu, Z., Yao, T., Mei, T.: Learning spatio-temporal representation with pseudo-3D residual networks. In: ICCV (2017)
48. Feichtenhofer, C., Pinz, A., Wildes, R.: Spatiotemporal residual networks for video action recognition. In: Neural Information Processing Systems (NIPS) (2016)
49. Yao, J., Fidler, S., Urtasun, R.: Describing the scene as a whole: joint object detection, scene classification and semantic segmentation. In: CVPR (2012)
50. Kumar, M.P., Koller, D.: Efficiently selecting regions for scene understanding. In: CVPR (2010)
51. Russell, B.C., Freeman, W.T., Efros, A.A., Sivic, J., Zisserman, A.: Using multiple segmentations to discover objects and their extent in image collections. In: CVPR (2006)
52. Santoro, A., et al.: A simple neural network module for relational reasoning. In: Neural Information Processing Systems (NIPS) (2017)
53. Battaglia, P., Pascanu, R., Lai, M., Rezende, D.J., et al.: Interaction networks for learning about objects, relations and physics. In: Neural Information Processing Systems (NIPS) (2016)
54. Watters, N., Tacchetti, A., Weber, T., Pascanu, R., Battaglia, P., Zoran, D.: Visual interaction networks. In: Neural Information Processing Systems (NIPS) (2017)
55. Ma, C.Y., Kadav, A., Melvin, I., Kira, Z., AlRegib, G., Graf, H.P.: Attend and interact: higher-order object interactions for video understanding. In: CVPR (2018)
56. Gkioxari, G., Girshick, R., Malik, J.: Actions and attributes from wholes and parts. In: ICCV (2015)
57. Ni, B., Yang, X., Gao, S.: Progressively parsing interactional objects for fine grained action detection. In: CVPR (2016)

58. Wang, X., Girshick, R., Gupta, A., He, K.: Non-local neural networks. In: CVPR (2018)
59. Lafferty, J., McCallum, A., Pereira, F.C.: Conditional random fields: probabilistic models for segmenting and labeling sequence data. In: International Conference on Machine Learning (ICML) (2001)
60. Krähenbühl, P., Koltun, V.: Efficient inference in fully connected CRFs with Gaussian edge potentials. In: Neural Information Processing Systems (NIPS) (2011)
61. Chen, L.C., Papandreou, G., Kokkinos, I., Murphy, K., Yuille, A.L.: Semantic image segmentation with deep convolutional nets and fully connected CRFs. arXiv:1412.7062 (2014)
62. Zheng, S., et al.: Conditional random fields as recurrent neural networks. In: International Conference on Computer Vision (ICCV) (2015)
63. Chandra, S., Usunier, N., Kokkinos, I.: Dense and low-rank Gaussian CRFs using deep embeddings. In: International Conference on Computer Vision (ICCV) (2017)
64. Schwing, A.G., Urtasun, R.: Fully connected deep structured networks. arXiv preprint arXiv:1503.02351 (2015)
65. Krähenbühl, P., Koltun, V.: Efficient inference in fully connected CRFs with Gaussian edge potentials. In: NIPS (2011)
66. Harley, A., Derpanis, K., Kokkinos, I.: Segmentation-aware convolutional networks using local attention masks. In: International Conference on Computer Vision (ICCV) (2017)
67. Liu, S., De Mello, S., Gu, J., Zhong, G., Yang, M.H., Kautz, J.: Learning affinity via spatial propagation networks. In: Neural Information Processing Systems (NIPS) (2017)
68. Scarselli, F., Gori, M., Tsoi, A.C., Hagenbuchner, M., Monfardini, G.: The graph neural network model. IEEE Trans. Neural Netw. **20**, 61–80 (2009)
69. Li, Y., Tarlow, D., Brockschmidt, M., Zemel, R.: Gated graph sequence neural networks. In: ICLR (2016)
70. Marino, K., Salakhutdinov, R., Gupta, A.: The more you know: using knowledge graphs for image classification. In: CVPR (2017)
71. Yan, S., Xiong, Y., Lin, D.: Spatial temporal graph convolutional networks for skeleton-based action recognition. In: AAAI (2018)
72. Alayrac, J.B., Sivic, J., Laptev, I., Lacoste-Julien, S.: Joint discovery of object states and manipulation actions. In: ICCV (2017)
73. Wu, Z., Fu, Y., Jiang, Y.G., Sigal, L.: Harnessing object and scene semantics for large-scale video understanding. In: CVPR (2016)
74. Heilbron, F.C., Barrios, W., Escorcia, V., Ghanem, B.: SCC: semantic context cascade for efficient action detection. In: CVPR (2017)
75. Brendel, W., Todorovic, S.: Learning spatiotemporal graphs of human activities. In: ICCV (2011)
76. Chen, C.Y., Grauman, K.: Efficient activity detection with max-subgraph search. In: CVPR (2012)
77. Jain, A., Zamir, A.R., Savarese, S., Saxena, A.: Structural-RNN: deep learning on spatio-temporal graphs. In: CVPR (2016)
78. Yuan, Y., Liang, X., Wang, X., Yeung, D.Y., Gupta, A.: Temporal dynamic graph LSTM for action-driven video object detection. In: ICCV (2017)
79. Ren, S., He, K., Girshick, R., Sun, J.: Faster R-CNN: towards real-time object detection with region proposal networks. In: Neural Information Processing Systems (NIPS) (2015)
80. Girshick, R.: Fast R-CNN. In: International Conference on Computer Vision (ICCV) (2015)

81. He, K., Gkioxari, G., Dollár, P., Girshick, R.: Mask R-CNN. In: International Conference on Computer Vision (ICCV) (2017)
82. Girshick, R., Radosavovic, I., Gkioxari, G., Dollár, P., He, K.: Detectron (2018). https://github.com/facebookresearch/detectron
83. Lin, T.Y., Dollár, P., Girshick, R., He, K., Hariharan, B., Belongie, S.: Feature pyramid networks for object detection. In: Computer Vision and Pattern Recognition (CVPR) (2017)
84. Lin, T.Y., et al.: Microsoft COCO: common objects in context. In: Fleet, D., Pajdla, T., Schiele, B., Tuytelaars, T. (eds.) ECCV 2014. LNCS, vol. 8693, pp. 740–755. Springer, Cham (2014). https://doi.org/10.1007/978-3-319-10602-1_48
85. Vaswani, A., et al.: Attention is all you need. In: Neural Information Processing Systems (NIPS) (2017)
86. Ba, J.L., Kiros, J.R., Hinton, G.E.: Layer normalization. arXiv preprint arXiv:1607.06450 (2016)
87. Russakovsky, O., et al.: ImageNet large scale visual recognition challenge. Int. J. Comput. Vis. (IJCV) **115**, 211–252 (2015)
88. Kay, W., et al.: The kinetics human action video dataset. arXiv:1705.06950 (2017)
89. Simonyan, K., Zisserman, A.: Very deep convolutional networks for large-scale image recognition. In: International Conference on Learning Representations (ICLR) (2015)
90. Hinton, G.E., Srivastava, N., Krizhevsky, A., Sutskever, I., Salakhutdinov, R.R.: Improving neural networks by preventing co-adaptation of feature detectors. arXiv:1207.0580 (2012)
91. Goyal, P., et al.: Accurate, large minibatch SGD: training imageNet in 1 hour. arXiv:1706.02677 (2017)
92. Kendall, D.G.: A survey of the statistical theory of shape. Stat. Sci. **4**, 87–99 (1989)
93. Sigurdsson, G.A., Divvala, S., Farhadi, A., Gupta, A.: Asynchronous temporal fields for action recognition. In: Computer Vision and Pattern Recognition (CVPR) (2017)

Unified Perceptual Parsing for Scene Understanding

Tete Xiao[1(✉)], Yingcheng Liu[1], Bolei Zhou[2], Yuning Jiang[3], and Jian Sun[4]

[1] Peking University, Beijing, China
jasonhsiao97@pku.edu.cn
[2] MIT CSAIL, Cambridge, USA
[3] Bytedance Inc., Beijing, China
[4] Megvii Inc., Beijing, China

Abstract. Humans recognize the visual world at multiple levels: we effortlessly categorize scenes and detect objects inside, while also identifying the textures and surfaces of the objects along with their different compositional parts. In this paper, we study a new task called Unified Perceptual Parsing, which requires the machine vision systems to recognize as many visual concepts as possible from a given image. A multi-task framework called UPerNet and a training strategy are developed to learn from heterogeneous image annotations. We benchmark our framework on Unified Perceptual Parsing and show that it is able to effectively segment a wide range of concepts from images. The trained networks are further applied to discover visual knowledge in natural scenes (Models are available at https://github.com/CSAILVision/unifiedparsing).

Keywords: Deep neural network · Semantic segmentation
Scene understanding

1 Introduction

The human visual system is able to extract a remarkable amount of semantic information from a single glance. We not only instantly parse the objects contained within, but also identify the fine-grained attributes of objects, such as their parts, textures and materials. For example in Fig. 1, we can recognize that this is a living room with various objects such as a coffee table, a painting, and walls inside. At the same time, we identify that the coffee table has legs, an apron and top, as well as that the coffee table is wooden and the surface of the sofa is knitted. Our interpretation of the visual scene is organized at multiple levels, from the visual perception of the materials and textures to the semantic perception of the objects and parts.

Great progress in computer vision has been made towards human-level visual recognition because of the development of deep neural networks and large-scale

T. Xiao, Y. Liu and B. Zhou—Equal contribution.

V. Ferrari et al. (Eds.): ECCV 2018, LNCS 11209, pp. 432–448, 2018.
https://doi.org/10.1007/978-3-030-01228-1_26

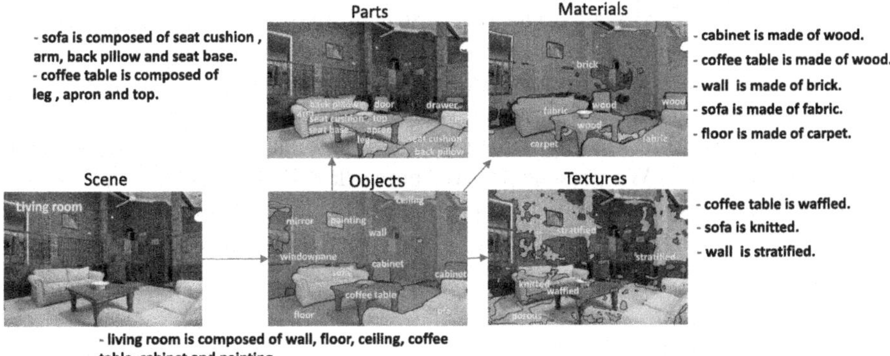

Fig. 1. Network trained for Unified Perceptual Parsing is able to parse various visual concepts at multiple perceptual levels such as scene, objects, parts, textures, and materials all at once. It also identifies the compositional structures among the detected concepts.

image datasets. However, various visual recognition tasks are mostly studied independently. For example, human-level recognition has been reached for object classification [1] and scene recognition [2]; objects and stuff are parsed and segmented precisely at pixel-level [2,3]; Texture and material perception and recognition have been studied in [4] and [5]. Since scene recognition, object detection, texture and material recognition are intertwined in human visual perception, this raises an important question for the computer vision systems: is it possible for a neural network to solve several visual recognition tasks simultaneously? This motives our work to introduce a new task called Unified Perceptual Parsing (UPP) along with a novel learning method to address it.

There are several challenges in UPP. First, there is no single image dataset annotated with all levels of visual information. Various image datasets are constructed only for specific task, such as ADE20K for scene parsing [2], the Describe Texture Dataset (DTD) for texture recognition [4], and OpenSurfaces for material and surface recognition [6]. Next, annotations from different perceptual levels are heterogeneous. For example, ADE20K has pixel-wise annotations while the annotations for textures in the DTD are image-level.

To address the challenges above we propose a framework that overcomes the heterogeneity of different datasets and learns to detect various visual concepts jointly. On the one hand, at each iteration, we randomly sample a data source, and only update the related layers on the path to infer the concepts from the selected source. Such a design avoids erratic behavior that the gradient with respect to annotations of a certain concept may be noisy. On the other hand, our framework exploits the hierarchical nature of features from a single network, *i.e.*, for concepts with higher-level semantics such as scene classification, the classifier is built on the feature map with the higher semantics only; for lower-level semantics such as object and material segmentation, classifiers are built on feature maps fused across all stages or the feature map with low-level semantics only. We further propose a training method that enables the network to predict pixel-wise texture labels using only image-level annotations.

Our contributions are summarized as follows: (1) We present a new parsing task Unified Perceptual Parsing, which requires systems to parse multiple visual concepts at once. (2) We present a novel network called UPerNet with hierarchical structure to learn from heterogeneous data from multiple image datasets. (3) The model is shown to be able to jointly infer and discover the rich visual knowledge underneath images.

1.1 Related Work

Our work is built upon the previous work of semantic segmentation and multi-task learning.

Semantic Segmentation. To generate pixel-wise semantic predictions for a given image, image classification networks [1,7–9] are extended to generate semantic segmentation masks. Pioneering work by Chen *et al.* [10], based on structure prediction, uses conditional random field (CRF) to refine the activations of the final feature map of CNNs. The most prevalent framework designed for this pixel-level classification task is the Fully Convolutional Network (FCN) [11], which replaces fully-connected layers in classification networks with convolutional layers. Noh *et al.* [12] propose a framework which applies deconvolution [13] to up-sample low resolution feature maps. Yu and Vladlen [14] propose an architecture based on dilated convolution which is able to exponentially expand the receptive field without loss of resolution or coverage. More recently, RefineNet [15] uses a coarse-to-fine architecture which exploits all information available along the down-sampling process. The Pyramid Scene Parsing Network (PSPNet) [16] performs spatial pooling at several grid scales and achieves remarkable performance on several segmentation benchmarks [2,17,18].

Multi-task Learning. Multi-task learning, which aims to train models to accomplish multiple tasks at the same time, has attracted attention since long before the era of deep learning. For example, a number of previous research works focus on the combination of recognition and segmentation [19–21]. More recently, Elhoseiny *et al.* [22] have proposed a model that performs pose estimation and object classification simultaneously. Eigen and Fergus [23] propose an architecture that jointly addresses depth prediction, surface normal estimation, and semantic labeling. Teichmann *et al.* [24] propose an approach to perform classification, detection, and semantic segmentation via a shared feature extractor. Kokkinos proposes the UberNet [25], a deep architecture that is able to do seven different tasks relying on diverse training sets. Another recent work [3] proposes a partially supervised training paradigm to scale up the segmentation of objects to $3,000$ objects using box annotations only. Comparing our work with previous works on multi-task learning, only a few of them perform multi-task learning on heterogeneous datasets, *i.e.*, a dataset that does not necessarily have all levels of annotations over all tasks. Moreover, although tasks in [25] are formed from low level to high level, such as boundary detection, semantic segmentation and object detection, these tasks do not form the hierarchy of visual concepts. In Sect. 4.2, we further demonstrate the effectiveness of our proposed tasks and frameworks in discovering the rich visual knowledge from images.

2 Defining Unified Perceptual Parsing

We define the task of Unified Perceptual Parsing as the recognition of many visual concepts as possible from a given image. Possible visual concepts are organized into several levels: from scene labels, objects, and parts of objects, to materials and textures of objects. The task depends on the availability of different kinds of training data. Since there is no single image dataset annotated with all visual concepts at multiple levels, we first construct an image dataset by combining several sources of image annotations.

2.1 Datasets

In order to accomplish segmentation of a wide range of visual concepts from multiple levels, we utilize the Broadly and Densely Labeled Dataset (Broden) [26], a heterogeneous dataset that contains various visual concepts. Broden unifies several densely labeled image datasets, namely ADE20K [2], Pascal-Context [27], Pascal-Part [28], OpenSurfaces [6], and the Describable Textures Dataset (DTD) [4]. These datasets contain samples of a broad range of scenes, objects, object parts, materials and textures in a variety of contexts. Objects, object parts and materials are segmented down to pixel level while textures and scenes are annotated at image level.

The Broden dataset provides a wide range of visual concepts. Nevertheless, since it is originally collected to discover the alignment between visual concepts and hidden units of Convolutional Neural Networks (CNNs) for network interpretability [26,29], we find that samples from different classes are unbalanced. Therefore we standardize the Broden dataset to make it more suitable for training segmentation networks. First, we merge similar concepts across different datasets. For example, objects and parts annotations in ADE20K, Pascal-Context, and Pascal-Part are merged and unified. Second, we only include object classes which appear in at least 50 images *and* contain at least 50,000 pixels in the whole dataset. Also, object parts which appear in at least 20 images can be considered valid parts. Objects and parts that are conceptually inconsistent are manually removed. Third, we manually merge under-sampled labels in OpenSurfaces. For example, *stone* and *concrete* are merged into *stone*, while *clear plastic* and *opaque plastic* are merged into *plastic*. Labels that appear in less than 50 images are also filtered out. Fourth, we map more than 400 scene labels from the ADE20K dataset to 365 labels from the Places dataset [30].

Table 1 shows some statistics of our standardized Broden, termed as Broden+. It contains 57,095 images in total, including 22,210 images from ADE20K,

Table 1. Statistics of each label type in the Broden+ dataset. Evaluation metrics for each type of labels are also listed.

Category	Classes	Sources	Eval. metrics
Scene	365	ADE [2]	top-1 acc
Object	335	ADE [2], Pascal-Context [27]	mIoU & pixel acc
Object w/part	77	ADE [2], Pascal-Context [27]	-
Part	152	ADE [2], Pascal-Part [28]	mIoU (bg) & pixel acc
Material	26	OpenSurfaces [6]	mIoU & pixel acc
Texture	47	DTD [4]	top-1 acc

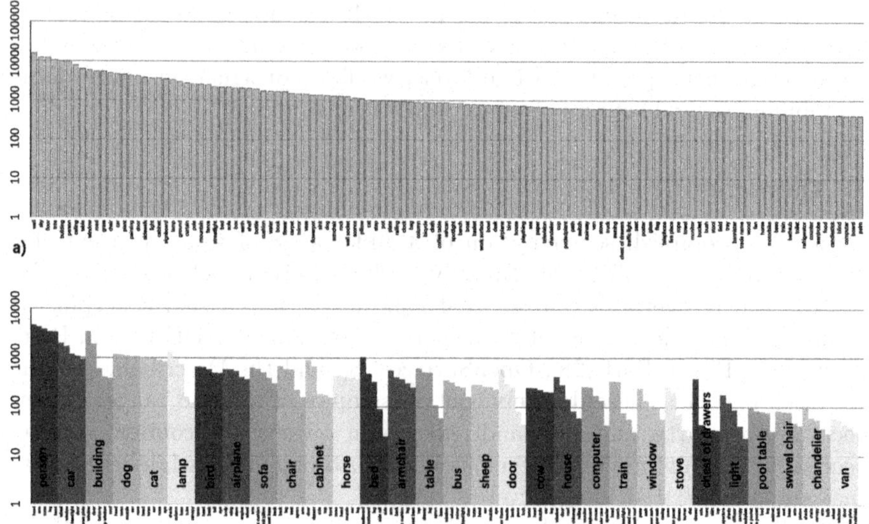

Fig. 2. (a) Sorted object classes by frequency: we show top 120 classes selected from the Broden+. Object classes that appear in less than 50 images or contain less than 50,000 pixels are filtered. (b) Frequency of parts grouped by objects. We show only top 30 objects with their top 5 frequent parts. The parts that appear in less than 20 images are filtered.

10,103 images from Pascal-Context and Pascal-Part, 19,142 images from OpenSurfaces and 5,640 images from DTD. Figure 2 shows the distribution of objects as well as parts grouped by the objects to which they belong. We also provide examples from each source of the Broden+ dataset in Fig. 3.

2.2 Metrics

To quantify the performance of models, we set different metrics based on the annotations of each dataset. Standard metrics to evaluate semantic segmentation

Fig. 3. Samples from the Broden+ dataset. The ground-truth labels for scene and texture are image-level annotations, while for object, part and material are pixel-wise annotations. Object and part are densely annotated, while material is partially annotated. Images with texture labels are mostly such localized object regions.

tasks include Pixel Accuracy (P.A.), which indicates the proportion of correctly classified pixels, and mean IoU (mIoU), which indicates the intersection-over-union (IoU) between the predicted and ground truth pixels, averaged over all object classes. Note that since there might be unlabeled areas in an image, the mIoU metric will not count the predictions on unlabeled regions. This would encourage people to exclude the background label during training. However, it is not suitable for the evaluation of tasks like part segmentation, because for some objects the regions with part annotations only account for a small number of pixels. Therefore we use mIoU, but count the predictions in the background regions, denoted as mIoU-bg, in certain tasks. In this way, excluding background labels during training will boost P.A. by a small margin. Nonetheless, it will significantly downgrade mIoU-bg performance.

For object and material parsing involving ADE20K, Pascal-Context, and OpenSurfaces, the annotations are at pixel level. Images in ADE20K and Pascal-Context are fully annotated, with the regions that do not belong to any pre-defined classes categorized into an unlabeled class. Images in OpenSurfaces are partially annotated, *i.e.*, if several regions of material occur in a single image, more than one region may not be annotated. We use P.A. and mIoU metrics for these two tasks.

For object parts we use P.A. and mIoU-bg metrics for the above mentioned reason. The IoU of each part is first averaged within an object category, then averaged over all object classes. For scene and texture classification we report top-1 accuracy. Evaluation metrics are listed in Table 1.

To balance samples across different labels in different categories we first randomly sample 10% of original images as the validation set. We then randomly choose an image both from the training and validation set, and check if the annotations in pixel level are more balanced towards 10% after swapping these two images. The process is performed iteratively. The dataset is split into 51,617 images for training and 5,478 images for validation.

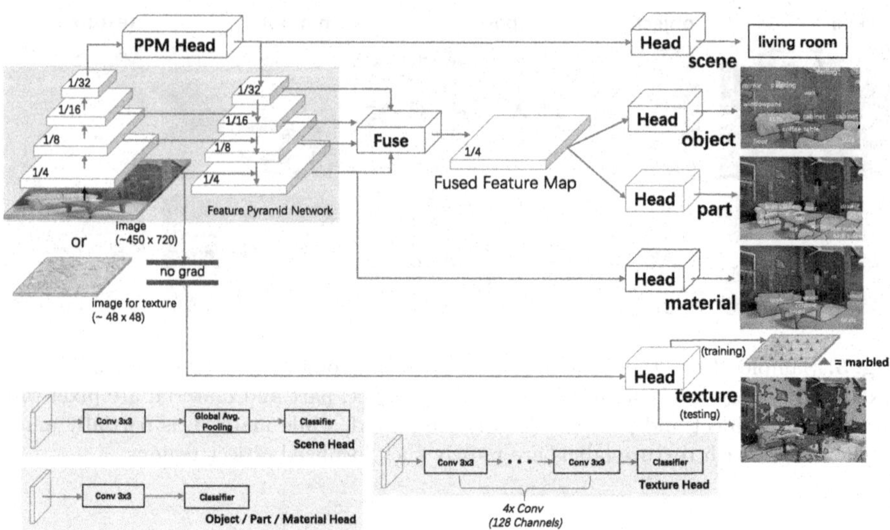

Fig. 4. UPerNet framework for Unified Perceptual Parsing. Top-left: The Feature Pyramid Network (FPN) [31] with a Pyramid Pooling Module (PPM) [16] appended on the last layer of the back-bone network before feeding it into the top-down branch in FPN. Top-right: We use features at various semantic levels. Scene head is attached on the feature map directly after the PPM since image-level information is more suitable for scene classification. Object and part heads are attached on the feature map fused by all the layers put out by FPN. Material head is attached on the feature map in FPN with the highest resolution. Texture head is attached on the Res-2 block in ResNet [1], and fine-tuned after the whole network finishes training on other tasks. Bottom: The illustrations of different heads. Details can be found in Sect. 3.

3 Designing Networks for Unified Perceptual Parsing

We demonstrate our network design in Fig. 4, termed as **UPerNet** (**U**nified **Per**ceptual Parsing **Net**work), based on the Feature Pyramid Network (FPN) [31]. FPN is a generic feature extractor which exploits multi-level feature representations in an inherent and pyramidal hierarchy. It uses a top-down architecture with lateral connections to fuse high-level semantic information into middle and low levels with marginal extra cost. To overcome the issue raised by Zhou *et al.* [32] that although the theoretical receptive field of deep CNN is large enough, the empirical receptive field of deep CNN is relatively much smaller [33], we apply a Pyramid Pooling Module (PPM) from PSPNet [16] on the last layer of the backbone network before feeding it into the top-down branch in FPN. Empirically we find that the PPM is highly compatible with the FPN architecture by bringing effective global prior representations. For further details on FPN and PPM, we refer the reader to [31] and [16].

With the new framework, we are able to train a single network which is able to unify parsing of visual attributes at multiple levels. Our framework is based on Residual Networks [1]. We denote the set of last feature maps of each stage in ResNet as $\{C_2, C_3, C_4, C_5\}$, and the set of feature maps put out by FPN as $\{P_2, P_3, P_4, P_5\}$, where P_5 is also the feature map directly following PPM. The down-sampling rates are $\{4, 8, 16, 32\}$, respectively. *Scene label*, the highest-level attribute annotated at image-level, is predicted by a global average pooling of P_5 followed by a linear classifier. It is worth noting that, unlike frameworks based on a dilated net, the down-sampling rate of P_5 is relatively large so that the features after global average pooling focus more on high-level semantics. For *object label*, we empirically find that fusing all feature maps of FPN is better than only using the feature map with the highest resolution (P_2). *Object parts* are segmented based on the same feature map as objects. For *materials*, intuitively, if we have prior knowledge that these areas belong to the object "cup", we are able to make a reasonable conjecture that it might be made up of paper or plastics. This context is useful, but we still need local apparent features to decide which one is correct. It should also be noted that an object can be made up of various materials. Based on the above observations, we segment materials on top of P_2 rather than fused features. *Texture label*, given at the image-level, is based on non-natural images. Directly fusing these images with other natural images is harmful to other tasks. Also we hope the network can predict texture labels at pixel level. To achieve such a goal, we append several convolutional layers on top of C_2, and force the network to predict the texture label at every pixel. The gradient of this branch is prevented from back-propagating to layers of backbone networks, and the training images for texture are resized to a smaller size ($\sim 64 \times 64$). The reasons behind these designs are: (1) Texture is the lowest-level perceptual attribute, thus it is purely based on apparent features and does not need any high-level information. (2) Essential features for predicting texture correctly are implicitly learned when trained on other tasks. (3) The receptive field of this branch needs to be small enough, so that the network is able to predict different labels at various regions when an image at normal scale is fed in the network. We only fine-tune the texture branch for a few epochs after the whole network finishes training on other tasks.

When only trained on object supervision, without further enhancements, our framework yields almost identical performance as the state-of-the-art PSPNet, while requiring only 63% of training time for the same number of epochs. It is worth noting that we do not even perform deep supervision or data augmentations used in PSPNet other than scale jitter, according to the experiments in their paper [16]. Ablation experiments are provided in Sect. 4.1.

3.1 Implementation Details

Every classifier is preceded by a separate convolutional head. To fuse the layers with different scales such as $\{P_2, P_3, P_4, P_5\}$, we resize them via bilinear interpolation to the size of P_2 and concatenate these layers. A convolutional layer is then applied to fuse features from different levels as well as to reduce channel dimensions. All extra non-classifier convolutional layers, including those in FPN, have batch normalization [34] with 512-channel output. ReLU [35] is applied after batch normalization. Same as [36], we use the "poly" learning rate policy where the learning rate at current iteration equals the initial learning rate multiplying $(1 - \frac{iter}{max\_iter})^{power}$. The initial learning rate and power are set to 0.02 and 0.9, respectively. We use a weight decay of 0.0001 and a momentum of 0.9. During training the input image is resized such that the length of its shorter side is randomly chosen from the set $\{300, 375, 450, 525, 600\}$. For inference we do not apply multi-scale testing for fair comparison, and the length is set to 450. The maximum length of the longer side is set to 1200 in avoidance of GPU memory overflow. The layers in the backbone network are initialized with weights pre-trained on ImageNet [37].

During each iteration, if a mini-batch is composed of images from several sources on various tasks, the gradient with respect to a certain task can be noisy, since the real batch size of each task is in fact decreased. Thus we randomly sample a data source at each iteration based on the scale of each source, and only update the path to infer the concepts related to the selected source. For object and material, we do not calculate loss on unlabeled area. For part, as mentioned in Sect. 2.2, we add background as a valid label. Also the loss of a part is applied only inside the regions of its super object.

Due to physical memory limitations a mini-batch on each GPU involves only 2 images. We adopt synchronized SGD training across 8 GPUs. It is worth noting that batch size has proven to be important to generate accurate statistics for tasks like classification [38], semantic segmentation [16] and object detection [39]. We implement batch normalization such that it is able to synchronize across multiple GPUs. We do not fix any batch norm layer during training. The number of training iterations of ADE20k (with $\sim 20k$ images) alone is $100k$. If trained on a larger dataset, we linearly increase training iterations based on the number of images in the dataset.

3.2 Design Discussion

State-of-the-art segmentation networks are mainly based on fully convolutional networks (FCNs) [11]. Due to a lack of sufficient training samples, segmentation networks are usually initialized from networks pre-trained for image classification [7,8,37]. To enable high-resolution predictions for semantic segmentation, dilated convolution [14], a technique which removes the stride of convolutional layers and adds holes between each location of convolution filters, has been proposed to ease the side effect of down-sampling while maintaining the expansion rate for receptive fields. The dilated network has become the *de facto* paradigm for semantic segmentation.

We argue that such a framework has major drawbacks for the proposed Unified Perceptual Parsing task. First, recently proposed deep CNNs [1,40], which have succeeded on tasks such as image classification and semantic segmentation usually have tens or hundreds of layers. These deep CNNs are intricately designed such that the down-sampling rate grows rapidly in the early stage of the network for the sake of a larger receptive field and lighter computational complexity. For example, in the ResNet with 100 convolutional layers in total,

Table 2. Detailed analysis of our framework based on ResNet-50 *v.s.* state-of-the-art methods on ADE20K dataset. Our results are obtained without multi-scale inference or other techniques. FPN baseline is competitive while requiring much less computational resources. Further increasing resolution of feature maps brings consistent gain. PPM is highly compatible with FPN. Empirically we find that fusing features from all levels of FPN yields best performance. *: A stronger reference for DilatedNet reported in [16]. †: Training time is based on our reproduced models. We also use the same codes in FPN baseline.

Method	Mean IoU(%)	Pixel acc.(%)	Overall(%)	Time(hr)
FCN [11]	29.39	71.32	50.36	-
SegNet [42]	21.64	71.00	46.32	-
DilatedNet [14]	32.31	73.55	52.93	-
CascadeNet [2]	34.90	74.52	54.71	-
RefineNet (Res-152) [15]	40.70	-	-	-
DilatedNet*†(Res-50) [16]	34.28	76.35	55.32	53.9
PSPNet†(Res-50) [16]	**41.68**	**80.04**	**60.86**	61.1
FPN (/16)	34.46	76.04	55.25	18.1
FPN (/8)	34.99	76.54	55.77	20.2
FPN (/4)	35.26	76.52	55.89	21.2
FPN + PPM (/4)	40.13	79.61	59.87	27.8
FPN + PPM + Fusion (/4)	41.22	79.98	60.60	38.7

there are 78 convolutional layers in the Res-4 and Res-5 blocks combined, with down-sampling rates of 16 and 32, respectively. In practice, in a dilated segmentation framework, dilated convolution needs to be applied to both blocks to ensure that the maximum down-sampling rate of all feature maps do not exceed 8. Nevertheless, due to the feature maps within the two blocks are increased to 4 or 16 times of their designated sizes, both the computation complexity and GPU memory footprint are dramatically increased. The second drawback is that such a framework utilizes only the deepest feature map in the network. Prior works [41] have shown the hierarchical nature of the features in the network, *i.e.*, lower layers tend to capture local features such as corners or edge/color conjunctions, while higher layers tend to capture more complex patterns such as parts of some object. Using the features with the highest-level semantics might be reasonable for segmenting high-level concepts such as objects, but it is naturally unfit to segment perceptual attributes at multiple levels, especially the low-level ones such as textures and materials. In what follows, we demonstrate the effectiveness and efficiency of our UPerNet.

4 Experiments

The experiment section is organized as follows: we first introduce the quantitative study of our proposed framework on the original semantic segmentation task

Table 3. Results of Unified Perceptual Parsing on the Broden+ dataset. O: Object. P: Part. S: Scene. M: Material. T: Texture. mI.: mean IoU. P.A.: pixel accuracy. mI.(bg): mean IoU including background. T-1: top-1 accuracy.

Training data					Object		Part		Scene	Material		Texture
+O	+P	+S	+M	+T	mI.	P.A.	mI.(bg)	P.A.	T-1	mI.	P.A.	T-1
✓					24.72	78.03	-	-	-	-	-	-
			✓		-	-	-	-	-	52.78	84.32	-
✓	✓				23.92	77.48	30.21	48.30	-	-	-	-
✓	✓	✓			23.83	77.23	30.10	48.34	71.35	-	-	-
✓	✓	✓	✓		23.36	77.09	28.75	46.92	70.87	54.19	84.45	-
✓	✓	✓	✓	✓	23.36	77.09	28.75	46.92	70.87	54.19	84.45	35.10

and the UPP task in Sect. 4.1. Then we apply the framework to discover visual common sense knowledge underlying scene understanding in Sect. 4.2.

4.1 Main Results

Overall Architecture. To demonstrate the effectiveness of our proposed architecture on semantic segmentation, we report the results trained on ADE20K using object annotations under various settings in Table 2. In general, FPN demonstrates competitive performance while requiring much less computational resources for semantic segmentation. Using the feature map up-sampled only once with a down-sampling rate of 16 (P_4), it reaches mIoU and P.A. of 34.46/76.04, almost identical to the strong baseline reference reported in [16] while only taking about 1/3 of the training time for the same number of iterations. Performance improves further when the resolution is higher. Adding the Pyramid Pooling Module (PPM) boosts performance by a 4.87/3.09 margin, which demonstrates that FPN also suffers from an insufficient receptive field. Empirically we find that fusing features from all levels of FPN yields best performance, a consistent conclusion also observed in [43] (Table 3).

The performance of FPN is surprising considering its simplicity with feature maps being simply up-sampled by bilinear interpolation instead of time-consuming deconvolution, and the top-down path is fused with bottom-up path by an 1×1 convolutional layer followed by element-wise summation without any complex refinement module. It is the simplicity that accomplishes its efficiency. We therefore adopt this design for Unified Perceptual Parsing.

Multi-task Learning with Heterogeneous Annotations. We report the results trained on separate or fused different sets of annotations. The baseline of object parsing is the model trained on ADE20K and Pascal-Context. It yields mIoU and P.A. of 24.72/78.03. This result, compared with the results for ADE20K, is relatively low because Broden+ has many more object classes. The baseline of material is the model trained on OpenSurfaces. It yields mIoU and P.A. of 52.78/84.32. Joint training of object and part parsing yields 23.92/77.48 on object and 30.21/48.30 on part. The performance on object parsing trained plus part annotations is almost identical to that trained only on object annotations. After adding a scene prediction branch it yields top-1 accuracy of 71.35% on scene classification, with negligible downgrades of object and part performance. When jointly training material with object, part, and scene classification, it yields a performance of 54.19/84.45 on material parsing, 23.36/77.09 on object parsing, and 28.75/46.92 on part parsing. It is worth noting that the object and part both suffer a slight performance degrade due to heterogeneity, while material enjoys a boost in performance compared with that trained only on OpenSurfaces. We conjecture that it is attributed to the usefulness of information in object as priors for material parsing. As mentioned above, we find that directly fusing texture images with other natural images is harmful to other tasks, since there are nontrivial differences between images in DTD and natural images. After fine-tuning on texture images using the model trained with all other tasks, we can obtain the quantitative texture classification results by picking the most frequent pixel-level predictions as an image-level prediction. It yields classification accuracy of 35.10. The performance on texture indicates that only fine-tuning the network on texture labels is not optimal. However, this is a necessary step to overcome the fusion of natural and synthetic data sources. We hope future research can discover ways to better utilize such image-level annotations for pixel-level predictions.

Qualitative Results. We provide qualitative results of UPerNet, as visualized in Fig. 5. UPerNet is able to unify compositional visual knowledge and efficiently predicts hierarchical outputs simultaneously.

4.2 Discovering Visual Knowledge in Natural Scenes

Unified Perceptual Parsing requires a model that is able to recognize as many visual concepts as possible from a given image. If a model successfully achieves this goal, it could discover rich visual knowledge underlying the real world, such as answering questions like "What are the commonalities between living rooms and bedrooms?" or "What are the materials that make a cup?" The discovery or even the reasoning of visual knowledge in natural scenes will enable future vision systems to understand its surroundings better. In this section, we demonstrate that our framework trained on the Broden+ is able to discover compositional visual knowledge at multiple levels. That is also the special application for the network trained on heterogeneous data annotations. We use the validation set of Places-365 [30] containing 36, 500 images from 365 scenes as our testbed, since the Places dataset contains images from a variety of scenes and is closer to real world. We define several relations in a hierarchical way, namely *scene-object* relation, *object-part* relation, *object-material* relation, *part-material* relation and *material-texture* relation. Note that only the object-part relations can be directly read out from the ground-truth annotations, other types of relations can only be extracted from the network predictions.

Fig. 5. Predictions on the validation set using UPerNet (ResNet-50). From left to right: scene classification, and object, part, material, and texture parsing.

Scene-Object Relations. For each scene, we count how many objects show up normalized by the frequency of this scene. According to [44], we formulate the relation as a bipartite graph $G = (V, E)$ comprised of a set $V = V_s \cup V_o$ of scene nodes and object nodes together with a set E of edges. The edge with a weight from v_s to v_o represents the percent likelihood that object v_o shows up in scene v_s. No edge connects two nodes that are both from V_s or both from V_o. We filter the edges whose weight is lower than a threshold and run a clustering algorithm to form a better layout. Due to space limitations, we only sample dozens of nodes and show the visualization of the graph in Fig. 6(a). We can clearly see that the indoor scenes mostly share objects such as ceiling, floor, chair, or windowpane while the outdoor scenes mostly share objects such as sky, tree, building, or mountain. What is more interesting is that even in the set of scenes, human-made and natural scenes are clustered into different groups. In the layout, we are also able to locate a common object appearing in various scenes, or find the objects in a certain scene. The bottom-left and bottom-right pictures in Fig. 6(a) illustrate an example in which we can reasonably conclude that the shelf often appears in shops, stores, and utility rooms; and that in a heliport there are often trees, fences, runways, persons, and of course, airplanes.

Object(part)-Material Relations. Apart from scene-object relations, we are able to discover object-material relations as well. Thanks to the ability of our model to predict a label of both object and material at each pixel, it is straightforward to align objects with their associated materials by counting at each pixel what percentage of each material is in every object. Similar to the scene-object relationship, we build a bipartite graph and show its visualization in the left of

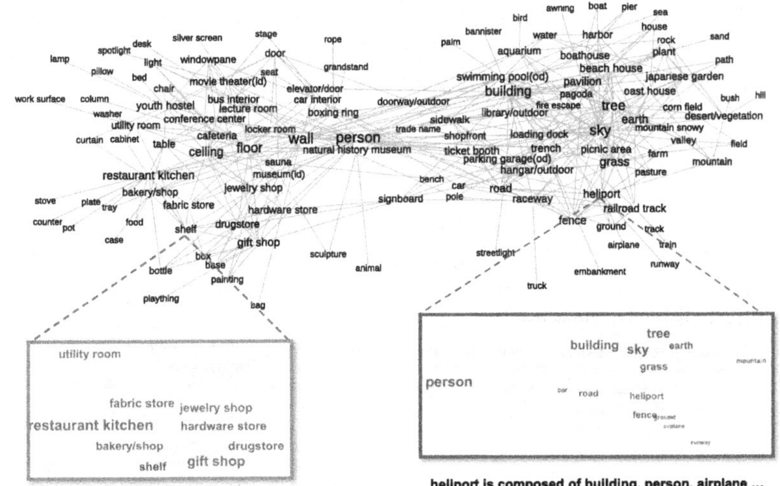

(a) Visualization of scene-object relations. Indoor scenes and outdoor scenes are clustered into different groups (left part of top image and right part of top image). We are also able to locate a common object appearing in various scenes, or find the objects in a certain scene (bottom left and bottom right).

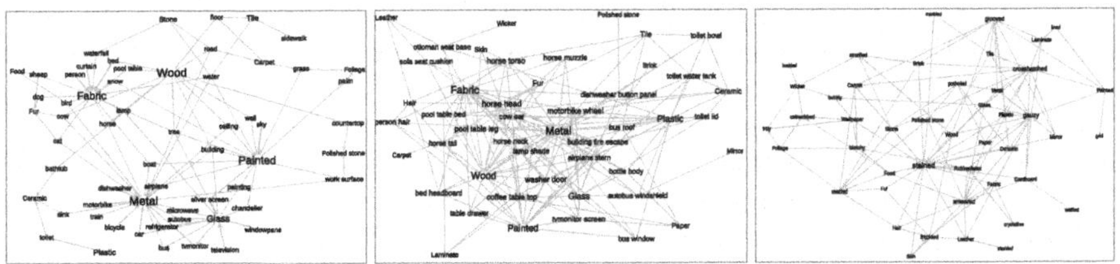

(b) From left to right: visualizations of object-material relations, part-material relations and material-texture relations. We are able to discover knowledge such as some sinks are ceramic while others are metallic. We can also find out what can be used to describe a material.

Fig. 6. Visualizing discovered compositional relations between various concepts.

Fig. 6(b). Using this graph we can infer that some sinks are ceramic while others are metallic; different floors have different materials, such as wood, tile, or carpet. Ceiling and wall are painted; the sky is also "painted", more like a metaphor. However, we can also see that most of the bed is fabric instead of wood, a misalignment due to the actual objects on the bed. Intuitively, the material of a part in an object will be more monotonous. We show the part-material visualization in the middle of Fig. 6(b).

Material-Texture Relations. One type of material may have various kinds of textures. But what is the visual description of a material? We show the visualization of material-texture relations in the right of Fig. 6(b). It is worth noting that although there is a lack of pixel-level annotations for texture labels, we can still generate a reasonable relation graph. For example, a carpet can be described as matted, blotchy, stained, crosshatched and grooved.

5 Conclusion

This work studies the task of Unified Perceptual Parsing, which aims at parsing visual concepts across scene categories, objects, parts, materials and textures from images. A multi-task network and training strategy of handling heterogeneous annotations are developed and benchmarked. We further utilize the trained network to discover visual knowledge among scenes.

References

1. He, K., Zhang, X., Ren, S., Sun, J.: Deep residual learning for image recognition. In: Proceedings of the IEEE Conference on Computer Vision and Pattern Recognition, pp. 770–778 (2016)
2. Zhou, B., Zhao, H., Puig, X., Fidler, S., Barriuso, A., Torralba, A.: Scene parsing through ADE20K dataset. In: Proceedings of CVPR (2017)
3. Hu, R., Dollár, P., He, K., Darrell, T., Girshick, R.: Learning to segment every thing. arXiv preprint arXiv:1711.10370 (2017)
4. Cimpoi, M., Maji, S., Kokkinos, I., Mohamed, S., Vedaldi, A.: Describing textures in the wild. In: 2014 IEEE Conference on Computer Vision and Pattern Recognition (CVPR), pp. 3606–3613. IEEE (2014)
5. Liu, C., Sharan, L., Adelson, E.H., Rosenholtz, R.: Exploring features in a Bayesian framework for material recognition. In: Proceedings of CVPR (2010)
6. Bell, S., Upchurch, P., Snavely, N., Bala, K.: OpenSurfaces: a richly annotated catalog of surface appearance. ACM Trans. Graph. (TOG) **32**(4), 111 (2013)
7. Krizhevsky, A., Sutskever, I., Hinton, G.E.: Imagenet classification with deep convolutional neural networks. In: Advances in Neural Information Processing Systems, pp. 1097–1105 (2012)
8. Simonyan, K., Zisserman, A.: Very deep convolutional networks for large-scale image recognition (2015)
9. Szegedy, C., et al.: Going deeper with convolutions. In: CVPR (2015)
10. Chen, L.C., Papandreou, G., Kokkinos, I., Murphy, K., Yuille, A.L.: Semantic image segmentation with deep convolutional nets and fully connected CRFs. In: International Conference on Learning Representations (ICLR) (2014)
11. Long, J., Shelhamer, E., Darrell, T.: Fully convolutional networks for semantic segmentation. In: Proceedings of the IEEE Conference on Computer Vision and Pattern Recognition, pp. 3431–3440 (2015)
12. Noh, H., Hong, S., Han, B.: Learning deconvolution network for semantic segmentation. In: Proceedings of the IEEE International Conference on Computer Vision, pp. 1520–1528 (2015)
13. Zeiler, M.D., Taylor, G.W., Fergus, R.: Adaptive deconvolutional networks for mid and high level feature learning. In: 2011 IEEE International Conference on Computer Vision (ICCV), pp. 2018–2025. IEEE (2011)
14. Yu, F., Koltun, V.: Multi-scale context aggregation by dilated convolutions. In: International Conference on Learning Representations (ICLR) (2016)

15. Lin, G., Milan, A., Shen, C., Reid, I.: RefineNet: multi-path refinement networks for high-resolution semantic segmentation. In: IEEE Conference on Computer Vision and Pattern Recognition (CVPR) (2017)
16. Zhao, H., Shi, J., Qi, X., Wang, X., Jia, J.: Pyramid scene parsing network. In: IEEE Conference on Computer Vision and Pattern Recognition (CVPR), pp. 2881–2890 (2017)
17. Everingham, M., Van Gool, L., Williams, C.K., Winn, J., Zisserman, A.: The pascal visual object classes (VOC) challenge. Int. J. Comput. Vis. **88**(2), 303–338 (2010)
18. Cordts, M., et al.: The cityscapes dataset for semantic urban scene understanding. In: Proceedings of the IEEE Conference on Computer Vision and Pattern Recognition, pp. 3213–3223 (2016)
19. Keeler, J.D., Rumelhart, D.E., Leow, W.K.: Integrated segmentation and recognition of hand-printed numerals. In: Advances in Neural Information Processing Systems, pp. 557–563 (1991)
20. Kokkinos, I., Maragos, P.: An expectation maximization approach to the synergy between image segmentation and object categorization. In: 2005 Tenth IEEE International Conference on Computer Vision, ICCV 2005, vol. 1, pp. 617–624. IEEE (2005)
21. Maire, M., Stella, X.Y., Perona, P.: Object detection and segmentation from joint embedding of parts and pixels. In: 2011 IEEE International Conference on Computer Vision (ICCV), pp. 2142–2149. IEEE (2011)
22. Elhoseiny, M., El-Gaaly, T., Bakry, A., Elgammal, A.: Convolutional models for joint object categorization and pose estimation. arXiv preprint arXiv:1511.05175 (2015)
23. Eigen, D., Fergus, R.: Predicting depth, surface normals and semantic labels with a common multi-scale convolutional architecture. In: Proceedings of the IEEE International Conference on Computer Vision, pp. 2650–2658 (2015)
24. Teichmann, M., Weber, M., Zoellner, M., Cipolla, R., Urtasun, R.: MultiNet: real-time joint semantic reasoning for autonomous driving. arXiv preprint arXiv:1612.07695 (2016)
25. Kokkinos, I.: UberNet: training a universal convolutional neural network for low-, mid-, and high-level vision using diverse datasets and limited memory. In: IEEE Conference on Computer Vision and Pattern Recognition (CVPR) (2017)
26. Bau, D., Zhou, B., Khosla, A., Oliva, A., Torralba, A.: Network dissection: quantifying interpretability of deep visual representations. In: Proceedings of CVPR (2017)
27. Mottaghi, R., et al.: The role of context for object detection and semantic segmentation in the wild. In: IEEE Conference on Computer Vision and Pattern Recognition (CVPR) (2014)
28. Chen, X., Mottaghi, R., Liu, X., Fidler, S., Urtasun, R., Yuille, A.: Detect what you can: detecting and representing objects using holistic models and body parts. In: IEEE Conference on Computer Vision and Pattern Recognition (CVPR) (2014)
29. Zhou, B., Bau, D., Oliva, A., Torralba, A.: Interpreting deep visual representations via network dissection. In: IEEE Trans. Pattern Anal. Mach. Intell. (2018)
30. Zhou, B., Lapedriza, A., Xiao, J., Torralba, A., Oliva, A.: Learning deep features for scene recognition using places database. In: Advances in Neural Information Processing Systems, pp. 487–495 (2014)
31. Lin, T.Y., Dollár, P., Girshick, R., He, K., Hariharan, B., Belongie, S.: Feature pyramid networks for object detection. In: CVPR, vol. 1, p. 4 (2017)

32. Zhou, B., Khosla, A., Lapedriza, A., Oliva, A., Torralba, A.: Object detectors emerge in deep scene CNNs. In: International Conference on Learning Representations (ICLR) (2015)
33. Zhou, B., Khosla, A., Lapedriza, A., Oliva, A., Torralba, A.: Learning deep features for discriminative localization. In: 2016 IEEE Conference on Computer Vision and Pattern Recognition (CVPR), pp. 2921–2929. IEEE (2016)
34. Ioffe, S., Szegedy, C.: Batch normalization: accelerating deep network training by reducing internal covariate shift. In: International Conference on Machine Learning, pp. 448–456 (2015)
35. Nair, V., Hinton, G.E.: Rectified linear units improve restricted Boltzmann machines. In: Proceedings of the 27th International Conference on Machine Learning (ICML 2010), pp. 807–814 (2010)
36. Chen, L.C., Papandreou, G., Kokkinos, I., Murphy, K., Yuille, A.L.: DeepLab: semantic image segmentation with deep convolutional nets, atrous convolution, and fully connected CRFs. arXiv preprint arXiv:1606.00915 (2016)
37. Deng, J., Dong, W., Socher, R., Li, L.J., Li, K., Fei-Fei, L.: ImageNet: a large-scale hierarchical image database. In: 2009 IEEE Conference on Computer Vision and Pattern Recognition, CVPR 2009, pp. 248–255. IEEE (2009)
38. Ioffe, S.: Batch renormalization: towards reducing minibatch dependence in batch-normalized models. In: Advances in Neural Information Processing Systems, pp. 1942–1950 (2017)
39. Peng, C., et al.: MegDet: a large mini-batch object detector. arXiv preprint arXiv:1711.07240 (2017)
40. Xie, S., Girshick, R., Dollár, P., Tu, Z., He, K.: Aggregated residual transformations for deep neural networks. In: 2017 IEEE Conference on Computer Vision and Pattern Recognition (CVPR), pp. 5987–5995. IEEE (2017)
41. Zeiler, M.D., Fergus, R.: Visualizing and understanding convolutional networks. In: Fleet, D., Pajdla, T., Schiele, B., Tuytelaars, T. (eds.) ECCV 2014. LNCS, vol. 8689, pp. 818–833. Springer, Cham (2014). https://doi.org/10.1007/978-3-319-10590-1_53
42. Badrinarayanan, V., Kendall, A., Cipolla, R.: SegNet: a deep convolutional encoder-decoder architecture for image segmentation. IEEE Trans. Pattern Anal. Mach. Intell. **39**(12), 2481–2495 (2017)
43. Kirillov, A., He, K., Girshick, R., Dollár, P.: Mscoco challenge 2017: stuff segmentation, team fair (2017)
44. Brandes, U., Robins, G., McCranie, A., Wasserman, S.: What is network science? Netw. Sci. **1**(1), 1–15 (2013)

Synthetically Supervised Feature Learning for Scene Text Recognition

Yang Liu[1(✉)], Zhaowen Wang[2], Hailin Jin[2], and Ian Wassell[1]

[1] Computer Laboratory, University of Cambridge, Cambridge, UK
{yl504,ijw24}@cam.ac.uk
[2] Adobe Research, San Jose, CA, USA
{zhawang,hljin}@adobe.com

Abstract. We address the problem of image feature learning for scene text recognition. The image features in the state-of-the-art methods are learned from large-scale synthetic image datasets. However, most methods only rely on outputs of the synthetic data generation process, namely realistically looking images, and completely ignore the rest of the process. We propose to leverage the parameters that lead to the output images to improve image feature learning. Specifically, for every image out of the data generation process, we obtain the associated parameters and render another "clean" image that is free of select distortion factors that are applied to the output image. Because of the absence of distortion factors, the clean image tends to be easier to recognize than the original image which can serve as supervision. We design a multi-task network with an encoder-discriminator-generator architecture to guide the feature of the original image toward that of the clean image. The experiments show that our method significantly outperforms the state-of-the-art methods on standard scene text recognition benchmarks in the lexicon-free category. Furthermore, we show that without explicit handling, our method works on challenging cases where input images contain severe geometric distortion, such as text on a curved path.

Keywords: Scene text recognition · Deep learning · Neural networks Feature learning · Synthetic data · Multi-task learning

1 Introduction

Scene text recognition, the problem of recognizing text in natural scene images, has always occupied a special place in image understanding and Computer Vision, because of the importance of text in the way that people communicate with each other. It has a wide range of practical applications including autonomous driving, robots and drones, mobile e-commerce, and helping visually impaired people. Image features play a crucial role in scene text recognition. Early methods use hand-crafted features and break the problem into subproblems such as character detection [34,36,38]. The state-of-the-art methods use convolutional neural networks and train from images directly to text in an end-to-end fashion [17,27].

V. Ferrari et al. (Eds.): ECCV 2018, LNCS 11209, pp. 449–465, 2018.
https://doi.org/10.1007/978-3-030-01228-1_27

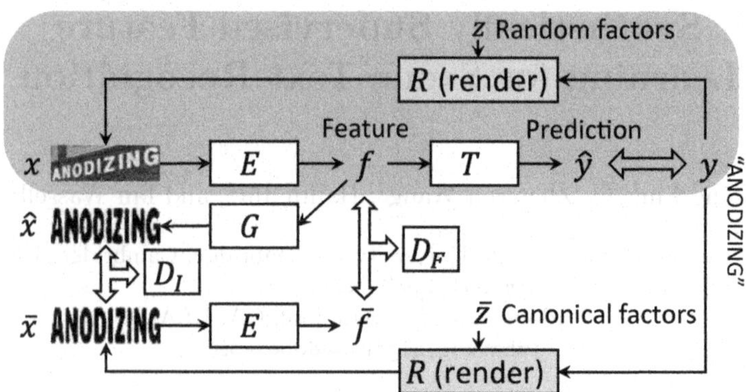

Fig. 1. The proposed text feature learning framework. The blue shaded box at the top contains a generic text recognition pipeline, with an input image $\mathbf{x}$ going through a feature encoder E and a text decoder T, resulting in a predicted text string $\hat{y}$. By a synthetically-supervised approach, we use the true text label y to render not only a noisy input image $\mathbf{x}$, but also a clean image $\bar{\mathbf{x}}$ with the canonical rendering parameter $\bar{\mathbf{z}}$. The encoded feature $\mathbf{f} = E(\mathbf{x})$ is trained to match its clean counterpart $\bar{\mathbf{f}}=E(\bar{\mathbf{x}})$, as well as to reproduce the clean image through an image generator G. Adversarial matching losses are imposed on both image and feature domains by discriminators D_I and D_F. (Color figure online)

One of the key factors in the state-of-the-art methods is the use of large-scale synthetic image datasets to train convolutional neural networks [17]. The ability to use synthetic data is special in the text recognition problem. Thanks to the fact that text is *not* a natural object, we are able to generate an unlimited amount of labeled images that resemble real-world images. In the generation process, we can manipulate nuisance factors such as font, lighting, shadow, border, background, image noise, geometric deformation, and compression artifacts. As a result, image features trained on synthetic data with these factors will be robust to their variations, leading to a significant improvement of recognition accuracy.

There is a fundamental difference between real images and synthetic images which is that synthetic images are obtained through a process that is controllable to a Machine Learning algorithm. This process provides not only an unlimited amount of training data (images and labels) but also parameters that are associated with the data. This difference has been completely ignored in the literature. For instance, most state-of-the-art methods follow a simple training procedure and only exploit the abundance of synthetic data to train image features. The key idea of this work is that we can leverage the difference between real and synthetic images, namely the controllability of the generation process, and control the generation process to generate paired training data. Specifically, for every synthetic image out of the generation process with aforementioned nuisance factors, we obtain the associated rendering parameters, manipulate the parameters, and generate a corresponding *clean* image where we remove part or all of the nuisance factors. For instance, the original image may have a perspective warp and the clean image does not contain any geometric deformation. Because of the absence of nuisance factors, the text in the clean image is generally easier to recognize and can therefore serve as supervision. By training on synthetic images both with and without nuisance factors, we expect to learn a more robust text recognition feature that is invariant to undesired nuisance factors.

The overall framework of our proposed method, which we call synthetically supervised feature learning, is shown in the Fig. 1. We use cleans image as supervision at both the pixel level and the feature level in a generative way, and design auxiliary training losses that can be combined with conventional training objectives of any deep network model for text recognition. We follow two principles – *invariance* and *completeness* – to learn a good text feature encoder $E(\cdot)$, which usually consists of the first several convolutional layers in the recognition model. Feature invariance requires that the encoder extracts the same feature for any input image $\mathbf{x}$ and its corresponding clean image $\bar{\mathbf{x}}$: $E(\mathbf{x}) = E(\bar{\mathbf{x}})$. Feature completeness requires all text label information to be contained in $E(\mathbf{x})$. It is equivalent to require the existence of an inverse mapping, or an image generator $G(\cdot)$, that can transform the encoded feature back to the deterministic clean image: $G(E(\mathbf{x})) = \bar{\mathbf{x}}$. Since the supervision from the clean image is applied on image and feature domains, it is tempting to employ generative adversarial networks (GANs) [7] to help the feature learning in addition to the use of basic ℓ_1 or ℓ_2 losses. Therefore, we also explore using discriminators $D_I(\cdot)$ and $D_F(\cdot)$ to encourage the generated image and feature to be more similar to their clean counterparts, respectively. Our experiment results show that, with the right combination, the invariance, completeness and adversarial losses all contribute to a text feature that is more robust to nuisance factors.

The main contributions of this paper are threefold: 1. We propose to leverage the controllability of the data generation process and introduce clean images that are free byproducts as the auxiliary training data for scene text recognition. Otherwise, our method does not require information of other nuisance factors in the generation process which is less structured and harder to use. We propose a general algorithm to use clean images as additional supervision that can be applied to most deep learning based text recognition models. 2. We design a novel scene text recognition algorithm that learns a descriptive and robust text representation (image feature) through image generation, feature matching and adversarial training. We conduct a detailed ablation study by examining the effectiveness of each proposed component. 3. Our method achieves the state-of-the-art performance on various scene text recognition benchmarks and significantly outperforms the state-of-the-art in the lexicon-free category. Moreover, Our approach generalizes to irregular text recognition, such as perspective text and curved text recognition.

2 Related Work

Scene text recognition is an important area in image understanding and Computer Vision. There is a sizable body of literature on this topic. We will only discuss closely related work here and refer the reader to recent surveys [34,36,38] for more thorough expositions. [14,15,32] are among the early works in using deep convolutional neural networks as image features for scene text recognition. [17] formulates the problem as a 90K-class convolutional neural network, where each class corresponds to an English word. One of the key contributions of [17] is that it proposes a large-scale synthetic dataset as existing image datasets are not sufficient to train deep convolutional neural networks. This synthetic dataset is later adopted by follow-up works. To overcome the problem of using a fixed lexicon in training, [16] proposes a joint graphical model and [27] propose an end-to-end sequence recognition network where images and texts are separately encoded as patch sequences and character sequences. A lexicon can be introduced at the test time if necessary. [4,5,20] are among the latest approaches which adopt attention-based networks to handle complicated text distortion and low-quality images. Our method follows the general direction of using convolutional neural networks and sequence recognition for the problem. Our contribution lies in using the rendering parameters in the synthetic data generation process to obtain new clean reference images. We leverage both original images and clean images to guide image feature learning. To the best of our knowledge, this is the first work in scene text recognition to use auxiliary reference images to improve feature learning, sharing similar philosophy with other generative multi-task learning works [24,30,35]. We show that our method can correct geometric distortion present in input images. This is related to [28] which uses a spatial transformer network to rectify the image before the recognition pipeline. However, [28] employs a hand-designed architecture that only works for geometric distortion while our method applies to arbitrary distortion in a unified way. As long as the synthetic data generation process can simulate a distortion, our method can potentially correct it through feature learning.

3 Method

We build a synthetically-supervised feature learning framework for text recognition as shown in Fig. 1. It consists of a text image renderer R, a feature encoder E, a text decoder T, an image generator G, and two discriminators D_I and D_F. We discuss each of these components and their interactions in the following.

Renderer: We use a standard text renderer R to synthesize a text image $\mathbf{x}=R(y,\mathbf{z})$ with a text string y and rendering parameters $\mathbf{z}$. $\mathbf{z}$ describes how nuisance factors are added in the rendered image, and is drawn randomly from a distribution covering the combinations of various factors including font, outline, color, shading, background, perspective warping, and imaging noise. The clean image $\bar{\mathbf{x}}$ for text y is synthesized as $R(y,\bar{\mathbf{z}})$ by fixing the rendering parameters to a canonical value $\bar{\mathbf{z}}$. In our case, $\bar{\mathbf{z}}$ corresponds to a standard font and zero noise perturbation, yielding a clean image $\bar{\mathbf{x}}$ as illustrated in Fig. 1. The renderer provides training triplets $\{(\mathbf{x},\bar{\mathbf{x}},y)\}$ in our framework, and it is not trainable.

Encoder and Text Decoder: The encoder E takes an input image $\mathbf{x}$ to extract its image feature $\mathbf{f}$, which is further fed into the text decoder T to predict the text character sequence $\hat{y}$. The cross-modal encoder-decoder structure represents a generic deep network design for scene text recognition. We follow the prior work of [27] to build these two components.

Specifically, E is a multi-layer fully convolutional network that extracts a 3D feature map $\mathbf{f}$, and T is a two-layer Bidirectional Long-Short Term Memory (BLSTM) network [10,11] that predicts text by solving a sequence labeling problem. The feature map $\mathbf{f}$ is first transformed to a sequence $\{\mathbf{f}^1, ..., \mathbf{f}^N\}$ by flattening N feature segments sliced from $\mathbf{f}$ horizontally from left to right. Due to the translation-invariant property of CNN, each feature frame $\mathbf{f}^n$ corresponds to the n-th local image region which may contain one or part of a text glyph. With the feature sequence as input, the BLSTM decoder T analyzes the dependency among the feature frames and predicts a character probability distribution π^n corresponding to each $\mathbf{f}^n$. The probability space of π^n includes all English alphanumeric characters as well as a blank token for word separation. Finally, the per-frame predictions $\{\pi^1, ..., \pi^T\}$ are translated into the text prediction $\hat{y}$ through beam search.

As in [27], the network branch of E and T can be trained by minimizing the discrepancy between the probability sequence $\{\pi^1, ..., \pi^T\}$ and the true text y using the Connectionist Temporal Classification (CTC) technique [9]. CTC aligns the variable length character sequence of y with the fixed length probability sequence so that the conditional probability of y can be evaluated based on $\{\pi^1, ..., \pi^T\}$. The training loss given by the direct supervision from y can be summarized as

$$\min_{E,T} \mathcal{L}_y = p(y|T(E(\mathbf{x}))) = \sum_{\tilde{y}:\mathcal{B}(\tilde{y})=y} \prod_{t=1}^{T} \pi^t(\tilde{y}^t), \tag{1}$$

where $\mathcal{B}$ is the CTC mapping for sequences of length T, and $\tilde{y}^t$ denotes the t-th token in $\tilde{y}$.

Feature Matching and Image Generator: Our motivation of utilizing the clean image $\bar{\mathbf{x}}$ is to learn a good text feature encoder E that is both invariant to nuisance factors and complete in describing text content. In terms of invariance, we explicitly minimize the difference between the features extracted from $\mathbf{x}$ and $\bar{\mathbf{x}}$, since the two images share the same text label y:

$$\min_{E} \mathcal{L}_f = \|E(\mathbf{x}) - E(\bar{\mathbf{x}})\|_2 . \tag{2}$$

In terms of completeness, we require all information in the clean image $\bar{\mathbf{x}}$ to be captured by feature $E(\mathbf{x})$. Equivalently, there should exist an image generator G that can reconstruct $\bar{\mathbf{x}}$ given $E(\mathbf{x})$. To generate images, we construct G as a deconvolutional network, which is trained jointly with the encoder E to minimize the ℓ_1 image reconstruction loss:

$$\min_{E,G} \mathcal{L}_g = \|G(E(\mathbf{x})) - \bar{\mathbf{x}}\|_1 . \tag{3}$$

Adversarial Discriminators: As the supervision from the clean image $\bar{\mathbf{x}}$ is applied on image and feature domains, we thus also explore the idea of generative adversarial network (GAN) [7] to help improve the distributional similarity between $G(E(\mathbf{x}))/E(\mathbf{x})$ and their clean counterparts $\bar{\mathbf{x}}/E(\bar{\mathbf{x}})$. We design an image discriminator D_I and a feature discriminator D_F that try to distinguish between noise and clean input sources. The two discriminators are both convolutional networks with binary classification outputs, and they are trained against E and G in an adversarial minimax style:

$$\min_{E,G} \max_{D_I} \mathcal{L}_{ga} = \log D_I(\bar{\mathbf{x}}|\mathbf{x}) + \log(1 - D_I(G(E(\mathbf{x}))|\mathbf{x})), \tag{4}$$

$$\min_{E} \max_{D_F} \mathcal{L}_{fa} = \log D_F(E(\bar{\mathbf{x}})) + \log(1 - D_F(E(\mathbf{x}))). \tag{5}$$

Note that the image discriminator D_I in Eq. (4) is formulated as a conditional GAN [22] conditioned on the original input image $\mathbf{x}$. This encourages the image generated by G to not only look realistic but also have the same text content as $\mathbf{x}$.

With all the above loss terms combined together, we come to the overall training objective for our synthetically-supervised text recognition model:

$$\min_{E,T,G} \max_{D_I,D_F} \mathbb{E}_{\mathbf{x},\bar{\mathbf{x}},y} \left[\mathcal{L}(\mathbf{x}, \bar{\mathbf{x}}, y)\right], \ \mathcal{L} = \lambda_y \mathcal{L}_y + \lambda_f \mathcal{L}_f + \lambda_g \mathcal{L}_g + \lambda_{ga} \mathcal{L}_{ga} + \lambda_{fa} \mathcal{L}_{fa}, \tag{6}$$

where all the λ's are weighting coefficients. The effect of each individual loss and their best combinations will be discussed in the experiments.

4 Experiments

In this section, we evaluate our model on a number of benchmarks for scene text recognition. The network structure and implementation details are provided in Sect. 4.1. We present an ablation study in Sect. 4.2 to explore how the performance of the proposed method is affected by different model configurations, including different types of clean image $\bar{\mathbf{x}}$ and different combinations of model components. A comprehensive comparison on general recognition benchmarks is reported in Sect. 4.3. Finally, to further demonstrate the generalization capability of our proposed model, we verify its robustness on two benchmarks created especially for irregular text recognition in Sect. 4.4.

4.1 Implementation Details

Network Structure: Detailed information of the network structure is provided in Table 1. For the design of encoder E and text decoder T, we follow the configuration in [27] to enable a fair comparison. The BLSTM has 256 memory blocks and 37 output units (26 letters, 10 digits and 1 EOS symbol). The batch-normalization is applied after the 5th and 6th convolutional layers. Since the stability of the adversarial training suffers if sparse gradient layers are used,

Table 1. Network structure for our scene text recognition algorithm

Layer	Filter/stride	Output size	Layer	Filter/stride	Output size
Encoder			Image generator		
Input	-	$32 \times 100 \times 3$			
Conv1	$3 \times 3/2 \times 2$	$16 \times 50 \times 64$	FConv7	$2 \times 2/2 \times 1$	$2 \times 25 \times 512$
Conv2	$3 \times 3/2 \times 2$	$8 \times 25 \times 128$	FConv6	$3 \times 3/2 \times 1$	$4 \times 25 \times 512$
Conv3	$3 \times 3/1 \times 1$	$8 \times 25 \times 256$	FConv5	$3 \times 3/1 \times 1$	$4 \times 25 \times 256$
Conv4	$3 \times 3/2 \times 1$	$4 \times 25 \times 256$	FConv4	$3 \times 3/2 \times 1$	$8 \times 25 \times 256$
Conv5	$3 \times 3/1 \times 1$	$4 \times 25 \times 512$	FConv3	$3 \times 3/1 \times 1$	$8 \times 25 \times 256$
Conv6	$3 \times 3/2 \times 1$	$2 \times 25 \times 512$	FConv2	$3 \times 3/2 \times 2$	$16 \times 50 \times 128$
Conv7	$2 \times 2/2 \times 1$	$1 \times 25 \times 512$	FConv1	$3 \times 3/2 \times 2$	$32 \times 100 \times 3$
Feature discriminator			Image discriminator		
ConvF1	$1 \times 1/1 \times 1$	$1 \times 25 \times 256$	ConvI1	$3 \times 3/2 \times 2$	$16 \times 50 \times 64$
ConvF2	$1 \times 1/1 \times 1$	$1 \times 25 \times 128$	ConvI2	$3 \times 3/2 \times 2$	$8 \times 25 \times 128$
ConvF3	$1 \times 1/1 \times 1$	$1 \times 25 \times 64$	ConvI3	$3 \times 3/2 \times 1$	$4 \times 25 \times 256$
ConvF4	$1 \times 1/1 \times 1$	$1 \times 25 \times 32$	ConvI4	$3 \times 3/2 \times 1$	$2 \times 25 \times 256$
ConvF5	$1 \times 1/1 \times 1$	$1 \times 25 \times 1$	ConvI5	$2 \times 2/2 \times 1$	$1 \times 25 \times 1$
AvgPool	$1 \times 25/1 \times 1$	$1 \times 1 \times 1$	AvgPool	$1 \times 25/1 \times 1$	$1 \times 1 \times 1$
Text decoder					
BLSTM1	256	25×512			
BLSTM2	256	25×512			
Output	37	25×37			

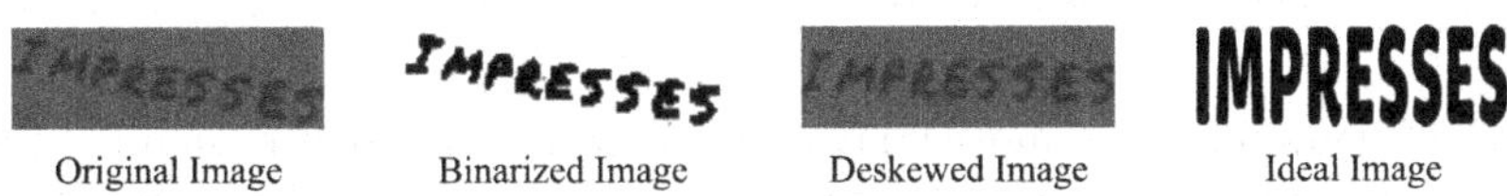

Fig. 2. Example of different formations of clean images.

we replace MaxPool and ReLu with stride convolution and leaky rectified linear unit respectively. The image generator G contains a series of fractional-stride convolutions [2] to generate an image with the same size of the original input. The discriminators D_I and D_F both contain five fully convolutional layers.

Training Details: For all the experiments for scene text recognition, we use the synthetic dataset (Synth90) released by Jaderberg et al. [14] as the training data. The dataset contains 8 million images and their corresponding ground truth text labels. Different types of clean images are leveraged to supervise feature learning, and their effectiveness is analyzed in Sect. 4.2. Our network is trained on Synth90 and tested on all other real-world test datasets without any fine-tuning. Detailed information about real-world test benchmarks is provided in

Sects. 4.3 and 4.4. Following [27], images are resized to 32×100 in both training and testing. The image intensities are linearly scaled to the range of $[-1, 1]$. The batch size is set to 32. All weights are initialized from a zero-mean normal distribution with a standard deviation of 0.01. The Adam optimizer [19] is used with a learning rate of 0.002 and momentum 0.5. The parameters in the objective function (6) are determined by 5-fold cross-validation. For testing, in the process of unconstrained text recognition (lexicon-free), we straightforwardly select the most probable character. While in constrained text recognition, we calculate the conditional probability distributions for all lexicon words, and take the one with the highest probability as output result.

4.2 Ablation Study

In this section, we empirically investigate how the performance of the proposed method is affected by different model settings on the Street View Text dataset [31]. We study mainly in two aspects: the formation of clean image and the contribution of network components.

Formation of Clean Images: One of the main contributions of this paper is that we explore using clean image as auxiliary supervision to guide feature learning. To enable a fair comparison with existing works, our training data are the pre-rendered images from Synth90 [14], with the text labels being the only accessible rendering parameter. To evaluate the effects of removing different nuisance factors, besides rendering a clean image without any noise perturbation, we post-process the original input images to simulate the formation of different types of "less clean" images, as shown in Fig. 2, in the following ways.

Binarized Images: To remove image color variation, we convert an input image to gray-scale and then binarize the gray-scale image by thresholding. The threshold is set to be the mean value of the input image. The output binary image has 0 (black) for all pixels with intensity less than the mean value and 255 (white) otherwise.

Deskewed Images: To remove text orientation variation, we first detect the text baseline in the input image using a pre-trained neural network model for text detection [37]. Then we compute the angle of the text and rotate the text to the horizontal orientation.

Ideal Images: We render a new image which matches the ground truth text label while removing all the other nuisance factors. More specifically, we use the FreeType library [12] to render the corresponding text in black with font style 'Brevia Black Regular'. The font size is set as 64. The text is arranged horizontally in a clean white background. After rendering, we re-scale the synthesized image to 32×100, which has the same size as the original input image.

Table 2. Text recognition accuracy on SVT [31] using different types of clean images.

Clean image	Recognition accuracy (%)
None [27]	80.8
Binarized images	85.8
Deskewed images	84.7
Ideal images	**87.0**

Table 3. Text recognition accuracies for different variants of our model, compared with CRNN [27] baseline. The corresponding training losses are shown.

Model variant	Training losses	Accuracy (%)
CRNN [27]	$\mathcal{L}_y$	80.8
Image generation	$\mathcal{L}_y + \mathcal{L}_g$	86.1
Adversarial generation	$\mathcal{L}_y + \mathcal{L}_g + \mathcal{L}_{ga}$	84.7
Feature matching	$\mathcal{L}_y + \mathcal{L}_f$	85.1
Adversarial matching	$\mathcal{L}_y + \mathcal{L}_g + \mathcal{L}_f + \mathcal{L}_{fa}$	**87.0**

The performances of our model using 3 types of clean images are shown in Table 2, together with the CRNN model [27] trained without using any auxiliary clean data as a baseline. To enable a fair comparison, we use the same model architecture for all the clean image variants, and the configurations of our encoder and text decoder match those used in [27]. As shown in Table 2, introducing auxiliary clean data boosts the performance significantly. The reason is that removing part or all the nuisance factors from the original image makes text recognition easier. We further observe that leveraging the ideal image leads to the highest accuracy, which outperforms the baseline by over 6%. We attribute this improvement to that the ideal image makes the learned feature resilient to all the nuisance factors. The learned feature is optimized with respect to the text information while being invariant to other undesired nuisance factors, which is critical for scene text recognition. We use the ideal image as auxiliary supervision throughout the rest of the experiments.

Architectural Variants: We conduct a detailed ablation study by examining the effectiveness of each proposed component in our network structure. We evaluate and compare each of the following module configurations:

CRNN Model [27]: built with components E and T, and trained only with a CTC loss, corresponding to $\mathcal{L}_y$ in our framework.

Image Generation: built with E, T, and G, and trained with $\mathcal{L}_y$ and $\mathcal{L}_g$ losses.

Adversarial Generation: built with E, T, G and D_I, and trained with $\mathcal{L}_y$, $\mathcal{L}_g$ and $\mathcal{L}_{ga}$. Previous approaches have found it to be beneficial to mix the GAN objective with the ℓ_1 loss [13]. The encoder and the image generator work cooperatively to compete with the image discriminator.

Feature Matching: built with E and T, and trained with $\mathcal{L}_y$ and $\mathcal{L}_f$.

Adversarial Matching: built with E, T, G and D_F, and trained with $\mathcal{L}_y$, $\mathcal{L}_g$, $\mathcal{L}_f$ and $\mathcal{L}_{fa}$. The encoder not only tries to make the features of the original input and its corresponding clean image pair similar, but also to fool the feature discriminator. The adversarial game is conducted between the encoder and the feature discriminator. We also impose ℓ_1 reconstruction loss at pixel level.

The performances of the above 5 models are listed in Table 3. The CRNN model [27] serves as a baseline in the comparison. The 4 different variants of the proposed model all boost recognition performance compared to the baseline. Adding either feature consistency loss $\mathcal{L}_f$ or image generation loss $\mathcal{L}_g$ improves the performance by over 5%, which verifies the effectiveness of leveraging the clean data as auxiliary supervision in feature learning. Also, it is observed that the image generation loss $\mathcal{L}_g$ contributes to the most performance gain as an individual module. It indicates that reconstructing the clean image, or preserving the text content, is the most important task when learning the feature representation.

Another interesting observation is that compared with image generation using the $\mathcal{L}_g$ loss only, adding the adversarial training in the image generation does not bring a significant improvement to the scene recognition performance. One possible reason may be revealed in the second example in Fig. 3, which has ground truth label 'coffee'. Although the image generated by the adversarial training looks more realistic than using $\mathcal{L}_g$ alone, as shown in Fig. 3, it interprets the last second character as 'l' instead of 'e', which leads to an incorrect prediction. This misunderstanding can be observed in both the generated image and the final prediction. Although using the image discriminator degrades the performance a little, it does provide us with a new possibility. With the help of the image discriminator, we can obtain a confidence score of the final prediction, which indicates the quality of generated images. The confidence score is close to 1 when a generated image looks realistic and to 0 otherwise. It is plotted in the last column of Fig. 3 for 25 local image regions from left to right. This confidence score has a correlation with character recognition accuracy and may be used in the lexicon-based word search. Since the image discriminator does not provide noticeable improvement in the recognition performance, in the following experiments, we disable the image discriminator unless otherwise specified.

On the other hand, adding the feature discriminator and adversarial training in the feature domain further boosts the recognition accuracy to 87%. It means that the adversarial training between the encoder and feature discriminator acts as a critical role in aligning the distribution between the features of the original

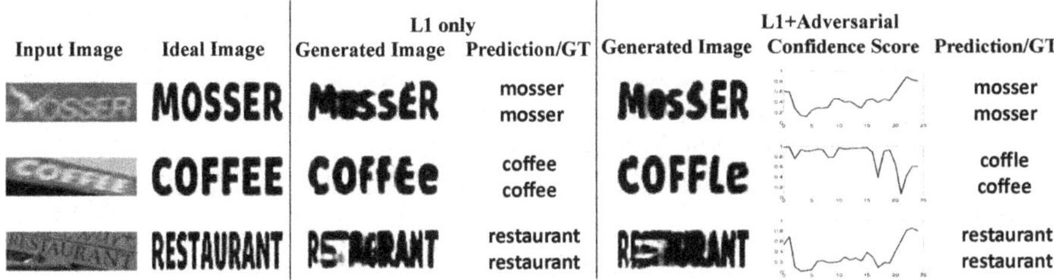

Fig. 3. Examples showing the generated images and their corresponding confidence scores. The first column shows the original input images and their paired 'clean' images. The middle column shows the generated images by using L_1 loss only and the corresponding prediction. The right column shows the generated images using L_1 loss with adversarial training, the corresponding confidence score and predictions. The confidence score corresponds to 25 local image regions which may contain one or part of a text glyph horizontally from left to right. The confidence score is close to 1 when it looks realistic and to 0 otherwise.

input image and the corresponding clean image. It makes the learned feature representation more exclusive or invariant to other nuisance factors.

4.3 Results and Comparisons on General Benchmarks

We evaluate our proposed method on the benchmarks that are designed for general scene text recognition, which mostly contain regular text although irregular text occasionally exists. The benchmark datasets are:

- **IIIT 5K-Words** [23]: (IIIT5K) contains 3000 cropped word images in its test set, which is collected from the Internet. Each image specifies a 50-word lexicon and a 1k-word lexicon.
- **Street View Text** [31]: (SVT) contains 647 test images, which are cropped from 249 Google Street View images. Many images in SVT suffer from severe noise and blur or have a very low resolution. Each image is associated with a 50-word lexicon.
- **ICDAR 2003** [21]: (IC03) contains 251 scene images labeled with text bounding boxes. For fair comparison [31], we discard the images contain non-alphanumeric characters or those having less than three characters. The resulting dataset contains 867 cropped images. Each cropped image is associated with a 50-word lexicon defined by Wang et al. [31] and a full lexicon which combines all lexicon words.
- **ICDAR 2013** [18]: (IC13) inherits most of its samples from IC03. After filtering samples as done in IC03, the dataset contains 857 samples. No lexicon is specified.

In Table 4, we report the performances of our synthetically-supervised feature learning model and compare them with 16 existing methods on the general

Table 4. Recognition rates (%) on standard scene text recognition benchmarks. '50' and '1k' refer to the lexicon sizes, 'Full' indicates the combined lexicon of all images in the benchmarks, and 'None' means unconstrained lexicon-free. Our method achieves the state-of-the-art performance across different benchmarks and significantly outperforms the state-of-the-art in the lexicon-free category.

Method	IIIT5K			SVT		IC03			IC13
	50	1K	None	50	None	50	Full	None	None
ABBEY [31]	24.3	-	-	35.0	-	56.0	55.0	-	-
SYNTH+PLEX [31]	-	-	-	57.0	-	76.0	62.0	-	-
Mishra et al. [10]	64.1	57.5	-	73.2	-	81.8	67.8	-	-
Wang et al. [32]	-	-	-	70.0	-	90.0	84.0	-	-
wDTW [6]	-	-	-	77.3	-	89.7	-	-	-
PhotoOCR [3]	-	-	-	90.4	78.0	-	-	-	87.6
Almazan et al. [1]	91.2	82.1	-	89.2	-	-	-	-	-
Strokelets [33]	80.2	69.3	-	75.9	-	88.5	80.3	-	-
Su and Lu [29]	-	-	-	83.0	-	92.0	82.0	-	-
Gordo [8]	93.3	86.6	-	91.8	-	-	-	-	-
Jaderberg et al. [17]	97.1	92.7	-	95.4	80.7	98.7	98.6	93.1	90.8
Jaderberg et al. [16]	95.5	89.6	-	93.2	71.7	97.8	97.0	89.6	81.8
CRNN [27]	97.6	94.4	78.2	96.4	80.8	98.7	97.6	89.4	86.7
RARE [28]	96.2	93.8	81.9	95.5	81.9	98.3	96.2	90.1	88.6
R^2AM [20]	96.8	94.4	78.4	96.3	80.7	97.9	97.0	88.7	90.0
FAN [4]	**99.3**	**97.5**	87.4	**97.1**	85.9	**99.2**	97.3	94.2	93.9
Ours	97.3	96.1	**89.4**	96.8	**87.1**	98.1	**97.5**	**94.7**	**94.0**

text recognition benchmarks. On unconstrained recognition tasks (recognizing without a lexicon), our method shows a significant improvement in all cases by using the clean image as supervision at both pixel level and at feature level in a generative way. More specifically, since CRNN [27] and our proposed method share the same encoder and text decoder network structure, thus it can serve as a strong baseline for fair comparison without adopting any auxiliary clean image for supervision. Our method outperforms CRNN by around 7% on average. This demonstrates the effectiveness and superiority of leveraging the auxiliary clean image. On constrained recognition tasks, we use a standard lexicon searching algorithm as in [27], and also achieve state-of-the-art or highly competitive results.

Compared with the method proposed in FAN [4], our method achieves competitive accuracies without using deep resent-based encoder or any attention mechanism as is done in FAN [4]. In addition, in the lexicon-free setting, our method significantly outperforms FAN on IIIT5K, SVT and performs comparably to the performance on IC03 and IC13. From our observations, we found that

Table 5. Recognition rates (%) on irregular text recognition benchmarks.

Method	SVT-Perspective	Curved text
Jaderberg et al. [17]	-	42.7
CRNN [27]	66.8	54.9
RARE [28]	71.8	59.2
Ours	**73.9**	**62.5**

IIIT5K and SVT contains more irregular text, especially curved text and has very low resolution images. Our method has an advantage in dealing with irregular text which have a large variance in their appearance. This may be because the learned text representation in our proposed method is largely invariant of the other nuisance factors, thus makes different text images are maximally distinguishable. In order to further verify the robustness and generalization capability of our proposed method, we provide more testing of our method on challenging irregular text recognition tasks in 4.4.

4.4 Results and Comparisons on Irregular Text Benchmarks

In this section, we evaluate our proposed algorithm on the irregular text scenarios to verify its effectiveness. We use the same model trained on the Synth90 dataset without fine-tuning. All models are evaluated without a lexicon. The two standard irregular text benchmark datasets are SVT-Perspective [25] and CUTE80 [26].

SVT-Perspective: (SVT-Perspective) contains 639 cropped images for testing, which is specially designed for evaluating the performance of perspective text recognition. Test samples are selected from side view angles in Google Street View. Thus most of them are heavily deformed by perspective distortion.

CUTE80: (CUTE80) contains 288 cropped word images for testing, which is collected from 80 high-resolution images taken in the natural scene. This dataset is specially designed for evaluating curved text recognition.

Table 5 summarizes the recognition performance on the SVT-Perspective and CUTE80 datasets. In comparison with other existing methods, which use the same training set, our method outperforms them by a large margin in all cases. Furthermore, recall the results in Table 4, compared with the baseline CRNN model, on SVT-Perspective our proposed method outperforms CRNN by an even larger margin than it does for SVT benchmark. The reason is that the SVT-Perspective dataset mainly consists of the perspective text, which is more challenging and inappropriate for direct recognition. Our synthetically-supervised feature learning can significantly alleviate this problem.

It worth noting that we achieve a significant improvement over RARE [28], which is a method designed specifically for irregular text. Our proposed model is simple and effective to address various kinds of irregular text in a unified way by learning from auxiliary 'clean' image. In addition, our methods does not need to detect the fiducial points and rectify the images before the image recognition procedure as is done in RARE. This further indicates that the learned text feature in our model is more robust to the variance of nuisance factors, i.e., the curved shape or the perspective angles. We also present some visual examples to compare the quality of the rectified images by RARE and generated image by our proposed method in Fig. 4. For given input examples listed in the first column, the second column represents the rectified images achieved by RARE, and the third column shows the generated images obtained by our image generator. We observe that our generated image is closer to a canonical view of the original input image, which eliminates off most of the appearance variance of the nuisance factors. In contrast to the RARE method, we do not use the generated image as a pre-processed step before the sequential text recognition. The generation of 'clean' image only aims to guide the feature learning.

In Fig. 5, we present some interesting examples to show some challenging and failure cases. Figure 5(a) shows some challenging examples our model makes a correct prediction, which shows that our model is robust to the undesired occlusion, background variation, geometric deformation in both the image generation and text decoding task. Figure 5(b) demonstrates some failure cases, which reveals that the prediction accuracy is always linked to the quality of the generated image closely. For instance, for the word 'phil', the second character in our generated image is similar to the character 'i', which is misclassified to 'i' in the prediction. For the input image 'i8', we predict its label to '18', which shows our model implicitly understands that numbers always appear together, which might comes from the bias in the training samples. In most cases, the predict result is consistent with the characters appears in the generated image. Most misclassified samples contain a short text or has a very low resolution.

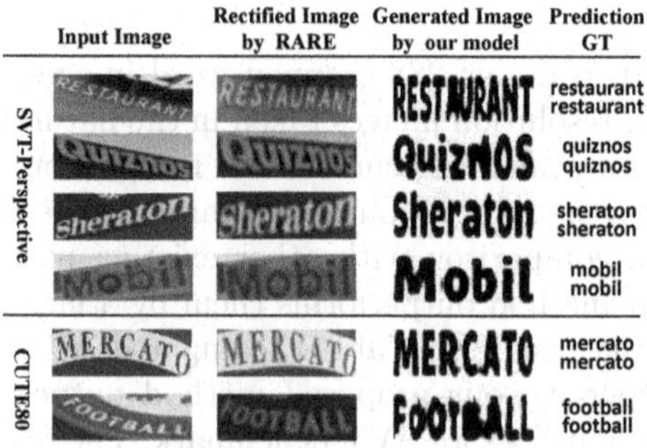

Fig. 4. Comparison of image rectification effects using our generative model versus the transformation model of RARE [28]. Our model correctly recognizes all these challenging examples.

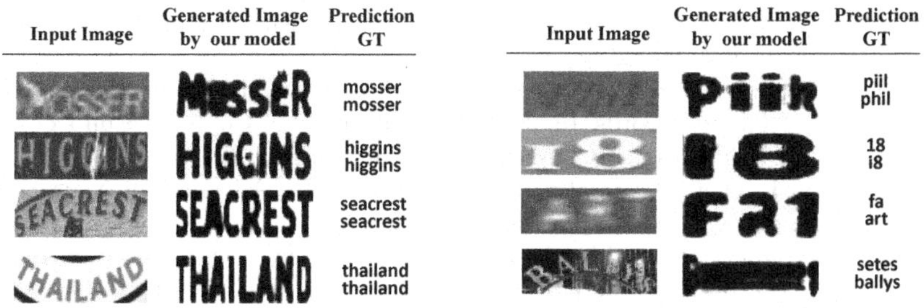

Input Image	Generated Image by our model	Prediction GT
		mosser mosser
		higgins higgins
		seacrest seacrest
		thailand thailand

(a) Successful Cases

Input Image	Generated Image by our model	Prediction GT
		piil phil
		18 i8
		fa art
		setes ballys

(b) Failure Cases

Fig. 5. Examples showing the images our model generated and the recognition results. In each sub-figure, the left column is the input images; the middle column is the generated image; the right column is the recognized text and the ground truth text. Blue and red characters are correctly and mistakenly recognized characters. (Color figure online)

5 Conclusions

We have presented a novel algorithm for scene text recognition. The core novelties of our method are the use of "clean" images that are readily available from the synthetic data generation process and a novel multi-task network with an encoder-generator-discriminator-decoder architecture that guides image feature learning by using clean images. We show that our method significantly outperforms the state-of-the-art methods on standard scene text recognition benchmarks. Furthermore, we show that without explicit handling, our method works on challenging cases where input images contain severe geometric distortion, such as text on a curved path. Future work might include studies on how different clean images may affect the performance of the recognition algorithm, how to use other parameters of the data generation process, such as font, as auxiliary data for feature learning, and how to train end-to-end systems that combine both text detection and recognition in this framework.

References

1. Almazán, J., Gordo, A., Fornés, A., Valveny, E.: Word spotting and recognition with embedded attributes. IEEE Trans. Pattern Anal. Mach. Intell. **36**(12), 2552–2566 (2014)
2. Berthelot, D., Schumm, T., Metz, L.: Began: boundary equilibrium generative adversarial networks. arXiv preprint arXiv:1703.10717 (2017)
3. Bissacco, A., Cummins, M., Netzer, Y., Neven, H.: PhotoOCR: reading text in uncontrolled conditions. In: 2013 IEEE International Conference on Computer Vision (ICCV), pp. 785–792. IEEE (2013)
4. Cheng, Z., Bai, F., Xu, Y., Zheng, G., Pu, S., Zhou, S.: Focusing attention: towards accurate text recognition in natural images. In: 2017 IEEE International Conference on Computer Vision (ICCV), pp. 5086–5094. IEEE (2017)

5. Ghosh, S.K., Valveny, E., Bagdanov, A.D.: Visual attention models for scene text recognition. In: ICDAR (2017)
6. Goel, V., Mishra, A., Alahari, K., Jawahar, C.: Whole is greater than sum of parts: recognizing scene text words. In: 2013 12th International Conference on Document Analysis and Recognition (ICDAR), pp. 398–402. IEEE (2013)
7. Goodfellow, I., et al.: Generative adversarial nets. In: Advances in Neural Information Processing Systems, pp. 2672–2680 (2014)
8. Gordo, A.: Supervised mid-level features for word image representation. In: Proceedings of the IEEE Conference on Computer Vision and Pattern Recognition, pp. 2956–2964 (2015)
9. Graves, A., Fernández, S., Gomez, F., Schmidhuber, J.: Connectionist temporal classification: labelling unsegmented sequence data with recurrent neural networks. In: Proceedings of the 23rd International Conference on Machine Learning, pp. 369–376. ACM (2006)
10. Graves, A., Mohamed, A.R., Hinton, G.: Speech recognition with deep recurrent neural networks. In: 2013 IEEE International Conference on Acoustics, Speech and Signal Processing (ICASSP), pp. 6645–6649. IEEE (2013)
11. Hochreiter, S., Schmidhuber, J.: Long short-term memory. Neural Comput. **9**(8), 1735–1780 (1997)
12. https://www.freetype.org
13. Isola, P., Zhu, J.Y., Zhou, T., Efros, A.A.: Image-to-image translation with conditional adversarial networks. arXiv preprint (2017)
14. Jaderberg, M., Simonyan, K., Vedaldi, A., Zisserman, A.: Synthetic data and artificial neural networks for natural scene text recognition. In: NIPS Deep Learning Workshop (2014)
15. Jaderberg, M., Vedaldi, A., Zisserman, A.: Deep features for text spotting. In: Fleet, D., Pajdla, T., Schiele, B., Tuytelaars, T. (eds.) ECCV 2014. LNCS, vol. 8692, pp. 512–528. Springer, Cham (2014). https://doi.org/10.1007/978-3-319-10593-2_34
16. Jaderberg, M., Simonyan, K., Vedaldi, A., Zisserman, A.: Deep structured output learning for unconstrained text recognition. In: International Conference on Learning Representations (2015)
17. Jaderberg, M., Simonyan, K., Vedaldi, A., Zisserman, A.: Reading text in the wild with convolutional neural networks. Int. J. Comput. Vis. **116**(1), 1–20 (2016)
18. Karatzas, D., et al.: ICDAR 2013 robust reading competition. In: 2013 12th International Conference on Document Analysis and Recognition (ICDAR), pp. 1484–1493. IEEE (2013)
19. Kingma, D.P., Ba, J.: Adam: a method for stochastic optimization. In: ICLR (2015)
20. Lee, C.Y., Osindero, S.: Recursive recurrent nets with attention modeling for ocr in the wild. In: Proceedings of the IEEE Conference on Computer Vision and Pattern Recognition, pp. 2231–2239 (2016)
21. Lucas, S.M., et al.: ICDAR 2003 robust reading competitions: entries, results, and future directions. Int. J. Doc. Anal. Recognit. (IJDAR) **7**(2–3), 105–122 (2005)
22. Mirza, M., Osindero, S.: Conditional generative adversarial nets. arXiv preprint arXiv:1411.1784 (2014)
23. Mishra, A., Alahari, K., Jawahar, C.: Scene text recognition using higher order language priors. In: BMVC 2012–23rd British Machine Vision Conference. BMVA (2012)
24. Peng, X., Yu, X., Sohn, K., Metaxas, D.N., Chandraker, M.: Reconstruction-based disentanglement for pose-invariant face recognition. Intervals **20**, 12 (2017)

25. Phan, T.Q., Shivakumara, P., Tian, S., Tan, C.L.: Recognizing text with perspective distortion in natural scenes. In: 2013 IEEE International Conference on Computer Vision (ICCV), pp. 569–576. IEEE (2013)
26. Risnumawan, A., Shivakumara, P., Chan, C.S., Tan, C.L.: A robust arbitrary text detection system for natural scene images. Expert. Syst. Appl. **41**(18), 8027–8048 (2014)
27. Shi, B., Bai, X., Yao, C.: An end-to-end trainable neural network for image-based sequence recognition and its application to scene text recognition. IEEE Trans. Pattern Anal. Mach. Intell. **39**(11), 2298–2304 (2017)
28. Shi, B., Wang, X., Lyu, P., Yao, C., Bai, X.: Robust scene text recognition with automatic rectification. In: Proceedings of the IEEE Conference on Computer Vision and Pattern Recognition, pp. 4168–4176 (2016)
29. Su, B., Lu, S.: Accurate scene text recognition based on recurrent neural network. In: Cremers, D., Reid, I., Saito, H., Yang, M.-H. (eds.) ACCV 2014. LNCS, vol. 9003, pp. 35–48. Springer, Cham (2015). https://doi.org/10.1007/978-3-319-16865-4_3
30. Tran, L., Yin, X., Liu, X.: Disentangled representation learning GAN for pose-invariant face recognition. In: CVPR (2017)
31. Wang, K., Babenko, B., Belongie, S.: End-to-end scene text recognition. In: 2011 IEEE International Conference on Computer Vision (ICCV), pp. 1457–1464. IEEE (2011)
32. Wang, T., Wu, D.J., Coates, A., Ng, A.Y.: End-to-end text recognition with convolutional neural networks. In: ICPR (2012)
33. Yao, C., Bai, X., Shi, B., Liu, W.: Strokelets: a learned multi-scale representation for scene text recognition. In: Proceedings of the IEEE Conference on Computer Vision and Pattern Recognition, pp. 4042–4049 (2014)
34. Ye, Q., Doermann, D.: Text detection and recognition in imagery: a survey. IEEE Trans. Pattern Anal. Mach. Intell. **37**(7), 1480–1500 (2015)
35. Yim, J., Jung, H., Yoo, B., Choi, C., Park, D., Kim, J.: Rotating your face using multi-task deep neural network. In: Proceedings of the IEEE Conference on Computer Vision and Pattern Recognition, pp. 676–684 (2015)
36. Yin, X.C., Zuo, Z.Y., Tian, S., Liu, C.L.: Text detection, tracking and recognition in video: a comprehensive survey. IEEE Trans. Image Process. **25**(6), 2752–2773 (2016)
37. Zhou, X., et al.: East: an efficient and accurate scene text detector. arXiv preprint arXiv:1704.03155 (2017)
38. Zhu, Y., Yao, C., Bai, X.: Scene text detection and recognition: recent advances and future trends. Front. Comput. Sci. **10**, 19–36 (2016)

Probabilistic Video Generation Using Holistic Attribute Control

Jiawei He[1(✉)], Andreas Lehrmann[2], Joseph Marino[3], Greg Mori[1], and Leonid Sigal[4]

[1] Simon Fraser University, Burnaby, Canada
jha203@sfu.ca
[2] Disney Research, Pittsburgh, USA
[3] California Institute of Technology, Pasadena, USA
[4] The University of British Columbia, Vancouver, Canada

Abstract. Videos express highly structured spatio-temporal patterns of visual data. A video can be thought of as being governed by two factors: (i) temporally invariant (*e.g.*, person identity), or slowly varying (*e.g.*, activity), attribute-induced appearance, encoding the persistent content of each frame, and (ii) an inter-frame motion or scene dynamics (*e.g.*, encoding evolution of the person executing the action). Based on this intuition, we propose a generative framework for video generation and future prediction. The proposed framework generates a video (short clip) by decoding samples sequentially drawn from a latent space distribution into full video frames. Variational Autoencoders (VAEs) are used as a means of encoding/decoding frames into/from the latent space and RNN as a way to model the dynamics in the latent space. We improve the video generation *consistency* through temporally-conditional sampling and *quality* by structuring the latent space with attribute controls; ensuring that attributes can be both inferred and conditioned on during learning/generation. As a result, given attributes and/or the first frame, our model is able to generate diverse but highly consistent sets of video sequences, accounting for the inherent uncertainty in the prediction task. Experimental results on three challenging datasets, along with detailed comparison to the state-of-the-art, verify effectiveness of the framework.

1 Introduction

Deep generative models, such as variational autoencoders (VAEs) [4] and generative adversarial networks (GANs) [5], have recently received increased attention [6–9] due to their probabilistic and unsupervised nature and their ability to synthesize large numbers of interdependent variables from compact representations. Impressive results have been achieved in a broad range of domains,

J. He—Work conducted at Disney Research.

Electronic supplementary material The online version of this chapter (https://doi.org/10.1007/978-3-030-01228-1_28) contains supplementary material, which is available to authorized users.

V. Ferrari et al. (Eds.): ECCV 2018, LNCS 11209, pp. 466–483, 2018.
https://doi.org/10.1007/978-3-030-01228-1_28

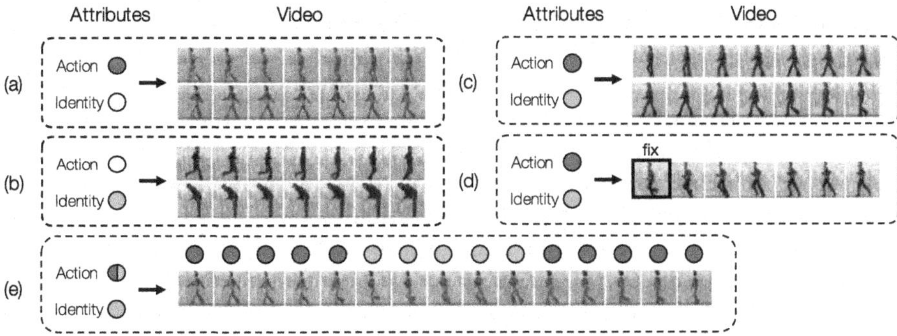

Fig. 1. Video generation using attribute control. Our framework uses a semi-supervised latent space containing a fixed number of control signals to steer the generation. Setting one (a–b) or both (c) of the attributes 'action' and 'identity' to a desired or inferred category (colored circles) constrains the generative process, but takes advantage of the remaining degrees of freedom to synthesize diverse video samples. In (d), conditioning on both attributes as well as the first frame effectively removes all uncertainty (degrees of freedom) in the generation process. In (e) attribute transition from 'walking' to 'running' and back to 'walking' is induced at the 6th and 11th frame, resulting in the illustrated corresponding transition within the generated video. (Color figure online)

including image generation [10], text synthesis [11], and text-based image synthesis [12,13].

Despite the impressive progress towards better image generation, including controlled attribute-based models [13,14], it still remains a challenge to generate videos. Video generation models are inherently useful for building spatio-temporal priors, forecasting [7,9,15], and unsupervised feature learning [16]. Although a video can usually be represented as a sequence of temporally coherent images, the extension from image generation to video generation is surprisingly difficult.

In videos, in addition to individual frames containing plausible object/scene arrangements, the motions of those objects and scene elements, over time, need to be coherent and plausible as well. This is complicated because some motions might be very local (smile on a face), while others global (waves running onto a beach). Further, there are inherent ambiguities in the potential resulting motion patterns. Meaning, given the same input (*e.g.*, first frame of a person standing) a multitude of plausible futures may realistically unfold (*e.g.*, he/she may continue to stand, may start walking, may walk and then sit). Nevertheless, each one of those future predictions is self consistent. For example, once we start predicting that a person is walking, he/she should continue to walk for some nominal number of frames before a transition is plausible. Therefore a generative video model should have the following properties: (1) it should be able to model diversity of future predictions; (2) each future prediction, which corresponds to a sample from the generative model, should be self-consistent.

We introduce a novel framework **VideoVAE** based on variational autoencoders (VAEs). At each time-step, the VAE encodes the visual input into a high-dimensional latent distribution. This distribution is passed to a long short-term memory (LSTM) to encode the motion expressed in the latent space. At every time-step the resulting latent distribution can be sampled and decoded back into a full image. In order to improve the consistency within a generated sequence and also to control the generation process, we expand the latent space in VAEs into a structured latent space with holistic attribute control. The holistic attribute control can be specified or inferred from data; it can be fixed over time, or can exhibit sparse transitions (see Fig. 1). The hierarchical conditional posterior distributions proposed in the structured latent space thus make predictions conditioned on multiple crucial information sources. In addition, conditional sampling is proposed to utilize the previous samples to generate temporally-coherent sequences. Experiments on three challenging data sets show that these techniques effectively address criteria (1) and (2) above and can generate promising videos of plausible objects with various motions.

2 Related Work

We build upon research in style-content models, deep generative models, semantic latent representations, and video synthesis.

Style-Content Models. Our approach is implicitly related to the rich literature on style-content separation (a problem introduced in [17]); in our case a distribution over the *content*, in each frame, is being parameterized by attribute factors that affect the latent state and *style* is modelled by the motion patterns that result from dynamics encoded by an RNN. Bilinear [17], nonlinear [18,19] and factored models [20] have been used in the past, but assumed deterministic linear dynamics in the latent space (*e.g.*, GPDM [19]) and relatively simple temporal signals (*e.g.*, motion capture sequences [19,20] or foreground segmentations [18]).

Deep Generative Models. Deep generative models (DGMs) use unlabeled data to learn parameters of a deep topology with compact features. As a prominent member, variational autoencoders (VAEs) optimize the well-known encoder-decoder architecture [4,21] using a variational objective, possibly conditioned on an auxiliary input [22]. Their principled design, as well as generative capabilities, have led to a fast adoption and impressive extensions along several axes: A semi-supervised VAE was proposed in [23]. Hierarchical versions aim at increasing the capacity of VAEs and include [11] and [10]. The expressiveness of the approximate posterior can be increased through normalizing flows [24] and its derivatives [25]. Recurrent frameworks using VAEs as a base model [26] are inherently close to our work. However, previous works do not model the non-trivial nature of videos: objects/scenes remain the same within a short video clip. Also, prior methods usually only aim to model synthesized objects with simple motions.

Semantic Latent Representations. Semantic latent spaces are interesting, useful, and have a long history in vision and graphics [27]. Recently, [28] utilized the *graphics code* (a set of pre-defined latent codes) for interpretable representation learning. However, the predefined graphics code constrains the system to the parameterized renderable class of objects. Alternatively, [6] uses mutual information to enforce correspondence between parts of the latent space and attributes. In an unsupervised effort, [29] up-weights the KL divergence term in the variational lower bound; when combined with a standard factorized Gaussian prior, this encourages additional independence between the latent variables. Similarly, [8] uses a hierarchy of latent variables to learn a set of independent hierarchical features. Finally, in [13] a disentangled latent representation is used to generate images conditioned on attributes.

Video Synthesis. Several very recent works have been proposed to tackle video synthesis. For example, [9,15] predict uncertain future frames from a static image input. However, such (extremely) short-term predictions are unable to model motion. In a somewhat different task, [30] uses GANs to model motions, and [31] uses VAE to predict trajectories of pedestrians. Related, [32] uses RNNs in the encoder and decoder, as well as a feedforward network in the prior, to model video and other dynamic data, particularly for counter-factual reasoning. In [33], the authors use a VAE to encode linear dynamics in the latent space for videos of basic physics phenomena; [34] uses an additional set of discrete latent variables to model linear dynamics in the latent space. Finally, [35] proposes a probabilistic video model that estimates the discrete joint distribution of the raw pixel values in a video. However, these models lack a natural latent structure to capture semantic-level information.

Contributions. Our key contribution is a novel generative video model – **VideoVAE**. VideoVAE is based on the variational autoencoder (VAE), which provides probabilistic methods of encoding/decoding full frames into/from a compact latent state. The motion of the resulting distribution in the latent space, accounting for the motion in the video, is modeled using an LSTM. At every time-step the structured latent distribution can be sampled and decoded back into a full frame. To improve the quality of the inference and generation, we propose a factoring of the latent space into holistic attribute controls and residual information; control variables can either be observed (specified) or inferred from the first frame or snippet of the video (allowing semi-supervised training). Further, since both dynamics and appearance can be multimodal, to avoid jumps among the modes, we propose conditional sampling which facilitates self-consistent sequence generation. Experiments on three challenging datasets show that our proposed model can generate plausible videos that are quantifiably better than state-of-the-art.

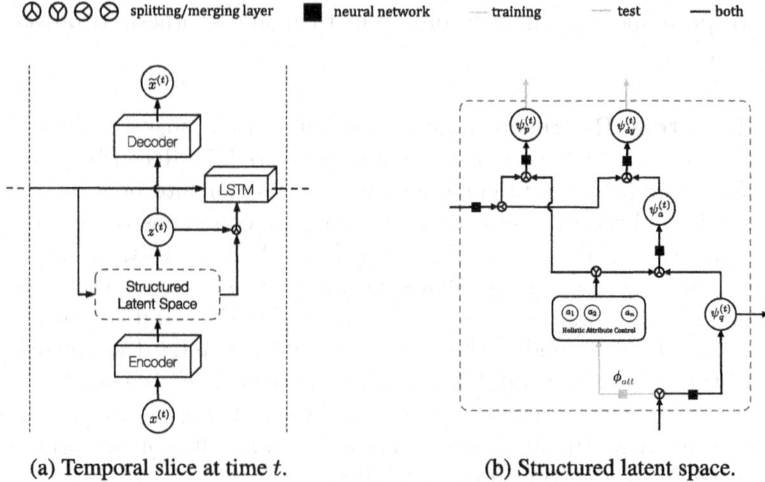

(a) Temporal slice at time t.

(b) Structured latent space.

Fig. 2. Overview. (a) A structured latent representation of a variational autoencoder (VAE; [4]) encodes a conditional approximate posterior that is propagated through time with the help of a long short-term memory (LSTM; [36]). (b) Detailed view of the dashed box in (a): In a hierarchical process, holistic attributes are first merged with the variational approximate posterior and then integrated with temporal information from the LSTM, effectively resulting in a doubly-conditional dynamic approximate posterior. We denote the parameters of these distributions as $\psi_\bullet^{(t)} := [\mu_\bullet^{(t)}, \sigma_\bullet^{(t)}]$, where $\mu_\bullet^{(t)}$ and $\sigma_\bullet^{(t)}$ are the mean and covariance of a multivariate Gaussian, respectively. Information flow only available during specific phases is highlighted as ↑ for training and ↑ for testing. The prior distribution $\psi_p^{(t)}$, for instance, is only used to calculate the KL-loss at training time but as a sampling distribution for $z^{(t)}$ at test time.

3 Probabilistic Video Generation

We will now describe our proposed model (Fig. 2). At a high level, VideoVAE models spatio-temporal sequences by building upon VAE as a spatial model and LSTM as a temporal model, *i.e.*, each frame is encoded into a latent distribution (representing appearance dependencies within a frame) that is fed into a recurrent neural network (modeling motion dynamics across frames). We will first provide a brief summary of the two base models (Sect. 3.1) and then discuss our contributions that result in coherent and controllable video generation: a structured latent space with holistic attribute control (Sect. 3.2) and a conditional variational posterior (Sect. 3.3).

3.1 Background: Base Models

Variational Autoencoder (VAE). A VAE [4] describes an instance of a generative process with simple prior $p_\theta(z)$ (*e.g.*, Gaussian) and complex likelihood $p_\theta(x|z)$ (*e.g.*, a neural network) in which z is a latent and x is an observed variable. Approximating the intractable posterior $p_\theta(z|x)$ with a variational neural network $q_\phi(z|x)$, we can jointly optimize over θ and ϕ by maximizing the variational lower bound $\mathcal{L}$ on the marginal likelihood $p_\theta(x^{(t)})$ of a video frame $x^{(t)}$,

$$\begin{aligned} \log p_\theta(x^{(t)}) &= \mathrm{KL}(q_\phi \| p_\theta) + \mathcal{L}(\theta, \phi) \\ &\geq \mathcal{L}(\theta, \phi) = -\mathbb{E}_{q_\phi}\left[\log \frac{q_\phi(z|x^{(t)})}{p_\theta(z, x^{(t)})}\right]. \end{aligned} \tag{1}$$

From an autoencoder point of view, we can think of the approximate posterior q_ϕ as an encoder and the likelihood p_θ as a decoder. Generating a video frame corresponds to decoding a sample from the prior.

Long Short-Term Memory (LSTM). While VAEs are a powerful framework for modeling static video frames, they fail to model the motion dynamics between frames in a video. Long short-term memory (LSTM) [36], a form of a recurrent neural network, is able to capture such dynamic dependencies. An LSTM consists of two components: (1) a transition function f_h that determines the evolution of an internal hidden state; (2) a mapping from the internal hidden state to an output. The transition function of a standard LSTM is entirely deterministic,

$$h^{(t)} = f_h(v^{(t)}, h^{(t-1)}), \tag{2}$$

where $v^{(t)}$ and $h^{(t)}$ are the LSTM input and hidden state at time t, respectively.

3.2 Spatial Model

Frames in a video typically exhibit both transient and persistent characteristics. For example, identity and action of a subject are likely to remain fixed (persistent) in a short clip, while the limbs of the person are likely to move (transient) as he/she performs the action. Modeling video using a simple VAE+RNN [26] combination effectively models all frame appearance at the temporal granularity of a frame. This often leads to artifacts during generation, like undesired identity changes. To address this, we structure the latent space by introducing *holistic attribute controls.* The key benefit of such control variables is that they are persistent, meaning that they either stay fixed or change extremely infrequently with respect to the frame rate of the video. The following two paragraphs describe holistic attribute controls in more detail and show their hierarchical integration with residual and temporal information (Fig. 2b).

Holistic Attribute Control. Holistic attributes $\mathbf{a} = (a_i)_i$ are a set of predefined attributes that do not change with time.[1] Examples include the person identities in human action sequences or the scene labels in generic video clips. These fixed attribute variables $\mathbf{a}$ cast holistic control on the entire generated

[1] They do not change with time unless explicitly asked to, *e.g.*, to control the temporal content of a synthesized clip, as demonstrated in Fig. 4.

video sequence and can, in general, be of various types: categorical, discrete or continuous. Their state can be clamped to a desired value, inferred from data, or even derived from some external data source. In this work, the controls are inferred in a semi-supervised manner at training time and set as fixed during generation.

Training. Since the VAE encoder ϕ_{enc} already maps the input images $x^{(1:T)}$ to a set of latent features $\phi_{enc}\left(x^{(1:T)}\right)$, we infer the attributes a_i from those representations by adding a small classification network $\phi_{att}^{(i)}$ for each attribute after the encoder.[2] This is illustrated by the lower orange arrow in Fig. 2b and can be expressed as

$$a_i = \phi_{att}^{(i)}\left(\phi_{enc}\left(x^{(1:T)}\right)\right). \tag{3}$$

The image encoder ϕ_{enc} and attribute classifiers $\boldsymbol{\phi}_{att} = \{\phi_{att}^{(i)}\}_i$ are learned independently, which allows easy pretraining of the attribute inference and quick adaption to new attributes. Another advantage of this setting is that it makes it possible to utilize a subset of labeled training data to learn $\boldsymbol{\phi}_{att}$ and generalize to the remaining (unlabeled) training instances with the same attributes, leading to a semi-supervised training scenario. In general, we observed that label information for about 20% of the training data is sufficient to infer the remaining attributes. Once the attributes are inferred for each video in the training set, they are used as fixed controls during VideoVAE training (Sect. 4).

Testing. The attributes are set as fixed to cast holistic control over the generation process. They could be a single label (*e.g.*, "walking") or a sequence of labels (*e.g.*, "walking" – "running"– "skipping") associated with specific frames to cast transient control.

Conditional Approximate Posterior. Traditional VAEs encode the data into an approximate posterior distribution and sample from a prior to synthesize novel data. This works well in image generation, since each synthesized image can be sampled independently. However, in video generation, successive samples should be temporally coherent. In other words, samples should be drawn conditioned on previous information and also the order of the samples matters. The latent code z should combine this type of frame-level consistency with the sequence-level consistency provided by the holistic control variables discussed above.

Based on these observations, we propose the following structured latent space, which comprises a set of hierarchical approximate posterior distributions (Fig. 2b):

(1) an initial approximate posterior distribution, $\mathcal{N}(\mu_q^{(t)}, \sigma_q^{(t)})$, conceptually modeling residual information not captured by holistic attributes;

[2] Each network consists of two fully-connected layers with a central ReLU unit, connected in time by an LSTM. This LSTM for attribute inference is independent of the main LSTM modelling motion dynamics.

(2) a conditional approximate posterior, $\mathcal{N}(\mu_a^{(t)}, \sigma_a^{(t)})$, encoding the full appearance of the frame, combining holistic attribute control with the residual posterior above;
(3) a dynamic approximate posterior, $\mathcal{N}(\mu_{dy}^{(t)}, \sigma_{dy}^{(t)})$, which further incorporates motion information and enforces a temporally coherent trajectory. Please refer to Sect. 3.3 for more details on the integration of temporal information.

The three distributions can be expressed in terms of the encoded input, the attributes, and the LSTM state,

$$\begin{aligned}\psi_q^{(t)} &= [\mu_q^{(t)}, \sigma_q^{(t)}] = \phi_\tau(\phi_{enc}(x^{(t)})),\\ \psi_a^{(t)} &= [\mu_a^{(t)}, \sigma_a^{(t)}] = \phi_\tau(\psi_q^{(t)}, \mathbf{a}),\\ \psi_{dy}^{(t)} &= [\mu_{dy}^{(t)}, \sigma_{dy}^{(t)}] = \phi_\tau(\psi_a^{(t)}, \phi_\tau(h^{(t-1)})).\end{aligned} \tag{4}$$

Here, ϕ_τ refers to a neural network with an architecture similar to the attribute inference network (two fully-connected layers with a central ReLU unit, but no LSTM). Separate instances of ϕ_τ (black boxes in Fig. 2b) along the hierarchical chain of our structured latent space share this architecture but have different weights.

3.3 Temporal Model

VideoVAE contains a VAE at each timestep and propagates information between timesteps with an LSTM to capture the motion dynamics in videos. The following two paragraphs discuss the integration of this temporal information with respect to the encoder and decoder of the VAE at time t. An illustration of this interaction is depicted in Fig. 2a.

Decoder. The latent variational representations at time-step t are conditioned on the state variable $h^{(t-1)}$ of the LSTM. This additional dependency takes advantage of the fact that videos are highly temporally consistent and prevents the content and motion between two consecutive frames from changing too quickly. As the prior distribution $\psi_p^{(t)}$ represents the model's prediction and belief at timestep t given all previous information, it should not be a fixed Gaussian (as is the case in static VAEs) but follow the distribution

$$[\mu_p^{(t)}, \sigma_p^{(t)}] = \phi_\tau(\phi_\tau(h^{(t-1)}), \mathbf{a}), \tag{5}$$

where $\mu_p^{(t)}$ and $\sigma_p^{(t)}$ denote the parameters of the prior distribution at timestep t. With this setting, under the assumption that the LSTM hidden state $h^{(t-1)}$ contains all necessary information from $x^{(<t)}$, the prior distribution at timestep t becomes $p(z^{(t)}|x^{(<t)})$. This distribution changes with time and effectively represents the *prediction* of the current time-step given previous information.

Similarly, the output distribution is updated according to

$$\begin{aligned} z^{(t)} &\sim \mathcal{N}(\mu_{dy}^{(t)}, \sigma_{dy}^{(t)}), \\ [\mu_x^{(t)}, \sigma_x^{(t)}] &= \phi_{dec}(z^{(t)}), \\ \tilde{x}^{(t)} | z^{(t)} &\sim \mathcal{N}(\mu_x^{(t)}, \sigma_x^{(t)}), \end{aligned} \tag{6}$$

where $\mu_x^{(t)}, \sigma_x^{(t)}$ denote the parameters of the output distribution and $\tilde{x}^{(t)}$ the reconstruction of the input $x^{(t)}$ at time t.

Encoder. At each timestep, the frame input $x^{(t)}$ is mapped by the encoder function ϕ_{enc} to the hierarchical latent space (Fig. 2b), from which the decoder samples

$$z^{(t)} | x^{(t)} \sim \mathcal{N}(\mu_{dy}^{(t)}, \sigma_{dy}^{(t)}), \tag{7}$$

where the dynamic approximate posterior is given by Eq. (4).

Conditional Sampling. In the temporal framework described thus far, only the distribution $\mathcal{N}(\mu_q^{(t)}, \sigma_q^{(t)})$ is passed to the LSTM. In other words, the samples at each time-step are not passed along time, and are thus independent, resulting in temporally inconsistent sequences (*e.g.*, in terms of the attributes expressed in a decoded RGB frame). Following intuition from LSTM-based language decoders [37], we introduce conditional sampling to address this problem. In addition to the initial approximate posterior distribution $\mathcal{N}(\mu_q^{(t)}, \sigma_q^{(t)})$, sample $z^{(t)}$ is also passed to the LSTM (Fig. 2a). The hidden state of the LSTM is therefore updated according to

$$h^{(t)} = f_h(\psi_q^{(t)}, z^{(t)}, h^{(t-1)}). \tag{8}$$

In this way, based on the past information, a reasonable initial guess of where the sample $z^{(t+1)}$ should be in $\mathcal{N}(\mu_{dy}^{(t+1)}, \sigma_{dy}^{(t+1)})$ is provided. Notably, due to the VAE structure of our model, this change requires no changes to the architecture itself, as compared to, for example, language translation models. The effectiveness of this conditional sampling scheme to improve the consistency of the generated sequences will be shown in Sect. 5.

4 Learning and Synthesis

4.1 Learning

We follow a two-stage training strategy. As discussed in Sect. 3.2, we first use approximately 20% of the training data to train the holistic attribute classifiers $\boldsymbol{\phi}_{att}$ using a cross entropy loss. Once $\boldsymbol{\phi}_{att}$ is trained, it is used to infer the holistic attributes for the rest of the training set. This part of the training process is thus semi-supervised. The inferred attributes are then considered as fixed during training of the VideoVAE model, the objective function of which becomes a timestep-wise variational lower bound,

$$\mathcal{L} = \mathbb{E}_{q(z^{(\leq t)}|x^{(\leq t)})}[\sum_{t=1}^{T}(\log p(x^{(t)}|z^{(\leq t)}, x^{(<t)}) \\ -\mathrm{KL}(q(z^{(t)}|x^{(\leq t)}, z^{(<t)}))||p(z^{(t)}|x^{(<t)}, z^{(<t)})]. \tag{9}$$

We optimize Eq. (9) using a pixel-wise L_1-loss with standard SGD techniques [38]. The first part is the log-likelihood of the generated data distribution and the second part is the KL divergence between the prior distribution and the approximate posterior distribution at time-step t. A full derivation of the objective function is included in the supplementary material.

4.2 Synthesis

In order to generate a video, *i.e.*, at test time, we adapt the architecture described in Sect. 3 as illustrated in Fig. 2: First, the holistic attributes are not inferred from the input data, as is the case during training, because there is no input data at test time. Instead, we choose and fix a set of desired holistic attributes to steer the generative process. Second, the sample is not drawn from the dynamic approximate posterior distribution, but from the prior distribution at each time-step, following standard VAE practice. The samples are then decoded into an output frame and fed back into the network.

We further propose two different methods to initialize the generative process:

- **Holistic attribute controls only:** in this setting, only partial or full holistic attribute controls are provided (Fig. 1(a)–(c)). The initial LSTM state $h^{(0)}$ is randomly initialized and the first generated frame is sampled and decoded from the distribution $[\mu_p^{(1)}, \sigma_p^{(1)}] = \phi_\tau(\phi_\tau(h^{(0)}), \mathbf{a})$.
- **Holistic attribute controls & first frame:** in this setting, in addition to the holistic attribute controls, the first frame is also provided (Fig. 1(d)). The first generated frame, in this case, is the reconstruction of the input, and the rest of the generation follows Eq. 5. Typically, conditioning on the first frame improves the generation quality as it provides the framework more precise information.

5 Experiments

We conduct qualitative and quantitative experiments on multiple datasets to evaluate the proposed framework. After a brief description of the datasets (Sect. 5.1), we describe our evaluation metrics (Sect. 5.2) and validate our contributions in an ablation study and a comprehensive comparison to various baseline models (Sect. 5.3).

5.1 Datasets

We evaluate our model on three datasets: Chair CAD [1], Weizmann Human Action [2], and YFCC [3] – MIT Flickr [16]. These datasets contains various kinds of motion patterns, such as simple rotation, structured human action, or complicated scene-related motions.

Chair CAD [1]**.** The dataset contains 1393 chair-CAD models. We follow [39] and use a subset of 809 chair models in our experiments. Each chair model is rendered from 31 azimuth angles and 2 elevation angles at a fixed distance to the virtual camera. The rendered images are cropped to have a small border and resized to a common size of $64 \times 64 \times 3$ pixels by [39]. In our experiments, we divide the length-31 sequence into 2 length-16 sequences starting from the 16th frame. Altogether, there are four video sequences per chair model. We randomly pick three of them for training, and the last is used for testing generation (conditioned on the first frame).

Weizmann Human Action [2]**.** This dataset contains 90 videos of 9 people performing 10 actions. We cropped each frame to center on the person and resize the frames to the size of $64 \times 64 \times 3$. In order to perform generation conditioned on first frame, we first split each video into training and test subset. The first 2/3 frames of the video are treated as training sequences, and the last 1/3 frames of the video are treated as test sequences. Then we sample 20 mini-clips of length-10 from each training video to form a final training set.

YFCC [3] – **MIT Flickr** [16]**.** The dataset contains 35 million clips and we use a pre-processed subset of this dataset provided by [16], of witch the videos have been stabilized by SIFT+RANSAC and each video clip contains 32 frames. We use two scene categories *beach* and *golf* provided in [16]. Note that these scene categories are filtered by a pre-trained Place-CNN model, so the labels are not as accurate as the labels in other datasets.

5.2 Evaluation Metrics

Quantitative evaluation of generative models is an inherently challenging task. A good generative model should synthesize samples that are both realistic and diverse. Recently, the *Inception Score (I-score)* [40] has been proposed as an evaluation measure reflecting both these criteria. For static images x, it is defined as

$$I = \exp\left(\mathbb{E}_x\left[\mathrm{KL}\left[\rho(y|x)\|\rho(y)\right]\right]\right), \tag{10}$$

where $\rho(y|x)$ is the conditional label distribution of an inception model [41] pre-trained on ImageNet [42]. The entropy of this first term in the KL-divergence measures the confidence of the classifier and the entropy of the second term

$\rho(y)$ measures the diversity of the marginal label distribution over all generated samples.

However, in the video generation field, the lack of a standard model structure and large datasets makes it hard to come up with a universal classifier. Therefore, we pre-train individual classifiers on each dataset. We also believe that the first term $\rho(y|x)$ in Eq. (10) is more important for video generation tasks, since it measures the quality of a generated sequence. Therefore, in addition to the I-score, we analyze both terms separately as follows:

Intra Entropy. Intra-entropy measures the conditional label entropy of a set $\{x_i\}_i$ of generated video sequences. Specifically, we use the pre-trained classifier to obtain a conditional distribution over the attributes $\mathbf{a}$ and compute

$$S_{\text{intra}} = \sum_i \mathrm{H}\left[\rho(\mathbf{a}|x_i)\right]. \tag{11}$$

A smaller value of S_{intra} means that the pre-trained classifier is more confident to classify the generated videos, which indicates that they are more similar to real videos.

Inter Entropy. Inter-Entropy measures the label entropy of a set $\{x_i\}_i$ of generated video sequences. The pre-trained classifier assigns a label $a_j \in \mathbf{a}$ to each sequence, which allows us to compute the entropy of the induced distribution $p(\mathbf{a})$ over the labels,

$$S_{\text{inter}} = \mathrm{H}\left[\rho\left(\mathbf{a}\right)\right]. \tag{12}$$

A larger value of S_{inter} indicates that the distribution over the label space is more uniform, which implies that the generative model can produce diverse samples.

Table 1. Ablation study on Chair CAD [39]. We evaluate our contributions individually and in combination. $+C$ and $+S$ indicate conditional sampling and a structured latent space, respectively. The proposed videoVAE model uses both elements ($+C+S$; last column). Arrows indicate whether lower (↓) or higher (↑) scores are better.

		Bound	Static	$-C$		$+C$	
				$-S$	$+S$	$-S$	$+S$
Intra-E	↓	1.98	40.33	17.64	7.79	14.81	**5.50**
Inter-E	↑	1.39	0.42	0.73	1.35	1.02	**1.37**
I-Score	↑	4.01	1.28	1.83	3.63	2.56	**3.94**

5.3 Video Synthesis

Ablation Study. In order to demonstrate the contribution and effectiveness of each component of our model, we conduct an ablation study on Chair CAD.

Variants. We distinguish five different variations of our model: The static model uses a standard VAE to generate chair images. This model is trained with individual frames in the Chair-CAD dataset. 15 consecutively generated images are then treated as one video sequence. A standard VAE plus temporal model in the form of an LSTM is referred to as $(-C-S)$ in Table 1. An illustration of such a model can be obtained from Fig. 2a by omitting conditional sampling and replacing the structured latent space with a single approximate posterior. Previous VAE-based temporal generative models [26] are of this type. The $(+C-S)$ model adds conditional sampling at each time-step to the temporal model. Specifically, the sample $z^{(t)}$ at time-step t is concatenated with the parameters $\psi_q^{(t)}$ of the latent distribution; the merged information is then treated as the input of the LSTM. The $(-C+S)$ model replaces the latent space in the temporal model with our proposed structured latent space with holistic attribute control. With structured latent space, this model should show superior consistency in a generated video compared with the previous models. Finally, we obtain our full pipeline when both conditional sampling and a structured latent space are used; this is the model shown in Fig. 2. A detailed setup of the individual layers is given in the supplementary material.

Results. As shown in Table 1, each part of our model plays an important role. The static version cannot capture the motion patterns, making it impossible to generate consistent sequences. The $(-C-S)$ variant has an LSTM as a temporal model and can generate relatively consistent video sequences. The performance measures show much better results. However, the single approximate posterior distribution in the latent space cannot separate between different modes. As a consequence, attributes such as actions or identities may change along time. It also tends to generate similar sequences, since the latent space is not uniformly distributed and one or a few modes may take up the majority of the latent space. The structured latent space in the $(-C+S)$ model introduces additional information (holistic attribute control) to the model, and therefore the consistency within a generated video (represented by *Intra-E*) is improved by a large margin. In addition, the attribute control disentangles the latent space to some degree, which empirically prevents the modes from collapsing. The conditional sampling in the $(+C-S)$ model improves the consistency between consequent frames. Finally, the $(+C+S)$ model achieves the best result by combining the benefits of both structured latent space and conditional sampling. Visualizations of all models are included in the supplementary material.

Baseline Comparison. We compare our method to three baseline methods. Since some of the baseline models do not provide their detailed training setup, we only conduct comparison with them on the dataset they reported in the paper. Specifically, we use Deep Rotator [39] as the baseline model for Chair-CAD,

Table 2. Quantitative results. We report Intra-E, Inter-E, and I-Score on three different datasets. All scores are calculated on attribute classifiers pre-trained on each dataset; comparison across datasets is therefore meaningless. The bounds are calculated by utilizing those classifiers on the actual test videos, *i.e.*, they reflect the statistics of real videos. Depending on the baseline protocol, we compute VideoVAE results for de-novo synthesis (○) and/or prediction given the first frame (◉). Arrows indicate whether lower (↓) or higher (↑) scores are better.

		Chair CAD [1,39]		
		Bound	Deep Rot. [39]	VideoVAE (ours)
			◉	◉
Intra-E	↓	1.98	14.68	**5.50**
Inter-E	↑	1.39	1.34	**1.37**
I-Score	↑	4.01	3.39	**3.94**

		Weizmann Human Action [2]			
		Bound	MoCoGAN [7]	VideoVAE (ours)	
			○	○	◉
Intra-E	↓	0.63	23.58	9.53	**9.44**
Inter-E	↑	4.49	2.91	**4.37**	**4.37**
I-Score	↑	89.12	13.87	69.55	**70.10**

		YFCC [3] — MIT Flickr [16]			
		Bound	VGAN [16]	VideoVAE (ours)	
			○	○	◉
Intra-E	↓	30.34	46.96	44.03	**38.20**
Inter-E	↑	0.693	**0.692**	0.691	**0.692**
I-Score	↑	1.87	1.58	1.62	**1.81**

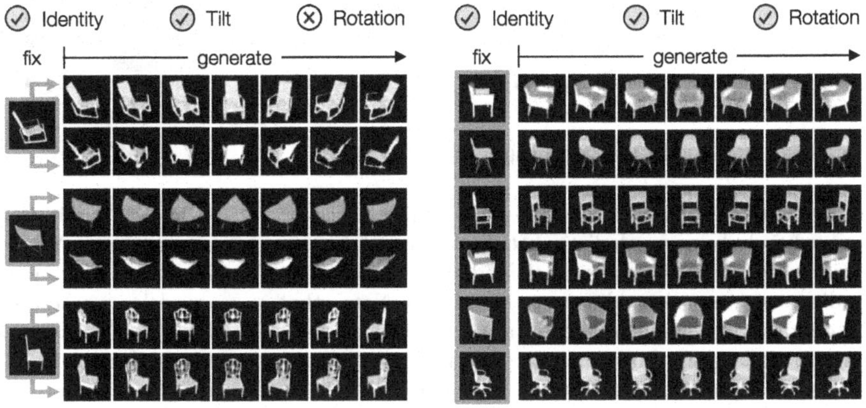

(a) Partial control.

(b) Full control.

Fig. 3. Qualitative results on chair CAD.

MoCoGAN [7] for Weizmann Human Action and VGAN [16] for YFCC-MIT Flickr.

Baseline Models. Deep Rotator uses a simple autoencoder and LSTM structure to generate rotating chairs. However, this framework is limited to simple motions and difficult to generalize. MoCoGAN decomposes the noise vector in GAN models into motion noise and identity noise to separate identity from motion. There are two major drawbacks with this approach: (1) it shows severe mode collapsing, *i.e.*, focuses on a few major motions only; (2) the decomposition limits the approach to scenes with a clear person-action foreground. VGAN uses a two-stream process to generate foreground and background content separately, then combines them into the final video. Although this framework generates prominent foreground objects, the motion and appearance of these objects are usually distorted, unrealistic and exaggerated. VGAN also requires training a model on each category independently.

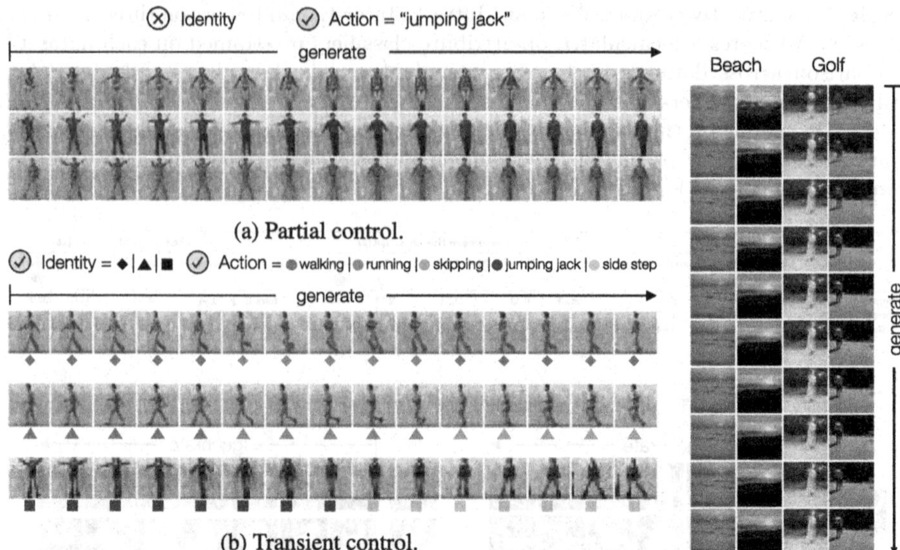

Fig. 4. Qualitative results on Weizmann Human Action. (a) Conditioned on one holistic attribute control (action = "jumping jack"), our model generates the corresponding action using different identities. Note that the identity of a person within a sequence is consistent. (b) Providing both holistic controls but changing the action attribute during the generation process results in smooth transitions between actions. See supplementary material for full-sized video sequences.

Fig. 5. Qualitative results on YFCC – MIT Flickr. Our model generates realistic clips of both scene types. Each column is one sequence. Refer to the supplementary material for additional visualizations.

In our comparison, we use the pre-trained models provided by Deep Rotator and VGAN to generate videos. Since a pre-trained MoCoGAN model is not available, we follow exactly the protocol in [7] to train the model. If the baseline model is deterministic [16,39], we generate an equal number of videos for each class for fair comparison. Since the imperfect quality of the generated sequences lowers the classification accuracy, Inter-E and bound are not the same.

Results. Our quantitative comparisons with the baseline models are given in Table 2. The proposed VideoVAE model consistently and with a large margin (*e.g.*, inception score: 13.87 (MoCoGAN [7]) vs. 69.55 (ours)) outperforms the baseline models by generating high quality but diverse video sequences. The upper/lower bounds on performance (2nd column in Tables 2/1) are calculated by utilizing the pre-trained attribute classifiers on each dataset's real test set; they represent the statistics of real videos. In addition, Fig. 3 shows the generated sequences on Chair-CAD in various control scenarios: given partial attribute control (chair ID and tilt angle in this case), the model generates chairs rotating to different directions (since direction is unspecified), as shown in Fig. 3a; providing all attribute controls removes the remaining degree of freedom corresponding to direction, resulting in the (unimodal) samples shown in Fig. 3b. Figure 4 shows the generated sequences on the human action dataset. In Fig. 4a, we fix the action but leave the identity unspecified (partial control), resulting in videos containing different people performing the same 'jumping jack' action. Also note that holistic controls do not have to be static: Replacing the static controls with a set of time-varying controls (*e.g.*, 'walking-running-walking' instead of 'walking'), we can steer the generative process and synthesize video sequences with smooth transitions between actions, shown in Fig. 4b. Finally, Fig. 5 shows synthetic sequences for two scene types in YFCC-MIT Flickr, illustrating our models capability to handle unconstrained scenes as well. More full-size visualizations and comparisons are provided in the supplementary material.

6 Conclusion

We propose a novel probabilistic generative framework for video generation and future prediction. The proposed framework generates a video (short clip) by decoding samples sequentially drawn from the latent space distribution into full video frames. VAE is used as a means of encoding/decoding frames into/from the latent space and LSTM as a way to model the distribution dynamics in the latent space. We improve the video generation *consistency* through temporally-conditional sampling and *quality* by structuring the latent space with attribute controls. An ablation study illustrates the importance of our contributions and algorithmic choices. Extensive experiments on three challenging datasets show that our proposed model *significantly* outperforms state-of-the-art approaches in video generation; it also enables controlled generation.

References

1. Aubry, M., Maturana, D., Efros, A., Russell, B., Sivic, J.: Seeing 3D chairs: exemplar part-based 2D–3D alignment using a large dataset of CAD models. In: CVPR (2014)
2. Blank, M., Gorelick, L., Shechtman, E., Irani, M., Basri, R.: Actions as space-time shapes. In: ICCV (2005)
3. Thomee, B., et al.: YFCC100M: the new data in multimedia research. ACM (2016)
4. Kingma, D.P., Welling, M.: Auto-encoding variational bayes. In: ICLR (2014)
5. Goodfellow, I., et al.: Generative adversarial nets. In: NIPS (2014)
6. Chen, X., Duan, Y., Houthooft, R., Schulman, J., Sutskever, I., Abbeel, P.: InfoGAN: interpretable representation learning by information maximizing generative adversarial nets. In: NIPS (2016)
7. Tulyakov, S., Liu, M., Yang, X., Kautz, J.: MoCoGAN: decomposing motion and content for video generation. CoRR (2017)
8. Zhao, S., Song, J., Ermon, S.: Learning hierarchical features from deep generative models. In: ICML (2017)

9. Xue, T., Wu, J., Bouman, K., Freeman, B.: Visual dynamics: probabilistic future frame synthesis via cross convolutional networks. In: NIPS (2016)
10. Sønderby, C.K., Raiko, T., Maaløe, L., Sønderby, S.K., Winther, O.: Ladder variational autoencoders. In: NIPS (2016)
11. Serban, I.V., et al.: A hierarchical latent variable encoder-decoder model for generating dialogues. In: AAAI (2017)
12. Reed, S., Akata, Z., Yan, X., Logeswaran, L., Schiele, B., Lee, H.: Generative adversarial text to image synthesis. In: NIPS (2016)
13. Yan, X., Yang, J., Sohn, K., Lee, H.: Attribute2Image: conditional image generation from visual attributes. In: Leibe, B., Matas, J., Sebe, N., Welling, M. (eds.) ECCV 2016. LNCS, vol. 9908, pp. 776–791. Springer, Cham (2016). https://doi.org/10.1007/978-3-319-46493-0_47
14. Mathieu, M., Zhao, J., Sprechmann, P., Ramesh, A., LeCun, Y.: Disentangling factors of variation in deep representations using adversarial training. In: NIPS (2016)
15. Walker, J., Doersch, C., Gupta, A., Hebert, M.: An uncertain future: forecasting from static images using variational autoencoders. In: Leibe, B., Matas, J., Sebe, N., Welling, M. (eds.) ECCV 2016. LNCS, vol. 9911, pp. 835–851. Springer, Cham (2016). https://doi.org/10.1007/978-3-319-46478-7_51
16. Vondrick, C., Pirsiavash, H., Torralba, A.: Generating videos with scene dynamics. In: NIPS (2016)
17. Tenenbaum, J., Freeman, W.: Separating style and content with bilinear models. Neural Comput. **12**, 1247–1283 (2000)
18. Elgammal, A., Lee, C.S.: Separating style and content on a nonlinear manifold. In: CVPR (2004)
19. Wang, J.M., Fleet, D.J., Hertzmann, A.: Gaussian process dynamical models. In: NIPS (2005)
20. Wang, J.M., Fleet, D.J., Hertzmann, A.: Multifactor Gaussian process models for style-content separation. In: ICML (2007)
21. Rezende, D.J., Mohamed, S., Wierstra, D.: Stochastic backpropagation and approximate inference in deep generative models. In: ICML (2014)
22. Sohn, K., Lee, H., Yan, X.: Learning structured output representation using deep conditional generative models. In: NIPS (2015)
23. Kingma, D.P., Mohamed, S., Rezende, D.J., Welling, M.: Semi-supervised learning with deep generative models. In: NIPS (2014)
24. Rezende, D.J., Mohamed, S.: Variational inference with normalizing flows. In: ICML (2015)
25. Kingma, D.P., Salimans, T., Jozefowicz, R., Chen, X., Sutskever, I., Welling, M.: Improving variational inference with inverse autoregressive flow. In: NIPS (2016)
26. Chung, J., Kastner, K., Dinh, L., Goel, K., Courville, A.C., Bengio, Y.: A recurrent latent variable model for sequential data. In: NIPS (2015)
27. Matusik, W., Pfister, H., Brand, M., McMillan, L.: A Data-driven reflectance model. ACM ToG (2002)
28. Kulkarni, T.D., Whitney, W.F., Kohli, P., Tenenbaum, J.: Deep convolutional inverse graphics network. In: NIPS (2015)
29. Higgins, I., et al.: beta-VAE: learning basic visual concepts with a constrained variational framework. In: ICLR (2017)
30. Zhou, Y., Berg, T.L.: Learning temporal transformations from time-lapse videos. In: Leibe, B., Matas, J., Sebe, N., Welling, M. (eds.) ECCV 2016. LNCS, vol. 9912, pp. 262–277. Springer, Cham (2016). https://doi.org/10.1007/978-3-319-46484-8_16

31. Lee, N., Choi, W., Vernaza, P., Choy, C.B., Torr, P.H.S., Chandraker, M.K.: DESIRE: distant future prediction in dynamic scenes with interacting agents. CoRR (2017)
32. Krishnan, R.G., Shalit, U., Sontag, D.: Deep Kalman filters. In: WS on Black Box Learning and Inference (2015)
33. Karl, M., Soelch, M., Bayer, J., van der Smagt, P.: Deep variational bayes filters: unsupervised learning of state space models from raw data. In: ICLR (2017)
34. Johnson, M., Duvenaud, D.K., Wiltschko, A., Adams, R.P., Datta, S.R.: Composing graphical models with neural networks for structured representations and fast inference. In: NIPS (2016)
35. Kalchbrenner, N., et al.: Video pixel networks. CoRR (2016)
36. Hochreiter, S., Schmidhuber, J.: Long short-term memory. Neural Comput. **9**, 1735–1780 (1997)
37. Vinyals, O., Toshev, A., Bengio, S., Erhan, D.: Show and tell: a neural image caption generator. In: CVPR (2015)
38. Kingma, D., Ba, J.: Adam: a method for stochastic optimization. In: ICLR (2014)
39. Yang, J., Reed, S.E., Yang, M.H., Lee, H.: Weakly-supervised disentangling with recurrent transformations for 3D view synthesis. In: NIPS (2015)
40. Salimans, T., et al.: Improved techniques for training GANs. In: NIPS (2016)
41. Szegedy, C., Vanhoucke, V., Ioffe, S., Shlens, J., Wojna, Z.: Rethinking the inception architecture for computer vision. In: CVPR (2016)
42. Russakovsky, O., et al.: ImageNet large scale visual recognition challenge. IJCV **115**, 211–252 (2015)

Learning Rigidity in Dynamic Scenes with a Moving Camera for 3D Motion Field Estimation

Zhaoyang Lv[1(✉)], Kihwan Kim[2], Alejandro Troccoli[2], Deqing Sun[2], James M. Rehg[1], and Jan Kautz[2]

[1] Georgia Institute of Technology, Atlanta, USA
{zhaoyang.lv,rehg}@gatech.edu
[2] NVIDIA, Santa Clara, USA
{kihwank,atroccoli,deqings,jkautz}@nvidia.com

Abstract. Estimation of 3D motion in a dynamic scene from a temporal pair of images is a core task in many scene understanding problems. In real-world applications, a dynamic scene is commonly captured by a moving camera (i.e., panning, tilting or hand-held), increasing the task complexity because the scene is observed from different viewpoints. The primary challenge is the disambiguation of the camera motion from scene motion, which becomes more difficult as the amount of rigidity observed decreases, even with successful estimation of 2D image correspondences. Compared to other state-of-the-art 3D scene flow estimation methods, in this paper, we propose to *learn* the rigidity of a scene in a supervised manner from an extensive collection of dynamic scene data, and directly infer a rigidity mask from two sequential images with depths. With the learned network, we show how we can effectively estimate camera motion and projected scene flow using computed 2D optical flow and the inferred rigidity mask. For training and testing the rigidity network, we also provide a new semi-synthetic dynamic scene dataset (synthetic foreground objects with a real background) and an evaluation split that accounts for the percentage of observed non-rigid pixels. Through our evaluation, we show the proposed framework outperforms current state-of-the-art scene flow estimation methods in challenging dynamic scenes.

Keywords: Rigidity estimation · Dynamic scene analysis
Scene flow · Motion segmentation

1 Introduction

The estimation of 3D motion from images is a fundamental computer vision problem, and key to many applications such as robot manipulation [3], dynamic

Z. Lv—This work started during an internship that the author did at NVIDIA.

Electronic supplementary material The online version of this chapter (https://doi.org/10.1007/978-3-030-01228-1_29) contains supplementary material, which is available to authorized users.

V. Ferrari et al. (Eds.): ECCV 2018, LNCS 11209, pp. 484–501, 2018.
https://doi.org/10.1007/978-3-030-01228-1_29

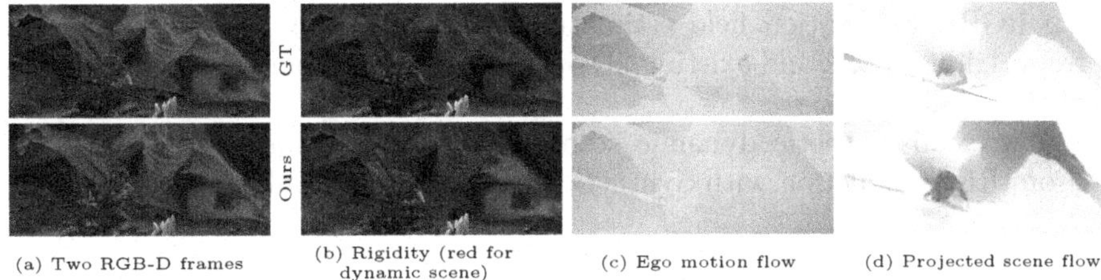

Fig. 1. Our estimated rigidity (b), Ego-motion Flow (c) and Projected scene flow (d) (bottom row) compared to the ground truth (top row). The rigidity mask allows us to solve for the relative camera transform and compute the 3D motion field given the optical flow.

scene reconstruction [14,23], autonomous driving [8,27,29,44], action recognition [43], and video analysis [13]. This task is commonly referred as *3D motion field* or *scene flow estimation*. 3D motion field estimation in a dynamic environment is, however, a challenging and still open problem when the scene is observed from different view points and the amount of coverage of moving objects in each image is significant. This is mainly because the disambiguation of camera motion (ego-motion) from object motion requires the correct identification of *rigid static structure* of a scene. Unlike other methods solving the problem with piecewise rigid motion [9,19,41], clustering local motions [16], and semantic segmentation [32,45], our network can infer per-pixel rigidity by jointly learning rigidity and the relative camera transform from large-scale dynamic scene data. A brief example of our results is shown in Fig. 1.

Our framework, shown in Fig. 2, takes a sequential image pair with color and depth (RGBD) as the input and mainly focuses on dynamic scenes with a moving camera (e.g., panning), where camera motion and objects motions are entangled in each observation. To solve for 2D correspondences, our framework relies on 2D optical flow, and is not tied to any particular algorithm. We use the method by Sun et al. [33], which we evaluate together with the rigidity network to estimate both ego-motion and scene-motions. The network that learns the per-pixel rigidity also solves for the relative camera pose between two images, and we can accurately refine the pose as a least square problem with the learned dense flow correspondences and rigidity region. To provide better supervision during training and encourage generalization, we develop a tool and methodology that enables the creation of a scalable semi-synthetic RGB-D dynamic scene dataset, which we call *REFRESH*. This dataset combines real-world static rigid background with non-rigid synthetic human motions [36] and provides ground truth color, depth, rigidity, optical flow and camera pose.

In summary, our major contributions are:

1. A learning-based rigidity and pose estimation algorithm for dynamic scenes with a moving camera.

2. An RGBD 3D motion field estimation framework that builds on inference from rigidity, pose, and existing 2D optical flow, which outperforms the state-of-the-art methods.
3. A new semi-synthetic dynamic scene data and its creation tool: REal 3D From REconstruction with Synthetic Humans (REFRESH).

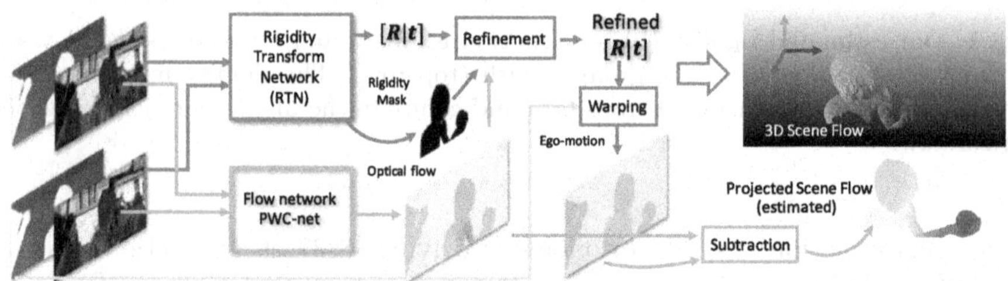

Fig. 2. An overview of our proposed inference architecture for 3D motion field estimation. Our method takes two RGB-D frames as inputs independently processed by two networks. The Rigidity Transform Network (RTN) estimates the relative camera transform and rigid/non-rigid regions. The flow network [33] computes dense flow correspondences. We further refine the relative pose with dense flow over the rigid region. With the refined pose, we compute 3D motion field and projected scene flow from the egomotion flow.

2 Related Work

Scene Flow: Scene flow estimation in dynamic scenes brings together fundamental computer vision algorithms in optical flow, and pose estimation of camera and objects. Vedula et al. [37] defined the 3D motion field as *scene flow*, and proposed a method to compute *dense non-rigid* 3D motion fields from a fixed multi-view set-up. Its extension to a moving camera case needs to disambiguate the camera ego-motion from object scene motions in 3D. Due to the intrinsic complexity of such task, existing methods often address it with known camera parameters [1,35] or assume scene motions are piecewise rigid [9,19,21,39,40,42]. When depth is known, scene flow can be more accurately estimated. Quiroga et al. estimates RGB-D scene flow as a rigid flow composited with a non-rigid 6DoF transforms [25]. Sun et al. estimates scene flow as a composition of finite rigid moving objects [32]. Jaimez et al. separately solve rigid region as visual odometry and non-rigid regions as moving clustered patches conditioned on rigidity segmentation [16]. They solve the rigidity segmentation based on the robust residuals of two frame alignment, similar to [18,23] for camera tracking in dynamic environments. All of these approaches use rigidity as a prior, but can fail as the complexity of the dynamic scene increases. None of these methods use learned models. We show that the 3D motion field can be more accurately estimated using learned models for rigidity and optical flow.

Learning Camera Transform and Rigidity: Recently, various learning-based methods have been introduced for the joint estimation of camera transform and depth (or rigid structure) [34,38,49], and rigid motion tracking [3]. Most of them assume that the scene is either static [34], quasi-static (scene motions are minimal and can be dealt as outliers) [49], or that the camera remains static when a rigid scene motion occurs [3]. More recently, a few approaches [45,47] demonstrated the importance of learning *rigidity* to handle dynamic scenes. Wulff et al. [45] assume the rigidity can be learned by finetuning the semantic segmentation network from a single image, while we posit that rigidity correlates spatially to the epipolar geometry. Yin and Shi [47] unsupervised learn the non-rigid flow residual in the 3D urban scene. We are interested in more general dynamic scenes with unconstrained scene motions observed from moving cameras, and we address this by directly learning the per-pixel rigidity in the supervised manner which can generalize to unseen scenes.

3 Rigidity, Scene Flow and Moving Camera

We focus on solving for the 3D motion field in the physical scene observed from a moving camera, commonly termed as scene flow [16,37]. Here we define the relationship between 2D image correspondences and scene flow in physical 3D scenes with object motions and camera motion derived from relative camera poses between two temporal views.

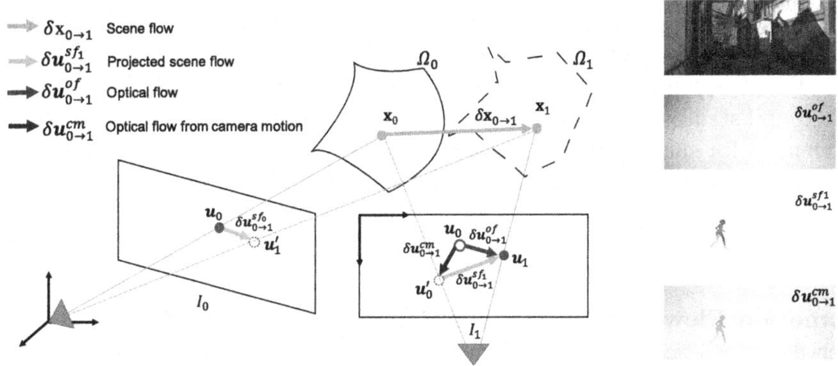

Fig. 3. The geometry of two-frame scene flow, where the camera moves from I_0 to I_1, and point $\mathbf{x}_0$ moves to $\mathbf{x}_1$ (green circles), and their projections in the two images are shown as $\mathbf{u}_0, \mathbf{u}_1$ respectively (red circles). Note that $\mathbf{u}'_0$ is a projected location of $\mathbf{x}_0$ in I_1, as if $\mathbf{x}_0$ were observed by I_1, and can be computed by camera motion as $\delta\mathbf{u}^{cm}_{0\to1}$, and $\mathbf{u}_0$ in I_1 is visualizing the pixel location it had in I_0. If the camera was static and observed both $\mathbf{x}_0$ and $\mathbf{x}_1$ at the position of I_1, optical flow $\delta\mathbf{u}^{of}_{0\to1}$ would be same to a projected scene flow $\delta\mathbf{u}^{sf_1}_{0\to1}$. The right image shows each flow in I_1 of dynamic scene under camera panning. (Color figure online)

Let $\mathbf{x}_t \in \mathbb{R}^3$ be the location of a point $\mathbf{x}$ on a non-rigid surface Ω_t of a moving object with respect to a fixed world coordinate system at time t. We define $\delta\mathbf{x}_{t\rightarrow t+1}$ as the 3D motion vector of $\mathbf{x}$ from time t to time $t+1$, also referred as scene flow in this paper. When $\mathbf{x}_t$ is observed by a camera with known intrinsics, we define $\pi(\mathbf{x}_t)$ to be the projection of $\mathbf{x}_t$ to image coordinates $\mathbf{u}_t$, and $\pi^{-1}(\mathbf{u}_t, z_t)$ the inverse projection into 3D camera coordinates given the known depth z_t in the camera reference frame.

Scene flow, 2D Optical Flow, and Camera Pose Optical flow offers direct 2D associations of measurements in I_t and I_{t+1}. Suppose $\mathcal{C}_t$ is the known camera extrinsics matrix for I_t, then the optical flow $\delta\mathbf{u}_{t\rightarrow t+1}$ from I_t to I_{t+1} can be defined as follows:

$$\delta\mathbf{u}^{of}_{t\rightarrow t+1} = \pi(\mathcal{C}_{t+1}(\mathbf{x}_t + \delta\mathbf{x}_{t\rightarrow t+1})) - \pi(\mathcal{C}_t\mathbf{x}_t) \tag{1}$$

Equation 1 states the two-view geometric relationship between 2D optical flow and 3D scene flow. We can simplify it by considering the camera's relative motion from I_0 to I_1, i.e. assuming $t = 0$ and setting $\mathcal{C}_0$ to identity:

$$\delta\mathbf{u}^{of}_{0\rightarrow 1} = \pi(\mathcal{C}_1(\mathbf{x}_0 + \delta\mathbf{x}_{0\rightarrow 1})) - \pi(\mathbf{x}_0) \tag{2}$$

Given the optical flow $\delta\mathbf{u}^{of}_{0\rightarrow 1}$ and the depth from the RGBD data, the 3D scene flow vector can be computed as:

$$\delta\mathbf{x}_{0\rightarrow 1} = \mathcal{C}_1^{-1}\pi^{-1}(\mathbf{u}_0 + \delta\mathbf{u}^{of}_{0\rightarrow 1}, z_1) - \pi^{-1}(\mathbf{u}_0, z_0) \tag{3}$$

Note that $\mathcal{C}_1$ can be computed from 2D correspondences that follow two-view epipolar geometry [11], and the corresponding points should lie on the rigid and static background structure. This is especially challenging when the scene contains dynamic components (moving objects) as well as a rigid and stationary background structure. As such, identifying inliers and outliers using *rigidity* is a key element for successful relative camera pose estimation, and thus is necessary to achieve reaching accurate scene flow estimation in a dynamic scene [16], which we will discuss in Sect. 4.

Egomotion Flow from a Moving Camera in a Static Scene: When an observed $\mathbf{x}$ in a scene remains static between the two frames, $\delta\mathbf{x}_{0\rightarrow 1} = \mathbf{0}$ and therefore $\mathbf{x}_1 = \mathbf{x}_0$. Then, the observed optical flow is purely induced by the camera motion and we refer it as a camera egomotion flow:

$$\delta\mathbf{u}^{cm}_{0\rightarrow 1} = \pi(\mathcal{C}_1\mathbf{x}_0) - \pi(\mathbf{x}_0) \tag{4}$$

Projected Scene Flow and Rigidity: As described in Fig. 3, the projected scene flow is a projection of a 3D scene flow $\delta\mathbf{x}_{0\rightarrow 1}$ in I_1 if $\mathbf{x}_0$ was observed from I_1, which can be computed from camera ego-motion and optical flow:

$$\delta\mathbf{u}^{sf}_{0\rightarrow 1} = \delta\mathbf{u}^{of}_{0\rightarrow 1} - \delta\mathbf{u}^{cm}_{0\rightarrow 1} \tag{5}$$

The projected scene flow (in a novel view) is also referred as non-rigid residual [25,47]. All locations with zero values in projected scene flow indicate the rigidity region in ground truth data. As demonstrated in Fig. 3, the projected scene flow is a useful tool to evaluate the results of dense scene flow estimation in the 2D domain which requires accurate estimation of both camera pose and optical flow. Thus, we use it as the evaluation metric in Sect. 6.

4 3D Motion Field Estimation Pipeline

We introduce a framework that refines the relative camera transform and the optical flow with a rigidity mask for accurate scene flow estimation. Figure 2 shows the overview of our proposed pipeline. Given a temporal pair of RGB-D images, we concurrently run the optical flow and rigidity-transform network. The optical flow network [33] offers the 2D correspondence association between frames, and our proposed rigidity-transform network provides an estimate of the camera transform and the rigidity mask.

4.1 Rigidity-Transform Network

Previous work on camera pose estimation using CNNs focused on either static or quasi-static scenes, where scene motions are absent or their amount is minimal [34,38,49]. In dynamic scenes with a moving camera, camera pose estimation can be challenging due to the ambiguity induced by the camera motion and scene (object) motion. Although existing approaches leverage prior information in motion or semantic knowledge [16,25,28,32] to disambiguate the two, the priors are usually not general for different scenes.

We propose to infer the rigidity from epipolar geometry by a fully-convolutional network that jointly learns camera motion and segmentation of the scene into dynamic and static regions from RGB-D inputs. We represent this rigidity segmentation as a binary mask with the static scene masked as rigid. The rigid scene components will obey the rigid transform constraints induced by the camera ego-motion and serve as the regions of *attention of the camera transform*. We name it rigidity-transform network (RTN), shown in Fig. 4.

RTN: Given a pair of RGB-D frames, we pre-process each frame into a 6 channel tensor $[(u-c_x)/f_x, (v-c_y)/f_y, 1/d, r, g, b]$, from camera intrinsic parameters $[f_x, f_y, c_x, c_y]$ and the depth d. Due to the range of depth values, this representation is numerical stable in training and delivers good generalization performance. We truncate $1/d$ to the range $[1e-4, 10]$, which can cover scenes of various scales. We concatenate the two-frame tensors to a 12-channel tensor as input to our network. The network is composed of an encoder followed by pose regression and a decoder followed by the rigidity segmentation.

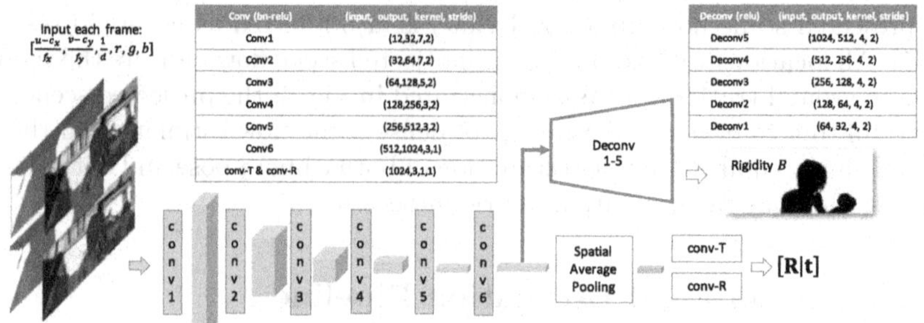

Fig. 4. Rigidity-Transform network (RTN) architecture The inputs to the RTN are 12 channel tensors encoded with $[(u-c_x)/f_x, (v-c_y)/f_y, 1/d, r, g, b]$ computed from a pair of RGB-D images and their intrinsics. It is a fully convolutional encoder-decoder architecture predicting pose as a translation and euler angles, and scene rigidity as a binary mask.

Encoder: We use five stride-2 conv-layers which gradually reduce spatial resolution and one stride-1 convolution as the conv-6 layer. Each convolution is followed by a batchnorm and ReLU layer. In the bottleneck layer, the target is to predict the camera relative translation $\mathbf{t}$ and rotation Θ. After the conv-6 layer, we use a spatial-average pooling (SAP) to reduce the feature into a $1024D$ vector. With two 1×1 convolution layers that output 3 channels, we separately estimate the $\mathbf{t}$ and Θ. We assume the relative camera transformation between two frames is small and thus we represent the rotation $\mathbf{R}(\alpha, \beta, \gamma) = \mathbf{R}_x(\alpha)\mathbf{R}_y(\beta)\mathbf{R}_z(\gamma)$ with Euler angles $\Theta = [\alpha, \beta, \gamma]$. The regression loss is a weighted combination of the robust Huber loss $\rho(\cdot)$ for translation and rotation as:

$$\mathcal{L}_p = \rho(\mathbf{t} - \mathbf{t}^\star) + w_\Theta \rho(\Theta - \Theta^\star) \tag{6}$$

Decoder: The decoder network is composed of five deconvolution (transpose convolution) layers which gradually upsample the conv-6 feature into input image scale and reshape it into the original image resolution. We estimate the rigidity attention as a binary segmentation problem with binary cross-entropy loss $\mathcal{L}_r$. The overall loss is a weighted sum of both loss functions: $\mathcal{L}_c = w_p\mathcal{L}_p + \mathcal{L}_r$.

Enforcing Learning from Two Views: We enforce the network to capture both scene structures and epipolar constraints using two views rather than a single-view short-cut. First, our network is fully convolutional, and we regress the camera pose from the SAP layer which preserves feature distributions spatially. Features for rigidity segmentation and pose regression can interact directly with each other spatially across each feature map. We do not use any skip layer connections. Our experiments in Sect. 6 show that joint learning of camera pose and rigidity can help RTN to achieve better generalization in complex scenes. Second, we randomly use two identical views as input, and a fully rigid mask as output with 20% probability during data augmentation, which prevents the network from only using a single view for its prediction.

4.2 Pose Refinement from Rigidity and Flow

To solve for the 3D motion field accurately from two views from Eq. 3, we require a precise camera transformation. Moreover, the pose output from RTN may not always precisely generalize to new test scenes. To overcome this, we propose a refinement step based on the estimated rigidity B and bidirectional dense optical flow $\delta\mathbf{u}^{of}_{0\to1}$ and $\delta\mathbf{u}^{of}_{1\to0}$ (with forward and backward pass). We view the estimation of $\mathcal{C}_1$ as a robust least square problem as:

$$\underset{\mathcal{C}_1}{\operatorname{argmin}} \sum_{\{\mathbf{x}_0,\mathbf{x}_1\}\in\Omega(B)} [\mathbf{I}]\rho(\mathcal{C}_1\mathbf{x}_0 - \mathbf{x}_1) \tag{7}$$

where $\mathbf{x}_i = \pi^{-1}(\mathbf{u}_i, z_i)$ in all background regions B, predicted by the RTN. $[\mathbf{I}]$ is an Iverson bracket for all the inlier correspondences. We filter the inlier correspondences in several steps. We first use forward-backward consistency check for bidirectional optical flow with a threshold of 0.75 to remove all flow correspondences which are not consistent. The removed region approximates the occlusion map O. We use a morphological operator with patch size 10 to dilate B and O to further remove the outliers on boundaries. From all correspondences, we uniformly sample bidirectional flow correspondences with a stride of 4 and select 1e4 points among them that are closest to the camera viewpoint. These help to solves the optimization more efficiently and numerically stable. We also use the Huber norm $\rho(\cdot)$ as a robust way to handle the remaining outliers. We solve Eq. 7 efficiently via Gauss-Newton with $\mathcal{C}_1$ initialized from the RTN output. Note that in most cases correspondences are mostly accurate, the initialization step trivially helps but can also be replaced by an identity initialization.

5 REFRESH Dataset

Training our network requires a sufficient amount of dynamic RGB-D images over scenes and ground truth in the form of known camera pose, rigidity mask, and optical flow. However, acquiring such ground truth from the real-world data is difficult or even infeasible. Existing dataset acquisition tools include rendered animations like SINTEL [2] and Monka [20], and frames captured from games [26]. SINTEL [2] has a small number of frames, so we use it for testing instead of training. Most approaches render scenes using rigid 3D object models [7,20,31] with the concept. Among all existing tools and datasets, only Things3D [20] provides sufficient 3D training samples for learning 3D flow with moving camera ground truth. However, it only uses a small set of 3D objects with textured images at infinity as static scene context and rigid objects as the dynamic scene, which does not provide realistic 3D scene structure for motion estimation that can generalize well.

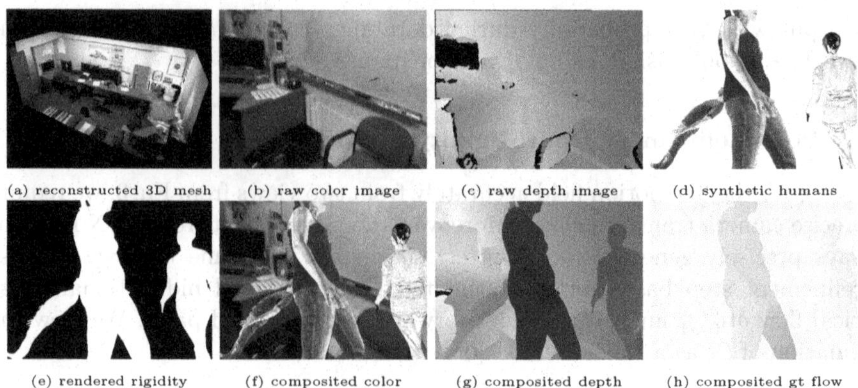

(a) reconstructed 3D mesh (b) raw color image (c) raw depth image (d) synthetic humans

(e) rendered rigidity (f) composited color (g) composited depth (h) composited gt flow

Fig. 5. REFRESH dataset creation pipeline With a captured RGB-D trajectory, the scene is reconstructed as a 3D mesh by BundleFusion [5] (a), with raw RGB-D input as (b) and (c). With sampled frames from the camera trajectory, we load synthetic human models [36] with motions randomly into the 3D as (d), and render the rigidity mask (e), Finally we composite the rendered synthetic ground truth with its corresponding rendered 3D views and the final semi-synthetic RGB-D views (f) and (h), with optical flow ground truth as (i).

To overcome the dataset issue, we propose a semi-synthetic scene flow dataset: REal 3D from REconstruction with Synthetic Humans, which we name as **REFRESH**. For this task we leverage the success of state of the art 3D reconstruction systems [5,10,46], which directly provide dense 3D meshes and optimized camera trajectories. We use a pre-captured RGB-D dataset and create dynamic 4D scenes by rendering non-rigid 3D moving objects with pre-defined trajectories. We overlay synthetic objects over the original footage to obtain a composite image with the ground truth as shown in Fig. 5.

Real 3D Reconstructed Scenes: We use the 3D meshes created with BundleFusion [5]. The authors released eight reference 3D meshes with the 25 K input RGB-D images, camera intrinsic and extrinsic parameters.

Synthetic Humans: We create non-rigid scene elements with the method introduced in SURREAL [36]. Each synthetic body is created from realistic articulated human body models [17] and pose actions are from the CMU MoCap database [15] with more than 20 K sequences of 23 action categories. The human textures are composed of SMPL CAESAR scans and real clothing registered with 4Cap [24]. We create each synthetic human with random gender, body shape, cloth texture, action and their positions in the 3D scene which guarantees the diversity of dynamic scenes. We control the visibility of human models along the trajectory by putting the pelvis point of each human model in the free space w.r.t. the ego-centric viewpoint from a selected frame along the trajectory. The free space is sampled by the corresponding depth. For every 100 frames, we select n frames (n sample from $\sim \mathcal{N}(15, 5)$) and insert n human models into the scene.

Rendering and Ground-Truth Generation: We use Cycles from the Blender[1] suite as our rendering engine. The lighting is created using spherical harmonics, as in Varol et al. [36]. First, we set the virtual camera using the same 3D scene camera intrinsic and spatial resolution. The camera extrinsic follows the real-data trajectory (computed from BundleFusion [5]). Thus, we can use the raw color image rather than rendered image as background texture which is photo-realistic and contains artifacts such as motion blur. With the same camera settings, we separately render the 3D reconstructed static mesh and the synthetic humans, and composite them using alpha-matting. Different from the color image, the depth map is rendered from the 3D mesh, which is less noisy and more complete than raw depth. Since the camera movement during the 3D acquisition is small between frames, we sub-sample frames at intervals of [1,2,5,10,20] to create larger motions. We employ a multi-pass rendering approach to generate depth, optical flow and rigidity mask as our ground truth.

6 Experiments

We implemented the RTN in PyTorch, and the pose refinement in C++ with GTSAM 4.0 [6]. The PWCNet [33] is trained in Caffe. We integrate all the modules through Python. We use 68 K images from our REFRESH dataset for training[2]. We train RTN from scratch using weight initialization from He et al. [12] and Adam optimizer ($\beta_1 = 0.9$ and $\beta_2 = 0.999$, learning rate of $2e^{-4}$) on 3 GPUs for 12 epochs. During training, the rigidity mask loss is accumulated over 5 different scales with balanced weights, and we choose $w_\Theta = 100$. We follow the same training as PWC-net Sun et al. [33]. We will release our code, datasets and REFRESH toolkit[3].

We evaluate our approach under various settings to show the performance of rigidity and pose estimation and their influence on scene flow estimation. For the effective analysis in scenes with different levels of non-rigid motions, we create a new test split from SINTEL data [2] based on the non-rigid number of pixels percentage. In Sect. 6.1, we provide a comparison of the performance with different settings for RTN, refinement and other state-of-the-arts methods. In Sect. 6.2, we qualitative evaluate of our method using real world images. Please also refer to our video for more qualitative evaluations.

6.1 Quantitative Evaluations

We first evaluate our approach on the challenging SINTEL dataset [2], which is a 3D rendered animation containing a sequence of 23 dynamic scenes with

[1] Blender: https://www.blender.org/.

[2] More details about the dataset are included in the supplementary materials.

[3] Code repository: https://github.com/NVlabs/learningrigidity.git.

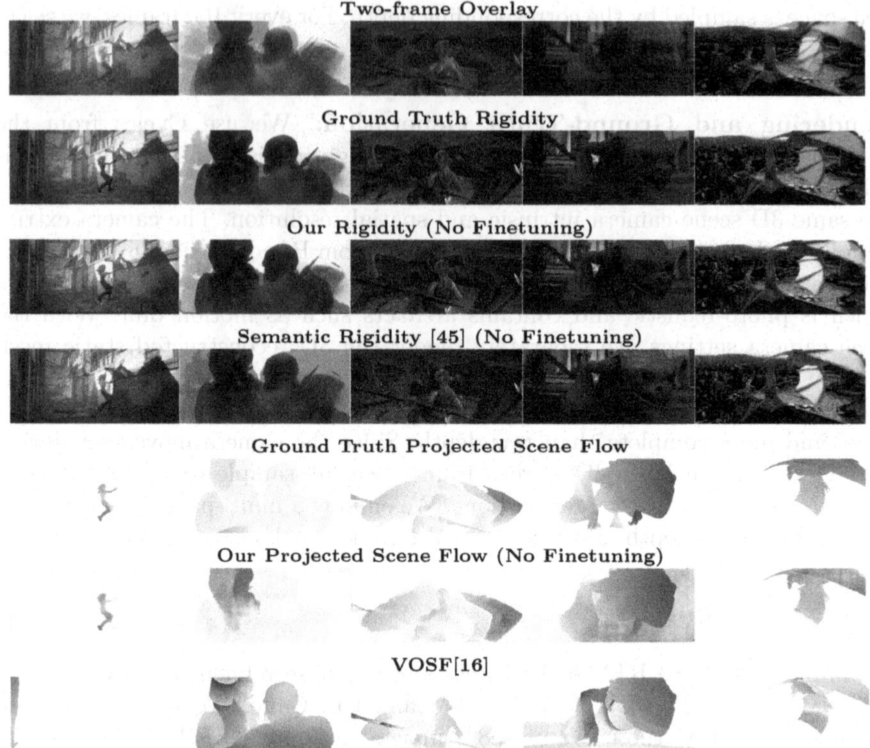

Fig. 6. Qualitative visualization on our SINTEL test split. We compare our rigidity prediction with the output using semantic rigidity [45] trained on our REFRESH dataset and our projected scene flow with output of VOSF [16].

cinematic camera motion. The dataset has two versions with different rendering settings: *clean* and *final*. The latter set contains motion blur and depth of field effects, which are not present in the *clean* set. Since the official SINTEL test dataset does not provide RGB-D 3D flow evaluation, we split the SINTEL training set into train, validation, and test split. For the test split, to effectively evaluate and analyze the impact of different levels of non-rigid motions in the estimation, we choose *alley_2*(1.8%), *temp_2*(5.8%), *market_5*(27.04%), *ambush_6*(38.96%), *cave_4*(47.10%), where (·) indicates the average non-rigid regions in each scene sequence. These examples also contain a sufficient amount of camera motion. We use the first 5 frames in the rest of the 18 scenes as a validation set, and the remaining images for training in our finetuning setting.

We show our quantitative evaluations using flow metric in Table 1, relative pose metric in Table 2, and the rigidity IOU in Table 3. We list the end-point-error (EPE) in the ego-motion flow (EF) and projected scene flow (PSF) as defined in Sect. 3. Our proposed metrics overcomes the traditional difficulty of 3D motion flow evaluation. We compare our method to two state-of-art

Table 1. Quantitative evaluation in flow residuals using SINTEL dataset on our test split. The ratio of Nonrigid (NR) Region indicates the average ratio of pixels in the scene which represents the complexity of dynamic motion in the scene. We report the EPE in egomotion flow (EF) and projected scene flow (PSF). For all the baseline methods in both non-finetuning (NO FT) and finetuning (FT) setting, we use the same optical flow network trained as our method. The lowest residual under the same setting (e.g. NO FT, clean set) is highlighted as **bold**.

		NR Region<10%				NR Region 10%−40%				NR Region>40%		All Test	
		alley_2		temple_2		market_5		ambush_6		cave4		Average	
		EF	PSF	EF	PSF	EF	PSF	EF	PSF	EF	PSF	EF	PSF
	CLEAN (no motion blur)												
	(a) SRSF [25]	4.24	7.25	7.59	16.55	25.26	31.67	17.84	37.21	10.77	11.82	12.47	18.57
	(b) VOSF [16]	6.53	1.13	5.13	10.36	16.02	35.24	13.39	28.31	6.05	9.30	8.86	15.24
NO FT	(c) Refine only	0.29	0.48	0.90	2.95	8.81	22.34	3.59	14.39	2.18	5.88	3.09	8.47
	(d) Semantic [45]+Refine	0.25	0.53	1.07	3.87	5.77	15.74	1.70	9.58	0.85	4.34	1.96	6.42
	(e) RANSAC+Flow	0.31	0.57	0.47	2.73	7.36	19.19	3.86	14.89	2.17	5.94	2.69	7.78
	(f) RTN (use Things [20])+Refine	0.34	0.60	1.47	3.98	7.21	18.73	21.84	23.97	1.17	4.90	4.20	5.85
	(g) RTN (no-pose)+Refine	**0.13**	**0.45**	0.49	2.79	5.78	16.24	3.72	16.92	1.67	5.37	2.07	7.09
	(h) **RTN+Refine**	0.18	0.48	**0.46**	**2.72**	**1.61**	**11.86**	**0.97**	**8.61**	**0.63**	**4.05**	**0.74**	**5.10**
FT	(i) Semantic [45]+Refine	0.19	**0.46**	0.50	2.73	2.73	13.45	1.13	9.94	2.07	5.87	1.35	5.98
	(j) **RTN+Refine**	**0.18**	0.47	**0.42**	**2.64**	**1.69**	**11.53**	**0.47**	**7.74**	**0.91**	**4.34**	**0.77**	**5.03**
	FINAL (with motion blur)												
	(k) SRSF [25]	4.33	7.78	7.59	15.51	24.93	31.29	17.26	39.08	10.80	13.29	12.37	18.86
	(l) VOSF [16]	6.29	1.54	5.69	8.91	15.99	35.17	13.37	24.02	6.23	9.28	8.96	14.61
NO FT	(m) Refine only	0.28	0.57	0.90	3.77	8.80	20.64	3.59	20.41	2.18	6.52	3.09	8.95
	(n) Semantic [45]+refine	0.25	0.52	0.96	3.83	>100	>100	20.23	35.46	11.05	12.81	>100	>100
	(o) RANSAC+Flow	0.36	0.61	0.62	3.41	4.68	18.69	5.79	20.86	2.28	6.55	2.31	8.47
	(p) RTN (use Things [20])+Refine	0.25	0.52	5.06	9.82	4.88	16.99	33.44	52.21	1.05	5.07	5.44	11.88
	(q) RTN (no-pose)+Refine	0.19	0.48	**0.82**	**3.58**	2.15	13.97	3.34	20.02	1.52	5.72	1.36	7.14
	(r) **RTN+Refine**	**0.18**	**0.47**	0.88	3.93	**0.79**	**11.87**	**2.82**	**19.42**	**0.66**	**4.66**	**0.82**	**6.29**
FT	(s) Semantic [45]+Refine	**0.19**	**0.48**	1.91	5.19	1.58	13.02	2.58	19.11	2.13	6.50	1.55	7.39
	(t) **RTN+Refine**	0.21	**0.48**	**0.66**	**3.27**	**0.97**	**11.35**	**2.34**	**19.08**	**0.74**	**4.75**	**0.79**	**6.12**

Table 2. Quantitative evaluation in relative camera transform using on our SINTEL test split. We report the relative pose error [30] (RPE) composed of translation (t) error and rotation error (r) in Euler angles (degree) in SINTEL depth metric averaged on from outputs using *clean* and *final* pass.

	NR Region <10%				NR Region 10% – 40%				NR Region >40%		All Test	
	alley_2		temple_2		market_5		ambush_6		cave4		AVERAGE	
	RPE(t)	RPE(r)	RPE(t)	RPE(r)	RPE(t)	RPE(r)	RPE(t)	RPE(r)	RPE(t)	RPE(r)	RPE(t)	RPE(r)
ORB-SLAM [22]	0.0300	0.0190	0.1740	0.0220	0.1500	0.0160	0.0550	0.0280	0.0167	0.0277	0.0894	0.0218
SRSF [25]	0.0487	0.0141	0.1763	0.0117	0.1566	0.0105	0.0672	0.0729	0.0218	0.0150	0.0980	0.0180
VOSF [16]	0.1043	0.0316	0.1055	0.0155	0.0605	**0.0006**	0.0375	0.0190	0.0438	0.0046	0.0750	0.0136
Registration [1]	0.0400	0.0094	0.3990	0.0381	0.0269	0.0073	0.0698	0.0225	0.0551	0.0076	0.1251	0.0162
RANSAC+Flow	0.0026	0.0047	0.0258	0.0033	0.0446	0.0043	0.0318	0.0082	0.0318	0.0411	0.0267	0.0039
Our RTN Pose	0.0349	0.0237	0.1589	0.0120	0.1520	0.0208	0.0455	0.0493	0.0233	0.0212	0.0883	0.0220
Ours (no ft)	**0.0015**	**0.0036**	**0.0215**	**0.0010**	**0.0059**	**0.0009**	**0.0153**	**0.0061**	**0.0053**	**0.0009**	**0.0091**	**0.0020**

Table 3. Evaluation of rigidity using mean IOU of rigid and nonrigid scenes.

Mean IOU	REFRESH val	SINTEL clean val	SINTEL final val
Semantic Rigidity [2] trained on REFRESH	0.934	0.392	0.446
RTN trained on Things [4]	-	0.283	0.286
RTN trained on our REFRESH	**0.956**	**0.542**	**0.627**

optimization-based RGB-D scene flow solutions: SRSF [25] and VO-SF [16] which estimate the camera pose as part of the solution to flow correspondence. In addition, we evaluate three types of baselines. The first one solves the refinement stage from flow without any inputs from RTN (*Refine Only*), which assumes rigidity often dominates the scene [16, 18, 23]. Secondly, we use three-point RANSAC to calculate the camera pose from the flow. Third, to fairly evaluate the rigidity of (RTN) and its generalization, we compare it to semantic rigidity estimation [45], which assumes that the non-rigid motion can be predicted from its semantic labeling. We follow Wulff et al. [45] and use the DeepLab [4] architecture initialized from the pre-trained MS-COCO model, but trained over the same data we used for our model. In the pose refinement stage, we substitute our rigidity from RTN with the semantic rigidity. For the fine-tuned evaluation on SINTEL, we re-train both our RTN and the semantic rigidity network. All methods use the same optical flow network and weights, and all use the same depth from SINTEL ground truth. The qualitative comparison is shown in Fig. 6.

The Flow Metrics in Table 1 show that: (1) compared to SRSF [25] and VOSF [16], our proposed algorithm with learned rigidity can improve scene flow accuracy by a significant margin with no further fine-tuning (NO FT) (rows (a),(b)vs(h); (k),(l)vs(r)); (2) the rigidity mask from our RTN performs better than the single-view semantic segmentation based approach [45], particularly in the more realistic *final pass* with no fine-tuning (row (d)vs(g),(h); (n)vs(q),(r)); (3) as shown in *RTN+refine*, the simultaneous learning of rigidity with pose transform achieves better generalization than learning rigidity alone (row (g)vs(h); (q)vs(r)); (4) RTN trained on our dataset generalizes better compared to the same RTN trained using Things3D [20] (row (f)vs(h); (p)vs(r)); and (5) the final approaches consistently outperforms all baselines. Note that the semantic rigidity [45] can achieve better performance (from Table 1) relying on fine-tuning on SINTEL, our learned rigidity can generalize to unseen complex scenes and perform as well as the fine-tuned model. Our rigidity prediction can capture unseen objects well, as shown by the dragon in Fig. 6.

The Pose Metrics evaluations in Table 2 include two other baselines: depth-based ORB-SLAM [22] and point cloud registration [48]. As mentioned, the accuracy of all relevant methods in dynamic scenes with moving camera highly relies on the ability ignore the non-rigid surfaces. As shown in the table, our pose directly predicted from RTN can achieve same or better accuracy with all relevant methods, and our final solution *without fine-tunning* can out-perform all state-of-the-art methods by a significant margin.

The Rigidity Metric in Table 3 further shows the generalization in rigidity estimation. Our approach trained on our dataset generalizes significant better compared to the same approach trained using Things3D [20] and the semantic rigidity [45] using the same data.

6.2 Evaluation on Real-World Images

To test our algorithm in real-world dynamic scenarios, we use three TUM RGB-D sequences [30] which contains dynamic motions observed from a moving Kinect camera. The depth input is noisy with missing observations and the color images contain severe motion blur. We use the raw color and depth input with provided calibrated camera intrinsics as input, and mark the regions as invalid region when the depth value is not within [0.1, 8]. In invalid regions, we ignore the rigidity prediction and treat the flow correspondence as outliers. Considering there is no 3D motion flow ground truth for our real data, we visualize the rigidity prediction and projected scene flow to qualitatively show the performance in Fig. 7. Our results show that our trained model on semi-synthetic data can also generalize well to real noisy RGB-D data with significant motion blur.

Fig. 7. Qualitative visualization of dynamic sequences in TUM [30] sequences.

7 Conclusion and Future Work

We have presented a learning-based approach to estimate the rigid regions in dynamic scenes observed by a moving camera. Furthermore, we have shown that our framework can accurately compute the 3D motion field (scene flow), and the relative camera transform between two views. To provide better supervision to the rigidity learning task and encourage the generalization of our model, we created a novel semi-synthetic dynamic scene dataset, REFRESH, which contains real-world background scenes together with synthetic foreground moving objects. Through various tests, we have shown that our proposed method can outperform state-of-the-art solutions. We also included a new guideline for dynamic scene evaluation regarding the amount of scene motion and camera motion.

We observed some cases where the rigidity mask deviates from the ground-truth. We noticed that in these situations the moving object size is small, or the temporal motions between the two frames are small. In these cases, the error and deviations scales are small, which does not significantly affect the 3D scene flow computed as a result. Note that the success of this method also depends on the accuracy of optical flow. In scenarios when the optical flow fails or produces a noisy result, the errors in the correspondences will also propagate to 3D motion field. In future work, we can address these problems by exploiting rendering more diverse datasets to encourage generalization in different scenes. We will also incorporate both rigidity and optical flow to refine the correspondence estimation and explore performance improvements with end-to-end learning, including correspondence refinement and depth estimation from RGB inputs.

Acknowledgment. This work was partially supported by the National Science Foundation and National Robotics Initiative (Grant # IIS-1426998).

References

1. Basha, T., Moses, Y., Kiryati, N.: Multi-view scene flow estimation: a view centered variational approach. In: IEEE Conference on Computer Vision and Pattern Recognition (CVPR), pp. 1506–1513 (2010)
2. Butler, D.J., Wulff, J., Stanley, G.B., Black, M.J.: A naturalistic open source movie for optical flow evaluation. In: Fitzgibbon, A., Lazebnik, S., Perona, P., Sato, Y., Schmid, C. (eds.) ECCV 2012. LNCS, vol. 7577, pp. 611–625. Springer, Heidelberg (2012). https://doi.org/10.1007/978-3-642-33783-3_44
3. Byravan, A., Fox, D.: SE3-nets: learning rigid body motion using deep neural networks. In: IEEE International Conference on Robotics and Automation (ICRA), pp. 173–180. IEEE (2017)
4. Chen, L.C., Papandreou, G., Kokkinos, I., Murphy, K., Yuille, A.L.: DeepLab: semantic image segmentation with deep convolutional nets, atrous convolution, and fully connected CRFs. arXiv:1606.00915 (2016)
5. Dai, A., Nießner, M., Zollöfer, M., Izadi, S., Theobalt, C.: BundleFusion: real-time globally consistent 3D reconstruction using on-the-fly surface re-integration. ACM Trans. Graph. (TOG) (2017)
6. Dellaert, F.: Factor graphs and GTSAM: a hands-on introduction. Technical report, GT-RIM-CP&R-2012-002, GT RIM, September 2012. https://research.cc.gatech.edu/borg/sites/edu.borg/files/downloads/gtsam.pdf
7. Dosovitskiy, A., et al.: FlowNet: learning optical flow with convolutional networks. In: International Conference on Computer Vision (ICCV), pp. 2758–2766 (2015)

8. Geiger, A., Lauer, M., Wojek, C., Stiller, C., Urtasun, R.: 3D traffic scene understanding from movable platforms. IEEE Trans. Pattern Anal. Mach. Intell. **36**, 1012–1025 (2014)
9. Golyanik, V., Kim, K., Maier, R., Nießner, M., Stricker, D., Kautz, J.: Multiframe scene flow with piecewise rigid motion. In: International Conference on 3D Vision, Qingdao, China, October 2017
10. Handa, A., Whelan, T., McDonald, J., Davison, A.: A benchmark for RGB-D visual odometry, 3D reconstruction and SLAM. In: IEEE International Conference on Robotics and Automation (ICRA), Hong Kong, China, May 2014
11. Hartley, R.I., Zisserman, A.: Multiple View Geometry in Computer Vision, 2nd edn. Cambridge University Press, Cambridge (2004). ISBN 0521540518
12. He, K., Zhang, X., Ren, S., Sun, J.: Delving deep into rectifiers: surpassing human-level performance on imagenet classification. In: Proceedings of the 2015 IEEE International Conference on Computer Vision (ICCV), pp. 1026–1034. IEEE Computer Society (2015). https://doi.org/10.1109/ICCV.2015.123
13. Hung, C.H., Xu, L., Jia, J.Y.: Consistent binocular depth and scene flow with chained temporal profiles. Int. J. Comput. Vis. **102**(1–3), 271–292 (2013)
14. Innmann, M., Zollhöfer, M., Nießner, M., Theobalt, C., Stamminger, M.: VolumeDeform: real-time volumetric non-rigid reconstruction. In: Leibe, B., Matas, J., Sebe, N., Welling, M. (eds.) ECCV 2016. LNCS, vol. 9912, pp. 362–379. Springer, Cham (2016). https://doi.org/10.1007/978-3-319-46484-8_22
15. Ionescu, C., Papava, D., Olaru, V., Sminchisescu, C.: Human3.6M: large scale datasets and predictive methods for 3D human sensing in natural environments. IEEE Trans. Pattern Anal. Mach. Intell. **36**(7), 1325–1339 (2014)
16. Jaimez, M., Kerl, C., Gonzalez-Jimenez, J., Cremers, D.: Fast odometry and scene flow from RGB-D cameras based on geometric clustering. In: IEEE International Conference on Robotics and Automation (ICRA) (2017)
17. Loper, M., Mahmood, N., Romero, J., Pons-Moll, G., Black, M.J.: SMPL: a skinned multi-person linear model. SIGGRAPH Asia **34**(6), 248:1–248:16 (2015)
18. Lv, Z.: KinfuSeg: a dynamic SLAM approach based on kinect fusion. Master's thesis, Imperial College London (2013)
19. Lv, Z., Beall, C., Alcantarilla, P.F., Li, F., Kira, Z., Dellaert, F.: A continuous optimization approach for efficient and accurate scene flow. In: Leibe, B., Matas, J., Sebe, N., Welling, M. (eds.) ECCV 2016. LNCS, vol. 9912, pp. 757–773. Springer, Cham (2016). https://doi.org/10.1007/978-3-319-46484-8_46
20. Mayer, N., et al.: A large dataset to train convolutional networks for disparity, optical flow, and scene flow estimation. In: IEEE Conference on Computer Vision and Pattern Recognition (CVPR), pp. 4040–4048 (2016)
21. Menze, M., Geiger, A.: Object scene flow for autonomous vehicles. In: IEEE Conference on Computer Vision and Pattern Recognition (CVPR), pp. 3061–3070 (2015)
22. Mur-Artal, R., Tardós, J.D.: ORB-SLAM2: an open-source SLAM system for monocular, stereo and RGB-D cameras. IEEE Trans. Robot. **33**(5), 1255–1262 (2017). https://doi.org/10.1109/TRO.2017.2705103
23. Newcombe, R.A., Fox, D., Seitz, S.M.: DynamicFusion: reconstruction and tracking of non-rigid scenes in real-time. In: IEEE Conference on Computer Vision and Pattern Recognition (CVPR), June 2015
24. Pons-Moll, G., Romero, J., Mahmood, N., Black, M.J.: Dyna: a model of dynamic human shape in motion. SIGGRAPH **34**(4), 120:1–120:14 (2015)

25. Quiroga, J., Brox, T., Devernay, F., Crowley, J.: Dense semi-rigid scene flow estimation from RGBD images. In: Fleet, D., Pajdla, T., Schiele, B., Tuytelaars, T. (eds.) ECCV 2014. LNCS, vol. 8695, pp. 567–582. Springer, Cham (2014). https://doi.org/10.1007/978-3-319-10584-0_37
26. Richter, S.R., Hayder, Z., Koltun, V.: Playing for benchmarks. In: International Conference on Computer Vision (ICCV) (2017)
27. Scharwächter, T., Enzweiler, M., Franke, U., Roth, S.: Stixmantics: a medium-level model for real-time semantic scene understanding. In: Fleet, D., Pajdla, T., Schiele, B., Tuytelaars, T. (eds.) ECCV 2014. LNCS, vol. 8693, pp. 533–548. Springer, Cham (2014). https://doi.org/10.1007/978-3-319-10602-1_35
28. Sevilla-Lara, L., Sun, D., Jampani, V., Black, M.J.: Optical flow with semantic segmentation and localized layers. In: IEEE Conference on Computer Vision and Pattern Recognition (CVPR), June 2016
29. Shashua, A., Gdalyahu, Y., Hayun, G.: Pedestrian detection for driving assistance systems: single-frame classification and system level performance. In: IEEE Intelligent Vehicles Symposium (IV), pp. 1–6, June 2004
30. Sturm, J., Engelhard, N., Endres, F., Burgard, W., Cremers, D.: A benchmark for the evaluation of RGB-D SLAM systems. In: IEEE/RSJ International Conference on Intelligent Robots and Systems (IROS), October 2012
31. Su, H., Qi, C.R., Li, Y., Guibas, L.J.: Render for CNN: viewpoint estimation in images using CNNs trained with rendered 3D model views. In: International Conference on Computer Vision (ICCV), December 2015
32. Sun, D., Sudderth, E.B., Pfister, H.: Layered RGBD scene flow estimation. In: IEEE Conference on Computer Vision and Pattern Recognition (CVPR), pp. 548–556. IEEE (2015)
33. Sun, D., Yang, X., Liu, M.Y., Kautz, J.: PWC-Net: CNNs for optical flow using pyramid, warping, and cost volume. In: IEEE Conference on Computer Vision and Pattern Recognition (CVPR) (2018)
34. Ummenhofer, B., et al.: DeMoN: depth and motion network for learning monocular stereo. In: IEEE Conference on Computer Vision and Pattern Recognition (CVPR) (2017)
35. Valgaerts, L., Bruhn, A., Zimmer, H., Weickert, J., Stoll, C., Theobalt, C.: Joint estimation of motion, structure and geometry from stereo sequences. In: Daniilidis, K., Maragos, P., Paragios, N. (eds.) ECCV 2010. LNCS, vol. 6314, pp. 568–581. Springer, Heidelberg (2010). https://doi.org/10.1007/978-3-642-15561-1_41
36. Varol, G., et al.: Learning from synthetic humans. In: IEEE Conference on Computer Vision and Pattern Recognition (CVPR) (2017)
37. Vedula, S., Baker, S., Rander, P., Collins, R., Kanade, T.: Three-dimensional scene flow. In: International Conference on Computer Vision (ICCV), vol. 2, pp. 722–729 (1999)
38. Vijayanarasimhan, S., Ricco, S., Schmid, C., Sukthankar, R., Fragkiadaki, K.: SfM-Net: learning of structure and motion from video. arXiv abs/1704.07804 (2017)
39. Vogel, C., Schindler, K., Roth, S.: 3D scene flow estimation with a rigid motion prior. In: International Conference on Computer Vision (ICCV), pp. 1291–1298 (2011)
40. Vogel, C., Schindler, K., Roth, S.: Piecewise rigid scene flow. In: International Conference on Computer Vision (ICCV), pp. 1377–1384 (2013)
41. Vogel, C., Schindler, K., Roth, S.: 3D scene flow estimation with a piecewise rigid scene model. Int. J. Comput. Vis. **115**(1), 1–28 (2015)

42. Vogel, C., Roth, S., Schindler, K.: View-consistent 3D scene flow estimation over multiple frames. In: Fleet, D., Pajdla, T., Schiele, B., Tuytelaars, T. (eds.) ECCV 2014. LNCS, vol. 8692, pp. 263–278. Springer, Cham (2014). https://doi.org/10.1007/978-3-319-10593-2_18
43. Wang, P., Li, W., Gao, Z., Zhang, Y., Tang, C., Ogunbona, P.: Scene flow to action map: a new representation for RGB-D based action recognition with convolutional neural networks. In: IEEE Conference on Computer Vision and Pattern Recognition (CVPR), July 2017
44. Wedel, A., Brox, T., Vaudrey, T., Rabe, C., Franke, U., Cremers, D.: Stereoscopic scene flow computation for 3D motion understanding. Int. J. Comput. Vis. **95**(1), 29–51 (2011)
45. Wulff, J., Sevilla-Lara, L., Black, M.J.: Optical flow in mostly rigid scenes. In: IEEE Conference on Computer Vision and Pattern Recognition (CVPR), July 2017
46. Xiao, J., Owens, A., Torralba, A.: SUN3D: a database of big spaces reconstructed using SfM and object labels. In: International Conference on Computer Vision (ICCV), pp. 1625–1632. IEEE Computer Society (2013)
47. Yin, Z., Shi, J.: GeoNet: unsupervised learning of dense depth, optical flow and camera pose. In: IEEE Conference on Computer Vision and Pattern Recognition (CVPR) (2018)
48. Zhou, Q.-Y., Park, J., Koltun, V.: Fast global registration. In: Leibe, B., Matas, J., Sebe, N., Welling, M. (eds.) ECCV 2016. LNCS, vol. 9906, pp. 766–782. Springer, Cham (2016). https://doi.org/10.1007/978-3-319-46475-6_47
49. Zhou, T., Brown, M., Snavely, N., Lowe, D.G.: Unsupervised learning of depth and ego-motion from video. In: IEEE Conference on Computer Vision and Pattern Recognition (CVPR) (2017)

Unsupervised CNN-Based Co-saliency Detection with Graphical Optimization

Kuang-Jui Hsu[1,2](✉), Chung-Chi Tsai[1,3], Yen-Yu Lin[1], Xiaoning Qian[3], and Yung-Yu Chuang[1,2]

[1] Research Center for Information Technology Innovation, Academia Sinica, Taipei, Taiwan
{kjhsu,yylin}@citi.sinica.edu.tw

[2] Computer Science and Information Engineering, National Taiwan University, Taipei, Taiwan
cyy@csie.ntu.edu.tw

[3] Electrical and Computer Engineering, Texas A&M University, College Station, USA
{chungchi,xqian}@ece.tamu.edu

Abstract. In this paper, we address co-saliency detection in a set of images jointly covering objects of a specific class by an unsupervised convolutional neural network (CNN). Our method does not require any additional training data in the form of object masks. We decompose co-saliency detection into two sub-tasks, *single-image saliency detection* and *cross-image co-occurrence region discovery* corresponding to two novel unsupervised losses, *the single-image saliency (SIS) loss* and *the co-occurrence (COOC) loss*. The two losses are modeled on a graphical model where the former and the latter act as the unary and pairwise terms, respectively. These two tasks can be jointly optimized for generating co-saliency maps of high quality. Furthermore, the quality of the generated co-saliency maps can be enhanced via two extensions: map sharpening by self-paced learning and boundary preserving by fully connected conditional random fields. Experiments show that our method achieves superior results, even outperforming many supervised methods.

Keywords: Co-saliency detection · Unsupervised learning
Convolutional neural networks · Deep learning · Graphical model

1 Introduction

Co-saliency detection refers to searching for visually salient objects repetitively appearing in multiple given images. For its superior scalability, co-saliency has been applied to help various applications regarding image content understanding, such as image/video co-segmentation [1–3], object co-localization [4], content-aware compression [5], etc.

The success of co-saliency detection relies on robust feature representations of co-salient objects against appearance variations across images. Engineered

V. Ferrari et al. (Eds.): ECCV 2018, LNCS 11209, pp. 502–518, 2018.
https://doi.org/10.1007/978-3-030-01228-1_30

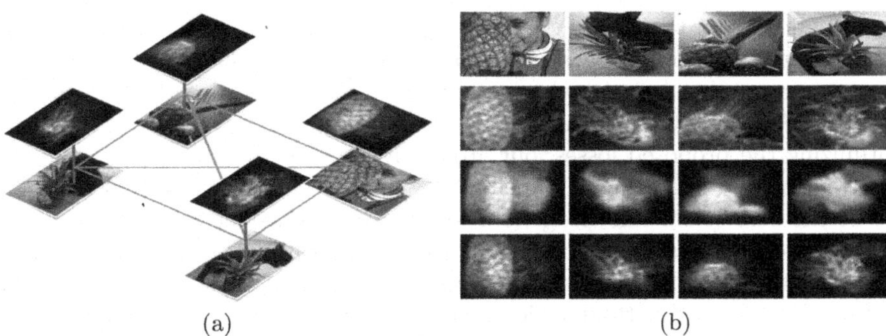

Fig. 1. Motivation of our method. (a) Our method optimizes an objective function defined on a graph where single-image saliency (SIS) detection (red edges) and cross-image co-occurrence (COOC) discovery (blue edges) are considered jointly. (b) The first row displays the images for co-saliency detection. The following three rows show the detected saliency maps by using COOC, SIS, and both of them, respectively. (Color figure online)

features, such as color histograms, Gabor filtered texture features, and SIFT [6] are widely used in conventional co-saliency methods [7–10]. Deep learning (DL) has recently emerged and demonstrated success in many computer vision applications. DL-based features have been adopted for co-saliency detection, such as those extracted from a pre-trained convolutional neural network (CNN) [11] or from unsupervised semantic feature learning with restricted Boltzmann machines (RBMs) [12]. However, feature extraction and co-saliency detection are treated as separate steps in these approaches [7–12], leading to suboptimal performance. In contrast, the supervised methods, by metric learning [13] or DL [14], enable the integration of feature learning and co-saliency detection. However, they require additional training data in the form of object masks, often manually drawn or delineated by tools with intensive user interaction. Such heavy annotation cost makes these methods less practical as pointed out in other applications, such as semantic segmentation [15] and saliency detection [16]. Furthermore, their learned models may not perform well for unseen object categories in testing, since the models do not adapt themselves to unseen categories.

In this work, we address the aforementioned issues by proposing an unsupervised CNN-based method for joint adaptive feature learning and co-saliency detection for given images, hence making a good compromise between the performance and the annotation requirement. In the proposed method, co-saliency detection is decomposed into two complementary parts, *single-image saliency detection* and *cross-image co-occurrence region discovery*. The former detects the saliency object in a single image, which may not repetitively appear across images. The latter discovers regions repetitively appearing across images, which may not be visually salient. To this end, we design two novel losses, *the single-image saliency (SIS) loss* and *the co-occurrence (COOC) loss*, to capture the two different but complementary sources of information. These two losses measure the quality of the saliency maps by referring to individual images and the co-occurrence regions for each image pair, respectively. They are further integrated on a graphical model whose unary and pairwise terms correspond to the proposed SIS and COOC losses respectively, as illustrated in Fig. 1(a). Through optimizing the proposed losses, our approach can generate co-saliency maps of high quality by integrating SIS and COOC cues, as shown in Fig. 1(b).

To the best of our knowledge, our method represents the first unsupervised CNN model for co-saliency detection. Compared with unsupervised methods including those using engineered features [3,7–10] and those using DL-based features [11,12], our method achieves better performance by joint adaptive feature learning and co-saliency detection based on CNNs. Compared with the supervised method [13,17], our method can reach comparable or even slightly better performance and does not suffer from the high annotation cost of labeling object masks as training data. We comprehensively evaluate our method on three benchmarks for co-saliency detection, including *the MSRC dataset* [18], *the iCoseg dataset* [19], and *the Cosal2015 dataset* [12]. The results show that our approach remarkably outperforms the state-of-the-art unsupervised methods and even surpasses many supervised DL-based saliency detection methods.

2 Related Work

2.1 Single-Image Saliency Detection

Single-image saliency detection is to distinguish salient objects from the background by either unsupervised [20–25] or supervised [26–30] methods based on color appearance, spatial locations, as well as various supplementary higher-level priors, including objectness. These approaches can handle well images with single salient objects. However, they may fail when the scenes are more complex, for example when multiple salient objects are presented with intra-image variations. By exploiting co-occurrence patterns when common objects appearing in multiple images, co-saliency detection is expected to perform better. However, the appearance variations of common objects across images could also make co-saliency detection a more challenging task.

2.2 Co-saliency Detection

Co-saliency detection discovers common and salient objects across multiple images using different strategies. The co-saliency detection methods have been developed within the bottom-up frameworks based on different robust features, including low-level handcrafted features [3,7–10,17,31,32] and high-level DL-based semantic features [11,12] to catch intra-image visual stimulus as well as inter-image repetitiveness. However, there are no features adopted suitable for all visual variations, and they treat the separate steps of feature extraction and co-saliency detection, leading to suboptimal performance. Data-driven methods [13,14,17] directly learn the patterns of co-salient objects to overcome the limitation of bottom-up methods. For instance, the transfer-learning-based method [17] uses the object masks to train a stacked denoising autoencoder (SDAE) to learn the intra-image contrast evidence, and propagate this knowledge to catch inter-image coherent foreground representations. Despite their impressive results, the performance might drop dramatically once the transferred knowledge on feature representations is not satisfactory as the separation of feature extraction and co-saliency detection may potentially impede the performance. Recently, Wei *et al.* [14] and Han *et al.* [13] have proposed unified learning-based methods to learn semantic features and detect co-salient objects jointly. Despite the improved performance, their methods rely on a large number of training object masks. It reduces the generalizability of their approaches to unseen images. However, our method can perform the adaptive and unified learning for given images in an unsupervised manner, and hence no aforementioned issues exist in our approach.

2.3 Graphical Models with CNNs

Deep learning has demonstrated success in many computer vision applications. For better preserving spatial consistency, graphical models have been integrated with CNNs when requiring structured outputs, such as depth estimation [33], stereo matching [34], semantic segmentation [35–37], image denoising, and optical flow estimation [38]. Although showing promise in preserving spatial consistency and modeling pairwise relationships, these methods have three major limitations when extending to co-saliency detection. First, their graphical models are built on single images, and hence can not be directly applied to co-saliency detection with multiple images. Second, the pairwise terms in these graphical models often act as regularization terms to ensure spatial consistency but can not work alone by themselves. Finally, they require training data to train the model. For the inter-image graphical models, Hayder *et al.* [39] and Yuan *et al.* [40] respectively integrated fully-connected CRFs into CNNs for object proposal co-generation and object co-segmentation, where each node is an object proposal. However, their methods still suffer from the last two limitations. In comparison, our method integrates the merits from graphical models for co-saliency detection without aforementioned issues.

3 Our Approach

We first describe the proposed formulation for co-saliency detection. Next, we propose a couple of enhancements by self-paced learning and fully connected conditional random fields. Finally, the optimization process and the implementation details are provided.

3.1 The Proposed Formulation

Given a set of N images $\{I_n\}_{n=1}^{N}$, co-saliency detection aims to detect the salient objects of a category commonly present in these images. We accomplish the

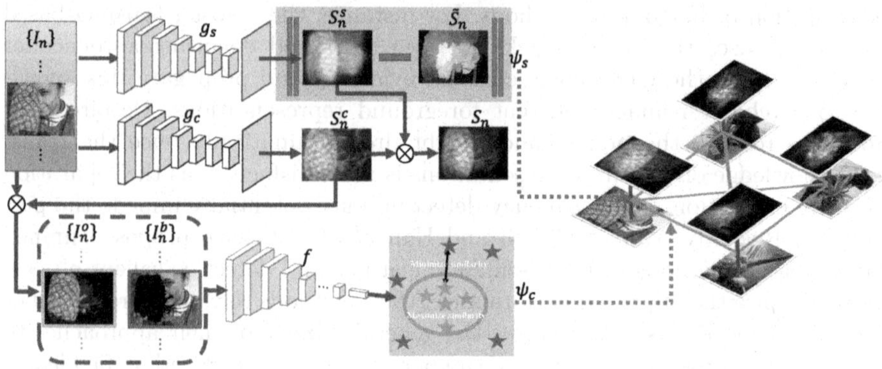

Fig. 2. Overview of our approach to co-saliency detection. It optimizes an objective function defined on a graph by learning two collaborative FCN models g_s and g_c which respectively generates single-image saliency maps and cross-image co-occurrence maps.

task by decomposing it into two sub-tasks, *single-image saliency detection* and *cross-image co-occurrence discovery*. The former detects the salient regions in a single image, without considering whether the detected regions are commonly present across images. The latter discovers the regions repetitively occurring across images, while disregarding whether the discovered regions stand out visually. Co-saliency detection, finding the salient co-occurrence regions, can then be carried out by performing and integrating the two tasks on a graph whose two types of edges respectively correspond to the two tasks, as shown in Fig. 1(a). The proposed objective function on the graph is defined by

$$E(\mathbf{w}) = \sum_{n=1}^{N} \psi_s(I_n; \mathbf{w}) + \sum_{n=1}^{N} \sum_{m \neq n} \psi_c(I_n, I_m; \mathbf{w}), \tag{1}$$

where the unary term $\psi_s(I_n; \mathbf{w})$ focuses on saliency detection for the image I_n, the pairwise term $\psi_c(I_n, I_m; \mathbf{w})$ accounts for co-occurrence discovery for the image pair (I_n, I_m), and $\mathbf{w}$ is the set of model parameters.

As shown in Fig. 2, we learn two fully convolutional network (FCN) [41] models, g_s and g_c, to optimize the unary term ψ_s and the pairwise term ψ_c in Eq. (1), respectively. For image I_n, FCN g_s investigates intra-image clues and generates its *saliency map* S_n^s. In contrast, FCN g_c discovers cross-image evidence and produces its *co-occurrence map* S_n^c, where the repetitively occurring regions are highlighted. The resultant *co-saliency map*, highlighting the co-occurrence and salient regions, is yielded by $S_n = g_s(I_n) \otimes g_c(I_n) = S_n^s \otimes S_n^c$, where $\otimes$ denotes the element-wise multiplication operator.

Let $\mathbf{w}_s$ and $\mathbf{w}_c$ denote the learnable parameter sets of FCNs g_s and g_c, respectively. We learn g_s and g_c jointly by optimizing $E(\mathbf{w} = \mathbf{w}_s \cup \mathbf{w}_c)$ in Eq. (1). The unary term ψ_s and the pairwise term ψ_c in Eq. (1) are described below.

3.2 Unary Term ψ_s

This term aims to identify the salient regions in a single image. It guides the training of FCN g_s, which produces saliency map S_n^s for image I_n, i.e., $S_n^s = g_s(I_n)$. Inspired by Zhang *et al.* [42], we apply an existing unsupervised method for saliency detection to image I_n, and use its output saliency map $\tilde{S}_n$ as the desired target for learning FCN g_s. In this work, we adopt MILP [25] to generate $\tilde{S}_n$. Specifically, the unary term $\psi_s(I_n; \mathbf{w}_s)$ applied to image I_n is defined by

$$\psi_s(I_n; \mathbf{w}_s) = \sum_{i \in I_n} R_n(i) |S_n^s(i) - \tilde{S}_n(i)|^2, \tag{2}$$

where i is the index of the pixels in I_n, $S_n^s(i)$ and $\tilde{S}_n(i)$ are respectively the saliency values of maps S_n^s and $\tilde{S}_n$ at pixel i, and $R_n(i)$ represents the importance of pixel i. Pixels in map $\tilde{S}_n$ can be divided into the salient and non-salient groups by using the mean value of $\tilde{S}_n$ as the threshold. $R_n(i)$ is introduced here to deal with the potential size unbalance between the two groups. Let δ be ratio of salient pixels over the whole image I_n. $R_n(i)$ takes the value $1 - \delta$ if pixel i belongs to the salient group, and δ otherwise. In this way, the salient and non-salient groups contribute equally in Eq. (2).

3.3 Pairwise Term ψ_c

The pairwise term ψ_c seeks the regions simultaneously appearing across images. It serves as the objective to learn FCN g_c. The regions should look similar across images but distinctive from surrounding non-detected regions. Thus, two criteria are jointly considered in the design of ψ_c, including (1) high cross-image similarity between the detected co-occurrence regions and (2) high intra-image distinctness between the detected co-occurrence regions and the rest of the image. The second criterion is auxiliary but crucial to avoid trivial solutions.

As shown in Fig. 2, FCN g_c produces the co-occurrence map S_n^c for image I_n, i.e., $S_n^c = g_c(I_n)$. The sigmoid function is used as the activation function in the last layer of g_c. Thus, the value of the co-occurrence map at each pixel i, $S_n^c(i)$, is between 0 and 1. With S_n^c, image I_n is decomposed into two masked images,

$$I_n^o = S_n^c \otimes I_n \text{ and } I_n^b = (1 - S_n^c) \otimes I_n, \tag{3}$$

where $\otimes$ denotes element-wise multiplication. The masked image I_n^o keeps the detected co-occurrence regions of I_n, while image I_n^b contains the rest.

To measure the similarity between images, we employ a feature extractor f to compute the features of a given image. In this work, the extractor f can be a pre-trained CNN model for image classification, e.g., AlexNet [43] or VGG-19 [44], with the softmax function and the last fully connected layer removed. We apply the extractor f to all masked images $\{I_n^o, I_n^b\}_{n=1}^N$ and obtain their features $\{f(I_n^o) \in \mathbb{R}^c, f(I_n^b) \in \mathbb{R}^c\}_{n=1}^N$, where c is the feature dimension. With these extracted features, the pairwise term $\psi_c(I_n, I_m; \mathbf{w}_c)$ applied the image pair I_n and I_m is defined by

$$\psi_c(I_n, I_m; \mathbf{w}_c) = -\log(p_{nm}), \tag{4}$$

where p_{nm} is the score estimating the quality of the detected co-occurrence regions in I_n and I_m. The score p_{nm} is defined below,

$$p_{nm} = \frac{\exp(-d_{nm}^+)}{\exp(-d_{nm}^+) + \exp(-d_{nm}^-)}, \text{ where} \tag{5}$$

$$d_{nm}^+ = \frac{1}{c}\|f(I_n^o) - f(I_m^o)\|^2 \text{ and} \tag{6}$$

$$d_{nm}^- = \frac{1}{2c}\|f(I_n^o) - f(I_n^b)\|^2 + \frac{1}{2c}\|f(I_m^o) - f(I_m^b)\|^2. \tag{7}$$

Equation (6) measures the inter-image distance between the detected co-occurrence regions in images I_n and I_m (criterion 1). Equation (7) evaluates the intra-image distance between the detected co-occurrence regions and the rest of the image (criterion 2). By minimizing the pairwise term $\psi_c(I_n, I_m; \mathbf{w}_c)$ in Eq. (4) for each image pair (I_n, I_m), the resultant FCN g_c will produce the co-occurrence maps where the inter-image distances between the detected co-occurrence regions are minimized while the intra-image distances between the detected co-occurrence regions and the rest of the images are maximized. After learning FCNs g_s and g_c jointly through the unary and pairwise terms in Eq. (1), the resultant co-saliency map S_n of a given image I_n is produced via $S_n = g_s(I_n) \otimes g_c(I_n)$.

Note that the pairwise term in Eq. (4) is defined by referring to the co-occurrence maps produced by FCN g_c, i.e., S_n^c and S_m^c. In practice, we found that the performance of co-saliency detection can be further improved if co-saliency maps S_n and S_m are also taking into account in the pairwise term. In our implementation, we extend the pairwise term in Eq. (4) to

$$\psi_c(I_n, I_m; \mathbf{w}_c) = -\lambda_c \log(p_{nm}) - \lambda_{\tilde{c}} \log(\tilde{p}_{nm}), \tag{8}$$

where like p_{nm}, $\tilde{p}_{nm}$ is computed in the same way but by referring to co-saliency maps S_n and S_m. Constants λ_c and $\lambda_{\tilde{c}}$ are used in Eq. (8) for weighting the corresponding terms. In the following, we will show that the quality of the co-saliency maps can be further improved via two extensions, including map enhancement by self-paced learning and postprocessing by fully connected conditional random fields (or DenseCRFs) [45].

3.4 Co-saliency Map Enhancement

The self-paced learning with CNNs is proposed to make salience map sharper. Then, fully connected conditional random fields are adopted to preserve co-salient objects' boundaries. The details of these two extensions are given below.

Co-saliency Map Enhancement by Self-paced Learning. The co-saliency maps obtained by optimizing Eq. (1) are sometimes over smooth, because both FCNs g_s and g_c do not take into account the information regarding object boundaries. To address this issue, we oversegment each image I_n into superpixels $Q_n = \{q_n^k\}_{k=1}^K$, where q_n^k is the kth superpixel and K is the number of superpixels. Pixels in a superpixel tend to belong to either a salient object or the background all together. This property can be leveraged to propagate information from pixels of high confidence to those of low confidence within the same superpixel. We divide superpixels into three groups, i.e., $Q_n = O_n \cup B_n \cup T_n$. The first two groups, O_n and B_n, contain superpixels that likely belong to the object and the background, respectively. The third group T_n covers the rest. Given the co-saliency map S_n, the three groups are yielded by

$$q_n^k \in \begin{cases} O_n, & \text{if } \mu_n^k > \mu_n + \sigma_n, \\ B_n, & \text{if } \mu_n^k < \mu_n - 0.25 * \sigma_n, \\ T_n, & \text{otherwise,} \end{cases} \quad \text{for } k = 1, 2, ..., K, \tag{9}$$

where μ_n^k is the mean saliency value of superpixel q_n^k, while μ_n and σ_n are the mean and the standard deviation of $\{\mu_n^k\}_{k=1}^K$. In addition, we follow the background seed sampling strategy used in previous work [20,46], and add superpixels on the image boundary to the set B_n. Superpixels in O_n and B_n are confident to be assigned to either the salient regions or the background. Those in T_n are ambiguous, so they are not taken into account here. With O_n and B_n of image I_n, another FCN g_e for co-saliency map **e**nhancement is trained by optimizing

$$\psi_e(I_n; \mathbf{w}_e) = w_o \sum_{q \in O_n} \sum_{i \in q} |S_n^e(i) - 1|^2 + w_b \sum_{q \in B_n} \sum_{i \in q} |S_n^e(i) - 0|^2, \tag{10}$$

where map $S_n^e = g_e(I_n)$ is generated by FCN g_e, and i the index of pixels in I_n. Constants $w_o = \frac{|B_n|}{|O_n|+|B_n|}$ and $w_b = \frac{|O_n|}{|O_n|+|B_n|}$ are the weights used to balance the contributions of O_n and B_n, where $|O_n|$ and $|B_n|$ are the numbers of pixels in O_n and B_n, respectively.

The term in Eq. (10) enhances the consensus within superpixels of high confidence. If it is turned on, the objective is extended from that in Eq. (1) to

$$E(\mathbf{w}) = \sum_{n=1}^{N} \psi_s(I_n; \mathbf{w}_s) + \lambda_e \psi_e(I_n; \mathbf{w}_e) + \sum_{n=1}^{N-1} \sum_{m=n+1}^{N} \psi_c(I_n, I_m; \mathbf{w}_c), \tag{11}$$

where λ_e is a weight, and $\mathbf{w} = \mathbf{w}_s \cup \mathbf{w}_e \cup \mathbf{w}_c$ is the union of the learnable parameter sets of FCNs g_s, g_e, and g_c. After optimizing the objective function in Eq. (11), the co-saliency map S_n of image I_n is generated by $S_n = g_s(I_n) \otimes g_e(I_n) \otimes g_c(I_n) = S_n^s \otimes S_n^e \otimes S_n^c$.

Postprocessing Using DenseCRFs. The co-saliency maps obtained by optimizing the objective in Eq. (11) can be further improved by enforcing spatial coherence and preserving object boundaries. To this end, we follow previous work [28,47] and adopt DenseCRFs [45] to postprocess the co-saliency map S_n of a given image I_n. We use the DenseCRFs code implemented by Li and Yu [47] in this work.

3.5 Optimization

To reduce memory consumption and speed up the training, the proposed method is optimized by using a two-stage procedure. At the first stage, we respectively learn FCNs g_s and g_c by using the objective functions in Eqs. (2) and (4) with all images for 20 epochs. The co-saliency maps $\{S_n = g_s(I_n) \otimes g_c(I_n)\}_{n=1}^N$ become stable enough. Thus, we divide the superpixels of each image into three groups via Eq. (9). FCN g_e is then trained with the objective in Eq. (10) with all images for 20 epochs. At the second stage, we turn on all the three terms in Eq. (11) where the extended pairwise term in Eq. (8) is adopted. The three FCNs, g_s, g_e, and g_c, are optimized jointly for 20 epochs. Note that at the second stage, we optimize only the parameters in the last two convolutional layers and the skip connections of each FCN model.

The objectives in Eqs. (1) and (11) are defined on a fully-connected graph. It is difficult to directly optimize either objective with all images at the same time due to the limited memory size. Thereby, we adopt the *piecewise training* scheme [48]. Namely, we consider only the sub-graph yielded by a subset of images at each time. The learning rate is set to 10^{-6} at the first stage and is reduced to 10^{-8} at the second stage. The weight decay and momentum are set to 0.0005 and 0.9, respectively. The objective function in Eq. (11) is differentiable. We choose ADAM [49] as the optimization solver for its rapid convergence. The gradients with respect to the optimization variables can be derived straightforward, so we omit their derivation here.

3.6 Implementation Details

The proposed method is implemented using `MatConvNet` [50]. The same network architecture is used in all the experiments. ResNet-50 [51] is adopted as the feature extractor f for the pairwise term, because AlexNet [43] and VGG-16/19 [44] sometimes lead to the problem of vanishing gradients in our application. The feature extractor f is pre-trained on ImageNet [52] and fixed during the optimization process. The features extracted by f are the inputs to the last fully connected layer of f. The feature dimension, i.e., c in Eqs. (6) and (7), is set to 2,048. All FCNs, including g_s, g_e and g_c, are developed based on the VGG-16 [44] setting of FCN [41]. We replace the activation function *softmax* in the last layer with the *sigmoid* function. SLIC [53] is adopted to generate superpixels because of its computational efficiency, better compactness and regularity. The models pre-trained on the ImageNet [54] dataset for classification are required. Following previous co-saliency detection methods [11,12], we determine the values of hyperparameters empirically and keep them fixed in all the experiments.

4 Experimental Results

In this section, we first describe the datasets and evaluation metrics. Next, we compare our method with a set of state-of-the-art methods. Finally, we investigate contributions of different components by reporting ablation studies.

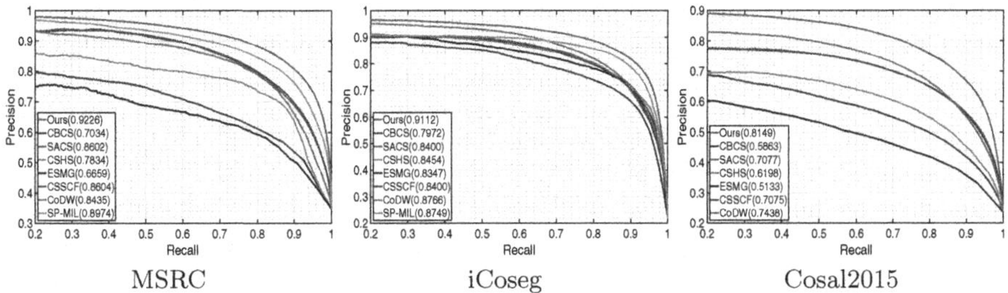

Fig. 3. Comparison with the state-of-the-art methods with the same setting in terms of PR curves on three benchmark datasets. The numbers in parentheses are AP values.

4.1 Datasets and Evaluation Metrics

Datasets. We evaluated the proposed approach on three public benchmark datasets: *iCoseg* [19], *MSRC* [18] and *Cosal2015* [12]. *iCoseg* consists of 38 groups of total 643 images, and each group has 4–42 images. The images of *iCoseg* contain single or multiple similar objects in various poses and sizes with complex backgrounds. *MSRC* contains 7 groups of total 240 images, and each group has 30–53 images. Compared to *iCoseg*, objects in *MSRC* exhibit greater appearance variation. *Cosal2015* is a more recent and more challenging dataset than the other two. It has 50 groups and a total of 2015 images. Each group contains 26 to 52 images, with various poses and sizes, appearance variations and even more complex backgrounds. Because the images of *iCoseg* and *Cosal2015* have larger sizes than the ones of *MSRC*, different batch sizes and resolutions were used. The batch size is 3 and the resolution is 512 × 512 for *iCoseg* and *Cosal2015*, while the batch size is 5 and the resolution is 320 × 320 for *MSRC*.

Evaluation Metrics. To evaluate the performance of co-saliency detection, we consider three metrics, *average precision* (AP), *F-measure* (F_β), and *structure measure* (S_α). AP is computed from the area under the Precision-Recall (PR) curve, which is produced by binarizing saliency maps with every integer threshold in the range of $[0, 255]$. *F-measure* denotes the harmonic mean of the precision and recall values obtained by a self-adaptive threshold $T = \mu + \sigma$, where μ and σ are respectively the mean and standard deviation of the saliency map. With the precision and recall values, the *F-measure* is computed by $F_\beta = \frac{(1+\beta^2)\times precision \times recall}{\beta^2 \times precision + recall}$, where $\beta^2 = 0.3$ to emphasize more on recall as suggested in previous work [11,12,56]. The *structure measure* (S_α) [57] is adopted to evaluate the spatial structure similarities of saliency maps based on both region-aware structural similarity S_r and object-aware structural similarity S_o, defined as $S_\alpha = \alpha * S_r + (1 - \alpha) * S_o$, where $\alpha = 0.5$ following [57].

4.2 Comparison with State-of-the-Art Methods

To have a thorough comparison with state-of-the-art methods, we divide them into four groups, i.e., the unsupervised saliency [20,22–25,42] and co-

Table 1. The performance of co-saliency detection on three benchmark datasets. SI and CS denote the single-image saliency and co-saliency methods, respectively. US and S indicate the unsupervised and supervised methods, respectively. The numbers in red and green respectively indicate the best and the second best results of the unsupervised co-saliency methods (CS+US), the group which the proposed method belongs to.

Method	Setting	MSRC			iCoseg			Cosal2015		
		AP	F_β	S_α	AP	F_β	S_α	AP	F_β	S_α
DIM [17]	CS+S	-	-	-	0.8773	0.7918	0.7583	-	-	-
UMLBF [13]	CS+S	0.9160	0.8410	-	-	-	-	0.8210	0.7120	-
CBCS [7]	CS+US	0.7034	0.5910	0.4801	0.7972	0.7408	0.6580	0.5863	0.5579	0.5439
SACS [31]	CS+US	0.8602	0.7877	0.7074	0.8400	0.7973	0.7523	0.7077	0.6923	0.6938
CSHS [8]	CS+US	0.7834	0.7118	0.6661	0.8454	0.7549	0.7502	0.6198	0.6181	0.5909
ESMG [32]	CS+US	0.6659	0.6245	0.5804	0.8347	0.7766	0.7677	0.5133	0.5114	0.5446
CSSCF [3]	CS+US	0.8604	0.8005	0.7383	0.8400	0.7811	0.7404	0.7075	0.6815	0.6710
CoDW [12]	CS+US	0.8435	0.7724	0.7129	0.8766	0.7985	0.7500	0.7438	0.7046	0.6473
SP-MIL [11]	CS+US	0.8974	0.8029	0.7687	0.8749	0.8143	0.7715	-	-	-
MVSRC [55]	CS+US	0.8530	0.7840	-	0.8680	0.8100	-	-	-	-
Ours	CS+US	0.9226	0.8404	0.7948	0.9112	0.8497	0.8200	0.8149	0.7580	0.7506
LEGS [26]	SI+S	0.8479	0.7701	0.6997	0.7924	0.7473	0.7529	0.7339	0.6926	0.7068
DCL [47]	SI+S	0.9065	0.8259	0.7742	0.9003	0.8444	0.8606	0.7815	0.7386	0.7591
DSS [28]	SI+S	0.8700	0.8313	0.7435	0.8802	0.8386	0.8483	0.7745	0.7509	0.7579
UCF [29]	SI+S	0.9217	0.8114	0.8175	0.9292	0.8261	0.8754	0.8081	0.7194	0.7790
Amulet [30]	SI+S	0.9219	0.8159	0.8162	0.9395	0.8381	0.8937	0.8201	0.7384	0.7856
GMR [20]	SI+US	0.8092	0.7460	0.6547	0.7990	0.7805	0.7068	0.6649	0.6605	0.6599
GP [22]	SI+US	0.8200	0.7422	0.6844	0.7821	0.7495	0.7198	0.6847	0.6576	0.6714
MB+ [23]	SI+US	0.8367	0.7817	0.7200	0.7868	0.7706	0.7272	0.6710	0.6689	0.6724
MST [24]	SI+US	0.8057	0.7491	0.6460	0.8019	0.7659	0.7292	0.7096	0.6669	0.6676
MILP [25]	SI+US	0.8334	0.7776	0.6871	0.8182	0.7883	0.7514	0.6797	0.6734	0.6752
SVFSal [42]	SI+US	0.8669	0.7934	0.7688	0.8376	0.8056	0.8271	0.7468	0.7120	0.7604

saliency [3,7,8,11,12,31,32,55] detection methods as well as supervised saliency [26,28–30,47,58] and co-saliency [13,17] detection methods. The overall performance statistics are compared in Table 1 and Fig. 3. Please note that all compared supervised single-image saliency detection methods are CNN-based. Among unsupervised single-image saliency methods, SVFSal [42] is CNN-based. When available, we used the publicly released source code with default parameters provided by the authors to reproduce the experimental results. For methods without releasing source code, we either evaluated metrics on their pre-generated co-saliency maps (SP-MIL [11], CoDW [12] and DIM [17]), or directly copied the numbers reported in their papers (UMLBF [13] and MVSRC [55]).

From Table 1, our method outperforms all methods with the same unsupervised co-saliency detection setting by a significant margin. Most approaches of this category take feature extraction and co-salient object detection as

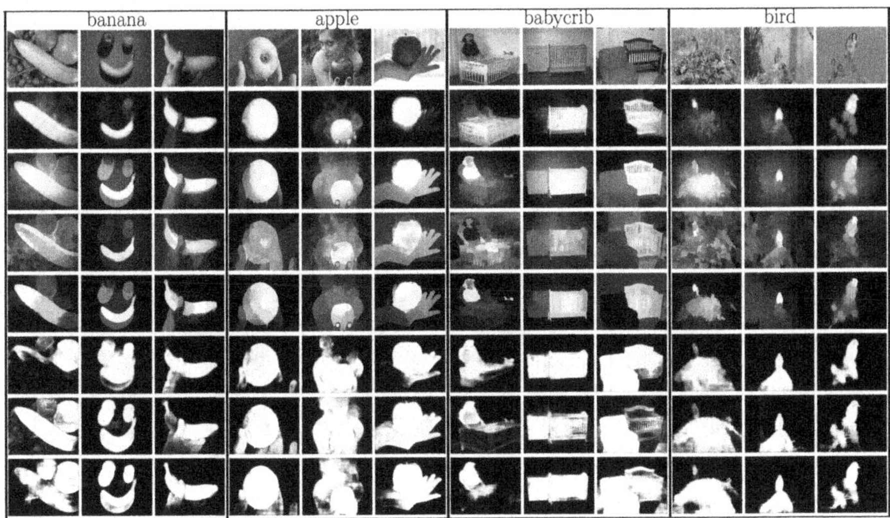

Fig. 4. Example saliency maps generated by our method and some state-of-the-art methods. From the top to the bottom, they are the given images, ours, CSSCF [3], CoDW [12], MILP [25], SVFSal [42], UCF [29] and Amulet [30].

separating steps. Our approach excels them by performing these steps simultaneously and adopting CNN models. Comparing with the group of the supervised co-saliency method, UMLBF [13] and DIM [17], our method yields comparable or even slightly better performance without expensive object annotations. Although both with the unsupervised setting, by taking advantage of additional information within an image set, our method clearly outperforms the group of unsupervised single-image saliency detection methods. It's worth mentioning that our method also outperforms the unsupervised CNN-based single-saliency method, SVFSal [42] that requires saliency proposal fusion for generating high-quality pseudo ground-truth as training data. In general, the supervised CNN-based single-image saliency methods perform the best among four groups of methods as they better utilize the object annotations. Even so, our method still outperforms many of the methods in this group by exploiting cross-image referencing and adaptive feature learning. From the PR curves in Fig. 3, the proposed method outperforms the state-of-the-arts by a large margin.

Figure 4 shows example saliency maps produced by our method and some state-of-the-art methods, including unsupervised co-saliency detection methods (CSSCF [3], CoDW [12]), unsupervised single-image saliency methods (MILP [25] and SVFSal [42]), and supervised CNN-based methods (UCF [29] and Amulet [30]). Without referring to other images in the given image set, single-image saliency methods could detect the visually salient objects that do not repetitively appear in other images, such as the orange and the apple in the second image of the banana set or the woman in the first image of the babycrib set. Co-saliency detection methods perform better in this regard. The competing co-saliency

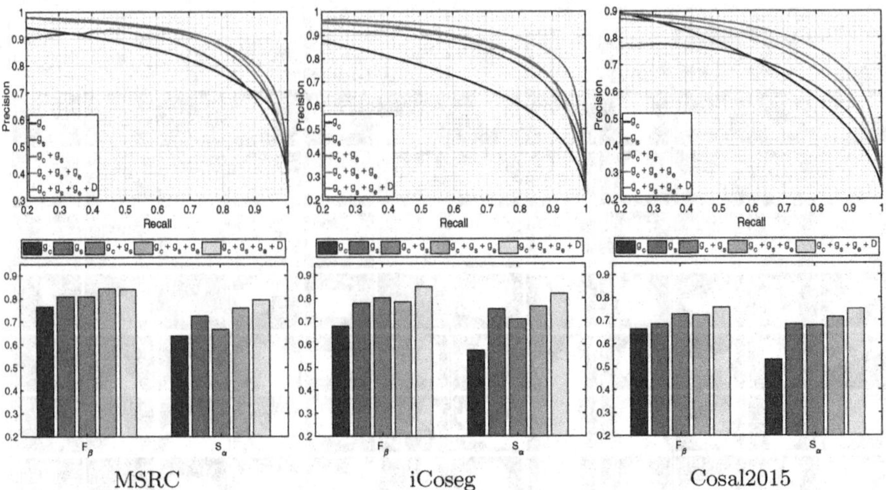

Fig. 5. Ablation studies on three benchmarks. The top row plots the PR curves, while the bottom row shows the performance in F_β and S_α.

methods, CSSCF [3] and CoDW [12], cannot perform well for images with low figure-ground discrepancies or highly-textured backgrounds, such as the second and third images of the babycrib set or the first and second images of the bird set. The major drawback of their approaches is to treat feature extraction as a separate step. Thus, they cannot find the most discriminative features across images. Our method addresses the problem by performing adaptive feature learning and co-saliency detection jointly.

4.3 Ablation Studies

We have performed ablation studies to investigate the contributions of individual components, g_c, g_s, g_e and DenseCRFs. Figure 5 reports the results with different metrics. +D denotes the results refined by DenseCRFs. For both AP and F_β, the integration of g_c and g_s outperforms either alone. It is not the case for S_α measuring the structure of the detected objects. It will be explained later. Both self-paced learning and DenseCRFs further improve the results.

Figure 6 gives example co-saliency maps for ablation studies. They demonstrate that g_c and g_s can be complementary to each other. Taking the butterfly set as an example, g_s highlights both butterflies and flowers in the first, third and fourth images. After integrating the co-occurrence information discovered by g_c, the flowers are mostly removed and lightened in $g_c + g_s$. As mentioned above, $g_c + g_s$ could perform worse in terms of S_α. It is because g_c tends to have less certainty, particularly inside objects or ambiguous background regions, as illustrated in the second row of Fig. 6. Thus, $g_c + g_s$ usually generates fuzzier maps than g_s alone. For example, the cattle have lower saliency values in $g_c + g_s$ (the fourth row of Fig. 6) than g_s (the third row of Fig. 6). By propagating

Fig. 6. Example co-saliency maps generated by combinations of different components. From the top to the bottom, they are the given images, g_c, g_s, $g_c + g_s$, $g_c + g_s + g_e$ and $g_c + g_s + g_e + \mathrm{D}$, respectively.

information from regions with high confidence, g_e improves the certainty of the results of $g_c + g_s$. Although with less gain in AP and F_β, it brings large improvement in S_α since objects are more highlighted and the backgrounds are further lightened as shown in the fifth row of Fig. 6. Finally, the DenseCRF enhances spatial coherence and boundary preservation, thus improving both quantitative and qualitative results.

5 Conclusions

In this paper, we have presented an unsupervised method for co-saliency detection using CNNs. To the best of our knowledge, it is the first one to address this problem with an unsupervised CNN. Our method decomposes the problem into two sub-tasks, *single-image saliency detection* and *cross-image co-occurrence region discovery*, by modeling the corresponding novel losses: *single-image saliency (SIS) loss* and *co-occurrence (COOC) loss*. The graphical model is adopted to integrate these two losses with unary and pairwise terms corresponding to the SIS and COOC losses, respectively. By optimizing the energy function associated with the graph, two networks are learnt jointly. The quality of co-saliency maps is further improved by self-paced learning and postprocessing by DenseCRFs. Experiments on three challenging benchmarks show that the proposed method outperforms the state-of-the-art unsupervised methods. In the future, we plan to generalize our method to other applications, such as semantic correspondence [59], image co-localization [14] and object co-segmentation [60] that also require learning among multiple images.

Acknowledgments. This work was supported in part by Ministry of Science and Technology (MOST) under grant 105-2221-E-001-030-MY2 and MOST Joint Research

Center for AI Technology and All Vista Healthcare under grant 107-2634-F-002-007. This work was partially supported by Awards #1547557 and #1553281 from the National Science Foundation.

References

1. Fu, H., Xu, D., Zhang, B., Lin, S., Ward, R.: Object-based multiple foreground video co-segmentation via multi-state selection graph. TIP **24**, 3415–3424 (2015)
2. Fu, H., Xu, D., Lin, S., Liu, J.: Object-based RGBD image co-segmentation with mutex constraint. In: CVPR (2015)
3. Jerripothula, K., Cai, J., Yuan, J.: Image co-segmentation via saliency co-fusion. TMM **18**, 1896–1909 (2016)
4. Jerripothula, K.R., Cai, J., Yuan, J.: CATS: co-saliency activated tracklet selection for video co-localization. In: Leibe, B., Matas, J., Sebe, N., Welling, M. (eds.) ECCV 2016. LNCS, vol. 9911, pp. 187–202. Springer, Cham (2016). https://doi.org/10.1007/978-3-319-46478-7_12
5. Xue, J., Li, C., Zheng, N.: Proto-object based rate control for JPEG2000: an approach to content-based scalability. IEEE Trans. Image Process. **20**(4), 1177–1184 (2011)
6. Lowe, D.: Distinctive image features from scale-invariant keypoints. IJCV **60**, 91–110 (2004)
7. Fu, H., Cao, X., Tu, Z.: Cluster-based co-saliency detection. TIP **22**, 3766–3778 (2013)
8. Liu, Z., Zou, W., Li, L., Shen, L., Meur, O.L.: Co-saliency detection based on hierarchical segmentation. SPL **21**, 88–92 (2014)
9. Tsai, C.C., Qian, X., Lin, Y.Y.: Segmentation guided local proposal fusion for co-saliency detection. In: ICME (2017)
10. Tsai, C.C., Qian, X., Lin, Y.Y.: Image co-saliency detection via locally adaptive saliency map fusion. In: ICASSP (2017)
11. Zhang, D., Meng, D., Han, J.: Co-saliency detection via a self-paced multiple-instance learning framework. TPAMI **39**(5), 865–878 (2017)
12. Zhang, D., Han, J., Li, C., Wang, J., Li, X.: Detection of co-salient objects by looking deep and wide. IJCV **120**, 215–232 (2016)
13. Han, J., Cheng, G., Li, Z., Zhang, D.: A unified metric learning-based framework for co-saliency detection. TCSVT (2017)
14. Wei, L., Zhao, S., Bourahla, O., Li, X., Wu, F.: Group-wise deep co-saliency detection. In: IJCAI (2017)
15. Hsu, K.J., Lin, Y.Y., Chuang, Y.Y.: Augmented multiple instance regression for inferring object contours in bounding boxes. TIP **23**, 1722–1736 (2014)
16. Hsu, K.J., Lin, Y.Y., Chuang, Y.Y.: Weakly supervised saliency detection with a category-driven map generator. In: BMVC (2017)
17. Zhang, D., Han, J., Han, J., Shao, L.: Cosaliency detection based on intrasaliency prior transfer and deep intersaliency mining. TNNLS **27**, 1163–1176 (2016)
18. Winn, J., Criminisi, A., Minka, T.: Object categorization by learned universal visual dictionary. In: ICCV (2005)
19. Batra, D., Kowdle, A., Parikh, D., Luo, J., Chen, T.: iCoseg: interactive co-segmentation with intelligent scribble guidance. In: CVPR (2010)
20. Yang, C., Zhang, L., Lu, H., Ruan, X., Yang, M.M.: Saliency detection via graph-based manifold ranking. In: CVPR (2013)

21. Huan, C.R., Chang, Y.J., Yang, Z.X., Lin, Y.Y.: Video saliency map detection by dominant camera motion removal. TCSVT **24**, 1336–1349 (2014)
22. Jiang, P., Vasconcelos, N., Peng, J.: Generic promotion of diffusion-based salient object detection. In: ICCV (2015)
23. Zhang, J., Sclaroff, S., Lin, Z., Shen, X., Price, B., Mech, R.: Minimum barrier salient object detection at 80 fps. In: ICCV (2015)
24. Tu, W.C., He, S., Yang, Q., Chien, S.Y.: Real-time salient object detection with a minimum spanning tree. In: CVPR (2016)
25. Huang, F., Qi, J., Lu, H., Zhang, L., Ruan, X.: Salient object detection via multiple instance learning. TIP **26**, 1911–1922 (2017)
26. Wang, L., Lu, H., Ruan, X., Yang, M.H.: Deep networks for saliency detection via local estimation and global search. In: CVPR (2015)
27. Liu, N., Han, J.: DHSNet: deep hierarchical saliency network for salient object detection. In: CVPR (2016)
28. Hou, Q., Cheng, M.-M., Hu, X., Borji, A., Tu, Z., Torr, P.: Deeply supervised salient object detection with short connections. In: CVPR (2017)
29. Zhang, P., Wang, D., Lu, H., Wang, H., Yin, B.: Learning uncertain convolutional features for accurate saliency detection. In: ICCV (2017)
30. Zhang, P., Wang, D., Lu, H., Wang, H., Ruan, X.: Amulet: aggregating multi-level convolutional features for salient object detection. In: ICCV (2017)
31. Cao, X., Tao, Z., Zhang, B., Fu, H., Feng, W.: Self-adaptively weighted co-saliency detection via rank constraint. TIP **23**, 4175–4186 (2014)
32. Li, Y., Fu, K., Liu, Z., Yang, J.: Efficient saliency-model-guided visual co-saliency detection. SPL **22**, 588–592 (2015)
33. Liu, F., Shen, C., Lin, G.: Deep convolutional neural fields for depth estimation from a single image. In: CVPR (2015)
34. Knobelreiter, P., Reinbacher, C., Shekhovtsov, A., Pock, T.: End-to-end training of hybrid CNN-CRF models for stereo. In: CVPR (2017)
35. Chandra, S., Usunier, N., Kokkinos, I.: Dense and low-rank Gaussian CRFs using deep embeddings. In: ICCV (2017)
36. Shen, F., Gan, R., Yan, S., Zeng, G.: Semantic segmentation via structured patch prediction, context CRF and guidance CRFs. In: ICCV (2017)
37. Zheng, S., et al.: Conditional random fields as recurrent neural networks. In: ICCV (2015)
38. Wang, S., Fidler, S., Urtasun, R.: Proximal deep structured models. In: NIPS (2016)
39. Hayder, Z., He, X., Salzmann, M.: Learning to co-generate object proposals with a deep structured network. In: CVPR (2016)
40. Yuan, Z., Lu, T., Wu, Y.: Deep-dense conditional random fields for object co-segmentation. In: IJCAI (2017)
41. Long, J., Shelhamer, E., Darrell, T.: Fully convolutional models for semantic segmentation. In: CVPR (2015)
42. Zhang, D., Han, J., Zhang, Y.: Supervision by fusion: towards unsupervised learning of deep salient object detector. In: ICCV (2017)
43. Krizhevsky, A., Sutskever, I., Hinton, G.: ImageNet classification with deep convolutional neural networks. In: NIPS (2012)
44. Simonyan, K., Zisserman, A.: Very deep convolutional networks for large-scale image recognition. In: ICLR (2015)
45. Krahenbuhl, P., Koltun, V.: Efficient inference in fully connected CRFs with Gaussian edge potentials. In: NIPS (2011)

46. Jiang, B., Zhang, L., Lu, H., Yang, C., Yang, M.M.: Saliency detection via absorbing Markov chain. In: ICCV (2013)
47. Li, G., Yu, Y.: Deep contrast learning for salient object detection. In: CVPR (2016)
48. Sutton, C., McCallum, A.: Piecewise training for structured prediction. Mach. Learn. **77**(2–3), 165–194 (2009)
49. Kingma, D., Ba, J.: ADAM: a method for stochastic optimization. In: ICLR (2014)
50. Vedaldi, A., Lenc, K.: MatConvNet - convolutional neural networks for MATLAB. In: ACMMM (2015)
51. He, K., Zhang, X., Ren, S., Sun, J.: Deep residual learning for image recognition. In: CVPR (2016)
52. Deng, J., Dong, W., Socher, R., Li, L.J., Li, K., Fei-Fei, L.: ImageNet: a large-scale hierarchical image database. In: CVPR (2009)
53. Achanta, R., Shaji, A., Smith, K., Lucchi, A., Fua, P., Süsstrunk, S.: SLIC superpixels compared to state-of-the-art superpixel methods. TPAMI **34**, 2274–2282 (2012)
54. Russakovsky, O., et al.: ImageNet large scale visual recognition challenge. IJCV **115**, 211–252 (2015)
55. Yao, X., Han, J., Zhang, D., Nie, F.: Revisiting co-saliency detection: a novel approach based on two-stage multiview spectral rotation co-clustering. TIP **26**, 3196–3209 (2017)
56. Borji, A., Cheng, M.M., Jiang, H., Li, J.: Salient object detection: a benchmark. TIP **24**, 5706–5722 (2015)
57. Fan, D.P., Cheng, M.M., Liu, Y., Li, T., Borji, A.: Structure-measure: a new way to evaluate foreground maps. In: ICCV (2017)
58. Zhao, R., Ouyang, W., Li, H., Wang, X.: Saliency detection by multi-context deep learning. In: CVPR (2015)
59. Hsu, K.J., Lin, Y.Y., Chuang, Y.Y.: Robust image alignment with multiple feature descriptors and matching-guided neighborhoods. In: CVPR (2015)
60. Hsu, K.J., Lin, Y.Y., Chuang, Y.Y.: Co-attention CNNs for unsupervised object co-segmentation. In: IJCAI (2018)

Mutual Learning to Adapt for Joint Human Parsing and Pose Estimation

Xuecheng Nie[1(✉)], Jiashi Feng[1], and Shuicheng Yan[1,2]

[1] ECE Department, National University of Singapore, Singapore, Singapore
niexuecheng@u.nus.edu, elefjia@nus.edu.sg
[2] Qihoo 360 AI Institute, Beijing, China
yanshuicheng@360.cn

Abstract. This paper presents a novel *Mutual Learning to Adapt* model (MuLA) for joint human parsing and pose estimation. It effectively exploits mutual benefits from both tasks and simultaneously boosts their performance. Different from existing post-processing or multi-task learning based methods, MuLA predicts dynamic task-specific model parameters via recurrently leveraging guidance information from its parallel tasks. Thus MuLA can fast adapt parsing and pose models to provide more powerful representations by incorporating information from their counterparts, giving more robust and accurate results. MuLA is implemented with convolutional neural networks and end-to-end trainable. Comprehensive experiments on benchmarks LIP and extended PASCAL-Person-Part demonstrate the effectiveness of the proposed MuLA model with superior performance to well established baselines.

Keywords: Human pose estimation · Human parsing
Mutual learning

1 Introduction

Human parsing and pose estimation are two crucial yet challenging tasks for human body configuration analysis in 2D monocular images, which aim at segmenting human body into semantic parts and allocating body joints for human instances respectively. Recently, they have drawn increasing attention due to their wide applications, *e.g.*, human behavior analysis [9,22], person-identification [20,29] and video surveillance [14,30]. Although analyzing human body from different perspectives, these two tasks are highly correlated and could provide beneficial clues for each other. Human pose can offer structure information for body part segmentation and labeling, and on the other hand human parsing can facilitate localizing body joints in difficult scenarios. Figure 1 gives examples where considering such mutual guidance information between the two tasks can correct labeling and localization errors favorably, as highlighted in Fig. 1(b), and improve parsing and pose estimation results, as shown in Fig. 1(c).

V. Ferrari et al. (Eds.): ECCV 2018, LNCS 11209, pp. 519–534, 2018.
https://doi.org/10.1007/978-3-030-01228-1_31

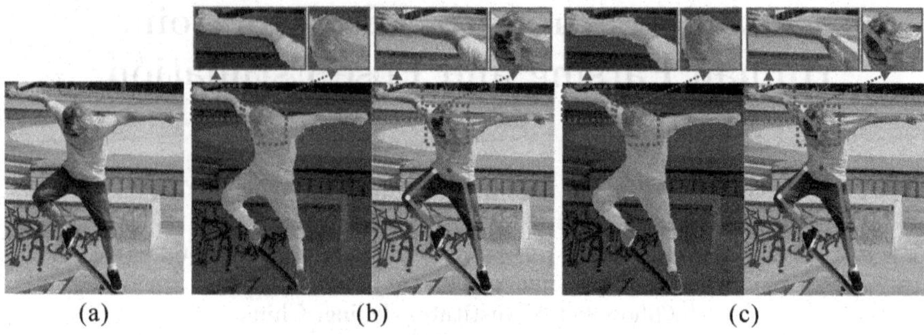

Fig. 1. Illustration of our motivation for joint human parsing and pose estimation. (a) Input image. (b) Results from independent models. (c) Results of the proposed MuLA model. MuLA can leverage mutual guidance information between human parsing and pose estimation to improve performance of both tasks, as shown with highlighted body parts and joints. Best viewed in color

Motivated by the above observation, some efforts [8,10,12,24–26] have been made to extract and use such guidance information to improve performance of the two tasks mutually. However, existing methods usually train the task-specific models separately and leverage the guidance information for post-processing, suffering several drawbacks. First, they heavily rely on hand-crafted features extracted from outputs of one task to assist the other, in an *ad hoc* manner. Second, they only utilize guidance information in inference procedure and fail to enhance model capacity during training. Third, they are one-stop solutions and too rigid to fully utilize enhanced models and iteratively improve the results. Last but not least, the models are not end-to-end learnable.

Targeting at these drawbacks, we propose a novel *Mutual Learning to Adapt* (MuLA) model to sufficiently and systematically exploit mutual guidance information between human parsing and pose estimation. In particular, our MuLA has a carefully designed interweaving architecture that enables effective between-task cooperation and mutual learning. Moreover, instead of simply fusing learned features from two tasks as in existing works, MuLA introduces a *learning to adapt* mechanism where the guidance information from one task can be effectively transferred to modify model parameters for the other parallel task, leading to augmented representation and better performance. In addition, MuLA is capable of recurrently performing model adaption by transforming estimation results to the representation space and thus can continuously refine semantic part labels and body joint locations based on enhanced models in the previous iteration.

Specifically, the MuLA model includes a representation encoding module, a mutual adaptation module and a classification module. The representation encoding module encodes input images into preliminary representations for human parsing and pose estimation individually, and meanwhile provides guidance for model adaptation. With such guidance information, the mutual adaptation module learns to dynamically predict model parameters for augmenting representations by incorporating useful prior learned from the other task, enabling effective between-task interaction and cooperation in model training. Introducing such a mutual adaptation module improves the learning process of one task towards benefiting the other, providing easily transferable information between tasks. In addition, these dynamic parameters are efficiently learned in a one-shot manner according to different inputs, leading to fast and robust model adaptation. MuLA fuses mutually-tailored representations with the preliminary ones in a residual manner to produce augmented representations for making final prediction, through the classification modules. MuLA also allows for iterative model adaption and improvement by transforming estimation results to the representation space, which serve as enhanced input for the next stage. The proposed MuLA is implemented with deep Convolutional Neural Networks and is end-to-end learnable.

We evaluate the proposed MuLA model on Look into Person (LIP) [10] and extended PASCAL-Person-Part [24] benchmarks. The experiment results well demonstrate its superiority over existing methods in exploiting mutual guidance information for joint human parsing and pose estimation. Our contributions are summarized in four aspects. First, we propose a novel end-to-end learnable model for jointly learning human parsing and pose estimation. Second, we propose a novel mutual adaptation module for dynamic interaction and cooperation between two tasks. Third, the proposed model is capable of iteratively exploiting mutual guidance information to consistently improve performance of two tasks. Fourth, we achieve new state-of-the-art on LIP dataset, and outperform the previous best model for joint human parsing and pose estimation on extended PASCAL-Person-Part dataset.

2 Related Work

Due to their close correlations, recent works have exploited human parsing (human pose estimation) to assist human pose estimation (human parsing) or leveraged their mutual benefits to jointly improve the performance for both tasks.

In [12], Ladicky *et al.* proposed to utilize body parts as additional constraint for the pose estimation model. Given locations of all joints, they introduced a body part mask component to predict labels of pixels belonging to each body part, which can be optimized with the overall model together. In [25], Xia *et al.* proposed to exploit pose estimation results to guide human parsing by leveraging joint locations to extract segment proposals for semantic parts, which are selected and assembled using an And-Or graph to output a parse of the person. In [10], Gong *et al.* proposed to improve human parsing with pose estimation in a self-supervised structure-sensitive manner through weighting segmentation loss with joint structure loss. Similar to [10], Zhao *et al.* [28] proposed to improve human parsing via regarding human pose structure from a global perspective for feature aggregation considering the importance of different positions. Yamaguchi *et al.* [26] proposed to optimize human parsing and pose estimation and improve the performance of two tasks in an alternative manner: utilizing pose estimation

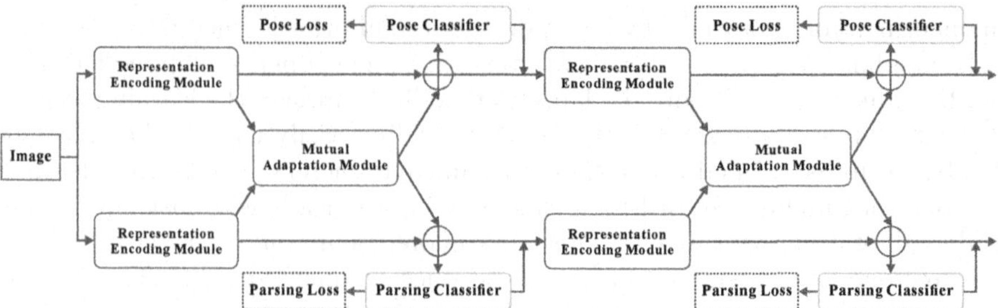

Fig. 2. Illustration of overall architecture of the proposed Mutual Learning to Adapt model (MuLA) for joint human parsing and pose estimation. Given an input image, MuLA utilizes the novel *mutual adaptation* module to build dynamic interaction and cooperation between parsing and pose estimation models in an iterative way for fully exploiting their mutual benefits to simultaneously improve their performance

results to generate body part locations for human parsing and then exploiting human parsing results to update appearance features in the pose estimation model for refining joint locations. Dong *et al.* [8] proposed a Hybrid Parsing Model for unified human parsing and pose estimation under the And-Or graph framework. They utilized body joints to assist human parsing via constructing the mixture of joint-group templates for body part representation, and exploited body parts to improve human pose estimation through forming parselets to constrain the position and co-occurrence of body joints. In [24], Xia *et al.* proposed to utilize deep learning models for joint human parsing and pose estimation. They utilized parsing results for hand-crafted features to assist pose estimation by considering relationships of body joints and parts, and then exploited the generated pose estimation results to construct joint label maps and skeleton maps for refining human parsing. With the powerful deep learning models, they achieved superior performance over previous methods.

Despite previous success, existing methods suffer from limitations of hand-crafted features relying on estimation results for exploiting guidance information to improve the counterpart models. In contrast, the proposed Mutal Learning to Adapt model can mutually learn to fast adapt the model of one task conditioned on representations of the other for specific inputs. In addition, MuLA utilizes the guidance information in both training and inference phases for joint human parsing and pose estimation. Moreover, it is end-to-end learnable via implementation with CNNs.

3 The Proposed Approach

3.1 Formulation

For an RGB image $I \in \mathbb{R}^{H\times W\times 3}$ with height H and width W, we use $S = \{s_i\}_{i=1}^{H\times W}$ to denote the human parsing result of I, where $s_i \in \{0,\dots,P\}$ is the semantic part label of the ith pixel and P is the total number of semantic part categories. Specially, 0 represents the background category. We use $J = \{(x_i, y_i)\}_{i=1}^N$ to denote body joint locations of the human instance in I, where (x_i, y_i) represents the spatial coordinates of the ith body joint and N is the number of joint categories. Our goal is to design a unified model for simultaneously predicting human parsing S and pose J via fully exploiting their mutual benefits to boost performance for both tasks.

Existing methods for joint human parsing and pose estimation usually extract hand-crafted features from the output of one task to assist the other task at post-processing. They can neither extract powerful features nor strengthen the models. Targeting at such limitations, we propose a *Mutual Learning to Adapt* (MuLA) model to substantially exploit mutual benefits from human parsing and pose estimation towards effectively improving performance of the counterpart models, through learning to adapt model parameters. In the following, we use $g_{[\psi,\psi_*]}(\cdot)$ and $h_{[\phi,\phi_*]}(\cdot)$ to denote the parsing and pose models respectively, with parameters specified in the subscripts. Specifically, ψ_* and ϕ_* denote parameters that are adaptable to the other task. Then, our proposed MuLA is formulated as following recurrent learning process:

$$\begin{aligned} S^{(t)} &= g_{[\psi^{(t)},\psi_*^{(t)}]}(F_S^{(t)}), \text{ where } \psi_*^{(t)} = h'(F_J^{(t)}, \hat{J}), \\ J^{(t)} &= h_{[\phi^{(t)},\phi_*^{(t)}]}(F_J^{(t)}), \text{ where } \phi_*^{(t)} = g'(F_S^{(t)}, \hat{S}), \end{aligned} \tag{1}$$

where t is the iteration index, $\hat{S}$ and $\hat{J}$ are parsing and pose annotations for the input image I, and $F_S^{(t)}$ and $F_J^{(t)}$ denote the extracted features for parsing and pose prediction respectively. Note, at the beginning, $F_S^{(1)} = F_J^{(1)} = I$.

The above formulation in Eq. (1) highlights the most distinguishing feature of MuLA from existing methods: MuLA explicitly adapts some model parameters of one task (*e.g.* parsing model parameter ψ_*) to the guidance information of the other task (*e.g.* pose estimation) via adapting functions $h'(\cdot,\cdot)$ and $g'(\cdot,\cdot)$. In this way, the adaptive parameters $\psi_*^{(t)}$ and $\phi_*^{(t)}$ encode useful information from the parallel tasks. With these parameters, the MuLA model can learn complementary representations and boost performance for both human parsing and pose estimation tasks, by more flexibly and effectively exploiting interaction and cooperation between them. In addition, MuLA bases $\psi_*^{(t)}$ and $\phi_*^{(t)}$ on the input images. Different inputs would modify the model parameters dynamically, making the model robust to various testing senarios. Moreover, MuLA has the ability to iteratively exploit mutual guidance information between two tasks via the recurrent learning process and thus continuously improves both models.

The overall architecture of MuLA is shown in Fig. 2. Concretely, MuLA presents an interweaving architecture and consists of three components: a *representation encoding* module, a *mutual adaptation* module and a *classification* module. The representation encoding module consists of two encoders $E^S_{\psi_e^{(t)}}(\cdot)$ and $E^J_{\phi_e^{(t)}}(\cdot)$ for transforming inputs $F_S^{(t)}$ and $F_J^{(t)}$ into high-level preliminary representations for human parsing and pose estimation.

The mutual adaptation module targets at adapting parameters $\psi_*^{(t)}$ and $\phi_*^{(t)}$ to augment preliminary representations from $E^S_{\psi_e^{(t)}}(\cdot)$ and $E^J_{\phi_e^{(t)}}(\cdot)$ by leveraging auxiliary guidance information from the parallel tasks. Inspired by the "Learning to Learn" framework [2], for achieving fast and effective adaptation, within functions $g'(\cdot,\cdot)$ and $h'(\cdot,\cdot)$, we design two learnable adapters $A_{\psi_a^{(t)}}(\cdot)$ and $A_{\phi_a^{(t)}}(\cdot)$ to learn to predict these adaptive parameters. For reliable and robust parameter prediction, we take the highest-level representation from $E^S_{\psi_e^{(t)}}(\cdot)$ and $E^J_{\phi_e^{(t)}}(\cdot)$ as mutual guidance information. Namely, $A_{\psi_a^{(t)}}(\cdot)$ and $A_{\phi_a^{(t)}}(\cdot)$ take $E^S_{\psi_e^{(t)}}(F_S^{(t)})$ and $E^J_{\phi_e^{(t)}}(F_J^{(t)})$ as inputs and output $\phi_*^{(t)}$ and $\psi_*^{(t)}$. Formally,

$$\begin{aligned} \psi_*^{(t)} &= h'(F_J^{(t)}, \hat{J}) := A_{\phi_a^{(t)}}\left(E^J_{\phi_e^{(t)}}(F_J^{(t)})\right), \\ \phi_*^{(t)} &= g'(F_S^{(t)}, \hat{S}) := A_{\psi_a^{(t)}}\left(E^S_{\psi_e^{(t)}}(F_S^{(t)})\right). \end{aligned} \tag{2}$$

Here $\psi_*^{(t)}$ and $\phi_*^{(t)}$ can tailor preliminary representations extracted by $\psi_e^{(t)}$ and $\phi_e^{(t)}$ for better human parsing and pose estimation via leveraging their mutual guidance information. We utilize the tailored representations extracted by $\psi_e^{(t)}$ and $\phi_e^{(t)}$ together with $\psi_*^{(t)}$ and $\phi_*^{(t)}$ for making final predictions, and use $E^S_{[\psi_e^{(t)},\psi_*^{(t)}]}(\cdot)$ and $E^J_{[\phi_e^{(t)},\phi_*^{(t)}]}(\cdot)$ to denote the derived adaptive encoders in MuLA. The mutual adaptation module allows for dynamic interaction and cooperation between two tasks within MuLA for fully exploiting their mutual benefits.

MuLA uses two classifiers $C^S_{\psi_w^{(t)}}(\cdot)$ and $C^J_{\phi_w^{(t)}}(\cdot)$ following the mutual adaptation module for predicting human parsing $S^{(t)}$ and pose $J^{(t)}$. Specifically, $[\psi_e^{(t)}, \psi_w^{(t)}]$ and $[\phi_e^{(t)}, \phi_w^{(t)}]$ together instantiate parameters $\psi^{(t)}$ and $\phi^{(t)}$ in Eq. (1), respectively. For iteratively exploiting mutual guidance information, we design two mapping modules $M^S_{\psi_m^{(t)}}(\cdot,\cdot)$ and $M^J_{\phi_m^{(t)}}(\cdot,\cdot)$ to map representations from $E^S_{[\psi_e^{(t)},\psi_*^{(t)}]}(\cdot)$ and $E^J_{[\phi_e^{(t)},\phi_*^{(t)}]}(\cdot)$ together with prediction results $S^{(t)}$ and $J^{(t)}$ into inputs $F_S^{(t+1)}$ and $F_J^{(t+1)}$ for the next stage. Namely,

$$F_S^{(t+1)} = M^S_{\psi_m^{(t)}}(E^S_{[\psi_e^{(t)},\psi_*^{(t)}]}(F_S^{(t)}), S^{(t)}) \text{ and } F_J^{(t+1)} = M^J_{\phi_m^{(t)}}(E^J_{[\phi_e^{(t)},\phi_*^{(t)}]}(F_J^{(t)}), J^{(t)}). \tag{3}$$

By the definition in Eq. (3), $F_S^{(t)}$ and $F_J^{(t)}$ provide preliminary representations at the start of the next stage and avoid learning from scratch at each stage. In addition, $S^{(t)}$ and $J^{(t)}$ offer additional guidance information for generating better prediction results and alleviate learning difficulties in subsequent stages [15,23].

To train MuLA, we add groundtruth supervision $\hat{S}$ and $\hat{J}$ for human parsing and pose estimation at each stage, and define the following loss function:

$$\mathcal{L} = \sum_{t=1}^{T}\left(\mathcal{L}^S\left(C^S_{\psi_w^{(t)}}(E^S_{[\psi_e^{(t)},\psi_*^{(t)}]}(F_S^{(t)})), \hat{S}\right) + \beta\mathcal{L}^J\left(C^J_{\phi_w^{(t)}}(E^J_{[\phi_e^{(t)},\phi_*^{(t)}]}(F_J^{(t)})), \hat{J}\right)\right) \tag{4}$$

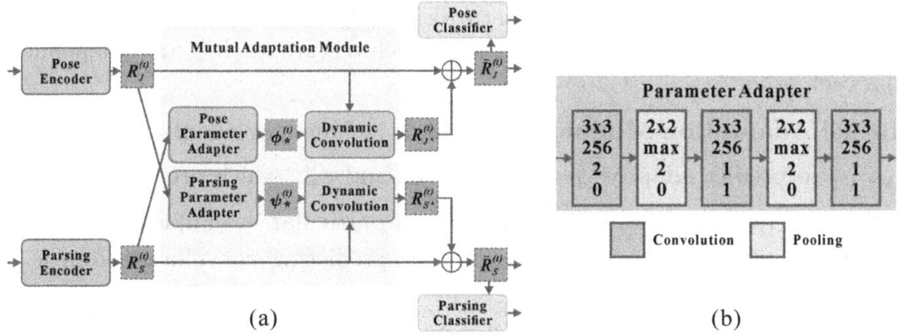

Fig. 3. (a) The CNN implementation of MuLA for one stage. Given inputs $F_S^{(t)}$ and $F_J^{(t)}$ at stage t, the parsing and pose encoders generate preliminary representations $R_S^{(t)}$ and $R_J^{(t)}$. Then, the parameter adapters predict dynamic parameters $\psi_*^{(t)}$ and $\phi_*^{(t)}$ for learning complementary representations $R_{S*}^{(t)}$ and $R_{J*}^{(t)}$ via dynamic convolutions, which are exploited to tailor preliminary representations via addition in a residual manner for producing refined representations $\bar{R}_S^{(t)}$ and $\bar{R}_J^{(t)}$. Finally, MuLA feeds $\bar{R}_S^{(t)}$ and $\bar{R}_J^{(t)}$ to classifiers for parsing and pose estimation, respectively. (b) The network architecture of parameter adapter, consisting of three convolution and two pooling layers. For each layer, the kernel size, the number of channel/pooling types, stride and padding size are specified from top to bottom

where T denotes the total number of iterations in MuLA, $\mathcal{L}^S(\cdot,\cdot)$ and $\mathcal{L}^J(\cdot,\cdot)$ represent loss functions for human parsing and pose estimation, respectively, and β is a weight coefficient for balancing $\mathcal{L}^S(\cdot,\cdot)$ and $\mathcal{L}^J(\cdot,\cdot)$. In next subsection, we will provide details on implementation of MuLA.

3.2 Implementation

We implement MuLA with deep Convolutional Neural Networks (CNNs), and show architecture details in Fig. 3(a).

Representation Encoding Module. This module is composed of two encoders $E^S_{\psi_e^{(t)}}(\cdot)$ and $E^J_{\phi_e^{(t)}}(\cdot)$, targeting at encoding inputs $F_S^{(t)}$ and $F_J^{(t)}$ into discriminative representations $R_S^{(t)}$ and $R_J^{(t)}$ for estimating parsing and pose results, as well as for predicting adaptive parameters. We implement $E^S_{\psi_e^{(t)}}(\cdot)$ and $E^J_{\phi_e^{(t)}}(\cdot)$ with two different state-of-the-art architectures: the VGG network [19] and Hourglass network [15]. VGG network is a general architecture widely applied in various vision tasks [5,18]. We utilize its fully convolutional version with 16 layers, denoted as VGG16-FCN, for both tasks. In addition, we modify VGG16-FCN to reduce the total stride from 32 to 8 via removing the last two max-pooing layers, aiming to enlarge feature maps for improving part labeling and joint localization accuracy. The Hourglass network has a U-shape architecture which is initially designed for human pose estimation. We extend it to parsing by making the output layer aim for semantic part labeling instead of joint confidence regression.

Other configurations of Hourglass network exactly follow [15]. Note that paring and pose encoders need not have the same architecture as they are independent from each other.

Mutual Adaptation Module. This module includes two adapters $A_{\phi_a^{(t)}}(\cdot)$ and $A_{\psi_a^{(t)}}(\cdot)$ to predict adaptive parameters $\psi_*^{(t)}$ and $\phi_*^{(t)}$ which are used to tailor preliminary representations $R_S^{(t)}$ and $R_J^{(t)}$. In particular, we implement $A_{\psi_a^{(t)}}(\cdot)$ and $A_{\phi_a^{(t)}}(\cdot)$ with the same small CNN for predicting convolution kernels of counterpart models, as shown in Fig. 3(b). The adapter networks take $R_S^{(t)}$ and $R_J^{(t)}$ as inputs and output tensors $\phi_*^{(t)} \in \mathbb{R}^{h\times h\times c}$ and $\psi_*^{(t)} \in \mathbb{R}^{h\times h\times c}$ as convolution kernels, where h is the kernel size and $c = c_i \times c_o$ is the number of kernels with input and output channel number c_i and c_o, respectively.

However, it is not feasible to directly predict all the convolution kernels due to their large scale. To reduce the number of kernels to predict by adapters $A_{\psi_a^{(t)}}(\cdot)$ and $A_{\phi_a^{(t)}}(\cdot)$, we follow [2] to use a way analogous to SVD for decomposing parameters $\psi_*^{(t)}$ and $\phi_*^{(t)}$ via

$$\psi_*^{(t)} = U_S^{(t)} \otimes \widetilde{\psi}_*^{(t)} \otimes_{\mathrm{c}} V_S^{(t)} \text{ and } \phi_*^{(t)} = U_J^{(t)} \otimes \widetilde{\phi}_*^{(t)} \otimes_{\mathrm{c}} V_J^{(t)}, \tag{5}$$

where $\otimes$ denotes convolution operation, $\otimes_{\mathrm{c}}$ denotes channel-wise convolution operation, $U_S^{(t)}/U_J^{(t)}$ and $V_S^{(t)}/V_J^{(t)}$ are auxiliary parameters and can be viewed as parameter bases, and $\widetilde{\psi}_*^{(t)} \in \mathbb{R}^{h\times h\times c_i}$ and $\widetilde{\phi}_*^{(t)} \in \mathbb{R}^{h\times h\times c_i}$ are the actual parameters to predict by $A_{\phi_a^{(t)}}(\cdot)$ and $A_{\psi_a^{(t)}}(\cdot)$. In this way, the number of predicted parameters can be reduced by an order of magnitude.

For tailoring preliminary representations with adaptive parameters, we utilize *dynamic convolution layers* for directly applying $\psi_*^{(t)}$ and $\phi_*^{(t)}$ to conduct convolution operations on $R_S^{(t)}$ and $R_J^{(t)}$, which is implemented by just replacing static convolution kernels with the predicted dynamic ones in the traditional convolution layer:

$$\begin{aligned} R_{S*}^{(t)} &= \psi_*^{(t)} \otimes R_S^{(t)} = U_S^{(t)} \otimes \widetilde{\psi}_*^{(t)} \otimes_{\mathrm{c}} V_S^{(t)} \otimes R_S^{(t)}, \\ R_{J*}^{(t)} &= \phi_*^{(t)} \otimes R_J^{(t)} = U_J^{(t)} \otimes \widetilde{\phi}_*^{(t)} \otimes_{\mathrm{c}} V_J^{(t)} \otimes R_J^{(t)}, \end{aligned} \tag{6}$$

where $R_{S*}^{(t)}$ and $R_{J*}^{(t)}$ are dynamic representations learned from the guidance information of task counterparts, overcoming drawbacks of existing methods with hand-crafted features from estimation results. In addition, $R_{S*}^{(t)}$ and $R_{J*}^{(t)}$ are efficiently generated in a one-shot manner, avoiding the time-consuming iterative updating scheme utilized by traditional methods for representation learning. We implement $U_S^{(t)}/U_J^{(t)}$ and $V_S^{(t)}/V_J^{(t)}$ with 1×1 convolutions and apply them together with $\widetilde{\psi}_*^{(t)}/\widetilde{\phi}_*^{(t)}$ sequentially on $R_S^{(t)}/R_J^{(t)}$ to produce $R_{S*}^{(t)}/R_{J*}^{(t)}$.

Through leveraging mutual benefits between human parsing and pose estimation, $R_{S*}^{(t)}$ and $R_{J*}^{(t)}$ can provide powerful complementary cues to tailor $R_S^{(t)}$ and $R_J^{(t)}$ for better labeling semantic parts and localizing body joints. We fuse complementary representations and preliminary ones via addition in a residual manner for generating tailored representations $\bar{R}_S^{(t)}$ and $\bar{R}_J^{(t)}$ for final predictions:

$$\bar{R}_S^{(t)} = R_S^{(t)} + R_{S*}^{(t)} \text{ and } \bar{R}_J^{(t)} = R_J^{(t)} + R_{J*}^{(t)}. \tag{7}$$

Classification Module. Given representations $\bar{R}_S^{(t)}$ and $\bar{R}_J^{(t)}$, we apply two linear classifiers $C^S_{\psi_w^{(t)}}(\cdot)$ and $C^J_{\phi_w^{(t)}}(\cdot)$ for predicting semantic part probability maps $S^{(t)}$ and body joint confidence maps $J^{(t)}$, respectively. In particular, we implement classifiers with 1×1 convolution layers.

After getting $S^{(t)}$ and $J^{(t)}$, the mapping modules $M^S_{\psi_m^{(t)}}(\cdot,\cdot)$ and $M^J_{\phi_m^{(t)}}(\cdot,\cdot)$ transform them and tailored representations $\bar{R}_S^{(t)}$ and $\bar{R}_J^{(t)}$ into inputs $F_S^{(t+1)}$ and $F_J^{(t+1)}$ for the next stage. Following [15], we use 1×1 convolutions on $S^{(t)}$ and $J^{(t)}$ to map predictions into the representation space. We also apply 1×1 convolutions on $\bar{R}_S^{(t)}$ and $\bar{R}_J^{(t)}$ to map highest-level representations of the previous stage into preliminary representations for the following stage. We integrate these two representations via addition for obtaining $F_S^{(t+1)}$ and $F_J^{(t+1)}$.

Training and Inference. As exhibited in the loss function in Eq. (4), we apply both parsing and pose supervision at each mutual learning stage for training the MuLA model. In particular, we utilize CrossEntropy loss and Mean Square Error loss for parsing and pose models respectively. MuLA is end-to-end trainable by gradient back propagation.

At the inference phase, MuLA simultaneously estimates parsing and pose for an input image in one forward pass. The semantic part probability maps $S^{(T)}$ and body joint confidence maps $J^{(T)}$ from the last stage of MuLA are used for final predictions. In particular, for human parsing, the category with maximum probability at each position of $S^{(T)}$ is output as the semantic part label. For pose estimation, in the single-person case, we take the position with maximum confidence for each confidence map in $J^{(T)}$ as the location of each type of body joints; in the multi-person case, we perform Non-Maximum Suppression (NMS) on each confidence map in $J^{(T)}$ for generating joint candidates.

4 Experiments

4.1 Experimental Setup

Datasets. We evaluate the proposed MuLA model on two benchmarks for simultaneous human parsing and pose estimation: the Look into Person (LIP) dataset [10] and extended PASCAL-Person-Part dataset [24]. The LIP dataset includes 50,462 single-person images collected from various realistic scenarios, with pixel-wise annotations provided for 19 categories of semantic parts and location annotations for 16 types of body joints. In particular, LIP images are split into 30,462 for training, 10,000 for validation and 10,000 for testing. The extended PASCAL-Person-Part is a challenging multi-person dataset, containing annotations for 14 body joints and 6 semantic parts. In total, there are 3,533 images, which are split into 1,716 for training and 1,817 for testing.

Data Augmentation. We conduct data augmentation strategies commonly used in previous works [3,28] for both human parsing and pose estimation, including random rotation in $[-40°, 40°]$, random scaling in $[0.8, 1.5]$, random cropping based on the person center with translational offset in $[-40\text{px}, 40\text{px}]$, and random horizontally mirroring. We resize and pad augmented training samples into 256×256 as input to CNNs.

Implementation. We train MuLA from scratch for LIP and extended PASCAL-Person-Part datasets with their own training samples, separately. For multi-person pose estimation on extended PASCAL-Person-Part dataset, we follow the method proposed in [16]. It partitions joint candidates into corresponding persons via a dense regression branch in the pose model of MuLA for transforming joint candidates into the centroid embedding space. We implement MuLA with PyTorch [17] and use RMSProp [21] as the optimizer. We set the initial learning rate as 0.0025 and drop it with multiplier 0.5 at the 150th, 170th, 200th and 230th epochs. We train MuLA for 250 epochs in total. We perform multi-scale testing to produce final predictions for both human parsing and pose estimation. Our codes and pre-trained models will be made available.

Metrics. Following conventions, Mean Intersection-over-Union (mIOU) [10] is used for evaluating human parsing performance. We use PCK [27] and Mean Average Precision (mAP) [11,16] for measuring accuracy of single- and multi-person pose estimation, respectively.

4.2 Results on LIP Dataset

Ablation Analysis. We evaluate the proposed MuLA model with two kinds of backbone architectures, *i.e.*, the VGG16-FCN and Hourglass networks, for both human parsing and pose estimation as mentioned in Sect. 3.2.

Firstly, we conduct ablation experiments on LIP validation set with VGG16-FCN based model, denoted as VGG16-FCN-MuLA, to investigate efficacy of MuLA on leveraging mutual guidance information to simultaneously improve parsing and pose performance. The results are shown in Table 1. To demonstrate effectiveness of the adaptive representations learned by MuLA, we compare with prevalent strategies that directly fuse representations from parallel models, including addition, multiplication, concatenation. We denote these baselines as VGG16-FCN-Add/Multi/Concat respectively. To evaluate the advantages of the interweaving architecture of MuLA, we also compare it with traditional multi-task learning framework for joint human parsing and pose estimation, implemented by adding both parsing and pose supervision on a single VGG16-FCN, denoted as VGG16-FCN-MTL. To investigate effects of the residual architecture followed by the adaptation modules, we wipe off mutual interaction between tasks through replacing dynamic convolution layers with traditional

Table 1. VGG16-FCN based ablation studies on LIP validation set

Methods	PCK	mIOU
VGG16-FCN	69.1	34.5
VGG16-FCN-Add	69.7	36.5
VGG16-FCN-Multi	69.4	35.8
VGG16-FCN-Concat	69.5	36.1
VGG16-FCN-MTL	65.3	31.2
VGG16-FCN-Self	69.8	36.1
VGG16-FCN-LA-Pose	75.0	32.1
VGG16-FCN-LA-Parsing	66.5	40.0
VGG16-FCN-MuLA	**76.0**	**40.2**

Table 2. Hourglass network based ablation studies on LIP validation set

Methods	PCK	mIOU
HG-0s-1u-MuLA	78.8	38.5
HG-1s-1u-MuLA	82.2	43.5
HG-2×1u	80.8	41.3
HG-2s-1u-MuLA (1st Stage)	82.8	45.5
HG-2s-1u-MuLA (2nd Stage)	83.1	45.6
HG-2s-1u-MuLA	84.4	46.9
HG-3s-1u-MuLA	85.0	47.8
HG-4s-1u-MuLA	85.1	48.9
HG-5s-1u-MuLA	**85.4**	**49.3**

convolution layers. Such a variant is denoted as VGG16-FCN-Self. To validate advantages of bidirectionally utilizing guidance information between two tasks, we simplify MuLA by alternatively removing parsing and pose adapters, resulting in single-direction adaptation models, denoted as VGG16-FCN-LA-Pose and VGG16-FCN-LA-Parsing.

From Table 1, we can see that the proposed VGG16-FCN-MuLA significantly improves performance of baseline VGG16-FCN by a large margin on both human parsing and pose estimation, from 34.5% to 40.2% mIoU and 69.1% to 76.0% PCK, respectively. These results clearly show efficacy of MuLA on exploiting mutual benefits to jointly enhance model performance. We can also observe direct fusion of representations from both models as VGG16-FCN-Add/Multi/Concat cannot sufficiently utilize guidance information, resulting in very limited performance improvement. In contrast to these naive fusion strategies, VGG16-FCN-MuLA can learn more powerful representations via dynamically adapting parameters. Traditional multi-task learning framework VGG16-FCN-MTL suffers performance decline for both parsing and pose estimation, due to limitations brought by its tied architecture trying to learn single representation for both tasks. In contrast, MuLA learns separate representations for each task, providing a flexible and effective model for multi-task learning. Adding a residual architecture to the adaptation modules only slightly improves performance for both tasks, revealing performance gain is not simply from network architecture engineering. Instead, MuLA indeed learns useful complementary representations.

Single-direction learning to adapt variants VGG16-FCN-LA-Pose/Parsing can successfully leverage parsing (or pose) information to adapt pose (or parsing respectively) models, leading to performance improvement. This verifies effectiveness of our proposed learning to adapt module in exploiting guidance information from parallel models. However, we can also observe such single-direction learning harms performance of "source" tasks, due to over-concentration on

Table 3. Comparison with state-of-the-arts on LIP for human pose estimation task

Methods	PCK
Hybrid pose machine	77.2
BUPTMM-POSE	80.2
Pyramid stream network	82.1
Chou *et al.* [7]	87.4
Our model	**87.5**

Table 4. Comparison with state-of-the-arts on LIP for human parsing task

Methods	PixelAcc	MeanAcc	mIoU
SegNet [1]	69.0	24.0	18.2
FCN-8s [13]	76.1	36.8	28.3
DeepLabV2 [4]	82.7	51.6	41.6
Attention [5]	83.4	54.4	42.9
Attention+SSL [10]	84.4	54.9	44.7
SS-NAN [28]	87.6	56.0	47.9
Our model	**88.5**	**60.5**	**49.3**

the "target" tasks. It demonstrates the necessity of mutual learning for simultaneously boosting performance of human parsing and pose estimation.

To evaluate the power of MuLA on iteratively exploiting mutual benefits between human parsing and pose estimation, we further perform ablation studies with the Hourglass based model. The results are summarized in Table 2. We use HG-ms-nu-MuLA to denote the model containing m stages each with n-unit depth (32-layer per unit depth per Hourglass module is the basic configuration in [15]). Specially, HG-0s-1u-MuLA denotes independent Hourglass networks (without mutual learning to adapt) are utilized for the two tasks. We purposively make all stages have the same architecture for disentangling effects of architecture variations on performance. In particular, HG-2s-1u-MuLA (1st/2nd Stage) denotes ablation cases of HG-2s-1u-MuLA where only the 1st or 2nd stage contains the module for mutual-learning to adapt. We use HG-$k\times n$u to denote standard Hourglass network with k stacked Hourglass modules of n-unit depth.

From Table 2, we can observe that increasing the number of stages in MuLA from 0 to 5 can continuously improve the performance for both tasks, from 38.5% to 49.3% mIoU for human parsing and 78.8% to 85.4% PCK for pose estimation. Comparing HG-2s-1u-MuLA with HG-2×1u, we can find the proposed MuLA model can learn valuable representations from model counterparts rather than benefiting from stacking Hourglass modules. Comparing HG-2s-1u-MuLA with HG-2s-1u-MuLA (1st/2nd Stage), we can see that removing mutual-learning process at any stage will always harm the performance for both parsing and pose estimation, demonstrating that the proposed adaptation module is effective at leveraging mutual guidance information and necessary to be applied for all the stages in MuLA. In addition, we find using more than 5 stages for MuLA will not bring observable improvement. Hence, we set $T = 5$ for efficiency.

Comparisons with State-of-the-Arts. We compare our model HG-5s-1u-MuLA with state-of-the-arts for both human parsing and pose estimation on LIP dataset. The results are shown in Tables 3 and 4.

For human pose estimation, the method in [7] wins the first place in Human Pose Estimation track in the 1st LIP Challenge. It extensively exploits adversar-

Table 5. Results on the PASCAL-Person-Part dataset for human pose estimation

Methods	mAP
Chen and Yuille [6]	21.8
Insafutdinov *et al.* [11]	28.6
Xia *et at.* [24]	39.2
Our baseline (w/o MuLA)	38.6
Our model	**39.9**

Table 6. Results on the PASCAL-Person-Part dataset for human parsing

Methods	mIoU
Attention+SSL [10]	59.4
SS-NAN [28]	62.4
Xia *et al.* [24]	64.4
Our baseline (w/o MuLA)	62.9
Our model	**65.1**

ial training strategies. The pyramid stream network introduces top-down pathway and lateral connections to combine features of different levels for recurrently refining joint confidence maps. BUPTMM-POSE and Hybrid Pose machines are from combining the Hourglass network and Convolutional Pose Machines. From Table 3, we can find our model achieves superior accuracy over all these strong baselines. It achieves new state-of-the-art 87.5% PCK on the LIP dataset.

Table 4 shows comparison with state-of-the-arts for human parsing. In addition to mIoU, we also report pixel accuracy and mean accuracy, following conventions [5,10,28]. In particular, the methods in [10,28] utilize human pose information as extra supervision to assist human parsing via introducing a structure-sensitive loss based on body joint locations. We can observe that our model outperforms all previous methods consistently for all the evaluation metrics. It gives new state-of-the-art 88.5% pixel accuracy, 60.5% mean accuracy and 49.3% mIoU. This demonstrates our learning to adapt module indeed provides a more effective way for exploiting human pose information to guide human parsing than the other sophisticated strategies like structure-sensitive loss in [10,28].

Qualitative Results. Figure 4(a) shows qualitative results to visually illustrate the efficacy of MuLA in mutually boosting human parsing and pose estimation. We can observe that MuLA can exploit body part information from human parsing to constrain body joint locations, *e.g.*, from the 1st and 2nd examples. On the other hand, MuLA can use human pose to provide structure information to benefit human parsing by improving accuracy of semantic part labeling, as shown in the 3rd and 4th examples. Moreover, we can see that MuLA simultaneously improves both parsing and pose quality for all the examples.

4.3 Results on PASCAL-Person-Part Dataset

Different from LIP dataset, the extended PASCAL-Person-Part dataset presents more challenging pose estimation problems due to existence of multiple persons. As mentioned in Sect. 4.1, we utilize the model in [16] as the pose model in MuLA for partitioning joint candidates to corresponding person instances. We exploit Hourglass network based MuLA with 5 stages for experiments. The results are shown in Tables 5 and 6.

We can see that our baseline models achieves 38.6% mAP and 62.9% mIoU for multi-person pose estimation and human parsing. With the proposed MuLA model, the performance for two tasks can be improved to 39.9% mAP and 65.1% mIoU, respectively. We also observe that our model achieves superior performance over previous methods for both tasks. In particular, [24] presents the state-of-the-art model for joint human parsing and pose estimation via exploiting hand-crafted features from estimation results as post-processing. The superior performance of our model over [24] further demonstrates the effectiveness of learning to adapt with mutual guidance information for enhancing models for joint human parsing and pose estimation.

We visualize human parsing and multi-person pose estimation results in Fig. 4(b). We can see that MuLA can use body joint information to recover missing detected parts, *e.g.*, left arm of left person in the 1st example and right arm of right person in the 2nd example. In addition, MuLA can also utilize semantic part information to constrain body joint location, *e.g.*, right knee of the right person in the 1st example and left ankle of the left person in the 2nd example.

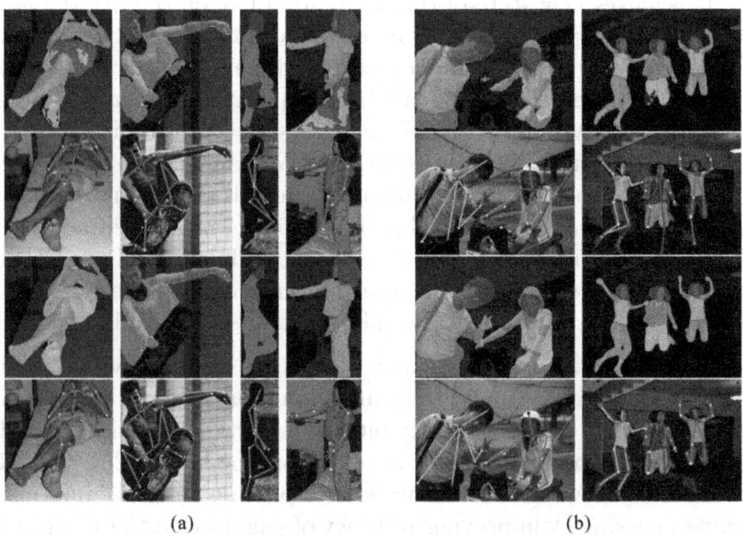

Fig. 4. Qualitative results on (a) LIP and (b) extended PASCAL-Person-Part dataset. For each column, the first two rows are results of the baseline model HG-5×1u without exploiting mutual guidance information and the last two rows are results of the proposed model HG-5s-1u-MuLA. Best viewed in color

5 Conclusion

In this paper, we present a novel Mutual Learning to Adapt (MuLA) model for solving the challenging joint human parsing and pose estimation problem. MuLA uses a new interweaving architecture to leverage their mutual guidance information to boost their performance simultaneously. In particular, MuLA achieves dynamic interaction and cooperation between these two tasks by mutually learning to adapt parameters of parallel models for tailoring their preliminary representations by injecting information from the other one. MuLA can iteratively weave mutual guidance information for continuously improving performance for both tasks. It effectively overcomes limitations of previous works that exploit mutual benefits between two tasks through using hand-crafted features in the post-processing. Comprehensive experiments on benchmarks have clearly verified the efficacy of MuLA for joint human parsing and pose estimation. In particular, MuLA achieved new state-of-the-art for both human parsing and pose estimation tasks on the LIP dataset, and outperformed all previous methods devoted to jointly performing these two tasks on PASCAL-Person-Part dataset.

Acknowledgement. Jiashi Feng was partially supported by NUS IDS R-263-000-C67-646, ECRA R-263-000-C87-133 and MOE Tier-II R-263-000-D17-112.

References

1. Badrinarayanan, V., Kendall, A., Cipolla, R.: SegNet: a deep convolutional encoder-decoder architecture for image segmentation. IEEE Trans. Pattern Anal. Mach. Intell. **39**(12), 2481–2495 (2017)
2. Bertinetto, L., Henriques, J.F., Valmadre, J., Torr, P., Vedaldi, A.: Learning feed-forward one-shot learners. In: NIPS (2016)
3. Cao, Z., Simon, T., Wei, S.E., Sheikh, Y.: Realtime multi-person 2D pose estimation using part affinity fields. In: CVPR (2017)
4. Chen, L.C., Papandreou, G., Kokkinos, I., Murphy, K., Yuille, A.L.: DeepLab: semantic image segmentation with deep convolutional nets, atrous convolution, and fully connected CRFs. In: ICLR (2015)
5. Chen, L.C., Yang, Y., Wang, J., Xu, W., Yuille, A.L.: Attention to scale: scale-aware semantic image segmentation. In: CVPR (2016)
6. Chen, X., Yuille, A.: Parsing occluded people by flexible compositions. In: 2015 IEEE Conference on Computer Vision and Pattern Recognition (CVPR) (2015)
7. Chou, C.J., Chien, J.T., Chen, H.T.: Self adversarial training for human pose estimation. In: CVPR Workshops (2017)
8. Dong, J., Chen, Q., Shen, X., Yang, J., Yan, S.: Towards unified human parsing and pose estimation. In: CVPR (2014)
9. Gan, C., Lin, M., Yang, Y., de Melo, G., Hauptmann, A.G.: Concepts not alone: exploring pairwise relationships for zero-shot video activity recognition. In: AAAI (2016)
10. Gong, K., Liang, X., Shen, X., Lin, L.: Look into person: self-supervised structure-sensitive learning and a new benchmark for human parsing. In: CVPR (2017)
11. Insafutdinov, E., Pishchulin, L., Andres, B., Andriluka, M., Schiele, B.: DeeperCut: a deeper, stronger, and faster multi-person pose estimation model. In: Leibe, B., Matas, J., Sebe, N., Welling, M. (eds.) ECCV 2016. LNCS, vol. 9910, pp. 34–50. Springer, Cham (2016). https://doi.org/10.1007/978-3-319-46466-4_3
12. Ladicky, L., Torr, P.H., Zisserman, A.: Human pose estimation using a joint pixel-wise and part-wise formulation. In: CVPR (2013)

13. Long, J., Shelhamer, E., Darrell, T.: Fully convolutional networks for semantic segmentation. In: CVPR (2015)
14. Lu, Y., Boukharouba, K., Boonært, J., Fleury, A., Lecoeuche, S.: Application of an incremental SVM algorithm for on-line human recognition from video surveillance using texture and color features. Neurocomputing **126**, 132–140 (2014)
15. Newell, A., Yang, K., Deng, J.: Stacked hourglass networks for human pose estimation. In: Leibe, B., Matas, J., Sebe, N., Welling, M. (eds.) ECCV 2016. LNCS, vol. 9912, pp. 483–499. Springer, Cham (2016). https://doi.org/10.1007/978-3-319-46484-8_29
16. Nie, X., Feng, J., Xing, J., Yan, S.: Generative partition networks for multi-person pose estimation. arXiv preprint arXiv:1705.07422 (2017)
17. Paszke, A., Gross, S., Chintala, S.: PyTorch (2017)
18. Ren, S., Kaiming, H., Girshick, R., Sun, J.: Faster R-CNN: towards real-time object detection with region proposal networks. In: NIPS (2015)
19. Simonyan, K., Zisserman, A.: Very deep convolutional networks for large-scale image recognition. In: ICLR (2015)
20. Su, C., Li, J., Zhang, S., Xing, J., Gao, W., Tian, Q.: Pose-driven deep convolutional model for person re-identification. In: CVPR (2017)
21. Tieleman, T., Hinton, G.: Lecture 6.5-rmsprop: divide the gradient by a running average of its recent magnitude. COURSERA: Neural Networks for Machine Learning (2012)
22. Wang, C., Wang, Y., Yuille, A.L.: An approach to pose-based action recognition. In: CVPR (2013)
23. Wei, S.E., Ramakrishna, V., Kanade, T., Sheikh, Y.: Convolutional pose machines. In: CVPR (2016)
24. Xia, F., Wang, P., Chen, X., Yuille, A.: Joint multi-person pose estimation and semantic part segmentation. In: CVPR (2017)
25. Xia, F., Zhu, J., Wang, P., Yuille, A.L.: Pose-guided human parsing by an and/or graph using pose-context features. In: AAAI (2016)
26. Yamaguchi, K., Kiapour, M.H., Ortiz, L.E., Berg, T.L.: Parsing clothing in fashion photographs. In: CVPR (2012)
27. Yang, Y., Ramanan, D.: Articulated human detection with flexible mixtures of parts. IEEE Trans. Pattern Anal. Mach. Intell. **35**(12), 2878–2890 (2013)
28. Zhao, J., et al.: Self-supervised neural aggregation networks for human parsing. In: CVPR Workshops (2017)
29. Zhao, R., Ouyang, W., Wang, X.: Unsupervised salience learning for person re-identification. In: CVPR (2013)
30. Zhou, X., Zhu, M., Leonardos, S., Derpanis, K.G., Daniilidis, K.: Sparseness meets deepness: 3D human pose estimation from monocular video. In: CVPR (2016)

DCAN: Dual Channel-Wise Alignment Networks for Unsupervised Scene Adaptation

Zuxuan Wu[1(✉)], Xintong Han[2], Yen-Liang Lin[3], Mustafa Gökhan Uzunbas[3], Tom Goldstein[1], Ser Nam Lim[4], and Larry S. Davis[1]

[1] University of Maryland, College Park, USA
zxwu@cs.umd.edu
[2] Malong Technologies, Shenzhen, China
[3] GE Global Research, Niskayuna, USA
[4] Facebook, Menlo Park, USA

Abstract. Harvesting dense pixel-level annotations to train deep neural networks for semantic segmentation is extremely expensive and unwieldy at scale. While learning from synthetic data where labels are readily available sounds promising, performance degrades significantly when testing on novel realistic data due to domain discrepancies. We present Dual Channel-wise Alignment Networks (DCAN), a simple yet effective approach to reduce domain shift at both pixel-level and feature-level. Exploring statistics in each channel of CNN feature maps, our framework performs channel-wise feature alignment, which preserves spatial structures and semantic information, in both an image generator and a segmentation network. In particular, given an image from the source domain and unlabeled samples from the target domain, the generator synthesizes new images on-the-fly to resemble samples from the target domain in appearance and the segmentation network further refines high-level features before predicting semantic maps, both of which leverage feature statistics of sampled images from the target domain. Unlike much recent and concurrent work relying on adversarial training, our framework is lightweight and easy to train. Extensive experiments on adapting models trained on synthetic segmentation benchmarks to real urban scenes demonstrate the effectiveness of the proposed framework.

1 Introduction

Deep neural networks have driven recent advances in computer vision. However, significant boosts in accuracy achieved by high-capacity deep models require large corpora of manually labeled data such as ImageNet [1] and COCO [2]. The need to harvest clean and massive annotations limits the ability of these

Electronic supplementary material The online version of this chapter (https://doi.org/10.1007/978-3-030-01228-1_32) contains supplementary material, which is available to authorized users.

V. Ferrari et al. (Eds.): ECCV 2018, LNCS 11209, pp. 535–552, 2018.
https://doi.org/10.1007/978-3-030-01228-1_32

approaches to scale, especially for fine-grained understanding tasks like semantic segmentation, where dense annotations are extremely costly and time-consuming to obtain. One possible solution is to learn from synthetic images rendered by modern computer graphics tools (*e.g.*, video game engines), such that ground-truth labels are readily available. While synthetic data have been exploited to train deep networks for a multitude of tasks like depth estimation [3], object detection [4], *etc.*, the resulting models usually suffer from poor generalization when exposed to novel realistic samples. The reasons are mainly two-folds: (1) the realism of synthesized images is limited—inducing an inherent gap between synthetic and real image distributions; (2) deep networks are prone to overfitting in the training stage, which leads to limited generalization ability.

Learning a discriminative model that reduces the disparity between training and testing distributions is typically known as domain adaptation; a more challenging setting is unsupervised domain adaptation that aims to bridge the gap without accessing labels of the testing domain during training. Most existing work seeks to align features in a deep network of the *source* domain (training sets) and the *target* domain (testing sets) by either explicitly matching feature statistics [5–7] or implicitly making features domain invariant [8,9]. Recent work also attempts to minimize domain shift in the pixel space to make raw images look alike [10–12] with adversarial training. While good progress has been made for classification, generalizing these ideas to semantic segmentation has been shown to be less effective [13], possibly due to the fact that high-dimensional feature maps are more challenging to align compared to features used for classification from fully-connected layers.

In this paper, we study unsupervised domain adaptation for semantic segmentation, which we refer as unsupervised scene adaptation. We posit that channel-wise alignment of high-level feature maps is important for adapting segmentation models, as it is able to preserve spatial structures and consider semantic information like attributes and concepts encoded in different channels [14] independently, which implicitly helps transfer feature distributions between the corresponding concepts across domains. In particular, we build upon recent advances of instance normalization [15] due to its effectiveness and simplicity for style transfer [15–17]. Instance normalization is motivated by the fact that mean and standard deviation in each channel of CNN feature maps contain the style information of an image, and hence they are used to translate feature maps of a source image into a normalized version based on a reference image for each channel. In addition to being able to match feature statistics, the ability to maintain spatial structures in feature maps with channel-wise normalization makes it appealing for tasks like segmentation.

Motivated by these observations, we propose to reduce domain differences at both low-level and high-level through channel-wise alignment. In particular, we normalize features of images from the source domain with those of images from the target domain by matching their channel-wise feature statistics. Nevertheless, such alignment is on a per image basis with each target sample serving as a reference for calibration. When multiple images exist in the target domain, a straightforward way is to enumerate all of them to cover all possible variations, which is computationally expensive. In contrast, we stochastically sample from the target domain for alignment. The randomization strategy is not only efficient, but more importantly, provides a form of regularization for training in similar spirit to stochastic depth [18], data transformation [19,20], and dropout [21].

To this end, we present, Dual Channel-wise Alignment Networks (DCAN), a simple yet effective framework optimized in an end-to-end manner. The main idea is leveraging images from the target domain for channel-wise alignment, which not only enables minimizing the low-level domain discrepancies in pixel space (*e.g.*, color, texture, lighting conditions, *etc.*), but also, simultaneously normalizes high-level feature maps of source images specific to those of target images for improved segmentation. Figure 1 gives an overview of the framework. In particular, we utilize an image generator to map an image from the source domain to multiple representations with the same content as the input but in different styles, determined by unlabeled images randomly selected from the target set. These synthesized images, resembling samples from the target domain, together with sampled target images, are further input into a segmentation network, in which channel-wise feature alignment is performed once more to refine features for the final segmentation task.

The key contributions of DCAN are summarized as follows: (1) we present an end-to-end learning framework, guided by feature statistics of images from the target domain, to synthesize new images as well as normalize features on-the-fly for unsupervised scene adaptation; (2) we demonstrate that channel-wise feature alignment, preserving spatial structures and semantic concepts, is a simple yet effective way to reduce domain shift in high-level feature maps. With this, our method departs from much recent and concurrent work, which uses adversarial training for distribution alignment; (3) we conduct extensive experiments by transferring models trained on synthetic segmentation benchmarks, *i.e.*, SYNTHIA [22] and GTA5 [23], to real urban scenes, CITYSCAPES [24], and demonstrate DCAN outperforms state-of-the-art methods with clear margins and it is compatible with several modern segmentation networks.

2 Related Work

There is a large body of work on domain adaptation (see [25,26] for a survey), and here we focus only on the most relevant literatures.

Unsupervised Domain Adaptation. Most existing work focuses on classification problems and falls into two categories: feature-level and pixel-level adaptation. Feature-level adaptation seeks to align features by either explicitly minimizing the distance measured by Maximum Mean Discrepancies (MMD) [27,28], covariances [6], *etc.*, between source and target distributions or implicitly optimizing adversarial loss functions in the forms of reversed gradient [29,30], domain confusion [31], or Generative Adversarial Network [8,9,32,33], such that features are domain-invariant. In contrast, pixel-level domain adaptation attempts to remove low-level differences like color and texture by stylizing source images to resemble target images [10,34–36]. Compared to a large amount of work on classification problems, limited effort has been made for semantic segmentation. In [9], adversarial training is utilized to align features in fully convolutional networks for segmentation, and the idea is further extended for both pixel-level and feature-level adaptation jointly using cycle consistency [11]. A curriculum learning strategy is proposed in [13] by leveraging information from global label distributions and local super-pixel distributions. Our work differs from previous work in two aspects: (1) we introduce channel-wise alignment for unsupervised scene adaption, which preserves spatial information and semantic information of each channel when normalizing high-level feature maps for alignment; (2) we avoid adversarial training, which "remains remarkably difficult to train" [37], yet achieves better performance.

Image Synthesis. Generative Adversarial Networks (GANs) [38], consisting of a generator and a discriminator optimized to compete with each other, are one of the most popular deep generative models for image synthesis [36,39,40]. Various prior information, including labels [41], text [42], attributes [43], images [44,45] has been explored to condition the generation process. GANs have also been further extended to the problem of image-to-image translation, which maps a given image to another one in a different style, using cycle consistency [46] or a shared latent space [47]. This line of work aims to learn a joint distribution of images from two domains using images from the marginal distributions of each domain. As previously mentioned, adversarial loss functions are hard to train, and hence generating high resolution images is still a challenging problem that could take days [48]. A different direction of image-to-image translation is neural style transfer [17,49–52]. Though style transfer can be seen as a special domain adaptation problem with each style as a domain [53], our goal in this work is different: we focus on unsupervised scene adaption, by jointly synthesizing images and performing segmentation with the help of images from the target domain for channel-wise distribution alignment.

3 Approach

Given labeled images from a source domain and unlabeled samples from a target domain, our goal is to reduce domain discrepancies at both pixel-level and feature-level. In particular, we leverage unlabeled target images for channel-wise alignment—synthesizing photo-realistic samples to appear as if from the target set, and simultaneously normalizing feature maps of source images, upon which segmentation classifiers directly rely. The resulting segmentation model can then be readily applied to the novel target domain. To this end, we consider each image from the target domain as a unique reference sample, whose feature representations are used to normalize those of images from the source domain. In addition, given an image from the source domain, instead of considering every single target image, we sample from the target set for alignment stochastically, serving as regularization to improve generalization. Figure 1 gives an overview of this framework.

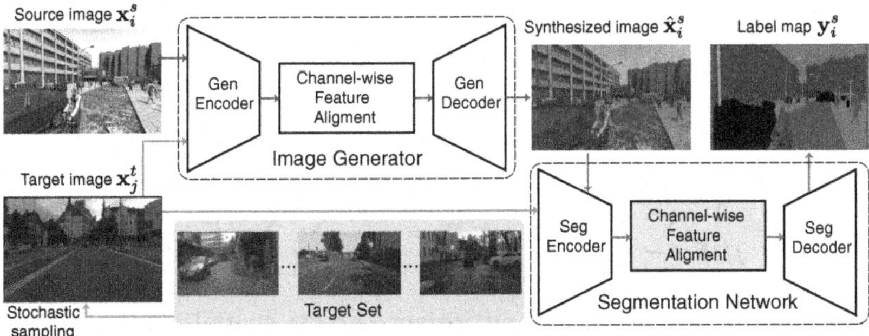

Fig. 1. An overview of the proposed framework. It contains an image generator and a segmentation network, in both of which channel-wise alignment is performed. The generator synthesizes a new image, reducing low-level appearance differences, which is further input to the semantic segmentation network. Features directly used for segmentation are refined before producing prediction maps. During testing, we turn off the alignment (shaped in blue) and the segmentation network can be readily applied. (Color figure online)

More formally, let $\mathbf{X}^s = \{\mathbf{x}_i^s, \mathbf{y}_i^s\}_{i \in [N^s]}$ denote the source domain with N^s images $\mathbf{x}_i^s \in \mathbb{R}^{3 \times H \times W}$ and the corresponding label maps $\mathbf{y}_i^s \in \{0, 1\}^{C \times H \times W}$, where H and W represent the height and width of the image, respectively and C denotes the number of classes. The target domain, on the other hand, has N^t images $\mathbf{X}^t = \{\mathbf{x}_j^t\}_{j \in [N^t]}$ of the same resolution without labels. For each image $\mathbf{x}_i^s$ in the source domain, we randomly select one sample $\mathbf{x}_j^t$ from the target domain (we use one image here for the ease of description, but it can be a set of images as will be shown in experiments). A synthesized image $\hat{\mathbf{x}}_i^s$ is generated with the content of $\mathbf{x}_i^s$ and style of $\mathbf{x}_j^t$ by channel-wise alignment of feature statistics. This image is then fed into a segmentation network, where domain shift in high-level feature maps is further minimized for segmentation.

In the following, we first revisit channel-wise alignment (Sect. 3.1), and then we present DCAN (Sect. 3.2), which contains an image generator, synthesizing new images to minimize low-level differences like color and texture, and a segmentation network, refining high-level feature maps that are critical in the final segmentation task. Finally, we introduce the learning strategy (Sect. 3.3).

3.1 Channel-Wise Feature Alignment

The mean and standard deviation of each channel in CNN feature maps have been shown to capture the style information of an image [15–17], and hence channel-wise alignment of feature maps is adopted for fast style transfer with a simple instance normalization step. Here, due to its effectiveness and simplicity, we use adaptive instance normalization [17], to match the mean and standard deviation of images from two different domains. In particular, given feature maps F_i^s and F_j^t of the same size $\mathbb{R}^{\hat{C} \times \hat{H} \times \hat{W}}$ ($\hat{C}$, $\hat{H}$, $\hat{W}$ represents the channel, height and width respectively) from the source and target domain, adaptive instance normalization h produces a new representation of the source image as:

$$\hat{F_i^s} = h(F_i^s, F_j^t) = \sigma(F_j^t)\left(\frac{F_i^s - \mu(F_i^s)}{\sigma(F_i^s)}\right) + \mu(F_j^t), \tag{1}$$

$$\mu_c(F) = \frac{1}{\hat{H}\hat{W}}\sum_{h=1}^{\hat{H}}\sum_{w=1}^{\hat{W}} F_{chw},\ \sigma_c^2(F) = \frac{1}{\hat{H}\hat{W}}\sum_{h=1}^{\hat{H}}\sum_{w=1}^{\hat{W}}(F_{chw} - \mu_c(F))^2,$$

where μ_c and σ_c denotes mean and variance across spatial dimensions for the c-th channel. This simple operation normalizes features of a source image to have similar statistics with those of a target image for each channel, which is appealing for segmentation tasks, since it is spatially invariant, *i.e.*, relative locations of pixels are fixed. In addition, such channel-wise alignment ensures semantic information like attributes encoded in different channels [14] is processed independently. In our work, we adopt channel-wise feature alignment in both our image generator for synthesizing photo-realistic samples, and segmentation network to refine features used for segmentation. Note that channel-wise feature alignment is generic and can be plugged into different layers of networks.

3.2 Dual Channel-Wise Alignment Networks

Image Generator. Our image generator contains an encoder and a decoder with channel-wise alignment in between. The encoder, denoted as f_{gen}, is truncated from a pre-trained VGG19 network [54] by taking layers up till `relu4`. We fix the weights of the encoder, following [17,55], to map images $\mathbf{x}_i^s$ and $\mathbf{x}_j^t$ into fixed representations: $F_i^s = f_{gen}(\mathbf{x}_i^s)$ and $F_j^t = f_{gen}(\mathbf{x}_j^t)$, respectively. F_i^s is further normalized to produce a new representation $\hat{F_i^s}$ according to Eq. (1). Given the aligned source representation, a decoder, represented by g_{gen}, is applied to synthesize a new image $\hat{\mathbf{x}}_i^s = g_{gen}(\hat{F_i^s})$, in the style of samples from the target set. This is achieved by minimizing the following image generation loss function:

$$\ell_{gen} = \|f_{gen}(\hat{\mathbf{x}}_i^s) - \hat{F_i^s}\|_2 + \sum_{l=1}^{4}\|G(f_{gen}^l(\hat{\mathbf{x}}_i^s)) - G(f_{gen}^l(\mathbf{x}_j^t))\|_2. \tag{2}$$

Here, the first term is the content loss measuring the discrepancies between features from the stylized image $\hat{\mathbf{x}}_i^s$ and the aligned features of the source image (weights of f_{gen} are fixed), forcing the synthesized image to contain the same contents as the original one. The second term matches the style information, by penalizing the differences of Gram matrices between $\hat{\mathbf{x}}_i^s$ and the target image $\mathbf{x}_j^t$ using features from the first four layers (with l denoting the layer index) in the encoder [49]. More specifically, given a reshaped feature map $F \in \mathbb{R}^{\hat{C}\times\hat{H}\hat{W}}$ with its original channel, height and width being $\hat{C}$, $\hat{H}$, $\hat{W}$ respectively, the gram matrix can be computed as: $G(F) = \sum_{k=1}^{\hat{H}\hat{W}} F_{ik}F_{jk} \in \mathbb{R}^{\hat{C}\times\hat{C}}$.

Segmentation Network. A new image $\hat{\mathbf{x}}_i^s$ synthesized with our generator, resembling target samples with similar low-level details like color, texture, lighting, *etc.*, is ready for semantic segmentation. Instead of sending $\hat{\mathbf{x}}_i^s$ to any off-the-shelf segmentation engine for the task, we leverage the target style image $\mathbf{x}_j^t$ once more to calibrate features of $\hat{\mathbf{x}}_i^s$ with channel-wise alignment, such that they possess similar statistics and its spatial information is preserved for segmentation. Here, the intuition is to remove undesired mismatches in higher-level feature maps that might still exist after minimizing low-level differences in the first stage. Therefore, DCAN explicitly performs another round of alignment in the segmentation network, refining features tailored for pixel-level segmentation. To this end, we divide a fully convolutional network (FCN) based model into an encoder f_{seg} and a decoder g_{seg}, with alignment in between. In particular, the segmentation decoder produces a prediction map: $\mathbf{p}_i^s = g_{seg}(h(f_{seg}(\hat{\mathbf{x}}_i^s), f_{seg}(\mathbf{x}_j^t)))$ and the segmentation loss ℓ_{seg} takes the form:

$$\ell_{seg} = -\sum_{m=1}^{H\times W}\sum_{c=1}^{C}\mathbf{y}_i^{mc}\texttt{log}(\mathbf{p}_i^{mc}), \tag{3}$$

which is essentially a multi-class cross-entropy loss summed over all pixels (superscript s denoting the source domain is omitted here). Note that state-of-the-art segmentation networks like DeepLab [56], FCN [57], PSPNet [58], GCN [59], *etc.*, are usually built upon top-performing models on ImageNet like VGG [54] or ResNet [60]; these networks differ in depth but have similar configurations, *i.e.*, five groups of convolution. In this case, we utilize the first three convolution groups from a segmentation model as our encoder and the remaining part as the decoder. For encoder-decoder based segmentation networks like SegNet [61], the simple idea could be directly applied.

In summary, DCAN works in the following way: given a source image, a target image is randomly selected whose style information is used for dual channel-wise alignment in both image synthesis and segmentation phases. The image generator first synthesizes a new image on-the-fly to appear similar as samples from the target domain, reducing low-level domain discrepancies in pixel space (*e.g.*, color, texture, lighting conditions, *etc.*), which is further input into the segmentation network. In the segmentation model, features from the synthesized image are further normalized specific to the sampled target image while preserving spatial structures and semantic information before producing label maps.

At test time, a novel image from the target domain is input into the segmentation network (segmentation encoder and then decoder) to predict its semantic map. The channel-wise feature alignment in the segmentation network is turned off since the network is already trained to match the feature statistics between two domains and thus can be directly applied for testing as shown in Fig. 1.

3.3 Optimization

One could train the framework by selecting each sample in the source domain and normalizing it with the style information of each image in the target domain, which leads to N^t copies of the original image; the new dataset $\hat{\mathbf{X}}^s$ with the size of $N^s N^t$ can then be used for training by minimizing:

$$\mathcal{L} = \frac{1}{N^s}\sum_{i=1}^{N^s}\frac{1}{N^t}\sum_{j=1}^{N^t}(\ell_{seg}(\mathbf{x}_i^s, \mathbf{x}_j^t, \mathbf{y}_i^s; \Theta_{seg}) + \lambda\ell_{gen}(\mathbf{x}_i^s, \mathbf{x}_j^t; \Theta_{gen})), \tag{4}$$

where Θ_{seg} and Θ_{gen} denote the parameters for the segmentation network and the image generator, respectively, and λ balances the two losses. However, enumerating all targets would be computationally expensive, as the cost grows linearly with the number of images in the target domain. It is worth noting that when there are infinite target images, Eq. (4) can be re-written as:

$$\mathcal{L} = \frac{1}{N^s}\sum_{i=1}^{N^s}\mathbb{E}_{\mathbf{x}_j^t\sim\mathbf{X}^t}[\ell_{seg}(\mathbf{x}_i^s, \mathbf{x}_j^t, \mathbf{y}_i^s; \Theta_{seg}) + \lambda\ell_{gen}(\mathbf{x}_i^s, \mathbf{x}_j^t; \Theta_{gen})]. \tag{5}$$

Here, the expected mean can be computed by stochastic sampling during training. The intuition is to introduce "uncertainties" to the learning processes as opposed to summing over all target styles deterministically, making the derived model more robust to noise and to generalize better on the target domain. It is a type of regularization similar in spirit to SGD for fast convergence [62], stochastic depth [18] and dropout [21,63,64]. Another way to view this is randomized data augmentation to improve generalization ability [54,65]. Unlike PixelDA [10] which generates new samples conditioned on a noise vector, we augment data using feature statistics of images randomly sampled from the target domain. It is also worth noting that the idea of sampling is in line with stochastic gradient descent, which loops over the training set by sampling batches of images, and hence can be easily implemented in current deep learning frameworks.

4 Experiments

In this section, we first introduce the experimental setup and implementation details. Then, extensive experimental results are presented to demonstrate the effectiveness of our method. Finally, an ablation study is conducted to evaluate the contribution of different components of DCAN.

4.1 Experimental Setup

Datasets and Evaluation Metrics. We train DCAN on two source datasets, SYNTHIA [22] and GTA5 [23] respectively, and then evaluate the models on CITYSCAPES [24]. CITYSCAPES is a real-world dataset, capturing street scenes of 50 different cities, totaling 5,000 images with pixel-level labels. The dataset is divided into a training set with 2,975 images, a validation set with 500 images and a testing set with 1,525 images. SYNTHIA is a large-scale synthetic dataset automatically generated for semantic segmentation of urban scenes. As in [9,13], we utilize SYNTHIA-RAND-CITYSCAPES, a subset that contains 9,400 images paired with CITYSCAPES, sharing 16 common classes. We randomly select 100 images for validation and use the remaining 9,300 images for training. GTA5 contains 24,966 high-resolution images, automatically annotated into 19 classes. The dataset is rendered from a modern computer game, Grand Theft Auto V, with labels fully compatible with those of CITYSCAPES. We randomly pick 1,000 images for validation and use the remaining 23,966 images for training.

Following [9,13], to train our model, we utilize *labeled* images from the training set of either SYNTHIA or GTA5, as well as *unlabeled* images from the training set of CITYSCAPES serving as references for distribution alignment. Then we evaluate the segmentation model on the validation set of CITYSCAPES, and report mean intersection-over-union (mIoU) to measure the performance. These two adaptation settings are denoted as SYNTHIA $\rightarrow$ CITYSCAPES and GTA5 $\rightarrow$ CITYSCAPES, respectively.

Network Architectures. For the image generator, its encoder is based on a VGG19 network; the detailed architecture of the decoder can be found in the supplemental material. To verify the effectiveness of DCAN in state-of-the-art segmentation networks, we experiment with three top-performing architectures, FCN-8s-VGG16 [57], FCN-8s-ResNet101, and PSPNet [58]. In particular, FCN8s-VGG16 and FCN8s-ResNet101 respectively adapt a pre-trained VGG16 and a ResNet101 network into fully convolutional networks and use skip connections for detailed segmentations. PSPNet is built upon a ResNet50 model with a novel pyramid pooling module to obtain representations of multiple sub-regions for per-pixel prediction [58]. These networks are pre-trained on ImageNet.

Implementation Details. We adopt PyTorch for implementation and use SGD as the optimizer with a momentum of 0.99. The learning rate is fixed to $1e-3$ for both FCN8s-ResNet101 and PSPNet, and $1e-5$ for FCN8s-VGG16. We adopt a batch size of three and optimize for 100,000 iterations, and we fix λ to 0.1. Given each sample in the training set, we randomly sample 2 images and 1 image from the target image set for experiments on SYNTHIA and GTA5 respectively. This is to achieve efficient training on GTA5, for its size is three times larger than SYNTHIA, and we will analyze the effect of the number of sampled images below. We use a crop of 512×1024 during training, and for evaluation we upsample the prediction map by a factor of 2 and then evaluate mIoU.

4.2 Main Results

We compare DCAN to state-of-the-art methods on unsupervised domain adaptation for semantic segmentation, including "FCN in the wild" [9] and "Curriculum Adaptation" [13]. In particular, FCN in the wild uses an adversarial loss to align fully connected layers (adapted to convolution layers) of a VGG16 model, and additionally leverages multiple instance learning to transfer spatial layout [9]. Curriculum Adaptation infers properties of the target domain using label distributions of images and superpixels [13]. The results of SYNTHIA $\rightarrow$ CITYSCAPES and GTA5 $\rightarrow$ CITYSCAPES are summarized in Table 1.

Table 1. Results and comparisons on CITYSCAPES when adapted from SYNTHIA and GTA5, respectively. Here, "Source" denotes source only methods, "Oracle" denotes results from supervised training, and A, B, C represent FCN8s-VGG16, FCN8s-ResNet101 and PSPNet. A/d uses dilation in VGG16 for segmentation.

SYNTHIA → CITYSCAPES																		
Method	network	road	sidewalk	building	wall	fence	pole	traffic light	traffic sign	vegetation	sky	person	rider	car	bus	motorbike	bike	mIOU	mIOU gain
Source [9]	A/d	6.40	17.7	29.7	1.20	0.00	15.1	0.00	7.20	30.3	66.8	51.1	1.50	47.3	3.90	0.10	0.00	17.4	
[9]	A/d	11.5	19.6	30.8	4.40	0.00	20.3	0.10	11.7	42.3	68.7	51.2	3.80	54.0	3.20	0.20	0.60	20.2	2.80
Source [13]	A	5.60	11.2	59.6	8.00	0.50	21.5	8.00	5.30	72.4	75.6	35.1	9.00	23.6	4.50	0.50	18.0	22.0	
[13]	A	65.2	26.1	74.9	0.10	0.50	10.7	3.50	3.00	76.1	70.6	47.1	8.20	43.2	20.7	0.70	13.1	29.0	7.00
Source	A	10.8	11.4	66.6	1.60	0.10	16.9	5.50	14.1	74.2	76.2	46.0	11.5	45.4	15.1	6.00	13.4	25.9	-
DCAN	A	79.9	30.4	70.8	1.60	0.60	22.3	6.70	23.0	76.9	73.9	41.9	16.7	61.7	11.5	10.3	38.6	**35.4**	**9.5**
Source	B	57.9	17.0	72.7	0.20	0.00	10.4	0.00	0.00	73.5	75.4	37.8	9.30	59.3	21.7	0.40	12.3	28.0	
DCAN	B	81.5	33.4	72.4	7.90	0.20	20.0	8.60	10.5	71.0	68.7	51.5	18.7	75.3	22.7	12.8	28.1	**36.5**	**8.5**
Source	C	56.0	24.6	76.5	5.00	0.20	19.0	5.70	7.80	77.5	78.9	44.7	7.70	35.3	7.90	1.50	24.0	29.5	
DCAN	C	82.8	36.4	75.7	5.08	0.06	25.8	8.04	18.7	74.7	76.9	51.1	15.9	77.7	24.8	4.11	37.3	**38.4**	**8.9**
Oracle	A	96.4	70.3	85.9	44.4	35.8	31.5	41.5	54.2	87.5	88.9	64.1	40.8	88.5	66.1	35.5	60.3	62.0	-
	B	97.3	76.7	88.1	44.4	46.9	35.3	44.5	55.9	88.6	91.2	67.7	41.6	89.9	73.3	44.7	63.1	65.6	-
	C	97.8	78.6	89.6	56.7	57.8	39.9	61.3	65.2	89.9	91.5	73.4	56.0	89.9	84.1	54.2	69.5	72.2	-

GTA5 → CITYSCAPES																						
Method	network	road	sidewalk	building	wall	fence	pole	traffic light	traffic sign	vegetation	terrain	sky	person	rider	car	truck	bus	train	motorbike	bike	mIOU	mIOU gain
Source [9]	A/d	31.9	18.9	47.7	7.40	3.10	16.0	10.4	1.00	76.5	13.0	58.9	36.0	1.00	67.1	9.50	3.70	0.00	0.00	0.00	21.2	
[9]	A/d	70.4	32.4	62.1	14.9	5.40	10.9	14.2	2.70	79.2	21.3	64.6	44.1	4.20	70.4	8.00	7.30	0.00	3.50	0.00	27.1	5.90
Source [13]	A	18.1	6.80	64.1	7.30	8.70	21.0	14.9	16.8	45.9	2.40	64.4	41.6	17.5	55.3	8.40	5.0	6.90	4.30	13.8	22.3	
[13]	A	74.9	22.0	71.7	6.00	11.9	8.40	16.3	11.1	75.7	13.3	66.5	38.0	9.30	55.2	18.8	18.9	0.00	16.8	16.6	28.9	6.6
Source	A	72.5	25.1	71.2	6.60	13.4	12.3	11.0	4.70	76.1	16.4	67.7	43.1	8.00	70.4	11.3	4.80	0.00	13.9	0.40	27.8	
DCAN	A	82.3	26.7	77.4	23.7	20.5	20.4	30.3	15.9	80.9	25.4	69.5	52.6	11.1	79.6	24.9	21.2	1.30	17.0	6.70	**36.2**	**8.4**
Source	B	44.5	12.7	71.1	9.40	17.7	15.3	24.3	11.9	80.5	14.3	80.0	50.3	7.70	45.4	30.5	30.8	5.50	9.80	3.50	29.8	
DCAN	B	88.5	37.4	79.3	24.8	16.5	21.3	26.3	17.4	80.8	30.9	77.6	50.2	19.2	77.7	21.6	27.1	2.70	14.3	18.1	**38.5**	**8.7**
Source	C	69.9	22.3	75.6	15.8	20.1	18.8	28.2	17.1	75.6	8.00	73.5	55.0	2.90	66.9	34.4	30.8	0.00	18.4	0.00	33.3	
DCAN	C	85.0	30.8	81.3	25.8	21.2	22.2	25.4	26.6	83.4	36.7	76.2	58.9	24.9	80.7	29.5	42.9	2.50	26.9	11.6	**41.7**	**8.4**
Oracle	A	96.4	70.3	85.9	44.4	35.8	31.5	41.5	54.2	87.5	51.9	88.9	64.1	40.8	88.5	55.8	66.1	44.9	35.5	60.3	60.2	-
	B	97.3	76.7	88.1	44.4	46.9	35.3	44.5	55.9	88.6	55.9	91.2	67.7	41.6	89.9	60.1	73.3	54.4	44.7	63.1	64.2	-
	C	97.8	78.6	89.6	56.7	57.8	39.9	61.3	65.2	89.9	58.9	91.5	73.4	56.0	89.9	75.8	84.1	78.8	54.2	69.5	72.0	-

We observe that these domain adaptation methods, although different in design, can indeed lead to improvements over the source only method (denoted as source), which simply trains a model on the source domain and then directly applies it to the target domain. In particular, DCAN outperforms its corresponding source only baseline with clear margins, around 8 and 9 absolute percentage points, using all three different networks on both datasets. This confirms the effectiveness of DCAN, which not only reduces domain differences for improved performance but also is general for multiple network architectures. Furthermore, with PSPNet, DCAN achieves 41.7% and 38.4% on CITYSCAPES when adapted from GTA5 and SYNTHIA, respectively. Compared to [9,13], with the same backbone VGG16 architecture, DCAN offers the best mIoU value as well the largest relative mIoU gain (9.5% and 8.4% trained from SYNTHIA and GTA5 respectively). Note that although the backbone network is the same, source only baselines are different due to different experimental settings. A dilated VGG16 network is adopted in [9] and the network is additionally pre-trained on PASCAL-CONTEXT in [13]. In addition, it uses a crop size of 320 × 640 during training. Our model is initialized on ImageNet and we choose 512 × 1024 for training since large resolution offers better performance as observed in [58], which is also consistent with state-of-the-art supervised methods on CITYSCAPES [24]. It is worth noting that DCAN improves a stronger baseline by 36% relatively (25.9% to 35.4%). With the same image size as in [13], DCAN improves the source only baseline from 23.6% to 33.0% (*v.s.*, 22.0% to 29.0% in [13]; see Table 2).

Among three different networks, PSPNet gives the best results on both datasets, mainly resulting from the pyramid pooling module that considers difference scales. Figure 2 illustrates sampled results of PSPNet under the GTA5 → CITYSCAPES setting, and its comparison with the source only method. Comparing across datasets, models trained on GTA5 produce better accuracies than those learned from SYNTHIA. The reasons are two-folds: (1) a large number of images from SYNTHIA are rendered at night, incurring significant domain differences since images from CITYSCAPES are captured during day time; (2) there are more training samples in GTA5. In addition, oracle results, which are produced with traditional supervised training using annotations from the target domain, are also listed for reference. We can see there is still significant performance gaps between domain adaptation methods and oracle supervised training, highlighting the challenging nature of this problem.

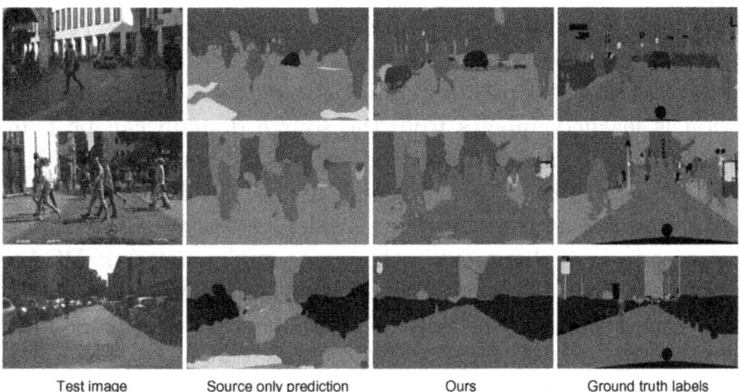

Fig. 2. Sampled prediction results of PSPNet and its corresponding source only model under the GTA5 → CITYSCAPES setting using testing images from CITYSCAPES. Our model improves the generalization ability of the trained segmentation network.

Table 2. Results of FCN8s-VGG16 using three different image resolutions.

SYNTHIA → CITYSCAPES			
Resolution	Method	mIoU	Gain
256 × 512	Source	21.2	8.4
	DCAN	29.6	
320 × 640	Source	23.6	9.4
	DCAN	33.0	
512 × 1024	Source	25.9	9.5
	DCAN	35.4	

Table 3. Training with and without feature alignment in FCN8s-VGG16 using different image synthesis methods.

SYNTHIA → CITYSCAPES	
Method	mIoU
CycleGAN [46]	30.4
CycleGAN w. FeatureAlignment	31.7
UNIT [55]	31.6
UNIT w. FeatureAlignment	32.7
DCAN w/o FeatureAlignment	33.8
DCAN (two stage)	33.7
DCAN (end-to-end)	35.4

4.3 Discussions

In this section, we run a number of experiments to analyze DCAN in the SYNTHIA → CITYSCAPES setting, and provide corresponding results and discussions.

Image Resolution. Top performing approaches on CITYSCAPES typically use a high resolution for improved performance [24]. For example, GCN and FRRN utilize a resolution of 800 × 800 [59] and 512 × 1024 [66], respectively. Here, we report the results of DCAN adapted from SYNTHIA using FCN8s-VGG16 with three different resolutions, and compare with the corresponding source only method in Table 2. DCAN offers significant performance gains for all resolutions, and a larger resolution is indeed better for unsupervised domain adaptation.

Different Image Synthesis Methods. We compare with two different image synthesis methods: (1) CycleGAN [46] and (2) UNIT [47], both of which attempt to learn a distribution mapping function between two domains. Once the mapping function is learned, images from the source domain can be translated to the style of the target domain. Therefore, we use the translated images from the source domain to train the segmentation network. Table 3 presents the results. For fair comparisons, we compare them under two settings, with and without the channel-wise feature alignment in the segmentation network. DCAN achieves better results than both GAN-based image synthesis methods in both scenarios. To justify the advantage of an end-to-end framework, we also compare with a two-stage training strategy, which simply trains a segmentation network using pre-synthesized images without end-to-end training. In this case, image synthesis is not optimized using gradients from the segmentation network. DCAN improves the two-stage training by 1.7% mIOU, demonstrating the importance of guiding the synthesis process with useful information from the final task.

Figure 3 further compares images produced by different synthesis methods. DCAN is able to generate images that conform to the style of images from the target set, containing fewer artifacts than CycleGAN and UNIT. In addition, both CycleGAN and UNIT seek to align distributions at a dataset level, and once the mapping is learned, the translation from the source to the target is fixed (a fixed output given an input image). Learning such a transformation function on high resolution images is a non-trivial task and might not perfectly cover all possible variations. Instead, DCAN performs image translation at an instance level, and in the regime of stochastic sampling, it is able to cover sufficient styles from the target set for distribution alignment. One can further increase the variations of synthesized images by compositing feature maps of source images and target images (see Supple. for details). It is also worth noting that feature alignment can improve segmentation results regardless of synthesis methods. We also experimented with other GAN-based approaches like PixelDA [10] for image synthesis; however, conditioning on a noise vector rather than label maps [67] fails to produce photo-realistic images in high resolution.

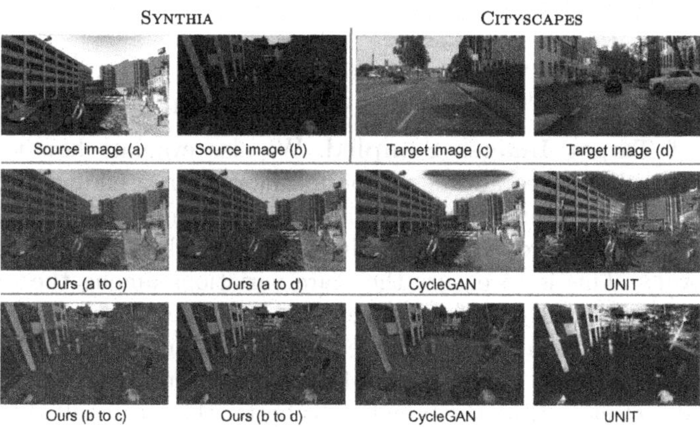

Fig. 3. Images from SYNTHIA synthesized in the style of CITYSCAPES with CycleGAN [46], UNIT [47] and DCAN.

Channel-Wise Feature Alignment for Segmentation. We now analyze the effect of channel-wise alignment in the segmentation network (Table 4) with FCN8s-VGG16. We compare with Adversarial Discriminative Domain Adaptation [8], which leverages an adversarial loss to make features from two domains indistinguishable without considering spatial structures explicitly. DCAN outperforms ADDA by 1.4%, and also converges faster during training. We also implemented MMD [27] and CORAL [6] loss to align features, but their results are worse than source only methods. This is consistent with observations in [13]. We further investigate where to align in the segmentation network and found that alignment after the `Conv3` layer gives the best results, possibly due to it contains both sufficient number of channels and relatively large feature maps. In addition, aligning features maps with more detailed spatial information (`Conv2` and `Conv4`) is also better than `Conv6` and `Conv7` (convolution layers adapted

Table 4. Comparisons of different feature alignment methods in the segmentation network.

SYNTHIA → CITYSCAPES	
Alignment method	mIoU
ADDA [8]	34.0
Ours-w/o alignment	33.8
Ours–Conv2	34.0
Ours–Conv4	34.4
Ours–Conv6	33.2
Ours–Conv7	32.7
Ours–Conv3	35.4

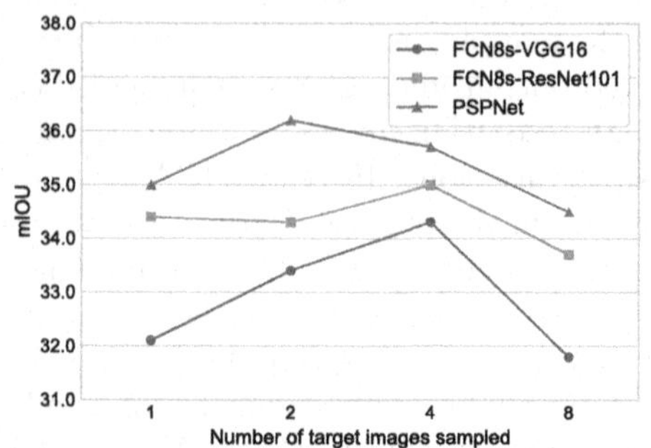

Fig. 4. Effect of using different number of target images for each training sample.

from fully connected layers, whose feature maps are smaller). This confirms the importance to consider detailed spatial information explicitly for alignment.

Number of Target Images Sampled. We also evaluate how the number of sampled target images affects the performance. Since enumerating around 3, 000 samples for each image in the training set is computationally prohibitive, we create a pseudo-target set with 8 images randomly selected from 8 cities in CITYSCAPES. This is to ensure there are variations among the targets and it is computationally feasible for enumerating all targets. We then analyze the effect of the number of target images used during training by randomly selecting 1, 2, 4 samples from SYNTHIA. Figure 4 presents the results. We observe that stochastically selecting from the target set is better than using all of them for all three networks. This might result from two reasons: (1) translating one image to multiple different representations in one-shot is hard to optimize; (2) stochastic sampling acts as regularization to improve generalization, which is similar to the case that stochastic gradient is better than full batch gradient descent. Interestingly, for PSPNet and FCN8s-ResNet101, sampling one image achieves competitive results, and this is very appealing when the number of samples in the target domain is limited.

5 Conclusion

In this paper, we have presented, DCAN, a simple yet effective approach to reduce domain shift at both pixel-level and feature-level for unsupervised scene adaptation. In particular, our framework leverages channel-wise feature alignment in both the image generator for synthesizing photo-realistic samples, appearing as if drawn from the target set, and the segmentation network, which simultaneously normalizes feature maps of source images. In contrast to recent work that makes extensive use of adversarial training, our framework is lightweight and easy to train. We conducted extensive experiments by transferring models learned on synthetic segmentation datasets to real urban scenes, and demonstrated the effectiveness of DCAN over state-of-the-art methods and its compatibility with modern segmentation networks.

Acknowledgment. The research is based upon work supported by the Office of the Director of National Intelligence (ODNI), Intelligence Advanced Research Projects Activity (IARPA), via DOI/IBC Contract Number D17PC00287. The views and conclusions contained herein are those of the authors and should not be interpreted as necessarily representing the official policies or endorsements, either expressed or implied, of the ODNI, IARPA, or the U.S. Government. The U.S. Government is authorized to reproduce and distribute reprints for Governmental purposes notwithstanding any copyright annotation thereon.

References

1. Deng, J., Dong, W., Socher, R., Li, L.J., Li, K., Fei-Fei, L.: ImageNet: a large-scale hierarchical image database. In: CVPR (2009)
2. Lin, T.Y., et al.: Microsoft COCO: common objects in context. In: Fleet, D., Pajdla, T., Schiele, B., Tuytelaars, T. (eds.) ECCV 2014. LNCS, vol. 8693, pp. 740–755. Springer, Cham (2014). https://doi.org/10.1007/978-3-319-10602-1_48
3. Varol, G., et al.: Learning from synthetic humans. In: CVPR (2017)
4. Peng, X., Sun, B., Ali, K., Saenko, K.: Learning deep object detectors from 3D models. In: ICCV (2015)
5. Sun, B., Feng, J., Saenko, K.: Return of frustratingly easy domain adaptation. In: AAAI (2016)
6. Sun, B., Saenko, K.: Deep CORAL: correlation alignment for deep domain adaptation. In: Hua, G., Jégou, H. (eds.) ECCV 2016. LNCS, vol. 9915, pp. 443–450. Springer, Cham (2016). https://doi.org/10.1007/978-3-319-49409-8_35
7. Xu, H., Zheng, J., Chellappa, R.: Bridging the domain shift by domain adaptive dictionary learning. In: BMVC (2015)
8. Tzeng, E., Hoffman, J., Saenko, K., Darrell, T.: Adversarial discriminative domain adaptation. In: CVPR (2017)
9. Hoffman, J., Wang, D., Yu, F., Darrell, T.: FCNs in the wild: pixel-level adversarial and constraint-based adaptation. CoRR (2016)
10. Bousmalis, K., Silberman, N., Dohan, D., Erhan, D., Krishnan, D.: Unsupervised pixel-level domain adaptation with generative adversarial networks. In: CVPR (2017)
11. Hoffman, J., et al.: Cycada: cycle-consistent adversarial domain adaptation. In: ICML (2018)
12. Bousmalis, K., et al.: Using simulation and domain adaptation to improve efficiency of deep robotic grasping. In: ICRA (2018)
13. Zhang, Y., David, P., Gong, B.: Curriculum domain adaptation for semantic segmentation of urban scenes. In: ICCV (2017)
14. Chen, L., et al.: SCA-CNN: spatial and channel-wise attention in convolutional networks for image captioning. In: CVPR (2017)
15. Ulyanov, D., Vedaldi, A., Lempitsky, V.S.: Instance normalization: the missing ingredient for fast stylization. CoRR (2016)

16. Dumoulin, V., Shlens, J., Kudlur, M.: A learned representation for artistic style. In: ICLR (2016)
17. Huang, X., Belongie, S.: Arbitrary style transfer in real-time with adaptive instance normalization. In: ICCV (2017)
18. Huang, G., Sun, Y., Liu, Z., Sedra, D., Weinberger, K.Q.: Deep networks with stochastic depth. In: Leibe, B., Matas, J., Sebe, N., Welling, M. (eds.) ECCV 2016. LNCS, vol. 9908, pp. 646–661. Springer, Cham (2016). https://doi.org/10.1007/978-3-319-46493-0_39
19. Ciregan, D., Meier, U., Schmidhuber, J.: Multi-column deep neural networks for image classification. In: CVPR (2012)
20. Sajjadi, M., Javanmardi, M., Tasdizen, T.: Regularization with stochastic transformations and perturbations for deep semi-supervised learning. In: NIPS (2016)
21. Srivastava, N., Hinton, G., Krizhevsky, A., Sutskever, I., Salakhutdinov, R.: Dropout: a simple way to prevent neural networks from overfitting. JMLR **15**, 1929–1958 (2014)
22. Ros, G., Sellart, L., Materzynska, J., Vazquez, D., Lopez, A.M.: The synthia dataset: a large collection of synthetic images for semantic segmentation of urban scenes. In: CVPR (2016)
23. Richter, S.R., Vineet, V., Roth, S., Koltun, V.: Playing for data: ground truth from computer games. In: Leibe, B., Matas, J., Sebe, N., Welling, M. (eds.) ECCV 2016. LNCS, vol. 9906, pp. 102–118. Springer, Cham (2016). https://doi.org/10.1007/978-3-319-46475-6_7
24. Cordts, M., et al.: The cityscapes dataset for semantic urban scene understanding. In: CVPR (2016)
25. Pan, S.J., Yang, Q.: A survey on transfer learning. IEEE TKDE **22**, 1345–1359 (2010)
26. Csurka, G.: A comprehensive survey on domain adaptation for visual applications. In: Csurka, G. (ed.) Domain Adaptation in Computer Vision Applications. ACVPR, pp. 1–35. Springer, Cham (2017). https://doi.org/10.1007/978-3-319-58347-1_1
27. Long, M., Cao, Y., Wang, J., Jordan, M.I.: Learning transferable features with deep adaptation networks. In: ICML (2015)
28. Bousmalis, K., Trigeorgis, G., Silberman, N., Krishnan, D., Erhan, D.: Domain separation networks. In: NIPS (2016)
29. Ganin, Y., Lempitsky, V.S.: Unsupervised domain adaptation by backpropagation. In: ICML. (2015)
30. Ganin, Y., et al.: Domain-adversarial training of neural networks. JMLR **17**, 2030–2096 (2016)
31. Tzeng, E., Hoffman, J., Darrell, T., Saenko, K.: Simultaneous deep transfer across domains and tasks. In: ICCV (2015)
32. Sankaranarayanan, S., Balaji, Y., Jain, A., Lim, S.N., Chellappa, R.: Unsupervised domain adaptation for semantic segmentation with gans. In: CVPR (2018)
33. Zhang, Y., Qiu, Z., Yao, T., Liu, D., Mei, T.: Fully convolutional adaptation networks for semantic segmentation. In: CVPR (2018)
34. Shrivastava, A., Pfister, T., Tuzel, O., Susskind, J., Wang, W., Webb, R.: Learning from simulated and unsupervised images through adversarial training. In: CVPR (2017)
35. Taigman, Y., Polyak, A., Wolf, L.: Unsupervised cross-domain image generation. In: ICLR (2017)
36. Liu, M.Y.L., Tuzel, O.: Coupled generative adversarial networks. In: NIPS (2016)

37. Arjovsky, M., Bottou, L.: Towards principled methods for training generative adversarial networks. In: ICLR (2017)
38. Goodfellow, I., et al.: Generative adversarial nets. In: NIPS (2014)
39. Yoo, D., Kim, N., Park, S., Paek, A.S., Kweon, I.S.: Pixel-level domain transfer. In: Leibe, B., Matas, J., Sebe, N., Welling, M. (eds.) ECCV 2016. LNCS, vol. 9912, pp. 517–532. Springer, Cham (2016). https://doi.org/10.1007/978-3-319-46484-8_31
40. Radford, A., Metz, L., Chintala, S.: Unsupervised representation learning with deep convolutional generative adversarial networks. In: ICLR (2016)
41. Odena, A., Olah, C., Shlens, J.: Conditional image synthesis with auxiliary classifier gans. In: ICML (2017)
42. Reed, S., Akata, Z., Yan, X., Logeswaran, L., Schiele, B., Lee, H.: Generative adversarial text to image synthesis. In: ICML (2016)
43. Shen, W., Liu, R.: Learning residual images for face attribute manipulation. In: CVPR (2017)
44. Isola, P., Zhu, J.Y., Zhou, T., Efros, A.A.: Image-to-image translation with conditional adversarial networks. In: CVPR (2017)
45. Ledig, C., et al.: Photo-realistic single image super-resolution using a generative adversarial network. In: CVPR (2017)
46. Zhu, J.Y., Park, T., Isola, P., Efros, A.A.: Unpaired image-to-image translation using cycle-consistent adversarial networks. In: ICCV (2017)
47. Liu, M.Y., Breuel, T., Kautz, J.: Unsupervised image-to-image translation networks. In: NIPS (2017)
48. Karras, T., Aila, T., Laine, S., Lehtinen, J.: Progressive growing of gans for improved quality, stability, and variation. In: ICLR (2018)
49. Gatys, L.A., Ecker, A.S., Bethge, M.: Image style transfer using convolutional neural networks. In: CVPR (2016)
50. Ulyanov, D., Lebedev, V., Vedaldi, A., Lempitsky, V.S.: Texture networks: feed-forward synthesis of textures and stylized images. In: ICML (2016)
51. Perarnau, G., van de Weijer, J., Raducanu, B., Álvarez, J.M.: Invertible conditional gans for image editing. In: NIPS Workshop (2016)
52. Johnson, J., Alahi, A., Fei-Fei, L.: Perceptual losses for real-time style transfer and super-resolution. In: Leibe, B., Matas, J., Sebe, N., Welling, M. (eds.) ECCV 2016. LNCS, vol. 9906, pp. 694–711. Springer, Cham (2016). https://doi.org/10.1007/978-3-319-46475-6_43
53. Li, Y., Wang, N., Liu, J., Hou, X.: Demystifying neural style transfer. In: IJCAI (2018)
54. Simonyan, K., Zisserman, A.: Very deep convolutional networks for large-scale image recognition. In: ICLR (2015)
55. Li, Y., Fang, C., Yang, J., Wang, Z., Lu, X., Yang, M.H.: Universal style transfer via feature transforms. In: NIPS (2017)
56. Chen, L.C., Papandreou, G., Kokkinos, I., Murphy, K., Yuille, A.L.: DeepLab: semantic image segmentation with deep convolutional nets, atrous convolution, and fully connected CRFs. IEEE TPAMI **40**, 834–848 (2018)
57. Long, J., Shelhamer, E., Darrell, T.: Fully convolutional networks for semantic segmentation. In: CVPR (2015)
58. Zhao, H., Shi, J., Qi, X., Wang, X., Jia, J.: Pyramid scene parsing network. In: CVPR (2017)
59. Peng, C., Zhang, X., Yu, G., Luo, G., Sun, J.: Large kernel matters - improve semantic segmentation by global convolutional network. In: CVPR (2017)
60. He, K., Zhang, X., Ren, S., Sun, J.: Deep residual learning for image recognition. In: CVPR (2016)

61. Badrinarayanan, V., Kendall, A., Cipolla, R.: SegNet: a deep convolutional encoder-decoder architecture for image segmentation. IEEE TPAMI (2017)
62. Bottou, L.: Large-scale machine learning with stochastic gradient descent. In: Lechevallier, Y., Saporta, G. (eds.) COMPSTAT. Physica-Verlag HD (2010). https://doi.org/10.1007/978-3-7908-2604-3_16
63. Han, B., Sim, J., Adam, H.: Branchout: regularization for online ensemble tracking with convolutional neural networks. In: CVPR (2017)
64. Wan, L., Zeiler, M., Zhang, S., Cun, Y.L., Fergus, R.: Regularization of neural networks using dropconnect. In: ICML (2013)
65. Krizhevsky, A., Sutskever, I., Hinton, G.E.: ImageNet classification with deep convolutional neural networks. In: NIPS (2012)
66. Pohlen, T., Hermans, A., Mathias, M., Leibe, B.: Full-resolution residual networks for semantic segmentation in street scenes. In: CVPR (2017)
67. Wang, T.C., Liu, M.Y., Zhu, J.Y., Tao, A., Kautz, J., Catanzaro, B.: High-resolution image synthesis and semantic manipulation with conditional gans. In: CVPR (2018)

View-Graph Selection Framework for SfM

Rajvi Shah(✉), Visesh Chari, and P. J. Narayanan

CVIT, Kohli Center for Intelligent Systems, IIIT Hyderabad, Hyderabad, India
rajvi.shah@research.iiit.ac.in

Abstract. View-graph selection is a crucial step for accurate and efficient large-scale structure from motion (SfM). Most SfM methods remove undesirable images and pairs using several fixed heuristic criteria, and propose tailor-made solutions to achieve specific reconstruction objectives such as efficiency, accuracy, or disambiguation. In contrast to these disparate solutions, we propose an optimization based formulation that can be used to achieve these different reconstruction objectives with task-specific cost modeling and construct a very efficient network-flow based formulation for its approximate solution. The abstraction brought on by this selection mechanism separates the challenges specific to datasets and reconstruction objectives from the standard SfM pipeline and improves its generalization. This paper mainly focuses on application of this framework with standard SfM pipeline for accurate and ghost-free reconstructions of highly ambiguous datasets. To model selection costs for this task, we introduce new disambiguation priors based on local geometry. We further demonstrate versatility of the method by using it for the general objective of accurate and efficient reconstruction of large-scale Internet datasets using costs based on well-known SfM priors.

Keywords: View-graph · Structure from motion · Disambiguation

1 Introduction

View-graph is a crucial input structure for large-scale structure from motion (SfM). Nodes in this graph represent images (also called cameras/views) and edges represent relative motion or epipolar geometries (EGs) between the nodes. View-graphs help in 'organizing' unordered image collections useful to, (i) select a core set of images for reconstruction, and (ii) identify noisy EGs that might degrade the quality of reconstruction. State-of-the-art SfM methods like incremental [17,22,32], hierarchical [3,7,18,28], or global [1,2,13,14,21], all rely on a view-graph based initial pruning step for efficient and accurate reconstruction.

Large community photo collections often display point-of-view bias, as some viewing angles are more popular than others. Using the full view-graph for SfM is

Electronic supplementary material The online version of this chapter (https://doi.org/10.1007/978-3-030-01228-1_33) contains supplementary material, which is available to authorized users.

V. Ferrari et al. (Eds.): ECCV 2018, LNCS 11209, pp. 553–568, 2018.
https://doi.org/10.1007/978-3-030-01228-1_33

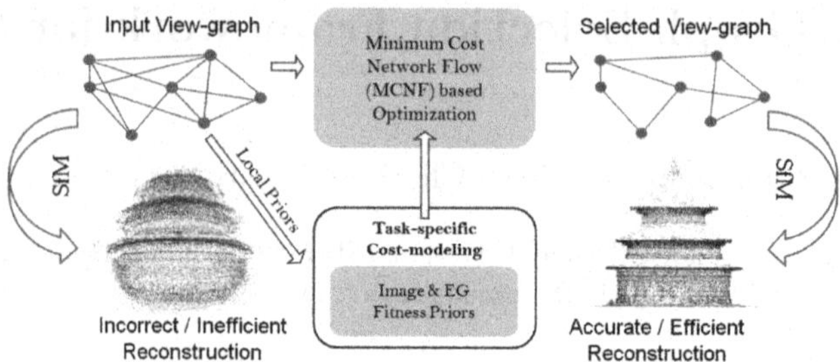

Fig. 1. Outline of the proposed selection framework. With appropriately modeled costs, the framework can select view-graphs that meet desired reconstruction objectives.

often computationally expensive and unnecessary due to high redundancy. Also, for closely clustered images, narrow baselines increase the uncertainty of triangulation, causing large re-projection errors. While isolated erroneous EGs can be overcome by robust averaging (global SfM) and repeated bundle adjustment (incremental SfM), large number of incorrect EGs can degrade reconstruction. Hence, it is crucial to select 'good' images and more importantly 'good' pairs for accuracy. Standard SfM methods apply fixed heuristics such as inliers, baselines, homography, loop closure for conservative selection/pruning of images and pairs. While these heuristics work well for a large variety of datasets, they are insufficient to identify and remove consistent noise that arise in ambiguous scenes.

Ambiguity in pairwise matching arises because man-made structures often comprise of repetitions (windows, arches), symmetries (circular structures, similar facades), and large duplicate elements (minarets, domes). While standard SfM pipelines are robust to handle a large number of inaccurate EGs in isolation, for scenes with high ambiguity, such wrong EGs form consistent sets, resulting in mis-registered cameras, 'phantom' structures, or structures incorrectly folded along symmetry. Previous works propose tailor-made solutions to handle such scenes with local/global steps for 'reasoning' ambiguity [10,11,16,29,33,34]. While these methods show good results on challenging datasets, they do not operate within the framework of standard SfM pipelines. We believe that these challenges can be addressed under the same umbrella of 'selecting' a complete, consistent and noise-free view-graph for accurate and efficient reconstruction.

The main motivation of our work is to formalize the core problem of view-graph selection to meet different objectives within a unified framework. We pose this as an optimization problem with image and pair selection costs and propose a novel network-flow based approximation for its efficient solution. This abstraction allows different objectives to be achieved by plugging in task-specific costs while keeping the overall selection and reconstruction framework the same. Figure 1 shows an outline of this framework. We mainly focus on the application of this framework for accurate and ghost-free reconstructions of highly ambiguous datasets and show how pairwise selection cost can be modeled using local priors, and also introduce a new context-based prior. Additionally, we also show its usefulness for accurate and efficient reconstruction of general large-scale Internet landmarks datasets with costs modeled using commonly used local heuristics.

To the best of our knowledge, this is the first attempt at systematizing view-graph selection. The proposed framework brings greater flexibility and generalization to standard SfM pipelines and its application is not limited to the specified use-cases. A unified framework also lands optimal view-graph selection as a learning problem if and when task-specific ground-truth data becomes available.

2 Related Work

In SfM literature, view-graph selection is not dealt with in a unified sense, instead, specific methods are designed to meet specific selection objectives. For efficiency and completeness, incremental/hierarchical SfM methods compute spanning subgraphs [8,15,24,28], with different criteria and selection strategies. For global methods, optimality of a subgraph is often related to consistency and robustness goals [5,13,14,27,31,35]. Our framework is not a one-size-fits-all replacement to specialized methods, but provides a mechanism to express different objectives using task-specific image and pairwise selection costs. Here, we revisit prior works related to the general objective of accuracy and the specific objective of disambiguation, and discuss their relevance to our work.

Implicit View-Graph Filtering in SfM Methods. Pruning undesirable images/pairs from input view-graph is implicit to both incremental and global SfM methods and is often done using thresholds on various criteria. Accuracy of incremental SfM hinges on seed pairwise reconstruction and next best view selection. Wide baseline seed pair selection is ensured using criteria based on epipolar inliers (that don't fit a homography) [22,23], or inlier ratios (to detect pairwise motion as planar, rotational, or general) [17]. For next best view selection, triangulation angle, inliers, or correspondence distribution are used as criteria [17,22].

Global SfM methods first use relative rotations to estimate global rotations followed by global translations estimation [1,2,13,21,27,30]. In [2], to reduce the state space of camera parameters for MRF based estimation, relative twist and unusual aspect ratios are used as view filtering criteria. Methods that use lie-algebraic averaging of relative rotations [1,4,5,13,14,27,35] often discard images with unknown calibration and handle outlier EGs with loop consistency checks [13,14,35] and robust cost functions.

Many of these heuristics are easy to incorporate as image and pairwise selection costs into our framework. Other heuristics that employ global reasoning (such as loop consistency) can be potentially remodeled as a pairwise heuristic.

SfM Methods for Disambiguation. Initial methods for disambiguation focused on inferring missing correspondences [34] and using it as a prior with global objectives of camera pose inference [16] or consistent view-graph expansion [11]. Other methods consist of social network principles based track refinement [29], geometry-aware feature matching [19], triplet-consistent graph expansion [20], and geodesic manifold based ambiguity detection and correction [33]. A post-reconstruction approach to disambiguation uses back-projected 3D points to identify conflicting observations [9,10]. In contrast to these specialized algorithms, we use our selection framework with costs modeled as a combination of disambiguation priors. We also propose a new context based pairwise selection prior that is based on both, missing correspondences and conflicting observations and unlike [9], it can be computed pre-reconstruction. Our solution is more general and very efficient as compared to prior methods and still recovers correct structures for a variety of ambiguous datasets.

3 Posing View-Graph Selection as Optimization

Let the input view-graph be $\mathcal{G} = (\mathcal{V}, \mathcal{E})$, where the set of vertices (nodes) $\mathcal{V}$ represents the images and the set of edges $\mathcal{E}$ represents the pairwise epipolar geometries (EGs). The goal is to select a subset of nodes $\mathcal{V}'$ and a subset of edges $\mathcal{E}'$ (a subgraph $\mathcal{G}' = (\mathcal{V}', \mathcal{E}')$) that meets a desired objective. We denote the indicator variables for image selection as δ_i and pair selection as δ_{ij}. Here, each δ_i, δ_{ij} correspond to the image vertex $v_i \in \mathcal{V}$ and the pairwise edge $e_{ij} \in \mathcal{E}$. Intuitively, this problem can be represented as a minimization of the form,

$$\arg\min \quad f(\delta) = \sum_i q_i \delta_i + \sum_i \sum_j q_{ij} \delta_{ij} \tag{1}$$

$$\text{subject to} \quad \sum \delta_i \leq N, \sum \delta_{ij} \leq M \tag{2}$$

$$\delta_{ij} \leq \delta_i, \; \delta_{ij} \leq \delta_j$$

$$\text{where} \quad \forall i \in \mathcal{V}, \; \forall (i,j) \in \mathcal{E}, \delta_i, \delta_{ij} \in \{0,1\},$$

$$N < |\mathcal{V}|, \; M < |\mathcal{E}| \tag{3}$$

Activation of indicator variables δ_i and δ_{ij} imply selection of corresponding image v_i and pair e_{ij}. q_i is the cost of selecting the view v_i and q_{ij} is the cost of selecting the edge e_{ij} and these costs assumed to be negative in the minimization sense. N and M indicate thresholds on maximum number of selected images and pairs and ensure that the subgraph selection is non-trivial (Eq. 2). Selection of image pair (i, j) requires that both images i and j constituting the pair also must be selected (Eq. 3).

Modeling these costs appropriately can express different objectives for view-graph selection. In this paper, we discuss cost modeling for accurate and ghost-free reconstructions using a few relevant priors. However, this can be used to achieve other objectives using a variety of other priors known in the literature or even learned costs.

This minimization problem can be formulated as a binary integer linear program (BILP), which is NP-complete. To find an exact optimal solution, stock solvers for BILP use branch-and-bound like techniques to intelligently iterate through all possible solutions. However, owing to the NP-complete nature of the problem, it is infeasible to compute the exact optimal solution for many problems of our interest. In fact, in our experiments, the computation time for a branch-and-bound based ILP solver was very high even for toy-sized problems. A standard trick to achieve efficient solutions with some approximation is to use a linear programming (LP) relaxation with rounding to obtain an integer solution. However, in preliminary experiments, the solutions obtained using this approach seemed too inaccurate to be useful. Furthermore, this formulation does not take into account connectivity of the selected subgraph. To tackle both these problems, we pose view-graph selection as a minimum cost network-flow (MCNF) problem (see supplementary material for more discussion) that guarantees us a binary solution in polynomial time and encourages connectivity in the selected sub-graph. The proposed MCNF formulation is explained in the next section.

4 View-Graph Selection as MCNF Problem

The network in MCNF problems is a directed graph with at least one source and one sink nodes. We denote the network as $\mathcal{T} = (\mathcal{N}, \mathcal{A})$, where $\mathcal{N}$ represents the set of nodes and $\mathcal{A}$ represents the set of directed edges/arcs. Each edge (i, j) in the network has a cost c_{ij} associated to let across one unit of flow, and the cost incurred by an edge is proportional to the flow (x_{ij}) through it. Each edge also has a lower and an upper bound (l_{ij}, u_{ij}) on the amount of flow (x_{ij}) that can pass through it, known as capacity constraints (**c.c**). The source sends a certain units of flow that the sink node must receive. At all other nodes, flow must be conserved. Let us denote the total flow as F and the remainder flow at a node i as b_i, then $b_i = F$ when i is source, $b_i = -F$ when i is sink, and $b_i = 0$ otherwise. These constraints are known as equal flow constraints (**e.f.c**). The MCNF problem is about sending the total flow from source to sink at a minimum cost, without violating the capacity and flow constraints. This minimization with flow and capacity constraints can be described as,

$$\text{minimize} \sum_{(i,j)\in\mathcal{A}} c_{ij}x_{ij} \tag{5}$$

$$\text{subject to,} \sum_{\{j:(i,j)\in\mathcal{A}\}} x_{ij} - \sum_{\{j:(j,i)\in\mathcal{A}\}} x_{ji} = b_i \qquad \forall i \in \mathcal{N} \quad \textbf{e.f.c} \tag{6}$$

$$l_{ij} \leq x_{ij} \leq u_{ij} \qquad \forall (i,j) \in \mathcal{A} \quad \textbf{c.c} \tag{7}$$

Network Construction. To pose view-graph selection as an MCNF problem, we construct the network as follows. All indicator variables corresponding to image/pair selection $\{\delta_i\}$, $\{\delta_{ij}\}$ are represented using arcs $(i, j) \in \mathcal{A}$ in the network, source and sink nodes are auxiliary. Since view selection variables are represented as arcs, each vertex i in the view-graph corresponds to two nodes, $(2i-1, 2i)$ in the network. Each odd node $(2i-1)$ corresponding to the vertex i in the view-graph is connected to the source node and similarly each even node $(2i)$ is connected to the sink node. The arcs corresponding to the pairwise selection variables $\{\delta_{ij}\}$, join the even node of the lower index image with the odd node of the higher index image. This choice prevents cycle formation in the network.

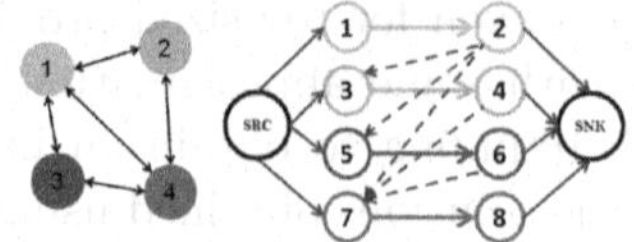

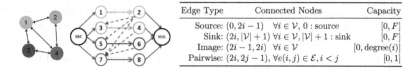

Edge Type	Connected Nodes	Capacity
Source:	$(0, 2i-1)$ $\forall i \in \mathcal{V}$, 0 : source	$[0, F]$
Sink:	$(2i, \lvert\mathcal{V}\rvert+1)$ $\forall i \in \mathcal{V}$, $\lvert\mathcal{V}\rvert+1$: sink	$[0, F]$
Image:	$(2i-1, 2i)$ $\forall i \in \mathcal{V}$	$[0, \text{degree}(i)]$
Pairwise:	$(2i, 2j-1)$, $\forall e(i,j) \in \mathcal{E}, i < j$	$[0, 1]$

Fig. 2. Network construction for a sample view-graph is shown on the left. Image nodes and selection arcs in are color-coded to match vertices in the view-graph. Pairwise selection arcs are depicted by black dashed lines. Arc connections and their capacities are described in the table shown on the right. (Color figure online)

Summarizing, the network has $|\mathcal{N}| = 2|\mathcal{V}| + 2$ nodes and $|\mathcal{A}| = |3\mathcal{V}| + |\mathcal{E}|$ arcs. These arc connections are summarized in Fig. 2 along with a pictorial example.

Equal Flow and Capacity Constraints. At source and sink the sent and received flow is equal to the total flow. Equal flow constraints require that in and out flow at every other node remain equal. In our formulation, capacity constraints - lower and upper bounds on flow through an arc are specified based on the edge type as mentioned in Fig. 2.

To understand the choice of these capacities, consider the vertex v_1 in the depicted view-graph. The arc corresponding to v_1's selection variable δ_1 in the network is $a(1,2)$. Corresponding to v_1's degree in the view-graph, the node n_2 in the network has three outgoing arcs $a(2,3)$, $a(2,5)$, and $a(2,7)$ for pairwise selection variables δ_{12}, δ_{13}, and δ_{14}. The flow starting from source node, after passing through $a(1,2)$, should plausibly be able to pass through all three outgoing arcs. Since flow can only be divided in integer units, the minimum capacity of image selection arc $a(1,2)$ has to be at least 3 ($deg(v_i)$). Under minimum cost solution, the flow at any node will continue to take the path of least resistance (cost). Now, suppose that the cost assigned to $a(2,3)$ is the least amongst the three outgoing arcs and its max. capacity is 3 units (or any value $1 < k < deg(v_i)$). In this scenario, $a(2,3)$ being the lowest cost arcs will pull all 3 units of flow from $a(1,2)$, starving the other arcs of any flow and preventing the corresponding view-graph edges from ever getting selected. To avoid this, we restrict the maximum flow through pairwise selection arcs to 1.

Effect of Cost Normalization and Flow on Solution. In minimization sense, negative costs provide encouragement for flow to pass through an arc, whereas positive costs provide discouragement. Suppose, all costs are negative, then total flow F of 1 unit will select the lowest cost chain in the network (often the longest). As we increase the value of total flow, more paths get explored and when $F = |\mathcal{E}|$ all images and EGs get selected. When costs are both encouraging and discouraging, many positive cost arcs will act as barriers for the flow. As a result, at some value of total flow F the selection will (nearly) saturate and may never select the full view-graph. For the proposed applications, we use only encouraging costs ($-1 \leq c_{ij} \leq 0$), while flow remains the only free parameter.

Tuning Flow Parameter. To systematically understand the effect of total flow on image and pair selection, we created synthetic view-graphs with varying number

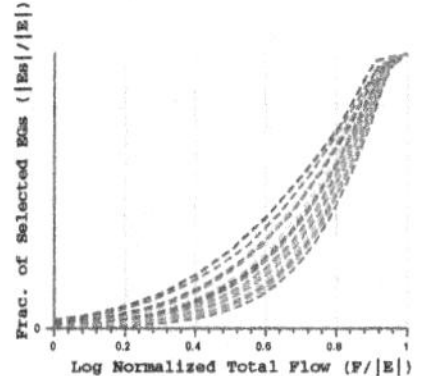

Fig. 3. Effect of total flow on edge selection: selected edges increase monotonically with flow.

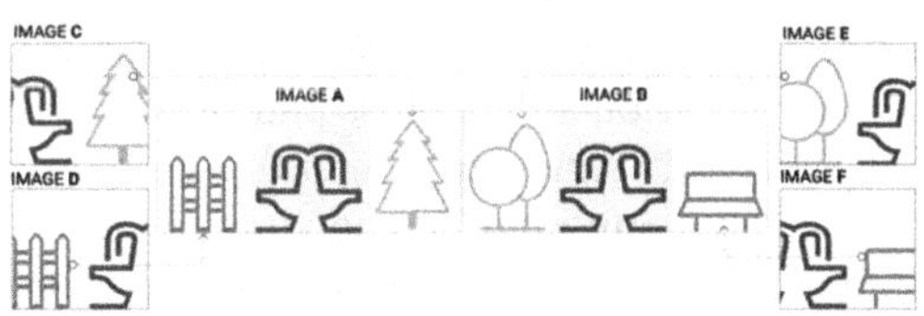

Fig. 4. Image pair (A,B) capture a scene with duplicate elements. Though duplicate elements in the images yield many matches, elements in context regions tend to find matches with non-intersecting sets of images.

of vertices, varying degrees of connectivity simulated using Gaussian assumptions on neighborhood, and randomly assigned (negative) costs (discussed in detail in the suppl. material). We performed sub-graph selection on ~100 such synthetic view-graphs using the proposed MCNF approach for increasing values of total flow and observed a consistent pattern in selection behavior. Figure 3 shows the plot for fraction of total edges selected vs. normalized total flow. It can be seen that for negative costs, the relation between total flow and selected vertices and edges is logarithmic in nature. This relation is also observed on real-world (Internet) datasets with well-connected view-graphs (see supplementary material). Depending on the fraction of total vertices and edges we want to be selected, the logarithmic dependence allows us to find the desired sub-graph by a binary search of the flow parameter over the [0,1] interval with a logarithmic scale. Such an iterative search is particularly effective in view of the extremely low computational time of the MCNF algorithm. In fact, the combined processing time of the whole search procedure is still an insignificant fraction of the total time required for SfM, and is thus far from being the computational bottleneck.

Running Time. A crucial advantage of this formulation is that it can be solved very efficiently. Constructing the network and solving for MCNF takes less than a second even for graphs with ~1000 nodes and ~100K edges.

5 Applications and Cost Modeling

To show that the proposed framework can address different concerns using task-specific costs, we tackle two use-cases. We first discuss cost modeling for reconstruction of highly ambiguous datasets using local disambiguation priors. Later, we discuss cost modeling for the general use-case of accurate and efficient reconstruction of large-scale Internet datasets using common SfM priors.

5.1 Cost Modeling for Ambiguous Datasets

We propose that even for highly ambiguous datasets, with conservative selection of an input view-graph such that it consists of a higher fraction of 'true' EGs, correct reconstruction can be recovered without any change in the reconstruction pipeline. To achieve this, we use three pairwise measures that act as strong priors for disambiguation and express pair selection cost as a linear combination of these three priors (with uniform weights). These priors are based on local geometry and can be easily computed at the time of initial view-graph construction without significant overhead. Note that $c^k(e_{ij})$ denotes the contribution of prior k to the total cost c for the pair e_{ij}, and g denotes a normalization function that distributes raw prior value to the desired cost range.

Context Similarity. Missing correspondences (matches in a pair, not matching the third image in a triplet) are a useful prior for disambiguation. However, by itself, this prior is not very effective for disambiguation and it is commonly used in an inference framework with other priors or with a global objective [11,16,34]. Track covisibility statistics [29] are also useful for disambiguation, but it is not straightforward to apply this prior to describe pairwise fitness. In a post-reconstruction disambiguation approach [10], reconstructed 3D points are back-projected into image pairs and conflicting observations in unmatched regions (context) are identified. However, this measure is also not directly useful as our approach is a pre-process to SfM reconstruction. Motivated by these priors, we propose a new, context based pairwise prior that is suitable to our framework.

For image pair $(\mathrm{I_i}, \mathrm{I_j})$, the sets of all matched features (matched with any image) are S_i, S_j and the sets of features that match between $(\mathrm{I_i}, \mathrm{I_j})$ are M_i, M_j. The difference sets $U_i = S_i \setminus M_i$, $U_j = S_j \setminus M_j$ consist of unique features in $\mathrm{I_i}$ and $\mathrm{I_j}$. Suppose images I_i and I_j are looking at a scene with duplicate instances of a structure. The features in the match sets M_i, M_j will most likely lie on the duplicate elements. We consider the unique feature sets U_i, U_j to belong to the context regions. If two images are truly looking at the same instance, the context features of both images would have matched similar set of images. On the other hand, if two images are looking at duplicate instances, the context features would be distributed over different sets of images (see Fig. 4). We find distribution of features in U_i and U_j over all N images in the collection based on their matches and make an N dimensional description of the context space. Context feature of image I_i w.r.t. image I_j can be described as,

$$\mathbf{w}_{ij} = [w_i^1, w_i^2, \ldots, w_i^N] \quad w_i^j = 0 \tag{8}$$

$$w_i^k = |\{u \in U_i \mid u \leftrightarrow u', u' \in S_k, k \neq j\}| \tag{9}$$

This measure is slightly biased against pairs with very low visual overlap, however, combined with the other two measures, it works effectively for selection. We compared the context features of a pair using cosine similarity or hamming distance (after binarization) and found them to be working similarly. The context similarity can be defined as, $c^k(e_{ij}) = g(\mathbf{w}_{ij}^\top \mathbf{w}_{ji})$.

Loop Consistency. Loop consistency suggests that rotations in an EG triplet when chained should yield identity [6]. We find all triplets in the view-graph and label them as consistent or inconsistent. For each EG, we count the total number of consistent EGs it participates in and use this as a measure of its fitness. Though it is not same as explicitly enforcing loop consistency, it is a convenient way to incorporate a non-local (pairwise) geometric cue as a pairwise prior. $c^k(e_{ij}) = g(\frac{\#\text{ consistent triplets on } (i,j)}{median(\#\text{ consistent triplets on any}(i,j))})$.

Multiple Motions. We model this prior to disambiguate image pairs capturing repetitive or duplicate instances of some scene elements. We remove the correspondences that satisfy the estimated EG from the initial set of matches and estimate the secondary relative pose using the leftover matches. If sufficient inliers are found, we decompose the relative pose into rotation and translation. We estimate the angular difference between primary and secondary rotations (ΔR_θ) and also the angle between the both position vectors ($\arccos(\Delta \mathrm{C}_{ij}^\mathsf{T} \Delta \mathrm{C}_{ij})$). If the difference angles are small, the secondary motion is most possibly arising due to threshold sensitivity and measurement drift, otherwise, these indicate presence of correspondences on ambiguous structures. Examples of these scenarios are shown in Fig. 5. $c^k(e_{ij}) = g(\Delta R_\theta, \arccos(\Delta \mathrm{C}_{ij}^\mathsf{T} \Delta \mathrm{C}_{ij}))$. When secondary motion is detected, the value of this prior is very effective in disambiguating (except for the instances when camera is purely translating along the direction of repetition). However, this prior alone is insufficient for disambiguation, as for many incorrect pairs secondary geometry is not detected. We combine this prior with the other two priors only for the pairs where secondary geometry is detected.

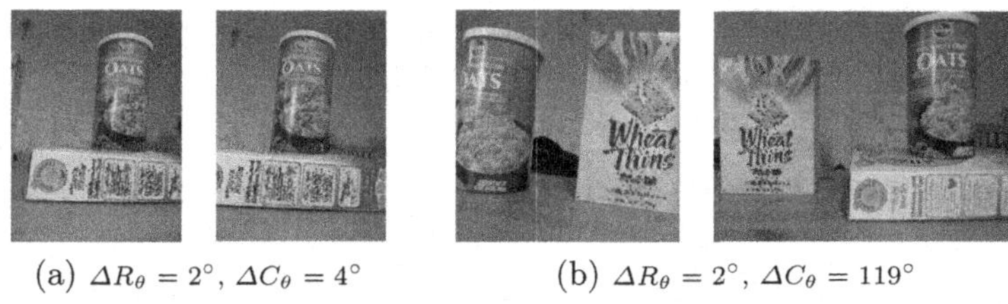

(a) $\Delta R_\theta = 2°$, $\Delta C_\theta = 4°$ (b) $\Delta R_\theta = 2°$, $\Delta C_\theta = 119°$

Fig. 5. Multiple motion detection: for correctly matched pair (a) both motions are in agreement, while for pair (b) matches due to ambiguity cause large position difference.

5.2 Cost Modeling for General Datasets

View-graph selection for general datasets is typically done to achieve complete reconstructions with smaller re-projection errors and shorter run-time. For these goals, we use simple priors based on graph-connectivity and local geometry that express common-knowledge selection heuristics and criteria of general SfM methods in form of image and pairwise selection costs, suitable for our framework.

Image Selection Priors. For the purposes of accurate and complete reconstruction, we consider three image priors, (i) degree of an image node in the view-graph, (ii) fraction of an image's features that participates in tracks, (iii) local clustering coefficient of an image node in the view-graph. First two measures favor selecting images with many observations and connections to support longer tracks useful for accurate triangulation. Since Internet photo collections often suffer from point of view bias, using only connectivity based priors could lead to selections within popular components. To compensate for this effect, we include local clustering coefficient (lcc) of a vertex as an image prior to prefer images that provide connections across components than within components. Image selection cost is a linear combination of these priors with uniform weights.

Pairwise Selection Priors. Fitness of a pair in traditional SfM pipelines is measured using two common criteria, baseline and number of EG inliers. We use four pairwise priors, (i) number of inliers, (ii) median triangulation angle of pairwise reconstructed features, (iii) overlap (area of a convex hull of the matched features), and (iv) infinite homography, that are reflective of this selection criteria. While the usefulness of first three priors is evident, detecting infinite homography is useful in discouraging pairs with panoramic motion (rotation around a fixed center). Despite a high overlap, such pairs are undesirable as they lead to degenerate or ill-conditioned EG. Simply using homography inliers also rejects valid EGs due to planar regions. We use the fact that calibration normalized infinite homographies are basically rotations [6]. Hence, $\mathrm{H}^{\mathsf{T}}\mathrm{H}$ should be close to identity for such pairs and we model this prior as, $||\mathrm{H}_{ij}^{\mathsf{T}}\mathrm{H}_{ij} - \mathrm{I}||_{\mathrm{F}}$.

A more detailed expression of the priors discussed in this section is provided in supplementary material along with other implementation details such as choice of thresholds and normalization (g) for different priors.

6 Results and Discussion

We apply our view-graph (henceforth mentioned as VG for brevity) selection framework for the two use-cases discussed and show results on a variety of datasets. Implementation details are provided in the supplementary material along with additional analysis and results. Code can be found at, https://cvit.iiit.ac.in/research/projects/cvit-projects/viewgraphselection.

6.1 Ambiguous Datasets Reconstruction

We show successful reconstruction results on 12 highly ambiguous datasets consisting of small-scale lab-style scenes [16], and large-scale urban scenes [10,20] with the standard incremental SfM pipeline and VGs selected using our approach. Details of these datasets and selection statistics are given in Table 1a.

Qualitative Comparison. Figure 7 shows reconstruction results for small-scale ambiguous scenes [16]. With selected VGs, we are able to recover true structures for all datasets. Figure 8 shows reconstruction results for large-scale urban ambiguous scenes [10,20]. Our method is able to recover comparable splits to the method of [10] and successful reconstruction for TOH dataset. Our result for ANC dataset is incomplete as compared to [10,33] (shown in supplementary material).

Ablation of Priors. To highlight the effectiveness of disambiguation specific priors, we also reconstruct these datasets for VGs selected using random costs (fails on all datasets), baseline priors based costs (fails on all but the 'books' dataset), and combination of all costs based on priors for general reconstruction and disambiguation (fails on 'cup' and 'cereal' datasets). Among the disambiguation priors, context similarity based prior is the most effective standalone. To further evaluate the effectiveness of the disambiguation priors and their combinations, we study the range of flow values for which the given prior based selection results in successful reconstruction (see Fig. 6). We observed Context+Loop prior combination to be the most robust in this ablation study but empirically observed benefits of using multiple motions based prior on larger datasets. Qualitative results for the ablation study are provided in supplementary material.

Runtime Comparison. Method proposed in [10] operates post-reconstruction to split incorrectly merged model parts and takes ∼16 to ∼85 min to process for these datasets. Our framework pre-selects the VG and reconstruction is performed without any additional processing. Recently proposed method of [33] also tackles the disambiguation problem as a pre-process to SfM but their method takes 2–11 min on these datasets. Our subgraph selection framework is extremely efficient taking 1–2 s for constructing and solving the MCNF problem for these and even larger datasets. Moreover, our framework is intended to be general purpose with disambiguation as one of the specific objectives.

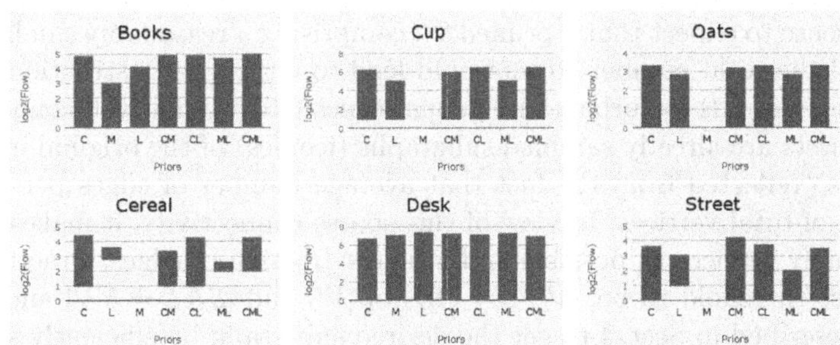

Fig. 6. Range of flow values ($y-$axis on log scale) for which given prior combinations ($x-$axis) lead to correct reconstructions. Priors that lead to correct reconstruction for higher values of flow are better at disambiguation and more robust, since this behavior implies selection of smaller fraction of outlier EGs. Since multiple motions are detected for a smaller fraction of pairs. For most datasets, context prior performs better than loop prior. Combination of all priors performs equivalently for practical purposes.

Criteria for Flow Parameter Search. As can be seen in Table 1a, for the lab-style datasets, the full VG is generally quite dense, with an average vertex degree (edges

Table 1. (a) shows details of ambiguous datasets and selection statistics. t_{sel} shows the combined running time for all search iterations of MCNF solver. Abbreviated labels correspond to: ANC – Alexander Nevsky Cathedral, ADT – Arc de Triomphe, BG – Brandenburg Gate, CSB – Church on Splilled Blood, RDC – Radcliff Camera, TOH – Temple of Heaven; (b) top rows show results reported by other methods on small-scale ambiguous datasets (1 to 6) where – implies results not reported, *[16] succeeds on these sets only with time-stamp info. Bottom rows show results of our selection method with various prior based costs for given flow.

Sr.	Dataset	$\|\mathcal{V}\|$	$\|\mathcal{E}\|$	F	$\|\mathcal{V}_s\|$	$\|\mathcal{E}_s\|$	t_{sel}
1	Cereal	25	228	4	25	49	0.0137
2	Cup	64	1217	16	64	265	0.0268
3	Oats	24	220	4	24	49	0.0137
4	Street	19	95	2	19	26	0.0089
5	Books	21	161	4	21	41	0.0135
6	Desk	31	261	4	31	64	0.0138
7	ANC	448	5037	512	416	2497	0.1288
8	ADT	381	3627	512	340	2148	0.0940
9	RDC	271	3378	128	258	1498	0.0717
10	BG	161	2003	128	129	848	0.0522
11	CSB	277	5191	128	233	1380	0.0743
12	ToH	341	50332	32	341	1990	0.2372

(a) Datasets and selection details

		1	2	3	4	5	6
Other Methods	Roberts et al. [16]*	✗	✗	✗	✗	✗	✗
	Jiang et al. [11]	✓	✗	✓	✓	✓	✓
	Wilson and Snavely [29]	✗	✗	✗	✓	✗	✗
	Heinly et al. [10]	✓	–	–	–	–	✓
	Shen et al. [20]	–	✓	✓	✓	–	✗
	Yan et al. [33]	–	✓	–	–	✓	–
Ours with diff. priors	Baseline	✗	✗	✗	✗	✓	✗
	General+Disamb.	✗	✗	✓	✓	✓	✓
	Context	✓	✓	✓	✓	✓	✓
	Loop	✗	✓	✓	✓	✓	✓
	MM	✗	✗	✗	✗	✓	✓
	Context+Loop	✓	✓	✓	✓	✓	✓
	Context+MM	✓	✓	✓	✓	✓	✓
	Loop+MM	✓	✓	✓	✓	✓	✓
	Context+Loop+MM	✓	✓	✓	✓	✓	✓

(b) Comparison and Ablation

per vertex) ~32% of total vertices. However, due to the very high ambiguity in the scenes, large number of pairs are expected to be outliers. Therefore, it makes intuitive sense to expect that a pruned VG comprising a reasonably small fraction (~25%) of the total number edges would lead to a good reconstruction. On the other hand, the VGs for urban ambiguous scenes [10] are not well-connected, as these datasets are already sampled subgraphs (iconics) of the original image set. This is also reflected from the fact that average number of edges per vertex is only ~5% of total vertices. In view of this sparse connectivity, it makes sense to keep as many vertices as possible and a bigger fraction of edges. Practically, we chose these threshold to be, $|\mathcal{V}_s| >= 80\%$ of $|\mathcal{V}|$, and $|\mathcal{E}_s| >= 5|\mathcal{V}|$ and use the method described in Sect. 4 to get the desired sub-graph by efficiently searching for the appropriate flow value.

6.2 General Datasets Reconstruction

We show that the proposed framework is versatile and can also be used for the general goals of accuracy and efficiency for reconstruction of standard SfM datasets, by modeling image and pair selection costs with well-known and commonly used SfM priors. For this task, we show the results on two datasets, *(i)* MVS benchmark [25], and *(ii)* Internet landmarks [12,22]. These datasets are reconstructed with incremental [32] and global SfM [26] pipelines, using both, full VGs and VGs selected by our method.

Table 2. Selection and reconstruction statistics for general datasets. Labels 'S' and 'F' show selected and full VGs, $|\mathcal{V}|$, $|\mathcal{E}|$ – vertices and edges, N_c – #reconstructed cameras, R_{err}, T_{err}, and r_{err} – median rotation, translation, and reprojection errors, t_{sel} and t_{sfm} – runtime for VG selection (cumulative) and SfM reconstruction.

Dataset	VG	$\|\mathcal{V}\|$	$\|\mathcal{E}\|$	Incremental SfM R_{err}	Incremental SfM T_{err}	Incremental SfM r_{err}	Global SfM R_{err}	Global SfM T_{err}	Global SfM r_{err}
Castle	S	30	49	2.44	0.15	0.38	2.21	1.29	1.01
	F		118	2.22	0.22	0.34	2.17	7.49	1.14
Fountain	S	11	21	2.90	0.01	0.29	2.82	0.29	0.35
	F		25	2.90	0.01	0.72	2.82	0.27	0.59
Herzjesu	S	25	55	2.36	0.03	0.50	2.38	0.75	1.18
	F		128	2.38	0.02	0.43	2.39	0.56	1.71

(a) MVS dataset statistics

Dataset	VG	$\|\mathcal{V}\|$	$\|\mathcal{E}\|$	t_{sel}	N_c	r_{err}	R_{err}	T_{err}	t_{sfm}
Notre Dame	S	659	16970	1.744	628	1.41	0.072	0.195	1151
	F	714	46746	–	682	1.53	0.089	0.217	1760
Pantheon	S	761	15975	3.721	754	1.06	0.098	0.310	1785
	F	781	139630	–	775	1.31	0.125	0.309	3601
St. Peters	S	1132	39640	2.864	1095	1.341	0.037	0.517	1147
	F	1155	119977	–	1111	1.458	0.028	0.496	1367

(b) Internet landmarks datasets statistics

MVS benchmark consists of three toy-sized datasets with ground-truth (GT) camera positions. Table 2a shows that, for both SfM methods, the selected VGs based reconstructions are comparable to the full VGs based reconstructions. Flow parameter for these selections was chosen such that all vertices are selected (for GT comparisons). For large-scale Internet landmarks datasets, we reconstruct the scenes using selected VGs and full VGs with global SfM pipeline (typically slightly less robust than incremental SfM methods) in order to compare the reconstruction accuracy w.r.t. incremental SfM based baseline reconstructions

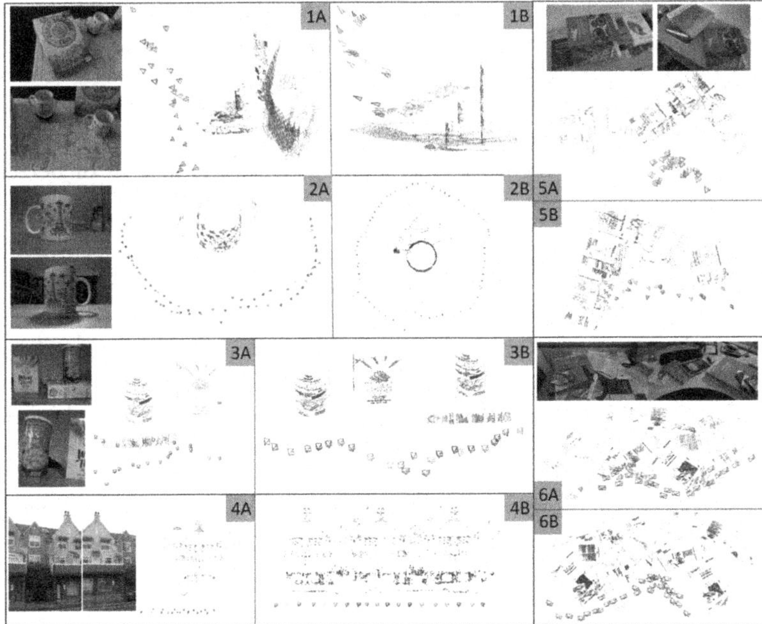

Fig. 7. Reconstructions for small ambiguous datasets (numbered as per Table 1a): (A) indicate full VG based reconstructions, (B) indicate selected VG based reconstructions.

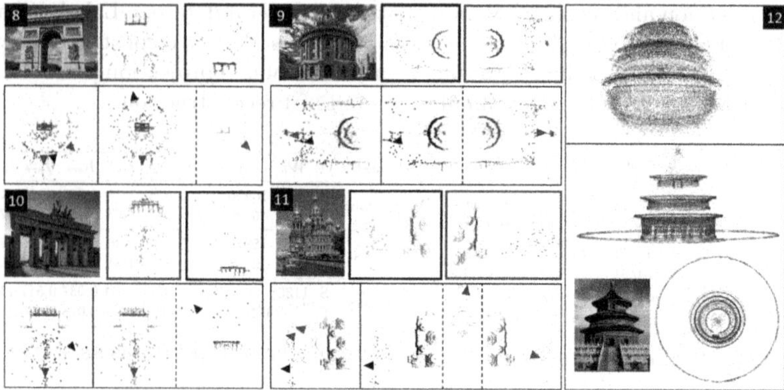

Fig. 8. Comparison of our reconstruction results on large ambiguous datasets (numbered as per Table 1a). For 8 to 11, bottom left – incorrect model with full VG, bottom right – result of correctly split models using the post-reconstruction pipeline of [10], and top row – our result (color-coded to match the splits of [10]. For 12, top – full VG result, bottom – result with our selection. (Color figure online)

(in absence of ground-truth). Table 2b shows the selection and reconstruction statistics for these datasets. It can be seen that the reconstructions with selected VGs are comparable or more accurate as compared to those with full VGs and SfM run-time with selected VGs is notably shorter. For completeness of the recovered structure, it is desirable to have as many vertices as possible in the subgraph. For efficiency, it is desirable to select fewer edges, however too few edges (low vertex degree) can lead to many short feature tracks and high reprojection errors. With these considerations, we keep $|\mathcal{V}_s| = 90\%$ of $|\mathcal{V}|$ and $|\mathcal{E}_s| = 20|\mathcal{V}|$ as flow search criteria. The selected VG reconstructions are qualitatively similar or better than full VG reconstructions (shown in supplementary material).

7 Conclusions and Future Work

We presented a novel and efficient, unified framework for selecting subgraphs from initial view-graphs that can achieve different selection objectives with appropriately modeled image and pairwise selection costs. This mechanism provides an interesting way to separate dataset and task specific challenges from the standard SfM pipeline, thereby improving its generality. We demonstrated utility and potential of this framework by achieving satisfactory results for two objectives. One interesting way to achieve even further abstraction to this problem would be to replace hand-designed costs by a weighted combination ($c_i = \sum_k \alpha_k f_k(i)$) of a number of known and designed priors. Cost formulation of this form would be expressive enough to cater to a wide variety of selection objectives. The problem of modeling costs to meet the desired objective then translates to that of devising new priors to add to the combination and finding the right weights for prior combination. In future, we wish to explore this direction for extending our framework. While this is non-trivial, it can lead to interesting directions of research for searching/learning new priors and the combination weights.

Acknowledgement. We thank Google India PhD Fellowship and India Digital Heritage Project of Department of Science and Technology, Govt. of India for funding this work.

References

1. Chatterjee, A., Govindu, V.M.: Efficient and robust large-scale rotation averaging. In: Proceedings IEEE ICCV (2013)
2. Crandall, D., Owens, A., Snavely, N., Huttenlocher, D.: Discrete-continuous optimization for large-scale structure from motion. In: Proceedings IEEE CVPR (2011)
3. Gherardi, R., Farenzena, M., Fusiello, A.: Improving the efficiency of hierarchical structure-and-motion. In: Proceedings IEEE CVPR (2010)
4. Govindu, V.M.: Lie-algebraic averaging for globally consistent motion estimation. In: Proceedings IEEE CVPR (2004)
5. Govindu, V.M.: Robustness in motion averaging. In: Narayanan, P.J., Nayar, S.K., Shum, H.-Y. (eds.) ACCV 2006. LNCS, vol. 3852, pp. 457–466. Springer, Heidelberg (2006). https://doi.org/10.1007/11612704_46
6. Hartley, R., Zisserman, A.: Multiple View Geometry in Computer Vision. Cambridge University Press, Cambridge (2003)
7. Havlena, M., Torii, A., Knopp, J., Pajdla, T.: Randomized structure from motion based on atomic 3D models from camera triplets. In: Proceedings IEEE CVPR (2009)
8. Havlena, M., Torii, A., Pajdla, T.: Efficient structure from motion by graph optimization. In: Daniilidis, K., Maragos, P., Paragios, N. (eds.) ECCV 2010. LNCS, vol. 6312, pp. 100–113. Springer, Heidelberg (2010). https://doi.org/10.1007/978-3-642-15552-9_8
9. Heinly, J., Dunn, E., Frahm, J.-M.: Recovering correct reconstructions from indistinguishable geometry. In: Proceedings 3D Vision (3DV) (2014)
10. Heinly, J., Dunn, E., Frahm, J.-M.: Correcting for duplicate scene structure in sparse 3D reconstruction. In: Fleet, D., Pajdla, T., Schiele, B., Tuytelaars, T. (eds.) ECCV 2014. LNCS, vol. 8692, pp. 780–795. Springer, Cham (2014). https://doi.org/10.1007/978-3-319-10593-2_51
11. Jiang, N., Tan, P., Cheong, L.F.: Seeing double without confusion: structure-from-motion in highly ambiguous scenes. In: Proceedings IEEE CVPR (2012)
12. Li, Y., Snavely, N., Huttenlocher, D.P.: Location recognition using prioritized feature matching. In: Daniilidis, K., Maragos, P., Paragios, N. (eds.) ECCV 2010. LNCS, vol. 6312, pp. 791–804. Springer, Heidelberg (2010). https://doi.org/10.1007/978-3-642-15552-9_57
13. Moulon, P., Monasse, P., Marlet, R.: Global fusion of relative motions for robust, accurate and scalable structure from motion. In: Proceedings IEEE ICCV (2013)
14. Olsson, C., Enqvist, O.: Stable structure from motion for unordered image collections. In: Heyden, A., Kahl, F. (eds.) SCIA 2011. LNCS, vol. 6688, pp. 524–535. Springer, Heidelberg (2011). https://doi.org/10.1007/978-3-642-21227-7_49
15. Raguram, R., Wu, C., Frahm, J.-M., Lazebnik, S.: Modeling and recognition of landmark image collections using iconic scene graphs. Int. J. Comput. Vis. **95**(3), 213–239 (2011)

16. Roberts, R., Sinha, S.N., Szeliski, R., Steedly, D.: Structure from motion for scenes with large duplicate structures. In: Proceedings IEEE CVPR (2011)
17. Schonberger, J.L., Frahm, J.M.: Structure-from-motion revisited. In: Proceedings IEEE CVPR (2016)
18. Shah, R., Deshpande, A., Narayanan, P.J.: Multistage SFM: revisiting incremental structure from motion. In: Proceedings 3D Vision (3DV) (2014)
19. Shah, R., Srivastava, V., Narayanan, P.J.: Geometry-aware feature matching for structure from motion applications. In: Proceedings IEEE Winter Conference on Applications of Computer Vision (2015)
20. Shen, T., Zhu, S., Fang, T., Zhang, R., Quan, L.: Graph-based consistent matching for structure-from-motion. In: Leibe, B., Matas, J., Sebe, N., Welling, M. (eds.) ECCV 2016. LNCS, vol. 9907, pp. 139–155. Springer, Cham (2016). https://doi.org/10.1007/978-3-319-46487-9_9
21. Sinha, S.N., Steedly, D., Szeliski, R.: A multi-stage linear approach to structure from motion. In: Kutulakos, K.N. (ed.) ECCV 2010. LNCS, vol. 6554, pp. 267–281. Springer, Heidelberg (2012). https://doi.org/10.1007/978-3-642-35740-4_21
22. Snavely, N., Seitz, S.M., Szeliski, R.: Photo tourism: exploring photo collections in 3D. ACM Trans. Graph. **25**(3), 835–846 (2006)
23. Snavely, N., Seitz, S.M., Szeliski, R.: Modeling the world from internet photo collections. Int. J. Comput. Vision **80**(2), 189–210 (2008)
24. Snavely, N., Seitz, S.M., Szeliski, R.: Skeletal graphs for efficient structure from motion. In: Proceedings IEEE CVPR, (2008)
25. Strecha, C., Von Hansen, W., Van Gool, L., Fua, P., Thoennessen, U.: On benchmarking camera calibration and multi-view stereo for high resolution imagery. In: Proceedings IEEE CVPR (2008)
26. Sweeney, C.: Theia Multiview Geometry Library: Tutorial & Reference. University of California Santa Barbara (2015)
27. Sweeney, C., Sattler, T., Hollerer, T., Turk, M., Pollefeys, M.: Optimizing the viewing graph for structure-from-motion. In: Proceedings IEEE ICCV (2015)
28. Toldo, R., Gherardi, R., Farenzena, M., Fusiello, A.: Hierarchical structure-and-motion recovery from uncalibrated images. Comput. Vis. Image Underst. **140**, 127–143 (2015)
29. Wilson, K., Snavely, N.: Network principles for SfM: disambiguating repeated structures with local context. In: Proceedings IEEE ICCV (2013)
30. Wilson, K., Snavely, N.: Robust global translations with 1DSfM. In: Fleet, D., Pajdla, T., Schiele, B., Tuytelaars, T. (eds.) ECCV 2014. LNCS, vol. 8691, pp. 61–75. Springer, Cham (2014). https://doi.org/10.1007/978-3-319-10578-9_5
31. Wilson, K., Bindel, D., Snavely, N.: When is rotations averaging hard? In: Leibe, B., Matas, J., Sebe, N., Welling, M. (eds.) ECCV 2016. LNCS, vol. 9911, pp. 255–270. Springer, Cham (2016). https://doi.org/10.1007/978-3-319-46478-7_16
32. Wu, C.: Towards linear-time incremental structure from motion. In: Proceedings 3D Vision (3DV) (2013)
33. Yan, Q., Yang, L., Zhang, L., Xiao, C.: Distinguishing the indistinguishable: exploring structural ambiguities via geodesic context. In: Proceedings IEEE CVPR, July 2017
34. Zach, C., Irschara, A., Bischof, H.: What can missing correspondences tell us about 3D structure and motion? In: Proceedings IEEE CVPR (2008)
35. Zach, C., Klopschitz, M., Pollefeys, M.: Disambiguating visual relations using loop constraints. In: Proceedings IEEE CVPR (2010)

Selfie Video Stabilization

Jiyang Yu(✉) and Ravi Ramamoorthi

University of California, San Diego, USA
jiy173@eng.ucsd.edu, ravir@cs.ucsd.edu

Abstract. We propose a novel algorithm for stabilizing selfie videos. Our goal is to automatically generate stabilized video that has optimal smooth motion in the sense of both foreground and background. The key insight is that non-rigid foreground motion in selfie videos can be analyzed using a 3D face model, and background motion can be analyzed using optical flow. We use second derivative of temporal trajectory of selected pixels as the measure of smoothness. Our algorithm stabilizes selfie videos by minimizing the smoothness measure of the background, regularized by the motion of the foreground. Experiments show that our method outperforms state-of-the-art general video stabilization techniques in selfie videos.

1 Introduction

Selfie video has become one of the major video types thanks to the recent development of social media. However, selfie videos taken by amateurs are usually shaky due to the lack of stabilizing equipment. Recent state-of-the-art works have been developed for general video stabilization tasks and integrated into commercial tools such as Adobe Warp Stabilizer [1] and the YouTube video stabilizer [2]. However, selfie videos usually have properties that create difficulties for existing methods. We show several example frames from typical selfie videos in Fig. 1, in which these properties are demonstrated:

(a) Large non-rigid occlusion from face and body close to the camera;
(b) Selfie videos usually come with strong motion blur/out-of-focus background;
(c) Foreground motion does not coincide with background motion.

General video stabilization methods fail in selfie videos for several reasons. First, most of these works depend on tracking 2D feature points. Existing 3D stabilization approaches require Structure from Motion (SfM) to estimate an initial camera path and build a sparse 3D scene. 2D methods also need to find frame motion using features. Therefore these methods are sensitive to inaccurate tracking of feature points. In Fig. 1(b), we show the example frames with blurred

Electronic supplementary material The online version of this chapter (https://doi.org/10.1007/978-3-030-01228-1_34) contains supplementary material, which is available to authorized users.

V. Ferrari et al. (Eds.): ECCV 2018, LNCS 11209, pp. 569–584, 2018.
https://doi.org/10.1007/978-3-030-01228-1_34

Fig. 1. Selfie videos have several properties that cause difficulties for traditional video stabilization methods: (a) face and body significantly occludes the background; (b) bad feature detection caused by motion blur/out of focus, insets show areas where feature points are hard to track accurately; (c) foreground and background motion mismatch; the foreground motion (red) can be different from background motion (blue) due to the dynamics of face and body; our method uses (d) a 3D face model to analyze the motion in the foreground and (e) optical flow to analyze the motion in the background. The video is stabilized with respect to both foreground and background. (Color figure online)

background and lack of sharp corners. In these videos, feature point detection is less reliable and the subsequent feature tracking is error-prone.

Second, it is also difficult to obtain long and error-free feature tracks in selfie videos with strong shake. The feature tracking becomes brittle due to the significant occlusion imposed by human face and body. Having noticed feature tracking as a general shortcoming in video stabilization, some methods tried to avoid using features by analyzing the pixel profiles using optical flow [3]. However, optical flow based algorithms still have failure cases when the occluding object dominates the foreground, which is likely to happen in selfie videos (Fig. 1(a)). Our algorithm takes advantage of optical flow to track the background pixels. Unlike Liu et.al [3] which uses optical flow to synthesize new frames, we only warp the frame with 2D projective transformations and a grid-based warp field. This guarantees the rigidity over the entire frame. To avoid tracking points and generating long trajectories, we only use small segments of these trajectories so that the foreground occlusion has minimal impact on the stabilization. We further discuss the advantages of the strategy in Sect. 7.

Third, general video stabilization only stabilizes with respect to part of the scene. This is not always desired in selfie videos. Both foreground (face and body) and background are important regions that need to be stabilized. To our knowledge, ours is the first method that utilizes the face geometry information in the video stabilization task (Fig. 1(d)). Our algorithm can automatically plan the optimal motion so that both the foreground and background motion are smoothed (Fig. 1(d) and (e)). In summary, our contributions include:

Foreground Motion from 3D Face Model: We utilize 3D human face information to gain knowledge about foreground motion in selfie videos (Sect. 4).

Novel Background Motion Tracking: Our method uses optical flow to find dense correspondences on the background, and therefore does not require good feature detection and tracking. We only use temporal motion information and are robust to occlusions in the scene (Sect. 5).

Optimal Foreground/Background Stabilization: By considering foreground motion, our method can stabilize selfie videos with respect to foreground and background simultaneously (Sect. 6).

Labeled Selfie Video Dataset: We provide a selfie video dataset (Fig. 7) of 33 videos, labeled with properties such as dynamic occlusion and lack of background features (Fig. 9) that significantly affect the video stabilization task. The dataset can be used to compare different methods, and will be a useful resource for the field. We make the dataset, code and benchmark per Fig. 9 publicly available online at http://viscomp.ucsd.edu/projects/ECCV18VideoStab.

2 Related Work

General video stabilization can be broadly categorized into 2D methods and 3D methods, according to their proposed camera motion models.

2D Stabilization. General 2D video stabilization techniques compute 2D motion and generate stabilized video by applying the smoothed motion to original video frames. Some approaches use simple camera motion models. Grundmann et al. [2] proposed a constrainable L1-optimization framework which solves the smoothed camera path composed of constant, linear and parabolic motion. Gleicher and Liu [4] assume the scene is largely planar and use homography to synthesize new frames. Liu et al. [5] divide the frame space into a grid mesh and allow spatially-variant motion. Some methods smooth the motion by imposing non-trivial constraints. Liu et al. [6] smooth 2D feature tracks by enforcing low-dimensional subspace constraints. Wang et al. [7] smoothes feature tracks while maintaining the spatial relations among them. Goldstein and Fattal [8] uses epipolar constraints when warping the video frames into synthesized frames. There are also explorations of non feature-point based approaches: Liu et al. [3] solves for a smooth per-frame optical flow field and stabilizes the video by smoothing pixel profiles instead of smoothing feature tracks.

3D Stabilization. Some methods sparsely reconstruct the 3D scene. The sparse 3D information is used to guide the synthesis of new frames. These methods generate better results than 2D methods by modeling physically accurate 3D camera motions but are less robust under non-ideal conditions, e.g. large occlusion, motion blur, and rolling shutter. Liu et al. [1] first uses structure from motion to find feature points' 3D positions, reprojects them onto the smoothed camera path and warps the original frames according to reprojected feature points.

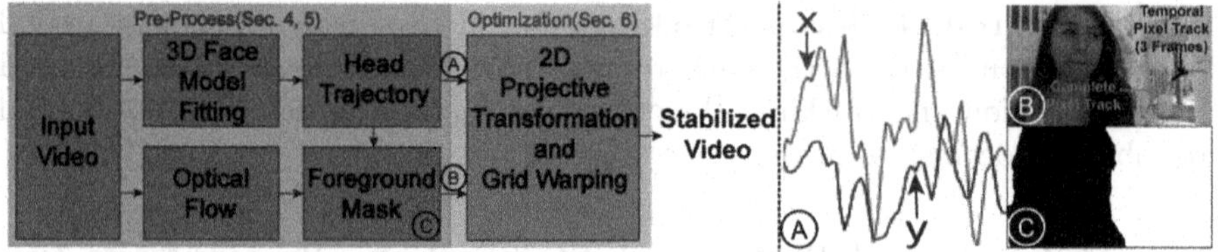

Fig. 2. Pipeline of our method. Ⓐ: By fitting a 3D face model, we find the head trajectory in the selfie video (Sect. 4); Ⓑ: Optical flow is used to track background pixels for 3 neighboring frames; Ⓒ: The foreground mask is computed from the head trajectory and is used to find the background pixels (Sect. 5). The 2D projective transformation and a grid-based warp field is estimated to remove the undesired motion of both foreground and background (Sect. 6).

There are also methods that render new frames using 3D information: Buehler et al. [9] uses image-based rendering to synthesize new views; Smith et al. [10] utilize the light field camera to stabilize video; Sun [11] uses depth information. Due to the non-rigid occlusion in selfie videos (Fig. 1(a)), 3D methods that are based on structure from motion can be error-prone. 3D methods that use depth information are also not directly applicable to selfie videos, since depth is not available in most cases.

Face Modeling. Human face modeling has been intensely studied. We will only summarize works that are closely related to our work. A widely used early work (Blanz and Vetter [12]) models face shape across people as a parametric PCA space learned from a database of laser scans. Cao et al. [13] models faces by assembling Kinect face scans as a tensor with identity and expression dimensions. Many follow-up works apply these models in image manipulation (Cao et al. [13], Fried et al. [14]), image/video re-animation (Blanz et al. [15], Thies et al. [16]), face tracking (Cao et al. [17]), facial performance capture (Cao et al. [18], Shi and Tomasi [19]), face reconstruction and rigging (Garrido et al. [20], Ichim et al. [21]). However, these works mainly focus on images/videos captured under ideal conditions (still or stable camera). Our work explores the possibility of utilizing 3D face models in the analysis of selfie videos captured with camera shake. We blend the models in Blanz and Vetter [12] and Cao et al. [13], to use as the reference model for the face fitting process, which will be discussed in Sect. 4.

3 Overview

In this section, we provide an overview of our approach for stabilizing selfie videos (Fig. 2). We seek to stabilize the selfie video with respect to both foreground and background. We analyze the foreground motion by modeling the face using a 3D face model, and analyze the background motion by optical flow. Fitting the 3D face model to selfie videos provides the head trajectory. We transform each frame according to the head positions so that the foreground regions are roughly aligned across the entire video. Since the foreground regions are aligned, the accumulated motion in this region will be smaller than background regions. Therefore the foreground and background regions can be separated. Details regarding this process will be discussed in Sect. 4. The background is defined as the white region in the foreground mask shown in Fig. 2. We randomly select pixels in the background that satisfy certain conditions, and use the optical flow to track their motion. Because of occlusion, our method only tracks pixels for 3 neighboring frames. We discuss details of pixel selection and tracking in Sect. 5.

The goal of video stabilization is to warp the original video frame so that the undesired frame motions are cancelled. We model the frame motion as a combination of global motion and local motion. The global motion refers to the 2D projective transformation of a frame. Since the frame content is the result of multiple factors, e.g., camera projection, camera distortion, rolling shutter and the 3D structure of the scene, simple 2D projective transformation cannot represent the camera motion accurately. Therefore, we use local motion to refer to any residual motion. Motivated by this analysis, we design our stabilization algorithm as a single joint optimization that simutaneously stabilizes foreground head motion and the background's global and local motion. We will describe details of our joint optimization algorithm in Sect. 6.

4 Foreground Tracking

Since the head and body are attached, we believe that the head motion can well represent the entire foreground motion. We don't explicitly track the body in this work, but implicitly separate the foreground and background by accumulating the optical flow. Details will be discussed in Sect. 5. Here we seek to find the position of the head in each frame. Since multiple faces could exist in the selfie video, we only track the dominant face in the video. A regular 2D face detector can provide the face bounding box for each frame, but is not accurate enough for tracking the exact head position. A 2D facial landmark detector provides more accurate detection of the face, but is easily affected by head rotation and facial expression. To find the actual head

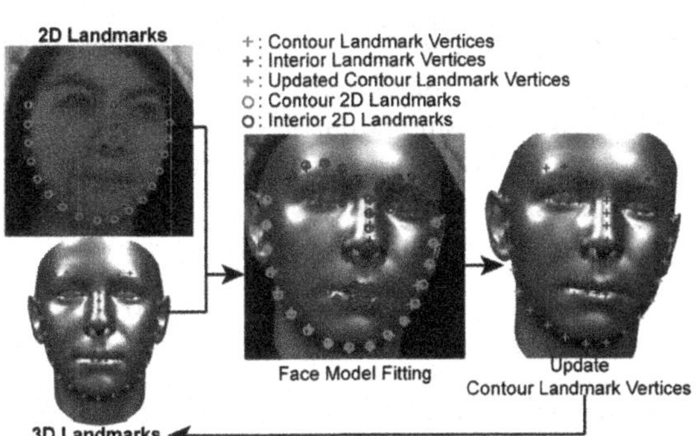

Fig. 3. The vertices used as contour 3D landmarks are fixed in the fitting process. The fitted face is rendered and new contour 2D landmarks are detected. The projected vertices closest to the detected 2D contour landmarks are selected as 3D contour landmarks for the next iteration.

position invariant to head rotation and facial expression, we use the 3D position of the head and reproject it to the image space as the head position. This requires modeling the face and gaining knowledge about the shape of the face in the selfie video.

3D Face Model. We utilize the linear face model proposed by Blanz and Vetter [12] and the bilinear face model proposed by Cao et al. [13]. Note that although the bilinear face model is more widely used in recent researches, their model was built based on a head mesh with relatively sparse vertices compared to Blanz and Vetter [12]. Our facial landmark based algorithm, which we will discuss later in this section, needs a dense face mesh in the face fitting algorithm. Therefore, we extend the linear face model of Blanz and Vetter [12] by transferring the expressions from Cao et al. [13]. Our extended linear face model is parameterized as follows:

$$\boldsymbol{F} = \boldsymbol{\mu} + \boldsymbol{U}_s \boldsymbol{\Sigma}_s \boldsymbol{c}_s + \boldsymbol{U}_e \boldsymbol{\Sigma}_e \boldsymbol{c}_e \tag{1}$$

where $\boldsymbol{\mu}$ encodes the vertex position of the mean face, $\boldsymbol{U}_s$ are the principal components of face shape, diagonal matrix $\boldsymbol{\Sigma}_s$ contains standard deviations of principal components and $\boldsymbol{c}_s$ is the weight vector that combines principal components. In (1), the third term $\boldsymbol{U}_e$ represents the expression principal components. It is generated as follows: we average the shape dimension of the bilinear face model [13] and use deformation transfer [22] to deform the mean linear face model with the bilinear face model's expressions. We extract principal components $\boldsymbol{U}_e$ of these expression deformed face meshes using regular PCA.

Face Fitting Algorithm. Our face model fitting algorithm is a purely landmark based algorithm. For a video with T frames, we detect facial landmarks L_t in each frame using Bulat and Tzimiropoulos [23]. The unknown parameters include the 3D rotation $\boldsymbol{R}_t \in SO(3)$, the 3D translation $\boldsymbol{T}_t \in \mathbb{R}^3$, per-frame facial expression coefficient $\boldsymbol{c}_{e,t}$ and the shape parameter $\boldsymbol{c}_s$. We also assume a simple perspective camera projection:

$$\boldsymbol{P} = \begin{bmatrix} f & 0 & w/2 \\ 0 & f & h/2 \\ 0 & 0 & 1 \end{bmatrix} \tag{2}$$

where we assume same unknown focal length in horizontal and vertical direction, known fixed optical center at the center of the frame (w and h represents frame width and height respectively), and zero skew. Denoting the 3D transformation matrix as $\boldsymbol{K}_t = [\boldsymbol{R}_t \ \boldsymbol{T}_t]$ where $\boldsymbol{R}_t \in \mathbb{R}^{3\times3}$ and $\boldsymbol{T}_t \in \mathbb{R}^3$, the 3D face model is fitted by solving:

$$\min_{\substack{\boldsymbol{P},\boldsymbol{R}_t,\boldsymbol{T}_t,\\ \boldsymbol{c}_s,\boldsymbol{c}_{e,t}}} \sum_{t=0}^{T-1} \left(\left\| L_t - \boldsymbol{P}\boldsymbol{K}_t \widehat{\boldsymbol{F}}_t \right\|^2 + \lambda_1 \left\| \boldsymbol{c}_{e,t} \right\|^2 \right) + \lambda_2 T \left\| \boldsymbol{c}_s \right\|^2 \tag{3}$$

where $\widehat{\boldsymbol{F}}_t$ represents the landmark vertices controlled by $\boldsymbol{c}_s$ and $\boldsymbol{c}_{e,t}$ as in (1), and λ_1 and λ_2 are regularization values that prevent the optimization from getting in local minima. The optimization can be easily solved as an unconstrained non-linear least squares problem. We use all the 199 shape principal components and 46 expression principal components in the fitting process. We use $\lambda_1 = 5$ and $\lambda_2 = 5$ in our experiment. The centroids of fitted face meshes are projected using the solved projection matrix $\boldsymbol{P}$, resulting in the head trajectory.

Facial landmark update. In Bulat and Tzimiropoulos [23], the contour 2D landmarks are defined by the face silhouette. The face silhouette depends on the pose of the head; therefore the corresponding contour landmark vertices need to be updated during optimization (3). However, this requires computing and rendering the whole mesh for facial landmark detection. To avoid this cost, we only update the contour landmark vertices between two iterations of optimization: we first fix the landmark vertices and use them in the face model fitting, then fix the estimated parameters and update the contour landmark vertices. The update of landmark vertices is demonstrated in Fig. 3. We first render the current face mesh, and detect 2D landmarks using the rendered image. We update the landmark vertices' indices by projecting all the visible vertices to the image plane and find the closest ones to the detected 2D landmarks. These closest vertices are used as contour landmark vertices in the next iteration. Note that the 2D-3D correspondence is established by finding vertices closest to landmarks. Therefore, a denser mesh will result in more accurate correspondence. This explains why we extend the denser linear face model (Blanz and Vetter [12]) instead of using the sparse bilinear face model (Cao et al. [13]) directly.

Disscussion. General video stabilization methods have difficulties when occlusion occurs in the video. Some methods either try to exclude the occlusion region by detecting discontinuity in motions (Liu et al. [3]) or let users remove features belonging to the foreground (Bai et al. [24]). The novelty of our method is that it also considers the motion in the foreground. Due to the dynamics of faces, feature based analysis is easily affected by head poses and facial expressions. We use the 3D face model to track the foreground face, so that the foreground can be analyzed even with large non-rigidity. In Fig. 4 we show that by implementing the contour landmark update scheme, our face fitting algorithm also achieves results comparable to the methods that use 3D facial land-

Fig. 4. Comparison of our 3D face fitting result to Shi et al. [19] and Thies et al. [16]. Our method achieves comparable results without using complex structure-from-motion and shading constraints.

marks estimated using non-rigid structure-from-motion (Shi et al. [19]) or 2D facial landmarks with additional light and shading constraints (Thies et al. [16]). Note that our method uses only 2D landmarks and thus is simpler than state-of-the-art methods.

5 Background Tracking

While we can track the foreground motion using a 3D face model, we also need to analyze the background motion so that both these regions can be considered in the stabilization process. We use the optical flow proposed by Kroeger et al. [25] to track a group of background pixels in each frame. The optical flow can be inaccurate in specific regions due to motion blur/out-of-focus and occlusion. However, minor inaccuracies in small regions can be ignored since our goal is to analyze the global camera motion. In addition, to minimize the impact of occlusion in the scene, we only track each pixel for 3 neighboring frames. We will discuss how this temporal motion information is used in our stabilization process in Sect. 6.

Not all pixels can be used to track the background motion. Obviously, pixels falling in the foreground region should not be selected. Face fitting described in Sect. 4 provides the head positions in each frame. We first translate all the frames so that the head positions in each frame are aligned to the same point, which leads to a head-aligned video. We perform optical flow between each frame of the head-aligned video. The accumulated optical flow forms a map that encodes the accumulated motion magnitude of each pixel. Since the video is aligned with respect to head position, the accumulated magnitude of optical flow will be smaller in the face and body region, but larger in the background region.

We show an example of a motion map in Fig. 5A. After computing the motion map, we use K-means to divide the pixels into two clusters. The cluster with smaller values is considered as foreground. The randomly selected pixels in this cluster will not be used in the stabilization.

Fig. 5. Ⓐ: Accumulated optical flow. A large value indicates the background area. Ⓑ: Example moving standard deviation of optical flow. Large values indicate the edges of objects in the scene.

Moreover, pixels near the occluding boundary should not be selected. Although our method does not require long feature tracks, we still need to track pixels using optical flow. The downside of tracking with optical flow is that tracking loss caused by occlusion is not easily detectable. To tackle this problem, we want to remove the pixels that are near the occluding boundary.

The objects in the scene can be distinguished by the direction of their motions. We use the standard deviation of the optical flow σ_F in a 21×21 neighborhood to measure the local variation in the optical flow. An example of standard deviation of the optical flow is shown in Fig. 5B. The foreground boundary has a larger variation in terms of the optical flow direction. In the stabilization, we only use the pixels with σ_F smaller than a threshold value. We use 0.3 as the threshold in all of our tests.

6 Stabilization

The goal of video stabilization is to warp the original video frame so that the undesired frame motions are cancelled. We model the frame motion as a combination of global motion and local motion. The global motion refers to the 2D projective transformation of a frame. Since the frame content is the result of multiple factors, e.g. camera projection, camera distortion, rolling shutter and the 3D structure of the scene, a simple 2D projective transformation cannot represent the camera motion accurately. Therefore, we use local motion to refer to any residual motion.

Motivated by this analysis, we design our algorithm to stabilize the global motion using the whole frame 2D projective transformation and stabilize the local motion using the per-frame grid warping.

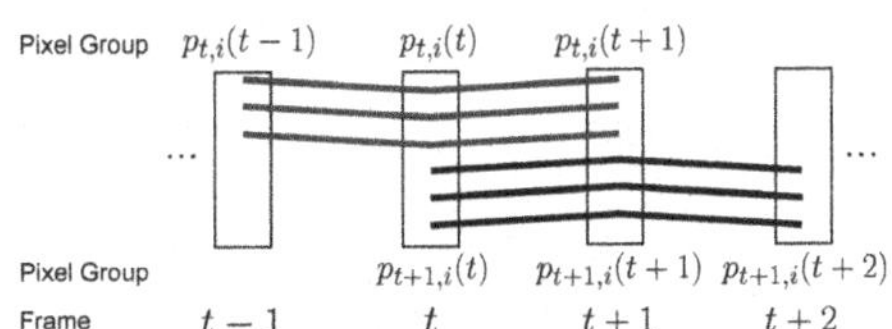

Fig. 6. Our method tracks background pixels for 3 neighboring frames.

Smoothness Measure. In selfie videos, the human appears as a large occlusion near the camera, making the trajectory of a pixel fragile. As a consequence, obtaining long feature tracks is difficult. Instead of tracking a pixel over multiple frames, we only track a pixel for 3 frames that are necessary for estimating the second derivative at time t. To demonstrate our idea, we use a single pixel in the scene as an example. Assume a pixel p is tracked over a time period. The trajectory it forms is denoted by $p(t)$. To evaluate the smoothness of this trajectory, we use the integral of squared second derivative or acceleration over the time period. This metric is commonly used in cubic spline fitting algorithms for optimal smoothness. By using this metric, we allow the frames to move to some extent but not try to completely eliminate the low frequency shake. This also helps in generating a larger output frame size when the camera motion is large, which is very common in selfie videos. Details of this effect will be discussed in Sect. 7. For a set of selected background pixels (which pixels we choose for this purpose is discussed in Sect. 5), the smoothness of the background motion can be written as:

$$E_s(t) = \sum_{i=1}^{N_t} \|\widehat{p}_{t,i}(t+1) - 2\widehat{p}_{t,i}(t) + \widehat{p}_{t,i}(t-1)\|^2 \tag{4}$$

where $p_{t,i}$ is the ith pixel tracked from $t-1$ to $t+1$, and $\widehat{p}$ is the new trajectory formed by transforming the original trajectory p. To guarantee the robustness, we track N_t pixels that are randomly selected in the frame at time $t-1$. We illustrate the tracking of background pixels in Fig. 6.

Frame Transformation. We seek to find a per-frame 2D projective transformation along with a per-frame grid warp field to transform $p_{t,i}$ to $\widehat{p}_{t,i}$ so that the objective (4) is minimized.

For the grid warping, we use the same bilinear interpolation representation as Liu et al. [1]. Each point is represented by a combination of four vertices of its enclosing grid cell:

$$p_{t,i} = w_{t,i}^T V_t \tag{5}$$

where V_t is a vector of the four vertices of the original grid cell that $p(t)$ is in; and w_t is the weight which sums to 1. Denote the output grid as $\widehat{V}$ and the 2D projective transformation as H. The warped scene point $\widehat{p}$ can be calculated using the same weights:

$$\widehat{p}_{t,i} = w_{t,i}^T H_t \widehat{V}_t \tag{6}$$

Regularization. In selfie videos, the foreground that contains face and body should also be stabilized. The motion of the foreground is not always consistent with the motion of the background. To account for the foreground motion, we also consider the head trajectory:

$$E_h(t) = N_t \left\| \widehat{h}(t+1) - \widehat{h}(t) \right\|^2 \tag{7}$$

where $h(t)$ is the head trajectory and $\widehat{h}(t)$ is the transformed head trajectory at time t. The head trajectory was obtained via fitting a 3D face model to the video as described in Sect. 4.

Moreover, to avoid undesired deformation caused by grid warping, we use the Laplacian of the grid to measure the rigidity of the warping:

$$E_V(t) = \Delta(\widehat{V}_t) \tag{8}$$

Optimization. Our final objective function is a combination of the smoothness measure and the regularization term:

$$\min_{H_t, \widehat{V}_t} \sum_{t=1}^{T-2} E_s(t) + \lambda_a E_h(t) + \lambda_b E_V(t) \tag{9}$$

Due to the high degree of freedom of the unknowns, the objective function has a complex landscape. Therefore, we first fix the grid $\widehat{V}_t$ and solve for 2D perspective transformation H_t, then use the result as an initialization and refine by running the full optimization (9).

Fig. 7. Example video stills from our dataset. The labels represent the example indices in Fig. 9.

Fig. 8. Visual comparison of input video, our result, Grundmann et al. [2] result and Liu et al. [1] result. The video stills are scaled by the same factor. Our method generates results with larger field of view and does not introduce visible distortion. We recommend readers to watch the accompanying video for more visual comparison. Labels represent example indices in Fig. 9.

We use Matlab's nonlinear least-squares solver to solve this optimization problem. For each frame at time t, the error terms E_s, E_h and E_V are only affected by 3 frames at $t-1$, t and $t+1$. This leads to a sparse jacobian matrix. Therefore this problem can be efficiently solved.

7 Results

In this section, we show example frames of selfie video stabilization, along with the visual comparison of the input video, our result, Liu et al. [1] and Grundmann et al. [2]. We also show that our method achieves better quantitative results than the comparison methods. Finally we discuss the advantages of our method over general video stabilization methods. Our results are generated with fixed parameters $\lambda_a = 1$ and $\lambda_b = 5$. On average, our Matlab code takes 15 min in all: 3 min for head fitting, 1 min for optical flow, 8 min for optimization and 3 min for warping and rendering the video on a desktop computer with an Intel i7-5930K CPU@ 3.5 GHz. We did not focus on speed in this work and we believe that our optimization can be implemented on the GPU in future.

Test Set. We collected 33 selfie video clips from the Internet, which is the first such dataset of selfie videos. A subset of our example clips are shown in Fig. 7. We label each video with properties that affect video stabilization: dynamic occlusion, multiple faces, large foreground motion, lack of background features, dynamic background and motion/defocus blur (Fig. 9). We will make our test set available publicly for comparison of different methods, and believe it will be a useful resource for the community.

Visual Comparison. In Fig. 8, the video stills are scaled by the same factor so that their sizes can be compared. Our results have a larger field of view compared to Liu et al. [1] and Grundmann et al. [2], which is often desired in stabilizing selfie videos. This is because the movement of the camera is large in these examples. The methods proposed by Liu et al. [1] and Grundmann et al. [2] over-stabilize the background, resulting in a small overlap region among frames. To obtain a rectangular video, most of the regions have to be cropped. Our method considers the foreground and background motion together and allows the frame to move in a low frequency sense. Therefore we avoid over-stabilization with respect to either foreground or background. Also note that our result preserves the original shape of the face and body, while the Liu et al. [1] result contains large distortions on the face. Since the dynamics are hard to show with images, we recommend readers to watch the accompanying video for the visual comparison of the results.

Our method is not sensitive to λ_b, but by changing the head regularization value λ_a in (9), we can control the algorithm to mainly stabilize the foreground or the background. We also included an example stabilized with different λ_a values in the accompanying video.

Quantitative Comparision. To evaluate the level of smoothness of the videos, we compute the average squared magnitude of second derivative of tracks of all pixels in each frame. The smoothness measure is defined as:

$$S = \frac{1}{|\Omega|} \sum_{t=1}^{T-2} \sum_{i} \|\omega_{t,i}(t+1) - 2\omega_{t,i}(t) + \omega_{t,i}(t-1)\|^2 \tag{10}$$

where we track all the pixels $\boldsymbol{\omega}_t = \{\omega_{t,1}, \omega_{t,2}...\}$ in the frame at time t, and Ω is the set of all the pixels $\{\boldsymbol{\omega}_1, \boldsymbol{\omega}_2 ... \boldsymbol{\omega}_{T-1}\}$. Since we sum the second derivatives of all the pixel tracks, a smaller smoothness measure indicates that the frames are changing in a more stabilized way. In (10), we use the optical flow to track the pixels. To eliminate the effect of different video sizes, we normalize the optical flow with the frame size on horizontal and vertical directions respectively. We show smoothness comparison for these examples in Fig. 9. Note that a lower bar indicates a better result. For better comparison, we sorted the examples by their original smoothness value. Our final results achieve better smoothness compared to the results of Liu et al. [1] and Grundmann et al. [2] in all of the examples.

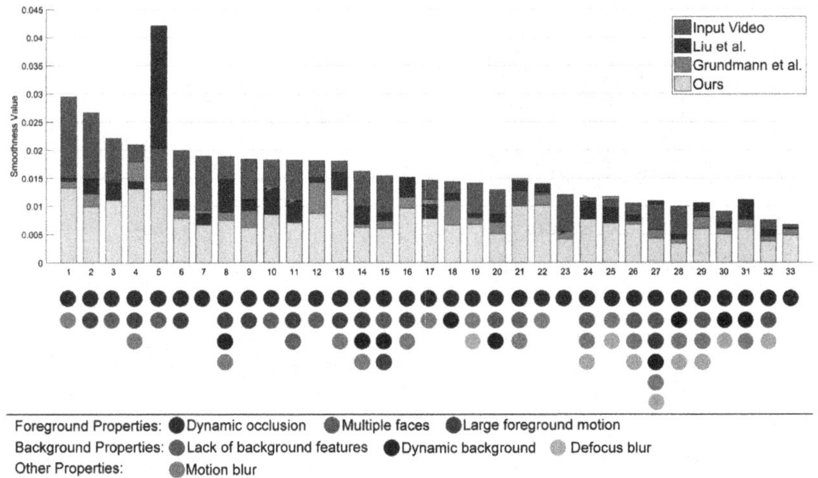

Fig. 9. Smoothness comparison of input video, our result, Liu et al. result [1] and Grundmann et al. result [2]. The horizontal axis represents the examples, and the height of the bar represents the smoothness value. Colored arrows are added where the bars overlap. The labeled properties are visualized as colored dots below each example. (Color figure online)

Advantages. Our method has some advantages over other general video stabilization methods in the selfie video case. Traditional 2D and 3D methods usually rely on feature tracks [1,2,6,10], making them vulnerable to insufficient feature counts in selfie videos. Since our method uses optical flow to track the motion, we achieve significantly better result in videos with few background features (examples 3, 5, 10, 11, 12, 21, 24, 26 and 29 in Fig. 9). Note that the feature point based general video stabilization methods fail in some of the low feature count cases (examples 5, 21 and 29 in Fig. 9), resulting in an even higher smoothness value than the input video. Our method is also robust to videos with motion blur and defocus blur, which are very common properties in selfie videos.

It is hard to obtain long feature tracks in selfie videos with large foreground motion. Note that 3D methods like Liu et al. [1] cannot perform accurate structure from motion when there is dynamic occlusion. Therefore Liu et al. [1] in general does not perform well in large foreground motion cases (examples 2, 4, 6, 8, 9, 11, 13, 14, 15, 16 and 27 in Fig. 9). Using only fragments of pixel trajectories over 3 frames, our method is robust to large occlusions near the camera. This strategy also helps handle dynamic background (examples 8, 14, 15, 18, 20, 27, 28, 30 and 31 in which multiple non-dominant faces or moving objects exist).

Finally, our method provides a novel application of 3D face modeling: track the foreground motion in selfie videos. Current 2D video stabilization methods focus on detecting non-rigid regions and do not consider the motion in these regions. In selfie videos, the foreground occupies a large portion of the frames and cannot be ignored. Our method automatically plans the motion so that

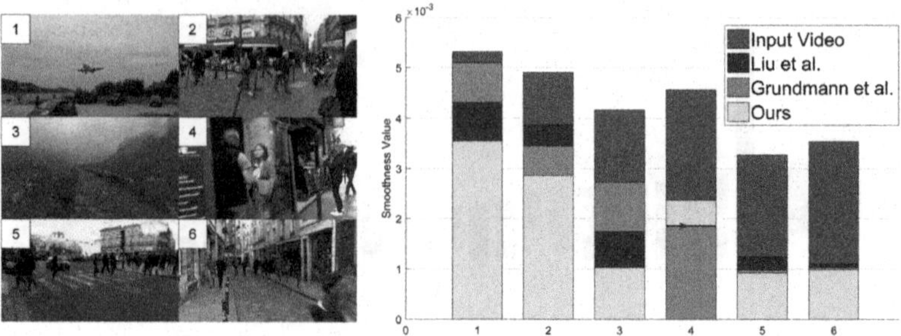

Fig. 10. Example video stills from our test set, and smoothness comparison on general videos, showing our result, Liu et al. [1] result and Grundmann et al. [2] result. Numbers on video stills indicate the example indices on the bar graph. Colored arrows are added where the bars overlap. (Color figure online)

both foreground and background motion are smoothed. The foreground motion also helps regularize the video stabilization process. In all of the examples, our method avoids over stabilizing the background and produces results with significantly larger field of view.

Generalization. Our method also applies to stabilizing general videos. We can simply ignore the E_h term in (9) and perform the optimization for the entire background region. We also collect 6 general videos shown in Fig. 10 and compare the smoothness of our result against Liu et al. [1] and Grundmann et al. [2]. Note that we only use 3 neighbouring frames to track the frame motion and only local motion information is available. Therefore, our method faces a harder problem in general video stabilization. However, Fig. 10 shows that our method still achieves comparable results in general video cases.

Failure Cases. Our frame motion model does not apply to videos with complex motions, e.g. strong rolling shutter effect and fisheye effect. We also include a selfie video taken with a fisheye camera in the accompanying video, in which our method does not perform well. Our method does not explicitly correct motion blur. Therefore our results on videos with strong motion blur (mostly because of low illumination) will have unsatisfactory appearance. Our result of example 4 in the selfie video dataset belongs to this category. Note that Fig. 9 shows that we still generate better results for example 4 compared to Liu et al. [1] and Grundmann et al. [2].

8 Conclusion, Limitations and Future Work

We proposed a novel video stabilization technique for selfie videos. Our method analyzes the motion of foreground (face and body) using a 3D face model and the motion of background by temporally tracking the pixels using optical flow. We achieve visually and quantatively better results than the state-of-the-art general video stabilization methods. Our method also exhibits robustness under different situations (e.g., large foreground occlusion, blur due to motion or out-of-focus and foreground/background motion mismatch).

Our method requires optical flow to track pixels in the video, and therefore suffers from the overhead of computing optical flow for neighboring frames. Another limitation of our method is that we require that facial landmarks can be detected in most of the frames. In our experiments, we linearly interpolate the head position for frames in which no face was detected. If the faces are undetectable in many consecutive frames, simply interpolating head positions will yield inaccurate estimation of the foreground motion. These limitations can be resolved by applying a more efficient optical flow technique and a more robust facial landmark detector. Our frame motion model does not apply to videos with complex motion. Our method also does not correct motion blur. Therefore for night-time videos or videos taken under dark lighting conditions, our method does not produce satisfactory results.

Since our method utilizes the 3D face model in selfie videos, one future work would be using 3D information to estimate 3D camera motion, so that the 3D video stabilization can be applied to selfie videos with large dynamic occlusions. The 3D face model also enables other future works, including manipulating the shape and expression of the face in selfie videos or high quality 3D reconstruction of face and body from selfie videos.

Acknowledgements. We thank Nima Khademi Kalantari for the supplementary video voice over. This work was supported in part by Sony, the Ronald L. Graham endowed Chair, and the UC San Diego Center for Visual Computing.

References

1. Liu, F., Gleicher, M., Jin, H., Agarwala, A.: Content-preserving warps for 3D video stabilization. ACM Trans. Graph. **28**(3), 44 (2009)
2. Grundmann, M., Kwatra, V., Essa, I.: Auto-directed video stabilization with robust l1 optimal camera paths. In: IEEE CVPR (2011)
3. Liu, S., Yuan, L., Tan, P., Sum, J.: SteadyFlow: spatially smooth optical flow for video stabilization. In: IEEE CVPR (2014)
4. Gleicher, M.L., Liu, F.: Re-cinematography: improving the camerawork of casual video. ACM Trans. Multimed. Comput. Commun. Appl. **5**(1), 2 (2008)
5. Liu, S., Yuan, L., Tan, P., Sun, J.: Bundled camera paths for video stabilization. ACM Trans. Graph. **32**(4), 78 (2013)
6. Liu, F., Gleicher, M., Wang, J., Jin, H., Agarwala, A.: Subspace video stabilization. ACM Trans. Graph. **30**(1), 4 (2011)
7. Wang, Y.S., Liu, F., Hsu, P.S., Lee, T.Y.: Spatially and temporally optimized video stabilization. IEEE Trans. Vis. Comput. Graph. **19**(8), 1354–1361 (2013)
8. Goldstein, A., Fattal, R.: Video stabilization using epipolar geometry. ACM Trans. Graph. **31**(5), 126 (2012)
9. Buehler, C., Bosse, M., McMillan, L.: Non-metric image-based rendering for video stabilization. In: IEEE CVPR (2001)

10. Smith, B.M., Zhang, L., Jin, H., Agarwala, A.: Light field video stabilization. In: IEEE ICCV (2009)
11. Sun, J.: Video stabilization with a depth camera. In: IEEE CVPR (2012)
12. Blanz, V., Vetter, T.: A morphable model for the synthesis of 3D faces. In: ACM SIGGRAPH (1999)
13. Cao, C., Weng, Y., Zhou, S., Tong, Y., Zhou, K.: Facewarehouse: a 3D facial expression database for visual computing. IEEE Trans. Vis. Comput. Graph. **20**(3), 413–425 (2014)
14. Fried, O., Shechtman, E., Goldman, D.B., Finkelstein, A.: Perspective-aware manipulation of portrait photos (2016)
15. Blanz, V., Basso, C., Poggio, T., Vetter, T.: Reanimating faces in images and video. In: Computer Graphics Forum, vol. 22, no. 3 (2003)
16. Thies, J., Zollhöfer, M., Stamminger, M., Theobalt, C., Nießner, M.: Face2Face: real-time face capture and reenactment of RGB videos. In: IEEE CVPR (2016)
17. Cao, C., Hou, Q., Zhou, K.: Displaced dynamic expression regression for real-time facial tracking and animation. ACM Trans. Graph. **33**(4), 43 (2014)
18. Cao, C., Bradley, D., Zhou, K., Beeler, T.: Real-time high-fidelity facial performance capture. ACM Trans. Graph. **34**(4), 46 (2015)
19. Shi, F., Wu, H.T., Tong, X., Chai, J.: Automatic acquisition of high-fidelity facial performances using monocular videos (2014)
20. Garrido, P., Zollhöfer, M., Casas, D., Valgaerts, L., Varanasi, K., Pérez, P., Theobalt, C.: Reconstruction of personalized 3D face rigs from monocular video. ACM Trans. Graph. **35**(3), 28 (2016)
21. Ichim, A.E., Bouaziz, S., Pauly, M.: Dynamic 3D avatar creation from hand-held video input. ACM Trans. Graph. **34**(4), 45 (2015)
22. Sumner, R.W., Popović, J.: Deformation transfer for triangle meshes. In: ACM SIGGRAPH (2004)
23. Bulat, A., Tzimiropoulos, G.: How far are we from solving the 2D & 3D face alignment problem? (and a dataset of 230,000 3D facial landmarks). In: IEEE ICCV (2017)
24. Bai, J., Agarwala, A., Agrawala, M., Ramamoorthi, R.: User-assisted video stabilization. In: EGSR (2014)
25. Kroeger, T., Timofte, R., Dai, D., Van Gool, L.: Fast optical flow using dense inverse search. In: Leibe, B., Matas, J., Sebe, N., Welling, M. (eds.) ECCV 2016. LNCS, vol. 9908, pp. 471–488. Springer, Cham (2016). https://doi.org/10.1007/978-3-319-46493-0_29

CubeNet: Equivariance to 3D Rotation and Translation

Daniel Worrall([✉]) and Gabriel Brostow([✉])

Computer Science Department, University College London, London, UK
{d.worrall,g.brostow}@cs.ucl.ac.uk

Abstract. 3D Convolutional Neural Networks are sensitive to transformations applied to their input. This is a problem because a voxelized version of a 3D object, and its rotated clone, will look unrelated to each other after passing through to the last layer of a network. Instead, an idealized model would preserve a meaningful representation of the voxelized object, while explaining the pose-difference between the two inputs. An equivariant representation vector has two components: the invariant identity part, and a discernable encoding of the transformation. Models that can't explain pose-differences risk "diluting" the representation, in pursuit of optimizing a classification or regression loss function.

We introduce a Group Convolutional Neural Network with linear equivariance to translations *and* right angle rotations in three dimensions. We call this network *CubeNet*, reflecting its cube-like symmetry. By construction, this network helps preserve a 3D shape's global and local signature, as it is transformed through successive layers. We apply this network to a variety of 3D inference problems, achieving state-of-the-art on the ModelNet10 classification challenge, and comparable performance on the ISBI 2012 Connectome Segmentation Benchmark. To the best of our knowledge, this is the first 3D rotation equivariant CNN for voxel representations.

Keywords: Deep learning · Equivariance · 3D representations

1 Introduction

Convolutional neural networks (CNNs) are the go-to model for most prediction-based computer vision problems. However, most popularized CNNs are treated as black-boxes, lacking interpretability and simple properties concerning the data domains they act on. For instance, in 3D object recognition, we know that object categories are *invariant* to object pose, but convolutional neural network filters are orientation, scale, reflection, and parity (point reflection) selective. This means that every activation in any intermediate layer is sensitive to local pose, and ultimately the global output of the network is too. A simple solution to obtain this sought-after invariance is to augment the input data with transformed copies, spanning all possible variations, to which we seek to be invariant [2]. This

V. Ferrari et al. (Eds.): ECCV 2018, LNCS 11209, pp. 585–602, 2018.
https://doi.org/10.1007/978-3-030-01228-1_35

method is simple and effective, but relies on an efficient and realistic data augmentation pipeline. There is also the argument, why should we bother learning these invariances, if we can enforce them *a priori*? If successful, we would not need as much training data [8,50]. Indeed, convolutional neural networks already have (i) filter locality and (ii) translational weight-tying built directly into their architectures, which arguably could be learned using a multilayer perceptron with a enough computational budget and training data.

We introduce a CNN architecture, which is *linearly equivariant* (a generalization of invariance defined in the next section) to 3D rotations about patch centers. To the best of our knowledge, this paper provides the first example of a group-CNN [8] with linear equivariance to 3D rotations and 3D translations of voxelized data. By exploiting the symmetries of the classification task, we are able to reduce the number of trainable parameters using judicious weight tying. We also need less training and test time data augmentation, since some aspects of 3D geometry are already 'hard-baked' into the network. We demonstrate state-of-the-art and comparable performance on (i) the ModelNet10 classification challenge, which is a standard 3D classification benchmark task, and (ii) the ISBI 2012 connectome segmentation benchmark, which is a 3D anisotropic boundary segmentation problem. We have released our code at https://deworrall92.github.com.

2 Background

For completeness, we set out our terminology and definitions. We outline definitions of linear equivariance, invariance, groups, and convolution, and then combine these ideas into the group convolution, which is the workhorse of the paper. These definitions are not our contribution and can be found in textbooks such as [7], but we have tried to standardize them and simplify notation.

Definition 1 (Equivariance). *Consider a set of transformations G, where individual transformations are indexed as $g \in G$. Consider also a function or feature map $\boldsymbol{\Phi} : \mathcal{X} \to \mathcal{Y}$ mapping inputs $\boldsymbol{x} \in \mathcal{X}$ to outputs $\boldsymbol{y} \in \mathcal{Y}$. Transformations can be applied to any $\boldsymbol{x} \in \mathcal{X}$ using the operator $\mathcal{T}_g^{\mathcal{X}} : \mathcal{X} \to \mathcal{X}$, so that $\boldsymbol{x} \mapsto \mathcal{T}_g^{\mathcal{X}}[\boldsymbol{x}]$. The same can be done for the outputs with $\boldsymbol{y} \mapsto \mathcal{T}_g^{\mathcal{Y}}[\boldsymbol{y}]$. We say that $\boldsymbol{\Phi}$ is* equivariant *to G if*

$$\boldsymbol{\Phi}(\mathcal{T}_g^{\mathcal{X}}[\boldsymbol{x}]) = \mathcal{T}_g^{\mathcal{Y}}[\boldsymbol{\Phi}(\boldsymbol{x})], \qquad \forall g \in G. \tag{1}$$

Since $\mathcal{T}_g^{\mathcal{X}}$ and $\mathcal{T}_g^{\mathcal{Y}}$ are related via (1), they are essentially different *representations* of the same transformation. Due to this connection, it is customary to drop the $\mathcal{T}_g^{\bullet}$ notation and write

$$\boldsymbol{\Phi}(g\mathbf{x}) = g\boldsymbol{\Phi}(\mathbf{x}). \tag{2}$$

Equivariance is important, because it highlights an explicit relationship between input transformations and feature-space transformations, which in the context of deep learning is not well-understood. An example of an equivariant task is pose-detection, where g represents the sought-after pose. The kind of equivariant feature maps, we are interested in, are those where $\mathcal{T}^{\mathcal{X}}$ and $\mathcal{T}^{\mathcal{Y}}$ are linear. Such feature maps are known as *linearly equivariant.* A special case of equivariance is *invariance*, where we have

$$\boldsymbol{\Phi}(\mathbf{x}) = \boldsymbol{\Phi}(g\mathbf{x}), \tag{3}$$

that is, the feature-space transformation is just the identity. An example of an invariant task is object classification. Note when we use the term equivariant in the rest of the paper, we will generally refer to non-invariance.

Groups. Invertible transformations are members of a class of mathematical objects called *groups.* Groups are a mathematical abstraction, which are used to describe the compositional structure of mathematical operators, such as transformations. Groups have four main properties: for group elements $f, g, h \in G$

1. **closure**: chained transformations are transformations, e.g. $fg \in G$
2. **associativity**: f(gh) = (fg)h = fgh
3. **identity**: there exists a transformation $e \in G$ (sometimes written $\mathbf{0}$) such that $eg = ge = g, \forall g \in G$
4. **invertibility**: every transformation g has an inverse g^{-1}, so $gg^{-1} = g^{-1}g = e$. Rotations and translations are both examples of groups.

Convolution. The fundamental operation in convolutional neural networks is the convolution—technically CNNs perform cross-correlation, but we stick with the term 'convolution' to remain in sync with the literature $\star$. In 3D, convolution is the inner product of a *filter* $\mathbf{W} \in \mathbb{R}^{h \times w \times d}$ with patches extracted from an *activation tensor* or *feature map* $\mathbf{F} \in \mathbb{R}^{H \times W \times D}$ where h, w, d, H, W, D are the **h**eight, **w**idth, and **d**epth of the filter/activations respectively. The method of patch extraction is usually a translationally sliding window. So given a filter $\mathbf{W}$, the translated version is $g\mathbf{W}$, such that

$$[\mathbf{F} \star \mathbf{W}]_g = \sum_{\mathbf{x} \in \mathbb{Z}^3} [g\mathbf{W}]_{\mathbf{x}} \mathbf{F}_{\mathbf{x}} = \sum_{\mathbf{x} \in \mathbb{Z}^3} \mathbf{W}_{g^{-1}\mathbf{x}} \mathbf{F}_{\mathbf{x}}; \tag{4}$$

where to index elements of the filters/activations we have used the multi-index notation $\mathbf{W}_{\mathbf{x}} := \mathbf{W}_{x,y,z}$ for $\mathbf{x} = [x, y, z]^\top \in \mathbb{Z}^3$, and so in this example $\mathbf{W}_{g^{-1}\mathbf{x}} = \mathbf{W}_{x-g_x, y-g_y, z-g_z}$ for voxel-wise translation in 3D by $g = [g_x, g_y, g_z]^\top$. This sliding-window interpretation of convolution can be viewed as applying the same filter to different local regions of the inputs. Note that in reality, since the feature map is zero outside of a a certain neighborhood, we need not sum over all $\mathbb{Z}^3$. Note also how the output of the convolution is indexed by the transformation parameter g; that is, the gth activation corresponds to the response of a g-shifted filter $g\mathbf{W}$. We have used the notation $[\mathbf{F} \star \mathbf{W}]_g$ to emphasize that $[\mathbf{F} \star \mathbf{W}]$ is an indexable object like $\mathbf{W}$ or $\mathbf{F}$, and it can be viewed as a vector (see Fig. 1). CNNs usually have multiple *channels* k per activation tensor, so in general we really have

$$[\mathbf{F} \star \mathbf{W}]_g^k = \sum_{i=1}^{I} \sum_{\mathbf{x} \in \mathbb{Z}^3} [g\mathbf{W}]_{\mathbf{x}}^{ik} \mathbf{F}_{\mathbf{x}}^i, \tag{5}$$

where the dummy index i is over input channels with output channel k.

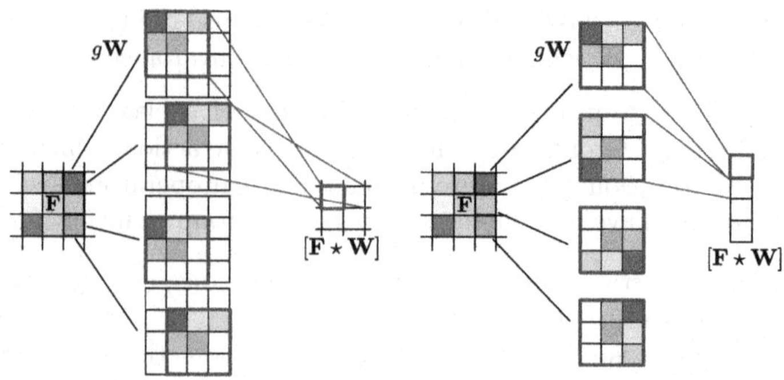

Fig. 1. (Best viewed in color) On the left we show the standard 2D convolution of Eq. 4 between a sliding filter $\mathbf{W}$ and an input patch $\mathbf{F}$. On the right we show the 2D right-angle rotation convolution (called Z_4-convolution) acting on an input where $G = \mathbb{Z}^2$.

One can show (c.f. [8,11] and Eqs. 8 and 9) that the standard translational convolution is equivariant to translations; that is, translations of the input to the convolution result in translations in the feature space representation $[\mathbf{F} \star \mathbf{W}]$. The extension of this translational equivariance to other groups of transformation is embodied in the *group convolution* [8], which we show next. This has been proven [29] to be the only operator which is equivariant to (compact) group-structured transformations.

Definition 2 (Group Convolution). *A group convolution between a filter* $\boldsymbol{W}$ *and a single-channel feature map* $\boldsymbol{F}$ *over a group of transformations* G *is*

$$[\boldsymbol{F} \star \boldsymbol{W}]_g = \sum_{h \in G} [g\,\boldsymbol{W}]_h \boldsymbol{F}_h = \sum_{h \in G} \boldsymbol{W}_{g^{-1}h} \boldsymbol{F}_h. \tag{6}$$

The extension to multichannel activations parallels Eq. (5).

We see that the main difference between the standard convolution of Eq. 4 and the group convolution of Eq. 6 is that we have replaced the domain of summation from $\mathbb{Z}^3$ to the group G. So the sliding inner product could generalize to a sliding-and-rotating inner-product, or sliding-and-flipping inner product, or even sliding-and-scaling inner product depending on the choice of group G. A simple example is shown in Fig. 1, where we show a 2D translational convolution and a first layer 2D right-angle rotational convolution (called Z_4-convolution). In this example, the domain of the Z_4-convolution is $G = \mathbb{Z}^2$, the standard 2D image domain, but the output is over the group of four 2D rotations, Z_4. This amounts to taking an inner product of the kernel $\mathbf{W}$ rotated four times, with each individual response being stacked into a vector. If we were to then convolve a kernel over the response of this first Z_4-convolution, the domain of that convolution would be $G = Z_4$. Stacks of group convolutions turn out to be equivariant as well.

Note that the dimensionality of the convolutional responses is linear in the number of elements of the group G. At each layer, it is common to choose the size of the group to be the same, or smaller if we include pooling. To maintain a transformation invariant output, we using average over the group at the final layer of the network, which is an extension of global average pooling to groups.

In this paper, we are interested in the group of 3D roto-translations. The group convolution for this group will involve us convolving an activation tensor with rotated and shifted copies of a filter $[g\mathbf{W}]_{\mathbf{x}} = \mathbf{W}_{g^{-1}\mathbf{x}} = \mathbf{W}_{\mathbf{R}_g^{-1}\mathbf{x}-\mathbf{z}_g}$, where $\mathbf{R}_g$ is a 3D rotation matrix and $\mathbf{z}_g$ is a translational offset.

3 Related Work

Recently there has been an explosion of interest into CNNs with predefined transformation equivariances, beyond translation [8,9,11,14–16,18,19,22,25,26, 28,29,31,33,36,42,48–50,55]. However, with the exception of Cohen and Welling [9] (projections on sphere), Kondor [28] (point clouds), and Thomas et al. [48] (point clouds), these have mainly focused on the 2D scenario. There are also examples of CNNs, which have explicit regularization to learn equivariance [30, 40,43,51]. To the best of our knowledge, *we are the first to develop a 3D rotation equivariant CNN architecture for voxelized data.*

Handcrafted Equivariance. There are many computer vision models that exhibit equivariance properties. Perhaps the first notable instance is the scale-space [13], which specifically displays equivariance to isotropic scale, later extended to affine equivariance by Lindeberg [34]. In the presence of continuous transformations, Freeman and Adelson famously [17] (and less famously Lenz [32]), shored up the theory of *steerable filters*, which are a set of bandlimited linear filters $\mathbf{w}_\theta \in \mathbb{R}^{H \times W}$, which can be synthesized *exactly* at any rotation θ as a *finite* linear combination of basis filters

$$w_\theta(\mathbf{x}) = \sum_{n=1}^{N} \alpha_n(\theta)\phi_n(\mathbf{x}). \tag{7}$$

These are attractive because their expressiveness is controlled by the number of coefficients N, rather than the spatial size of the filter. These have been applied to scale-spaces/pyramids in Simoncelli et al. [44], and have been placed on firm theoretical ground by Teo [47] in his PhD thesis. It has also been shown that for certain transformations, such as scalings (or more generally non-compact groups), exact steering is only possible if $N = \infty$. In this case, Perona [37] showed that he could approximate Eq. 7 using an SVD formulation. Like our method, all these works display handcrafted linear equivariance to a predefined set of transformations.

2D Rotation Invariant Neural Networks. For CNNs, as mentioned, most works have focussed on 2D rotations. Fasel and Gatica-Perez [16], Laptev et al. [31], and Gonzalez et al. [19] average classifier predictions on multiple rotated copies of an input. Sifre and Mallat [42] and Oyallon and Mallat [36] use a scattering network [5] for roto-translation invariant classification. Every layer of these networks is locally (patch-wise) rotation invariant, performing a pre-determined wavelet transform averaging responses over rotation. Cotter and Kingsbury [12] recently suggested, however, that these networks lack discriminativeness, partially from the phase removal and partially from the fact that the wavelet transforms are not optimized per-task, which our method can handle.

2D Rotation Equivariant Neural Networks. Henriques and Vedaldi [22] and Esteves et al. [15] perform a log-polar transform of the input, which converts scalings and rotations about a single point into a translation. Applying a standard translation equivariant CNN to this representation is then equivariant to rotations and scalings about the image center. This is only equivariant to global rotations, and does not generalize to 3D. For locally equivariant methods Dieleman et al. [14] maintain multiple rotated feature maps at every layer of a network; whereas, Cohen and Welling [8] rotate the filters. In the same paper, Cohen and Welling also extended this method to finite groups and later generalized this to arbitrary compact groups in [11]. Worrall et al. [50] generalized the filter rotation method to continuous rotations, using circular Fourier transforms to compute continuous rotation responses with a finite number of filters. At the same time Zhou et al. [55] extended the filter rotation method to non-90° rotations using bilinear interpolation. Gonzalez et al. [18] do similar, but also pool over rotations and use a representation similar to [50]. Weiler et al. [49] so far have the best solution to rotate filters, using steerable filters to solve the interpolation problem. Our method can be seen as an instance of Cohen and Welling [8] adapted to 3D rotation and translation.

Deeply Learned Equivariance. There are many papers which also focus on learning equivariance. Tangent Prop by Simard et al. [43] is a classic example of an invariance inducing regularizer. Hinton et al. [23] introduced the transforming autoencoder to build latent spaces with equivariant structure. More recently, Worrall et al. [51] extended this method by imposing explicit transformation rules on the latent space. Papers such as InfoGAN by Chen et al. [6] and the Deep Convolutional Inverse Graphics Network of Kulkarni et al. [30] seek to learn equivariant structure in unsupervised fashion unsupervised. Most recently Sabour et al. [40] and Hinton et al. [24] achieved highly impressive results on the MNIST dataset with capsule networks by learning approximations to affine equivariance. While these methods are very flexible, they require lots of training data

3D Methods. For classification, the most straightforward CNNs operating on 3D voxel data use 3D convolutions as of Eq. 4 such as Maturana and Scherer [35] or 3D Convolutional Deep Belief Network as in Wu et al. [53]. Brock et al. [4] take this to the extreme, designing an ensemble of six 45-layer deep inception- and resnet-style networks trained with a lot of data-augmentation and rotation averaging. Sedaghat et al. [41] rely less on brute force, augmenting the prediction task with orientation estimation. For 3D rotation equivariant methods, Cohen and Welling introduce the Spherical CNN [10], which operates on images projected onto the sphere, while Kondor [28] and Thomas et al. [48] operate on point clouds. All three methods use variants of a 3D extension of Worrall et al. [50], which introduced continuous rotation equivariance into CNNs, by use of the shifting property of Fourier transforms.

4 Method

We have introduced the concept of groups as a way to model transformations, and as a way to extend standard convolution to these transformations. Here, we chart out three different discrete 3D rotation groups; namely, Klein's four-group, the tetrahedral group and the cube group. We then show how to apply these groups in a group equivariant CNN using Cayley tables to build three different 3D rotation equivariant CNNs. We do not consider equivariant to continuous 3D rotations in this paper, leaving it for future work.

Cube Group. The set of all right-angle rotations of a cubic filter $\mathbf{F}_{\mathbf{x}} \in \mathbb{R}^{N\times N\times N}$ forms a group. There are 24 such rotations, going by the name of the *cube group*[1] S_4. Each of the 24 rotations applied to a cube is shown in Fig. 2. The group is non-commutative, so $\mathbf{F}_{(g_1 g_7)^{-1}\mathbf{x}} \neq \mathbf{F}_{(g_7 g_1)^{-1}\mathbf{x}}$ for rotations g_1 and g_7, for example.

Tetrahedral Group. Using 24 copies of the same filter increases the computational overhead 24 times. A cheaper subsampling is the rotations of the tetrahedron. This has 12 states, and goes by the name of the *rotational tetrahedral group* T_4. T_4 is formally a subgroup[2] of the cube group, comprised of all even rotations (i.e. all rotations which can be made by two 90°-rotations). It is shown as the 12 cube rotations wrapped in thin blue in Fig. 2.

Klein's Four-Group. The smallest subsampling of rotations, which can be seen as rotations about 3 independent axes is Klein's *Vierergruppe* V or *four-group.* It has four rotations as can be seen in Fig. 3. This group is a subgroup of the rotational tetrahedral group and the cube group. Interestingly, it is commutative and also the smallest non-cyclic group. It is shown as the 4 rotations wrapped in dashed red in Fig. 2.

[1] Other names are the subgroup O of the octohedral group; symmetric group S_4; and full tetrahedral group T_d.

[2] A subgroup H is any subset of G, which satisfies the four group axioms, which we introduced in the background section.

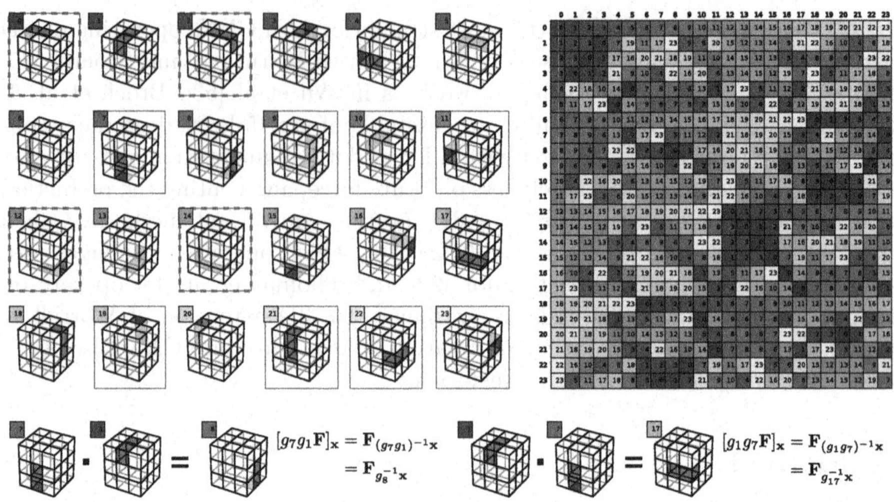

Fig. 2. (Best viewed in color) LEFT: The 24 rotations of the cube group S_4, applied to the a cube $\mathbf{F}_{\mathbf{x}}$ are shown. For instance, rotation g_{22} applied to the cube returns $\mathbf{F}_{g_{22}^{-1}\mathbf{x}}$, shown by the #22 in the bottom row. The 12 cubes wrapped in thin blue boxes are the rotational tetrahedral group T_4. The 4 cubes wrapped in thick dashed red lines are the Klein four-group V. RIGHT: The Cayley table of the cube group, representing how rotations are composed. For instance, on the BOTTOM LEFT, we have the example of composing rotation g_7 with rotation g_1. The composition is performed by (i) first applying g_7 to the cube to yield $\mathbf{F}_{g_7^{-1}\mathbf{x}}$ then (ii) applying g_1 to $\mathbf{F}_{g_7^{-1}\mathbf{x}}$, returning $\mathbf{F}_{g_1^{-1}g_7^{-1}\mathbf{x}}$. The first transformation is easy to visualize - it is by #7 in the grid of cubes. The transformation g_1 is a rotation by 90° counter-clockwise about the vertical axis, thus for the composition we rotate $\mathbf{F}_{g_7^{-1}\mathbf{x}}$ 90° counter-clockwise about the z-axis. This results in $F_{g_8^{-1}\mathbf{x}}$. This result is stored in the Cayley table by placing the first rotation down the left column and the second rotation along the top row. The intersection of row **7** with column **1** is the rotation **8**. On the BOTTOM RIGHT, we show the composition $g_7 g_1 = g_{17} \neq g_8 = g_1 g_7$, demonstrating the non-commutativity property of the cube group and 3D rotations in general.

4.1 Cayley Tables

Knowing how a rotation of the input will permute the convolutional response can be figured out from the group *Cayley table*. This is a multiplication table enumerating every composition of transformations. For Klein's four-group, we label the rotations as g_0 (the identity), g_1, g_2, & g_3. The Cayley table with instructions of how to read it are given in Table 1. The Cayley table is useful for determining how to perform the group convolution in deeper layers. We can see why this is the case because looking to the expression for the group convolution $\sum_{h \in G} \mathbf{W}_{g^{-1}h} \mathbf{F}_h$, we see a product $g^{-1}h$ in the indices of $\mathbf{W}$. We can use the Cayley table to ascertain the single transformation that is the result of the product. Looking closely at a Cayley table we see that all the rows/columns are permutations of one another, this will be important for understanding how input rotations affect the group-convolutional response.

Table 1. The Cayley table for Klein's four-group. The product g_2g_3 (a g_2-rotation followed by a g_3-rotation) can be found by looking down the left column for the first transformation g_2, then finding the second transformation g_3 in the top row. The cell at the intersection of row-g_2 and column-g_3 (shaded in yellow) is g_1, so $g_2g_3 = g_1$.

$\bullet$	g_0	g_1	g_2	g_3
g_0	g_0	g_1	g_2	g_3
g_1	g_1	g_0	g_3	g_2
g_2	g_2	g_3	g_0	g_1
g_3	g_3	g_2	g_1	g_0

4.2 Discrete Group Equivariance and Permutations

Rotating an input to a group convolution will lead to a transformation of its output. Specifically a rotation will lead to a permutation of the output, where we view the output as a vector of responses, with each dimension corresponding to a different group element/transformation $g \in G$. An example of this vectorized output can be seen in Fig. 1. For translations the permutation is a voxel-wise shift, but for the aforementioned 3D rotations the permutations are much more complicated. If we apply a transformation p to the input features $\mathbf{F}$, then

$$[[p\mathbf{F}] \star \mathbf{W}]_g = \sum_{h \in G} [g\mathbf{W}]_h [p\mathbf{F}]_h = \sum_{h \in G} \mathbf{W}_{g^{-1}h} \mathbf{F}_{p^{-1}h} \tag{8}$$

$$= \sum_{h' \in G} \mathbf{W}_{g^{-1}ph'} \mathbf{F}_{h'} = [\mathbf{F} \star \mathbf{W}]_{p^{-1}g} = [p[\mathbf{F} \star \mathbf{W}]]_g. \tag{9}$$

Here we have made the substitution $h' = p^{-1}h$ and noted that $p^{-1}G = G$ for $p \in G$, where $p^{-1}G := \{p^{-1}g \mid g \in G\}$. What lines 8 and 9 say is that the output of the group convolution is permuted whenever the input $\mathbf{F}$ is transformed by an element of the group G. The specific permutation of the output depends on the specific transformation and transformation group. Thinking of $\mathbf{F} \star \mathbf{W}$ and $[p\mathbf{F}] \star \mathbf{W}$ as vectors separated by a permutation, we can write

$$[p\mathbf{F}] \star \mathbf{W} = p[\mathbf{F} \star \mathbf{W}] = \mathbf{P}_p[\mathbf{F} \star \mathbf{W}], \tag{10}$$

where the first equality is from Eqs. 8 and 9 and in the second equality we have rewritten the permutation as multiplication with the *permutation matrix* $\mathbf{P}_p$. In fact $\mathbf{P}_p$ is the permutation matrix corresponding to the pth column of the Cayley table. Thus we see that group convolutions are *linearly* equivariant to transformations $p \in G$, as defined in Eq. 1. We see an example of this for Klein's four-group in Fig. 3, where we have labeled the four rotations as g_0 (the identity), g_1, g_2, & g_3.

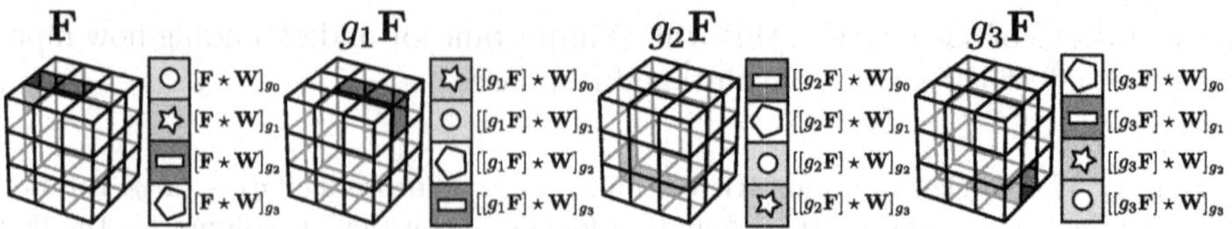

Fig. 3. Example of how the group convolution output permutes as a function of the input rotation. This example is for Klein's four-group V. Each cube represents a rotation from V and a corresponding example feature vector is given with each cube.

4.3 Implementation: Roto-Translational Group-Convolution

Now we show how to implement a group-convolution for a 3D roto-translation. In this example, we focus on the four-group to model rotations. A roto-translation can be synthesized from a rotation, followed by a translation. Roto-translations form a group, which can be seen as the product[3] of V and $\mathbb{Z}^3$. For our purposes, it is safe to assume that we can write the elements of this producted group as tr for $t \in \mathbb{Z}^3$ and $r \in V$. So,

$$[\mathbf{F} \star \mathbf{W}]_{tr} = \sum_{\tau \in \mathbb{Z}^3} \sum_{\rho \in V} [tr\mathbf{W}]_{\tau\rho} \mathbf{F}_{\tau\rho} = \sum_{\tau \in \mathbb{Z}^3} \sum_{\rho \in V} \left[t\,[r\mathbf{W}]_{\rho}\right]_{\tau} \mathbf{F}_{\tau\rho}. \tag{11}$$

The interpretation behind this equation is as follows. First we start with a filter $\mathbf{W}$. $\mathbf{W}$ has a different value for each voxel in its receptive field, indexed by the translation variable τ, and also for every input rotation ρ—it may be easier just to think of four 3D filters, $\mathbf{W}_{\rho_0}, \mathbf{W}_{\rho_1}, \mathbf{W}_{\rho_2}, \mathbf{W}_{\rho_3}$, one for each rotation in V. To convolve, we first rotate the kernel as $r\mathbf{W}_{\rho_\bullet}$, then we perform a translational shift $t[r\mathbf{W}_{\rho_\bullet}]$—this second part ends up as the standard convolution of Eq. 4, which is efficient on GPUs. The initial rotation of the filter $r\mathbf{W}_{\rho_\bullet}$ can be found from composing r and $\rho_\bullet$ using our Cayley tables. It is the rotation needed to rotate r into $\rho_\bullet$. When the input is a raw image, the input domain is just $\mathbb{Z}^3$, so the rotation of $\mathbf{W}$ is just r.

To compute gradient for backpropagation we leverage the power of automatic differention, which is available in most modern neural network libraries.

5 Experiments and Results

Here we describe two simple experiments we performed to demonstrate the effectiveness of group-convolutions on 3D voxelized data. We tested on the ModelNet10 classification challenge, which is a small 3D voxel dataset, and on the ISBI 2012 connectome segmentation challenge. In both examples, we found Klein's four-group to be the most effective group for the rotation-equivariant group-convolutions.

[3] Formally, this is a semi-direct product.

5.1 ModelNet10

The ModelNet 10 dataset [53] contains 4905 CAD models from 10 categories with a train:test split of 3991:914. Each model is aligned to a canonical frame and then rotated at 12 evenly-sampled orientations about the z-axis. These rotated models are then voxelized to a $32 \times 32 \times 32$ grid. We use the voxelized version of Maturana and Scherer [35]. While the dataset consists of vertically aligned models, rotated only about the z-axis, we posit that local features occur at all 3D rotations, and so a Cubenet is well positioned to operate on such as dataset. We use the four-group of rotations and the rotational tetrahedral group T_4, since we found the cube-group too large and slow to be trained practically multiple times during a model search.

We use a simple VGG-like [45] network architecture shown in Fig. 4. It consists of 10 group-convolutional layers followed by a 2-layer fully-connected network. Before every convolution, we combine multiplicative dropout with 0.1 standard deviation on the filter tensors, and after every convolution we add batch normalization. We use ReLU nonlinearities and global average pooling before two fully-connected layers at the end of the network. The loss function is the multi-class cross-entropy. We initialize all weights using the He method [20] and train the network with ADAM stochastic gradient descent [27], with a learning rate of 1e−3, which steps down by 1/5 every 5 epochs for 25 epochs.

The data augmentation is performed similar to the implementation found in Brock [4] with 12 stratified rotations about the z-axis, reflections in the x- and y-axis with uniform probability and uniformly random translations of up to ± 4 voxels along all three axes. We use this data augmentation to maintain a direct comparison with prior works. It should also be noted that rotational data augmentation cannot be avoided entirely, since our networks are only equivariant to subgroups of the full roto-translation group $SE(3)$, so we still need to augment for all angles in the quotient $SE(3)/G$, where G is the subgroup of interest. We also rescale the voxel values to $\{-1, 5\}$ instead of $\{0, 1\}$ as in [4], who showed it helps with sparse voxel volumnes. We show our results in Table 2. We compare the rotational tetrahedral group and the four-group models. For the four-group model, we compare the average single-view accuracy across 5 models for robustness, with rotation averaged accuracy and single-view accuracy for the best model. The single view accuracy is computed as the accuracy averaged over each of the 12 rotated test views; whereas, the rotation averaged accuracy is computed as the accuracy of the average of all 12 predictions.

For the single-model category, our four-group, rotation-averaged network attains state-of-the-art performance. Interestingly, our single-view result we obtain is very similar to ORION [41], which introduces an orientation estimation task along with the classification. We posit that the T_4-model does not perform as well as the V-model, because increasing the number of filter copies reduces the diversity of filters, when the number of total filters (number of learnable filters times number of copies) is constrained. Essentially there is a tradeoff between filter diversity and the extent of equivariance due to weight-tying. The Klein-group appears to achieve best in this situation. It is also interesting to see that rotation

Table 2. Results for the ModelNet 10 benchmark. We compare against other methods which operate on a voxel-representation of the data. The only model to beat us is Brock et al. 's ensemble of 6 models. If we just restrict to a single model, then we hold state-of-the-art accuracy.

Method	ModelNet10	# params ($\times 10^6$, 2 s.f.)
3D ShapeNets [53]	0.8354	12
Xu and Todovoric [54]	0.8800	0.080
3D-GAN [52]	0.9100	11
VRN [4]	0.9133	18
VoxNet [35]	0.9200	0.92
Fusion-Net [21]	0.9311	120
ORION [41]	0.9380	0.91
Ours T_4	0.9127	4.5
Our V (average)	0.9372	4.5
Ours V (best model single-view)	0.9420	4.5
Ours V (best model rotation averaged)	**0.9460**	4.5
VRN Ensemble [4]	0.9714	108

averaging improves performance slightly, compared to our single-view model. We suggest this is because we are averaging over rotations not covers by the four-group. Looking across the model sizes, we see that the group-convolutional models sit somewhere in the middle in terms of number of parameters. Speed-wise, we found that during development the four-group network only trained about 2× slower than non-group CNNs.

5.2 ISBI 2012 Challenge: Connectome Segmentation

The ISBI 2012 Challenge is a volumetric boundary segmentation benchmark. The task is to segment Drosophilia ventral nerve cords from a serial-section transmission electron microscopy (EM) image [1]. The training set is a single $2 \times 2 \times 1.5\,\mu\text{m}^3$ volume of anisotropic imaging resolution (high x-y resolution, low z resolution). Each voxel is $4 \times 4 \times 50\,\text{nm}^3$ so the full training image is $512 \times 512 \times 30$ voxels in shape. The test image is $512 \times 512 \times 30$ voxel, with withheld labels. Scoring is performed using the metrics V_{rand} and V_{info} described in [1]. Larger is better.

Here we are faced with two major issues, (a) small dataset, (b) high imaging anisotropy. We counter (a) with heavy data augmentation as per [38] and by noting that group convolutions reduce the number of trainable parameters through significant weight-tying. To counter the imaging anisotropy, we use Klein's four-group, which is not affected by stretching of one of the axes (Fig. 5).

Competing methods segment on a single 2D high-resolution slice at a time, but as a proof of concept we try segmentation as a 3D problem, feeding 3D

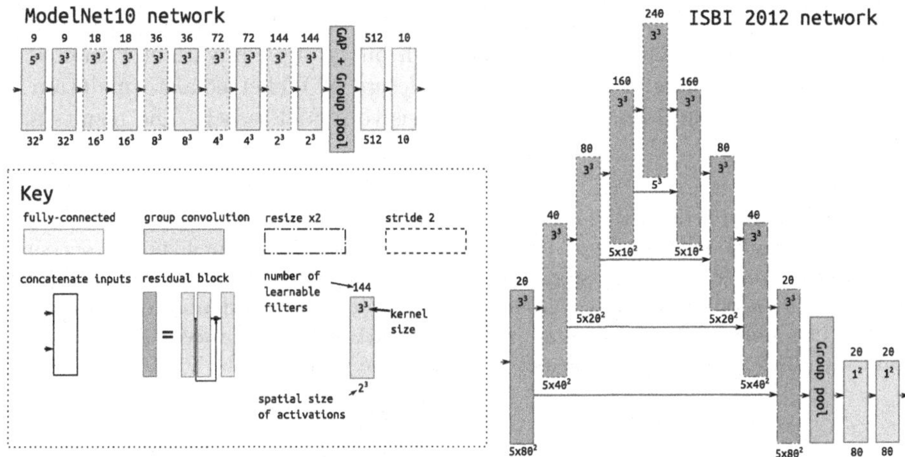

Fig. 4. (Best viewed in color) The architectures used in our experiments. We use a simple VGG-like architecture for the ModelNet10 classification challenge, and a UNet/FusionNet-like architecture for the ISBI2012 boundary segmentation benchmark.

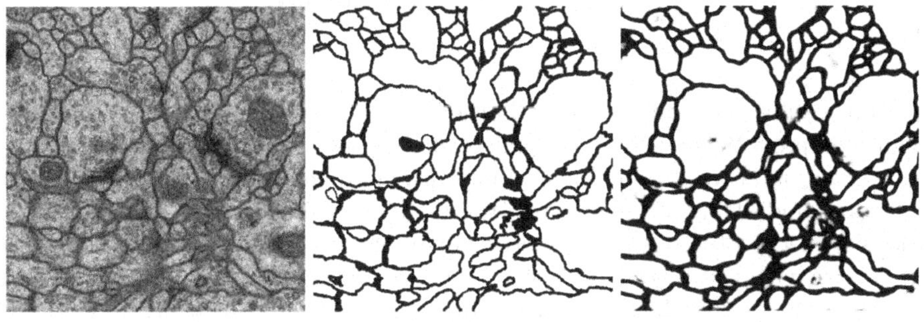

Fig. 5. Examples of 2D slices from the training volume, the associated label mask, and the prediction made by our network. The original volume contains small amounts of noise and certain structures within the volume are ambiguous in nature.

image chunks into a 3D network. We use an architecture as shown in Fig. 4, based on Weiler et al.'s steerable version [49] of the FusionNet [38]. It is a UNet [39] with added skip connections within the encoder and decoder paths to encourage better gradient flow. We place Gaussian multiplicative dropout [46] with standard deviation 0.1 before every convolution. By this we mean if x is an activation and $n \sim \text{Normal}(n; 1, 0.1^2)$ then the result of dropout is $x \cdot n$. We also place batch normalization after every convolution and use ReLU nonlinearities directly before each convolution, except on the input.

For the training set we extract random $100 \times 100 \times 5$ voxel patches from the training volume and predict the center slice. We reflection pad 10 voxels in the x-y plane, and constant pad up to 5 voxels in the z-direction if we sample at the upper or lower image boundaries. We then apply a random elastic distortion in the x-y-plane, and pass the patches through our group-equivariant FusionNet. We keep our implementation close to the design of Weiler et al. to maintain a close comparison, and do not perform extensive model search. The results are shown in Table 3.

Table 3. Results for the ISBI 2012 challenge. We have tried to keep our implementation as close as possible to Weiler et al. Unlike other methods, we perform no post-processing at all unlike Weiler et al. who use a lifting multi-cut [3] post-process, or UNet and Quan et al. who use rotation averaging. Quan also adds an optional median filtering to boost scores. This shows that we can adapt state-of-the-art models to process 3D volumetric data with little change in the competitiveness of the results.

Method	V_{rand}	V_{info}
UNet [39]	0.97276	0.98662
Quan et al. [38]	0.97804	0.98995
Ours	0.98018	0.98202
Weiler et al. [49]	0.98680	0.99144
IAL MC/LMC	0.98792	0.99183

Our results are comparable with other leading methods. Our V_{rand} metric is slightly improved over UNet and Quan et al., but not as good as Weiler et al., who use a 2D group convolutional neural network approach, with 17 rotations about the z-axis and lifting multicut post-process. The leading method uses the lifting multicut method too. Our V_{info} metric is not as good as the other methods, but we believe with sufficient model search, and extensive post-processing we could increase this number further. The main point of this experiment, as with the ModelNet10 experiment, was to demonstrate that we could get relatively good performance, without the need for extensive test-time rotation averaging.

6 Conclusion

We have presented a 3D convolutional neural network architecture, which is equivariant to right-angle rotations in three dimensions. This relies on an extension of the standard convolution to 3D rotations. On the ModelNet10 classification challenge, we have achieved state-of-the-art for a single model, beating some much larger models, which rely on heavy data augmentation. Since our models are rotation in/equivariant by design, our CNNs need not learn to *overcome* rotations, the way a standard CNN does. In 3D, this is an especially important gain. As a result, our model is positioned to get better generalization with less data, while avoiding the need to perform time-costly rotation averaging at test-time.

Another perspective on our approach is to think of it as global average pooling over rotations, where we expose a new 'rotation-dimension'. Without adhering to a defined group, it would be challenging to disentangle or orient a feature space (at any one layer, or across multiple layers) with respect to such a rotation dimension. The trade-off is that we commit to a group and its corresponding CubeNet architecture, to avoid the considerable effort of learning to disentangle pose.

We leave it to future work to examine whether these models can be generalized to continuous rotations and other challenging transformations, such as scale. There is also the untouched challenge of finding 3D rotation groups, which are not aligned to the Cartesian voxel-grid.

References

1. Arganda-Carreras, I., et al.: Crowdsourcing the creation of image segmentation algorithms for connectomics. Front. Neuroanat. **9**, 142 (2015). https://doi.org/10.3389/fnana.2015.00142
2. Barnard, E., Casasent, D.: Invariance and neural nets. IEEE Trans. Neural Netw. **2**(5), 498–508 (1991). https://doi.org/10.1109/72.134287
3. Beier, T., Andres, B., Köthe, U., Hamprecht, F.A.: An efficient fusion move algorithm for the minimum cost lifted multicut problem. In: Leibe, B., Matas, J., Sebe, N., Welling, M. (eds.) ECCV 2016. LNCS, vol. 9906, pp. 715–730. Springer, Cham (2016). https://doi.org/10.1007/978-3-319-46475-6_44
4. Brock, A., Lim, T., Ritchie, J.M., Weston, N.: Generative and discriminative voxel modeling with convolutional neural networks (2016)
5. Bruna, J., Mallat, S.: Invariant scattering convolution networks. IEEE Trans. Pattern Anal. Mach. Intell. **35**(8), 1872–1886 (2013). https://doi.org/10.1109/TPAMI.2012.230
6. Chen, X., Duan, Y., Houthooft, R., Schulman, J., Sutskever, I., Abbeel, P.: InfoGAN: interpretable representation learning by information maximizing generative adversarial nets. In: Advances in Neural Information Processing Systems 29: Annual Conference on Neural Information Processing Systems 2016, 5–10 December 2016, Barcelona, Spain, pp. 2172–2180 (2016). http://papers.nips.cc/paper/6399-infogan-interpretable-representation-learning-by-information-maximizing-generative-adversarial-nets
7. Chirikjian, G.S.: Engineering Applications of Noncommutative Harmonic Analysis: With Emphasis on Rotation and Motion Groups. CRC Press, Abingdon (2000)
8. Cohen, T., Welling, M.: Group equivariant convolutional networks. In: Proceedings of the 33rd International Conference on Machine Learning, ICML 2016, New York City, NY, USA, 19–24 June 2016, pp. 2990–2999 (2016). http://jmlr.org/proceedings/papers/v48/cohenc16.html
9. Cohen, T.S., Geiger, M., Koehler, J., Welling, M.: Spherical CNNs (2018)
10. Cohen, T.S., Geiger, M., Köhler, J., Welling, M.: Spherical CNNs. CoRR (2018). http://arxiv.org/abs/1801.10130
11. Cohen, T.S., Welling, M.: Steerable CNNs. CoRR (2016). http://arxiv.org/abs/1612.08498
12. Cotter, F., Kingsbury, N.G.: Visualizing and improving scattering networks. In: 27th IEEE International Workshop on Machine Learning for Signal Processing, MLSP 2017, Tokyo, Japan, 25–28 September 2017, pp. 1–6 (2017). https://doi.org/10.1109/MLSP.2017.8168136

13. Crowley, J.L., Parker, A.C.: A representation for shape based on peaks and ridges in the difference of low-pass transform. IEEE Trans. Pattern Anal. Mach. Intell. **6**(2), 156–170 (1984). https://doi.org/10.1109/TPAMI.1984.4767500
14. Dieleman, S., Fauw, J.D., Kavukcuoglu, K.: Exploiting cyclic symmetry in convolutional neural networks. In: Proceedings of the 33rd International Conference on Machine Learning, ICML 2016, New York City, NY, USA, 19–24 June 2016, pp. 1889–1898 (2016). http://jmlr.org/proceedings/papers/v48/dieleman16.html
15. Esteves, C., Allen-Blanchette, C., Zhou, X., Daniilidis, K.: Polar transformer networks. CoRR (2017). http://arxiv.org/abs/1709.01889
16. Fasel, B., Gatica-Perez, D.: Rotation-invariant neoperceptron. In: 18th International Conference on Pattern Recognition (ICPR 2006), Hong Kong, China, 20–24 August 2006, pp. 336–339 (2006). https://doi.org/10.1109/ICPR.2006.1020
17. Freeman, W.T., Adelson, E.H.: The design and use of steerable filters. IEEE Trans. Pattern Anal. Mach. Intell. **13**(9), 891–906 (1991). https://doi.org/10.1109/34.93808
18. Gonzalez, D.M., Volpi, M., Komodakis, N., Tuia, D.: Rotation equivariant vector field networks. In: IEEE International Conference on Computer Vision, ICCV 2017, Venice, Italy, 22–29 October 2017, pp. 5058–5067 (2017). https://doi.org/10.1109/ICCV.2017.540
19. Gonzalez, D.M., Volpi, M., Tuia, D.: Learning rotation invariant convolutional filters for texture classification. In: 23rd International Conference on Pattern Recognition, ICPR 2016, Cancún, Mexico, 4–8 December 2016, pp. 2012–2017 (2016). https://doi.org/10.1109/ICPR.2016.7899932
20. He, K., Zhang, X., Ren, S., Sun, J.: Delving deep into rectifiers: surpassing human-level performance on imagenet classification. In: 2015 IEEE International Conference on Computer Vision, ICCV 2015, Santiago, Chile, 7–13 December 2015, pp. 1026–1034 (2015). https://doi.org/10.1109/ICCV.2015.123
21. Hegde, V., Zadeh, R.: FusionNet: 3D object classification using multiple data representations. CoRR (2016). http://arxiv.org/abs/1607.05695
22. Henriques, J.F., Vedaldi, A.: Warped convolutions: efficient invariance to spatial transformations. In: Proceedings of the 34th International Conference on Machine Learning, ICML 2017, Sydney, NSW, Australia, 6–11 August 2017, pp. 1461–1469 (2017). http://proceedings.mlr.press/v70/henriques17a.html
23. Hinton, G.E., Krizhevsky, A., Wang, S.D.: Transforming auto-encoders. In: Honkela, T., Duch, W., Girolami, M., Kaski, S. (eds.) ICANN 2011. LNCS, vol. 6791, pp. 44–51. Springer, Heidelberg (2011). https://doi.org/10.1007/978-3-642-21735-7_6
24. Hinton, G.E., Sabour, S., Frosst, N.: Matrix capsules with EM routing. In: International Conference on Learning Representations (2018). https://openreview.net/forum?id=HJWLfGWRb
25. Jacobsen, J.H., Oyallon, E., Mallat, S., Smeulders, A.W.M.: Hierarchical attribute CNNs. In: ICML Workshop on Principled Approaches to Deep Learning (2017). https://ivi.fnwi.uva.nl/isis/publications/2017/JacobsenPADL2017
26. Jacobsen, J., Brabandere, B.D., Smeulders, A.W.M.: Dynamic steerable blocks in deep residual networks. CoRR (2017). http://arxiv.org/abs/1706.00598
27. Kingma, D.P., Ba, J.: Adam: a method for stochastic optimization. CoRR (2014). http://arxiv.org/abs/1412.6980
28. Kondor, R.: N-body networks: a covariant hierarchical neural network architecture for learning atomic potentials (2018)
29. Kondor, R., Trivedi, S.: On the generalization of equivariance and convolution in neural networks to the action of compact groups (2018)

30. Kulkarni, T.D., Whitney, W.F., Kohli, P., Tenenbaum, J.B.: Deep convolutional inverse graphics network. In: Advances in Neural Information Processing Systems 28: Annual Conference on Neural Information Processing Systems 2015, Montreal, Quebec, Canada, 7–12 December 2015, pp. 2539–2547 (2015). http://papers.nips.cc/paper/5851-deep-convolutional-inverse-graphics-network
31. Laptev, D., Savinov, N., Buhmann, J.M., Pollefeys, M.: TI-POOLING: transformation-invariant pooling for feature learning in convolutional neural networks. In: 2016 IEEE Conference on Computer Vision and Pattern Recognition, CVPR 2016, Las Vegas, NV, USA, 27–30 June 2016, pp. 289–297 (2016). https://doi.org/10.1109/CVPR.2016.38
32. Lenz, R.: Group Theoretical Methods in Image Processing. Lecture Notes in Computer Science, vol. 413. Springer, Heidelberg (1990). https://doi.org/10.1007/3-540-52290-5
33. Li, J., Yang, Z., Liu, H., Cai, D.: Deep rotation equivariant network (2017)
34. Lindeberg, T.: Generalized Gaussian scale-space axiomatics comprising linear scale-space, affine scale-space and spatio-temporal scale-space. J. Math. Imaging Vis. **40**(1), 36–81 (2011). https://doi.org/10.1007/s10851-010-0242-2
35. Maturana, D., Scherer, S.: VoxNet: a 3D convolutional neural network for real-time object recognition. In: 2015 IEEE/RSJ International Conference on Intelligent Robots and Systems, IROS 2015, Hamburg, Germany, 28 September–2 October 2015, pp. 922–928 (2015). https://doi.org/10.1109/IROS.2015.7353481
36. Oyallon, E., Mallat, S.: Deep roto-translation scattering for object classification. In: IEEE Conference on Computer Vision and Pattern Recognition, CVPR 2015, Boston, MA, USA, 7–12 June 2015, pp. 2865–2873 (2015). https://doi.org/10.1109/CVPR.2015.7298904
37. Perona, P.: Deformable kernels for early vision. In: IEEE Computer Society Conference on Computer Vision and Pattern Recognition, CVPR 1991, Lahaina, Maui, Hawaii, USA, 3–6 June 1991, pp. 222–227 (1991). https://doi.org/10.1109/CVPR.1991.139691
38. Quan, T.M., Hildebrand, D.G.C., Jeong, W.: FusionNet: a deep fully residual convolutional neural network for image segmentation in connectomics. CoRR (2016). http://arxiv.org/abs/1612.05360
39. Ronneberger, O., Fischer, P., Brox, T.: U-Net: convolutional networks for biomedical image segmentation. In: Navab, N., Hornegger, J., Wells, W.M., Frangi, A.F. (eds.) MICCAI 2015. LNCS, vol. 9351, pp. 234–241. Springer, Cham (2015). https://doi.org/10.1007/978-3-319-24574-4_28
40. Sabour, S., Frosst, N., Hinton, G.E.: Dynamic routing between capsules. In: Advances in Neural Information Processing Systems 30: Annual Conference on Neural Information Processing Systems 2017, Long Beach, CA, USA, 4–9 December 2017, pp. 3859–3869 (2017). http://papers.nips.cc/paper/6975-dynamic-routing-between-capsules
41. Sedaghat, N., Zolfaghari, M., Brox, T.: Orientation-boosted voxel nets for 3D object recognition. CoRR (2016). http://arxiv.org/abs/1604.03351
42. Sifre, L., Mallat, S.: Rotation, scaling and deformation invariant scattering for texture discrimination. In: 2013 IEEE Conference on Computer Vision and Pattern Recognition, Portland, OR, USA, 23–28 June 2013, pp. 1233–1240 (2013). https://doi.org/10.1109/CVPR.2013.163

43. Simard, P.Y., Victorri, B., LeCun, Y., Denker, J.S.: Tangent prop - a formalism for specifying selected invariances in an adaptive network. In: Advances in Neural Information Processing Systems 4, NIPS Conference, Denver, Colorado, USA, 2–5 December 1991, pp. 895–903 (1991). http://papers.nips.cc/paper/536-tangent-prop-a-formalism-for-specifying-selected-invariances-in-an-adaptive-network
44. Simoncelli, E.P., Freeman, W.T., Adelson, E.H., Heeger, D.J.: Shiftable multiscale transforms. IEEE Trans. Inf. Theory **38**(2), 587–607 (1992). https://doi.org/10.1109/18.119725
45. Simonyan, K., Zisserman, A.: Very deep convolutional networks for large-scale image recognition. CoRR (2014). http://arxiv.org/abs/1409.1556
46. Srivastava, N., Hinton, G.E., Krizhevsky, A., Sutskever, I., Salakhutdinov, R.: Dropout: a simple way to prevent neural networks from overfitting. J. Mach. Learn. Res. **15**(1), 1929–1958 (2014). http://dl.acm.org/citation.cfm?id=2670313
47. Teo, P.C.: Theory and applications of steerable functions. Ph.D. thesis, Department of Computer Science, Stanford University, March 1998
48. Thomas, N., et al.: Tensor field networks: rotation- and translation-equivariant neural networks for 3D point clouds (2018)
49. Weiler, M., Hamprecht, F.A., Storath, M.: Learning steerable filters for rotation equivariant CNNs. CoRR (2017). http://arxiv.org/abs/1711.07289
50. Worrall, D.E., Garbin, S.J., Turmukhambetov, D., Brostow, G.J.: Harmonic networks: deep translation and rotation equivariance. In: 2017 IEEE Conference on Computer Vision and Pattern Recognition, CVPR 2017, Honolulu, HI, USA, 21–26 July 2017, pp. 7168–7177 (2017). https://doi.org/10.1109/CVPR.2017.758
51. Worrall, D.E., Garbin, S.J., Turmukhambetov, D., Brostow, G.J.: Interpretable transformations with encoder-decoder networks. In: IEEE International Conference on Computer Vision, ICCV 2017, Venice, Italy, 22–29 October 2017, pp. 5737–5746 (2017). https://doi.org/10.1109/ICCV.2017.611
52. Wu, J., Zhang, C., Xue, T., Freeman, B., Tenenbaum, J.: Learning a probabilistic latent space of object shapes via 3D generative-adversarial modeling. In: Advances in Neural Information Processing Systems 29: Annual Conference on Neural Information Processing Systems 2016, Barcelona, Spain, 5–10 December 2016, pp. 82–90 (2016). http://papers.nips.cc/paper/6096-learning-a-probabilistic-latent-space-of-object-shapes-via-3d-generative-adversarial-modeling
53. Wu, Z., et al.: 3D ShapeNets: a deep representation for volumetric shapes. In: IEEE Conference on Computer Vision and Pattern Recognition, CVPR 2015, Boston, MA, USA, 7–12 June 2015, pp. 1912–1920 (2015). https://doi.org/10.1109/CVPR.2015.7298801
54. Xu, X., Todorovic, S.: Beam search for learning a deep convolutional neural network of 3D shapes. In: 23rd International Conference on Pattern Recognition, ICPR 2016, Cancún, Mexico, 4–8 December 2016, pp. 3506–3511 (2016). https://doi.org/10.1109/ICPR.2016.7900177
55. Zhou, Y., Ye, Q., Qiu, Q., Jiao, J.: Oriented response networks. In: 2017 IEEE Conference on Computer Vision and Pattern Recognition, CVPR 2017, Honolulu, HI, USA, 21–26 July 2017, pp. 4961–4970 (2017). https://doi.org/10.1109/CVPR.2017.527

YouTube-VOS: Sequence-to-Sequence Video Object Segmentation

Ning Xu[1(✉)], Linjie Yang[2], Yuchen Fan[3], Jianchao Yang[2], Dingcheng Yue[3], Yuchen Liang[3], Brian Price[1], Scott Cohen[1], and Thomas Huang[3]

[1] Adobe Research, San Jose, USA
{nxu,bprice,scohen}@adobe.com
[2] Snapchat Research, Venice, USA
{linjie.yang,jianchao.yang}@snap.com
[3] University of Illinois at Urbana-Champaign, Illinois, USA
{yuchenf4,dyue2,yliang35,t-huang1}@illinois.edu

Abstract. Learning long-term spatial-temporal features are critical for many video analysis tasks. However, existing video segmentation methods predominantly rely on static image segmentation techniques, and methods capturing temporal dependency for segmentation have to depend on pretrained optical flow models, leading to suboptimal solutions for the problem. End-to-end sequential learning to explore spatial-temporal features for video segmentation is largely limited by the scale of available video segmentation datasets, i.e., even the largest video segmentation dataset only contains 90 short video clips. To solve this problem, we build a new large-scale video object segmentation dataset called YouTube Video Object Segmentation dataset (YouTube-VOS). Our dataset contains 3,252 YouTube video clips and 78 categories including common objects and human activities (This is the statistics when we submit this paper, see updated statistics on our website). This is by far the largest video object segmentation dataset to our knowledge and we have released it at https://youtube-vos.org. Based on this dataset, we propose a novel sequence-to-sequence network to fully exploit long-term spatial-temporal information in videos for segmentation. We demonstrate that our method is able to achieve the best results on our YouTube-VOS test set and comparable results on DAVIS 2016 compared to the current state-of-the-art methods. Experiments show that the large scale dataset is indeed a key factor to the success of our model.

Keywords: Video object segmentation · Large-scale dataset
Spatial-temporal information

1 Introduction

Learning effective spatial-temporal features has been demonstrated to be very important for many video analysis tasks. For example, Donahue *et al.* [9] propose long-term recurrent convolution network for activity recognition and video

V. Ferrari et al. (Eds.): ECCV 2018, LNCS 11209, pp. 603–619, 2018.
https://doi.org/10.1007/978-3-030-01228-1_36

captioning. Srivastava *et al.* [37] propose unsupervised learning of video representation with a LSTM autoencoder. Tran *et al.* [41] develop a 3D convolutional network to extract spatial and temporal information jointly from a video. Other works include learning spatial-temporal information for precipitation prediction [45], physical interaction [13], and autonomous driving [46].

Video segmentation plays an important role in video understanding, which fosters many applications, such as accurate object segmentation and tracking, interactive video editing and augmented reality. Video object segmentation, which targets at segmenting a particular object instance throughout the entire video sequence given only the object mask on the first frame, has attracted much attention from the vision community recently [5,7,10,18,21,31,40,43,49]. However, existing state-of-the-art video object segmentation approaches primarily rely on single image segmentation frameworks [5,31,43,49]. For example, Caelles *et al.* [5] propose to train an object segmentation network on static images and then fine-tune the model on the first frame of a test video over hundreds of iterations, so that it remembers the object appearance. The fine-tuned model is then applied to all following individual frames to segment the object without using any temporal information. Even though simple, such an online learning or one-shot learning scheme achieves top performance on video object segmentation benchmarks [20,32]. Although some recent approaches [7,10,40] have been proposed to leverage temporal consistency, they depend on models pretrained on other tasks such as optical flow [19,34] or motion segmentation [39], to extract temporal information. These pretrained models are learned from separate tasks, and therefore are suboptimal for the video segmentation problem.

Learning long-term spatial-temporal features directly for video object segmentation task is, however, largely limited by the scale of existing video object segmentation datasets. For example, the popular benchmark dataset DAVIS [33] has only 90 short video clips, which is barely sufficient to learn an end-to-end model from scratch like other video analysis tasks. Even if we combine all the videos from available datasets [4,12,14,20,25,29], its scale is still far smaller than other video analysis datasets such as YouTube-8M [1] and ActivityNet [16]. To solve this problem, we present the first large-scale video object segmentation dataset called YouTube-VOS (YouTube Video Object Segmentation dataset) in this work. Our dataset contains 3,252 YouTube video clips featuring 78 categories covering common animals, vehicles, accessories and human activities. Each video clip is about 3–6 s long and often contains multiple objects, which are manually segmented by professional annotators. Compared to existing datasets, our dataset contains a lot more videos, object categories, object instances and annotations, and a much longer duration of total annotated videos. Table 1 provides quantitative scale comparisons of our new dataset against existing datasets. We retrain existing algorithms on YouTube-VOS and benchmark their performance on our test set which contains 322 videos. In addition, our test set contains 10 categories unseen in the training set and are used to evaluate the generalization ability of existing approaches.

Table 1. Scale comparison between YouTube-VOS and existing datasets. "Annotations" denotes the total number of object annotations. "Duration" denotes the total duration (in minutes) of the annotated videos.

Scale	JC	ST	YTO	FBMS	DAVIS		YouTube-VOS
	[12]	[25]	[20]	[29]	[32]	[33]	(Ours)
Videos	22	14	96	59	50	90	**3,252**
Categories	14	11	10	16	-	-	**78**
Objects	22	24	96	139	50	205	**6,048**
Annotations	6,331	1,475	1,692	1,465	3,440	13,543	**133,886**
Duration	3.52	0.59	9.01	7.70	2.88	5.17	**217.21**

Based on Youtube-VOS, we propose a new sequence-to-sequence learning algorithm to explore spatial-temporal modeling for video object segmentation. We utilize a convolutional LSTM [45] to learn long-term spatial-temporal information for segmentation. At each time step, the convolutional LSTM accepts last hidden states and an encoded image frame, it then outputs encoded spatial-temporal features which are decoded into a segmentation mask. Our algorithm is different from existing approaches in that it fully exploits the long-term spatial-temporal information in an end-to-end manner and does not depend on existing optical flow or motion segmentation models. We evaluate our algorithm on both YouTube-VOS and DAVIS 2016 and it achieves better or comparable results compared to the current state of the arts.

The rest of our paper is organized as follows. In Sect. 2 we briefly introduce the related works. In Sects. 3 and 4 we describe our YouTube-VOS dataset and the proposed algorithm in detail. Experimental results are presented in Sect. 5. Finally we conclude the paper in Sect. 6.

2 Related Work

In the past decades, several datasets [4,12,14,20,25,29] have been created for video object segmentation. All of them are in small scales which usually contain only dozens of videos. In addition, their video content is relatively simple (*e.g.* no heavy occlusion, camera motion or illumination change) and sometimes the video resolution is low. Recently, a new dataset called DAVIS [32,33] was published and has become the benchmark dataset in this area. Its 2016 version contains 50 videos with a single foreground object per video while the 2017 version has 90 videos with multiple objects per video. In comparison to previous datasets [4,12,14,20,25,29], DAVIS has both higher-quality of video resolutions and annotations. In addition, their video content is more complicated with multi-object interactions, camera motion, and occlusions.

Early methods [4,11,20,27,30] for video object segmentation often solve some spatial-temporal graph structures with hand-crafted energy terms, which are usually associated with features including appearance, boundary, motion and optical flows. Recently, deep-learning based methods were proposed due to its great success in image segmentation tasks [6,35,47,48]. Most of these methods [5, 7,10,31,43,49] build their model based on an image segmentation network and do not involve sequential modeling. Online learning [5] is commonly used to improve their performance. To make the model temporally consistent, the predicted mask of the previous frame is used as a guidance in [18,31,49]. Other methods have been proposed to leverage spatial-temporal information. Jampani *et al.* [21] use spatial-temporal consistency to propagate object masks over time. Tokmakov *et al.* [40] use a two-stream network to model objects' appearance and motion and use a recurrent layer to capture the evolution. However, due to the lack of training videos, they use a pretrained motion segmentation model [39] and optical-flow model [19], which leads to suboptimal results since the model is not trained end-to-end to best capture spatial-temporal features.

3 YouTube-VOS

To create our dataset, we first carefully select a set of object categories including animals (*e.g. ant, eagle, goldfish, person*), vehicles (*e.g. airplane, bicycle, boat, sedan*), accessories (*e.g. eyeglass, hat, bag*), common objects (*e.g. potted plant, knife, sign, umbrella*), and humans in various activities (*e.g. tennis, skateboarding, motorcycling, surfing*). The videos containing human activities have diversified appearance and motion, so instead of treating human videos as one class, we divide different activities into different categories. Most of these videos contain interactions between a person and a corresponding object, such as tennis racket, skateboard, motorcycle, etc. The entire category set includes 78 categories that covers diverse objects and motions, and should be representative for everyday scenarios.

We then collect many high-resolution videos with the selected category labels from the large-scale video classification dataset YouTube-8M [1]. This dataset consists of millions of YouTube videos associated with more than 4,700 visual entities. We utilize its category annotations to retrieve candidate videos that we are interested in. Specifically, up to 100 videos are retrieved for each category in our segmentation category set. There are several advantages to using YouTube videos to create our segmentation dataset. First, YouTube videos have very diverse object appearances and motions. Challenging cases for video object segmentation, such as occlusions, fast object motions and change of appearances, commonly exist in YouTube videos. Second, YouTube videos are taken by both professionals and amateurs and thus different levels of camera motions are shown in the crawled videos. Algorithms trained on such data could potentially handle camera motion better and thus are more practical. Last but not the least, many YouTube videos are taken by today's smart phone devices and there are demanding needs to segment objects in those videos for applications such as video editing and augmented reality.

Fig. 1. The ground truth annotations of sample video clips in our dataset. Different objects are highlighted with different colors.

Since the retrieved videos are usually long (several minutes) and have shot transitions, we use an off-the-shelf video shot detection algorithm[1] to automatically partition each video into multiple video clips. We first remove the clips from the first and last 10% of the video, since these clips have a high chance of containing introductory subtitles and credits lists. We then sample up to five clips with appropriate lengths (3–6 s) per video and manually verify that these clips contain the correct object categories and are useful for our task (*e.g.* no scene transition, not too dark, shaky, or blurry). After the video clips are collected, we ask human annotators to select up to five objects of proper sizes and categories per video clip and carefully annotate them (by tracing their boundaries instead of rough polygons) every five frames in a 30fps frame rate, which results in a 6fps sampling rate. Given a video and its category, annotators are first required to annotate objects belonging to that category. If the video contains other objects that belong to our 78 categories, we ask the annotators to label them as well, so that each video has multiple objects annotated. In human activity videos, both the human subject and the object he/she interacts with are labeled, *e.g.*, both the person and the skateboard are required to be labeled in a "skateboarding" video. Some annotation examples are shown in Fig. 1. Unlike dense per-frame annotation in previous datasets [12,32,33], we believe that the temporal correlation between five consecutive frames is sufficiently strong that annotations can be omitted for intermediate frames to reduce the annotation efforts. Such a skip-frame annotation strategy allows us to scale up the number of videos and objects under the same annotation budget, which are important factors for better performance. We find empirically that our dataset is effective in training different segmentation algorithm.

As a result, our dataset YouTube-VOS consists of 3,252 YouTube video clips and 133,886 object annotations, 33 and 10 times more than the best of the existing video object segmentation datasets, respectively (See Table 1). YouTube-VOS is the largest dataset for video object segmentation to date.

[1] http://johmathe.name/shotdetect.html.

4 Sequence-to-Sequence Video Object Segmentation

Based on our new dataset, we propose a new sequence-to-sequence video object segmentation algorithm. Different from existing approaches, our algorithm learns long-term spatial-temporal features directly from training data in an end-to-end manner, and the offline trained model is capable of propagating an initial object segmentation mask accurately by memorizing and updating the object charactersitics, including appearance, location and scale, and temporal movements, automatically over the entire video sequence.

4.1 Problem Formulation

Let us denote a video sequence with T frames as $\{\mathbf{x}_t | t \in [0, T-1]\}$ where $\mathbf{x}_t \in \mathbb{R}^{H \times W \times 3}$ is the RGB frame at time step t, and denote an initial binary object mask at time step 0 as $\mathbf{y}_0 \in \mathbb{R}^{H \times W}$. The target of video object segmentation is to predict the object mask automatically for the remaining frames from time step 1 to $T-1$, *i.e.* $\{\hat{\mathbf{y}}_t | t \in [1, T-1]\}$.

To obtain a predicted mask $\hat{\mathbf{y}}_t$ for $\mathbf{x}_t$, many existing deep learning methods only leverage information at time step 0 (*e.g.* online learning or one-shot learning [5]) or time step $t-1$ (*e.g.* optical flow [31]) while the long-term history information is totally dismissed. Their frameworks can be formulated as $\hat{\mathbf{y}}_t = \arg\max_{\forall \bar{\mathbf{y}}_t} \mathbb{P}(\bar{\mathbf{y}}_t | \mathbf{x}_0, \mathbf{y}_0, \mathbf{x}_t)$ or $\hat{\mathbf{y}}_t = \arg\max_{\forall \bar{\mathbf{y}}_t} \mathbb{P}(\bar{\mathbf{y}}_t | \mathbf{x}_0, \mathbf{y}_0, \mathbf{x}_t, \mathbf{x}_{t-1})$. They are effective when the object appearance is similar between time 0 and time t or when the object motion from time $t-1$ to t can be accurately measured. However, these assumptions will be violated when the object has drastic appearance variation and rapid motion, which is often case in many real-world videos. In such cases, the history information of the object in all previous frames becomes critical and should be leveraged in an effective way. Therefore, we propose to solve a different objective function, *i.e.* $\hat{\mathbf{y}}_t = \arg\max_{\forall \bar{\mathbf{y}}_t} \mathbb{P}(\bar{\mathbf{y}}_t | \mathbf{x}_0, \mathbf{x}_1, \ldots, \mathbf{x}_t, \mathbf{y}_0)$, which can be transformed into a sequence-to-sequence learning problem.

4.2 Our Algorithm

Recurrent Neural Networks (RNN) has been adopted by many sequence-to-sequence learning problems because it is capable to learn long-term dependency from sequential data. LSTM [17] as a special RNN structure solves vanishing or exploding gradients issue [3]. A convolutional variant of LSTM (convolutional LSTM) [45] is later proposed to preserve the spatial information of the data in the hidden states of the model.

Our algorithm is inspired by the convolutional encoder-decoder LSTM structure [8,38] which has achieved much success in machine translation, where an input sentence in language A is first encoded by a encoder LSTM and its outputs are fed into a decoder LSTM which can generate the desired output sentence in language B. In video object segmentation, it is essential to capture the object characteristics over time. To generate the initial states for our convolutional LSTM (*ConvLSTM*), we use a feed-forward neural network to encode both the

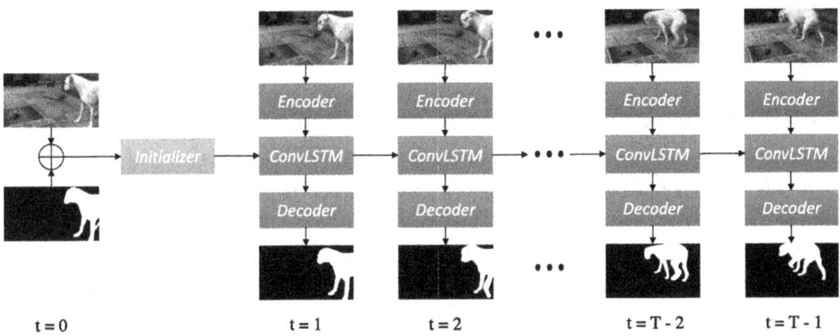

Fig. 2. The framework of our algorithm. The initial information at time 0 is encoded by *Initializer* to initialize *ConvLSTM*. The new frame at each time step is processed by *Encoder* and the segmentation result is decoded by *Decoder*. *ConvLSTM* is automatically updated over the entire video sequence.

first image frame and the segmentation mask. Specifically, we concatenate the initial frame $\mathbf{x}_0$ and segmentation mask $\mathbf{y}_0$ and feed it into a trainable network, denoted as *Initializer*, which outputs the initial memory state $\mathbf{c}_0$ and hidden state $\mathbf{h}_0$. These initial states capture object appearance, object location and scale. And they are feed into *ConvLSTM* for sequence learning.

At time step t, frame $\mathbf{x}_t$ is first processed by a convolutional encoder, denoted as *Encoder*, to extract feature maps $\tilde{\mathbf{x}}_t$. Then $\tilde{\mathbf{x}}_t$ is sent as the inputs of *ConvLSTM*. The internal states $\mathbf{c}_t$ and $\mathbf{h}_t$ are automatically updated given the new observation $\tilde{\mathbf{x}}_t$, which capture the new characteristics of the object. The output $\mathbf{h}_t$ is passed into a convolutional decoder, denoted as *Decoder*, to get the full-resolution segmentation results $\hat{\mathbf{y}}_t$. Binary cross-entropy loss is computed between $\hat{\mathbf{y}}_t$ and $\mathbf{y}_t$ during training process. The entire model is trained end-to-end using back-propagation to learn parameters for the *Initializer* network, the *Encoder* and *Decoder* networks, and *ConvLSTM* network. Figure 2 illustrates our sequence learning algorithm for video object segmentation. The learning process can be formulated as follows:

$$\mathbf{c}_0, \mathbf{h}_0 = Initializer(\mathbf{x}_0, \mathbf{y}_0) \tag{1}$$

$$\tilde{\mathbf{x}}_t = Encoder(\mathbf{x}_t) \tag{2}$$

$$\mathbf{c}_t, \mathbf{h}_t = ConvLSTM(\tilde{\mathbf{x}}_t, \mathbf{c}_{t-1}, \mathbf{h}_{t-1}), \tag{3}$$

$$\hat{\mathbf{y}}_t = Decoder(\mathbf{h}_t) \tag{4}$$

$$\mathcal{L} = -(\mathbf{y_t} \log(\hat{\mathbf{y}}_\mathbf{t})) + ((1 - \mathbf{y_t}) \log(1 - \hat{\mathbf{y}}_\mathbf{t})) \tag{5}$$

4.3 Implementation Details

Model Structures. Both our *Initializer* and *Encoder* use VGG-16 [36] network structures. In particular, all the convolution layers and the first fully connected layer of VGG-16 are used as backbone for the two networks. The fully connected layer is transformed to a 1 × 1 convolution layer to make our model fully convolutional. On top of it, *Initializer* has two additional convolution layers with ReLU [28] activation to produce $\mathbf{c}_0$ and $\mathbf{h}_0$ respectively. Each convolution layer has 512 1 × 1 filters. The *Encoder* has one additional convolution layer with ReLU activation which has 512 1×1 filters. The VGG-16 layers of the *Initializer* and *Encoder* are initialized with pre-trained VGG-16 parameters while the other layers are randomly initialized by Xavier [15].

All the convolution operations of the *ConvLSTM* layer use 512 3 × 3 filters, initialized by Xavier. Sigmoid activation is used for gate outputs and ReLU is used for state outputs (empirically we find ReLU activation produces better results than tanh activation for our model). Following [22], we set the bias of the forget gate to be 1s at initialization.

The *Decoder* has five upsampling layers with 5 × 5 kernel size and 512, 256, 128, 64 and 64 filters respectively. The last layer of the *Decoder* produces segmentation results, which has one 5 × 5 filter with sigmoid activation. All the parameters are initialized by Xavier.

Training. Our algorithm is trained on the YouTube-VOS training set. At each training iteration, our algorithm first randomly samples an object and T (5–11) frames from a random training video sequence. Then the original RGB frames and annotations are resized to 256 × 448 for memory and speed concern. At the early stage of training, we only select frames with ground truth annotation as our training samples so that the training loss can be computed and backpropagated at each time step. When the training losses become stable, we added frames without annotations to training data. For those frames without ground truth annotations, loss is set to be 0. Adam [23] is used to train our network and the initial learning rate is set to 10^{-5}, and our model converges in 80 epochs.

Inference. Our offline-trained model is able to learn features for general object characteristics effectively. It is able to produce good segmentation results by directly applying it to a new test video with unseen categories. This is in contrast to recent state-of-the-art approaches, which have to fine-tune their models on each new test video over hundreds of iterations. In our experiments, we show that our algorithm without online learning can achieve comparable or better results compared to previous state of the arts with online learning, which implies much faster inference speed for practical applications. Neverthless, we find that the performance of our model can be further improved with online learning.

Online Learning. Given a test video, we generate random pairs of online training examples $\{(\mathbf{x}^0, \mathbf{y}^0), (\mathbf{x}^1, \mathbf{y}^1)\}$ through affine transformations from $(\mathbf{x}_0, \mathbf{y}_0)$. We treat $(\mathbf{x}^0, \mathbf{y}^0)$ as the initial frame and mask and $(\mathbf{x}^1, \mathbf{y}^1)$ as the first frame and ground truth mask. We then fine tune our *Initializer*, *Encoder* and *Decoder* networks on such randomly generated pairs. The parameters of *ConvLSTM* are fixed as it models long-term spatial-temporal dependency that should be independent of object categories.

5 Experiments

In this section, we first evaluate our algorithm and recent state-of-the-art algorithms on our YouTube-VOS dataset. Then we compare our results on the DAVIS 2016 validation dataset [32], which is an existing benchmark dataset for video object segmentation. Finally, we do an ablation study to explore the effect of data scale and model variants to our method.

5.1 Experiment Settings

We split the YouTube-VOS dataset of 3,252 videos into training (2,796), validation (134) and test (322) sets. To evaluate the generalization ability of existing approaches on unseen categories, the test set is further split into test-seen and test-unseen subsets. We first select 10 categories (*i.e. ant, bull riding, butterfly, chameleon, flag, jellyfish, kangaroo, penguin, slopestyle, snail*) as unseen categories during training and treat their videos as test-unseen set. The validation and test-seen subsets are created by sampling two and four videos per category, respectively. The rest of videos are the training set. We use the region similarity $\mathcal{J}$ and the contour accuracy $\mathcal{F}$ as the evaluation metrics as in [32].

5.2 YouTube-VOS

For fair comparison, we re-train previous methods (*i.e.* SegFlow [7], OSMN [49], MaskTrack [31], OSVOS [5] and OnAVOS [43]) on our training set with the same settings as our algorithm. One difference is that other methods leverage post-processing steps to achieve additional gains while our models do not.

The results are presented in Table 2. All the comparison methods use static image segmentation models and four of them (*i.e.* SegFlow, MaskTrack, OSVOS and OnAVOS) require online learning. Our algorithm leverages long-term spatial-temporal characteristics and achieves better performance even without online learinng (the second last row in Table 2), which effectively demonstrates the importance of long-term spatial-temporal information for video object segmentation. With online learning, our model is further improved and achieves around 8% absolute improvement over the best previous method OSVOS on $\mathcal{J}$ mean. Our method also outperforms previous methods on contour accuracy and decay rate with a large margin. Surprisingly, OnAVOS which is the best performing method on DAVIS does not achieve good results on our dataset. We believe the drastic appearance changes and complex motion patterns in our dataset makes the online adaptation fail in many cases. Figure 3 visualizes the changes of $\mathcal{J}$ mean over the duration of video sequences. Without online learning, our method is worse than online learning methods such as OSVOS at the first few frames since the object appearance usually has not changed too much from the initial frame and online learning is effective under such scenario. However, our method degrades slower than the other methods and starts to outperform OSVOS at around 25% of the videos, which demonstrates that our method

Table 2. Comparisons of our approach and other methods on YouTube-VOS test set. The results in each cell show the test results for seen/unseen categories. "OL" denotes online learning. The best results are highlighted in bold.

Method	$\mathcal{J}$ mean↑	$\mathcal{J}$ recall↑	$\mathcal{J}$ decay↓	$\mathcal{F}$ mean↑	$\mathcal{F}$ recall↑	$\mathcal{F}$ decay↓
SegFlow [7]	40.4/38.5	45.4/41.7	**7.2/8.4**	35.0/32.7	35.3/32.1	**6.9/9.1**
OSVOS [5]	59.1/58.8	66.2/64.5	17.9/19.5	63.7/63.9	69.0/67.9	20.6/23.0
MaskTrack [31]	56.9/60.7	64.4/69.6	13.4/16.4	59.3/63.7	66.4/73.4	16.8/19.8
OSMN [49]	54.9/52.9	59.7/57.6	10.2/14.6	57.3/55.2	60.8/58.0	10.4/13.8
OnAVOS [43]	55.7/56.8	61.6/61.5	10.3/9.4	61.3/62.3	66.0/67.3	13.1/12.8
Ours (w/o OL)	60.9/60.1	70.3/71.2	7.9/12.9	64.2/62.3	73.0/71.4	9.3/14.5
Ours (with OL)	**66.9/66.8**	**78.7/76.5**	10.2/9.5	**74.1/72.3**	**82.8/80.5**	12.6/13.4

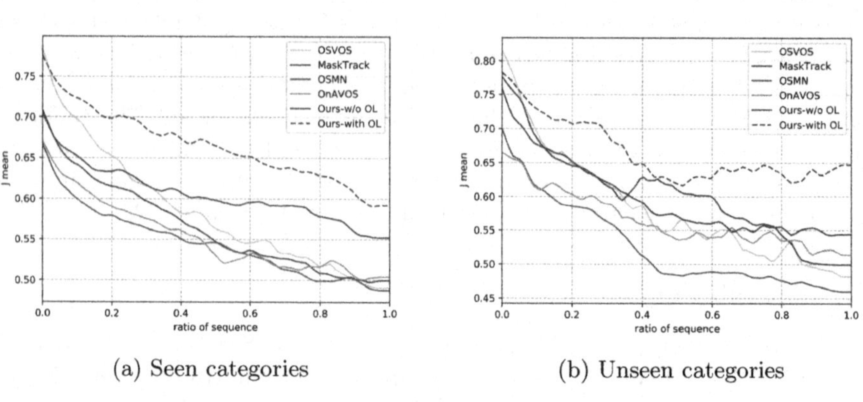

(a) Seen categories

(b) Unseen categories

Fig. 3. The changes of $\mathcal{J}$ mean values over the length of video sequences.

indeed propagates object segmentations more accurately over time than previous methods. With the help of online learning, our method outperforms previous methods in most parts of the video sequences, while maintaining a small decay rate.

Next we compare the generalization ability of existing methods on unseen categories in Table 2. Most methods have better performance on seen categories than unseen categories, which is expected. But the differences are not obvious, *e.g.* usually within 2% absolute differences on each metric. On one hand, it suggests that existing methods are able to alleviate the mismatch issue between training and test categories by approaches such as online learning. On the other hand, it also demonstrates the diverse training categories in YouTube-VOS helps different methods to generalize to new categories. Experiments on dataset scale in Sect. 5.4 further suggests the power of data scale on our model. Compared to other single-frame based methods, OSMN has a more obvious degradation on unseen categories since it does not use online learning. Our method without online learning does not have the issue since it leverages spatial-temporal information which is more robust to unseen categories. MaskTrack and OnAVOS

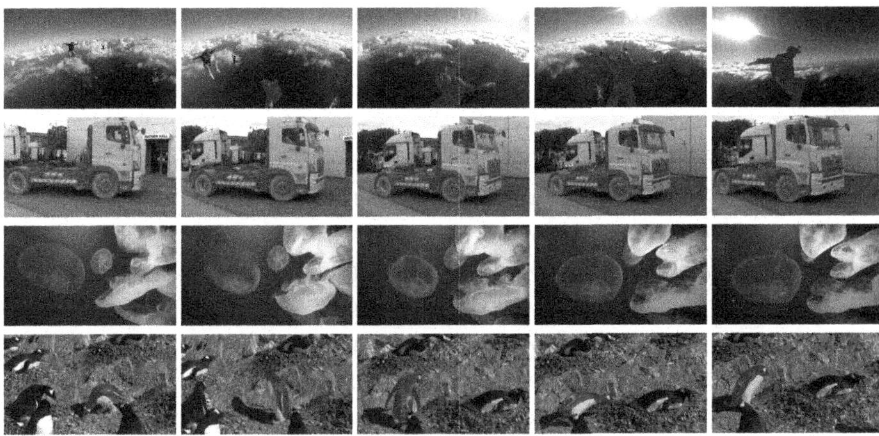

Fig. 4. Some visual results produced by our model without online learning on the YouTube-VOS test set. The first column shows the initial ground truth object segmentation (green color) while the second to the last column are predictions. (Color figure online)

have better performance on unseen than seen categories. We believe that they benefit from the guidance of previous segmentation or online adaption, which have advantages to deal with videos with slow motion. There are indeed several objects with slow motion in the unseen categories such as *snail* and *chameleon*.

Some test results produced by our model without online learning are visualized in Fig. 4. The first two rows are from seen categories while the last two rows are from unseen categories. In addition, each example represents some challenging cases in video object segmentation. For example, the person in the first example has large changes in appearance and illumination. The second and third examples both have multiple similar objects and heavy occlusions. The last example has strong camera motion and the penguin changes its pose frequently. Our model obtains accurate results on all the examples, which demonstrates the effectiveness of spatial-temporal features learned from large-scale training data.

5.3 DAVIS 2016

DAVIS 2016 is a popular prior benchmark dataset for video object segmentation. To evaluate our algorithm, we first fine-tune our pretrained model in 200 epochs on the DAVIS training set which contains 30 videos. The comparison results between our fine-tuned models and previous methods are shown in Table 3.

BVS and OFL are based on hand-crafted features and graphical models, while the rest are all deep learning based methods. Among the methods [5,31,43,49] using image segmentation frameworks, OnAVOS achieves the best performance. However, its online adaption process makes the inference pretty slow (~13 s per frame). Our model without online learning (the second last row) achieves comparable results to other online learning methods without post-processing (*e.g.*

Table 3. Comparisons of our approach and previous methods on the DAVIS 2016 dataset. Different components used in each algorithm are marked. "OL" denotes online learning. "PP" denotes post processing by CRF [24] or Boundary Snapping [5]. "OF" denotes optical flows. "RNN" denotes RNN and its variants.

Method	OL	PP	OF	RNN	Mean IoU(%)	Speed(s)
BVS [42]	-	✗	✗	-	60.0	0.37
OFL [26]	-	✓	✓	-	68.0	42.2
SegFlow [7]	✓	✓	✓	✗	76.1	7.9
MaskTrack [31]	✓	✓	✗	✗	79.7	12
OSVOS [5]	✓	✓	✗	✗	79.8	10
OnAVOS [43]	✓	✓	✗	✗	**85.7**	13
OSMN [49]	✗	✗	✗	✗	74.0	**0.14**
VPN [21]	✗	✗	✗	✗	70.2	0.63
ConvGRU [40]	✗	✓	✓	✓	75.9	20
Ours	✗	✗	✗	✓	76.5	0.16
Ours	✓	✗	✗	✓	79.1	9

Fig. 5. The comparison results between our model without online learning (upper row) and with online learning (bottom row). Each column shows predictions of the two models at the same frame.

MaskTrack 69.8% and OSVOS 77.4%), but with a significant speed-up (60 times faster). Previous methods using spatial-temporal information including SegFlow, VPN and ConvGRU get inferior results compared to ours. Among them, ConvGRU is most related to ours since it also incorporates RNN memory cells in its model. However, it is an unsupervised methods to only segment moving foreground, while our method can segment arbitrary objects given the mask supervision. Finally, online learning helps our model segment object boundary more accurately. Figure 5 shows such an example.

To demonstrate the scale limitation of existing datasets, we train our models on three different settings and evaluate on DAVIS 2016.

- Setting 1: We train our model from scratch on the 30 training videos.
- Setting 2: We train our model from scratch on the 30 training videos, plus all the videos from the SegTrackv2, JumpCut and YoutubeObjects datasets, which results in a total of 192 training videos.

Table 4. The effect of data scale on our algorithm. We use different portions of training data to train our models and evaluate on the YouTube-VOS test set.

Scale	$\mathcal{J}$ mean↑	$\mathcal{J}$ recall↑	$\mathcal{J}$ decay↓	$\mathcal{F}$ mean↑	$\mathcal{F}$ recall↑	$\mathcal{F}$ decay↓
25%	46.7/40.1	53.5/45.6	8.3/13.6	46.7/40.0	52.2/41.6	8.5/13.2
50%	51.5/50.3	59.2/58.8	10.3/13.1	51.8/50.2	59.5/55.8	11.1/13.3
75%	56.8/56.0	65.7/67.1	7.6/10.0	59.6/56.3	68.8/64.1	8.5/11.1
100%	60.9/60.1	70.3/71.2	7.9/12.9	64.2/62.3	73.0/71.4	9.3/14.5

- Setting 3: Following the idea of ConvGRU, we use a pretrained object segmentation model DeepLab [6] as our *Encoder* and train the other parts of our model on the 30 training videos.

Our models trained on setting 1 and 2 only get 51.3% and 51.9% mean IoU, which suggests that existing video object segmentation datasets do not have sufficient data to train our models. Therefore our YouTube-VOS dataset is one of the key elements for the success of our algorithm. In addition, there is only little improvement by adding videos from the SegTrackv2, JumpCut and YoutubeObjects datasets, which suggests that the small scale is not the only problem for previous datasets. For example, videos in the three datasets usually only have one main foreground. SegTrackv2 has low-resolution videos. The annotation of YoutubeObjects videos is not accurate along object boundaries, *etc.* However, our YouTube-VOS dataset is carefully created to avoid all these problems. Setting 3 is a common detour for existing methods to bypass the data-insufficiency issue, *i.e.* using pre-trained models on other large-scale datasets to reduce the parameters to be learned for their models. However, our model using this strategy gets even worse results (45.6%) than training from scratch, which suggests that spatial-temporal features cannot be trivially transfered from representations learned from static images. Thus large scale training data such as our dataset is essential to learn spatial-temporal representation for video object segmentation.

5.4 Ablation Study

In this subsection, we perform an ablation study on the YouTube-VOS dataset to evaluate different variants of our algorithm.

Dataset Scale. Since the dataset scale is very important to our models, we train several models on different portions of the training set of YouTube-VOS to explore the effect of data. Specifically, we randomly select 25%, 50% and 75% of the training set and retrain our models from scratch. The results are listed in Table 4. It can be seen that using only 25% of the training videos (∼700 videos) drops the performance almost 30% from the original model. In addition, the performance of the model on unseen categories are much worse than its performance on seen categories, which suggests that the model fails to capture general features for objectness. Since the scale of adding all the videos from all existing datasets is still much less than 700 videos, there is no doubt that existing datasets cannot satisfy the needs of our algorithm. With more and more training videos, our algorithm is improved rapidly, which well demonstrates the importance of large-scale data on our algorithm. We can see the trend of accuracies for 100% data still have not reached a plateau. We are working on collecting more data to explore the impact of data on the algorithm further.

Initializer Variants. The *Initializer* in our original model is a VGG-16 network which encodes a RGB frame and an object mask and outputs initial hidden states of *ConvLSTM*. We would like to explore using the object mask directly as the initial hidden states of *ConvLSTM*. We train an alternative model by removing the *Initializer* and directly using the object mask as the hidden states, *i.e.* the object mask is reshaped to match the size of the hidden states. The $\mathcal{J}$ mean of the adapted model are 45.1% on the seen categories and 38.6% on the unseen categories. This suggests that the object mask alone does not have enough information for localizing the object.

Encoder Variants. The *Encoder* in our original model receives a RGB frame as input at each time step. Alternatively, we can use the segmentation mask of the previous step as additional inputs to explicitly provide extra information to the model, similar to MaskTrack [31]. In this way, our *Initializer* and *Encoder* can be replaced with a single VGG-16 network since the inputs at every time step have same dimensions and similar meaning. However, such a framework potentially has the error-drifting issue since segmentation mistakes made at previous steps will be propagated to the current step.

In the early stage of training, the model is unable to predict good segmentation results. Therefore we use the ground truth annotation of the previous step as the input. Such strategy is known as teacher forcing [44] which can make the training faster. After the training losses become stable, we replace the ground truth annotation with the model's prediction of the previous step so that the model is forced to correct its own mistakes. Such a strategy is known as curriculum learning [2]. Empirically we find that both the two strategies are important to make the model to work well. The $\mathcal{J}$ mean results of the model are 59.4% on the seen categories and 60.7% on the unseen categories, which is similar to our original model.

6 Conclusion

In this work, we introduce the largest video object segmentation dataset (YouTube-VOS) to date. The new dataset, much larger than existing datasets in terms of number of videos and annotations, allows us to design a new deep learning algorithm to explicitly model long-term spatial-temporal dependency from videos for segmentation in an end-to-end learning framework. Thanks to the large scale dataset, our new algorithm achieves better or comparable results compared to existing state-of-the-art approaches. We believe the new dataset will foster research on video-based computer vision in general.

Acknowledgement. This research was partially supported by a gift funding from Snap Inc. and UIUC Andrew T. Yang Research and Entrepreneurship Award to Beckman Institute for Advanced Science & Technology, UIUC.

References

1. Abu-El-Haija, S., et al.: YouTube-8M: a large-scale video classification benchmark. arXiv preprint arXiv:1609.08675 (2016)
2. Bengio, S., Vinyals, O., Jaitly, N., Shazeer, N.: Scheduled sampling for sequence prediction with recurrent neural networks. In: Advances in Neural Information Processing Systems, pp. 1171–1179 (2015)
3. Bengio, Y., Simard, P., Frasconi, P.: Learning long-term dependencies with gradient descent is difficult. IEEE Trans. Neural Netw. **5**(2), 157–166 (1994)
4. Brox, T., Malik, J.: Object segmentation by long term analysis of point trajectories. In: Daniilidis, K., Maragos, P., Paragios, N. (eds.) ECCV 2010. LNCS, vol. 6315, pp. 282–295. Springer, Heidelberg (2010). https://doi.org/10.1007/978-3-642-15555-0_21
5. Caelles, S., Maninis, K.K., Pont-Tuset, J., Leal-Taixé, L., Cremers, D., Van Gool, L.: One-shot video object segmentation. In: CVPR (2017)
6. Chen, L., Papandreou, G., Kokkinos, I., Murphy, K., Yuille, A.L.: DeepLab: semantic image segmentation with deep convolutional nets, atrous convolution, and fully connected CRFs. In: IEEE T-PAMI, vol. 40, pp. 834–848 (2018)
7. Cheng, J., Tsai, Y.H., Wang, S., Yang, M.H.: SegFlow: joint learning for video object segmentation and optical flow. In: IEEE International Conference on Computer Vision (ICCV) (2017)
8. Cho, K., et al.: Learning phrase representations using RNN encoder-decoder for statistical machine translation. arXiv preprint arXiv:1406.1078 (2014)
9. Donahue, J., et al.: Long-term recurrent convolutional networks for visual recognition and description. In: CVPR (2015)
10. Dutt Jain, S., Xiong, B., Grauman, K.: FusionSeg: learning to combine motion and appearance for fully automatic segmentation of generic objects in videos. In: The IEEE Conference on Computer Vision and Pattern Recognition (CVPR), July 2017
11. Faktor, A., Irani, M.: Video segmentation by non-local consensus voting. In: BMVC (2014)
12. Fan, Q., Zhong, F., Lischinski, D., Cohen-Or, D., Chen, B.: JumpCut: non-successive mask transfer and interpolation for video cutout. ACM Trans. Graph. **34**(6) (2015)
13. Finn, C., Goodfellow, I., Levine, S.: Unsupervised learning for physical interaction through video prediction. In: Advances in Neural Information Processing Systems, pp. 64–72 (2016)
14. Galasso, F., Nagaraja, N.S., Cárdenas, T.J., Brox, T., Schiele, B.: A unified video segmentation benchmark: annotation, metrics and analysis. In: ICCV. IEEE (2013)
15. Glorot, X., Bengio, Y.: Understanding the difficulty of training deep feedforward neural networks. In: Proceedings of the Thirteenth International Conference on Artificial Intelligence and Statistics, pp. 249–256 (2010)
16. Heilbron, F.C., Escorcia, V., Ghanem, B., Niebles, J.C.: ActivityNet: a large-scale video benchmark for human activity understanding. In: 2015 IEEE Conference on Computer Vision and Pattern Recognition (CVPR), pp. 961–970. IEEE (2015)

17. Hochreiter, S., Schmidhuber, J.: Long short-term memory. Neural Comput. **9**(8), 1735–1780 (1997)
18. Hu, Y.T., Huang, J.B., Schwing, A.: MaskRNN: instance level video object segmentation. In: NIPS (2017)
19. Ilg, E., Mayer, N., Saikia, T., Keuper, M., Dosovitskiy, A., Brox, T.: FlowNet 2.0: evolution of optical flow estimation with deep networks. In: CVPR (2017)
20. Jain, S.D., Grauman, K.: Supervoxel-consistent foreground propagation in video. In: Fleet, D., Pajdla, T., Schiele, B., Tuytelaars, T. (eds.) ECCV 2014. LNCS, vol. 8692, pp. 656–671. Springer, Cham (2014). https://doi.org/10.1007/978-3-319-10593-2_43
21. Jampani, V., Gadde, R., Gehler, P.V.: Video propagation networks. In: CVPR (2017)
22. Jozefowicz, R., Zaremba, W., Sutskever, I.: An empirical exploration of recurrent network architectures. In: International Conference on Machine Learning, pp. 2342–2350 (2015)
23. Kingma, D.P., Ba, J.: Adam: a method for stochastic optimization. arXiv preprint arXiv:1412.6980 (2014)
24. Krähenbühl, P., Koltun, V.: Efficient inference in fully connected CRFs with Gaussian edge potentials. In: NIPS, pp. 109–117 (2011)
25. Li, F., Kim, T., Humayun, A., Tsai, D., Rehg, J.M.: Video segmentation by tracking many figure-ground segments. In: ICCV (2013)
26. Märki, N., Perazzi, F., Wang, O., Sorkine-Hornung, A.: Bilateral space video segmentation. In: CVPR (2016)
27. Nagaraja, N.S., Schmidt, F.R., Brox, T.: Video segmentation with just a few strokes. In: ICCV, pp. 3235–3243 (2015)
28. Nair, V., Hinton, G.E.: Rectified linear units improve restricted Boltzmann machines. In: Proceedings of the 27th International Conference on Machine Learning (ICML 2010), pp. 807–814 (2010)
29. Ochs, P., Malik, J., Brox, T.: Segmentation of moving objects by long term video analysis. IEEE Trans. Pattern Anal. Mach. Intell. **36**(6), 1187–1200 (2014)
30. Papazoglou, A., Ferrari, V.: Fast object segmentation in unconstrained video. In: 2013 IEEE International Conference on Computer Vision (ICCV), pp. 1777–1784. IEEE (2013)
31. Perazzi, F., Khoreva, A., Benenson, R., Schiele, B., Sorkine-Hornung, A.: Learning video object segmentation from static images. In: CVPR (2017)
32. Perazzi, F., Pont-Tuset, J., McWilliams, B., Van Gool, L., Gross, M., Sorkine-Hornung, A.: A benchmark dataset and evaluation methodology for video object segmentation. In: CVPR (2016)
33. Pont-Tuset, J., Perazzi, F., Caelles, S., Arbeláez, P., Sorkine-Hornung, A., Van Gool, L.: The 2017 davis challenge on video object segmentation. arXiv:1704.00675 (2017)
34. Revaud, J., Weinzaepfel, P., Harchaoui, Z., Schmid, C.: EpicFlow: edge-preserving interpolation of correspondences for optical flow. In: CVPR (2015)
35. Shelhamer, E., Long, J., Darrell, T.: Fully convolutional networks for semantic segmentation. IEEE Trans. Pattern Anal. Mach. Intell. **39**(4), 640–651 (2017)
36. Simonyan, K., Zisserman, A.: Very deep convolutional networks for large-scale image recognition. arXiv preprint arXiv:1409.1556 (2014)
37. Srivastava, N., Mansimov, E., Salakhudinov, R.: Unsupervised learning of video representations using LSTMs. In: International Conference on Machine Learning (2015)

38. Sutskever, I., Vinyals, O., Le, Q.V.: Sequence to sequence learning with neural networks. In: Advances in Neural Information Processing Systems, pp. 3104–3112 (2014)
39. Tokmakov, P., Alahari, K., Schmid, C.: Learning motion patterns in videos. In: CVPR (2017)
40. Tokmakov, P., Alahari, K., Schmid, C.: Learning video object segmentation with visual memory. In: ICCV (2017)
41. Tran, D., Bourdev, L., Fergus, R., Torresani, L., Paluri, M.: Learning spatiotemporal features with 3D convolutional networks. In: ICCV (2015)
42. Tsai, Y.H., Yang, M.H., Black, M.J.: Video segmentation via object flow. In: CVPR (2016)
43. Voigtlaender, P., Leibe, B.: Online adaptation of convolutional neural networks for video object segmentation. arXiv preprint arXiv:1706.09364 (2017)
44. Williams, R.J., Zipser, D.: A learning algorithm for continually running fully recurrent neural networks. Neural Comput. **1**(2), 270–280 (1989)
45. Xingjian, S., Chen, Z., Wang, H., Yeung, D.Y., Wong, W.K., Woo, W.C.: Convolutional LSTM network: a machine learning approach for precipitation nowcasting. In: Advances in Neural Information Processing Systems, pp. 802–810 (2015)
46. Xu, H., Gao, Y., Yu, F., Darrell, T.: End-to-end learning of driving models from large-scale video datasets. In: CVPR (2017)
47. Xu, N., Price, B., Cohen, S., Yang, J., Huang, T.: Deep grabcut for object selection. arXiv preprint arXiv:1707.00243 (2017)
48. Xu, N., Price, B., Cohen, S., Yang, J., Huang, T.S.: Deep interactive object selection. In: Proceedings of the IEEE Conference on Computer Vision and Pattern Recognition, pp. 373–381 (2016)
49. Yang, L., Xiong, X., Wang, Y., Yang, J., Katsaggelos, A.K.: Efficient video object segmentation via network modulation. In: CVPR (2018)

PPF-FoldNet: Unsupervised Learning of Rotation Invariant 3D Local Descriptors

Haowen Deng[1,2,3], Tolga Birdal[1,2(✉)], and Slobodan Ilic[1,2]

[1] Technische Universitat München, Munich, Germany
tolga.birdal@tum.de
[2] Siemens AG, Munich, Germany
[3] National University of Defense Technology, Changsha, China

Abstract. We present PPF-FoldNet for unsupervised learning of 3D local descriptors on pure point cloud geometry. Based on the folding-based auto-encoding of well known point pair features, PPF-FoldNet offers many desirable properties: it necessitates neither supervision, nor a sensitive local reference frame, benefits from point-set sparsity, is end-to-end, fast, and can extract powerful rotation invariant descriptors. Thanks to a novel feature visualization, its evolution can be monitored to provide interpretable insights. Our extensive experiments demonstrate that despite having six degree-of-freedom invariance and lack of training labels, our network achieves state of the art results in standard benchmark datasets and outperforms its competitors when rotations and varying point densities are present. PPF-FoldNet achieves 9% higher recall on standard benchmarks, 23% higher recall when rotations are introduced into the same datasets and finally, a margin of >35% is attained when point density is significantly decreased.

Keywords: 3D deep learning · Local features · Descriptors
Rotation invariance

1 Introduction

Local descriptors are one of the essential tools used in computer vision, easing the tasks of object detection, pose estimation, SLAM or image retrieval [23, 27]. While being well established in the 2D domain, 3D local features are still known to lack good discriminative power and repeatibility. With the advent of deep learning, many areas in computer vision shifted from hand crafted labor towards a problem specific end-to-end learning. Local features are of course no exception. Already in 2D, learned descriptors significantly outperform their engineered counterparts [28,49]. Thus, it was only natural for the scholars to tackle the task of 3D local feature extraction employing similar approaches [8,

Electronic supplementary material The online version of this chapter (https://doi.org/10.1007/978-3-030-01228-1_37) contains supplementary material, which is available to authorized users.

V. Ferrari et al. (Eds.): ECCV 2018, LNCS 11209, pp. 620–638, 2018.
https://doi.org/10.1007/978-3-030-01228-1_37

18, 51]. However, due to the inherent ambiguities and less informative nature of sole geometry, extracting 3D descriptors on point sets still poses an unsolved problem, even for learning-based methods.

Up until now, deep learning of local features in 3D has suffered from one or more of the following: (**a**) being supervised and requiring an abundant amount of labels in form of pairs, triplets or N-tuples [8, 51], (**b**) being sensitive to 6DoF rotations [8, 51], (**c**) involving significant hand-crafted input preparation [18] and (**d**) unsatisfactory performance [18, 30]. In this paper, we map out an elegant architecture to tackle all of these problems and present PPF-FoldNet: an unsupervised, high-accuracy, 6DoF transformation invariant, sparse and fast 3D local feature learning network. PPF-FoldNet operates directly on point sets, taking into account the point sparsity and permutation invariant set property, deals well with density variations, while significantly outperforming its rotation-variant counterparts even based on the standard benchmarks.

Our network establishes theoretical rotation invariance inspired by use a point pair feature (PPF) [3, 4, 8] encoding of the local 3D geometry into patches. In contrast to PPFNet [8], we do not incorporate the original points or normals into the encoding. The collection of these 4D PPFs are then sent to a FoldingNet-like end to end auto-encoder (AE) [48], trained to auto-reconstruct the PPFs, using a set distance. Our encoder is simpler than in FoldingNet and for decoding, we propose a similar folding scheme, where a low dimensional 2D grid lattice is folded onto a 4D PPF space and monitor the network evolution by a novel lossless visualization of the PPF space. Our overall architecture is based on PointNet [30] to achieve permutation invariance and to fully utilize the sparsity. Training our AE is far easier than training, for example, 3DMatch [51], because we do not need to sample pairs or triplets from a pre-annotated large dataset and we benefit from linear time complexity to the number of patches.

Extensive evaluations demonstrate that PPF-FoldNet outperforms the state of the art across the standard benchmarks in which severe rotations are avoided. When arbitrary rotations are introduced into the input, our descriptors outperform related approaches by a large margin including even the best competitor, Khoury et al.'s CGF [18]. Moreover, we report better performance as the input sparsifies, as well as good generalization properties. Our qualitative evaluations will uncover how our network operates and give valuable interpretations. In a nutshell, our contributions can be summarized as:

- An auto-encoder, that unifies a PointNet encoding with a FoldingNet decoder,
- Use of well established 4D PPFs in this modified auto-encoder to learn rotation invariant 3D local features without supervision.
- A novel look at the invariance of point pair features and derived from it, a new way of visualizing PPFs and monitoring the network progress.

2 Prior Art

Following their hand-crafted counterparts [10, 16, 34, 35, 40], 3D deep learning methods started to enjoy a deep-rooted history. Initial attempts to learn from 3D

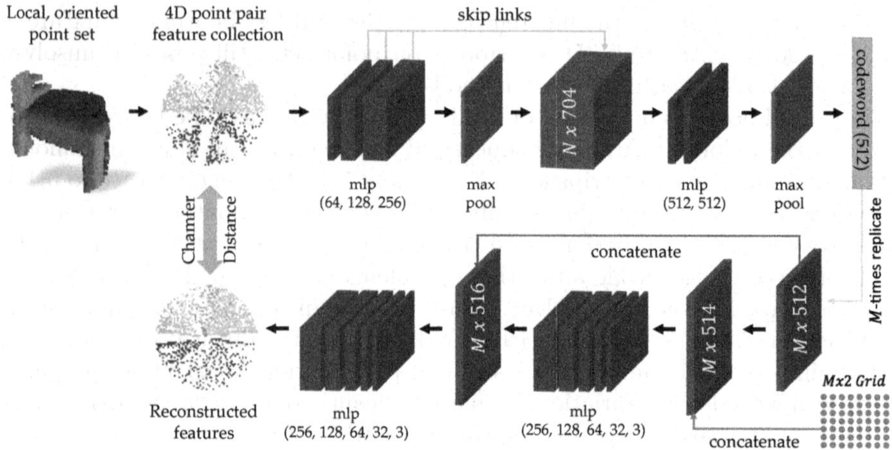

Fig. 1. PPF-FoldNet: The point pair feature folding network. The point cloud local patches are first converted into PPF representations, and then sent into the encoder to get compressed codewords. The decoder tries to reconstruct full PPFs from these codewords by folding. This forces the codewords to keep the most critical and discriminative information. The learned codewords are proven to be robust and effective as we will show across extensive evaluations.

data used the naive dense voxel grid representation [11,26,46,51]. While being straightforward extensions of 2D architectures, such networks did not perform as efficiently and robustly as 2D CNNs [21]. Hence, they are superseded by networks taking into account the spatial sparsity by replacing the dense grids with octrees [33,38,43] or kd-trees [20].

Another family of works acknowledges that 3D surfaces live on 2D submanifolds and seek to learn projections rather than the space of actual input. A reduction of dimension to two makes it possible to benefit from developments in 2D CNNs such as Res-Nets [13]: LORAX [9] proposes a *super-point* to depth map projection. Kehl et al. [17] operate on the RGB-D patches that are natural projections onto the camera plane. Huang et al. [15] anchor three local cameras to each 3D keypoint and collect multi-channel projections to learn a semi-global representation. Cao et al. [7] use spherical projections to aid object classification. Tatarchenko et al. propose convolutions in the tangent space as a way of operating on the local 2D projection [39].

Point clouds can be treated as graphs by associating edges among neighbors. This paves the way to the appliance of graph convolutional networks [25]. FoldingNet [48] employs graph-based encoding layers. Wang et al. [44] tackle the segmentation tasks on point sets via graph convolutions networks (GCNs), while Qi et al. [32] apply GCNs to RGB-D semantic segmentation. While showing a promising direction, the current efforts involving graphs on 3D tasks are still supervised, try to imitate CNNs and cannot really outperform their unstructured point-processing counterparts.

Despite all developments in 3D deep learning, there are only a handful of methods that explicitly learn generic local descriptors on 3D data. One of the first methods that learns 3D feature matching, also known as correspondence, is 3DMatch [51]. It uses dense voxel grids to summarize the local geometry and learning is performed via contrastive loss. 3DMatch is weakly supervised by task, does not learn generic descriptors, and is not invariant to rotations. PointNet [30] and PointNet++ [31] work directly on the unstructured point clouds and minimize a multi-task loss, resulting in local and global features. Similar to [51], invariance is not of concern and weak supervision is essential. CGF [18] combines a hand-crafted input preparation with a deep dimensionality-reduction and still uses supervision. However, the input features are not learned but only the embedding. PPFNet [8] improves over all these methods by incorporating global context, but still fails to achieve full invariance and expects supervision.

2.1 Background

From all of the aforementioned developments, we will now pay particular attention to three: PointNet, FoldingNet and PPFNet which combined, give our network its name.

PointNet [30]. Direct consumption of unstructured point input in the form of a set within deep networks began by PointNet. Qi et al. proposed to use a point-wise multi layer perceptron (MLP) and aggregated individual feature maps into a global feature by a permutation-invariant max pooling. Irrespective of the input ordering, PointNet can generate per-point local descriptors as well as a global one, which can be combined to solve different problems such as keypoint extraction, 3D segmentation or classification. While not being the most powerful network, it clearly sets out a successful architecture giving rise to many successive studies [2,29,31,36].

FoldingNet [48]. While PointNet can work with point clouds, it is still a supervised architecture, and constructing unsupervised extensions like an auto-encoder on points is non-trivial as the upsampling step is required to interpolate sets [31,50]. Yang et al. offer a different perspective and instead of resorting to costly voxelizations [45], propose *folding*, as a strong decoder alternative. Folding warps an underlying low-dimensional grid towards a desired set, specifically a 3D point cloud. Compared to other unsupervised methods, including GANs [45], FoldingNet achieves superior performance in common tasks such as classification and therefore, in PPF-FoldNet we benefit from its decoder structure, though in a slightly altered form.

PPFNet [8]. Proposes to learn local features informed by the global context of the scene. To do so, an N-tuple loss is designed, seeking to find correspondences jointly between all patches of two fragments. Features learned in this way are shown to be superior than prior methods and PPFNet is reported to be the state-of-the-art local feature descriptor. However, even if Deng et al. stress the importance of learning permutation and rotation invariant features, the authors only manage to improve the resilience to Euclidean isometries slightly by concatenating PPF to the point set. Moreover, the proposed N-tuple loss still requires supervision. Our work improves on both of these aspects: It is capable of using PPFs only and operating without supervision.

3 PPF-FoldNet

PPF-FoldNet is based on the idea of auto-encoding a rotation invariant but powerful representation of the point set (PPFs), such that the learned low dimensional embedding can be truly invariant. This is different to training the network with many possible rotations of the same input and forcing the output to be a canonical reconstruction. The latter would both be approximate and much harder to learn. Input to our network are local patches which, unlike PPFNet, are individually auto-encoded. The latent low dimensional vector of the auto-encoder, *codeword*, is used as the local descriptor attributed to the point around which the patch is extracted.

3.1 Local Patch Representation

Our input point cloud is a set of oriented points $\mathbf{X} = \{\mathbf{x}_i \in \mathbb{R}^6\}$, meaning that each point is decorated with a local normal (e.g. tangent space) $\mathbf{n} \in \mathbb{R}^3$: $\mathbf{x} = \{\mathbf{p}, \mathbf{n}\} \in \mathbb{R}^6$. A local patch is a subset of the input $\boldsymbol{\Omega}_{\mathbf{x}_r} \subset \mathbf{X}$ center around a reference point $\mathbf{x}_r$. We then encode this patch as a collection of pair features, computed between a central reference and all the other points:

$$\mathbf{F}_{\boldsymbol{\Omega}} = \{\mathbf{f}(\mathbf{x}_r, \mathbf{x}_1) \cdots \mathbf{f}(\mathbf{x}_r, \mathbf{x}_i) \cdots \mathbf{f}(\mathbf{x}_r, \mathbf{x}_N)\} \in \mathbb{R}^{4 \times N-1}, \, i \neq r \tag{1}$$

The features between any pair (point pair features) are then defined to be a map $\mathbf{f} : \mathbb{R}^{12} \rightarrow \mathbb{R}^4$ sending two oriented points to three angles and the pair distance:

$$\mathbf{f} : (\mathbf{x}_r^T, \mathbf{x}_i^T)^T \rightarrow (\angle(\mathbf{n}_r, \mathbf{d}), \angle(\mathbf{n}_i, \mathbf{d}), \angle(\mathbf{n}_r, \mathbf{n}_i), \|\mathbf{d}\|_2)^T \tag{2}$$

$\mathbf{d} = \mathbf{p}_r - \mathbf{p}_i$. An angle computation for non-normalized vectors is given in [3]. Such encoding of the local geometry resembles that of PPFNet [8], but differs in the fact that we ignore the points and normals as they are dependent on the orientation and local reference frame. We instead use pure point pair features, thereby avoiding a canonical frame computation. Note that the dimensionality of this feature is still irreducible without data loss.

Proposition 1. *PPF representation* $\mathbf{f}$ *around* $\mathbf{x}_r$ *explains the original oriented point pair up to a rotation and reflection about the normal of the reference point.*

Proof. Let us consider two oriented points $\mathbf{x}_1$ and $\mathbf{x}_2$. We can always write the components of the associated point pair feature $\mathbf{f}(\mathbf{x}_1, \mathbf{x}_2)$ as follows:

$$\mathbf{n}_1^T \mathbf{n}_2 = f_1 \qquad \mathbf{n}_1^T \mathbf{d}_n = f_2 \qquad \mathbf{n}_2^T \mathbf{d}_n = f_3 \tag{3}$$

where $\mathbf{d}_n = \mathbf{d}/\|\mathbf{d}\|$. We now try to recover the original pair given its features. First, it is possible to write:

$$\begin{bmatrix} \mathbf{n}_1^T \\ \mathbf{n}_2^T \\ \mathbf{d}_n^T \end{bmatrix} \begin{bmatrix} \mathbf{n}_1 & \mathbf{n}_2 & \mathbf{d}_n \end{bmatrix} = \begin{bmatrix} 1 & f_1 & f_2 \\ f_1 & 1 & f_3 \\ f_2 & f_3 & 1 \end{bmatrix} \tag{4}$$

given that all vectors are of unit length. In matrix notation, Eq. 4 can be written as $\mathbf{A}^T\mathbf{A} = \mathbf{K}$. Then, by singular value decomposition, $\mathbf{K} = \mathbf{USV}^T$ and thus $\mathbf{A} = \mathbf{US}^{1/2}\mathbf{V}^T$. Note that, any orthogonal matrix (rotation and reflection) $\mathbf{R}$ can now be applied to $\mathbf{A}$ without changing the outcome: $(\mathbf{RA})^T\mathbf{RA} = \mathbf{A}^T\mathbf{R}^T\mathbf{RA} = \mathbf{A}^T\mathbf{A} = \mathbf{K}$. Hence, such decomposition is up to finite-dimensional linear isometries: rotations and reflections. Since we know that the local patch is centered at the reference point $\mathbf{p}_r = \mathbf{0}$, we are free to choose an $\mathbf{R}$ such that the normal vector of $\mathbf{p}_r$ ($\mathbf{n}_r$) is aligned along one of the canonical axes, say $+\mathbf{z} = [0, 0, 1]^T$ (freely chosen):

$$\mathbf{R} = \mathbf{I} + [\mathbf{v}]_x + [\mathbf{v}_x]^2 \frac{1 - n_r^z}{\|v\|} \tag{5}$$

where $\mathbf{v} = \mathbf{n}_r \times \mathbf{z}$, n_r^z is the z component of $\mathbf{n}_r$ and $\mathbf{I}$ is identity. $[\cdot]_x$ denotes skew symmetric cross product matrix. Because now $\mathbf{Rn}_r = \mathbf{z}$, any rotation θ and reflection ϕ about $\mathbf{z}$ would result in the same vector $\mathbf{z} = \mathbf{R}_z(\theta, \phi)\mathbf{z}$, $\forall\theta, \phi \in \mathbb{R}$. Any paired point can then be found in the canonical frame, uniquely up to two parameters as $\mathbf{p}_r \leftarrow \|\mathbf{d}\|\mathbf{R}_z(\theta.\phi)\mathbf{Rd}_n$, $\mathbf{n}_r \leftarrow \mathbf{R}_z(\theta, \phi)\mathbf{Rn}_r$. □

In the case where reflections are ignored (as they are unlikely to happen in a 3D world), this leaves a single degree of freedom, rotation angle around the normal. Also note once again that for the given local representation, the reference point $\mathbf{p}_r$ is common to all the point pairs.

Visualizing PPFs. PPFs exist in a 4D space and thus it is not trivial to visualize them. While simple solutions such as PCA would work, we prefer a more geometrically meaningful and simpler solution. Proposition 1 allows us to compute a signature of a set of point pairs by orienting the vectors $(\mathbf{n}_1, \mathbf{n}_2, \mathbf{d})$ individually for all points in order to align the difference vectors $\{\mathbf{d}_i\}$ with the $x - z$ plane by choosing an appropriate $\mathbf{R}_z(\theta.\phi)$. Such a transformation would not alter the features as shown. In this way, the paired points can be transformed onto a common plane (image), where the location is determined by the difference vector, in polar coordinates. The normal of the second point would not lie in this plane but can be encoded as colors in that image. Hence, it is possible to obtain a 2D visualization, without any data loss, i.e. all components of the vector contribute to the visualization. In Fig. 2 we provide a variety of local patch and PPF visualizations from the datasets of concern.

3.2 PPF Auto-Encoder and Folding

PPF-FoldNet employs a PointNet-like encoder with skip-links and a FoldingNet-like decoding scheme. It is designed to operate on 4D-PPFs, as summarized in Fig. 1.

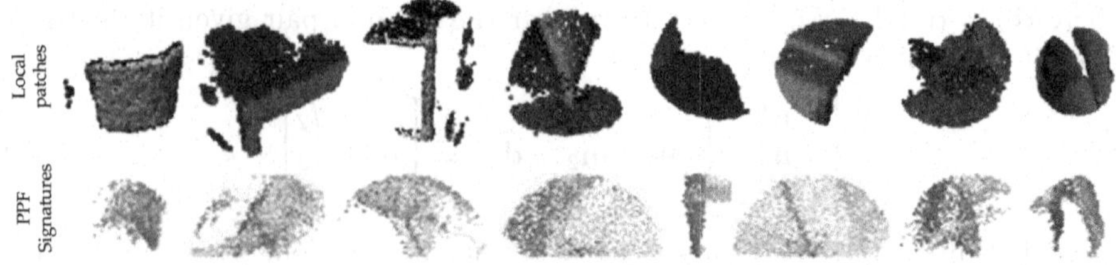

Fig. 2. Visualisation of some local patches and their correspondent PPF signatures. (Color figure online)

Encoder. The input to our network, and thus to the encoder, is $\mathbf{F}_{\Omega}$, a local PPF representation, as in Sect. 3.1. A three-layer, point-wise MLP (Multi Layer Perceptron) follows the input layer and subsequently a max-pooling is performed to aggregate the individual features into a global one, similar to PointNet [30]. The low level features are then concatenated with this global feature using skip-links. This results in a more powerful representation. Another two-layer MLP finally redirects these features to a final encoding, the codeword, which is of dimension 512.

Proposition 2. *The encoder structure of PPF-FoldNet is permutation invariant.*

Sketch of the Proof. The encoder is composed of per-data-point functions (MLP), RELU layers and max-pooling, all of which either do not affect the point order or are individually shown to be permutation invariant [30, 48]. Moreover, it is shown that composition of functions is also invariant [48] and so is our encoder. We refer the reader to the references for further details. □

In summary, altering the order of the PPF set will not affect the learned representation.

Decoder. Our decoder tries to reconstruct the whole set of point PPFs using a single codeword, which in return, also forces the codeword to be informative and distill the most distinctive information from the high-dimensional input space. However, inspired by FoldingNet, instead of trying to upsample or interpolate point sets, the decoder will try to deform a low-dimensional grid structure guided by the codeword. Each grid point is concatenated to a replica of the codeword, resulting in an $M \times 514$ vector as input to what is referred as *folding operation* [48]. Folding can be a highly non-linear operation and is thus performed by two consecutive MLPs: the first folding results in a deformed grid, which is appended once again to the codewords and propagates through the second MLP, reconstructing the input PPFs. Moreover, in contrast to FoldingNet [48], we try to reconstruct a higher dimensional set, 4D vs 3D (2D manifold); we are better off using a deeper MLP - 5-layer as opposed to the 3-layer of [48].

Other than simplifying and strengthening the decoding, the folding is also beneficial in making the network interpretable. For instance, it is possible to monitor the grid during subsequent iterations and envisage how the network evolves.

To do so, Sect. 4.4 will trace the PPF sets by visualizing them as described in Sect. 3.1.

Chamfer Loss. Note that as size of the grid M, is not necessarily the same as the size of the input N, and the correspondences in 4D PPF space are lost when it comes to evaluating the loss. This requires a distance computation between two unequal cardinality point pair feature sets, which we measure via the well known Chamfer metric:

$$d(\mathbf{F}, \hat{\mathbf{F}}) = \max\left\{ \frac{1}{|\mathbf{F}|} \sum_{\mathbf{f}\in\mathbf{F}} \min_{\hat{\mathbf{f}}\in\hat{\mathbf{F}}} \|\mathbf{f} - \hat{\mathbf{f}}\|_2, \; \frac{1}{|\hat{\mathbf{F}}|} \sum_{\mathbf{f}\in\hat{\mathbf{F}}} \min_{\mathbf{f}\in\mathbf{F}} \|\mathbf{f} - \hat{\mathbf{f}}\|_2 \right\} \tag{6}$$

where $\hat{}$ operator refers to the reconstructed (estimated) set.

Implementation Details. PPF-FoldNet uses Tensorflow framework [1]. The initial values of all variables are initialized randomly by Xavier's algorithm. Global loss is minimized with an ADAM optimizer [19]. Learning rate starts at 0.001 and exponentially decays after every 10 epochs, truncated at 0.0001. We use batches of size 32.

4 Experimental Evaluation

4.1 Datasets and Preprocessing

To fully drive the network towards learning varieties of local 3D geometries and gain robustness to different noises present in real data, we use the 3DMatch Benchmark Dataset [51]. This dataset is a large ensemble of the existing ones such as Analysis-by-Synthesis [41], 7-Scenes [37], SUN3D [47], RGB-D Scenes v.2 [22] and Halber and Funkhouser [12]. It contains 62 scenes in total, and we reserve 54 of them for training and validation. 8 are for benchmarking. 3DMatch already provided fragments fused from 50 consecutive depth frames of the 8 test scenes, and we follow the same pipeline to generate fragments from the training scenes. Test fragments lack the color information and therefore we resort to using only the 3D shape. This also makes our network insensitive to illumination changes.

Prior to operation, we downsample the fused fragments with spatial uniformity [5] and compute surface normals using [14] in a 17-point neighborhood. A reference point and its neighbors within 30 cm vicinity form a local patch. The number of points in a local patch is thus flexible, which makes it difficult to organize data into regular batches. To facilitate training as well as to increase the representation robustness to noises and different point densities, each local patch is down-sampled. For a fair comparison with other methods in the literature, we use 2048 points, but also provide an extended version that uses 5K since we are not memory bound, as for example, PPFNet [8] is. The preparation stage ends with the PPFs calculated for the assembled local patches.

4.2 Accuracy Assessment Techniques

Let us assume that a pair of fragments $\mathbf{P} = \{\mathbf{p}_i \in \mathbb{R}^3\}$ and $\mathbf{Q} = \{\mathbf{q}_i \in \mathbb{R}^3\}$ are aligned by an associated rigid transformation $\mathbf{T} \in SE(3)$, resulting in a certain overlap. We then define a non-linear feature function $g(\cdot)$ for mapping from input points to feature space, and in our case, this summarizes the PPF computation and encoding as a codeword. The feature for point $\mathbf{p}_i$ is $g(\mathbf{p}_i)$, and $g(\mathbf{P})$ is the pool of features extracted for the points in $\mathbf{P}$. To estimate the rigid transformation between $\mathbf{P}$ and $\mathbf{Q}$, the typical approach finds a set of matching pairs in each fragment and associates the correspondences. The inter point pair set $\mathbf{M}$ is formed by the pairs $(\mathbf{p}, \mathbf{q})$ that lie mutually close in the feature space by applying nearest neighbor search NN:

$$\mathbf{M} = \{\{\mathbf{p}_i, \mathbf{q}_i\}, g(\mathbf{p}_i) = NN(g(\mathbf{q}_i), g(\mathbf{P})), \, g(\mathbf{q}_i) = NN(g(\mathbf{p}_i), g(\mathbf{Q}))\,\} \tag{7}$$

True matches set $\mathbf{M}_{gnd}$ is the set of point pairs with a Euclidean distance below a threshold τ_1 under ground-truth transformation $\mathbf{T}$.

$$\mathbf{M}_{gnd} = \{\{\mathbf{p}_i, \mathbf{q}_i\} : (\mathbf{p}_i, \mathbf{q}_i) \in \mathbf{M}, ||\mathbf{p}_i - \mathbf{T}\mathbf{q}_i||_2 < \tau_1\} \tag{8}$$

We now define an inlier ratio for $\mathbf{M}$ as the percentage of true matches in $\mathbf{M}$ as $r_{in} = |\mathbf{M}_{gnd}|/|\mathbf{M}|$. To successfully estimate the rigid transformation based on $\mathbf{M}$ via registration algorithms, r_{in} needs to be greater than τ_2. For example, in a common RANSAC pipeline, achieving 99.9% confidence in the task of finding a subset with at least 3 correct matches $\mathbf{M}$, with an inlier ratio $\tau_2 = 5\%$ requires at least 55258 iterations. Theoretically, given $r_{in} > \tau_2$, it is highly probable a reliable local registration algorithm would work, regardless of the robustifier. Therefore instead of using the local registration results to judge the quality of features, which would be both slow and not very straightforward, we define $\mathbf{M}$ with $r_{in} > \tau_2$ votes for a correct match of two fragments.

Each scene in the benchmark contains a set of fragments. Fragment pairs $\mathbf{P}$ and $\mathbf{Q}$ having an overlap above 30% under the ground-truth alignment are considered to match. Together they form the set of fragment pairs $\mathbf{S} = \{(\mathbf{P}, \mathbf{Q})\}$ that are used in evaluations. The quality of features is measured by the recall R of fragment pairs matched in $\mathbf{S}$:

$$R = \frac{1}{|\mathbf{S}|} \sum_{i=1}^{|\mathbf{S}|} \mathbb{1}\left(r_{in}(\mathbf{S}_i = (\mathbf{P}_i, \mathbf{Q}_i)) > \tau_2 \right) \tag{9}$$

4.3 Results

Feature Quality Evaluation. We first compare the performance of our features against the well-accepted works on the 3DMatch benchmark with $\tau_1 = 10$ cm and $\tau_2 = 5\%$. Table 1 tabulates the findings. The methods selected for comparison comprise 3 handcrafted features (Spin Images [16], SHOT [35], FPFH [34]) and 4 state-of-the-art deep learning based methods (3DMatch [51], CGF [18],

Table 1. Our results on the standard 3DMatch benchmark. *Red Kitchen* data is from 7-scenes [37] and the rest imported from SUN3D [47].

	Spin image [16]	SHOT [35]	FPFH [34]	3DMatch [51]	CGF [18]	PPFNet [8]	FoldNet [48]	Ours	Ours-5K
Kitchen	0.1937	0.1779	0.3063	0.5751	0.4605	**0.8972**	0.5949	0.7352	0.7866
Home 1	0.3974	0.3718	0.5833	0.7372	0.6154	0.5577	0.7179	0.7564	**0.7628**
Home 2	0.3654	0.3365	0.4663	**0.7067**	0.5625	0.5913	0.6058	0.625	0.6154
Hotel 1	0.1814	0.208	0.2611	0.5708	0.4469	0.5796	0.6549	0.6593	**0.6814**
Hotel 2	0.2019	0.2212	0.3269	0.4423	0.3846	0.5769	0.4231	0.6058	**0.7115**
Hotel 3	0.3148	0.3889	0.5000	0.6296	0.5926	0.6111	0.6111	0.8889	**0.9444**
Study	0.0548	0.0719	0.1541	0.5616	0.4075	0.5342	**0.7123**	0.5753	0.6199
MIT Lab	0.1039	0.1299	0.2727	0.5455	0.3506	**0.6364**	0.5844	0.5974	0.6234
Average	0.2267	0.2382	0.3589	0.5961	0.4776	0.6231	0.6130	0.6804	**0.7182**

PPFNet [8], FoldingNet [48]). Note that FoldingNet has never been tested on local descriptor extraction before. It is apparent that, overall, our PPF-FoldNet could match far more fragment pairs in comparison to the other methods, except for scenes *Kitchen* and *Home*, where PPFNet and 3DMatch achieve a higher recall respectively. In all the other cases, PPF-FoldNet outperforms the state of the art by a large margin, >9% on average. PPF-FoldNet has a recall of 68.04% when using 2K sample points (the same as PPFNet), while PPFNet remains on 62.32%. Moreover, because PPF-FoldNet has no memory bottleneck, it can achieve an additional 3% improvement in comparison with the 2K version, when 5K points are used. Interestingly, FPFH is also constructed from a type of PPF features [34], but in a form of manual histogram summarization. Compared to FPFH, PPF-FoldNet has 32.15% and 35.93% higher recall using 2K and 5K points respectively. It demonstrates the unprecedented strength of our advanced method in compressing the PPFs. In order to optimally reconstruct PPFs in the decoder, the network forces the bottleneck codeword to be compact as well as distilling the most critical and distinctive information in PPFs.

Table 2. Our results on the rotated 3DMatch benchmark. *Red Kitchen* data is from 7-scenes [37] and the rest imported from SUN3D [47].

	Spin image [16]	SHOT [35]	FPFH [34]	3DMatch [51]	CGF [18]	PPFNet [8]	FoldNet [48]	Ours	Ours-5K
Kitchen	0.1779	0.1779	0.2905	0.004	0.4466	0.002	0.0178	0.7352	**0.7885**
Home 1	0.4487	0.3526	0.5897	0.0128	0.6667	0.0000	0.0321	0.7692	**0.7821**
Home 2	0.3413	0.3365	0.4712	0.0337	0.5288	0.0144	0.0337	0.6202	**0.6442**
Hotel 1	0.1814	0.2168	0.3009	0.0044	0.4425	0.0044	0.0133	0.6637	**0.6770**
Hotel 2	0.1731	0.2404	0.2981	0.0000	0.4423	0.0000	0.0096	0.6058	**0.6923**
Hotel 3	0.3148	0.3333	0.5185	0.0096	0.6296	0.0000	0.0370	0.9259	**0.963**
Study	0.0582	0.0822	0.1575	0.0000	0.4178	0.0000	0.0171	0.5616	**0.6267**
MIT Lab	0.1169	0.1299	0.2857	0.026	0.4156	0.0000	0.0260	0.6104	**0.6753**
Average	0.2265	0.2337	0.364	0.0113	0.4987	0.0026	0.0233	0.6865	**0.7311**

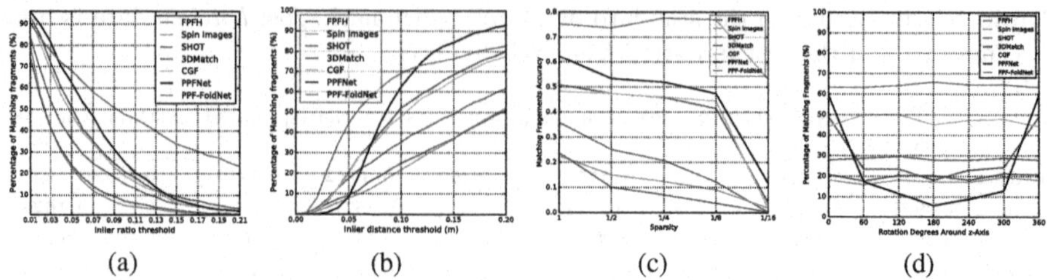

(a) (b) (c) (d)

Fig. 3. Evaluations on 3DMatch benchmark: (a) Results of different methods under varying inlier ratio threshold (b) Results of different methods under varying point distance threshold (c) Evaluating robustness again point density (d) Evaluations against rotations around z-axis

To illustrate that parameters in the evaluation metric are not tuned for our own good, we also repeat the experiments with different τ_1 and τ_2 values. The results are shown in Fig. 3(a) and (b). In Fig. 3(a), τ_1 is fixed at 10 cm, τ_2 increases gradually from 1% to 20%. When τ_2 is above 4%, PPF-FoldNet always has a higher recall than the other methods. Below 4%, some other methods may obtain a higher recall but this is too strict for most of the registration algorithms anyway. It is further noteworthy that when τ_2 is set to 20%, the point where PPF-FoldNet still gets a recall above 20%, the performance of the other methods falls below 5%. This justifies that PPF-FoldNet is capable of generating many more sets of matching points with a high inlier ratio r_{in}. This offers a tremendous benefit for the registration algorithms. In Fig. 3(b), τ_2 is fixed at 5%, τ_1 increases gradually from 0 cm to 20 cm. When τ_1 is smaller than 12 cm, PPF-FoldNet consistently generates higher recall. This finding indicates that PPF-FoldNet matches more point pairs with a small distance error in the Euclidean space, which could efficiently decrease the rigid transformation estimation errors.

Tests on Rotation Invariance. To demonstrate the outstanding rotation-invariance property of PPF-FoldNet, we take random fragments out of the evaluation set and gradually rotate them around the z-axis from 60° to 360° in steps of 60°. The matching results are shown in Fig. 3(d). As expected, both PPFNet and 3DMatch perform poorly as they operate on rotation-variant input representations. Hand crafted features or CGF also demonstrate robustness to rotations thanks to the reliance on the local reference frame (LRF). However, PPF-FoldNet stands out as the best approach with a much higher recall which furthermore does not require computation of local reference frames.

To further test how those methods perform under situations with severe rotations, we rotate all the fragments in 3DMatch benchmark with randomly sampled axes and angles over the whole rotation space, and introduce a new benchmark – *Rotated 3DMatch Benchmark*. The same evaluation is once again conducted on this new benchmark. Keeping the accuracy evaluations identical, our results are shown in Table 2. 3DMatch and PPFNet completely failed under this new benchmark because of the variables introduced by large rotations. Once again, PPF-FoldNet, surpasses all other methods, achieving the best results in all the scenes, predominates the runner-up CGF by large margins of 18.78% and 23.24% respectively when using 2K and 5K points.

Sparsity Evaluation. Thanks to the sparse representation of our input, PPF-FoldNet is also robust in respect of the changes in point cloud density and noise. Figure 3(c) shows the performance of different methods when we gradually decrease the points in the fragment from 100% to only 6.25%. We can see that PPF-FoldNet is least affected by the decrease in point cloud density. In particular, when only 6.25% points are left in the fragments, the recall for PPF-FoldNet is still greater than 50% while PPFNet remains around 12% and the other methods almost fail. The results of PPFNet and PPF-FoldNet together demonstrate that PPF representation offers more robustness in respect of point densities, which is a common problem existing in many point cloud representations.

Table 3. Accuracy comparison of different PPF representations.

	Kitchen	Home 1	Home 2	Hotel 1	Hotel 2	Hotel 3	Study	MIT Lab	Average
PPFH	0.534	0.622	0.486	0.341	0.346	0.574	0.233	0.351	0.436
Bobkov1	0.514	0.635	0.510	0.403	0.433	0.611	0.281	0.481	0.483
Our-PPF	0.506	0.635	0.495	0.350	0.385	0.667	0.267	0.403	0.463

Can PPF-FoldNet Operate with Different PPF Constructions? We now study 3 identical networks, trained for 3 different PPF formulations: ours, PPFH (the PPF used in FPFH [34]) and Bobkov1 et al. [6]. The latter has an added component of *occupancy ratio* based on grid space. We use a subset of 3DMatch benchmark to train all networks for a fixed number of iterations and test on the rotated fragments. Table 3 presents our findings: all features perform similarly. Thus, we do not claim the superiority of our PPF representation, but stress that it is simple, easy to compute, intuitive and easy to visualize. Due to the voxelization, *Bobkov1* is significantly slower than the other methods, and due to the lack of an LRF, our PPF is faster than *PPFH*'s. Using stronger pair primitives would favor PPF-FoldNet as our network is agnostic to the PPF construction.

Runtime. We run our algorithm on a machine loaded with NVIDIA TitanX Pascal GPU and an Intel Core i7 3.2 GHz CPU. On this hardware, computing features of an entire fragment via FPFH [34] takes 31.678 s, whereas PPF-FoldNet achieves a 10× speed-up with 3.969 s, despite having similar theoretical complexity. In particular, our input preparation for PPF extraction runs in 2.616 s, and the inference in 1.353. This is due to (1) PPF-FoldNet requiring only a single pass over the input, (2) our efficient network accelerated on GPU powered Tensorflow.

Fig. 4. Qualitative results of matching across different fragments and for different methods. When severe transformations are present, only hand-crafted algorithms, CGF and our method achieves satisfactory matches. However, for PPF-FoldNet, the number of matches are significantly larger.

4.4 Qualitative Evaluations

Visualizing the Matching Result. From the quantitative results, PPF-FoldNet is expected to have better and more correct feature matches, especially when arbitrary rigid transformations are applied. To show this visually, we run dif-

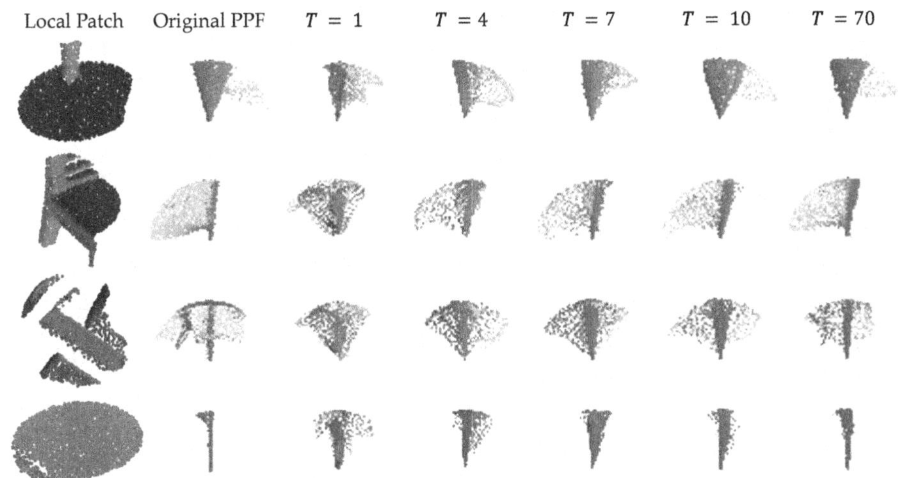

Fig. 5. Visualizing signatures of reconstructed PPFs. As the training converges, the reconstructed PPF signatures become closer to the original signatures. Our network reveals the underlying structure of the PPF space.

ferent methods and ours across several fragments undergoing varying rotations. In Fig. 4 we show the matching regions, over uniformly sampled [5] keypoints on these fragments. It is clear that our algorithm performs the best among all others in discovering the most correct correspondences.

Monitoring Network Evolution. As our network is interpretable, it is tempting to qualitatively analyze the progress of the network. To do that we record the PPF reconstruction output at discrete time steps and visualize the PPFs as explained in Sect. 3.1. Figure 5 shows such a visualization for different local patches. First, thanks to the representation power, our network achieves high fidelity recovery of PPFs. Note that even though the network starts from a random initialization, it can quickly recover a desired point pair feature set, even after only a small number of iterations. Next, for similar local patches (top and bottom rows), the reconstructions are similar, while for different ones, different.

Visualizing the Latent Space. We now attempt to visualize the learned latent space and assess whether the embedding is semantically meaningful. To do so, we compute a set of codewords and the associated PPF signatures. We then run the Barnes Hut T-SNE algorithm [24, 42] on the extracted codewords and form a two-dimensional embedding space, as shown in Fig. 6. At each 2D location we paint the PPF signature and thereby illustrate the distribution of PPFs along the manifold. We also plot the original patches which generated the codewords and their corresponding signatures as cutouts. Presented in Fig. 6, whenever the patches are geometrically and semantically close, the computed descriptors are close, and whenever the patches have less physical similarity, they are embedded into different parts of the space. This provides insight into the good performance

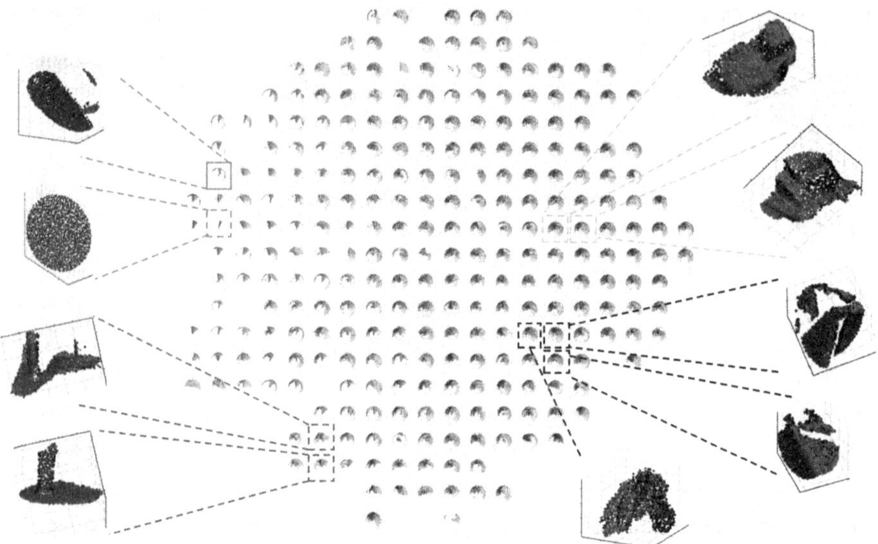

Fig. 6. Visualization of the latent space of codewords, associated PPFs and samples of clustered local 3D patches using TSNE [24,42].

Fig. 7. Visualization of the latent feature space on fragments fused from different views. To map each feature to a color on the fragment, we use TSNE embedding [24]. We reduce the dimension to three and associate each low dimensional vector with an RGB color. (Color figure online)

and meaningfulness in the relationships our network could learn. In a further experiment, we extract a feature at each location of the point cloud. Then, we reduce the dimension of the latent space to three via TSNE [24], and colorize each point by the reduced feature vector. Qualitatively justifying the repeatibility of our descriptors, the outcome is shown in Fig. 7. Note that, descriptors extracted by the proposed approach lead to similar colors in matching regions among the different fragments.

5 Concluding Remarks

We have presented PPF-FoldNet, an unsupervised, rotation invariant, low complexity, intuitive and interpretable network in order to learn 3D local features solely from point geometry information. Our network is built upon its contemporary ancestors, PointNet, FoldingNet & PPFNet and it inherits best attributes of all. Despite being rotation invariant, we have outperformed all the state-of-the-art descriptors, including supervised ones even in the standard benchmarks under challenging conditions with varying point density. We believe PPF-FoldNet offers a promising new approach to the important problem of unsupervised 3D local feature extraction and see this as an important step towards unsupervised revolution in 3D vision.

Our architecture can be extended in many directions. One of the most promising of those would be to adapt our features towards tasks like classification and object pose estimation. We conclude with the hypothesis that the generalizability in our unsupervised network should transfer easily into solving other similar problems, giving rise to an open application domain.

References

1. Abadi, M., et al.: TensorFlow: large-scale machine learning on heterogeneous distributed systems. arXiv preprint arXiv:1603.04467 (2016)
2. Achlioptas, P., Diamanti, O., Mitliagkas, I., Guibas, L.: Learning Representations and generative models for 3D point clouds. In: International Conference on Machine Learning (ICML) (2018)
3. Birdal, T., Ilic, S.: Point pair features based object detection and pose estimation revisited. In: 3D Vision, pp. 527–535. IEEE (2015)
4. Birdal, T., Ilic, S.: CAD priors for accurate and flexible instance reconstruction. In: 2017 IEEE International Conference on Computer Vision (ICCV), pp. 133–142. IEEE (2017)
5. Birdal, T., Ilic, S.: A point sampling algorithm for 3D matching of irregular geometries. In: International Conference on Intelligent Robots and Systems (IROS 2017). IEEE (2017)
6. Bobkov, D., Chen, S., Jian, R., Iqbal, M.Z., Steinbach, E.: Noise-resistant deep learning for object classification in three-dimensional point clouds using a point pair descriptor. IEEE Robot. Autom. Lett. **3**(2), 865–872 (2018)
7. Cao, Z., Huang, Q., Karthik, R.: 3D object classification via spherical projections. In: 2017 International Conference on 3D Vision (3DV), pp. 566–574. IEEE (2017)
8. Deng, H., Birdal, T., Ilic, S.: PPFNet: global context aware local features for robust 3D point matching. In: Computer Vision and Pattern Recognition (CVPR), vol. 1. IEEE (2018)
9. Elbaz, G., Avraham, T., Fischer, A.: 3D point cloud registration for localization using a deep neural network auto-encoder. In: The IEEE Conference on Computer Vision and Pattern Recognition (CVPR), July 2017
10. Guo, Y., Sohel, F.A., Bennamoun, M., Wan, J., Lu, M.: RoPS: a local feature descriptor for 3D rigid objects based on rotational projection statistics. In: 2013 1st International Conference on Communications, Signal Processing, and their Applications (ICCSPA), pp. 1–6. IEEE (2013)
11. Hackel, T., Savinov, N., Ladicky, L., Wegner, J.D., Schindler, K., Pollefeys, M.: SEMANTIC3D.NET: a new large-scale point cloud classification benchmark. In: ISPRS Annals of the Photogrammetry, Remote Sensing and Spatial Information Sciences, vol. IV-1-W1, pp. 91–98 (2017)

12. Halber, M., Funkhouser, T.: Fine-to-coarse global registration of RGB-D scans. In: Proceedings of the IEEE Conference on Computer Vision and Pattern Recognition (CVPR) (2017)
13. He, K., Zhang, X., Ren, S., Sun, J.: Deep residual learning for image recognition. In: Proceedings of the IEEE conference on computer vision and pattern recognition, pp. 770–778 (2016)
14. Hoppe, H., DeRose, T., Duchamp, T., McDonald, J., Stuetzle, W.: Surface reconstruction from unorganized points, vol. 26, no. 2. ACM (1992)
15. Huang, H., Kalogerakis, E., Chaudhuri, S., Ceylan, D., Kim, V.G., Yumer, E.: Learning local shape descriptors from part correspondences with multiview convolutional networks. ACM Trans. Graph. **37**(1) (2017)
16. Johnson, A.E., Hebert, M.: Using spin images for efficient object recognition in cluttered 3D scenes. IEEE Trans. Pattern Anal. Mach. Intell. **21**(5), 433–449 (1999)
17. Kehl, W., Milletari, F., Tombari, F., Ilic, S., Navab, N.: Deep learning of local RGB-D patches for 3D object detection and 6D pose estimation. In: Leibe, B., Matas, J., Sebe, N., Welling, M. (eds.) ECCV 2016. LNCS, vol. 9907, pp. 205–220. Springer, Cham (2016). https://doi.org/10.1007/978-3-319-46487-9_13
18. Khoury, M., Zhou, Q.Y., Koltun, V.: Learning compact geometric features. In: The IEEE International Conference on Computer Vision (ICCV), October 2017
19. Kinga, D., Adam, J.B.: A method for stochastic optimization. In: International Conference on Learning Representations (ICLR) (2015)
20. Klokov, R., Lempitsky, V.: Escape from cells: deep KD-networks for the recognition of 3D point cloud models. In: 2017 IEEE International Conference on Computer Vision (ICCV), pp. 863–872. IEEE (2017)
21. Krizhevsky, A., Sutskever, I., Hinton, G.E.: Imagenet classification with deep convolutional neural networks. In: Pereira, F., Burges, C.J.C., Bottou, L., Weinberger, K.Q. (eds.) Advances in Neural Information Processing Systems, vol. 25, pp. 1097–1105. Curran Associates, Inc. (2012)
22. Lai, K., Bo, L., Fox, D.: Unsupervised feature learning for 3D scene labeling. In: 2014 IEEE International Conference on Robotics and Automation (ICRA), pp. 3050–3057. IEEE (2014)
23. Lowe, D.G.: Object recognition from local scale-invariant features. In: The Proceedings of the Seventh IEEE International Conference on Computer Vision, vol. 2, pp. 1150–1157. IEEE (1999)
24. van der Maaten, L., Hinton, G.: Visualizing data using t-SNE. J. Mach. Learn. Res. **9**(Nov), 2579–2605 (2008)
25. Manessi, F., Rozza, A., Manzo, M.: Dynamic graph convolutional networks. arXiv preprint arXiv:1704.06199 (2017)
26. Maturana, D., Scherer, S.: VoxNet: a 3D convolutional neural network for real-time object recognition. In: 2015 IEEE/RSJ International Conference on Intelligent Robots and Systems (IROS), pp. 922–928. IEEE (2015)
27. Mur-Artal, R., Montiel, J.M.M., Tardos, J.D.: ORB-SLAM: a versatile and accurate monocular SLAM system. IEEE Trans. Robot. **31**(5), 1147–1163 (2015)
28. Noh, H., Araujo, A., Sim, J., Weyand, T., Han, B.: Large-scale image retrieval with attentive deep local features. In: The IEEE International Conference on Computer Vision (ICCV), October 2017
29. Qi, C.R., Liu, W., Wu, C., Su, H., Guibas, L.J.: Frustum pointnets for 3D object detection from RGB-D data. In: The IEEE Conference on Computer Vision and Pattern Recognition (CVPR), June 2018

30. Qi, C.R., Su, H., Mo, K., Guibas, L.J.: PointNet: deep learning on point sets for 3D classification and segmentation. In: Proceedings of the Computer Vision and Pattern Recognition (CVPR), vol. 1, no. 2, p. 4 (2017)
31. Qi, C.R., Yi, L., Su, H., Guibas, L.J.: PointNet++: deep hierarchical feature learning on point sets in a metric space. In: Guyon, I., et al. (eds.) Advances in Neural Information Processing Systems, vol. 30, pp. 5099–5108. Curran Associates, Inc. (2017)
32. Qi, X., Liao, R., Jia, J., Fidler, S., Urtasun, R.: 3D graph neural networks for RGBD semantic segmentation. In: The IEEE International Conference on Computer Vision (ICCV), October 2017
33. Riegler, G., Ulusoy, O., Geiger, A.: OctNet: learning deep 3D representations at high resolutions. In: IEEE Conference on Computer and Pattern Recognition (CVPR), July 2017
34. Rusu, R.B., Blodow, N., Beetz, M.: Fast point feature histograms (FPFH) for 3D registration. In: 2009 IEEE International Conference on Robotics and Automation, ICRA 2009, pp. 3212–3217. IEEE (2009)
35. Salti, S., Tombari, F., Di Stefano, L.: SHOT: unique signatures of histograms for surface and texture description. Comput. Vis. Image Underst. **125**, 251–264 (2014)
36. Shen, Y., Feng, C., Yang, Y., Tian, D.: Neighbors do help: deeply exploiting local structures of point clouds. ArXiv e-prints, December 2017
37. Shotton, J., Glocker, B., Zach, C., Izadi, S., Criminisi, A., Fitzgibbon, A.: Scene coordinate regression forests for camera relocalization in RGB-D images. In: Proceedings of the IEEE Conference on Computer Vision and Pattern Recognition, pp. 2930–2937 (2013)
38. Tatarchenko, M., Dosovitskiy, A., Brox, T.: Octree generating networks: efficient convolutional architectures for high-resolution 3D outputs. In: IEEE International Conference on Computer Vision (ICCV) (2017)
39. Tatarchenko, M., Park, J., Koltun, V., Zhou, Q.Y.: Tangent convolutions for dense prediction in 3D. In: IEEE Conference on Computer Vision and Pattern Recognition (CVPR) (2018)
40. Tombari, F., Salti, S., Di Stefano, L.: Unique shape context for 3D data description. In: Proceedings of the ACM Workshop on 3D Object Retrieval, pp. 57–62. ACM (2010)
41. Valentin, J., et al.: Learning to navigate the energy landscape. In: 2016 Fourth International Conference on 3D Vision (3DV), pp. 323–332. IEEE (2016)
42. van der Maaten, L.: Barnes-Hut-SNE. ArXiv e-prints, January 2013
43. Wang, P.S., Liu, Y., Guo, Y.X., Sun, C.Y., Tong, X.: O-CNN: octree-based convolutional neural networks for 3D shape analysis. ACM Trans. Graph. (TOG) **36**(4), 72 (2017)
44. Wang, Y., Sun, Y., Liu, Z., Sarma, S.E., Bronstein, M.M., Solomon, J.M.: Dynamic graph CNN for learning on point clouds. ArXiv e-prints, January 2018
45. Wu, J., Zhang, C., Xue, T., Freeman, B., Tenenbaum, J.: Learning a probabilistic latent space of object shapes via 3D generative-adversarial modeling. In: Advances in Neural Information Processing Systems, pp. 82–90 (2016)
46. Wu, Z., et al.: 3D ShapeNets: a deep representation for volumetric shapes. In: Proceedings of the IEEE Conference on Computer Vision and Pattern Recognition, pp. 1912–1920 (2015)
47. Xiao, J., Owens, A., Torralba, A.: SUN3D: a database of big spaces reconstructed using SFM and object labels. In: Proceedings of the IEEE International Conference on Computer Vision, pp. 1625–1632 (2013)

48. Yang, Y., Feng, C., Shen, Y., Tian, D.: FoldingNet: point cloud auto-encoder via deep grid deformation. In: The IEEE Conference on Computer Vision and Pattern Recognition (CVPR), June 2018
49. Yi, K.M., Trulls, E., Lepetit, V., Fua, P.: LIFT: learned invariant feature transform. In: Leibe, B., Matas, J., Sebe, N., Welling, M. (eds.) ECCV 2016. LNCS, vol. 9910, pp. 467–483. Springer, Cham (2016). https://doi.org/10.1007/978-3-319-46466-4_28
50. Yu, L., Li, X., Fu, C.W., Cohen-Or, D., Heng, P.A.: PU-Net: point cloud upsampling network. In: The IEEE Conference on Computer Vision and Pattern Recognition (CVPR), June 2018
51. Zeng, A., Song, S., Nießner, M., Fisher, M., Xiao, J., Funkhouser, T.: 3DMatch: learning local geometric descriptors from RGB-D reconstructions. In: CVPR (2017)

In the Eye of Beholder: Joint Learning of Gaze and Actions in First Person Video

Yin Li[1], Miao Liu[2(✉)], and James M. Rehg[2]

[1] Carnegie Mellon University, Pittsburgh, USA
yinl2@andrew.cmu.edu
[2] College of Computing and Center for Behavioral Imaging, Georgia Institute of Technology, Atlanta, USA
{mliu328,rehg}@gatech.edu

Abstract. We address the task of jointly determining what a person is doing and where they are looking based on the analysis of video captured by a headworn camera. We propose a novel deep model for joint gaze estimation and action recognition in First Person Vision. Our method describes the participant's gaze as a probabilistic variable and models its distribution using stochastic units in a deep network. We sample from these stochastic units to generate an attention map. This attention map guides the aggregation of visual features in action recognition, thereby providing coupling between gaze and action. We evaluate our method on the standard EGTEA dataset and demonstrate performance that exceeds the state-of-the-art by a significant margin of 3.5%.

1 Introduction

Our daily interaction with objects is guided by a sequence of carefully orchestrated fixations. Therefore, "where we look" reveals important information about "what we do." Consider the examples in Fig. 1, where only small regions around the first person's point of gaze are shown. What is this person doing? We can easily identify the actions as "squeeze liquid soap into hand" and "cut tomato," in spite of the fact that more than 80% of the pixels are missing. This is possible because egocentric gaze serves as an index into the critical regions of the video that define the action. Focusing on these regions eliminates the potential distraction of irrelevant background pixels, and allows us to focus on the key elements of the action.

There have been several recent works that use human gaze for action recognition [7,24,31]. Only our previous effort [7] attempted to model attention and action simultaneously. This paper is focused on the joint modeling of gaze estimation and action recognition in First Person Vision (FPV), where gaze, action and video are aligned in the same egocentric coordinate system. In this case, attention is naturally embodied in the camera wearer's actions. Thus, FPV provides the ideal vehicle for studying the joint modeling of attention and action.

Y. Li—This work was done when Y. Li was at Georgia Tech.

V. Ferrari et al. (Eds.): ECCV 2018, LNCS 11209, pp. 639–655, 2018.
https://doi.org/10.1007/978-3-030-01228-1_38

Fig. 1. *Can you tell what the person is doing?* With only 20% of the pixels visible, centered around the point of gaze, we can easily recognize the camera wearer's actions. The gaze indexes key regions containing interactions with objects. We leverage this intuition and develop a model to jointly infer gaze and actions in First Person Vision.

A major challenge for the joint modeling task is the uncertainty in gaze measurements. Around 25% [11] of our gaze within daily actions are saccades—rapid gaze jumps during which our vision system receives no inputs [3]. Within the gaze events that remain, it is not clear what portion of the fixations correspond to overt attention and are therefore meaningfully-connected to actions [14]. In addition, there are small but non-negligible measurement errors in the eye-tracker itself [10]. It follows that a joint model of attention and actions must account for the uncertainty of gaze. What model should we use to represent this uncertainty?

Our inspiration comes from the observation that gaze can be characterized by a *latent* distribution of attention in the context of an action, represented as an attention map in egocentric coordinates. This map identifies image regions that are salient to the current action, such as hands, objects, and surfaces. We model gaze measurements as samples from the attention map distribution. Given gaze measurements obtained during the production of actions, we can directly learn a model for the attention map, which can in turn guide action recognition. Our action recognition model can then focus on action-relevant regions to determine what the person is doing. The attention model is tightly coupled with the recognition of actions. Building on this intuition, we develop a deep network with a latent variable attention model and an attention mechanism for recognition.

To this end, we propose a novel deep model for joint gaze estimation and action recognition in FPV. Specifically, we model the latent distribution of gaze as stochastic units in a deep network. This representation allows us to sample attention maps. These maps are further used to selectively aggregate visual features in space and time for action recognition. Our model thus both encodes the uncertainty in gaze measurement, and models visual attention in the context of actions. We train the model in an end-to-end fashion using action labels and noisy gaze measurements as supervision. At testing time, our model receives only an input video and is able to infer both gaze and action.

We test our model on the EGTEA dataset—the largest public benchmark for FPV gaze and actions [19]. As a consequence of jointly modeling gaze and actions, we obtain results for action recognition that outperform state-of-the-art deep models by a significant margin (3.5%). Our gaze estimation accuracy is also comparable with strong baseline methods. To the best of our knowledge, this is the first work to model *uncertainty* in gaze measurements for action recognition, and the first deep model for *joint* gaze estimation and action recognition in FPV.

2 Related Works

First Person Vision. The advent of wearable cameras has led to growing interest in First Person Vision (FPV)—the automatic analysis of first person videos (see a recent survey in [1]). Here we focus on gaze and actions in FPV.

- **FPV Gaze.** Gaze estimation is well studied in computer vision [2]. Recent works have addressed egocentric gaze estimation. Our previous work [18] estimated egocentric gaze using hand and head cues. Zhang et al. [47] predicted future gaze by estimating gaze from predicted future frames. Park et al. [25] considered 3D social gaze from multiple camera wearers. However, these works did not model egocentric gaze in the context of actions.
- **FPV Actions.** FPV action has been the subject of many recent efforts. Spriggs et al. [37] proposed to segment and recognize daily activities using a combination of video and wearable sensor data. Kitani et al. [17] used a global motion descriptor to discover egocentric actions. Fathi et al. [6] presented a joint model of objects, actions and activities. Pirsiavash and Ramanan [27] further advocated for an object-centric representation of FPV activities. Other efforts included the modeling of conversations [5] and reactions [46] in social interactions. Several recent works have developed deep models for FPV action recognition. Ryoo et al. [30] developed a novel pooling method for deep models. Poleg et al. [28] used temporal convolutions on motion fields for long-term activity recognition. In contrast to our approach, these prior works did not consider the exploitation of egocentric gaze for action recognition.
- **FPV Gaze and Actions.** There have been a few works that incorporated egocentric gaze for FPV action recognition. For example, our previous work [19] showed the benefits of gaze-indexed visual features in a comprehensive benchmark. Both Singh et al. [35] and Ma et al. [22] explored the use of multi-stream networks to capture egocentric attention. These works have clearly demonstrated the advantage of using egocentric gaze for FPV actions. However, they all model FPV gaze and actions *separately* rather than jointly, and they do not address the uncertainty in gaze. Moreover, these methods require *side information* in addition to the input image at testing time, e.g., hand masks [19,35] or object information [22]. In contrast, our method jointly models gaze and action, captures the uncertainty of gaze, and requires only video inputs during testing.

Our previous work [7] presented a joint model for egocentric gaze and actions. This work extends [7] in multiple aspects: (1) we propose an end-to-end deep model rather than using hand crafted features; (2) we explicitly model "noise" in gaze measurements while [7] did not; (3) we infer gaze and action jointly through a single pass during testing while [7] used iterative inference. In a nutshell, we model gaze as a stochastic variable via a novel deep architecture for joint gaze estimation and action recognition. Our model thus combines the benefits of latent variable modeling with the expressive power of a learned feature representation.

Consequently, we show that our method can outperform state-of-the-art deep models [4] for FPV action recognition.

Action Recognition. There is a large body of literature on action recognition (see [41] for a survey). We discuss relevant work that targets the development of deep models and the use of attentional cues for recognizing actions.

- **Deep Models for Actions.** Deep models have demonstrated recent success for action recognition. Simonyan and Zisserman [34] proposed two-stream networks that learn to recognize an action from both optical flow and RGB frames. Wang et al. [44] extended two-stream networks to model multiple temporal segments within the video. Tran et al. [40] replaced 2D convolution with spatiotemporal convolution and trained a 3D convolutional network for action recognition. Carreira and Zisserman further proposed two-stream 3D networks for action recognition [4]. A similar idea is also explored in [42]. Our model builds on the latest development of two-stream 3D convolutional networks [4] to recognize actions in FPV. Our technical novelty is to incorporate stochastic units to model egocentric gaze.
- **Attention for Actions.** Human gaze provides useful signals for the location of actions, and this intuition has been explored for action recognition in domains outside of FPV. Mathe and Sminchesescu [24] proposed to recognize actions by sampling local descriptors from a predicted saliency map. Shapovalova et al. [31] presented a method that uses human gaze for learning to localize actions. However, these methods did not use deep models. Recently, Sharma et al. [32] incorporated soft attention into a deep recurrent network for recognizing actions. However, their notion of attention is defined by discriminative image regions that are not derived from gaze measurements, and therefore they can't support the joint inference of egocentric gaze and actions.

Our method shares a key intuition with [24,31]: the use of predicted gaze to select visual features. However, our attention model is built within a deep network and trained from end-to-end. Our model is similar to [32] in that we also design a attention mechanism that facilitates end-to-end training. However, attention is modeled as stochastic units in our network and receives supervision from noisy human gaze measurements.

3 Method

We denote an input first person video as $x = (x^1, ..., x^t)$ with its frames x^t indexed by time t. Our goal is to predict the action category y for x. We assume egocentric gaze measurements $g = (g^1, ..., g^t)$ are available during training yet need to be inferred during testing. g^t are measured as a single 2D gaze point at time t defined on the image plane of x^t. For our model, it is helpful to reparameterize g^t as a 2D saliency map $g^t(m,n)$, where the value of the gaze position are set to one and all others are zero. And thus $\Sigma_{m,n} g^t(m,n) = 1$. In this case, $g^t(m,n)$ defines a proper probabilistic distribution of 2D gaze.

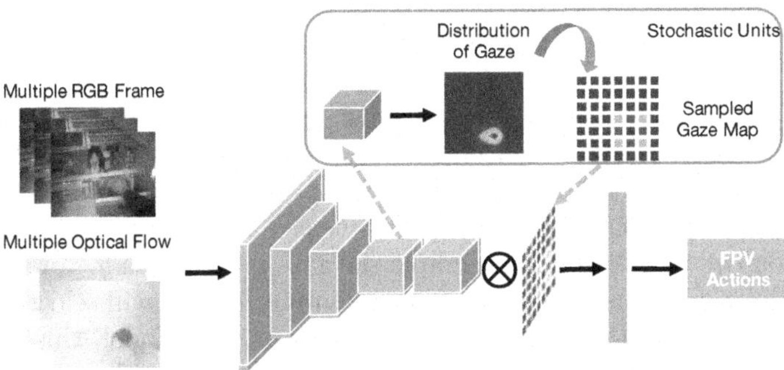

Fig. 2. Overview of our model. Our network takes multiple RGB and flow frames as inputs, and outputs a set of parameters defining a distribution of gaze in the middle layers. We then sample a gaze map from this distribution. This map is used to selectively pool visual features at higher layers of the network for action recognition. During training, our model receives action labels and noisy gaze measurement. Once trained, the model is able to infer gaze and recognize actions in FPV. We show that this network builds a probabilistic model that naturally accounts for the uncertainty of gaze and captures the relationship between gaze and actions in FPV.

Figure 2 presents an overview of our model. We'd like to draw an analogy between our model and the well-known R-CNN framework for object detection [9,29]. Our model takes a video x as input and outputs the distribution of gaze q as an intermediate result. We then sample the gaze map g from this predicted distribution. g encodes location information for actions and thus can be viewed as a source of action proposals—similar to the object proposals generated in R-CNN. Finally, we use the attention map to select features from the network hierarchy for recognition. This can be viewed as Region of Interest (ROI) pooling in R-CNN, where visual features in relevant regions are selected for recognition.

3.1 Modeling Gaze with Stochastic Units

Our main idea is to model $g(m,n)$ as a probabilistic variable to account for its uncertainty. More precisely, we model the conditional probability of $p(y|x)$ by

$$p(y|x) = \int_g p(y|g,x)p(g|x)dg. \tag{1}$$

Intuitively, $p(g|x)$ estimates gaze g given the input video x. $p(y|g,x)$ further uses the predicted gaze g to select visual features from input video x to predict the action y. Moreover, we want to use high capacity models, such as deep networks, for both $p(g|x)$ and $p(y|g,x)$. While this model is appealing, the learning and inference tasks are intractable for high dimensional video inputs x.

Our solution, inspired by [16,36], is to approximate the intractable posterior $p(g|x)$ with a carefully designed $q_\pi(g|x)$. Specifically, we define $q(m,n)$ on a 2D image plane of the same size $M \times N$ as x. q is parameterized by $\pi_{m,n}$, where

$$q(m,n) = q(g_{m,n} = 1|x) = \frac{\pi_{m,n}}{\sum_{m,n} \pi_{m,n}}. \tag{2}$$

$\pi = q_\psi(X)$ is the output from a deep neural network q_ψ. $q(g|x)$ thus models the probabilistic distribution of egocentric gaze. Thus, our deep network creates a 2D map of $\pi_{m,n}$. π defines an approximation q_π to the distribution of the latent attention map. Specifically, $q(m,n)$ can be viewed as the expectation of the gaze g at position (m,n). We can then sample the gaze map $\tilde{g}$ from q_π for recognition.

Given a sampled gaze map $\tilde{g}$, our attention mechanism will selectively aggregate visual features $\phi(x)$ defined by network ϕ. In our model, this is simply a weighted average pooling, where the weights are defined by the gaze map $\tilde{g}$. We then send pooled features to the recognition network f. We further constrain f to have the form of a linear classifier, followed by a softmax function. This design is important for approximate inference. Now we have

$$p(y|g,x) = f(\Sigma_{m,n}\tilde{g}_{m,n}\phi(x)_{m,n}) = softmax\left(W_f^T(\Sigma_{m,n}\tilde{g}_{m,n}\phi(x)_{m,n})\right). \tag{3}$$

The sum operation is equivalent to spatially re-weighting individual feature channels. By doing so, we expect that the network will learn to attend to discriminative regions for action recognition. Note that this is a soft attention mechanism that allows back-propagation. Thus, top-down modulation of gaze can be achieved through gradients from action labels.

Our model thus includes three sub-networks: $q_\psi(x)$ that outputs parameters for the attention map, $\phi(x)$ that extracts visual representations for x, and $f(g,x)$ that pools features and recognizes actions. All three sub-networks share the same backbone network with their separate heads, and thus our model is realized as a single feed forward deep network. Due to the sampling process introduced in modeling, learning the parameters of the network is challenging. We overcome this challenge by using variational learning and optimizing a lower bound. We now present our training objective and inference method.

3.2 Variational Learning

During training, we make use of the input video x, its action label y and human gaze measurements g sampled from a distribution $p(g|x)$. Intuitively, our learning process has two major goals. First, our predicted gaze distribution parameterized by $q_\psi(x)$ should match the noisy observations of gaze. Second, the final recognition error should be minimized. We achieve these goals by maximizing the lower bound of $\log p(y|x)$, given by

$$\log p(y|x) \geq -\mathcal{L} = E_{g\sim q(g|x)}[\log p(y|g,x)] - KL[q(g|x)||p(g|x)], \tag{4}$$

where $KL(p||q)$ is the Kullback–Leibler (KL) divergence between distribution p and q, and E denotes the expectation.

Noise Pattern of Egocentric Gaze. Computing $KL(p||q)$ requires the prior knowledge of $p(g|x)$. In our case, given x, we observe gaze g drawn from $p(g|x)$.

Thus, $p(g|x)$ is the noise pattern of the gaze measurement g. We adapt a simple noise model of gaze. For all tracked fixation points, we assume a 2D isotropic Gaussian noise, where the standard deviation of the Gaussian is selected based on the average tracking error of modern eye trackers. When the gaze point is a saccade (or is missing), we set $p(g|x)$ to the 2D uniform distribution, allowing attention to be allocated to any location on the image plane.

Loss Function. Given our noise model of gaze $p(g|x)$, we now minimize our loss function as the negative of the empirical lower bound, given by

$$-\sum_g \log p(y|g,x) + KL[q(g|x)||p(g|x)]. \tag{5}$$

During training, we sample the gaze map $\tilde{g}$ from the predicted distribution $q(g|x)$, apply the map for recognition ($p(y|\tilde{g},x) = f(\tilde{g},x)$) and compute its negative log likelihood—the same as the cross entropy loss for a categorical variable y. Our objective function thus has two terms: (a) the negative log likelihood term as the cross entropy loss between the predicated and the ground-truth action labels using the sampled gaze maps; and (b) the KL divergence between the predicted distribution $q(g|x)$ and the gaze distribution $p(g|x)$.

Reparameterization. Our model is fully differentiable except for the sampling of $\tilde{g}$. To allow end-to-end back propagation, we re-parameterize the discrete distribution $q(m,n)$ using the Gumbel-Softmax approach as in [15,23]. Specifically, instead of sampling from $q(m,n)$ directly, we sample the gaze map $\tilde{g}$ via

$$\tilde{g}_{m,n} \sim \frac{\exp((\log \pi_{m,n} + G_{m,n})/\tau)}{\sum_{m,n} \exp((\log \pi_{m,n} + G_{m,n})/\tau)}, \tag{6}$$

where τ is the temperature that controls the "sharpness" of the distribution. We set $\tau = 2$ for all of our experiments. The softmax normalization ensures that $\sum_{m,n} \tilde{g}(m,n) = 1$, such that it is a proper gaze map. G follows the Gumbel distribution $G = -\log(-\log U)$, where U is the uniform distribution on $[0,1)$. This Concrete distribution separates out the sampling into a random variable from a uniform distribution and a set of parameters π, and thus allows the direct back-propagation of gradients to π.

3.3 Approximate Inference

During testing, we feed an input video x forward through the network to estimate the gaze distribution $q(g|x)$. Ideally, we should sample multiple gaze maps $\tilde{g}$ from q, pass them into our recognition network $f(g,x)$, and average all predictions. This is, however, prohibitively expensive. Since $f(g,x)$ is nonlinear and g has hundreds of dimensions, we will need many samples $\tilde{g}$ to approximate the expectation $E_g[f(g,x)]$, where each sample requires us to recompute $f(\tilde{g},x)$. We take a shortcut by feeding q_π into f to avoid the sampling. We note that q_π is the expectation of $\tilde{g}$, and thus our approximation is $E_g[f(g,x)] \approx f(E[g],x)$.

This shortcut does provide a good approximation. Recall that our recognition network f is a softmax linear classifier. Thus, f is convex (even with the weight decay on W_f). By Jensen's Inequality, we have $E_g[f(g,x)] \geq f(E[g],x)$. Thus, our approximation $f(E[g],x)$ is indeed a lower bound for the sample averaged estimate of $E_g[f(g,x)]$. Using this deterministic approximation during testing also eliminates the randomness in the results due to sampling. We have empirically verified the effectiveness of our approximation.

3.4 Discussions

For further insights, We connect our model to the technique of Dropout and the model of Conditional Variational AutoEncoder (CVAE).

Connection to Dropout. Our sampling procedure during learning can viewed as an alternative to Dropout [38], and thus helps to regularize the learning. In particular, we sample the gaze map $\tilde{g}$ to re-weight features. This map will have a single peak and many close-to-zero values due to the softmax function. If a position (m,n) has a very small weight, the features at that position are "dropped out". The key difference is that our sampling is guided by the predicted gaze distribution of q_ψ instead of random masking used by Dropout.

Connection to Conditional Variational Autoencoder. Our model is also connected to CVAE [36]. Both models use stochastic variables for discriminative tasks. Yet these two models are different: (1) our stochastic unit—the 2D gaze distribution, is discrete. In contrast, CVAE employs a continuous Gaussian variable, leading to a different reparameterization technique. (2) our stochastic unit—the gaze map is physically meaningful and *receives supervision* during training, while CVAE's is latent. (3) our model approximates the posterior with $q_\psi(x)$ and uses one forward pass for approximated inference, while CVAE models the posterior as a function of both x and y and thus requires recurrent updates.

3.5 Network Architecture

Our model builds on two-stream I3D networks [4]. Similar to its base Inception network [39], I3D has 5 convolutional blocks and the network uses 3D convolutions to capture the temporal dynamics of videos. Specifically, our model takes both RGB frames and optical flow as inputs, and feeds them into an RGB or a flow stream, respectively. We fuse the two streams at the end of the 4th convolutional block for gaze estimation, and at the end of the 5th convolutional block for action recognition. The fusion is done using element-wise summation as suggested by [8]. We used 3D max pooling to match the predicted gaze map to the size of the feature map at the 5th convolutional block for weighted pooling.

Our model takes the inputs of 24 frames, outputs action scores and a gaze map at a temporal stride of 8. Our output gaze map will have the spatial resolution of 7×7 (downsampled by 32x). During testing, we average the clip-level actions scores to recognizing actions in a video.

4 Experiments

We now present our experiments and results. We first introduce the dataset, the evaluation criteria and implementation details for FPV gaze estimation and action recognition. We then present our experiments on gaze and actions. Our main results are divided into three parts. First, we present an ablation study of our model. Second, we demonstrate our main results on FPV action recognition and compare our results to several state-of-the-art methods. Finally, we show results on gaze estimation and compare to a set of strong baselines. Our model achieves strong results for both action recognition and gaze estimation.

4.1 Dataset and Benchmark

Dataset. We use the Extended GTEA Gaze+ dataset.[1] This dataset contains 29 h of first person videos from 86 unique sessions. These sessions come from 32 subjects performing 7 different meal preparation tasks in a naturalistic kitchen environment. The videos have a resolution of 1280×960 at 24 Hz with gaze tracking at every frame. The dataset also comes with action annotations of 10321 instances from 106 classes with an average duration of 3.2 s.

EGTEA poses a challenge of fine grained action recognition in FPV. Example action categories include "Move Around pot", "Spread condiment (on) bread (using) eating utensil". Moreover, these action instances follow a long-tailed distribution. The frequent classes, such as "open fridge" have a few hundred samples and the classes on the tail, such as "crack egg" have only around 30 samples. We use the first split (8299 for training, 2022 for testing) of the dataset and evaluate the performance of gaze estimation and action recognition.

Evaluation Metric. We use standard metrics for both gaze and actions.

- **Gaze:** We consider gaze estimation as binary classification. We evaluate all fixation points and ignore untracked gaze or saccade in action clips. We report the Precision and Recall values and their corresponding F1 score.
- **Action:** We treat action recognition as multi-class classification. We report mean class accuracy at the clip level (24 frames) and at the video level.

Note that our gaze output is down-sampled both spatially (x32) and temporally (x8). When evaluating gaze, we aggregate fixation points within 8 frames and project them into a downsampled 2D map. This time interval (300 ms) is equal to the duration of a fixation (around 250 ms) and thus this temporal aggregation should preserve the location of gaze.

Implementation Details. We downsample all video frames to 320×256 and compute optical flow using FlowNet V2 [12]. We empirically verify that FlowNet V2 gives satisfactory motion estimation in egocentric videos. The flow map is

[1] Available at http://cbi.gatech.edu/fpv.

truncated in the range of $[-20, 20]$ and rescaled to $[0, 255]$ as [34,44]. During training, we randomly crop 224×224 regions from 24 frames. We then feed the RGB frames and flow maps into our networks. We also perform random horizontal flip and color jittering for data augmentation. For testing, we send the frames with a resolution of 320×256 and their flipped version. For action recognition, we average pool scores of all clips within a video. For gaze estimation, we flip back the gaze map and take the average.

Training Details. All our models are trained using SGD with momentum of 0.9 and weight decay of 0.00004. The initial weights for 3D convolutional networks are restored from Kinectcs pre-trained models [4]. For training two stream-networks, we use a batch size of 40, paralleled over 4 GPUs. We use a initial learning rate of 0.032, which matches the same learning rate from [4]. We decay the learning rate by a factor of 10 at 40th epoch and end the training at 60 epochs. We enable batch normalization [13] during training and set the decay rate for its parameters to 0.9, allowing faster aggregation of dataset statistics. By default, dropout with rate of 0.7 is attached for fully connected layer during training, as suggested in [44]. We disable dropout for our proposed model.

Table 1. Ablation study on backbone networks and probabilistic modeling. We show F1 scores for gaze estimation and mean class accuracy for action recognition.

Networks	Action Acc (Clip)	Action Acc (Video)
I3D RGB	43.69	47.26
I3D Flow	32.08	38.31
I3D Fusion	N/A	48.84
I3D Joint	46.42	49.79

(a) **Backbone Network**: We compare RGB, Flow, late fusion and joint training of I3D for action recognition. Joint training works the best.

Methods	Gaze F1	Action Acc
I3D Joint	N/A	49.79
Gaze MLE	24.68	51.12
Soft-Atten	10.27	50.30
Ours (Prob.)	32.97	53.30
Ours w. Dropout	32.66	52.12

(b) **Probabilistic Modeling**: We compare our model to its deterministic version (Gaze MLE). We also study the effect of Dropout.

4.2 Ablation Study

We start with a comprehensive study of our model on the EGTEA Gaze dataset. Our model consists of (1) the backbone network for feature presentation; (2) the probabilistic modeling; and (3) the attention guided action recognition. We separate out these components and test them independently.

Backbone Network: RGB vs. Flow. We evaluate different network architectures on EGTEA dataset for FPV action recognition. Our goal is to understand which network performs the best in the egocentric setting. Concretely, we tested

RGB and flow streams of I3D [4], the late fusion of two streams, and the joint training of two streams [8]. The results are summarized in Table 1a. Overall, EGTEA dataset is very challenging, even the strongest model has an accuracy below 50%. To help calibrate the performance, we note that the same I3D model achieved 36% on Charades [33,45], 74% on Kinetics and 99% on UCF [4].

Unlike Kinetics or UCF, where flow stream performs comparably to RGB stream, the performance of I3D flow stream on EGTEA is significantly lower than its RGB counterpart. This is probably because of the frequent motion of the camera in FPV. It is thus more difficult to capture motion cues. Finally, the joint training of RGB and flow streams performs the best in the experiment. Thus, we choose this network as our backbone for the rest of our experiments.

Modeling: Probabilistic vs. Deterministic. We then test the probabilistic modeling part of our method. We focus on the key question: "What is the benefit of probabilistic modeling of gaze?" To this end, we present a deterministic version of our model that uses maximum likelihood estimation for gaze. We denote this model as *Gaze MLE*. Instead of sampling, this model learns to directly output a gaze map, and apply the map for recognition. During training, the gaze map is supervised by human gaze using a pixel-wise sigmoid cross entropy loss. We keep the model architecture and the training procedure the same as our model. And we disable the loss for gaze when fixation is not available.

We compare our model with Gaze MLE for gaze and actions, and present the results in Table 1b. Our probabilistic model outperforms its deterministic version by 2.2% for action recognition and 8.3% for gaze estimation. We attribute this significant gain to the modeling. If the supervisory signal is highly noisy, allowing the network to adapt the stochasticity will facilitate the learning.

Regularization: Sampling vs. Dropout. To further test our probabilistic component, we compare our sampling of gaze map to the dropout of features. As we discussed in Sect. 3.4, the sampling procedure in our model can be viewed as a way of "throwing away" features. Thus, we experiment with enabling Dropout directly after the attention pooled feature map in the model. Specifically, we compare two models with the same architecture, yet one trained with Dropout and one without. The results are in Table 1b. When Dropout is disabled, the network performs slightly better for action recognition (+1.2%) and gaze estimation (+0.3%). In contrast, removing Dropout from the backbone I3D will slightly decrease the accuracy [44]. We postulated that with regularization from our sampling, further dropping out the features will hurt the performance.

Attention for Action Recognition. Finally, we compare our method to a soft attention model (*Soft-Atten* in Table 1b) using the same backbone networks. Similar to our model, this method fuses the two streams at the end of the 4th and 5th conv blocks. Soft attention map is produced by 1x1 convolution with Sigmoid activations from the fused features at the 4th conv block. This map is further used to pool the fused features (by weighted averaging) at the 5th conv block for recognition. Thus, this soft attention map receives no supervision of gaze. A similar soft attention mechanism was used in a concurrent work [20].

For action recognition, *Soft-Atten* is worse than gaze supervised models by 0.8–3%, yet outperforms the base I3D model by 0.5%. These results suggest that (1) soft attention helps to improve action recognition even without explicit supervision of gaze; and (2) adding human gaze as supervision provides a significant performance gain. For gaze estimation, *Soft-Atten* is worse (−14%) than any gaze supervised models, as it does not receive supervision of gaze.

4.3 FPV Action Recognition

We now describe our experiments on FPV action recognition. We introduce our baselines and compare their results to our full model. These results discussed.

Table 2. Action Recognition and Gaze Estimation. For action recognition, we report mean class accuracy at both clip and video level. For gaze estimation, we show F1 scores and their corresponding precision and recall scores.

Methods	Clip Acc	Video Acc
EgoIDT+Gaze† [19]	N/A	46.50
I3D+Gaze†	46.77	51.21
EgoConv+I3D [35]	N/A	48.93
Gaze MLE	47.41	51.12
Our Model	**47.71**	**53.30**

(a) **Action Recognition Results**: Our method outperforms previous methods by at least 3.5%, and even beats the deep model that uses human gaze at test time (I3D+Gaze) by 2.1%. †: methods use human gaze during testing.

Methods	F1	Prec	Recall
EgoGaze [18]	16.63	16.63	16.63*
Simple Gaze	30.10	25.14	37.48
Deep Gaze [47]	**33.51**	**28.04**	41.62
Gaze MLE†	24.68	18.55	36.86
Our Model†	32.97	27.01	**42.31**

(b) **Gaze Estimation Results**: Our model is comparable to the state-of-the-art methods. †: methods jointly model gaze and actions. This joint modeling does not benefit gaze estimation. *: see Sec 4.4 for discussions.

Baselines. We consider a set of strong baselines for FPV action recognition.

- **EgoIDT+Gaze** [19] combines egocentric features with dense trajectory descriptors [43]. These features are further selected by gaze points, and encoded using Fisher vectors [26] for action recognition.
- **I3D+Gaze** is inspired by [7,19], where the ground truth human gaze is used to pool features from the last convolutional outputs of the network. For this method, we use the same I3D joint backbone and the same attention mechanism as our model, yet use human gaze for pooling features. When human gaze is not available, we fall back to average pooling.
- **EgoConv+I3D** [35] adds a stream of egocentric cues for FPV action recognition. This egocentric stream encodes head motion and hand masks, and its outputs are fused with RGB and flow streams. We use Fully Convolutional

Network (FCN) [21] for hand segmentation, and late fuse the score of egocentric stream with I3D for a fair comparison. This model is trained from scratch.

- **Gaze MLE** is the same model in our ablation study, where the gaze is estimated using maximum likelihood. It provides a simple baseline of multi-task learning of gaze and actions within a single deep network.

Unfortunately, we are unable to compare against relevant methods in [7,22]. These methods require additional object annotations for training, which is not presented in EGTEA dataset. And we do want to emphasis that our method does not need object or hand information for training or testing.

Results. Our results for action recognition are shown in Table 2a. Not surprisingly, all deep models outperform EgoIDT+Gaze [19], which uses hand crafted features. Moreover, EgoConv+I3D only slightly improves the I3D late fusion results (+0.1%). This is because [35] was designed to capture actions defined by "gross body motion", such as "take" vs. "put". And our setting requires fine grained recognition of actions, e.g., "take cup" vs. "take plate".

Surprisingly, even using human gaze at test time, I3D+Gaze is only slightly better than Gaze MLE (+0.1%). And finally, our full model outperforms all baseline methods by a significant margin, including those use human gaze during testing. Our model reaches the accuracy of **53.30%**. We argue that these results provide a strong evidence to our modeling of uncertainty in gaze measurements. A model must learn to account for this uncertainty to avoid misleading gaze points, which will distract the model to action irrelevant regions.

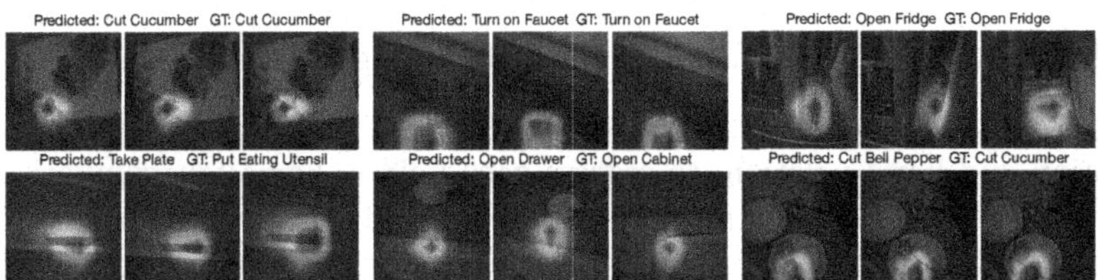

Fig. 3. Visualization of our gaze estimation and action recognition. For each 24-frame snippet, we plot the output gaze heat map at a temporal stride of 8 frames. We also print the predicted action labels and ground-truth labels above the images. Both successful (first row) and failure cases (second row) are presented.

Analysis and Discussion. Going beyond the scores, we provide more results to help understand our model. Specifically, we compare the confusion matrix of our model with backbone I3D Joint network and second best I3D+Gaze in Fig. 4. Our model achieves the highest accuracy among the three for 31 out of 106 classes. These classes include actions where the temporal sequencing is critical, such as "take/turn on object" vs "put/turn off object". These actions have been previously considered challenging in FPV setting [19].

Finally, we visualize the outputs of gaze estimation and action labels from our model in Fig. 3. Our gaze outputs often attend to foreground objects that the person is interacting with. We believe this is why the model is able to better recognize egocentric actions. Moreover, we find these visualizations helpful for diagnosing the error of action recognition. A good example is the first failure case in the second row of Fig. 3, where our model outputs the action of "take plate" when the actually action has not happened yet. Another example is the last failure case in Fig. 3, where the recognition model is confused due to the appearance similarity between cucumbers and bell peppers.

4.4 FPV Gaze Estimation

We now present our baselines and results for FPV gaze estimation.

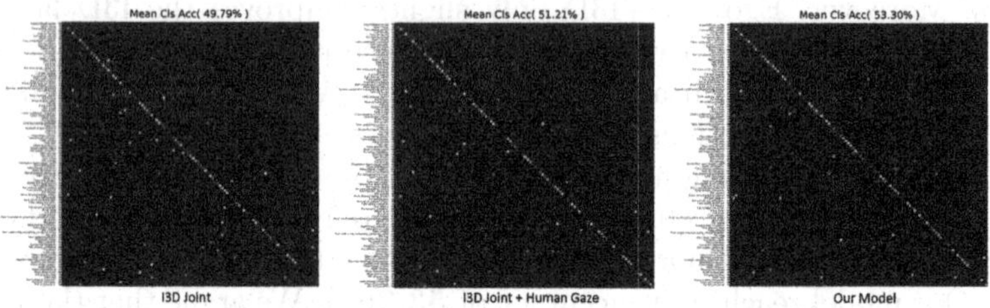

Fig. 4. Confusion matrix for action recognition. We compare our model (right) with I3D Joint (left) and I3D+Gaze (middle). Among the three methods, our method achieves the best accuracy of 31 out of 106 classes, including the challenging cases that require distinguishing actions like "turn on faucet" vs. "turn off faucet".

Baselines. We compare our model to the following baseline methods.

- **EgoGaze** [18] makes use of hand crafted egocentric features, such as head motion and hand position, to regress gaze points. For a fair comparison, we use the FlowNet V2 for motion estimation and hand masks from FCN for hand positions (same as our method). EgoGaze outputs a single gaze point per frame. With a single ground-truth gaze, EgoGaze will have equal numbers of false positives and false negative. Thus, its precision, recall and F1 scores are the same.
- **Simple Gaze** is a deep model inspired by our previous work [7]. Specifically, we directly estimate the gaze map using maximum likelihood (sigmoid cross entropy loss). We use the same backbone network (I3D Joint) as our model and keep the output resolution the same.
- **Deep Gaze** [47] is the FPV gaze prediction module from [47], where a 3D convolutional network is combined with a KL loss. Again, we use I3D Joint as the backbone network and keep the output resolution. Note that this model can be considered as a special case of our model by removing the sampling, the attention mechanism and the recognition network.
- **Gaze MLE** is the deterministic version of our joint model.

Results. Our gaze estimation results are shown in Table 2b. We report F1 scores and their corresponding precision and recall values. Again, deep models outperform hand crafted features by a large margin. We also observe that models with KL loss are consistently better than those use cross entropy loss. This impact is more significant for joint modeling, mostly likely due to the difficulty in balancing between the losses for two tasks. Moreover, the joint models slightly decrease the gaze estimation performance when compared to gaze-only models.

Discussion. Our results suggest that the top-down, task-relevant attention is not captured in these models, even though the top-down modulation can be achieved via back-propagation. This is thus an interesting future direction for the community to explore. Finally, we note that the benchmark of gaze estimation uses noisy human gaze as ground truth. We argue that even though these gaze measurements are noisy, they largely correlate with the underlie signal of attention. And thus the results of the benchmark are still meaningful.

5 Conclusion

We presented a novel deep model for jointly estimating gaze and recognizing actions in FPV. Our core innovation is to model the noise in human gaze measurement using stochastic units embedded in a deep neural network. Our model predicts a probabilistic representation of gaze, and uses it to select features for recognition. The method thus learns to account for the uncertainty within the supervisory signal of human gaze. We provide extensive experiments that demonstrate the effectiveness of our method. Our results surpass state-of-the-art methods for FPV action recognition and remain on par with strong baselines for gaze estimation. Going beyond FPV, our method provides a novel means of encoding the uncertainty present in training signals. We believe this capability is an important step in developing more expressive probabilistic deep models.

Acknowledgments. This research was supported in part by the Intel Science and Technology Center on Pervasive Computing.

References

1. Betancourt, A., Morerio, P., Regazzoni, C.S., Rauterberg, M.: The evolution of first person vision methods: a survey. IEEE Trans. Circuits Syst. Video Technol. **25**(5), 744–760 (2015)
2. Borji, A., Itti, L.: State-of-the-art in visual attention modeling. IEEE Trans. Pattern Anal. Mach. Intell. **35**(1), 185–207 (2013)
3. Bridgeman, B., Hendry, D., Stark, L.: Failure to detect displacement of the visual world during saccadic eye movements. Vis. Res. **15**(6), 719–722 (1975)
4. Carreira, J., Zisserman, A.: Quo vadis, action recognition? A new model and the kinetics dataset. In: CVPR (2017)
5. Fathi, A., Hodgins, J.K., Rehg, J.M.: Social interactions: a first-person perspective. In: CVPR (2012)

6. Fathi, A., Farhadi, A., Rehg, J.M.: Understanding egocentric activities. In: ICCV (2011)
7. Fathi, A., Li, Y., Rehg, J.M.: Learning to recognize daily actions using gaze. In: Fitzgibbon, A., Lazebnik, S., Perona, P., Sato, Y., Schmid, C. (eds.) ECCV 2012. LNCS, vol. 7572, pp. 314–327. Springer, Heidelberg (2012). https://doi.org/10.1007/978-3-642-33718-5_23
8. Feichtenhofer, C., Pinz, A., Zisserman, A.: Convolutional two-stream network fusion for video action recognition. In: CVPR (2016)
9. Girshick, R., Donahue, J., Darrell, T., Malik, J.: Rich feature hierarchies for accurate object detection and semantic segmentation. In: CVPR (2014)
10. Hansen, D.W., Ji, Q.: In the eye of the beholder: a survey of models for eyes and gaze. IEEE Trans. Pattern Anal. Mach. Intell. **32**(3), 478–500 (2010)
11. Henderson, J.M.: Human gaze control during real-world scene perception. Trends Cogn. Sci. **7**(11), 498–504 (2003)
12. Ilg, E., Mayer, N., Saikia, T., Keuper, M., Dosovitskiy, A., Brox, T.: FlowNet 2.0: evolution of optical flow estimation with deep networks. In: ICCV (2017)
13. Ioffe, S., Szegedy, C.: Batch normalization: accelerating deep network training by reducing internal covariate shift. In: ICML (2015)
14. Itti, L., Koch, C.: Computational modelling of visual attention. Nat. Rev. Neurosci. **2**(3), 194 (2001)
15. Jang, E., Gu, S., Poole, B.: Categorical reparameterization with gumbel-softmax. In: ICLR (2017)
16. Kingma, D.P., Welling, M.: Auto-encoding variational bayes. In: ICLR (2014)
17. Kitani, K.M., Okabe, T., Sato, Y., Sugimoto, A.: Fast unsupervised ego-action learning for first-person sports videos. In: CVPR (2011)
18. Li, Y., Fathi, A., Rehg, J.M.: Learning to predict gaze in egocentric video. In: ICCV (2013)
19. Li, Y., Ye, Z., Rehg, J.M.: Delving into egocentric actions. In: CVPR (2015)
20. Liu, S., Johns, E., Davison, A.J.: End-to-end multi-task learning with attention. arXiv preprint arXiv:1803.10704 (2018)
21. Long, J., Shelhamer, E., Darrell, T.: Fully convolutional networks for semantic segmentation. In: CVPR (2015)
22. Ma, M., Fan, H., Kitani, K.M.: Going deeper into first-person activity recognition. In: CVPR (2016)
23. Maddison, C.J., Mnih, A., Teh, Y.W.: The concrete distribution: a continuous relaxation of discrete random variables. In: ICLR (2017)
24. Mathe, S., Sminchisescu, C.: Dynamic eye movement datasets and learnt saliency models for visual action recognition. In: Fitzgibbon, A., Lazebnik, S., Perona, P., Sato, Y., Schmid, C. (eds.) ECCV 2012. LNCS, pp. 842–856. Springer, Heidelberg (2012). https://doi.org/10.1007/978-3-642-33709-3_60
25. Park, H.S., Jain, E., Sheikh, Y.: 3D social saliency from head-mounted cameras. In: Pereira, F., Burges, C.J.C., Bottou, L., Weinberger, K.Q. (eds.) NIPS, pp. 422–430. Curran Associates, Inc., Red Hook (2012)
26. Perronnin, F., Sánchez, J., Mensink, T.: Improving the fisher kernel for large-scale image classification. In: Daniilidis, K., Maragos, P., Paragios, N. (eds.) ECCV 2010. LNCS, vol. 6314, pp. 143–156. Springer, Heidelberg (2010). https://doi.org/10.1007/978-3-642-15561-1_11
27. Pirsiavash, H., Ramanan, D.: Detecting activities of daily living in first-person camera views. In: CVPR (2012)
28. Poleg, Y., Ephrat, A., Peleg, S., Arora, C.: Compact CNN for indexing egocentric videos. In: WACV (2016)

29. Ren, S., He, K., Girshick, R., Sun, J.: Faster R-CNN: towards real-time object detection with region proposal networks. In: Cortes, C., Lawrence, N.D., Lee, D.D., Sugiyama, M., Garnett, R. (eds.) NIPS, pp. 91–99. Curran Associates, Inc., Red Hook (2015)
30. Ryoo, M.S., Rothrock, B., Matthies, L.: Pooled motion features for first-person videos. In: CVPR (2015)
31. Shapovalova, N., Raptis, M., Sigal, L., Mori, G.: Action is in the eye of the beholder: eye-gaze driven model for spatio-temporal action localization. In: Burges, C.J.C., Bottou, L., Welling, M., Ghahramani, Z., Weinberger, K.Q. (eds.) NIPS, pp. 2409–2417. Curran Associates, Inc., Red Hook (2013)
32. Sharma, S., Kiros, R., Salakhutdinov, R.: Action recognition using visual attention. In: ICLR Workshop (2016)
33. Sigurdsson, G.A., Varol, G., Wang, X., Farhadi, A., Laptev, I., Gupta, A.: Hollywood in homes: crowdsourcing data collection for activity understanding. In: Leibe, B., Matas, J., Sebe, N., Welling, M. (eds.) ECCV 2016. LNCS, vol. 9905, pp. 510–526. Springer, Cham (2016). https://doi.org/10.1007/978-3-319-46448-0_31
34. Simonyan, K., Zisserman, A.: Two-stream convolutional networks for action recognition in videos. In: Ghahramani, Z., Welling, M., Cortes, C., Lawrence, N.D., Weinberger, K.Q. (eds.) NIPS, pp. 568–576. Curran Associates, Inc., Red Hook (2014)
35. Singh, S., Arora, C., Jawahar, C.: First person action recognition using deep learned descriptors. In: CVPR (2016)
36. Sohn, K., Lee, H., Yan, X.: Learning structured output representation using deep conditional generative models. In: Cortes, C., Lawrence, N.D., Lee, D.D., Sugiyama, M., Garnett, R. (eds.) NIPS, pp. 3483–3491. Curran Associates, Inc., Red Hook (2015)
37. Spriggs, E.H., De La Torre, F., Hebert, M.: Temporal segmentation and activity classification from first-person sensing. In: CVPR Workshops (2009)
38. Srivastava, N., Hinton, G., Krizhevsky, A., Sutskever, I., Salakhutdinov, R.: Dropout: a simple way to prevent neural networks from overfitting. J. Mach. Learn. Res. **15**, 1929–1958 (2014)
39. Szegedy, C., et al.: Going deeper with convolutions. In: CVPR (2015)
40. Tran, D., Bourdev, L., Fergus, R., Torresani, L., Paluri, M.: Learning spatiotemporal features with 3D convolutional networks. In: ICCV (2015)
41. Turaga, P., Chellappa, R., Subrahmanian, V.S., Udrea, O.: Machine recognition of human activities: a survey. IEEE Trans. Circuits Syst. Video Technol. **18**(11), 1473–1488 (2008)
42. Varol, G., Laptev, I., Schmid, C.: Long-term temporal convolutions for action recognition. IEEE Trans. Pattern Anal. Mach. Intell. **40**(6), 1510–1517 (2017)
43. Wang, H., Kläser, A., Schmid, C., Liu, C.L.: Action recognition by dense trajectories. In: CVPR (2011)
44. Wang, L., et al.: Temporal segment networks: towards good practices for deep action recognition. In: Leibe, B., Matas, J., Sebe, N., Welling, M. (eds.) ECCV 2016. LNCS, vol. 9912, pp. 20–36. Springer, Cham (2016). https://doi.org/10.1007/978-3-319-46484-8_2
45. Wang, X., Girshick, R.B., Gupta, A., He, K.: Non-local neural networks. In: CVPR (2018)
46. Yonetani, R., Kitani, K.M., Sato, Y.: Recognizing micro-actions and reactions from paired egocentric videos. In: CVPR (2016)
47. Zhang, M., Teck Ma, K., Hwee Lim, J., Zhao, Q., Feng, J.: Deep future gaze: gaze anticipation on egocentric videos using adversarial networks. In: CVPR (2017)

Double JPEG Detection in Mixed JPEG Quality Factors Using Deep Convolutional Neural Network

Jinseok Park[1], Donghyeon Cho[2], Wonhyuk Ahn[1], and Heung-Kyu Lee[1(✉)]

[1] School of Computing, Korea Advanced Institute of Science and Technology (KAIST), Daejeon, South Korea
jspark@mmc.kaist.ac.kr, {whahnize,heunglee}@kaist.ac.kr
[2] Electrical Engineering, Korea Advanced Institute of Science and Technology (KAIST), Daejeon, South Korea
cdh12242@gmail.com

Abstract. Double JPEG detection is essential for detecting various image manipulations. This paper proposes a novel deep convolutional neural network for double JPEG detection using statistical histogram features from each block with a vectorized quantization table. In contrast to previous methods, the proposed approach handles mixed JPEG quality factors and is suitable for real-world situations. We collected real-world JPEG images from the image forensic service and generated a new double JPEG dataset with 1120 quantization tables to train the network. The proposed approach was verified experimentally to produce a state-of-the-art performance, successfully detecting various image manipulations.

Keywords: Image forensics · Image manipulation · Fake images Double JPEG · Convolutional neural networks

1 Introduction

With the development of digital cameras and relevant technology, digital images can be captured from anywhere, posted online, or sent directly to friends through various social network services. People tend to think that all such immediately posted digital images are real, but many images are fake, having been generated by image-editing programs such as Photoshop.

Image manipulation is easy but can have significant impact. The left two images of Fig. 1 show normal and spliced images implying an unrelated person may have been present somewhere. It is difficult to determine whether the spliced image is real or not by the naked eye. Such artificially created images spread distorted information and can cause various societal effects. Politicians and entertainers, for example, are particularly vulnerable to image manipulation, where persons can use composite images to undermine their reputation. The right two images of Fig. 1 show another manipulation example. The specific region of the image was replaced by different colors, which gives a different impression to the original image.

V. Ferrari et al. (Eds.): ECCV 2018, LNCS 11209, pp. 656–672, 2018.
https://doi.org/10.1007/978-3-030-01228-1_39

(a) Normal (b) Manipulated (c) Normal (d) Manipulated

Fig. 1. Two examples of image manipulations. The left two images show normal and spliced images. A soldier was extracted from another image and pasted into the normal image. The right two images show normal and color-modified images. The color of some tulips has been changed. (Color figure online)

Thus, image manipulations can be applied to any image, and it is not easy to authenticate the image visually. Researchers have been developing image forensic techniques for many years to distinguish fake images to overcome these problems and restore digital image credibility [1,2].

Image forensic technology is categorized into two types. The first type target a specific manipulation and detects it. Many studies have developed detection methods for various manipulations, such as splicing [3–7], copy-move [8–11], color modification [12,13], and face morphing [14]. Detection techniques based on these operation types are well suited to specific situations, where the target manipulation(s) has been applied. However, they cannot be applied generally because there are many image transformations aside from those considered, and images are often subject to multiple manipulations, where the order of operation is also significant.

The second approach detects remaining traces that occur when capturing the image by digital camera. In the digital image process, light passes through the camera lens and multiple filters and impacts on a capture array to produce pixel values that are stored electronically. Thus, the images include traces with common characteristics. Several image manipulation detection methods have been proposed to detect such traces [15–17], including detecting the interpolation operation generated by the color filter array [18,19] and resampling traces generated during image manipulation [20–22].

Image forensic techniques using image acquisition traces have the advantage that they can be commonly applied to various image manipulations. However, the approach is almost impossible to use in a real image distribution environment. Although various traces are evident in uncompressed images, they are all high-frequency signals. Most digital images are JPEG compressed immediately when taken or compressed when they are uploaded online, which eliminates or modifies high frequency signals within the image.

Although JPEG compression removes many subtle traces, quantization, an essential part of the JPEG compression process, also leaves traces, and methods have been proposed to use these traces to detect image manipulations. Since JPEG is a lossy compression, image data differs between single and double image compression because the quantization tables are not unique (e.g., they strongly depend on the compression quality setting) [23].

Lukas et al. showed that the first compression quantization table could be estimated to some extent from a doubly compressed JPEG image and used to detect image manipulation [24]. Various double JPEG detection methods have been subsequently proposed. However, existing double JPEG detection methods only consider specific situations rather than a general solution. Therefore, this paper proposes detecting double JPEG compression for general cases with mixed quality factors to detect image manipulations.

The contributions can be summarized as follows. (1) We created a new double JPEG dataset suitable for real situations based on JPEG images obtained from two years of an image forensic service. (2) We propose a novel deep convolutional neural network (CNN, or ConvNet) structure that distinguishes between single and double JPEG blocks with high accuracy under mixed quality factor conditions. (3) We show that the proposed system can detect various image manipulations under a situation similar to one in the real-world.

2 Related Work

This section introduces current double JPEG methods and describes their limitations.

Early Double JPEG Detection: Early double JPEG detection methods extracted hand-crafted features from discrete cosine transformation (DCT) coefficients to distinguish between single and double JPEG images. Fu et al. found that Benford's rule occurs for JPEG coefficients and suggested it could be used to verify image integrity [25]. Li et al. proposed a method to detect double JPEG images by analyzing the first number of DCT coefficients [26].

In contrast to previous methods that assessed a double JPEG using the entire image, Lin et al. proposed a method to detect image manipulations from the DCT coefficients for each block [27], and Farid et al. proposed a method to detect partial image manipulations through JPEG ghost extraction [28]. These methods exploited the fact that manipulated JPEG images have different characteristics for each block.

Figure 2 shows how some blocks are single or double JPEG across a manipulated image. JPEG compression is quantized in 8×8 block units. If the first and the second quantization tables are different, the distribution of the corresponding DCT coefficients differs from the distribution of the DCT coefficients of the JPEG compressed once. When the image is saved to JPEG format after changing the value of a specific region of a JPEG image, the distribution of the DCT coefficients in the region becomes similar to the DCT coefficient of the single JPEG. This is because when the pixels of the region are changed, the quantization interval of the DCT coefficient that already exists disappears.

Bianchi et al. investigated various double JPEG block detection aspects, and proposed an image manipulation detection method based on analyzing DCT coefficients [29]. They also discovered that double JPEG effects could be classified

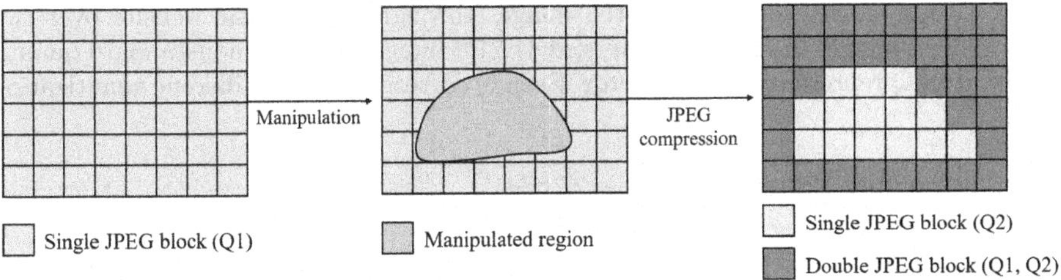

Fig. 2. The detection of image manipulations using double JPEG detection algorithm. The normal image ordinarily has single JPEG characteristics of quantization Table 1 (Q1). If the normal image is manipulated and re-compressed with quantization Table 2 (Q2), the manipulated region has the single JPEG characteristics of Q2. In contrast, the other part has double compression characteristics. We can find the suspicious area by separating single JPEG blocks and double JPEG blocks.

into two cases, aligned and non-aligned [30]. Chen et al. showed that periodic patterns appear in double JPEG spatial and frequency domains and proposed an image manipulation detection method based on this effect [31].

Double JPEG Detection Using ConvNets: Two neural network based methods have been recently proposed to improve current hand-crafted feature based double JPEG detection performance.

Wang et al. showed double JPEG blocks can be detected using ConvNets. They experimentally demonstrated that CNNs could distinguish single and double JPEG blocks with high accuracy when histogram features were inserted into the network after extracting from the DCT coefficients [32]. Subsequently, Barni et al. found that ConvNets could detect double JPEG block with high accuracy when the CNNs took noise signal or histogram features as input [33].

Limitations of Current Double JPEG Detecting Methods: Although double JPEG detection performance has greatly improved, current detection methods have major drawbacks for application in real image manipulation environments. Current methods can only perform double JPEG detection for specific JPEG quality factor states such as in the case where the first JPEG quality (Q1) is 90 and the second JPEG quality (Q2) is 80. However, actual distributed JPEG images can have very different characteristics with a very diverse mixture of JPEG quality parameters. Images are JPEG compressed using not only the standard quality factor (SQ) but also each individual program's JPEG quality factor.

3 Real-World Manipulated Images

We have operated a public forensic website for two years to provide a tool for determining image authenticity. Thus, we could characterize real-world manipulated images. This section introduces the characteristics of requested images

Table 1. Summarization of requested images through the forensic website over two years. 77.95% images of JPEG format, and 41.77% images with the nonstandard quantization table. Q represents quality factor. Each Q corresponds to a different quantization table.

The number of images	127,874			
Manipulation type and region	Unknown			
File type	JPG(+JPEG)	PNG	BMP	TIF(+TIFF)
Percent (%)	77.95	20.67	1.21	0.18
JPEG quality type	Standard Q (0-100)		Nonstandard Q	
Percent (%)	58.22		41.77	
The number of Q types	1170			

and the method employed to generate the new dataset used to develop the generalized double JPEG detection algorithms.

3.1 Requested Images

Table 1 shows a total of 127,874 images were requested to inspect authenticity over two years. As a result of analyzing the requested image data, the JPEG format was found to be the most requested (77.95%), followed by PNG (20.67%).

JPEG Images: As discussed above, JPEG compression quantizes DCT coefficients using a predefined 8×8 JPEG quantization table. Previous studies have assumed that all JPEG images are compressed with standard quality factors, but even Photoshop, the most popular image-editing program, does not use the standard quality factor. Rather, Photoshop uses 12-step quantization tables that do not include the standard quality factor. Among the 99,677 JPEG images from the forensics website, only 58.22% had standard quality factors from 0 to 100, with 41.78% using nonstandard quantization tables. In total, 1170 quantization tables were identified, including 101 different standard quantization tables.

3.2 Generating New Datasets

We generated single and double JPEG blocks of 256×256 in size using collected quantization tables extracted from 99,677 collected JPEG images[1]. Since images with standard quality factors of less than 50 degraded severely, we only considered standard quality factors from 51 to 100; that is, we created a compressed image using a total of 1120 quantization tables.

Since it was not known in what state the collected JPEG images were uploaded, they could not be directly used to generate datasets. For this reason, we used 18,946 RAW images from 15 different camera models in the three raw image datasets [34–36] and split the images into a total of 570,215 blocks.

[1] https://sites.google.com/view/jspark/home/djpeg.

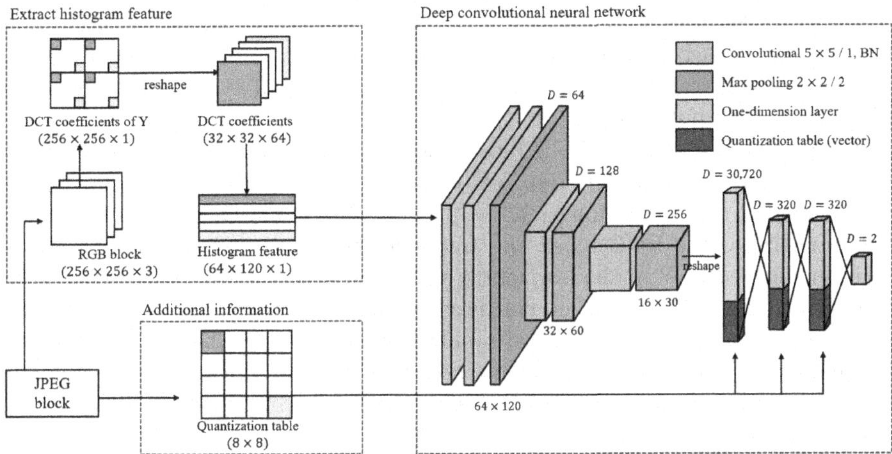

Fig. 3. A network architecture to distinguish between single and double JPEG blocks. The block is transformed in the DCT domain of the Y channel, and its histogram feature is forwarded to the network. The quantization table from the JPEG header is concatenated with the fully connected layer.

The single JPEG blocks were produced by compressing each RAW block with a randomly chosen quantization table, and the double JPEG blocks were produced by further compression with another random quantization table.

Comparison with Existing Double JPEG Datasets: Current double JPEG detection methods were developed from data generated from a very limited range of JPEG quality factors, from 50 to 100, with predefined first quality factors, rather than mixed quality factors. In contrast, the double JPEG dataset we created differs from previous datasets as follows.

- We collected 1120 different quantization tables from actual requested images.
- The images were compressed using 1120 quantization tables.
- Data was generated by mixing all quality factors.

4 Double JPEG Block Detection

This section introduces the new double JPEG block detection method using a CNN and describes the detection of manipulated regions within an image.

4.1 Architecture

The proposed CNN takes histogram features and quantization tables as inputs. We first explain how to construct the input data and then provide the CNN details.

Histogram Features: Since JPEG compression changes the statistical properties of each block rather than the semantic information of the entire image, DCT coefficient statistical characteristics were employed rather than the RGB image as CNN input [33].

Figure 3 shows how the RGB blocks were converted into histogram features. RGB blocks were converted into YCbCr color space and DCT coefficients of the Y channel calculated for each 8×8 block. Thus, the DCT coefficients had the same size as the RGB block and frequency information was saved for every position skipped by 8 in the horizontal and vertical directions. This is the same as JPEG compression. We then collected data D with the same frequency component for each channel. The total number of channels was 64 (one DC and 63 AC channels), where each channel is represented by D_c. The process to calculate D from Y can be accomplished in a single convolutional (stride is 8) operation as below:

$$D = conv_8(Y, B), \tag{1}$$

where B is a $8 \times 8 \times 64$ matrix set of 8×8 DCT basis functions. D has a 1/8 width and height (N_W and N_H, respectively) compared to the input block and 64 channels. Thus, the size of D is $32 \times 32 \times 64$.

After calculating D, we extracted histogram features from each channel. The chosen histogram feature was the percentage of values in each channel relative to the total amount of data, where we set the histogram range as $b = [-60, 60]$, which was determined experimentally to provide the best performance. To extract histogram features, we first subtracted b from D_c and applied the sigmoid function after multiplying by γ, which provided a sufficiently large positive value if each $D_c - b$ was positive and a sufficiently large negative value if each $D_c - b$ was negative. Thus, we set $\gamma = 10^6$. Therefore,

$$S_{c,b} = sigmoid(\gamma * (D_c - b)), \tag{2}$$

where $S_{c,b}$ has the same width and height as D_c, and each value of $S_{c,b}$ is close to zero or one.

We then calculated $a_{c,b}$ by averaging $S_{c,b}$ and generated H features for all b and c,

$$a_{c,b} = \frac{1}{N_W * N_H} \sum_{i=1}^{N_H} \sum_{j=1}^{N_W} S_{c,b}(i, j), \tag{3}$$

and

$$H = \{h | h_{c,b} = a_{c,b+1} - a_{c,b}, \quad \forall c, b\}, \tag{4}$$

where H is a two-dimensional $|c| \times |b|$ matrix and each raw of H is a histogram of channel c of the DCT coefficients. This operation was not part of learning, because there were no weights, but was implemented as a network operation for end-to-end learning.

Quantization Table: The JPEG image file's header contain the quantization table in the form of an 8×8 matrix, which is used for the quantization

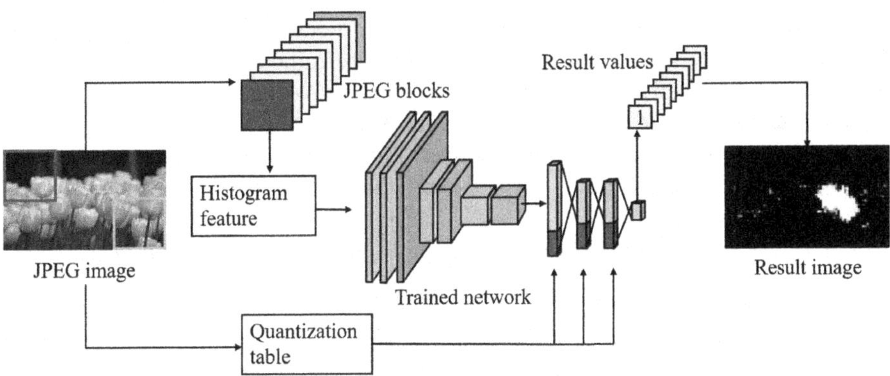

Fig. 4. The process of detecting the manipulated regions in a JPEG image. Through the sliding window, the manipulated regions are identified by detecting single and double JPEG blocks.

and dequantization of DCT coefficients. Quantization table information is not required for conventional double JPEG detection, since the JPEG quality factor is usually fixed. However, this paper considers mixed JPEG quality factors; thus, the quantization table will facilitate single and double JPEG assessment. For a double JPEG image, only the second quantization table is stored in the file.

To input the quantization table into the network, we reshaped it into a vector and then merged the vector with the activations of the last max pooling layer and two fully connected layers as shown in Fig. 3 (right block). The ability of the network to distinguish between single and double JPEG blocks was dramatically improved by including quantization table information.

Deep ConvNet: The deep ConvNet received the histogram features and quantization table inputs and assessed if the corresponding data was single or double JPEG compressed. The network consisted of four convolutional layers, three max pooling layers, and three fully connected layers, as shown in Fig. 3 (right block). The quantization table vector was combined with the last max pooling layer and two fully connected layer activations. The final network output was a 2×1 vector, y, where $y = [1; 0]$ for a single block and $y = [0; 1]$ for a double block. The loss, L, was calculated from cross entropy,

$$L = -(1-p) * log(\frac{e^{y_0}}{e^{y_0} + e^{y_1}}) - p * log(\frac{e^{y_1}}{e^{y_0} + e^{y_1}}), \quad (5)$$

where $p = 0$ if the input data is a single JPEG and $p = 1$ for a double JPEG.

4.2 Manipulated Region Detection

As mentioned in Fig. 2, when a specific part of a JPEG image was manipulated and then stored as JPEG again, the specific region had a single JPEG block property and the other region had a double JPEG block property.

Using this principle, to find the manipulated area, we extracted blocks from the whole image using a sliding window and determined if the block was single or double compressed using the trained deep ConvNet, as shown in Fig. 4. The sliding window's stride size had to be a multiple of 8 because the compression process was conducted in 8×8 block units. Thus, the compression traces aligned with the 8×8 blocks, and if we extracted blocks randomly they would have different properties.

Let $y(i,j)$ be the network output of the input block of location (i,j), then

$$R = \left\{ r | r_{i,j} = \frac{e^{y_0(i,j)}}{e^{y_0(i,j)} + e^{y_1(i,j)}}, \quad \forall i,j \right\}, \tag{6}$$

where, r is the probability the block was compressed once. R could be visualized, and where some regions appeared single compressed, and others appeared double compressed, only the single-compressed portion had been manipulated.

5 Experiments

This section compares the classification accuracy to detect double JPEG blocks using several state-of-the-art methods and compares the results of detecting manipulated images.

5.1 Comparison with the State-of-the-Art

We divided double JPEG block detection into three parts: first, double JPEG detection using VGGNet [37], which has shown good performance in many computer vision applications; second, two networks specialized for double JPEG detection by Wang [32], and Barni [33]; third, detection results for the proposed network.

The experiments were performed using the dataset generated in Sect. 3, comprising 1,026,387 blocks for training and 114,043 blocks for testing. All experiments were conducted using TensorFlow 1.5.0 and GeForce GTX 1080, with an initial learning rate of 0.001 and an Adam optimizer.

VGG-16Net: Table 2, part 1 shows VGG-16Net detection performance directly using RGB blocks to distinguish between single and double JPEG blocks. VGG-16Net has previously shown good performance for object category classification, but could not distinguish between single compressed and double compressed JPEG blocks. This is because it is necessary to distinguish the statistical characteristics of DCT coefficients to detect double JPEG, but VGG-16Net uses the semantic information rather than the statistical characteristics of DCT coefficients.

Networks Using Histogram Features: Two methods have been proposed with CNNs and histogram features to distinguish double JPEG. Wang et al. proposed histogram features for DCT values $[-5, 5]$ from nine DCT channels,

Table 2. Performance comparison between double JPEG detection ConvNets. All variants of proposed methods outperformed previous networks. ACC, TPR, and TNR represent the accuracy, true positive rate, and true negative rate, respectively, and positive means classifying a block as double JPEG. The network with the highest accuracy for each part is highlighted in red.

Method	Type	ACC(%)	TPR(%)	TNR(%)
VGG-16 [37]	RGB pixels	50.00	00.00	100.00
Wang [32]	Range - $[-5, 5]$	73.05	67.74	78.37
Barni [33]	Range - $[-50, 50]$	83.47	77.47	89.43
	Range - $[-60, 60]$	84.46	78.35	90.53
	Range - $[-70, 70]$	82.87	75.80	89.90
	Range - $[-80, 80]$	83.90	76.41	91.39
	Range - $[-90, 90]$	83.44	75.65	91.19
	Range - $[-100, 100]$	82.30	79.64	84.92
Proposed (+ Q table)	Last conv output	89.89	86.95	92.81
	First FC ouput	89.95	83.73	96.15
	Second FC output	86.79	82.90	90.67
	All three outputs	90.37	84.84	95.88
Proposed (# of conv layers)	4 conv layers	91.83	87.16	96.50
	5 conv layers	91.33	90.19	92.43
	6 conv layers	91.72	85.93	96.10
	7 conv layers	91.02	85.93	96.10
Proposed*	Optimization	92.76	90.90	94.59

comprising two one-dimensional convolutional layers, two max pooling layers, and three fully connected layers. Barni et al. also used histogram features but the network calculated histogram features within the ConvNets, collecting DCT values $[-50, 50]$ from 64 DCT channels, and comprising three convolutional layers, three max pooling layers, and three fully connected layers.

Table 2, parts 2 and 3 shows that the Wang and Barni network classified single or double JPEG blocks with 73.05% and 83.47% accuracy, respectively. The Barni method extracts histograms over a wider range; thus, it has over 10% better performance due to the larger number of network layers. Compared with the VGG-16Net results, it is critical to use histograms with statistical features for double JPEG detection.

Additional experiments were conducted with the Barni network to investigate how accuracy varied with the histogram range. We tried to increase the histogram range to $[-100, 100]$, but we found that the accuracy was lower if the range was over $[-60, 60]$. Based on this phenomenon, it was estimated that most DCT coefficients were less than 60.

Proposed Networks: The most important point of the proposed network is to include quantization table information in the neural network. We constrained the network structure to match the Barni network that has a $[-60, 60]$ histogram range and inserted quantization table information at three different locations to determine the optimal insertion point: each output of the final convolutional layer, of the first fully connected layer, and of second fully connected layer, as shown in Table 2, part 4. Even though only the quantization table was inserted, the accuracy was 5.43%, 5.52%, and 2.33% higher than the Barni network that had a $[-60, 60]$ histogram range network according to the insertion points. We also inserted the quantization table into all three locations, as shown in the final row of Table 2, part 4, producing the best accuracy (90.37%).

Table 2, part 5 compares the proposed network performance according to convolutional layer depth. Since the previous network used three convolutional layers, we increased the depth from four to seven layers. Increasing the number of convolutional layers to four provided a significant increase in accuracy (1.46% improvement), but there was no subsequent significant improvement for five or more layers because the histogram feature already compressed the statistical data characteristics sufficiently.

The final optimal network had four 5×5 convolutional layers, three max pooling layers and three fully connected layers as shown in Fig. 3. The quantization table information was combined with the output of the last max pooling layer, the output of the first fully connected layer, and the output of the second fully connected layer. All convolutional layers were used with batch normalization [38]. The optimization network reached 92.76% accuracy, as shown in Table 2, part 6.

5.2 Manipulated Region Detection

This section shows the results of image manipulation detection using the proposed network. The 14 images used in the experiments were manipulated in the following order. First, we generated single JPEG images using 1120 different randomly selected quantization tables. Second, we manipulated images by splicing, copy-move, color changing, brightness changing, interpolation, blurring, and resizing using Photoshop. Third, we saved the manipulated images using different randomly selected quantization tables apart from the first one. All manipulated region detection experiments were performed in 32 strides.

Results for Copy-Move and Splicing Manipulations: Figure 5 shows the six results for the copy-move and splicing manipulations. The top two lines show the copy-move manipulations and detection results. Two manipulated images were made by copying the windows and cherry blossoms in the image and then pasting them to another location in the same image. Because copy-move operations are performed within the same image, natural manipulation is possible. The proposed network found single JPEG blocks near the ground truth; however, the Barni network incorrectly detected many double JPEG blocks as single JPEG blocks.

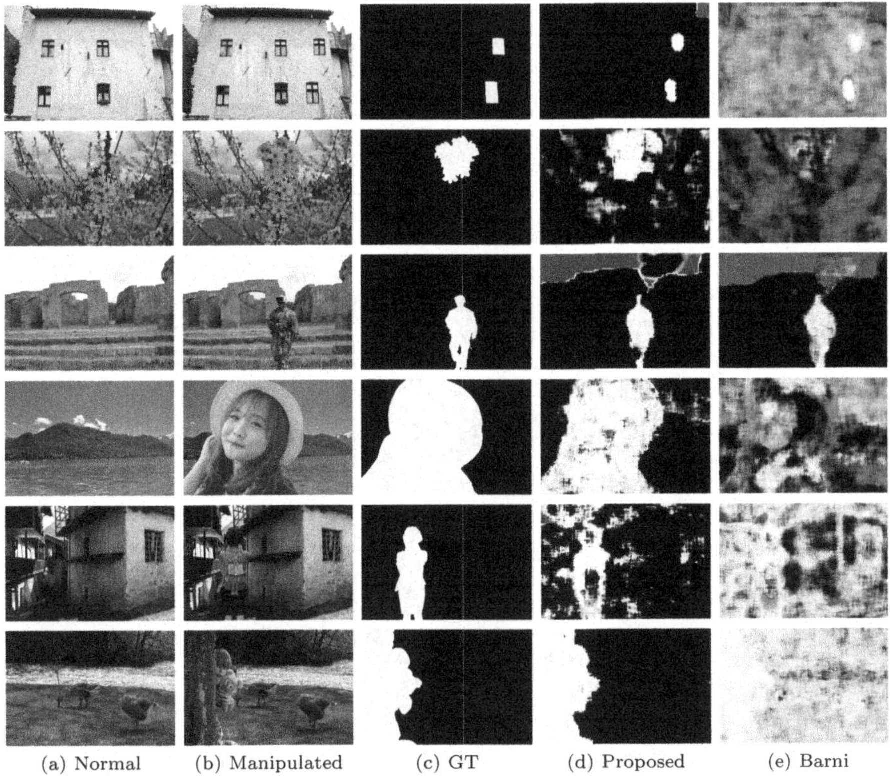

Fig. 5. Examples of copy-move and image splicing detection. (a) and (b) are normal and manipulated images, (c) is the ground truth, (d) is the results of the proposed network, and (e) is the results of the Barni network. The top two rows of images show the copy-move manipulation. The bottom fourth-row images show the image splicing manipulation.

The bottom four lines show the splicing manipulations and detection results. Splicing is one of the most important detection operations because it can completely change the meaning of an image. We pasted four people into four images that were not related to them and applied the blur filter to object edges. The proposed network properly detected four manipulated regions, but, the Barni network detected only one region.

Results for Local Manipulations: Figure 6 shows six results for local manipulations. The top three line of manipulated images were made by color transformation and changing the brightness. Each image became other images with completely different information by changing the color of the tulips, houses, and cars. In the case of the tulip image, the proposed network correctly found a single JPEG area, whereas the Barni network determined that all areas were a

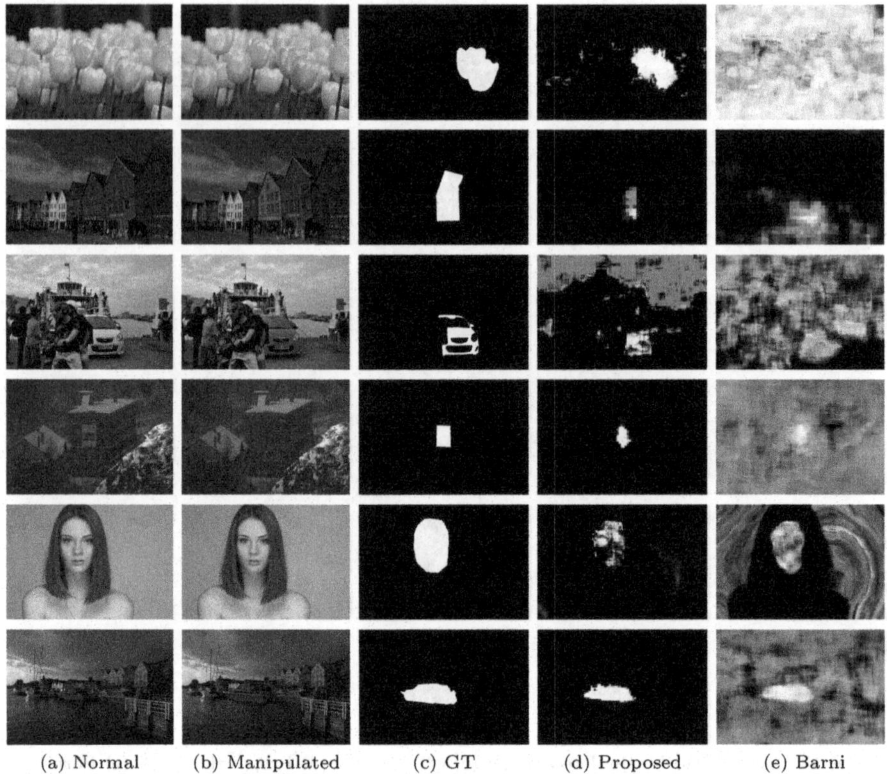

Fig. 6. Examples of local manipulation detection. (a) and (b) are normal and manipulated images, (c) is the ground truth, (d) is the results of the proposed network, and (e) is the results of the Barni network. The top third-row images underwent a change in color, and the bottom third-row images were changed by other local manipulations.

single JPEG. The proposed network showed better performance for the second and third manipulated images.

We erased the banner photos in the building using a content-aware interpolation method, blurred a model's face, and resized the boat. The Barni network distinguished some of the manipulated regions, but there were many false negatives. On the other hand, the proposed network detected single JPEG regions with much high accuracy.

F-measure: To numerically compare the manipulation region detection capabilities, we conducted quantitative experiments on two manipulations–copy-move and blurring. We generated 2100 images of 1024×1024 in size for each manipulation with raw image datasets [34–36]. In the case of the copy-move manipulation, a patch of 544×544 in a random position was copied and pasted into a random location in the same image. In the case of the blur manipulation, a blur filter ($\sigma = 2$) was applied to a 544×544 area of a random position in the image. JPEG

Table 3. F-measures for two manipulations using the proposed network and the Barni network, respectively.

	Proposed	Barni [33]
Copy-move (F-measure)	0.7595	0.6323
Blurring (F-measure)	0.7783	0.6450

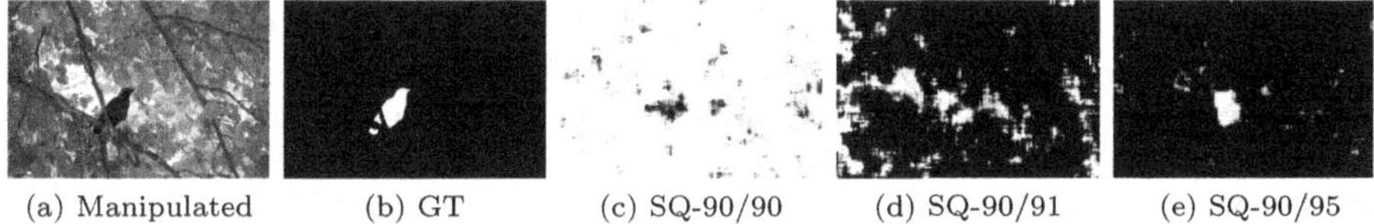

(a) Manipulated (b) GT (c) SQ-90/90 (d) SQ-90/91 (e) SQ-90/95

Fig. 7. Detecting results according to changing the second quality factor. (a) is a manipulated image by changing the color of a bird, (b) is the ground truth and, (c)–(e) are the detection results for images generated according to each quality factor.

compression was performed using 1120 quantization tables in the same manner as 14 representative manipulation images. Table 3 shows the detection results (F-measure) for the copy-move and blur manipulations. That of the proposed network was approximately 0.12 higher than that of the Barni network.

Failure Results and Analysis: In some cases, manipulation regions were not properly detected. The second line of Fig. 5 shows that both the proposed and the Barni networks had false negatives because the pixel values in the sky were saturated and only low frequencies were present. In addition, if single JPEG quality and double JPEG quality were the same or there was little difference, it was impossible to detect the operation area. Because the DCT coefficients of a single JPEG block and a double JPEG block were almost identical, the network could not distinguish between the two classes. Figure 7 shows the detection results according to changing the second quality factor (standard quality factor). Although it was impossible to detect image manipulation with the same quality factor, as the quality factor difference increased, the proposed network could detect the manipulation region.

6 Conclusion

Current double JPEG detection methods only work in very limited situations and cannot be applied to real situations. To overcome this limits, we have created a new dataset using JPEG quantization tables from actual forensic images and designed a novel deep CNN for double JPEG detection using statistical histogram features from each block with a vectorized quantization table. We have also proven that the proposed network can detect various manipulations with mixed JPEG quality factors.

Acknowledgements. This work was supported by the Institute for Information & communications Technology Promotion (IITP) grant funded by the Korean government (MSIP) (2017-0-01671, Development of high reliability image and video authentication service for smart media environment).

References

1. Piva, A.: An overview on image forensics. ISRN Sig. Process. **2013**, 22 p. (2013). https://doi.org/10.1155/2013/496701. Article ID 496701
2. Stamm, M.C., Wu, M., Liu, K.R.: Information forensics: an overview of the first decade. IEEE Access **1**, 167–200 (2013)
3. Shi, Y.Q., Chen, C., Chen, W.: A natural image model approach to splicing detection. In: Proceedings of the 9th Workshop on Multimedia & Security, pp. 51–62. ACM (2007)
4. Chen, W., Shi, Y.Q., Su, W.: Image splicing detection using 2-D phase congruency and statistical moments of characteristic function. In: Security, Steganography, and Watermarking of Multimedia Contents IX, vol. 6505, p. 65050R. International Society for Optics and Photonics (2007)
5. Cozzolino, D., Poggi, G., Verdoliva, L.: Splicebuster: a new blind image splicing detector. In: 2015 IEEE International Workshop on Information Forensics and Security (WIFS), pp. 1–6. IEEE (2015)
6. Rao, Y., Ni, J.: A deep learning approach to detection of splicing and copy-move forgeries in images. In: 2016 IEEE International Workshop on Information Forensics and Security (WIFS), pp. 1–6. IEEE (2016)
7. Chen, C., McCloskey, S., Yu, J.: Image splicing detection via camera response function analysis. In: Proceedings of the IEEE Conference on Computer Vision and Pattern Recognition, pp. 5087–5096 (2017)
8. Fridrich, A.J., Soukal, B.D., Lukáš, A.J.: Detection of copy-move forgery in digital images. In: in Proceedings of Digital Forensic Research Workshop. Citeseer (2003)
9. Ryu, S.-J., Lee, M.-J., Lee, H.-K.: Detection of copy-rotate-move forgery using Zernike moments. In: Böhme, R., Fong, P.W.L., Safavi-Naini, R. (eds.) IH 2010. LNCS, vol. 6387, pp. 51–65. Springer, Heidelberg (2010). https://doi.org/10.1007/978-3-642-16435-4_5
10. Li, J., Li, X., Yang, B., Sun, X.: Segmentation-based image copy-move forgery detection scheme. IEEE Trans. Inf. Forensics Secur. **10**(3), 507–518 (2015)
11. Zhou, Z., Wang, Y., Wu, Q.J., Yang, C.N., Sun, X.: Effective and efficient global context verification for image copy detection. IEEE Trans. Inf. Forensics Secur. **12**(1), 48–63 (2017)
12. Choi, C.H., Lee, H.Y., Lee, H.K.: Estimation of color modification in digital images by CFA pattern change. Forensic Sci. Int. **226**(1–3), 94–105 (2013)
13. Hou, J.U., Lee, H.K.: Detection of hue modification using photo response nonuniformity. IEEE Trans. Circ. Syst. Video Technol. **27**(8), 1826–1832 (2017)
14. Zhou, P., Han, X., Morariu, V.I., Davis, L.S.: Two-stream neural networks for tampered face detection. In: 2017 IEEE Conference on Computer Vision and Pattern Recognition Workshops (CVPRW), pp. 1831–1839. IEEE (2017)
15. Swaminathan, A., Wu, M., Liu, K.R.: Digital image forensics via intrinsic fingerprints. IEEE Trans. Inf. Forensics Secur. **3**(1), 101–117 (2008)
16. Cao, H., Kot, A.C.: Accurate detection of demosaicing regularity for digital image forensics. IEEE Trans. Inf. Forensics Secur. **4**(4), 899–910 (2009)

17. Stamm, M.C., Liu, K.R.: Forensic detection of image manipulation using statistical intrinsic fingerprints. IEEE Trans. Inf. Forensics Secur. **5**(3), 492–506 (2010)
18. Popescu, A.C., Farid, H.: Exposing digital forgeries in color filter array interpolated images. IEEE Trans. Sig. Process. **53**(10), 3948–3959 (2005)
19. Ferrara, P., Bianchi, T., De Rosa, A., Piva, A.: Image forgery localization via fine-grained analysis of CFA artifacts. IEEE Trans. Inf. Forensics Secur. **7**(5), 1566–1577 (2012)
20. Popescu, A.C., Farid, H.: Exposing digital forgeries by detecting traces of resampling. IEEE Trans. Sig. Process. **53**(2), 758–767 (2005)
21. Kirchner, M., Gloe, T.: On resampling detection in re-compressed images. In: First IEEE International Workshop on Information Forensics and Security, WIFS 2009, pp. 21–25. IEEE (2009)
22. Mahdian, B., Saic, S.: Blind authentication using periodic properties of interpolation. IEEE Trans. Inf. Forensics Secur. **3**(3), 529–538 (2008)
23. Pennebaker, W.B., Mitchell, J.L.: JPEG: Still Image Data Compression Standard. Springer, New York (1992)
24. Lukáš, J., Fridrich, J.: Estimation of primary quantization matrix in double compressed JPEG images. In: Proceedings of Digital Forensic Research Workshop, pp. 5–8 (2003)
25. Fu, D., Shi, Y.Q., Su, W.: A generalized Benford's law for jpeg coefficients and its applications in image forensics. In: Security, Steganography, and Watermarking of Multimedia Contents IX, vol. 6505, p. 65051L. International Society for Optics and Photonics (2007)
26. Li, B., Shi, Y.Q., Huang, J.: Detecting doubly compressed JPEG images by using mode based first digit features. In: 2008 IEEE 10th Workshop on Multimedia Signal Processing, pp. 730–735. IEEE (2008)
27. Lin, Z., He, J., Tang, X., Tang, C.K.: Fast, automatic and fine-grained tampered JPEG image detection via DCT coefficient analysis. Pattern Recognit. **42**(11), 2492–2501 (2009)
28. Farid, H.: Exposing digital forgeries from JPEG ghosts. IEEE Trans. Inf. Forensics Secur. **4**(1), 154–160 (2009)
29. Bianchi, T., Piva, A.: Analysis of non-aligned double jpeg artifacts for the localization of image forgeries. In: 2011 IEEE International Workshop on Information Forensics and Security (WIFS), pp. 1–6. IEEE (2011)
30. Bianchi, T., De Rosa, A., Piva, A.: Improved DCT coefficient analysis for forgery localization in JPEG images. In: 2011 IEEE International Conference on Acoustics, Speech and Signal Processing (ICASSP), pp. 2444–2447. IEEE (2011)
31. Chen, Y.L., Hsu, C.T.: Detecting recompression of JPEG images via periodicity analysis of compression artifacts for tampering detection. IEEE Trans. Inf. Forensics Secur. **6**(2), 396–406 (2011)
32. Wang, Q., Zhang, R.: Double JPEG compression forensics based on a convolutional neural network. EURASIP J. Inf. Secur. **2016**(1), 23 (2016)
33. Barni, M., et al.: Aligned and non-aligned double JPEG detection using convolutional neural networks. J. Vis. Commun. Image Represent. **49**, 153–163 (2017)
34. Dang-Nguyen, D.T., Pasquini, C., Conotter, V., Boato, G.: Raise: a raw images dataset for digital image forensics. In: Proceedings of the 6th ACM Multimedia Systems Conference, pp. 219–224. ACM (2015)
35. Gloe, T., Böhme, R.: The dresden image database for benchmarking digital image forensics. J. Digit. Forensic Pract. **3**(2–4), 150–159 (2010)

36. Bas, P., Filler, T., Pevný, T.: "Break our steganographic system": the ins and outs of organizing BOSS. In: Filler, T., Pevný, T., Craver, S., Ker, A. (eds.) IH 2011. LNCS, vol. 6958, pp. 59–70. Springer, Heidelberg (2011). https://doi.org/10.1007/978-3-642-24178-9_5
37. Simonyan, K., Zisserman, A.: Very deep convolutional networks for large-scale image recognition. arXiv preprint arXiv:1409.1556 (2014)
38. Ioffe, S., Szegedy, C.: Batch normalization: accelerating deep network training by reducing internal covariate shift. In: International Conference on Machine Learning, pp. 448–456 (2015)

Wasserstein Divergence for GANs

Jiqing Wu[1(✉)], Zhiwu Huang[1], Janine Thoma[1], Dinesh Acharya[1], and Luc Van Gool[1,2]

[1] Computer Vision Lab, ETH Zurich, Zürich, Switzerland
{jwu,zhiwu.huang,jthoma,vangool}@vision.ee.ethz.ch, acharyad@student.ethz.ch

[2] VISICS, KU Leuven, Leuven, Belgium

Abstract. In many domains of computer vision, generative adversarial networks (GANs) have achieved great success, among which the family of Wasserstein GANs (WGANs) is considered to be state-of-the-art due to the theoretical contributions and competitive qualitative performance. However, it is very challenging to approximate the k-Lipschitz constraint required by the Wasserstein-1 metric (W-met). In this paper, we propose a novel Wasserstein divergence (W-div), which is a relaxed version of W-met and does not require the k-Lipschitz constraint. As a concrete application, we introduce a Wasserstein divergence objective for GANs (WGAN-div), which can faithfully approximate W-div through optimization. Under various settings, including progressive growing training, we demonstrate the stability of the proposed WGAN-div owing to its theoretical and practical advantages over WGANs. Also, we study the quantitative and visual performance of WGAN-div on standard image synthesis benchmarks, showing the superior performance of WGAN-div compared to the state-of-the-art methods.

Keywords: Wasserstein metric · Wasserstein divergence · GANs Progressive growing

1 Introduction

Over the past few years, we have witnessed the great success of generative adversarial networks (GANs) [1] for a variety of applications. GANs are a useful family of generative models that expresses generative modeling as a zero-sum game between two networks: A generator network produces plausible samples given some noise, while a discriminator network distinguishes between the generator's output and real data. There are numerous works inspired by the original GANs, [2–5] to name a few. While GANs can produce visually pleasing samples, they lack a reliable way of measuring the difference between fake and real data distribution, which leads to unstable training.

Electronic supplementary material The online version of this chapter (https://doi.org/10.1007/978-3-030-01228-1_40) contains supplementary material, which is available to authorized users.

V. Ferrari et al. (Eds.): ECCV 2018, LNCS 11209, pp. 673–688, 2018.
https://doi.org/10.1007/978-3-030-01228-1_40

To address this issue, [6] introduced the Wassestein-1 metric (W-met) to the GAN framework. Compared to the Jensen-Shannon (JS) or the Kullback-Leibler (KL) divergence, W-met is considered to be more sensible for distributions supported by low dimensional manifolds. Given that the primal form of W-met is intractable to compute, [6] proposed to use the dual form of W-met, which requires the k-Lipschitz constraint. A series of ideas [6–9] were proposed to approximate the dual W-met and achieved impressive results compared to the non-Wasserstein based GANs. However, they generally suffer from unsatisfying regularization for the k-Lipschitz constraint, mainly because it is a very strict constraint and non-trivial to approximate [9,10].

Other studies have tackled the stability issue from different angles. For example, [10] proposed a gradient-based regularizer associated with the $\mathfrak{f}$-divergence [11] to address the dimensional misspecification. In order to stabilize the training towards high resolution images, [12,13] applied deep stack architectures by incorporating extra information. Recently, building upon the dual W-met objective of [7,14] presented a sophisticated progressive growing training scheme and obtained excellent high resolution images.

In this paper, we propose to resolve the k-Lipschitz constraint by introducing a relaxed version of W-met and incorporating it in the GAN framework. Our contributions can be summarized as follows:

1. We introduce a novel Wasserstein divergence (W-div) and prove that the proposed W-div is a symmetric divergence. Moreover, we explore the connection between the proposed W-div and W-met.
2. Benefiting from the non-challenging constraint required by the W-div, we introduce Wasserstein divergence GANs (WGAN-div) as its practical application. The proposed objective can faithfully approximate the corresponding W-div through optimization.
3. We demonstrate the stability of WGAN-div under various settings including progressive growing training. Also, we conduct various experiments on standard image synthesis benchmarks and present superior results of WGAN-div compared to the state-of-the-art methods, both quantitatively and qualitatively.

2 Background

Imagine there are two players in a game. One player (Generator) intends to generate visually plausible images, aiming to fool its opponent, while the opponent (Discriminator) attempts to discriminate real images from synthetic images. Such adversarial competition is the key idea behind GAN models. To measure the distance between real and fake data distributions, [1] proposed the objective

$$L_{\mathrm{JS}}(\mathbb{P}_r, \mathbb{P}_g) = \mathop{\mathbb{E}}_{\boldsymbol{x}\sim\mathbb{P}_r}[\ln(f(\boldsymbol{x}))] + \mathop{\mathbb{E}}_{\tilde{\boldsymbol{x}}\sim\mathbb{P}_g}[\ln(1 - f(\tilde{\boldsymbol{x}}))], \tag{1}$$

which can be interpreted as the JS divergence up to a constant [15] and where f is a discriminative function. The model can thus be defined as a min-max optimization problem:

$$\min_G \max_D \mathop{\mathbb{E}}_{\boldsymbol{x}\sim\mathbb{P}_r}[\ln(D(\boldsymbol{x}))] + \mathop{\mathbb{E}}_{G(\boldsymbol{z})\sim\mathbb{P}_g}[\ln(1-D(G(\boldsymbol{z})))], \tag{2}$$

where G is the generator parametrized by a neural network and D is the discriminative neural network parametrizing f. Usually, we let $\boldsymbol{z}$ be low dimensional random noise, and $\boldsymbol{x}, G(\boldsymbol{z})$ are the real and fake data satisfying the probability measures $\mathbb{P}_r, \mathbb{P}_g$.

Wasserstein GANs (WGANs). The rise of the Wasserstein-1 metric (W-met) in GAN models is primarily motivated by unstable training caused by the gradient vanishing problem [6]. Given two probability measures $\mathbb{P}_r, \mathbb{P}_g$, the W-met [16] is defined as

$$\mathcal{W}_1(\mathbb{P}_r, \mathbb{P}_g) = \sup_{f\in \mathrm{Lip}_1} \mathop{\mathbb{E}}_{\boldsymbol{x}\sim\mathbb{P}_r}[f(\boldsymbol{x})] - \mathop{\mathbb{E}}_{\tilde{\boldsymbol{x}}\sim\mathbb{P}_g}[f(\tilde{\boldsymbol{x}})], \tag{3}$$

where Lip_1 is the function space of all f satisfying the 1-Lipschitz constraint $\|f\|_L \leq 1$. It is worth mentioning that $\mathcal{W}_1$ is invariant up to a positive scalar k if the Lipschitz constraint is modified to be k. $\mathcal{W}_1$ is believed to be more sensible to distributions supported by low dimensional manifolds such as image, video, etc. Generally, the existing Wasserstein GANs (WGANs) fall into two categories:

Weight Constraints. To approximately satisfy the Lipschitz constraint, [6] proposed a weight clipping method that imposes a hard threshold $c > 0$ on the weights $\boldsymbol{w}$ of the discriminator D, which parametrizes f in Eq. 3:

$$\boldsymbol{w}' = \begin{cases} \boldsymbol{w} & \text{if } |\boldsymbol{w}| < c \\ c & \text{if } \boldsymbol{w} \geq c \\ -c & \text{if } \boldsymbol{w} \leq -c \end{cases} \tag{4}$$

This approach was proven to be unsatisfactory by [7], since through weight clipping, the neural network tends to learn oversimplified functions. Later, [8] proposed spectral normalization GANs (SNGANs). To impose the 1-Lipschitz constraint, SNGANs normalize the weights $\boldsymbol{w}_i$ of each layer i by the L_2 matrix norm,

$$\boldsymbol{w}_i' = \frac{\boldsymbol{w}_i}{\|\boldsymbol{w}_i\|_2}. \tag{5}$$

Because the set of functions satisfying the local 1-Lipschitz constraint is merely a subset of the function space Lip_1, such a constraint inevitably narrows the effective search space and entails a sub-optimal solution.

Gradient Constraints. To overcome the disadvantages of weight clipping, [7] introduced a gradient penalty term to Wasserstein GANs (WGAN-GP). The objective is defined as

$$L_{\mathrm{GP}} = \underbrace{\mathop{\mathbb{E}}_{\boldsymbol{x}\sim\mathbb{P}_r}[f(\boldsymbol{x})] - \mathop{\mathbb{E}}_{\tilde{\boldsymbol{x}}\sim\mathbb{P}_g}[f(\tilde{\boldsymbol{x}})]}_{\text{Wasserstein term}} + k \underbrace{\mathop{\mathbb{E}}_{\hat{\boldsymbol{x}}\sim\mathbb{P}_y}[(\|\nabla f(\hat{\boldsymbol{x}})\|_2 - 1)^2]}_{\text{gradient penalty}}, \tag{6}$$

where ∇ is the gradient operator and $\mathbb{P}_y$ is the distribution obtained by sampling uniformly along straight lines between points from the real and fake data distributions $\mathbb{P}_r$ and $\mathbb{P}_g$. As pointed out by [9,10], with a finite number of training iterations on limited input samples, it is very difficult to guarantee the k-Lipschitz constraint for the whole input domain. Thus, [9] further proposed Wasserstein GANs with a consistency term (CTGANs). Inspired by the original 1-Lipschitz constraint, CTGANs add the following term to Eq. 6,

$$\mathrm{CT}|_{\boldsymbol{x}_1,\boldsymbol{x}_2} = \mathbb{E}_{\boldsymbol{x}_1,\boldsymbol{x}_2}[\max(0, \frac{d(f(\boldsymbol{x}_1), f(\boldsymbol{x}_2))}{d(\boldsymbol{x}_1,\boldsymbol{x}_2)} - c)], \tag{7}$$

where $\boldsymbol{x}_1, \boldsymbol{x}_2$ are two data points, d is a metric and c is a threshold. Recently, to improve stability and image quality, [14] proposed a training scheme in which GANs are grown progressively. In addition to progressive growing, [14] also proposed an objective $L_{\mathrm{PG}} = L_{\mathrm{GP}} + \mathrm{PG}$, where

$$\mathrm{PG} = \begin{cases} \underset{\hat{\boldsymbol{x}}\sim\mathbb{P}_y}{\mathbb{E}} [(\|\nabla f(\hat{\boldsymbol{x}})\|_2 - 750)^2/750^2] & \text{for CIFAR-10} \\ 0.001 \underset{\hat{\boldsymbol{x}}\sim\mathbb{P}_y}{\mathbb{E}} [\|\nabla f(\hat{\boldsymbol{x}})\|_2^2] & \text{for other datasets} \end{cases} \tag{8}$$

$\mathfrak{f}$-GANs. Outside the family of Wasserstein metrics, there is another important family of divergences—the $\mathfrak{f}$-divergences. [11] argued that $\mathfrak{f}$-divergence can be used for training generative samplers and proposed $\mathfrak{f}$-GANs. Since the $\mathfrak{f}$-GANs are vulnerable to the dimension mismatch between fake and real data, [10] proposed a gradient-based regularizer to stabilize the training and gave an example based on JS-divergence:

$$\begin{aligned} L_{\mathrm{RJS}}(\mathbb{P}_r, \mathbb{P}_g) &= \underset{\boldsymbol{x}\sim\mathbb{P}_r}{\mathbb{E}} [\ln(f(\boldsymbol{x}))] + \underset{\tilde{\boldsymbol{x}}\sim\mathbb{P}_g}{\mathbb{E}} [\ln(1 - f(\tilde{\boldsymbol{x}}))] - k\Omega(\mathbb{P}_r, \mathbb{P}_g) \\ \Omega(\mathbb{P}_r, \mathbb{P}_g) &:= \underset{\boldsymbol{x}\sim\mathbb{P}_r}{\mathbb{E}} \left[(1 - f(\boldsymbol{x}))^2 \|\nabla f(\boldsymbol{x})\|^2\right] + \underset{\tilde{\boldsymbol{x}}\sim\mathbb{P}_g}{\mathbb{E}} \left[f(\tilde{\boldsymbol{x}})^2 \|\nabla f(\tilde{\boldsymbol{x}})\|^2\right]. \end{aligned} \tag{9}$$

Information Geometry. In information geometry, [17] studied the connections between the Wasserstein distance and the Kullback-Leibler (KL) divergence employed by early GANs. They exploit the fact that by regularizing the Wasserstein distance with entropy, the entropy relaxed Wasserstein distance introduces a divergence and naturally defines certain geometrical structures from the information geometry viewpoint.

3 Proposed Method

As discussed above, it is very challenging to approximate the W-met. This is due to the gap between limited input samples on the one hand and the strict 1-Lipschitz constraint on the whole input sample domain [9,18] on the other hand. At the same time, it is natural to ask whether there exists an optimal f^* for

W-met (Eq. 3). According to [19], by solving a family of minimization problems given $p > 0$

$$f_p = \operatorname*{argmin}_{f \in W_c^{1,p}} \mathop{\mathbb{E}}_{\boldsymbol{x} \sim \mathbb{P}_r} [f(\boldsymbol{x})] - \mathop{\mathbb{E}}_{\tilde{\boldsymbol{x}} \sim \mathbb{P}_g} [f(\tilde{\boldsymbol{x}})] + \frac{1}{p} \mathop{\mathbb{E}}_{\hat{\boldsymbol{x}} \sim \mathbb{P}_u} [\|\nabla f(\hat{\boldsymbol{x}})\|^p], \tag{10}$$

where $\mathbb{P}_u$ is a Radon probability measure and $W_c^{1,p}$ is the Sobolev space containing all the functions f in L^p space with first order weak derivatives and compact support, we can find a sequence $p_k \to \infty$ such that $f_{p_k} \to -f^*$.

3.1 Wasserstein Divergence

The connection between Eq. 10 and W-met inspires us to propose a novel Wasserstein divergence (W-div) and we prove that it is indeed a valid symmetric divergence.

Theorem 1 *(Wasserstein divergence). Let $\Omega \subset \mathbb{R}^n$ be an open, bounded, connected set and S be the set of all the Radon probability measures on Ω. If for some $p \neq 1, k > 0$ we define*

$$\begin{aligned} \mathcal{W}'_{p,k} &: S \times S \to \mathbb{R}^- \cup \{0\} \\ &(\mathbb{P}_r, \mathbb{P}_g) \to \inf_{f \in C_c^1(\Omega)} \mathop{\mathbb{E}}_{\boldsymbol{x} \sim \mathbb{P}_r} [f(\boldsymbol{x})] - \mathop{\mathbb{E}}_{\tilde{\boldsymbol{x}} \sim \mathbb{P}_g} [f(\tilde{\boldsymbol{x}})] + k \mathop{\mathbb{E}}_{\hat{\boldsymbol{x}} \sim \mathbb{P}_u} [\|\nabla f(\hat{\boldsymbol{x}})\|^p], \end{aligned} \tag{11}$$

where $C_c^1(\Omega)$ is the function space of all the first order differentiable functions on Ω with compact support, then $\mathcal{W}'_{p,k}$ is a symmetric divergence (up to the negative sign).

Proof. See supplementary material.

By imposing the $C_c^1(\Omega)$ function space, we rule out pathological functions with weak derivatives. Compared to the k-Lipschitz constraint, $f \in C_c^1(\Omega)$ is less restrictive, since $\|\nabla f\|$ does not need to be bounded by a hard threshold k. Given the universal approximation theorem and the modern architecture of neural networks—stacking differentiable layers to form a nonlinear differentiable function—$f \in C_c^1(\Omega)$ can easily be parameterized by a neural network.

In the following we further explore the connection between the proposed W-div and the original W-met in Eq. 3.

Remark 1 *(Upper bound). Given Radon probability measures $\mathbb{P}_r, \mathbb{P}_g, \mathbb{P}_u$ on Ω, let*

$$\mathcal{W}'_{\mathbb{P}_u}(\mathbb{P}_r, \mathbb{P}_g) := \inf_{f \in C_c^\infty(\Omega)} \mathop{\mathbb{E}}_{\boldsymbol{x} \sim \mathbb{P}_r} [f(\boldsymbol{x})] - \mathop{\mathbb{E}}_{\tilde{\boldsymbol{x}} \sim \mathbb{P}_g} [f(\tilde{\boldsymbol{x}})] + \frac{1}{2} \mathop{\mathbb{E}}_{\hat{\boldsymbol{x}} \sim \mathbb{P}_u} [(\|\nabla f(\hat{\boldsymbol{x}})\|^2], \tag{12}$$

where C_c^∞ is the function space of all the smooth functions f with compact support. There exists an optimal f^* for $\mathcal{W}_1$ (Eq. 3) such that

$$\mathcal{W}_1(\mathbb{P}_r, \mathbb{P}_g) = \mathop{\mathbb{E}}_{\boldsymbol{x} \sim \mathbb{P}_r} [f^*(\boldsymbol{x})] - \mathop{\mathbb{E}}_{\tilde{\boldsymbol{x}} \sim \mathbb{P}_g} [f^*(\tilde{\boldsymbol{x}})], \tag{13}$$

and a $\mathcal{W}^{'}_{\mathbb{P}_{u^*}}$ *determined by* f^* *such that*

$$\mathcal{W}^{'}_{\mathbb{P}_{u^*}}(\mathbb{P}_r, \mathbb{P}_g) = \sup_{\mathbb{P}_u \in S} \mathcal{W}^{'}_{\mathbb{P}_u}(\mathbb{P}_r, \mathbb{P}_g). \tag{14}$$

Please see the detailed discussion in [19].

Remark 1 indicates that $\mathcal{W}^{'}_{\mathbb{P}_{u^*}}$, which is determined by the optimal f^*, is the upper bound of our W-div $\mathcal{W}^{'}_{\mathbb{P}_u}$ [1].

Given the similarities between our proposed W-div and L_{GP} (Eq. 6), it may be interesting to know if there exists a divergence corresponding to L_{GP}. In general, the answer is no.

Remark 2. *If for* $n > 0$ *we let*

$$\mathcal{W}^{''}_{p,k,n}(\mathbb{P}_r, \mathbb{P}_g) := \inf_{f \in C^1_c(\Omega)} \mathop{\mathbb{E}}_{\boldsymbol{x} \sim \mathbb{P}_r}[f(\boldsymbol{x})] - \mathop{\mathbb{E}}_{\tilde{\boldsymbol{x}} \sim \mathbb{P}_g}[f(\tilde{\boldsymbol{x}})] + k \mathop{\mathbb{E}}_{\hat{\boldsymbol{x}} \sim \mathbb{P}_u}[(\|\nabla f(\hat{\boldsymbol{x}})\| - n)^p], \tag{15}$$

then $\mathcal{W}^{''}_{p,k,n}$ *is* ***not*** *a divergence in general.*

Counterexample. Assuming $\Omega = (-1, 1)$ and $p = 2$, it suffices to show that $\mathcal{W}^{''}_{2,k,n}(\mathbb{P}_r, \mathbb{P}_g) \neq 0$ for $\mathbb{P}_r = \mathbb{P}_g$ almost everywhere. Since $\mathbb{E}_{\boldsymbol{x} \sim \mathbb{P}_r}[f(\boldsymbol{x})]$ and $\mathbb{E}_{\tilde{\boldsymbol{x}} \sim \mathbb{P}_g}[f(\tilde{\boldsymbol{x}})]$ cancel out, in order to guarantee $\mathcal{W}^{''}_{2,k,n}(\mathbb{P}_r, \mathbb{P}_g) = 0$, $\|\nabla f(\hat{\boldsymbol{x}})\|$ must be equal to n on $(-1, 1)$, which implies that f is affine and contradicts the compact support constraint. For m-dimensional sets such as $(-1, 1)^m$ and an even integer p we need to employ the uniqueness argument of the Picard-Lindelöf Theorem to show that f can only be affine.

Remark 2 implies that the plausible statistic distance $\mathcal{W}^{''}_{2,k,1}$ corresponding to Eq. 6 is neither a divergence, nor a valid metric.

3.2 Wasserstein Divergence GANs

Although W-met enjoys the tempting property of providing useful gradients, in practice, the original formulation $\mathbb{E}_{\boldsymbol{x} \sim \mathbb{P}_r}[f(\boldsymbol{x})] - \mathbb{E}_{\tilde{\boldsymbol{x}} \sim \mathbb{P}_g}[f(\tilde{\boldsymbol{x}})]$ of W-met cannot be directly applied as an objective without imposing the strict 1-Lipschitz constraint. In contrast, it is very straightforward to use our proposed W-div as an objective. Therefore, we introduce Wasserstein divergence GANs (WGAN-div). Our objective can be smoothly derived as

$$L_{\text{DIV}} = \mathop{\mathbb{E}}_{\boldsymbol{x} \sim \mathbb{P}_r}[f(\boldsymbol{x})] - \mathop{\mathbb{E}}_{\tilde{\boldsymbol{x}} \sim \mathbb{P}_g}[f(\tilde{\boldsymbol{x}})] + k \mathop{\mathbb{E}}_{\hat{\boldsymbol{x}} \sim \mathbb{P}_u}[\|\nabla f(\hat{\boldsymbol{x}})\|^p], \tag{16}$$

which is identical to the formulation of W-div without the infimum. Minimizing L_{DIV} faithfully approximates $\mathcal{W}^{'}_{p,k}$, in a sense that the decrease of L_{DIV} indicates a better approximation of $\mathcal{W}^{'}_{p,k}$. In comparison, lowering L_{GP} does not

[1] $\mathcal{W}^{'}_{\mathbb{P}_u}$ is a family of special cases of Eq. 11 with a more restrictive function space C^{∞}_c.

Algorithm 1. The proposed WGAN-div algorithm

Require: Batch size m, generator G and discriminator D, power p, coefficient k, training iterations n, and other hyperparameters

for $i \leftarrow 1$ to n **do**

  Sample real data $\boldsymbol{x}_1, \ldots, \boldsymbol{x}_m$ from $\mathbb{P}_r$

  Sample Gaussian noise $\boldsymbol{z}_1, \ldots, \boldsymbol{z}_m$ from $\mathcal{N}(0, 1)$

  Sample vector $\boldsymbol{\mu} = (\mu_1, \ldots, \mu_m)$ from uniform distribution $U[0, 1]$ such that

  $\hat{\boldsymbol{x}}_j = (1 - \mu_j)\boldsymbol{x}_j + \mu_j G(\boldsymbol{z}_j)$

  Update the weights $\boldsymbol{w}_G$ of G by descending:
  $\boldsymbol{w}_G \leftarrow \mathrm{Adam}(\nabla_{\boldsymbol{w}_G}(\frac{1}{m}\sum_{j=1}^{m} D(G(\boldsymbol{z}_j))), \boldsymbol{w}_G, \alpha, \beta_1, \beta_2)$

  Update the weights $\boldsymbol{w}_D$ of D by descending:
  $\boldsymbol{w}_D \leftarrow \mathrm{Adam}(\nabla_{\boldsymbol{w}_D}(\frac{1}{m}\sum_{j=1}^{m} D(\boldsymbol{x}_j) - D(G(\boldsymbol{z}_j))$
  $+k\|\nabla_{\hat{\boldsymbol{x}}_j} D(\hat{\boldsymbol{x}}_j)\|^p), \boldsymbol{w}_D, \alpha, \beta_1, \beta_2)$

end for

Table 1. The default architecture of WGAN-div for 64×64 image generation

Generator	Kernel size	Resampling	Output shape
Noise	-	-	128
Linear	-	-	$512 \times 4 \times 4$
Residual block	$[3 \times 3] \times 2$	Up	$512 \times 8 \times 8$
Residual block	$[3 \times 3] \times 2$	Up	$256 \times 16 \times 16$
Residual block	$[3 \times 3] \times 2$	Up	$128 \times 32 \times 32$
Residual block	$[3 \times 3] \times 2$	Up	$64 \times 32 \times 32$
Conv, tanh	3×3	-	$3 \times 64 \times 64$
Discriminator			
Conv	3×3	-	$64 \times 64 \times 64$
Residual block	$[3 \times 3] \times 2$	Down	$128 \times 32 \times 32$
Residual block	$[3 \times 3] \times 2$	Down	$256 \times 16 \times 16$
Residual block	$[3 \times 3] \times 2$	Down	$512 \times 8 \times 8$
Residual block	$[3 \times 3] \times 2$	Down	$512 \times 4 \times 4$
Linear	-	-	1

Table 2. Visual and FID comparison for generated samples (green dots) and real samples (yellow dots) on Swiss Roll, 8 Gaussians and 25 Gaussians. The value surfaces of the discriminators are also plotted.

WGAN-GP			CTGAN			**WGAN-div**		
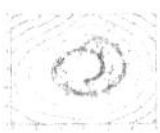 0.02	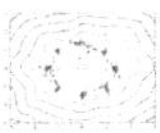 0.04	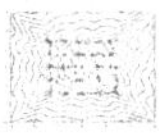 0.04	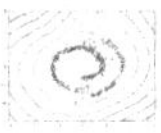 0.02	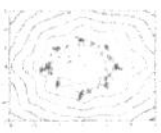 0.03	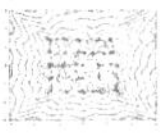 0.03	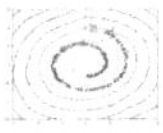 **0.01**	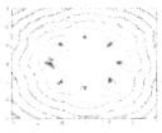 **0.02**	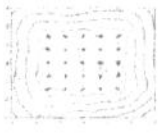 **0.01**

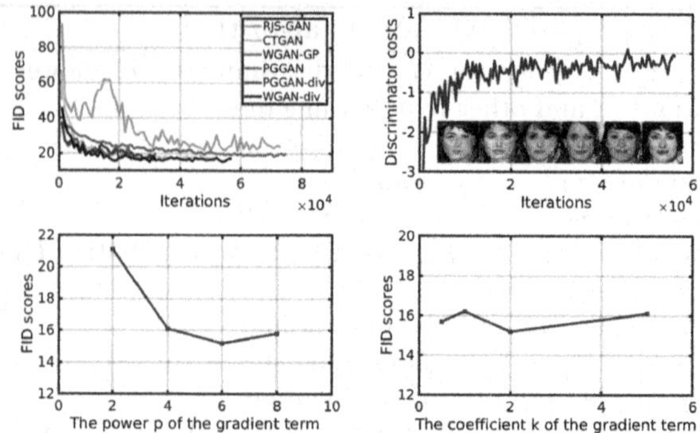

Fig. 1. Curves of FID vs. iteration (top left), Discriminator cost vs. iteration (top right), FID vs. power p (bottom left), and FID vs. coefficient k (bottom right) for WGAN-div on CelebA.

necessarily imply that L_{GP} approximates $\mathcal{W}_1$ better, since L_{GP} can be decreased at the cost of violating the gradient penalty term (Eq. 6).

By incorporating our objective L_{DIV} in the GAN framework, together with parameterizing $f \in C_c^1$ by a discriminator D and the fake data distribution $\mathbb{P}_g$ by a generator G, our min-max optimization problem can be written as

$$\min_G \max_D \mathop{\mathbb{E}}_{G(\boldsymbol{z})\sim\mathbb{P}_g}[D(G(\boldsymbol{z}))] - \mathop{\mathbb{E}}_{\boldsymbol{x}\sim\mathbb{P}_r}[D(\boldsymbol{x})] - k \mathop{\mathbb{E}}_{\hat{\boldsymbol{x}}\sim\mathbb{P}_u}[\|\nabla_{\hat{\boldsymbol{x}}} D(\hat{\boldsymbol{x}})\|^p], \tag{17}$$

where $\boldsymbol{z}$ is random noise, $\boldsymbol{x}$ is the real data, and $\hat{\boldsymbol{x}}$ is sampled as a linear combination of real and fake data points. For more studies of sampling strategies we refer readers to our supplementary material. The final algorithm is obtained as shown in Algorithm 1. Following the good practice of [7], our building blocks for D and G are residual blocks [20]. The default architecture of WGAN-div is presented in Table 1. We apply Adam optimization [21] to update G and D. We study the crucial hyperparameters such as the coefficient k and the power p in the next section.

4 Experiments

In this section, we evaluate WGAN-div on toy datasets and three widely used image datasets—CIFAR-10, CelebA [22] and LSUN [23]. As a preliminary evaluation, we use low-dimensional datasets such as Swiss roll, 8 Gaussians and 25 Gaussians to justify that our proposed W-div can be more effectively learned than W-met used by WGAN-GP and CTGAN, in terms of more meaningful value surfaces of discriminator D i.e. f, and better generated data distribution (Table 2). Meanwhile, the three large scale datasets highlight a variety of challenges that WGAN-div should address and evaluation on them is adequate to support the advantages of WGAN-div.

Recently, [24] pointed out that the inception score (IS) [25] is not reliable because it does not incorporate the statistics of real image samples. As an alternative, they introduced the Fréchet inception distance (FID) to measure the difference between real and fake data distributions. Experiments verified that the FID score is consistent with visual judgment by humans. Later, [26] conducted a comprehensive study of the state-of-the-art GANs based on FID, which confirmed that FID provides fairer assessment. Hence, we consider the FID score as the major criterion for evaluating our method. Also, visual results are provided as a complementary form of verification.

We compare our WGAN-div to the state-of-the-art DCGAN [2], WGAN-GP [7], RJS-GAN [18], CTGAN [9], SNGAN [8], and PGGAN [14]. For each method, we apply the default architectures and hyperparamters recommended by their papers. The default architectures for G and D of WGAN-div follow the ResNet design [20] as presented in Table 1. We use Adam optimization [21] for updating G and D with a learning rate of 0.0002 for all three datasets. The number of training steps are 100000 for CelabA and CIFAR-10, and 200000 for LSUN. By cross validation we determine the number of iterations for D per training step to be 4 for CelebA and LSUN, and 5 for CIFAR-10.

4.1 Hyperparameter Study

We demonstrate the impact of two important hyperparameters—the power p and the coefficient k—on our WGAN-div method. Both of them control the gradient term of L_{DIV}. We report the obtained FID scores on the 64×64 CelebA dataset in the bottom row of Fig. 1. For a fixed optimal $p = 6$ and varying k, Fig. 1 shows that L_{DIV} is not sensitive to changes of k, with the FID score fluctuating mildly around 16. On the other hand, for a fixed $k = 2$ and changing p, we obtain the optimal FID at $p = 6$, which differs from the common choice $p = 2$ applied in WGAN methods. The fact that f_p (Eq. 10) converges to the optimal discriminator when p becomes larger may explain why L_{DIV} favors a larger power p. To summarize, our default p, k are determined to be $p = 6$ and $k = 2$.

4.2 Stability Study

In this section we evaluate the stability of our method to changes in architecture and compare it to other approaches. In this light, we apply various architecture settings for WGAN-div, WGAN-GP, and RJS-GAN, which represent three types of statistical distances: W-div, W-met, and $\mathfrak{f}$-divergence. We train these methods with two standard architectures—ConvNet as used by DCGAN [2] and ResNet [20], which is used by WGAN-GP [7]. Since batch normalization [27] (BN) is considered to be a key ingredient in stabilizing the training process [2], we also evaluate the FID without BN. In total, we use four settings: ResNet, ResNet without BN, ConvNet, and ConvNet without BN. As shown in Table 3, each column reports the visual and FID results obtained under the same architecture. Our WGAN-div achieves the best FID scores for all four settings. Table 3

Table 3. FID scores and qualitative comparison of various architectures on CelebA.

	ResNet	ResNet without BN	ConvNet	ConvNet without BN
WGAN-GP	18.4 	20.3 	21.2 	24.6 
RJS-GAN	21.4 	23.2 	21.7 	22.4 
WGAN-div	**15.2** 	**18.6** 	**17.5** 	**21.5** 

also features corresponding visual results. Compared to WGAN-GP and RJS-GAN, WGAN-div produces more visually pleasing images and the visual quality remains more stable under changing settings. This experimental study confirms the advantages gained by our W-div and its identical objective L_{DIV}.

4.3 Evaluation on the Standard Training Scheme

In this experiment, we intend to fairly compare the performance of various GANs by ruling out the impact caused by fine-tuned training strategies. For this purpose, we follow the standard, i.e. non-growing, training scheme, which fixes the size and architecture of the discriminator and generator through the whole training process. We compute the FID scores for DCGAN, WGAN-GP, RJS-GAN, CTGAN, and WGAN-div. The configurations of the compared methods are set according to the recommendations from the authors. The results are reported in Table 4. WGAN-div reaches the best FID scores among the compared approaches, which quantitatively confirms the advantages of our method.

While the FID score of WGAN-div mildly outperforms the state-of-the-art methods on the dataset CIFAR-10, it demonstrates clearer improvements on the larger scale datasets CelebA and LSUN. Similarly, the facial results shown in Fig. 2 tell us that WGAN-div is better than the compared methods with regard to diversity and semantics. For example, Fig. 2 shows diverse faces generated by

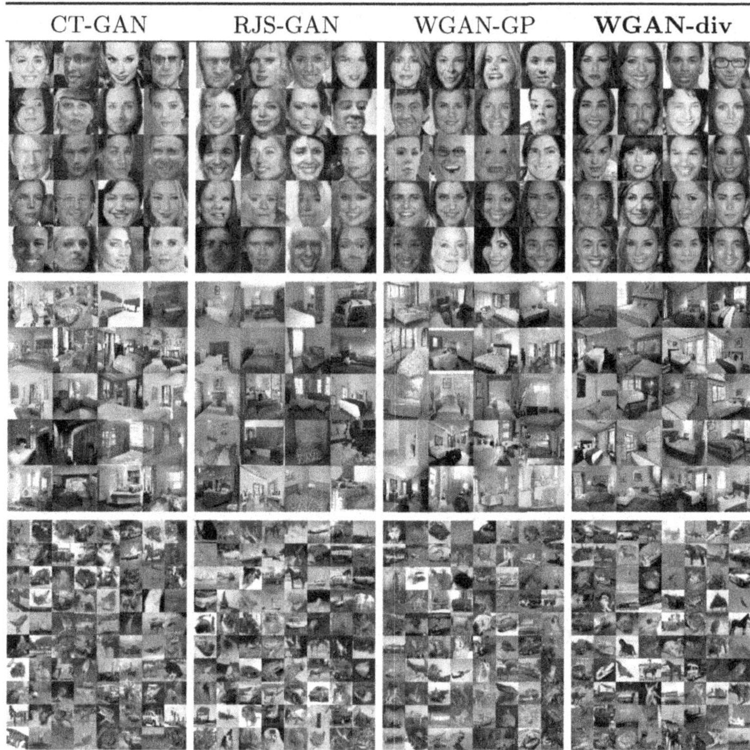

Fig. 2. Visual results of WGAN-div and compared methods on CelebA (top row), LSUN (middle row), and CIFAR-10 (bottom row).

WGAN-div in terms of gender, age, facial expression and makeup. We can make the same conclusions on LSUN. The proposed WGAN-div outperforms the compared methods with a considerable margin both quantitatively and qualitatively. For example, WGAN-div achieves an FID score of 15.9 on LSUN, which is 4.4 lower than CTGAN, which is already an improved version of WGAN-GP, that introduced an extra regularizer to enhance WGAN-GP.

The examples of visually plausible bedrooms shown in Fig. 2 further highlight the advantages gained by introducing W-div in the GAN model. For the interpolation results in the latent space please check our supplementary material.

The top row of Fig. 1 reports the learning curve of the compared methods showing that the training process of our WGAN-div is comparatively stable and converges fast. It achieves top FID scores with less than 60 K iterations. The top right plot of Fig. 1 illustrates the meaningful correlation between image quality and discriminator cost. It is worth mentioning that [24] proposed a two time-scale update method to generally improve the training of a variety of GANs. We believe that WGAN-div can also benefit from such a sophisticated update rule. However, due to the space limit, this is left for further studies.

Table 4. FID comparison between WGAN-div and the state-of-the-art methods. The result with a * was taken from the original paper [8].

	CIFAR-10	CelebA	LSUN
DCGAN [2]	30.9	52.0	61.1
WGAN-GP [7]	18.8	18.4	26.8
RJS-GAN [10]	19.6	21.4	16.7
CTGAN [9]	18.6	16.4	20.3
SNGAN [8]	21.7*	-	-
WGAN-div	**18.1**	**15.2**	**15.9**

Table 5. FID comparison between PGGAN-div and PGGAN at different resolutions.

	Resolution	CelebA	LSUN
PGGAN	64×64	16.3	17.8
PGGAN-div	64×64	**16.0**	**16.5**
PGGAN	128×128	14.1	**15.4**
PGGAN-div	128×128	**13.5**	15.5
PGGAN	256×256	-	15.1
PGGAN-div	256×256	-	**14.9**

4.4 Evaluation on the Progressive Growing Training Scheme

Inspired by the success of PGGAN [14], which trained a W-met based GAN model in a progressive growing fashion, we evaluate how our objective L_{DIV} performs with this sophisticated training scheme. More specifically, we replace L_{PG} with our L_{DIV} while following the default configurations suggested in [14] and propose PGGAN-div. However, computing the FID scores for this experimental setting is challenging, as it is non-trivial to adapt existing FID models for evaluating higher resolution generated images. Since [14] does not specify the details of how their FID scores were computed for higher resolution images, we propose to downscale higher resolution images to 64×64 resolution and then compute the FID score. The resulting scores are reported in Table 5.

Interestingly, Table 5 shows that, for low resolution images, the FID score of PGGAN is slightly worse than the one of some top methods reported in Table 4, including WGAN-div. We believe that this phenomenon is not surprising. Since it is comparatively easy to learn a data distribution in low dimensional space, applying the standard training scheme suffices to achieve good FID scores. There is no need to introduce the sophisticated progressive growing strategy during the low dimensional phase. For higher resolution images (128×128 and 256×256) on the other hand, the FID scores for both PGGAN and PGGAN-div decrease with non-negligible margin. It is worth mentioning that our PGGAN-div slightly improves the FID scores over the original PGGAN, demonstrating the stability of our objective L_{DIV} under a sophisticated training scheme.

Fig. 3. Visual results of PGGAN (top), PGGAN-div (bottom) on CelebA-HQ.

We also present the 256×256 visual results for CelebA-HQ (Fig. 3) and LSUN (Fig. 4). Since CelebA-HQ was generated by post-processing CelebA [14], we do not report its FID scores due to the distribution shift introduced by the artificial

Fig. 4. Visual results of PGGAN (top), PGGAN-div (bottom) on 256 × 256 LSUN.

post-processing algorithms. The visual results in Figs. 3 and 4 demonstrate that our PGGAN-div is very competitive compared to the original PGGAN for both datasets. To summarize, we demonstrate the stability of our W-div objective under this training scheme.

5 Conclusion

In this paper, we introduced a novel Wasserstein divergence which does not require the 1-Lipschitz constraint. As a concrete example, we equip the GAN model with our Wasserstein divergence objective, resulting in WGAN-div. Both FID score and qualitative performance evaluation demonstrate the stability and superiority of the proposed WGAN-div over the state-of-the-art methods.

Acknowledgment. We would like to thank Nvidia for donating the GPUs used in this work.

References

1. Goodfellow, I., et al.: Generative adversarial nets. In: NIPS (2014)
2. Radford, A., Metz, L., Chintala, S.: Unsupervised representation learning with deep convolutional generative adversarial networks. arXiv preprint arXiv:1511.06434 (2015)
3. Berthelot, D., Schumm, T., Metz, L.: BEGAN: boundary equilibrium generative adversarial networks. arXiv preprint arXiv:1703.10717 (2017)
4. Mao, X., Li, Q., Xie, H., Lau, R.Y., Wang, Z., Smolley, S.P.: Least squares generative adversarial networks. arXiv preprint arXiv:1611.04076 (2016)
5. Zhao, J., Mathieu, M., LeCun, Y.: Energy-based generative adversarial network. arXiv preprint arXiv:1609.03126 (2016)
6. Arjovsky, M., Chintala, S., Bottou, L.: Wasserstein generative adversarial networks. In: ICML (2017)
7. Gulrajani, I., Ahmed, F., Arjovsky, M., Dumoulin, V., Courville, A.: Improved training of wasserstein GANs. In: NIPS, pp. 5767–5777 (2017)
8. Miyato, T., Kataoka, T., Koyama, M., Yoshida, Y.: Spectral normalization for generative adversarial networks. arXiv preprint arXiv:1802.05957 (2018)
9. Wei, X., Gong, B., Liu, Z., Lu, W., Wang, L.: Improving the improved training of wasserstein GANs: a consistency term and its dual effect. In: ICLR (2018)
10. Roth, K., Lucchi, A., Nowozin, S., Hofmann, T.: Stabilizing training of generative adversarial networks through regularization. In: NIPS, pp. 2015–2025 (2017)
11. Nowozin, S., Cseke, B., Tomioka, R.: f-GAN: training generative neural samplers using variational divergence minimization. In: NIPS, pp. 271–279 (2016)
12. Zhang, H., et al.: StackGAN: text to photo-realistic image synthesis with stacked generative adversarial networks. In: ICCV (2017)
13. Huang, X., Li, Y., Poursaeed, O., Hopcroft, J., Belongie, S.: Stacked generative adversarial networks. arXiv preprint arXiv:1612.04357 (2016)
14. Karras, T., Aila, T., Laine, S., Lehtinen, J.: Progressive growing of GANs for improved quality, stability, and variation. arXiv preprint arXiv:1710.10196 (2017)
15. Arjovsky, M., Bottou, L.: Towards principled methods for training generative adversarial networks. In: NIPS Workshop, vol. 2016 (2017)
16. Villani, C.: Optimal Transport: Old and New, vol. 338. Springer, Heidelberg (2008). https://doi.org/10.1007/978-3-540-71050-9
17. Karakida, R., Amari, S.: Information geometry of wasserstein divergence. In: Nielsen, F., Barbaresco, F. (eds.) GSI 2017. LNCS, vol. 10589, pp. 119–126. Springer, Cham (2017). https://doi.org/10.1007/978-3-319-68445-1_14

18. Rothe, R., Timofte, R., Gool, L.V.: Deep expectation of real and apparent age from a single image without facial landmarks. Int. J. Comput. Vis. (IJCV) **126**(2–4), 144–157 (2016)
19. Evans, L.C.: Partial differential equations and monge-kantorovich mass transfer. Curr. Dev. Math. **1997**(1), 65–126 (1997)
20. He, K., Zhang, X., Ren, S., Sun, J.: Deep residual learning for image recognition. In: CVPR, pp. 770–778 (2016)
21. Kingma, D., Ba, J.: Adam: a method for stochastic optimization. arXiv preprint arXiv:1412.6980 (2014)
22. Liu, Z., Luo, P., Wang, X., Tang, X.: Deep learning face attributes in the wild. In: ICCV (2015)
23. Yu, F., Seff, A., Zhang, Y., Song, S., Funkhouser, T., Xiao, J.: LSUN: construction of a large-scale image dataset using deep learning with humans in the loop. arXiv preprint arXiv:1506.03365 (2015)
24. Heusel, M., Ramsauer, H., Unterthiner, T., Nessler, B., Hochreiter, S.: GANs trained by a two time-scale update rule converge to a local nash equilibrium. In: NIPS, pp. 6629–6640 (2017)
25. Salimans, T., Goodfellow, I., Zaremba, W., Cheung, V., Radford, A., Chen, X.: Improved techniques for training GANs. In: NIPS, pp. 2234–2242 (2016)
26. Lucic, M., Kurach, K., Michalski, M., Gelly, S., Bousquet, O.: Are GANs created equal? A large-scale study. arXiv preprint arXiv:1711.10337 (2017)
27. Ioffe, S., Szegedy, C.: Batch normalization: accelerating deep network training by reducing internal covariate shift. arXiv preprint arXiv:1502.03167 (2015)

Semi-supervised FusedGAN for Conditional Image Generation

Navaneeth Bodla[1(✉)], Gang Hua[2], and Rama Chellappa[1]

[1] University of Maryland, College Park, USA
{nbodla,rama}@umiacs.umd.edu
[2] Microsoft Research, Redmond, USA
ganghua@microsoft.com

Abstract. We present FusedGAN, a deep network for conditional image synthesis with controllable sampling of diverse images. Fidelity, diversity and controllable sampling are the main quality measures of a good image generation model. Most existing models are insufficient in all three aspects. The FusedGAN can perform controllable sampling of diverse images with very high fidelity. We argue that controllability can be achieved by disentangling the generation process into various stages. In contrast to stacked GANs, where multiple stages of GANs are trained separately with full supervision of labeled intermediate images, the FusedGAN has a single stage pipeline with a built-in stacking of GANs. Unlike existing methods, which require full supervision with paired conditions and images, the FusedGAN can effectively leverage more abundant images without corresponding conditions in training, to produce more diverse samples with high fidelity. We achieve this by fusing two generators: one for unconditional image generation, and the other for conditional image generation, where the two partly share a common latent space thereby disentangling the generation. We demonstrate the efficacy of the FusedGAN in fine grained image generation tasks such as text-to-image, and attribute-to-face generation.

1 Introduction

Recent development of deep generative models has spurred a lot of interest in synthesizing realistic images. Generative adversarial networks (GANs) [2] and Variational Autoencoders (VAEs) [6] have been extensively adopted in various applications, such as generating super-resolution images from low resolution images, image inpainting, text-to-image synthesis, attribute to face synthesis, sketch to face synthesis, and style transfer [4,5,19], etc. While synthesizing images by random sampling is interesting, conditional image generation is of

Part of the work done during Navaneeth Bodla's internship at Microsoft Research.

Electronic supplementary material The online version of this chapter (https://doi.org/10.1007/978-3-030-01228-1_41) contains supplementary material, which is available to authorized users.

V. Ferrari et al. (Eds.): ECCV 2018, LNCS 11209, pp. 689–704, 2018.
https://doi.org/10.1007/978-3-030-01228-1_41

Fig. 1. The illustration of sampling with controlled diversity for both low and high resolution images: StackGAN can only generate random images given the corresponding texts as shown in A. In addition to this, our method can generate samples with controlled diversity such as in B, we show examples interpolated between two styles with the same posture, in C we fix the posture and generate samples with varying details and backgrounds. In D, we fix the posture and generate samples of birds with varying styles as defined by the descriptions. Examples in 1 correspond to sampling of low resolution images and 2 corresponds to high resolution images. (Color figure online)

more practical value. For example, generating faces given a particular set of attributes has a lot of practical usage in forensics applications, which makes it easy to make a portrait of a potential suspect. Generating a fine-grained bird image given its description may be of interest in both education and research in biology.

CGAN [8] has been widely adopted for synthesizing an image given a condition [1,17,18]. A good and effective image generation model needs to possess the following three properties: (1) fidelity (2) diversity, and (3) controllability in sampling. Controlled sampling refers to the process of sampling images by controlled change of factors such as posture, style, background, and fine-grained details, etc. By controlling one or more of these factors, diverse images can be generated. For example, one can generate diverse images by keeping a constant background, or generate images with diverse styles by keeping the same posture. Controllability in sampling is directly related to the representation produced from a certain network architecture. We argue that it is equally important to fidelity and diversity, since it can support more practical applications, such as the case we discussed above in generating the portraits of criminal suspects based on describable attributes (Fig. 1).

Using text to birds image generation as an example, controllable factors include styles, postures, the amount of fine grained details, and background. Using the StackGAN [18], it is possible to generate birds images with high fidelity, but we have control only over the styles (*i.e.*, text descriptions) in the sampling process. To achieve more control in sampling, we need to better

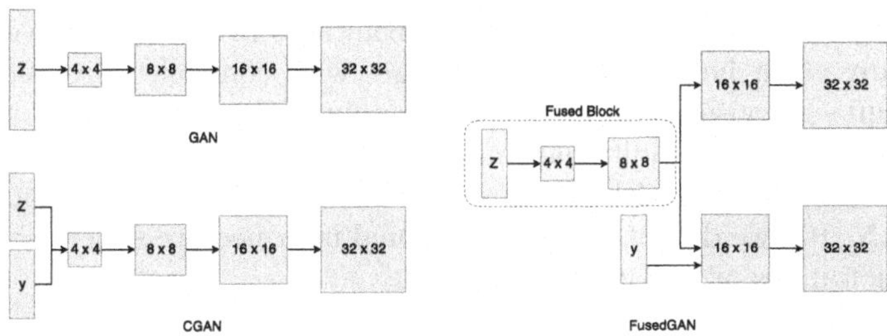

Fig. 2. Illustration of FusedGAN by fusing GAN and CGAN for a 32 × 32 image synthesis.

disentangle the different factors in the latent space. In attribute2image [17], Yan *et al.* have disentangled the foreground and background generation, and thereby achieving controlled sampling by keeping either one of them fixed and varying the other.

We propose a way to disentangle the structures (which capture the posture and the shape) and the styles (which capture fined-grained appearances of both foreground and background) to perform image synthesis with high fidelity, diversity and controllability in sampling. Instead of trying to learn a standalone conditional generator, we propose to derive it from an unconditional generator.

We illustrate our approach by a simple thought experiment. Consider the task of painting a bird given a text description, such as "a yellow bird with black wings and a red tail". The most intuitive way of doing this is to first sketch an outline of a bird with a specific posture and shape of the wings, crown, beak and tail. Then, per the description, subsequently paint the wings as black, the body as yellow, and the tail as red. Note that the initial sketch of the bird is independent of the condition, *i.e.*, the text description which defines the style. It is only needed in the later stages of painting the bird.

Motivated by this intuitive process of drawing, and the success of previous stacked deep generative models [16,18,20], we propose to disentangle the image generation process such that we learn two cascaded generators. The first unconditional generator produces a structure prior (akin to the initial sketch of the bird) which is independent of the condition, and the second conditional generator further adds style to it and creates an image that matches the condition (check Sect. 3 for details). In other words, we fuse two generators by cascading them, as shown in Fig. 2, where the fused block acts as a structure prior.

By disentangling the generation process, an added advantage of our method is that we can train the unconditional generator using just the images without corresponding conditions. This enables us to exploit semi-supervised data during training. It facilitates in learning a better structure prior (the fused block shown in Fig. 2) which in turn contributes to generating better and diverse conditional images.

Our proposed model, referred to as FusedGAN, is unique in the sense that it enjoys the strengths of stacking in a single stage, which can be effectively trained with semi-supervised data. The advantages of our model over existing methods are: (1) it helps in sampling images with controlled diversity. (2) We can use semi-supervised data during our training. This implies that along with usual paired data for conditional image generation such as text to image, we can also leverage images without paired conditions. (3) Unlike FashionGAN [20] and S^2GAN [16], we do not require additional intermediate supervision such as segmentation maps or surface normals.

2 Related Work

We briefly summarize related works in text-to-image generation, and stacking in deep generative models.

Text-to-Image Generation. Reed *et al.* [12], were the first to propose a model called GAN-INT for text to image generation, where they used a conditional GAN to generate images. In their follow-up work GAWWN [11], they leveraged additional supervision in terms of bounding boxes and keypoints to generate birds in a more controlled setup. Zhang *et al.* [18] extended the idea of conditional GAN to two stage conditional GAN, where two GANs are stacked to progressively generate high resolution images from a low resolution image generated from the first stage. The StackGAN is able to produce high resolution 256×256 images with very good visual quality. Instead of single-shot image generation, Gregor *et al.* [3] proposed DRAW, which generates images pixel by pixel using a recurrent network.

The key problems, that both GAN-INT [12] and StackGAN [18] attempted to address, are diversity and discontinuity of the latent space. Due to the very high dimensionality of the latent space and limited availability of text data, the latent space tends to be highly discontinuous which makes it difficult for the generator to synthesize meaningful images. While GAN-INT proposes a manifold interpolation method during training, StackGAN proposed condition augmentation to sample the text embeddings from a Gaussian distribution. We further analyze the contribution of condition augmentation in our method, and show that it models the diversity in fine-grained details of the generated birds (check Sect. 5 for details).

Stacking. The core idea behind the proposed FusedGAN model is to disentangle the generation process by stacking. Stacking allows each stage of the generative model to focus on smaller tasks, and disentangling supports more flexible sampling. We briefly summarize previous works addressing disentangling and stacking.

Stacked image generation has shown to be effective in many image synthesis tasks. At a high level, stacked image generation pipelines often have two separate consecutive stages. The first stage generates an intermediate image (such as a segmentation map, or a map of surface normals). Then, the second stage takes the intermediate image as an input to generate a final conditional image.

For example, the S^2 GAN [16] synthesizes images by first generating the shape structure (*i.e.*, surface normals), and then generates the final image of the

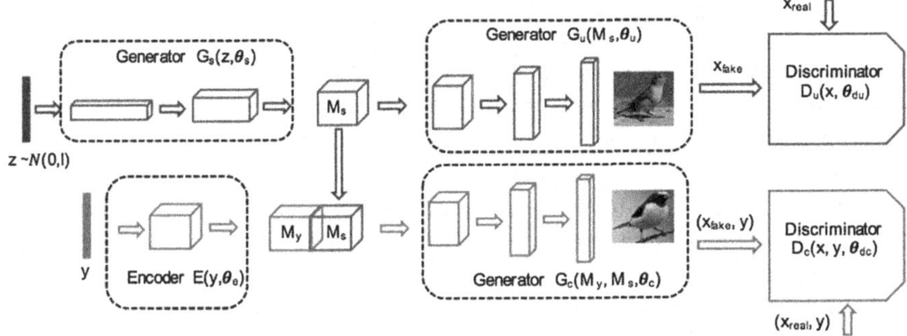

Fig. 3. The end to end pipeline of the proposed method. Blue and orange blocks correspond to the unconditional and conditional image generation pipelines respectively. (Color figure online)

scene in the second stage. StackGAN [18] first generates a low resolution image conditioned on the text embedding ϕ_t, and subsequently uses it to generate the high resolution image. In fashionGAN [20], Zhu *et al.* have used the first stage to generate a segmentation map conditioned on the design encoding ϕ_d and then used it to generate a new fashion image in the second stage.

We use stacking as a way of learning disentangled representations. Different from these existing work, the stages in our model are implicit. Specifically, in our model, stage one performs unconditional image generation and stage two performs conditional image generation. Moreover, both stages share a set of high level filters. As a result, the two stages are literally fused into a single stage, which is trained end to end.

Similar to S^2GAN, our model disentangles style and structure. But different from S^2GAN [16], we do not require any additional supervision in terms of surface normals, nor do we require separate training of stages. Similarly, FashionGAN [20] and attribute2image [17] both require additional intermediate supervision in the form of segmentation maps, which are not needed in our case.

3 The FusedGAN: Formulation

In order to disentangle the generation of structure and style, our method comprises of two fused stages. The first stage performs an unconditional image generation, and produces a feature map which acts as a structure prior for the second stage. The second stage then generates the final conditional image (*i.e.*, the image that match the style defined by the text description) using this structure prior and the condition as the inputs. It must be noted that there is no explicit hierarchy in stage one and stage two. Both stages can be trained simultaneously using alternating optimization. We use text-to-image synthesis as an example for providing the details of our approach which can be easily extended to other tasks such as attribute-to-face synthesis.

3.1 Stage One: Learning a Structure Prior

Our first stage is a GAN which generates bird images from a random noise vector, and also in the process produces a intermediate representation serving as a structure prior for the second stage. It contains a generator G_1 and a discriminator D_u, which are pitched against each other in a two player min-max game. In the min-max game, the generator tries to fool the discriminator by generating birds as close to real as possible, whereas the discriminator tries to differentiate between them.

G_1 and D_u are both differentiable functions such as deep neural networks and the training is done by optimizing the min-max loss function

$$\min_{G_1} \max_{D_u} V(D_u, G_1) = \mathbb{E}_{x \sim p_{data}}[\log D_u(x)] + \mathbb{E}_{z \sim p_z}[\log(1 - D_u(G_1(z)))]. \quad (1)$$

Since we would like to first generate a structure prior, we split the generator G_1 of stage one into two modules: G_s and G_u. G_s takes a noise vector z as the input. After a series of convolution and upsampling operations, it generates a structure prior M_s. G_u then takes the structure prior as input and again after a series of upsampling and convolutions, generates the final image. Accordingly, G_1 in the min-max objective function as presented in Eq. 1, is further decomposed to G_s and G_u, *i.e.*,

$$M_s = G_s(z), \; G_1(z) = G_u(M_s). \quad (2)$$

where M_s is an intermediate representation. It captures all the required high level information for creating a bird such as the posture and structure. Therefore, it acts as a structure prior that dictates the final shape of the bird. Since the posture and structure information is independent of the style, it could be reused in the second stage to synthesize a bird that matches the description. The advantage of this first stage is that it does not require any paired training data. It can be trained using large datasets containing just the images of the target concept, such as birds for example, which helps in learning an improved structure prior.

3.2 Stage Two: Stylzing with the Structure Prior

In the second stage, we use a CGAN for generating birds that match the description. Different from the traditional CGAN pipelines, whose input include the condition (*i.e.*, the text description) and the random noise vector, we feed the structure prior M_s from stage one and the text description as inputs to the conditional generator G_c. Similar to CGAN, the discriminator D_c of stage two takes an image and condition as inputs to ensure that G_c generates images that match the description.

The M_s acts as a template and provides additional signal to the generator of stage two. This forces the generator to synthesize birds that not only match the description but also preserve the structure information contained in it. Therefore, instead of learning from scratch, G_c builds on top of M_s by adding styles to it using the text description. Note that the M_s could also have its own style information from stage one. However, because both the generator and discriminator in stage two takes the text description as inputs, the G_c ensures that the style of the generated image is that of the description and not M_s

In this way, the tasks are divided among G_s, G_u and G_c, where G_s is responsible to learn the overall image structure, and G_u and G_c focus on taking the structure information and generating unconditional and conditional images, respectively. The overall pipeline is shown in Fig. 3. The conditional GAN is trained by optimizing the following objective function, *i.e.*,

$$\min_{G_c}\max_{D_c} V(D_c, G_c) = \mathbb{E}_{x\sim p_{data}}[\log D_c(x|y)] + \mathbb{E}_{z\sim p_z}[\log(1 - D_c(G_c(G_u(z)|y)))]. \tag{3}$$

4 The FusedGAN: Learning and Inference

In this section, we provide the details of training our FusedGAN pipeline, as well as the inference procedures. We first present the notation used to describe the training algorithm and then details of the architecture and the inference steps.

Learning. Let $\mathbf{z} \in \mathbb{R}^{\mathrm{d}\times 1}$ be a noise vector sampled from a normal distribution, *i.e.*, $z \sim \mathcal{N}(0, I)$, where d is the dimensionality of the latent space; $G_s(z, \theta_s)$ be the generator that generates the structure prior $M_s \in \mathbb{R}^{\mathrm{s}\times\mathrm{s}\times\mathrm{k}}$; $G_u(M_s, \theta_u)$ be the unconditional image generator that takes the structure prior M_s as input and generates a target image x_{uf}; and $D_u(x, \theta_{du})$ be the unconditional image discriminator that takes a real image x_r or a generated image x_{uf} as inputs.

For the conditional image generation pipeline, let $E(\theta_e, y)$ be the text encoder that takes a text embedding $y \in \mathbb{R}^{\mathrm{p}\times 1}$ as the input, and produces a tensor $M_y \in \mathbb{R}^{\mathrm{s}\times\mathrm{s}\times\mathrm{q}}$. To achieve this, inspired by the StackGAN [18], condition augmentation is performed to sample latent variables $\hat{c} \in \mathbb{R}^{\mathrm{q}\times 1}$ from an independent Gaussian distribution $N(\mu(y), \Sigma(y))$ around the text embedding. The $\hat{c}$ is then spatially repeated to match the spatial dimension of M_s to produce M_y.

We denote $G_c(M_y, M_s, \theta_c)$ as the conditional generator that takes M_y and M_s as inputs to generate x_{cf}, the conditional image. Similarly, $D_c(x, y, \theta_{dc})$ is the conditional image discriminator which takes a real image x_{cr}, or a conditional image x_{cf} along with the condition y as inputs. Both real or generated images are of size $\mathbb{R}^{\mathrm{N}\times\mathrm{N}\times 3}$.

The standard alternating optimization method is used to train our model. We train the conditional and unconditional pipelines in alternating steps till the model converges. The model parameters are updated by optimizing the combined GAN and CGAN objectives, *i.e.*,

$$\begin{aligned} \mathcal{L}_{G_u} &= \log D_u(G_u(z)), \quad \mathcal{L}_{D_u} = \log D_u(x), \quad \mathcal{L}_{D_c} = \log D_c(x, y), \\ \mathcal{L}_{G_c} &= \log D_c(G_c(M_y, M_s), y) + \lambda D_{KL}(N(\mu(y), \Sigma(y))||N(0, I)) \end{aligned} \tag{4}$$

Inference. During inference, for generating a conditional image, we first draw a noise sample z from $N(0, I)$, which is passed through G_s to generate the structure prior M_s. M_s then takes two paths, one through the generator G_u to produce an unconditional image x_{uf}. In the second path, we first send the text input through the encoder E, which draws a sample from the Gaussian around the text embedding. The output of E and M_s are concatenated, and passed through G_c to generate the conditional image x_{cf}.

Note in this process, we have two random noise vectors from (1) $N(0, I)$ and (2) the distribution of the input text $N(\mu(y), \Sigma(y))$, which are two control factors over the sampling procedure. In other words, in one inference step, we synthesize two images: x_{cf} the conditional image and x_{uf} the unconditional image, a byproduct of our model which helps to analyze and better understand our proposed model and the results.

Further details about the architecture and algorithm are presented in the supplementary material.

5 Experiments

We present results and analysis of our method in two conditional image generation use cases: (1) text-to-image synthesis using birds as a case study, and (2) attributes-to-image synthesis using faces as a case study. For evaluation of our method we perform both qualitative and quantitative analysis. The qualitative analysis is done by performing user study. For quantitative results, we use the inception score [13].

5.1 Text-to-Image Synthesis

The CUB birds dataset [15] contains 11,788 images. For each image, 10 descriptions and a 1024 dimensional text encodings are provided by Reed *et al.* [10]. The dataset is partitioned into class disjoint train and test splits of 8,855 and 2,933 images, respectively, as mentioned in [12]. Since our approach can handle semi-supervised data, we augment this dataset with the nabirds dataset [14] which contains 48,562 images of the birds without any corresponding text descriptions. We use a total of 57,417 images for our stage one structure prior generation and 8,855 image and text pairs for training the stage two conditional image generator. As a pre-processing step, we crop the images to make sure that object-image size ratio is greater than 0.75 [18].

Results and Analysis. In this section, we present the usefulness of our method in various controlled sampling use cases and compare the performance with baseline methods: StackGAN stage-I, StackGAN stage-II, GAN-INT-CLS and GAWWN. We provide a detailed ablation analysis on the contributions of various components in our pipeline. Since synthesizing high resolution images is not the main contribution of our work, we perform the ablation experiments by analyzing 64×64 synthesized images.

Fixed Posture with Varying Styles: Many birds with varying style could have the same posture. We show how to generate them with the FusedGAN.

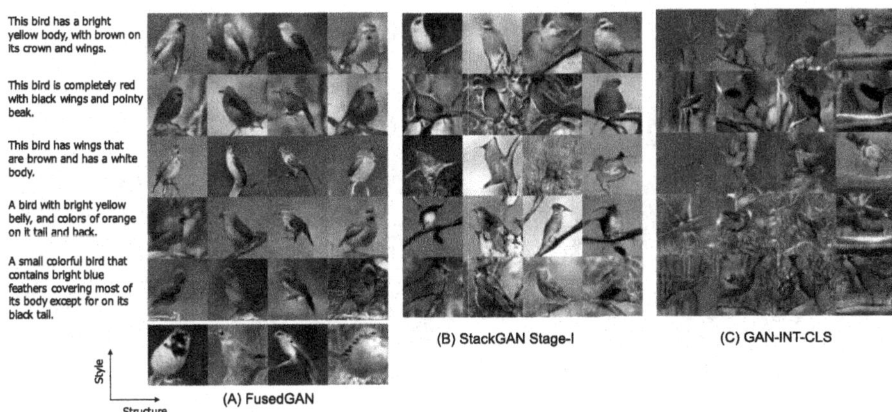
This bird has a bright yellow body, with brown on its crown and wings.
This bird is completely red with black wings and pointy beak.
This bird has wings that are brown and has a white body.
A bird with bright yellow belly, and colors of orange on it tail and back.
A small colorful bird that contains bright blue feathers covering most of its body except for on its black tail.
Style
Structure
(A) FusedGAN
(B) StackGAN Stage-I
(C) GAN-INT-CLS

Fig. 4. Example birds synthesized from our FusedGAN model, StackGAN stage-I and GAN-INT-CLS. For FusedGAN, the first five rows correspond to the images generated by the respective text descriptions shown on the left and the last row corresponds to the unconditional images generated by our model. (Color figure online)

An illustration with visual results are presented in Fig. 4 on the left. We also analyze the contribution of the structure prior in the overall conditional image generation process. For this we consider 5 text descriptions t_i where $i = 1, 2, .., 5$ of birds and sample 4 images per description with the same posture in every column as shown in Fig. 4 on the left.

In order to control the posture, *i.e.*, to generate birds of various styles (text descriptions) with same posture, we keep the z constant and vary the text descriptions. For example, consider the first column in Fig. 4 of FusedGAN. To generate these birds, we sample a z from $N(0, I)$ and pass it through G_s which produces a structure prior M_s. We then use the same M_s with 5 of our text description samples to produce the respective conditional images as shown in the first five rows. Notice that they all have the same posture, because the structure prior is the same for them. This demonstrates that the pose and structure information is successfully captured in M_s, and the style information is left to G_c.

We further examine the contribution of the structure prior by visualizing the unconditional images, as shown in the last row of Fig. 4 for FusedGAN. For the third column, all the birds seem to have a distinct long tail which can also be seen in the unconditional image. Also in the fourth column, we can observe that the unconditional image has a large breast, which is clearly transferred to the yellow, red and orange birds. These results strongly support that M_s is able to successfully capture and transfer significant amount of information about the structure of the bird into the conditional generated bird images of various descriptions.

We further compare the controlled sampling approach with StackGAN and GAN-INT-CLS, as shown in Fig. 4. For both methods, we try to control the

Fig. 5. (a) Generated bird images of various styles but varying amount of fine-grained details. (b) Interpolation between birds of six text descriptions by keeping the same posture (Color figure online)

posture by using the same z as the input to each image in a column, but with varying text descriptions. The GAN-INT-CLS seems to be able to control the posture across all the columns, whereas the StackGAN is not. Although for some results of StackGAN, such as the second column, it seems to have preserved the posture across all styles but for the other columns it does not. For example, in the third column, we can clearly observe that the posture of the last two birds are completely flipped. This indicates that the style and structure are not completely disentangled. In contrast, in results from our FusedGAN, we observe that the structure prior explicitly ensures that the posture is consistently preserved.

Fixed Posture with Varying Details: A bird with a particular posture and style could still have a lot of diversity in terms of fine-grained details and background. In this experiment, we show a way to sample them. This also shows the role and usefulness of condition augmentation in our model.

To keep the posture to be the same, as mentioned in the previous section, we sample a z and generate M_s which is held constant for this experiment. To vary the fine details, we consider a particular text description and pass it through E and draw 5 samples from the Gaussian distribution around the text embedding applying the condition augmentation. Each of these 5 samples produce birds with the same posture (and style) but with varying amount of fine details and backgrounds as shown in Fig. 5a.

It can be observed from the second row of Fig. 5a that for the red bird with black on its wing, even though all the birds have the same posture, no two birds are exactly the same. They all have varying amount of black on their wings and the length of the tail. Similar behavior can be seen in the fourth row, where all the birds are orange but with varying color saturation. This demonstrates that condition augmentation is positively adding to diversity by modeling the finer details of the birds in our model.

Table 1. Inception scores and average human ranks

Model	Inception score	Human rank
GAN-INT-CLS (64×64)	$2.88 \pm .04$	1.60
StackGAN stage-I (64×64)	$2.95 \pm .02$	1.91
FusedGAN(ours) (64×64)	$\mathbf{3.00 \pm .03}$	**3.12**
GAWWN (128×128)	$3.62 \pm .07$	-
StackGAN stage-II (256×256)	$3.70 \pm .04$	-
FusedGAN + high-res(ours) (256×256)	$\mathbf{3.92 \pm .05}$	-

The GAN-INT-CLS does not have any additional control over sampling of text embedding. While the StackGAN shows that the condition augmentation helps in general in improving the diversity, it does not have a way to leverage it for controlled sampling. Using condition augmentation, our model can both improve the diversity and perform controlled sampling of birds with varying fine-grained details.

Interpolation with the Same Posture but Varying Styles: Our method also allows to interpolate between various styles by keeping the posture constant, as shown in Fig. 5b. To achieve this, we take two text-samples t_1 and t_2 and then pass them through E to draw two samples from their respective Gaussian distributions. We obtain two samples each of 1×128 dimensions. Then, we interpolate between them to uniformly pick 8 samples, such that the first sample corresponds to t_1 and last one corresponds to t_2. We then draw a z and generate a M_s which is held constant for these 8 samples.

As described in our earlier sections and inference process, M_s and the interpolated samples are given as inputs to G_c to generate the conditional images. In Fig. 5b, we show some results of this interpolation experiment. The first and last image of each row correspond to the two styles. All the images in between are interpolated. Moreover, the first image of each row is the same as the last image of the previous row. In this way, we interpolate between 5 different styles keeping the same posture. Note that the rows are interpolation between: $t_1 \rightarrow t_2$, $t_2 \rightarrow t_3$, $t_3 \rightarrow t_4$, $t_4 \rightarrow t_5$ and $t_5 \rightarrow t_1$ to complete the full cycle.

High Resolution Image Synthesis: Since the main contribution of our work is synthesizing images with controlled sampling, we presented a model to synthesize 64×64 images. However image resolution is not a limitation of our model and it can be seamlessly stacked with a high resolution generator, similar to stackGAN stage-II to synthesize better high resolution images. We show some of the visual results of stacking G_c with high resolution generator in Fig. 6. These visual results verify that high resolution images can be generated without loosing the controlled image synthesis ability akin to Figs. 4 and 5. We provide further details about the high resolution generator pipeline in the supplementary material.

Qualitative and Quantitative Comparison: To quantitatively compare the results of our method with StackGAN, GAN-INT-CLS and GAWWN, we use

Table 2. FusedGAN-FS refers to training FusedGAN with full supervision on CUB birds dataset alone. FusedGAN(ours) refers to semi-supervised training.

Metric	StackGAN-I	FusedGAN-FS	FusedGAN(ours)
Inception score	2.95 ± .02	2.69 ± .02	**3.00 ± .03**

the publicly available models from respective authors and compute the inception scores as shown in Table 1. We randomly sample 30k images for each model and compute the inception scores using the pre-trained model on CUB birds test set provided by StackGAN. Table 1 shows the performance of various methods in both high resolution and low resolution setups. For the low resolution 64 × 64 image synthesis, our method obtains a slightly better inception score than that of StackGAN, and beats GAN-INT-CLS with a significant margin. Since inception score has its own limitations in terms of fully evaluating fidelity and diversity, we also perform a user study to compare the results of our method with the two competing methods.

For this user study we randomly select 100 text descriptions and sample 8 images for every model. We show these images to 10 different people and ask them to score the fidelity of the birds. None of the authors were part of the user study. The results of the user study shows that birds generated by our method have better visual quality compared to stage-I of StackGAN and GAN-INT-CLS. This can be partly attributed to the fact that our proposed model can leverage more training images with no paired text description, due to semi-supervised nature of our model.

Fig. 6. (First row corresponds to low resolution FusedGAN (64 × 64) and second row corresponds to high resolution FusedGAN (256 × 256). A and B are two examples

Table 1 high resolution image synthesis performance shows that our FusedGAN with high resolution generator achieves state of the art performance compared to published works on text-to-image synthesis using CUB dataset. More details about user study are presented in the supplementary material. In addition to the limited visual results presented in Fig. 4, we provide more visual results in supplementary material.

Evaluating Semi-supervised Training: Since by design, our FusedGAN supports training with semi-supervised data, without the need for the entire dataset to have corresponding text captions. This lets us use unpaired images in training which is expected to learn a better generator G_s and in turn learn a better structure prior M_s. To quantitatively evaluate and show that semi-supervised training indeed helps in generating better images, we compare the inception score

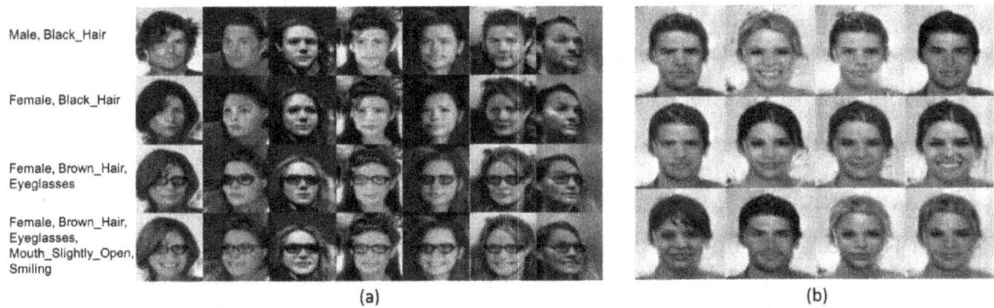

Fig. 7. Generated visual examples illustrating the disentangling of style and structure in face synthesis.

by training our model on CUB dataset alone, without any data augmentation with nabirds. Also, since StackGAN stage-I is trained only on CUB dataset with full supervision, it serves as another baseline to compare with. Table 2 shows that semi-supervised training helps in improving the inception score and hence synthesizes better images compared to fully supervised training, which can not leverage more aboundant unpaired images.

5.2 Attribute-to-Face Generation

To further analyze the importance of disentangling and the structure prior, we evaluate its usefulness on attribute-to-face synthesis as shown in Fig. 7. For this experiment, we use the CelebA [7] dataset that has a 40 dimensional binary attribute vector annotated with each face image. We follow the same training protocol for building our proposed model, except that we do not augment the dataset with any more images without paired attributes. That is because CelebA already has over 200k images, which are sufficient. We use the standard DCGAN architecture [9] for training and more details on this are provided in the supplementary material.

Results and Analysis: Sampling with the Same Structure but Varying Attributes. Similar to the experiment in birds generation, in this experiment, we draw a z from $N(0, I)$ and keep the structure prior constant. We then give various attribute vectors as inputs to synthesize faces as shown in Fig. 7. For every column in Fig. 7, all the rows have the same pose and structure, but the synthesized faces vary as per the attributes. For every row, by default all the attributes are off and only the attributes that are shown next to each row are on.

We make several interesting observations from Fig. 7a. For example, in the first column, for the first two images, when the attribute for gender is switched from male to female, not only the pose but also some other characteristics of the face, such as hair style is also roughly preserved. Similarly, for the second and third images in the same column, the faces look very similar. A closer inspection of these images reveal that there are subtle differences around the mouth and jaw bone areas, which distinguishes between male and female. More over, in the last column, it can be observed that the structure is preserved even for extreme poses. This further reaffirms that our model is able to successfully disentangle the style and structure.

Figure 7b presents a batch of faces generated from various random attributes but with the same structure prior. We can observe how different faces are generated with varying attributes, such as color and style of the hair, wearing a hat or not, skin tone, gender, etc., but they all look alike. Controlled sampling like this finds its use case in forensic science to synthesize similarly looking faces with varying attributes, which helps in making a portrait of a potential suspect.

To quantitatively measure the performance of our method, we compare with attribute2image. Attr2Image uses additional supervision of segmentation maps during training whereas our method doesn't require any such supervision. They performed experiments on LFW dataset because of availability of segmentation maps. However, there are no ground truth attribute vectors for LFW and the authors have used attributes from a pretrained model which are not reliable. Instead we performed our experiments on CelebA which provides ground truth attribute vectors. Therefore, merely comparing the visual quality of images from two different setups is not very useful. For the sake of completeness, we compare the performance of our model with attr2image by evaluating inception score (using the model in [17]). We observe a score of 1.87 ± 0.01 for attr2image and 2.63 ± 0.03 for FusedGAN.

6 Conclusion

We presented FusedGAN, a new deep generative model architecture for conditional image generation by fusing two generators, where one of them generates an unconditional image and the other generates a conditional image. The unconditional image generation can leverage additional training images without the corresponding conditions to learn a good structure prior. This in turn helps in synthesizing a better conditional image, as it takes the structure prior as part of its input in addition to the condition. The proposed model enjoys the strengths of stacking and disentangling without the need for separate training of stages or additional intermediate image supervision. Extensive analysis and experiments on text-to-image synthesis and attribute-to-face synthesis show that the model is able to successfully learn a disentangled representation for style and structure, and hence generate birds and faces with high fidelity, diversity, and more controllability in sampling.

Acknowledgement. The work of Navaneeth Bodla and Rama Chellappa is supported by IARPA JANUS effort. This research is based upon work supported by the Office of the Director of National Intelligence (ODNI), Intelligence Advanced Research Projects Activity(IARPA), via IARPA R&D Contract No. 2014-14071600012. The views and conclusions contained herein are those of the authors and should not be interpreted as necessarily representing the official policies or endorsements, either expressed or implied, of the ODNI, IARPA, or the U.S. Government. The U.S. Government is authorized to reproduce and distribute reprints for Governmental purposes notwithstanding any copyright annotation thereon. Gang Hua's work is partly supported by National Natural Science Foundation of China under Grant 61629301.

References

1. Dai, B., Lin, D., Urtasun, R., Fidler, S.: Towards diverse and natural image descriptions via a conditional GAN. arXiv preprint arXiv:1703.06029 (2017)
2. Goodfellow, I., et al.: Generative adversarial nets. In: Advances in Neural Information Processing Systems, pp. 2672–2680 (2014)
3. Gregor, K., Danihelka, I., Graves, A., Rezende, D.J., Wierstra, D.: Draw: a recurrent neural network for image generation. arXiv preprint arXiv:1502.04623 (2015)
4. Gulrajani, I., Ahmed, F., Arjovsky, M., Dumoulin, V., Courville, A.: Improved training of wasserstein GANs. arXiv preprint arXiv:1704.00028 (2017)
5. Isola, P., Zhu, J.Y., Zhou, T., Efros, A.A.: Image-to-image translation with conditional adversarial networks. arXiv (2016)
6. Kingma, D.P., Welling, M.: Auto-encoding variational bayes. arXiv preprint arXiv:1312.6114 (2013)
7. Liu, Z., Luo, P., Wang, X., Tang, X.: Deep learning face attributes in the wild. In: Proceedings of International Conference on Computer Vision (ICCV), December 2015
8. Mirza, M., Osindero, S.: Conditional generative adversarial nets. arXiv preprint arXiv:1411.1784 (2014)
9. Radford, A., Metz, L., Chintala, S.: Unsupervised representation learning with deep convolutional generative adversarial networks. arXiv preprint arXiv:1511.06434 (2015)
10. Reed, S., Akata, Z., Lee, H., Schiele, B.: Learning deep representations of fine-grained visual descriptions. In: Proceedings of the IEEE Conference on Computer Vision and Pattern Recognition, pp. 49–58 (2016)
11. Reed, S., Akata, Z., Mohan, S., Tenka, S., Schiele, B., Lee, H.: Learning what and where to draw. In: Advances in Neural Information Processing Systems (2016)
12. Reed, S., Akata, Z., Yan, X., Logeswaran, L., Schiele, B., Lee, H.: Generative adversarial text to image synthesis. arXiv preprint arXiv:1605.05396 (2016)
13. Salimans, T., Goodfellow, I., Zaremba, W., Cheung, V., Radford, A., Chen, X.: Improved techniques for training GANs. In: Advances in Neural Information Processing Systems, pp. 2234–2242 (2016)
14. Van Horn, G., et al.: Building a bird recognition app and large scale dataset with citizen scientists: the fine print in fine-grained dataset collection. In: Proceedings of the IEEE Conference on Computer Vision and Pattern Recognition, pp. 595–604 (2015)
15. Wah, C., Branson, S., Welinder, P., Perona, P., Belongie, S.: The Caltech-UCSD Birds-200-2011 Dataset. Technical report, CNS-TR-2011-001, California Institute of Technology (2011)
16. Wang, X., Gupta, A.: Generative image modeling using style and structure adversarial networks. In: Leibe, B., Matas, J., Sebe, N., Welling, M. (eds.) ECCV 2016. LNCS, vol. 9908, pp. 318–335. Springer, Cham (2016). https://doi.org/10.1007/978-3-319-46493-0_20
17. Yan, X., Yang, J., Sohn, K., Lee, H.: Attribute2Image: conditional image generation from visual attributes. corr abs/1512.00570 (2015)

18. Zhang, H., et al.: StackGAN: text to photo-realistic image synthesis with stacked generative adversarial networks. arXiv preprint arXiv:1612.03242 (2016)
19. Zhu, J.Y., Park, T., Isola, P., Efros, A.A.: Unpaired image-to-image translation using cycle-consistent adversarial networks. arXiv preprint arXiv:1703.10593 (2017)
20. Zhu, S., Fidler, S., Urtasun, R., Lin, D., Loy, C.C.: Be your own prada: fashion synthesis with structural coherence (2017)

Pose Partition Networks for Multi-person Pose Estimation

Xuecheng Nie[1(✉)], Jiashi Feng[1], Junliang Xing[2], and Shuicheng Yan[1,3]

[1] ECE Department, National University of Singapore, Singapore, Singapore
niexuecheng@u.nus.edu, elefjia@nus.edu.sg, yanshuicheng@360.cn
[2] Institute of Automation, Chinese Academy of Sciences, Beijing, China
jlxing@nlpr.ia.ac.cn
[3] Qihoo 360 AI Institute, Beijing, China

Abstract. This paper proposes a novel Pose Partition Network (PPN) to address the challenging multi-person pose estimation problem. The proposed PPN is favorably featured by low complexity and high accuracy of joint detection and partition. In particular, PPN performs dense regressions from global joint candidates within a specific embedding space, which is parameterized by centroids of persons, to efficiently generate robust person detection and joint partition. Then, PPN infers body joint configurations through conducting graph partition for each person detection locally, utilizing reliable global affinity cues. In this way, PPN reduces computation complexity and improves multi-person pose estimation significantly. We implement PPN with the Hourglass architecture as the backbone network to simultaneously learn joint detector and dense regressor. Extensive experiments on benchmarks MPII Human Pose Multi-Person, extended PASCAL-Person-Part, and WAF show the efficiency of PPN with new state-of-the-art performance.

Keywords: Multi-person pose estimation · Pose partition
Dense regression

1 Introduction

Multi-person pose estimation aims to localize body joints of multiple persons captured in a 2D monocular image [7,22]. Despite extensive prior research, this problem remains very challenging due to the highly complex joint configuration, partial or even complete joint occlusion, significant overlap between neighboring persons, unknown number of persons and more critically the difficulties in allocating joints to multiple persons. These challenges feature the uniqueness of multi-person pose estimation compared with the simpler single-person setting [18,27]. To tackle these challenges, existing multi-person pose estimation

Electronic supplementary material The online version of this chapter (https://doi.org/10.1007/978-3-030-01228-1_42) contains supplementary material, which is available to authorized users.

V. Ferrari et al. (Eds.): ECCV 2018, LNCS 11209, pp. 705–720, 2018.
https://doi.org/10.1007/978-3-030-01228-1_42

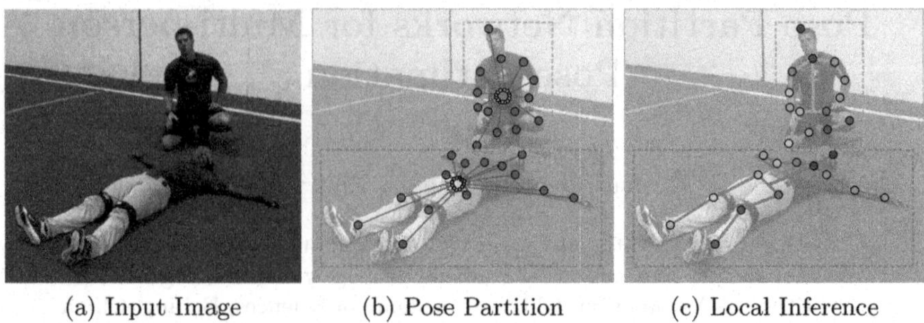

Fig. 1. Pose Partition Networks for multi-person pose estimation. (a) Input image. (b) Pose partition. PPN models person detection and joint partition as a regression process inferred from joint candidates. (c) Local inference. PPN performs local inference for joint configurations conditioned on generated person detections with joint partitions

approaches usually perform joint detection and partition *separately*, mainly following two different strategies. The *top-down* strategy [7,8,13,20,23] first detects persons and then performs pose estimation for each single person individually. The *bottom-up* strategy [3,11,12,15,16,22], in contrast, generates all joint candidates at first, and then tries to partition them to corresponding person instances.

The top-down approaches directly leverage existing person detection models [17,24] and single-person pose estimation methods [18,27]. Thus they effectively avoid complex joint partitions. However, their performance is critically limited by the quality of person detections. If the employed person detector fails to detect a person instance accurately (due to occlusion, overlapping or other distracting factors), the introduced errors cannot be remedied and would severely harm performance of the following pose estimation. Moreover, they suffer from high joint detection complexity, which linearly increases with the number of persons in the image, because they need to run the single-person joint detector for each person detection sequentially.

In contrast, the bottom-up approaches detect all joint candidates at first by globally applying a joint detector for only once and then partition them to corresponding persons according to joint affinities. Hence, they enjoy lower joint detection complexity than the top-down ones and better robustness to errors from early commitment. However, they suffer from very high complexity of partitioning joints to corresponding persons, which usually involves solving NP-hard graph partition problems [11,22] on densely connected graphs covering the whole image.

In this paper, we propose a novel solution, termed the *Pose Partition Network* (PPN), to overcome essential limitations of the above two types of approaches and meanwhile inherit their strengths within a unified model for efficiently and effectively estimating poses of multiple persons in a given image. As shown in Fig. 1, PPN solves multi-person pose estimation problem by simultaneously (1) modeling person detection and joint partition as a regression process over all joint candidates and (2) performing local inference for obtaining joint categorization and association conditioned on the generated person detections.

In particular, PPN introduces a dense regression module to generate person detections with partitioned joints via votes from joint candidates in a carefully designed embedding space, which is efficiently parameterized by person centroids. This pose partition model produces joint candidates and partitions by running a joint detector for only one feed-forward pass, offering much higher efficiency than top-down approaches. In addition, the produced person detections from PPN are robust to various distracting factors, *e.g.*, occlusion, overlapping, deformation, and large pose variation, benefiting the following pose estimation. PPN also introduces a local greedy inference algorithm by assuming independence among person detections for producing optimal multi-person joint configurations. This local optimization strategy reduces the search space of the graph partition problem for finding optimal poses, avoiding high joint partition complexity challenging the bottom-up strategy. Moreover, the local greedy inference algorithm exploits reliable global affinity cues from the embedding space for inferring joint configurations within robust person detections, leading to performance improvement.

We implement PPN based on the Hourglass network [18] for learning joint detector and dense regressor, simultaneously. Extensive experiments on MPII Human Pose Multi-Person [1], extended PASCAL-Person-Part [28] and WAF [7] benchmarks evidently show the efficiency and effectiveness of the proposed PPN. Moreover, PPN achieves new state-of-the-art on all these benchmarks.

We make following contributions. (1) We propose a new one feed-forward pass solution to multi-person pose estimation, totally different from previous top-down and bottom-up ones. (2) We propose a novel dense regression module to efficiently and robustly partition body joints into multiple persons, which is the key to speeding up multi-person pose estimation. (3) In addition to high efficiency, PPN is also superior in terms of robustness and accuracy on multiple benchmarks.

2 Related Work

Top-Down Multi-person Pose Estimation. Existing approaches following top-down strategy sequentially perform person detection and single-person pose estimation. In [9], Gkioxari *et al.* proposed to adopt the Generalized Hough Transform framework to first generate person proposals and then classify joint candidates based on the poselets. Sun *et al.* [25] presented a hierarchical part-based model for jointly person detection and pose estimation. Recently, deep learning techniques have been exploited to improve both person detection and single-person pose estimation. In [13], Iqbal and Gall adopted Faster-RCNN [24] based person detector and convolutional pose machine [27] based joint detector for this task. Later, Fang *et al.* [8] utilized spatial transformer network [14] and Hourglass network [18] to further improve the quality of joint detections and partitions. Despite remarkable success, they suffer from limitations from

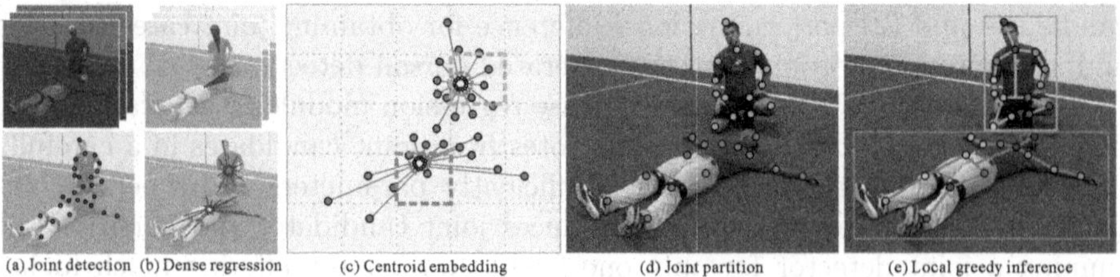

Fig. 2. Overview of the proposed Pose Partition Network for multi-person pose estimation. Given an image, PPN first uses a CNN to predict (a) joint confidence maps and (b) dense joint-centroid regression maps. Then, PPN performs (c) centroid embedding for all joint candidates in the embedding space via dense regression, to produce (d) joint partitions within person detections. Finally, PPN conducts (e) local greedy inference to generate joint configurations for each joint partition locally, giving pose estimation results of multiple persons

early commitment and high joint detection complexity. Differently, the proposed PPN adopts a one feed-forward pass regression process for efficiently producing person detections with partitioned joint candidates, offering robustness to early commitment as well as low joint detection complexity.

Bottom-Up Multi-person Pose Estimation. The bottom-up strategy provides robustness to early commitment and low joint detection complexity. Previous bottom-up approaches [3,11,19,22] mainly focus on improving either the joint detector or joint affinity cues, benefiting the following joint partition and configuration inference. For joint detector, fully convolutional neural networks, *e.g.*, Residual networks [10] and Hourglass networks [18], have been widely exploited. As for joint affinity cues, Insafutdinov *et al.* [11] explored geometric and appearance constraints among joint candidates. Cao *et al.* [3] proposed part affinity fields to encode location and orientation of limbs. Newell and Deng [19] presented the associative embedding for grouping joint candidates. Nevertheless, all these approaches partition joints based on partitioning the graph covering the whole image, resulting in high inference complexity. In contrast, PPN performs local inference with robust global affinity cues which is efficiently generated by dense regressions from the centroid embedding space, reducing complexity for joint partitions and improving pose estimation.

3 Approach

3.1 Pose Partition Model

The overall pipeline for the proposed Pose Partition Network (PPN) model is shown in Fig. 2. Throughout the paper, we use following notations. Let $\mathbf{I}$ denote an image containing multiple persons, $\mathbf{p}=\{\mathbf{p}_1, \mathbf{p}_2, \dots, \mathbf{p}_N\}$ denote spatial coordinates of N joint candidates from all persons in $\mathbf{I}$ with $\mathbf{p}_v=(x_v, y_v)^\top, \forall v=1, \dots, N$, and $\mathbf{u}=\{u_1, u_2, \dots, u_N\}$ denote the labels of corresponding joint candidates, in which $u_v \in \{1, 2, \ldots, K\}$ and K is the number of joint categories. For allocating joints via local inference, we also consider the proximities between joints, denoted as $\mathbf{b} \in \mathbb{R}^{N \times N}$. Here $\mathbf{b}_{(v,w)}$ encodes the proximity between the vth joint candidate $(\mathbf{p}_v, u_v)$ and the wth joint candidate $(\mathbf{p}_w, u_w)$, and gives the probability for them to be from the same person.

The proposed PPN with learnable parameters Θ aims to solve the multi-person pose estimation task through learning to infer the conditional distribution $\mathbb{P}(\mathbf{p}, \mathbf{u}, \mathbf{b}|\mathbf{I}, \Theta)$. Namely, given the image $\mathbf{I}$, PPN infers the joint locations $\mathbf{p}$, labels $\mathbf{u}$ and proximities $\mathbf{b}$ providing the largest likelihood probability. To this end, PPN adopts a regression model to *simultaneously* produce person detections with joint partitions implicitly and infers joint configuration $\mathbf{p}$ and $\mathbf{u}$ for each person detection locally. In this way, PPN reduces the difficulty and complexity of multi-person pose estimation significantly. Formally, PPN introduces latent variables $\mathbf{g} = \{\mathbf{g}_1, \mathbf{g}_2, \ldots, \mathbf{g}_M\}$ to encode joint partitions, and each $\mathbf{g}_i$ is a collection of joint candidates (without labels) belonging to a specific person detection, and M is the number of joint partitions. With these latent variables $\mathbf{g}$, $\mathbb{P}(\mathbf{p}, \mathbf{u}, \mathbf{b}|\mathbf{I}, \Theta)$ can be factorized into

$$\mathbb{P}(\mathbf{p}, \mathbf{u}, \mathbf{b}|\mathbf{I}, \Theta) = \sum_{\mathbf{g}} \mathbb{P}(\mathbf{p}, \mathbf{u}, \mathbf{b}, \mathbf{g}|\mathbf{I}, \Theta) = \sum_{\mathbf{g}} \underbrace{\mathbb{P}(\mathbf{p}|\mathbf{I}, \Theta)\mathbb{P}(\mathbf{g}|\mathbf{I}, \Theta, \mathbf{p})}_{\text{partition generation}} \underbrace{\mathbb{P}(\mathbf{u}, \mathbf{b}|\mathbf{I}, \Theta, \mathbf{p}, \mathbf{g})}_{\text{joint configuration}}, \tag{1}$$

where $\mathbb{P}(\mathbf{p}|\mathbf{I}, \Theta)\mathbb{P}(\mathbf{g}|\mathbf{I}, \Theta, \mathbf{p})$ models the joint partition generation process within person detections based on joint candidates. Maximizing the above likelihood probability gives optimal pose estimation for multiple persons in $\mathbf{I}$.

However, directly maximizing the above likelihood is computationally intractable. Instead of maximizing *w.r.t.* all possible partitions $\mathbf{g}$, we propose to maximize its lower bound induced by a single "optimal" partition, inspired by the EM algorithm [6]. Such approximation could reduce the complexity significantly without harming performance. Concretely, based on Eq. (1), we have

$$\mathbb{P}(\mathbf{p}, \mathbf{u}, \mathbf{b}|\mathbf{I}, \Theta) \geq \mathbb{P}(\mathbf{p}|\mathbf{I}, \Theta) \left\{ \max_{\mathbf{g}} \mathbb{P}(\mathbf{g}|\mathbf{I}, \Theta, \mathbf{p}) \right\} \mathbb{P}(\mathbf{u}, \mathbf{b}|\mathbf{I}, \Theta, \mathbf{p}, \mathbf{g}). \tag{2}$$

Here, we find the optimal solution by maximizing the above induced lower bound $\mathbb{P}(\mathbf{p}, \mathbf{u}, \mathbf{b}, \mathbf{g}|\mathbf{I}, \Theta)$, instead of maximizing the summation. The joint partitions $\mathbf{g}$ disentangle independent joints and reduce inference complexity— only the joints falling in the same partition have non-zero proximities $\mathbf{b}$. Then $\mathbb{P}(\mathbf{p}, \mathbf{u}, \mathbf{b}, \mathbf{g}|\mathbf{I}, \Theta)$ is further factorized as

$$\mathbb{P}(\mathbf{p}, \mathbf{u}, \mathbf{b}, \mathbf{g}|\mathbf{I}, \Theta) = \mathbb{P}(\mathbf{p}, \mathbf{g}|\mathbf{I}, \Theta) \times \prod_{\mathbf{g}_i \in \mathbf{g}} \mathbb{P}(\mathbf{u}_{\mathbf{g}_i}|\mathbf{I}, \Theta, \mathbf{p}, \mathbf{g}_i)\mathbb{P}(\mathbf{b}_{\mathbf{g}_i}|\mathbf{I}, \Theta, \mathbf{p}, \mathbf{g}_i, \mathbf{u}), \tag{3}$$

where $\mathbf{u}_{\mathbf{g}_i}$ denotes the labels of joints falling in the partition $\mathbf{g}_i$ and $\mathbf{b}_{\mathbf{g}_i}$ denotes their proximities. In the above probabilities, we define $\mathbb{P}(\mathbf{p}, \mathbf{u}, \mathbf{b}, \mathbf{g}|\mathbf{I}, \Theta)$ as a Gibbs distribution:

$$\mathbb{P}(\mathbf{p}, \mathbf{u}, \mathbf{b}, \mathbf{g}|\mathbf{I}, \Theta) \propto \exp\{-E(\mathbf{p}, \mathbf{u}, \mathbf{b}, \mathbf{g})\}, \tag{4}$$

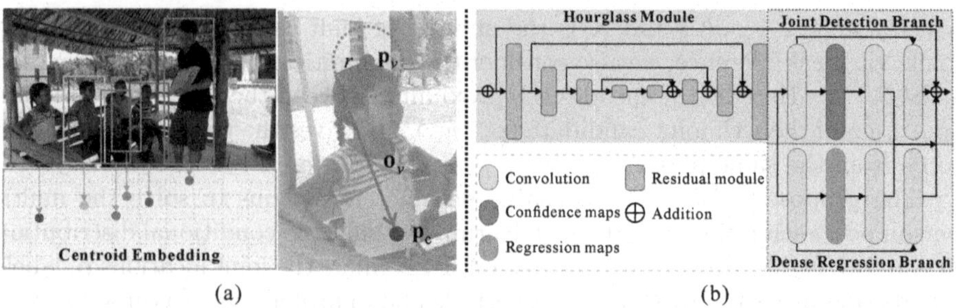

Fig. 3. (a) Centroid embedding via dense joint regression. Left image shows centroid embedding results for persons and right one illustrates construction of the regression target for a pixel (Sect. 3.3). (b) Architecture of Pose Partition Network. Its backbone is an Hourglass module (in blue block), followed by two branches: joint detection (in green block) and dense regression for joint partition (in yellow block) (Color figure online)

where $E(\mathbf{p}, \mathbf{u}, \mathbf{b}, \mathbf{g})$ is the energy function for the joint distribution $\mathbb{P}(\mathbf{p}, \mathbf{u}, \mathbf{b}, \mathbf{g}|\mathbf{I}, \Theta)$. Its explicit form is derived from Eq. (3) accordingly:

$$E(\mathbf{p}, \mathbf{u}, \mathbf{b}, \mathbf{g}) = -\varphi(\mathbf{p}, \mathbf{g}) - \sum_{\mathbf{g}_i \in \mathbf{g}} \Big(\sum_{\mathbf{p}_v \in \mathbf{g}_i} \psi(\mathbf{p}_v, u_v) + \sum_{\mathbf{p}_v, \mathbf{p}_w \in \mathbf{g}_i} \phi(\mathbf{p}_v, u_v, \mathbf{p}_w, u_w) \Big). \tag{5}$$

Here, $\varphi(\mathbf{p}, \mathbf{g})$ scores the quality of joint partitions $\mathbf{g}$ generated from joint candidates $\mathbf{p}$ for the input image $\mathbf{I}$, $\psi(\mathbf{p}_v, u_v)$ scores how the position $\mathbf{p}_v$ is compatible with label u_v, and $\phi(\mathbf{p}_v, u_v, \mathbf{p}_w, u_w)$ represents how likely the positions $\mathbf{p}_v$ with label u_v and $\mathbf{p}_w$ with label u_w belong to the same person, *i.e.*, characterizing the proximity $\mathbf{b}_{(v,w)}$. In the following subsections, we will give details for detecting joint candidates $\mathbf{p}$, generating optimal joint partitions $\mathbf{g}$, inferring joint configurations $\mathbf{u}$ and $\mathbf{b}$ along with the algorithm to optimize the energy function.

3.2 Joint Candidate Detection

To reliably detect human body joints, we use confidence maps to encode probabilities of joints presenting at each position in the image. The joint confidence maps are constructed by modeling the joint locations as Gaussian peaks, as shown in Fig. 2(a). We use $\mathbf{C}_j$ to denote the confidence map for the jth joint with $\mathbf{C}_j^i$ being the confidence map of the jth joint for the ith person. For a position $\mathbf{p}_v$ in the given image, $\mathbf{C}_j^i(\mathbf{p}_v)$ is calculated by $\mathbf{C}_j^i(\mathbf{p}_v) = \exp\left(-\|\mathbf{p}_v - \mathbf{p}_j^i\|_2^2/\sigma^2\right)$, where $\mathbf{p}_j^i$ denotes the groundtruth position of the jth joint of the ith person, and σ is an empirically chosen constant to control variance of the Gaussian distribution and set as 7 in the experiments. The target confidence map, which the proposed PPN model learns to predict, is an aggregation of peaks of all the persons in a single map. Here, we choose to take the maximum of confidence maps rather than average to remain distinctions between close-by peaks [3], *i.e.* $\mathbf{C}_j(\mathbf{p}_v) = \max_i \mathbf{C}_j^i(\mathbf{p}_v)$. During testing, we first find peaks with confidence scores greater than a given threshold τ (set as 0.1) on predicted confidence maps $\tilde{\mathbf{C}}$ for all types of joints. Then we perform Non-Maximum Suppression (NMS) to find the joint candidate set $\tilde{\mathbf{p}}=\{\mathbf{p}_1, \mathbf{p}_2, \ldots, \mathbf{p}_N\}$.

3.3 Pose Partition via Dense Regression

Our proposed pose partition model performs dense regression over all the joint candidates to localize centroids of multiple persons and partitions joints into different person instances accordingly, as shown in Fig. 2(b) and (c). It learns to transform all the pixels belonging to a specific person to an identical single point in a carefully designed embedding space, where they are easy to cluster into corresponding persons. Such a dense regression framework enables partitioning joints by one single feed-forward pass, reducing joint detection complexity that troubles top-down solutions.

To this end, we propose to parameterize the joint candidate embedding space by the human body centroids, as they are stable and reliable to discriminate difference person instances even in presence of some extreme poses. We denote the constructed embedding space as $\mathcal{H}$. In $\mathcal{H}$, each person corresponds to a single point (*i.e.*, the centroid), and each point $\mathbf{h}_*\in\mathcal{H}$ represents a hypothesis about centroid location of a specific person instance. An example is given in the left image of Fig. 3(a).

Joint candidates are densely transformed into $\mathcal{H}$ and can collectively determine the centroid hypotheses of their corresponding person instances, since they are tightly related with articulated kinematics, as shown in Fig. 2(c). For instance, a candidate of the head joint would add votes for the presence of a person's centroid to the location just below it. A single candidate does not necessarily provide sufficient evidence for the exact centroid of a person instance, but the population of joint candidates can vote for the correct centroid with large probability and determine the joint partitions correctly. In particular, the probability of generating joint partition $\mathbf{g}_*$ at location $\mathbf{h}_*$ is calculated by summing the votes from different joint candidates together, *i.e.*

$$\mathbb{P}(\mathbf{g}_*|\mathbf{h}_*) \propto \sum_j w_j \Big(\sum_{\mathbf{p}_v\in\tilde{\mathbf{p}}} \mathbb{1}[\tilde{\mathbf{C}}_j(\mathbf{p}_v) \geq \tau] \exp\{-\|f_j(\mathbf{p}_v) - \mathbf{h}_*\|_2^2\}\Big), \tag{6}$$

where $\mathbb{1}[\cdot]$ is the indicator function and w_j is the weight for the votes from jth joint category. We set w_j=1 for all joints assuming all kinds of joints equally contribute to the localization of person instances in view of unconstrained shapes of human body and uncertainties of presence of different joints. The function $f_j : \mathbf{p} \rightarrow \mathcal{H}$ learns to densely transform *every* pixel in the image to the embedding space $\mathcal{H}$. For learning f_j, we build the target regression map $\mathbf{T}_j^i$ for the jth joint of the ith person as follows:

$$\mathbf{T}_j^i(\mathbf{p}_v) = \begin{cases} \mathbf{o}_{j,v}^i/Z & \text{if } \mathbf{p}_v \in \mathcal{N}_j^i \\ 0 & \text{otherwise,} \end{cases}, \quad \mathbf{o}_{j,v}^i = (\mathbf{p}_c^i - \mathbf{p}_v) = (x_c^i - x_v, y_c^i - y_v), \tag{7}$$

where $\mathbf{p}_c^i$ denotes the centroid position of the ith person, Z=$\sqrt{H^2+W^2}$ is the normalization factor, H and W denote the height and width of image $\mathbf{I}$,

$\mathcal{N}_j^i = \{\mathbf{p}_v | \ \|\mathbf{p}_v - \mathbf{p}_j^i\|_2 \leq r\}$ denotes the neighbor positions of the jth joint of the ith person, and r is a constant to define the neighborhood size, set as 7 in our experiments. An example is shown in right image of Fig. 3(a) for construction of a regression target of a pixel in a given image. Then, we define the target regression map $\mathbf{T}_j$ for the jth joint as the average for all persons by

$$\mathbf{T}_j(\mathbf{p}_v) = \frac{1}{N_v} \sum_i \mathbf{T}_j^i(\mathbf{p}_v), \tag{8}$$

where N_v is the number of non-zero vectors at position $\mathbf{p}_v$ across all persons. During testing, after predicting the regression map $\tilde{\mathbf{T}}_j$, we define transformation function f_j for position $\mathbf{p}_v$ as $f_j(\mathbf{p}_v) = \mathbf{p}_v + Z\tilde{\mathbf{T}}_j(\mathbf{p}_v)$. After generating $\mathbb{P}(\mathbf{g}_*|\mathbf{h}_*)$ for each point in the embedding space, we calculate the score $\varphi(\mathbf{p}, \mathbf{g})$ as $\varphi(\mathbf{p}, \mathbf{g}) = \sum_i \log \mathbb{P}(\mathbf{g}_i|\mathbf{h}_i)$.

Then the problem of joint partition generation is converted to finding peaks in the embedding space $\mathcal{H}$. As there are no priors on the number of persons in the image, we adopt the Agglomerative Clustering [2] to find peaks by clustering the votes, which can automatically determine the number of clusters. We denote the vote set as $\mathbf{h} = \{\mathbf{h}_v | \mathbf{h}_v = f_j(\mathbf{p}_v), \tilde{\mathbf{C}}_j(\mathbf{p}_v) \geq \tau, \mathbf{p}_v \in \tilde{\mathbf{p}}\}$, and use $\mathcal{C} = \{\mathcal{C}_1, \ldots, \mathcal{C}_M\}$ to denote the clustering result on $\mathbf{h}$, where $\mathcal{C}_i$ represents the ith cluster and M is the number of clusters. We assume the set of joint candidates casting votes in each cluster corresponds to a joint partition $\mathbf{g}_i$, defined by

$$\mathbf{g}_i = \{\mathbf{p}_v | \mathbf{p}_v \in \tilde{\mathbf{p}}, \tilde{\mathbf{C}}_j(\mathbf{p}_v) \geq \tau, f_j(\mathbf{p}_v) \in \mathcal{C}_i\}. \tag{9}$$

3.4 Local Greedy Inference for Pose Estimation

According to Eq. (4), we maximize the conditional probability $\mathbb{P}(\mathbf{p}, \mathbf{u}, \mathbf{b}, \mathbf{g}|\mathbf{I}, \Theta)$ by minimizing energy function $E(\mathbf{p}, \mathbf{u}, \mathbf{b}, \mathbf{g})$ in Eq. (5). We optimize $E(\mathbf{p}, \mathbf{u}, \mathbf{b}, \mathbf{g})$ in two sequential steps: (1) generate joint partition set based on joint candidates; (2) conduct joint configuration inference in each joint partition locally, which reduces the joint configuration complexity and overcomes the drawback of bottom-up approaches.

After getting joint partition according to Eq. (9), the score $\varphi(\mathbf{p}, \mathbf{g})$ becomes a constant. Let $\tilde{\mathbf{g}}$ denote the generated partition set. The optimization is then simplified as

$$\tilde{\mathbf{u}}, \tilde{\mathbf{b}} = \arg\min_{\mathbf{u}, \mathbf{b}} \Big(- \sum_{\mathbf{g}_i \in \tilde{\mathbf{g}}} \Big(\sum_{\mathbf{p}_v \in \mathbf{g}_i} \psi(\mathbf{p}_v, u_v) + \sum_{\mathbf{p}_v, \mathbf{p}_w \in \mathbf{g}_i} \phi(\mathbf{p}_v, u_v, \mathbf{p}_w, u_w) \Big) \Big). \tag{10}$$

Pose estimation in each joint partition is independent, thus inference over different joint partitions becomes separate. We propose the following local greedy inference algorithm to solve Eq. (10) for multi-person pose estimation. Given a joint partition $\mathbf{g}_i$, the unary term $\psi(\mathbf{p}_v, u_v)$ is the confidence score at $\mathbf{p}_v$ from the u_vth joint detector: $\psi(\mathbf{p}_v, u_v) = \tilde{\mathbf{C}}_{u_v}(\mathbf{p}_v)$. The binary term $\phi(\mathbf{p}_v, u_v, \mathbf{p}_w, u_w)$

Algorithm 1. Local greedy inference for multi-person pose estimation

input : joint candidates $\tilde{\mathbf{p}}$, joint partitions $\tilde{\mathbf{g}}$, joint confidence maps $\tilde{\mathbf{C}}$, dense regression maps $\tilde{\mathbf{T}}$, τ.
output: multi-person pose estimation $\mathcal{R}$
initialization: $\mathcal{R} \leftarrow \varnothing$
for $\mathbf{g}_i \in \tilde{\mathbf{g}}$ **do**
  while $\mathbf{g}_i \neq \varnothing$ **do**
    Initialize single-person pose estimation $\mathcal{P} \leftarrow \varnothing$
    for *jth joint category*, $j = 1$ *to* K **do**
      if $\mathcal{P} = \varnothing$ **then**
        Find root joint candidate in $\mathbf{g}_i$ for $\mathcal{P}$ by:
        $\mathbf{p}_* \leftarrow \arg\max_{\mathbf{p}_v \in \mathbf{g}_i} \tilde{\mathbf{C}}_j(\mathbf{p}_v)$
      else
        Find joint candidate closest to centroid $\mathbf{c}$:
        $\mathbf{p}_* \leftarrow \arg\max_{\mathbf{p}_v \in \mathbf{g}_i} \frac{\mathbb{1}[\tilde{\mathbf{C}}_j(\mathbf{p}_v) \geq \tau]}{\exp\{\|f_j(\mathbf{p}_v) - \mathbf{c}\|_2^2\}}$
      end
      if $\tilde{\mathbf{C}}_j(\mathbf{p}_*) \geq \tau$ **then**
        Update $\mathcal{P} \leftarrow \mathcal{P} \cup \{(\mathbf{p}_*, j)\}$, $\mathbf{g}_i \leftarrow \mathbf{g}_i \backslash \{\mathbf{p}_*\}$ Update $\mathbf{c}$ by averaging the person centroid hypotheses: $\mathbf{c} \leftarrow \sum_{(\mathbf{p}_v, n) \in \mathcal{P}} f_n(\mathbf{p}_v)/|\mathcal{P}|$
      end
    end
    Update $\mathcal{R} \leftarrow \mathcal{R} \cup \{\mathcal{P}\}$
  end
end

is the similarity score of votes of two joint candidates based on the global affinity cues in the embedding space:

$$\phi(\mathbf{p}_v, u_v, \mathbf{p}_w, u_w) = \mathbb{1}[\tilde{\mathbf{C}}_{u_v}(\mathbf{p}_v) \geq \tau]\mathbb{1}[\tilde{\mathbf{C}}_{u_w}(\mathbf{p}_w) \geq \tau] \exp\{-\|\mathbf{h}_v - \mathbf{h}_w\|_2^2\}, \quad (11)$$

where $\mathbf{h}_v = \mathbf{p}_v + Z\tilde{\mathbf{T}}_{u_v}(\mathbf{p}_v)$ and $\mathbf{h}_w = \mathbf{p}_w + Z\tilde{\mathbf{T}}_{u_w}(\mathbf{p}_w)$.

For efficient inference in Eq. (10), we adopt a greedy strategy which guarantees the energy monotonically decreases and eventually converges to a lower bound. Specifically, we iterate through each joint one by one, first considering joints around torso and moving out to limb. We start the inference with neck. For a neck candidate, we use its embedding point in $\mathcal{H}$ to initialize the centroid of its person instance. Then, we select the head top candidate closest to the person centroid and associate it with the same person as the neck candidate. After that, we update person centroid by averaging the derived hypotheses. We loop through all other joint candidates similarly. Finally, we get a person instance and its associated joints. After utilizing neck as root for inferring joint configurations of person instances, if some candidates remain unassigned, we utilize joints from torso, then from limbs, as the root to infer the person instance. After all candidates find their associations to persons, the inference terminates. See details in Algorithm 1.

4 Learning Joint Detector and Dense Regressor with CNNs

PPN is a generic model and compatible with various CNN architectures. Extensive architecture engineering is out of the scope of this work. We simply choose the state-of-the-art Hourglass network [18] as the backbone of PPN. Hourglass network consists of a sequence of Hourglass modules. As shown in Fig. 3(b), each Hourglass module first learns down-sized feature maps from the input image, and then recovers full-resolution feature maps through up-sampling for precise joint localization. In particular, each Hourglass module is implemented as a fully convolutional network. Skipping connections are added between feature maps with the same resolution symmetrically to capture information at every scale. Multiple Hourglass modules are stacked sequentially for gradually refining the predictions via reintegrating the previous estimation results. Intermediate supervision is applied at each Hourglass module.

Hourglass network was proposed for *single*-person pose estimation. PPN extends it to *multi*-person cases. PPN introduces modules enabling simultaneous joint detection (Sect. 3.2) and dense joint-centroid regression (Sect. 3.3), as shown in Fig. 3(b). In particular, PPN utilizes the Hourglass module to learn image representations and then separates into two branches: one produces the dense regression maps for detecting person centroids, via one 3×3 convolution on feature maps from the Hourglass module and another 1×1 convolution for classification; the other branch produces joint detection confidence maps. With this design, PPN obtains joint detection and partition in one feed-forward pass. When using multi-stage Hourglass modules, PPN feeds the predicted dense regression maps at every stage into the next one through 1×1 convolution, and then combines intermediate features with features from the previous stage.

For training PPN, we use ℓ_2 loss to learn both joint detection and dense regression branches with supervision at each stage. The losses are defined as

$$\begin{aligned} L^t_{\text{joint}} &\triangleq \sum_j \sum_v \|\tilde{\mathbf{C}}^t_j(\mathbf{p}_v) - \mathbf{C}_j(\mathbf{p}_v)\|^2_2 \\ L^t_{\text{regression}} &\triangleq \sum_j \sum_v \|\tilde{\mathbf{T}}^t_j(\mathbf{p}_v) - \mathbf{T}_j(\mathbf{p}_v)\|^2_2, \end{aligned} \tag{12}$$

where $\tilde{\mathbf{C}}^t_j$ and $\tilde{\mathbf{T}}^t_j$ represent predicted joint confidence maps and dense regression maps at the tth stage, respectively. The groundtruth $\mathbf{C}_j(\mathbf{p}_v)$ and $\mathbf{T}_j(\mathbf{p}_v)$ are constructed as in Sects. 3.2 and 3.3 respectively. The total loss is given by $L{=}\sum_{t=1}^{T}(L^t_{\text{joint}} + \alpha L^t_{\text{regression}})$, where $T{=}8$ is the number of Hourglass modules (stages) used in implementation and weighting factor α is empirically set as 1.

5 Experiments

5.1 Experimental Setup

Datasets. We evaluate the proposed PPN on three widely adopted benchmarks: MPII Human Pose Multi-Person (MPII) dataset [1], extended PASCAL-Person-Part dataset [28], and "We Are Family" (WAF) dataset [7]. The MPII dataset

Table 1. Comparison with state-of-the-arts on the full testing set of MPII Human Pose Multi-Person dataset (AP)

Method	Head	Shoulder	Elbow	Wrist	Hip	Knee	Ankle	Total	Time [s]
Iqbal and Gall [13]	58.4	53.9	44.5	35.0	42.2	36.7	31.1	43.1	10
Insafutdinov *et al.* [11]	78.4	72.5	60.2	51.0	57.2	52.0	45.4	59.5	485
Levinkov *et al.* [16]	89.8	85.2	71.8	59.6	71.1	63.0	53.5	70.6	-
Insafutdinov *et al.* [12]	88.8	87.0	75.9	64.9	74.2	68.8	60.5	74.3	-
Cao *et al.* [3]	91.2	87.6	77.7	66.8	75.4	68.9	61.7	75.6	1.24
Fang *et al.* [8]	88.4	86.5	78.6	70.4	74.4	73.0	65.8	76.7	1.5
Newell and Deng [19]	92.1	89.3	78.9	69.8	76.2	71.6	64.7	77.5	-
PPN (Ours)	**92.2**	**89.7**	**82.1**	**74.4**	**78.6**	**76.4**	**69.3**	**80.4**	**0.77**

consists of 3,844 and 1,758 groups of multiple interacting persons for training and testing respectively. Each person in the image is annotated for 16 body joints. It also provides more than 28,000 training samples for single-person pose estimation. The extended PASCAL-Person-Part dataset contains 3,533 challenging images from the original PASCAL-Person-Part dataset [4], which are split into 1,716 for training and 1,817 for testing. Each person is annotated with 14 body joints shared with MPII dataset, without pelvis and thorax. The WAF dataset contains 525 web images (350 for training and 175 for testing). Each person is annotated with 6 line segments for the upper-body.

Data Augmentation. We follow conventional ways to augment training samples by cropping original images based on the person center. In particular, we augment each training sample with rotation degrees sampled in $[-40°, 40°]$, scaling factors in $[0.7, 1.3]$, translational offset in $[-40\text{px}, 40\text{px}]$ and horizontally mirror. We resize each training sample to 256×256 pixels with padding.

Implementation. For MPII dataset, we reserve 350 images randomly selected from the training set for validation. We use the rest training images and all the provided single-person samples to train the PPN for 250 epochs. For evaluation on the other two datasets, we follow the common practice and finetune the PPN model pretrained on MPII for 30 epochs. To deal with some extreme cases where centroids of persons are overlapped, we slightly perturb the centroids by adding small offset to separate them. We implement our model with PyTorch [21] and adopt the RMSProp [26] for optimization. The initial learning rate is 0.0025 and decreased by multiplying 0.5 at the 150th, 170th, 200th, 230th epoch. In testing, we follow conventions to crop image patches using the given position and average person scale of test images, and resize and pad the cropped samples to 384×384 as input to PPN. We search for suitable image scales over 5 different choices. Specially, when testing on MPII, following previous works [3,19], we apply a single-person model [18] trained on MPII to refine the estimations. We use the standard Average Precision (AP) as performance metric on all the datasets, as suggested by [11,28]. Our codes and pre-trained models will be made available.

Table 2. Comparison with state-of-the-arts on the testing set of the extended PASCAL-Person-Part dataset (AP)

Method	Head	Shoulder	Elbow	Wrist	Hip	Knee	Ankle	Total
Chen and Yuille [5]	45.3	34.6	24.8	21.7	9.8	8.6	7.7	21.8
Insafutdinov et al. [11]	41.5	39.3	34.0	27.5	16.3	21.3	20.6	28.6
Xia et at. [28]	58.0	52.1	43.1	37.2	22.1	30.8	31.1	39.2
PPN (Ours)	**66.9**	**60.0**	**51.4**	**48.9**	**29.2**	**36.4**	**33.5**	**46.6**

Table 3. Comparison with state-of-the-arts on testing set of WAF dataset (AP)

Method	Head	Shoulder	Elbow	Wrist	Total
Chen and Yuile [5]	83.3	56.1	46.3	35.5	55.3
Pishchulin *et al.* [22]	76.6	80.8	73.7	73.6	76.2
Insafutdinov *et al.* [11]	92.6	81.1	75.7	78.8	82.0
PPN (Ours)	**93.1**	**82.9**	**83.5**	**79.9**	**84.8**

5.2 Results and Analysis

MPII. Table 1 shows the evaluation results on the full testing set of MPII. We can see that the proposed PPN achieves overall 80.4% AP and significantly outperforms previous state-of-the-art achieving 77.5% AP [19]. In addition, the proposed PPN improves the performance for localizing all the joints consistently. In particular, it brings remarkable improvement over rather difficult joints mainly caused by occlusion and high degrees of freedom, including wrists (74.4% vs 69.8% AP), ankles (69.3% vs 64.7% AP), and knees (with absolute 4.8% AP increase over [19]), confirming the robustness of the proposed pose partition model and global affinity cues to these distracting factors. These results clearly show PPN is outstandingly effective for multi-person pose estimation. We also report the computational speed of PPN[1] in Table 1. PPN is about 2 times faster than the bottom-up approach [3] with state-of-the-art speed for multi-person pose estimation. This demonstrates the efficiency of performing joint detection and partition simultaneously in our model.

PASCAL-Person-Part. Table 2 shows the evaluation results. PPN provides absolute 7.4% AP improvement (46.6% vs 39.2% AP) over the state-of-the-art [28]. Moreover, the proposed PPN brings significant improvement on difficult joints, such as wrist (48.9% vs 37.2% AP). These results further demonstrate the effectiveness and robustness of our model for multi-person pose estimation.

WAF. As shown in Table 3, PPN achieves overall 84.8% AP, bringing 3.4% improvement over the best bottom-up approach [11]. PPN achieves the best

[1] The runtime time is measured on CPU Intel I7-5820K 3.3GHz and GPU TITAN X (Pascal). The time is counted with 5 scale testing, not including the refinement time by single-person pose estimation.

Table 4. Ablation experiments on MPII validation set (AP)

Method	Head	Shoulder	Elbow	Wrist	Hip	Knee	Ankle	Total	InferTime [ms]
PPN-Full	94.4	90.0	81.3	72.1	77.8	72.7	64.7	79.0	1.9
PPN-w/o-Partition	93.2	89.3	79.9	70.1	78.8	73.1	65.7	78.6	3.4
PPN-w/o-LGI	93.1	89.1	79.5	68.5	79.0	71.4	64.4	77.8	-
PPN-w/o-Refinement	90.4	86.8	79.3	69.8	77.5	69.3	61.9	76.4	-
PPN-256 × 256	91.0	87.1	78.6	70.2	76.7	70.5	60.0	76.3	-
PPN-Vanilla	90.5	86.4	77.1	69.4	72.2	67.7	60.2	74.8	-

performance for all upper-body joints. In particular, it gives the most significant performance improvement on the elbow, about 10.3% higher than previous best results. These results verify the effectiveness of the proposed PPN for tackling the multi-person pose estimation problem.

Qualitative Results. Visualization examples of pose partition, local inference, and multi-person pose estimation by the proposed PPN on these three datasets are provided in the supplemental materials.

5.3 Ablation Analysis

We conduct ablation analysis for the proposed PPN model using the MPII validation set. We evaluate multiple variants of our proposed PPN model by removing certain components from the full model ("PPN-Full"). "PPN-w/o-Partition" performs inference on the whole image without using obtained joint partition information, which is similar to the pure bottom-up approaches. "PPN-w/o-LGI" removes the local greedy inference phase. It allocates joint candidates to persons through finding the most activated position for each joint in each joint partition. This is similar to the top-down approaches. "PPN-w/o-Refinement" does not perform refinement by using single-person pose estimator. We use "PPN-256 × 256" to denote testing over 256 × 256 images and "PPN-Vanilla" to denote single scale testing without refinement.

From Table 4, "PPN-Full" achieves 79.0% AP and the joint partition inference only costs 1.9ms, which is very efficient. "PPN-w/o-Partition" achieves slightly lower AP (78.6%) with slower inference speed (3.4ms). The results confirm effectiveness of generating joint partitions by PPN—inference within each joint partition individually reduces complexity and improves pose estimation over multi-persons. Removing the local greedy inference phase as in "PPN-w/o-LGI" decreases the performance to 77.8% AP, showing local greedy inference is beneficial to pose estimation by effectively handling false alarms of joint candidate detection based on global affinity cues in the embedding space. Comparison of "PPN-w/o-Refinement"(76.4% AP) with the full model demonstrates that single-person pose estimation can refine joint localization. "PPN-Vanilla" achieves 74.8% AP, verifying the stableness of our approach for multi-person pose estimation even in the case of removing refinement and multi-scale testing.

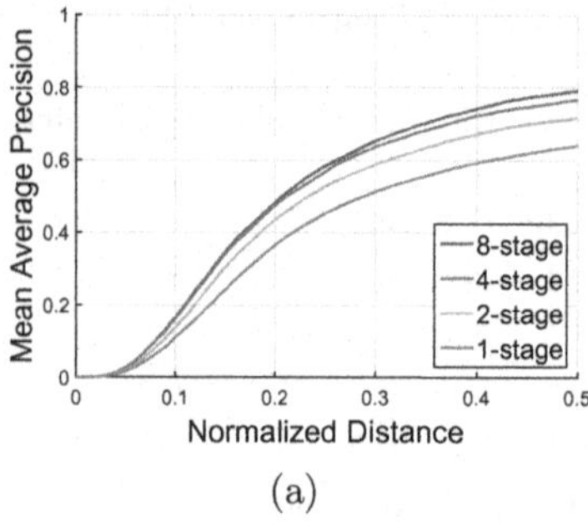

(a)

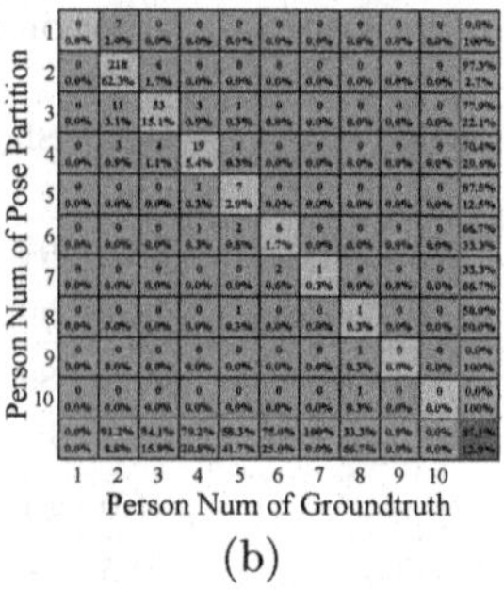

(b)

Fig. 4. (a) Ablation study on multi-stage Hourglass network. (b) Confusion matrix on person number inferred from pose partition (Sect. 3.3) with groundtruth. Mean square error is 0.203. Best viewed in color and 2× zoom

We also evaluate the pose estimation results from 4 different stages of the PPN model and plot the results in Fig. 4(a). The performance increases monotonically when traversing more stages. The final results achieved at the 8th stage give about 23.4% improvement comparing with the first stage (79.0% vs 64.0% AP). This is because the proposed PPN can recurrently correct errors on the dense regression maps along with the joint confidence maps conditioned on previous estimations in the multi-stage design, yielding gradual improvement on the joint detections and partitions for multi-person pose estimation.

Finally, we evaluate the effectiveness of pose partition model for partition person instances. In particular, we evaluate how its produced partitions match the real number of persons. The confusion matrix is shown in Fig. 4(b). We can observe the proposed pose partition model can predict very close number of persons with the groundtruth, with mean square error as small as 0.203.

6 Conclusion

We presented the Pose Partition Network (PPN) to efficiently and effectively address the challenging multi-person pose estimation problem. PPN solves the problem by simultaneously detecting and partitioning joints for multiple persons. It introduces a new approach to generate partitions through inferring over joint candidates in the embedding space parameterized by person centroids. Moreover, PPN introduces a local greedy inference approach to estimate poses for person instances by utilizing the partition information. We demonstrate that PPN can provide appealing efficiency for both joint detection and partition, and it can significantly overcome limitations of pure top-down and bottom-up solutions on three benchmarks multi-person pose estimation datasets.

Acknowledgement. Jiashi Feng was partially supported by NUS IDS R-263-000-C67-646, ECRA R-263-000-C87-133 and MOE Tier-II R-263-000-D17-112.

References

1. Andriluka, M., Pishchulin, L., Gehler, P., Schiele, B.: 2D human pose estimation: New benchmark and state of the art analysis. In: CVPR (2014)
2. Bourdev, L., Malik, J.: Poselets: body part detectors trained using 3D human pose annotations. In: ICCV (2009)
3. Cao, Z., Simon, T., Wei, S.E., Sheikh, Y.: Realtime multi-person 2D pose estimation using part affinity fields. In: CVPR (2017)
4. Chen, X., Mottaghi, R., Liu, X., Fidler, S., Urtasun, R., Yuille, A.L.: Detect what you can: detecting and representing objects using holistic models and body parts. In: CVPR (2014)
5. Chen, X., Yuille, A.L.: Parsing occluded people by flexible compositions. In: CVPR (2015)
6. Dempster, A.P., Laird, N.M., Rubin, D.B.: Maximum likelihood from incomplete data via the EM algorithm. J. Roy. Stat. Soc. B. **39**(1), 1–38 (1977)
7. Eichner, M., Ferrari, V.: We are family: joint pose estimation of multiple persons. In: Daniilidis, K., Maragos, P., Paragios, N. (eds.) ECCV 2010. LNCS, vol. 6311, pp. 228–242. Springer, Heidelberg (2010). https://doi.org/10.1007/978-3-642-15549-9_17
8. Fang, H., Xie, S., Tai, Y., Lu, C.: RMPE: regional multi-person pose estimation. In: ICCV (2017)
9. Gkioxari, G., Hariharan, B., Girshick, R., Malik, J.: Using k-poselets for detecting people and localizing their keypoints. In: CVPR (2014)
10. He, K., Zhang, X., Ren, S., Sun, J.: Deep residual learning for image recognition. In: CVPR (2016)
11. Insafutdinov, E., Pishchulin, L., Andres, B., Andriluka, M., Schiele, B.: DeeperCut: a deeper, stronger, and faster multi-person pose estimation model. In: Leibe, B., Matas, J., Sebe, N., Welling, M. (eds.) ECCV 2016. LNCS, vol. 9910, pp. 34–50. Springer, Cham (2016). https://doi.org/10.1007/978-3-319-46466-4_3
12. Insafutdinov, E., Andriluka, M., Pishchulin, L., Tang, S., Andres, B., Schiele, B.: Articulated multi-person tracking in the wild. In: CVPR (2017)
13. Iqbal, U., Gall, J.: Multi-person pose estimation with local joint-to-person associations. In: Hua, G., Jégou, H. (eds.) ECCV 2016. LNCS, vol. 9914, pp. 627–642. Springer, Cham (2016). https://doi.org/10.1007/978-3-319-48881-3_44
14. Jaderberg, M., Simonyan, K., Zisserman, A., et al.: Spatial transformer networks. In: NIPS (2015)
15. Ladicky, L., Torr, P.H., Zisserman, A.: Human pose estimation using a joint pixel-wise and part-wise formulation. In: CVPR (2013)
16. Levinkov, E., et al.: Joint graph decomposition & node labeling: problem, algorithms, applications. In: CVPR (2017)
17. Liu, W., et al.: SSD: single shot MultiBox detector. In: Leibe, B., Matas, J., Sebe, N., Welling, M. (eds.) ECCV 2016. LNCS, vol. 9905, pp. 21–37. Springer, Cham (2016). https://doi.org/10.1007/978-3-319-46448-0_2
18. Newell, A., Yang, K., Deng, J.: Stacked hourglass networks for human pose estimation. In: Leibe, B., Matas, J., Sebe, N., Welling, M. (eds.) ECCV 2016. LNCS, vol. 9912, pp. 483–499. Springer, Cham (2016). https://doi.org/10.1007/978-3-319-46484-8_29
19. Newell, A., Deng, J.: Associative embedding: end-to-end learning for joint detection and grouping. In: NIPS (2017)

20. Papandreou, G., et al.: Towards accurate multi-person pose estimation in the wild. In: CVPR (2017)
21. Paszke, A., Gross, S., Chintala, S.: PyTorch (2017)
22. Pishchulin, L., et al.: DeepCut: joint subset partition and labeling for multi person pose estimation. In: CVPR (2016)
23. Pishchulin, L., Jain, A., Andriluka, M., Thormählen, T., Schiele, B.: Articulated people detection and pose estimation: Reshaping the future. In: CVPR (2012)
24. Ren, S., He, K., Girshick, R., Sun, J.: Faster R-CNN: towards real-time object detection with region proposal networks. In: NIPS (2015)
25. Sun, M., Savarese, S.: Articulated part-based model for joint object detection and pose estimation. In: ICCV (2011)
26. Tieleman, T., Hinton, G.: Lecture 6.5-rmsprop: divide the gradient by a running average of its recent magnitude. COURSERA: Neural Networks for Machine Learning (2012)
27. Wei, S.E., Ramakrishna, V., Kanade, T., Sheikh, Y.: Convolutional pose machines. In: CVPR (2016)
28. Xia, F., Wang, P., Chen, X., Yuille, A.L.: Joint multi-person pose estimation and semantic part segmentation. In: CVPR (2017)

Understanding Degeneracies and Ambiguities in Attribute Transfer

Attila Szabó[1], Qiyang Hu[1(✉)], Tiziano Portenier[1], Matthias Zwicker[2], and Paolo Favaro[1]

[1] University of Bern, Bern, Switzerland
{szabo,hu,portenier,favaro}@inf.unibe.ch
[2] University of Maryland, College Park, USA
zwicker@cs.umd.edu

Abstract. We study the problem of building models that can transfer selected attributes from one image to another without affecting the other attributes. Towards this goal, we develop analysis and a training methodology for autoencoding models, whose encoded features aim to disentangle attributes. These features are explicitly split into two components: one that should represent attributes in common between pairs of images, and another that should represent attributes that change between pairs of images. We show that achieving this objective faces two main challenges: One is that the model may learn degenerate mappings, which we call shortcut problem, and the other is that the attribute representation for an image is not guaranteed to follow the same interpretation on another image, which we call reference ambiguity. To address the shortcut problem, we introduce novel constraints on image pairs and triplets and show their effectiveness both analytically and experimentally. In the case of the reference ambiguity, we formally prove that a model that guarantees an ideal feature separation cannot be built. We validate our findings on several datasets and show that, surprisingly, trained neural networks often do not exhibit the reference ambiguity.

1 Introduction

One way to simplify the problem of classifying or regressing attributes of interest from data is to build an intermediate representation, a feature, where the information about the attributes is better separated than in the input data. Better separation means that some entries of the feature vary only with respect to one and only one attribute. In this way, classifiers and regressors would not need to build invariance to many nuisance attributes. Instead, they could devote more capacity to discriminating the attributes of interest, and possibly achieve better performance. We call this task *disentangling factors of variation*, and we speak interchangeably of attributes and factors. In addition to facilitating classification and regression, this task is beneficial to image synthesis. One could build

A. Szabó and Q. Hu—Equal contribution.

V. Ferrari et al. (Eds.): ECCV 2018, LNCS 11209, pp. 721–736, 2018.
https://doi.org/10.1007/978-3-030-01228-1_43

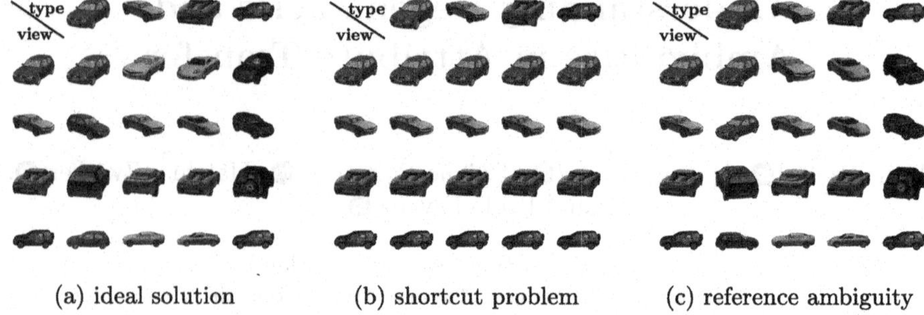

(a) ideal solution (b) shortcut problem (c) reference ambiguity

Fig. 1. Illustration of the challenges of attribute transfer. Consider a feature split into two parts, one representing the viewpoint, the other the car type. For all subfigures, the viewpoint feature is taken from the leftmost column and the car type feature is taken from the topmost row. (a) Ideal solution: the viewpoint and the car type are transferred correctly. (b) Shortcut problem: the car type is not transferred. The car type information from the image on the top row is ignored. (c) Reference ambiguity: the blue car has a different viewpoint orientation interpretation compared to the other car types.

a model to transfer attributes between images by rendering images where some elements of the input vary only one attribute of the output at a time.

When labeling is possible and available, supervised learning can be used to solve this task. In general, however, some attributes may not be easily quantifiable (*e.g.* style). Therefore, we consider using *weak labeling*, where we only know what attribute has changed between two images, although we do not know by how much. This type of labeling may be readily available in many cases without manual annotation. For example, objects in image pairs from a stereo system are automatically labeled with an unknown viewpoint change. A practical model that can learn from these labels is an autoencoder (*i.e.*, an encoder-decoder pair) subject to a reconstruction constraint. In this model the weak labels can be used to define similarities between subsets of the feature obtained from two input images. However, training such a model faces two fundamental challenges: one is that it may learn degenerate encodings, which we call the *shortcut problem*, and the other is that attributes extracted from one image must be interpreted in the same way on another image (*e.g.*, the attribute about the viewpoint of a car may be mapped to different angles in different car models), which we call the *reference problem*. These challenges are illustrated in Fig. 1.

Our contributions can be summarized as follows: *(1)* We introduce a novel adversarial training of autoencoders to solve the disentangling task when only weak labels are available. The discriminator network in the adversarial training takes image pairs as input. In contrast to [15], our discriminator is not conditioned on class labels, so the number of parameters in our model can be kept constant; *(2)* We show analytically and experimentally that our training method fully addresses the *shortcut problem*, where all the information is encoded only in one part of the feature (see Fig. 1b); *(3)* We show analysis on the *reference ambiguity*, and prove that it is unavoidable in the disentangling task when only weak labels are used. In Fig. 1c images are characterized by two car attributes: the viewpoint and the type. In this case, the reference ambiguity means that the viewpoint extracted from one image can have a different meaning than that of a different car type. Surprisingly, this ambiguity seems to occur rarely, typically only when the data dependence on the attribute of interest is complex.

2 Related Work

In this paper we use autoencoders as the main model to build features and to synthesize new data. Therefore, we briefly review methods related to autoencoders. Since we train our model with an adversarial scheme, we also give a brief overview of some of the recent developments in this area. Finally, we discuss prior work on disentangling factors of variation that closely relates to our aims.

Autoencoders. Autoencoders [1,2,9] learn to reconstruct the input data as $\mathbf{x} = \text{Dec}(\text{Enc}(\mathbf{x}))$, where $\text{Enc}(\mathbf{x})$ is the internal image representation (the encoder) and Dec (the decoder) reconstructs the input of the encoder. Variational autoencoders [10] use instead a generative model $p(\mathbf{x}, \mathbf{z}) = p(\mathbf{x}|\mathbf{z})p(\mathbf{z})$, where $\mathbf{x}$ is the observed data (images), and $\mathbf{z}$ are latent variables. The encoder estimates the parameters of the posterior, $\text{Enc}(\mathbf{x}) = p(\mathbf{z}|\mathbf{x})$, and the decoder estimates the conditional likelihood, $\text{Dec}(\mathbf{z}) = p(\mathbf{x}|\mathbf{z})$. Transforming autoencoders [8] are trained with transformed image input pairs. The relative transformation parameters are also fed to the network. Because the internal representation explicitly represents the objects presence and location, the network can learn their absolute position. One important aspect of the autoencoders, which we exploit, is that they encourage latent representations to keep as much information about the input as possible.

GAN. Generative Adversarial Nets [7] learn to sample realistic images with two competing neural networks. The generator Dec creates images $\mathbf{x} = \text{Dec}(\mathbf{z})$ from a random noise sample $\mathbf{z}$ and tries to fool a discriminator Dsc, which has to decide whether the image is sampled from the generator p_g or from real images p_{real}. After a successful training the discriminator cannot distinguish real from generated samples. Adversarial training is often used to enforce (implicit) constraints on random variables as we do. For instance, BIGAN [6] learns a feature representation with adversarial nets by training an encoder Enc, such that $\text{Enc}(\mathbf{x})$ is Gaussian, when $\mathbf{x} \sim p_{real}$. CoGAN [13] learns the joint distribution of multi-domain images by having generators and discriminators in each domain, and sharing their weights. They can transform images between domains without being given correspondences. InfoGan [4] learns a subset of factors of variation by reproducing parts of the input vector with the discriminator.

Disentangling Factors of Variation. Many recent methods use neural networks for disentangling factors of variation. A lot of them are fully supervised [11,16,18,19,22], *i.e.*, they use labels for all factors they aim to disentangle. For example, Peng *et al.* [16] disentangle the face identities and poses using multiple source of labels including identity, pose and landmarks. With identity and pose labels Tran *et al.* [22] can learn pose invariant features and synthesize frontalized faces from any pose. In deep visual analogy making [19] the supervisory signal is an image. The feature representation is split into two parts to represent different factors. The combination of these parts from different inputs are fed to the decoder, which has to reconstruct the target image. We also use the same feature swapping technique as in [19], but we do not need the ground truth target image for our training. Semi-supervised methods use labels of only part of the data samples. Siddharth *et al.* [21] propose a hybrid generative model to combine structured graphical models and unstructured random variables, thus enabling semi-supervised disentanglement. Our main focus is weakly supervised learning, where not all attributes come with labels. Shu *et al.* [20] disentangle intrinsic image factors (albedo and normal map) by modeling the physics of the image formation in their network. They use a 3D morphable model prior to guide the training. DrNet [5] disentangles the pose and content from videos. Assuming that the subsequent frames contain the same object, they can eliminate the content information from the pose, using an adversarial term on the features. Mathieu *et al.* [15] also use the feature swapping as in [19]. They use a GAN to avoid using the ground truth target images. In our work we do not use any prior information like in [20]. Compared to [5], our adversarial term allows for higher dimensional features, and unlike [15], we do not condition our GAN on class labels, thus we can keep the number of parameters constant. Moreover, with our adversarial term we can provably avoid the shortcut problem.

3 Disentangling Attributes

We are interested in the design and training of two models. One should map a data sample (*e.g.*, an image) to a feature that is explicitly partitioned into subvectors, each associated with a specific attribute. The other model should map this feature back to an image. We call the first model the *encoder* and the second one the *decoder*. For example, given the image of a car as input we would like the encoder to output a feature with two subvectors: one related to the car viewpoint, and the other to the car type. This separation should simplify classification or regression of the attributes (the car viewpoint and type in the example). It should also be very useful for the advanced editing of images through the decoder. For example, the transfer of the viewpoint or car types from an image to another can be achieved by swapping the corresponding subvectors. Next, we introduce our model of the data and the definitions of our encoder and decoder (see Fig. 2).

Data Model. We assume that observed data $\mathbf{x}$ is generated through an unknown deterministic invertible and smooth process f that depends on the factors $\mathbf{v}$ and $\mathbf{c}$, so that $\mathbf{x} = f(\mathbf{v}, \mathbf{c})$. In our earlier example, $\mathbf{x}$ is an image, $\mathbf{v}$ is a viewpoint, $\mathbf{c}$ is a car type, and f is the rendering engine. It is reasonable to assume that f is invertible, as for most cases the factors are readily apparent from the image. f is smooth, because we assume that a small change in the factors results in a

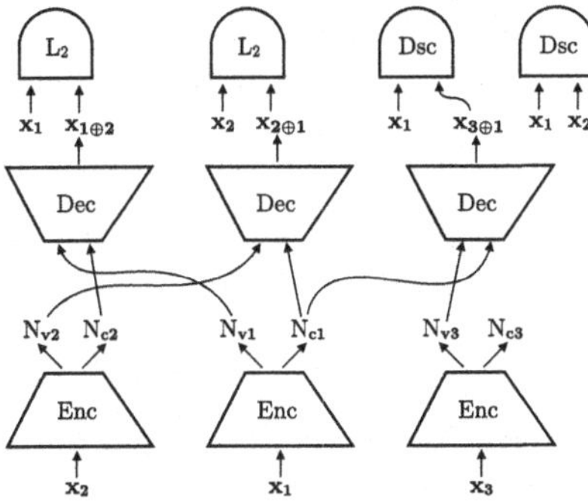

Fig. 2. Learning to disentangle factors of variation. The scheme above shows how the encoder (Enc), the decoder (Dec) and the discriminator (Dsc) are trained with input triplets. The components with the same name share weights.

small change in the image and vice versa. We denote the inverse of the rendering engine as $f^{-1} = [f_{\mathbf{v}}^{-1}, f_{\mathbf{c}}^{-1}]$, where the subscript refers to the recovered factor.

Weak Labeling. In the training we are given pairs of images $\mathbf{x}_1$ and $\mathbf{x}_2$, which differ in $\mathbf{v}$ (varying factor), but have the same $\mathbf{c}$ (common factor). We also assume that the two varying factors and the common factor are sampled independently, $\mathbf{v}_1 \sim p_{\mathbf{v}}$, $\mathbf{v}_2 \sim p_{\mathbf{v}}$ and $\mathbf{c} \sim p_{\mathbf{c}}$. The images are generated as $\mathbf{x}_1 = f(\mathbf{v}_1, \mathbf{c})$ and $\mathbf{x}_2 = f(\mathbf{v}_2, \mathbf{c})$. We call this labeling weak, because we do not know the absolute values of either the $\mathbf{v}$ or $\mathbf{c}$ factors or even relative changes between $\mathbf{v}_1$ and $\mathbf{v}_2$. All we know is that the image pairs share the same common factor $\mathbf{c}$.

The Encoder. Let Enc be the encoder that maps images to features. For simplicity, we consider features split into only two column subvectors, $N_{\mathbf{v}}$ and $N_{\mathbf{c}}$, one associated to the varying factor $\mathbf{v}$ and the other associated to the common factor $\mathbf{c}$. Then, we have that $\text{Enc}(\mathbf{x}) = [N_{\mathbf{v}}(\mathbf{x}), N_{\mathbf{c}}(\mathbf{x})]$. Ideally, we would like to find the inverse of the image formation function, $[N_{\mathbf{v}}, N_{\mathbf{c}}] = f^{-1}$, which separates and recovers the factors $\mathbf{v}$ and $\mathbf{c}$ from data samples $\mathbf{x}$, *i.e.*,

$$N_{\mathbf{v}}(f(\mathbf{v}, \mathbf{c})) = \mathbf{v} \qquad N_{\mathbf{c}}(f(\mathbf{v}, \mathbf{c})) = \mathbf{c}. \tag{1}$$

In practice, these equations are not usable because all our constraints include the decoder, which can undo any bijective transformation of $\mathbf{v}$ and $\mathbf{c}$ and produce the same output $\mathbf{x}$. Therefore, we aim to find $N_{\mathbf{v}}$ and $N_{\mathbf{c}}$ that satisfy

$$R_{\mathbf{v}}(N_{\mathbf{v}}(f(\mathbf{v}, \mathbf{c}))) = \mathbf{v} \qquad R_{\mathbf{c}}(N_{\mathbf{c}}(f(\mathbf{v}, \mathbf{c}))) = \mathbf{c}, \tag{2}$$

which we call the *feature disentangling* properties, for all $\mathbf{v}$, $\mathbf{c}$, and some bijective functions $R_{\mathbf{v}}$ and $R_{\mathbf{c}}$, so that $N_{\mathbf{v}}$ is invariant to $\mathbf{c}$ and $N_{\mathbf{c}}$ is invariant to $\mathbf{v}$.

The Decoder. Let Dec be the decoder that maps features to images. The sequence encoder-decoder is constrained to form an *autoencoder*, so

$$\text{Dec}(N_{\mathbf{v}}(\mathbf{x}), N_{\mathbf{c}}(\mathbf{x})) = \mathbf{x}, \qquad \forall \mathbf{x}. \tag{3}$$

To use the decoder to synthesize images, where different factors are transferred from different images, we can define the combined image as

$$\mathbf{x}_{1\oplus 2} \triangleq \text{Dec}(N_{\mathbf{v}}(\mathbf{x}_1), N_{\mathbf{c}}(\mathbf{x}_2)). \tag{4}$$

The ideal decoder should satisfy for all $\mathbf{x}_1$ and $\mathbf{x}_2$ the *data disentangling* properties

$$f_{\mathbf{v}}^{-1}(\mathbf{x}_{1\oplus 2}) = f_{\mathbf{v}}^{-1}(\mathbf{x}_1) \qquad f_{\mathbf{c}}^{-1}(\mathbf{x}_{1\oplus 2}) = f_{\mathbf{c}}^{-1}(\mathbf{x}_2) \tag{5}$$

In the next section we describe our training method for disentangling. We introduce a novel adversarial term that does not need to be conditioned on the common factor, but rather uses only image pairs, so the number of model parameters are constant. Then, we address the two main challenges of disentangling, the *shortcut problem* and the *reference ambiguity.* We discuss which disentanglement properties can be provably achieved by our, or any other, method.

3.1 Model Training

In our training procedure we use two terms in the objective function: an *autoencoder loss* and an *adversarial loss.* We describe these losses in functional form, however the components are implemented using neural networks. In all our terms we use the following sampling of independent factors

$$\mathbf{c}_1, \mathbf{c}_3 \sim p_{\mathbf{c}}, \quad \mathbf{v}_1, \mathbf{v}_2, \mathbf{v}_3 \sim p_{\mathbf{v}}. \tag{6}$$

The images are formed as $\mathbf{x}_1 = f(\mathbf{v}_1, \mathbf{c}_1)$, $\mathbf{x}_2 = f(\mathbf{v}_2, \mathbf{c}_1)$ and $\mathbf{x}_3 = f(\mathbf{v}_3, \mathbf{c}_3)$. The images $\mathbf{x}_1$ and $\mathbf{x}_2$ share the same common factor, and $\mathbf{x}_1$ and $\mathbf{x}_3$ are independent. In our objective functions, we use either pairs or triplets of the above images.

Autoencoder Loss. In this term, we use images $\mathbf{x}_1$ and $\mathbf{x}_2$ with the same common factor $\mathbf{c}_1$. We feed both images to the encoder. Since both images share the same $\mathbf{c}_1$, we impose that the decoder should reconstruct $\mathbf{x}_1$ from the encoder subvectors $N_{\mathbf{v}}(\mathbf{x}_1)$ and $N_{\mathbf{c}}(\mathbf{x}_2)$. Similarly $\mathbf{x}_2$ is reconstructed from $N_{\mathbf{v}}(\mathbf{x}_2)$ and $N_{\mathbf{c}}(\mathbf{x}_1)$. The autoencoder loss is thus defined as

$$\mathcal{L}_{AE} \triangleq \mathrm{E}_{\mathbf{x}_1,\mathbf{x}_2}\Big[\big|\mathbf{x}_1 - \text{Dec}(N_{\mathbf{v}}(\mathbf{x}_1), N_{\mathbf{c}}(\mathbf{x}_2))\big|^2 + \big|\mathbf{x}_2 - \text{Dec}(N_{\mathbf{v}}(\mathbf{x}_2), N_{\mathbf{c}}(\mathbf{x}_1))\big|^2\Big]. \tag{7}$$

Adversarial Loss. We introduce an adversarial training where the *generator* is our encoder-decoder pair and the *discriminator* Dsc is a neural network, which takes image pairs as input. The discriminator learns to distinguish between real image pairs $[\mathbf{x}_1, \mathbf{x}_2]$ and fake ones $[\mathbf{x}_1, \mathbf{x}_{3\oplus 1}]$, where $\mathbf{x}_{3\oplus 1} \triangleq \text{Dec}(N_{\mathbf{v}}(\mathbf{x}_3), N_{\mathbf{c}}(\mathbf{x}_1))$. The generator learns to fool the discriminator, so that $\mathbf{x}_{3\oplus 1}$ looks like the random variable $\mathbf{x}_2$ (the common factor is $\mathbf{c}_1$ and the varying factor is independent of $\mathbf{v}_1$). The adversarial loss function is then defined as

$$\mathcal{L}_{GAN} \triangleq \mathrm{E}_{\mathbf{x}_1,\mathbf{x}_2}\Big[\log(\text{Dsc}(\mathbf{x}_1, \mathbf{x}_2))\Big] + \mathrm{E}_{\mathbf{x}_1,\mathbf{x}_3}\Big[\log(1 - \text{Dsc}(\mathbf{x}_1, \mathbf{x}_{3\oplus 1}))\Big]. \tag{8}$$

Composite Loss. Finally, we optimize the weighted sum of the two losses $\mathcal{L} = \mathcal{L}_{AE} + \lambda\mathcal{L}_{GAN}$,

$$\min_{\text{Dec,Enc}} \max_{\text{Dsc}} \mathcal{L}_{AE}(\text{Dec}, \text{Enc}) + \lambda\mathcal{L}_{GAN}(\text{Dec}, \text{Enc}, \text{Dsc}) \tag{9}$$

where λ regulates the relative importance of the two losses.

3.2 The Shortcut Problem

Ideally, at the global minimum of $\mathcal{L}_{AE}$, $N_{\mathbf{v}}$ relates only to the factor $\mathbf{v}$ and $N_{\mathbf{c}}$ only to $\mathbf{c}$. However, the encoder may map a complete description of its input into $N_{\mathbf{v}}$ and the decoder may completely ignore $N_{\mathbf{c}}$. We call this challenge the *shortcut problem*. When this occurs, the decoder is invariant to its second input, thus the data disentanglement property for $\mathbf{c}$ Eq. (5) does not hold, and we have

$$\text{Dec}(N_{\mathbf{v}}(\mathbf{x}_3), N_{\mathbf{c}}(\mathbf{x}_1)) = \mathbf{x}_3. \tag{10}$$

The shortcut problem can be addressed by reducing the dimensionality of $N_{\mathbf{v}}$, so that the encoder cannot build a complete representation of all input images. This also forces the encoder and decoder to make use of $N_{\mathbf{c}}$ for the common factor. However, this strategy may not be convenient as it leads to a time consuming trial-and-error procedure to find the correct dimensionality, which is unknown. In the next proposition we show that a better way to address the shortcut problem is instead to use adversarial training through the losses (8) and (9).

Proposition 1. *Let* $\mathbf{x}_1$, $\mathbf{x}_2$ *and* $\mathbf{x}_3$ *be data samples satisfying (6), where the factors* $\mathbf{c}_1, \mathbf{c}_3, \mathbf{v}_1, \mathbf{v}_2, \mathbf{v}_3$ *are jointly independent, and let* $\mathbf{x}_{3\oplus 1} \triangleq$ *Dec*$(N_{\mathbf{v}}(\mathbf{x}_3), N_{\mathbf{c}}(\mathbf{x}_1))$. *When the global optimum of the composite loss (9) is reached, the* $\mathbf{c}$ *factor has been disentangled, i.e.,* $f_{\mathbf{c}}^{-1}(\mathbf{x}_{3\oplus 1}) = \mathbf{c}_1$.

Proof. At the global optimum of (9), the distributions of $[\mathbf{x}_1, \mathbf{x}_2]$ and $[\mathbf{x}_1, \mathbf{x}_{3\oplus 1}]$ image pairs are identical. We compute statistics of the inverse of the common factor $f_{\mathbf{c}}^{-1}$ on the data. For the images $\mathbf{x}_1$ and $\mathbf{x}_2$ we obtain

$$E_{\mathbf{x}_1,\mathbf{x}_2}\left[|f_{\mathbf{c}}^{-1}(\mathbf{x}_1) - f_{\mathbf{c}}^{-1}(\mathbf{x}_2)|^2\right] = E_{\mathbf{c}_1}\left[|\mathbf{c}_1 - \mathbf{c}_1|^2\right] = 0 \tag{11}$$

by construction (of $\mathbf{x}_1$ and $\mathbf{x}_2$). For the images $\mathbf{x}_1$ and $\mathbf{x}_{3\oplus 1}$ we obtain

$$E_{\mathbf{x}_1,\mathbf{x}_3}\left[|f_{\mathbf{c}}^{-1}(\mathbf{x}_1) - f_{\mathbf{c}}^{-1}(\mathbf{x}_{3\oplus 1})|^2\right] = E_{\mathbf{v}_1,\mathbf{c}_1,\mathbf{v}_3,\mathbf{c}_3}\left[|\mathbf{c}_1 - \mathbf{c}_{3\oplus 1}|^2\right] \geq 0, \tag{12}$$

where $\mathbf{c}_{3\oplus 1} = f_{\mathbf{c}}^{-1}(\mathbf{x}_{3\oplus 1})$. We achieve equality if and only if $\mathbf{c}_1 = \mathbf{c}_{3\oplus 1}$ for all samples (in the support of $p_{\mathbf{c}}$). □

3.3 The Reference Ambiguity

When the varying attribute (*e.g.*, the viewpoint) is transferred from an image to another, the numerical value of the varying attribute is interpreted in a reference frame, and the reference frame can depend on the common attribute (car type). Let us consider a practical example, where $\mathbf{v} \sim \mathcal{U}[-\pi, \pi]$ is the (continuous) viewpoint (the azimuth angle) and $\mathbf{c} \sim \mathcal{B}(1/2)$ is the car type, where $\mathcal{U}$ denotes the uniform distribution and $\mathcal{B}(1/2)$ the Bernoulli distribution with probability $p_\mathbf{c}(\mathbf{c}=0) = p_\mathbf{c}(\mathbf{c}=1) = 1/2$ (*i.e.*, there are only 2 car types). We can define a function $T(\mathbf{v}, \mathbf{c}) = \mathbf{v}(2\mathbf{c}-1)$ so that the mapping of $\mathbf{v}$ is mirrored as we change the car type. By construction $T(\mathbf{v}, \mathbf{c}) \sim \mathcal{U}[-\pi, \pi]$ for any $\mathbf{c}$ and $T(\mathbf{v}, \mathbf{c}_1) \neq T(\mathbf{v}, \mathbf{c}_2)$ for $\mathbf{v} \neq 0$ and $\mathbf{c}_1 \neq \mathbf{c}_2$. The encoder $N_\mathbf{v}(f(\mathbf{v}, \mathbf{c})) = T(\mathbf{v}, \mathbf{c})$ is feasible and reverses the ordering of the azimuth of car 1 with respect to car 0. Each car has its own reference system, and thus it is not possible to transfer the viewpoint from one system to the other, as illustrated in Fig. 1c. Below we prove that it is possible to disentangle $\mathbf{c}$, but not $\mathbf{v}$, as the task itself gives rise to this ambiguity.

Let us consider the ideal case where we observe the space of all images. Given the weak labels, we also know what images $\mathbf{x}_1$ and $\mathbf{x}_2$ share the same $\mathbf{c}$ factor (*e.g.*, which images have the same car). This labeling is equivalent to defining the probability density function $p_\mathbf{c}$ and the joint $p_{\mathbf{x}_1,\mathbf{x}_2}$. In the following proposition, we show that the labeling allows a learning algorithm to satisfy the feature disentangling property (2) for $\mathbf{c}$, but in Proposition 3 we show that this is not true for $\mathbf{v}$ (the reference ambiguity holds). The key step is that weak labels allow one to impose stricter constraints on $N_\mathbf{c}$, than on $N_\mathbf{v}$.

Proposition 2. *Given weak labels, the data is sampled according to* $[\mathbf{x}_1, \mathbf{x}_2] \sim p_{\mathbf{x}_1,\mathbf{x}_2}$. *Then, the feature disentangling property (2), for* $\mathbf{c}$, *can be satisfied.*

Proof. For any $[\mathbf{x}_1, \mathbf{x}_2] \sim p_{\mathbf{x}_1,\mathbf{x}_2}$, one can impose $N_\mathbf{c}(\mathbf{x}_1) = N_\mathbf{c}(\mathbf{x}_2)$, which implies that $N_\mathbf{c}$ is invariant to $\mathbf{v}$. Thus, $\forall \mathbf{c}$ let us define $C(\mathbf{c}) \triangleq N_\mathbf{c}(\mathbf{x}_1)$ as a function that depends only on $\mathbf{c}$. One can impose $f_\mathbf{c}^{-1}(\mathbf{x}_{a \oplus b}) = f_\mathbf{c}^{-1}(\mathbf{x}_b)$ (see Proposition 1), then images with the same $\mathbf{v}$, but different $\mathbf{c}$ must also result in different features, $C(\mathbf{c}_a) = N_\mathbf{c}(f(\mathbf{v}, \mathbf{c}_a)) \neq N_\mathbf{c}(f(\mathbf{v}, \mathbf{c}_b)) = C(\mathbf{c}_b)$. Then, there exists a bijective function $R_\mathbf{c} = C^{-1}$ such that property (2) is satisfied for $\mathbf{c}$. □

We now introduce a definition that we need to formalize the reference ambiguity.

Definition 1. *We say that a function g reproduces the data distribution, when it generates samples* $[\mathbf{y}_1, \mathbf{y}_2]$, *where* $\mathbf{y}_1 = g(\mathbf{v}_1, \mathbf{c})$ *and* $\mathbf{y}_2 = g(\mathbf{v}_2, \mathbf{c})$, *that have the same distribution as the data* $[\mathbf{x}_1, \mathbf{x}_2]$. *Formally,* $[\mathbf{y}_1, \mathbf{y}_2] \sim p_{\mathbf{x}_1,\mathbf{x}_2}$, *where the latent factors are independent, i.e.,* $\mathbf{v}_1 \sim p_\mathbf{v}$, $\mathbf{v}_2 \sim p_\mathbf{v}$ *and* $\mathbf{c} \sim p_\mathbf{c}$.

The next proposition illustrates the second main result in this paper: The reference ambiguity of the varying factor $\mathbf{v}$ occurs when a decoder reproduces the data without satisfying the disentangling properties. This implies that we cannot provably disentangle all the factors of variation from weakly labeled data, even if we had access to all the data and knew the distributions $p_\mathbf{v}$ and $p_\mathbf{c}$.

Proposition 3. *Let $p_\mathbf{v}$ assign the same probability value to at least two different instances of $\mathbf{v}$. Then, there exists a decoder that reproduces the data distribution, but does not satisfy the disentangling properties for $\mathbf{v}$ in Eqs. (2) and (5).*

Proof. Let us choose $N_\mathbf{c} \triangleq f_\mathbf{c}^{-1}$, the inverse of the rendering engine. Now we look at defining $N_\mathbf{v}$ and the decoder. Let us denote with $\mathbf{v}_a \neq \mathbf{v}_b$ two varying factors such that $p_\mathbf{v}(\mathbf{v}_a) = p_\mathbf{v}(\mathbf{v}_b)$. Then, let the encoder for $\mathbf{v}$ be defined as

$$N_\mathbf{v}(f(\mathbf{v},\mathbf{c})) \triangleq \begin{cases} \mathbf{v} & \text{if } \mathbf{v} \neq \mathbf{v}_a, \mathbf{v}_b \text{ or } \mathbf{c} \in \mathcal{C} \\ \mathbf{v}_a & \text{if } \mathbf{v} = \mathbf{v}_b \text{ and } \mathbf{c} \notin \mathcal{C} \\ \mathbf{v}_b & \text{if } \mathbf{v} = \mathbf{v}_a \text{ and } \mathbf{c} \notin \mathcal{C} \end{cases} \tag{13}$$

and $\mathcal{C}$ is a subset of the domain of $\mathbf{c}$, where $\int_\mathcal{C} p_\mathbf{c}(\mathbf{c})d\mathbf{c} \notin \{0,1\}$. Therefore, $N_\mathbf{v}(f(\mathbf{v},\mathbf{c})) \sim p_\mathbf{v}$ and $N_\mathbf{v}(f(\mathbf{v},\mathbf{c}_1)) \neq N_\mathbf{v}(f(\mathbf{v},\mathbf{c}_2))$ for $\mathbf{v} \in \{\mathbf{v}_a, \mathbf{v}_b\}$, $\mathbf{c}_1 \in \mathcal{C}$, and $\mathbf{c}_2 \notin \mathcal{C}$. Finally, we define the decoder as

$$\text{Dec}(\mathbf{v},\mathbf{c}) \triangleq \begin{cases} f(\mathbf{v},\mathbf{c}) & \text{if } \mathbf{v} \neq \mathbf{v}_a, \mathbf{v}_b \text{ or } \mathbf{c} \in \mathcal{C} \\ f(\mathbf{v}_a,\mathbf{c}) & \text{if } \mathbf{v} = \mathbf{v}_b \text{ and } \mathbf{c} \notin \mathcal{C} \\ f(\mathbf{v}_b,\mathbf{c}) & \text{if } \mathbf{v} = \mathbf{v}_a \text{ and } \mathbf{c} \notin \mathcal{C}. \end{cases} \tag{14}$$

Notice that $N_\mathbf{v}(f(\mathbf{v},\mathbf{c}))$ depends on $\mathbf{c}$ functionally, but is statistically independent from it. In fact, because $p_\mathbf{v}(\mathbf{v}_a) = p_\mathbf{v}(\mathbf{v}_b)$ we have

$$\begin{aligned} p_{N_\mathbf{v},\mathbf{c}}(\mathbf{v},\mathbf{c}) &= p_{N_\mathbf{v}|\mathbf{c}}(\mathbf{v}|\mathbf{c})p_\mathbf{c}(\mathbf{c}) \\ &= \left[\mathbf{1}_\mathcal{C}(\mathbf{c})p_\mathbf{v}(\mathbf{v}) + \mathbf{1}_{\overline{\mathcal{C}}}(\mathbf{c})\left[\delta(\mathbf{v}-\mathbf{v}_a)p_\mathbf{v}(\mathbf{v}_b) + \delta(\mathbf{v}-\mathbf{v}_b)p_\mathbf{v}(\mathbf{v}_a)\right]\right]p_\mathbf{c}(\mathbf{c}) \\ &= \left[\mathbf{1}_\mathcal{C}(\mathbf{c})p_\mathbf{v}(\mathbf{v}) + \mathbf{1}_{\overline{\mathcal{C}}}(\mathbf{c})\left[\delta(\mathbf{v}-\mathbf{v}_a)p_\mathbf{v}(\mathbf{v}_a) + \delta(\mathbf{v}-\mathbf{v}_b)p_\mathbf{v}(\mathbf{v}_b)\right]\right]p_\mathbf{c}(\mathbf{c}) \\ &= p_\mathbf{v}(\mathbf{v})p_\mathbf{c}(\mathbf{c}). \end{aligned} \tag{15}$$

Thus, no statistical constraint on the encoded factors $N_\mathbf{v}, N_\mathbf{c}$ will allow distinguishing them from the original factors $\mathbf{v},\mathbf{c}$. Finally, we can substitute in $[\text{Dec}(N_\mathbf{v}(\mathbf{x}_1), N_\mathbf{c}(\mathbf{x}_1)), \text{Dec}(N_\mathbf{v}(\mathbf{x}_2), N_\mathbf{c}(\mathbf{x}_2))]$ and reproduce the data distribution, *i.e.*, $[\text{Dec}(\mathbf{v}_1,\mathbf{c}), \text{Dec}(\mathbf{v}_2,\mathbf{c})] \sim p_{\mathbf{x}_1,\mathbf{x}_2}$. The feature disentanglement property is not satisfied because $N_\mathbf{v}(f(\mathbf{v}_a,\mathbf{c}_1)) = \mathbf{v}_a \neq \mathbf{v}_b = N_\mathbf{v}(f(\mathbf{v}_a,\mathbf{c}_2))$, when $\mathbf{c}_1 \in \mathcal{C}$ and $\mathbf{c}_2 \notin \mathcal{C}$. Similarly, the data disentanglement property does not hold, because $f_\mathbf{v}^{-1}(\text{Dec}(N_\mathbf{v}(f(\mathbf{v}_a,\mathbf{c}_1)),\mathbf{c}_1)) \neq f_\mathbf{v}^{-1}(\text{Dec}(N_\mathbf{v}(f(\mathbf{v}_a,\mathbf{c}_1)),\mathbf{c}_2))$. □

3.4 Implementation

In our implementation we use convolutional neural networks for all the models. We denote with θ the parameters associated to each network. Then, the optimization of the composite loss can be written as

$$\hat{\theta}_\text{Dec}, \hat{\theta}_\text{Enc}, \hat{\theta}_\text{Dsc} = \arg\min_{\theta_\text{Dec},\theta_\text{Enc}} \max_{\theta_\text{Dsc}} \mathcal{L}(\theta_\text{Dec}, \theta_\text{Enc}, \theta_\text{Dsc}). \tag{16}$$

We choose $\lambda = 1$ and also add regularization to the adversarial loss so that each logarithm has a minimum value. We define $\log_\epsilon \text{Dsc}(\mathbf{x}_1,\mathbf{x}_2) = \log(\epsilon + \text{Dsc}(\mathbf{x}_1,\mathbf{x}_2))$

Table 1. Network architectures. In the encoder and discriminator we used convolutional layers with a kernel size 4 and stride 2. After each convolutional layer we added normalization and a leaky ReLU layer with a leak coefficient of 0.2. In the decoder we used deconvolutional layers with kernel size 4 and stride 2 followed by a ReLU. *c* stands for convolutional, *d* for deconvolutional and *f* for fully connected layers, and the numbers indicate the number of channels.

	ShapeNet, CelebA, CUB	MNIST	Sprites
Enc	c64-c128-c256-c512-c512-f	c64-c128-c256-f	c64-c128-c256-c512-f
Dec	f-d512-d512-d256-d128-d3	f-d512-d256-d128-d3	f-d512-d256-d128-d3
Dsc	c64-c128-c256-c512-f	c64-c128-c256-f	c64-c128-c256-c512-f

Table 2. Nearest neighbor classification on viewpoint and car type features using different normalization techniques on ShapeNet cars. The performance is measured in mean average precision.

Normalization	Viewpoint	Car type
None	0.47	0.13
Batch	0.50	0.08
Instance	0.50	0.20

(and similarly for the other logarithmic term) and use $\epsilon = 10^{-12}$. The main components of our neural network are shown in Fig. 2. The architecture of the encoder, decoder and the discriminator were taken from DCGAN [17], with slight modifications. We added fully connected layers at the output of the encoder and to the input of the decoder. As the input to the discriminator is an image pair, we concatenate them along the color channels. The details of the architecture is described in Table 1 for all datasets we experimented on.

Normalization. In our architecture both the encoder and the decoder networks use blocks with a convolutional layer, a nonlinear activation function (ReLU/leaky ReLU) and a normalization layer, typically, batch normalization (BN). As an alternative to BN we consider *instance normalization* (IN) [23]. The main difference between BN and IN is that the latter just computes the mean and standard deviation across the spatial domain of the input and not along the batch dimension. Thus, the shift and scaling for the output of each layer is the same at every iteration for the same input image. We compared the different normalization choices for the ShapeNet dataset in Table 2, where we report the performance on the nearest neighbor classification task. The feature dimensions were fixed at 1024 for both $N_\mathbf{v}$ and $N_\mathbf{c}$ in all normalization cases. We can see that both batch and instance normalization perform equally well on viewpoint classification and no normalization is slightly worse. For the car type classification instance normalization is clearly better.

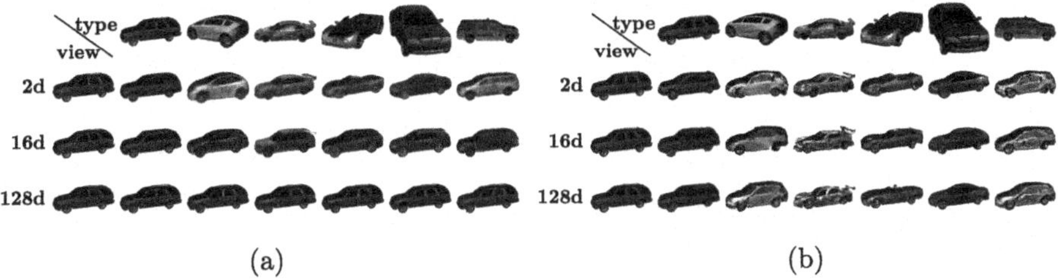

Fig. 3. Attribute transfer on ShapeNet. (a) Synthesized images with $\mathcal{L}_{AE}$, where the top row shows images from which the car type is taken. The second, third and fourth row show the decoder renderings using 2, 16 and 128 dimensions for the feature $N_{\mathbf{v}}$. (b) Images synthesized with $\mathcal{L}_{AE} + \mathcal{L}_{GAN}$. The setting for the inputs and feature dimensions are the same as in (a).

4 Experiments

We tested our method on the MNIST, Sprites, CelebA, CUB and ShapeNet datasets and performed ablation studies on the shortcut problem using ShapeNet cars. We focused on the effect of the feature dimensionality and having the adversarial term (*i.e.*, $\mathcal{L}_{AE} + \mathcal{L}_{GAN}$) or not (*i.e.*, only $\mathcal{L}_{AE}$). We also show that in most cases the reference ambiguity does not arise in practice (MNIST, Sprites, CelebA, CUB, ShapeNet cars and motorcycles), we can only observe it when the data is more complex (ShapeNet chairs and vessels).

The Shortcut Problem. The ShapeNet dataset [3] contains 3D objects than we can render from different viewpoints. We consider only one category (cars) and a set of fixed viewpoints. Cars have high intraclass variability and they do not have rotational symmetries. We used approximately 3K car types for training and 300 for testing. We rendered 24 possible viewpoints around each object in a full circle, resulting in 80K images in total. The elevation was fixed to 15 degrees and azimuth angles were spaced 15 degrees apart. We normalized the size of the objects to fit in a 100×100 pixel bounding box, and placed it in the middle of a 128×128 pixel image. Figure 3 shows the attribute transfer on the ShapeNet cars. We compare the methods $\mathcal{L}_{AE}$ and $\mathcal{L}_{AE} + \mathcal{L}_{GAN}$ with different feature dimension of $N_{\mathbf{v}}$. The size of the common feature $N_{\mathbf{c}}$ was fixed to 1024 dimensions. We can observe that the transferring performance degrades for $\mathcal{L}_{AE}$, when we increase the feature size of $N_{\mathbf{v}}$. This illustrates the shortcut problem, where the autoencoder tries to store all the information into $N_{\mathbf{v}}$. The model $\mathcal{L}_{AE}+\mathcal{L}_{GAN}$ instead renders images without loss of quality, independently of the feature dimension. In Fig. 4 we visualize the t-SNE embeddings of the $N_{\mathbf{v}}$ features for several models using different feature sizes. For the $2D$ case, we do not modify the data. We can see that both $\mathcal{L}_{AE}$ with 2 dimensions and $\mathcal{L}_{AE}+\mathcal{L}_{GAN}$ with 128 dimensions separate the viewpoints well, but the lone $\mathcal{L}_{AE}$ with 128 dimensions does not separate the viewpoints well due to the shortcut problem. We investigate the effect of dimensionality of the $N_{\mathbf{v}}$ features on the nearest neighbor classification task. The performance is measured by the mean

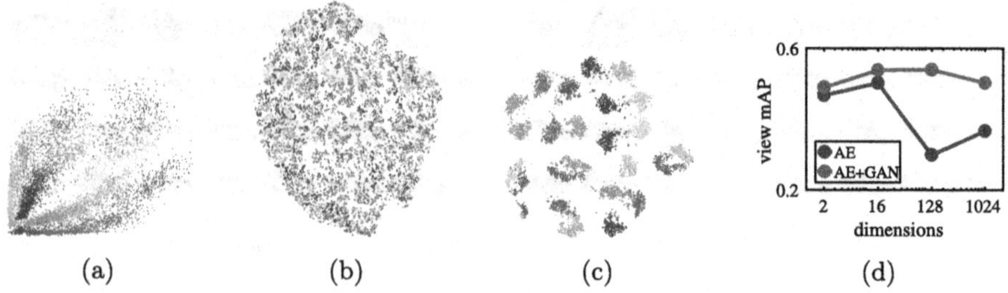

(a) (b) (c) (d)

Fig. 4. The effect of dimensions and objective function on $N_{\mathbf{v}}$ features. (a), (b), (c) t-SNE embeddings on $N_{\mathbf{v}}$ features. Colors correspond to the ground truth viewpoint. The objective functions and the $N_{\mathbf{v}}$ dimensions are: (a) $\mathcal{L}_{AE}$ 2 dim, (b) $\mathcal{L}_{AE}$ 128 dim, (c) $\mathcal{L}_{AE} + \mathcal{L}_{GAN}$ 128 dim. (d) Mean average precision curves for the viewpoint prediction from the viewpoint feature using different models and dimensions for $N_{\mathbf{v}}$.

average precision. For $N_{\mathbf{v}}$ we use the viewpoint as ground truth. Figure 4 also shows the results on $\mathcal{L}_{AE}$ and $\mathcal{L}_{AE} + \mathcal{L}_{GAN}$ models with different $N_{\mathbf{v}}$ feature dimensions. The dimension of $N_{\mathbf{c}}$ was fixed to 1024 for this experiment. One can now see quantitatively that $\mathcal{L}_{AE}$ is sensitive to the size of $N_{\mathbf{v}}$, while $\mathcal{L}_{AE}+\mathcal{L}_{GAN}$ is not. $\mathcal{L}_{AE} + \mathcal{L}_{GAN}$ also achieves a better performance.

The Reference Ambiguity. We rendered the ShapeNet chairs, vessels and motorcycles with the same settings (viewpoints, image size) as the cars. There are 3500 chair, 1500 vessel and 300 motorcycle types for training, which provide between 7K and 84K images for each category. We trained our network with the full objective $\mathcal{L}_{AE} + \mathcal{L}_{GAN}$ and with the same settings as in the case of ShapeNet cars. In Fig. 5 we show the attribute transfer results. We can see that the object type is transferred correctly in all cases, and we can observe the reference ambiguity in two out of four categories. Some of the rendered chairs are flipped. The most interesting case is the vessel category, where the viewpoint angle is interpreted in two different ways depending on the boat type. We may be inclined to conclude that objects with a similar shape tend to share the same reference for the varying attribute (in the case of vessels, large boats seem to transfer the viewpoint between each other, but not with thinner boats).

MNIST Evaluation. The MNIST dataset [12] contains handwritten grayscale digits of size 28×28 pixel. There are 60K images of 10 classes for training and 10K for testing. The common factor is the digit class and the varying factor is the intraclass variation. We take image pairs that have the same digit for training, and use our full model $\mathcal{L}_{AE}+\mathcal{L}_{GAN}$ with dimensions 64 for $N_{\mathbf{v}}$ and 64 for $N_{\mathbf{c}}$. In Fig. 6(a) and (b) we show the transfer of varying factors. Qualitatively, both our method and [15] perform well. We observe neither the reference ambiguity nor the shortcut problem in this case, probably due to the high similarity of objects within the same category.

Sprites Evaluation. The Sprites dataset [19] contains 60 pixel color images of animated characters (sprites). There are 672 sprites, 500 for training, 100 for

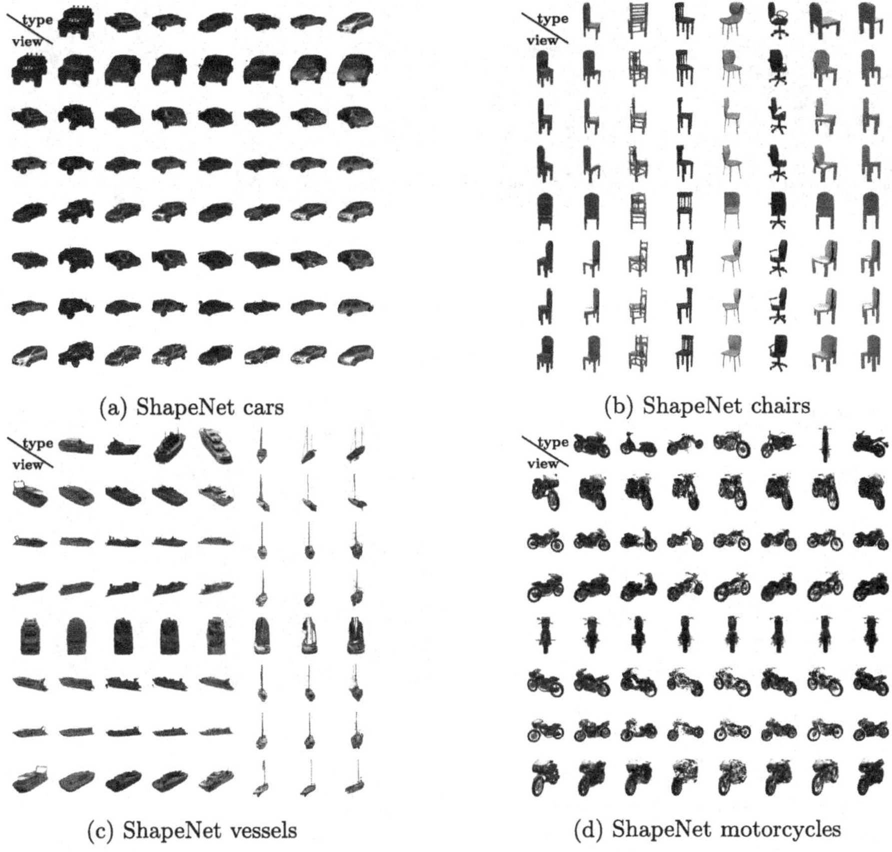

Fig. 5. Attribute transfer on ShapeNet categories. For all subfigures the object type is taken from the topmost row and the viewpoint is taken from the leftmost column.

testing and 72 for validation. Each sprite has 20 animations and 178 images, so the full dataset has 120K images in total. There are many changes in the appearance of the sprites, they differ in their body shape, gender, hair, armour, arm type, greaves, and weapon. We consider character identity as the common factor and the pose as the varying factor. We train our system using image pairs of the same sprite and do not exploit labels on their pose. We train the $\mathcal{L}_{AE} + \mathcal{L}_{GAN}$ model with dimensions 64 for $N_{\mathbf{v}}$ and 448 for $N_{\mathbf{c}}$. Figure 6(c) and (d) show results on the attribute transfer task. Both our method and [15] transfer the identity of the sprites correctly, the reference ambiguity does not arise.

CUB Evaluation. The CUB birds dataset [24] contains 12K images of 200 bird species. In our model we choose the bird species as the common factor and used the same settings as for ShapeNet. The results on attribute transfer can be seen on Fig. 7a.

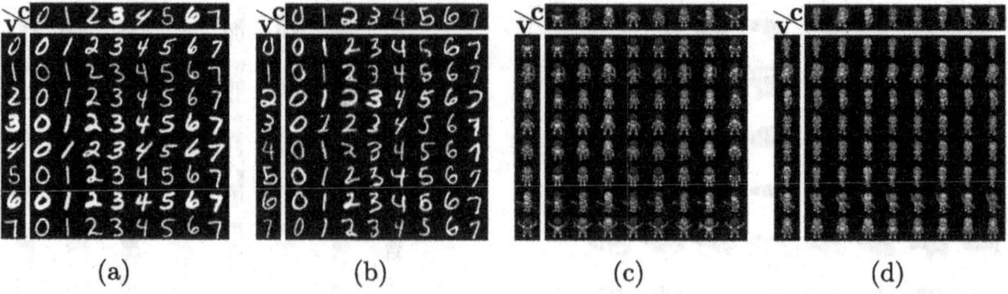

Fig. 6. Renderings of transferred features. In all figures the varying factor is transferred from the left column and the common factor from the top row. (a) MNIST [15]; (b) MNIST (ours); (c) Sprites [15]; (d) Sprites (ours).

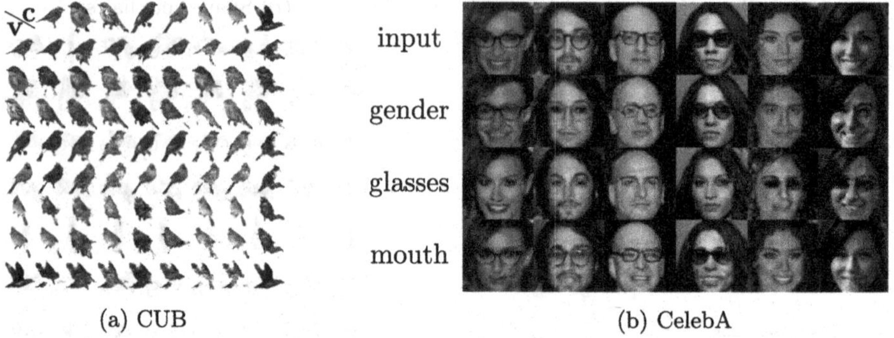

(a) CUB (b) CelebA

Fig. 7. Attribute transfer on CUB and CelebA datasets. (a) CUB birds, where the pose is taken from the leftmost column and the species is taken from the topmost row. (b) CelebA, the first row shows the original image and each subsequent row shows the change of the following attributes: gender, glasses, mouth-open.

CelebA Evaluation. The CelebA dataset [14] contains 200K face images. It contains labelled binary attributes such as male/female, old/young and so on. We used the same settings as for ShapeNet, and trained separate models, where the common attribute was one of the labelled ones. The results on attribute transfer can be seen in Fig. 7b.

5 Conclusions

In this paper we studied two fundamental challenges of disentangling factors of variation: the shortcut problem and the reference ambiguity. The shortcut problem occurs when all information is stored in only one feature subvector, while the other is ignored. The reference ambiguity means that the reference in which a factor is interpreted, may depend on other factors. This makes the attribute transfer ambiguous. We introduced a novel training of autoencoders to solve disentangling using image triplets. We showed theoretically and experimentally how to avoid the shortcut problem through adversarial training. Moreover, our method allows using arbitrarily large feature dimensions, which simplifies the design of the autoencoder model. We proved that the reference ambiguity is inherently present in the disentangling task when weak labels are used. Most importantly this can be stated independently of the learning algorithm. We demonstrated that training and transfer of factors of variation may not be guaranteed. However, in practice we observe that some trained models work well on many datasets and exhibit good attribute transfer capabilities.

Acknowledgements. QH, TP and AS have been supported by the Swiss National Science Foundation (SNSF) grants 200021_149227 and 200021_156253.

References

1. Bengio, Y., Courville, A., Vincent, P.: Representation learning: a review and new perspectives. IEEE Trans. Pattern Anal. Mach. Intell. **35**(8), 1798–1828 (2013)
2. Bourlard, H., Kamp, Y.: Auto-association by multilayer perceptrons and singular value decomposition. Biol. Cybern. **59**(4), 291–294 (1988)
3. Chang, A.X., Funkhouser, T., Guibas, L., Hanrahan, P., Huang, Q., Li, Z., Savarese, S., Savva, M., Song, S., Su, H., Xiao, J., Yi, L., Yu, F.: ShapeNet: An Information-Rich 3D Model Repository. arXiv:1512.03012 (2015)
4. Chen, X., Duan, Y., Houthooft, R., Schulman, J., Sutskever, I., Abbeel, P.: Info-GAN: interpretable representation learning by information maximizing generative adversarial nets. In: NIPS (2016)
5. Denton, E.L., Birodkar, V.: Unsupervised learning of disentangled representations from video. In: NIPS (2017)
6. Donahue, J., Krähenbühl, P., Darrell, T.: Adversarial feature learning. In: ICLR (2014)
7. Goodfellow, I., Pouget-Abadie, J., Mirza, M., Xu, B., Warde-Farley, D., Ozair, S., Courville, A., Bengio, Y.: Generative adversarial nets. In: NIPS (2014)
8. Hinton, G.E., Krizhevsky, A., Wang, S.D.: Transforming auto-encoders. In: International Conference on Artificial Neural Networks, pp. 44–51 (2011)
9. Hinton, G.E., Salakhutdinov, R.R.: Reducing the dimensionality of data with neural networks. Science **313**(5786), 504–507 (2006)
10. Kingma, D.P., Welling, M.: Auto-encoding variational bayes. In: ICLR (2014)
11. Lample, G., Zeghidour, N., Usunier, N., Bordes, A., Denoyer, L., Ranzato, M.A.: Fader networks: manipulating images by sliding attributes. In: NIPS (2017)
12. LeCun, Y., Bottou, L., Bengio, Y., Haffner, P.: Gradient-based learning applied to document recognition. Proc. IEEE **86**(11), 2278–2324 (1998)
13. Liu, M.Y., Tuzel, O.: Coupled generative adversarial networks. In: NIPS (2016)
14. Liu, Z., Luo, P., Wang, X., Tang, X.: Deep learning face attributes in the wild. In: ICCV (2015)
15. Mathieu, M.F., Zhao, J.J., Zhao, J., Ramesh, A., Sprechmann, P., LeCun, Y.: Disentangling factors of variation in deep representation using adversarial training. In: NIPS (2016)
16. Peng, X., Yu, X., Sohn, K., Metaxas, D.N., Chandraker, M.: Reconstruction-based disentanglement for pose-invariant face recognition. In: ICCV (2017)
17. Radford, A., Metz, L., Chintala, S.: Unsupervised representation learning with deep convolutional generative adversarial networks. arXiv:1511.06434 (2015)

18. Reed, S., Sohn, K., Zhang, Y., Lee, H.: Learning to disentangle factors of variation with manifold interaction. In: ICML (2014)
19. Reed, S.E., Zhang, Y., Zhang, Y., Lee, H.: Deep visual analogy-making. In: NIPS (2015)
20. Shu, Z., Yumer, E., Hadap, S., Sunkavalli, K., Shechtman, E., Samaras, D.: Neural face editing with intrinsic image disentangling. In: CVPR (2017)
21. Siddharth, N., Paige, T.B., van de Meent, J.W., Desmaison, A., Goodman, N., Kohli, P., Wood, F., Torr, P.: Learning disentangled representations with semi-supervised deep generative models. In: NIPS (2017)
22. Tran, L., Yin, X., Liu, X.: Disentangled representation learning GAN for pose-invariant face recognition. In: CVPR (2017)
23. Ulyanov, D., Vedaldi, A., Lempitsky, V.S.: Improved texture networks: Maximizing quality and diversity in feed-forward stylization and texture synthesis. In: CVPR (2017)
24. Wah, C., Branson, S., Welinder, P., Perona, P., Belongie, S.: The Caltech-UCSD Birds-200-2011 Dataset. Technical report (2011)

Reinforced Temporal Attention and Split-Rate Transfer for Depth-Based Person Re-identification

Nikolaos Karianakis[1(✉)], Zicheng Liu[1], Yinpeng Chen[1], and Stefano Soatto[2]

[1] Microsoft, Redmond, USA
nikarian@microsoft.com
[2] University of California, Los Angeles, USA

Abstract. We address the problem of person re-identification from commodity depth sensors. One challenge for depth-based recognition is data scarcity. Our *first* contribution addresses this problem by introducing *split-rate* RGB-to-Depth transfer, which leverages large RGB datasets more effectively than popular fine-tuning approaches. Our transfer scheme is based on the observation that the model parameters at the bottom layers of a deep convolutional neural network can be directly shared between RGB and depth data while the remaining layers need to be fine-tuned rapidly. Our *second* contribution enhances re-identification for video by implementing temporal attention as a Bernoulli-Sigmoid unit acting upon frame-level features. Since this unit is stochastic, the temporal attention parameters are trained using reinforcement learning. Extensive experiments validate the accuracy of our method in person re-identification from depth sequences. Finally, in a scenario where subjects wear unseen clothes, we show large performance gains compared to a state-of-the-art model which relies on RGB data.

Keywords: Person re-identification from depth
Reinforced temporal attention · Split-rate transfer

1 Introduction

Person re-identification is a fundamental problem in automated video surveillance and has attracted significant attention in recent years [7,23,78]. When a person is captured by cameras with non-overlapping views, or by the same camera but over many days, the objective is to recognize them across views among a large number of imposters. This is a difficult problem because of the visual ambiguity in a person's appearance due to large variations in illumination, human pose, camera settings and viewpoint. Additionally, re-identification systems have to be robust to partial occlusions and cluttered background. Multi-person association has wide applicability and utility in areas such as robotics, multimedia, forensics, autonomous driving and cashier-free shopping.

V. Ferrari et al. (Eds.): ECCV 2018, LNCS 11209, pp. 737–756, 2018.
https://doi.org/10.1007/978-3-030-01228-1_44

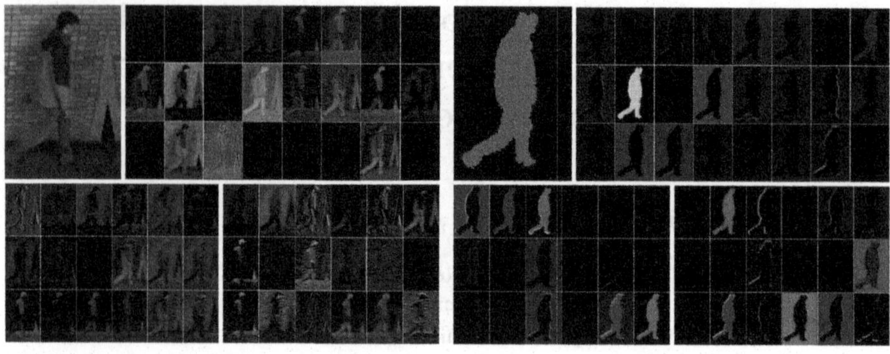

(a) Person ReID from RGB [82]

(b) Person ReID from Depth

Fig. 1. Filter responses from "conv1" (upper right), "conv2" (bottom left) and "conv3" (bottom right) layers for a given frame from the TUM GAID data using (a) a framework for person re-identification from RGB [82] and (b) the feature embedding f_{CNN} of our framework, which is drawn in Fig. 3 and exclusively utilizes depth data.

1.1 Related Work

Existing methods of person re-identification typically focus on designing invariant and discriminant features [10,22,24,38,43,46,50,87,100], which can enable identification despite nuisance factors such as scale, location, partial occlusion and changing lighting conditions. In an effort to improve their robustness, the current trend is to deploy higher-dimensional descriptors [43,47] and deep convolutional architectures [1,17,40,45,65,73,79,82,83,89,101,109].

In spite of the ongoing quest for effective representations, it is still challenging to deal with very large variations such as ultra wide-baseline matching and dramatic changes in illumination and resolution, especially with limited training data. As such, there is vast literature in learning discriminative distance metrics [5,19,35,42,43,48,51,53,55,61,77,91,105,108] and discriminant subspaces [15,43,46,47,63,64,84,94,107]. Other approaches handle the problem of pose variability by explicitly accounting for spatial constraints of the human body parts [12,39,96,97] or by predicting the pose from video [16,72].

However, a key challenge to tackle within both distance learning and deep learning pipelines in practical applications is the *small sample size* problem [14, 94]. This issue is exacerbated by the lack of large-scale person re-identification datasets. Some new ones have been released recently, such as CUHK03 [40] and MARS [102], a video extension of the Market-1501 dataset [103]. However, their training sets are in the order of 20,000 positive samples, i.e. two orders of magnitude smaller than Imagenet [66], which has been successfully used for object recognition [37,69,75].

The small sample size problem is especially acute in person re-identification from temporal sequences [9,26,54,86,110], as the feature dimensionality increases linearly in the number of frames that are accumulated compared to the single-shot representations. On the other hand, explicitly modeling temporal dynamics and using multiple frames help algorithms to deal with noisy measurements, occlusions, adverse poses and lighting.

Regularization techniques, such as Batch Normalization [30] and Dropout [27], help learning models with larger generalization capability. Xiao et al. [82] achieved top accuracy on several benchmarks by leveraging on their proposed "domain-guided dropout" principle. After their model is trained on a union of datasets, it is further enhanced on individual datasets by adaptively setting the dropout rate for each neuron as a function of its activation rate in the training data.

Haque et al. [26] designed a *glimpse* layer and used a 4D convolutional autoencoder in order to compress the 4D spatiotemporal input video representation, while the next spatial location (glimpse) is inferred within a recurrent attention framework using reinforcement learning [56]. However, for small patches (at the glimpse location), the model loses sight of the overall body shape, while for large patches, it loses the depth resolution. Achieving a good *trade-off* between visibility and resolution within the objective of compressing the input space to tractable levels is hard with limited data. Our algorithm has several key differences from this work. First, observing that there are large amount of RGB data available for training frame-level person ReID models, we transfer parameters from pre-trained RGB models with an improved transfer scheme. Second, since the input to our frame-level model is the entire body region, we do not have any visibility constraints at a cost of resolution. Third, in order to better utilize the temporal information from video, we propose a novel reinforced temporal attention unit on top of the frame-level features which is *guided* by the task in order to predict the weights of individual frames into the final prediction.

Our method for transferring a RGB Person ReID model to the depth domain is based on the key observation that the model parameters at the bottom layers of a deep convolutional neural network can be directly shared between RGB and depth data while the remaining upper layers need to be fine-tuned. At first glance, our observation is inconsistent with what was reported in the RGB-D object recognition approach by Song et al. [71]. They reported that the bottom layers cannot be shared between RGB and depth models and it is better to retrain them from scratch. Our conjecture is that this behavior is in part specific to the HHA depth encoding [25], which is not used in our representation.

Some recent works in natural language processing [11,49] explore temporal attention in order to keep track of long-range structural dependencies. Yao et al. [88] in video captioning use a soft attention gate inside their Long Short-term memory decoder, so that they estimate the relevance of current features in the input video given all the previously generated words. One key difference of our approach is that our attention unit is exclusively dependent on the frame-level feature embedding, but not on the hidden state, which likely makes it less prone to error drifting. Additionally, our temporal attention is not differentiable so we resort to reinforcement learning techniques [80] for binary outcome. Being inspired by the work of Likas [44] in online clustering and Kontoravdis et al. [36]

in exploration of binary domains, we model the weight of each frame prediction as a *Bernoulli-sigmoid* unit. We review our model in detail in Sect. 2.2.

Depth-based methods that use measurements from 3D skeleton data have emerged in order to infer anthropometric and human gait criteria [2,3,21,57,60]. In an effort to leverage the full power of depth data, recent methods use 3D point clouds to estimate motion trajectories and the length of specific body parts [29,95]. It is worthwhile to point out that skeleton information is not always available. For example, the skeleton tracking in Kinect SDK can be ineffective when a person is in side view or the legs are not visible.

On top of the above-mentioned challenges, RGB-based methods are challenged in scenarios with significant lighting changes and when the individuals change clothes. These factors can have a big impact on the effectiveness of a system that, for instance, is meant to track people across different areas of a building over several days where different areas of a building may have drastically different lighting conditions, the cameras may differ in color balance, and a person may wear clothes of different patterns. This is our *key motivation* for using depth silhouettes in our scenario, as they are insensitive to these factors.

Our contributions can be summarized as follows:

(i) We propose novel reinforced temporal attention on top of the frame-level features to better leverage the temporal information from video sequences by learning to adaptively weight the predictions of individual frames based on a task-based reward. In Sect. 2.2 we define the model, its end-to-end training is described in Sect. 2.3, and comparisons with baselines are shown in Sect. 3.5.

(ii) We tackle the data scarcity problem in depth-based person re-identification by leveraging the large amount of RGB data to obtain stronger frame-level features. Our *split-rate* RGB-to-depth transfer scheme is drawn in Fig. 4. We show in Fig. 5 that our method outperforms a popular fine-tuning method by more effectively utilizing pre-trained models from RGB data.

(iii) Extensive experiments in Sect. 3.5 not only show the superiority of our method compared to the state of the art in depth-based person re-identification from video, but also tackle a challenging application scenario where the persons wear clothes that were unseen during training. In Table 2 we demonstrate the robustness of our method compared to its RGB-based counterpart and the mutual gains when jointly using the person's head information.

2 Our Method

2.1 Input Representation

The input for our system is raw depth measurements from the Kinect V2 [68]. The input data are depth images $\mathbf{D} \in \mathbb{Z}^{512\times 424}$, where each pixel $D[i,j], i \in [1,512], j \in [1,424]$, contains the Cartesian distance, in millimeters, from the image plane to the nearest object at the particular coordinate (i,j).

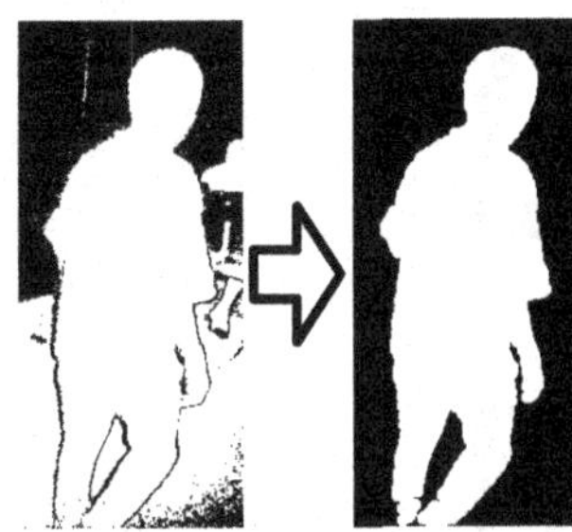

Fig. 2. The cropped color image (left), the grayscale depth representation $\mathbf{D_p^g}$ (center) and the result after background subtraction (right) using the body index information $\mathbf{B_p}$ from skeleton tracking.

In "default range" setting, the intervals $[0, 0.4\,m)$ and $(8.0\,m, \infty)$ are classified as unknown measurements, $[0.4, 0.8)[m]$ as "too near", $(4.0, 8.0][m]$ as "too far" and $[0.8, 4.0][m]$ as "normal" values. When skeleton tracking is effective, the *body index* $\mathbf{B} \in \mathbb{Z}^{512 \times 424}$ is provided by the Kinect SDK, where 0 corresponds to background and a positive integer i for each pixel belonging to the person i.

After extracting the person region $\mathbf{D_p} \subset \mathbf{D}$, the measurements within the "normal" region are normalized in the range $[1, 256]$, while the values from "too far" and "unknown" range are set as 256, and values within the "too near" range as 1. In practice, in order to avoid a concentration of the values near 256, whereas other values, say on the floor in front of the subject, span the remaining range, we introduce an offset $t_o = 56$ and normalize in $[1, 256 - t_o]$. This results in the "grayscale" person representation $\mathbf{D_p^g}$. When the body index is available, we deploy $\mathbf{B_p} \subset \mathbf{B}$ as mask on the depth region $\mathbf{D_p}$ in order to achieve background subtraction before applying range normalization (see Fig. 2).

2.2 Model Structure

The problem is formulated as *sequential decision proccss* of an agent that performs human recognition from a partially observed environment via video sequences. At each time step, the agent observes the environment via depth camera, calculates a feature vector based on a deep Convolutional Neural Network (CNN) and actively infers the importance of the current frame for the re-identification task using novel Reinforced Temporal Attention (RTA). On top of the CNN features, a Long Short-Term Memory (LSTM) unit models short-range temporal dynamics. At each time step the agent receives a reward based on the success or failure of its classification task. Its objective is to maximize the sum of rewards over time. The agent and its components are detailed next, while the training process is described in Sect. 2.3. The model is outlined in Fig. 3.

Agent: Formally, the problem setup is a Partially Observable Markov Decision Process (POMDP). The true state of the environment is unknown. The agent

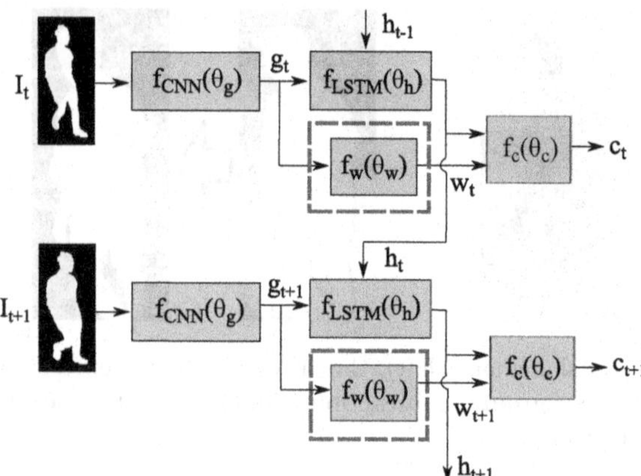

Fig. 3. Our model architecture consists of a frame-level feature embedding f_{CNN}, which provides input to both a recurrent layer f_{LSTM} and the Reinforced Temporal Attention (RTA) unit f_w (highlighted in red). The classifier is attached to the hidden state h_t and its video prediction is the weighted sum of single-frame predictions, where the weights w_t for each frame t are predicted by the RTA unit. (Color figure online)

learns a stochastic policy $\pi((w_t, c_t)|s_{1:t};\theta)$ with parameters $\theta = \{\theta_g, \theta_w, \theta_h, \theta_c\}$ that, at each step t, maps the past history $s_{1:t} = I_1, w_1, c_1, \ldots, I_{t-1}, w_{t-1}, c_{t-1}, I_t$ to two distributions over discrete actions: the frame weight w_t (sub-policy π_1) and the class posterior c_t (sub-policy π_2). The weight w_t is sampled stochastically from a binary distribution parameterized by the RTA unit $f_w(g_t;\theta_w)$ at time t: $w_t \sim \pi_1(\cdot|f_w(g_t;\theta_w))$. The class posterior distribution is conditioned on the classifier module, which is attached to the LSTM output h_t: $c_t \sim \pi_2(\cdot|f_c(h_t;\theta_c))$. The vector h_t maintains an internal state of the environment as a summary of past observations. Note that, for simplicity of notation, the input image at time t is denoted as I_t, but the actual input is the person region $D^g_{p,t}$ (see Sect. 2.1).

Frame-Level Feature Embedding $f_{CNN}(\theta_g)$: Given that there is little depth data but a large amount of RGB data available for person re-identification, we would like to leverage the RGB data to train depth models for frame-level feature extraction. We discovered that the parameters at the bottom convolutional layers of a deep neural network can be directly shared between RGB and depth data (*cf.* Sect. 2.3) through a simple depth encoding, that is, each pixel with depth D is replicated to three channels and encoded as (D, D, D), which corresponds to the three RGB channels. This motivates us to select a pre-trained RGB model.

RGB-based person re-identification has progressed rapidly in recent years [1,40,73,79,82,89]. The deep convolutional network introduced by Xiao et al. [82] outperformed other approaches on several public datasets. Therefore, we decide to adopt their model for frame-level feature extraction. This network is similar in nature to *GoogleNet* [75]; it uses batch normalization [30] and includes 3 × 3 convolutional layers [69], followed by 6 Inception modules [75], and 2 fully connected layers. In order to make this network applicable to our scenario, we introduce two small modifications. First, we replace the top classification layer with a $256 \times N$ fully connected layer, where N is the number of subjects at the target dataset and its weights are initialized at random from a zero-mean Gaussian distribution with standard deviation 0.01. Second, we add dropout regularization between the fully-connected layers. In Sect. 2.3 we demonstrate an effective way to transfer the model parameters from RGB to Depth.

Recurrent Module $f_{LSTM}(\theta_h)$: We use the efficient Long Short-Term Memory (LSTM) element units as described in [92], which have been shown by Donahue et al. [20] to be effective in modeling temporal dynamics for video recognition and captioning. In specific, assuming that $\sigma()$ is sigmoid, $g[t]$ is the input at time frame t, $h[t-1]$ is the previous output of the module and $c[t-1]$ is the previous cell, the implementation corresponds to the following updates:

$$i[t] = \sigma(W_{gi}g[t] + W_{hi}h[t-1] + b_i) \tag{1}$$
$$f[t] = \sigma(W_{gf}g[t] + W_{hf}h[t-1] + b_f) \tag{2}$$
$$z[t] = tanh(W_{gc}g[t] + W_{hc}h[t-1] + b_c) \tag{3}$$
$$c[t] = f[t] \odot c[t-1] + i[t] \odot z[t] \tag{4}$$
$$o[t] = \sigma(W_{go}g[t] + W_{ho}h[t-1] + b_o) \tag{5}$$
$$h[t] = o[t] \odot tanh(c[t]) \tag{6}$$

where W_{sq} is the weight matrix from source s to target q for each gate q, b_q are the biases leading into q, $i[t]$ is the input gate, $f[t]$ is the forget gate, $z[t]$ is the input to the cell, $c[t]$ is the cell, $o[t]$ is the output gate, and $h[t]$ is the output of this module. Finally, $x \odot y$ denotes the element-wise product of vectors x and y.

Reinforced Temporal Attention $f_w(\theta_w)$: At each time step t the RTA unit infers the *importance* w_t of the image frame I_t, as the latter is represented by the feature encoding g_t. This module consists of a linear layer which maps the 256×1 vector g_t to one scalar, followed by Sigmoid non-linearity which squashes real-valued inputs to a $[0, 1]$ range. Next, the output w_t is defined by a Bernoulli random variable with probability mass function:

$$f(w_t; f_w(g_t; \theta_w)) = \begin{cases} f_w(g_t; \theta_w), & w_t = 1 \\ 1 - f_w(g_t; \theta_w), & w_t = 0 \end{cases} \tag{7}$$

The Bernoulli parameter is conditioned on the Sigmoid output $f_w(g_t; \theta_w)$, shaping a Bernoulli-Sigmoid unit [80]. During training, the output w_t is sampled *stochastically* to be a binary value in $\{0, 1\}$. During evaluation, instead of sampling from the distribution, the output is deterministically decided to be equal to the Bernoulli parameter and, therefore, $w_t = f_w(g_t; \theta_w)$.

Classifier $f_c(\theta_c)$ and Reward: The classifier consists of a sequence of a rectified linear unit, dropout with rate $r = 0.4$, a fully connected layer and Softmax. The parametric layer maps the 256×1 hidden vector h_t to the $N \times 1$ class posterior vector c_t, which has length equal to the number of classes N. The multi-shot prediction with RTA attention is the weighted sum of frame-level predictions c_t, as they are weighted by the normalized, RTA weights $w'_t = \frac{f_w(g_t;\theta_w)}{\sum_{t=1}^{T} f_w(g_t;\theta_w)}$.

The Bernoulli-Sigmoid unit is stochastic during training and therefore we resort to the REINFORCE algorithm in order to obtain the gradient for the backward pass. We describe the details of the training process in Sect. 2.3, but here we define the required reward function. A straightforward definition is:

$$r_t = \mathcal{I}(arg\,max(c_t) = g_t) \tag{8}$$

where r_t is the raw reward, $\mathcal{I}$ is the indicator function and g_t is the ground-truth class for frame t. Thus, at each time step t, the agent receives a reward r_t, which equals to 1 when the frame is correctly classified and 0 otherwise.

2.3 Model Training

In our experiments we first pre-train the parameters of the frame-level feature embedding, and afterwards we attach LSTM, RTA and the new classifier in order to train the whole model (*cf.* Fig. 3). At the second step the weights of the embedding are frozen while the added layers are initialized at random. We adopt this modular training so that we provide both single-shot and multi-shot evaluation, but the entire architecture can well be trained end to end from scratch if processing video sequences is the sole objective. Next, we first describe our transfer learning for the frame-level embedding and following the hybrid supervised training algorithm for the recursive model with temporal attention.

Split-Rate Transfer Learning for Feature Embedding $f_{CNN}(\theta_g)$: In order to leverage on vast RGB data, our approach relies on transferring parameters θ_g from a RGB pre-trained model for initialization. As it is unclear whether and which subset of RGB parameters is beneficial for depth embedding, we first gain insight from work by Yosinski et al. [90] in CNN feature transferability. They showed that between two almost equal-sized splits from Imagenet [66], the most effective model adaptation is to transfer and slowly fine-tune the weights of the bottom convolutional layers, while re-training the top layers. Other works that tackle model transfer from a large to a small-sized dataset (*e.g.* [33]) copy and slowly fine-tune the weights of the whole hierarchy except for the classifier which is re-trained using a higher learning rate.

Inspired by both approaches, we investigate the model transferability between RGB and depth. Our method has three differences compared to [90]. First, we found that even though RGB and depth are quite different modalities (*cf.* Fig. 1), the bottom layers of the RGB models can be shared with the depth data (without fine-tuning). Second, fine-tuning parameters transferred from RGB works better than training from scratch for the top layers. Third, using slower (or zero) learning rate for the bottom layers and higher for the top layers is more effective than using uniform rate across the hierarchy. Thus, we term our method as *split-rate* transfer. This first and third remarks also consist key differences with [33], as firstly they fine-tune all layers and secondly they deploy higher learning rate only

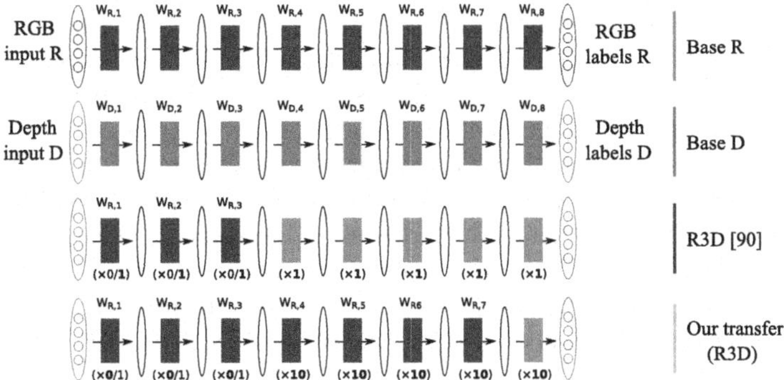

Fig. 4. Our split-rate RGB-to-Depth transfer compared with Yosinski et al. [90]. At the top, the two models are trained from scratch with RGB and Depth data. Next we show the "R3D" instances (i.e. the bottom 3 layers' weights from RGB remain frozen or slowly changing) for both methods, following the notation of [90]. The color of each layer refers to the initialization and the number below is the relative learning rate (the best performing one in bold). The key differences are summarized in the text.

for the classifier. Our approach is visualized in Fig. 4 and ablation studies are shown in Sect. 3.4 and Fig. 5, which support the above-mentioned observations.

Hybrid Learning for CNN-LSTM and Reinforced Temporal Attention: The parameters $\{\theta_g, \theta_h, \theta_c\}$ of CNN-LSTM are learned by minimizing the classification loss that is attached on the LSTM unit via backpropagation backward through the whole network. We minimize the cross-entropy loss as customary in recognition tasks, such as face identification [74]. Thus, the objective is to maximize the conditional probability of the true label given the observations, i.e. we maximize $\log \pi_2(c_t^*|s_{1:t}; \theta_g, \theta_h, \theta_c)$, where c_t^* is the true class at step t.

The parameters $\{\theta_g, \theta_w\}$ of CNN and RTA are learned so that the agent maximizes its total reward $R = \sum_{t=1}^{T} r_t$, where r_t has defined in Eq. 8. This involves calculating the expectation $J(\theta_g, \theta_w) = \mathbb{E}_{p(s_{1:T};\theta_g,\theta_w)}[R]$ over the distribution of all possible sequences $p(s_{1:T}; \theta_g, \theta_w)$, which is intractable. Thus, a sample approximation, known as the REINFORCE rule [80], can be applied on the Bernoulli-Sigmoid unit [36,44], which models the sub-policy $\pi_1(w_t|f_w(g_t; \theta_w))$. Given probability mass function $\log \pi_1(w_t; p_t) = w_t \log p_t + (1 - w_t) \log(1 - p_t)$ with Bernoulli parameter $p_t = f_w(g_t; \theta_w)$, the gradient approximation is:

$$\nabla_{\theta_g,\theta_w} J = \sum_{t=1}^{T} \mathbb{E}_{p(s_{1:T};\theta_g,\theta_w)}[\nabla_{\theta_g,\theta_w} \log \pi_1(w_t|s_{1:t}; \theta_g, \theta_w)(R_t - b_t)] \tag{9}$$

$$\approx \frac{1}{M} \sum_{i=1}^{M} \sum_{t=1}^{T} \frac{w_t^i - p_t^i}{p_t^i(1 - p_t^i)} (R_t^i - b_t) \tag{10}$$

where sequences i, $i \in \{1, \ldots, M\}$, are obtained while running the agent for M episodes and $R_t^i = \sum_{\tau=1}^{t} r_\tau^i$ is the cumulative reward at episode i acquired after collecting the sample w_t^i. The gradient estimate is biased by a baseline reward b_t in order to achieve lower variance. Similarly to [26,56], we set $b_t = \mathbb{E}_\pi[R_t]$, as the mean square error between R_t^i and b_t is also minimized by backpropagation.

At each step t, the agent makes a prediction w_t and the reward signal R_t^i evaluates the effectiveness of the agent for the classification task. The REINFORCE update increases the log-probability of an action that results in higher than the expected accumulated reward (i.e. by increasing the Bernoulli parameter $f_w(g_t;\theta_w)$). Otherwise, the log-probability decreases for sequence of frames that lead to low reward. All in all, the agent jointly optimizes the accumulated reward and the classification loss, which constitute a *hybrid* supervised objective.

3 Experiments

3.1 Depth-Based Datasets

DPI-T (Depth-Based Person Identification from Top). Being recently introduced by Haque et al. [26], it contains 12 persons appearing in a total of 25 sequences across many days and wearing 5 different sets of clothes on average. Unlike most publicly available datasets, the subjects appear from the top, which is a common scenario in automated video surveillance. The individuals are captured in daily life situations where they hold objects such as handbags, laptops and coffee.

BIWI. In order to explore sequences with varying human pose and scale, we use BIWI [58], where 50 individuals appear in a living room. 28 of them are re-recorded in a different room with new clothes and walking patterns. We use the full training set, while for testing we use the *Walking* set. From both sets we remove the frames with no person or a person heavily occluded from the image boundaries or too far from the sensor, as they provide no skeleton information.

IIT PAVIS. To evaluate our method when shorter video sequences are available, we use IIT PAVIS [6]. This dataset includes 79 persons that are recorded in 5-frame walking sequences twice. We use *Walking1* and *Walking2* sequences as the training and testing set, respectively.

TUM-GAID. To evaluate on a large pool of identities, we use the *TUM-GAID* database [28], which contains RGB and depth video for 305 people in three variations. A subset of 32 people is recorded a second time after three months with different clothes, which makes it ideal for our application scenario in Sect. 3.6. In our experiments we use the "normal" sequences (n) from each recording.

3.2 Evaluation Metrics

Top-k accuracy equals the percentage of test images or sequences for which the ground-truth label is contained within the first k model predictions. Plotting the top-k accuracy as a function of k gives the *Cumulative Matching Curve* (CMC).

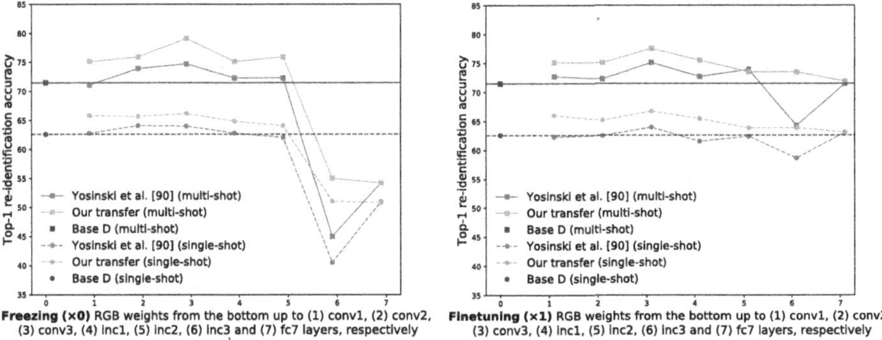

Fig. 5. Comparison of our RGB-to-Depth transfer with Yosinski et al. [90] in terms of top-1 accuracy on DPI-T. In this ablation study the x axis represents the number of layers whose weights are frozen (left) or fine-tuned (right) starting from the bottom.

Integrating the area under the CMC curve and normalizing over the number of IDs produces the normalized *Area Under the Curve* (nAUC).

In single-shot mode the model consists only of the f_{CNN} branch with an attached classifier (see Fig. 3). In multi-shot mode, where the model processes sequences, we evaluate our CNN-LSTM model with (or without) RTA attention.

3.3 Experimental Setting

The feature embedding f_{CNN} is trained in Caffe [31]. Consistent with [82], the input depth images are resized to be 144×56. SGD mini-batches of 50 images are used for training and testing. Momentum $\mu = 0.5$ yielded more stable training. The momentum effectively multiplies the size of the updates by a factor of $\frac{1}{1-\mu}$ after several iterations, so lower values result in smaller updates. The weight decay is set to $2 * 10^{-4}$, as it is common in Inception architecture [75]. We deploy modest base learning rate $\gamma_0 = 3 \times 10^{-4}$. The learning rate is reduced by a factor of 10 throughout training every time the loss reaches a "plateau".

The whole model with the LSTM and RTA layers in Fig. 3 is implemented in Torch/Lua [18]. We implemented customized Caffe-to-Torch conversion scripts for the pre-trained embedding, as the architecture is not standard. For end-to-end training, we use momentum $\mu = 0.9$, batch size 50 and learning rate that linearly decreases from 0.01 to 0.0001 in 200 epochs up to 250 epochs maximum duration. The LSTM history consists of $\rho = 3$ frames.

3.4 Evaluation of the Split-Rate RGB-to-Depth Transfer

In Fig. 5 we show results of our split-rate RGB-to-Depth transfer (which is described in Sect. 2.3) compared to [90]. We show the top-1 re-identification accuracy on DPI-T when the bottom CNN layers are frozen (left) and slowly fine-tuned (right). The top layers are transferred from RGB and rapidly fine-tuned in our approach, while they were re-trained in [90]. Given that the CNN

Table 1. Single-shot and multi-shot person re-identification performance on the test set of DPI-T, BIWI and IIT PAVIS. Dashes indicate that no published result is available

Mode	Method	Top-1 accuracy (%)		
		DPI-T	BIWI	IIT PAVIS
	Random	8.3	2.0	1.3
Single-shot	Skeleton (NN) [58]	–	21.1	28.6
	Skeleton (SVM) [59]	–	13.8	35.7
	3D RAM [26]	47.5	**30.1**	41.3
	Our method (CNN)	**66.8**	25.4	**43.0**
Multi-shot	Skeleton (NN) [58]	–	39.3	–
	Skeleton (SVM) [59]	–	17.9	–
	Energy volume [70]	14.2	25.7	18.9
	3D CNN + Avg Pooling [8]	28.4	27.8	27.5
	4D RAM [26]	55.6	45.3	43.0
	Our method (CNN-LSTM + Avg Pooling)	75.5	45.7	50.1
	Our method with attention from [88]	75.9	46.4	50.6
	Our method with RTA attention	**76.3**	**50.0**	**52.4**

architecture has 7 main layers before the classifier, the x axis is the number of layers that are frozen or fine-tuned counting from the bottom.

Evidently, transferring and freezing the three bottom layers, while rapidly fine-tuning the subsequent "inception" and fully-connected layers, brings in the best performance on DPI-T. Attempting to freeze too many layers leads to performance drop for both approaches, which can been attributed to feature *specificity*. Slowly fine-tuning the bottom layers helps to alleviate *fragile co-adaptation*, as it was pointed out by Yosinski et al. [90], and improves generalization, especially while moving towards the right of the x axis. Overall, our approach is more accurate in our setting across the x axis for both treatments.

3.5 Evaluation of the End-to-End Framework

In Table 1 we compare our framework with depth-based baseline algorithms. First, we show the performance of guessing uniformly at random. Next, we report results from [6,59], who use hand-crafted features based on biometrics, such as distances between skeleton joints. A 3D CNN with average pooling over time [8] and the gait energy volume [70] are evaluated in multi-shot mode. Finally, we provide the comparisons with 3D and 4D RAM models [26].

In order to evaluate our model in multi-shot mode without temporal attention, we simply average the output of the classifier attached on the CNN-LSTM output across the sequence (*cf.* Fig. 3). In the last two rows we show results that leverage temporal attention. We compare our RTA attention with the *soft*

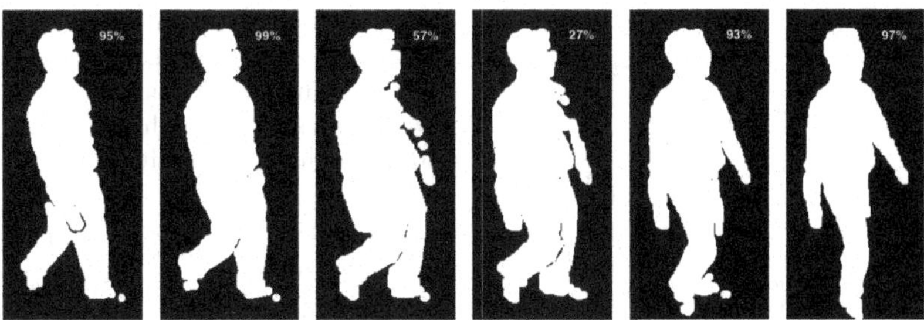

Fig. 6. Example sequence with the predicted Bernoulli parameter printed.

attention in [88], which is a function of both the hidden state h_t and the embedding g_t, whose projections are added and passed through a *tanh* non-linearity.

We observe that methods that learn end-to-end re-identification features perform significantly better than the ones that rely on hand-crafted biometrics on all datasets. Our algorithm is the top performer in multi-shot mode, as our RTA unit effectively learns to re-weight the most effective frames based on classification-specific reward. The split-rate RGB-to-Depth transfer enables our method to leverage on RGB data effectively and provides discriminative depth-based ReID features. This is especially reflected by the single-shot accuracy on DPI-T, where we report 19.3% better top-1 accuracy compared to 3D RAM. However, it is worth noting that 3D RAM performs better on BIWI. Our conjecture is that the spatial attention mechanism is important in datasets with significant variation in human pose and partial body occlusions. On the other hand, the spatial attention is evidently less critical on DPI-T, which contains views from the top and the visible region is mostly uniform across frames.

Next in Fig. 6 we show a testing sequence with the predicted Bernoulli parameter $f_w(g_t; \theta_w)$ printed. After inspecting the Bernoulli parameter value on testing sequences, we observe large variations even among neighboring frames. Smaller values are typically associated with noisy frames, or frames with unusual pose (*e.g.* person turning) and partial occlusions.

3.6 Application in Scenario with Unseen Clothes

Towards tackling our key motivation, we compare our system compared to a state-of-the-art RGB method in scenario where the individuals change clothes between the recordings for training and test set. We use the TUM-GAID database at which 305 persons appear in sequences $n01$–$n06$ from session 1, and 32 among them appear with new clothes in sequences $n07$–$n12$ from session 2.

Following the official protocol, we use the Training IDs to perform RGB-to-Depth transfer for our CNN embedding. We use sequences $n01$–$n04$, $n07$–$n10$ for training, and sequences $n05$–$n06$ and $n11$–$n12$ for validation. Next, we deploy the Testing IDs and use sequences $n01$–$n04$ for training, $n05$–$n06$ for validation and $n11$–$n12$ for testing. Thus, our framework has *no access* to data from the

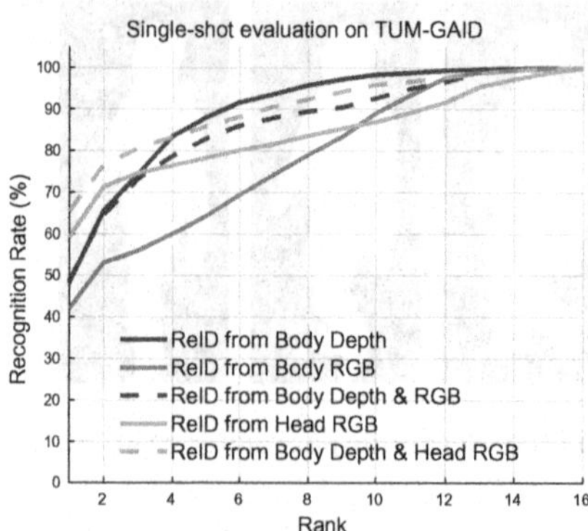

Fig. 7. Cumulative Matching Curves (CMC) on TUM-GAID for the scenario that the individuals wear clothes which are not provided during training.

Table 2. Top-1 re-identification accuracy (top-1, %) and normalized Area Under the Curve (nAUC, %) on TUM-GAID in new-clothes scenario with single-shot (*ss*) and multi-shot (*ms*) evaluation

Modality	Top-1	nAUC
Body RGB (ss) [82]	41.8	74.3
Body depth (ss)	48.0	**85.0**
Body depth & RGB (ss)	48.6	81.9
Head RGB (ss)	59.4	79.5
Body depth & Head RGB (ss)	**65.4**	85.2
Body RGB (ms: LSTM & RTA)	50.0	79.9
Body depth (ms: LSTM)	56.3	87.7
Body depth (ms: LSTM & RTA)	59.4	**89.6**
Head RGB (ms: LSTM & RTA)	65.6	81.0
Body depth & Head RGB (ms: LSTM & RTA)	**75.0**	88.1

session 2 during training. However, we make the assumption that the 32 subjects that participate in the second recording are known for all competing methods.

In Table 2 we show that re-identification from body depth is more robust than from body RGB [82], presenting 6.2% higher top-1 accuracy and 10.7% larger nAUC in single-shot mode. Next, we explore the benefit of using head information, which is less sensitive than clothes to day-by-day changes. To that end, we transfer the RGB-based pre-trained model from [82] and fine-tune on the upper body part, which we call "Head RGB". This results in increased accuracy, individually and jointly with body depth. Finally, we show the mutual benefits in multi-shot performance for both body depth, head RGB and their linear combination in class posterior. In Fig. 7 we visualize the CMC curves for single-shot setting. We observe that ReID from body depth scales better than its counterparts, which is validated by the nAUC scores.

4 Conclusion

In the paper, we present a novel approach for depth-based person re-identification. To address the data scarcity problem, we propose split-rate RGB-depth transfer to effectively leverage pre-trained models from large RGB data and learn strong frame-level features. To enhance re-identification from video sequences, we propose the Reinforced Temporal Attention unit, which lies on top of the frame-level features and is not dependent on the network architecture. Extensive experiments show that our approach outperforms the state of the art in depth-based person re-identification, and it is more effective than its RGB-based counterpart in a scenario where the persons change clothes.

Acknowledgments. This work was supported in part by ARO W911NF-15-1-0564/66731-CS, ONR N00014-13-1-034, and AFOSR FA9550-15-1-0229.

References

1. Ahmed, E., Jones, M., Marks, T.K.: An improved deep learning architecture for person re-identification. In: CVPR (2015)
2. Albiol, A., Oliver, J., Mossi, J.: Who is who at different cameras: people re-identification using depth cameras. IET Comput. Vis. **6**, 378–387 (2012)
3. Andersson, V., Dutra, R., Araújo, R.: Anthropometric and human gait identification using skeleton data from kinect sensor. In: ACM Symposium on Applied Computing (2014)
4. Bai, S., Bai, X., Tian, Q.: Scalable person re-identification on supervised smoothed manifold. In: CVPR (2017)
5. Bak, S., Carr, P.: One-shot metric learning for person re-identification. In: CVPR (2017)
6. Barbosa, I.B., Cristani, M., Del Bue, A., Bazzani, L., Murino, V.: Re-identification with RGB-D sensors. In: Fusiello, A., Murino, V., Cucchiara, R. (eds.) ECCV 2012. LNCS, vol. 7583, pp. 433–442. Springer, Heidelberg (2012). https://doi.org/10.1007/978-3-642-33863-2_43
7. Bedagkar-Gala, A., Shah, S.K.: A survey of approaches and trends in person re-identification. Image Vis. Comput. **32**, 270–286 (2014)
8. Boureau, Y.L., Ponce, J., LeCun, Y.: A theoretical analysis of feature pooling in visual recognition. In: ICML (2010)
9. Castro, F.M., Marín-Jiménez, M.J., Guil, N., Pérez de la Blanca, N.: Automatic learning of gait signatures for people identification. In: Rojas, I., Joya, G., Catala, A. (eds.) IWANN 2017. LNCS, vol. 10306, pp. 257–270. Springer, Cham (2017). https://doi.org/10.1007/978-3-319-59147-6_23
10. Castro, F.M., Marín-Jimenez, M.J., Medina-Carnicer, R.: Pyramidal fisher motion for multiview gait recognition. In: ICPR (2014)
11. Chan, W., Jaitly, N., Le, Q.V., Vinyals, O.: Listen, attend and spell. In: ICASSP (2016)
12. Chen, D., Yuan, Z., Chen, B., Zheng, N.: Similarity learning with spatial constraints for person re-identification. In: CVPR (2016)
13. Chen, J., Wang, Y., Qin, J., Liu, L., Shao, L.: Fast person re-identification via cross-camera semantic binary transformation. In: CVPR (2017)
14. Chen, L.F., Liao, H.Y.M., Ko, M.T., Lin, J.C., Yu, G.J.: A new LDA-based face recognition system which can solve the small sample size problem. Pattern Recognit. **33**, 1713–1726 (2000)
15. Chen, W., Chen, X., Zhang, J., Huang, K.: Beyond triplet loss: a deep quadruplet network for person re-identification. In: CVPR (2017)
16. Cho, Y.J., Yoon, K.J.: Improving person re-identification via pose-aware multi-shot matching. In: CVPR (2016)
17. Chung, D., Tahboub, K., Delp, E.J.: A two stream siamese convolutional neural network for person re-identification. In: ICCV (2017)
18. Collobert, R., Kavukcuoglu, K., Farabet, C.: Torch7: a matlab-like environment for machine learning. In: BigLearn, NIPS Workshop (2011)
19. Ding, S., Lin, L., Wang, G., Chao, H.: Deep feature learning with relative distance comparison for person re-identification. Pattern Recognit. **48**, 2993–3003 (2015)

20. Donahue, J., et al.: Long-term recurrent convolutional networks for visual recognition and description. In: CVPR (2015)
21. Dubois, A., Charpillet, F.: A gait analysis method based on a depth camera for fall prevention. In: IEEE Engineering in Medicine and Biology Society (2014)
22. Farenzena, M., Bazzani, L., Perina, A., Murino, V., Cristani, M.: Person re-identification by symmetry-driven accumulation of local features. In: CVPR (2010)
23. Gong, S., Cristani, M., Yan, S., Loy, C.C.: Person Re-identification. Springer, Heidelberg (2014). https://doi.org/10.1007/978-1-4471-6296-4
24. Gray, D., Tao, H.: Viewpoint invariant pedestrian recognition with an ensemble of localized features. In: Forsyth, D., Torr, P., Zisserman, A. (eds.) ECCV 2008. LNCS, vol. 5302, pp. 262–275. Springer, Heidelberg (2008). https://doi.org/10.1007/978-3-540-88682-2_21
25. Gupta, S., Girshick, R., Arbeláez, P., Malik, J.: Learning rich features from RGB-D images for object detection and segmentation. In: Fleet, D., Pajdla, T., Schiele, B., Tuytelaars, T. (eds.) ECCV 2014. LNCS, vol. 8695, pp. 345–360. Springer, Cham (2014). https://doi.org/10.1007/978-3-319-10584-0_23
26. Haque, A., Alahi, A., Fei-Fei, L.: Recurrent attention models for depth-based person identification. In: CVPR (2016)
27. Hinton, G.E., Srivastava, N., Krizhevsky, A., Sutskever, I., Salakhutdinov, R.R.: Improving neural networks by preventing co-adaptation of feature detectors. Preprint arXiv:1207.0580 (2012)
28. Hofmann, M., Geiger, J., Bachmann, S., Schuller, B., Rigoll, G.: The TUM gait from audio, image and depth database: multimodal recognition of subjects and traits. J. Vis. Commun. Image Represent. **25**, 195–206 (2014)
29. Ioannidis, D., Tzovaras, D., Damousis, I.G., Argyropoulos, S., Moustakas, K.: Gait recognition using compact feature extraction transforms and depth information. IEEE Trans. Inf. Forensics Secur. **2**, 623–630 (2007)
30. Ioffe, S., Szegedy, C.: Batch normalization: accelerating deep network training by reducing internal covariate shift. In: ICML (2015)
31. Jia, Y., et al.: Caffe: convolutional architecture for fast feature embedding. In: Proceedings of the ACM International Conference on Multimedia (2014)
32. Kale, A., Cuntoor, N., Yegnanarayana, B., Rajagopalan, A.N., Chellappa, R.: Gait analysis for human identification. In: Kittler, J., Nixon, M.S. (eds.) AVBPA 2003. LNCS, vol. 2688, pp. 706–714. Springer, Heidelberg (2003). https://doi.org/10.1007/3-540-44887-X_82
33. Karayev, S., et al.: Recognizing image style (2014)
34. Kodirov, E., Xiang, T., Fu, Z., Gong, S.: Person re-identification by unsupervised ℓ_1 graph learning. In: Leibe, B., Matas, J., Sebe, N., Welling, M. (eds.) ECCV 2016. LNCS, vol. 9905, pp. 178–195. Springer, Cham (2016). https://doi.org/10.1007/978-3-319-46448-0_11
35. Koestinger, M., Hirzer, M., Wohlhart, P., Roth, P.M., Bischof, H.: Large scale metric learning from equivalence constraints. In: CVPR (2012)
36. Kontoravdis, D., Likas, A., Stafylopatis, A.: Enhancing stochasticity in reinforcement learning schemes: application to the exploration of binary domains. J. Intell. Syst. **5**, 49–77 (1995)
37. Krizhevsky, A., Sutskever, I., Hinton, G.E.: Imagenet classification with deep convolutional neural networks. In: NIPS (2012)
38. Kviatkovsky, I., Adam, A., Rivlin, E.: Color invariants for person re-identification. IEEE Trans. Pattern Anal. Mach. Intell. **35**, 1622–1634 (2013)

39. Li, D., Chen, X., Zhang, Z., Huang, K.: Learning deep context-aware features over body and latent parts for person re-identification. In: CVPR (2017)
40. Li, W., Zhao, R., Xiao, T., Wang, X.: DeepReID: deep filter pairing neural network for person re-identification. In: CVPR (2014)
41. Li, Y., Lin, G., Zhuang, B., Liu, L., Shen, C., van den Hengel, A.: Sequential person recognition in photo albums with a recurrent network. In: CVPR (2017)
42. Li, Z., Chang, S., Liang, F., Huang, T.S., Cao, L., Smith, J.R.: Learning locally-adaptive decision functions for person verification. In: CVPR (2013)
43. Liao, S., Hu, Y., Zhu, X., Li, S.Z.: Person re-identification by local maximal occurrence representation and metric learning. In: CVPR (2015)
44. Likas, A.: A reinforcement learning approach to online clustering. Neural Comput. **11**, 1915–1932 (1999)
45. Lin, J., Ren, L., Lu, J., Feng, J., Zhou, J.: Consistent-aware deep learning for person re-identification in a camera network. In: CVPR (2017)
46. Lisanti, G., Masi, I., Bagdanov, A.D., Del Bimbo, A.: Person re-identification by iterative re-weighted sparse ranking. IEEE Trans. Pattern Anal. Mach. Intell. **37**, 1629–1642 (2015)
47. Lisanti, G., Masi, I., Del Bimbo, A.: Matching people across camera views using kernel canonical correlation analysis. In: Proceedings of the International Conference on Distributed Smart Cameras. ACM (2014)
48. Liu, Z., Wang, D., Lu, H.: Stepwise metric promotion for unsupervised video person re-identification. In: ICCV (2017)
49. Luong, M.T., Pham, H., Manning, C.D.: Effective approaches to attention-based neural machine translation. In: EMNLP (2015)
50. Ma, B., Su, Y., Jurie, F.: Local descriptors encoded by fisher vectors for person re-identification. In: Fusiello, A., Murino, V., Cucchiara, R. (eds.) ECCV 2012. LNCS, vol. 7583, pp. 413–422. Springer, Heidelberg (2012). https://doi.org/10.1007/978-3-642-33863-2_41
51. Ma, L., Yang, X., Tao, D.: Person re-identification over camera networks using multi-task distance metric learning. IEEE Trans. Image Process. **23**, 3656–3670 (2014)
52. Mansur, A., Makihara, Y., Aqmar, R., Yagi, Y.: Gait recognition under speed transition. In: CVPR (2014)
53. Martinel, N., Das, A., Micheloni, C., Roy-Chowdhury, A.K.: Temporal model adaptation for person re-identification. In: Leibe, B., Matas, J., Sebe, N., Welling, M. (eds.) ECCV 2016. LNCS, vol. 9908, pp. 858–877. Springer, Cham (2016). https://doi.org/10.1007/978-3-319-46493-0_52
54. McLaughlin, N., Martinez del Rincon, J., Miller, P.: Recurrent convolutional network for video-based person re-identification. In: CVPR (2016)
55. Mignon, A., Jurie, F.: PCCA: a new approach for distance learning from sparse pairwise constraints. In: CVPR (2012)
56. Mnih, V., Heess, N., Graves, A., et al.: Recurrent models of visual attention. In: NIPS (2014)
57. Mogelmose, A., Moeslund, T.B., Nasrollahi, K.: Multimodal person re-identification using RGB-D sensors and a transient identification database. In: IEEE International Workshop on Biometrics and Forensics (2013)
58. Munaro, M., Basso, A., Fossati, A., Van Gool, L., Menegatti, E.: 3D reconstruction of freely moving persons for re-identification with a depth sensor. In: ICRA (2014)

59. Munaro, M., Fossati, A., Basso, A., Menegatti, E., Van Gool, L.: One-shot person re-identification with a consumer depth camera. In: Person Re-Identification (2014)
60. Munsell, B.C., Temlyakov, A., Qu, C., Wang, S.: Person identification using full-body motion and anthropometric biometrics from kinect videos. In: Fusiello, A., Murino, V., Cucchiara, R. (eds.) ECCV 2012. LNCS, vol. 7585, pp. 91–100. Springer, Heidelberg (2012). https://doi.org/10.1007/978-3-642-33885-4_10
61. Paisitkriangkrai, S., Shen, C., van den Hengel, A.: Learning to rank in person re-identification with metric ensembles. In: CVPR (2015)
62. Pathak, D., Girshick, R.B., Dollár, P., Darrell, T., Hariharan, B.: Learning features by watching objects move. In: CVPR (2017)
63. Pedagadi, S., Orwell, J., Velastin, S., Boghossian, B.: Local fisher discriminant analysis for pedestrian re-identification. In: CVPR (2013)
64. Prosser, B., Zheng, W.S., Gong, S., Xiang, T., Mary, Q.: Person re-identification by support vector ranking. In: BMVC (2010)
65. Qian, X., Fu, Y., Jiang, Y.G., Xiang, T., Xue, X.: Multi-scale deep learning architectures for person re-identification. In: ICCV (2017)
66. Russakovsky, O., et al.: ImageNet large scale visual recognition challenge. Int. J. Comput. Vis. **115**, 211–252 (2015)
67. Shi, H., et al.: Embedding deep metric for person re-identification: a study against large variations. In: Leibe, B., Matas, J., Sebe, N., Welling, M. (eds.) ECCV 2016. LNCS, vol. 9905, pp. 732–748. Springer, Cham (2016). https://doi.org/10.1007/978-3-319-46448-0_44
68. Shotton, J., et al.: Real-time human pose recognition in parts from single depth images. Commun. ACM **56**, 116–124 (2013)
69. Simonyan, K., Zisserman, A.: Very deep convolutional networks for large-scale image recognition. In: ICLR (2015)
70. Sivapalan, S., Chen, D., Denman, S., Sridharan, S., Fookes, C.: Gait energy volumes and frontal gait recognition using depth images. In: International Joint Conference on Biometrics (2011)
71. Song, X., Herranz, L., Jiang, S.: Depth CNNs for RGB-D scene recognition: learning from scratch better than transferring from RGB-CNNs. In: AAAI (2017)
72. Su, C., Li, J., Zhang, S., Xing, J., Gao, W., Tian, Q.: Pose-driven deep convolutional model for person re-identification. In: ICCV (2017)
73. Su, C., Zhang, S., Xing, J., Gao, W., Tian, Q.: Deep attributes driven multi-camera person re-identification. In: Leibe, B., Matas, J., Sebe, N., Welling, M. (eds.) ECCV 2016. LNCS, vol. 9906, pp. 475–491. Springer, Cham (2016). https://doi.org/10.1007/978-3-319-46475-6_30
74. Sun, Y., Wang, X., Tang, X.: Deep learning face representation from predicting 10,000 classes. In: CVPR (2014)
75. Szegedy, C., et al.: Going deeper with convolutions. In: CVPR (2015)
76. Tang, S., Andriluka, M., Andres, B., Schiele, B.: Multiple people tracking by lifted multicut and person re-identification. In: CVPR (2017)
77. Tao, D., Jin, L., Wang, Y., Yuan, Y., Li, X.: Person re-identification by regularized smoothing kiss metric learning. IEEE Trans. Circuits Syst. Video Technol. **23**, 1675–1685 (2013)
78. Vezzani, R., Baltieri, D., Cucchiara, R.: People re-identification in surveillance and forensics: a survey. ACM Comput. Surv. **46**, 29 (2013)
79. Wang, F., Zuo, W., Lin, L., Zhang, D., Zhang, L.: Joint learning of single-image and cross-image representations for person re-identification. In: CVPR (2016)

80. Williams, R.J.: Simple statistical gradient-following algorithms for connectionist reinforcement learning. Mach. Learn. **8**, 229–256 (1992)
81. Wu, A., Zheng, W.S., Yu, H.X., Gong, S., Lai, J.: RGB-infrared cross-modality person re-identification. In: ICCV (2017)
82. Xiao, T., Li, H., Ouyang, W., Wang, X.: Learning deep feature representations with domain guided dropout for person re-identification. In: CVPR (2016)
83. Xiao, T., Li, S., Wang, B., Lin, L., Wang, X.: Joint detection and identification feature learning for person search. In: CVPR (2017)
84. Xiong, F., Gou, M., Camps, O., Sznaier, M.: Person re-identification using kernel-based metric learning methods. In: Fleet, D., Pajdla, T., Schiele, B., Tuytelaars, T. (eds.) ECCV 2014. LNCS, vol. 8695, pp. 1–16. Springer, Cham (2014). https://doi.org/10.1007/978-3-319-10584-0_1
85. Xu, S., Cheng, Y., Gu, K., Yang, Y., Chang, S., Zhou, P.: Jointly attentive spatial-temporal pooling networks for video-based person re-identification. In: ICCV (2017)
86. Yan, Y., Ni, B., Song, Z., Ma, C., Yan, Y., Yang, X.: Person re-identification via recurrent feature aggregation. In: Leibe, B., Matas, J., Sebe, N., Welling, M. (eds.) ECCV 2016. LNCS, vol. 9910, pp. 701–716. Springer, Cham (2016). https://doi.org/10.1007/978-3-319-46466-4_42
87. Yang, Y., Yang, J., Yan, J., Liao, S., Yi, D., Li, S.Z.: Salient color names for person re-identification. In: Fleet, D., Pajdla, T., Schiele, B., Tuytelaars, T. (eds.) ECCV 2014. LNCS, vol. 8689, pp. 536–551. Springer, Cham (2014). https://doi.org/10.1007/978-3-319-10590-1_35
88. Yao, L., et al.: Describing videos by exploiting temporal structure. In: ICCV (2015)
89. Yi, D., Lei, Z., Liao, S., Li, S.Z.: Deep metric learning for person re-identification. In: ICPR (2014)
90. Yosinski, J., Clune, J., Bengio, Y., Lipson, H.: How transferable are features in deep neural networks? In: NIPS (2014)
91. Yu, H.X., Wu, A., Zheng, W.S.: Cross-view asymmetric metric learning for unsupervised person re-identification. In: ICCV (2017)
92. Zaremba, W., Sutskever, I.: Learning to execute. Preprint arXiv:1410.4615 (2014)
93. Zeng, W., Wang, C., Yang, F.: Silhouette-based gait recognition via deterministic learning. Pattern Recognit. **47**, 3568–3584 (2014)
94. Zhang, L., Xiang, T., Gong, S.: Learning a discriminative null space for person re-identification. In: CVPR (2016)
95. Zhao, G., Liu, G., Li, H., Pietikainen, M.: 3D gait recognition using multiple cameras. In: Automatic Face and Gesture Recognition (2006)
96. Zhao, H., et al.: Spindle net: person re-identification with human body region guided feature decomposition and fusion. In: CVPR (2017)
97. Zhao, L., Li, X., Zhuang, Y., Wang, J.: Deeply-learned part-aligned representations for person re-identification. In: ICCV (2017)
98. Zhao, R., Ouyang, W., Wang, X.: Person re-identification by salience matching. In: ICCV (2013)
99. Zhao, R., Ouyang, W., Wang, X.: Unsupervised salience learning for person re-identification. In: CVPR (2013)
100. Zhao, R., Ouyang, W., Wang, X.: Learning mid-level filters for person re-identification. In: CVPR (2014)
101. Zheng, K., et al.: Learning view-invariant features for person identification in temporally synchronized videos taken by wearable cameras. In: ICCV (2017)

102. Leibe, B., Matas, J., Sebe, N., Welling, M.: MARS: a video benchmark for large-scale person re-identification. In: Leibe, B., Matas, J., Sebe, N., Welling, M. (eds.) ECCV 2016. LNCS, vol. 9910, pp. 868–884. Springer, Cham (2016). https://doi.org/10.1007/978-3-319-46466-4_52
103. Zheng, L., Shen, L., Tian, L., Wang, S., Wang, J., Tian, Q.: Scalable person re-identification: a benchmark. In: ICCV (2015)
104. Zheng, L., Zhang, H., Sun, S., Chandraker, M., Yang, Y., Tian, Q.: Person re-identification in the wild. In: CVPR (2017)
105. Zheng, W.S., Gong, S., Xiang, T.: Re-identification by relative distance comparison. IEEE Trans. Pattern Anal. Mach. Intell. **35**, 653–668 (2013)
106. Zheng, Z., Zheng, L., Yang, Y.: Unlabeled samples generated by GAN improve the person re-identification baseline in vitro. In: ICCV (2017)
107. Zhong, Z., Zheng, L., Cao, D., Li, S.: Re-ranking person re-identification with k-reciprocal encoding. In: CVPR (2017)
108. Zhou, J., Yu, P., Tang, W., Wu, Y.: Efficient online local metric adaptation via negative samples for person re-identification. In: ICCV (2017)
109. Zhou, S., Wang, J., Wang, J., Gong, Y., Zheng, N.: Point to set similarity based deep feature learning for person re-identification. In: CVPR (2017)
110. Zhou, Z., Huang, Y., Wang, W., Wang, L., Tan, T.: See the forest for the trees: joint spatial and temporal recurrent neural networks for video-based person re-identification. In: CVPR (2017)

Scale Aggregation Network for Accurate and Efficient Crowd Counting

Xinkun Cao[1], Zhipeng Wang[1], Yanyun Zhao[1,2(✉)], and Fei Su[1,2]

[1] School of Information and Communication Engineering, Beijing University of Posts and Telecommunications, Beijing, China
{cc,wzpycg,zyy,sufei}@bupt.edu.cn

[2] Beijing Key Laboratory of Network System and Network Culture, Beijing University of Posts and Telecommunications, Beijing, China

Abstract. In this paper, we propose a novel encoder-decoder network, called *Scale Aggregation Network (SANet)*, for accurate and efficient crowd counting. The encoder extracts multi-scale features with scale aggregation modules and the decoder generates high-resolution density maps by using a set of transposed convolutions. Moreover, we find that most existing works use only Euclidean loss which assumes independence among each pixel but ignores the local correlation in density maps. Therefore, we propose a novel training loss, combining of Euclidean loss and local pattern consistency loss, which improves the performance of the model in our experiments. In addition, we use normalization layers to ease the training process and apply a patch-based test scheme to reduce the impact of statistic shift problem. To demonstrate the effectiveness of the proposed method, we conduct extensive experiments on four major crowd counting datasets and our method achieves superior performance to state-of-the-art methods while with much less parameters.

Keywords: Crowd counting · Crowd density estimation
Scale Aggregation Network · Local pattern consistency

1 Introduction

With the rapid growth of the urban population, crowd scene analysis [1,2] has gained considerable attention in recent years. In this paper, we focus on the crowd density estimation which could be used in crowd control for public safety in many scenarios, such as political rallies and sporting events. However, precisely estimating crowd density is extremely difficult, due to heavy occlusions, background clutters, large scale and perspective variations in crowd images.

Recently, CNN-based methods have been attempted to address the crowd density estimation problem. Some works [3–6] have achieved significant improvement by addressing the scale variation issue with multi-scale architecture. They use CNNs with different field sizes to extract features which are adaptive to the large variation in people size. The success of these works suggests that the multi-scale representation is of great value for crowd counting task. Besides, the crowd

V. Ferrari et al. (Eds.): ECCV 2018, LNCS 11209, pp. 757–773, 2018.
https://doi.org/10.1007/978-3-030-01228-1_45

density estimation based approaches aim to incorporate the spatial information of crowd images. As the high-resolution density maps contain finer details, we hold the view that it is helpful for crowd density estimation to generate the high-resolution and high-quality of density maps.

However, there exists two main drawbacks in recent CNN-based works. On the one hand, crowd density estimation benefits from the multi-scale representation of multi-column architecture, which uses multiple sub-networks to extract features at different scales. But the scale diversity is completely restricted by the number of columns (e.g. only three branches in multi-column CNN in [3]). On the other hand, only pixel-wise Euclidean loss is used in most works, which assumes each pixel is independent and is known to result in blurry images on image generation problems [7]. In [6], adversarial loss [8] has been applied to improve the quality of density maps and achieved good performance. Nevertheless, density maps may contain little high-level semantic information and the additional discriminator sub-network increases the computation cost.

To address these issues, we follow the two points discussed above and propose a novel encoder-decoder network, named *Scale Aggregation Network (SANet)*. The architecture of SANet is shown in Fig. 1. Motived by the achievement of Inception [9] structure in image recognition domain, we employ scale aggregation modules in encoder to improve the representation ability and scale diversity of features. The decoder is composed of a set of convolutions and transposed convolutions. It is used to generate high-resolution and high-quality density maps, of which the sizes are exactly same as input images. Inspired by [10], we use a combination of Euclidean loss and local pattern consistency loss to exploit the local correlation in density maps. The local pattern consistency loss is computed by SSIM [11] index to measure the structural similarity between the estimated density map and corresponding ground truth. The extra computation cost is negligible and the result shows it availably improves the performance.

We use Instance Normalization (IN) [12] layers to alleviate the vanishing gradient problem. Unfortunately, our patch-based model achieves inferior result when tested with images due to the difference between local (patch) and global (image) statistics. Thus, we apply a simple but effective patch-based training and testing scheme to diminish the impact of statistical shifts. Extensive experiments on four benchmarks show that the proposed method outperforms recent state-of-the-art methods.

To summarize, the main contributions of our work as follows:

- We propose a novel network, dubbed as *Scale Aggregation Network (SANet)* for accurate and efficient crowd counting, which improves the multi-scale representation and generates high-resolution density maps. The network can be trained end-to-end.
- We analyze the statistic shift problem caused by IN layers which are used to ease the training process. Then we propose a simple but effective patch-based train and test scheme to reduce its influence.
- We propose a novel training loss, combining Euclidean loss and local pattern consistency loss to utilize the local correlation in density maps. The former

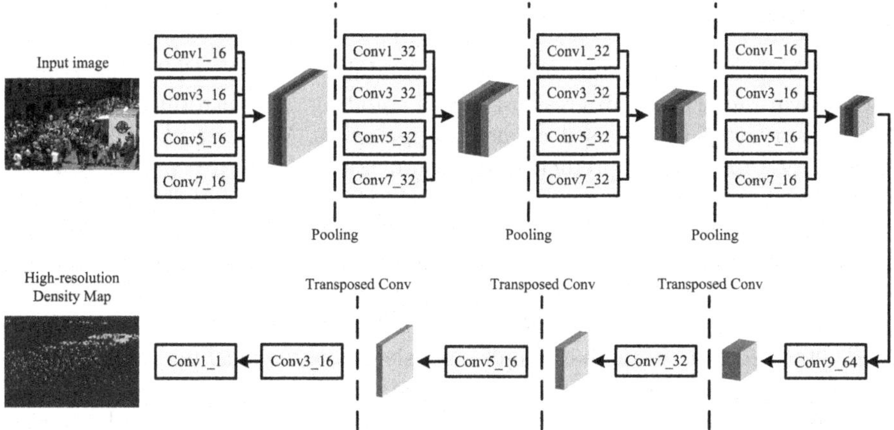

Fig. 1. The architecture of the SANet. A convolutional layer is denoted as "Conv(kernel size)_(number of channels)".

loss limits the pixel-wise error and the latter one enforces the local structural similarity between predicted results and corresponding ground truths.

- Extensive experiments conducted on four challenging benchmarks demonstrate that our method achieves superior performance to state-of-the-art methods with much less parameters.

2 Related Works

A variety of methods have been proposed to deal with crowd counting task. They can be briefly summarized into traditional methods and CNN-based approaches.

2.1 Traditional Approaches

Most of the early works [13,14] estimate crowd count via pedestrian detection [15–17], which use body or part-based detector to locate people in the crowd image and sum them up. However, these detection-based approaches are limited by occlusions and background clutters in dense crowd scenes. Researchers attempted regression-based methods to directly learn a mapping from the feature of image patches to the count in the region [18–20]. With similar approaches, Idrees *et al.* [21] proposed a method which fuses features extracted with Fourier analysis, head detection and SIFT [22] interest points based counting in local patches. These regression-based methods predicted the global count but ignored the spatial information in the crowd images. Lempitsky *et al.* [23] proposed a method to learn a linear mapping between features and object density maps in local region. Pham *et al.* [24] observed the difficulty of learning a linear mapping and used random forest regression to learn a non-linear mapping between local patch features and density maps.

2.2 CNN-Based Approaches

Due to the excellent representation learning ability of CNN, CNN-based works have shown remarkable progress for crowd counting. [25] introduced a comprehensive survey of CNN-based counting approaches. Wang *et al.* [26] modified AlexNet [27] for directly predicting the count. Zhang *et al.* [28] proposed a convolutional neural network alternatively trained by the crowd density and the crowd count. When deployed into a new scene, the network is fine-tuned using training samples similar to the target scene. In [29], Walach and Wolf made use of layered boosting and selective sampling methods to reduce the count estimation error. Different from the existing patch-based estimation methods, Shang *et al.* [30] used a network that simultaneously estimates local and global counts for whole input images. Boominathan *et al.* [31] combined shallow and deep networks for generating density map. Zhang *et al.* [3] designed multi-column CNN (MCNN) to tackle the large scale variation in crowd scenes. With similar idea, Onoro and Sastre [4] also proposed a scale-aware network, called Hydra, to extract features at different scales. Recently, inspired by MCNN [3], Sam *et al.* [5] presented Switch-CNN which trains a classifier to select the optimal regressor from multiple independent regressors for particular input patches. Sindagi *et al.* [6,32] explored methods to incorporate the contextual information by learning various density levels and generate high-resolution density maps. To improve the quality of density maps, they use adversarial loss to overcome the limitation of Euclidean loss. Li *et al.* [33] proposed CSRNet by combining VGG-16 [34] and dilated convolution layers to aggregate multi-scale contextual information.

However, by observing these recent state-of-the-art approaches, we found that: (1) Most works use multi-column architecture to extract features at different scales. As the issue discussed in Sect. 1, the multi-scale representation of this architecture might be insufficient to deal with the large size variance due to the limited scale diversity. (2) [5,6,32] require density level classifier to provide contextual information. However, these extra classifiers significantly increase the computations. In addition, the density level is related to specific dataset and is hard to be defined. (3) Most works use only pixel-wise Euclidean loss which assumes independence among each pixel. Though adversarial loss has shown improvement for density estimation, density maps may contain little high-level semantic information.

Based on the former observations, we propose an encoder-decoder network to improve the performance without extra classifier. Furthermore, we use a light-weight loss to enforce the local pattern consistency between the estimated density map and the corresponding ground truth.

3 Scale Aggregation Network

This section presents the details of the *Scale Aggregation Network (SANet)*. We first introduce our network architecture and then give descriptions of the proposed loss function.

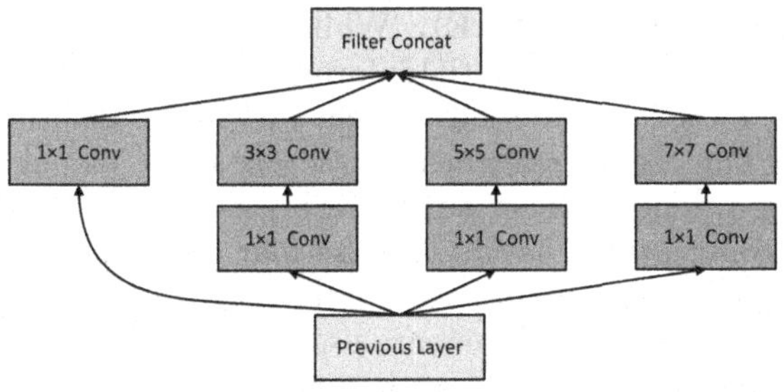

Fig. 2. The architecture of scale aggregation module.

3.1 Architecture

As shown in Fig. 1, we construct our SANet network based on two insights, i.e. multi-scale feature representations and high-resolution density maps. The SANet consists of two components: feature map encoder (FME) and density map estimator (DME). FME aggregates multi-scale features extracted from input image and DME estimates high-resolution density maps by fusing these features.

Feature Map Encoder (FME). Most previous works use the multi-column architecture to deal with the large variation in object sizes due to perspective effect or across different resolutions. MCNN [3] contains three sub-networks to extract features at different scales. However, as the drawback mentioned in Sect. 1, the scale diversity of features is limited by the number of columns.

To address the problem, we propose an scale aggregation module to break the independence of columns with concatenation operation, as shown in Fig. 2. This module is flexible and can be extended to arbitrary branches. In this paper, we construct it by four branches with the filter sizes of 1×1, 3×3, 5×5, 7×7. The 1×1 branch is used to reserve the feature scale in previous layer to cover small targets, while others increase respective field sizes. The output channel number of each branch is set equal for simplicity. In addition, we add a 1×1 convolution before the $3 \times 3, 5 \times 5$ and 7×7 convolution layers to reduce the feature dimensions by half. These reduction layers are removed in the first scale aggregation module. ReLU is applied after every convolutional layer.

The FME of SANet is constructed by scale aggregation modules stacked upon each other as illustrated in Fig. 1, with 2×2 max-pooling layers after each module to halve the spatial resolution of feature maps. The architecture exponentially increases the possible combination forms of features and enhances the representation ability and scale diversity of the output feature maps. In this paper, we stack four scale aggregation modules. The stride of output feature map is 8 pixels *w.r.t* the input image. Intuitively, FME might represent an ensemble of variable respective field sizes networks. The ensemble of different paths throughout the model would capture the multi-scale appearance of people in dense crowd, which would benefit the crowd density estimation.

Density Map Estimator (DME). While crowd density estimation based approaches take account of the spatial information, the output of most works is low-resolution and lose lots of details. To generate high-resolution density maps, we use a similar but deeper refinement structure to [6] as our DME, which is illustrated in Fig. 1. The DME of our SANet consists of a set of convolutional and transposed convolutional layers. We use four convolutions to progressively refine the details of feature maps, with filter sizes from 9×9 to 3×3. And three transposed convolutional layers are used to recover the spatial resolution, each of which increases the size of feature maps by a factor 2. ReLU activations are added after each convolutional and transposed convolutional layers. Then, a 1×1 convolution layer is used to estimate the density value at each position. Since the values of density maps are always non-negative, we apply a ReLU activation behind the last convolution layer. Finally, DME generates the high-resolution density maps with the same size as input, which could provide finer spatial information to facilitate the feature learning during training the model.

Normalization Layers. We observe a gradient vanishing problem which leads to non-convergence in training process when we combine FME and DME together. We attempt the Batch Normalization [35] (BN) and Instance Normalization [12] (IN) to alleviate the problem, but get worse results when using BN due to the unstable statistic with small batchsize. Hence, we apply IN layers, which use statistics of each instance in current batch at training and testing, after each convolutional and transposed convolutional layers. However, our model trained by small patches gets inferior results when tested with whole images. We think it is caused by the statistical shifts. Considering the last 1×1 convolution layer and the preceding IN layer, for a d-dimensional vector $\mathbf{x} = (x_1 \ldots x_d)$ of input feature maps, the output is

$$y = ReLU\left(\sum_{i=0}^{d} w_i \cdot ReLU\left(\gamma_i \cdot \frac{x_i - \mu_i}{\sqrt{\sigma_i^2 + \epsilon}} + \beta_i\right) + b\right), \tag{1}$$

where w and b are weight and bias term of the convolution layer, γ and β are weight and bias term of the IN layer, μ and σ^2 are mean and variance of the input. The output is a weighted combination of the features which are normalized by the IN layer. Therefore, it is sensitive to the magnitude of features. But we find the difference of σ^2 are relatively large in some feature dimension when input patches or images. Then the deviation is amplified by square root and reciprocal function, and finally causes wrong density value. Since it is crucial to train the deep network with patches in consideration of speed and data augmentation, we apply a simple but effective patch-based training and testing scheme to reduce the impact of statistic shift problem.

3.2 Loss Function

Most existing methods use pixel-wise Euclidean loss to train their network, which is based on the pixel independence hypothesis and ignores the local correlation of density maps. To overcome this issue, we use single-scale SSIM to measure the local pattern consistency and combine it with L_2 loss.

Euclidean Loss. The Euclidean loss is used to measure estimation error at pixel level, which is defined as follows:

$$L_E = \frac{1}{N} \|F(X; \Theta) - Y\|_2^2 \tag{2}$$

where Θ denotes a set of the network parameters, N is the number of pixels in density maps, X is the input image and Y is the corresponding ground truth density map, $F(X; \Theta)$ denotes the estimated density map (we omit X and Θ for notational simplicity in later part). The Euclidean loss is computed at each pixel and summed over. Considering the size of input image may be different in a dataset, the loss value of each sample is normalized by the pixel number to keep training stable.

Local Pattern Consistency Loss. Beyond the pixel-wise loss function, we also incorporate the local correlation in density maps to improve the quality of results. We utilize SSIM index to measure the local pattern consistency of estimated density maps and ground truths. SSIM index is usually used in image quality assessment. It computes similarity between two images from three local statistics, i.e. mean, variance and covariance. The range of SSIM value is from -1 to 1 and it is equal to 1 when the two image are identical. Following [11], we use an 11×11 normalized Gaussian kernel with standard deviation of 1.5 to estimate local statistics. The weight is defined by $W = \{W(\boldsymbol{p}) \mid \boldsymbol{p} \in \mathcal{P}, \mathcal{P} = \{(-5,-5), \cdots, (5,\ 5)\}\}$, where $\boldsymbol{p}$ is offset from the center and $\mathcal{P}$ contains all positions of the kernel. It is easily implemented with a convolutional layer by setting the weights to W and not updating it in back propagation. For each location $\boldsymbol{x}$ on the estimated density map F and the corresponding ground truth Y, the local statistics are computed by:

$$\mu_F(\boldsymbol{x}) = \sum_{\boldsymbol{p} \in \mathcal{P}} W(\boldsymbol{p}) \cdot F(\boldsymbol{x} + \boldsymbol{p}), \tag{3}$$

$$\sigma_F^2(\boldsymbol{x}) = \sum_{\boldsymbol{p} \in \mathcal{P}} W(\boldsymbol{p}) \cdot [F(\boldsymbol{x} + \boldsymbol{p}) - \mu_F(\boldsymbol{x})]^2, \tag{4}$$

$$\sigma_{FY}(\boldsymbol{x}) = \sum_{\boldsymbol{p} \in \mathcal{P}} W(\boldsymbol{p}) \cdot [F(\boldsymbol{x} + \boldsymbol{p}) - \mu_F(\boldsymbol{x})] \cdot [Y(\boldsymbol{x} + \boldsymbol{p}) - \mu_Y(\boldsymbol{x})], \tag{5}$$

where μ_F and σ_F^2 are the local mean and variance estimation of F, σ_{FY} is the local covariance estimation. μ_Y and σ_Y^2 are computed similarly to Eqs. 3 and 4. Then, SSIM index is calculated point by point as following:

$$SSIM = \frac{(2\mu_F \mu_Y + C_1)(2\sigma_{FY} + C_2)}{(\mu_F^2 + \mu_Y^2 + C_1)(\sigma_F^2 + \sigma_Y^2 + C_2)}, \tag{6}$$

where C_1 and C_2 are small constants to avoid division by zero and set as [11]. The local pattern consistency loss is defined below:

$$L_C = 1 - \frac{1}{N} \sum_{\boldsymbol{x}} SSIM(\boldsymbol{x}), \tag{7}$$

where N is the number of pixels in density maps. L_C is the local pattern consistency loss that measures the local pattern discrepancy between the estimated result and ground truth.

Final Objective. By weighting the above two loss functions, we define the final objective function as follows:

$$L = L_E + \alpha_C L_C, \tag{8}$$

where α_C is the weight to balance the pixel-wise and local-region losses. In our experiments, we empirically set α_C as 0.001.

4 Implementation Details

After alleviating the vanishing gradient problem with IN layers, our method can be trained end-to-end. In this section, we describe our patch-based training and testing scheme which is used to reduce the impact of statistic shift problem.

4.1 Training Details

In training stage, patches with 1/4 size of original image are cropped at random locations, then they are randomly horizontal flipped for data augmentation. Annotations for crowd image are points at the center of pedestrian head. It is required to convert these points to density map. If there is a point at pixel $\boldsymbol{x}_i$, it can be represented with a delta function $\delta(\boldsymbol{x} - \boldsymbol{x}_i)$. The ground truth density map Y is generated by convolving each delta function with a normalized Gaussian kernel G_σ:

$$Y = \sum_{\boldsymbol{x}_i \in S} \delta(\boldsymbol{x} - \boldsymbol{x}_i) * G_\sigma, \tag{9}$$

where S is the set of all annotated points. The integral of density map is equal to the crowd count in image. Instead of using the geometry-adaptive kernels [3], we fix the spread parameter σ of the Gaussian kernel to generate ground truth density maps.

We end-to-end train the SANet from scratch. The network parameters are randomly initialized by a Gaussian distributions with mean zero and standard deviation of 0.01. Adam optimizer [36] with a small learning rate of 1e-5 is used to train the model, because it shows faster convergence than standard stochastic gradient descent with momentum in our experiments. The implementation of our method is based on the Pytorch [37] framework.

4.2 Evaluation Details

Due to the statistic shift problem caused by the IN layers, the input need to be consistent during training and testing. For testing the model trained based on patches, we crop each test sample to patches 1/4 size of original image with 50% overlapping. For each overlapping pixels between patches, we only reserve the density value in the patch of which the center is the nearest to the pixel than others, because the center part of patches has enough contextual information to ensure accurate estimation.

For crowd counting, the count error is measured by two metrics, Mean Absolute Error (MAE) and Mean Squared Error (MSE), which are commonly used for quantitative comparison in previous works. They are defined as follows:

$$MAE = \frac{1}{N}\sum_{i=1}^{N}|C_i - C_i^{GT}|, \qquad MSE = \sqrt{\frac{1}{N}\sum_{i}^{N}|C_i - C_i^{GT}|^2}, \tag{10}$$

where N is the number of test samples, C_i and C_i^{GT} are the estimated and ground truth crowd count corresponding to the ith sample, which is given by the integration of density map. Roughly speaking, MAE indicates the accuracy of predicted result and MSE measures the robustness. Because MSE is sensitive to outliers and it would be large when the model poorly performs on some samples.

5 Experiments

In this section, we first introduce datasets and experiment details. Then an ablation study is reported to demonstrate the improvements of different modules in our method. Finally, we give the evaluation results and perform comparisons between the proposed method with recent state-of-the-art methods.

5.1 Datasets

We evaluate our SANet on four publicly available crowd counting datasets: ShanghaiTech [3], UCF_CC_50 [21], WorldExpo'10 [28] and UCSD [38].

ShanghaiTech. The ShanghaiTech dataset [3] contains 1198 images, with a total of 330,165 annotated people. This dataset is divided to two parts: Part A with 482 images and Part B with 716 images. Part A is randomly collected from the Internet and Part B contains images captured from streets views. We use the training and testing splits provided by the authors: 300 images for training and 182 images for testing in Part A; 400 images for training and 316 images for testing in Part B. Ground truth density maps of both subset are generated with fixed spread Gaussian kernel.

WorldExpo'10. The WorldExpo'10 dataset [28] consists of total 3980 frames extracted from 1132 video sequences captured with 108 surveillance cameras. The density of this dataset is relatively sparser in comparison to ShanghaiTech dataset. The training set includes 3380 frames and testing set contains 600 frames from five different scenes and 120 frames per scene. Regions of interest (ROI) are provided for all scenes. We use ROI to prune the feature maps of the last convolution layer. During testing, only the crowd estimation error in specified ROI is computed. This dataset also gives perspective maps. We evaluate our method by ground truth generated with and without perspective maps. We follow experiment setting of [6] to generate density maps with perspective maps.

UCF_CC_50. The UCF_CC_50 dataset [21] includes 50 annotated crowd images. There is a large variation in crowd counts which range from 94 to 4543. The limited number of images make it a challenging dataset for deep learning method. We follow the standard protocol and use 5-fold cross-validation to evaluate the performance of proposed method. Ground truth density maps are generated with fixed spread Gaussian kernel.

UCSD. The UCSD dataset [38] consists of 2000 frames with size of 158×238 collected from surveillance videos. This dataset has relatively low density with an average of around 25 people in a frame. The region of interest (ROI) is also provided to ignore irrelevant objects. We use ROI to process the annotations. MAE and MSE are evaluated only in the specified ROI during testing. Following the train-test split used by [38], frames 601 through 1400 are used as training set and the rest as testing set. We generate ground truth density maps with fixed spread Gaussian kernel.

5.2 Ablation Experiments

We implement the MCNN and train it with the ground truth generated by fixed-spread Gaussian kernel. The result is slightly better than that reported in [3]. Based on the MCNN model, several ablation studies are conducted on ShanghaiTech Part A dataset. The evaluation results are reported in Table 1.

Architecture. We separately investigate the roles of FME and DME in SANet. We first append a 1×1 convolution layer to our FME to estimate density maps, which are $1/8$ the size of input images. Both MCNN and FME output low-resolution density maps, but FME improves the scale diversity of features by the scale aggregation modules. Then, We combine DME with MCNN model to increase the resolution of density maps. With up-sampling by the transposed convolution layers in DME, the size of estimated density maps is the same as input images. Compared with MCNN baseline, both FME and DME substantially reduce the estimation error. Table 1a shows that FME lowers MAE by 19.9 points and MSE by 32.4 points, while DME decreases 26.1 points of MAE and 26.9 points of MSE than baseline. This result demonstrate that the multi-scale feature representation and the high-resolution density map are extremely beneficial for the crowd density estimation task.

Table 1. Ablation experiment results on ShanghaiTech Part A. Models are trained with patches and using only Euclidean loss unless otherwise noted

(a) **Modules**: Comparison the estimation error of different network configurations. MCNN∗ refers to our reimplementation

Model	MAE	MSE
MCNN [3]	110.2	173.2
MCNN∗	109.4	161.6
FME	90.5	**129.2**
MCNN+DME	**83.3**	134.7

(b) **Instance Normalization layers**: Estimation error of the models trained with or without IN layers. '-' indicates that the model fails to converge

Model	IN	MAE	MSE
MCNN+DME	×	83.3	134.7
MCNN+DME	✓	77.6	111.5
SANet	×	-	-
SANet	✓	**71.0**	**107.5**

(c) **Loss function and Test Scheme**: Estimation error of SANet trained with different loss functions and tested with different samples. L_E refers to Euclidean loss and L_C refers to local pattern consistency loss

Loss function	Test sample	MAE	MSE
L_E	image	116.8	180.4
L_E	patch	71.0	107.5
L_E, L_C	image	88.1	134.3
L_E, L_C	patch	**67.0**	**104.5**

Instance Normalization. Considering the vanishing gradient problem, we apply IN layers to both MCNN+DME and SANet. As illustrated in Table 1b, the IN layer can ease training process and boost the performance by a large margin. For MCNN+DME, IN layers decrease MAE by 5.7 points and MSE by 23.2 points. This result indicates that the model tends to fall into local minima without the normalization layers. Meanwhile, SANet with IN layers converges during training and achieves competitive results, with MAE of 71.0 and MSE of 107.5. The result would encourage attempts to use deeper network in density estimation problem.

Test Scheme. We evaluated the SANet trained with patches by different input samples, i.e. images and patches. As shown in Table 1c, we can see that the SANet obtains promising results when testing with patches, but the performance is significantly dropped when testing with images. It verifies the statistic shift problem caused by IN layers. Therefore, it is indispensable to apply the patch-based test scheme.

Local Pattern Consistency Loss. The result by using the combination of Euclidean loss and local pattern consistency loss is given in the Table 1c. We can observe that the model trained with the loss combination results in lower estimation error than using only L_E, which indicates this light-weight loss can improve the accuracy and robustness of model. Furthermore, the local pattern consistency loss significantly increases the performance when testing with images, which shows that the loss can enhance the insensitivity to statistic shift. We

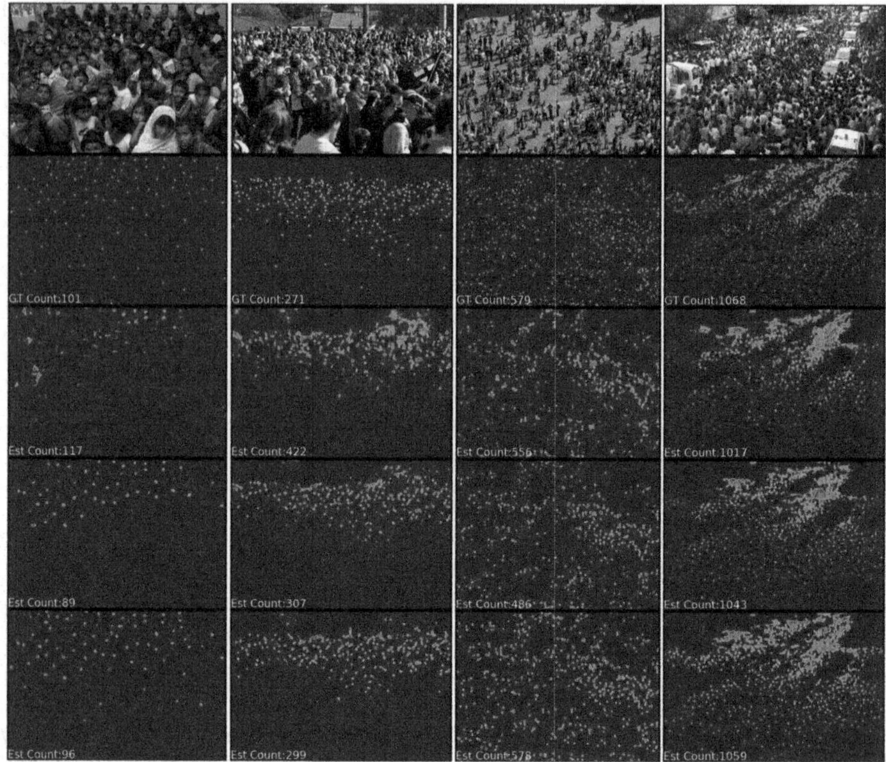

Fig. 3. Visualization of estimated density maps. First row: sample images from ShanghaiTech Part A. Second row: ground truth. Third row: estimated density maps by MCNN [3], which are resized to the same resolution as input images. Four row: estimated density maps by SANet trained with Euclidean loss only. Five row: estimated density maps by SANet trained with the combination of Euclidean loss and the local pattern consistency loss.

think it could smooth changes in the local region and reduce the statistical discrepancy between patches and images

Qualitative Analysis. Estimated density maps from MCNN and our SANet with or without local pattern consistency loss on sample input images are illustrated in Fig. 3. We can see that our method obtains lower count error and generates higher quality density maps with less noise than MCNN. Moreover, the use of additional local pattern consistency loss further reduce the estimation error and improve the quality.

5.3 Comparisons with State-of-the-Art

We demonstrate the efficiency of our proposal method on four challenging crowd counting datasets. Tables 2, 3, 4 and 5 report the results on ShanghaiTech,

Table 2. Comparison with state-of-the-art methods on ShanghaiTech dataset [3]

	Part A		Part B	
Method	MAE	MSE	MAE	MSE
Zhang *et al.* [28]	181.8	277.7	32.0	49.8
MCNN [3]	110.2	173.2	26.4	41.3
Cascaded-MTL [32]	101.3	152.4	20.0	31.1
Huang *et al.* [39]	-	-	20.2	35.6
Switch-CNN [5]	90.4	135.0	21.6	33.4
CP-CNN [6]	73.6	106.4	20.1	30.1
CSRNet [33]	68.2	115.0	10.6	16.0
SANet(ours)	**67.0**	**104.5**	**8.4**	**13.6**

Table 3. Comparison with state-of-the-art methods on WorldExpo'10 dataset [28]. Only MAE is computed for each scene and then averaged to evaluate the overall performance

Method	Scene1	Scene2	Scene3	Scene4	Scene5	Average
Zhang *et al.* [28]	9.8	14.1	14.3	22.2	3.7	12.9
MCNN [3]	3.4	20.6	12.9	13.0	8.1	11.6
Huang *et al.* [39]	4.1	21.7	11.9	11.0	3.5	10.5
Switch-CNN [5]	4.4	15.7	10.0	11.0	5.9	9.4
CP-CNN [6]	2.9	14.7	10.5	**10.4**	5.8	8.9
CSRNet [33]	2.9	**11.5**	**8.6**	16.6	3.4	8.6
SANet(ours) with perspective	2.8	14.0	10.2	12.5	3.5	8.6
SANet(ours) w/o perspective	**2.6**	13.2	9.0	13.3	**3.0**	**8.2**

Table 4. Comparison with state-of-the-art methods on UCF_CC_50 dataset [21]

Method	MAE	MSE
Idrees *et al.* [21]	419.5	541.6
Zhang *et al.* [28]	467.0	498.5
MCNN [3]	377.6	509.1
Huang *et al.* [39]	409.5	563.7
Hydra-2s [4]	333.7	425.3
Cascaded-MTL [32]	322.8	341.4
Switch-CNN [5]	318.1	439.2
CP-CNN [6]	295.8	**320.9**
CSRNet [33]	266.1	397.5
SANet(ours)	**258.4**	334.9

Table 5. Comparison with state-of-the-art methods on UCSD dataset [38]

Method	MAE	MSE
Zhang *et al.* [28]	1.60	3.31
MCNN [3]	1.07	1.35
Huang *et al.* [39]	**1.00**	1.40
CCNN [4]	1.51	-
Switch-CNN [5]	1.62	2.10
CSRNet [33]	1.16	1.47
SANet(ours)	1.02	**1.29**

Table 6. Number of parameters (in millions)

Method	MCNN [3]	Switch-CNN [5]	CP-CNN [6]	CSRNet [33]	**SANet**
Parameters	0.13	15.11	68.4	16.26	**0.91**

WorldExpo'10, UCF_CC_50 and UCSD respectively. They show that the proposed method outperforms all other state-of-the-art methods from all tables, which indicates our method works not only in dense crowd images but also relatively sparse scene.

As shown in Table 2, our method obtains the lowest MAE on both subset of ShanghaiTech. On WorldExpo'10 dataset, our approaches with and without perspective maps, both are able to achieve superior result compared to the other methods in Table 3. In addition, the method without perspective maps gets better result than using it and acquires the best MAE in two scenes. In Table 4, our SANet also attains the lowest MAE and a comparable MSE comparing to other eight state-of-the-art methods, which states our SANet also has decent performance in the case of small dataset. Table 5 shows that our method outperforms other state-of-the-art methods even in sparse scene. These superior results demonstrate the effectiveness of our proposed method.

As shown in Table 6, the parameters number of our proposed SANet is the least except MCNN. Although CP-CNN and CSRNet have comparable result with our method, CP-CNN has almost 75× parameters and CSRNet has nearly 17× parameters than ours. Our method achieves superior results than other state-of-the-art methods while with much less parameters, which proves the efficiency of our proposed method.

6 Conclusion

In this work, we propose a novel encoder-decoder network for accurate and efficient crowd counting. To exploit the local correlation of density maps, we propose the local pattern consistency loss to enforce the local structural similarity between density maps. By alleviating the vanishing gradient problem and statistic shift problem, the model can be trained end-to-end. Extensive experiments show that our method achieves the superior performance on four major crowd counting benchmarks to state-of-the-art methods while with much less parameters.

Acknowledgement. This work was supported by Chinese National Natural Science Foundation Projects No. 61532018 and No. 61471049.

References

1. Zhan, B., Monekosso, D.N., Remagnino, P., Velastin, S.A., Xu, L.Q.: Crowd analysis: a survey. Mach. Vis. Appl. **19**(5–6), 345–357 (2008)
2. Li, T., Chang, H., Wang, M., Ni, B., Hong, R., Yan, S.: Crowded scene analysis: a survey. IEEE Trans. Circuits Syst. Video Technol. **25**(3), 367–386 (2015)
3. Zhang, Y., Zhou, D., Chen, S., Gao, S., Ma, Y.: Single-image crowd counting via multi-column convolutional neural network. In: Proceedings of the IEEE Conference on Computer Vision and Pattern Recognition, pp. 589–597 (2016)
4. Oñoro-Rubio, D., López-Sastre, R.J.: Towards perspective-free object counting with deep learning. In: Leibe, B., Matas, J., Sebe, N., Welling, M. (eds.) ECCV 2016. LNCS, vol. 9911, pp. 615–629. Springer, Cham (2016). https://doi.org/10.1007/978-3-319-46478-7_38
5. Sam, D.B., Surya, S., Babu, R.V.: Switching convolutional neural network for crowd counting. In: Proceedings of the IEEE Conference on Computer Vision and Pattern Recognition, vol. 1, p. 6 (2017)
6. Sindagi, V.A., Patel, V.M.: Generating high-quality crowd density maps using contextual pyramid CNNS. In: 2017 IEEE International Conference on Computer Vision (ICCV), pp. 1879–1888. IEEE (2017)
7. Isola, P., Zhu, J.Y., Zhou, T., Efros, A.A.: Image-to-image translation with conditional adversarial networks. In: Proceedings of the IEEE Conference on Computer Vision and Pattern Recognition, pp. 1125–1134 (2017)
8. Goodfellow, I., et al.: Generative adversarial nets. In: Advances in Neural Information Processing Systems, pp. 2672–2680 (2014)
9. Szegedy, C., et al.: Going deeper with convolutions. IEEE (2015)
10. Zhao, H., Gallo, O., Frosio, I., Kautz, J.: Loss functions for neural networks for image processing. IEEE Trans. Comput. Imaging (2017)
11. Wang, Z., Bovik, A.C., Sheikh, H.R., Simoncelli, E.P.: Image quality assessment: from error visibility to structural similarity. IEEE Trans. Image Process. **13**(4), 600–612 (2004)
12. Huang, X., Belongie, S.: Arbitrary style transfer in real-time with adaptive instance normalization. CoRR, abs/1703.06868 (2017)
13. Ge, W., Collins, R.T.: Marked point processes for crowd counting. In: IEEE Conference on Computer Vision and Pattern Recognition, CVPR 2009, pp. 2913–2920. IEEE (2009)
14. Li, M., Zhang, Z., Huang, K., Tan, T.: Estimating the number of people in crowded scenes by mid based foreground segmentation and head-shoulder detection. In: 19th International Conference on Pattern Recognition, ICPR 2008, pp. 1–4. IEEE (2008)

15. Dollar, P., Wojek, C., Schiele, B., Perona, P.: Pedestrian detection: an evaluation of the state of the art. IEEE Trans. Pattern Anal. Mach. Intell. **34**(4), 743–761 (2012)
16. Felzenszwalb, P.F., Girshick, R.B., McAllester, D., Ramanan, D.: Object detection with discriminatively trained part-based models. IEEE Trans. Pattern Anal. Mach. Intell. **32**(9), 1627–1645 (2010)
17. Leibe, B., Seemann, E., Schiele, B.: Pedestrian detection in crowded scenes. In: IEEE Computer Society Conference on Computer Vision and Pattern Recognition, CVPR 2005. vol. 1, pp. 878–885. IEEE (2005)
18. Chan, A.B., Vasconcelos, N.: Bayesian poisson regression for crowd counting. In: IEEE 12th International Conference on Computer Vision, pp. 545–551. IEEE (2009)
19. Chen, K., Loy, C.C., Gong, S., Xiang, T.: Feature mining for localised crowd counting. In: BMVC, vol. 1, p. 3 (2012)
20. Ryan, D., Denman, S., Fookes, C., Sridharan, S.: Crowd counting using multiple local features. In: Digital Image Computing: Techniques and Applications, DICTA 2009, pp. 81–88. IEEE (2009)
21. Idrees, H., Saleemi, I., Seibert, C., Shah, M.: Multi-source multi-scale counting in extremely dense crowd images. In: 2013 IEEE Conference on Computer Vision and Pattern Recognition (CVPR), pp. 2547–2554. IEEE (2013)
22. Ng, P.C., Henikoff, S.: Sift: predicting amino acid changes that affect protein function. Nucleic Acids Res. **31**(13), 3812–3814 (2003)
23. Lempitsky, V., Zisserman, A.: Learning to count objects in images. In: Advances in Neural Information Processing Systems, pp. 1324–1332 (2010)
24. Pham, V.Q., Kozakaya, T., Yamaguchi, O., Okada, R.: Count forest: co-voting uncertain number of targets using random forest for crowd density estimation. In: Proceedings of the IEEE International Conference on Computer Vision, pp. 3253–3261 (2015)
25. Sindagi, V.A., Patel, V.M.: A survey of recent advances in cnn-based single image crowd counting and density estimation. Pattern Recognit. Lett. **107**, 3–16 (2017)
26. Wang, C., Zhang, H., Yang, L., Liu, S., Cao, X.: Deep people counting in extremely dense crowds. In: Proceedings of the 23rd ACM International Conference on Multimedia, pp. 1299–1302. ACM (2015)
27. Krizhevsky, A., Sutskever, I., Hinton, G.E.: Imagenet classification with deep convolutional neural networks. In: Advances in Neural Information Processing Systems, pp. 1097–1105 (2012)
28. Zhang, C., Li, H., Wang, X., Yang, X.: Cross-scene crowd counting via deep convolutional neural networks. In: 2015 IEEE Conference on Computer Vision and Pattern Recognition (CVPR), pp. 833–841. IEEE (2015)
29. Walach, E., Wolf, L.: Learning to count with CNN boosting. In: Leibe, B., Matas, J., Sebe, N., Welling, M. (eds.) ECCV 2016. LNCS, vol. 9906, pp. 660–676. Springer, Cham (2016). https://doi.org/10.1007/978-3-319-46475-6_41
30. Shang, C., Ai, H., Bai, B.: End-to-end crowd counting via joint learning local and global count. In: 2016 IEEE International Conference on Image Processing (ICIP), pp. 1215–1219. IEEE (2016)
31. Boominathan, L., Kruthiventi, S.S., Babu, R.V.: Crowdnet: a deep convolutional network for dense crowd counting. In: Proceedings of the 2016 ACM on Multimedia Conference, pp. 640–644. ACM (2016)

32. Sindagi, V.A., Patel, V.M.: CNN-based cascaded multi-task learning of high-level prior and density estimation for crowd counting. In: 2017 14th IEEE International Conference on Advanced Video and Signal Based Surveillance (AVSS), pp. 1–6. IEEE (2017)
33. Li, Y., Zhang, X., Chen, D.: CSRNET: dilated convolutional neural networks for understanding the highly congested scenes. In: Proceedings of the IEEE Conference on Computer Vision and Pattern Recognition (2018)
34. Simonyan, K., Zisserman, A.: Very deep convolutional networks for large-scale image recognition. arXiv preprint arXiv:1409.1556 (2014)
35. Ioffe, S., Szegedy, C.: Batch normalization: Accelerating deep network training by reducing internal covariate shift. In: International Conference on Machine Learning, pp. 448–456 (2015)
36. Kingma, D.P., Ba, J.: Adam: a method for stochastic optimization. In: ICLR (2015)
37. Paszke, A., et al.: Pytorch: tensors and dynamic neural networks in python with strong GPU acceleration, May 2017
38. Chan, A.B., Liang, Z.S.J., Vasconcelos, N.: Privacy preserving crowd monitoring: counting people without people models or tracking. In: IEEE Conference on Computer Vision and Pattern Recognition, CVPR 2008, pp. 1–7. IEEE (2008)
39. Huang, S., et al.: Body structure aware deep crowd counting. IEEE Trans. Image Process. **27**(3), 1049–1059 (2018)

Deep Shape Matching

Filip Radenović(✉), Giorgos Tolias, and Ondřej Chum

Visual Recognition Group, FEE, CTU in Prague, Prague, Czech Republic
{filip.radenovic,giorgos.tolias,chum}@cmp.felk.cvut.cz

Abstract. We cast shape matching as metric learning with convolutional networks. We break the end-to-end process of image representation into two parts. Firstly, well established efficient methods are chosen to turn the images into edge maps. Secondly, the network is trained with edge maps of landmark images, which are automatically obtained by a structure-from-motion pipeline. The learned representation is evaluated on a range of different tasks, providing improvements on challenging cases of domain generalization, generic sketch-based image retrieval or its fine-grained counterpart. In contrast to other methods that learn a different model per task, object category, or domain, we use the same network throughout all our experiments, achieving state-of-the-art results in multiple benchmarks.

Keywords: Shape matching · Cross-modal recognition and retrieval

1 Introduction

Deep neural networks have recently become very popular for computer-vision problems, mainly due to their good performance and generalization. These networks have been first used for image classification by Krizhevsky *et al.* [3], then their application spread to other related problems. A standard architecture of a classification network starts with convolutional layers followed by fully connected layers. Convolutional neural networks (CNNs) became a popular choice of learning image embeddings, *e.g.* in efficient image matching – image retrieval. It has been observed that the convolutional part of the classification network captures well *colours*, *textures* and *structures* within the receptive field.

In a number of problems, the colour and/or the texture is not available or misleading. Three examples are shown in Fig. 1. For sketches or outlines, there is no colour or texture available at all. For artwork, the colour and texture is present, but often can be unrealistic to stimulate certain impression rather than exactly capture the reality. Finally, in the case of extreme illumination changes, such as a day-time versus night images, the colours may be significantly distorted and the textures weakened. On the other hand, the image discontinuities in colour or texture, as detected by modern edge detectors, and especially their shapes, carry the information about the content, independent of, or insensitive to, the illumination changes, artistic drawing and outlining.

V. Ferrari et al. (Eds.): ECCV 2018, LNCS 11209, pp. 774–791, 2018.
https://doi.org/10.1007/978-3-030-01228-1_46

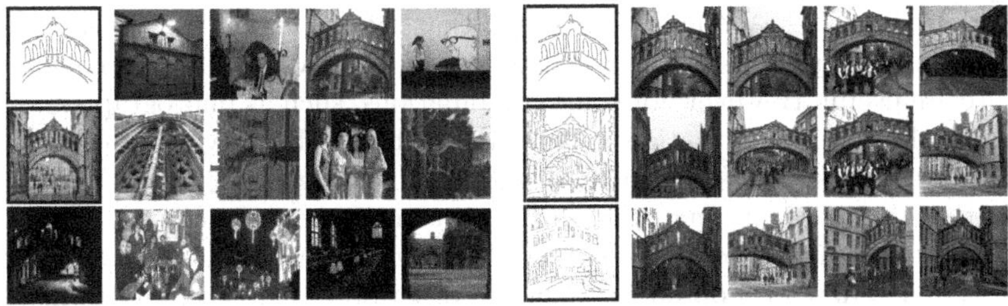

Fig. 1. Three examples where **shape** is the only relevant information: sketch, artwork, extreme illumination conditions. Top retrieved images from the Oxford Buildings dataset [1]: CNN with an RGB input [2] (left), and our shape matching network (right). Query images are shown with black border.

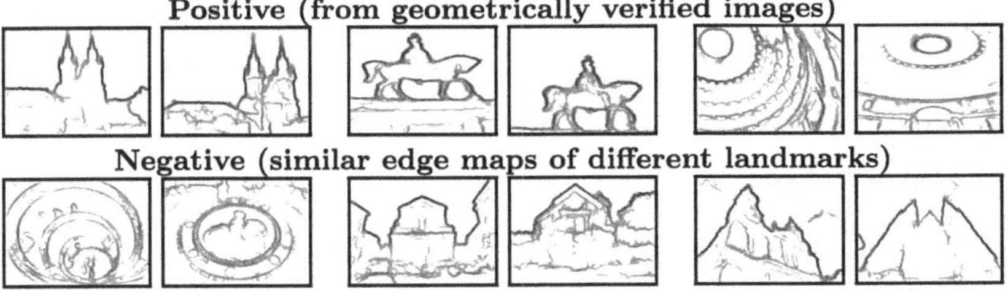

Fig. 2. Edge maps extracted from matching and non-matching image pairs that serve as training data for our network.

This work is targeting at shape matching, in particular the goal is to extract a descriptor that captures the shape depicted in the input. The shape descriptors are extracted from image edge maps by a CNN. Sketches, black and white line drawings or cartoons are simply considered as a special type of an edge map.

The network is trained without any human supervision or image, sketch or shape annotation. Starting from a pre-trained classification network stripped off the fully connected layers, the CNN is fine-tuned using a simple contrastive loss function. Matching and non-matching training pairs are extracted from automatically generated 3D models of landmarks [2]. Edge maps detected on these images provide training data for the network. Examples of positive and negative pairs of edge maps are shown in Fig. 2.

We show the importance of shape matching on two problems: (1) modality invariant representation, *i.e.* classification for domain generalization, and (2) cross modality matching of sketches to images.

In the domain generalization, some of the domains are available, but some are completely unseen during the training phase. We evaluate on domain generalization by performing object recognition. We extract the learned descriptors and train a simple classifier on the seen domains, which is later used to classify images of the unseen domain. We show, that for some combinations of seen-unseen domains, such as artwork and photograph, descriptors using colour and texture are useful. However, for some combinations, such as photograph and line drawing, the shape information is crucial. Combining both types of descriptors outperforms the state-of-the-art approach in all settings.

In the cross modality matching task, it is commonly assumed that annotated training data is available for both modalities. Even for this task, we apply the domain generalization approach, using the descriptors learned on edge maps of building images. We evaluate the cross modality matching on sketch based image retrieval datasets. Modern sketch-based image retrieval take the path of object recognition from human sketches. Rather than performing shape matching, the networks are trained to recognize simplified human drawings. Such an approach requires very large number of annotated images and drawn sketches for each category of interest. Even though the proposed network is *not trained* to recognize human-drawn object sketches, our experiments show that it performs well on standard benchmarks.

2 Related Work

Shape matching is shown useful in several computer vision tasks such as object recognition [4], object detection [5], 3D shape matching [6,7] and cross-modal retrieval [8,9]. In this section we review prior work related to sketch-based image retrieval, a particular flavor of cross-modal retrieval, where we apply the proposed representation. Finally, we discuss domain generalization approaches since our method is directly applicable on this problem handling it simply by learning shape matching.

Sketch-based image retrieval has been, until recently, handled with hand-crafted descriptors [10–19]. Deep learning methods have been applied to the task of sketch-based retrieval [20–26] much later than to the related task of image retrieval. We attribute the delay to the fact that the training data acquisition for sketch-based retrieval is much more tedious compared to image-based retrieval because it not only includes labeling the images, but also sketches must be drawn in large quantities. Methods with no learning typically carry no assumptions on the depicted categories, while the learning based methods often include category recognition into training. The proposed method aims at generic sketch-based retrieval, not limited to a fixed set of categories; it is, actually, not even limited to objects.

Learning-free methods have followed the same initial steps as in the traditional image search. These include the construction of either global [12,16,27] or local [11,14,28–30] image and/or sketch representations. Local representations are also using vector quantization to create a Bag-of-Words model [31]. Further cases are symmetry-aware and flip invariant descriptors [30], descriptors that are based on local contours [29] or line segments [14], and kernel descriptors [19]. Transformation invariance is often sacrificed for the sake of scalability [8,9]. In contrast, the method proposed in this paper is fully translation invariant, and scalable, because it reduces to a nearest-neighbor search in a descriptor space.

Learning-based methods require annotated data in both domains, typically for a fixed set of object categories, making the methods [6,20–26,32] to be category specific. End-to-end learning methods are applied to both category level [25,26] and to fine-grained, *i.e.* sub-category level retrieval [22–24,32], while sometimes a different model per category has to be learned [22,32–34]. A sequence of different learning and fine-tuning stages is applied [22–26], involving massive manual annotation effort. For example, the Sketchy dataset [23] required collectively 3,921 h of sketching. On the contrary, our proposed fine-tuning does not require any manual annotation.

Domain generalization is handled in a variety of ways, ranging from learning domain invariant features [35,36] to learning domain invariant classifiers [37,38] or both [39,40]. Several methods focus on one-way shift between two domains, such as sketch-based retrieval described earlier or learning on real photos and testing on art [41,42]. An interesting benchmark is released in the work of Li *et al.* [39], where four domains of increasing visual abstraction are used, namely *photos*, *art*, *cartoon*, and *sketches* (PACS). Prior domain generalization methods [35–37] are shown effective on PACS, while simply training a CNN on all the available (seen) domains is a very good baseline [39]. We tackle this problem from the representation point of view and focus on the underlined shapes. Our shape descriptor is extracted and the labels are used only to train a linear classifier. In this fashion, we are able to train on a single domain and test on all the rest, while common domain generalization approaches require different domains present in the training set.

3 Method

In this section we describe the proposed approach. The process of fine-tuning the CNN is described in Sect. 3.1, while the final representation and the way it is used for retrieval and classification is detailed in Sect. 3.2.

We break the end-to-end process of image description into two parts. In the first part, the images are turned into edge maps. In particular, throughout all our experiments we used the edge detector of Dollár and Zitnick [43] due to its great trade-off between efficiency and accuracy, and the tendency not to consider textured regions as edges. Our earlier experiments on sketch-based image retrieval with a CNN-based edge detector [44] did not show any significant changes in the performance. An image is represented as an edge map, which is a 2D array containing the edge strength in each image pixel. The edge strength is in the range of $[0, 1]$, where 0 represents background. Sketches, in the case of sketch-to-image retrieval, are represented as a special case of an edge map, where the edge strength is either 0 for the background or 1 for a contour.

The second part is a fully convolutional network extracting a global image descriptor. The two part approach allows, in a simple manner, to unify all modalities at the level of edge maps. Jointly training these two parts, *e.g.* in the case of a CNN-based edge detector [44], can deliver an image descriptor too. However, this descriptor may not be based on shapes. It is unlikely that such an optimization would end in a state where the representation between the two parts actually corresponds to edges. Enforcing this with additional training data in the form of edge maps and a loss on the output of the first part is exactly what we are avoiding and improving in this work.

3.1 Training

We use a network architecture previously proposed for image classification [45], in particular, we use all convolutional layers and the activations of the very last one, *i.e.*, the network is stripped of the fully-connected layers. The CNN is initialized by the parameters learned on a large scale annotated image dataset, such as ImageNet [46]. This is a fairly standard approach adopted in a number of problems, including image search [2,47,48]. The network is then fine-tuned with pairs of image edge maps.

The Network. The image classification network expects an RGB input image, while the edge maps are only two dimensional. We sum the first convolution filters over RGB. Unlike in RGB input, no mean pixel subtraction is performed to the input data. To obtain a compact, shift invariant descriptor, a global max-pooling [49] layer is appended after the last convolutional layer. This approach is also known as Maximum Activations of Convolutions (MAC) vector [50]. After the MAC layer, the vectors are ℓ_2 normalized.

Edge Filtering. A typical output of edge detectors is a strength of an edge in every pixel. We introduce an edge filtering layer to address two frequent issues with edge responses. First, the background often contains close-to-zero responses, which typically introduce noise into the representation. This issue is commonly handled by thresholding the response function. Second, the strength of the edges provides ordering, *i.e.* higher edge response implies that the edge is more likely to be present, however its value typically does not have practical interpretation. Prior to the first convolution layer, a continuous and differentiable function is pre-pended. This layer is trained together with the rest of the network

Fig. 3. Sample images, the output of the edge detector, the filtered edge map, and the edge-filtering function.

to transform the edge detector output with soft thresholding by a sigmoid and power transformation. Denote the edge strength by $w \in [0, 1]$. Edge filtering is performed as

$$f(w) = \frac{w^p}{1 + e^{\beta(\tau - w)}}, \tag{1}$$

where p controls the contrast between strong and weak edges, τ is the threshold parameter, and β is the scale of the sigmoid choosing between hard thresholding and a softer alternative. The final function (1) with learned parameters is plotted in Fig. 3 (right). The figure also visually demonstrates the effect of application of the filtering. The weak edges are removed on the background and the result appearance is closer to a rough sketch, while the uncertainty in edges is still preserved.

Fine Tuning. The CNN is trained with Stochastic Gradient Descent in a Siamese fashion with contrastive loss [51]. The positive training pairs are edge maps of matching images (similarity of the edge maps is not considered), while the negative pairs are similar edge maps (according to the current state of the network) of non-matching images.

Given a pair of vectors $\mathbf{x}$ and $\mathbf{y}$, the loss is defined as their squared Euclidean distance $||\mathbf{x} - \mathbf{y}||^2$ for positive examples, and as $\max\{(m - ||\mathbf{x} - \mathbf{y}||)^2, 0\}$ for negative examples. Hard-negative mining is performed several times per epoch which has been shown to be essential [2,48].

Training Data. The training images for fine tuning the network are collected in a fully automatic way. In particular, we use the publicly available dataset used in Radenovic *et al.* [2] and follow the same methodology, briefly reviewed in the following. A large unordered image collection is passed through a 3D reconstruction system based on local features and Bag-of-Words retrieval [52, 53]. The outcome consists of a set of 3D models which mostly depict outdoor landmarks and urban scenes. For each landmark, a maximum of 30 six-tuples of images are being selected. The six-tuple consists of: one image as the training query, then one matching image to the training query, and five similar non-matching images. This gives arise to one positive and five negative pairs. The geometry of the 3D models, including camera positions, allows to mine matching images, *i.e.* those that share adequate visual overlap. Negative-pair mining is facilitated by the 3D models, too: negative images are chosen only if they belong to a different model.

Data Augmentation. A standard data-augmentation, *i.e.* random horizontal flipping (mirroring) procedure is applied to introduce further variance in the training data and to avoid over-fitting. The training query and the positive example are jointly mirrored with 50% probability. Negative examples are sought after eventual flipping. We propose an additional augmentation technique for the selected training queries. Their edge map responses are thresholded with a random threshold uniformly chosen from $[0, 0.2]$ and the result is binarized. Matching images (in positive examples) are left unchanged; negative images are selected after the transformation. This augmentation process is applied with a probability of 50%. It offers a level of shape abstraction and mimics the asymmetry of sketch-to-edge map matching. The randomized threshold can be also seen as an approximation of the stroke removal in [22].

3.2 Representation, Search and Classification

We use the trained network to extract image and sketch descriptors capturing the underlying shapes, which are then used to perform cross-modal image retrieval, in particular sketch-based, and object recognition via transfer learning, in particular domain generalization.

Representation. The input to the descriptor extraction process is always resized to a maximum dimensionality of 227×227 pixels. A multi-scale representation is performed by processing at 5 fixed scales, *i.e.*, re-scaling the original input by a factor of $1/2, 1/\sqrt{2}$, 1, $\sqrt{2}$, 2, and, with the additional mirroring, 10 final instances are produced. *Images* undergo edge detection and the resulting edge map [43] is fed to the CNN[1]. *Sketches* come in the form of strokes, thin line drawings, or brush drawings, depending on the input device or the dataset. To unify the sketch input, a simple morphological filter is applied to a binary sketch image. Specifically, a morphological thinning followed by dilation is performed. After the pre-processing, the sketch is treated as an edge map. As a consequence of the rescaling and mirroring, an image/sketch is mapped to 10 high dimensional vectors. We refer to these ℓ_2 normalized vectors as EdgeMAC descriptors. They are subsequently sum-aggregated or indexed separately, depending on the evaluation benchmark, see Sect. 4 for more details.

Search. An image collection is indexed by simply extracting and storing the corresponding EdgeMAC descriptors for each image. Search is performed by nearest-neighbors search of the query descriptor in the database. This makes retrieval compatible with approximate methods [54,55] that can speed up search and offer memory savings.

Classification. We extract EdgeMAC descriptors from labeled images and train a multi-class linear classifier [56] to perform object recognition. This is especially useful for transfer learning when the training domain is different from the target/testing one. In this case, no labeled images of the training domain are available during the training of our network and no labeled images of the target domain are available during classifier training.

3.3 Implementation Details

In this section we discuss implementation details. The training dataset used to train our network is presented. We train a single network, which is then used for different tasks. Training sets provided for specific tasks are not exploited.

Training Data. We use the same training set as in the work of Radenovic *et al.* [2][2] which comprises landmarks and urban scenes. There are around 8k

[1] We perform zero padding by 30 pixels to avoid border effects.

[2] Training data available at cmp.felk.cvut.cz/cnnimageretrieval.

tuples. Due to the overlap of landmarks contained in the training set and one of the test sets involved in our evaluation, we manually excluded these landmarks from our training data. We end up with with 5,969 tuples for training and 1,696 for validation. Hard negatives are re-mined 3 times per epoch [2] from a pool of around 22k images.

Training Implementation. We use the MatConvNet toolbox [57] to implement the learning. We initialize the convolutional layers by VGG16 [45] (results in 512D EdgeMAC descriptor) trained on ImageNet and sum the filters of the first layer over the feature maps dimension to accommodate for the 2D edge map input instead of the 3D image. The edge-filtering layer is initialized with values $p = 0.5$, $\tau = 0.1$ and β is fixed and equal to 500 so that it always approximates hard thresholding. Additionally, the output of the egde-filtering layer is linearly scaled from $[0, 1]$ to $[0, 10]$. Initial learning rate is $l_0 = 0.001$ with an exponential learning rate decay $l_0\text{exp}(-0.1j)$ over epoch j; momentum is 0.9; weight decay is 0.0005; contrastive loss margin is 0.7; and batch size is equal to 20 training tuples. All training images are resized so that the maximum extent is 200 pixels, while keeping the original aspect ratio.

Training Time. Training is performed for at most 20 epochs and the best network is chosen based on the performance on validation tuples. The whole training takes about 10 h on a single GeForce GTX TITAN X (Maxwell) GPU with 12GB of memory.

4 Experiments

We evaluate EdgeMAC descriptor on domain generalization and sketch-based image retrieval. We train a single network and apply it on both tasks proving the generic nature of the representation.

4.1 Domain Generalization Through Shape Matching

We extract EdgeMAC descriptors from labeled images, sum-aggregate descriptors of rescaled and mirrored instances and ℓ_2 normalize to produce one descriptor per image, and train a linear classifier [56] to perform object recognition. We evaluate on domain generalization to validate the effectiveness of our representation on shape matching.

PACS dataset was recently introduced by Li *et al.* [39]. It consists of images coming from 4 domains with varying level of abstraction, namely, *art* (painting), *cartoon*, *photo*, and *sketch*. Images are labeled according to 7 categories, namely, dog, elephant, giraffe, guitar, horse, house, and person. Each time, one domain is considered unseen, otherwise called target or test domain, while the image of the other 3 are used for training. Finally, multi-class accuracy is evaluated on the unseen domain. In our work, we additionally perform classifier training using a single domain and then test on the rest. We find this scenario to be realistic, especially in the case of training on photos and testing on the rest. The domain

Table 1. Multi-class accuracy on PACS dataset for 4 different descriptors. The combined descriptor (pre-trained + ours) is constructed via concatenation. A: Art, C: Cartoon, P: Photo, S: Sketch, 3: all 3 other domains.

	Pre-trained (RGB)				Siamese [2] (RGB)				Ours (edge map)				Pre-trained+Ours			
Test →	A	C	P	S	A	C	P	S	A	C	P	S	A	C	P	S
Train A	N/A	59.2	95.0	33.1	N/A	59.5	86.3	42.9	N/A	55.9	61.2	65.6	N/A	61.6	94.9	38.4
Train C	71.7	N/A	86.8	37.0	61.0	N/A	77.0	51.6	45.2	N/A	57.3	74.8	69.3	N/A	85.0	55.3
Train P	72.5	33.3	N/A	24.8	66.0	38.0	N/A	31.9	45.4	42.3	N/A	46.3	73.3	34.0	N/A	27.61
Train S	31.9	49.5	42.5	N/A	38.7	49.3	44.4	N/A	34.8	63.0	43.3	N/A	33.7	59.3	43.4	N/A
Train 3	78.0	68.0	94.4	47.1	71.5	64.3	85.1	56.0	53.8	67.9	64.5	74.7	80.0	68.7	93.7	62.7
Mean 3	71.9				69.2				65.2				76.2			

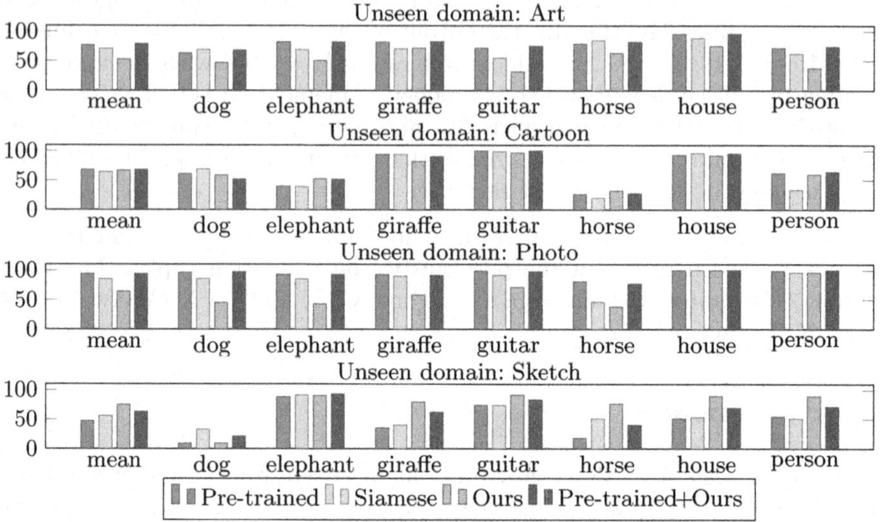

Fig. 4. Classification accuracy on PACS dataset with different descriptors. Testing is performed on 1 unseen domain each time, while training is performed on the other 3.

of realistic photos is the richest in terms of annotated data, while others such as sketches and cartoons are very sparsely annotated.

Baselines. We are interested in translation invariant representations and consider the two following baselines. First, MAC [50] descriptors extracted using a network that is pre-trained on ImageNet. Second, MAC descriptors extracted by a network that is fine-tuned for image retrieval in a siamese manner [2]. These two baselines have the same descriptor extraction complexity as ours. They are extracted on RGB images, while ours on edge maps. Note, that we treat all domains as images with our approach and extract edge maps, *i.e.* we do not perform any special treatment on sketches as in the case of sketch retrieval.

Performance Comparison. We evaluate our descriptor, the two baselines, and the concatenated version of ours and the descriptor of the pre-trained baseline network, and report results in Table 1. Our representation significantly improves

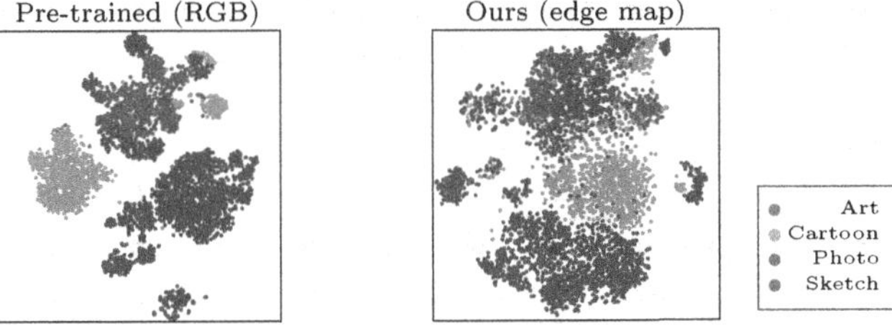

Fig. 5. Visualization of PACS images with t-SNE (more overlap is better).

sketch recognition while training on a single or all seen domains. Similar improvements are observed for cartoon recognition when training on photos or sketches, while when training on artwork the color information appears to be beneficial. We consider the case of training only on photos and testing on other domains to be the most interesting and realistic one. In this scenario, we provide improvements, compared to the baselines, for sketch recognition (15% and 22%) and cartoon recognition (4% and 9%). Finally, the combined descriptor reveals the complementarity of the representations in several cases, such as artwork and cartoon recognition while training on all seen domains, or training on single domain when artwork is involved, *e.g.* train on P (or A) and test on A (or C). The best reported score on PACS is 69.2 [39] by fine-tuning AlexNet on PACS. The achieved score by our descriptor with fine-tuned VGG (PACS not used during network training) is 76.2, which is significantly higher. The same experiment with AlexNet achieves 70.9. Performance is reported per category in Fig. 4. Our descriptor achieves significant improvements on most categories for sketch recognition, while the combined is a safe choice in several cases. Interestingly, our experiments reveal that the siamese baseline slightly improves shape matching, despite being trained on RGB images.

Visualization with t-SNE. We use t-SNE [58] to reduce the dimensionality of descriptors to 2 and visualize the result for the pre-trained baseline and our descriptor in Fig. 5. The different modalities are brought closer with our descriptor. Observe how separated is the sketch modality with the pre-trained network that receives an RGB image for input.

4.2 Sketch-Based Image Retrieval

We extract EdgeMAC descriptors to index an image collection, treat sketch queries as described in Sect. 3.2 and perform sketch-based image retrieval via simple nearest neighbor search.

Test Datasets and Evaluation Protocols. The method is evaluated on two standard sketch-based image retrieval benchmarks.

Flickr15k [11] consists of 15k database images and 330 sketch queries that are related to 33 categories. Categories include particular object instances (Brussels Cathedral, Colosseum, Arc de Triomphe, *etc.*), generic objects (airplane, bicycle,

Table 2. Performance evaluation of the different components of our method on Flickr15k dataset. Network: off-the-shelf (O), fine-tuned (F).

Component	Network							
	O	O	F	F	F	F	F	F
Train/Test: Edge filtering		■	■	■	■	■	■	■
Train: Query binarization				■	■	■	■	■
Test: Mirroring					■		■	■
Test: Multi-scale						■	■	■
Test: Diffusion								■
mAP	25.9	27.9	38.4	41.9	43.4	45.6	46.1	68.9

bird, *etc.*), and shapes (circle shape, star shape, heart, balloon, *etc.*). The performance is measured via mean Average Precision (mAP) [1]. We sum-aggregate descriptors of rescaled and mirrored instances and ℓ_2 normalize to produce one descriptor per image. Search is performed by a cosine similarity nearest-neighbor search.

Shoes/Chairs/Handbags [22,32] datasets contain images from one category only, *i.e.* shoe/chair/handbag category respectively. It consists of pairs of a photo and a corresponding hand-drawn detailed sketch of this photo. There are 419, 297, and 568 sketch–photo pairs of shoes, chairs, and handbags, respectively. Out of these, 304, 200, and 400 pairs are selected for training, and 115, 97, and 168 for testing shoes, chairs, and handbags, respectively. The performance is measured via the matching accuracy at the top K retrieved images, denoted by acc.@K. The underlying task is quite different compared to Flickr15k. The photograph used to generate the sketch is to be retrieved, while all other images are considered false positives. The search protocol used in [22] is as follows: Descriptors are extracted from 5 image crops (corners and center) and their horizontally mirrored counterparts. This holds for database images and the sketch query. During search, these 10 descriptors are compared one-to-one and their similarity is averaged. For fair comparison, we adopt this protocol and do not use a single descriptor per image/sketch for this benchmark. However, instead of image crops, we extract descriptors at 5 image scales and their horizontally mirrored counterparts, as these are defined in Sect. 3.2.

Impact of Different Components. Table 2 shows the impact of different components on the final performance of the proposed method as measured on Flickr15k dataset. Direct application of the off-the-shelf CNN on edge maps already outperforms most prior hand-crafted methods (see Table 3). Adding the edge-filtering layer to the off-the-shelf network improves the precision. The initial parameters for filtering are used. Fine-tuning brings significant jump to 38.4 mAP, which is already the state-of-the-art on this dataset. Random training-query binarization and multi-scale with mirroring representation further improve the mAP score to 46.1. Finally, we boost the recall of our sketch-based retrieval

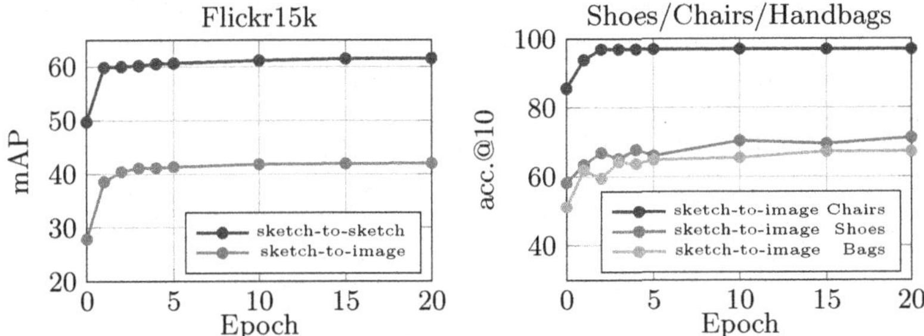

Fig. 6. Performance evaluation of the fine-tuned network over training epochs for the single-scale representation. All shown datasets and their evaluation protocols are described in Sect. 4.2.

by global diffusion, as recently proposed by Iscen *et al.* [59]. We construct the neighborhood graph by combining kNN-graphs built on two different similarities [60,61]: edge map similarity with EdgeMAC and image similarity with CroW descriptors [62]. This increases the performance to 68.9.

Performance Evolution During Learning. We report the performance of the fine-tuned network at different stages (epochs) of training. The same network is evaluated for all datasets as we train a single network for all tasks. The performance is shown in Fig. 6 for both benchmarks. On all datasets, the fine-tuning significantly improves the performance already from the first few epochs.

As a sanity check, we also perform a non-standard sketch-to-sketch evaluation. On the Flickr15k dataset, each of the 330 sketches is used to query the other 329 sketches (the query sketch is removed from the evaluation), which attempts to retrieve sketches of the same category. The evolution of the performance shows similar behavior as the sketch-to-image search, *i.e.*, the learning on edge maps improves the performance on sketch-to-sketch retrieval, see Fig. 6.

Comparison with the State of the Art. We extensively compare our method to the state-of-the-art performing methods on both benchmarks. Whenever code and trained models are publicly available, we additionally evaluate them on test sets they were not originally applied on. In cases that the provided code is used for evaluation on Flickr15k we center and align the sketches appropriately in order to achieve high scores, while our method is translation invariant so there is no such need. First we give a short overview of the best performing and most relevant methods to ours. Finally, a comparison via quantitative results is given.

Shoes/Chairs/Handbags networks [22,32] are trained from scratch based on the Sketch-a-Net architecture [63]. This is achieved by the following steps [22][3]: (i) Training with classification loss for 1k categories from ImageNet-1K data with edge maps input. (ii) Training with classification loss for 250 categories of TU-Berlin [64] sketch data. (iii) Training a triplet network with shared weights and ranking loss on TU-Berlin sketches and ImageNet images. (iv) Finally, training

[3] Networks/code available at github.com/seuliufeng/DeepSBIR.

Table 3. Performance comparison via mean Average Precision (mAP) with the state-of-the-art sketch-based image retrieval on the Flickr15k dataset. Best result is highlighted in red, second best in **bold**. Query expansion methods are shown below the horizontal line and are highlighted separately. Our evaluation of the methods that do not originally report results on Flickr15 is marked with †.

Hand-crafted methods

Method	Dim	mAP
GF-HOG [11]	n/a	12.2
S-HELO [12]	1296	12.4
HLR+S+C+R [14]	n/a	17.1
GF-HOG extended [15]	n/a	18.2
PerceptualEdge [16]	3780	18.4
LKS [17]	1350	24.5
AFM [19]	243	30.4
AFM+QE [19]	755	**57.9**

CNN-based methods

Method	Dim	mAP
Sketch-a-Net+EdgeBox [20]	5120	27.0
Shoes network [22]†	256	29.9
Chairs network [22]†	256	29.8
Sketchy network [23]†	1024	34.0
Quadruplet network [24]	1024	32.2
Triplet no-share network [26]	128	**36.2**
⋆ EdgeMAC	512	**46.1**
Sketch-a-Net+EdgeBox+GraphQE [20]	n/a	32.3
⋆ EdgeMAC+Diffusion	n/a	**68.9**

separate networks for fine-grain instance-level ranking using the Shoes/Chairs//Handbags training datasets. This approach is later improved [32] by adding an attention module with a coarse-fine fusion (CFF) into the architecture, and by extending the triplet loss with a higher order learnable energy function (HOLEF). Such a training involves various datasets, with annotation at different levels, and a variety of task-engineered loss functions. Note that the two models available online achieve higher performance than the ones reported in [22], due to parameter retuning. We compare our results to their best performing models.

Sketchy network [23] consists of two asymmetric sketch and image branches, both initialized with GoogLeNet. The training involves the following steps[4]: (i) Training for classification on TU-Berlin sketch dataset. (ii) Separate training of the sketch branch with classification loss on 125 categories of Sketchy dataset and training of the image branch with classification loss on the same categories with additional 1000 Flickr photos per category. (iii) Training both branches in a triplet network with ranking loss on the Sketchy sketch–photo pairs. The last part involves approximately 100k positive and a billion negative pairs.

Quadruplet network [24] tackles the problem in a similar way as Sketchy network, however, they use ResNet-18 [65] architecture with shared weights for both sketch and image branches. The training involves the following steps: (i) Training with classification loss on Sketchy dataset. (ii) Training a network with triplet loss on Sketchy dataset, while mining three different types of triplets.

Triplet no-share network [26] consists of asymmetric sketch and image branches initialized by Sketch-a-Net and AlexNet [3], respectively. The training involves: (i) Separate training of the sketch branch with classification loss on TU-Berlin and training of the image branch with classification loss on ImageNet. (ii) Training a triplet network with ranking loss on TU-Berlin sketches augmented with 25k corresponding photos harvested from the Internet. (iii) Training a triplet network with ranking loss on the Sketchy dataset.

[4] Network/code available at github.com/janesjanes/sketchy.

Table 4. Performance comparison via accuracy at rank K (acc.@K) with the state-of-the-art sketch-based image retrieval on the Shoes/Chairs test datasets. Best result is highlighted in red, second best in **bold**. Note that [22] and [32] train a separate network per object category. †We evaluate the publicly available networks, because the performance is higher than the one originally reported in [22].

Method	Dim	Shoes		Chairs		Handbags	
		acc.@1	acc.@10	acc.@1	acc.@10	acc.@1	acc.@10
BoW-HOG + rankSVM [22]	500	17.4	67.8	28.9	67.0	2.4	10.7
Dense-HOG + rankSVM [22]	200K	24.4	65.2	52.6	93.8	15.5	40.5
Sketch-a-Net + rankSVM [22]	512	20.0	62.6	47.4	82.5	9.5	44.1
CCA-3V-HOG + PCA [18]	n/a	15.8	63.2	53.2	90.3	–	–
Shoes net [22]†	256	52.2	**92.2**	65.0	92.8	23.2	59.5
Chairs net [22]†	256	30.4	75.7	72.2	**99.0**	26.2	58.3
Handbags net [32]	256	–	–	–	–	39.9	82.1
Shoes net + CFF + HOLEF [32]	512	**61.7**	**94.8**	–	–	–	–
Chairs net + CFF + HOLEF [32]	512	–	–	**81.4**	95.9	–	–
Handbags net + CFF + HOLEF [32]	512	–	–	–	–	**49.4**	**82.7**
⋆ EdgeMAC	512	40.0	76.5	**85.6**	95.9	35.1	70.8
⋆ EdgeMAC + whitening	512	**54.8**	**92.2**	**85.6**	**97.9**	**51.2**	**85.7**

Performance Comparison. We compare our network with other methods on both benchmarks. Methods that have not reported scores on a particular datasets are evaluated by ourselves while using the publicly available networks.

Results on the Flickr15k dataset are presented in Table 3, where our method significantly outperforms both hand-crafted descriptors and CNN-based that are learned on a variety of training data. This holds for both plain search with the descriptors, and for methods using re-ranking techniques, such as query expansion [66] and diffusion [59].

Results on the fine-grained Shoes/Chairs/Handbags benchmark are shown in Table 4. In this experiment, we also report the performance after applying descriptor whitening which is learned in a supervised way [2] by using the descriptors of the training images of this benchmark. A single whitening transformation is learned for all three datasets. Such a process takes only a few seconds once descriptors are given. It is orders of magnitude faster than using the training set to perform network fine-tuning. We achieve the top performance in 2 out of 3 categories and the second best in the other one. The approach of [22] and [32] train a separate network per category (3 in total), which is clearly not scalable to many objects. In contrast our approach uses a single generic network. An additional drawback is revealed when we evaluate the publicly available Shoes and Chairs networks on the category they were not trained on. We observe a significant drop in performance, see Table 4.

The Number of Parameters. Our reported results use the VGG16 network stripped off the fully connected layers (FC), leaving ~15M parameters. The number of parameters of Sketch-A-Net [63] is ~8.5M parameters, while when used for SBIR in two different branches (Shoes, Chairs, Handbags [22]) there is ~17M parameters. Triplet no-share network [26] uses two branches (Sketch-a-Net with additional FC layer and AlexNet [3]) leading to ~115M, and Sketchy [23] uses 2× GoogLeNet leading to ∼26M parameters. Our network has the smallest number of parameters from the competing methods.

5 Conclusions

We have introduced an approach to learn shape matching by training a CNN with edge maps of matching images. The training stage does not require any manual annotation, achieved by following the footsteps of image retrieval [2], where image pairs are automatically mined from large scale 3D reconstruction.

The generic applicability of the representation is proven by validating on a variety of cases. It achieves state-of-the-art results on standard benchmarks for sketch-based image retrieval, while we have further demonstrated the applicability beyond sketch-based image retrieval. Promising results were achieved for queries with different modality (artwork) and significant change of illumination (day-night retrieval). The descriptor is shown beneficial for object recognition via transfer learning, especially to classify images of unseen domains, such as cartoons and sketches, where the amount of annotated data is limited. Remarkably, the same network is applied in all the different tasks. Training data, trained models, and code are publicly available at cmp.felk.cvut.cz/cnnimageretrieval.

Acknowledgements. This work was supported by the MSMT LL1303 ERC-CZ grant and the OP VVV funded project CZ.02.1.01/0.0/0.0/16_019/0000765 "RCI".

References

1. Philbin, J., Chum, O., Isard, M., Sivic, J., Zisserman, A.: Object retrieval with large vocabularies and fast spatial matching. In: CVPR (2007)
2. Radenović, F., Tolias, G., Chum, O.: CNN image retrieval learns from BoW: unsupervised fine-tuning with hard examples. In: Leibe, B., Matas, J., Sebe, N., Welling, M. (eds.) ECCV 2016. LNCS, vol. 9905, pp. 3–20. Springer, Cham (2016). https://doi.org/10.1007/978-3-319-46448-0_1
3. Krizhevsky, A., Sutskever, I., Hinton, G.E.: Imagenet classification with deep convolutional neural networks. In: NIPS (2012)
4. Belongie, S., Malik, J., Puzicha, J.: Shape matching and object recognition using shape contexts. PAMI (2002)
5. Ferrari, V., Fevrier, L., Jurie, F., Schmid, C.: Groups of adjacent contour segments for object detection. PAMI (2008)
6. Wang, F., Kang, L., Li, Y.: Sketch-based 3D shape retrieval using convolutional neural networks. In: CVPR (2015)
7. Tabia, H., Laga, H.: Covariance-based descriptors for efficient 3D shape matching, retrieval, and classification. IEEE Trans. Multimed. **17**(9), 1591–1603 (2015)
8. Cao, Y., Wang, C., Zhang, L., Zhang, L.: Edgel index for large-scale sketch-based image search. In: CVPR (2011)
9. Sun, X., Wang, C., Xu, C., Zhang, L.: Indexing billions of images for sketch-based retrieval. In: ACM Multimedia (2013)
10. Eitz, M., Richter, R., Boubekeur, T., Hildebrand, K., Alexa, M.: Sketch-based shape retrieval. ACM Trans. Graph. (2012)

11. Hu, R., Collomosse, J.: A performance evaluation of gradient field hog descriptor for sketch based image retrieval. CVIU **117**(7), 790–806 (2013)
12. Saavedra, J.M.: Sketch based image retrieval using a soft computation of the histogram of edge local orientations (S-HELO). In: ICIP (2014)
13. Parui, S., Mittal, A.: Similarity-invariant sketch-based image retrieval in large databases. In: Fleet, D., Pajdla, T., Schiele, B., Tuytelaars, T. (eds.) ECCV 2014. LNCS, vol. 8694, pp. 398–414. Springer, Cham (2014). https://doi.org/10.1007/978-3-319-10599-4_26
14. Wang, S., Zhang, J., Han, T.X., Miao, Z.: Sketch-based image retrieval through hypothesis-driven object boundary selection with HLR descriptor. IEEE Trans. Multimed. **17**(7), 1045–1057 (2015)
15. Bui, T., Collomosse, J.: Scalable sketch-based image retrieval using color gradient features. In: ICCV (2015)
16. Qi, Y., et al.: Making better use of edges via perceptual grouping. In: CVPR (2015)
17. Saavedra, J.M., Barrios, J.M., Orand, S.: Sketch based image retrieval using learned keyshapes (LKS). In: BMVC (2015)
18. Xu, P., et al.: Cross-modal subspace learning for fine-grained sketch-based image retrieval. Neurocomputing **278**, 75–86 (2017)
19. Tolias, G., Chum, O.: Asymmetric feature maps with application to sketch based retrieval. In: CVPR (2017)
20. Bhattacharjee, S.D., Yuan, J., Hong, W., Ruan, X.: Query adaptive instance search using object sketches. In: ACM Multimedia (2016)
21. Qi, Y., Song, Y.Z., Zhang, H., Liu, J.: Sketch-based image retrieval via siamese convolutional neural network. In: ICIP (2016)
22. Yu, Q., Lie, F., Song, Y.Z., Xian, T., Hospedales, T., Loy, C.C.: Sketch me that shoe. In: CVPR (2016)
23. Sangkloy, P., Burnell, N., Ham, C., Hays, J.: The sketchy database: learning to retrieve badly drawn bunnies. ACM Trans. Graph. **35**(4), 119 (2016)
24. Seddati, O., Dupont, S., Mahmoudi, S.: Quadruplet networks for sketch-based image retrieval. In: ICMR (2017)
25. Liu, L., Shen, F., Shen, Y., Liu, X., Shao, L.: Deep sketch hashing: Fast free-hand sketch-based image retrieval. In: CVPR (2017)
26. Bui, T., Ribeiro, L., Ponti, M., Collomosse, J.: Generalisation and sharing in triplet convnets for sketch based visual search. arXiv:1611.05301 (2016)
27. Chalechale, A., Naghdy, G., Mertins, A.: Sketch-based image matching using angular partitioning. IEEE Trans. Syst. Man Cybern. **35**(1), 28–41 (2005)
28. Eitz, M., Hildebrand, K., Boubekeur, T., Alexa, M.: An evaluation of descriptors for large-scale image retrieval from sketched feature lines. Comput. Graph. **34**(5), 482–498 (2010)
29. Riemenschneider, H., Donoser, M., Bischof, H.: Image retrieval by shape-focused sketching of objects. In: CVWW (2011)
30. Cao, X., Zhang, H., Liu, S., Guo, X., Lin, L.: Sym-fish: a symmetry-aware flip invariant sketch histogram shape descriptor. In: ICCV (2013)
31. Ma, C., Yang, X., Zhang, C., Ruan, X., Yang, M.H., Coporation, O.: Sketch retrieval via dense stroke features. In: BMVC (2013)
32. Song, J., Yu, Q., Song, Y.Z., Xiang, T., Hospedales, T.: Deep spatial-semantic attention for fine-grained sketch-based image retrieval. In: ICCV (2017)
33. Li, Y., Hospedales, T.M., Song, Y.Z., Gong, S.: Fine-grained sketch-based image retrieval by matching deformable part models. In: BMVC (2014)

34. Song, J., Song, Y.Z., Xiang, T., Hospedales, T., Ruan, X.: Deep multi-task attribute-driven ranking for fine-grained sketch-based image retrieval. In: BMVC (2016)
35. Ghifary, M., Bastiaan Kleijn, W., Zhang, M., Balduzzi, D.: Domain generalization for object recognition with multi-task autoencoders. In: ICCV (2015)
36. Muandet, K., Balduzzi, D., Schölkopf, B.: Domain generalization via invariant feature representation. In: ICML (2013)
37. Xu, Z., Li, W., Niu, L., Xu, D.: Exploiting low-rank structure from latent domains for domain generalization. In: Fleet, D., Pajdla, T., Schiele, B., Tuytelaars, T. (eds.) ECCV 2014. LNCS, vol. 8691, pp. 628–643. Springer, Cham (2014). https://doi.org/10.1007/978-3-319-10578-9_41
38. Khosla, A., Zhou, T., Malisiewicz, T., Efros, A.A., Torralba, A.: Undoing the damage of dataset bias. In: Fitzgibbon, A., Lazebnik, S., Perona, P., Sato, Y., Schmid, C. (eds.) ECCV 2012. LNCS, vol. 7572, pp. 158–171. Springer, Heidelberg (2012). https://doi.org/10.1007/978-3-642-33718-5_12
39. Li, D., Yang, Y., Song, Y.Z., Hospedales, T.M.: Deeper, broader and artier domain generalization. In: ICCV (2017)
40. Bousmalis, K., Trigeorgis, G., Silberman, N., Krishnan, D., Erhan, D.: Domain separation networks. In: NIPS (2016)
41. Crowley, E., Zisserman, A.: The state of the art: object retrieval in paintings using discriminative regions. In: BMVC (2014)
42. Crowley, E.J., Zisserman, A.: The art of detection. In: Hua, G., Jégou, H. (eds.) ECCV 2016. LNCS, vol. 9913, pp. 721–737. Springer, Cham (2016). https://doi.org/10.1007/978-3-319-46604-0_50
43. Dollár, P., Zitnick, C.L.: Structured forests for fast edge detection. In: ICCV (2013)
44. Kokkinos, I.: Pushing the boundaries of boundary detection using deep learning. In: ICLR (2016)
45. Simonyan, K., Zisserman, A.: Very deep convolutional networks for large-scale image recognition. In: ICLR (2014)
46. Dong, W., Socher, R., Li-Jia, L., Li, K., Fei-Fei, L.: ImageNet: a large-scale hierarchical image database. In: CVPR (2009)
47. Arandjelović, R., Gronat, P., Torii, A., Pajdla, T., Sivic, J.: NetVLAD: CNN architecture for weakly supervised place recognition. In: CVPR (2016)
48. Gordo, A., Almazán, J., Revaud, J., Larlus, D.: Deep image retrieval: learning global representations for image search. In: Leibe, B., Matas, J., Sebe, N., Welling, M. (eds.) ECCV 2016. LNCS, vol. 9910, pp. 241–257. Springer, Cham (2016). https://doi.org/10.1007/978-3-319-46466-4_15
49. Razavian, A.S., Sullivan, J., Carlsson, S., Maki, A.: Visual instance retrieval with deep convolutional networks. ITE Trans. MTA **4**(3), 251–258 (2016)
50. Tolias, G., Sicre, R., Jégou, H.: Particular object retrieval with integral max-pooling of CNN activations. In: ICLR (2016)
51. Chopra, S., Hadsell, R., LeCun, Y.: Learning a similarity metric discriminatively, with application to face verification. In: CVPR (2005)
52. Schönberger, J.L., Radenović, F., Chum, O., Frahm, J.M.: From single image query to detailed 3D reconstruction. In: CVPR (2015)
53. Radenović, F., Schönberger, J.L., Ji, D., Frahm, J.M., Chum, O., Matas, J.: From dusk till dawn: modeling in the dark. In: CVPR (2016)
54. Muja, M., Lowe, D.G.: Fast approximate nearest neighbors with automatic algorithm configuration. In: VISAPP (2009)
55. Johnson, J., Douze, M., Jégou, H.: Billion-scale similarity search with GPUs. arXiv:1702.08734 (2017)

56. Perronnin, F., Akata, Z., Harchaoui, Z., Schmid, C.: Towards good practice in large-scale learning for image classification. In: CVPR (2012)
57. Vedaldi, A., Lenc, K.: MatConvNet: convolutional neural networks for MATLAB. In: ACM Multimedia (2015)
58. Maaten, L.V.D., Hinton, G.: Visualizing data using t-SNE. JMLR **9**, 2579–2605 (2008)
59. Iscen, A., Tolias, G., Avrithis, Y., Furon, T., Chum, O.: Efficient diffusion on region manifolds: recovering small objects with compact CNN representations. In: CVPR (2017)
60. Bai, S., Sun, S., Bai, X., Zhang, Z., Tian, Q.: Smooth neighborhood structure mining on multiple affinity graphs with applications to context-sensitive similarity. In: Leibe, B., Matas, J., Sebe, N., Welling, M. (eds.) ECCV 2016. LNCS, vol. 9906, pp. 592–608. Springer, Cham (2016). https://doi.org/10.1007/978-3-319-46475-6_37
61. Zhang, S., Yang, M., Cour, T., Yu, K., Metaxas, D.N.: Query specific fusion for image retrieval. In: Fitzgibbon, A., Lazebnik, S., Perona, P., Sato, Y., Schmid, C. (eds.) ECCV 2012. LNCS, pp. 660–673. Springer, Heidelberg (2012). https://doi.org/10.1007/978-3-642-33709-3_47
62. Kalantidis, Y., Mellina, C., Osindero, S.: Cross-dimensional weighting for aggregated deep convolutional features. In: Hua, G., Jégou, H. (eds.) ECCV 2016. LNCS, vol. 9913, pp. 685–701. Springer, Cham (2016). https://doi.org/10.1007/978-3-319-46604-0_48
63. Yu, Q., Yang, Y., Song, Y.Z., Xiang, T., Hospedales, T.M.: Sketch-a-Net that beats humans. In: BMVC (2015)
64. Eitz, M., Hays, J., Alexa, M.: How do humans sketch objects? ACM Trans. Graph. (2012)
65. He, K., Zhang, X., Ren, S., Sun, J.: Deep residual learning for image recognition. In: CVPR (2016)
66. Chum, O., Philbin, J., Sivic, J., Isard, M., Zisserman, A.: Total recall: automatic query expansion with a generative feature model for object retrieval. In: ICCV (2007)

Eigendecomposition-Free Training of Deep Networks with Zero Eigenvalue-Based Losses

Zheng Dang[1,2(✉)], Kwang Moo Yi[3], Yinlin Hu[4], Fei Wang[1,2], Pascal Fua[4], and Mathieu Salzmann[4]

[1] National Engineering Laboratory for Visual Information Processing and Application, Xi'an Jiaotong University, 99 Yanxiang Road, Xi'an 710054, Shaanxi, China
dangzheng713@stu.xjtu.edu.cn, wfx@mail.xjtu.edu.cn

[2] School of Electronic and Information Engineering, Xi'an Jiaotong University, 28 West Xianning Road, Xi'an 710049, Shaanxi, China

[3] Visual Computing Group, University of Victoria, Victoria, Canada
kyi@uvic.ca

[4] CVLab, EPFL, Lausanne, Switzerland
{yinlin.hu, pascal.fua, mathieu.salzmann}@epfl.ch

Abstract. Many classical Computer Vision problems, such as essential matrix computation and pose estimation from 3D to 2D correspondences, can be solved by finding the eigenvector corresponding to the smallest, or zero, eigenvalue of a matrix representing a linear system. Incorporating this in deep learning frameworks would allow us to explicitly encode known notions of geometry, instead of having the network implicitly learn them from data. However, performing eigendecomposition within a network requires the ability to differentiate this operation. While theoretically doable, this introduces numerical instability in the optimization process in practice.

In this paper, we introduce an eigendecomposition-free approach to training a deep network whose loss depends on the eigenvector corresponding to a zero eigenvalue of a matrix predicted by the network. We demonstrate on several tasks, including keypoint matching and 3D pose estimation, that our approach is much more robust than explicit differentiation of the eigendecomposition. It has better convergence properties and yields state-of-the-art results on both tasks.

Keywords: End-to-end learning · Eigendecomposition
Singular value decomposition · Geometric vision

1 Introduction

In traditional Computer Vision, many tasks can be solved by finding the singular- or eigen-vector corresponding to the smallest, often zero, singular- or eigen-value

V. Ferrari et al. (Eds.): ECCV 2018, LNCS 11209, pp. 792–807, 2018.
https://doi.org/10.1007/978-3-030-01228-1_47

of the matrix encoding a linear system. Examples include estimating essential matrices or homographies from matched keypoints and computing pose from 3D to 2D correspondences.

In the era of Deep Learning, there is growing interest in embedding these methods within a deep architecture to allow end-to-end training. For example, it has recently been shown that such an approach can be used to train networks to detect and match keypoints in image pairs while accounting for the global consistency of the correspondences [37]. More generally, this approach would allow us to explicitly encode notions of geometry within deep networks, thus sparing the network the need to re-learn what has been known for decades and making it possible to learn from smaller amounts of training data.

One way to implement this approach is to design a network whose output defines a matrix and train it so that the smallest singluar- or eigen-vector of the matrices it produces are as close as possible to ground-truth ones. This is the strategy used in [37] to simultaneously establish correspondences and compute the corresponding Essential Matrix: The network's outputs are weights discriminating inlier correspondences from outliers and are used to assemble an auxiliary matrix whose smallest eigenvector is the sought-for Essential Matrix.

The main obstacle to implementing this approach is that it requires being able to differentiate the singular value decomposition (SVD) or the eigendecomposition (ED) in a stable manner to train the network, a non-trivial problem that has already received considerable attention [9,16,26]. As a result, these decompositions are already part of standard Deep Learning frameworks, such as TensorFlow [1] or PyTorch [27]. However, they ignore two key practical issues. First, when optimizing with respect to the matrix itself or with respect to parameters defining it, the vector corresponding to the smallest singular value or eigenvalue may switch abruptly as the relative magnitudes of these values change, which is essentially non-differentiable. This is illustrated in the example of Fig. 1, discussed in detail in Sect. 2. Second, computing the gradient requires dividing by the difference between two singular values or eigenvalues, which could be zero. While a solution to the latter was proposed in [26], the former is unavoidable.

In this paper, we therefore introduce an approach to training a deep network whose loss depends on the eigenvector corresponding to a zero eigenvalue of a matrix $\mathbf{M}$, which is either the output of the network or a function of it, *without* explicitly performing an SVD or ED. Our loss is fully differentiable, does *not* suffer from the instabilities the above-mentioned problems can cause, and can be naturally incorporated in a deep learning architecture. In practice, because image measurements are never perfect, the eigenvalue is never strictly zero. This, however, does not affect the computation either, which makes our approach robust to noise.

To demonstrate this in a Deep Learning context, we evaluate our approach on the tasks of training a network to find globally-consistent keypoint correspondences using the essential matrix and training another to remove outliers for pose estimation when solving the Perspective-n-Point (PnP) problem. In both cases, our approach delivers state-of-the-art results, whereas using the standard

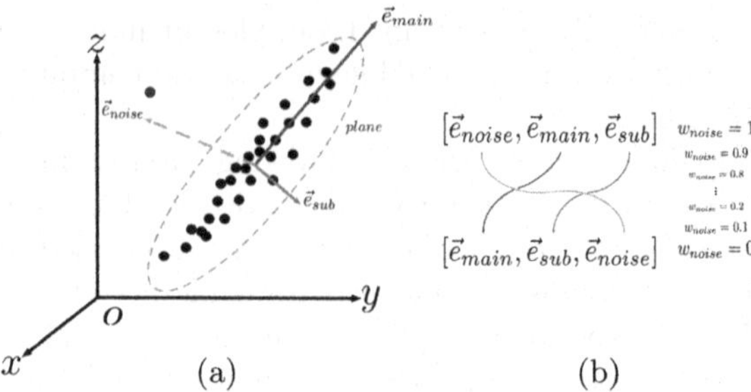

Fig. 1. Eigenvector switching. (a) 3D points lying on a plane in black and distant outlier in red. (b) When the weights assigned to all the points are one, the eigenvector corresponding to the smallest eigenvalue is $\mathbf{e}_{sub}$, the vector shown in blue in (a), and on the right in the top portion of (b), where we sort the eigenvectors by decreasing eigenvalue. As the optimization progresses and the weight assigned to the outlier decreases, the eigenvector corresponding to the smallest eigenvalue switches to $\mathbf{e}_{noise}$, the vector shown in green in (a), which introduces a sharp change in the gradient values. (Color figure online)

implementation of singular- and eigen-value decomposition provided in TensorFlow results in either the learning procedure not converging or in significantly worse performance.

2 Motivation

To illustrate the problems associated with differentiating eigenvectors and eigenvalues, consider the outlier rejection toy example depicted by Fig. 1. The inputs are 3D points lying on a plane and drawn in black, and an outlier 3D point shown in red, which we assume to be very far from the plane. Suppose we want to assign a binary weight to each point (1 for inliers, 0 for outliers) such that the eigenvector corresponding to the smallest eigenvalue of the weighted covariance matrix is close to the ground-truth one in the least-square sense. When the weight assigned to the outlier is 0, it would be $\mathbf{e}_{noise}$, which is also the normal to the plane and is shown in green. However, if at some point during optimization, typically at initialization, we assign the weight 1 to the outlier, $\mathbf{e}_{noise}$ will correspond to the largest eigenvalue instead of the smallest, and the eigenvector corresponding to the smallest eigenvalue will be the vector $\mathbf{e}_{sub}$ shown in blue, which is perpendicular to $\mathbf{e}_{noise}$. As a result, if we initially set all weights to 1 and optimize them so that the smallest eigenvector approaches the plane normal, the gradient values will depend on the coordinates of $\mathbf{e}_{sub}$. At one point during the optimization, if everything goes well, the weight assigned to the outlier will become small enough so that the smallest eigenvector switches from being $\mathbf{e}_{sub}$ to being $\mathbf{e}_{noise}$, which introduces a large jump in the gradient vector whose values will now depend on the coordinates of $\mathbf{e}_{noise}$ instead of $\mathbf{e}_{sub}$.

In this simple case, this kind of instability does not preclude eventual convergence. However, in more complex situations, we found that it does, as evidenced by our experiments. This problem was already noted in [37] in the context of learning keypoint correspondences. To circumvent this issue, the algorithm in [37] had to first rely on a classification loss to determine the potential inlier correspondences before incorporating the loss based on the essential matrix to impose geometric constraints, which requires eigendecomposition. This ensured that the network weights were already good enough to prevent eigenvector switching when starting to minimize the geometry-based loss.

3 Related Work

In recent years, the need to integrate geometric methods and mathematical tools into Deep Learning frameworks has led to the reformulation of a number of them in network terms. For example, [17] considers spatial transformations of image regions with CNNs. The set of such transformations is extended in [10]. In a different context, [24] derives a differentiation of the Cholesky decomposition that could be integrated in Deep Learning frameworks.

Unfortunately, the set of geometric Computer Vision problems that these methods can handle remains relatively limited. In particular, there is no widely accepted deep-learning way to solve the many geometric problems that reduce to finding least-square solution of linear systems. In this work, we consider two such problems: Computing the essential matrix from keypoint correspondences in an image pair and estimating the 3D pose of an object from 3D-to-2D correspondences, both of which we briefly discuss below.

Estimating the Essential Matrix from Correspondences. The eigenvalue-based solution to this problem has been known for decades [11,12,23] and remains the standard way to compute Essential matrices [25]. The real focus of research in this area has been to establish reliable keypoint correspondences and to eliminate outliers. In this context, variations of RANSAC [7], such as MLESAC [33] and Least median of squared (LMeds) [29], and very recently GMS [2], have become popular. For a comprehensive study of such methods, we refer the interested reader to [28]. With the emergence of Deep Learning, there has been a trend towards moving away from this decades-old knowledge and apply instead a black-box approach where a Deep Network is trained to directly estimate the rotation and translation matrices [34,38] without *a priori* geometrical knowledge. The very recent work of [37] attempts to reconcile these two opposing trends by embedding the geometric constraints into a Deep Net and has demonstrated superior performance for this task when the correspondences are hard to establish.

Estimating 3D Pose from 3D-to-2D Correspondences. This is known as the Perspective-n-Point (PnP) problem. It has also been investigated for decades and is also amenable to an eigendecomposition-based solution [11], many variations of which have been proposed over the years [6,19,21,40]. DSAC [3] is the only approach we know of that integrates the PnP solver into a Deep Network. As explicitly differentiating through the PnP solver is not optimization friendly, the authors apply the log trick used in the reinforcement learning literature. This amounts to using a numerical approximation of the derivative from random samples, which is not ideal, given that an analytical alternative exists. Moreover, DSAC only works for grid configurations and known scenes. By contrast, the method we propose in this work has an analytical form, with no need for stochastic sampling.

Differentiating the Eigen- and Singular Value Decomposition. Whether computing the essential matrix, estimating 3D pose, or solving any other least-squares problem, incorporating an eigendecomposition-solver into a deep network requires differentiating the eigendecomposition. Expressions for such derivatives have been given in [9,26] and reformulated in terms that are compatible with back-propagation in [16]. Specifically, as shown in [16], for a matrix $\mathbf{M}$ written as $\mathbf{M} = \mathbf{U\Sigma U}^T$, the variations of the eigenvectors $\mathbf{U}$ with respect to the matrix, used to compute derivatives, are

$$d\mathbf{U} = 2\mathbf{U}\left(\mathbf{K} \odot (\mathbf{U}^T d\mathbf{M}\mathbf{U})_{sym}\right), \tag{1}$$

where $\mathbf{S}_{sym} = \frac{1}{2}(\mathbf{S}^T + \mathbf{S})$, and

$$\mathbf{K}_{ij} = \begin{cases} \frac{1}{\sigma_i - \sigma_j}, & i \neq j \\ 0, & i = j \end{cases}. \tag{2}$$

As can be seen from Eq. 2, if two eigenvalues are equal, that is, $\sigma_i = \sigma_j$, the denominator becomes 0, thus creating numerical instabilities. The same can be said about singular value decomposition.

A solution to this was proposed in [26], and singular- and eigen-value decomposition have been used within deep networks for problems where all the singular values are used and their order is irrelevant [14,15]. In the context of spectral clustering, the approach of [20] also proposed a solution that eliminates the need for explicit eigendecomposition. This solution, however, was dedicated to the scenario where one seeks to use all non-zero eigenvalues, assuming a matrix of constant rank.

Here, by contrast, we tackle problems where what matters is a single eigen- or singular-value. In this case, the order of the eigenvalues is important. However, this order can change during training, which results in a non-differentiable switch from one eigenvector to another, as in the toy example of Sect. 2. In turn, this leads to numerical instabilities, which can prevent convergence. In [37], this problem is finessed by first training the network using a classification loss that does not depend on eigenvectors. Only once a sufficiently good solution is found, that is, a solution close enough to the correct one for vector switching not to happen anymore, is the loss term that depends on the eigenvector associated to the smallest eigenvalue turned on. As we will show later, we can achieve state-of-the-art results without the need for such a heuristic, by deriving a more robust, eigendecomposition-free loss function.

4 Our Approach

We introduce an approach that enables us to work with eigenvectors corresponding to zero eigenvalues within an end-to-end learning formalism, while being subject to neither the gradient instabilities due to vector switching discussed in Sect. 2 nor to difficulties caused by repeated eigenvalues. To this end, we derive a loss function that directly operates on the matrix whose eigen- or singular-vectors we are interested in but without explicitly performing an SVD or ED.

Below, we first discuss the generic scenario in which the matrix of interest directly is the output of the network. We then consider the slightly more involved case where the network predicts weights that themselves define the matrix, which corresponds to our application scenarios. Note that, while we discuss our approach in the context of Deep Learning, it is applicable to *any* optimization framework where one seeks to optimize a loss function based on the smallest eigenvector of a matrix with respect to the parameters that defining this matrix.

4.1 Generic Scenario

Given an input measurement $\mathbf{x}$, let us denote by $f_\theta(\mathbf{x})$ the output of a deep network with parameters θ. Here, we consider the case where the output of the network is a matrix, which we write as $\mathbf{A}_\theta = f_\theta(\mathbf{x})$. Our goal is to tackle problems where the loss function of the network depends on the smallest eigenvector $\mathbf{e}_\theta$ of $\mathbf{A}_\theta^T\mathbf{A}_\theta$, which ensures that the matrix is symmetric.

Typically, one can use an ℓ_2 loss of the form $\|\mathbf{e}_\theta - \tilde{\mathbf{e}}\|^2$, where $\tilde{\mathbf{e}}$ is the ground-truth smallest eigenvector. The standard approach to addressing this, as followed in [16,37], consists of explicitly differentiating this loss w.r.t. $\mathbf{e}_\theta$, then $\mathbf{e}_\theta$ w.r.t. $\mathbf{A}_\theta$ and finally $\mathbf{A}_\theta$ w.r.t. θ via backpropagation. As discussed above, however, this is not optimization friendly.

To overcome this, we propose to define a new loss motivated by the linear equation that defines eigenvectors and eigenvalues. Specifically, if $\mathbf{e}_\theta$ is an eigenvector of $\mathbf{A}_\theta^T\mathbf{A}_\theta$ with eigenvalue λ, it satisfies $\mathbf{A}_\theta^T\mathbf{A}_\theta\mathbf{e}_\theta = \lambda\mathbf{e}_\theta$. Since eigenvectors have unit-norm, i.e., $\mathbf{e}_\theta^T\mathbf{e}_\theta = 1$, multiplying both sides of this equation from the left by $\mathbf{e}_\theta^T$ yields

$$\mathbf{e}_\theta^T\mathbf{A}_\theta^T\mathbf{A}_\theta\mathbf{e}_\theta = \lambda. \tag{3}$$

In this paper, we consider zero eigenvalue problems, that is, $\lambda = 0$. Since $\mathbf{A}_\theta^T\mathbf{A}_\theta$ is positive semi-definite, we have that $\mathbf{e}^T\mathbf{A}_\theta^T\mathbf{A}_\theta\mathbf{e} \geq 0$ for any $\mathbf{e}$. Given the ground-truth eigenvector $\tilde{\mathbf{e}}$ that we seek to predict, this lets us define the loss function

$$L_{eig}(\theta) = \tilde{\mathbf{e}}^T\mathbf{A}_\theta^T\mathbf{A}_\theta\tilde{\mathbf{e}}. \tag{4}$$

Intuitively, this loss aims to find the parameters θ such that $\tilde{\mathbf{e}}$ is an eigenvector of the resulting matrix $\mathbf{A}_\theta^T\mathbf{A}_\theta$ with minimum eigenvalue, that is, zero in our case, assuming that we can truly reach the global minimum of our loss. However, this loss alone has multiple, globally-optimal solutions, including the trivial one $\mathbf{A}_\theta = 0$.

To address this, we note that this trivial solution has not only one zero eigenvalue corresponding to eigenvector $\tilde{\mathbf{e}}$, but that all its eigenvalues are zero. Since, in practice, we typically search for matrices that have a single zero eigenvalue, we propose to maximize the projection of the data along the directions orthogonal to $\tilde{\mathbf{e}}$. Such a projection can be achieved by making use of the orthogonal complement to $\tilde{\mathbf{e}}$, given by $(\mathbf{I} - \tilde{\mathbf{e}}\tilde{\mathbf{e}}^T)$, where $\mathbf{I}$ is the identity matrix. By defining $\bar{\mathbf{A}}_\theta = \mathbf{A}_\theta(\mathbf{I} - \tilde{\mathbf{e}}\tilde{\mathbf{e}}^T)$, we can then re-write our loss function as

$$\tilde{L}(\theta) = \tilde{\mathbf{e}}^T \mathbf{A}_\theta^T \mathbf{A}_\theta \tilde{\mathbf{e}} - \alpha \mathrm{tr}\left(\bar{\mathbf{A}}_\theta^T \bar{\mathbf{A}}_\theta\right), \tag{5}$$

where $\mathrm{tr}(\cdot)$ computes the trace of a matrix and α sets the relative influence of the two terms. Note that we can apply the same strategy to cases where multiple eigenvalues are zero, by reducing the orthogonal space to only the directions corresponding to non-zero eigenvalues, and introducing the first term for all eigenvectors whose eigenvalues we want to be zero.

For numerical stability, we further propose to bound the second term in the range $[0, 1]$. To do so, we therefore re-write our loss as

$$L(\theta) = \tilde{\mathbf{e}}^T \mathbf{A}_\theta^T \mathbf{A}_\theta \tilde{\mathbf{e}} + \alpha \exp\left(-\beta \mathrm{tr}\left(\bar{\mathbf{A}}_\theta^T \bar{\mathbf{A}}_\theta\right)\right), \tag{6}$$

where β is a scalar. This loss is fully differentiable, and can thus be used to learn the parameters θ of a deep network. Since it does not explicitly depend on performing an eigendecomposition at every iteration of the optimization, it suffers from neither the eigenvector switching problem, nor the non-unique eigenvalue problem.

4.2 Learning to Predict Weights

In practice, the problem of interest is often more constrained than training a network to directly output a matrix $\mathbf{A}_\theta$. In particular, in this paper, we consider problems where the goal is to predict a weight w_i for each element of the input. This typically leads to formulations where $\mathbf{A}_\theta^T \mathbf{A}_\theta$ has the form $\mathbf{X}^T\mathbf{W}\mathbf{X}$, with $\mathbf{X}$ a data matrix and $\mathbf{W}$ a diagonal matrix whose elements are the w_is. Below, we introduce the formulation for each of the applications in our experiments.

Outlier Rejection with 3D Points. To show that we can indeed back-propagate nicely through the proposed loss formulation where directly using the analytical gradient fails, we first briefly revisit the toy outlier rejection problem used to motivate our approach in Sect. 1. For this experiment, we do not train a Deep Network, or perform any learning procedure. Instead, given N 3D points $\mathbf{x}_i$, including inliers and outliers, we directly optimize the weight w_i of each point. At every step of optimization, given the current weight values, we compute the weighted mean of the points $\mu = \frac{1}{\sum_{i=1}^N w_i} \sum_{i=1}^N w_i \mathbf{x}_i$. Let $\mathbf{X}$ be the $3 \times N$ matrix of mean-subtracted 3D points. We then compute the weighted covariance matrix $\mathbf{C} = \mathbf{X}^T\mathbf{W}\mathbf{X}$, where $\mathbf{W}$ is a diagonal matrix whose elements are the w_is. The smallest eigenvector of $\mathbf{C}$ then defines the direction of noise.

Given the ground-truth such eigenvector $\tilde{\mathbf{e}}$, let $\bar{\mathbf{X}} = \mathbf{I} - \tilde{\mathbf{e}}\tilde{\mathbf{e}}^T$. We adapt the general formulation of Eq. 6 and formulate the outlier rejection problem as

$$\underset{\mathbf{W}}{\text{minimize}} \ \tilde{\mathbf{e}}^T \mathbf{X}^T \mathbf{W} \mathbf{X} \tilde{\mathbf{e}} \ + \alpha \exp\left(-\beta tr(\bar{\mathbf{X}}^T \mathbf{W} \bar{\mathbf{X}})\right). \quad (7)$$

Note that this translates directly to Eq. 6 by defining $\mathbf{A}_\theta = \mathbf{W}^{\frac{1}{2}} \bar{\mathbf{X}}$, where $\mathbf{W}^{\frac{1}{2}}$ is a diagonal matrix with elements $\sqrt{w_i}$.

Keypoint Matching with the Essential Matrix. For this task, to isolate the effect of the loss function only, we followed the same setup as in [37]. Specifically, we used the same network architecture as in [37], which takes C correspondences between two 2D points as input and outputs a C-dimensional vector of weights, that is, one weight for each correspondence. Formally, let

$$\mathbf{q}_i = \left[u_i, v_i, u_i', v_i'\right]^T, \quad (8)$$

encode the coordinates of correspondence i in the two images. Following the 8 points algorithm [23], we construct as matrix $\mathbf{X} \in \mathbb{R}^{C \times 9}$, each row of which is computed from one correspondence vector $\mathbf{q}_i$ as

$$\mathbf{X}^{(i)} = [u_i u_i', u_i v_i, u_i, v_i u_i', v_i v_i', v_i, u_i', v_i', 1], \quad (9)$$

where $\mathbf{X}^{(i)}$ denotes row i of $\mathbf{X}$. A weighted version of the 8 points algorithm [39] then computes the essential matrix as the smallest eigenvector of $\mathbf{X}^T \mathbf{W} \mathbf{X}$, with $\mathbf{W}$ the diagonal matrix of weights.

Let $\bar{\mathbf{X}} = \mathbf{X}(\mathbf{I} - \tilde{\mathbf{e}}\tilde{\mathbf{e}}^T)$, where $\tilde{\mathbf{e}}$ is the ground-truth eigenvector representing the true essential matrix. We write our eigendecomposition-free essential loss as

$$L(\mathbf{W}) = \tilde{\mathbf{e}}^T \mathbf{X}^T \mathbf{W} \mathbf{X} \tilde{\mathbf{e}} + \alpha \exp\left(-\beta \text{tr}\left(\bar{\mathbf{X}}^T \mathbf{W} \bar{\mathbf{X}}\right)\right). \quad (10)$$

Given a set of training samples, consisting of N image pairs with ground-truth essential matrices, we can then use this loss, instead of the classification loss or essential loss of [37], to train a network to predict the weights.

Note that, as suggested by [11] and done in [37], we use the 2D coordinates normalized to $[-1, 1]$ using the camera intrinsics as input to the network.

When calculating the loss, as suggested by [12], we move the centroid of the reference points to the origin of the coordinate system and scale the points so that their RMS distance to the origin is equal to $\sqrt{2}$. This means that we also have to scale and translate $\tilde{\mathbf{e}}$ accordingly.

3D-to-2D Correspondences for Pose Estimation. The goal of this problem, also known as the Perspective-n-Point (PnP) problem [21], is to determine the absolute pose (rotation and translation) of a calibrated camera, given known 3D points and corresponding 2D image points.

For this task, as we are still dealing with sparse correspondences, we use the same network architecture as for 2D-to-2D correspondences, except that we now have one additional input dimension, since we have *3D*-to-2D correspondences.

This network takes C correspondences between 3D and 2D points as input and outputs a C-dimensional vector of weights, one for each correspondence.

Mathematically, we can denote the input correspondences as

$$\mathbf{q}_i = [x_i, y_i, z_i, u_i, v_i]^T, \tag{11}$$

where x_i, y_i, z_i are the coordinates of a 3D point, and u_i, v_i denote the corresponding image location. According to [11], we have

$$f_{scale} \begin{bmatrix} u_i \\ v_i \\ 1 \end{bmatrix} = [\mathbf{R}, \mathbf{t}] \begin{bmatrix} x_i \\ y_i \\ z_i \\ 1 \end{bmatrix} = \begin{bmatrix} p_1 & p_2 & p_3 & p_4 \\ p_5 & p_6 & p_7 & p_8 \\ p_9 & p_{10} & p_{11} & p_{12} \end{bmatrix} \begin{bmatrix} x_i \\ y_i \\ z_i \\ 1 \end{bmatrix}. \tag{12}$$

To recover the pose, we then follow the Direct Linear Transform (DLT) method [11]. This consists of constructing the matrix $\mathbf{X} \in \mathbb{R}^{2C \times 12}$, every two rows of which are computed from one correspondence $\mathbf{q}_i$ as

$$\begin{bmatrix} \mathbf{X}^{(2i-1)} \\ \mathbf{X}^{(2i)} \end{bmatrix} = \begin{bmatrix} x_i \; y_i \; z_i \; 1 \; 0 & 0 & 0 & 0 & -u_i x_i & -u_i y_i & -u_i z_i & -u_i \\ 0 & 0 & 0 & 0 \; x_i \; y_i \; z_i \; 1 & -v_i x_i & -v_i y_i & -v_i z_i & -v_i \end{bmatrix}, \tag{13}$$

where $\mathbf{X}^{(i)}$ denotes row i of $\mathbf{X}$. Then, the solution of the weighted PnP problem can be obtained as the eigenvector of $\mathbf{X}^T\mathbf{W}\mathbf{X}$ corresponding to the smallest eigenvalue. Therefore, we can define a PnP loss similar to the one of Eq. 10 for 2D-to-2D correspondences, but with $\mathbf{X}$ defined as discussed above, and, given N training samples, each consisting of a set of 3D-to-2D correspondences with corresponding ground-truth eigenvector encoding the pose, train a network to predict weights such that we obtain the correct pose via DLT. As in the 2D-to-2D case, we use the normalized coordinate system for the 2D coordinates.

Note that the characteristics of the rotation matrix, that is, orthogonality and determinant 1, are not preserved by the DLT solution. Therefore, to make the result a valid rotation matrix, we refine the DLT results by the generalized Procrustes algorithm [8,30], which is a common post-processing technique for PnP algorithms. Note that this step is not involved during training, but only in the validation process to select the best model and at test time.

5 Experiments

We now present our results for the three tasks discussed above, that is, plane fitting as in Sect. 2, distinguishing good keypoint correspondences from bad ones, and solving the Perspective-n-Point (PnP) problem. We rely on a TensorFlow implementation using the Adam [18] optimizer, with a learning rate of 10^{-4}, unless stated otherwise, and default parameters. When training a network for keypoint matching and PnP, we used mini-batches of 32 samples and, in the plane fitting case, we also tested vanilla gradient descent.

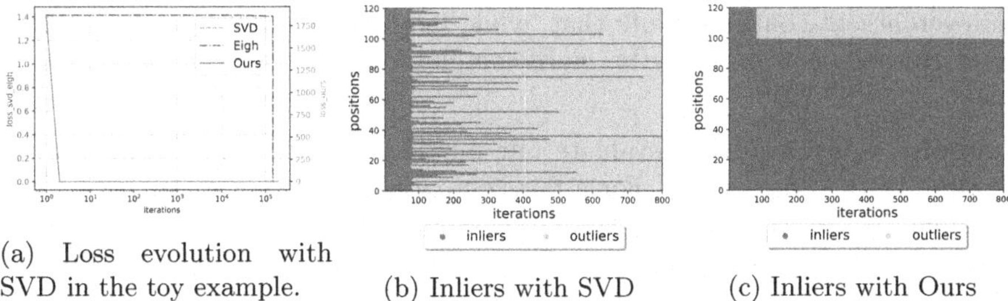

(a) Loss evolution with SVD in the toy example. (b) Inliers with SVD (c) Inliers with Ours

Fig. 2. Plane fitting in the presence of one or multiple outliers. We report results for Singular Value Decomposition (SVD), self-adjoint Eigendecomposition (Eigh), and for our loss function. For each loss, we tried multiple learning rates within the range $[10^{-5}, 1]$ and report the best results in terms of convergence. (a) Loss evolution with a single outlier. (b) With multiple outliers, the SVD baseline discards many inliers (Positions 1 to 100 are true inliers), while accepting outliers. By contrast, as shown in (c), our approach correctly rejects the outliers and accepts the inliers.

Plane Fitting. The setup is the one discussed in Sect. 2. We randomly sampled 100 3D points on the $z = 1$ plane. Specifically, we uniformly sampled $x \in [0, 40]$ and $y \in [0, 2]$. We then added zero-mean Gaussian noise with standard deviation 0.001 in the z dimension. We also generated outliers in a similar way, where x and y are uniformly sampled in the same range, and z is sampled from a Gaussian distribution with mean 50 and standard deviation 5. For the baselines that directly use the analytical gradients of SVD and ED, we take the objective function to be $\min \|\mathbf{e}_{min}(\mathbf{w}) \pm \mathbf{e}_{gt}\|_2$, where $\mathbf{e}_{min}(\mathbf{w})$ is the minimum eigenvector of $\mathbf{X}^\top \mathbf{W} \mathbf{X}$ in Eq. 7 and $\mathbf{e}_{gt}$ is the ground-truth noise direction, which is also the plane normal and is the vector $[0, 0, 1]$ in this case. Note that we consider both $+\mathbf{e}_{gt}$ and $-\mathbf{e}_{gt}$ and take the minimum distance, denoted by the $\pm$ and the min in the loss function. For this problem, both solutions are correct due to the sign ambiguity of ED, which should be taken into account.

We consider two ways of computing analytical gradients, one using the SVD and the other the self-adjoint eigendecomposition (Eigh), which both yield mathematically valid solutions. To implement our approach, we rely on Eq. 7.

Figure 2(a) shows the evolution of the loss as the optimization proceeds when using vanilla gradient descent and with a single outlier. Note that SVD and Eigh have exactly the same behavior because they constitute two equivalent ways of solving the same problem. Using gradient descent in conjunction with either one initially yields a very slow decrease in the loss function, until it suddenly drops to zero after millions of iterations, when a switch of the eigenvector with the smallest eigenvalue occurs. By contrast, our approach produces a much more gradual decrease in the loss.

We also evaluate the behavior of our method and the baselines in the presence of more outliers. Both our method and the baseline present the same convergence patterns as before, but, as shown in Fig. 2 (b and c), our approach correctly recovers the inliers and outliers, while the SVD baseline discards many outliers and even accepts outliers. Note that, while in this example the SVD- or Eigh-based methods converge, in the more complex cases below, this is not always true.

Keypoint Matching. To evaluate our method on a real-world problem, we use the SUN3D dataset [36]. For a fair comparison, we trained our network on the same data as [37], that is, the "brown-bm-3-05" sequence, and evaluate it on the test sequences used for testing in [34,37]. Additionally, to show that our method is not overfitting, we also test on a completely different dataset, the "fountain-P11" and "Herz-Jesus-P8" sequences of [32].

We follow the evaluation protocol of [37], which constitutes the state-of-the-art in keypoint matching, and only change the loss function to our own loss of Eq. 10. We use $\alpha = 10$ and $\beta = 10^{-3}$, which we empirically found to work well for 2D-to-2D keypoint matching. We compare our method against that of [37], both in its original implementation that involves minimizing a classification loss first and then without that initial step, which we denote as "Essential_Only". The latter is designed to show how critical the initial classification-based minimization of [37] is. In addition, we also compare against standard RANSAC [4], LMeds [31], MLESAC [33], and GMS [2] to provide additional reference points. We do this in terms of the performance metric used in [37] and referred to as mean Average Precision (mAP). This metric is computed by observing the ratio of accurately recovered poses given a certain maximum threshold, and taking the area under the curve of this graph.

We summarize the results in Fig. 3. Our approach performs on par with [37], the state-of-the-art method for keypoint matching, and outperforms all the other baselines, without the need of any pre-training. Importantly, "Essential_Only" severely underperforms and even often fails completely. In short, instead of having to find a workaround to the eigenvector switching problem as in [37], we can directly optimize our objective function, which is far more generally applicable. Furthermore, the workaround in [37] would converge to a sub-optimal solution, as it the classification loss depends on a user-selected decision boundary, that is, a heuristic definition of inliers. By contrast, our method can simply discover the inliers automatically while training, thanks to the second term in Eq. 6.

In the bottom row of Fig. 3, we compare the correspondences classified as inlier by our method to those of RANSAC on image pairs from the dataset of [32] and SUN3D, respectively. Note that even the correspondences that are misclassified as inliers by our approach are very close to being inliers. By contrast, RANSAC yields much larger errors.

PnP. Following standard practice for evaluating PnP algorithms [6,21], we generate a synthetic dataset composed of 3D-to-2D correspondences with noise and outliers. Each training example comprises two thousand 3D points, and we set the ground-truth translation of the camera pose $\mathbf{t}_{gt}$ to be their centroid. We then create a random ground-truth rotation $\mathbf{R}_{gt}$, and project the 3D points to the image plane of our virtual camera. As in REPPnP [6], we apply Gaussian noise with a standard deviation of 5 to these projections. We generate random outliers by assigning 3D points to arbitrary valid 2D image positions.

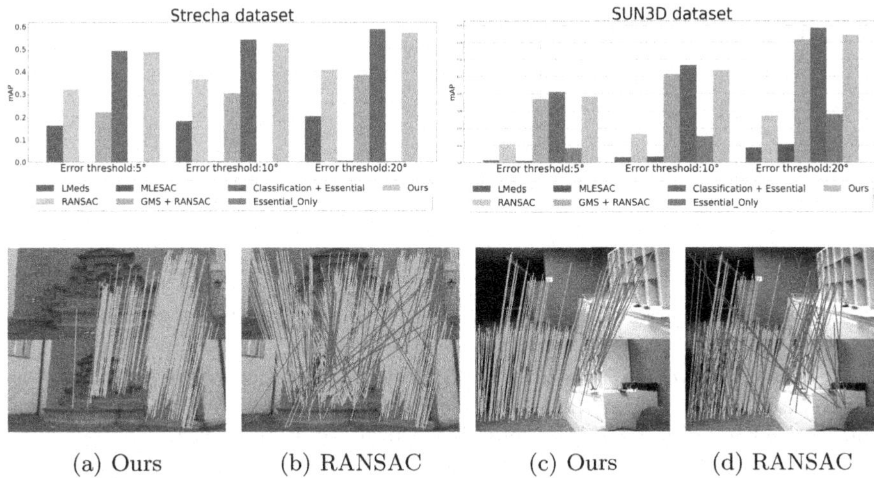

(a) Ours (b) RANSAC (c) Ours (d) RANSAC

Fig. 3. Results for the keypoint matching task. Note the significant performance gap between "Essential_Only", which utilizes eigendecomposition directly, and our approach. (Bottom left two images) Comparison of our results with RANSAC results on the "fountain-P11" image pair of [32]. (Bottom right two images) Similar comparison on the "brown-bm-3-05" image pair of SUN3D. We display the correspondences that the algorithms labeled as inliers. True positives are shown in green and false ones in red. The false positives of our approach are still close to being correct, while those of RANSAC are truly wrong. (Color figure online)

We train a neural network with the same architecture as in the keypoint matching case, except that it now takes 3D-to-2D correspondences as input. We empirically found that $\alpha = 1$ and $\beta = 5 \times 10^{-3}$ works well for this task. During training, to learn to be robust to outliers, we randomly select between 100 and 1000 of the two thousand matches and turn them into outliers. In other words, the two thousand training matches will contain a random number of outliers that our network will learn to filter out.

We compare our method against modern PnP methods, EPnP [21], OPnP [40], PPnP [8], RPnP [22] and REPPnP [6]. We also evaluate the DLT [11], since our loss formulation is based on it. Among these methods, REPPnP is the one most specifically designed to handle outliers. As in the keypoint matching case, we tried to compute the results of a network relying explicitly on eigendecomposition and minimizing the ℓ_2 norm of the difference between the ground-truth eigenvector and the predicted one. However, we found that such a network was unable to converge. We also report the performance of two commonly used baselines that leverage RANSAC [7], P3P [19]+RANSAC and EPnP+RANSAC. For other methods, RANSAC did not bring noticeable improvements, and we omitted them in the graph for better visual clarity.

For this comparison, we use standard rotation and translation error metrics [5]. Specifically, we report the closest arc distance in radians for the rotation

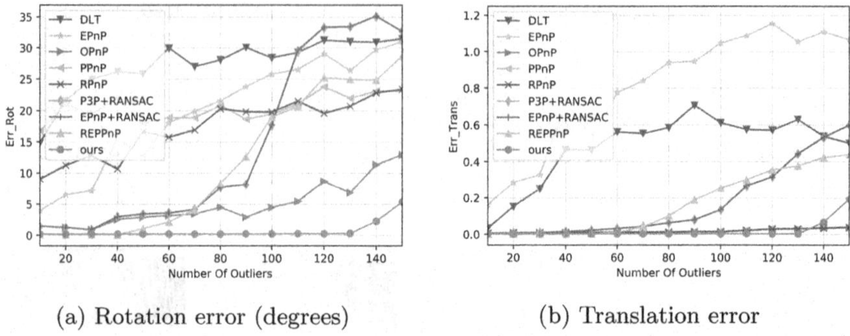

(a) Rotation error (degrees) (b) Translation error

Fig. 4. Quantitative PnP results. Rotation and translation errors for our method and several baselines. Our method gives extremely stable results despite the abundance of outliers, whereas all compared methods perform significantly worse as the number of outliers increases. Even when these methods perform well on either rotation or translation, they do not perform well on both. By contrast, Ours yields near zero errors for both measures up to 130 outliers (i.e., 65%).

matrix measured using quaternions, and the distance between the translation vectors normalized by the ground truth. To demonstrate the effect of outliers at test time, we fix the number of matches to 200 and vary the number of outliers from 10 to 150. We run each experiment 100 times and report the average.

Figure 4 summarizes the results. We outperform all other methods significantly, especially when the number of outliers increases. REPPnP is the one competing method that seems least affected. As long as the number of outliers is small, it is on a par with us but passed a certain point—when there are more than 40 outliers, that is, 20% of the total—its performance, particularly in terms of rotation error, decreases quickly whereas ours does not.

We evaluated our PnP approach on the real dataset of [13]. Specifically, the 3D points in this dataset were obtained using the SfM algorithm of [35], which also provides a rotation matrix and translation vector for each image. We treat these rotations and translations as ground truth to compare different PnP algorithms. Given a pair of images, we extract SIFT features at the reprojection of the 3D points in one image, and match these features to SIFT keypoints detected in the other image. This procedure produces erroneous correspondences, which a robust PnP algorithm should discard. In this example, we used the model trained on the synthetic data described before. Note that we apply the model **without any fine-tuning**, that is, the model is only trained with purely synthetic data. We observed that, except for EPnP+RANSAC, OPnP and P3P+RANSAC, the predictions of the baselines are far from the ground truth, which led to points reprojecting outside the image. In Fig. 5, we compare the reprojection of the 3D points on the input image after applying the rotation and translation obtained with our model and with EPnP+RANSAC. Note our better accuracy.

Fig. 5. Qualitive PnP results. Top: Two pairs of images (Left: Reichstag, Right: Notre-dame). For each pair, we seek to estimate the pose in the second image. Bottom: For each pair, we show in gray the reprojection of the 3D point cloud after applying the rotation and translation predicted by our model and EPnP+RANSAC, respectively. The red dots correspond to the ground-truth locations. Note that our model's predictions cover the ground truth much more closely than the baseline. (Color figure online)

6 Conclusion

We have introduced a novel approach to training deep networks that rely on losses computed from an eigenvector corresponding to a zero eigenvalue of a matrix defined by the network's output. Our loss does not suffer from the numerical instabilities of analytical differentiation of eigendecomposition, and converges to the correct solution much faster. Our approach achieves the state-of-the-art results on the tasks of keypoint matching and outlier rejection for the PnP problem.

Many Computer Vision tasks rely on least-square solutions to linear systems. We will therefore investigate the use of our approach for other ones. Furthermore, we hope that our work will contribute to imbuing Deep Learning techniques with traditional Computer Vision knowledge, thus avoiding discarding decades of valuable research, and develop more principled frameworks.

Acknowledgements. This research was partially supported by the National Natural Science Foundation of China: Grant 61603291, the program for introducing talents of discipline to university B13043 and the National Science, Technology Major Project: 2018ZX01008103, and by a grant from the Swiss Innovation Agency (CTI/InnoSuisse). This work was performed while Zheng Dang was visiting the CVLab at EPFL.

References

1. Abadi, M., et al.: TensorFlow: a system for large-scale machine learning. In: USENIX Conference on Operating Systems Design and Implementation, pp. 265–283 (2016)
2. Bian, J., Lin, W., Matsushita, Y., Yeung, S., Nguyen, T., Cheng, M.: GMS: grid-based motion statistics for fast, ultra-robust feature correspondence. In: CVPR (2017)

3. Brachmann, E., et al.: DSAC - differentiable RANSAC for camera localization. ArXiv (2016)
4. Cantzler, H.: RANdom Sample Consensus (RANSAC) (2005). cVonline
5. Crivellaro, A., Rad, M., Verdie, Y., Yi, K.M., Fua, P., Lepetit, V.: Robust 3D object tracking from monocular images using stable parts. PAMI **40**, 1465–1479 (2018)
6. Ferraz, L., Binefa, X., Moreno-noguer, F.: Very fast solution to the PnP problem with algebraic outlier rejection. In: CVPR, pp. 501–508 (2014)
7. Fischler, M., Bolles, R.: Random sample consensus: a paradigm for model fitting with applications to image analysis and automated cartography. Commun. ACM **24**(6), 381–395 (1981)
8. Garro, V., Crosilla, F., Fusiello, A.: Solving the PnP problem with anisotropic orthogonal procrustes analysis. In: 3DPVT, pp. 262–269 (2012)
9. Giles, M.: Collected matrix derivative results for forward and reverse mode algorithmic differentiation. In: Bischof, C.H., Bücker, H.M., Hovland, P., Naumann, U., Utke, J. (eds.) Advances in Automatic Differentiation. LNCSE, vol. 64, pp. 35–44. Springer, Heidelberg (2008). https://doi.org/10.1007/978-3-540-68942-3_4
10. Handa, A., Bloesch, M., Pătrăucean, V., Stent, S., McCormac, J., Davison, A.: GVNN: neural network library for geometric computer vision. In: Hua, G., Jégou, H. (eds.) ECCV 2016. LNCS, vol. 9915, pp. 67–82. Springer, Cham (2016). https://doi.org/10.1007/978-3-319-49409-8_9
11. Hartley, R., Zisserman, A.: Multiple View Geometry in Computer Vision. Cambridge University Press, Cambridge (2000)
12. Hartley, R.: In defense of the eight-point algorithm. PAMI **19**(6), 580–593 (1997)
13. Heinly, J., Schoenberger, J., Dunn, E., Frahm, J.M.: Reconstructing the world in six days. In: CVPR (2015)
14. Huang, G., Liu, Z., Weinberger, K., van der Maaten, L.: Densely connected convolutional networks. In: CVPR (2017)
15. Huang, Z., Wan, C., Probst, T., Gool, L.V.: Deep learning on lie groups for skeleton-based action recognition. In: CVPR, pp. 6099–6108 (2017)
16. Ionescu, C., Vantzos, O., Sminchisescu, C.: Matrix backpropagation for deep networks with structured layers (2015)
17. Jaderberg, M., Simonyan, K., Zisserman, A., Kavukcuoglu, K.: Spatial transformer networks. In: NIPS, pp. 2017–2025 (2015)
18. Kingma, D., Ba, J.: Adam: a method for stochastic optimisation. In: ICLR (2015)
19. Kneip, L., Scaramuzza, D., Siegwart, R.: A novel parametrization of the perspective-three-point problem for a direct computation of absolute camera position and orientation. In: CVPR, pp. 2969–2976 (2011)
20. Law, M., Urtasun, R., Zemel, R.S.: Deep spectral clustering learning. In: ICML, pp. 1985–1994 (2017)
21. Lepetit, V., Moreno-noguer, F., Fua, P.: EPnP: an accurate $o(n)$ solution to the PnP problem. IJCV (2009)
22. Li, S., Xu, C., Xie, M.: A robust O(n) solution to the perspective-n-point problem. PAMI **34**, 1444–1450 (2012)
23. Longuet-Higgins, H.: A computer algorithm for reconstructing a scene from two projections. Nature **293**, 133–135 (1981)
24. Murray, I.: Differentiation of the Cholesky decomposition. arXiv Preprint (2016)
25. Nister, D.: An efficient solution to the five-point relative pose problem. In: CVPR, June 2003

26. Papadopoulo, T., Lourakis, M.I.A.: Estimating the Jacobian of the singular value decomposition: theory and applications. In: Vernon, D. (ed.) ECCV 2000. LNCS, vol. 1842, pp. 554–570. Springer, Heidelberg (2000). https://doi.org/10.1007/3-540-45054-8_36
27. Paszke, A., et al.: Automatic differentiation in PyTorch. In: NIPS Autodiff Workshop (2017)
28. Raguram, R., Chum, O., Pollefeys, M., Matas, J., Frahm, J.M.: USAC: a universal framework for random sample consensus. PAMI **35**(8), 2022–2038 (2013)
29. Rousseeuw, P., Leroy, A.: Robust Regression and Outlier Detection. Wiley, New York (1987)
30. Schönemann, P.: A generalized solution of the orthogonal procrustes problem. Psychometrika **31**(1), 1–10 (1966)
31. Simpson, D.: Introduction to Rousseeuw (1984) least median of squares regression. In: Kotz, S., Johnson, N.L. (eds.) Breakthroughs in Statistics. SSS, pp. 433–461. Springer, New York (1997). https://doi.org/10.1007/978-1-4612-0667-5_18
32. Strecha, C., Hansen, W., Van Gool, L., Fua, P., Thoennessen, U.: On benchmarking camera calibration and multi-view stereo for high resolution imagery. In: CVPR (2008)
33. Torr, P., Zisserman, A.: MLESAC: a new robust estimator with application to estimating image geometry. CVIU **78**, 138–156 (2000)
34. Ummenhofer, B., et al.: DeMoN: depth and motion network for learning monocular stereo. In: CVPR (2017)
35. Wu, C.: Towards linear-time incremental structure from motion. In: 3DV (2013)
36. Xiao, J., Owens, A., Torralba, A.: SUN3D: a database of big spaces reconstructed using SFM and object labels. In: ICCV (2013)
37. Yi, K.M., Trulls, E., Ono, Y., Lepetit, V., Salzmann, M., Fua, P.: Learning to find good correspondences. In: CVPR (2018)
38. Zamir, A.R., Wekel, T., Agrawal, P., Wei, C., Malik, J., Savarese, S.: Generic 3D representation via pose estimation and matching. In: Leibe, B., Matas, J., Sebe, N., Welling, M. (eds.) ECCV 2016. LNCS, vol. 9907, pp. 535–553. Springer, Cham (2016). https://doi.org/10.1007/978-3-319-46487-9_33
39. Zhang, Z.: Determining the epipolar geometry and its uncertainty: a review. IJCV **27**(2), 161–195 (1998)
40. Zheng, Y., Kuang, Y., Sugimoto, S., Astrom, K., Okutomi, M.: Revisiting the PnP problem: a fast, general and optimal solution. In: ICCV (2013)

Visual Reasoning with Multi-hop Feature Modulation

Florian Strub[1(✉)], Mathieu Seurin[1], Ethan Perez[2,3], Harm de Vries[2], Jérémie Mary[4], Philippe Preux[1], Aaron Courville[2,5], and Olivier Pietquin[6]

[1] Univ. Lille, CNRS, Inria, UMR 9189 CRIStAL, Villeneuve-d'Ascq, France
florian.strub@inria.fr
[2] MILA, Université de Montréal, Montreal, Canada
[3] Rice University, Houston, USA
[4] Criteo, Paris, France
[5] CIFAR Fellow, Toronto, Canada
[6] Google Brain, Mountain View, USA

Abstract. Recent breakthroughs in computer vision and natural language processing have spurred interest in challenging multi-modal tasks such as visual question-answering and visual dialogue. For such tasks, one successful approach is to condition image-based convolutional network computation on language via Feature-wise Linear Modulation (FiLM) layers, i.e., per-channel scaling and shifting. We propose to generate the parameters of FiLM layers going up the hierarchy of a convolutional network in a multi-hop fashion rather than all at once, as in prior work. By alternating between attending to the language input and generating FiLM layer parameters, this approach is better able to scale to settings with longer input sequences such as dialogue. We demonstrate that multi-hop FiLM generation significantly outperforms prior state-of-the-art on the GuessWhat?! visual dialogue task and matches state-of-the art on the ReferIt object retrieval task, and we provide additional qualitative analysis.

Keywords: Deep learning · Computer vision · Multi-modal learning Natural language

1 Introduction

Computer vision has witnessed many impressive breakthroughs over the past decades in image classification [15,27], image segmentation [30], and object detection [12] by applying convolutional neural networks to large-scale, labeled datasets, often exceeding human performance. These systems give outputs such as class labels, segmentation masks, or bounding boxes, but it would be more natural for humans to interact with these systems through natural language. To this

Electronic supplementary material The online version of this chapter (https://doi.org/10.1007/978-3-030-01228-1_48) contains supplementary material, which is available to authorized users.

V. Ferrari et al. (Eds.): ECCV 2018, LNCS 11209, pp. 808–831, 2018.
https://doi.org/10.1007/978-3-030-01228-1_48

ReferIt	*GuessWhat?!*	
- The girl with a sweater	Is it a person?	Yes
- The fourth person	Is it a girl?	Yes
- The girl holding a white frisbee	Does she have a blue frisbee?	No

Fig. 1. The ReferIt and GuessWhat?! tasks. In ReferIt, a single expression identifies the selected object (with blue bounding box), while GuessWhat?! identifies objects through a sequence of yes/no questions. (Color figure online)

end, the research community has introduced various multi-modal tasks, such as image captioning [48], referring expressions [23], visual question-answering [1,34], visual reasoning [21], and visual dialogue [5,6].

These tasks require models to effectively integrate information from both vision and language. One common approach is to process both modalities independently with large unimodal networks before combining them through concatenation [34], element-wise product [25,31], or bilinear pooling [11]. Inspired by the success of attention in machine translation [3], several works have proposed to incorporate various forms of spatial attention to bias models towards focusing on question-specific image regions [47,48]. However, spatial attention sometimes only gives modest improvements over simple baselines for visual question answering [20] and can struggle on questions involving multi-step reasoning [21].

More recently, [38,44] introduced Feature-wise Linear Modulation (FiLM) layers as a promising approach for vision-and-language tasks. These layers apply a per-channel scaling and shifting to a convolutional network's visual features, conditioned on an external input such as language, *e.g.*, captions, questions, or full dialogues. Such feature-wise affine transformations allow models to dynamically highlight the key visual features for the task at hand. The parameters of FiLM layers which scale and shift features or feature maps are determined by a separate network, the so-called *FiLM generator*, which predicts these parameters using the external conditioning input. Within various architectures, FiLM has outperformed prior state-of-art for visual question-answering [38,44], multi-modal translation [7], and language-guided image segmentation [40].

However, the best way to design the FiLM generator is still an open question. For visual question-answering and visual reasoning, prior work uses single-hop FiLM generators that predict all FiLM parameters at once [38,44]. That is, a Recurrent Neural Network (RNN) sequentially processes input language tokens and then outputs all FiLM parameters via a Multi-Layer Perceptron (MLP). In this paper, we argue that using a *Multi-hop FiLM Generator* is better suited for tasks involving longer input sequences and multi-step reasoning such as dialogue. Even for shorter input sequence tasks, single-hop FiLM generators can require a large RNN to achieve strong performance; on the CLEVR visual reasoning task [21] which only involves a small vocabulary and templated questions, the FiLM generator in [38] uses an RNN with 4096 hidden units that comprises almost 90% of the model's parameters. Models with Multi-hop FiLM Generators may thus be easier to scale to more difficult tasks involving human-generated language involving larger vocabularies and more ambiguity.

As an intuitive example, consider the dialogue in Fig. 1 through which one speaker localizes the second girl in the image, the one who does not "have a blue frisbee". For this task, a single-hop model must determine upfront what steps of reasoning to carry out over the image and in what order; thus, it might decide in a single shot to highlight feature maps throughout the visual network detecting either non-blue colors or girls. In contrast, a multi-hop model may first determine the most immediate step of reasoning necessary (*i.e.*, locate the girls), highlight the relevant visual features, and then determine the next immediate step of reasoning necessary (*i.e.*, locate the blue frisbee), and so on. While it may be appropriate to reason in either way, the latter approach may scale better to longer language inputs and/or to ambiguous images where the full sequence of reasoning steps is hard to determine upfront, which can even be further enhanced by having intermediate feedback while processing the image.

In this paper, we therefore explore several approaches to generating FiLM parameters in multiple hops. These approaches introduce an intermediate context embedding that controls the language and visual processing, and they alternate between updating the context embedding via an attention mechanism over the language sequence (and optionally by incorporating image activations) and predicting the FiLM parameters. We evaluate our approach on ReferIt [23] and GuessWhat?! [6], two vision-and-language tasks illustrated in Fig. 1. We show that Multi-hop FiLM generation significantly outperforms single-hop FiLM models and prior state-of-the-art. For GuessWhat?!, our best model only updates the context embedding using the language input, while for ReferIt, incorporating visual feedback to update the context embedding improves performance.

In summary, this paper makes the following contributions:

- We introduce the Multi-hop FiLM architecture and demonstrate that our approach significantly improves or matches the state-of-the-art on the GuessWhat?! Oracle task, GuessWhat?! Guesser task and ReferIt Guesser task.
- We show that the Multi-hop FiLM architecture outperforms single-hop models on vision-and-language tasks involving complex visual reasoning.
- We find that including visual feedback into the context embedding of the Multi-hop FiLM Generator is helpful for tasks that do not include object category labels, such as ReferIt.

2 Background

In this section, we explain the prerequisites to understanding our model: RNNs, attention mechanisms, and FiLM. We subsequently use these building blocks to propose a Multi-hop FiLM model.

2.1 Language Processing

One common approach in natural language processing is to use an RNN to encode some linguistic input sequence l into a fixed-size embedding. The input (such as a question or dialogue) consists of a sequence of words $\omega_{1:T}$ of length T, where each word ω_t is contained within a predefined vocabulary $\mathcal{V}$. We embed each input token via a learned look-up table e and obtain a dense word-embedding $\boldsymbol{e}_{\omega_t} = e(\omega_t)$. The sequence of embeddings $\{\boldsymbol{e}_{\omega_t}\}_{t=1}^{T}$ is then fed to a RNN, which produces a sequence of hidden states $\{\boldsymbol{s}_t\}_{t=1}^{T}$ by repeatedly applying a transition function f: $\boldsymbol{s}_{t+1} = f(\boldsymbol{s}_t, \boldsymbol{e}_{\omega_t})$ To better handle long-term dependencies in the input sequence, we use a Gated Recurrent Unit (GRU) [4] with layer normalization [2] as transition function. In this work, we use a bidirectional GRU, which consists of one forward GRU, producing hidden states $\overrightarrow{\boldsymbol{s}_t}$ by running from ω_1 to ω_T, and a second backward GRU, producing states $\overleftarrow{\boldsymbol{s}_t}$ by running from ω_T to ω_1. We concatenate both unidirectional GRU states $\boldsymbol{s}_t = [\overrightarrow{\boldsymbol{s}_t}; \overleftarrow{\boldsymbol{s}_t}]$ at each step t to get a final GRU state, which we then use as the compressed embedding $\boldsymbol{e}_l$ of the linguistic sequence l.

2.2 Attention Mechanism

The form of attention we consider was first introduced in the context of machine translation [3,33]. This mechanism takes a weighted average of the hidden states of an encoding RNN based on their relevance to a decoding RNN at various decoding time steps. Subsequent *spatial* attention mechanisms have extended the original mechanism to image captioning [48] and other vision-and-language tasks [24,47]. More formally, given an arbitrary linguistic embedding $\boldsymbol{e}_l$ and image activations $\boldsymbol{F}_{w,h,c}$ where w, h, c are the width, height, and channel indices, respectively, of the image features $\boldsymbol{F}$ at one layer, we obtain a final visual embedding $\boldsymbol{e}_v$ as follows:

$$\xi_{w,h} = MLP(g(\boldsymbol{F}_{\boldsymbol{w},\boldsymbol{h},\cdot}, \boldsymbol{e}_l)); \quad \alpha_{w,h} = \frac{\exp(\xi_{w,h})}{\sum_{w',h'} \exp(\xi_{w',h'})}; \ \boldsymbol{e}_v = \sum_{w,h} \alpha_{w,h} \boldsymbol{F}_{\boldsymbol{w},\boldsymbol{h},\cdot}, \tag{1}$$

where MLP is a multi-layer perceptron and $g(.,.)$ is an arbitrary fusion mechanism (concatenation, element-wise product, etc.). We will use Multi-modal Low-rank Bilinear (MLB) attention [24] which defines $g(.,.)$ as:

$$g(\boldsymbol{F}_{w,h,\cdot}, \boldsymbol{e}_l) = \tanh(\boldsymbol{U}^T \boldsymbol{F}_{w,h,\cdot}) \circ \tanh(\boldsymbol{V}^T \boldsymbol{e}_l), \tag{2}$$

where $\circ$ denotes an element-wise product and where $\boldsymbol{U}$ and $\boldsymbol{V}$ are trainable weight matrices. We choose MLB attention because it is parameter efficient and has shown strong empirical performance [22,24].

2.3 Feature-Wise Linear Modulation

Feature-wise Linear Modulation was introduced in the context of image stylization [8] and extended and shown to be highly effective for multi-modal tasks such as visual question-answering [7,38,44].

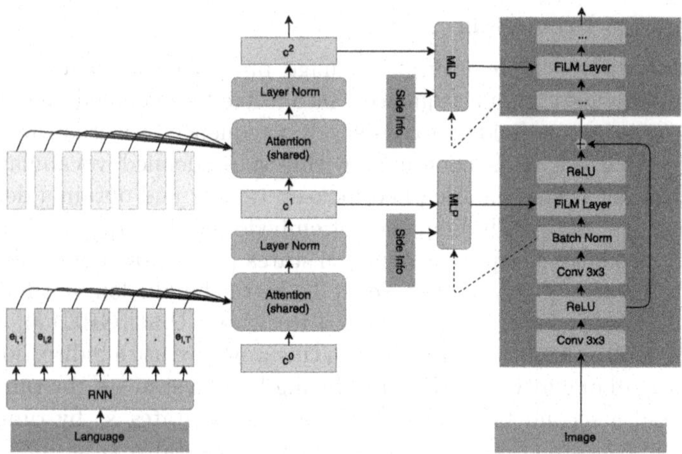

Fig. 2. Overview of the Multi-hop FiLM architecture for applying FiLM. Inputs, Layers, and activation are respectively colored in green, blue and purple. Note the initial FiLM architecture directly uses the $\boldsymbol{e}_{l,T}$ to predict the FiLM parameters. (Color figure online)

A Feature-wise Linear Modulation (FiLM) layer applies a per-channel scaling and shifting to the convolutional feature maps. Such layers are parameter efficient (only two scalars per feature map) while still retaining high capacity, as they are able to scale up or down, zero-out, or negate whole feature maps. In vision-and-language tasks, another network, the so-called FiLM generator h, predicts these modulating parameters from the linguistic input $\boldsymbol{e}_l$. More formally, a FiLM layer computes a modulated feature map $\hat{\boldsymbol{F}}_{w,h,c}$ as follows:

$$[\,\boldsymbol{\gamma}\,;\,\boldsymbol{\beta}\,] = h(\boldsymbol{e}_l); \qquad \hat{\boldsymbol{F}}_{.,.,c} = \gamma_c \boldsymbol{F}_{.,.,c} + \beta_c, \tag{3}$$

where $\boldsymbol{\gamma}$ and $\boldsymbol{\beta}$ are the scaling and shifting parameters which modulate the activations of the original feature map $\boldsymbol{F}_{.,.,c}$. We will use the superscript $k \in [1; K]$ to refer to the kth FiLM layer in the network.

FiLM layers may be inserted throughout the hierarchy of a convolutional network, either pre-trained and fixed [6] or trained from scratch [38]. Prior FiLM-based models [7,38,44] have used a single-hop FiLM generator to predict the FiLM parameters in all layers, *e.g.* an MLP which takes the language embedding $\boldsymbol{e}_l$ as input [7,38,44].

3 Multi-hop FiLM Architecture

In this section, we introduce the Multi-hop FiLM architecture (shown in Fig. 2) to predict the parameters of FiLM layers in an iterative fashion, to better scale to longer input sequences such as in dialogue. Another motivation was to better disantangle the linguistic reasoning from the visual one by iteratively attending to both pipelines.

We introduce a context vector $\boldsymbol{c}^k$ that acts as a controller for the linguistic and visual pipelines. We initialize the context vector with the final state of a bidirectional RNN $\boldsymbol{s}_T$ and repeat the following procedure for each of the FiLM layers in sequence (from lowest to highest convolutional layer): first, the context vector is updated by performing attention over RNN states (extracting relevant language information), and second, the context is used to predict a layer's FiLM parameters (dynamically modulating the visual information). Thus, the context vector enables the model to perform multi-hop reasoning over the linguistic pipeline while iteratively modulating the image features. More formally, the context vector is computed as follows:

$$\begin{cases} \boldsymbol{c}^0 = \boldsymbol{s}_T \\ \boldsymbol{c}^k = \sum_t \kappa_t^k(\boldsymbol{c}^{k-1}, \boldsymbol{s}_t)\boldsymbol{s}_t, \end{cases} \tag{4}$$

where:

$$\kappa_t^k(\boldsymbol{c}^{k-1}, \boldsymbol{s}_t) = \frac{\exp(\chi_t^k)}{\sum_t \exp(\chi_t^k)}; \qquad \chi_t^k(\boldsymbol{c}^{k-1}, \boldsymbol{s}_t) = MLP_{\text{Attn}}(g'(\boldsymbol{c}^k, \boldsymbol{s}_t)), \tag{5}$$

where the dependence of χ_t^k on $(\boldsymbol{c}^{k-1}, \boldsymbol{s}_t)$ may be omitted to simplify notation. MLP_{Attn} is a network (shared across layers) which aids in producing attention weights. g' can be any fusion mechanism that facilitates selecting the relevant context to attend to; here we use a simple dot-product following [33], thus $g'(\boldsymbol{c}^k, \boldsymbol{s}_t) = \boldsymbol{c}^k \circ \boldsymbol{s}_t$. Finally, FiLM is carried out using a layer-dependent neural network MLP^k_{FiLM}:

$$[\, \boldsymbol{\gamma}^k \,;\, \boldsymbol{\beta}^k \,] = MLP^k_{FiLM}(\boldsymbol{c}^k); \qquad \hat{\boldsymbol{F}}^k_{w,h,c} = \gamma^k_c \boldsymbol{F}^k_{\cdot,\cdot,c} + \beta^k_c. \tag{6}$$

As a regularization, we append a normalization-layer [2] on top of the context vector after each attention step.

External Information. Some tasks provide additional information which may be used to further improve the visual modulation. For instance, GuessWhat?! provides spatial features of the ground truth object to models which must answer questions about that object. Our model incorporates such features by concatenating them to the context vector before generating FiLM parameters.

Visual Feedback. Inspired by the co-attention mechanism [31,54], we also explore incorporating visual feedback into the Multi-hop FiLM architecture. To do so, we first extract the image or crop features $\boldsymbol{F}^k$ (immediately before modulation) and apply a global mean-pooling over spatial dimensions. We then concatenate this visual state into the context vector $\boldsymbol{c}^k$ before generating the next set of FiLM parameters.

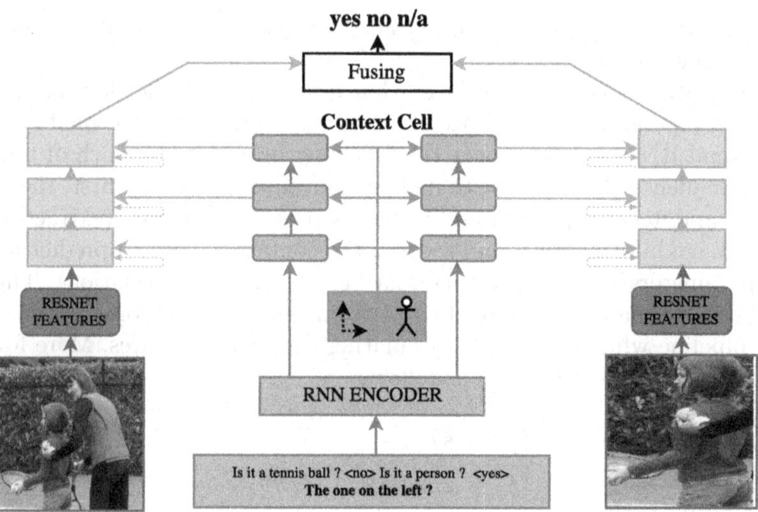

Fig. 3. Overall model. Consists of a visual pipeline (red and yellow) and linguistic pipeline (blue) and incorporates any additional contextual information (green). (Color figure online)

4 Experiments

In this section, we first introduce the ReferIt and GuessWhat?! datasets and respective tasks and then describe our overall Multi-hop FiLM architecture (Fig. 3)[1].

4.1 Dataset

ReferIt [23,51] is a cooperative two-player game. The first player (the Oracle) selects an object in a rich visual scene, for which they must generate an expression that refers to it (*e.g.* "the person eating an ice-cream"). the second player (the Guesser) must then select an object within the image. There are four ReferIt datasets exist: RefClef, RefCOCO, RefCOCO+ and RefCOCOg. The first dataset contains 130K references over 20K images from the ImageClef dataset [35], while the three other datasets respectively contain 142K, 142K and 86K references over 20K, 20k and 27K images from the MSCOCO dataset [29]. Each dataset has small differences. RefCOCO and RefClef were constructed using different image sets. RefCOCO+ forbids certain words to prevent object references from being too simplistic, and RefCOCOg only relies on images containing 2–4 objects from the same category. RefCOCOg also contains longer and more complex sentences than RefCOCO (8.4 vs. 3.5 average words). Here, we will show results on both the Guesser and Oracle tasks.

[1] The code and hyperparameters are available at https://github.com/GuessWhatGame.

GuessWhat?! [6] is a cooperative three-agent game in which players see the picture of a rich visual scene with several objects. One player (the Oracle) is randomly assigned an object in the scene. The second player (Questioner) aims to ask a series of yes-no questions to the Oracle to collect enough evidence to allow the third player (Guesser) to correctly locate the object in the image. The GuessWhat?! dataset is composed of 131K successful natural language dialogues containing 650k question-answer pairs on over 63K images from MSCOCO [29]. Dialogues contain 5.2 question-answer pairs and 34.4 words on average. Here, we will focus on the Guesser and Oracle tasks.

4.2 Task Descriptions

Game Features. Both games consist of triplets $(\mathcal{I}, l, o)$, where $\mathcal{I} \in \mathbb{R}^{3\times M\times N}$ is an RGB image and l is some language input (i.e. a series of words) describing an object o in $\mathcal{I}$. The object o is defined by an object category, a pixel-wise segmentation, an RGB crop of $\mathcal{I}$ based on bounding box information, and hand-crafted spatial information $\boldsymbol{x}_{spatial}$, where

$$\boldsymbol{x}_{spatial} = [x_{min}, y_{min}, x_{max}, y_{max}, x_{center}, y_{center}, w_{box}, h_{box}] \tag{7}$$

We replace words with two or fewer occurrences with an <*unk*> token.

The Oracle Task. Given an image $\mathcal{I}$, an object o, a question q, and a sequence δ of previous question-answer pairs $(\boldsymbol{q}, a)_{1:\delta}$ where $a \in \{\text{Yes}, \text{No}, \text{N/A}\}$, the oracle's task is to produce an answer a that correctly answers the question q. In our experiments, we will use the symbol (D) when the previous question-answer pairs are concatenated with the question q to obtain a single sequence of tokens s. Similarly, we will use the symbol (Q) when dropping the previous question-answers. The oracle is trained using cross-entropy loss.

The Guesser Task. Given an image $\mathcal{I}$, a list of objects $O = o_{1:\Phi}$, a target object $o^* \in O$ and the dialogue $\mathcal{D}$, the guesser needs to output a probability σ_ϕ that each object o_ϕ is the target object o^*. Following [17], the Guesser is evaluated by selecting the object with the highest probability of being correct. Note that even if the individual probabilities σ_ϕ are between 0 and 1, their sum can be greater than 1. More formally, the Guesser loss and error are computed as follows:

$$L_{Guesser} = \frac{-1}{N_{games}} \sum_{n}^{N_{games}} \frac{1}{\Phi^n} \sum_{\phi}^{\Phi} \log(p(o^* | \mathcal{I}^n, o_\phi^n, \mathcal{D}^n)) \tag{8}$$

$$E_{Guesser} = \frac{-1}{N_{games}} \sum_{n}^{N_{games}} \mathbb{1}(o^* \neq o_{\text{argmax}_\phi \, \sigma_\phi^n}) \tag{9}$$

where $\mathbb{1}$ is the indicator function and Φ^n the number of objects in the nth game.

4.3 Model

We use similar models for both ReferIt and GuessWhat?! and provide its architectural details in this subsection.

Object Embedding. The object category is fed into a dense look-up table $\boldsymbol{e}_{cat}$, and the spatial information is scaled to $[-1; 1]$ before being up-sampled via non-linear projection to $\boldsymbol{e}_{spat}$. We do not use the object category in ReferIt models.

Visual Pipeline. We first resized the image and object crop to 448×448 before extracting $14 \times 14 \times 1024$ dimensional features from a ResNet-152 [15] (block3) pre-trained on ImageNet [41]. Following [38], we feed these features to a 3×3 convolution layer with Batch Normalization [19] and Rectified Linear Unit [37] (ReLU). We then stack four modulated residual blocks (shown in Fig. 2), each producing a set of feature maps $\boldsymbol{F}^k$ via (in order) a 1×1 convolutional layer (128 units), ReLU activations, a 3×3 convolutional layer (128 units), and an untrainable Batch Normalization layer. The residual block then modulates $\boldsymbol{F}^k$ with a FiLM layer to get $\hat{\boldsymbol{F}}^k$, before again applying ReLU activations. Lastly, a residual connection sums the activations of both ReLU outputs. After the last residual block, we use a 1×1 convolution layer (512 units) with Batch Normalization and ReLU followed by MLB attention [24] (256 units and 1 glimpse) to obtain the final embedding $\boldsymbol{e}_v$. Note our model uses two independent visual pipeline modules: one to extract modulated image features $\boldsymbol{e}_v^{img}$, one to extract modulated crop features $\boldsymbol{e}_v^{crop}$.

To incorporate spatial information, we concatenate two coordinate feature maps indicating relative x and y spatial position (scaled to $[-1, 1]$) with the image features before each convolution layer (except for convolutional layers followed by FiLM layers). In addition, the pixel-wise segmentations $S \in \{0, 1\}^{M \times N}$ are rescaled to 14×14 floating point masks before being concatenated to the feature maps.

Linguistic Pipeline. We compute the language embedding by using a word-embedding look-up (200 dimensions) with dropout followed by a Bi-GRU (512×2units) with Layer Normalization [2]. As described in Sect. 3, we initialize the context vector with the last RNN state $\boldsymbol{c}^0 = \boldsymbol{s}_T$. We then attend to the other Bi-GRU states via an attention mechanism with a linear projection and ReLU activations and regularize the new context vector with Layer Normalization.

FiLM Parameter Generation. We concatenate spatial information $\boldsymbol{e}_{spat}$ and object category information $\boldsymbol{e}_{cat}$ to the context vector. In some experiments, we also concatenate a fourth embedding consisting of intermediate visual features $\boldsymbol{F}^k$ after mean-pooling. Finally, we use a linear projection to map the embedding to FiLM parameters.

Final Layers. We first generate our final embedding by concatenating the output of the visual pipelines $\boldsymbol{e}_{final} = [\boldsymbol{e}_v^{img}; \boldsymbol{e}_v^{crop}]$ before applying a linear projection (512 units) with ReLU and a softmax layer.

Training Process. We train our model end-to-end with Adam [26] (learning rate 3.10^{-4}), a dropout ratio of 0.5, weight decay of 5.10^{-6} for convolutional network

Table 1. ReferIt Guesser test error.

Referit Split by	RefCOCO (unc)			RefCOCO+ (unc)			RefCOCOg (google)
Report on	Valid	TestA	TestB	Valid	TestA	TestB	Val
MMI [36]	-	71.7%	71.1%	-	58.4%	51.2%	59.3%
visDif + MMI [51]	-	74.6%	76.6%	-	59.2%	55.6%	64.0%
NEG Bag [36]	-	75.6%	78.0%	-	-	-	68.4%
Joint-SLR [52]	78.9%	78.0%	80.7%	61.9%	64.0%	59.2%	-
PLAN [54]	81.7%	80.8%	81.3%	64.2%	66.3%	61.5%	69.5%
MAttN [50]	**85.7%**	85.3%	**84.6%**	71.0%	75.1%	**66.2%**	-
Baseline + MLB	77.6%	79.6%	77.2%	60.8%	59.7%	66.2%	63.1%
Single-hop FiLM	83.4%	85.8%	80.9%	72.1%	77.3%	63.9%	67.8%
Multi-hop FiLM	83.5%	86.5%	81.3%	73.4%	77.7%	64.5%	69.8%
Multi-hop FiLM (+img)	84.9%	**87.4%**	83.1%	**73.8%**	**78.7%**	65.8%	**71.5%**

layers, and a batch size of 64. We report results after early stopping on the validation set with a maximum of 15 epochs.

4.4 Baseline Models

In our experiments, we re-implement several baseline models to benchmark the performance of our models. The standard *Baseline* is a straightforward concatenation of the image and object crop features after mean pooling, the linguistic embedding, and the spatial embedding and the category embedding (GuessWhat?! only), followed by the same final layers described in our proposed model. We refer to a model which uses the MLB attention mechanism to pool the visual features as *Baseline+MLB*. We also implement a *Single-hop FiLM* mechanism which is equivalent to setting all context vectors equal to the last state of the Bi-GRU $\boldsymbol{e}_{l,T}$. Finally, we experiment with injecting intermediate visual features into the FiLM Generator input, and we refer to the model as *Multi-hop FiLM (+img)*.

4.5 Results

ReferIt Guesser. We report the best test error of the outlined methods on the ReferIt Guesser task in Table 1. Note that RefCOCO and RefCOCO+ split test sets into TestA and TestB, only including expression referring towards people and objects, respectively. We do not report [50] and [52] scores on RefCOCOg as the authors use a different split (umd). Our initial baseline achieves 77.6%, 60.8%, 63.1%, 73.4% on the RefCOCO, RefCOCO+, RefCOCOg, RefClef datasets, respectively, performing comparably to state-of-the-art models. We observe a significant improvements using a FiLM-based architecture, jumping to 84.9%, 87.4%, 73.8%, 71.5%, respectively, and outperforming most prior methods and achieving comparably performance with the concurrent MAttN [50] model. Interestingly, MAttN and Multi-hop FiLM are built in two different manners; while

Table 2. GuessWhat?! Oracle test error.

Oracle models	Quest.	Dial.	Object	Image	Crop	Test error
Dominant class (no)	✗	✗	✗	✗	✗	50.9%
Question only [6]	✓	✗	✗	✗	✗	41.2%
Image only [6]	✗	✗	✗	✓	✗	46.7%
Crop only [6]	✗	✗	✗	✗	✓	43.0%
No-Vision (Q) [6]	✓	✗	✓	✗	✗	21.5%
No-Vision (D)	✗	✓	✓	✗	✗	20.6%
Baseline (Q)	✓	✗	✓	✓	✓	23.3%
Baseline (D)	✗	✓	✓	✓	✓	22.4%
Baseline + MLB (Q)	✓	✗	✓	✓	✓	21.8%
Baseline + MLB (D)	✗	✓	✓	✓	✓	21.1%
MODERN [44]	✓	✗	✓	✗	✓	19.5%
Single-hop FiLM (Q)	✓	✗	✓	✓	✓	17.8%
Single-hop FiLM (D)	✗	✓	✓	✓	✓	17.6%
Multi-hop FiLM	✗	✓	✓	✓	✓	**16.9%**
Multi-hop FiLM (+img)	✗	✓	✓	✓	✓	17.1%

the former has three specialized reasoning blocks, our model uses a generic feature modulation approach. These architectural differences surface when examining test splits: MAttN achieves excellent results on referring expression towards objects while Multi-hop FiLM performs better on referring expressions towards people.

GuessWhat?! Oracle. We report the best test error of several variants of GuessWhat?! Oracle models in Table 2. First, we baseline any visual or language biases by predicting the Oracle's target answer using only the image (46.7% error) or the question (41.1% error). As first reported in [6], we observe that the baseline methods perform worse when integrating the image and crop inputs (21.1%) rather than solely using the object category and spatial location (20.6%). On the other hand, concatenating previous question-answer pairs to answer the current question is beneficial in our experiments. Finally, using Single-hop FiLM reduces the error to 17.6% and Multi-hop FiLM further to 16.9%, outperforming the previous best model by 2.4%.

GuessWhat?! Guesser. We provide the best test error of the outlined methods on the GuessWhat?! Guesser task in Table 3. As a baseline, we find that random object selection achieves an error rate of 82.9%. Our initial model baseline performs significantly worse (38.3%) than concurrent models (36.6%), highlighting that successfully jointly integrating crop and image features is far from trivial. However, Single-hop FiLM manages to lower the error to 35.6%. Finally, Multi-hop FiLM architecture outperforms other models with a final error of 30.5%.

Table 3. GuessWhat?! Guesser test error.

Guesser Error	Test Error
Random	82.9%
LSTM [6]	38.7%
LSTM + Img [6]	39.5%
PLAN [54]	36.6%
MLB-Baseline (crop)	38.3%
Single-hop FiLM	35.6%
Multi-hop FiLM	**30.5%**

Guesser Error	Crop	Image	Crop/Img
Baseline	38.3%	40.0%	45.1%
Single-hop FiLM	35.3%	35.7%	35.6%
Multi-hop FiLM	32.3%	35.0%	**30.5%**
Multi-hop FiLM (no cat.)	33.1%	40%	33.4%

5 Discussion

Single-hop FiLM vs. Multi-hop FiLM. In the GuessWhat?! task, Multi-hop FiLM outperforms Single-hop FiLM by 6.1% on the Guesser task but only 0.7% on the Oracle task. We think that the small performance gain for the Oracle task is due to the nature of the task; to answer the current question, it is often not necessary to look at previous question-answer pairs, and in most cases this task does not require a long chain of reasoning. On the other hand, the Guesser task needs to gather information across the whole dialogue in order to correctly retrieve the object, and it is therefore more likely to benefit from multi-hop reasoning. The same trend can be observed for ReferIt. Single-hop FiLM and Multi-hop FiLM perform similarly on RefClef and RefCOCO, while we observe 1.3% and 2% gains on RefCOCO+ and RefCOCOg, respectively. This pattern of performance is intuitive, as the former datasets consist of shorter referring expressions (3.5 average words) than the latter (8.4 average words in RefCOCOg), and the latter datasets also consist of richer, more complex referring expressions due *e.g.* to taboo words (RefCOCO+). In short, our experiments demonstrate that Multi-hop FiLM is better able reason over complex linguistic sequences.

Reasoning Mechanism. We conduct several experiments to better understand our method. First, we assess whether Multi-hop FiLM performs better because of increased network capacity. We remove the attention mechanism over the linguistic sequence and update the context vector via a shared MLP. We observe that this change significantly hurts performance across all tasks, *e.g.*, increasing the Multi-hop FiLM error of the Guesser from 30.5 to 37.3%. Second, we investigate how the model attends to GuessWhat?! dialogues for the Oracle and Guesser tasks, providing more insight into how to the model reasons over the language input. We first look at the top activation in the (crop) attention layers to observe where the most prominent information is. Note that similar trends are observed for the image pipeline. As one would expect, the Oracle is focused on a specific word in the last question 99.5% of the time, one which is crucial to answer the question at hand. However, this ratio drops to 65% in the Guesser task, suggesting the model is reasoning in a different way. If we then extract the top 3 activations per layer, the attention points to <*yes*> or <*no*> tokens (respectively) at least once, 50% of the time for the Oracle and Guesser, showing that the attention is able to correctly split the dialogue into question-answer

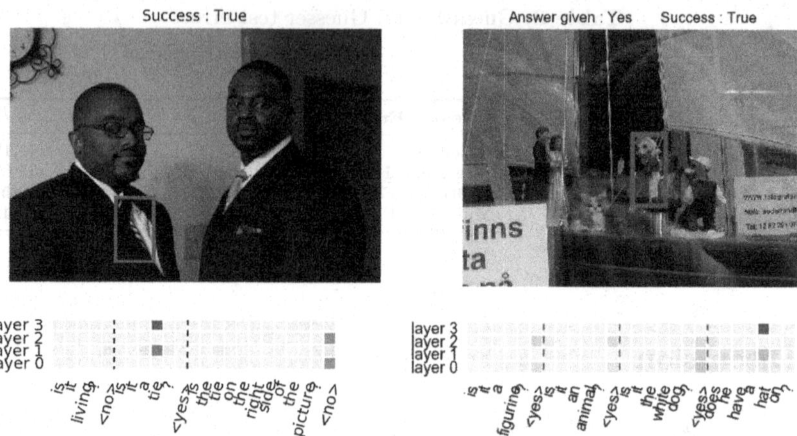

Fig. 4. Guesser and Oracle attention mechanism in the crop visual pipeline.

pairs. Finally, we plot the attention masks for each FiLM layer to have a better intuition of this reasoning process in Fig. 4.

Crop vs. Image. We also evaluate the impact of using the image and/or crop on the final error for the Guesser task Table 3. Using the image alone (while still including object category and spatial information) performs worse than using the crop. However, using image and crop together inarguably gives the lowest errors, though prior work has not always used the crop due to architecture-specific GPU limitations [44].

Visual Feedback. We explore whether adding visual feedback to the context embedding improves performance. While it has little effect on the GuessWhat?! Oracle and Guesser tasks, it improves the accuracy on ReferIt by 1–2%. Note that ReferIt does not include class labels of the selected object, so the visual feedback might act as a surrogate for this information. To further investigate this hypothesis, we remove the object category from the GuessWhat?! task and report results in Table 5 in the supplementary material. In this setup, we indeed observe a relative improvement 0.4% on the Oracle task, further confirming this hypothesis.

Pointing Tasks. In GuessWhat?!, the Guesser must select an object among a list of items. For the task to be natural, the system should directly point out the object as a human would might. Thus, we provide an initial baseline that scores up to 84.0% error in the supplementary material in Table 7.

6 Related Work

The ReferIt game [23] has been a testbed for various vision-and-language tasks over the past years, including object retrieval [32,36,50–52,54], semantic image segmentation [16,39], and generating referring descriptions [32,51,52]. To tackle object retrieval, [36,50,51] extract additional visual features such as relative object locations and [32,52] use reinforcement learning to iteratively train the object retrieval and description generation models. Closer to our work, [17,54] use the full image and the object crop to locate the correct object. While some previous work relies on task-specific modules [50,51], our approach is general and can be easily extended to other vision-and-language tasks.

The GuessWhat?! game [6] can be seen as a dialogue version of the ReferIt game, one which additionally draws on visual question answering ability. [28,42,53] make headway on the dialogue generation task via reinforcement learning. However, these approaches are bottlenecked by the accuracy of Oracle and Guesser models, despite existing modeling advances [44,54]; accurate Oracle and Guesser models are crucial for providing a meaningful learning signal for dialogue generation models, so we believe the Multi-hop FiLM architecture will facilitate high quality dialogue generation as well.

A special case of Feature-wise Linear Modulation was first successfully applied to image style transfer [8], whose approach modulates image features according to some image style (*i.e.*, cubism or impressionism). [44] extended this approach to vision-and-language tasks, injecting FiLM-like layers along the entire visual pipeline of a pre-trained ResNet. [38] demonstrates that a convolutional network with FiLM layers achieves strong performance on CLEVR [21], a task that focuses on answering reasoning-oriented, multi-step questions about synthetic images. Subsequent work has demonstrated that FiLM and variants thereof are effective for video object segmentation where the conditioning input is the first image's segmentation (instead of language) [49] and language-guided image segmentation [40]. Even more broadly, [9] overviews the strength of FiLM-related methods across machine learning domains, ranging from reinforcement learning to generative modeling to domain adaptation.

There are other notable models that decompose reasoning into different modules. For instance, Neural Turing Machines [13,14] divide a model into a controller with read and write units. Memory networks use an attention mechanism to answer a query by reasoning over a linguistic knowledge base [43,45] or image features [46]. A memory network updates a query vector by performing several attention hops over the memory before outputting a final answer from this query vector. Although Multi-hop FiLM computes a similar context vector, this intermediate embedding is used to predict FiLM parameters rather than the final answer. Thus, Multi-hop FiLM includes a second reasoning step over the image.

Closer to our work, [18] designed networks composed of Memory, Attention, and Control (MAC) cells to perform visual reasoning. Similar to Neural Turing Machines, each MAC cell is composed of a control unit that attends over the language input, a read unit that attends over the image and a write unit that fuses both pipelines. Though conceptually similar to Multi-hop FiLM models, Compositional Attention Networks differ structurally, for instance using a dynamic neural architecture and relying on spatial attention rather than FiLM.

7 Conclusion

In this paper, we introduce a new way to exploit Feature-wise Linear Modulation (FiLM) layers for vision-and-language tasks. Our approach generates the parameters of FiLM layers going up the visual pipeline by attending to the language input in multiple hops rather than all at once. We show Multi-hop FiLM Generator architectures are better able to handle longer sequences than their single-hop counterparts. We outperform state-of-the-art vision-and-language models with significant performance gains on the ReferIt object retrieval task and GuessWhat?! visual dialogue task. Finally, we believe that this Multi-hop FiLM Generator approach is generic and can extended to a variety of vision-and-language tasks, particularly those requiring complex visual reasoning.

Acknowledgements. The authors would like to acknowledge the stimulating research environment of the SequeL Team. We also thank Vincent Dumoulin for helpful discussions. We acknowledge the following agencies for research funding and computing support: CHISTERA IGLU and CPER Nord-Pas de Calais/FEDER DATA Advanced data science and technologies 2015–2020, NSERC, Calcul Québec, Compute Canada, the Canada Research Chairs and CIFAR.

Additional Results

ReferIt ImageClef

See Table 4.

Table 4. ReferIt Guesser test error.

Referit	RefClef (berkeley) test
SCRC [17]	72.7%
Baseline + MLB	74.6%
Single-hop FiLM	84.0%
Multi-hop FiLM	84.3%
Multi-hop FiLM +(img)	**85.1%**

Category-Less Oracle

Table 5. GuessWhat?! Oracle test error without category.

Oracle models	Quest.	Dial.	Spat.	Image	Crop	Test error
Baseline + MLB	✗	✓	✓	✓	✓	26.7%
Single-hop FiLM	✗	✓	✓	✓	✓	19.5%
Multi-hop FiLM	✗	✓	✓	✓	✓	18.9%
Multi-hop FiLM (+img loop)	✗	✓	✓	✓	✓	**18.4%**

Category-Less Guesser

See Table 6.

Table 6. GuessWhat?! Guesser test error without category.

Guesser error	Crop	Image	Crop/Img
PLAN [54]	-	-	40.3%
Multi-hop FiLM	35.3%	39.8%	33.9%
Multi-hop FiLM (+img)	34.3%	40.1%	**33.2%**

Guesser Pointing

Table 7. Guesser pointing errors for different IoU thresholds.

Guesser model	IoU > 0.3	IoU >0.5	IoU > 0.7
Baseline	81.4%	92.0%	98.2%
FiLM	74.0%	85.9%	94.7%
Multi-hop FiLM	73.4%	84.6%	93.7%
Multi-hop FiLM (+img)	**71.9%**	**84.0%**	**93.6%**

So far, the guesser has selected its answer among a provided list of objects. A more natural task would be for the guesser to directly point out the object as a human might. Thus, we introduce such a pointing task as a new benchmark for GuessWhat?!. This task is to locate the intended object based on a series of questions and answers, but instead of selecting the object from a list, the guesser must output a bounding box around the object of its guess. This box is defined as the 4-tuple (x, y, width, height), where (x, y) is the coordinate of the top left corner of the box, within the original image $\mathcal{I}$, given an input dialogue. Note that this new task is more difficult, as the model does not have access to the list of objects. The original task also includes important side information, namely object category and (x, y)-position [6] which ease the object retrieval.

We assess bounding box accuracy using the Intersection Over Union (IoU) metric: the area of the intersection of predicted and ground truth bounding boxes, divided by the area of their union. In prior literature [10,12], an object is usually considered found if the IoU is greater than 0.5.

$$\mathbf{IoU} = \frac{|\text{bboxA} \cap \text{bboxB}|}{|\text{bboxA} \cup \text{bboxB}|} = \frac{|\text{bboxA} \cap \text{bboxB}|}{|\text{bboxA}| + |\text{bboxB}| - |\text{bboxA} \cap \text{bboxB}|} \tag{10}$$

We report model error in Table 7. Interestingly, the baseline obtains 92.0% error while Multi-hop FiLM Generator obtains 84.0% error. As previously discussed, we also note that re-injecting visual features into the Multi-hop FiLM Generator's context cell is also beneficial. The error rates are relatively high, though also in line with those of similar pointing tasks such as SCRC [16,17] (around 90%) on ReferIt.

Attention Mask

See Figs. 5, 6, 7, 8 and 9.

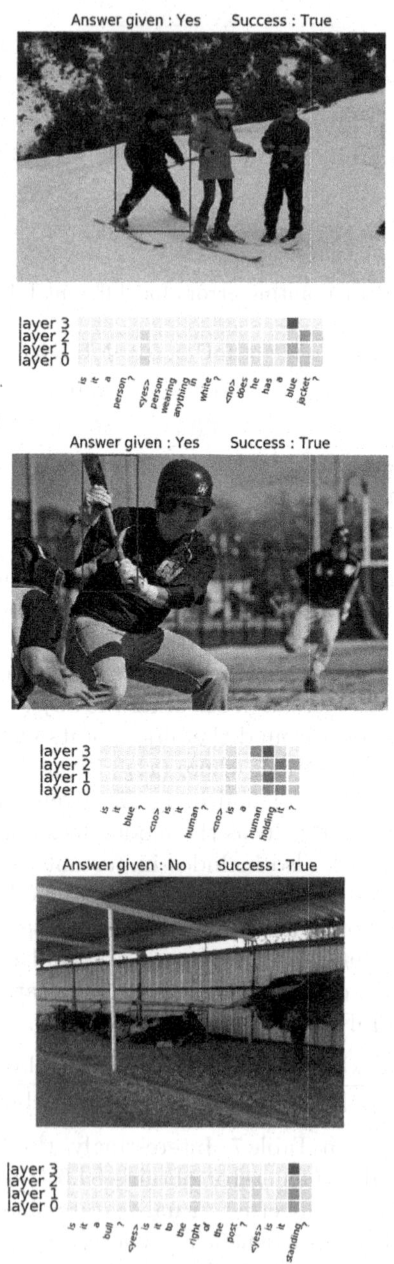

Fig. 5. Oracle attention masks with attention on the last question (crop pipeline)

Fig. 6. Oracle attention masks with complex reasoning (crop pipeline)

Fig. 7. Oracle attention masks with negative results (crop pipeline)

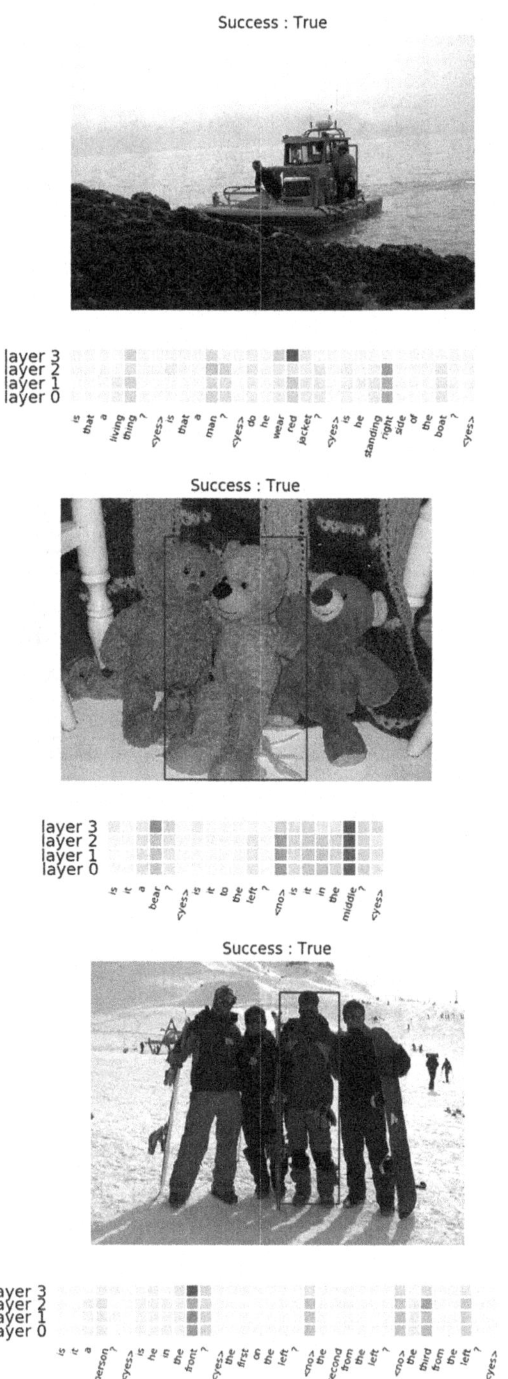

Fig. 8. Guesser attention masks with positive results (crop pipeline)

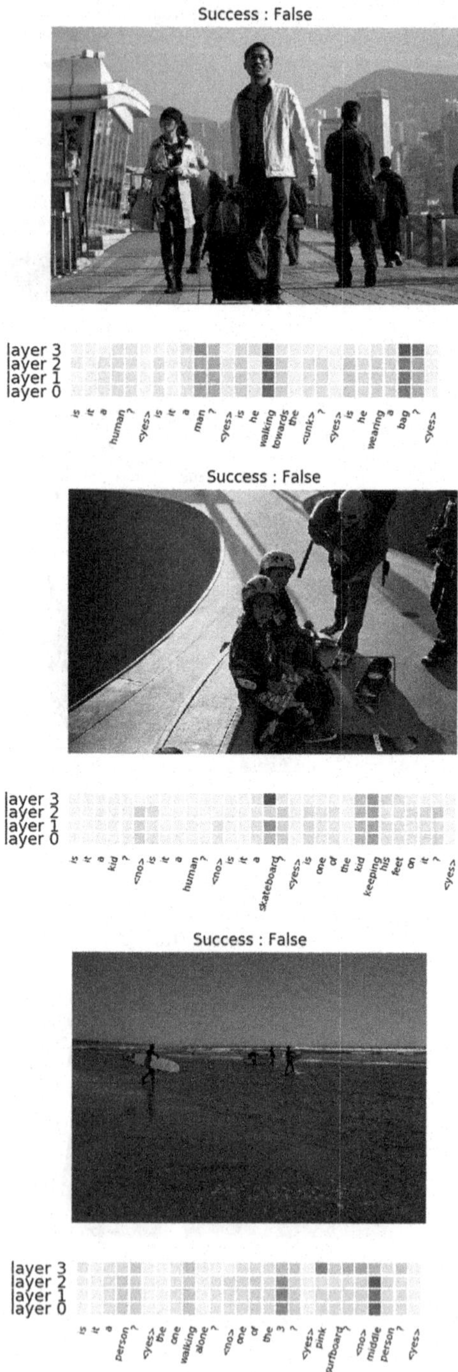

Fig. 9. Guesser attention masks with negative results (crop pipeline).

References

1. Antol, S., et al.: VQA: visual question answering. In: Proceedings of ICCV (2015)
2. Ba, J.L., Kiros, J.R., Hinton, G.E.: Layer normalization. In: Deep Learning Symposium (NIPS) (2016)
3. Bahdanau, D., Cho, K., Bengio, Y.: Neural machine translation by jointly learning to align and translate. In: Proceedings of ICLR (2015)
4. Chung, J., Gulcehre, C., Cho, K., Bengio, Y.: Empirical evaluation of gated recurrent neural networks on sequence modeling. In: Proceedings of ICML (2015)
5. Das, A., et al.: Visual dialog. In: Proceedings of CVPR (2017)
6. De Vries, H., Strub, F., Chandar, S., Pietquin, O., Larochelle, H., Courville, A.: Guesswhat?! Visual object discovery through multi-modal dialogue. In: Proceedings of CVPR (2017)
7. Delbrouck, J.B., Dupont, S.: Modulating and attending the source image during encoding improves multimodal translation. In: Visually-Grounded Interaction and Language Workshop (NIPS) (2017)
8. Dumoulin, V., Shlens, J., Kudlur, M.: A learned representation for artistic style. In: Proceedings of ICLR (2017)
9. Dumoulin, V., et al.: Feature-wise transformations. Distill (2018). https://doi.org/10.23915/distill.00011, https://distill.pub/2018/feature-wise-transformations
10. Everingham, M., Van Gool, L., Williams, C.K., Winn, J., Zisserman, A.: The pascal visual object classes (VOC) challenge. Int. J. Comput. Vis. **88**(2), 303–338 (2010)
11. Fukui, A., Park, D.H., Yang, D., Rohrbach, A., Darrell, T., Rohrbach, M.: Multimodal compact bilinear pooling for visual question answering and visual grounding. In: Proceedings of EMNLP (2016)
12. Girshick, R., Donahue, J., Darrell, T., Malik, J.: Rich feature hierarchies for accurate object detection and semantic segmentation. In: Proceedings of of CVPR (2014)
13. Graves, A., Wayne, G., Danihelka, I.: Neural turing machines. arXiv preprint arXiv:1410.5401 (2014)
14. Graves, A., et al.: Hybrid computing using a neural network with dynamic external memory. Nature **538**(7626), 471 (2016)
15. He, K., Zhang, X., Ren, S., Sun, J.: Deep residual learning for image recognition. In: Proceedings of CVPR (2016)
16. Hu, R., Rohrbach, M., Darrell, T.: Segmentation from natural language expressions. In: Leibe, B., Matas, J., Sebe, N., Welling, M. (eds.) ECCV 2016. LNCS, vol. 9905, pp. 108–124. Springer, Cham (2016). https://doi.org/10.1007/978-3-319-46448-0_7
17. Hu, R., Xu, H., Rohrbach, M., Feng, J., Saenko, K., Darrell, T.: Natural language object retrieval. In: Proceedings of CVPR (2016)
18. Hudson, D.A., Manning, C.D.: Compositional attention networks for machine reasoning. In: Proceedings of ICL (2018)
19. Ioffe, S., Szegedy, C.: Batch normalization: accelerating deep network training by reducing internal covariate shift. In: Proceedings of ICML (2015)
20. Jabri, A., Joulin, A., van der Maaten, L.: Revisiting visual question answering baselines. In: Leibe, B., Matas, J., Sebe, N., Welling, M. (eds.) ECCV 2016. LNCS, vol. 9912, pp. 727–739. Springer, Cham (2016). https://doi.org/10.1007/978-3-319-46484-8_44
21. Johnson, J., Hariharan, B., van der Maaten, L., Fei-Fei, L., Zitnick, C.L., Girshick, R.: CLEVR: a diagnostic dataset for compositional language and elementary visual reasoning. In: Proceedings of CVPR (2017)

22. Kafle, K., Kanan, C.: Visual question answering: datasets, algorithms, and future challenges. Comput. Vis. Image Underst. **163**, 3–20 (2017)
23. Kazemzadeh, S., Ordonez, V., Matten, M., Berg, T.: ReferitGame: referring to objects in photographs of natural scenes. In: Proceedings of EMNLP (2014)
24. Kim, J.H., On, K.W., Lim, W., Kim, J., Ha, J.W., Zhang, B.T.: Hadamard product for low-rank bilinear pooling. In: Proceedings of ICLR (2017)
25. Kim, J.H., et al.: Multimodal residual learning for visual QA. In: Proceedings of NIPS (2016)
26. Kingma, D.P., Ba, J.: Adam: a method for stochastic optimization. In: Proceedings of ICLR (2014)
27. Krizhevsky, A., Sutskever, I., Hinton, G.E.: Imagenet classification with deep convolutional neural networks. In: Proceedings of of NIPS (2012)
28. Lee, S.W., Heo, Y.J., Zhang, B.T.: Answerer in questioner's mind for goal-oriented visual dialogue. In: Visually-Grounded Interaction and Language Workshop (NIPS) (2018)
29. Lin, T.-Y., et al.: Microsoft COCO: common objects in context. In: Fleet, D., Pajdla, T., Schiele, B., Tuytelaars, T. (eds.) ECCV 2014. LNCS, vol. 8693, pp. 740–755. Springer, Cham (2014). https://doi.org/10.1007/978-3-319-10602-1_48
30. Long, J., Shelhamer, E., Darrell, T.: Fully convolutional networks for semantic segmentation. In: Proceedings of CVPR (2015)
31. Lu, J., Yang, J., Batra, D., Parikh, D.: Hierarchical question-image co-attention for visual question answering. In: Proceedings of NIPS (2016)
32. Luo, R., Shakhnarovich, G.: Comprehension-guided referring expressions. In: Proceedings of CVPR (2017)
33. Luong, M.T., Pham, H., Manning, C.D.: Effective approaches to attention-based neural machine translation. In: Proceedings of EMNLP (2015)
34. Malinowski, M., Rohrbach, M., Fritz, M.: Ask your neurons: a neural-based approach to answering questions about images. In: Proceedings of ICCV (2015)
35. Mller, H., Clough, P., Deselaers, T., Caputo, B.: ImageCLEF: Experimental Evaluation in Visual Information Retrieval. Springer, Heidelberg (2012). https://doi.org/10.1007/978-3-642-15181-1
36. Nagaraja, V.K., Morariu, V.I., Davis, L.S.: Modeling context between objects for referring expression understanding. In: Leibe, B., Matas, J., Sebe, N., Welling, M. (eds.) ECCV 2016. LNCS, vol. 9908, pp. 792–807. Springer, Cham (2016). https://doi.org/10.1007/978-3-319-46493-0_48
37. Nair, V., Hinton, G.E.: Rectified linear units improve restricted Boltzmann machines. In: Proceedings of ICML (2010)
38. Perez, E., Strub, F., De Vries, H., Dumoulin, V., Courville, A.: Film: visual reasoning with a general conditioning layer. In: Proceedings of AAAI (2018)
39. Rohrbach, A., Rohrbach, M., Hu, R., Darrell, T., Schiele, B.: Grounding of textual phrases in images by reconstruction. In: Leibe, B., Matas, J., Sebe, N., Welling, M. (eds.) ECCV 2016. LNCS, vol. 9905, pp. 817–834. Springer, Cham (2016). https://doi.org/10.1007/978-3-319-46448-0_49
40. Rupprecht, C., Laina, I., Navab, N., Hager, G.D., Tombari, F.: Guide me: interacting with deep networks. In: Proceedings of CVPR (2018)
41. Russakovsky, O., et al.: Imagenet large scale visual recognition challenge. Int. J. Comput. Vis. **115**(3), 211–252 (2015)
42. Strub, F., De Vries, H., Mary, J., Piot, B., Courville, A., Pietquin, O.: End-to-end optimization of goal-driven and visually grounded dialogue systems. In: Proceedings of IJCAI (2017)

43. Sukhbaatar, S., Weston, J., Fergus, R., et al.: End-to-end memory networks. In: Proceedings of NIPS (2015)
44. de Vries, H., Strub, F., Mary, J., Larochelle, H., Pietquin, O., Courville, A.C.: Modulating early visual processing by language. In: Proceedings of NIPS (2017)
45. Weston, J., Chopra, S., Bordes, A.: Memory networks. arXiv preprint arXiv:1410.3916 (2014)
46. Xiong, C., Merity, S., Socher, R.: Dynamic memory networks for visual and textual question answering. In: Proceedings of ICML (2016)
47. Xu, H., Saenko, K.: Ask, attend and answer: exploring question-guided spatial attention for visual question answering. In: Leibe, B., Matas, J., Sebe, N., Welling, M. (eds.) ECCV 2016. LNCS, vol. 9911, pp. 451–466. Springer, Cham (2016). https://doi.org/10.1007/978-3-319-46478-7_28
48. Xu, K., et al.: Show, attend and tell: neural image caption generation with visual attention. In: Proceedings of ICML (2015)
49. Yang, L., Wang, Y., Xiong, X., Yang, J., Katsaggelos, A.K.: Efficient video object segmentation via network modulation. In: Proceedings of CVPR (2018)
50. Yu, L., et al.: MAttNet: modular attention network for referring expression comprehension. In: Proceedings of CVPR (2018)
51. Yu, L., Poirson, P., Yang, S., Berg, A.C., Berg, T.L.: Modeling context in referring expressions. In: Leibe, B., Matas, J., Sebe, N., Welling, M. (eds.) ECCV 2016. LNCS, vol. 9906, pp. 69–85. Springer, Cham (2016). https://doi.org/10.1007/978-3-319-46475-6_5
52. Yu, L., Tan, H., Bansal, M., Berg, T.L.: A joint speakerlistener-reinforcer model for referring expressions. In: Proceedings of CVPR (2016)
53. Zhu, Y., Zhang, S., Metaxas, D.: Reasoning about fine-grained attribute phrases using reference games. In: Visually-Grounded Interaction and Language Workshop (NIPS) (2017)
54. Zhuang, B., Wu, Q., Shen, C., Reid, I.D., van den Hengel, A.: Parallel attention: a unified framework for visual object discovery through dialogs and queries. In: Proceedings of CVPR (2018)

Author Index